WILDLIFE *of* BRITAIN

THE DEFINITIVE VISUAL GUIDE

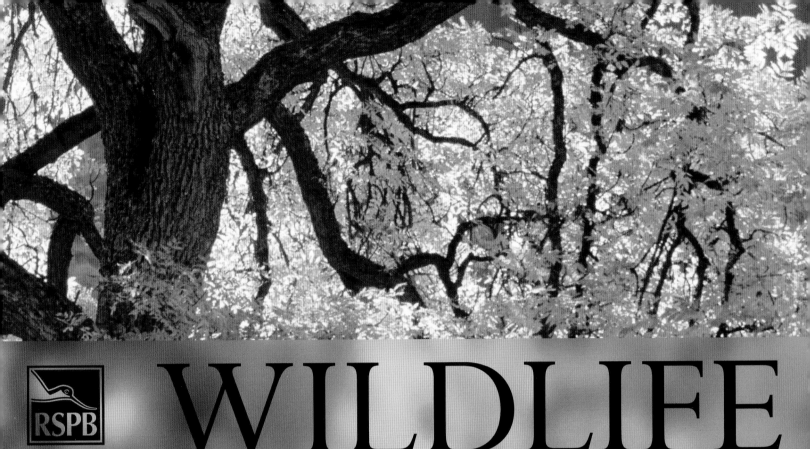

RSPB

DK

WILDLIFE *of* BRITAIN

THE DEFINITIVE VISUAL GUIDE

DK

LONDON • NEW YORK • MELBOURNE
MUNICH • DELHI

DK LONDON

Senior Art Editor Ina Stradins
Senior Editor Angeles Gavira
Art Editor Mark Lloyd
Project Editor Ruth O'Rourke
Editors Gill Pitts, Claire Tennant-Scull,
Miezan van Zyl, Rebecca Warren
Production Editor Tony Phipps
Designers Sonia Barbate, Duncan Turner
Editorial Assistant Tamlyn Calitz

Cartographer David Roberts
Picture Researchers Emily Hedges,
David Penrose, Richard Philpott
Illustrators Jane Durston, Sandra Pond

Senior Managing Art Editor Phil Ormerod
Managing Editor Sarah Larter
Art Director Bryn Walls
Reference Publisher Jonathan Metcalf

DK DELHI

Designers Ivy Roy, Neerja Rawat,
Neha Ahuja, Govind Mittal
DTP Pushpak Tyagi, Harish Aggarwal,
Jagtar Singh, Dheeraj Arora
DTP Co-ordinator Balwant Singh
Editors Saloni Talwar, Kingshuk Ghoshal
Editorial Manager Dipali Singh
Design Manager Arunesh Talapatra
Art Director Shefali Upadhyay

CONTRIBUTORS

Habitats Ben Hoare, Ben Morgan,
Steve Parker
Mammals Chris Gibson
Birds Jonathan Elphick,
Rob Hume, John Woodward
Fish Kim Dennis-Bryan
Butterflies & Moths Andrew Mackay,
Chris Pellant, Paul Sterry
Invertebrates George McGavin

Trees Allen Coombes
Wild Flowers Neil Fletcher
Other Plants David Burnie,
Helen Pellant, Joyce Pitt
Fungi Shelley Evans, Geoffrey Kibby
Conservation Richard Beatty,
Neil Fletcher, Tim Halliday, Rob
Houston, Rob Hume, Michelle Payne,
Chris Pellant, Graham Scholey

First published in Great Britain in 2008 by
Dorling Kindersley Limited, 80 Strand, London, WC2R 0RL
Penguin Group (UK)
This edition published in 2011
2 4 6 8 10 9 7 5 3 1
001 – CD238 – Apr/2011
Copyright © 2008, 2011 Dorling Kindersley Limited

A CIP catalogue record for this book is available from the British Library.

ISBN 978 1 4053 6709 7

Reproduced by Colourscan, Singapore
Printed and bound by Hung Hing, China

Keep safe, and remember to follow the Countryside Code, available at
www.countrysideaccess.gov.uk. Culinary, herbal, or medicinal uses of wild plants
mentioned in the book are purely anecdotal. They are not recommendations
of the author or the publisher and should not be undertaken. Many fungi are
poisonous, with effects ranging from stomach upset to organ failure and
death. Collection for consumption is entirely at the reader's own risk.

Discover more at
www.dk.com

CONTENTS

△ **Greylag Geese**
Britain is a focal point for millions of migrating birds, including wild geese, from Arctic Canada, Europe, Asia, and Africa.

FOREWORD

Our rather small, intricate islands have exceptional wildlife riches. The variety of geology and geography, the strong seasonal changes and mild winters, and the human activity that influences Britain's landscape, provide great scope for the inquisitive naturalist to discover an amazing diversity of wildlife within a small area. This book explores the varied habitats of the British Isles and the flora and fauna that inhabits them, giving you all you need to enjoy and understand their marvels, from soaring eagles to minute spiders, bumbling badgers to darting dragonflies, and insectivorous bog plants to ancient forests.

While we do not have high mountains like other parts of Europe, our moderate peaks offer spectacular cliffs and tundra-like plateaux. Lower down, extensive acidic moors and some of the finest watery peatlands in the world can be found, as well as forests with endangered Wildcats and rare Pine Martens, and dry heaths with warmth-loving reptiles. Chalk downlands add specialist wild flowers and butterflies that are not found in other habitats. Britain's wetlands, including reedbeds, swamps, lakes and rivers, and more recently-flooded gravel pits, provide marvellous wildlife-watching opportunities. Coastal marshes and estuaries are fantastic wildlife hotspots on lower-lying coasts, and cliffs and islands come into their own in summer, when millions of seabirds breed.

Britain is a gardening nation, too, and wildlife likes comfortable places close to home – much of it coming in from nearby woods. In short, there is wildlife to be discovered anywhere and everywhere in Britain, from the town centre to the most remote offshore rock. All you need to do is to get out, if you can, to discover it for yourself. It is a fantastically rewarding occupation.

Rob Hume.

THREE CLIFFS West of Swansea in South Wales, the picturesque Gower Peninsula extends into the ever-widening Bristol Channel. At the centre of the peninsula's south coast is more than a kilometre of rippled sands, Oxwich Bay to the west and Three Cliffs to the east. They meet at the estuary of a small river, the Pennard Pill, which has trickled past limestone features, the ruins of Pennard Castle, the sand dunes and salt marshes of Pennard Burrows, and a crossing of stepping stones on its way out into the bay. The Three Cliffs themselves are a row of pointed mounds of sedimentary rock jutting out to the south-west. They are favourites with rock climbers, while at low tide walkers can stroll through the natural arches in the peak bases, as riders gallop their horses along the wide sweeping sands. The bay is also popular with surfers, the waves being best between mid- and high tide, but beware of the strong rip-tides.

DORSET DOWNS The downlands of
Southern England are a restful and
distinctive set of habitats – unique
products of centuries spent grazing
sheep, cattle, and other livestock, and
planting light crops, such as hay grasses
and grains. The hallmark of downland,
as beautifully portrayed by the Dorset
Downs south of Sherborne, is a rolling
landscape of rounded chalky hills
infiltrated by shallow valleys harbouring
clay-based soils. On steeper slopes,
erosion has revealed outcrops of chalk,
while gentler slopes maintain a thin
covering of well-drained soil, which
supports the characteristic springy turf.
Patches of woodland called hangers
dot the slopes and are typically rich in
beech and ash, but also contain Wych
Elm, yew, and lime. Well-managed
Dorset downlands are home to all six
native British reptile species, and a
flora that can exceed 50 plant species
per square metre.

GIANT'S CAUSEWAY Just west of
Ireland's northernmost point, near
Bushmills, the Giant's Causeway has
fascinated people for centuries. This
impressive geological feature, declared a
UNESCO World Heritage Site in 1986, is
named for its legendary builder, Irish
giant Fionn Mac Cumhaill (Finn McCool).
The story goes that Fionn wished to
walk the 25 or so kilometres across the
North Channel of the Irish Sea to
Kintyre, to challenge the Scottish giant
Benandonner. Less romantically, flows
of molten lava erupted millions of years
ago, and as they cooled they contracted,
forming columns. Most of the columns
are six-sided and form stepping stones
that descend below the waves. Several
large weathered column formations
have names such as the Pipe Organ and
Shepherd's Steps. Fulmars, petrels,
redshanks, and other birds frequent the
area, which supports flora such as
Vernal Squill and Hare's-foot Clover.

NORFOLK MEADOW Far from being as flat as some people imagine, the huge "bread basket" fields of Norfolk, East Anglia, are cropped intensively for beet sugar, oilseed rape, peas, beans, and sunflowers, as well as the mainstays of wheat, barley, and other grains. Yet here and there, occasional meadows and pastures survive the incessant annual routine of ploughs, seed drills, and harvesters, as measures are taken to preserve habitats that are rich in wildflower species. In late spring and early summer these fields come alive with brilliant blooms, such as the black-centred, bright red bowls of Common Poppy, a specialist of recently disturbed land, and the yellow-centred, pure white rays of Oxeye Daisy. Open-country birds abound, from Skylarks to Common Buzzards and Red Kites, and even the occasional Marsh Harrier straying from the nearby wetter landscapes of the broads and fens.

BUTTERMERE In the massive rocky dome that comprises Cumbria's Lake District National Park, long, narrow meres (lakes) form a 'wagon-wheel', radiating from a hub just north of Grasmere. The wheel's 10 o'clock 'spoke' is Buttermere (shown here upper left), with its twin of Crummock Water just beyond. Buttermere Fell's slope broods above the north-eastern shore, with the pyramid of Fleetworth Pike in the foreground. The Lake District is home to England's highest hills and deepest waters, with a complex geology spanning 500 million years – igneous rocks such as granite formed from magma, limestone sediments were laid on ancient sea beds, and sandstones accumulated during periods of drought. In the last million years, repeated glaciations carved out smooth-sided valleys. Heathers and bracken cloak the upper slopes, with oak woods and pines lower down, and cattle graze the valley floor.

COTSWOLD WOOD Leaves glow with reds, yellows, and golds in the autumn's weakening sun at Painswick – Queen of the Cotswolds – just north of Stroud, Gloucestershire. The Cotswold Hills stretch north-east from Bath, onwards between Gloucester and Cirencester, as far as Moreton-in-Marsh. This is one of the most picturesque and quintessentially English regions. The stone blocks used in its quaint dwellings and historic buildings reflect the changing colour of the limestone, from honeyed browns in the north to paler creams farther south. As England's largest Area of Outstanding Natural Beauty, almost one-tenth of the Cotswolds is wooded. The woodland occurs mainly along the escarpments – as here in Longridge Wood – and in the valleys. The original forests were rich in beech, along with oak, ash, and elm. Replantings in recent decades mean conifers will now lend green tinges to the forthcoming winter landscape.

RANNOCH MOOR Looking north from Black Mount across the waters of Lochan na h-Achlaise and Loch Bà, the slopes of Rannoch Moor rise to the 739-metre highpoint of Stob na Cruaiche, with the snow-capped Black Corries behind. This is border country between Scotland's Highland and Perth and Kinross regions, south-east of Fort William. Rannoch's mound-like granite plateau is surrounded by higher, steeper, craggier uplands. It was once covered with Scots Pine, which flourishes in well-drained soils, and remnants of that forest still occur around the moor's fringes. Today, heathers paint the late summer purple as the air shimmers with the fragrant yet insect-repelling scent of Bog Myrtle (Sweet Gale). Rannoch is noted for its range of peat-based habitats, such as blanket bogs. As a Site of Special Scientific Interest, it is the only British home of the delicate Rannoch Rush with its yellow-green flowers and seeds.

HABITATS

GEOLOGY OF THE BRITISH ISLES

G reat Britain has a fascinating geology – its wide range of rock types, and their interaction with the climate, shapes local topography, soil formation, the dominant types of vegetation, which in turn influences the kinds of animals that survive.

The oldest and hardest rock formations in the British Isles are in the north and west, mainly comprised of granite and other igneous (once molten) rocks such as basalt. Granite underlies much of the Scottish Highlands, and forms spectacular headlands and cliffs around Scotland and the north of Ireland.

To the south and east of Britain are younger, softer rocks, mainly sedimentary (formed from tiny particles). They grade from Welsh slates in the west to central sandstones, great chalk beds along the south coast, to the loose sands and clays of East Anglia.

A defining event for Britain was the last Ice Age, which started about 30,000 years ago. Ice sheets smoothed the jagged peaks of the uplands and gouged U-shaped valleys across north and central Britain and Ireland. As the ice retreated (about 10,000 years ago), it left much of today's topography, although it was largely bare land, ready to be colonized by wildlife – and people.

❸ Ben Bulben, or "Jaw Peak" near Drumcliff, County Sligo, is Ireland's "Table Mountain". It is a flat-topped feature known as a mesa, some 525 metres high. It was formed from a limestone block that was more resistant to erosion than the surrounding rock, shaped mainly during the last Ice Age. Its dominating presence has inspired numerous folk tales.

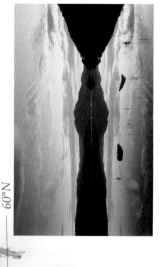

❶ In the Orkney Islands, wind-whipped waves and winter storms continually eat into the sandstone cliffs. The undercut cliff collapses into rubble here and there, leaving features such as arches and stacks (isolated columns), of which the 137-metre Old Man of Hoy (above) is a well-known example.

❷ Granite dominates much of the Scottish Highlands, as here at Loch Achray, north-east of Loch Lomond. British mountains are relatively old in geological terms, and most of their peaks and ridges have long been smoothed by ice. Many Scottish lochs were formed during the ice ages, as narrow valleys were scraped again by glacial gouging.

❹ Limestone country has characteristic formations. Rain containing minute amounts of natural carbonic acid, which often becomes more acidic as it passes through soil, reacts to dissolve the rock. Streams eat away potholes and underground caverns. Trickling rainwater erodes joints and cracks, forming limestone pavement, as seen here at Malham Lings, in the Yorkshire Dales north of Skipton.

SCALE 1:5 000 000

0 km   50   100   150

Unst
Yell
Shetland Islands
Mainland
60°N

Stronsay
Sanday
Westray   Mainland
Orkney Islands
Hoy ❶
4°W

58°N

2°W

The Minch
Isle of Lewis
Harris   The Little Minch
North Uist
South Uist
Isle of Skye
Rhum
Coll
Sea of the Hebrides
Inner Hebrides
Tiree
Colonsay
Islay
Isle of Mull
Loch Awe
Isle of Arran
Kintyre
Loch Tay
Clyde
Loch Lomond ❷
North West Highlands
Grampian Mountains
Sidlaw Hills
Cairngorm Mountains
Dee
Tay
Loch Ness
Ochil Hills
Pentland Hills
Southern Uplands
Tweed
Cheviot
Holy Island
56°N

Outer Hebrides
8°W
6°W
58°N

OCEAN
ATLANTIC

7 England's south coast displays a series of towering chalk cliffs, mostly formed during the Cretaceous Period (145–65 million years ago, *creta* being Latin for chalk). At the eastern end of the South Downs, Beachy Head, at 162 metres is Britain's tallest chalk cliff, but exposure to the elements is constantly eroding the rockface.

6 Much of Dartmoor National Park in Devon is underlain by granite. The copious rainfall does not drain easily through the granite, which also resists erosion. This gives rise to typical moorland scenery, with acidic, boggy soils dotted with rocky outcrops known as tors.

5 Glyder Fawr, at 643 metres, is the highest peak in the Glyderau range of Snowdonia National Park, Wales. From the summit there are stunning views of distorted, eroded slates, and other exposed, layered rocks, including this, the spiky Castell y Gwynt (Castle of the Wind).

Map labels

NORTH SEA

The Broads
Yare
East Anglia
Isle of Sheppey
Strait of Dover
Isle of Wight
New Forest
The Weald
North Downs
South Downs
Thames
Great Ouse
Nene
Chiltern Hills
Kennet
Salisbury Plain
Avon
The Fens
Rutland Water
The Wolds
Trent
Don
Derwent
Peak District
Wharfe
Ouse
Swale
Ribble
Derwent
North York Moors
Tees
Wear
Ullswater
Cumbrian Mtns
Lake Windermere District
Yorkshire Dales
Pennines
Britain
Cotswold Hills
Severn
Malvern Hills
Black Mtns
Brecon Beacons
Wye
Cambrian Mountains
Gower
Mendip Hills
Quantock Hills
Avon
Bristol Channel
Exe
Exmoor
Dartmoor
Bodmin Moor
Lundy
Isles of Scilly
Mersey
Snowdonia
Anglesey
Holy Island
Isle of Man
Irish Sea
Celtic Sea
St George's Channel
Strangford Lough
Lough Neagh
Mourne Mtns
Sperrin Mtns
Stack
Lower Lough Erne
Upper Lough Erne
Dartry Mtns
Iron Mtns
Slieve Gamph
Ireland
Shannon
Lough Corrib
Burren
Slieve Aughty Mtns
Lough Derg
Slieve Bloom Mtns
Lough Ree
Wicklow Mountains
Liffey
Barrow
Nore
Suir
Galty Mtns
Blackwater
Partry Mtns
Connemara
Caha Mountains

ATLANTIC

MAP KEY

Sedimentary rocks
- unconsolidated sand and shell banks
- clay
- chalk
- oolitic limestone
- massive limestone
- friable sandstone
- hard sandstone
- greywacke and slate
- mixed hard sediments
- coal measures

Igneous rocks
- extrusive (volcanic), such as lava and basalt
- intrusive, such as granite

Metamorphic rocks
- gneiss, schist, and quartzite

Exposed to hot sun, gales, lashing rain, and salty sea spray, cliffs are among Britain's **harshest** habitats. Yet **specialized** animals and plants eke out an existence.

SEA KALE

CLIFFS

Coastal cliffs form where rocky land faces the sea. The incessant pounding waves cut ever-changing profiles of different shapes and steepness, depending not only on the rock's hardness and integral strength, but also on a complex interaction of the prevailing winds – which affect the force of the breaking waves – along with the tidal range, direction of currents, and exposure to sun. Hard rocks, such as granite, are resistant to erosion and form looming, forbidding, often sheer masses with few cracks and ledges. Softer limestones and shales erode more easily, are undercut faster by waves, and may collapse to give a low, sloping, jumbled profile. Chalks can also form tumbledown mounds, although in some areas – such as the white cliffs along the English Channel – continual small-scale undercutting and disintegration by waves leave high, almost vertical faces.

Plant cover, too, is shaped by degree of exposure to tides, wind, sun, rain, spray, altitude above sea level, and rock type. Limestones usually have a wider array of species than acidic rocks such as granite. Hardy plants such as Stonecrop, Rock Samphire, and Buckshorn Plantain find rootholds in tiny cracks and crevices, especially if seabirds nest and leave their guano (dung) as fertilizer. Nearer the cliff top, as the land flattens out, floral diversity increases with Spring Squill, Hoary Stock, Thrift (Sea Pink), and various springy, tufted grasses. Only birds, bats, occasionally lizards, and buzzing insects, such as bees and wasps, reach the precipitous slopes, so cliff plants are relatively free of herbivore interference.

safety

CLIFFS ARE EXCELLENT FOR OBSERVING NESTING AND FISHING BIRDS, AND SEA-GOING MAMMALS SUCH AS SEALS, BUT THEY ARE ALSO AMONG THE MOST HAZARDOUS HABITATS.

Rocks and soils can be slippery when damp or coated with algal growth. They can also suddenly crumble.

The burrows of clifftop-nesting birds such as puffins, and mammals such as rabbits, can be a trip hazard or unexpectedly give way when trodden on.

Strong winds can dehydrate you and also mask the pain of developing sunburn.

A sudden gust of wind can easily unbalance you, or at least whisk away a field guide, notebook, or map.

A safe position is lying down, once you have found a secure spot with a good view.

Be careful not to inch forwards to get a better view, do this several times, and you might find yourself unwittingly approaching too close to the edge.

SPRING

▷ **Sand Martin**
At their traditional cliff nest sites of consolidated sand-banks and soft sandstones, Sand Martins arrive from Africa in spring and use their claws to renovate last year's burrows.
See page 143.

▷ **Roseroot**
As spring fades into summer, cushions of Roseroot push up yellow flowers from among their fleshy leaves, which have adapted to hold moisture against sun and wind. *See page 365.*

The limestone cliffs of Pembrokeshire, South Wales, reveal the first pale shoots of early-flowering plants, patchworked with the light green coatings of hardy lichens. The prevailing south-westerly winds whipping in from the Atlantic Ocean raise up breakers that have eroded long expanses of limestone cliff into fascinating shapes such as arches, stacks, and caves, providing myriad micro-habitats for varied plant growth.

◁ Rock Pipit
Rock Pipits avoid the most exposed cliff faces as they glean insects from vegetation, and also swoop down to peck along the shoreline for gnats and sandhoppers. See page 144.

◁ Kittiwake
Kittiwakes make their bowl-shaped nests of seaweed, moss, and other plant matter, glued together with droppings, on projecting ledges. See page 137.

SUMMER

△ Common Guillemot
Guillemots have the densest breeding colonies of almost any similar-size bird, jostling on crowded, guano-stained ledges as the single egg of each pair hatches into a hungry chick. See page 139.

▽ Sand Digger Wasp
Loose clifftop soils are ideal for Sand Digger Wasps. Each wasp digs a burrow, stocked with stung flies to feed larva. See page 285.

In early summer the cliff ledges and crests burst into colour as flower petals unfurl. At the sheltered headland of Wembury Bay, on the mouth of the River Yealm near Plymouth, the cliffs are covered in Thrift (Sea Pink, above), Sea Rush, and Red Fescue. Birds and butterflies flit among the blooms, gathering nectar and spreading pollen.

AUTUMN

▷ Shag
Shags perch on natural rock ledges as they dry out their wings; their close cousins, the Cormorants, often utilize man-made objects, such as marker buoys. See page 117.

△ Raven
The world's largest perching bird, the Raven swoops and soars along the coast on the lookout for carrion, including dead fish on the shoreline. See page 158.

As flowers wither, along the chalk clifftops of East Sussex's Seven Sisters Heritage Coast, floral colours fade to pale greens, yellows, and browns. Noisy breeding birds have dispersed, leaving an empty clifftop silence, apart from the ever present wind, and the waves echoing below. Insects find nooks for overwintering as autumn storms blow in.

WINTER

△ Puffin
The colourful breeding bill of the puffin fades for winter as these birds head out to sea, or occasionally get driven onto freshwater habitats inland. See page 139.

▷ Peregrine Falcon
Even skilled fliers such as the Peregrine Falcon struggle in winter gales. Many take refuge on coastal marshes. See page 126.

The season of storms throws raging elements at the towering granite cliffs near Aberdeen, Scotland. The narrow clifftop zones of peatland and heath die back and many birds have moved along the coast to low mudflats and saltmarshes, or inland to lakes and woods. Cliff collapses alter the shoreline and expose new surfaces for colonization in spring.

▽ **Springtail**
Simple types of wingless insects, springtails are tiny enough to hide in the smallest cracks and emerge to search for any edible particles. *See page 234.*

▽ **Rock Samphire**
Preparing to bloom by late spring, Rock Samphire grows on arid rocks, sand, and shingle banks and stores water in its fleshy leaves. *See page 388.*

▽ **Common Sea Urchin**
Globular relatives of starfish, urchins glide across rocks on their long, thin, flexible tube feet, as they graze on tiny plants and animals. *See page 309.*

Wave-cut concave curves form where storm-hurled boulders smash against the low granite cliff near The Brisons, a group of offshore rocks about 1.5 kilometres from Cape Cornwall near St Just, Cornwall. The winter's Atlantic breakers have rolled the rocky lumps against the land, eroding everything into smoothly rounded shapes. On an exposed coast such as this, even strong-cased shellfish are in danger of being smashed open. Few shore animals can survive unless they retreat with the tide.

▷ **Black-headed Gull**
These gulls consume almost anything, including rotting flesh and refuse thrown up along the high tide mark. *See page 135.*

△ **Sandhopper**
Flattened from side to side, this mini-crustacean lives among seaweed, eats almost anything and jumps like a flea when disturbed. *See page 304.*

Rockpools are harsh environments, as the sun warms, evaporates, and concentrates the salty water, then a sudden shower cools and dilutes the conditions. Starfish are slow but powerful predators able to pull apart the two valves (shell halves) of bivalves such as mussels. The razorshell on the left has been stranded by the tide.

△ **Beadlet Anemone**
The most common British anemone, beadlets vary in colour from red, orange, yellow, and brown, to green. *See page 308.*

△ **Kelp**
Kelp seaweeds such as these at Whitby, Yorkshire, have broad, tough fronds that absorb wave energy and provide calm shelter for many animals. *See page 440.*

As days shorten, and seas roughen, Grey Seals haul themselves onto the rocks for a rest, and the bulls (adult males) begin ritualized contests to establish their breeding territories. Britain hosts both the larger "roman-nosed" Grey Seals, and Common Seals, with almost half of the world population of the former.

Physical and chemical conditions can alter dramatically in minutes on rocky shores, with the changing of the tidal flow.

HERMIT CRAB

ROCKY BEACHES

Plants and animals of rocky shores must cope with battering waves slamming down tonnes of water, rocks being flung and splintered by the breakers, periods of hot summer sun that threaten dehydration, freezing winds in winter, downpours of fresh water that contrast enormously with the sea's salty immersion, and the relentless tidal ebb and flow. Yet many species have adapted and even thrive here, despite these legion hazards. Molluscs range from limpets and whelks to cuttlefish and octopus; crustaceans, from small shrimps to crabs and heavy-clawed lobsters; starfish and other echinoderms, as well as simpler creatures like sponges, worms and anemones.

Among the survival strategies deployed, animals may try to remain either in one place or maintain constant mobility. Mussels anchor by using silky filaments, limpets have enormous sucker power, and barnacles – crustacean cousins of crabs – cement themselves to bare patches of rock as young larvae, then develop hard protective plates, resembling miniature volcanoes. Anemones withdraw their tentacles as the tide recedes, but some can also shuffle along on their stalk bases to find more favourable sites. Starfish are also slow sliders, taking shelter under overhangs or in crevices when the waves get too rough. Much more mobile are crabs, shrimps, prawns, tough-skinned fish such as gobies and Butterfish, which slip between the stones or splash from one rockpool to another, and of course the gulls, Oystercatchers, and other birds that search for food along the shore.

key sites

WONDERFUL STRETCHES OF ROCKY AND BOULDER-STREWN SHORES EDGE BRITAIN, ESPECIALLY IN THE WEST AND SOUTH, WHERE PREVAILING WINDS AND THE ATLANTIC BREAKERS CRACK THE COAST.

The Menai Straits, a narrow channel of the Irish Sea between the Welsh mainland and the Isle of Anglesey, have unusual tidal conditions, with shelter from the large waves, and strong currents that come from two directions. The distinct zoning of sponges and seaweeds offshore reflects this strange configuration.

Sandness Coast on the west of mainland Shetland has wide lichen zones, species-rich rockpools, and dense seaweed beds.

Lyme Regis and Charmouth to Seatown, on the Dorset coast, are a mix of tall cliffs and tumbling boulders that yield dinosaur, and other fossils, on this famous Jurassic Coast.

Robin Hood's Bay, south of Whitby, North Yorkshire, on the North York Moors Heritage Coast, provides a marvellous variety of habitats, from low shelving beaches, through stony piles, to steeper cliffs.

WINTER

On the east coast on the Isle of Arran, Blackwaterfoot overlooks Drumadoon Bay and the Kilbrannan Sound, with prospects westwards to Campbeltown and the Mull of Kintyre. Loose boulders roll around in the large wintry waves, so shore feeders such as gulls, foxes, and otters give the shore a wide berth in rough weather.

△ **Otter**
A European Otter on a rock, eats its crab prey. Scotland's west coasts are the otter's UK stronghold, due to the relative abundance of food and mainly undisturbed coastlines. *See pages 92–94.*

▷ **Ringed Plover**
After a summer nesting on shingle beaches, plovers fly to varied shores for the winter. *See page 128.*

COASTAL | HABITATS

Wide-open sands may seem a great place for humans to spend a day at the **seaside,** but plants and animals require a range of **specialized** adaptations to survive there.

COMMON STARFISH

SANDY BEACHES

S andy beaches, bays and coves form where waves, tides, and currents have previously slowed enough to drop boulders and pebbles, and then linger to deposit the sand grains they carry, but are not so sluggish that they cannot still remove smaller particles of mud and silt. This natural size-sorting, or grading, leads to a constantly shifting habitat where hardly any plants can gain a hold among the rolling grains. Animal foods must be imported, most basically in the form of tiny plants and creatures delivered by sea water. These nourish the burrowing filter-feeders that hide below the surface at low tide and extend various body parts into the current as the waters rise. A stroll along the sand reveals marks and tracks that betray the presence of the animals beneath, especially the squiggly casts of lugworms and small conical depressions formed by razorshells.

As on mudflats and estuaries, beach sand-dwellers face plenty of dangers. At low tide, birds flock to the exposed flats to prod and probe, while fish, crabs, cuttlefish, and other aquatic creatures ride the rising tide, to search for prey. There is nowhere to hide but under the surface. At the high tide mark, the strandline carries its fragments of rotting seaweed, decomposing animal corpses, shells, driftwood, and other natural debris left by the waves, plus of course human refuse such as scraps of plastic. This line attracts its share of hunters and scavengers too, from foxes and otters to birds and even lizards.

The Gower Peninsula in South Wales is famed for its picturesque coastlines. At the western end is Rhossil Bay, seen here looking north from Worms Head Foreland, with Rhossil Down to the right. As the tide retreats, it leaves wet sand that slowly drains and dries in the spring sun. As the sand temperature gradually rises, it rouses invertebrates such as shellfish and worms, which have been largely dormant through the colder months.

key sites

BRITAIN HAS HUNDREDS OF KILOMETRES OF EXTENSIVE SANDS. SOME ARE DEVELOPED FOR LEISURE AND TOURISM, BUT MANY AREAS ARE QUIET, AND THRONG WITH BIRDS AND OTHER WILDLIFE, ESPECIALLY OUT OF THE MAIN HOLIDAY SEASON.

Newborough, Anglesey, sees spectacular sweeps of sand merge into an internationally recognized important dune system, the largest in Wales, with managed conifer forests and other habitats. Part of the area carries SSSI (Special Site of Scientific Interest) status.

Lincolnshire's Coastline has more than 60 kilometres of almost uninterrupted sandy beaches and flats stretching between Cleethorpes and Skegness.

At Saunton Sands and Braunton Burrows, North Devon a vast five-kilometre beach is backed by the massive Burrows, Britain's largest dune system.

Dornoch Firth, Highland Dornoch, and Whiteness Sands and their dune areas complement the area's estuarine habitats with their diverse animal and plant life.

SPRING

▷ **Sea-Buckthorn**
A seaside shrub, this bare ground colonizer stabilizes higher shores of sand and shingle. It produces small green spring blossoms and in September, orange berries, relished by migratory birds.
See page 320.

▷ **Pod Razorshell**
Named for its similarity in appearance to the old-fashioned "cut-throat" razor, this bivalve mollusc is one of the fastest burrowers on any shoreline.
See page 308.

SUMMER

△ **Bog Pimpernel**
A lover of damp dune dips, its summer flowers open in sunshine but close when clouds block the sun's rays.

▽ **Creeping Willow**
This low-growing shrub tolerates the dryness and salt spray of costal dunes.

June and July are peak pupping (birthing) times for Common Seals, which gather on suitable coastal flats. Often they "strand" themselves by allowing the high tide to leave them on the upper beach, where they can rest and sunbathe, unless disturbed – when they quickly wriggle or hump down to the water's edge for a fast getaway.

AUTUMN

△ **Lugworm sand casts**
The worm's coiled casts are sand that has been eaten, digested for any form of nourishment, and excreted to the surface in the manner of earthworm soil casts on garden lawns. See page 309.

▷ **Rabbit**
The dry sandy soil of dunes is ideal for digging warrens, while the landward rough vegetation provides plenty of food. See page 86.

Newborough Warren is a beach-fringed patchwork of dunes, mudflats, salt marshes and other coastal habitats at the southern tip of the Isle of Anglesey, North Wales. As autumn takes hold, the pioneer plant stablizer of dune systems, Marram Grass, has stems and blades that fade from green and grey to yellow and brown.

WINTER

△ **Dab**
The smallest British flatfish, rarely exceeding 500 grams, the Dab is superbly camouflaged when lying on the sandy sea bed.

▷ **Seaweed**
Different species of wracks and other green algae are often torn from their intertidal rocks by waves and washed up on the sand. See page 442.

As winds and storms increase, birds such as Herring Gulls (above) may forsake the coast and fly inland for easier pickings on farm fields and rubbish tips. Other birds, including various waders, move from their wetland breeding areas – which freeze over in winter – to the shore, where there is a year-round supply of food under the sand.

◁ **Common Lizard**
Although well adapted to a variety of habitats, sand dunes are a favoured territory of this small reptile, shown here regenerating its tail as it basks in the spring sunshine. See page 167.

◁ **Oystercatcher**
Wintering flocks of this wader, with its distinctive chisel-like orange bill, break up in spring as the birds begin their courtship and mating. See page 127.

Flocks of Brent Geese and other wildfowl swoop across the autumn skies of the Thames Estuary. These are the dark-bellied variety, arriving from Arctic Russia for the winter. Coastal flats and estuaries have a complex interchange of birds with the seasons, as some flocks leave while others arrive, and still others rest briefly and perhaps feed, as passage migrants.

P 266

AUTUMN

◁ **Sea Bass**
This powerful predator hunts small fish and crustaceans when young, then moves onto larger prey such as pilchards and herring.
See page 182.

◁ **Baltic Tellin**
An estuary specialist, this bivalve extends two long tubes, siphons, to the surface as inlet and outlet for filter-feeding.
See page 308.

▷ **Osprey**
Also commonly known as the Fish Hawk, Ospreys, when seen around English coasts, are usually passing through on their migration paths.
See page 119.

▷ **Grey Mullet**
Tolerant of pollution, mullet feed in an unusual way by swallowing mud and then digesting any nutritious particles it may contain.
See page 179.

SPRING

△ **Algae**
Green algae find the shifting mud a difficult home, but can form temporary colonies in depressions or on embedded stones. See page 443.

Norfolk's lengthy coastline has dozens of expansive miles of sand, silt, and mud which are home to numerous waders. The largest UK resident species is the Curlew (see page 133). As spring proceeds these birds will leave the flats where they have fed during the winter, and head inland to breed on moors and marshes.

▽ **Bar-tailed Godwit**
The Godwit moults its greyish winter plumage for a summer finery of browns and russets. See page 131.

SUMMER

▷ **Sea Aster**
These asters thrive on the salt marshes found at the upper reaches of estuaries, as well as on coastal cliffs. See page 413.

▽ **Freshwater Shrimp**
Shrimps pick their way delicately over the sea bed, grasping food with the pincer-ended front two pairs of legs. See page 304.

The strong sun warms the shallows of the Axe estuary as it joins the Bristol Channel near Clevedon, Somerset. The raised temperatures of sea and sediment mean this is a frantic breeding time for invertebrate mud dwellers. Many simply cast their eggs freely into the water. This in turn attracts predatory fish and birds.

COCKLE SHELL

MUDFLATS AND ESTUARIES

F ew habitats may look as unpromising as the coastal features known as mudflats, which can include sandbanks and shingle spits – strips of shingle that grow out from the coast where the coastline abruptly changes direction. Such features are often found where a slow-moving river widens into its estuary and meets the sea. As the water currents slow, they deposit their load of fine sediments, from sand grains to mud and silt. Tidal mudflats are covered and uncovered by the tide twice a day and algae and eelgrass are among the few plants that can withstand such conditions. Yet these seemingly barren, flat, glistening stretches also harbour a wealth of wildlife. Alongside millions of microscopic creatures, larger lifeforms include burrowing molluscs of many kinds, from bivalves such as clams, cockles, and tellins, to curly-shelled spireshells, towershells, and necklace-shells. There are plenty of crustaceans, too, in the form of burrowing shrimps, prawns, and crabs, as well as various types of sea urchins, and worms such as ragworms and lugworms settled into the mud.

These innumerable invertebrates feed on the tiny fragments of nutrients and detritus in the sediments, or filter the sea water as the tide comes in for floating edible particles, or simply prey on each other. In turn, they become the prey of major groups of vertebrates. As the tide retreats, waders, wildfowl, gulls, and other birds throng the flats, probing and pecking below the surface. As the tide rises, a wide variety of hungry fish follow the waterline and begin their search of the sea bed. They include a range of blennies, gobies, sand-Eels, flatfish such as plaice and Flounder, mullet, whiting, and the voracious Sea Bass.

WINTER

▷ **Dunlin**
The most numerous wintering waders on British estuaries, Dunlin probe with speedy "rat-a-tat" prods into the mud. See page 130.

▽ **Redshank**
Nicknamed the "sentinel", the Redshank is often first to spot danger and let out its piping alert call. See page 345.

Freiston Shore, Lincolnshire, is on the Wash – Britain's most important site for wintering birds. This vast mosaic of coastal and marine wetland habitats supports more than a million waders, wildfowl, and other birds during the coldest months. Winter visitors include Brent Geese, and flocks of Twite (a type of finch) on the salt marshes.

Apparently empty tidal flats conceal a wealth of wildlife just below the surface – as waders and fish well know.

watching

ESTUARIES AND FLATS ARE IDEAL PLACES TO APPRECIATE THE SPECTACULAR SWIRLING FLOCKS OF BIRDS FROM AFAR, AND OBSERVE THEIR INTRICATE FEEDING METHODS AT CLOSER RANGE.

Many coastal areas have suitably constructed and camouflaged hides set against a backdrop of sand dunes, rocky shores, or low cliffs.

Take up a position against a background where you are less likely to be noticed by animals looking landward from the sea.

Check the orientation of the coast (North, South, East, or West) when the sun is in a favourable position. For example, on an east-facing coast, the sun shines from the west at evening time. This illuminates the scene from over the shoulder to best effect, rather than glaring into the eyes and throwing the scene and its inhabitants into deep shadows.

Look out for any warning signs and check guides that are specific to the area you are visiting. See also the safety notes on how to avoid the dangers of soft mud and incoming tides on page 34.

COASTAL | HABITATS

FLOWERING
RUSHES

Part shifting sediment, and part **brackish,** or slightly salty water, salt marsh is a **continuously changing** mosaic of hummocks, muddy channels, and meadowlike stretches.

SALT MARSHES

S alt marshes tend to form in sheltered coastal areas. Seaward, they are usually protected from the force of bigger waves by natural barriers such as sand dunes or a shingle spit. Landward, there is generally a river bringing its load of nutrient-bearing sediments from the woods and fields beyond. The river may split into several deep channels that scour their walls. But twice daily the rising tide flows the opposite way, and brings salty water that floods the area, trickling in along a complex system of small creeks that continually redistribute the mud and silt. The sediments provide plenty of nourishment for plant growth, but other conditions make the salt marsh a difficult habitat. Vegetation needs to cope with both fresh and salty water, especially as the sun warms and evaporates some of the water from pools, leaving a much higher salt concentration. Plants also need to spread plentiful roots into the shifting mud, and their leaves and stems must resist clogging by shrugging off the sediment particles.

Despite these difficulties, salt marshes support a wide range of wildlife. Perennial shrubs such as Sea Purslane grow deep roots down to the more stable lower layers of sediment, where the salt concentrations are less varied. Prostrate Glasswort relies on its fleshy leaves to store reserves of water that counteract the salt's dehydrating effect. Vegetation zones develop according to the length of time the plants are immersed by the tide, from Sea Asters on the hummocks, to Sea Purslane along the channels, and Thrift and Red Fescue at higher levels.

watching

SALT MARSHES ARE EXCELLENT PLACES TO SEE FLOWERS AND WHEELING FLOCKS OF BIRDS, AND TO STUDY THE PLANT COLONIZATION OF SEDIMENTS. BUT IN COMMON WITH OTHER "SOFT" COASTAL HABITATS, LIKE MUD AND SAND, THERE ARE SERIOUS HAZARDS.

Make sure you keep to the firm ground around the edge of the marsh.

Carefully observe the way that the tide flows in, check tide tables, and make a proper note of the high and low tide times.

Look up and around regularly to survey the scene, check the weather, and make sure you know an accessible route back.

Usually patches of marsh with plenty of vegetation are firmest for walking. Avoid indiscriminate trampling of plants, especially less common species.

Getting stuck in the mud is a real risk, and potentially fatal. Do not venture any further if the ground becomes soft. Avoid jumping, as a heavy landing can force footwear deep into the mud.

Seemingly too late in the year, at last the salt marsh comes alive with yellows, blues, purples, and pinks – here at Afon Glaslyn River and Glaslyn Marshes, a Site of Special Scientific Interest (SSSI). The late blooming of the vegetation is partly due to the lower tidal range during this season, which means the flowering plants are less at risk of being flooded and ruined, yet there are still enough active insects necessary for pollination.

SPRING

△ **Shore Fly**
As temperatures rise in late spring, clouds of dark-bodied, red-eyed Shore Flies swarm over the marsh plants as they hunt tiny gnats and midges. *See page 277.*

△ **Glasswort**
Also called Marsh Samphire, each of the plant's fleshy sections is two leaves fused to a central woody stem. *See page 346.*

Many salt marsh plants do not flower until late summer or early autumn, so spring sees mainly renewed growth of the marsh's greenery. This attracts birds such as the Meadow Pipit, which breeds in all kinds of open habitats and may make its nest along the channel edges at the higher reaches of the salt marsh.

▽ **Skylark**
The Skylark's insistent, clear, warbling song is characteristic of open habitats. Small parties often move from inland towards the coast. *See page 143.*

▷ **Marsh Mallow**
Growing up to 1.5 metres in height, Marsh Mallow can tolerate brackish (part-salty) conditions, and may still be in flower in October. *See page 379.*

◁ **Wasp Spider**
The powerful *Agriope bruennichi*, or Wasp Spider, with its yellow and black abdominal markings, spins a large, strong orb web between the taller stems of vegetation. *See page 293.*

▽ **Common Shore Crab**
One of the hardiest shore creatures, this crab is found high up the saltmarsh and even in freshwater pools and streams. *See page 304.*

SUMMER

△ **Common Sea-lavender**
Sea-lavender, or *Latifolia,* flowers towards late summer, bearing clusters of lilac–blue flowers on its many branches. *See page 393.*

▽ **Common Tern**
Not Britain's most common tern, but the most widespread, these birds "dive-bomb" humans who intrude on their early summer nesting areas. *See page 137.*

While other habitats are bright with colourful blooms in early summer, most salt marshes remain stubbornly green. Teifi Marsh near Cardigan is one of Wales' finest wetlands, where the River Piliau wanders through a deep cut in the valley floor. The reserve boasts some impressive exotic imports – resident water buffalo.

WINTER

△ **Greylag Goose**
Greylags are the ancestors of domestic geese, and have been reintroduced to southern areas of Britain from their strongholds farther north. *See page 105.*

▽ **Pintail**
Mainly a winter visitor, Pintails join other wildfowl on coastal marshes as the inland waters freeze over. Pairing takes place during this time. *See page 108.*

Frost and snow covers the died-back annuals and hardy perennials of the salt marsh at Jenny Brown's Point, near Silverdale on the Cumbria–Lancashire border. The moderating effect on temperatures of the sea air, and the seawater itself, means that winter freezes rarely last long on coastal marshes.

key sites

BRITAIN HAS AN EXCELLENT VARIETY OF WATERWAYS, FROM RUSHING RAPIDS IN THE NORTH, TO SLUGGISH, SHALLOW RIVERS FARTHER SOUTH.

Hampshire's River Test is a 65-kilometre chalk watercourse with an international reputation for trout fishing. It rises in downlands near Basingstoke and meets the sea at Southampton Water.

At 350 kilometres long, and with a fall of 600 metres, the Severn is Britain's longest river and has the most copious flow. It shows the full range of watercourse habitats from the Cambrian Mountains of Wales to its huge estuary into the Bristol Channel.

The River Spey, Scotland's second longest river, flows from the loch of the same name near Fort Augustus, for 100 kilometres through the large deep valley of Strathspey, north-east to the coast between Lossiemouth and Buckie. It is famed for its tortured course and the fast flow that actually increases as it nears the sea. As one of the most unpolluted rivers in Britain it also has huge numbers of salmon and trout.

A river is not just one habitat but many, from a young **bubbling stream** to a slow, wide **meander** along its course, from the source to the sea.

MALLARD
DUCK FEATHER

RIVERS AND CANALS

Each waterway has its unique twists and turns, slopes, and meanders. These are goverened by local climate, especially rainfall, and the type of bedrock and topography. In general, however, most large rivers define a series of habitats, as they make their way downhill. At the source, whether rain- or spring-fed, the waters tend to run fast, cold, and clear, as brooks, streams, and burns rushing down steep slopes. The speedy current scours the bottom of smaller particles, so the stream bed is comprised of pebbles or shingle. Few plants can gain a roothold here, and animal life is likewise dominated by the fast current. Stonefly nymphs, squat in shape with powerful, low-slung legs, are one of the few small creatures that can hang on. The Dipper submerges itself completely to walk upstream, its angled body and uptilted tail keeping it pressed down in the current.

As streams merge and the slope eases, the river enters a more mature phase of its development. The current slows and drops sediments, mainly large particles such as small gravels and sand. More fish, crustaceans, and shellfish appear. At bends, the flow is faster around the outside, so the bank here has less marginal vegetation and tends to erode more quickly. The slower inside bend receives sediment deposits which nourish reeds, rushes, and other bankside plants, whose roots in turn stabilize the sediments. In this way, river bends slowly grow more acute. Eventually the water may break through where the land dips to start a new route, especially when helped by floods.

△ **Dipper**
Short-tailed, with head bobbing, the Dipper plunges into fast streams to pick up worms, tadpoles, insect larvae, and other small creatures. *See page 148.*

▽ **Weeping Willow**
Spring sees willow catkins dangle from twigs as the long, slim, slightly serrated leaves unfurl. *See page 337.*

SPRING

As river life awakens after its winter slumber, birds take the opportunity to consume the first flush of food and form breeding pairs. Young cygnets obediently follow their mother, the pen, on their first forays from the nest. The cob, or male, accompanies them and is ready to repel any threats with a fierce forward surge.

△ **White Water-lily**
The lily's stems may extend more than three metres down to the roots. The flowers open only for the middle part of the day, then close and sink slightly around dusk. *See page 351.*

△ **Finger-net Caddisfly**
The nymph (larva) makes a net-textured, finger-shaped silk tube as a body covering that also filters tiny food particles from the water. *See page 380.*

△ **Common Skimmer**
Known as the Four-spotted Skimmer, this dragonfly has a typically darting flight, with periods of hovering interspersed by low skims and fast dashes after small insect prey. *See page 237.*

SUMMER

△ **Water Rail**
One of the most secretive riverside birds, the Water Rail has long toes to spread its weight on floating leaves, and a slim body to slip between reedy thickets. *See page 127.*

As the waters warm, the river level falls, and currents slow, hosts of aquatic insect larvae change into adults and emerge as flying adults. Mayflies swarm over the surface on warm evenings, as damselflies, dragonflies, and caddisflies make breeding flights. Trout prefer clean, cool, well-oxygenated water running over a gravelly bed, as they feed voraciously on the aquatic larvae and make spectacular leaps for the adult insects.

△ **Kingfisher**
Unmistakable, in its plumage of glittering blue-green upper parts and chestnut-orange underside, the Kingfisher is nevertheless hard to spot as it quickly flashes past to its secretive perch. *See page 142.*

The mature river flows slower as the land flattens towards the coast, forming wide meanders with a variety of vegetation along the gently shelving banks. Smaller particles of sediment such as mud accumulate. Occasionally the waters are swollen by winter rain, or spring snowmelts from the upland source, and they spill onto the surrounding land spreading sediments across the floodplain. Wildlife increases in number and variety. Rushes, reeds, sedges, and water-loving trees such as willow and alder thrive. Emergent vegetation such as water lilies, Water-milfoil, and Water-starwort line the shallows. Longer food chains build up as crustaceans and smaller fish such as Minnows, Gudgeon, and young Roach feed on the multitude of worms, snails, and insect larvae, and in turn become prey for Chub, Perch, Pike, and Barbel. Tench and carp grub for food along the bottom, while River Mussels and other molluscs filter tiny edible particles from the flow. Bird life includes Kingfishers, grebes, and a great variety of wildfowl, from Common Mallards to stately swans.

As the river comes of age, its slowing current drops the finest sediments of silt. There is less turbulence and the banks may become choked with fringing vegetation. A typical fish here is the Bream, sucking up small food items from the mud using its protrusible tube-like mouth. As the river nears the sea, it begins to feel the influence of tides and salt water, and it widens into a series of different habitats – the salt marshes, mudflats, and sandbanks of the estuary.

▷ **Pied Wagtail**
Also called the Water Wagtail, this bird is well named, as it bobs and flicks its tail while searching for insects or similar small prey. *See page 145.*

▽ **Sallow Kitten Moth**
A second generation of Sallow Kittens flies in late summer and early autumn, having eaten leaves of Sallow (willow), aspens, and poplars. *See page 216.*

▽ **Water-cress**
A member of the cabbage family, Water-cress likes clean water and plenty of sunlight, and may flower into the middle of autumn. *See page 360.*

▽ **Chinese Water Deer**
Found mainly around the Broads and Fens of eastern England, the male has no antlers, but has long, tusk-like teeth. *See page 97.*

▽ **Black Poplar**
Up to 30 metres tall, a specimen Black Poplar has a large, full crown with a domed top, and flourishes alongside watercourses. *See page 336.*

▽ **Water Shrew**
This shrew hunts underwater for fish, worms, snails, and water grubs, and forages on land for spiders and insects. *See page 79.*

In mixed oak woodland alongside the River Wye, near Rhayader in Mid Wales, the leaves begin to turn colour and fall, and are carried away by the current. Autumn rains begin to swell the flow that rises up the banks after the summer lull. Fruits and seeds also drop into the water, where they are seized upon by wildfowl, or are deposited along the banks to be found by herbivores such as Water Voles and deer.

The Cuillin Hills of Scotland's Isle of Skye, form a backdrop to a torrent of water flowing over almost bare rocks. Winter downpours have dramatically swollen the river, and swept away all the smaller boulders. Many fish have retreated downstream to the calmer reaches, while insect larvae hide under rocks and stones. There is no risk of ice, as even slow-moving rivers rarely freeze in winter.

△ Pike
The predatory Pike is an opportunist feeder that lurks in reeds and weeds, waiting to attack any passing victim. *See page 178.*

▽ Wigeon
Wigeon numbers are boosted by autumn arrivals from continental Europe. *See page 106.*

▽ Red-eared Terrapin
Now common in some areas, this non-native species prepares to spend winter in a torpor on the lake bed. *See page 168.*

▽ Wild Angelica
As its late summer flowers fade, smooth-stemmed angelica produces its dry, flattened, winged fruits for wind dispersal. *See page 387.*

AUTUMN

Yellows and browns replace greens around Grasmere, in the Rothay Valley near the centre of the Lake District, Cumbria. This is one of the region's smaller bodies of water, less than two kilometres long and about 23 metres deep. Even so, there is enough surface area for the wind to build up considerable waves that break against the downwind shores to restrict plant growth and produce stony beaches.

SPRING

△ Grass Snake
An expert swimmer, the Grass Snake can gulp small prey such as tadpoles underwater, but drags ashore a larger catch to swallow it. *See page 167.*

▽ Great Crested Grebe
Courting pairs of grebes rise from the water breast-to-breast, and give each other "gifts" such as waterweeds. *See page 115.*

Warming temperatures come first to Britain's southern counties, such as this Sussex lake. Canada Geese construct their bankside nest in a hollow lined with grasses, leaves, and down, as many other birds court and nest. The spring abundance of water plants provides the goose's main food, but it also feeds on insects and other animal matter.

SUMMER

△ Water Scavenger Beetle
Also called the Silver Water Beetle, this is Britain's largest beetle species. Air bubbles trapped on its underside give it a silvery sheen. *See page 258.*

▷ Reed Mace
Often misidentified as a Bulrush, the tall Reed Mace produces its feathery yellow male flowerhead above the brown, female one. *See page 432.*

As puddles, ditches, and small ponds dry in the hot sun, animals such as deer are driven to drink from permanent bodies of water. Water lilies are now in full bloom and their floating leaves provide welcome shade for fish resting near the shore. The lake's surface waters are warmed, but the deeper regions remain cool.

A single lake provides a host of small-scale wildlife **environments,** from steep or gentle banks, to shelving shallows or sudden dips, to **darker depths.**

PINK-BARRED
SALLOW

LAKES

At first glance the huge range of habitats provided by lakes, meres, and freshwater lochs may not be as obvious as, say, rivers with their differing courses and currents. On a calm day, the water may seem quite undisturbed, yet even in an isolated lake, with no incoming stream or river, and no outflow, there are currents. Upper water layers warm in direct sun, stimulating movement. Stormy weather mixes the layers, as do wind-whipped waves, which greatly affect the types of plants growing along the banks.

In higher, cooler, more mountainous lakes, inflowing water has picked up few nutrients from the surrounding resistant rocks and thin soil. Such lakes are nutrient-poor with limited aquatic life, termed oligotrophic ("few feeding"). But a lack of particles means the water can be exceptionally clear, allowing plant growth at considerable depth. In contrast, many warmer lowland lakes are cloudy, or turbid, from washed-in, nutrient-loaded sediments. This may restrict plant growth to the banks, but overall there is a higher level of productivity, known as eutrophic ("good feeding").

Bird life may be easily seen at a lake, but under the surface is a hidden world of fish, from small sticklebacks to massive carp, as well as frogs and other amphibians. Crustaceans range from tiny freshwater shrimps, to hard-cased crayfish. Freshwater snails, cockles, mussels and other molluscs can be found, plus insect nymphs, flatworms, bloodworms, and Horsehair Worms, among other invertebrates.

WINTER

△ **Water Vole**
Sometimes mistaken for a swimming Brown Rat, the Water Vole has a blunter nose, wider face, and small ears almost hidden by its fur. *See page 87.*

◁ **Grey Heron**
As lakes ice over in winter, the patient Grey Heron may divert its hunt from fish to mammals such as mice and voles, and smaller birds. *See page 118.*

Snow and ice grip Marbury Big Mere and its skeleton-like offshore trees in Cheshire. The water near the lake shore may freeze, but wind-driven waves and currents keep the main area clear. Fish and other cold-blooded inhabitants are inactive on, or near the bottom.

watching

LAKES PROVIDE A PEACEFUL SCENE FOR WILDLIFE OBSERVATION, ALTHOUGH ANY HABITAT INVOLVING WATER PRESENTS CERTAIN HAZARDS.

A screen of low reeds or similarly dense plants in the shallows is an aid to staying unseen from the lake.

Good binoculars or a fieldscope help to bring the faraway banks closer. If there is no stand or tripod, the low branch of a lakeside tree makes a good substitute, helping to steady the scene and also save aching arms.

Bridges are often useful, allowing a vertical view down into the water, which helps to cut reflections and glare. Also, on hot sunny days, fish and other creatures take advantage of the bridge's shade.

A slow stroll along the lakeside often reveals prints and tracks of creatures in the mud. These include visitors such as deer, and the imprints of waterfowl such as, Coot and Moorhen.

Keep a safe distance from the bank as reeds and grasses can mask the water's edge.

Marshes, swamps, mires, bogs, fens, and carrs offer a **diversity of wildlife**, where **land and water intermingle** in mosaics of hummocks, pools, and channels.

SOUTHERN HAWKER
DRAGONFLY

WETLANDS

W herever water is slowed on its journey, wetlands develop. They vary depending on climate and rainfall, topography, and local soils. Some higher, more northerly areas of Britain have fairly flat regions underlain by impermeable rock, where high rainfall has produced waterlogged blanket bogs. The main plants here are bog mosses such as Sphagnum, which forms spongy mounds with yielding peaty layers beneath. The conditions are acidic, and few other plants grow, apart from some tough rushes, sedges, and tussock grasses. Reduced oxygen levels in the water support limited animal life.

At lower altitudes, with a wider range of terrain and a water inflow higher in nutrients, valley bogs and marshes occur. Plants like Bog Asphodel, Marsh Pennywort, and Bog Pimpernel grow, along with a greater variety of rushes and reeds. Trees may start to colonize, especially willows and alders. Plant roots trap more sediment, and build up organic matter. Gradually the pools and channels fill. A characteristic habitat is alder carr, (a wooded wetland) with alders and shade-tolerant flowers interspersed with open pools, according to the season.

Where the ground water is more alkaline or base-rich, wetlands have greater diversity. Reeds and rushes gradually spread from the shores, sheltering aquatic creatures and a multitude of birds. As the open water reduces, shrubs and trees take hold in the drier areas. Fen carr can be quite dense, with willows and alders, then birch and other tree species arrive as the wetland slowly becomes dry land.

key sites

WETLANDS MAY SEEM FORBIDDING PLACES, WITH DIFFICULT TERRAIN, WHETHER ON FOOT OR IN BOATS. BUT HOWEVER CHALLENGING, OBSERVING THEIR WILDLIFE CAN BE WONDERFULLY REWARDING.

The Broads of south-east Norfolk and adjoining Suffolk lie inland from the North Sea coast. Britain's largest nationally protected wetland, at more than 300 square kilometres, its stretches of reeds, marshes, and open water are home to many unusual species, such as Swallowtail butterflies, rare Norfolk Hawker dragonflies, and Bittern.

Slimbridge Wetland Centre, on the Severn Estuary south-east of Gloucester, is the headquarters of the Wildfowl and Wetlands Trust with a worldwide reputation for conservation and research. Both native and exotic species such as flamingos are hosted in 325 hectares of protected wetlands.

The Lewis peatlands of Scotland's western Isle of Lewis are among the world's most extensive areas of blanket bog. The site is a Special Area of Conservation and listed by the Ramsar Convention, an international treaty on wetland conservation.

This flock of Knot birds coming in to roost from the Wash, in Lincolnshire seems to flash on and off, from dark – as the birds' upper parts show – to pale, as they all wheel around as one to reveal their undersides. The scene is typical of the wetland in late summer when many creatures are at their busiest, as bird chicks grow and fledge, and the reeds and rushes flower and develop seedheads, which will provide food for migrating birds in autumn.

SUMMER

▽ **Eel**
This sinuous, snake-like fish, a nocturnal predator of any small animals, was once a common inhabitant of lowland rivers, fens, ditches, and canals, but its numbers have dropped in recent years.
See page 178.

▷ **Yellow Flag**
Growing in a range of habitats, from damp ground to shallow water, the yellow "petals" of this iris are actually sepals, petals and styles, blooming from June to August.

SPRING

Lengthening days and warming temperatures renew wetland plant growth and stir creatures into breeding condition. East Anglia has many marshes, swamps, and fens, criss-crossed by naturally shifting river channels and regularly cleared drainage ditches, as here at Cley-next-the-Sea, west of Sheringham, north Norfolk.

△ **Bream**
The deep-bodied freshwater bream prefers slow and still waters, with rich sediments containing plenty of worms, snails, and insect nymphs. *See page 175.*

▷ **Marsh Cinquefoil**
Unlike yellow-flowering cinquefoils, this marsh species, also known as Bog Strawberry, has reddish blooms and thrives in both bogs and fens. *See page 369.*

AUTUMN

Both spring and autumn see flurries of avian activity in wetlands, as wading, and other migrant birds arrive and depart. Yet many animals manage to remain elusive, especially the endangered Bittern, as it hunts among the reeds for fish and amphibians – although the male's booming mating and territorial calls indicate its presence.

△ **Marsh Harrier**
The female of this species, also known by the old name of Swamp Hawk, is the largest harrier, and has distinctive pale forewings. *See page 119.*

▽ **Palmate Newt**
The smallest British newt, the Palmate Newt copes well with cool temperatures and is often found near boggy moorland. *See page 169.*

WINTER

With many birds and mammals having left for shelter on the lower slopes, cold mist envelops a woodland bog on Rothiemurchus Estate, near Aviemore in the heart of the Cairngorms National Park, Scotland. Wetlands are quiet during the coldest months, with most animal life suspended, as creatures hide among roots and in the mud.

△ **Rudd**
The red-finned Rudd surface feeds on insects such as mayflies and crane flies during warmer months, then retreats to deeper waters in the winter.

▽ **Goldeneye**
Most Goldeneye are winter visitors from northern Europe and Asia. They often form single sex large flocks on lakes and marshes. *See page 110.*

◁ **Sedge Warbler**
A bird of reedbeds, sedge tussocks, and marshy shrubs, Sedge Warblers hunt insects in dense cover and are most active at dawn and dusk. *See page 151.*

▷ **Swallowtail**
Limited to East Anglia's Broads, the Swallowtail – Britain's largest butterfly – is on the wing mainly during June and July. Eggs are laid singly on Milk Parsley, the species' food plant. *See page 189.*

Being fairly small bodies of water by volume, but often having a relatively large surface area for heat exchange, ponds change temperature not only throughout the seasons, but also through each day. As the water starts to warm in spring, amphibians arrive, including Common Toads, as here, as well as various species of frogs and newts. The male toad positions himself on the female's back and grips her around the underside with his front legs, a mating position called amplexus.

SPRING

◁ **Broad-leaved Pondweed**
The long, ribbon-shaped, submerged leaves grow first in spring, followed by the more oval, floating leaves, and small green flowers. *See page 424.*

▽ **Reed Bunting**
The all-black head of the male contrasts with the female's browner head, as they build their cup-shaped nest among reed stems and grasses.
See page 162.

▷ **Marsh Fritillary**
The black spotted caterpillars of this endangered species feed on Devil's-bit Scabious, plantains, and wild honeysuckle before the adults fly from May into June. *See page 201.*

▷ **Alder Buckthorn**
On pond margins with peaty soil, this small bushy tree, also called Black Dogwood, bears tiny, green-white flowers in the leaf axils in late spring and early summer.
See page 331.

SUMMER

Many ponds come into full flower in early summer, like the striking yellow Flag Iris, here accompanied by Floating Sweet Grass. Most of the adult amphibians have spawned, and are preparing to leave, while their tadpoles are well on the way to growing legs, and in the case of frogs and toads, shrinking their tails.

△ Common Frog
The adults and new froglets leave the pond in June or July, depending on the water level and temperature, to live among damp vegetation. *See page 168.*

▽ Water Springtail
These wingless insects feed mainly on decaying matter, and feed on the bottom or breed near the surface. *See page 234.*

AUTUMN

Many pond plants receive an influx of nutrients in autumn, in the form of leaves falling from overhanging branches, or blowing in from the surroundings. However, too many rotting leaves can choke a small pond and cause a temporary oxygen deficit, as can too much excrement from Mallards and other water birds.

△ Little Grebe
This smallest of British grebes, also called the Dabchick, begins to lose its reddish face in autumn as it develops its browner winter plumage. *See page 115.*

△ Water Avens
A close cousin of Herb Bennet, Water Avens produces its nodding pink flowers into September. The beak-shaped, upright fruits have feathery tips. *See page 268.*

WINTER

As ice covers the pond, most fish, insects, snails, and other pond dwellers lie in a dormant state on the bottom, or in the mud. The ice prevents fresh oxygen from passing into the water, but the inactive animals are able to survive with very little, and may only be in danger if the ice freezes down to the mud.

△ Stickleback
Britain's smallest freshwater fish, sticklebacks are hardy and can tolerate moderate pollution and brackish waters. *See page 183.*

▽ Great Diving Beetle
Often the top predator in a small pond, the males of this water beetle fly powerfully at night. *See page 259.*

GREAT CRESTED NEWT

Plants, herbivores, predators, and top hunters – the pond is **an ecosystem in miniature.**

PONDS

P onds, puddles, and similar small bodies of water provide a fascinating insight into the workings of nature. There is no official difference between a pond and a lake, although a common distinction is that ponds can support bottom-rooted plants across their area, while lakes are too deep or extensive. In most cases, ponds have still, or very slow-moving water, while water flowing through a wide, deep portion of a small river is usually termed a pool.

Within these miniature ecosystems, the basis for pond life is its plant growth. The types of pond plants present depends on factors such as the water's depth, temperature, clarity, and nutrient content. They range from microscopic plant-like organisms, which are food of the ubiquitous Daphnia Pond Flea (not an insect, but a tiny crustacean cousin of crayfish), to slimy growths of algae (simple non-flowering plants) such as Blanket Weed, to the beautiful flowers of yellow Flag Irises and water lilies. These plants are food for all manner of small pond creatures, such as snails, and the young forms of insects called nymphs (larvae). Ponds are sometimes called "insect nurseries" as many types spend their early stages there as nymphs, and then emerge to become winged adults such as damselflies and dragonflies. Larger pond inhabitants include amphibians, fish such as Roach and sticklebacks, and birds like Coots, Moorhens, and many other kinds of waterfowl. Dead plants and animals fall to the pond bottom as food for scavengers and detritus feeders, and gradually their nutrients are recycled into fresh plant growth.

watching

OBSERVING THE INTRICATE COMINGS AND GOINGS IN A POND IS A SIMPLE ACTIVITY THAT CAN BE CARRIED OUT DURING THE DAY OR NIGHT AND IS BOTH INSTRUCTIVE AND FASCINATING.

Find a comfortable, but discreet place on the bank thats is firm and stable, and unlikely to collapse.

Many water animals can see shadows and through the surface to shapes against the sky, so it helps to have a fixture like a tree above and behind.

Lying prone and keeping still not only helps you to avoid visual detection, but also prevents you from causing vibrations in the ground, which pass to the water and are sensed by many aquatic creatures.

Reflections and glare from the surface can sometimess make observation difficult. A bucket or wooden box with a transparent base such as clear plastic, or even clingfilm, fixed in place by a waterproof seal, makes an excellent underwater viewer. The base is dipped just below the surface to reveal the creatures and plant life beneath.

Spectacular mountain scenery lifts the human spirit, but also presents harsh, variable, and demanding conditions for its plants and wild creatures.

COWBERRY

MONTANE

Hills and mountains are not only higher than their surrounding lowlands, but also cooler and windier, and often wetter. The temperature falls by an average of 0.5°C for each 100 metres of altitude, so a 1,000-metre peak is about 5°C colder than nearby sea level. These conditions bring about many different montane (mountainous) habitats, often in small patchworks, according to factors such as the steepness of slope, the underlying rock type, exposure to the sun's rays, and to the prevailing winds, as well as climatic effects like the rain shadow. There is no generally recognized standard height at which a hill becomes a mountain. The former usually has a rounded top, while the latter should rise to an identifiable peak. In Britain, a working definition of 600 metres above sea level is common, or less than this, as low as 300 metres, if the peak rises abruptly from surrounding lowlands.

Many mountain plants grow low in a creeping, or cushion-like habit, to reduce wind exposure. Their leaves are tough, and may have a hairy surface to reduce moisture loss and keep the worst of the frost and ice at bay. Trees are generally evergreen, with needle-like leaves to withstand freezing, and sloping branches that shed snow easily, rather than breaking under its accumulating weight. Warm-blooded animals, from Red Deer and Wild Cats, to Ptarmigan and Capercaillie, need thicker fur or feather insulation than their lowland counterparts. Montane insects tend to complete their life cycles rapidly, due to the short summer, and over-winter as frost-resistant eggs.

safety

MOUNTAINS PROVIDE MAJESTIC VIEWS, AND RARE PLANTS AND CREATURES, BUT THEY CAN ALSO BE DANGEROUS.

Follow countryside and trekking guidelines, such as letting someone know details of your route and when you expect to return. Do not rely on a mobile phone as many hills and mountains have no signal coverage.

Never go alone – three is a good minimum number – if one person is injured, then another can stay and take care of the casualty, while a third goes for help

Take several layers of warm clothing with you, which can be added or removed to stay comfortable, plus a waterproof outergarment.

Distances on a flat map look different in mountains. Allow at least 5 kilometres per hour plus 10 minutes for each 100 metres height gain.

Carry items such as a torch, whistle, phone, and emergency food in a backpack, leaving both hands free in case of stumbles or trips.

Check weather forecasts before you set off and do not go if conditions are at all doubtful.

SPRING

Spring comes late to the uplands. At Llyn (Lake) Idwal, in the Glyderau Range of Snowdonia, North Wales, the turf begins to sprout new green blades. Some of these may be the rare Snowdon Lily, in Welsh, *Brwynddail y Mynydd* ("rush leaves of the mountain"), which will not open its white flowers until June.

△ **Wild Cat**
The elusive Wild Cat is confined to Scotland, mainly the Highlands. In May, the female usually produces her litter of around 2–6 kittens. *See page 94.*

▽ **Capercaillie**
Males strut in their courtship display, making a call that begins as a rattle, then an explosive *"klop"* and rustling hiss. *See page 114.*

Dusk sees the last light on Latrigg, one of the Lake District's lowest fells, at 368 metres altitude. A less challenging climb, this is also a popular site due to its location just north of the busy Lakeland centre of Keswick. Above the forested tree zone, the autumn grasses shade from green to brown, and most upland blooms have been and gone, in contrast to the moor heathers that are starting to flower.

△ **Rowan**
Also known as the Mountain Ash, the Rowan tree produces a glorious early autumn display of bright red berry clusters before its leaves turn deep orange. *See page 332.*

▽ **Scotch Argus**
The last of these butterflies warm themselves in pockets of early morning sunshine, as their caterpillars prepare for winter hibernation. *See page 205.*

▷ **Red Squirrel**
Autumn is feast and caching time for these protected rare squirrels, natives of conifer woods, as they collect and bury a wide variety of nuts and seeds. *See page 87.*

▽ **Norway Maple**
This hardy, frost-resistant tree has become naturalized, and shows fine autumn colours as the leaves turn to yellows, browns, and dark scarlet. *See page 316.*

SUMMER

△ **Pine Marten**
These cousins of the Stoat mate in July or August, but the female's pregnancy does not begin until the following January. *See page 91.*

▽ **Mountain Ringlet**
This alpine butterfly can be seen flying on sunny days in the Lake District and Scottish Highlands. *See page 205.*

Even in midsummer, moist south-westerly winds can rise over the peaks and condense into heavy grey clouds – here over the peaks of the Cairngorms, viewed looking south across a forested valley of the River Spey, in north-east Scotland. The Scots pine in the foreground is greening up with new needles.

WINTER

North-west Scotland is the stronghold of the Ptarmigan. As winter sets in and the first snow flurries arrive, this is the only British bird to change its camouflage, from a summer plumage of brownish upper parts, to all-white feathers, except for the black tail and, in the male, as here, a distinctive black face patch.

△ **Mountain Hare**
The dense white winter coat helps with warmth and camouflage, as the Mountain Hare shelters among, and feeds on heathers. *See page 86.*

▷ **Golden Eagle**
Hares, Ptarmigan, and Grouse are among this eagle's prey. It also scavenges on carrion, as winter takes its toll on wildlife, and farm stock such as lambs. *See page 123.*

SPRING

△ Adder
A reptile of open habitats such as heaths, moors, and dunes, the Adder emerges in spring from its hibernating hole, where it may spend a communal winter with many of its kind. *See page 167.*

▽ Round-leaved Sundew
Sundews supplement what they obtain from their nutrient-poor environment by catching small insects on their red-haired, sticky leaves. *See page 363.*

The spring sunshine and lengthening days warm Bransdale Moor, North Yorkshire, almost in the centre of the North York Moors National Park, between Stokesley and Kirkbymoorside. The heathers begin to bud after winter inactivity, but colourful spring flowers are scarce on many moors because of the acidic, low-nutrient conditions.

AUTUMN

▷ Red-legged Partridge
Despite its apparently colourful plumage, this partridge blends well with heath vegetation as it darts among the plants. *See page 111.*

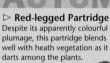

▽ The Blusher
The pinky-brown, scaly cap of this common fungus, growing larger than a hand, is found in many habitats, and pales to pink with age or damage. *See page 462.*

Shortening days, cooling temperatures, and even the first sharp frosts have little initial effect on the heather's flowering plants, although Bracken fronds begin to turn yellow, brown, and brittle. Many insects and spiders dig into the loose soil among the heather roots, where they will shelter from the cold weather.

WINTER

△ Hard Fern
Remaining stubbornly green all winter, Hard Fern fronds grow from a central rootstock. Each has 30–50 comb-like teeth on either side of the central stem. *See page 448.*

◁ Common Dodder
After flowering in early autumn, the Common Dodder's parasitic red stems still suck nutrients from hosts such as heather, thyme, and pea-family plants. *See page 389.*

A view towards the distinctive lop-sided summit of Roseberry Topping, a hill on the edge of the North York Moors, south-east of Middlesborough, shows thin patches of snow between the dense tussocky growths of brittle grasses. Boggy pools swell in winter, and in freezing snaps become covered with a treacherously thin layer of ice.

SUMMER

▽ Broom
With dense fibrous roots that grow well in dry, light soil, Broom thrives on sandy heaths. Its bright yellow pea-like flowers bloom from April onwards and turn into small black seed-pods. *See page 370.*

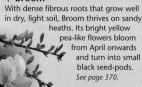

▷ Ghost Moth
This species is named because of the male's ghostly white colour. Groups of them hover around plants in the gathering late dusk of midsummer. *See page 225.*

As summer starts to fade, heathers approach their main blossom time and bring intense hues ranging from pinks through to deep "royal purple", on Dunwich Heath, near the coast of Suffolk, East Anglia. Among the heathers, gorse, and conifer plantations, the rare Dartford Warbler and Ant-lion insect are part of the heathland's summer wildlife. Various reptiles, including smooth snakes, Slow-worms, and Sand Lizards share this sandy, loose, and easily eroded habitat.

Heaths are named after their **principal plants – the short, woody-stemmed, heathers** – also called Ling, in some areas.

HIGH BROWN
FRITILLARY

UPLAND HEATH

Heaths and moors share a dominant common plant: heather. They have many other similarities, yet differences too. Heaths tend to have lighter, sandy soil, which drains easily and so stays relatively dry; they are found mainly in warmer parts of southern England. Moors are generally higher, colder, windier, and wetter; they occur chiefly in the north and west of Britain, where their shallow waterlogged soil covers bedrock. Despite the all-too-plentiful moisture, moorland plants suffer from stagnation in the acidic soil, where oxygen is used up by slowly rotting vegetation forming deep, peaty layers. The constant winds also have a drying effect, so heathers in these locations often suffer an apparent lack of water, similar to the sandy, dry heathlands. Soil nutrients for plant growth are scarce for similar reasons. On heaths they are washed away through the light soil, while on moors they are released only gradually by the very slow decay process.

Particular species of heathers favour different conditions. Common Heather, or Ling, likes heathy areas, Cross-leaved Heather is more characteristic of moors, and Bell Heather may be found in both habitats. These hardy plants form the base of many food chains and act as miniature jungles where spiders, insects, and reptiles fight for survival. Young heather shoots feed grouse and other birds, small mammals, and deer. The flower nectar is a welcome autumn food for many kinds of insects, especially bees, while the heather's seeds sustain numerous species of birds through the winter.

watching

IN SOUTHERN AND EASTERN ENGLAND, HEATHLAND HAS SOMETIMES BEEN TAKEN FOR GRANTED, AND AS A RESULT IS OFTEN UNDER PRESSURE FROM DEVELOPMENT.

Dunwich Heath, in coastal Suffolk, supports hundreds of hectares of prime heathland mixed with tree plantations, woods, coastal stretches of dunes and shingles, as well as the renowned RSPB Minsmere Bird Reserve.

Breckland or "The Brecks" covers almost 1,000 square kilometres across the western Norfolk–Suffolk border, with more than 40

Sites of Special Scientific Interest, and many heaths being restored to their ancient conditions. Rare plants include Bur Medick.

The Surrey Heathland Project around Woking aims to restore "Surrey's Last Wilderness" of heaths and commons amid this busy London commuter area.

Exmoor National Park on the north Devon–Somerset border, and Dartmoor National Park in south Devon, are vast and exceptionally valued upland mosaics of moor, heath, shrubland, and scattered woodlands.

◁ **Merlin**
The male Merlin, the UK's smallest bird of prey, hunts to feed its mate and chicks, flying low over moors, on the lookout for small birds, mice, lizards, and insects.
See page 126.

▷ **Pyramidal Orchid**
On chalky and limestone ground as well as heath, this orchid has bounteous nectar, and ranges in colour from pale to intense pink.
See page 437.

MOUNTAIN AND UPLAND | HABITATS

Southern England's downlands **reflect a heritage** of land clearance, feral grazing, and farming.

COWSLIP

DOWNLANDS

Many downs were once ancient beech forests that were felled for timber from Stone Age times, and later to create grazing land for horses, cattle, and especially sheep. Remnant beech copses or "hangers" remain on the slopes, or have been replanted, where they are often mixed with yew and ash. The introduction of rabbits from continental Europe for meat, from about the 12th century, brought another, now common herbivore to this mildly undulating countryside. The base of downland is chiefly chalk bedrock, which allows good drainage, so that only relatively thin soils accumulate. The grazers nibble tree shoots and saplings, which prevents them encroaching back into their former range. This gives the downs their short-turfed, airy nature.

Over the centuries, a dry, open habitat developed, attracting a characteristic set of plants and creatures. Orchids such as Autumn Lady's Tresses, and the pinkish mauve Monkey species, thrive where they are undisturbed. The Bee Orchid mimics the appearance of a female bee, so the male attends, in the process spreading the flower's pollen. Rockrose and Wild Thyme keep low to the ground, creeping among the grasses to contribute to the yielding turf. In summer, a variety of blue butterflies flutter between the flowers, as well as the Marbled-white butterfly and the Dark-green Fritillary, a large species whose caterpillar's favourite food plant is the violet. Wild Thyme is especially important as food for the caterpillar of the beautiful, impressive, but threatened Large Blue butterfly, subject of a reintroduction programme since the 1980s (see pages 194–95).

key sites

DOWNLANDS ARE HISTORIC, SPECIALIZED HABITATS, AND MANY ARE CAREFULLY MANAGED WITH GRAZING REGIMES. IT IS ESPECIALLY IMPORTANT TO FOLLOW THE COUNTRYSIDE CODES THERE, SO THAT LIVESTOCK DO NOT WANDER.

The 100-kilometre-long South Downs of West and East Sussex, just inland from Worthing, Brighton, and Newhaven, provide some of Britain's most magnificent downland scenery. The chalk meets the sea at the dramatic cliffs of Beachy Head which rise 162 metres above the English Channel.

Collard Hill, south of Street, Somerset, one of the National Trust's sites for reintroduction of the Large Blue butterfly. Grazing by cattle and Dartmoor ponies is carefully managed to encourage Wild Thyme and nests of the ants that shelter and "milk" the older caterpillars.

The Ridgeway is Britain's oldest road. It follows an ancient chalk path along the crest of the North Wessex Downs and Chiltern Hills. The route takes in many nature reserves – look out for Red Kites, which were reintroduced to the area in the 1980s.

Late spring and early summer, especially from late May and June, sees the chalk downlands of Hampshire ablaze with colour as a rich mix of flowering plants bloom. Bright yellow Cowslips nod in the breeze. They are visited by moths, bees, butterflies, moths, and other insects with mouthparts long enough to reach the nectar at the base of the tube formed by the petals. Orchids, thistles, and other species add to the profusion.

SUMMER

◁ **Small Heath**
A second generation of Small Heath adults appear in August, from eggs laid in May by butterflies that overwintered as caterpillars.
See page 204.

▷ **Hawthorn**
A master survivor, Hawthorn opens its white blossom around May and then gradually ripens its fleshy dark red berries, called haws.
See page 331.

SPRING

▷ **Stone Curlew**
From March, Stone Curlews arrive on southern downs, heaths, and drier arable lands, to court and nestbuild, sometimes with fragments of stone. *See page 129.*

▽ **Adonis Blue**
Taking to the wing around May, the males are perhaps the brightest of all the blue butterflies, while the female is light brown. *See page 193.*

Crops, pasture, and wild grasses renew growth on the South Downs of West and East Sussex. A view across Cuckmere Valley shows Firle Beacon, one of the highest points of the South Downs at 217 metres. Many such high points here are named after the ancient practice of lighting fires on hilltops as far-seen message beacons.

AUTUMN

△ **Silver Birch**
The Silver Birch favours well-drained soils with sand and gravel, but is hardy enough for other habitats. *See page 317.*

▽ **Springy Turf Moss**
Also known as Bent-leaved Moss, this non-flowering plant copes with grazing and grassy slopes.

Sheep graze in the autumn landscape of Martinsell Hill, south of Marlborough, Wiltshire, as the harvest is completed, and hay gathered for winter feed. From this prominent site at the south end of the Marlborough Downs there are views across the Vale of Pewsey, running along the northern flank of Salisbury Plain.

WINTER

△ **Goshawk**
Swooping from the trees of adjacent woodland, the Goshawk uses its broad wings to launch high-speed attacks on many kinds of bird prey, including pigeons and even crows. *See page 123.*

◁ **Chalk-hill Blue**
Adults fly in July and August, and like some other blue butterflies, they are attracted to sip essential salts and minerals from livestock dung puddles. *See page 193.*

▷ **Dwarf Thistle**
This ground-hugging thistle grows in a very low rosette, with the flower almost stemless. Its sharp leaves offer some protection from being consumed by animals. *See page 418.*

Wiltshire has vast tracts of downlands, not least Salisbury Plain, some 800 square kilometres of chalk plateau, one of the largest chalk-based grasslands in north-west Europe, and an Area of Outstanding Natural Beauty. Winter snow is soon blown from the ridges leaving a complex pattern in dips and furrows.

▷ **Common Box**
When not used as decorative hedging, box usually grows as a rounded bush or small evergreen tree. It can reach up to about 10 metres in height. *See page 318.*

Larch is one of the few deciduous conifers, losing its green needles as winter approaches – here near Montreathmont, Angus, in Scotland. With no protective canopy, snow coats the windward sides of the trunks, and carpets the ground vegetation, which is usually extensive under larch, and shelters creatures below from extremes of wind and temperature. Larch need space and light, and fare poorly in denser mixed woods.

WINTER

▽ **Common Juniper**
A long-lived conifer native to Britain, Juniper produces berries that are green in the first year, and slowly ripen to a deep blue–purple in the second year. *See page 319.*

◁ **Goldcrest**
One of Europe's smallest birds, the Goldcrest flits among the branches of tall conifers in its search for small insects, grubs, or spiders. *See page153.*

◁ **Gorse**
Prickly and evergreen, Gorse can produce its vibrant pea-like flowers almost all year round, and grows best on light soil, especially open, acidic uplands and heaths. *See page 370.*

◁ **Black Grouse**
With red head wattles, lyre-shaped tail, and mostly black plumage, the male Black Grouse prepares for his distinctive strutting courtship display in spring. *See page 114.*

SPRING

△ **Wall Brown**
Often known simply as the Wall, this brown butterfly overwinters as a caterpillar, and then pupates before its spring emergence. *See page 204.*

▽ **Brown-lipped Snail**
These banded, or *cepaea* snails are roused by spring warmth, after clustering in sheltered, frost-free places through the winter. *See page 306.*

Upland trees shoot and bud later than in the lowlands. So a spring scene may show an intensifying green carpet of mosses, ferns, and similar plants, with trees only just coming into leaf. The sun's warmth hatches the over-wintering eggs of insects and other creatures, as movements and sounds return after the cold spell.

SUMMER

△ **Sulphur Tuft**
This sulphur-yellow fungus, usually more orange in the central cap, grows in groups on all kinds of rotting wood. *See page 468.*

▽ **Holm Oak**
An evergreen species, spiky young leaves give this tree an alternative name of Holly Oak. *See page 324.*

Summer is mostly calm, but storms triggered by localized hot air rising, and then suddenly cooling, over the uplands may bring damaging high winds, as in this scene from the hillsides and conifer woods of Strathspey, Scotland. Deciduous trees in full leaf present considerable resistance to wind and may suffer broken branches or toppling.

AUTUMN

▷ **Red Kite**
Gliding over open hillsides, Red Kite scan for any kind of food, from carrion to small prey like Rabbits, voles, and songbirds. *See page 122.*

▽ **Common Beech**
Well adapted to shallow soil, beech trees change from yellows to oranges and then red-brown. *See page 321.*

The invasive and often troublesome ferns of Bracken "brown off", and birch leaves change colour in this river valley in Glen Strathfarrar, part of a national nature reserve area north-west of Loch Ness, Scotland. Downy Birch, with its greater tolerance of the cold and wet is more at home in this habitat than its close cousin, the Silver Birch.

Between the sheltered lowlands and the bleakly **exposed** mountains, the upland wood is usually open and airy, visited by **animals** from other habitats.

STAG BEETLE

UPLAND WOODS

Not all trees can grow at altitude. Upland trees require greater resistance than their lowland companions to high wind, frost, and snow. Also, surprisingly, they must be able to cope with drought. Rain may be plentiful on the upper slopes, but it soon drains downhill through the thin soil, so available moisture can be very limited. Juniper, yew, birch, some types of beech and oak, and ash, evergreen holly, and box can withstand these conditions, and are often to be found fringing forest conifer plantations of pines, spruces, and larches.

Temperature and humidity decrease with height, while wind speed and exposure to frost and ice increase. So the seasonal cycles on uplands tend to lengthen the winter months and shorten summer. Spring starts a couple of weeks later, and autumn commences a few weeks earlier than at lower altitudes. Many of the more mobile creatures, such as birds, and winged insects like butterflies, cope by making small-scale daily "vertical" migrations. On fine days they fly up to the higher woods, where there may well be fewer resident creatures and therefore less competition for food, returning to the lower levels towards dusk, for relative warmth and shelter at night. This strategy is also employed by Bullfinches, birds that are happy to feed in les s dense cover, and flit upwards during cold winter days to search for ash seeds and other morsels, then return a few hours later. Crossbills, another member of the finch family, have a similar routine in some areas, flying in gregarious parties to extract the seeds from pine and spruce cones.

watching

UPLAND HABITATS ARE IDEAL FOR VIEWING VALLEYS BELOW, AND WATCHING BIRD FLIGHT OR THE MOVEMENTS OF DEER, HARES, AND OTHER ANIMALS. BUT THERE ARE SAFETY ISSUES TO CONSIDER: FOR EXAMPLE, LOW TEMPERATURES AND THE RISK OF FALLS, SEE PAGE 46.

Many woods on upper slopes have wide spaces between the trees. This allows animals to spot humans from some distance, which gives them time to escape or hide – especially if the animal looks uphill to the sky through the tree trunks. It is best to avoid such

situations if you are observing wildlife. Keep to a dip in the ground and maintain a low profile.

A hide is especially useful in relatively open habitats. If a purpose-made one is unavailable, a temporary screen can be fashioned from loose pieces of wood and fronds of common plants such as Bracken.

Select time and weather carefully so that the sun is over your shoulder, and the wind is in your face. Then you will see a well illuminated scene, and you will not not alert creatures downwind by your scent.

SCOTS PINE
CONE

Britain's small area of truly native coniferous forest is one of the wildest habitats in the country – many plants and animals are found nowhere else in Britain.

CONIFEROUS FOREST

D ark swathes of coniferous forest are a familiar sight in the British Isles. Densely packed stands (groups of similar trees within a forest) of evergreen pines and firs exude a rich scent and cast a deep shade over a soft carpet of fallen needles, creating an environment popular with walkers and picnickers. Yet nearly all such forests are artificial plantations stocked with fast-growing non-native species.

For a brief period after the last Ice Age, coniferous forest covered most of Britain, forming the westernmost spur of the vast boreal forest ecosystem that encircles the Earth's northern latitudes. As the climate warmed, broadleaved deciduous trees invaded Britain from southern Europe, driving the conifers north. Today, only a small area of truly wild coniferous forest remains, hidden in the remote valleys of the Scottish Highlands. Known as the Caledonian Forest, this ancient wilderness is dominated by magnificent Scots Pine trees and provides a unique habitat for many species found nowhere else in Britain, including the Golden Eagle and the Scottish Crossbill (see page 163).

Unlike deciduous trees, which must shed their tender leaves in autumn, most conifers have tough, evergreen foliage that can function year round. The leaves have a distinctive needle shape that minimizes water loss and they bear a thick, waxy rind that further protects them from freezing and desiccation (drying out). In winter, when the ground is often frozen and roots are unable to draw water, conifer trees endure what is effectively a sub-zero drought.

key sites

LARGE AREAS OF NATIVE CONIFER FOREST CAN ONLY BE FOUND IN SCOTLAND, BUT SOME MANAGED CONIFER PLANTATIONS IN ENGLAND ARE ALSO RICH IN WILDLIFE.

Formby Squirrel Reserve in Merseyside is a coastal Scots Pine forest inhabited by some of the few remaining Red Squirrels in England.

Northumberland National Park includes large tracts of managed conifer plantations that are home to birds such as Common Crossbills and Goldcrests.

Glen Strathfarrar in the Western Highlands of Scotland is a large area of Caledonian Forest, with huge, gnarled Scots Pines.

Beinn Eighe Mountain near Kinlochewe was Britain's first national nature reserve. Its pinewoods are home to Red Deer, Golden Eagles, Pine Martens, and many rare plants.

The Cairngorms National Park in Scotland is the wildest part of Britain – a vast area of mountains, valleys, moorlands, and native coniferous forest. The tallest tree in the UK is a Douglas Fir in Reelig Glen near Inverness.

▷ **Great Spotted Woodpecker**
Woodpeckers can be heard drumming in spring as they build nesting holes, search for wood-boring insects, and signal to other birds. *See page 142.*

▽ **Wood Ant**
In May, winged queens and males fly from the nests of Wood Ants to mate. *See page 286.*

SPRING

△ **Short-eared Owl**
In summer, the migratory Short-eared Owl arrives in Scotland's Caledonian Forest to take advantage of seasonally abundant voles and mice. *See page 141.*

△ **Woodwasp**
The harmless Woodwasp is a common sight in conifer forests in July and August. Females drill holes into trees to lay eggs, and larvae feed on wood. *See page 281*

△ **Amethyst Deceiver**
Fungi such as the Amethyst Deceiver are active in the soil all year round. Their fruiting bodies (mushrooms and toadstools) appear from late summer onwards. *See page 475.*

▽ **Douglas Fir**
In late summer, the cones of Douglas Fir open to release their seeds. *See page 330.*

SUMMER

The cones of conifers, such as these female Sitka Spruce cones (above), take several years to mature. Male cones release pollen into the air in spring, fertilizing the tiny female cones. The towering Scots Pines by Loch-an-Eilein in Scotland's Cairngorms National Park (right) belong to one of Britain's largest remaining areas of native forest.

Throughout the summer, pine trees continuously shed and regrow their needles and ripened pine cones burst, releasing their seeds. The seedlings of the Scots Pine provide nutrition for Red Deer that inhabit the forest as they graze on the shoots and needles of the young trees. By summer the stags have nearly regrown the antlers that are produced each year in readiness for the autumn rut. Some trees can be damaged by the stags tearing at the bark in an effort to shed the velvet from their new antlers.

△ **Common Crossbill**
Common Crossbills sometimes flock to Britain from the Continent in autumn, fleeing poor crops of conifer seeds in European forests. *See page 161.*

▽ **Common Earwig**
The female Common Earwig lays eggs in the autumn in underground nests and remains with her brood until it hatches in the spring. *See page 245.*

▽ **Bilberry**
Bilberries thrive in acidic soil. The edible fruit is consumed by both wildlife and humans in the autumn. *See page 389.*

AUTUMN

△ **Coal Tit**
While birds such as thrushes and warblers leave Britain's conifer forests in autumn, Coal Tits remain and survive on a diet of insects and pine seeds. *See page 155*

While the soft leaves of deciduous trees decompose relatively quickly to produce a rich humus, conifer needles are so tough that they remain on the forest floor for years, decomposing slowly through the action of bacteria and fungi. The dense, springy mat of dead needles acidifies the soil, and the evergreen canopy casts year-round shade; as a result, thick conifer stands have few of the herbaceous or understorey plants that are common in deciduous woodlands.

Conifer needles are difficult for animals to digest, and only a few specialized species, including caterpillars and a type of grouse called the Capercaillie, can feed on them. The seeds released by mature cones, however, provide abundant food for many animals from Wood Mice and voles to Red Squirrels, and these in turn are food for Long-eared Owls and Pine Martens. Britain's sole endemic bird – the Scottish Crossbill – feeds on pine cones by using its twisted beak-tips to prise scales apart while reaching between them for seeds with its tongue.

Britain has only three native conifer trees: the Scots Pine, Juniper, and Yew. All can be found in the Caledonian Forest, mingled with deciduous trees such as birch, willow, Rowan, and Aspen. Together these trees create a diverse ecosystem, which is home to many native animals and plants. In contrast, areas of non-native trees in conifer plantations support fewer animals and plants, and forestry practices such as the removal of pests, dead wood, and invading saplings further discourage wildlife.

Much of the ancient Caledonian Forest is now fully protected as forestry policy has become more wildlife-friendly. Before the trees were cleared to make way for farmland, the Caledonian Forest covered an estimated 15,500 square kilometres of Scotland, of which only one per cent remains. There are now plans to enlarge its range, and there are hopes to reintroduce some of its lost animals, including the Elk, European Beaver, Grey Wolf, Wild Boar, the Eurasian Lynx, and the Brown Bear.

△ **Waxwing**
In winter, flocks of Waxwings migrate south from the conifer woodlands of northern Europe in search of food, particularly favouring large berries. *See page 145.*

▽ **Yew**
The fruit of the poisonous Yew tree is a welcome source of food in winter for birds, who eat the flesh and discard the toxic seed. *See page 338.*

WINTER

▽ **Ground Beetle**
The Violet Ground Beetle, can be found sheltering by day under forest floor debris, such as stones and fallen branches. *See page 256.*

Heather and Bilberry carpet the forest floor at Glenfeshie in the Cairngorms, the low plants thriving in the acid soil under a patchy canopy of ancient Scots Pines. In early autumn, a glut of bilberries provides essential calories for animals racing to build up fat reserves for winter. Bilberry foliage is highly palatable and provides food all year round to Capercaillies and Red Deer.

In winter, snow covers the slopes of Beinn Achaladair and Beinn an Dothaidh in the Scottish Highlands. Those animals that do not hibernate or leave for warmer climes in winter must draw on their fat reserves and search out whatever edible morsels are to be had. Red Squirrels survive on caches of pine seeds; Roe Deer strip bark from trees; and grouse and Capercaillie peck at the buds and stems of plants.

Deciduous forest reflects the rhythm of the seasons, with dramatic changes in colour and character throughout the year.

ENGLISH OAK
LEAF AND ACORN

DECIDUOUS FOREST

I f we abandoned the land, almost the whole of the British Isles would quickly revert to its natural state: deciduous forest. Deciduous trees – those that shed their foliage in winter rather than remaining evergreen – have dominated the British Isles for nearly 10,000 years. They colonized the land after the Ice Age, invading from southern Europe as the climate warmed. They were not the first plants to prosper here: as the glaciers retreated, tundra plants took hold, later giving way to the Great Caledonian pine forests, fragments of which still survive in the Scottish Highlands. Next the pines retreated, driven north by deciduous invaders: first hazel, around 9,300 years ago, then oak, elm, lime, holly, ash, beech, hornbeam, and maple.

Worldwide, deciduous forests make up one of our planet's major terrestrial ecosystems. They flourish in wet parts of the Earth's temperate belt, where seasons are marked but summers not to dry and winters not too cold. Unlike the tough, waxy needles of conifers, the broad leaves of deciduous trees are tender and wafer thin. They are not built to last: instead they are designed to capitalize with maximum speed and efficiency on the brief temperate growing season.

Life in deciduous forests is an endless cycle of renewal and death, its timing governed by the seasons. In early spring, woodland flowers burst into life on the forest floor, drawing on underground food reserves as they race to grow and flower before the awakening trees cast them into shade. With the advance of spring, a flush of vivid green spreads through

key sites

SMALL AREAS OF DECIDUOUS FOREST CAN BE FOUND ALL OVER THE BRITISH ISLES. SOME OF THE LARGER FORESTS ARE LISTED BELOW. IN OLD ENGLISH, "FOREST" SIMPLY MEANT HUNTING GROUND RATHER THAN WOODLAND.

Epping Forest, a 2,400-hectare area of deciduous forest to the north of London, is a fragment of an ancient woodland that once covered most of Essex. The trees were pollarded (cut back) in the medieval era, resulting in the peculiar shapes and thick canopy still visible today.

Windsor Great Park in Berkshire is a royal deer park established in the 13th century. It has the largest collection of ancient oaks in Great Britain, including one tree thought to be 1,300 years old and many at least 600 years old.

The Forest of Dean is a 11,000-hectare area of forest stretching across two great river valleys – from the Severn Vale in western Gloucestershire to the Wye Valley in Wales. Feral wild boar, once hunted in the forest by Norman royalty, have recently re-colonized the area after a three-century absence.

△ Holly Blue
This sky-blue butterfly overwinters as a chrysalis and emerges in spring. It can be seen basking in the sun on bushes as it warms its muscles ready for flight. *See page 192.*

△ Weasel
Weasels are active all year but raise their kits in spring when food is abundant. They hunt by following runways of mice and voles. *See page 91.*

△ Woodcock
Shy and secretive, Woodcocks nest on the forest floor in spring and rely on camouflage to hide from predators. *See page 131.*

▽ Horse Chestnut
In February or March, the Horse Chestnut's buds open to release large, oval leaves, the weight of which pulls down the branches and opens the crown. White or pink blossom emerges in April. *See page 325.*

SPRING

▷ Song Thrush
The male Song Thrush is one of the loudest and earliest singers in the dawn chorus, with a flute-like song. *See page 150.*

▽ White Admiral
The White Admiral emerges from its chrysalis in early summer and can be spotted in sunny glades feeding on Bramble nectar. *See page 203.*

SUMMER

Sparrowhawks hatch in early summer and are raised in tree-top nests that are sometimes fashioned from abandoned crow's nests. Small birds make up the bulk of their diet. These are typically caught on the wing, the adult hawk launching a surprise attack from a concealed perch and pursuing prey through trees and undergrowth.

Wild flowers of the forest floor, such as these Wood Anemones (see page 351) in the Peak District, emerge in early spring in order to capture the sun before the trees are in leaf. By early summer (below), oak woodland in the Lune Valley of Lancashire is bursting with greenery and the shade is deepening, yet Wild Garlic, or Ramsons, (see page 426) is still in flower.

◁ **Tawny owl**
The nocturnal Tawny Owl can be hard to spot when roosting in woodland because of its camouflaging plumage but it is often seen as a silhouette when hunting at night. *See page 141.*

AUTUMN

▽ **Nightingale**
A summer visitor to southeast England, the Nightingale prepares to depart in autumn for wintering grounds in Africa. *See page 148.*

▽ **Edible Dormouse**
Dormice hibernate in autumn. Their heart rate, breathing rate, and body temperature all drop drastically to conserve energy. *See page 88.*

▽ **Fly Agaric**
Fungi such as the Fly Agaric permeate the decaying matter of the forest floor all year, but it is only in autumn that their fruiting bodies are visible. *See page 462.*

the forest as tender new leaves open. Plant-eating insects emerge by the million to feast on the leaves, and migratory songbirds arrive to feast on the insects, their territorial songs filling the still morning air and giving us the dawn chorus. With the approach of winter, the forest begins to shut down: leaves fall, insects die or become dormant, summer visitors leave for warmer climes, and the skeletal trees fall silent.

A deciduous forest has a well-defined layered structure. At the top is the canopy, and beneath this is an understorey of shrubs such as hazel and Hawthorn, accompanied by saplings awaiting their turn at the top. Lower still is the herb layer made up of herbaceous wild flowers such as Bluebells, Foxgloves, and Wood Anemones; conspicuous in spring, they give way to ferns and Brambles as the seasons progress. All the plant life is nourished by a deep and very rich layer of soil formed from years of accumulated leaf litter.

Britain's ancient deciduous forests have a primeval quality that belies their true nature. None of them are truly wild or natural. For centuries they have been exploited by people, felled and replanted, moulded and managed. Vast areas were once run as hunting estates, their native carnivores exterminated as "vermin". Other areas were coppiced and pollarded, the trees regularly hacked back to stimulate regrowth of woody shoots useful for fencing, firewood, and making charcoal. The current distribution of tree species is a legacy of such practices. Ash, for example, was encouraged in southern forests because it provided a fast-growing timber crop; and oak was planted and harvested in royal forests during the ship-building centuries. Animal life too reflects a long history of human influence. Once-native mammals such as the Brown Bear, Wild Boar, Wolf, and Aurochs were driven to extinction long ago, while recently introduced alien species such as the American Mink, Grey Squirrel, and Muntjac Deer are now well-established residents.

WINTER

▷ **Wren**
Tiny but hardy, Wrens remain active in winter and endure severe frosts by roosting communally. *See page 148.*

▽ **Mistletoe**
A parasitic evergreen, Mistletoe feeds on the sap of trees. Its distinctive white berries ripen in winter. *See page 344.*

▽ **Roe Deer**
Red in summer, Roe Deer turn grey in winter and males lose their antlers so a new pair can grow by the next spring. *See page 97.*

In Autumn, deciduous forests, such as this beechwood near Arbroath, Angus, Scotland provide glorious displays of bright golds and warm browns. The Common Beech (see p.321) is known as "the Lady of the Woods" because of its graceful habit (shape), fine blue-grey bark, and delicate leaves. A beech forest provides rich pickings for mammals, such as squirrels, at this time of year as beech nuts ripen and emerge from their bristled husks.

Snow covers the bare branches of deciduous woods at Marshfield, Gloucestershire. The trees lie dormant in winter shedding their leaves as they channel all their stored nutrients into their roots, which are safely insulated underground. Growth is halted until the lengthening days signal the arrival of spring and new leaves begin to appear once again.

△ **Quaking Grass**
The pyramidal flowerheads of Quaking Grass rattle in the breeze and when dried make excellent floral decorations.

△ **Natterer's Bat**
This uncommon bat often roosts in farmyard buildings and old stone barns, emerging soon after sunset to hawk for insects. *See page 83.*

▽ **Carrion Crow**
Ubiquitous in farming areas, the Carrion Crow feeds on everything from earthworms to other birds' eggs and sheep carcasses.
See page 157.

▽ **Cow Parsley**
Dense patches of frothy white Cow Parsley have been likened to the crest of a breaking wave, and teem with insects. *See page 385.*

△ **Blue Tit**
Trees along field boundaries or standing alone in meadows are visited by several woodland birds, including tits and woodpeckers. *See page 155.*

▽ **Cornflower**
Brilliant azure-blue Cornflowers were once a common sight, but are now confined to a handful of areas in East Anglia and the south. *See page 419.*

Buzzing with insects and brightened by swathes of wild flowers, traditionally managed pasture creates a knee-high jungle in which nesting birds such as Skylarks and Lapwings can hide from predators. Close-cropped turf in chalk areas such as the South Downs is also a productive habitat, with up to 30 plant species per square metre of turf.

△ **Honey Fungus**
Clumps of this honey-coloured fungus can be seen on logs and tree stumps from July to December. *See page 477.*

▷ **Stock Dove**
The Stock Dove is smaller and smarter than a Woodpigeon, and nests in holes in trees. *See page 140.*

By August, meadow grasses have all set their seed and the once-verdant landscape is dominated by shades of gold, pink, brown, and white. Traditionally, the flowering of Yellow Rattle (see page 406) was the harbinger of autumn and a signal to cut the hay, but new fast-growing grass strains enable farmers to mow several times a year.

The working hay meadows of the Yorkshire Dales, Lake District, and North Pennines are carpeted with flowers in spring and summer. Different meadow grasses and herbs bloom in sequence through the growing season, until all the plants have completed their annual cycle and the grass is ready to cut. Enclosed by dry-stone walls, these hay fields may each have their own slightly different mix of plants and animals.

Grass is the hallmark of the British countryside, and **flower-rich turf** lies at the heart of our meadow ecosystem.

RED ADMIRAL

MEADOW AND PASTURE

A round 7,000 years ago, forest covered most of the British Isles and grassland was a relatively rare habitat confined to mountains, gorges, and coastal clifftops. Centuries of deforestation and grazing by cattle and sheep created the wide range of grassland habitats we see today, such as the lush pastures of the West Country, the upland hay meadows of northern England, the sheepwalks of Wales and Scotland, and the flood meadows of fertile river valleys. The long history of human influence on the British landscape has ensured that almost all grassland has at some time been grazed or burned.

Britain's mild, wet climate means that grass can grow for at least nine months of the year. More than 150 different wild species of grass are found in these islands, making grasses the largest family of flowering plants. But changing farming practices since World War II have transformed the character of meadows and pasture, with enormous consequences for plants and animals. The use of pesticides and fertilizers, destruction of field edges, and development of more vigorous grass varieties have produced a new type of farmland known as improved pasture, in which wild flowers – and thus insects – are few and far between. Instead of a mosaic of grasses and weeds that reverberates with the songs of Skylarks and Lapwings in summer, improved pasture is an unbroken blanket of bright green that supports little wildlife. The decline of formerly abundant flowers such as the Cornflower (see page 419), now endangered in the UK, has come to symbolize the scale of this change.

WINTER

△ **Pygmy Shrew**
Weighing about the same as a 5p coin, this tiny insect-eater remains active all winter in the surface "tunnels" it makes through long grass. *See page 79.*

▽ **Fieldfare**
Flocks of this well-built thrush, a winter visitor to the UK, announce their presence with harsh *chack chack* calls. *See page 150.*

In winter, upland pasture often seems deserted, whereas lowland grassland hosts flocks of Lapwings, gulls, finches, and thrushes, many of which have flown here from colder conditions in northern and eastern Europe. The short grass makes wildlife more visible and hunting easier for Barn Owls, which quarter the ground on silent wings.

watching

AS WITH ANY OPEN HABITAT, IT CAN BE DIFFICULT TO WATCH WILD ANIMALS IN PASTURE, BUT PERSISTENCE AND PLANNING WILL BRING THEIR REWARDS.

Buy a large-scale map to identify a circular walk that includes a variety of habitats, including open pasture, lanes, and copses. Farm ponds are always worth a look if there is public access.

Never enter fields with cattle or sheep unless you are sure there is a footpath, and make sure to close gates behind you.

A telescope is useful for scanning distant flocks of birds or scouring fields for hares.

Keep a low profile by walking alongside hedges or banks. This avoids your body being outlined against the sky, which could alert wildlife to your approach.

Get down on your knees to examine the turf for insects and flowers at ground level.

Some hay meadows are preserved as nature reserves. Access may be limited at times to protect ground-nesting birds and wild flowers.

WHEAT

Cultivated land has undergone **dramatic changes** in the past 60 years, yet arable land remains a **vital refuge** for many plants and animals.

ARABLE FARMLAND

Arable land is fields planted with crops, rather than pasture grazed by livestock. The first crops in Britain were harvested by Stone Age tribes over 5,000 years ago, and people have tilled the land ever since. For centuries, land under the plough was managed by a system known as the farming calendar – a continual cycle of sowing seeds, tending crops, harvesting, ploughing, and sowing, with fields left fallow every few years. In the 1940s, however, the need to feed the growing human population led to an agricultural revolution in which artificial fertilizers, herbicides, and mechanization became bywords for progress. Field sizes grew, and faster-growing crops enabled multiple plantings throughout the year, with autumn-sown "winter wheat" replacing the fields of stubble that used to lie empty over the winter.

Agricultural intensification has had a profound impact on the UK's wildlife, robbing once-common species such as Cirl Buntings, Tree Sparrows, and Harvest Mice of their traditional habitat. The Brown Hare is second only to the Water Vole as the British mammal that has shown the greatest decline in the last 100 years: recent surveys show that its numbers have crashed by more than 80 per cent. However, renewed interest in organic farming practices, together with the policy of "set-aside" (land that is left untreated with pesticides) has enabled some plants and animals to re-establish themselves. Wild flowers can grow undisturbed, invertebrate life becomes more prolific, and this in turn attracts feeding birds and small mammals.

watching

LOOK FOR A MIXED ARABLE LANDSCAPE OF SMALL FIELDS SOWN WITH DIFFERENT CROPS, BORDERED BY HEDGES AND UNCULTIVATED AREAS.

Respect agricultural land by following the "Countryside Code" – always keep to lanes or public footpaths and never trample on crops.

Learn to select set-aside fields, with their clumps of weeds and unkempt appearance. These attract flocks of finches and buntings in autumn and winter, and can be good for observing Barn Owl and Brown Hare.

Huge fields of cereals seldom have much wildlife, so it is best to look elsewhere.

In the early morning and at dusk, scan the woodland edge where it meets surrounding fields for a chance of spotting Roe Deer.

Stubble fields may be visited by flocks of geese in winter. In Norfolk, Pink-footed Geese feast on beet tops after the harvest.

Don't ignore common farmland animals such as Rabbits and Rooks – they can be just as fascinating to watch as rare species.

SPRING

Spring is a period of great vitality and change in farmland. Winter flocks of gulls and thrushes depart, and are replaced by an influx of summer visitors, such as Swallows. Overwintering insects emerge from hibernation, while for some animals, including Brown Hares and Red Foxes, the breeding season is already in full swing.

△ **Brown Hare**
The British stronghold of Brown Hares is in eastern arable areas, especially East Anglia. *See page 86.*

▽ **Pill Millipede**
Part of the hidden army of invertebrates in soil and leaf litter, Pill Millipedes eat decaying plant matter and thus help to return nutrients to the earth.
See page 302.

Ploughing breaks up compacted topsoil, buries weeds, and clears away dead vegetation, to give next season's seeds the best chance of growing. It also creates a short-lived feeding frenzy. Flocks of opportunist birds, such as Lapwings, Black-headed Gulls, Rooks, and Jackdaws, swoop onto the field to feast on the normally hidden creatures of the soil. They have learned to follow tractors, like seabirds trailing a fishing boat.

▷ **Rook**
Clusters of untidy Rook nests in bare treetops are a characteristic feature of the British countryside in winter. Rookeries are also used as winter roosts, and breeding pairs return to repair them. *See page 157.*

▽ **Pink Waxcap**
This beautiful but uncommon mushroom of grassy areas is sometimes likened to a ballerina's tutu. It is threatened by excessive pesticide use. *See page 478.*

▷ **Field Vole**
One of the most abundant mammals of farmland, Field Voles are usually nocturnal but in winter, to cope with food shortages they often forage during the day as well. *See page 87.*

▽ **Lapwing**
Flocks of Lapwings gather on recently ploughed fields, attracted by earthworms, millipedes, and Click Beetle larvae brought to the surface. *See page 128.*

△ **Field Mushroom**
The creamy white caps of this edible mushroom first appear in July and August after heavy rain, often sprouting in groups. *See page 467.*

◁ **Harvest Mouse**
Weighing less than a 2p coin, the Harvest Mouse is a superb acrobat, using its tail to cling to the stalks of wheat and long grass. *See page 89.*

Every field used to be carpeted with the flowers of arable weeds, and be alive with insect pollinators and small mammals during the summer months, but agricultural intensification has banished much wildlife. The traditional richness of arable farmland can still be experienced in fields left fallow as part of set-aside schemes.

The rolling grassland and wheat fields of Wiltshire's Salisbury Plain, pictured here at harvest time, support a number of nationally scarce species, including Stone Curlews. Food supplies for farmland wildlife are most abundant in autumn when there is corn stubble, spilt grain, and the fresh green shoots of winter wheat.

△ **Large White**
Caterpillars of the Large White are a major pest of cabbages and cauliflowers, although chemical pesticides now keep them under control. *See page 191.*

▷ **Pheasant**
Pheasants roost in hedgerows and copses at night, then spread out to feed along field margins during daylight hours. *See page 114.*

SPRING

▽ Cuckoo

In hedgerows most young Cuckoos are fostered by Dunnocks. The adult male Cuckoo's call is one of the most distinctive sounds of spring and early summer. *See page 140.*

▽ Lords-and-Ladies

The arrow-shaped leaves and purplish flower spikes of Lords-and-Ladies are a familiar sight on shady grassy banks in April and May. *See page 431.*

In early summer British hedgerows, such as this one in Cheshire's dairy-farming country, are festooned with the sweet-smelling, brilliant white blossom of Hawthorn, Blackthorn, Bird Cherry, and Crab Apple trees in spring. At this time of year hedges are alive with song, as birds compete to establish their breeding territories.

SUMMER

▷ Turtle Dove

A summer visitor to Britain, this dove has been hit hard by loss of hedgerows. *See page 140.*

▽ Glow-worm

Male glow-worms fly in search of the flashing lights of the wingless females on warm summer nights. *See page 263.*

An unsprayed hedgerow in summer will be full of caterpillars, shield bugs, chafers, bees, crane flies, hoverflies, and other invertebrates – all offering excellent feeding for families of small birds with the fledglings still in their juvenile plumage. Towards the summer's end, ripening blackberries provide a feast for Wood Mice and Hazel Dormice.

AUTUMN

△ Lesser Horseshoe Bat

This fast, low-flying bat can be seen hunting for insects at dusk along hedgerows in southern England until well into October, before it hibernates for the winter. *See page 82.*

◁ Spindle Tree

The fruits of this small hedgerow tree turn pink in autumn, then split open to reveal nutritious orange coloured seeds much loved by Robins and other birds. *See page 319.*

Insects are more scarce in autumn, but late-flowering plants such as ivy provide a final meal of nectar for Common Wasps and Red Admiral butterflies before they enter their winter torpor to overwinter in hedgerows as adults or larvae. Warblers feed on berries to fatten up for the long migration south, while Badgers eat any fallen fruit.

WINTER

▷ Bullfinch

Often the first sign of this shy finch is a soft mournful, whistled call, or the sudden flash of a white rump as it flies into leaf cover. It feeds on berries and supplements its diet by catching invertebrates from low bushes and sometimes from the ground. *See page 161.*

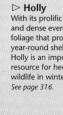

▷ Holly

With its prolific berries and dense evergreen foliage that provides year-round shelter, Holly is an important resource for hedgerow wildlife in winter. *See page 316.*

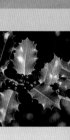

Dusted with snow after a blizzard, this well-established hedgerow in Herefordshire perfecty illustrates the way in which the trees on either side of a lane will eventually arch across to form a tunnel, if left untrimmed. The branches create an enclosed canopy attractive to a range of species normally associated with denser woodland, including woodpeckers, Tawny Owls, and Grey Squirrels.

Like ribbons of woodland **snaking across fields and meadows,** hedgerows give the British countryside its unique character.

BLACKBERRIES

HEDGEROW

H edgerows have played a central role in the agricultural and natural history of the British Isles. These tangled strips of trees, shrubs, and Brambles were originally planted to divide the land into fields and pen livestock, but have had a far-reaching impact on the country's wildlife. By creating a patchwork of open ground interwoven with hedges, generations have produced a more intimate and wildliferich rural landscape. Hedgerows provide a replacement habitat for the vast areas of forest that have been cut down over the centuries. Equally importantly, they link the remaining copses and woods, serving as a living network of green "highways" along which woodland plants and animals can travel and move into the open countryside.

Ancient hedgerows, usually defined as those in existence before the mid-18th century, support the greatest diversity of plants and animals. Some hedges, in Devon and elsewhere in the south-west and south Wales, may even follow field boundaries dating from as long ago as the late Iron Age. One sign of an ancient hedge is the presence of trees that spread very slowly, such as Hazel and Field Maple, or of typical woodland flowers such as Bluebell, Primrose, and Wood Anemone. Today, hedgerows are one of Britain's most valuable wildlife habitats. More than 500 species of plant have been recorded in our hedgerows, together with over 1,500 species of insect. In particular, hedgerows are a major habitat for butterflies, and are used by many nesting birds, including Yellowhammers and Whitethroats.

watching

FREQUENTLY OVERLOOKED AS A HABITAT IN THEIR OWN RIGHT, HEDGEROWS CAN BE THE MOST PRODUCTIVE PLACES FOR PLANTS AND ANIMALS IN FARMLAND AND ARE WORTH A VISIT AT ANY TIME OF YEAR.

Traditionally laid hedgerows with a mixture of full-sized trees and shrubs are the best for wildlife. Neat, tidy hedges are a poor relative.

The easiest way to explore hedgerows is to walk along a country lane, but even if it seems deserted stay alert for vehicles and always make sure that you step off the road when using binoculars.

Perennial plants such as orchids – and many fungi – die back at the end of each growing season to reappear in the same spot, so once located, can be enjoyed every year.

Look for clues left by secretive mammals – small burrows are likely to be the work of Field or Bank Voles, while a strand of grey hair caught on a thorn or barbed wire means a Badger passed earlier. You may also catch the pungent musky whiff of a Red Fox.

Listen carefully for the high-pitched squeaks of Common Shrews coming from the leaf litter – their calls are just within our hearing range.

◁ **Mistle Thrush**
Berry-covered holly and Hawthorn trees are often guarded by a resident Mistle Thrush, which drives away others to ensure its own supply. *See page 150.*

▷ **Woolly Milkcap**
The button-shaped fruiting bodies of Woolly Milkcap appear among the leaf litter on damp verges and banks, usually under Silver Birch trees. *See page 475.*

BRAMLEY APPLE

PARKS AND GARDENS

These green spaces may seem "tame" and devoid of interest for the nature watcher, but collectively they create a huge network of unofficial nature reserves that reaches deep into our towns and cities and which is just as important for wildlife as Britain's most famous wilderness areas. Close-mown lawns are of little value to animals, except for hungry flocks of Starlings and Black-headed Gulls: it is the wide variety of other features in parks and gardens, from flowerbeds to vegetable patches, compost heaps, hedges, parkland trees, and ponds, that make wonderful wildlife habitats. Parks and gardens are not only home to common species – several nationally scarce species can be found there too. On midsummer evenings the Stag Beetle is frequently spotted in gardens with mature trees in south-eastern England, while some suburban parks and golf courses have ponds with breeding populations of Great Crested Newts, which are in rapid decline across the UK.

The best gardens for wildlife are on the fringes of built-up areas, where woodland and farmland birds, amphibians, and even Badgers may turn up in search of food. But wildlife can also be attracted to the most unpromising, densely populated urban locations, especially if there is a pond. Apart from taking the decision to stop using pesticides and slug pellets, digging a pond is the single best thing any gardener can do for wildlife. Other simple steps are to plant native trees such as Silver Birch and Holly instead of exotic varieties, leave a patch of lawn unmown so daisies and buttercups flourish, and create a log pile for beetle larvae.

watching

MANY ANIMALS THAT ARE SHY IN THE COUNTRYSIDE ALLOW A CLOSER APPROACH IN PARKS AND GARDENS, SO THESE ARE GREAT PLACES TO DEVELOP IDENTIFICATION SKILLS AND STUDY THEIR BEHAVIOUR.

Try to visit parks with a mix of habitats, such as mature trees, overgrown shrubberies, a lake, and wildflower garden. Neat and tidy parks are less rewarding.

Explore quieter corners of the park, well away from the entrance and the disturbance caused by dog walkers and ball games.

Even a small garden pond is worth watching for half an hour in the morning and at dusk to see which birds and mammals come to drink. Keep a diary of seasonal changes in the wildlife that pay a visit.

Provide a variety of foods in your garden to attract different birds. Goldfinches and Siskins love niger seed, while a fat block may bring in a Nuthatch or Great Spotted Woodpecker.

Put out a little dry dog food in the evening to tempt hedgehogs to your garden (avoid milk and bread as it can make them unwell).

△ **Common Pipistrelle**
From mid-November until early April these bats hibernate together in churches and lofts. Sometimes they emerge briefly during spells of unusually mild winter weather. *See page 82.*

▽ **House Sparrow**
Sparrows are the most abundant garden birds, despite their numbers falling by over half since 1979. In towns, one of their main problems is a lack of suitable nest sites. *See page 158.*

▽ **Badger**
Like foxes, Badgers have adapted well to life in parks and gardens. Urban areas such as Birmingham, Bristol, Brighton, and London's outer suburbs have flourishing Badger populations. *See page 94.*

▽ **Wood Mouse**
This misleadingly named rodent is common in parks and leafy suburban gardens, often taking refuge in outbuildings. It starts breeding in late winter, usually in March. *See page 88.*

WINTER

SPRING

△ **Seven-spot Ladybird**
Having hibernated through the winter, ladybirds become active again on fine days in March and April and immediately start hunting for prey. *See page 265.*

▽ **Blackbird**
One of the finest singers in the bird world, the male Blackbird sings his heart out from the top of TV aerials, chimneys, and tall trees. *See page 150.*

The rising temperatures and lengthening days of spring trigger a frenetic round of activity in garden animals. Hedgehogs, bats, bumblebees, and beetles leave their hibernation sites, the year's first butterflies such as Small Tortoiseshells and Peacocks can be seen on the wing, and male birds erupt in song to establish nesting territories.

Urban foxes symbolize the remarkable adaptability of wild animals in our parks and gardens. During the 1920s and 1930s Red Foxes began moving into the UK's rapidly growing suburbs, taking advantage of the plentiful supply of rat and mice prey and scavenging household rubbish. They hid their earths under sheds or in cellars, sometimes becoming tame and even sleeping in the open. Today, one in seven British foxes live in urban areas.

SUMMER

△ Small Tortoiseshell
The caterpillars of this beautiful insect feed on stinging nettles, so it benefits from untidy areas left to grow wild. *See page 200.*

△ London Plane
Originally planted for its extreme resistance to air pollution, this is the typical tree of squares and roadsides in the capital. Squirrels feed on its seeds. *See page 330.*

Unsprayed herbaceous borders and vegetable patches are the rainforests of our towns and cities. They provide a major habitat for insects native to pasture and woodland, and in summer hum with a dozen or more species of bee, hoverfly, and butterfly. In turn the insects are eaten by Common Frogs, hedgehogs, and newly emerged fox cubs.

AUTUMN

Ornamental planting schemes support fewer animals than the UK's native woodland and hedgerows but produce an annual bounty each autumn: berries and nuts. Conkers are a major food for Grey Squirrels, and the brilliant red berries of Mountain Ash, Cotoneaster, and Pyracantha are devoured by flocks of thrushes.

△ Horse Chestnut
Avenues of golden-brown Horse Chestnuts make a spectacular sight in autumn. They are among the first trees to change colour. *See page 325.*

▽ Common Mole
Although moles are uncommon in towns, their telltale spoil heaps can be spotted in large parks and sports fields. *See page 78.*

Windowsills and parapets are no different from the ledges on a cliff-face as far as cliff-nesting birds are concerned, so a city offers thousands of potential nest sites. Nearly all British Rock Doves and Swifts nest on buildings, and growing numbers of Herring Gulls do too. Kittiwakes, normally one of the most marine gulls, have established a colony on the Tyne Bridge in central Newcastle (below), but the noise and mess they make has brought them into conflict with some local people.

SUMMER

◁ **Dandelion**
This fast-growing weed sprouts almost anywhere – between cracks in paving stones, on top of crumbling walls, or in the middle of roundabouts. *See page 421.*

◁ **Ivy**
Covering walls in a thick evergreen tangle, ivy is a wonderful microhabitat full of all kinds of spiders and insects. It also provides a secure nest site for Wrens and other birds. *See page 384.*

◁ **House Fly**
Usually seen as nothing more than a nuisance or pest, the humble House Fly is an important urban resident that recycles rubbish and leftovers. *See page 278.*

▷ **Common Poppy**
Poppies are just as likely to be seen growing in piles of rubble in urban wastelands as in fields, many of which are sprayed with weedkillers. *See page 356.*

The urban environment is **far from sterile.** It is home to thriving communities of plants and animals, often in the **most unexpected places.**

COCKROACH

URBAN

Almost 15 per cent of Britain's land surface was classed as urban in 2005 and this figure is increasing as sprawling towns and cities continue to grow, but the potential of this vast man-made habitat for plants and animals is often overlooked. The division between "town" and "country" is an artificial one for many species: winds blow wildflower seeds from the surrounding countryside into built-up areas, while roadside verges, railway lines, and canals provide green corridors along which animals can commute between rural and urban landscapes. Intensively managed farmland has few opportunities for wildlife, whereas urban waste ground can be a herbicide- and pesticide-free haven teeming with invertebrate life.

Derelict industrial or brownfield land is seldom protected but provides a refuge for a growing number of species declining in the countryside, including Common Toads, Grass Snakes, Kestrels, beetles, dragonflies, and several kinds of lizard. Rubbish dumps offer rich pickings for Red Foxes and huge flocks of gulls, and Peregrine Falcons nest in the heart of several cities, attracted by the abundant supply of pigeon prey. In even the most built-up city centres there is space for patches of wilderness, as demonstrated by an ecoroof project in east London to turn the flat roofs of office blocks into high-rise meadows suitable for rare Black Redstarts.

watching

THE URBAN JUNGLE IS NOT AS UNIFORM AS YOU THINK – THERE ARE ALWAYS PRODUCTIVE CORNERS FOR WILDLIFE, SUCH AS RUBBISH DUMPS, CANALS, ALLOTMENTS, DISUSED FACTORIES, AND CEMETERIES.

A street atlas will help you to find suitable green 'oases' for urban plants and animals, but make sure that there is public access before you start exploring.

Binoculars are just as useful in towns as in the countryside: try to get into the habit of taking them with you on urban walks.

Early mornings are best, because animals are more active and there is less disturbance from people and dogs being walked.

A higher viewpoint will allow you to scan the surrounding area. Footbridges are often good for watching canals, railway embankments, and roadside verges.

Leave traffic behind and you will have more chance of hearing bird song and calls.

High ledges and towers are worth a look for perched gulls, wagtails, and falcons.

SPRING

Pioneer plants such as Rosebay Willowherb – one of the most easily recognized flowers of waste ground – quickly take root in poor-quality soil, bringing a splash of colour to neglected urban areas. Later in the year other weeds burst into flower, providing nectar for butterflies, bees, hoverflies, and day-flying moths.

▽ **Groundsel**
Among the first weeds to flower in spring, Groundsel flourishes almost anywhere. Its seeds are eaten by House Sparrows. *See page 416.*

▽ **Slow Worm**
This legless lizard is common on open ground, frequently hiding under scrap metal and old tyres. It emerges from hibernation in April, when it can be spotted basking in the sun. *See page 167.*

AUTUMN

Wildflower seeds are a vital resource for animals in autumn, including Goldfinches and rodents such as this Harvest Mouse, feeding on the seed-head of an umbellifer. Harvest Mice avoid built-up areas but may move into undisturbed motorway verges – an ideal substitute for their usual habitat of traditionally managed pasture and cornfields.

▷ **Crane Fly**
In late summer and early autumn numbers of adult crane flies reach a peak in areas of long grass, while hordes of their larvae feed on the roots. *See page 270.*

▽ **Common Nettle**
Lush patches of stinging nettles are the classic vegetation of waste ground, and may flower well into September. *See page 344.*

WINTER

Towns and cities have several major advantages over the surrounding countryside in winter, when many animals face a battle for survival. There are more artificial food sources, fewer predators, and it is several degrees warmer at night due to the "heat pool" effect caused by the hot air escaping from engine exhausts and poorly insulated buildings.

▷ **Starling**
During winter flocks of Starlings, resplendent in spangled nonbreeding plumage, roost on tall buildings, pylons, and bridges. *See page 158.*

▽ **Rat**
Common Rats are able to breed year-round in towns, so it is possible to see young in every month of the year. Warmer winters are helping rat populations flourish. *See page 90.*

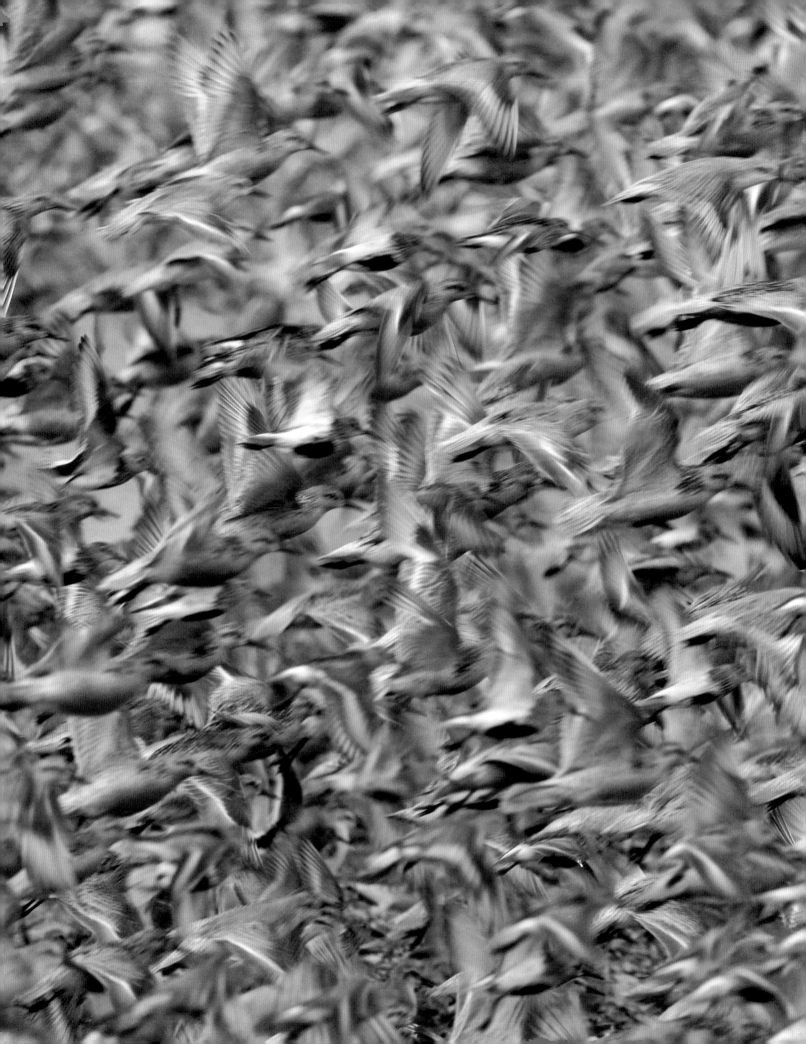

SPECIES

MAMMALS

Although among our most loved wildlife, the British Isles have relatively few mammals, a result of our island status and historic extinctions. Just half of all European species are found in Britain, and only 78 are native. Most important are Grey Seals – with about 60 per cent of the world population found on and around British coasts. We do, however, have a further 20 introduced species. Some, such as the Rabbit, which was introduced from the Mediterranean, are now ubiquitous, and Grey Squirrels give city dwellers their best chance to meet wildlife. Conservation is now active in restoring lost elements. There are, for example, plans to return the European Beaver and, much more controversially, the Brown Bear and Grey Wolf.

INSECTIVORES

Feeding on all manner of invertebrates, not just insects as their name might suggest, shrews, moles, and hedgehogs have elongated snouts, and sharp, pointed teeth for tackling their prey.

BATS

The only mammals capable of true flight, bats are mostly nocturnal, feeding on insects located by means of ultrasonic sonar, or echolocation. They often roost communally during the day and for hibernation.

RABBITS AND HARES

Small to medium-sized grazing animals, rabbits and hares have teeth and digestive systems that are adapted to eating and processing plant material. They have well-developed ears and hind legs.

RODENTS

Small and largely herbivorous, squirrels, voles, rats, and mice have teeth that are well adapted to their diet – a pair of chiselling incisors that can cope with nuts and seeds, and a row of grinding cheek-teeth.

CARNIVORES

Diverse in form and size, cats, dogs, and mustelids, such as stoats, ferrets, and otters, are linked by their meat-eating habits, although some have a more omnivorous diet; all have powerful teeth and jaws.

SEALS

Often classed with carnivores, seals breed on land, but feed at sea on fish and crustaceans. Strong swimmers, their limbs are modified into flippers and they have streamlined bodies for cutting through the water.

DOLPHINS

Dolphins, porpoises, and whales are truly aquatic mammals, their hairless, streamlined bodies, and flippers, fins, and tail flukes among their many adaptations to life in the sea.

DEER

Medium to large grazing and browsing animals, deer are grouped with other cloven-hooved mammals, such as pigs and goats. Males in particular often have paired antlers or horns.

Anatomy

Mammals are the only animals that are covered in fur, although only sparsely so in some groups, especially the aquatic ones. They are endothermic or "warm-blooded", and have the ability to maintain a constant internal body temperature, regardless of changing external conditions. All but a very few primitive species, which do not occur in Britain, bear live young. Most give birth to relatively advanced young, after a significant period of gestation; the exceptions are marsupials, which are not native to the British Isles.

female Rabbit suckling its young

YOUNG MAMMALS
A young mammal is nourished with its mother's milk. Parental care is one of the key features that sets mammals apart from other animals. Some mammals look after their young until they are several years old.

Basic Structure

Despite their diversity of form, mammals are made up of the same building blocks. Take the limbs – the ancestral pattern is to have five digits. Dolphins have flippers, but the bones reveal these developed from the five digit form. In deer, three digits have been lost or reduced, and the remaining two bear paired ("cloven") hooves. Even a bat's wing show the same characteristics.

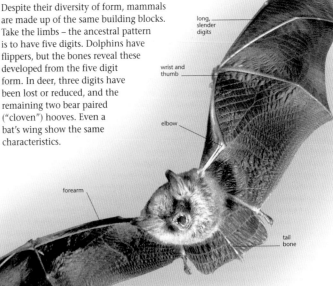

long, slender digits

wrist and thumb

elbow

forearm

tail bone

fifth finger

Fur Types

The fur of mammals has many functions, including insulation from extremes of temperature, physical defence and protection, camouflage, and visual communication. In many cases, including the examples below, there are specific adaptations to enable the fur to perform a particular role.

short fur

COMMON SEAL
Adult seals have short fur, keeping them streamlined. Seal pups have longer fur, for insulation, as they lack the adult's thick layers of blubber.

spines

HEDGEHOG
The modification of hairs into sharp spines, mean that Hedgehogs are relatively immune to predation; they also have insulating underfur.

guard hairs

BADGER
The outer hairs, or guard hairs, of a Badger are rather coarse, providing it with a degree of protection when squeezing through gaps or shrubs.

spots

FALLOW DEER
The spotted summer coat of a Fallow Deer provides good camouflage in its typical open woodland habitats, characterized by dappled shade.

Identification

Manny mammals are very shy and secretive, others are largely nocturnal, and a lot are rather rare. So seeing them can be difficult. However, you can increase your chances by taking a few simple steps. Firstly find the correct habitat – as with any plant or animal, mammals do have preferences. Then wait, and be patient, into the night if necessary: modern night-vision aids have revolutionized mammal watching. Be aware that animals have a keen sense of smell, so try and remain downwind of them.

OPEN FARMLAND

Rabbit

OPEN LOWLAND AND WATER

Bat

LOWLAND GRASSES

Hedgehog

Habitat and Distribution

Mammals can adapt more readily to different climatic conditions than reptiles or amphibians, and so are found in a wide range of habitats. Knowing which species to expect to see in a specific area is the first step to identification.

COASTS

Grey Seal

DRY GRASSLAND

Pygmy Shrew

DECIDUOUS WOODS

Dormouse

TALL GRASSLAND

Field Vole

OPEN WOODS

Red Deer

RIVERS

Otter

CONIFEROUS AND MIXED FOREST

Pine Marten

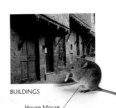

BUILDINGS

House Mouse

SHALLOW COASTAL WATERS

Harbour Porpoise

WOODLAND SCRUB

Wild Cat

WATERSIDE

American Mink

Tracks and Signs

Given the often secretive nature, and sometimes nocturnal habits, of many mammals, the best way of recognizing some species is from the signs they leave. These may include droppings, footprints, feeding signs, or distinctive places of shelter, protection, or breeding. Although not always providing conclusive proof of identity, such signs are an important part of the array of identification features.

TRACKS

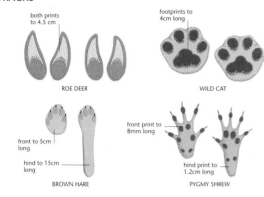

both prints to 4.5 cm

ROE DEER

footprints to 4cm long

WILD CAT

front to 5cm long

hind to 15cm long

BROWN HARE

front print to 8mm long

hind print to 1.2cm long

PYGMY SHREW

NESTS

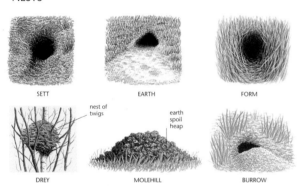

SETT

EARTH

FORM

nest of twigs

DREY

earth spoil heap

MOLEHILL

BURROW

FEEDING SIGNS

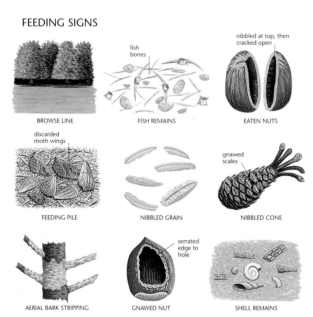

BROWSE LINE

fish bones

FISH REMAINS

nibbled at top, then cracked open

EATEN NUTS

discarded moth wings

FEEDING PILE

NIBBLED GRAIN

gnawed scales

NIBBLED CONE

AERIAL BARK STRIPPING

serrated edge to hole

GNAWED NUT

SHELL REMAINS

DROPPINGS

blackish droppings to 10cm long

OTTER DROPPINGS

tapered droppings to 5mm long

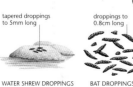

WATER SHREW DROPPINGS

droppings to 0.8cm long

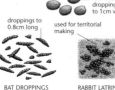

BAT DROPPINGS

rounded droppings to 1cm wide

used for territorial making

RABBIT LATRINE

Variations

Not all individuals in a species look the same. There may be differences between the sexes; young mammals may be very different from their parents; the appearance may change with the seasons. There may also be variations between animals from different parts of the geographical range. The entries in this book show some of the most common variations.

white winter coat

no antlers

STOAT
In the northern part of its range the Stoat's coat becomes white in winter, for camouflage. The tip of the tail remains black.

small antlers

black tail

brown coat

SEX DIFFERENCES
Adult male Roe Deer are distinguished from the females by their small antlers, and slightly larger stature.

Winter Behaviour

A few species hibernate through the colder months. True hibernation involves a reduction in the normal physiological processes including body temperature and breathing rate. However, many other mammals show reduced activity in winter, perhaps asleep but not so deeply as hibernators.

HEDGEHOG
The Hedgehog usually hibernates from late autumn, hidden within a collection of dead leaves or grass. Most individuals awaken from hibernation and move nests one or more times during the winter.

DORMOUSE
With one of the most extended hibernation periods of any British mammal, the Dormouse remains in its nest of grass, leaves and often Honeysuckle bark from October to April.

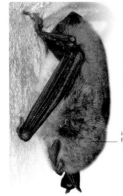

insulating fur

NATTERER'S BAT
Bats, being insectivorous, are not able to find food in winter. They hibernate in caves, tree cavities, and sometimes buildings, usually where the temperature is relatively constant to avoid being woken from their torpor.

SQUIRREL
Although making a series of winter nests, squirrels do not hibernate. They may remain inactive for several days in the coldest weather, but awaken regularly and replenish their energy reserves, eating the nuts cached in autumn.

SCALE MEASUREMENTS
Given the vast difference in sizes, two scale drawings, one of a human hand and one of an adult man, are used to convey a rough indication of the size of the species being described. The hand represents an average adult hand 18cm in height. The man represents an average adult man 1.8m (6ft) tall.

18cm

1.8m (6ft)

SYMBOLS
For clarity, symbols are used to denote males and females where these are visually distinct. ♀ *female* ♂ *male*

Common Mole

Talpa europaea (Insectivora)

Common Moles are rarely seen above ground, but their presence is easily noted from the spoil heaps (molehills) resulting from their burrowing activity, which continues day and night throughout the year. They are least visible in the heat of summer when their invertebrate prey is forced down to deeper, more moist soil levels. The dispersal of young animals is largely above ground, where they are especially vulnerable to predation by Red Foxes (p.90), Buzzards (p.122), and Grey Herons (p.118).

dark velvety fur

small, but open, eyes

large front feet

FAVOURS *grassland, cultivated areas, and deciduous woodland – almost to mountain top levels; avoids places that are prone to flooding.*

front to 4mm long, formed by claws only

hind to 2cm

spoil heap from tunnelling

MOLEHILL

SIZE *Body 11–16cm; tail 2–4cm.*
YOUNG *Usually a single litter of 3–4; May–June.*
DIET *Earthworms, insect larvae, and other subterranean invertebrates, often paralysed with a bite and stored alive for times of shortage. Rarely forage on surface.*
STATUS *Common.*
SIMILAR SPECIES *None.*

NOTE
Moles are adapted to burrowing, with a cylindrical body shape, spade-like forefeet, ears that do not project, and poor vision, but a keen sense of smell.

Western Hedgehog

Erinaceus europaeus (Insectivora)

Hedgehogs, characterized by their covering of protective spines up to 3cm long and short dark legs, are familiar animals, having colonized parks and gardens, even in the largest cities. There are three European species, with the Western Hedgehog being the only one in the British Isles and northwestern Europe. Its underside is clothed in uniformly coloured fur, which is dark in most hedgehogs found in the British Isles, but pale cream in those from southern France and Spain. A noisy forager and largely nocturnal, this hedgehog hibernates in nests of dry grass and leaves.

FOUND *in lowland grassland and open woods; very frequently in gardens where they perform a valuable role in pest control.*

hind to 3cm long

front to 2.5 cm long

droppings to 4cm long

NOTE
Spines are an effective defence against most predators – apart from motor vehicles. Sadly, road casualties are all too common.

face and limbs hidden

ROLLED DEFENSIVE POSTURE

covered in spines above

narrow spine-free "parting"

creamy brown spines, often dark-tipped

SIZE *Body 20–30cm; tail 1–4cm.*
YOUNG *One or two litters of up to six; June–September.*
DIET *Earthworms, slugs, woodlice, spiders, beetles, and other invertebrates; birds' eggs and nestlings; carrion; some plant material and fungi. Naturally control populations of slugs and snails in gardens.*
STATUS *Common.*
SIMILAR SPECIES *None.*

Common Shrew

Sorex araneus (Insectivora)

Like all shrews, the Common Shrew is a small, active but secretive animal, its elongated snout bearing long sensory bristles. Adults are distinctly three-coloured, with a brown back, creamy underside, and chestnut flanks. In contrast, juveniles have a less distinct flank coloration, a paler overall appearance, and a thicker tail, which bears tufts of bristly hair. Common Shrews are active by day and night, throughout the year, a consequence of their very high metabolic rate, which means they must eat more than 90 per cent of their body weight each day.

FREQUENTS *all habitats with significant ground cover, particularly rough grassland.*

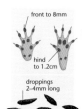

slender, pointed muzzle

front to 8mm

hind to 1.2cm

droppings 2–4mm long

NOTE
Shrews are relatively unpalatable, and so are frequently killed but not eaten by predators, such as cats. This provides a good opportunity for close examination of critical identification features.

pale underparts

dark brown back

small, inconspicuous eyes and ears

reddish flanks

SIZE *Body 5.5–9cm; tail 3–6cm.*
YOUNG *Up to four litters of 6–7; April–August.*
DIET *Worms, slugs, woodlice, spiders, beetles, and other ground-dwelling invertebrates, which it locates mainly through its sense of smell and hearing; small amounts of seed.*
STATUS *Common.*
SIMILAR SPECIES *Pygmy Shrew (p.79).*

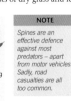

Pygmy Shrew

Sorex minutus (Insectivora)

The Pygmy Shrew is distinctly smaller than most other widespread shrews in Britain and Europe. Its upper fur is a relatively pale, medium brown colour, which merges into the whitish underside without a distinct flank colour. The tail is relatively long, greater than two-thirds of the head and body length, and broad, covered as it is by a dense clothing of hairs. Active by both day and night, with alternating periods of foraging and rest, the Pygmy Shrew is more diurnal than the Common Shrew (p.78), although more often heard squeaking than seen.

FOUND *in a very wide range of lowland and upland grassy heath and scrub habitats; more tolerant of shorter vegetation than the Common Shrew.*

brown fur

small eyes

more whitish underside

droppings to 4mm long

front print to 8mm long

hind print to 1.2cm long

no distinct flank colour

very small ears, hidden in fur

slender, pointed muzzle

NOTE

Teeth characteristics are useful for identifying shrews. In Europe, the Pygmy Shrew is unique in that its third single-cusped tooth in the upper jaw is longer than the second.

SIZE *Body 4–6cm; tail 3–4.6cm.*
YOUNG *Two litters of 4–7; April–August.*
DIET *Ground-dwelling invertebrates, especially beetles, spiders, and woodlice.*
STATUS *Common, though usually less abundant than Common Shrews in the same habitats.*
SIMILAR SPECIES *Common Shrew (p.78).*

Water Shrew

Neomys fodiens (Insectivora)

A large species, the Water Shrew is usually found in damp areas, as its name would suggest. It is a good swimmer, aided by fringes of hair on the feet and a keel of silvery hairs on the tail. When seen underwater, this shrew has a silvery appearance due to bubbles of air trapped in its fur. On land, it is black above and usually white below, with a sharp demarcation between the two. However, there is variation in the underside colour, and some individuals are black all over. Water Shrews are largely nocturnal foragers, leaving piles of food remains around their feeding sites. They build tunnels near water and live in nests made of dry grass and leaves.

LIVES *in a variety of aquatic habitats, from seaweed-covered boulders to mountain streams at high levels; rarely wanders to more terrestrial sites.*

shiny fur

black upperparts

small eyes

fringe of hair on feet

white underparts

hind print to 1.8cm long

front print to 1.2cm long

tapered droppings to 5mm long

NOTE

This is the most aquatic of European shrews, frequently hunting in water, where it feeds on fish and frogs after paralysing them with toxic saliva.

shells

FOOD REMAINS

SIZE *Body 6–9.5cm; tail 4.5–8cm.*
YOUNG *One or two litters of up to 15; April–September.*
DIET *Aquatic insects and crustaceans; small fish and amphibians.*
STATUS *Locally common.*
SIMILAR SPECIES *None.*

Greater White-toothed Shrew

Crocidura russula (Insectivora)

The white-toothed shrews are superficially similar to the red-toothed species, but can usually be told apart as a group by their prominent larger ears, not hidden in fur, and their shorter tail, covered with whiskery hair. But differentiation of species is more difficult, especially between Greater and Lesser White-toothed Shrews (*C. suaveolens*). Size is some indication, but there is considerable overlap, and details of the teeth may be needed for definite identification. The Greater White-toothed Shrew is the shrew that most frequently enters buildings, especially during the winter months.

SEEN *in lowland, dry grassland, woodland, and cultivated land; also gardens, houses, and farm buildings.*

pale below

mid-brown above

prominent ears

front print to 8mm

droppings 2–4mm long

hind print to 1cm

SIZE *Body 5.5–8.5cm; tail 2.5–4.5cm.*
YOUNG *Four or five litters of 3–4; February–November.*
DIET *Insects and other invertebrates; small vertebrates and carrion.*
STATUS *Common.*
SIMILAR SPECIES *Other White-toothed Shrews, especially Lesser (C. suaveolens), which lives in the Channel Islands, like the Greater White-toothed, but also on the Isles of Scilly.*

NOTE

This species may sometimes be seen "caravanning", when litters of young are led to safety by their mother, each grasping the tail of the animal in front with their teeth.

MAMMALS

GREATER HORSESHOE BAT

T he larger and rarer of Britain's two species of horseshoe bats, like its smaller relative, the Greater Horseshoe Bat has distinctive flaps and projections on its face, which act as part of its advanced sonar system. Although widespread across Eurasia, it is rare in western Europe. The small UK population declined in the 20th century, as a result of the loss of pasture, hedgerows, and woodland, the use of pesticides, and the destruction or disturbance of the bats' roosts and hibernation sites. The current population of 4,000–6,600 bats is fragmented, and based around one of 20–30 known "maternity colonies". Each colony is composed of up to a few hundred breeding females that roost in the roof spaces of old buildings. Females return to these birthplaces to raise their own young, and scientists are investigating how bats interbreed between the roosts and avoid isolation and inbreeding. To preserve these maternity sites, conservationists protect them from disturbance, maintaining the large entrance hole that horseshoe bats need, and even heating some roosts while the pups are growing. Hundreds of other caves, mines, and cellars, where the bats hibernate in the vicinity of the maternity roosts, are also protected. These and other conservation efforts have resulted in an increase in the Greater Horseshoe Bat population over the past few years.

Lesser Horseshoe-bat

Rhinolophus hipposideros (Chiroptera)

Often forming large communal roosts, the Lesser Horseshoe-bat is the smallest species of its group in Europe. Winter roosts, in which it hibernates between November and March, are largely underground, in caves, tunnels, and cellars, but breeding colonies are mostly to be found in buildings. As with other horseshoe-bats, the wings are wrapped around its body while at roost – completely so in the case of the Lesser and Greater (*R. ferrumequinum*) Horseshoe-bats. Individuals hang separately from the ceiling, without touching their neighbours.

FOUND *in well-wooded areas, usually associated with limestone geology; hunts close to the ground, usually below 5m.*

NOTE
The five European horseshoe-bats are characterized by complex folds of skin on the face, which are involved in the production of ultrasound for echolocation; they also differ in details of the sella and lancet.

wingspan 19–25 cm

wings enfold the body completely at rest

grey-brown above

greyish ears without a tragus

tapering sella

pale grey below

pale brown membrane

droppings to 8mm long

SIZE *Body 3.5–4.5cm; tail 2.5–3.3cm.*
YOUNG *Single young; June–August.*
DIET *Small insects and spiders.*
ECHOLOCATION *110kHz.*
STATUS *Vulnerable; scarce and declining.*
SIMILAR SPECIES *Greater Horseshoe-bat (R. ferrumequinum), which is much larger, with a butterfly-like flight.*

Brown Long-eared Bat

Plecotus auritus (Chiroptera)

Very long ears, up to 4cm long, serve to distinguish the long-eared bats from all other species. At rest, the ears are folded back over the body, although the long, narrowly triangular tragus remains erect. Its thumb is more than 6mm long. The ears and face of the Brown Long-eared Bat are pinkish brown, while the fur on its upperparts is pale brown, fading to whitish below. Its flight is graceful and swooping, often with well-controlled hovering as it gleans insects off the foliage of trees.

PREFERS *well-wooded, open areas, such as parks and gardens; roosts in buildings and trees throughout the year, and occasionally underground in winter.*

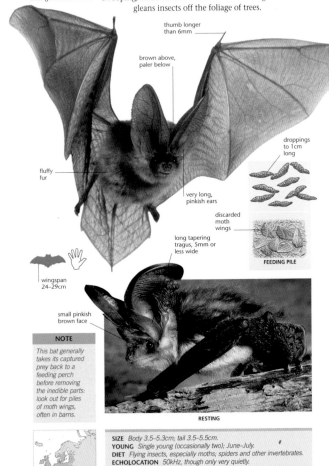

thumb longer than 6mm

brown above, paler below

droppings to 1cm long

fluffy fur

very long, pinkish ears

discarded moth wings

FEEDING PILE

long tapering tragus, 5mm or less wide

wingspan 24–29cm

small pinkish brown face

NOTE
This bat generally takes its captured prey back to a feeding perch before removing the inedible parts: look out for piles of moth wings, often in barns.

RESTING

SIZE *Body 3.5–5.3cm; tail 3.5–5.5cm.*
YOUNG *Single young (occasionally two); June–July.*
DIET *Flying insects, especially moths; spiders and other invertebrates.*
ECHOLOCATION *50kHz, though only very quietly.*
STATUS *Common.*
SIMILAR SPECIES *Grey Long-eared Bat (P. austriacus), a southern species with darker skin and underfur.*

Common Pipistrelle

Pipistrellus pipistrellus (Chiroptera)

OCCURS *in lowland habitats, including woodland, farmland, and urban areas, especially around water; roosts in buildings and trees, rarely in tunnels or caves.*

The commonest bat over most of Britain and Europe, Common Pipistrelle is also the smallest. This strongly colonial bat is a variable brown above and pale below, but each individual is generally uniform in colour. As with other pipistrelles, the wing membrane extends outside the calcar, but the thumb is relatively short. It is quite common to find maternity roosts of more than a thousand females. Its hunting flight is rather jerky, usually below 10m in height. Activity continues later into the autumn than most other bats, and midwinter emergence is not uncommon, when it feeds especially on Winter Moths.

NOTE
The Common Pipistrelle has recently been recognized as two species, the second being the Soprano Pipistrelle (P. pygmaeus), so called for its higher echolocation frequency of 55kHz. There are minor visible and perhaps distributional and ecological differences.

uniformly brown fur

long, blunt tragus

short thumb

short, rounded ears

wingspan 18–24cm

SOPRANO PIPISTRELLE

droppings to 0.8cm long

SIZE *Body 3.3–5.2cm; tail 2.5–3.6cm.*
YOUNG *Single litter of 1–2; May–August; mostly breed every other year.*
DIET *Small flying insects: midges, caddisflies, lacewings, and moths.*
STATUS *Common, though declining.*
ECHOLOCATION *45kHz.*
SIMILAR SPECIES *Other pipistrelles; Whiskered Bat (Myotis mystacinus), Brandt's Bat (M. brandtii), both of which have narrow ears and tragus.*

Daubenton's Bat

Myotis daubentonii (Chiroptera)

Small to medium-sized, Daubenton's Bat often feeds low over still or slow-moving water. It swims well and is capable of taking flight off the surface of water. In winter, it roosts in underground sites with high humidity, where torpid specimens often covered in dew are found. It occupies rock crevices and may also be found among screes on cave floors. One of the most abundant European bats, it is showing some signs of increase in population, perhaps as a result of climatic change.

INHABITS *open wooded areas, with access to water for feeding; summer roosts in cracks in trees and buildings, and under bridges.*

wingspan 23–27cm

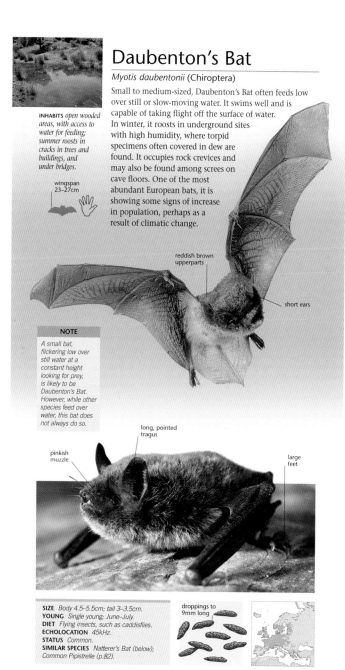

reddish brown upperparts

short ears

NOTE
A small bat, flickering low over still water at a constant height looking for prey, is likely to be Daubenton's Bat. However, while other species feed over water, this bat does not always do so.

long, pointed tragus

pinkish muzzle

large feet

SIZE *Body 4.5–5.5cm; tail 3–3.5cm.*
YOUNG *Single young; June–July.*
DIET *Flying insects, such as caddisflies.*
ECHOLOCATION *45kHz.*
STATUS *Common.*
SIMILAR SPECIES *Natterer's Bat (below); Common Pipistrelle (p.82).*

droppings to 9mm long

Natterer's Bat

Myotis nattereri (Chiroptera)

Natterer's Bat emerges just after sunset, and flies low with a slow, controlled flight, often hovering. In calm conditions it has a distinctive habit of flying with its tail pointed downwards. A medium-sized bat, it has a distinctly sinuous calcar (the bone supporting the tail membrane), and the rear margin of the tail has a dense fringe of hair.

FOUND *in open woodland and farmland, especially near wet habitats.*

wingspan 24–30cm

long, slim tragus

pink-tinged membranes

white underparts

ROOSTING

sinuous calcar

SIZE *Body 4–5cm; tail 4–5cm.*
YOUNG *Single young; June–July.*
DIET *Insects (flies, caddisflies, and beetles).*
ECHOLOCATION *45kHz.*
STATUS *Scarce or rare, but widespread.*
SIMILAR SPECIES *Other medium-sized Myotis bats, but none have the sinuous calcar.*

droppings to 1.1cm long

Noctule

Nyctalus noctula (Chiroptera)

The largest widespread British bat, Noctules are relatively visible as a result of their early emergence from roosts, up to an hour before dark. In such conditions, the distinctive red-brown colour of their upperparts can be clearly seen. Typically, they fly high (at 50m or more), but it is not difficult to find them even in the dark because the echolocation calls can be picked up on a bat detector at a range of 200m. Noctules also produce an audible (to most people) loud metallic chirp in flight.

FEEDS *over open woodland, pasture, and urban parks; summer roosts in tree holes, large winter roosts in rock crevices as well.*

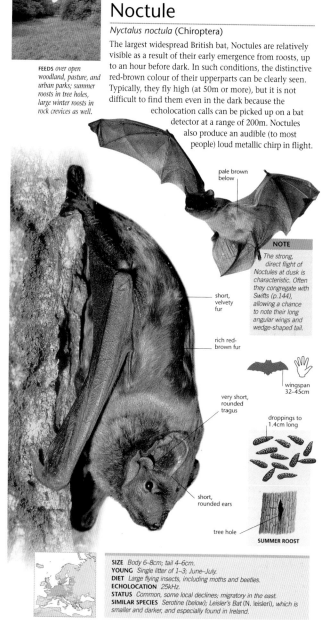

pale brown below

NOTE
The strong, direct flight of Noctules at dusk is characteristic. Often they congregate with Swifts (p.144), allowing a chance to note their long angular wings and wedge-shaped tail.

short, velvety fur

rich red-brown fur

wingspan 32–45cm

very short, rounded tragus

droppings to 1.4cm long

short, rounded ears

tree hole

SUMMER ROOST

SIZE *Body 6–8cm; tail 4–6cm.*
YOUNG *Single litter of 1–3; June–July.*
DIET *Large flying insects, including moths and beetles.*
ECHOLOCATION *25kHz.*
STATUS *Common, some local declines; migratory in the east.*
SIMILAR SPECIES *Serotine (below); Leisler's Bat (N. leisleri), which is smaller and darker, and especially found in Ireland.*

Serotine

Eptesicus serotinus (Chiroptera)

The Serotine is often seen feeding at dusk with Swifts (p.144), though at a somewhat lower level than Noctules (above). In reasonable light, the dark upperparts can be seen to contrast with the more yellowish underparts. At rest, the dark membranes and face are characteristic, together with its tragus. Its powerful teeth are necessary for tackling hard-bodied beetles.

FAVOURS *open and lightly wooded habitats in lowlands; roosts in buildings, occasionally tree holes, and in winter may be found underground.*

dark wing membranes

coarse droppings to 1cm long

short, narrow, and concave tragus

large teeth

wingspan 32–38cm

SIZE *Body 6–8cm; tail 4.5–5.5cm.*
YOUNG *Single young; June–August.*
DIET *Large flying insects, especially dung beetles and moths.*
ECHOLOCATION *25kHz.*
STATUS *Locally common.*
SIMILAR SPECIES *Noctule (above).*

Mountain Hare
Native to Britain, unlike the Brown Hare, the Mountain Hare's stronghold is the Scottish Highlands. It is associated with moorland, particularly that managed in traditional ways for Red Grouse.

Brown Hare

Lepus europaeus (Lagomorpha)

A widespread British species, Brown Hares have very long ears and large, powerful legs which can generate speeds of up to 75km per hour for short bursts. Unlike a Rabbit (right), with which a young, short-eared specimen may be confused, the tail is held depressed when running, so that the rump does not show as clear white, and the ears are tipped with black. Their activity takes place mostly at dusk and dawn, but they can be active at any time, especially during the springtime display period. Field signs include flattened patches of grass, or forms, where they rest by day and rear their young.

FREQUENTS *open agricultural fields and pastures, also hedgerows and woodland.*

LEVERET born and raised above ground

NOTE
"Mad March Hares" that are often seen chasing and boxing around open fields in the spring are actually the slightly larger females deterring the unwanted advances of males.

black tip
ears more than 8cm long
rich brown fur, reddening in winter
tail blackish above

front to 5cm long
hind to 15cm long

droppings 1cm wide

flattened grass
FORM

bark stripping
SAPLING DAMAGE

SIZE *Body 50–70cm; tail 7–10cm.*
YOUNG *About three litters of up to four; February–October.*
DIET *Grazes herbs, cereals, and grasses; browses low shrubs and strips bark.*
STATUS *Common, though declining in parts.*
SIMILAR SPECIES *Rabbit (right); Mountain Hare (below), which is a largely upland species with shorter ears.*

Rabbit

Oryctolagus cuniculus (Lagomorpha)

An ancient introduction for food and fur to much of Europe from its original home in Iberia, the Rabbit is now a familiar part of the British countryside, one which exerts a considerable influence on agriculture and natural habitats through grazing and other activities. Its fur is generally grey-brown above and paler below, but a wide range of colour variations from black to white can persist in the wild after escapes from captivity. The legs are relatively short, yet powerful, and the ears are long, though shorter than those of hares, and lack black tips. The tail is brown above and white below; when running, the tail is held erect to display the white fur to advantage, as a warning of danger to the social group.

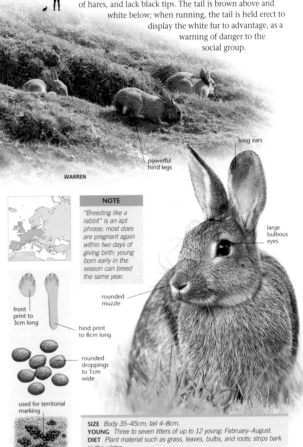

OCCUPIES *grassland and farmland, with hedges; look out for signs such as burrows, scrapes, and droppings in communal latrines.*

long ears
powerful hind legs
WARREN

NOTE
"Breeding like a rabbit" is an apt phrase; most does are pregnant again within two days of giving birth: young born early in the season can breed the same year.

front print to 3cm long
hind print to 8cm long

large bulbous eyes
rounded muzzle
rounded droppings to 1cm wide

used for territorial marking
LATRINE

SIZE *Body 35–45cm; tail 4–8cm.*
YOUNG *Three to seven litters of up to 12 young; February–August.*
DIET *Plant material such as grass, leaves, bulbs, and roots; strips bark in the winter.*
STATUS *Common.*
SIMILAR SPECIES *Brown Hare (left) and Mountain Hare (below), both of which have longer legs and ears and a more upright stance.*

Mountain Hare

Lepus timidus (Lagomorpha)

Also known as Blue Hare (due to its thick, insulating undercoat of dark-blue grey fur), the Mountain Hare's coat turns white in winter, and its feet are thick with fur. In lowland and agricultural areas, the hare has a brownish coat which does not turn white; the relatively short ears and wholly white tail are characteristic features to look out for. In Ireland, where the Brown Hare (above) is almost absent except as a local introduction, Mountain Hares are found in agricultural as well as montane habitats.

FAVOURS *montane grassland and woodland; sometimes found in lowland. Unlike other hares, it makes short burrows.*

front to 5cm long
droppings to 1cm wide
hind to 14cm long

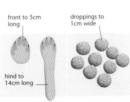

black tips to ears
white winter fur
WINTER COAT

grey-brown fur
ears less than 8cm long

SIZE *Body 45–60cm; tail 4–8cm.*
YOUNG *Two or three litters of up to five.*
DIET *Grasses, herbs, low shrubs, and bark.*
STATUS *Common in suitable habitats.*
SIMILAR SPECIES *Brown Hare (above), which is more bulky, with longer ears.*

Red Squirrel

Sciurus vulgaris (Rodentia)

A remarkably variable species over much of its range, the Red Squirrel can be any colour from red, through all shades of brown, to black, though always with white underparts. In winter, all variations assume a more greyish appearance and develop prominent ear-tufts. Red Squirrels are very agile and spend much of their time in the branches of trees, where the long bushy tail is used for balance. However, a considerable amount of foraging is done on the ground, where they move with a light, bounding gait.

OCCUPIES coniferous and deciduous woodland, where its nests (dreys) are built of twigs and leaves in the fork of a tree, normally close to the trunk.

brown or black upperparts

DARK FORM

ear-tufts

long bushy tail

front print to 3cm long

hind print to 5cm long

droppings to 8mm wide

white underparts

nest of twigs

DREY

scales removed whole

EATEN CONES

nibbled at top, then cracked open

EATEN NUTS

NOTE
One of the favoured foods of the Red Squirrel is pine seeds. A cone is held between the forefeet, and the scales are gnawed off to reveal the seeds. The core is then dropped, providing one of the most obvious field signs of Red Squirrels.

SIZE Body 18–25cm; tail 24–20cm.
YOUNG One or two litters of 3–5; March–September.
DIET Tree seeds, buds, bark, roots, fungi, birds' eggs, and nestlings.
STATUS Near-threatened; locally common, but declining where it overlaps with Grey Squirrels.
SIMILAR SPECIES Grey Squirrel (below), brighter individuals of which can approach the typical red colour of this species.

Grey Squirrel

Sciurus carolinensis (Rodentia)

The Grey Squirrel has displaced the Red Squirrel (above) from most of England and Wales. Less arboreal than Red Squirrels, they feed extensively on the ground, and hide caches of acorns and other fruit for future use. The grey fur is variable in colour and the ears are never strongly tufted. Field signs are similar to those of Red Squirrels.

INHABITS all kinds of woodland, parkland, and gardens with a ready supply of food.

whitish tail fringe

front print to 3cm

hind print to 5cm

droppings 8mm wide

DREY
stripped bark

TREE DAMAGE

reddish tone on flanks

SIZE Body 23–30cm; tail 20–24cm.
YOUNG One or two litters of 3–6; May–October.
DIET Seeds, bark, insects, eggs, and nestlings.
STATUS Introduced from North America; very common and still extending its range.
SIMILAR SPECIES Red Squirrel (above).

Water Vole

Arvicola terrestris (Rodentia)

A large, blunt-nosed vole with a furry tail, the Water Vole is usually found in or near aquatic habitats. The fur is variable in colour – usually brown, but a large proportion of voles can be almost black. Shredded bark, cut grass leaves, and irregularly gnawed nuts are often the best evidence of its presence, as it is largely active at twilight or before sunrise.

FOUND in freshwater habitats – listen for the "plop" as it dives for safety; also in meadows and pastures.

swims high in water

blunt muzzle

front to 2cm

hind to 3.5cm

green, with rounded ends

to 0.8cm

serrated edge to hole

GNAWED NUT

SIZE Body 12–22cm; tail 6–12cm.
YOUNG Two to five litters of 2–6, March–October.
DIET Wide range of plant material.
STATUS Locally common, but severely declining due to pollution and habitat loss.
SIMILAR SPECIES Other smaller voles.

Bank Vole

Clethrionomys glareolus (Rodentia)

This blunt-nosed vole climbs trees well, making it easier to observe than most other voles. As its activity is mostly under the cover of darkness, identification of its feeding signs is important. These range from small cones stripped of scales and seeds (less frayed than those eaten by squirrels) to hazelnuts with a large, neat, round hole, and no teeth marks outside the opening.

LIVES in scrubby grassland and in deciduous and mixed shrubby woodland.

large ears and eyes

russet-brown back

front to 1cm

hind to 1.8cm

droppings to 4mm

inner bark

AERIAL BARK STRIPPING

pale underparts

SIZE Body 8–11cm; tail 3.5–7cm.
YOUNG Four or five litters of 3–5; April–October, year round if conditions are good.
DIET Buds, leaves, fruit, seeds, and fungi; some invertebrates.
STATUS Common.
SIMILAR SPECIES Field Vole (below).

Field Vole

Microtus agrestis (Rodentia)

Also known as the Short-tailed Vole, the Field Vole has a tail that is shorter than many other voles, and is distinctly dark above. Its long, shaggy fur almost covers its small ears, which are partially hairy inside, especially at the base. Differentiation of the *Microtus* voles by their characteristic teeth details is of little value in the field, but useful for remains found in owl pellets.

FAVOURS marshes, tall grassland, and open woodland; shreds leaves and grass forming clear pathways.

front print to 1.2cm

hind print to 1.4cm

droppings to 4mm

in grassy tussock

NEST

dark grey-brown fur

short, rounded muzzle

SIZE Body 8–13cm; tail 2–5cm.
YOUNG Three to seven litters of 2–6 young.
DIET Grass, roots, fungi, and bark.
STATUS Common; may be a pest.
SIMILAR SPECIES Bank Vole (above); Common Vole (M. arvalis), only on Guernsey and Orkney.

MAMMALS

Hazel Dormouse

Muscardinus avellanarius (Rodentia)

A small, orange-brown, largely arboreal rodent, the Hazel or Common Dormouse is nocturnal and hibernates from October to April in a tightly curled position to conserve heat. It is rather sensitive to cold, and even during its active period, cold weather can induce periods of torpor. The nest is a spherical ball of woven grass, moss, and bark strips, positioned in dense undergrowth, or in tree forks or nesting boxes. As befits its climbing habit, its feet are prehensile for grasping branches, and have well-developed pads to enable it to grip well. Its long furry tail may occasionally have a white tip.

FAVOURS *deciduous, often coppiced, woodland, scrub, and thick hedges; rather elusive, so best located by looking for feeding signs, especially hazelnuts with a neat round hole.*

— pale below

SLEEPING

NOTE

A classic habitat for the Hazel Dormouse is coppiced Hazel, abundant Bramble, and Climbing Honeysuckle, the latter providing bark strips to line its nest with.

long whiskers

large eyes

orange-brown fur

furry tail

front to 1cm

hind to 1.5cm

droppings to 5mm

smooth inner margin

NIBBLED HAZELNUT

SIZE *Body 6–9cm; tail 5.5–8cm.*
YOUNG *One or two litters of 4–7; June–August.*
DIET *Flowers, insects, and fruit that is seasonally available in its habitat.*
STATUS *Near-threatened; scarce and declining due to habitat fragmentation.*
SIMILAR SPECIES *Harvest Mouse (p.89), which is a similar size and colour, but has a hairless tail.*

Fat Dormouse

Glis glis (Rodentia)

Also known as the Edible Dormouse, the Fat Dormouse puts on a thick layer of fat by eating nutritionally rich seeds and nuts in preparation for hibernation. For this reason, it has long been hunted and kept in captivity as a source of food and fur. This dormouse is nocturnal, its large size and grey fur can lead to it being mistaken for a Grey Squirrel (p.87), although the latter is larger and more active during the day. It has large eyes, their size exaggerated by the circles of black fur that surround them.

FOUND *in mature deciduous woodland, often of beech or Sweet Chestnut; does not require a shrub layer.*

moderately prominent ears

large eyes

grey fur, often tinged brown

NOTE

Search for nest sites for a glimpse of this dormouse: look for spherical nests of grass, leaves, and moss, often wedged in the fork of a branch or in holes in trees, buildings, or underground.

prehensile feet

round eyes

long, bushy tail

front to 1.5cm

hind to 3cm

SIZE *Body 13–19cm; tail 12–15cm.*
YOUNG *Single litter of 2–9; June–August.*
DIET *Nuts, seeds, fungi, bark, insects, and birds' eggs and nestlings.*
STATUS *Introduced in Britain.*
SIMILAR SPECIES *Grey Squirrel (p.87).*

Wood Mouse

Apodemus sylvaticus (Rodentia)

One of the commonest and most widespread of European mammals, the Wood Mouse is found throughout Britain and continental Europe. Although it is generally assumed that a mouse in a house is a House Mouse (p.89), very often it is a Wood Mouse, with larger ears, eyes, and feet to prove it. It is very agile, with a bounding, kangaroo-like gait across open ground, and climbs nimbly up trees. It sometimes has a yellowish chest spot, although if present at all, it is never as extensive as that of the Yellow-necked Mouse (p.89), and always longer than it is broad. Feeding signs to look out for are fir cones with scales neatly gnawed off, and hazelnuts with teeth marks around the outside of the hole.

OCCURS *in woodland, forest edges (Beech and Spruce), grassland, marshes, rocky areas, and cultivated land; frequently to be found in buildings.*

NOTE

Although largely a nocturnal species, the Wood Mouse is insensitive to infra-red light and can be clearly observed in filtered torchlight.

large ears

large, beady eyes

greyish white underparts

yellow-brown flanks

dark brown fur above

130–180 rings on tail

JUVENILE

front to 1.2cm

hind to 2cm

droppings to 6mm long

gnawed scales

NIBBLED CONE

teeth marks

NIBBLED NUT

SIZE *Body 8–11cm; tail 7–11.5cm.*
YOUNG *One or two litters of 4–8; March–October.*
DIET *Seeds (especially acorns, beech masts, hazelnuts), cereal crops, buds, and saplings; insects and snails.*
STATUS *Common.*
SIMILAR SPECIES *Yellow-necked Mouse (p.89); which always has a broad, yellowish chest spot.*

House Mouse

Mus domesticus (Rodentia)

FOUND *mainly in buildings, where it is active by night, usually making a bulky nest of shredded paper and fabric, leaving a distinctive musty smell; can occupy a wide range of semi-natural habitats.*

Worldwide the most widely distributed mammal, apart from humans, the House Mouse is typically grey-brown above and dusky grey below, and there is no sharp line between the colour of the upper- and underparts. There is some variation, to reddish brown above and paler brown below; pale individuals can occur in all populations, but are most frequent in the south. This mouse has relatively small eyes and ears. Its hairless, thick tail has 140–175 prominent rings and is as long as the head and body length. A distinctive feature of the teeth of the House Mouse is that the upper incisors have a notch at the tip.

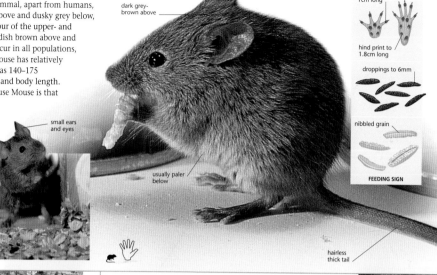

dark grey-brown above

small ears and eyes

usually paler below

hairless thick tail

front print to 1cm long

hind print to 1.8cm long

droppings to 6mm

nibbled grain

FEEDING SIGN

NOTE

Mice droppings can be confused with those of bats, especially since both can be found in houses and roof spaces. They are similar in shape and size, but those of bats crumble when rubbed between the fingers.

SIZE *Body 7–10cm; tail 7–9.5cm.*
YOUNG *Up to 10 litters of 4–8; year-round if sufficient food is available.*
DIET *Grain, stored food, and other plant matter; some invertebrates.*
STATUS *Common.*
SIMILAR SPECIES *Wood Mouse (p.88) and Yellow-necked Mouse (below) often enter human habitations, especially in the winter; both are larger and have longer ears and more prominent eyes.*

Yellow-necked Mouse

Apodemus flavicollis (Rodentia)

More robust than a Wood Mouse (p.88), the Yellow-necked Mouse is also a richer brown colour above and the brown is divided sharply from the pure white underparts. Its distinguishing feature is a yellow spot or collar on the chest. The amount of yellow on the neck is variable, but always more extensive than in the Wood Mouse. It is also a more arboreal species, often feeding nocturnally in the canopy of deciduous trees. It carries seeds and fruit to underground storage places, helping it to sustain itself and remain at least partially active during the winter months.

FAVOURS *deciduous woodland, hedges, orchards, and gardens; readily enters houses, especially during the winter.*

large ears

bulbous eyes

rich brown upperparts

white below

NOTE

The yellow chest mark, for which this rodent is named, is very variable; sometimes it forms a collar but if it is a spot, it is always more broad than it is long.

front to 1.5cm

hind to 2.5cm

droppings to 6mm

long tail, with 165–235 rings

SIZE *Body 9–13cm; tail 9–13cm.*
YOUNG *Three or four litters of up to eight; April–October.*
DIET *Seeds, seedlings, buds, fruit, fungi, and invertebrates.*
STATUS *Common.*
SIMILAR SPECIES *Wood Mouse (p.88); Alpine Mouse (A. alpicola), which has chest markings intermediate between those of Yellow-necked and Wood Mice and a relatively longer tail.*

Harvest Mouse

Micromys minutus (Rodentia)

The smallest European rodent, the Harvest Mouse is a very agile climber, using its feet with opposable outer toes to grip grass stems, and the semi-prehensile tail for additional support. The end 2cm of the tail can be curled around a stem, or held out straight for balance. Mainly nocturnal, it remains active throughout the year, although the winter months are spent largely on or below the ground. The soles of the feet of a Harvest Mouse are sensitive to vibration, and can thus alert them to oncoming danger.

OCCUPIES *grassland, scrub patches, river banks, edges of reedbeds, and among cereal crops.*

blunt snout

short hairy ears

whitish underparts

orange-brown fur above

front to 8mm

hind to 1.5cm

droppings to 2mm long

NEST

NOTE

The Harvest Mouse makes a distinctive nest of grass, woven into a ball up to 10cm wide and lodged in vegetation usually 30–60cm above the ground; given their small size and secretive nature, searching for nests in winter is the best way of establishing their presence on a site.

long, semi-prehensile tail

SIZE *Body 5–8cm; tail 5–7cm.*
YOUNG *Three to seven litters of up to eight; May–October.*
DIET *Grain and other seeds; buds, flowers, and fruit; insects and occasionally young birds and rodents.*
STATUS *Near-threatened; locally common but declining.*
SIMILAR SPECIES *Hazel Dormouse (p.88), which is only a little larger, but has a bushy tail, and is generally found in wooded areas.*

MAMMALS

Common Rat

Rattus norvegicus (Rodentia)

The Common Rat is also known as the Brown Rat. Its fur is generally a mid-brown colour, but there is some variability, although less than that shown by the Ship Rat *(R. rattus)*. A robust species, the Common Rat is further distinguished by its thicker tail, which is shorter than the head and body length, as well as being dark above and pale below, and its smaller, brownish, and hairy ears. Largely nocturnal, Common Rats are good swimmers and may be mistaken for Water Voles (p.87), although the smaller size and blunt muzzle of the voles are usually obvious. Small juvenile rats can be separated from mice by their disproportionately large feet.

OCCURS *in urban, industrial, and other developed areas, farms, refuse tips, sewage systems, and around natural river banks.*

NOTE

Common and Ship Rats (R. rattus) can be identified by their droppings: dividing the diameter by the length gives a value of more than 0.4 for Common Rat and less than 0.4 for the Ship Rat.

fleshy tail

pointed muzzle

mid-brown fur, lacking shaggy guard hairs

relatively small hairy ears

front print to 1.8cm

hind print to 3cm

droppings to 2cm

NIBBLED GRAIN

SIZE *Body 21–29cm; tail 17–23cm.*
YOUNG *Up to five litters of up to 15; year round.*
DIET *Seeds, grain, and other vegetable matter, invertebrates and small vertebrates; scavenges from human waste.*
STATUS *Introduced from Asia; common.*
SIMILAR SPECIES *Ship Rat (R. rattus), also known as Black Rat, is often darker and has a longer, thinner tail and larger ears; Water Vole (p.87).*

Red Fox

Vulpes vulpes (Carnivora)

Worldwide the most abundant and widespread carnivore, the Red Fox, as it name suggests, is usually a red-brown colour, although this can vary from sandy yellow to dark brown. Its underparts are usually white or pale, as is the tip of its long, bushy tail. The lower part of the legs and the backs of the erect, triangular ears are blackish. Predominantly crepuscular and nocturnal, the Red Fox is increasingly seen by day in areas where it is not persecuted. It is most easily noticed by its droppings, the musky odour of its urine, or its nocturnal high-pitched barks and screams.

OCCUPIES *a vast range of habitats, from woodland and farms to mountains and city centres; often secretive, look for its prominently displayed droppings.*

erect, pointed ears

CUBS

reddish brown fur

NOTE

Versatile and adaptable, the Red Fox is the only large carnivore that has successfully colonized urban areas, finding food and excavating burrows (earths) in parks and gardens.

darker fur patch on narrow muzzle

white upper lip and throat

front print to 5cm long

hind print smaller

tapered droppings 5–10cm long

spoil heap

EARTH

SIZE *Body 55–90cm; tail 30–45cm.*
YOUNG *Single litter of 4–5; March–May.*
DIET *Omnivorous: rabbits, rodents, hedgehogs, birds and their eggs; beetles, worms, and other ground invertebrates; crabs; fruit and berries; carrion and food scavenged from refuse tips and bins.*
STATUS *Common.*
SIMILAR SPECIES *None.*

Western Polecat

Mustela putorius (Carnivora)

The brown colour of this dark, slender predator is relieved only by its white face pattern, and where the outer coat is thinner on the flanks, the pale underfur may show through. As with most mustelids, the Western Polecat moves with a bounding gait, and readily adopts an alert posture, standing on its hind legs. Since it is largely nocturnal, it is not often seen, except all too often as a road casualty. However, its presence can be detected from the strong, musky scent it leaves as territorial marks on rocks and other landscape features.

FOUND *in lowland, often rocky woodland, river banks and marshes; around farms and buildings, particularly in winter.*

sinuous body

white ear fringes

whitish face pattern

dark brown outer fur

pale underfur, especially in winter

short legs

front to 3cm

hind to 4cm

tapered, twisted droppings to 7cm

DOMESTIC FERRET

NOTE

The Ferret is the domesticated form of this Polecat, and often escapes from captivity. Its dark and pale forms are distinctive, but those with a polecat pattern can only be differentiated on skull characteristics.

SIZE *Body 30–45cm; tail 12–14cm.*
YOUNG *Single litter of up to 12, May–July.*
DIET *Hunts rodents, rabbits, frogs, and birds; also takes insects, worms, and carrion.*
STATUS *Scarce, but increasing markedly, spreading out from its former Welsh heartland into central and northern Britain and Scotland.*
SIMILAR SPECIES *Domestic Ferret (M. furo).*

American Mink

Mustela vison (Carnivora)

An introduction in the 1920s, the American Mink has colonized Britain and Europe as a result of escapes from fur-farms. It has now occupied most of Britain and Ireland, and is considered to be a major factor in the recent decline in Water Vole (p.87) numbers. It is typically dark brown; other farmed colour forms that have escaped revert to dark brown after a few generations.

INHABITS *a variety of of waterside habitats, even rocky coasts; the droppings are similar to an Otter's but lack their "sweet" smell.*

front to 2.5cm

glossy dark brown fur

long, bushy tail

hind to 4m

twisted, tapering droppings to 8cm

partially webbed toes

white fur on lower lip

SIZE *Body 30–45cm; tail 13–20cm.*
YOUNG *Single litter of 4–6; April–May.*
DIET *Rodents, birds, amphibians, and fish.*
STATUS *Introduced from North America; locally common and spreading.*
SIMILAR SPECIES *Otter (p.94) is larger; Western Polecat (p.90) has a paler face.*

Weasel

Mustela nivalis (Carnivora)

In Britain, the Weasel is usually distinguishable from the similar Stoat (left) by its smaller size, and shorter tail with no black tip. However, the same is not true across its European range, where Weasels differ considerably in size and winter colour. An inquisitive predator, given its tiny size and high metabolic rate, it must eat several times a day; twenty-four hours without food would lead to starvation.

OCCURS *in all terrestrial habitats, from grassland to woodland, and coasts to mountain tops.*

chestnut fur

hind print to 3cm

white underparts

front print to 2cm

short tail

narrow, twisted droppings to 6cm long

SIZE *Body 13–30cm; tail 3–10cm.*
YOUNG *Single or double litters of 4–6; April–August.*
DIET *Rodents, Rabbits, and birds; needs up to 10 meals each day.*
STATUS *Common.*
SIMILAR SPECIES *Stoat (left).*

Stoat

Mustela erminea (Carnivora)

The rich chestnut upperparts of this slender, agile predator, contrast sharply with white below, and distinguish the Stoat from all its relatives, except the Weasel (right). However, the Weasel is generally smaller, and never has a black-tipped tail. In winter, all Stoats develop some white fur on the flanks and neck, but in more northerly areas, they assume the "ermine" coat – all white except the black tip to the tail.

FOUND *in most terrestrial habitats with sufficient cover, from woodland and grassland, to marshes and mountains.*

long, sinuous body

WINTER COAT

NOTE

Male Stoats are on an average about one-tenth larger than the females. Their diet varies accordingly: females specialize in hunting voles, whereas males also catch young rabbits and hares, and birds.

hind print to 3.5cm

front print to 2cm

droppings to 2cm

black tail-tip

chestnut upperparts

SIZE *Body 18–31cm; tail 9–14cm.*
YOUNG *Single litter of 6–12; April–May.*
DIET *Preys upon rodents (often pursued in their burrows), Rabbits, and birds.*
STATUS *Common.*
SIMILAR SPECIES *Weasel (right), which is smaller and does not have a black-tipped tail.*

Pine Marten

Martes martes (Carnivora)

The Pine Marten's sinuous shape, long legs, and long, bushy tail are useful features for its partly arboreal lifestyle – most of its hunting being done in trees. It climbs with agility despite its relative bulk. Largely nocturnal, it makes a den in a natural hole or crevice in rocks or trees. The most distinctive feature of its generally dark brown coat is the pale throat patch, which is rather variable in colour, from cream to pale orange.

LIVES *mainly in woodland (especially coniferous and mixed), but also colonizes scrub, rocky, and cliff habitats.*

pale patch

dark brown coat

long, bushy tail

hind print to 4cm

front print to 3cm

droppings to 10cm

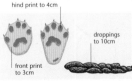

NOTE

Formerly found throughout the British Isles, Pine Martens were perscuted almost to extinction in the 19th century. They are now spreading again and have started to recolonize northern England and Wales, benefiting from the afforestation of the uplands.

SIZE *Body 40–55cm; tail 18–25cm.*
YOUNG *Single litter of 3–5; April–May.*
DIET *Rodents (mainly squirrels), frogs, birds, and eggs; fruit, berries, and fungi; honey.*
STATUS *Locally common.*
SIMILAR SPECIES *None, although Red Squirrel (p.87) may look similar but is smaller if glimpsed in the treetops.*

EUROPEAN OTTER

The European Otter population in Britain suffered significant decline from the late 1950s to the end of the 1970s. By then the otter was absent throughout most of England, rare in much of Wales, and was only found in any numbers in the north and west of Scotland. It is now clear that the probable cause of this crash in otter numbers was the use of toxic agricultural chemicals (now banned), which drained into rivers, and accumulated in the bodies of the animals through their main prey item, fish. In response to its precipitous decline, the otter received full protection under UK law in 1978. At the same time, a series of national surveys were begun, and recent studies have shown a significant recovery in the otter population. Recognized as a priority species for conservation, both government and voluntary organizations are involved in habitat restoration and protection of the species, while academic institutions have undertaken research into the ecology of the otter, and many landowners have improved riverside environments. Awareness of the otter's demise spawned a sustained effort to conserve the species, which continues today, and the otter has become a potent symbol of the conservation movement.

Otter

Lutra lutra (Carnivora)

A predominantly aquatic mammal, the Otter is generally seen in or near water. However, it will travel long distances overland at night, its main activity period: at such times, otters are frequently killed on roads. On land, it travels with an awkward, bounding gait, but in water it is very agile and playful. It swims low in the water, with just the head exposed, lower than any of the minks or large aquatic rodents with which it may be confused. When underwater, it has a silvery appearance due to bubbles of air trapped in the fur. It has whitish underparts and small ears.

sleek brown fur

whitish throat

fully webbed feet

JUVENILE

NOTE

Given their secretive nature, the best way to establish the presence of otters is to search for their spraints – oily, sweet-smelling droppings, usually containing fish scales and bones, mostly near water.

flattened head

long, thick, tapering tail

front to 7cm

hind to 9cm

blackish droppings to 10cm long

fish remains

FEEDING SITE

SIZE *Body 55–90cm; tail 35–50cm.*
YOUNG *Single litter of 2–5; May–August, but can be all year round.*
DIET *Fish, amphibians, rodents, water birds, and crustaceans; crabs and molluscs in coastal areas; carrion.*
STATUS *Generally scarce, though locally common.*
SIMILAR SPECIES *American Mink (p.91), often found in similar habitats, is smaller, darker brown in colour, and lacks the whitish throat patch.*

Badger

Meles meles (Carnivora)

The Badger is largely nocturnal and, therefore, rarely encountered, except as road casualties, unless actively sought out. However, its complex burrow system (sett) with an often extensive series of holes 20cm or more across is very obvious, and forms the focus of most surveys for the species. The characteristic black and white facial stripes are surprisingly visible even in twilight conditions, when most badgers are observed. Heavily built, the Badger has a small pointed head and short neck, widening to a powerful body, with short, strong limbs and a small tail.

NOTE

Badger field signs are many and varied, especially in the vicinity of the setts. These include spoil heaps, piles of bedding, dung pits, bark scratchings, and tufts of grey hair on barbed wire.

front to 12cm

hind to 10cm

brown droppings to 10cm

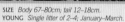

SETT

grey upperparts

small, white-fringed ears

black and white striped head

SIZE *Body 67–80cm; tail 12–18cm.*
YOUNG *Single litter of 2–4; January–March.*
DIET *Omnivorous; earthworms, insects, small mammals, amphibians, bulbs, grain, and carrion.*
STATUS *Common.*
SIMILAR SPECIES *None, although the Red Fox (p.90) has similar burrows, but in less extensive complexes and lacking the spoil heaps.*

Wild Cat

Felix sylvestris (Carnivora)

The size of a large domestic cat, Wild Cats can be very difficult to tell apart from feral tabbies and especially hybrids. Solitary and nocturnal, the Wild Cat is an agile climber, although it hunts mainly on the ground. Despite stalking and pouncing in the familiar cat manner, it displays no tendency to "play" with its prey. This species is relatively short-legged, and so is unable to tolerate snow deeper than 20cm for long periods.

NOTE

Definitive separation from some domestic cats, and especially hybrids, is very difficult and may rely on skull measurements.

footprints to 4cm long

droppings to 5cm long

irregular, blotchy stripes

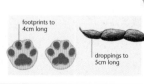

DOMESTIC TABBY

yellow-green eyes

dark markings forming stripes, not blotches

black-tipped, bushy tail with 3–5 dark rings

slender tail

SIZE *Body 48–65cm; tail 20–35cm.*
YOUNG *Single litter of 2–4; April–September.*
DIET *Rabbits, hares, rodents, birds, lizards, and frogs; exceptionally takes lambs.*
STATUS *Vulnerable, scarce and local, although some recent signs of increase; threatened by interbreeding with domestic cats.*
SIMILAR SPECIES *Domestic cats and hybrids.*

Grey Seal

Halichoerus grypus (Pinnipedia)

FOUND along coasts and in coastal marine waters; breeds on rocky islets and grassy coastal strips.

Male Grey Seals are very large, about a third larger than the females, and both sexes have variably blotchy grey upperparts and paler undersides. In profile, the forehead runs straight into the muzzle and the nostrils are widely separated. Pups are born white and remain on land for several weeks – Grey Seals, therefore, must breed above the high-tide mark. In water, they are capable of diving to depths of greater than 200m, remaining submerged for up to 30 minutes at a time. With a range extending across the north Atlantic and into the Baltic, almost half of the world population of Grey Seals breeds around the British coastline.

NOTE
The long, straight facial profile of this seal is especially characteristic of males; females and juveniles have a shorter muzzle, but never show the concave profile of most other European seal species.

wrinkled neck skin
elongated snout and broad muzzle
widely separated nostrils

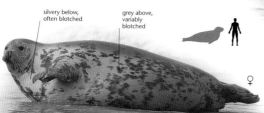

silvery below, often blotched
grey above, variably blotched

♀

white fur

SIZE Males 2.2–3m; females 2–2.5m.
YOUNG Single pup; normally October–February.
DIET Fish (including commercial species such as Salmon), crustaceans, and cuttlefish, squid, and octopus.
STATUS Locally common.
SIMILAR SPECIES Common Seal (below), which is smaller and has a dog-like facial profile.

JUVENILE

Common Seal

Phoca vitulina (Pinnipedia)

Also known as the Harbour Seal, the Common Seal is one of the smaller members of its family, with a grey or brownish coat speckled with black. Its nostrils form a V-shaped pattern. Pups are born with a colour similar to their parents, and are capable of swimming almost immediately after birth. Common Seals can, therefore, breed on tidal flats.

OCCUPIES shallow coastal waters and estuaries; rocks and sand banks at low tide; swims up rivers.

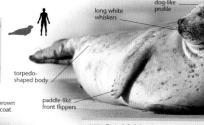

dog-like profile
long white whiskers
torpedo-shaped body
paddle-like front flippers

short muzzle
grey to brown mottled coat

SIZE Body 1.2–1.9m; females a little smaller than males.
YOUNG Single pup; June–July.
DIET Fish, shellfish, molluscs, crustaceans.
STATUS Locally common; numbers still recovering from recent viral epidemics.
SIMILAR SPECIES Grey Seal (above).

JUVENILE

Bottlenose Dolphin

Tursiops truncatus (Cetacea)

With resident populations off parts of the Scottish and Welsh coasts, this is the most frequently seen dolphin species. It has greyish upperparts, a short beak, and a long, curved dorsal fin. Despite its bulky appearance, it is very acrobatic, often leaping clear of the water, and it can be very inquisitive, approaching swimmers and boats closely.

OCCURS worldwide in tropical and temperate seas, from shallow estuaries to deep oceanic water.

grey-brown upperparts
short but distinct beak
large, recurved dorsal fin

SIZE 2.5–4m.
YOUNG Single calf; born usually April–September, at intervals of up to three years.
DIET Fish, cuttlefish, and squid.
STATUS Locally common.
SIMILAR SPECIES None.

Harbour Porpoise

Phocoena phocoena (Cetacea)

The commonest (and smallest) cetacean in European waters, the Harbour Porpoise is a relatively nondescript, steely grey above and whitish below, the pigmentation usually being asymmetric. The dorsal fin, often the only feature seen, is short and blunt, and located centrally down the back. It has a rounded head and spade-shaped teeth. Unlike most dolphins, the snout is not extended into a beak; nor is it typically as agile as a dolphin, as Harbour Porpoises do not leap clear of the water.

OCCURS in shallow coastal waters and estuaries right around Britain, including North Sea and Channel waters; aggregations can form in favoured feeding areas.

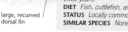

NOTE
Weather conditions influence the likelihood of viewing small cetaceans such as Harbour Porpoises; the merest hint of waves easily disguise the occasional fleeting dorsal fin.

diffuse line between upper and lower colours
whitish underparts
dark line from jaw to flipper

steely grey above
low, blunt dorsal fin

SIZE 1.4–1.8m.
YOUNG Single young; born May–August; not every year.
DIET Small fish, especially Herrings; also some crustaceans and cuttlefish.
STATUS Vulnerable; locally common, although populations in the southern North Sea and English Channel have declined substantially.
SIMILAR SPECIES None.

MAMMALS

Red Deer

Cervus elaphus (Artiodactyla)

A mature male Red Deer with a full set of antlers is a magnificent sight, each antler bearing five or more points, with two forward points near the base. These antlers and its noisy, bellowing rut behaviour, enable a dominant male to secure a considerable harem of breeding females. All adult animals can be distinguished by their uniform red-brown coat (young fawns are spotted with white), and their buff-coloured rump, without a black outline. These large deer leave many signs of their presence, including mud wallows, large black droppings, and damage to saplings and the bark of larger trees.

FAVOURS *open deciduous woodland, parkland, riverine marshes, open mountains and moorland; descends into woodland for the winter.*

NOTE

While the antlers of adult males are distinctive, younger animals have less developed antlers, and each antler is itself fully grown only from autumn to spring. There is, therefore, plenty of potential for confusion between deer species, except when adult males are in peak condition.

branched antlers

♂

large ears

white spots

JUVENILE

red-brown coat (greyer in winter)

hind print to 7cm long

front print to 8cm long

acorn-shaped droppings to 1.5cm long

teeth marks 1.6cm wide

GNAWED BARK

SIZE Body 1.6–2.6m; tail 10–15cm.
YOUNG Single young; born May–June.
DIET Grazes, and browses heather, conifers, birch, and other trees; strips bark.
STATUS Endangered (Corsican form); otherwise locally common.
SIMILAR SPECIES Sika Deer (below), which is smaller and has a white rump.

Fallow Deer

Dama dama (Artiodactyla)

A familiar and widespread deer, the Fallow Deer is found over much of Britain and Europe as a result of introductions and escapes; indeed, many free-ranging herds remain semi-domesticated. The ground colour of a Fallow Deer's coat is usually orange-brown, boldly spotted with white in summer and greyer and almost unspotted in winter. At all seasons, the white rump with a black border and long tail with a blackish upper surface are distinctive, as are the flattened, palmate antlers of an adult male. Look out for trampled rutting rings and a distinct browse line in its natural habitat.

OCCUPIES *open woodland and parkland, and adjacent agricultural habitats.*

♀

long tail

white rump patch

palmate antlers in adult male

front and hind prints to 6.5cm

♂

antlers with single basal point

pellets to 1.6cm

NOTE

The ground colour of the Fallow Deer ranges from black to white; the paler ones often lack the black border to the rump; the degree to which spots are lost in winter also varies.

white-spotted summer coat

BROWSE LINE

STRIPPED BARK

SIZE Body 1.3–1.6m; tail 16–20cm.
YOUNG Single young; born June–July.
DIET Grazes in open woodland or on nearby crops; browses saplings and larger trees; acorns and fruit; strips bark in the winter.
STATUS Native to the Mediterranean; widely introduced and common elsewhere, including most of the British Isles.
SIMILAR SPECIES Sika Deer (below), which has a shorter, white tail.

Sika Deer

Cervus nippon (Artiodactyla)

The Sika Deer can always be distinguished by its black-bordered white rump, and mostly white tail. In summer, adults are lightly spotted, although in winter the coat is greyer and the spots less obvious. Interbreeding between the Sika and Red Deer (above) represents a considerable risk to the genetic integrity of the native Red Deer. A young male Red Deer has similar antlers, though they are much larger with two forward points instead of one. Perhaps the Sika Deer's most distinctive feature is the sharp whistle of a rutting male.

FOUND *in deciduous and coniferous woodland, and adjacent open habitats.*

antlers with up to 4 points

heart-shaped white rump

lightly spotted summer coat

♂

each antler with up to 4 points

one forward-point

front to 6cm

hind to 6cm

droppings to 1.5cm

WINTER COAT

SIZE Body 1.2–1.4m; tail 12–15cm.
YOUNG Single young; May–June.
DIET Grass, herbs, low shrubs, and trees.
STATUS Introduced; locally common.
SIMILAR SPECIES Red Deer (above), which is larger, unspotted, and with larger antlers, when present; Fallow Deer (right), which is similarly sized, but more distinctly spotted and with palmate antlers.

Roe Deer

Capreolus capreolus (Artiodactyla)

The most widespread European deer, and the smallest native species, the Roe Deer is a secretive, solitary, and nocturnal woodland inhabitant, although it is increasingly found in suburban habitats. Red-brown above, turning grey in winter, its most distinctive feature is the white rump patch and short white tail. As with most deer, the fawns are spotted with white. The antlers of the male are short, with at most three points each.

FAVOURS *deciduous and coniferous woodland with dense shrubs, open farmland, reedbeds, and moorland.*

NOTE

Field signs of Roe Deer include frayed tree bark; it rubs against bark to help remove the "velvet" from its developing antlers, and also to act as a territorial marker for the rut.

unspotted red-brown coat

small antlers

white-spotted coat

♂

white upper lip and chin

front and hind prints to 4.5cm

front print splayed

droppings to 1.8cm

frayed bark

FIELD SIGN

FAWN

SIZE *Body 1–1.4m; tail 2–3cm.*
YOUNG *Single litter of one, occasionally two; May–June.*
DIET *Browses woodland-edge shrubs and low trees; also eats crops and autumn berries.*
STATUS *Common and increasing.*
SIMILAR SPECIES *Muntjac (below) and Chinese Water Deer (right), which are both a little smaller and have a different rump pattern.*

Chinese Water Deer

Hydropotes inermis (Artiodactyla)

The only European deer never to bear antlers, adult male Chinese Water Deer instead have upper canines elongated into tusks, up to 8cm long, which visibly protrude from the mouth. It is also the only species not to have a distinctly coloured rump patch. Its solitary nature, small size, and largely nocturnal habits make it difficult to see, though it does sometimes feed along with other deer in open, agricultural lands. Established in Europe and Britain in the 1940s, the population is still rather small, probably less than a thousand truly wild animals, with others free-ranging in parks.

FOUND *in deciduous, especially damp, woodland, marshes, and reedbeds.*

NOTE

This is a poorly known species, even in its native China, where it is classified as near-threatened. In this context, the introduced British population may have some global conservation significance.

droppings to 1.5cm

front and hind prints to 3cm

red-brown fur

large, broad ears

SIZE *Body 80–105cm; tail 4–8cm.*
YOUNG *Single litter of 1–2; May–July.*
DIET *Grazes grasses, sedges, and crops; browses shrubs and low trees.*
STATUS *Introduced; scarce but increasing.*
SIMILAR SPECIES *Muntjac (below), and Roe Deer (left), both of which have antlers.*

Muntjac

Muntiacus reevesi (Artiodactyla)

A very small deer, the Muntjac is generally dark brown above and white below, with a bushy tail that almost covers its white rump. When alarmed, it runs with the tail raised, revealing its white rump patch. Males have very short antlers, borne on skull projections which remain even after the antlers are shed. It is currently increasing, in southern Britain particularly, at an alarming rate, with resulting reports of damage to agricultural crops, gardens, and especially to forestry and woodland interests.

OCCURS *in dense woodland, especially deciduous; feeds in clearings, coppice plots, fields, and gardens.*

NOTE

This deer often eats the newly growing shoots on recently coppiced tree stumps. Although fences and brushwood piles are used in attempt to restrict access, they are rarely completely effective.

humped back

♀

skull projection

front to 3cm

rounded

short antlers

hind to 3cm

droppings to 1cm

dark face markings

red-brown coat

♂

SIZE *Body 90–105cm; tail 14–18cm.*
YOUNG *One or two litters of 1–2.*
DIET *Browses woodland shrubs, Bramble leaves, fruit, acorns, Bracken, and ivy.*
STATUS *Introduced, and locally common.*
SIMILAR SPECIES *Chinese Water Deer (right), which does not have antlers; Roe Deer (above).*

MAMMALS

Red Deer
Looking regal despite the inclement weather, this Red Deer stag shelters as best it can from the wind and rain on the open moorland. These deer are the largest native land mammal in Britain.

BIRDS

Britain's birdlife is enriched by its long coastline and varied habitats. From town centres to remote cliffs, birds are everywhere. Around 250 species are regular, but, being on one of the world's great flyways, Britain's list exceeds 600. In spring, millions of birds fly north from Africa, many to nest in Britain's woods and countryside, others passing through. In autumn, these birds return south, while millions more arrive from Arctic America, Europe, and Asia, and from continental Europe. Many head farther south, others stay the winter. In summer, Britain has more than half of the world population of some species of seabirds breeding on its cliffs and islands. In winter, British wetlands are hugely important for the survival of many of the world's wildfowl and wading birds.

WILDFOWL
Ducks, swans, and geese flock to Britain's marshes, lakes, flooded gravel pits, and innumerable estuaries from autumn to spring, taking advantage of the more temperate climate.

WADING BIRDS
Plovers, sandpipers, godwits, and other long-legged waders find Britain's mild winter conditions and beaches of mud and sand ideal from August to May, but breed much farther north in Europe.

BIRDS OF PREY
Buzzards, Kestrels, and Sparrowhawks are widespread, but Red Kites, Peregrines, and Marsh Harriers are making a comeback and even eagles and Ospreys nest in the British Isles.

WOODLAND BIRDS
Britain has huge numbers of common woodland birds, with residents such as the very familiar Robins, Wrens, tits and thrushes, and summer migrants including several warblers and flycatchers.

FARMLAND FLOCKS
Birds of the fields have declined in recent decades as farming has intensified, but the right conditions attract a variety of larks, finches, buntings, and sparrows in dramatic mixed flocks.

SEABIRDS
Rich coastal waters, islands, and sheer cliffs create ideal conditions for colonies of Gannets, Guillemots, Puffins, shearwaters, and Kittiwakes, among the finest bird spectacles in Europe.

Anatomy

While it is not necessary to know the details of anatomy to identify a bird, a little more knowledge adds to the interest and enjoyment. The correct terminology also adds precision to a verbal description: "a bit of colour on the wing" is vague, while "pale tips to the greater coverts" is a much more exact and useful description.

It is particularly useful to know how the bird "fits together": how wing feathers fold over one another as the bird closes its wing, or where a distinctive mark on the closed wing appears when the wing is spread. "Primaries" are the wingtip feathers that move out to the end of the open wing but are often hidden by feathers called tertials when the bird is perched. Tertials usually "stay where they are" when the wing is opened, and may even be hidden beneath the scapulars.

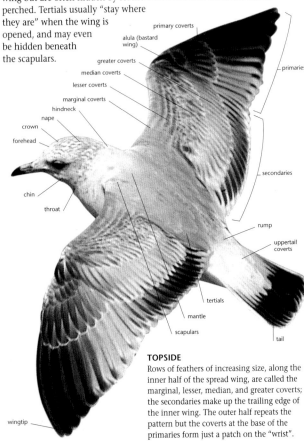

primary coverts
alula (bastard wing)
greater coverts
median coverts
lesser coverts
marginal coverts
hindneck
nape
crown
forehead
chin
throat
primaries
secondaries
rump
uppertail coverts
tertials
mantle
scapulars
tail
wingtip

TOPSIDE
Rows of feathers of increasing size, along the inner half of the spread wing, are called the marginal, lesser, median, and greater coverts; the secondaries make up the trailing edge of the inner wing. The outer half repeats the pattern but the coverts at the base of the primaries form just a patch on the "wrist".

UNDERSIDE
The coverts on the underside of a bird's wing form a smaller proportion of the wing area than they do on the upperside, but they are arranged in a similar regular pattern of overlapping rows. At the base of the wing, a triangular patch of feathers in the "wingpit" is formed by a group of feathers called the axillaries. The head, belly, breast, and flanks are covered by shorter, less flexible feathers.

axillaries
cheek (ear coverts)
bill
breast
belly
leg
wingtips
vent
undertail coverts
foot
flanks

HEAD MARKINGS
A bird's head markings may include a cap, various different kinds of stripes, such as a superciliary stripe over the eye and an eye-stripe through it, and a bib below the bill.

cap
superciliary stripe
eye-stripe
bib

FEATHER TYPES
Soft down feathers form an insulating underlayer. Over that, the head and body are covered with body, or contour, feathers. The wings have small, stiff feathers, wider on one side, called coverts, overlying the bases of the large flight feathers, which are also asymmetrical. The tail typically has 10 or 12 feathers.

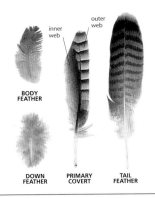

inner web
outer web
BODY FEATHER
DOWN FEATHER
PRIMARY COVERT
TAIL FEATHER

PLUMAGE
Feathers not only allow flight and keep a bird warm and dry but also add colour, pattern, and shape. This can be useful for mating and territorial displays, and for camouflage, especially for yong birds and those that nest and spend a lot of time on the ground, such as many gamebirds.

tail fanned in display
"beard" of spiky feathers
camouflaging pattern

CAPERCAILLIE

dark plumage prevents mistaken attack by territorial parent
white for long-distance visual contact

GANNET

bold breeding plumage
camouflaged non-breeding plumage

SNOW BUNTING

Identification

Identification of most birds becomes easier with experience: most of us can quickly identify a Robin or a House Sparrow. A familiar bird is like a familiar face in a crowd; an unfamiliar one is just as difficult as trying to find a person you have never seen before in a crowded street, based on a description in a book or from a small photograph. Identifying a bird is usually a process based on a range of information: the place, habitat, time of year, size and shape of the bird, colours, markings, the way it flies and moves, and its general behaviour.

Location

Similar species often live in different habitats, thus exploiting different feeding or nesting opportunities and avoiding competition with each other. Knowing this is helpful in identifying them. For example, Skylarks occur on open ground, rarely even close to a hedgerow, and may perch on a low fence but not on high wires. Woodlarks, by contrast, live along woodland edges and heaths, often close to bushy cover, and will perch high on a tree or wire.

WOODLARK
SKYLARK

Size

Judging size can be difficult but it is a useful clue to identification. If you see an unfamiliar bird, try to estimate its size against a more familiar one. Waders, for instance, range from tiny (Little Stint) or small (Dunlin) to middle-sized (Redshank), large (Bar-tailed Godwit) or very large (Curlew). More subtly, warblers range from tiny (Goldcrest) to small (Garden Warbler) or, for a warbler, large (Great Reed Warbler).

LITTLE STINT
12–14cm (4³/₄–5¹/₂in)

DUNLIN
16–20cm (6¹/₂–8in)

REDSHANK
27–29cm (10¹/₂–11¹/₂in)

BAR-TAILED GODWIT
33–42cm (13–16¹/₂in)

CURLEW
50–60cm (20–23¹/₂in)

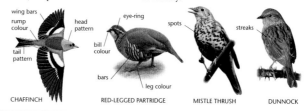

Body Shape

Judge a bird's overall shape if you can. Is it long and thin, short and squat, tall or short? The bill and leg lengths affect your judgement but use familiar birds, such as the Blue Tit (dumpy), Blackbird (round but longer-tailed), or Swallow (long-bodied, long-tailed) for comparison. Remember that even small, slim birds can look round and dumpy in cold weather.

small head

thickset body

tiny tail

round body

WILLOW GROUSE

WREN

Bill Shape

Is the bill long or short, thick or thin, straight or curved? Is it pointed, stubby, hooked, narrow, or broad and flattened at the tip? Getting a good idea of its shape will help you to put the bird into a smaller group, narrowing down the possibilities. Bill shape is generally related to the bird's diet, as indicated here.

worms and fruit

tiny insects and seeds

seeds and caterpillars

insects and spiders

BLACKBIRD

BLUE TIT

CHAFFINCH

REED WARBLER

tiny shrimps from water

fish

CURLEW

AVOCET

GREY HERON

birds, mammals, and carrion

grass and roots

big worms from deep mud

seeds and grain

GREYLAG GOOSE

MALLARD

GOLDEN EAGLE

Tail Shape

The tail helps a bird steer and brake in flight, but may also be developed for display. Its shape and proportions are invaluable in pinning down a bird to a family group and can be noted down almost immediately. Look for obvious features, such as a deep notch or fork, long outer or central feathers, or a diamond shape. Be aware, though, that tail shape can change dramatically, for example, a straight, narrow tail can be spread like a fan as the bird soars or lands.

GREAT TIT

medium length, square-ended

long spike, wide base

very long and narrow

LONG-TAILED TIT

PHEASANT

SWALLOW

short and rounded

long, deeply forked

notched, fanned, twisted

RED KITE

GREY PARTRIDGE

Wing Shape

The shape of a bird's wings depends on how it flies: for instance, gliders have longer, narrower wings than smaller, round-winged birds with whirring wing-beats. On most small, fast-moving birds wing shape is of little use because you cannot see much, but on bigger birds slower wing-beats allow a better view.

very broad and blunt

LAPWING

SPARROWHAWK

broad and rounded

angled, pointed

GREENSHANK

long, rounded

short, rounded

just a blur in flight

BLUE TIT

BUZZARD

KESTREL

SONG THRUSH

long, narrow, pointed

Colours and Markings

Preciseness is important: does the bird have streaks, bars, or spots? Are they on the wing, back, rump, or head? Head patterns can be very complex (see opposite). Look for wing and tail patterns, which may be revealed only when the bird opens its wings or spreads its tail. "Bare part" colours, such as those on the legs, around the eyes, or on the bill, can provide useful clues to a bird's identity.

wing bars

rump colour

head pattern

eye-ring

spots

streaks

tail pattern

bill colour

bars

leg colour

CHAFFINCH

RED-LEGGED PARTRIDGE

MISTLE THRUSH

DUNNOCK

Behaviour

The behaviour of a bird, subtle at first, quickly becomes a valuable aid: the way a Robin flicks its tail and cocks its head, or a Blackbird quickly raises and then slowly lowers its tail on landing are giveaway clues. In addition to such precise details, most birds have a hard-to-define "something" (which birdwatchers call jizz), most easily learned by repeated watching.

ALERT
The Great Tit is bold and active, with bouncy, jerky movements between perches.

HEAD DOWN
The Shelduck upends to reach food under water, taking food that it cannot exploit by dabbling with its bill at the surface.

CHIRPY
House Sparrows are lively, intensely sociable little birds. They spend much time chirruping endlessly and noisily in tight-packed groups.

UNOBTRUSIVE
Quiet and generally inconspicuous but not shy, the Dunnock shuffles mouse-like on the ground, flicking wings and tail. It usually stays close to bushes or other cover.

NERVOUS
The Green Sandpiper has the curious habit of frequently bobbing up and down as it stands at the water's edge. It frequently looks nervous, easily taking flight if disturbed.

INELEGANT
Barred Warblers have a distinctive habit of "crashing" heavily and clumsily through bushes, quite unlike the dainty progress of other, smaller warblers.

Flight

Sometimes, the only view you will get of a bird is in flight, when details of plumage and colour are often hard to see. In such cases, the way it flies may be your best clue to its identity. Birds have a host of different flight styles: they may fly with long glides on outstretched wings or with constant wing-beats, have shallow or deep beats, flat or arched wings, or hover or dive.

KESTREL HOVERING
Kestrels hunt from the air if there is no perch nearby, hovering as if suspended on a string.

RED KITE
The long, broad wings, with widely "fingered" tips, of this juvenile Red Kite are perfect for prolonged, energy-saving glides.

GOLDFINCH FLOCK
Goldfinches have a particularly light, airy, bouncing flight, with deep, swooping bounds.

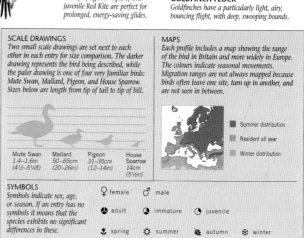

SCALE DRAWINGS
Two small scale drawings are set next to each other in each entry for size comparison. The darker drawing represents the bird being described, while the paler drawing is one of four very familiar birds: Mute Swan, Mallard, Pigeon, and House Sparrow. Sizes below are length from tip of tail to tip of bill.

| Mute Swan 1.4–1.6m (4½–5¼ft) | Mallard 50–65cm (20–26in) | Pigeon 31–35cm (12–14in) | House Sparrow 14cm (5½in) |

MAPS
Each profile includes a map showing the range of the bird in Britain and more widely in Europe. The colours indicate seasonal movements. Migration ranges are not always mapped because birds often leave one site, turn up in another, and are not seen in between.

■ Summer distribution
■ Resident all year
■ Winter distribution

SYMBOLS
Symbols indicate sex, age, or season. If an entry has no symbols it means that the species exhibits no significant differences in these.

♀ female   ♂ male

🐦 adult   🐦 immature   🐦 juvenile

⚓ spring   ☼ summer   🍂 autumn   ❄ winter

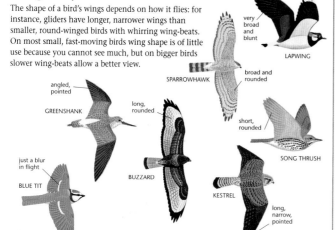

Mute Swan

Cygnus olor (Anatidae)

The huge, elegant Mute Swan is one of the most familiar of waterfowls. It holds its neck in a graceful curve, distinctive at long range, and has a longer tail than the two tundra-breeding swans. Territorial pairs are aggressive, driving off intruders with arched wings and loud hisses.

BREEDS *and feeds on lakes, reservoirs, rivers, estuaries, sheltered coasts, and marshes, as well as nearby fields and urban parks.*

outstretched neck

large black knob; smaller on female

all-white plumage

orange-red bill, angled down

long tail

grey-brown plumage

long, often curved neck

grey bill

VOICE *Strangled trumpeting, snorting, and hissing notes; wings throb loudly in flight.*
NESTING *Huge pile of vegetation at water's edge; 5–8 eggs; 1 brood; March–June.*
FEEDING *Plucks plants from short grass and shallow water; upends in deeper water.*
SIMILAR SPECIES *Bewick's Swan (below), Whooper Swan (below).*

Bean Goose

Anser fabalis (Anatidae)

This large, handsome, sociable goose is darker than other grey geese, with basically dark brown plumage marked with narrow, regular pale bars. There are two forms: one long-necked and long-billed, the other shorter-necked and looking more like a Pink-footed Goose (below). Sometimes it joins flocks of White-fronted Geese (below), when it can be picked out by its long, dark head and cleanly barred back.

WINTERS *on lakes and wet pasture, on sites used year after year. Breeds on northern bogs and tundra.*

dark brown head

broad, dark tail-band

orange band on black bill

brown back with cream bars

dark grey wings

yellow-orange legs

VOICE *Deep, two- or three-syllable trumpeting, ung-ung or unk-uk-uk.*
NESTING *Down-lined hollow near bog pool on tundra or in forest; 4–6 eggs; 1 brood; June.*
FEEDING *Grazes short grass, picks up grain and roots crops from fields.*
SIMILAR SPECIES *Pink-footed Goose (below), Greylag Goose (p.105).*

Bewick's Swan

Cygnus columbianus (Anatidae)

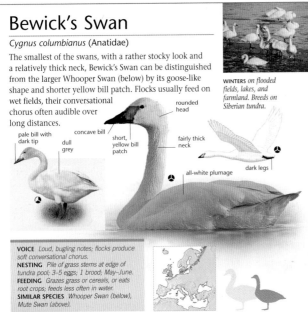

The smallest of the swans, with a rather stocky look and a relatively thick neck, Bewick's Swan can be distinguished from the larger Whooper Swan (below) by its goose-like shape and shorter yellow bill patch. Flocks usually feed on wet fields, their conversational chorus often audible over long distances.

WINTERS *on flooded fields, lakes, and farmland. Breeds on Siberian tundra.*

rounded head

pale bill with dark tip

concave bill

dull grey

short, yellow bill patch

fairly thick neck

all-white plumage

dark legs

VOICE *Loud, bugling notes; flocks produce soft conversational chorus.*
NESTING *Pile of grass stems at edge of tundra pool; 3–5 eggs; 1 brood; May–June.*
FEEDING *Grazes grass or cereals, or eats root crops; feeds less often in water.*
SIMILAR SPECIES *Whooper Swan (below), Mute Swan (above).*

Pink-footed Goose

Anser brachyrhynchus (Anatidae)

This round-headed, short-billed goose has a shorter neck than other geese, and a strong contrast between its very dark head and pale breast – features that are often obvious in flight. It occurs in tens of thousands at favoured sites, such as arable land near coast, feeding in dense flocks by day and making spectacular mass flights to its roosts in the evening.

ROOSTS *on estuaries, lakes, islands; feeds on marshes and coasts.*

small bill with pink band

dark underwings

dark, round head

white-barred, pale grey back

pale grey wings

dark bars on flanks

pale to rich pink legs

pale pinkish breast

VOICE *Resonant ahng-unk and frequent, higher wink-wink.*
NESTING *Down-lined nest on open tundra or rocky slope; 4–6 eggs; 1 brood; June–July.*
FEEDING *Eats grass, waste grain, sugar beet tops, carrots, and potatoes, feeding in flocks.*
SIMILAR SPECIES *Bean Goose (above), Greylag Goose (p.105).*

Whooper Swan

Cygnus cygnus (Anatidae)

As big as a Mute Swan (above), but with the goose-like look of Bewick's Swan (above), this is a wild, usually shy bird with a long, flat forehead and bill. It has more yellow on its bill than Bewick's Swan, and always holds its head horizontal and neck bolt upright when alert.

WINTERS *on large lakes, marshes, rivers, estuaries, and nearby fields. Breeds by tundra pools.*

long, slender neck

black bill tip

cream bill

yellow wedge extends beyond nostrils

all-white plumage

greyish body

VOICE *Loud, trumpeting call, often three or four syllables, whoop-whoop-whoop.*
NESTING *Big, domed structure of grass and reeds by water; 5–8 eggs; 1 brood; April–June.*
FEEDING *Plucks leaves and stems from dry ground, or digs roots from ploughed earth; feeds on aquatic plants in summer.*
SIMILAR SPECIES *Bewick's Swan (above).*

White-fronted Goose

Anser albifrons (Anatidae)

One of the more colourful and lively of the grey geese, the White-fronted Goose has a distinctive white patch at the front of its head and ragged black bars on its grey belly. The Siberian subspecies has a pink bill, while the larger, darker Greenland subspecies *(A. a. flavirostris)* has a longer, heavier orange bill. Both occur in large flocks at regular locations.

WINTERS *on pastures, coastal marshes, and estuaries. Breeds on northern tundra.*

broad, dark tail-band

white forehead blaze

grey on wings

no black bars

A.a.flavirostris

grey-brown body, with black bars on belly

bars broader

pale bars

VOICE *High, yodelling, yelping notes, kyu-yu, ku-yu-yu or lo-lyok.*
NESTING *Makes down-filled nest on the ground on tundra; 5–6 eggs; 1 brood; June.*
FEEDING *Grazes on firm ground during steady forward walk, taking grass, roots, some winter wheat, and grain.*
SIMILAR SPECIES *Greylag Goose (p.105).*

Greylag Goose

Anser anser (Anatidae)

The heaviest of the grey geese, the Greylag Goose looks pale in soft light but its colours look more contrasted in strong sun. It has a very pale forewing, and its white stern is often conspicuous. Its honking calls are familiar, betraying the fact that it is a direct ancestor of domestic geese.

FEEDS on coastal marshes, pastures, and farmland in winter. Breeds by lakes and coastal inlets.

- large orange bill
- very pale upperwings
- brown-grey above
- pale patch on under-wings
- pink legs
- white stern

VOICE Loud clattering and honking like farmyard goose, ahng-ahng-ahng, kang-ank.
NESTING Sparsely lined nest on ground, often on island; 4–6 eggs; 1 brood; May–June.
FEEDING Plucks grass and cereal shoots, digs for roots and waste grain.
SIMILAR SPECIES Pink-footed Goose, Bean Goose, and White-fronted Goose (p.104).

Barnacle Goose

Branta leucopsis (Anatidae)

Although clearly related to the Canada Goose, this highly social bird is easily identified by its creamy-white face, black breast, and beautifully barred back. Juveniles are duller, with less even barring. Large flocks winter on the same sites every year, often grazing at night.

WINTERS on pastures and salt marshes, on traditional sites. Breeds on northern coasts and Arctic tundra.

- pale grey wings
- stubby black bill
- glossy black neck and chest
- black and white bars
- black eye patch
- blue-grey back
- cream-tinged white face
- strongly contrasted below

VOICE Harsh, short bark, creating chattering, yapping chorus from flocks.
NESTING Feather-lined nest on ground or cliff ledge; 4–6 eggs; 1 brood; May–June.
FEEDING Large flocks graze on grass, clover, and similar vegetation.
SIMILAR SPECIES Brent Goose (below), Canada Goose (left).

Canada Goose

Branta canadensis (Anatidae)

A large goose with a black head and neck and a distinctive white "chinstrap", the Canada Goose is a native of North America that has become common and familiar in Britain and other parts of northern Europe. Originally migratory, this species is largely resident apart from annual movements to moulting grounds on quiet estuaries. Flocks of Canada Geese usually draw attention to themselves by their loud, honking calls.

LIVES on lakes, rivers, marshes, reservoirs, and surrounding grassland; also town parks and estuaries.

- white rump
- white chinstrap
- black bill
- black head and neck
- tail held high
- brown upperparts
- pale creamy-buff breast
- black legs
- white stern

VOICE Deep, loud, trumpeting ah-ronk! rising on second syllable; loud, honking effect from flock in flight.
NESTING Down-lined scrape on ground, often on small island left in flooded gravel pit; loosely colonial; 5–6 eggs; 1 brood; April–June.
FEEDING Grazes on grass and cereals in open meadows and fields close to water; takes some aquatic plants, including shoots of overhanging willows.
SIMILAR SPECIES Barnacle Goose (right).

Brent Goose

Branta bernicla (Anatidae)

This small, very dark goose occurs as two main races, dark-bellied and pale-bellied; the black-bellied North American race is a rare vagrant. All have black heads and a distinctive white neck patch. Flocks often feed on the water, upending like ducks to reach vegetation growing beneath the surface.

WINTERS on muddy estuaries and harbours, salt marshes, and nearby arable land. Breeds on tundra.

- black head
- black bill
- white patch on neck
- black chest
- pale bars on wings
- uniform wings
- **PALE-BELLIED**
- **DARK-BELLIED**
- dark grey-brown upperparts
- **DARK-BELLIED**
- brown underside
- bold white stern

VOICE Rhythmic, deep, throaty rronk rronk, in loud, murmuring chorus from flocks.
NESTING Feather-lined nest on ground near shallow pool; 4–6 eggs; 1 brood; May–June.
FEEDING Eats eel-grass and algae on coastal mudflats; increasingly cereals and grass.
SIMILAR SPECIES Barnacle Goose (above), Canada Goose (left).

Egyptian Goose

Alopochen aegyptiacus (Anatidae)

This large waterside bird, rather like a leggy intermediate between a duck and a goose, is a native of Africa. It was brought to eastern Britain as an ornamental bird. Its pale colours, short bill, dark face patch, and long, pale pink legs are distinctive, as is the large white wing patch when it takes flight.

PREFERS open water with scattered trees nearby, and feeds in the shallows or on muddy margins.

- dark brown face patch
- white forewing patch
- stubby pink bill
- pink legs
- dark bills in juveniles **GOSLINGS**
- pale coloured plumage

VOICE Staccato, guttural quacking notes; noisy if disturbed near nest.
NESTING Nests in tree hole up to 20m high; 6–10 eggs; 1 brood; May–June.
FEEDING Roots, shoots, seeds, and other vegetable matter, taken from shallow water and margins of fresh water.
SIMILAR SPECIES Juvenile Shelduck (p.106).

Shelduck

Tadorna tadorna (Anatidae)

Looking black and white at a distance, but revealing rich chestnut patches and a bright red bill at close range in breeding plumage, the Shelduck is a handsome, erect, rather goose-like duck that lives mainly on coasts and estuaries. In eclipse plumage, it is less distinctive, but still easy to identify. Usually seen in pairs or small, loose flocks, its bright white plumage is easily visible at great range against the dark mud of an estuary at low tide. Its pattern is also striking during its strong, fast, but rather heavy flight. Family groups gather together in late summer, when most of the adults fly to the North Sea to moult.

FEEDS and breeds on sandy or muddy shores, especially on sheltered estuaries; some breed near inland lakes and reservoirs.

NOTE

Shelducks in drab summer plumage can be confusing, but they usually retain traces of the distinctive chestnut chest band and black belly stripe.

bold black wingtips

brown-black cap

white below

pink or grey bill

black belly stripe

red knob

tawny orange band

no knob on bill

glossy, green-black head

bright red bill

broad chestnut-orange band around chest

black on wings

white lower neck

white body

pink legs ♂

VOICE Goose-like a-ank and growled grah grah; various whistling notes from male and rhythmic gagagagaga from female in spring.
NESTING In holes on ground, under brambles, between straw bales, in old buildings, and also in trees; 8–10 eggs; 1 brood; February–August.
FEEDING Typically sweeps bill from side to side over wet mud to gather algae, small aquatic snails, and small crustaceans; also grazes and upends in shallow water.
SIMILAR SPECIES Male Mallard (p.107).

Wigeon

Anas penelope (Anatidae)

Although it often nests far from the sea in its northern breeding grounds, the Wigeon is a characteristic duck of coastal estuaries and salt marshes in winter, where it can feed on short grasses like a miniature goose. The often large, colourful, grazing flocks advance across the ground in a tightly packed mass, all the birds usually facing in the same direction. Popular targets for wildfowlers, the flocks have good reason to be wary, and are quick to take to the wing, wheeling about as the males give their wonderfully wild, far-carrying, whistling calls. Squat and short-legged on the ground, Wigeon are transformed into swift and elegant birds in flight.

BREEDS on edges of moorland pools and lakes in Britain. Winters on estuaries, freshwater marshes, or around reservoirs.

dull grey wings

♀

sharp tail

reddish flanks contrast with white belly

bold white wing panel

yellow forehead

greyish bill with black tip

rounded grey body; paler than male Teal's

chestnut head and neck

♂✲

pinkish breast

black-and-white stern

white belly

white band on wings

NOTE

In flight, Wigeon are short-necked, with pointed wings and tail and a bulbous head on a pinched-in neck. The males' white wing panels flash prominently.

retains white on wing ♂☼

♀ mottled greyish to rust-brown body

round head

redder than female

VOICE Male has loud, explosive, musical whistling whee-oo; female gives deep, abrupt, harsh growls.
NESTING Down-lined hollow on ground among tallish vegetation, near water; 8–9 eggs; 1 brood; April–July.
FEEDING Grazes on short grasses, especially beds of eelgrass, often in dense flocks; also feeds by dabbling and upending in shallow water, taking mainly seeds, shoots, and roots.
SIMILAR SPECIES Male Teal (left), female Gadwall (p.107).

Teal

Anas crecca (Anatidae)

The Teal is the smallest of the common European surface-feeding ducks. Outside the breeding season, it is usually seen in smallish flocks. Taking off almost vertically, the fast-flying birds wheel and turn with great agility, co-ordinating their actions precisely like a flock of small waders.

LIVES in freshwater marshes and on boggy heathland and moorland. Winters mainly on fresh waters and estuaries.

♀

cream-edged green band

chestnut head

narrow, horizontal, white band along side

white midwing bars

white centre to underwings

♂✲

green patch

grey bill

♂✲

finely barred grey body

pale streak by tail

♀

streaked brown

VOICE Male has far-carrying, high-pitched, piping crik crik; female utters high quacks.
NESTING Down-lined hollow near water; 8–11 eggs; 1 brood; April–June.
FEEDING Dabbles and upends mainly for seeds, but also small snails, fly larvae, and other aquatic animals in breeding season.
SIMILAR SPECIES Male Wigeon (right).

Garganey

Anas querquedula (Anatidae)

Almost as small as the Teal (left), the Garganey is generally much scarcer; it is unique among ducks in Europe as it is only a summer visitor, wintering in Africa. Males in their breeding plumage are easy to distinguish from Teals, their white head stripe noticeable at long range, but mottled brown females and males in autumn are trickier to separate.

SEEN in wet, grassy marshes and flooded grassland with good cover; migrants are seen in small numbers in autumn on lakes.

two equal white bars on dark hindwings

♀

pale fore-wings

♂☙

dark leading edge

bold white crescent

pale spot

♀

pinkish brown

pale line

white spot

♂☙

chestnut breast and head

pale side

♂☙

blotchy brown

VOICE Male has brief, dry rattle; female may utter short, high quacks but is often silent.
NESTING Down-lined hollow in vegetation near water; 8–11 eggs; 1 brood; May–June.
FEEDING Eats insects, larvae, and other small invertebrates, or roots or seeds.
SIMILAR SPECIES Teal (left), female Shoveler (p.108).

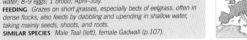

Gadwall

Anas strepera (Anatidae)

An elegant, exquisitely marked bird at close range, the Gadwall can appear rather drab-looking at a distance. It has a smaller, squarer head than the rather similar Mallard (right), which gives it a different character; the male also has a darker, greyer body than a Mallard or Wigeon (p.106). Gadwalls feed at the surface in shallow water, and in autumn and winter often flock on reservoirs and flooded pits, where they associate with Coots (p.127) to benefit from the food that the Coots bring up from the bottom when they dive. In spring, pairs are often seen flying over their territories, calling loudly.

FEEDS and breeds on lakes and rivers with reeds or wooded islands. Winters on open waters, such as large lakes, flooded pits, and reservoirs; more scarcely on quiet estuaries and salt marshes.

protruding head
♂❄
white belly
white patch near base of wings

white patch near base of wings
mottled brown body
♂☼
orange-sided bill
white patch

paler head than Mallard
white patch
dark bill with orange sides
♀

NOTE
Both the male and female Gadwall have a small square patch of white at the base of the hind-wing, which shows up well in flight and is often visible while the birds are settled on the water.

steep forehead
pale brown head
narrow, straight, black bill
♂❄
pale area
black stern

grey body
pale, yellowish orange legs

VOICE Male has high, nasal, whistling pee and deep, short, croaking ahrk; female gives loud quack, like female Mallard's but often higher.
NESTING Nest is down-lined hollow on ground near water; 8–12 eggs; 1 brood; April–June.
FEEDING Mostly feeds in shallow water, dabbling and upending for seeds, roots, and shoots of aquatic plants, plus insects and other small aquatic animals.
SIMILAR SPECIES Mallard (right), female Wigeon (p.106).

Mallard

Anas platyrhynchos (Anatidae)

Common, widespread, and adaptable, able to thrive in all kinds of environments from town parks to coastal marshes, the Mallard is the most familiar of all the ducks. The breeding male's glossy green head and white neck-ring are instantly recognizable, and both sexes sport a characteristic purple-blue wing patch or speculum throughout the year. Most farmyard ducks are derived from the Mallard, and interbreeding has produced a range of variants on the original plumage pattern that can be confusing. Yet they still have their basic Mallard character, and are often easy to identify.

FEEDS on arable land and near all kinds of waters, from urban ponds to remote moorland pools.

NOTE
Mallard plumage is very variable owing to interbreeding with domestic forms, but most of these hybrids retain the blue wing patch and male's curly tail.

white underwings
blue hindwings
♂
yellow bill
orange legs
blue hindwings
♂
glossy green head
♀
dark belly
curly central tail feathers
white neck-ring
pale body
brown breast
purple-blue, white-edged speculum

brown bill
streaked brown body
blue speculum
♀
brown head
becomes browner
♂☼
white tail

VOICE Male whistles quietly; female gives loud, raucous, descending quacks, quark quark quark.
NESTING Usually on ground in down-lined hollow, but sometimes in bush or tree; 9–13 eggs; 1 brood; January–August.
FEEDING Takes small aquatic invertebrates, seeds, roots, shoots, and grain from shallow water while upending or dabbling; also feeds on dry ground, such as stubble fields.
SIMILAR SPECIES Gadwall (left), Shoveler (p.108), Pintail (p.108).

Pochard

Aythya ferina (Anatidae)

Pochard often appear in large flocks on lakes in autumn, feed for a day or two and then move on. A winter male is striking, with a rich red head, black breast, and grey body; the female is greyish with pale "spectacles", but has a similar grey-patched bill. Often sleepy by day, they sit on the water in tight, frequently single-sex flocks.

WINTERS on open lakes and estuaries; breeds by reedy lakes, rivers, and marshes.

pale grey wingbars
♂❄
pale grey back
rich red head
dark bill with pale patch
peaked crown
dull grey-brown
dark cap
brown with pale flanks
♀
black breast
♂☼
dull head
brownish red head
♂⚘

VOICE Wheezing rise-and-fall call from displaying male; purring growl from female.
NESTING Pad of leaves and down on ground near water; 8–10 eggs; 1 brood; April–July.
FEEDING Dives from surface, taking seeds, shoots, and roots; often feeds at night.
SIMILAR SPECIES Scaup (p.109), female Tufted Duck (right).

Tufted Duck

Aythya fuligula (Anatidae)

The drooping crest and black-backed, pied plumage of the male Tufted Duck are distinctive in winter, but females and summer males are dark, dull, and easy to confuse with Scaup (p.109). A Tufted Duck has a larger black tip on the bill, which helps to identify it at close range.

BREEDS in long grass around lakes and rivers; winters in flocks on lakes and sheltered coastal waters.

♀
♂
bold white wingbars
golden eyes
slight tuft
dull brown body
♂☼
blue-grey bill with large black tip
long, wispy tuft on nape
black body with white flanks
♂❄
short crest
♀

VOICE Deep, grating growl; male gives nasal whistles during courtship.
NESTING Down-lined hollow concealed in dense, tall vegetation close to water; 8–11 eggs; 1 brood; May–June.
FEEDING Dives for molluscs and insects.
SIMILAR SPECIES Scaup (p.109), female Pochard (left).

Pintail

Anas acuta (Anatidae)

Arguably the most elegant of all the surface-feeding ducks, the Pintail is a big, slim, long-necked bird. It is generally scarcer than some of its relatives during winter, when birds from the main breeding populations in eastern and northern Europe disperse westwards to milder areas in Britain, often in ones or twos among large groups of more common ducks. Large flocks are found, however, on a few traditional wintering sites on estuaries and freshwater marshes. The striking breeding plumage of the males, acquired as with other ducks in winter, is unmistakable, but females and immatures need separating from those of other dabbling ducks. Good clues are the long neck, slim bill, and more pointed tail.

FEEDS at wintering sites on estuaries and fresh marshes; breeds by tundra and upland pools or lowland coastal marshes.

NOTE
The males' long central tail feathers are often raised, but may sometimes be lowered – as when the birds are upending for food or when they are nervous. In the autumn "eclipse" plumage, these are lost for a few weeks.

NOTE
In flight, female Pintails can be distinguished from females of other dabbling ducks by the bold white rear edge to the wings, visible at long range.

long, narrow, pointed wings
bold head pattern
long, pointed tail ♂❄
bold white trailing edge to wing
pointed tail
small head on long, slim neck ♀
chocolate-brown head
gleaming white neck-stripe and breast
long, spiky black and buff feathers
grey bill with black sides
black central tail feathers form long spike ♂❄

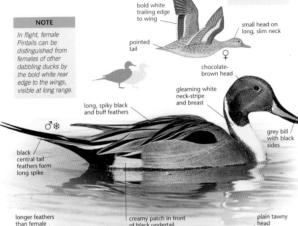

longer feathers than female
creamy patch in front of black undertail
plain tawny head ♀
dull greyish body
pale breast
two-tone bill
mottled grey-brown body
grey bill ♂❄

VOICE Male has low, short whistling call, lower-pitched than male Teal's (p.106); female has quack rather like that of female Mallard but quieter.
NESTING Hollow lined with leaves and down on ground among vegetation; 7–9 eggs; 1 brood; April–June.
FEEDING Mainly dabbles or upends for seeds, other vegetation, tiny snails, and other animals; also grazes on grass, marshes, and cereal fields for spilt grain and other crops.
SIMILAR SPECIES Mallard (p.107), female Gadwall (p.107).

Shoveler

Anas clypeata (Anatidae)

Male Shovelers in breeding plumage look superficially like male Mallards (p.107) with the colours rearranged into a different pattern. However, they are easily distinguished by their low-slung bodies, gleaming white breasts (visible at long range) that contrast with the dark green head and chestnut flanks, and above all, by their outsized, broad, shovel-like bill. The bill is also a feature of female Shovelers and, along with their body shape, helps separate them from females of Mallard and other dabbling ducks. Both sexes look front-heavy and short-tailed in their fast flight, in which they show pale forewings.

WINTERS on lakes, reservoirs, inland marshes, and sheltered estuaries with grassy salt marshes; feeds on and breeds by reedy pools, mainly in lowlands.

grey forewings
pale blue forewings
bold pattern on underparts ♀
♂
green head; looks black at distance
dark rufous flanks
striking yellow eyes
huge, long, broad bill
♂❄
dazzlingly white breast

streaked, pale brown body ♀
huge, shovel-like bill with orange sides
rufous-tinged flanks
dark head
pale crescent ♂❄

NOTE
Shovelers often feed in small groups that swim in circles. Each bird's bill almost touches the next one's tail, and is pushed through the water to sieve food particles from the sediment stirred up by the feet of the bird ahead. They also upend to feed, making their orange legs and pointed wings visible.

VOICE Often silent birds, although rival males give quiet, deep, gruff, nasal took took calls when they chase one another, and females may utter soft, deep quacks; wings make "woofing" noise on taking flight.
NESTING Hollow lined with down and sometimes with grasses or other leaves, in vegetation near water; 8–12 eggs; 1 brood; March–June.
FEEDING Dabbles on surface for seeds and invertebrates with bill thrust onto the water surface or beneath it with the bird's back almost awash.
SIMILAR SPECIES Mallard (p.107), female Garganey (p.106).

Common Scoter

Melanitta nigra (Anatidae)

A dark, large-bodied, slim-necked sea duck with a pointed tail, the Common Scoter gathers in large sociable groups out at sea, swimming buoyantly or flying low over the waves. The male is the only totally black duck; the female is browner with a pale face, but has no truly white body plumage.

WINTERS at sea around coasts, often well off-shore. Breeds on shores of moorland lakes and pools. Occurs in large flocks at regular sites.

dark cap
dark brown body ♀
grey face
black body with duller or paler wings
round head
pointed bill with yellow patch
long, pointed tail, often raised
thin neck ♂❄

pale tip to underwings ♂
slim neck

VOICE Male has musical, piping whistle; female makes deep growls.
NESTING Hollow near water, lined with leaves and down; often on islands; 6–8 eggs; 1 brood; March–June.
FEEDING Dives from surface to find shellfish, crustaceans, and worms.
SIMILAR SPECIES Velvet Scoter (right).

Velvet Scoter

Melanitta fusca (Anatidae)

With its large body and wedge-shaped face, the Velvet Scoter looks almost Eider-like (p.110), but much darker. It is usually seen in small numbers among flocks of the smaller Common Scoters (left), where it can be difficult to pick out – although the white wing-patches are distinctive. The white eye-spot of the black male is hard to see at long range.

WINTERS at sea off sheltered coasts. Breeds along northern coasts of Europe.

brown body
white spots ♀
white eye-spot
wedge-shaped face
thick neck
bill with yellow sides
black body ♂❄
red legs

white wing patch ♂

VOICE Male whistles, female growls, but generally quiet, especially in winter.
NESTING Down-lined hollow near the water; 6–8 eggs; 1 brood; May–July.
FEEDING Dives from surface to gather molluscs, crustaceans, and marine worms.
SIMILAR SPECIES Common Scoter (left), immature Goldeneye (p.110).

Scaup

Aythya marila (Anatidae)

Resembling the Tufted Duck (p.107), but with a rounder crown and no trace of a tuft, the Scaup is far more marine in its habits and only appears inland in small numbers. The black head of a breeding male has a green gloss in good light, while the back is a pale, marbled grey rather than black. Winter flocks of Scaup favour sheltered waters, where the clear white flanks of the males show up well against the dark sea.

WINTERS *in flocks on quiet coastal waters such as sea lochs and estuaries. Breeds in northern Europe.*

broad white wingbars

♂✿

pale patch at bill base

♀✿ pale cheeks

white blaze — rich brown head ♀✿

dull dark head — greyer back ♂✿

NOTE

A female Scaup is bigger than the very similar Tufted Duck. It also has a larger white area at the base of the bill, and the bill itself has a smaller black tip.

steep forehead — yellow eyes — black head with green gloss

blue-grey bill with black tip — pale grey back — white flanks — black around tail ♂✿

VOICE *Male produces low whistles in display, but is otherwise mostly silent; female has deep growl.*
NESTING *Uses hollow on ground, lined with feathers and down, near water; 8–11 eggs; 1 brood; April–June.*
FEEDING *Dives from surface in coastal shallows to find molluscs, crustaceans, and other invertebrates, as well as aquatic plants and waste grain on lakes and other fresh waters.*
SIMILAR SPECIES *Tufted Duck (p.107), male Pochard (p.107).*

Goosander

Mergus merganser (Anatidae)

The Goosander is the largest of the sawbills, with a thicker, more strongly-hooked bill than the more delicately built Red-breasted Merganser (below). The male is also much whiter with a salmon-pink tinge, and has a neater, drooping crest on its green-black head. The smaller female is mostly blue-grey with a dark rufous head and a white throat. It is much more of a freshwater bird than the Red-breasted Merganser; large flocks may gather on big lakes and reservoirs, with smaller numbers on flooded pits and rivers. Usually a shy, wary bird, the Goosander is easily scared off by intruders, even at long range.

FEEDS *mainly on fresh water, on reservoirs, lakes, and rivers. In summer, breeding pairs prefer upland reservoirs and shallower, fast-flowing, clear streams with plenty of boulders and stony shores.*

NOTE

A female Goosander can be reliably identified by the sharp division of colours on its neck; those of the Red-breasted Merganser (below) are blurred.

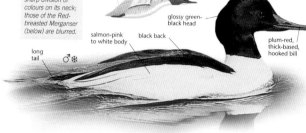

♂✿ large white wing patch

♀ — elongated look in flight — dark eyes

glossy green-black head

salmon-pink to white body — black back — plum-red, thick-based, hooked bill

long tail ♂✿

striped face — greyish body

dark brown head — smooth, downward-pointing crest — blue-grey body ♀ — sharp division between brown and white

NOTE

A male Goosander in eclipse plumage looks almost exactly like a female, but it has a redder bill and a clear division between its darker back and paler flanks. It also has more white on its wings, which shows up in flight and looks like a white flank streak on the water.

VOICE *Usually silent, but male gives frog-like double croaks during courtship, also twanging or bell-like notes; female makes cackling notes and harsh karrr.*
NESTING *Usually hole in tree near water, but may nest among heather, among rocks, or in hole in bank; 8–11 eggs; 1 brood; April–July.*
FEEDING *Dives from surface, travelling long distances underwater in large lakes, to take fish.*
SIMILAR SPECIES *Red-breasted Merganser (below), male Mallard (p.107).*

Smew

Mergellus albellus (Anatidae)

This is the smallest of the sawbilled ducks. The stunning winter male is a scarce bird over much of western Europe, including Britain, but immatures and females regularly winter at favoured sites. These "redheads" are quite distinctive, but the occasional adult male can be hard to spot in an active flock.

WINTERS *on coastal waters, and on lakes, pools, reservoirs, and estuaries. Breeds by forest lakes and rivers.*

brown cap — white cheeks ♀

orange-brown ♂✿

white crest — black nape — largely white plumage

black face patch

large white areas on wings ♂✿

black lines on plumage

♀

outstretched head ♂✿

VOICE *Silent in winter, but males often display with raised crests.*
NESTING *Tree hole near water; 4–6 eggs; 1 brood; April–June.*
FEEDING *Dives from surface to catch small fish and insect larvae.*
SIMILAR SPECIES *Female Goosander (right).*

Red-breasted Merganser

Mergus serrator (Anatidae)

A long, slim duck with a slender red bill, the Red-breasted Merganser is one of the fish-catching sawbills. The male is striking, with a dark head and a spiky crest; the female is very like a female Goosander (above), but has no sharp colour change on the neck. It is usually seen in small groups.

BREEDS *by northern coasts or along fast rivers; winters at sea, on sheltered coasts and estuaries.*

ginger-brown head ♀

white wing patch ♂✿

wispy crest on green-black head — slim, slightly upcurved red bill

black and white above — white collar

grey flanks

brown head ♂✿ — brownish grey body ♀

VOICE *Generally quiet, but may give a low, rolling croak or growl.*
NESTING *In long grass on ground, or among rocks; 8–11 eggs; 1 brood; April–June.*
FEEDING *Dives from surface to catch small fish and invertebrates.*
SIMILAR SPECIES *Female Goosander (above), male Mallard (p.107).*

Long-tailed Duck

Clangula hyemalis (Anatidae)

Many ducks feed both at sea and in freshwater, but the Long-tailed Duck is essentially a marine species that is found on lakes and similar waters only during the breeding season. Winter males are striking, with largely white plumage set off by blackish markings and a pair of long, dark central tail feathers. Females are darker above but pale below, with no long tail; summer males are similar, losing their long tails and becoming duller in late summer. Generally lively and active at sea, Long-tailed Ducks often fly low over the water, splash down, and take off again. They feed in flocks, often associating with scoters, and spend long periods underwater.

BREEDS *on lakes and pools on moorland and tundra. Winters at sea, typically well offshore but often drifting into bays and estuaries with tide, especially in early spring.*

NOTE

Winter male Long-tailed Ducks are distinctive, but other plumages can be confusing. The dark wings, dumpy body, and stubby dark bill are good clues.

dark wings

♀❄

white breast, dark in summer

♂❄

long, flexible tail point

♂❄

white and pale grey body

dark cheek patch

grey around eyes

pink band on stubby dark bill

blurred white band around eyes

◑❄

♀❄ pale flanks

dark cheek patch

♂☀ rich brown body

white face patch

♀☀

white neck

VOICE *Male makes loud, rhythmic, musical yodelling calls, a-ahulee; female gives low, barking quacks and growls.*
NESTING *Down-lined hollow on ground near water; 4–6 eggs; 1 brood; May–June.*
FEEDING *Dives from the surface to take molluscs, crustaceans, marine worms, and sea urchins; eats aquatic insects in summer on northern breeding grounds.*
SIMILAR SPECIES *Female Goldeneye (below), male Pintail (p.108).*

Eider

Somateria mollissima (Anatidae)

A big, bulky, entirely marine duck with a characteristic wedge-shaped head, the Eider is usually easy to identify. A winter male is boldly pied black and white, with green patches on its head and a pink flush on its breast. Females have brown plumage with close dark bars that provide superb camouflage on the nest. Highly sociable, Eiders often form large rafts offshore, but they are equally familiar around coastal rocks.

BREEDS *on low-lying northern coasts and islands with rocky shores and weedy bays. Winters at sea, often in sandy bays and over mussel beds.*

black outer wings

dark hindwings

white rear flanks

♂

black crown

♀

green patch

wedge-shaped bill

white upperparts

pale line above eye

brown, closely barred body

dark belly

♀

unbarred dark body, often piebald

♂☀

pale band over eye

black stern

pinkish breast

black underparts

white patch

♂❄

NOTE

The male Eider is the only duck that combines a white back and breast with black flanks and belly – features that are readily seen at long range.

VOICE *Male gives sensuous, cooing aa-ahooh; females respond with deep growls and a mechanical kok-kok-kok.*
NESTING *Hollow on ground, liberally lined with down, either exposed or well hidden; 4–6 eggs; 1 brood; April–June.*
FEEDING *Eats mainly molluscs, especially mussels, diving from surface to gather them from rocks; also crustaceans such as crabs and shrimps, starfish, and marine worms.*
SIMILAR SPECIES *Velvet Scoter (p.108), female Mallard (p.107).*

Goldeneye

Bucephala clangula (Anatidae)

A bulky, short-necked diving duck with a high-peaked head and triangular bill, the Goldeneye is an active, wary bird that spends most of its time on the water, repeatedly diving for food. The yellow eye is hard to see at a distance, but the winter male's pied plumage and bold white head patch are eye-catching. The female is basically grey with a chocolate-brown head and a white collar; summer males are similar, but without the collar. Feeding Goldeneyes are shy and easily disturbed, flying off in tight groups with a loud whistling noise from their wings. They fly fast and direct with deep wing beats, their large white wing patches showing up well.

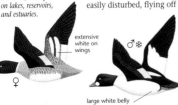

FEEDS *on coasts, lakes, reservoirs, large rivers, and estuaries; breeds in wooded areas beside cold freshwater lakes. In winter, widespread on lakes, reservoirs, and estuaries.*

extensive white on wings

♀

♂❄

large white belly

golden yellow eyes

high-peaked, triangular head

bold white spot

green-glossed black head plumage

black marks on sparkling white body

triangular dark bill

♂❄

face develops white spot in winter

gets whiter with age

◑♂

white collar

dark brown head

grey body

grey and yellow bill

♀

NOTE

As juvenile males and females look much like adult females, winter flocks naturally have a minority of immaculate adult males.

VOICE *Male gives frequent nasal, mechanical ze-zeee call in display; female has grating double note.*
NESTING *Cavity lined with down from female typically in tree hole, sometimes in abandoned rabbit hole or artificial nest box; 8–11 eggs; 1 brood; April–June.*
FEEDING *Dives constantly from the surface to gather molluscs, insect larvae, and crustaceans.*
SIMILAR SPECIES *Smew (p.109), Velvet Scoter (p.108).*

Red Grouse

Lagopus lagopus (Tetraonidae)

This is a thickset bird of heather-clad moors. It looks rather like a larger, darker partridge, but is more evenly mottled, rather than streaked and barred. In flight, it reveals darker wings and almost black sides to the short tail, and distinctive white underwings. Its echoing calls are a characteristic of upland moors. Red Grouse are hardy birds, but generally have poor breeding success in wet weather when many chicks die and adult birds succumb to disease. Successive cool, damp summers have led to widespread declines, especially in the west of Britain.

FOUND *mainly on dry heather moorland on northern hills of the British Isles.*

- short stout bill
- red wattle over eye
- short dark tail ♀
- neck outstretched
- red-brown, with paler feather edges
- stiff dark wing ♂
- plain dark wings
- short blackish tail ♂
- feathered feet
- yellow-brown plumage
- heavily mottled body ♀

NOTE

The Red Grouse has long been thought to be a species unique to Britain and Ireland, but is probably best considered a subspecies, of the Willow Grouse of northern Europe, which has white wings and plumage.

VOICE *Remarkable, deep, staccato calls that echo across the moors, kau-kau-kau-ka-ka-karrr-rrr-g'back, g'back, bak.*
NESTING *Sparsely lined scrape on ground in heather; 6–9 eggs; 1 brood; April–May.*
FEEDING *Plucks shoots and seeds from heather while standing or walking slowly over the ground; also takes a variety of berries and seeds; chicks feed on insects.*
SIMILAR SPECIES *Ptarmigan (right), Grey Partridge (right).*

Ptarmigan

Lagopus mutus (Tetraonidae)

Smaller than the Red Grouse (left), the Ptarmigan looks more delicate, but is in reality one of the hardiest of birds. It is difficult to see, being brilliantly camouflaged at all times of year and unwilling to fly. It "freezes" when approached but, if it does take to the air, reveals pure white wings. It lives on the highest hills and far northern peaks of mainland Scotland, where the ground lies under snow for much of the winter and is exposed to wind and rain in summer. The Ptarmigan population seems likely to decline as climate change reduces their habitat on northern hills and moors.

BREEDS *on high moors, boulder fields and rocky slopes well above the tree line.*

- bright red comb above eye
- delicate bill
- "salt and pepper" barring on grey upperparts
- grey head and body ♂✿
- white head and body ♂❄
- tail stays black
- white wings
- white belly ♂✿
- feathered legs
- red comb
- black line between bill and eye
- white plumage ♂❄
- yellow speckling on brown body
- white wings ♀✿
- no red comb or black line
- white plumage ♀❄

NOTE

A Ptarmigan is slightly smaller than a Red Grouse (left) and replaces it at higher altitudes, in surroundings that are similar to arctic tundra habitats.

VOICE *A variety of low, dry, croaking notes, especially a four-syllable arr-kar-ka-karrr; also a cackling "belch".*
NESTING *Nests in a scrape on the ground, lightly lined with grass; 5–9 eggs; 1 brood; May–July.*
FEEDING *Gathers food on the ground, taking shoots, leaves, buds, seeds, and berries of a variety of low-growing shrubs; also takes insects, which are an important food for chicks.*
SIMILAR SPECIES *Red Grouse (left).*

Red-legged Partridge

Alectoris rufa (Phasianidae)

An elegant gamebird with a bright red bill, the Red-legged Partridge is surprisingly well camouflaged and often hard to spot. It favours warm, open, stony slopes, or farmland with sandy soils. Its plumage looks unmistakable, but in many parts of its range, this bird is easily confused with hybrids resulting from crosses with the introduced Chukar Partridge (*A. chukar*).

BREEDS *on open slopes with bare ground and dry, sandy arable land; also on grassy heaths and coastal dunes.*

- plain pale brown above
- black, grey, and brown bars on flanks
- white stripe
- dark red-brown tail
- black-streaked "necklace"
- straight, stiff wings
- red legs
- rufous tail

VOICE *Deep, gobbling and hissing or chuckling mechanical calls, chuk-uk-ar, k'chuk-ar, k'chuk-ar.*
NESTING *Grass-lined scrape beneath low vegetation; 7–20 eggs; 1 brood; April–June.*
FEEDING *Takes leaves, shoots, berries, nuts, and seeds from ground; chicks eat insects.*
SIMILAR SPECIES *Grey Partridge (right).*

Grey Partridge

Perdix perdix (Phasianidae)

This neat gamebird is typical of old-fashioned farmland with hedges. It feeds secretively in long grass, in tight flocks, pausing to raise its head and look around. If disturbed, it rockets off with whirring wings, alternating with short glides on bowed wings.

LIVES *mainly on farmland, especially grassy meadows with rich insect life; also on heaths, low moorland, and dunes.*

- dull brown bill
- orange-brown face
- orange tail sides
- streaked back
- pale brown wings
- finely barred grey breast
- bold red-brown bars on flanks
- dull brown legs
- broad, brown belly patch ♂

VOICE *Distinctive low, rhythmic, mechanical, creaky kieeer-ik or ki-yik.*
NESTING *Well-hidden, shallow scrape on ground; 10–20 eggs; 1 brood; April–June.*
FEEDING *Takes seeds, leaves, and shoots from ground; feeds insects to chicks.*
SIMILAR SPECIES *Red-legged Partridge (left); juvenile Pheasant (p.114).*

Pheasant
There are few birds in Britain as flamboyantly coloured as the male Pheasant. With tail raised and wings spread, this male hopes to intimidate any potential rivals for his territory.

Black Grouse

Tetrao tetrix (Tetraonidae)

The glossy blue-black plumage, long, curved outer tail, and bright red comb of the male Black Grouse are unmistakable, particularly in display when the bird raises its tail to reveal a fan of white feathers. The smaller female is much less distinctive, although her notched tail is a useful clue. In spring, the males gather on communal display grounds (called leks) to compete for females with mock fights, spreading their feathers and calling with repetitive bubbling, cooing notes. They are easily disturbed at such times, and usually fly off and land far away if approached.

DISPLAYS *and lives on moorland edges, forest clearings, heaths, birch scrub, rough pastures, and young conifer plantations.*

NOTE

Black Grouse of both sexes have a large white area on their underwings. They also have an elongated look in flight, compared to Red Grouse (p.111), and generally fly higher when flushed.

big red comb

blue sheen on neck

small white shoulder spot

♂

white undertail feathers raised in display

curved, broad-tipped outer tail feathers

glossy black plumage

big, heavy, cockerel-like body

slightly notched tail

pale bar on mid-brown wings

♀

elongated shape

unique lyre-shaped tail

♂

bold white wingbar

dark-barred, yellow-brown or grey

♀

VOICE *Female has gruff bark; displaying male produces far-carrying, dove-like, rolling coo with regular rhythm, and explosive "sneeze".*
NESTING *Hollow on ground beneath heather or bracken, with little or no lining; 6–10 eggs; 1 brood; April–July.*
FEEDING *Wide variety of seeds, berries, buds, shoots, leaves, and flowers of many shrubs, sedges, and trees such as birch and hazel, changing with seasons; chicks eat insects.*
SIMILAR SPECIES *Capercaillie (right), female Red Grouse (p.111).*

Capercaillie

Tetrao urogallus (Tetraonidae)

The magnificent Capercaillie is by far the largest of the grouse. The male in particular is a massive, dark, turkey-like, aggressive bird; the female is much smaller, but still big in comparison with other grouse, with an orange breast and a broad tail. Males display competitively in spring, attracting females with their remarkable voices and wing-flapping leaps. Generally shy and secretive, the Capercaillie is sensitive to disturbance and is now seriously threatened in many parts of its range, including Scotland.

LIVES *in ancient pine forests and boggy forest clearings with bilberry, juniper, and heather; less often in mature pine plantations.*

short, stout, pale, hooked bill

red comb

♀

dark bars on orange tail

♂

big, rounded tail

brown wings

"beard" of spiky feathers

bold white shoulder spot

black tail, speckled with white

broad, round tail when fanned in display

huge, blackish body

♂

brown wings

dark bars on rufous-ginger body

cream with black and rufous bars

orange breast

♀

NOTE

Despite its size, the Capercaillie roosts in the trees, and often feeds up in the branches in winter. In summer, it is more likely to be found at ground level. It rarely allows a close approach, but sometimes sits tight until it is forced to burst up from underfoot in a cacophony of flapping wings.

VOICE *Pheasant-like crowing; male in spring utters bizarre "song" of clicks and belches, ending with cork-popping and wheezy gurgling.*
NESTING *Hollow on ground, often at base of tree, lined with grass, pine needles, and twigs; 5–8 eggs; 1 brood; March–July.*
FEEDING *Eats shoots, leaves, and buds of several shrubs and trees, berries of various herbs and shrubs, especially bilberry, and pine needles taken from treetops in winter.*
SIMILAR SPECIES *Female Black Grouse (left).*

Quail

Coturnix coturnix (Phasianidae)

A tiny, rounded, sharp-winged, secretive bird of long grass and dense crops, the Quail is often heard but rarely seen unless it ventures briefly into the open. Occasionally, it flies off on surprisingly long wings in a fast, low, short, arc before dropping back into thick cover.

BREEDS *and feeds in tracts of long grass or cereal fields, mainly in warm, dry areas. Migrants may rest in fields with sparse crops, or other open ground.*

striped crown

cream stripes on brown back

♂

short, dark, pointed tail

dark throat

pale throat

♀

small, striped head

long dark wings

dark stripes on flanks

VOICE *Song unique loud, far-carrying, full, liquid quick-we-wik, also quiet mewing notes.*
NESTING *Slight hollow, well hidden in grass or crops, lined with vegetation; up to 12 eggs; 1 brood; May–June.*
FEEDING *Takes seeds, shoots, and small insects from ground or foliage.*
SIMILAR SPECIES *Grey Partridge (p.111).*

Pheasant

Phasianus colchicus (Phasianidae)

The male pheasant is a conspicuous, noisy bird, although very variable, with or without a white neck-ring but always with a bold red wattle around the eye. The female is more anonymous-looking and secretive, but the long, pointed tail is very distinctive.

INHABITS *mainly in wood-land edge, arable land, reedbeds, heaths, and moorland edge.*

bare red skin

black markings

♀

long neck

white neck-ring

often has pale rump

tail longer than female's

♀

long pointed tail

white markings

PALE FORM

♂

orange-copper flanks

♂

DARK FORM

VOICE *Loud, explosive corr-kok! with sudden whirr of wings; loud clucking in flight.*
NESTING *Hollow on ground, beneath cover; 8–15 eggs; 1 brood; April–July.*
FEEDING *Takes a variety of food from ground, from seeds and berries to insects and lizards.*
SIMILAR SPECIES *Female like female Grey Partridge (p.111), Black Grouse (left).*

Red-throated Diver

Gavia stellata (Gaviidae)

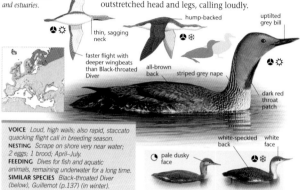

BREEDS *by remote moorland pools and lakes, but feeds at sea daily in parts of range. Winters on coasts and estuaries.*

As with other divers, this is a long-bodied, skilled swimmer and diver that usually has a low profile in the water, and is rarely seen on land except at the nest. The smallest diver, it is distinguished by its slimmer bill, held angled upwards. In summer, it is often seen commuting to and fro between its nest and the sea, flying high with outstretched head and legs, calling loudly.

thin, sagging neck

hump-backed

uptilted grey bill

faster flight with deeper wingbeats than Black-throated Diver

all-brown back

striped grey nape

dark red throat patch

white-speckled back

white face

pale dusky face

VOICE *Loud, high wails; also rapid, staccato quacking flight call in breeding season.*
NESTING *Scrape on shore very near water; 2 eggs; 1 brood; April–July.*
FEEDING *Dives for fish and aquatic animals, remaining underwater for a long time.*
SIMILAR SPECIES *Black-throated Diver (below), Guillemot (p.137) (in winter).*

Little Grebe

Tachybaptus ruficollis (Podicipedidae)

INHABITS *freshwater lakes, ponds, flooded pits, canals, and rivers. Winters on larger waters or sheltered coastal waters.*

The smallest European grebe, this dark, short-billed, rotund, and almost tailless bird swims buoyantly and dives often. Longer-necked and less portly in winter, it can look like a Black-necked Grebe (p.116). In summer, its whinnying trills are a good clue to its presence.

all-dark wings

trailing feet

blackish cap

rufous on face and neck

buff foreneck

pale yellow spot on short bill

buffish face

"sawn-off" rear end due to very short, buff tail

VOICE *When breeding, distinctive high-pitched, rapid trill that fades away.*
NESTING *Floating mound of weed, anchored to branch; 4–6 eggs; 1 brood; April–June.*
FEEDING *Dives to catch small fish, insects, and molluscs.*
SIMILAR SPECIES *Black-necked Grebe (p.116), Moorhen (p.127).*

Black-throated Diver

Gavia arctica (Gaviidae)

Easily distinguished in its beautifully patterned breeding plumage, the Black-throated Diver is duller in winter and harder to separate from the smaller Red-throated (above) or larger Great Northern Diver (below). Useful clues are the Black-throated's white flank patch, slim, straight bill, quite bulbous head, and greyish nape, paler than the back.

NESTS *mainly on islets in large, remote lakes. Winters in coastal waters and large estuaries, rarely inland.*

grey head

striped neck

black throat

head less sagging than Red-throated

oval patch of white bars on each side

dark above

grey nape

scaly back

dark cap

white flank patch

VOICE *Loud, wild, rhythmic wailing "song" and croaking calls in breeding season; silent in flight and during winter.*
NESTING *Shallow scrape by water's edge; 2 eggs; 1 brood; April–July.*
FEEDING *Catches fish in long, deep dives.*
SIMILAR SPECIES *Red-throated Diver (above), Great Northern Diver (below).*

Great Crested Grebe

Podiceps cristatus (Podicipedidae)

COURTS *and breeds on flooded gravel pits, reservoirs, or big lakes and rivers; winters on fresh waters or sheltered coastal waters.*

Largest of European grebes, this is a striking bird in spring and summer, when pairs use their spectacular head ruff and spiky head tufts in face-to-face head-shaking courtship displays. They also dive, surfacing with weed in their bills to offer one another. Winter birds are hard to distinguish from scarcer Red-necked Grebes (below).

black head plumes

dagger-like pink bill

unique ruff

slender white neck and white breast

drooping neck

two bold white patches

striped head

pink bill

pale greyish

white over eye

white foreneck

VOICE *Loud growls and barks while courting and nesting; juveniles make loud, fluty whistles.*
NESTING *Semi-floating pile of wet weed, anchored to vegetation; 3–4 eggs; 1 brood; February–June.*
FEEDING *Dives to catch mainly fish, also aquatic insect larvae and small amphibians.*
SIMILAR SPECIES *Red-necked Grebe (below).*

Great Northern Diver

Gavia immer (Gaviidae)

Largest of the common European divers, the Great Northern has boldly chequered upperparts and a black head in breeding plumage. In winter, it is best distinguished by its size, very broad body, heavy bill, thick neck, and big head with a steep forehead. It also has a dark nape and neck collar. It usually swims low in the water, its back often awash.

WINTERS *on coastal waters, including broad estuaries and bays, typically farther from shore than the two smaller divers.*

dark half-collar

chequered back

pale collar

dark crown

heavy, pale bill

broad body

white face

dark nape

MOULTING

flat head

chequered back

black head

barred back

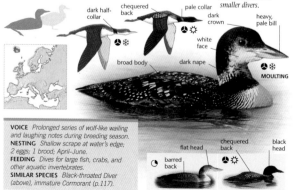

VOICE *Prolonged series of wolf-like wailing and laughing notes during breeding season.*
NESTING *Shallow scrape at water's edge; 2 eggs; 1 brood; April–June.*
FEEDING *Dives for large fish, crabs, and other aquatic invertebrates.*
SIMILAR SPECIES *Black-throated Diver (above), immature Cormorant (p.117).*

Red-necked Grebe

Podiceps grisegena (Podicipedidae)

A widespread and typical breeding bird of large fresh waters in northeast Europe, the Red-necked Grebe migrates in autumn to spend winter in western Europe. In the British Isles it is generally much scarcer than the usually slimmer-looking, paler Great Crested Grebe (above).

BREEDS *on reedy lakes or slow rivers; winters mainly on sheltered estuaries or coastal bays, sometimes on fresh waters inland.*

black cap extends below eye

yellow base to stout, dagger-like bill

grey face with white upper edge

white patches

dark chestnut neck and breast

slightly drooping neck

striped cheeks

dusky foreneck

VOICE *Growls, squeals, and wails when breeding; silent in winter.*
NESTING *Semi-floating heap of wet weed attached to stems; 3–4 eggs; 1 brood; April–June.*
FEEDING *Mainly fish caught by diving, also eats crustaceans and insects in summer.*
SIMILAR SPECIES *Great Crested Grebe (above).*

Slavonian Grebe

Podiceps auritus (Podicipedidae)

This handsome bird is easy to identify at its remote northern breeding sites in summer, but in winter is more difficult to distinguish from other small grebes, especially the Black-necked Grebe (right). Much more tied to coastal waters in winter, it has a different head shape, bill shape, and a sharper contrast between dark and white.

flat black crown

straight, pale-tipped bill

stiff golden wedge

rust-red neck

rust-red flanks

BREEDS *on remote, cold pools with some fringing vegetation. Winters mainly on muddy estuaries.*

white shoulder patch

white cheeks and foreneck

1ST

large white cheeks

black cap

VOICE *Fast, high, whistling trill when breeding; usually silent in winter.*
NESTING *Pile of wet weed anchored to stems; 4–5 eggs; 1 brood; April–July.*
FEEDING *Dives to catch small fish; eats mainly insects and crustaceans in summer.*
SIMILAR SPECIES *Black-necked Grebe (right), Red-necked Grebe (p.115).*

Black-necked Grebe

Podiceps nigricollis (Podicipedidae)

Widespread but very local as a breeding bird, since it is restricted to nutrient-rich, low-lying lakes, the Black-necked Grebe is more often seen on fresh water in winter than the Slavonian Grebe (left). It is best distinguished from the latter by its finer, slightly uptilted bill, peaked crown, and steep forehead.

NESTS *among dense vegetation on low-lying lakes and pools; winters on coastal bays, estuaries, and fresh waters.*

peaked crown

red eyes

fine, uptilted bill

fan-shaped golden ear plumes

black neck

coppery red flanks

dusky cheeks

white patch on slim wings

trailing legs

grey foreneck

pale "hook"

VOICE *Chattering and soft, high whistling calls in breeding season; silent in winter.*
NESTING *Mound of wet weed fixed to vegetation; 3–4 eggs; 1 brood; March–July.*
FEEDING *Catches insects, molluscs, and small fish in long dives underwater.*
SIMILAR SPECIES *Slavonian Grebe (left), Little Grebe (p.115).*

Storm Petrel

Hydrobates pelagicus (Hydrobatidae)

The tiny, delicate-looking Storm Petrel is little larger than a sparrow, yet spends most of its life far out at sea, enduring the most extreme conditions throughout the winter. Generally very dark, but with a bold white rump, it flies very low over the waves with constant, easy but fluttering wing-beats, rolling from side to side or turning and dipping to feed by snatching edible morsels from the surface. It often follows ships in small flocks, and may fly past them at surprising speed before swooping down to the water to investigate another potential meal. It is rarely seen on shore, since it returns to its breeding grounds only at night to avoid predatory gulls and skuas.

LIVES *well offshore at sea, only rarely being forced inshore by gales. Breeds on offshore islands and headlands, to which it returns only at night.*

white bar on underwings

swept-back wings

sooty-black head

sooty-black body

tube-nosed bill

short legs

steep forehead

rounded tail

all-dark upperwings

white rump

settles on water with wings raised

NOTE

The highly oceanic Storm Petrel rarely comes inshore, and is most likely to be seen from ships. Look for the white underwing bar and rounded tail that distinguish it from Leach's Petrel (right); the wingbar is the best clue, but is variable and often difficult to see. Apart from its white rump, the Storm Petrel is also very dark, with no pale patches on its upperwings.

VOICE *Soft, purring trill with abrupt ending, at nest; high-pitched squeaking from colonies at night.*
NESTING *Hole among rocks or in old wall, or small burrow made by animal such as rabbit; 1 egg; 1 brood; April–July.*
FEEDING *Picks up small planktonic invertebrates, tiny fish, fish oil, and scraps of fish offal discarded from ships; feeds in flight, taking food with bill while pattering across surface with feet.*
SIMILAR SPECIES *Leach's Petrel (right), House Martin (p.143).*

Leach's Petrel

Oceanodroma leucorhoa (Hydrobatidae)

Although slightly larger than the Storm Petrel (left), Leach's Petrel still seems far too fragile to live out on the open ocean, buffeted by Atlantic gales. It is browner than the Storm Petrel, with an obvious pale panel on each upper-wing, a "V"-shaped white rump, and a notched tail – although the notch is not always conspicuous. It has a quick, strong flight, more powerful than that of the Storm Petrel, and often makes erratic twists, turns, and changes of speed. While feeding, it dangles its legs, but is less likely to patter its feet on the surface. Storm-driven birds occasionally appear over reservoirs and large lakes far inland.

FEEDS *out at sea, well offshore throughout winter, but may be driven inshore or even inland by storms. Breeds on remote offshore islands.*

dark underwings

pale panel on upperwings

notched tail

long, angled, arched wings

"V" shaped white rump with central dark line

notch in tail hard to see

steep forehead

sooty-brown back

angular shape

paler wing plumage

NOTE

While the Storm Petrel (left) flies rather like a Swallow (p.144), Leach's Petrel is more tern-like, often holding its wings arched with the inner section raised and the tips pointing down to form a shallow "M". Its flight is buoyant, graceful, and extremely agile.

VOICE *Rattling, chattering coo at nest, plus cackling and screeching from breeding colonies at night.*
NESTING *Burrow or cavity among rocks, sometimes rabbit burrow; one bird incubates while the other is at sea, returning to nest only at night; 1 egg; 1 brood; April–July.*
FEEDING *Eats floating pieces of fish offal, fish oil, jellyfish, and other marine invertebrates, picking them from the surface at night.*
SIMILAR SPECIES *Storm Petrel (left), Black Tern (p.138).*

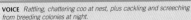

Fulmar

Fulmarus glacialis (Procellariidae)

Although it has gull-like plumage, the Fulmar is a tube-nosed petrel more closely related to the albatrosses. It holds its wings straight when gliding, unlike a gull, and has a distinctive thick neck and black eye-patch. Fulmars are often seen soaring on updraughts around coastal cliffs, although they spend much of their time at sea.

FEEDS *at sea; breeds on steep coastal cliffs or on remote grassy banks near sea.*

- black eye-patch
- yellowish white head
- short, thick neck
- tubular nostrils
- hooked bill
- pale patch
- stiff, straight wings
- grey wingtips
- pale grey rump and tail
- weak legs (cannot stand)

VOICE Loud, harsh, throaty cackling heard only at nesting ledge; generally silent at sea.
NESTING On cliff or earth ledge, or rarely on building; 1 egg; 1 brood; April–June.
FEEDING Takes mostly fish offal from trawlers, small fish, jellyfish, squid, and other marine animals.
SIMILAR SPECIES Herring Gull (p.135).

Manx Shearwater

Puffinus puffinus (Procellariidae)

Ungainly on land, shuffling along on its weak legs, aided by its bill and wings, this is a swift, elegant bird in the air. It is usually seen flying low over the sea with rapid, stiff-winged flaps between long glides, flashing alternately black and white as it banks from side to side.

FEEDS *over open sea, and breeds in colonies on islands and remote headlands. Widespread when migrating off coasts in autumn.*

- silvery white
- stiff wings
- blackish above; browner in strong sun
- thin dark bill
- white throat
- black cap
- white flank each side of rump

VOICE Loud, strangled wailing and chortling sounds at night around breeding colony.
NESTING Uses rabbit or Puffin (p.139) burrow or similar tunnel, or hole in scree; 1 egg; 1 brood; April–July.
FEEDING Flocks take fish and small squid, diving from surface or plunging from air.
SIMILAR SPECIES Razorbill (p.139).

Cormorant

Phalacrocorax carbo (Phalacrocoracidae)

Bigger and bulkier than a Shag (right), and slightly less snaky in shape, the Cormorant has a thicker bill, a low, flat forehead, and no crest. Its plumage is blackish, glossed with blue and bronze, and in spring it has white streaks on its head, a bold white throat, and white patches on its thighs. Often seen inland, even on small pools, Cormorants swim with their backs almost awash, and typically perch with their wings half-open. They fly strongly with long glides, often high up, in lines or "V" formations over coastal waters and wetlands.

LIVES *on coasts in sheltered estuaries and bays, and around harbours; also inland on lakes, rivers, and pools. Breeds on cliffs.*

- flat forehead
- hooked bill
- white on face
- yellow near bill
- blue gloss on head and neck
- white below
- neck kinked in flight
- blackish above, with bronze gloss
- bill tilted up
- brown above
- white below
- long, broad tail

NOTE
In flight, the neck of a Cormorant has an upward kink while the Shag's (right) neck is straight. Shags also tend to fly lower, often just above the waves.

VOICE Growling and cackling at nests and communal roosts, but otherwise a quiet bird.
NESTING Bulky nest of sticks in a tree or on a cliff ledge, often marked by white splashes beneath; 3–4 eggs; 1 brood; April–May.
FEEDING Catches fish, especially bottom-living flatfish and eels, in long underwater dive from surface, propelling itself with its feet; brings larger fish to surface before swallowing them.
SIMILAR SPECIES Shag (right), Great Northern Diver (p.115).

Shag

Phalacrocorax aristotelis (Phalacrocoracidae)

This large, long-bodied diving bird is very like the closely related Cormorant (left), but the adult is black overall with an oily green gloss, the only colour being the bright yellow patch at the base of its bill. In summer, both sexes sport a short curly crest. Winter birds are less distinctive and easier to confuse with Cormorants, but a certain slim snakiness gives the Shag a different character. Although sometimes solitary, Shags tend to feed in flocks, favouring the fast tide races and rough water under rocks and cliffs.

SEEN *off rocky coasts and islands; not common around harbours. Breeds on coastal cliffs.*

- short crest
- slim, slightly hooked bill
- narrow wings
- slender head and neck
- oily green-black plumage
- white chin
- paler below
- long, slim body
- long tail
- white spot
- dark brown above
- brown below
- low in water

NOTE
A Shag's head is a different shape from a Cormorant's (left), with a steep angle between its bill and its sloping forehead. An adult has no white on its face. It rarely strays inland, so any bird of this type seen away from the coast is likely to be a Cormorant.

VOICE Grunts, hisses, and coarse, frenzied rattling at nest; silent when feeding at sea.
NESTING Heap of grass, sticks, and seaweed on broad cliff ledge, or inside coastal cave; 3–4 eggs; 1 brood; May.
FEEDING Catches fish, mainly sandeels and herrings, by pursuing them underwater after dive from surface; often dives with quick, arching, forward leap.
SIMILAR SPECIES Cormorant (left), Black-throated Diver (p.115).

Gannet

Morus bassanus (Sulidae)

Largest of all European seabirds, the adult Gannet is typically seen offshore as a brilliant white bird with black wingtips, flying steadily, singly or in straggling lines, or circling and diving for fish with spectacular plunges. Juvenile birds, by contrast, are very dark with white specks, gradually becoming whiter over about five years, but their shape is always distinctive. At close range, the breeding adult's yellow-buff head is visible, as well as the dark markings on its face and fine lines on its big, sharp bill.

FEEDS *at sea, many moving south for the winter; breeds in dense, noisy colonies on rocky islands.*

long rear end and narrow, pointed tail

long, narrow wings

white band above tail

large black wingtips

protruding head

looks dark greyish at distance

dark above with white speckling

1ST

yellow-buff head

pale blue eyes

dagger-like bill with fine black lines

white plumage

black wingtips

webbing across all four toes

yellowish head

blackish above with white spots

piebald; turns white with age

NOTE

The protruding head, pointed bill, and narrow tail of a Gannet are quite unlike any gull's. Its long wings are much narrower, with more black on them.

VOICE *Rhythmic, throaty chorus of groans, barks, and croaks at nesting colony; otherwise silent, except for cackling from groups feeding at sea.*
NESTING *Pile of seaweed and debris on broad ledge high above sea, in dense, often very large colony; 1 egg; 1 brood; April–July.*
FEEDING *Catches fish such as mackerel and pollack underwater, in shallow and sloping dive from air, or vertical plunge dive from a greater height; also scavenges from fishing boats.*
SIMILAR SPECIES *Arctic Skua (p.134), Great Black-backed Gull (p.137).*

Little Egret

Egretta garzetta (Ardeidae)

This dazzling white bird is the most widespread of Europe's white herons. Found in both freshwater wetlands and along coasts, it is steadily spreading northwards in western Europe. It is much smaller than the Great White Egret. Often active and agile in search of prey, it also spends much time wading slowly or standing still.

SEEN *feeding in small loose flocks by or in water, from reedy lakes to rocky shores, but especially on open, muddy, or sandy shores.*

long plumes on nape

all-white plumage

rather bowed wings

no head or back plumes

slim, sharp dark bill

pointed breast plumes

black legs

yellow feet

VOICE *Usually silent except when breeding, when it utters snarling and croaking calls.*
NESTING *Stick nest in tree, often with other herons and cormorants; 3–4 eggs; 1 brood; April–July.*
FEEDING *Eats small fish, frogs, and snails.*
SIMILAR SPECIES *None in the British Isles, except other, very much rarer, egrets.*

Spoonbill

Platalea leucorodia (Threskiornithidae)

This big waterbird is unmistakable once its remarkable spatula-shaped bill is visible. Though rather like a large white egret, it is distinguished by its habit of striding with a strangely human-like walk through the shallows and sweeping its bill from side to side. Its head is outstretched in flight.

FEEDS *on saltpans, marshes, other shallow wetlands; breeds at reedy lakes with fringing bushes or trees.*

black wingtips

outstretched head

pinkish bill

white underwings

ochre on chin and base of neck

flattened, broad-tipped, black bill, yellow at end

long, thick black legs

VOICE *Normally silent.*
NESTING *Platform of sticks or reed in colony in reeds or tree; 3–4 eggs; 1 brood; April–July.*
FEEDING *Sweeps partly open bill through water from side to side to snap up small fish, molluscs, and crustaceans.*
SIMILAR SPECIES *Mute Swan (similar in flight) (p.104), Little Egret (above).*

Bittern

Botaurus stellaris (Ardeidae)

This very secretive, large, bulky bird is more often heard than seen, when males proclaim their territories by a remarkable booming "song", audible up to 5 km (3 miles) away. Restricted to large wet reedbeds, the Bittern is very local and scattered across its British range.

BREEDS *in large, wet reedbeds. More widespread in winter, when it may be forced by frost to feed in smaller patches of reed or open water.*

mottled brown body

blackish crown

broad, bowed wings

paler panel

black stripe

dagger-like bill

streaked neck

short legs and very long toes

VOICE *Repeated, deep, rhythmic boom, ker-whooomp! like the sound made by blowing over the top of a bottle; nasal flight call.*
NESTING *Broad nest of reed stems hidden in dense reedbed; 4–6 eggs; 1 brood; April–May.*
FEEDING *Catches fish, especially eels.*
SIMILAR SPECIES *Grey Heron (right).*

Grey Heron

Ardea cinerea (Ardeidae)

Standing still as a statue or walking slowly through the shallows, the Grey Heron will suddenly straighten its neck and grab a fish in its bill with lightning speed. Long-necked, long-legged, and mainly grey and white, it can however look hunched, with its neck drawn in. It flies with deeply bowed wings.

INHABITS *fresh and salt water habitats, from estuaries and rocky shores to lakes, floods, and even garden ponds.*

dagger-like yellowish bill; orange in spring

head with grey cap; lacks crest

grey sides of head and neck

wispy black plume

pale grey body

black streaks on white foreneck

broad, bowed, grey and black wings

long yellowish legs, reddish in spring

VOICE *Loud, harsh fraink; squawking, croaking, and bill-snapping at nest.*
NESTING *Large nest of stout sticks, usually in treetop colony; 4–5 eggs; 1 brood; January–May.*
FEEDING *Seizes fish, frogs, small mammals, and other prey, typically after long stalk.*
SIMILAR SPECIES *None in the British Isles.*

Osprey

Pandion haliaetus (Pandionidae)

A big, long-winged, eagle-like bird of prey, yet surprisingly like an immature gull at long range, the Osprey is uniquely equipped for diving into the water to catch fish. It is rarely seen far from water, but like many birds of prey it spends much of its time perched, when its white, black-banded head is usually obvious. Dark brown above, it is white below with a variable dark breastband and bold black wrist patch. It typically holds its wings at a marked angle, kinked at the wrist rather like a gull, and often hovers rather heavily before plunging headlong into the water for its prey.

CATCHES *fish in lakes, reservoirs, large rivers, estuaries, and in coastal waters. Breeds in tall trees or on cliffs near water.*

black patch on underwings
short, banded tail
variable breast-band
glides on kinked wings
black patch
dark brown above
white on head
whitish crown
black stripe through eye
long, broad wings
blackish band along middle of underwings
dark brown above; juvenile has bright buff feather edges
white underparts
close-feathered legs, like tight stockings
bluish grey feet
large, sharp claws

NOTE
An Osprey in flight can be confused with a gull at long range, but it has a shorter head and broader wings. A gull also has no dark wrist patches.

VOICE *Loud yelps and repeated, high, liquid, whistled pyew pyew pyew near nest.*
NESTING *Stick nest on tree or cliff, artificial platform or ruined building, re-used and added to each year until it reaches immense size; 2–3 eggs; 1 brood; April–July.*
FEEDING *Snatches fish from water using feet, after hovering and plunging in a steep dive; sometimes hunts from perch.*
SIMILAR SPECIES *Immature Great Black-backed Gull (p.137).*

Marsh Harrier

Circus aeruginosus (Accipitridae)

This is the biggest and heaviest of the harriers, and also the darkest – it can be taken for a dark Buzzard (p.122) when soaring. The male does have some grey in its plumage, but is much browner than a male Hen Harrier. The female is chocolate-brown above with cream head markings; a juvenile male is almost identical, but has no cream wing patch. Marsh Harriers hunt in classic harrier fashion, patrolling slowly at low level with their wings raised in a "V" when gliding, and dropping into reeds or long grass to seize their prey.

SEARCHES *for prey on marshland and coastal open country. Breeds in large reedbeds, among long grass, or tall crops.*

creamy cap and throat
cream patch on wings
very dark brown plumage
broad wings held in "V" when gliding
broad black wingtips
silver-grey
brown wing coverts
square grey tail

NOTE
Although harder to identify when soaring, Marsh Harrier has narrower wings than a Buzzard (p.122), and does not twist its tail in flight.

pale markings on head
pale head
brown back
grey on wings
dark belly
dark brown

VOICE *Shrill kee-yoo in display flight; hoarse chattering kyek-ek-ek-ek or kyi-yi-yi-yi, or high whistles.*
NESTING *Large platform of reed stems among dense reeds over water, or increasingly among crops; 4–5 eggs; 1 brood; April–July.*
FEEDING *Hunts low over marshes, diving to catch small birds, wildfowl, rabbits and other small mammals, and frogs; also takes eggs and chicks, and scavenges for carrion.*
SIMILAR SPECIES *Hen Harrier (left).*

Hen Harrier

Circus cyaneus (Accipitridae)

HUNTS *over heather moors in summer, coastal marshes or low-lying rough grassland in winter.*

Male and female Hen Harriers look very unlike one another, but very like the slimmer-winged Montagu's Harrier (right). The smaller, pale grey male is easier to identify than the female. Both glide on flatter wings than other harriers when hunting. The male is the only grey harrier to winter in Europe.

black wingtips
grey with dark bars
barred tail
pale grey head and body
dark brown
buff with streaks
white rump
whitish underside

VOICE *Near nest, irregular week-eek-ik-ik-ik from female; even chekekekekekek from male.*
NESTING *Nest of stems on ground in rushes or heather; 4–6 eggs; 1 brood; April–June.*
FEEDING *Hunts low over marshes, diving to catch small birds, ducks, rodents, and frogs.*
SIMILAR SPECIES *Montagu's Harrier (right), Short-eared Owl (p.141).*

Montagu's Harrier

Circus pygargus (Accipitridae)

BREEDS *on heaths, grassland, marshes, and in cereal fields; winters in Africa.*

Usually difficult to tell from a Hen Harrier (left), this is a slimmer, more delicate bird, often associated with arable fields. It has a distinctive black bar on the inner wing, obvious on the male, but the narrower, long-tipped wings are the best clue to its identity.

grey head
medium grey above
long, tapered black wingtips
wingtips angled back
black wingbar
small white rump
barred tail
rufous
pale crescents above and below eye
streaked below
streaked flanks

VOICE *High, clear yek-yek-yek from male, chek-ek-ek-ek from female.*
NESTING *Nest of stems and grasses on ground; 4–5 eggs; 1 brood; April–June.*
FEEDING *Catches small mammals, reptiles, and small birds on or near ground.*
SIMILAR SPECIES *Hen Harrier (left), female Marsh Harrier (above).*

BITTERN

B itterns live exclusively in freshwater reed swamps, where they feed on fish and frogs caught within the seclusion of dense vegetation. Reedbeds must be clean, with water deep enough for a thriving fish population in hidden pools, but such conditions tend to be temporary. Reeds grow in shallow water on fertile ground, but, as their tall, dense stems grow, die back, and fall as thick litter year by year, so the habitat dries out, and turns inevitably into willow thickets, then woodland. In a wilderness, new reedbeds replace lost ones, but in contemporary, controlled landscapes, this is unlikely. To conserve the Bittern, reedbeds must be managed: leaving them alone spells disaster for these specialized birds. Once common in Britain, especially in the East Anglian fens, Bitterns were driven out by drainage, hunting, and pollution. In the early 20th century they returned, and briefly increased in numbers, but by the 1990s only 11 breeding pairs remained. Since then, expensive restoration of reedbeds and the creation of new ones, has brought a recovery, but with only about 40 males each spring, numbers remain low, and careful management of their habitat will be essential to help the Bittern thrive in the future.

Red Kite

Milvus milvus (Accipitridae)

An agile, long-winged, aerobatic bird of prey, the Red Kite is exceptionally graceful in the air, with a light, buoyant, elastic flight style that has few equals. Identifying the Red Kite is no problem, for its rusty plumage, bold white wing patches, and contrasting black wingtips are distinctive. The forked tail often glows almost orange in bright sun. Where common, it may gather in large numbers to exploit good food sources.

WINTERS *at lower altitude, foraging around towns. Breeds in wooded valleys, hunting over open country.*

soars on bowed wings

pale eyes

whitish head

pale band on upperwings

black flight feathers

forked tail

pale tawny to rust-red body

whitish to pale red below tail

bold white patch

NOTE

At a distance, the long, narrow wings and flight style separate a kite from a Buzzard (below). White underwing patches and a reddish body identify a Red Kite.

paler than adult

paler upperwings

rusty-brown, forked tail

VOICE *High, long-drawn-out, wailing or squealing weieie-ee-ow, higher pitched than the call of a Buzzard.*
NESTING *Large nest of sticks, rags, earth, and rubbish in tree, usually well hidden; 2–4 eggs; 1 brood; March–June.*
FEEDING *Scavenges from the carcasses of dead animals such as rabbits or sheep; catches birds up to size of crow or gull in surprise dash; also feeds on insects, earthworms, and voles.*
SIMILAR SPECIES *Buzzard (below).*

Buzzard

Buteo buteo (Accipitridae)

SOARS *over, hunts, and breeds in wooded farmland, on moors, and mountains; also on coastal cliffs.*

One of the most common and widespread British birds of prey, the Buzzard is often seen soaring on broad wings in wavering, rising circles as it scans the ground for prey. Its plumage varies from pale cream to blackish brown, but from below its flight feathers are always pale with a dark trailing edge.

hunched shoulders

rich brown above

pale "U" below

cream head

soars with wings slightly raised

barred, pale underwings

PALE

pale, barred tail

short head

dark wrist patch

VOICE *Frequent, loud, high, ringing pee-yaah or weaker mew; calls often while flying.*
NESTING *Stick nest in tree, or beneath bush on cliff ledge; 2–4 eggs; 1 brood; March–June.*
FEEDING *Catches voles, rabbits, beetles, worms, and some birds; eats a lot of carrion.*
SIMILAR SPECIES *Honey Buzzard (right), Rough-legged Buzzard (right).*

Rough-legged Buzzard

Buteo lagopus (Accipitridae)

Named for its feathered legs, this big, broad-winged buzzard is easier to identify by its dark-tipped white tail and "frosted" upperparts. In western Europe, including Britain, it is usually a scarce visitor, but more appear when prey is scarce in the north.

HUNTS *over moorland, heaths, marshes, and dunes in winter. Breeds in far north on tundra.*

whitish patches

pale head

dark brown above

pale chest and blackish belly

"frosty" pale feather edges

dark bands on wings and tail

VOICE *Loud, low, plaintive squeal, pee-yow.*
NESTING *Stick nest on cliff or in tree; 2–4 eggs; 1 brood; March–June.*
FEEDING *Drops onto small mammals, especially voles and small rabbits, either from perch or from hovering flight.*
SIMILAR SPECIES *Buzzard (left), juvenile Golden Eagle (p.123).*

Honey Buzzard

Pernis apivorus (Accipitridae)

Not a true buzzard at all, this very variable relative of the kites specializes in raiding nests of bees and wasps, using its feet to dig out the grubs and, in the case of bees, the waxy honeycombs. Adults are typically greyish above – with dark trailing edges on the wings and three dark tail bands – and whitish below, with bold "tiger stripes" and dark wrist patches. Juveniles are browner. Elusive when breeding, Honey Buzzards are more often seen on migration, especially at narrow sea crossings like the Strait of Gibraltar.

BREEDS *and feeds in extensive forest or well-wooded hill country. Concentrates at sea crossings on migration.*

tiger-striped underwings and belly

soars with wings flat or drooped

dark head; often whiter on juvenile

yellow eyes; dark on juvenile

closed tail bulges at sides

dark wrist patches

three dark bands on tail

boldly striped below

NOTE

Difficult to identify by its very variable plumage, the Honey Buzzard's most distinctive feature is its narrow, tapered, weak-looking, Cuckoo-like head.

long tail, widest in centre

narrow, Cuckoo-like head

VOICE *Infrequent, plaintive, whistling peee-haa, or sometimes three-syllable pee-ee-aah.*
NESTING *Small platform of sticks and greenery high in a tree, often built on top of old nest of a crow or Buzzard; 1–3 eggs; 1 brood; April–June.*
FEEDING *Feeds mainly on wasp and bee grubs, beeswax, and honey, which it digs out with its feet; also eats some other adult insects, ant pupae, young birds, eggs, and small mammals and reptiles.*
SIMILAR SPECIES *Buzzard (left), Rough-legged Buzzard (above).*

Goshawk

Accipiter gentilis (Accipitridae)

Essentially a giant version of the Sparrowhawk (below), with the same adaptations for hunting in forests, the Goshawk – especially the Buzzard-sized (p.122) female – is powerful enough to kill a pheasant. The male is a lot smaller, about as big as a large female Sparrowhawk. The two can be hard to tell apart, but the Goshawk has longer wings, a bulkier, deeper body, and a less square-tipped tail. Often elusive in dense forest, Goshawks are best looked for in early spring when they soar over breeding territories in courtship display flights.

HUNTS *and breeds in well-wooded farmland, forests, and uplands; favours tall conifers. A few winter in more open country.*

brown above

broad wings

S-curve on hindwings

buff below with dark streaks

dark, drop-shaped streaks on warm buff underparts

flight feathers often only faintly barred

dark cap

pale stripe over eye

orange-red eyes

dark ear coverts

greyish to brownish above

white undertail coverts

whitish below with fine grey barring

NOTE

The Goshawk has much more obvious white undertail coverts than a Sparrowhawk (below), often visible when the birds are soaring overhead.

♂

VOICE *Woodpecker-like, chattering, nasal gek-gek-gek and mewing pi-aah from female begging food.*
NESTING *Remarkably large, flat-topped heap of sticks and greenery close to trunk of tall tree; 2–4 eggs; 1 brood; March–June.*
FEEDING *Hunts boldly in forest or clearings, catching birds from size of a thrush to crows, pigeons, gamebirds, and other birds of prey; also takes rabbits and squirrels.*
SIMILAR SPECIES *Sparrowhawk (below), Buzzard (p.122).*

Golden Eagle

Aquila chrysaetos (Accipitridae)

A huge, supremely elegant raptor, the Golden Eagle favours remote mountains and crags, and is rarely seen as more than a dot in the distance. Despite this, its wide, slow, circling flight is often sufficient to identify it. It holds its long, broad wings in a shallow "V" when soaring, the primaries swept up at the tips. An immature bird has extensive white areas on its wings and tail, which diminish and finally disappear as it grows older.

HUNTS *over remote peaks or upland forests and more rarely on steep coasts, far from settlements and roads.*

pale tawny to golden crown

soars with wings raised in shallow "V"

barred dark underwings

dark brown body plumage

white wing patches

white on tail

bulky body and wings

heavily feathered legs

long tail, paler at base

blacker than adult

NOTE

At a distance, when its size is not apparent, a Golden Eagle may be mistaken for a Buzzard (p.122). But it circles more slowly, has a longer tail, and its head protrudes more. At closer range, its underwings are broader, darker, and less patterned than a Buzzard's.

VOICE *Occasional shrill yelps and whistling twee-oo of alarm, but generally silent.*
NESTING *Immense pile of sticks, lined with wool and greenery, on broad cliff ledge or in old pine tree; 1–3 eggs, 1 brood; February–June.*
FEEDING *Hunts mainly for grouse, crows, hares, rabbits, and marmots, usually by diving from low-level flight; eats much carrion in winter, chiefly carcasses of dead sheep and deer.*
SIMILAR SPECIES *Buzzard (p.122), White-tailed Eagle (below).*

Sparrowhawk

Accipiter nisus (Accipitridae)

The short, broad wings and long tail give this bird great manoeuvrability in pursuing prey through forests. It often dashes to low level with a distinctive flap-flap-glide action, then jinks and swerves to disappear through a tight gap. At other times, it soars over the woods on fanned wings.

HUNTS *in wide variety of habitats, from dense forests to cities. Breeds in wooded farmland and forest; winters in more open country.*

short, small head

glaring yellow eyes gives fierce expression

orange on face

♂

orange bars

fine grey bars

pale line

broad wings

brown bars

long, thin, square tail

darker grey above

grey bars

♀

♂

long, thin, yellow legs

VOICE *Thin squealing peee-ee.*
NESTING *Platform of twigs close to tree trunk; 4–5 eggs; 1 brood; March–June.*
FEEDING *Hunts small birds, males take mainly tits and finches, larger females take thrushes and pigeons.*
SIMILAR SPECIES *Kestrel (p.126), Goshawk (above).*

White-tailed Eagle

Haliaeetus albicilla (Accipitridae)

A huge, heavy-billed bird with very long, broad, plank-like wings and a very short tail, the White-tailed Eagle has a distinctive flight silhouette. Adults have pale heads, yellow bills, and white tails, but immatures are darker overall. It has been reintroduced to its former range in Scotland.

WINTERS *mainly on large, coastal plains; hunts rocky coasts, estuaries, and remote marshes in summer.*

glides on flat wings

dark tail

head and neck protrude

pale head

saw-toothed trailing edge

big yellow bill

short white tail

pale and dark blotches

deeply fingered wingtips

VOICE *Shrill yaps near nest in summer, otherwise usually a silent bird.*
NESTING *Huge pile of sticks on cliff ledge or flat tree crown; 2 eggs; 1 brood; March–July.*
FEEDING *Picks dead and sick fish, and fish offal, from water with feet; catches seabirds and hares; takes carrion on land.*
SIMILAR SPECIES *Golden Eagle (above).*

BIRDS

WHITE-TAILED EAGLE

I n the Middle Ages, the White-tailed Eagle was almost as numerous as the Golden Eagle in Scotland, and bred in the swamps and fens of eastern Britain. It was the "common" eagle of coastal cliffs and lowland areas, and island groups such as the Orkneys and Shetlands. Birds of prey were, however, subject to intense persecution through the 17th, 18th, and 19th centuries, especially with the increase of sheep farming during the Highland Clearances, as a result White-tailed Eagles were reduced to a tiny remnant population. These, by their very rarity, then attracted Victorian egg- and stuffed-bird collectors, and the last pair nested in 1916. An attempt at reintroduction on Fair Isle in 1968 failed, but in 1975 a much more ambitious scheme, involving voluntary and government organizations in Britain and Norway, saw the establishment of a handful of Norwegian birds on Rhum, in the Inner Hebrides. Progress has been slow, but steady; 30 years later there were still under 30 pairs and few successful nests, but by 2007, the 200th chick was fledged from a Scottish nest. The centre of operations is now Mull, where people can see these magnificent birds from public viewpoints without risk of disturbance.

Kestrel

Falco tinnunculus (Falconidae)

A common and widespread falcon of open spaces, the Kestrel is familiar to most people as the bird that hovers over roadsides for long periods, as if suspended on a wire. In the north of its range, this hovering habit is almost unique: other raptors hover, but not for so long. The smaller male has a blue-grey head and tail while the female's upperparts are all brown, spotted with black. Both show a strong contrast between the pale inner and dark outer wing.

LIVES *in wide variety of habitats, from cities to remote mountains. Common around woodland, heaths, and over rough grassland.*

pale brown inner wings

paler outer wings than male

rufous inner wings

♀

short, round, blue-grey head

dark eyes

rufous back, spotted with black

♂

brown-black outer wings

dusky moustache stripe

buff below, spotted black

♂

blue-grey tail with black tip

black claws

black-barred back and inner wings

NOTE

A hovering Kestrel is usually unmistakable, especially when hovering head to wind as if on a string over a patch of grass, before dropping down onto a vole or mouse. But Kestrels are also capable of soaring high, and they often hunt from perches or catch small birds in sudden dashes, rather like Sparrowhawks (p.123).

♀

VOICE *Nasal, complaining, whining keee-eee-eeee and variants, especially near nest.*
NESTING *On bare ledges on cliffs, in quarries, on derelict buildings or high window-ledges, in disused crows' nests or tree holes; 4–6 eggs; 1 brood; March–July.*
FEEDING *Catches small mammals, especially voles, after hovering search; also eats beetles, lizards, earthworms, and small birds.*
SIMILAR SPECIES *Sparrowhawk (p.123), Merlin (below).*

Merlin

Falco columbarius (Falconidae)

A small, dynamic falcon of open country, the Merlin flies fast and low over the ground in pursuit of prey, with rapid flicks of its wings and a final agile rise to strike. The thrush-sized male is bluish grey above with a dark tail-band, while the bigger female is earthy-brown with a cream-barred tail.

BREEDS *on moorland, in north on tundra and conifer forests. Winters in lowlands on open pasture, and coastal marshes and fields.*

barred flight feathers

♀

small, square head

dark eyes

cream bands on tail

mud-brown above

bluish grey upperparts

♂

orange-buff with dark streaks below

♀

small, chunky body

pale tail with black band

dark, pointed wingtips

♂

VOICE *Male has quick chittering kik-kik-ki-kik; female has deeper, nasal kee-kee-kee.*
NESTING *Bare scrape on ground among heather, or in old crow's nest in tree; 3–6 eggs; 1 brood; April–June.*
FEEDING *Mostly eats small birds, caught in flight; also eats a variety of large aerial insects.*
SIMILAR SPECIES *Peregrine (right).*

Hobby

Falco subbuteo (Falconidae)

A dynamic aerial hunter with the speed and agility to catch dragonflies, swallows, and even swifts, the scythe-winged Hobby is like a smaller, slimmer version of the Peregrine (below). An adult is deep grey above, with a black cap and "moustache" that contrast sharply with its pale cheeks and throat. It has dense, dark streaks on its underside.

NESTS *in abandoned crows' nests; hunts over open ground, and especially areas with flooded pits where it can find flying insects to eat.*

browner than adult

buff cheeks

whitish cheeks and throat

deep grey upperparts

long, tapered wings

rufous thighs and undertail coverts

no red under tail

reddish under tail

dark head

yellow legs

short, narrow, plain tail

VOICE *Clear, musical, whistled kyu-kyu-kyu-kyu, especially near nest.*
NESTING *Uses old nest in tree, usually of crow family; 2–3 eggs; 1 brood; June–August.*
FEEDING *Catches fast-flying small birds in flight, and eats many large flying insects, such as dragonflies and airborne beetles.*
SIMILAR SPECIES *Peregrine (below).*

Peregrine

Falco peregrinus (Falconidae)

The big, powerfully built Peregrine is a bird-killing falcon, famous for the high-speed diving "stoop" that it often uses to kill its prey in mid-air. When hunting, it often patrols at great height, looking like a tiny black anchor in the sky. A closer view reveals its closely barred underparts, yellow legs, pale breast and throat, and the large dark "moustache" patches below its big, black, yellow-rimmed eyes. It spends much of its time perched, when it looks particularly bulky and broad-chested.

HUNTS *over estuaries and marshes in winter. Breeds on hills and rocky coasts with cliffs; also, increasingly in cities.*

dull black head

yellow eye-ring and bill base

white cheek patch

broad white breast

black lobes below eyes

blue-grey above

white below, closely barred with grey

darker wingtips

broad, pale rump

broad, pointed wings

blue base to bill

blue-grey upperparts

browner than adult with buff feather edges

NOTE

The arrival of a Peregrine overhead often causes panic among other birds, any of which may be potential prey. If you notice a sudden commotion, look up.

VOICE *Loud, raucous calls at nest include throaty haak-haak-haak-haak and whining kee-keee-eeeeee and wheeee-ip.*
NESTING *On broad ledge or earthy scrape on cliff, in quarry, or more rarely on building or on flatter ground; 2–4 eggs; 1 brood; March–June.*
FEEDING *Kills birds of sizes ranging from thrush to pigeon or grouse, sometimes larger, often rising to take them from beneath, chasing them in level flight, or diving from great height.*
SIMILAR SPECIES *Hobby (above), Kestrel (left), Merlin (left).*

Water Rail

Rallus aquaticus (Rallidae)

This is a skulking, secretive bird of dense reeds and water-side vegetation, often hard to see but readily identified by its long red bill. When venturing into the open, it soon slips out of sight between plant stems. It can often be detected at dawn or dusk by its squealing calls.

FEEDS *and breeds in wet reedbeds, swampy willow thickets, and overgrown riversides.*

dark streaked above

red eyes

red, slightly curved bill with black tip

grey chest and face

barred flanks

pink legs

dull legs

untidy bars below

slate-grey below

VOICE *Hard, repetitive, kipkipkipkipkip, extra-ordinary, loud, pig-like squealing, grunting.*
NESTING *Shallow nest of broad leaves and grasses in vegetation raised a little above water level; 6–11 eggs; 2 broods; May–August.*
FEEDING *Eats mainly insects and molluscs; also seeds, berries, voles, birds, and carrion.*
SIMILAR SPECIES *Spotted Crake (below).*

Moorhen

Gallinula chloropus (Rallidae)

Widespread and common on and near all kinds of waters from wet ditches to large lakes, the Moorhen is easily distinguished from the similar Coot (below) by its red and yellow bill and green legs. It has an oddly nervous manner, and usually runs or swims into cover at any hint of danger.

red eye

BREEDS *on small ponds with overgrown edges; feeds near ponds, lakes, and rivers, on open, wet, grassy ground.*

rich brown back

red bill with yellow tip

slate-grey below and on head

brown head; bill greenish yellow

white under tail

brown body

green legs

long green toes

diagonal white stripe

VOICE *Loud, throaty or metallic notes, kurruk or kittik, high kik, stuttering kik-kikikikik-ik.*
NESTING *Shallow bowl of leaves and stems in vegetation, usually just above water; 5–11 eggs; 2–3 broods; April–August.*
FEEDING *Picks seeds, fruit, shoots, snails, and insects from damp ground or shallows.*
SIMILAR SPECIES *Coot (below).*

Spotted Crake

Porzana porzana (Rallidae)

Although not exactly shy, the Spotted Crake is an elusive bird that typically feeds in dense vegetation, only rarely appearing in the open. It resembles a Water Rail (above), except that its bill is short and yellow instead of long and red. Its basically brown plumage is beautifully patterned when seen at close range.

BREEDS *in extensive flood-meadows; migrants feed in wet marshes, in reedy places, and at the edges of muddy pools.*

grey-buff neck with white spots

yellowish bill, red at base

white bars on flanks

browner on head and neck

VOICE *Repeated, rhythmic, whiplash sound or dripping hwit, hwit, hwit, at dusk or night.*
NESTING *Small saucer of leaves and stems, in upright stalks above water or in wet marsh; 8–12 eggs; 1 brood; May–July.*
FEEDING *Picks small insects and aquatic invertebrates from mud, water, and foliage.*
SIMILAR SPECIES *Water Rail (above).*

striped below

buff under tail

Coot

Fulica atra (Rallidae)

Bigger and sturdier than its relative the Moorhen (above), the quarrelsome Coot also differs in having lobed toes, like grebes. It forms larger, more cohesive feeding flocks, which dive often to feed underwater, bobbing up to the surface like corks.

WINTERS *on larger, more open lakes. Breeds mainly on lakes and flooded pits, with fringing vegetation or overhanging branches.*

pale trailing edge

white facial shield and bill

slate-black body

intensely black head

rounded rump

red eyes

yellowish bill

whitish face and throat

big grey feet with lobed toes

VOICE *Loud kowk! high-pitched, metallic pik or teuwk; juvenile gives loud whistles.*
NESTING *Heap of weed on bank or overhanging branch; 6–9 eggs; 1–2 broods; April–August.*
FEEDING *Eats grass, aquatic plants, seeds, tadpoles, and other small aquatic animals.*
SIMILAR SPECIES *Moorhen (above).*

Corncrake

Crex crex (Rallidae)

The rasping song of the corncrake used to be familiar throughout Britain, but is now heard mostly in northern Scotland where the grass is cut late enough to avoid its nests and chicks being destroyed. A slim, streaked bird, it is usually seen only fleetingly as it raises its head to check for danger.

BREEDS *in wet grass and late-harvested hayfields with dense cover in spring.*

soft grey and buff face

grey throat and breast

short, stout, pink bill

pink legs

narrow, rounded rufous wings

less grey

tawny back with black streaks

♂

♀

VOICE *Loud, repeated double note; at distance light, scratched crik crik, at close range hard, rattling, vibrating crrek crrek.*
NESTING *Small hollow on ground; 8–12 eggs; 1–2 broods; May–August.*
FEEDING *Picks insects, seeds, leaves, and shoots from foliage and ground.*
SIMILAR SPECIES *Spotted Crake (above).*

Oystercatcher

Haematopus ostralegus (Haematopodidae)

With its dazzling black and white plumage and stout, carrot-coloured, blade-like bill, the Oystercatcher is one of Britain's most unmistakable, and common, waders. A noisy bird, its loud, piercing calls are equally distinctive. The powerful bill is adapted for prising or hammering open cockles, mussels, and other bivalve molluscs.

ROOSTS *in often huge flocks. Breeds on sandy, muddy, and rocky shores; some inland on grass or river shingle.*

red eyes with orange eye-ring

portly, black and white body

big, bright orange-red bill

dark tip to bill

browner back

white "V"

white collar

broad white wingbar

bill with dark tip

short, sturdy, pale pink legs; duller in juvenile

VOICE *Loud, strident klip, kleep or kleep-a-kleep; shrill chorus from big flocks.*
NESTING *Shallow scrape in shingle or sand; 2–3 eggs; 1 brood; April–July.*
FEEDING *Probes for molluscs and marine worms; prises bivalve molluscs from rocks and seaweed; eats earthworms inland.*
SIMILAR SPECIES *Black-tailed Godwit (p.131).*

Little Ringed Plover

Charadrius dubius (Charadriidae)

The neat-looking Little Ringed Plover is a bird of fresh-water shores and open ground, where it feeds using the run-tilt-run technique typical of plovers. It resembles the more coastal Ringed Plover (below), but has a white line above a black forehead, no white wingbar, and less brightly coloured legs and bill.

BREEDS on shingly and sandy lake shores, dry shingly riverbeds, and also on waste ground, including mine or quarry waste.

white over eyes and forehead

plain wings

black forehead

bold yellow eye-ring

sandy brown above

broken breast-band

blurred pale area over eyes

long, tapered wingtips

stubby black bill

narrow black breast-band

clean white underside

dull legs

dull pink legs

VOICE *Short, abrupt, whistled* piw *or* p'ew; *song harsh* cree-cree-cree-crree *in flight.*
NESTING *Hollow on bare ground, usually hard to spot; 4 eggs; 1 brood; April–June.*
FEEDING *Picks small invertebrates from ground, using run, stop, tilt-forward action.*
SIMILAR SPECIES *Ringed Plover (below), Common Sandpiper (p.132).*

Golden Plover

Pluvialis apricaria (Charadriidae)

In winter, flocks of Golden Plover feed on lowland fields, often with Lapwings (below). Their winter plumage is like that of the Grey Plover (left), but lacks black "wingpits", and they have slimmer bills. In summer, birds from the north develop more black on the face and underside than those that stay to breed in Britain.

FEEDS on low-lying arable fields, pastures, and salt marshes in winter; breeds on high moorland and tundra.

mottled face

brownish black back

golden yellow, white, and black spangled

dark rump

weak white wingbars

white belly

pale yellow breast

buff-yellow spots

white-sided black belly

SOUTHERN RACE

white on underwings

VOICE *Plaintive, whistled* tleee, *higher* tlee, treeoleee; *song* phee-oo, pheee-oo *in flight.*
NESTING *Shallow scrape, lined with lichen and heather, on ground in heather or grass; 4 eggs; 1 brood; April–July.*
FEEDING *Takes insects in summer, mainly earthworms in winter.*
SIMILAR SPECIES *Grey Plover (left).*

Ringed Plover

Charadrius hiaticula (Charadriidae)

A small, pale plover with a striking head and breast pattern and bright orange legs, the Ringed Plover is typically found feeding on sandy beaches in summer, or in tight flocks with other waders at high tide. Migrants may move inland, especially in spring and autumn.

BREEDS on sandy and shingly beaches. Also locally but increasingly inland, on river banks or gravel pits.

black and orange bill

white wingbars

broad black breast-band

dull head

white over eyes

dull bill

weak band

orange legs

dull legs

VOICE *Characteristic fluty whistle, a bright, mellow* too-lit, *also a sharp* queep; *repeated* too-wee-a too-wee-a *in song-flight.*
NESTING *Shallow scrape lined with pebbles or grass; 4 eggs; 2–3 broods; April–August.*
FEEDING *Picks small insects and worms from ground, using run-tilt action.*
SIMILAR SPECIES *Little Ringed Plover (above).*

Lapwing

Vanellus vanellus (Charadriidae)

Distinguished by its unique wispy crest, the Lapwing is Britain's largest and most familiar plover. At a distance it looks black and white but a close view reveals glossy greenish upperparts. Very sociable, it breeds in loose colonies on undisturbed ground, males performing spectacular tumbling aerial displays while calling loudly. Outside the breeding season it forms large flocks on fields and pastures, often with Golden Plovers (above) and Black-headed Gulls (p.135). It gets its name from its flappy, instantly recognizable flight style, and has broad, rounded wings.

WINTERS on arable fields and salt marsh. Breeds on wet moors, riverside pastures, and upland fields.

white under-wing

broad, rounded wings

black cap extends into wispy crest

purple and copper gloss on dark green back

short crest

buff fringes to feathers

shorter crest than summer

green back with buffish feather edges

shorter crest than male

mottled throat

white underparts

dull pinkish legs

cinnamon patch under tail

NOTE
If a Lapwing dives at you in summer with a shrill weew-ee *call, it is trying to protect its eggs or young, so watch where you walk in case you step on them.*

VOICE *Nasal, strained* weet *or* ee-wit; *wheezy variations on this theme; passionate song in spring,* whee-er-ee, *a* wheep-wheep! *accompanied by loud throbbing from wings.*
NESTING *Shallow hollow on open ground, lined with grass; 3–4 eggs; 1 brood; April–June.*
FEEDING *Tilts forward to pick insects and spiders from ground, or pull earthworms from soil; often taps foot on ground to attract or reveal prey.*
SIMILAR SPECIES *None, this species is unmistakable.*

Grey Plover

Pluvialis squatarola (Charadriidae)

Like a silver version of the Golden Plover (right) in breeding plumage, but bigger and with a larger bill, the Grey Plover is a more coastal bird that typically feeds on mudflats, and roosts in rather static flocks on nearby fields at high tide. It is easily identified in flight by its black "wingpits".

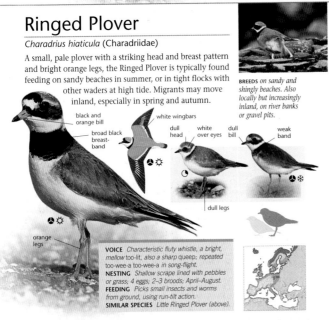

FEEDS on large muddy estuaries and other shores from autumn to spring; breeds on northern tundra.

bold white band from forehead to side of chest

bold white wingbars

white rump

spangled silver and black

black wingpits

patchy plumage

black underside

LATE MOULTING

mottled grey

pale below

VOICE *High, plaintive 3-syllabled* twee-oo-wee! *and loud, melancholic, fluted song.*
NESTING *Scrape on ground in short vegetation; 4 eggs; 1 brood; May–July.*
FEEDING *Pulls worms, molluscs, and crustaceans from mud in winter.*
SIMILAR SPECIES *Golden Plover (right), Knot (p.129).*

Dotterel

Charadrius morinellus (Charadriidae)

The Dotterel is one of the few British birds with reversed sexual roles: the female takes the lead in courtship and is bigger and brighter than the male in summer. Small flocks of spring and autumn migrants stop off at regular sites in the lowlands, where they are often unusually tame.

BREEDS *on tundra or on high, rolling or flat mountain-tops with lichens and other sparse cover, often with areas of bare rock and scree.*

black cap

broad white stripe over eye

sharper face pattern

pale "V"

rich rust-red with black belly

plain wings

duller than female

black belly (white in winter)

VOICE *Soft pip pip or sweet wit-ee-wee; migrants can give trilled piping on taking wing.*
NESTING *Shallow scraped hollow on ground, usually under cover of low vegetation; 3 eggs; 1 brood; May–August.*
FEEDING *Takes flies, beetles, earthworms, and similar invertebrates from ground.*
SIMILAR SPECIES *Golden Plover (p.128).*

Knot

Calidris canutus (Scolopacidae)

Marbled black, buff, and chestnut with coppery underparts, the Knot is among the most colourful of waders in spring and summer. In winter, it is a dull pale grey, yet it is still spectacular for it forms vast flocks of many thousands that often take to the sky in dramatic aerial manoeuvres.

pale grey rump and tail

pale stripe

ROOSTS *in dense flocks on muddy estuaries, and feeds on a wide variety of shores. Breeds on tundra.*

straight black bill

pale grey plumage

chestnut and copper

short grey legs

apricot-tinged below

VOICE *Rather quiet; dull, short nut, plus occasional bright, whistled note.*
NESTING *Shallow hollow on ground near water, on tundra; 3–4 eggs; 1 brood; May–July.*
FEEDING *Eats molluscs, crustaceans, and marine worms in winter.*
SIMILAR SPECIES *Grey Plover (left), Dunlin (p.130).*

Avocet

Recurvirostra avosetta (Recurvirostridae)

The Avocet is a distinctive wader, handsome and graceful, with a strongly upturned bill. Conservation and habitat management have helped provide it with its special needs: shallow, brackish water and oozy mud for feeding, and drier islands for nesting. As a result, it has thrived and spread.

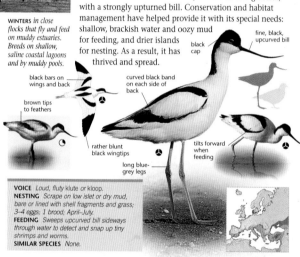

WINTERS *in close flocks that fly and feed on muddy estuaries. Breeds on shallow, saline coastal lagoons and by muddy pools.*

fine, black, upcurved bill

black cap

black bars on wings and back

brown tips to feathers

curved black band on each side of back

rather blunt black wingtips

tilts forward when feeding

long blue-grey legs

VOICE *Loud, fluty klute or kloop.*
NESTING *Scrape on low islet or dry mud, bare or lined with shell fragments and grass; 3–4 eggs; 1 brood; April–July.*
FEEDING *Sweeps upcurved bill sideways through water to detect and snap up tiny shrimps and worms.*
SIMILAR SPECIES *None.*

Sanderling

Calidris alba (Scolopacidae)

In winter, the Sanderling is by far the whitest of small waders. It has a unique feeding style: very quick and nimble, it darts back and forth along the edge of waves as they move in and out to snatch food carried by the surf. In spring and autumn, its back and breast are marbled chestnut, but its belly stays pure white.

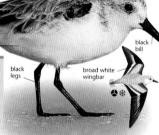

FEEDS *in flocks on broad sandy beaches and estuaries; scarce on other shores and inland. Breeds on northern tundra.*

black spangled grey

marbled chestnut

blackish patch on shoulder

pale back

bright white underparts

black legs

black bill

broad white wingbar

VOICE *Sharp, hard, short plit or twik twik.*
NESTING *Scrape on ground, lined with dead willow leaves; 4 eggs; 1 brood; May–July.*
FEEDING *Snatches marine worms, molluscs, and crustaceans such as sandhoppers and insects from the edge of waves.*
SIMILAR SPECIES *Dunlin (p.130), Little Stint (below).*

Stone-curlew

Burhinus oedicnemus (Burhinidae)

This semi-nocturnal wader is hard to locate by day, when it spends time standing or squatting stock-still, its camouflaging plumage blending into the background of soil, stones, or sand. If seen, it is easy to identify, with its big, pale, goggle-like eyes, long, strong, yellow legs, and two-tone bill. Breeding birds are very noisy after dark.

BREEDS *on heaths, arable fields with light, stony soil and sparse crops; most coastal populations extinct.*

staring yellow eyes

dark-streaked sandy brown body

pale tail

pale stripes above and below eye

pale yellow bill base

pale and dark bands

white spots

pale band

tail projects beyond wings

VOICE *Loud calls, Curlew- or Oystercatcher-like, but wilder, wailing: kur-li, klip, kee etc.*
NESTING *Shallow scrape on ground lined with stones etc; 2 eggs; 1–2 broods; April–August.*
FEEDING *Runs and tilts like plover to pick up beetles, worms, snails, lizards, or mice.*
SIMILAR SPECIES *Curlew (p.135), female Pheasant (p.114).*

Little Stint

Calidris minuta (Scolopacidae)

The smallest of the common waders, with a neat, rounded head and a fine, black bill, the Little Stint breeds in the far north but moves south in autumn. Most birds that turn up in western Europe are juveniles that forage frenetically in small parties on muddy shores, often with Dunlins (p.130).

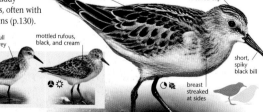

BREEDS *on tundra, but appears beside muddy pools and lagoons while on migration.*

cream lines on back

striking cream "V" on back

streaked cap

dull grey

mottled rufous, black, and cream

short, spiky black bill

breast streaked at sides

VOICE *Hard, dry, sharp tip or trip, or sometimes ti-ti-trip.*
NESTING *Small, shallow scrape on ground, close to water; 4 eggs; 1 brood; May–July.*
FEEDING *Catches tiny invertebrates and other animals; does not wade deeply.*
SIMILAR SPECIES *Sanderling (above), juvenile Dunlin (p.130).*

Curlew Sandpiper

Calidris ferruginea (Scolopacidae)

The Curlew Sandpiper follows the same migration pattern as the Little Stint (p.129), appearing with it in Britain as a passage migrant in spring and late summer. The superbly colourful spring adults are usually seen in southeastern Europe, while the birds that appear in Britain later in the year are moulting adults or juveniles. They often feed with Dunlins (right) but, being longer-legged and longer-billed, they can wade farther into the water and dig deeper. The more elongated shape of a Curlew Sandpiper gives it a more elegant appearance than a Dunlin, making it stand out in a mixed group. In flight, it shows a distinctive bold white rump.

FEEDS in shallow fresh water and marshes, and on coastal mudflats, in spring and autumn. Breeds on high Arctic tundra.

pale stripe over eyes

dark back with even, pale buff scales

long, slim, slightly down-curved bill

pale peachy-buff breast

white belly

long black legs

dark cap

long wings

bold white wingbars

white rump

copper-red plumage

pale eye-ring and chin

no streaks

NOTE
Apart from a few very much rarer sandpipers, the Curlew Sandpiper is the only bird of its group that sports a white rump. Obvious in flight, this can sometimes be spotted when the bird is feeding on the shore or in the water among other waders such as Dunlins (right), allowing it to be identified with near total certainty.

VOICE Flight call is a distinctive soft, trilling, rolled chirr-up, quite unlike the Dunlin's (right).
NESTING Simple shallow scrape on ground on tundra; 4 eggs; 1 brood; May–July.
FEEDING Uses its longer legs to wade into deeper water than the Dunlin, and probes softer mud with its longer bill to extract small worms, molluscs, and other invertebrates.
SIMILAR SPECIES Knot (p.129), juvenile Dunlin (right).

Dunlin

Calidris alpina (Scolopacidae)

Widespread and common on nearly all European shores in winter, the Dunlin often occurs in huge flocks that feed and roost together on mudflats and marshes, and perform spectacular, perfectly co-ordinated aerobatic flights. Its winter plumage is quite drab, but its thin white wingbar and white-sided, dark rump are useful clues. Breeding birds in summer are far more distinctive: rich chestnut and black above, with a unique squarish black patch on the belly. In silhouette, it has a rather hunched, round-shouldered look. There are three subspecies, with *C. a. alpina* of northern Scandinavia having the brightest breeding plumage and longest, most curved bill. The Greenland subsp. *arctica* is duller, with a short bill; the British and south Scandinavian *schinzii* is intermediate between the two.

WINTERS on large estuaries, inland marshes, and lake shores. Breeds on damp moorlands and tundra.

dark rump with white sides

thin white wingbars

hunched posture

grey-brown above

blurred pale streak over eye

very slightly downcurved, black bill

dull grey-streaked breast

white belly in winter

short dark legs

cream and black stripes on rufous back

chestnut and black back

black streaks below

black belly patch

dark-streaked, whitish breast

NOTE
In winter, the Dunlin is an anonymous-looking wader, with few really distinctive features. It does, however, occur in large flocks and this in itself is a useful clue to identification. In flight, the flocks move with tight precision, like starlings, dashing this way and that, and often sweeping way out over the sea and back again.

VOICE Thin, reedy shrree or rasping treerrr; song-flight develops this into longer, trilled/pulsating "pea whistle"; soft twitter from feeding flocks.
NESTING Small, grass-lined, shallow scoop on ground or in grassy tussock; 4 eggs; 1 brood; May–July.
FEEDING Feeds in flocks on muddy or drier shores, sometimes wading quite deeply, probing and picking up worms, insects, molluscs, and other invertebrates.
SIMILAR SPECIES Knot (p.129), Sanderling (p.129).

Purple Sandpiper

Calidris maritima (Scolopacidae)

Few waders are as tightly restricted to one habitat as this one. It spends most of its time at the very edge of the surf, searching through wave-washed, weed-covered rocks for its food. It is hard to see against the dark seaweed, particularly in its darker winter plumage, but its yellow-based, rather downcurved bill and yellow legs are useful clues to its identity.

FEEDS on rocky shores in winter; also around piers and groynes. Breeds on northern tundra.

rufous on head

slightly curved bill

very dark

scaly wing pattern

dark breast streaks

whitish and rufous edges to feathers

dull yellow

scaly dark back

dark streaks

VOICE Simple, low, liquid weet or weet-wit.
NESTING Slight scrape on ground, lined with leaves, on wide open tundra; 4 eggs; 1 brood; May–July.
FEEDING Takes a variety of insects, spiders, and other invertebrates in summer; chiefly periwinkles and similar molluscs in winter.
SIMILAR SPECIES Dunlin (right).

Ruff

Philomachus pugnax (Scolopacidae)

In spring, male Ruffs grow a huge ruff of feathers around the neck and curly crown-tufts, very varied in colour and pattern. These help them attract the much smaller females at communal mating grounds (leks). Winter adults are variable; the small head and drooping bill are distinctive features.

BREEDS in lowland wet meadows; migrants and wintering birds live by lakes, marshes, and coastal lagoons.

ruff of feathers ♂

head often white ♂

blotched back ♀

orange legs

short, barely curved bill

bright ochre-buff head and breast

white rump sides

bright buff feather edges

pale ochre to greenish legs

VOICE Usually silent; occasionally utters a low, gruff wek call.
NESTING Well hidden grass-lined scrape; 4 eggs; 1 brood; April–July.
FEEDING Probes into soft mud for worms, insects and their larvae; also eats some seeds.
SIMILAR SPECIES Redshank (p.132), Wood Sandpiper (p.132).

Jack Snipe

Lymnocryptes minimus (Scolopacidae)

The handsome little Jack Snipe is a secretive bird of dense vegetation, usually seen only when it explodes from almost underfoot and drops back into cover, often a short distance away. Much smaller than a Snipe (below), it has brighter cream stripes on its back, and its crown has a dark central stripe.

FEEDS *in deep cover in very wet grass, rushy places with standing water, reedbed edges, and upper edges of weedy salt marshes.*

cream-striped back with green gloss

broad, bright cream stripes

black stripe on centre of crown

shorter bill than Snipe

pale edge

streaked flanks

short greenish legs

NOTE

When disturbed, a Jack Snipe flies straight and low, landing quickly, while the Snipe (below) zigzags high into the air.

VOICE *Usually quiet, but muffled "galloping" in display flight.*
NESTING *Hollow in dry hummock of grass or moss in bog; 4 eggs; 1 brood; May–July.*
FEEDING *Walks with a bouncy, springy action, probing the ground for worms and seeds.*
SIMILAR SPECIES *Snipe (below), Dunlin (p.130).*

Snipe

Gallinago gallinago (Scolopacidae)

A heavily streaked wader with an extremely long bill, the Snipe can feed only in areas where soft, oozy mud allows it to probe deeply for prey. Less elusive than the Jack Snipe (above), it rises from cover with harsh, dry calls. In spring, males dive through the air with stiff outer tail feathers fanned to produce a strange bleating hum.

LIVES *in boggy heaths and wet freshwater marshes with soft mud, moving to coasts in freezing conditions.*

white tail tip

dark brown back with cream stripes

striped head with cream central stripe

streaked breast

very long bill

white belly

barred flanks

probes deep for food

rufous-centred tail

VOICE *Short, rasping* scaap; *in spring bright, musical* chip-per, chip-per, chip-per *from perch; also throbbing, wavering "bleat" from tail feathers during switchback display flight.*
NESTING *Grass-lined scrape in dense vegetation; 4 eggs; 1–2 broods; April–July.*
FEEDING *Probes soft mud for worms.*
SIMILAR SPECIES *Jack Snipe (above).*

Woodcock

Scolopax rusticola (Scolopacidae)

Its superbly camouflaged plumage ensures that the Woodcock is one of the hardest birds to spot on the ground. The best chance of seeing one is in spring and early summer when the male performs his "roding" display flight at dusk and dawn, as he patrols at just above treetop height, uttering strange croaking and sneezing calls.

BREEDS *in woodland of all types with soft, damp earth, ditches, and bogs nearby for feeding; in similar habitat in winter.*

black bars on angular head

broad wings and flickering wing-action

large eyes far back on head

dead-leaf pattern above

plump body

bill angled down

straight long bill

evenly barred pale underside

VOICE *In "roding" display flight, series of deep throaty croaks and sneezing* tsi-wip *calls.*
NESTING *Slight hollow among dead leaves or other cover; 4 eggs; 1 brood; March–August.*
FEEDING *Probes for worms, beetles, and seeds in leaf-mould, muddy ditches, and by the sides of streams.*
SIMILAR SPECIES *Snipe (above).*

Black-tailed Godwit

Limosa limosa (Scolopacidae)

This large, handsome wader is more localized than the Bar-tailed Godwit (below) at all times of year. Its longer legs and straighter bill help distinguish it in all plumages from its smaller relative. Unmistakable in flight, it reveals a bold white band along each wing, white underwings, and a broad white patch above its solidly black tail. Its bright summer plumage is quite unlike the grey of winter, but its striking wing and tail pattern remains the same all year. Unlike most wading birds, the Black-tailed Godwit is generally rather quiet, even in flight.

FREQUENTS *narrow, sheltered estuaries with long strips of rich mud in winter; breeds in wet meadows and flooded pastures.*

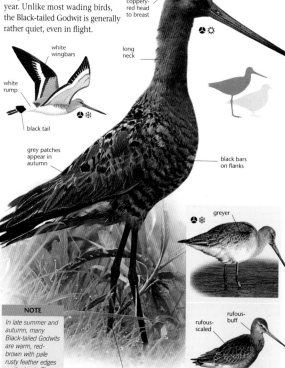

white wingbars

coppery-red head to breast

long neck

white rump

black tail

grey patches appear in autumn

black bars on flanks

greyer

rufous-scaled

rufous-buff

very long legs

NOTE

In late summer and autumn, many Black-tailed Godwits are warm, red-brown with pale rusty feather edges on the back. These are not adults losing summer plumage, but juveniles.

VOICE *Frequent nasal* weeka-weeka-weeka *calls when breeding; rapid* vi-vi-vi *flight calls.*
NESTING *Shallow scrape among dense vegetation; 3–4 eggs; 1 brood; May–July.*
FEEDING *Probes deeply for worms, molluscs, and seeds, often wading up to belly in water.*
SIMILAR SPECIES *Bar-tailed Godwit (below), in all seasons, Oystercatcher (p.127), only in flight.*

Bar-tailed Godwit

Limosa lapponica (Scolopacidae)

Although they breed only on the Arctic tundra, Bar-tailed Godwits are far more widespread on coasts of Britain in winter than the larger Black-tailed Godwits (above). Flocks disperse to probe for food in the mud; these often have a habit of rolling and twisting as they fly in to roost at high tide.

WINTERS *on broad estuaries and sheltered muddy and sandy beaches, rarely inland.*

streaked grey-brown and buff

long, slightly upcurved bill

coppery red below

plain upperwings with dark tips

pale buff breast

quite short, dark legs

barred tail

streaked bright buff

VOICE *Rapid, yelping* kirruk kirruk *flight call.*
NESTING *Shallow scrape on ground, on drier ridge or mound in mainly swampy tundra; 4 eggs; 1 brood; May–July.*
FEEDING *Probes in mud and sand for large marine worms and molluscs.*
SIMILAR SPECIES *Black-tailed Godwit (above), Curlew (p.133), Whimbrel (p.133).*

Spotted Redshank

Tringa erythropus (Scolopacidae)

The Spotted Redshank draws attention by its lively feeding actions – small groups are often seen leaping, running, upending, and diving for tiny fish in shallow water. Scarce in winter, they are typically seen on migration in late summer and autumn.

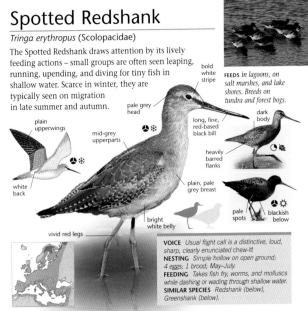

FEEDS *in lagoons, on salt marshes, and lake shores. Breeds on tundra and forest bogs.*

bold white stripe

pale grey head

plain upperwings

mid-grey upperparts

dark body

long, fine, red-based black bill

heavily barred flanks

white back

plain, pale grey breast

bright white belly

vivid red legs

pale spots

blackish below

> **VOICE** Usual flight call is a distinctive, loud, sharp, clearly enunciated chew-it!
> **NESTING** Simple hollow on open ground; 4 eggs; 1 brood; May–July.
> **FEEDING** Takes fish fry, worms, and molluscs while dashing or wading through shallow water.
> **SIMILAR SPECIES** Redshank (below), Greenshank (below).

Green Sandpiper

Tringa ochropus (Scolopacidae)

A larger and stockier bird than the Wood Sandpiper (below), often seen feeding in twos and threes on muddy shores, the Green Sandpiper usually looks very dark above and white below. It bobs like the Common Sandpiper (below), but not so continuously, and is quick to alarm and take to the air, flying off with loud calls and shooting around the sky.

INHABITS *shores of salt marsh creeks, pools, streams, and reservoirs. Breeds in boggy forests.*

pale line

dark wings

thick bars

diffuse buff spots

white-speckled, dark grey-brown upperparts

bright white below

greenish legs

> **VOICE** Loud, full-throated, liquid, almost yodelling tllu-eet, weet-weet!
> **NESTING** Old nest of thrush or similar, in tree near forest bog; 4 eggs; 1 brood; May–July.
> **FEEDING** Picks insects, crustaceans, and worms from water, often wading up to belly.
> **SIMILAR SPECIES** Common Sandpiper (below), Wood Sandpiper (below).

Redshank

Tringa totanus (Scolopacidae)

Very conspicuous, thanks to its loud voice and bold white upperwing bands, the Redshank is common on many coasts but scarcer inland in areas where drainage has destroyed wet grassland. A wary bird, it flies off with noisy calls, alerting other birds to danger.

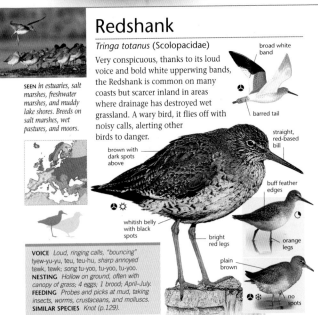

SEEN *in estuaries, salt marshes, freshwater marshes, and muddy lake shores. Breeds on salt marshes, wet pastures, and moors.*

broad white band

barred tail

straight, red-based bill

buff feather edges

brown with dark spots above

whitish belly with black spots

bright red legs

orange legs

plain brown

no spots

> **VOICE** Loud, ringing calls, "bouncing" tyew-yu-yu, teu, teu-hu, sharp annoyed tewk, tewk; song tu-yoo, tu-yoo, tu-yoo.
> **NESTING** Hollow on ground, often with canopy of grass; 4 eggs; 1 brood; April–July.
> **FEEDING** Probes and picks at mud, taking insects, worms, crustaceans, and molluscs.
> **SIMILAR SPECIES** Knot (p.129).

Wood Sandpiper

Tringa glareola (Scolopacidae)

Taller, slimmer, and more elegant than Common (below) and Green (above) Sandpipers, the Wood Sandpiper can be identified by its white rump, finely-barred tail, the pale stripe over its eye, and lack of white on its upperwings. It is a freshwater bird, often seen in weedy pools or paddling about on floating vegetation, and not on open seashores.

FEEDS *on muddy pools, weedy fringes of shallow lagoons, and salt pans, often near coast but not on estuarine mud.*

cream spots

brown back

pale spots

no white on upperwings

pale

long yellow-ochre legs

streaked breast

straight bill with dark tip

> **VOICE** Distinctive quick, sharp chiff-iff-iff-iff.
> **NESTING** Small, leaf-lined scrape on ground, occasionally old nest in tree; 4 eggs; 1 brood; May–July.
> **FEEDING** Steps delicately over vegetation, picking up small aquatic invertebrates.
> **SIMILAR SPECIES** Green Sandpiper (above), Redshank (left).

Greenshank

Tringa nebularia (Scolopacidae)

An elegant, delicate-looking wader, the Greenshank is a very active, dynamic feeder that often runs through the water, jinking and swerving in pursuit of prey. Rather larger than the Redshank (above), it looks heavier in flight; it has more white on its back but no white patches on its upperwings.

WINTERS *mainly on sheltered salt marsh creeks. Breeds near moorland pools; feeds on lake shores, wetlands, and estuaries.*

pale, scaly feather edges

pale head and neck

slightly upturned bill

clear white below

blackish spots

grey above

streaks on breast

white wedge on back

long grey-green legs

plain upperwings

> **VOICE** Loud, ringing, even-pitched tew-tew-tew; lacks "bounce"/hysteria of Redshank call.
> **NESTING** Scrape on ground, in grass or heather; 4 eggs; 1 brood; May–July.
> **FEEDING** Probes for worms, insects, and crustaceans in shallow water; chases fish.
> **SIMILAR SPECIES** Redshank (above).

Common Sandpiper

Actitis hypoleucos (Scolopacidae)

A small, slim, long-tailed wader, the Common Sandpiper can be recognized by the strong "hook" of white on its flank, and the way it bobs its head and swings its tail end up and down. It usually feeds in small, loose groups; when disturbed they fly off at low level with rapid, flickering wingbeats and stiff-winged glides, piping noisily.

BREEDS *on rocky streams and lakesides with shingle and grass banks. Migrants live in all waterside habitats, including estuaries.*

bold white bars

mottled, dark back; plainer in winter

mid-brown above

white crescent in front of wing

long tail

pale-flecked feather edges

greenish or ochre legs

> **VOICE** Loud, ringing, sharp tew-tew-tew or tyew-yu-yu; summer calls include fast, trilling teu-i teu-i teu-i, chip, tidledi tidledi tidledi.
> **NESTING** Small, grass-lined hollow on ground or bank; 4 eggs; 1 brood; April–July.
> **FEEDING** Skips and saunters along waterside snatching insects, worms, and molluscs.
> **SIMILAR SPECIES** Green Sandpiper (above).

Whimbrel

Numenius phaeopus (Scolopacidae)

This smaller cousin of the Curlew (below) is more compact and darker-plumaged, with a distinctively striped head. Unlike the common and widespread Curlew, the Whimbrel breeds only in northern Europe, being just a spring and autumn migrant elsewhere.

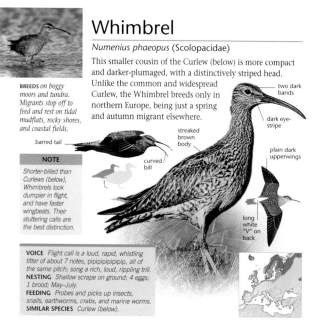

BREEDS *on boggy moors and tundra. Migrants stop off to feed and rest on tidal mudflats, rocky shores, and coastal fields.*

two dark bands

dark eye-stripe

streaked brown body

barred tail

plain dark upperwings

curved bill

long white "V" on back

NOTE
Shorter-billed than Curlews (below), Whimbrels look dumpier in flight, and have faster wingbeats. Their stuttering calls are the best distinction.

VOICE *Flight call is a loud, rapid, whistling titter of about 7 notes, pipipipipipipip, all of the same pitch; song a rich, loud, rippling trill.*
NESTING *Shallow scrape on ground; 4 eggs; 1 brood; May–July.*
FEEDING *Probes and picks up insects, snails, earthworms, crabs, and marine worms.*
SIMILAR SPECIES *Curlew (below).*

Curlew

Numenius arquata (Scolopacidae)

Britain's largest wader, the Curlew is widespread on all coasts and, especially when breeding, inland too, but it has declined dramatically on lowland farmland in England and Wales in recent years and is now mostly a breeding bird of northern moorland and bogs. With its very long, downcurved bill, distinctive calls, and lovely song, the Curlew is hard to mistake for any common bird apart from a Whimbrel (above), although distant flying birds can look rather like immature gulls. At long range on mudflats or roosting on sand spits, Curlews tend to look large and dark, but close views reveal a pale sandy-brown colour.

WINTERS *mainly on big, muddy estuaries; breeds on bogs, wet moorland or meadows, and northern shores and islands.*

two-tone upperwings

broad white "V"

gull-like wing shape

streaked brown above and on breast

white rump

long, evenly curved bill

quite short, greyish legs

whiter belly

spotted flanks

NOTE
Curlews look pale against a dark heather moor, or when well-lit on a muddy beach, but on a dull day on an estuary they tend to look very dark at long range. They stand motionless for long periods at high tide, often with Godwits and Redshanks nearby, and look much bigger than these.

VOICE *Loud whaup, whoy, cur-li; song starts slowly, accelerating to ecstatic bubbling trill.*
NESTING *Shallow hollow on ground, lined with grass; 4 eggs; 1 brood; April–July.*
FEEDING *Probes for and picks up worms, crabs, molluscs, starfish, and insects.*
SIMILAR SPECIES *Whimbrel (above), Bar-tailed Godwit (p.131).*

Turnstone

Arenaria interpres (Scolopacidae)

Most waders like to feed on soft mud or sand, but the stocky, short-billed Turnstone favours areas of stones, weed, or other debris that it can flick through in search of small animal food. Noisy, active, and often tame, it is colourful in summer but very dark above in winter, with a piebald look in flight.

bold black and white pattern on head

FEEDS *on sea coasts of all kinds, especially rocky shores and gravelly tidelines. Breeds on rocky northern coasts.*

white wing patch

black, white, and chestnut above

white wingbars

bold black breast-band

dull brown and black above

white below

short, vivid orange legs

VOICE *Fast, hard, abrupt, staccato calls, tukatukatuk, teuk, tchik.*
NESTING *Scantily lined scrape on ground close to shore on islands and rocky coasts; 4 eggs; 1 brood; May–July.*
FEEDING *Stirs up and turns seaweed, shells, and stones on beach to find invertebrates.*
SIMILAR SPECIES *Purple Sandpiper (p.130).*

Red-necked Phalarope

Phalaropus lobatus (Scolopacidae)

The tiny, delicate Red-necked Phalarope spends much of its time at sea, swimming with its head up, and tail and wings upswept. A very rare breeder in the far north, it is only a very scarce autumn migrant, usually in juvenile plumage, elsewhere in Britain. It is very like the Grey Phalarope (below) in winter, but its dark eye-patch curves down at the rear.

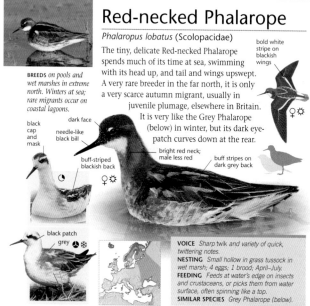

bold white stripe on blackish wings

BREEDS *on pools and wet marshes in extreme north. Winters at sea; rare migrants occur on coastal lagoons.*

black cap and mask

dark face

needle-like black bill

bright red neck; male less red

buff-striped blackish back

buff stripes on dark grey back

black patch grey

VOICE *Sharp twik and variety of quick, twittering notes.*
NESTING *Small hollow in grass tussock in wet marsh; 4 eggs; 1 brood; April–July.*
FEEDING *Feeds at water's edge on insects and crustaceans, or picks them from water surface, often spinning like a top.*
SIMILAR SPECIES *Grey Phalarope (below).*

Grey Phalarope

Phalaropus fulicarius (Scolopacidae)

Like the Red-necked Phalarope (above), the females of this species have brighter plumage than the males. These birds appears erratically on European coasts, usually in grey and white winter plumage, and look like tiny gulls when swimming on the sea.

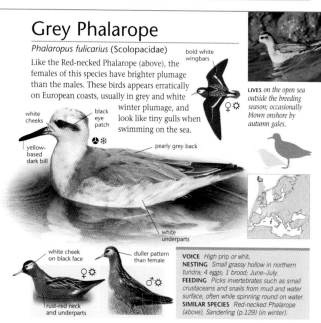

bold white wingbars

LIVES *on the open sea outside the breeding season; occasionally blown onshore by autumn gales.*

white cheeks

black eye patch

yellow-based dark bill

pearly grey back

white underparts

white cheek on black face

duller pattern than female

rust-red neck and underparts

VOICE *High prip or whit.*
NESTING *Small grassy hollow in northern tundra; 4 eggs; 1 brood; June–July.*
FEEDING *Picks invertebrates such as small crustaceans and snails from mud and water surface, often while spinning round on water.*
SIMILAR SPECIES *Red-necked Phalarope (above), Sanderling (p.129) (in winter).*

Pomarine Skua

Stercorarius pomarinus (Stercorariidae)

Resembling a larger, stouter, deeper-bellied version of the Arctic Skua (below), in both its pale and dark forms, the Pomarine Skua is distinguished in summer by its broad, spoon-like tail streamers. Juveniles can be mistaken for those of Arctic Skuas, but have clearer barring on the under- and upper-tail, and heavier, pale-based bills.

FEEDS *or rests on beaches after gales on migration, but mainly well out to sea. Breeds on Arctic tundra.*

black cap
yellow tint
brown back
patchy breast-band
PALE FORM
dark breast-band
DARK FORM
pale base to bill
blunt, spoon-shaped, twisted tail streamers
PALE FORM
blunt tail
broad bars
DARK FORM

VOICE *Loud, laughing waer-waer-waer on breeding sites; usually silent elsewhere.*
NESTING *Shallow scrape on open ground on Arctic tundra; 2 eggs; 1 brood; June.*
FEEDING *Eats lemmings and seabirds in summer; otherwise stolen fish and scraps.*
SIMILAR SPECIES *Arctic Skua (below), Great Skua (right), immature Herring Gull (p.135).*

Long-tailed Skua

Stercorarius longicaudus (Stercorariidae)

This small, slender skua has a graceful, almost tern-like flight, with frequent changes of course and height. Adults have long, whippy central tail streamers in summer. Juveniles lack these – most are paler than Arctic Skuas (left), but some are very similar. The best distinction is the shorter, thicker, pale-based bill.

BREEDS *on northern tundra; winters at sea, with migrants in coastal waters.*

black cap
grey-brown above
tiny pale flash
white breast
dark trailing edge
long central tail spike
dark belly
broad pale bars under tail
short, thick bill
thick-necked shape
narrow dark wings
DARK FORM

VOICE *Wailing, gull-like squeal and high alarm notes in summer; silent at sea.*
NESTING *Hollow in ground on tundra or high mountain; 2 eggs; 1 brood; June.*
FEEDING *Takes mostly lemmings, voles, and small birds in summer; fish in winter.*
SIMILAR SPECIES *Arctic Skua (left), Pomarine Skua (left).*

Arctic Skua

Stercorarius parasiticus (Stercorariidae)

FEEDS *near coasts on migration; winters out at sea. Breeds on coastal moorland and northern tundra. Generally the most commonly seen skua in Britain.*

The slender, sharp-winged Arctic Skua is a very variable but always elegant bird. Bigger and heavier than the Long-tailed Skua (right), but lighter than the Pomarine Skua (above), it is one of the most beautifully shaped seabirds in flight. It occurs in both pale and dark forms, which can be confusing, but its clean-cut profile is distinctive. It obtains a lot of its food by piracy, harassing terns and small gulls until they disgorge fish. The swift, acrobatic pursuit can be spectacular. On its northern breeding grounds, it has a fast, swooping, high display flight; it also attacks human intruders with great courage.

white wing flash
breast-band
PALE FORM
white wing flash
sharp central tail spike
DARK FORM
dark cap
brown back
grey-brown or yellowish breast-band
whitish underside
PALE FORM

NOTE

The long-winged Arctic Skua has a fast, fluent, rather erratic flight that can make it look rather falcon-like in the air, especially when it is in pursuit of other birds. Occasionally, it may even kill and eat small birds in flight like a true falcon, but it usually chases other birds to steal their food.

slimmer bill than juvenile Arctic or Long-tailed Skuas
sooty brown
DARK FORM

NOTE

The Arctic Skua has a variety of plumages, from pale to dark, with a range of intermediate forms. All have white flashes near the wingtips, both above and below, and the elongated central tail feathers of the adults are straight and pointed, rather than blunt like those of the Pomarine Skua (above). A juvenile has a very short pointed tail spike.

VOICE *Gives loud, nasal wailing in summer, ahh-yeow, eee-air, ka-wow; silent at sea.*
NESTING *Shallow scrape on ground in moss or heather, in small colony; 2 eggs; 1 brood; May–June.*
FEEDING *Robs terns and gulls of fish; also catches fish, small birds, and voles; eats some berries and insects.*
SIMILAR SPECIES *Pomarine Skua (above), immature Common Gull (p.136), immature Herring Gull (p.135).*

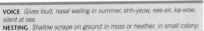

Great Skua

Stercorarius skua (Stercorariidae)

The largest, heaviest, boldest, and most predatory of the skuas, the Great Skua is always dark brown with pale buff streaks and big white wing patches. Able to steal from a Gannet (p.118) and kill a Kittiwake (p.137), its success in recent years has caused problems for other seabirds. Ironically, the decreasing numbers of fish that causes problems for commoner seabirds also puts extra pressure on them, as the Great Skua has to turn from stealing fish from other birds to a more predatory diet.

BREEDS *on northern moors near sea; at other times usually lives well offshore, but sometimes near coasts.*

bold white wing patch
dark cap
tapered wings
stout, hooked, dark bill
pale streaks on neck
streaked dark brown above
dark underparts
thick blackish legs

NOTE

Away from its Scottish breeding areas, the Great Skua is typically seen flying low over the sea from a headland in autumn, with a steady, unvarying progress.

VOICE *Barking uk-uk-uk, also deep tuk-tuk; silent at sea.*
NESTING *Simple hollow on ground on moorland, dives fearlessly at intruders into its nesting territory, including people; 2 eggs; 1 brood; May–June.*
FEEDING *Steals fish from other seabirds; kills birds, takes eggs, or scavenges for carrion.*
SIMILAR SPECIES *Pomarine Skua (left), Arctic Skua (left), immature Herring Gull (p.135).*

Little Gull

Larus minutus (Laridae)

The smallest of the gulls, this delicate, elegant, small-billed bird combines the "hooded gull" sequence of plumages with a strongly contrasted immature pattern like that of a Kittiwake (p.137). In summer plumage, its hood completely covers its head, with no pale eye-ring, unlike the larger Black-headed (right) and Mediterranean Gulls (below). It feeds over open fresh waters by dipping for prey like a Black Tern (p.138). Like the terns, it tends to appear over lakes and reservoirs in small groups in spring and autumn, but immatures may linger for weeks in the summer, often feeding alongside other gulls.

BREEDS *on marshland; at other times feeds on coasts, estuaries, coastal lagoons, lakes, and reservoirs.*

dark markings on head increase in spring

pale head

pale grey back

pale wingtips

delicate dark bill

black on underwings may be visible

no black on upperwings

blackish underwings with white rims

dark cap and ear patch

blackish zigzag on upperwings

dark ear spot

black hood

underwings paler than adult's

pearly grey

1ST

2ND

VOICE Low kek-kek-kek call, also hoarse, rapid, rather tern-like call, akar akar akar.
NESTING Grassy scrape on ground, or among dense marsh vegetation; 3 eggs; 1 brood; May–June.
FEEDING Mostly picks up insects, aquatic invertebrates, and small fish from surface of water in dipping flight.
SIMILAR SPECIES Black-headed Gull (right), Mediterranean Gull (below), immature Kittiwake (p.137).

Black-headed Gull

Larus ridibundus (Laridae)

Common and familiar, this is a small, agile, very white-looking gull. It is never truly "black-headed", because in breeding plumage its hood is dark chocolate brown and does not extend to the back of its head. In other plumages, it has a pale head with a dark ear spot. Its dark underwing gives a flickering effect in flight. It has always been a frequent bird inland, but numbers have increased still further in response to abundant food provided by refuse tips and safe roosting sites on reservoirs and flooded pits.

FEEDS *on coasts, lakes, reservoirs, farmland, refuse tips, and along rivers. Common in towns and cities. Breeds from coastal marshes to upland pools, widespread but local.*

dark brown hood

deep red bill

white eye-ring

very pale grey back

deep red legs

brown on neck and back

black-tipped

neck and back become grey

dark hind edge

1ST

1ST

dark grey underwings with white outer edge

white leading edge

black trailing edge

dark spot

vivid red bill with black tip

vivid red legs

VOICE Loud, harsh, squealing, laughing, and chattering calls, kwarrr, kee-arr, kwuk, kuk-kuk; particularly noisy at breeding colonies.
NESTING Pile of stems on ground in vegetation in marshland, in colony; 2–3 eggs; 1 brood; May–June.
FEEDING Takes worms, seeds, fish, and insects from ground and water, also catches insects in flight.
SIMILAR SPECIES Mediterranean Gull (left), Common Gull (p.136), Little Gull (left).

Mediterranean Gull

Larus melanocephalus (Laridae)

Although more common in southeast Europe, this beautiful gull has spread west, far beyond its original range. Bigger than the similar Black-headed Gull (above), with a heavier bill, it has white wingtips instead of black, and a jet-black rather than dark brown hood in summer.

WINTERS *on estuaries, beaches, and rarely on lakes. Breeds on shallow lagoons and coastal marshes.*

white wingtips

white underwings

dark patch around eye

mottled back

thick, red to black bill

red to black legs

black spots

2ND

black hood

VOICE Nasal, far-carrying, rising, and falling eeu-err eeu-err.
NESTING Grass-lined nest on sand, shingle, or in marsh; 3 eggs; 1 brood; May–June.
FEEDING Forages for fish, worms, aquatic invertebrates, and offal on beaches and land.
SIMILAR SPECIES Black-headed Gull (above), Common Gull (p.136).

Herring Gull

Larus argentatus (Laridae)

The big, noisy Herring Gull is mainly a bird of sea cliffs in summer, but roams over all kinds of shores and far inland in winter, when its white head and neck are streaked brownish. Paler than the Yellow-legged Gull (p.136), it has pink legs and fierce-looking pale eyes.

FEEDS *on beaches, estuaries, reservoirs, and refuse tips. Breeds on cliffs, islands, and rooftops.*

blotched brown

yellow bill with red spot

pale grey back

grey-brown streaks

white spots

pale pink legs

VOICE Loud, squealing notes, yelps, barks, kyow, kee-yow-yow-yow, ga-ga-ga, kuk-kuk.
NESTING Grass-lined nest on ground, cliff ledge, or building; 2–3 eggs; 1 brood; May.
FEEDING Takes fish, molluscs, insects, fish offal, and scraps from ground or water.
SIMILAR SPECIES Common Gull (p.136), Lesser Black-backed Gull (p.136).

Common Gull

Larus canus (Laridae)

Rather like the Herring Gull (p.135) in its general pattern, but much smaller, the Common Gull has a smaller bill with no red spot, a rounder head, and a dark eye, giving it a more gentle expression. Compared to the slightly smaller Black-headed Gull (p.135), it has no dark hood or ear spot, and no white leading edge on its outer wing. It is not as common as either species, with a curiously patchy, local distribution despite its wide range.

BREEDS *on coasts and moors; winters on coasts, farmland, lakes, and reservoirs.*

yellow-green bill with no red

grey-brown on head

mid-grey back

white spots on black wingtips

bold white crescent

1ST

brown wings, fading to buff

black band

dark brown

grey

brown wingtips

1ST

green to yellow-green legs

mid-grey back

buff-grey bill with black tip

wings fade paler

1ST

dark eye on white head

long, slim shape

green legs

large white spot on black wingtip

NOTE

At a distance, the Common Gull can be distinguished from the bigger Herring Gull (p.135) by the larger white patches on its black wingtips, and its more fluent, easy, relaxed flight style, with relatively little soaring or gliding.

all-white tail

VOICE Loud, shrill, nasal squealing kee-ee-ya, kee-ar-ar-ar-ar, higher-pitched than Herring Gull's calls; also a short gagagaga.
NESTING Pad of grass or seaweed on ground or on low stump, in colony; 2–3 eggs; 1 brood; May–June.
FEEDING Takes worms, insects, fish, and molluscs from ground or water; also scavenges for scraps.
SIMILAR SPECIES Herring Gull (p.135), Black-headed Gull (p.135), Mediterranean Gull (p.135).

Yellow-legged Gull

Larus (cachinnans) michahellis (Laridae)

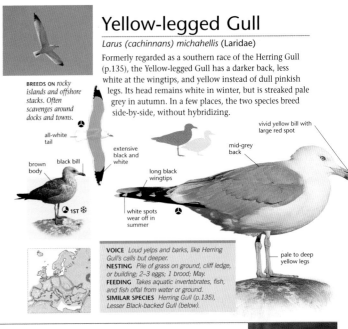

Formerly regarded as a southern race of the Herring Gull (p.135), the Yellow-legged Gull has a darker back, less white at the wingtips, and yellow instead of dull pinkish legs. Its head remains white in winter, but is streaked pale grey in autumn. In a few places, the two species breed side-by-side, without hybridizing.

BREEDS ON *rocky islands and offshore stacks. Often scavenges around docks and towns.*

all-white tail

extensive black and white

brown body

black bill

vivid yellow bill with large red spot

mid-grey back

long black wingtips

white spots wear off in summer

pale to deep yellow legs

VOICE Loud yelps and barks, like Herring Gull's calls but deeper.
NESTING Pile of grass on ground, cliff ledge, or building; 2–3 eggs; 1 brood; May.
FEEDING Takes aquatic invertebrates, fish, and fish offal from water or ground.
SIMILAR SPECIES Herring Gull (p.135), Lesser Black-backed Gull (below).

Lesser Black-backed Gull

Larus fuscus (Laridae)

A handsome bird in slate-grey and pure white with vivid yellow legs and bill, this gull is almost as big as the Herring Gull (p.135), but slimmer and darker. It used to be a summer visitor to western Europe, but has now established large wintering populations inland.

BREEDS *on cliffs, islands, moorland, and rooftops. Feeds on beaches, refuse tips, reservoirs, and fields.*

densely streaked, grey-brown head

slate-grey back

dark grey band on underwings

one white primary spot on black wingtip

mottled dark brown body

1ST YEAR

turns dark grey

black bill

2ND YEAR

white head

dull yellow legs

yellow bill with red spot

bright yellow

VOICE Deep, throaty, wailing calls, deeper than Herring Gull, as well as various barks and yelps.
NESTING Pile of grass or seaweed on ground; 2–3 eggs; 1 brood; May.
FEEDING Takes fish, worms, molluscs, crustaceans, and edible refuse; in summer feeds on other seabirds, their young, and eggs.
SIMILAR SPECIES Herring Gull (p.135).

Iceland Gull

Larus glaucoides (Laridae)

A large, handsome bird the size of a Herring Gull (p.135), the Iceland Gull breeds in Greenland but ranges south to Britain in winter. Its plumage is almost identical to that of the Glaucous Gull (right), but it has a rounder head, a slighter, shorter bill, and longer wingtips.

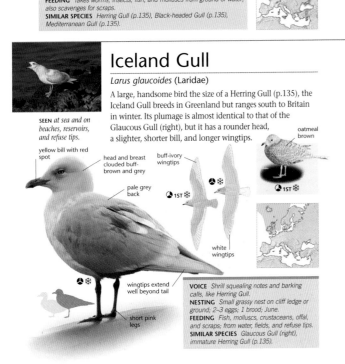

SEEN *at sea and on beaches, reservoirs, and refuse tips.*

oatmeal brown

yellow bill with red spot

head and breast clouded buff-brown and grey

buff-ivory wingtips

pale grey back

1ST

1ST

white wingtips

wingtips extend well beyond tail

short pink legs

VOICE Shrill squealing notes and barking calls, like Herring Gull.
NESTING Small grassy nest on cliff ledge or ground; 2–3 eggs; 1 brood; June.
FEEDING Fish, molluscs, crustaceans, offal, and scraps; from water, fields, and refuse tips.
SIMILAR SPECIES Glaucous Gull (right), immature Herring Gull (p.135).

Glaucous Gull

Larus hyperboreus (Laridae)

Bigger than the Iceland Gull (left), and distinctly fiercer-looking, the Glaucous Gull has a much larger, longer bill, and shorter wingtips at rest. In the British Isles, it is usually seen in its less immaculate winter plumage, before it heads north to breed in the Arctic.

FEEDS *around trawlers at sea, on beaches, reservoirs, and refuse tips. Breeds on northern coasts.*

white wingtips

1ST

buff wingtips

yellow bill with red spot

clouded grey-brown

barred oatmeal brown

pale pink bill with black tip

pale grey above

mottled brown

short white wingtips

1ST

1ST FADED

pale pink legs

VOICE Wailing and yapping notes, much like those of Herring Gull.
NESTING Pad of grass and stems on cliff ledge or ground; 2–3 eggs; 1 brood; May–June.
FEEDING Takes fish, invertebrates, offal, and scraps; more predatory in summer.
SIMILAR SPECIES Iceland Gull (left), immature Herring Gull (p.135).

Great Black-backed Gull

Larus marinus (Laridae)

Huge, powerful, heavy-billed, and fiercely predatory, the Great Black-backed is the world's largest gull. The size of its bill is a good guide to its identity even in immature plumages, when it resembles an oversized Herring Gull (p.135). Adults are blacker than the southern races of the Lesser Black-backed Gull (p.136), although the black plumage fades browner as it ages. It dominates other gulls, and preys on other seabirds and their young in summer.

FOUND *on rocky coasts with cliffs and stacks, often in flocks around coastal pools. Winters on beaches, harbours, reservoirs, and also on refuse tips.*

big, powerful yellow bill with red spot

faint markings on white head

black back

large white patch on wingtips

broad wings

white underside

pale greyish, whitish, or pink legs

NOTE

At long range, this gull can be told apart from the Lesser Black-backed (p.136) by the larger white patch on its wingtips, and its heavier flight.

black bill

whitish head

pale head

chequered back

pure white head

1ST

2ND

dark flight feathers

VOICE Deep barking notes, short hoarse yowk, gruff, guttural ow-ow-ow.
NESTING Shallow scrape on cliff ledge or pinnacle, lined with grass or weed; 3 eggs; 1 brood; May–June.
FEEDING Bold and predatory in summer, eating seabirds and voles; also catches fish, crustaceans, and other invertebrates; scavenges offal and edible scraps from sea, beaches, and refuse tips.
SIMILAR SPECIES Lesser Black-backed Gull (p.136), immature Herring Gull (p.135).

Common Tern

Sterna hirundo (Sternidae)

A typical black-capped, pale-bodied tern, the Common Tern is well named. It is widespread on coasts from spring to late autumn and is the most likely tern to be seen inland. It closely resembles the Arctic Tern (below), and often mixes with it, but is rather stouter, with a shorter tail and a longer red bill with a black tip. Towards the end of summer, the forehead of the adult turns white, and so resembles the Little Tern's (p.138), but since that is a much smaller and paler bird, there is little risk of confusion. It typically plunge-dives for prey with little hesitation, swallowing it or carrying it to the nest in its bill.

FEEDS *in coastal waters, rivers, and lakes. Breeds on coasts, islands, salt marshes, and locally on shingle or gravel banks by fresh waters. Migrants are widespread on coasts, some inland. Winters along coasts in Africa.*

long, black-tipped, bright red bill

black cap

pale grey upperparts

darker wingtip feathers

translucent underwing patch

long neck

forked white tail

white body

red legs, longer than Arctic Tern's

white forehead

dark shoulder

dark streaks on outer wings

dark nape

faint ginger bars

pale bill base

dark shoulder

NOTE

While very like the Arctic Tern (below), the Common Tern has a flatter head with a wider white line between its black cap and longer red bill. When seen in flight from below, only the inner primary feathers on its wings are translucent, creating a pale patch, whereas those of the Arctic Tern are all translucent apart from the dark trailing edge of the outer wing.

VOICE Grating, thin, falling kreee-yair of alarm, sharp kik kik, ringing keeer, rapid kirrikirrikirrik.
NESTING Scrape on ground, in sand, shingle, or dry earth, in colonies near water; 2–4 eggs; 1 brood; May–June.
FEEDING Dives into water for fish and aquatic invertebrates, after brief hover; also insects and fish from water surface in flight.
SIMILAR SPECIES Roseate Tern (p.138), Arctic Tern (below), Sandwich Tern (p.138).

Kittiwake

Larus tridactyla (Laridae)

One of the most maritime of gulls, the Kittiwake comes to land only to breed in noisy colonies on sheer cliffs. Its very white head and black wingtips are distinctive in flight, and its call is unmistakable. In winter, the adult has a grey nape and a dark ear patch.

BREEDS *on coastal cliffs. Winters at sea, when scarce on coasts. Rare but regular inland on migration.*

pale yellow-green bill

white head and breast

blue-grey back

pale outer wings

short blackish legs

1ST

black triangle

grey collar

black zigzag

1ST

dull plumage

black collar

black zigzag

dark spot

VOICE Ringing, nasal, rhythmic kiti-a-wake! often repeated; also high, thin, mewing note.
NESTING Nest of weed on ledge on cliff or seaside building; 2–3 eggs; 1 brood; May–June.
FEEDING Takes mostly fish in shallow dive or from surface; also fish offal from trawlers.
SIMILAR SPECIES Common Gull (p.136), Little Gull (p.135), Herring Gull (p.135).

Arctic Tern

Sterna paradisaea (Sternidae)

Similar to the Common Tern (above), the Arctic Tern is a more strictly maritime bird. Its wings have translucent outer primaries, and a narrow, more tapered dark trailing edge beneath. Uniquely, the Arctic Tern spends the northern winter in the Southern Ocean, thereby enjoying more summer daylight than any other bird.

LIVES *on northern offshore islands, and sandy and gravelly beaches. Winters in Southern Ocean, as far as Antarctic pack ice.*

very pale outer wings

bill shorter than Common Tern's

short neck

rounded head with black cap

grey back

short red bill

white forehead

black bill

dark crescents on back

long outer tail streamers

pale grey below

short red legs

VOICE Grating, sharp kee-yaah, rising pee-pee-pee, sharp kik, kreer.
NESTING Scrape in sand or shingle, hollow in rocks in colonies; 2 eggs; 1 brood; May–June.
FEEDING Plunge-dives for small fish; insects from freshwater pools and small crustaceans.
SIMILAR SPECIES Common Tern (above), Roseate Tern (p.138).

Roseate Tern

Sterna dougallii (Sternidae)

Named for the pink flush of its pale underparts in spring, the Roseate Tern is similar to the Common (p.137) and Arctic Terns (p.137), but paler, with longer tail streamers. It also has a longer, black bill, with a red base that becomes more extensive in late summer. Populations have declined much in recent years; the bird is now rare and local in Britain and Ireland.

SEEN *on beaches and vegetated islands, feeding at sea. Winters on West African coasts.*

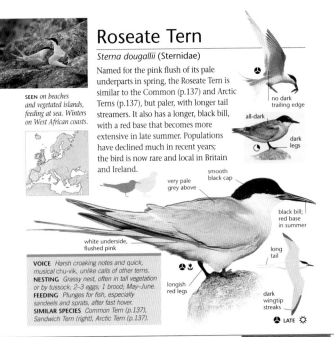

no dark trailing edge

all-dark

dark legs

smooth black cap

very pale grey above

black bill; red base in summer

white underside, flushed pink

long tail

longish red legs

dark wingtip streaks

● ↓ **LATE** ☼

VOICE *Harsh croaking notes and quick, musical chu-vik, unlike calls of other terns.*
NESTING *Grassy nest, often in tall vegetation or by tussock; 2–3 eggs; 1 brood; May–June.*
FEEDING *Plunges for fish, especially sandeels and sprats, after fast hover.*
SIMILAR SPECIES *Common Tern (p.137), Sandwich Tern (right), Arctic Tern (p.137).*

Sandwich Tern

Sterna sandvicensis (Sternidae)

The Sandwich Tern is a large, active, noisy bird with a spiky black crest, a long, sharp bill, and long, angular wings that it often holds away from its body, slightly drooped. It looks very white in the air, diving for fish from high up and hitting the water with a loud smack.

FOUND *on sand dunes, shingle beaches, and islands. Winters in coastal waters of Africa.*

long black bill, yellow at tip

black cap, spiky at rear

very pale silver-grey back

white underside

black legs

very pale silver-grey wings

short tail with shallow fork

white tail

dark chequers and bars on "saddle"

white forehead

dark streaks

dark tail corners

VOICE *Loud, harsh, rhythmic ker-ink, short kik or kear-ik!*
NESTING *Shallow scoop in sand or shingle; 1–2 eggs; 1 brood; May–June.*
FEEDING *Catches fish, especially sandeels, by plunge-diving from air.*
SIMILAR SPECIES *Common Tern (p.137), Black-headed Gull (p.135).*

Little Tern

Sterna albifrons (Sternidae)

The quick, nervous, and tiny Little Tern is usually easy to identify by its size alone, but it is also paler than other terns, with a white forehead all year round. Its wings have a black streak at the tip on the upper side, and the adult has a distinctive yellow dagger bill with a black tip. Although a widespread summer visitor, the Little Tern is becoming scarce on many coasts because it often breeds on popular leisure beaches; many colonies survive only because they are fenced off and protected. Rising sea levels may also be a threat, since extra-high tides often destroy its eggs and chicks.

BREEDS *on narrow sand and shingle coastal beaches; also inland in Spain and Portugal and eastern Europe. Winters along coasts of Africa.*

black streak at wingtips

pure white underside

short, white, forked tail

long, narrow wings

white forehead

black stripe through eye

black cap

black nape

sharp yellow bill with tiny dark tip

pale grey back

black wedge at wingtips

orange to yellow legs

streaky crown

dark chevrons on back

NOTE

The Little Tern is narrower-winged than other terns, and has a faster, more dashing, frenetic flight with rapid, flickering wingbeats, often calling noisily as it goes. It hovers often, low over the sea, with very quick, whirring wing-beats. So, even if a Little Tern is too distant to assess its size or distinguish its plumage, these features provide a clue to its identity.

VOICE *Sharp, high, rapid, irritated-sounding kirri-kirri-kirri and kitititit.*
NESTING *Shallow scoop on sand or shingle beach, often very near the water; 2–3 eggs; 1 brood; May–June.*
FEEDING *Plunge-dives for fish, often into breaking waves off steep shingle beach, with fast, abrupt smack into water, after a whirring hover that is often quite prolonged; repeats dives more quickly than other terns.*
SIMILAR SPECIES *Sandwich Tern (right), Common Tern (p.137), Arctic Tern (p.137).*

Black Tern

Chlidonias niger (Sternidae)

The marsh terns of the genus *Chlidonias* are smaller, more delicate birds than the sea terns, and customarily feed by dipping to the water surface instead of plunge-diving. The Black Tern is the most widespread species. It lives up to its name in summer by being mainly blackish and smoky grey, with white beneath its tail and pale underwings. It is more common in autumn, when its plumage is less distinctive: its body becomes patched with white, and the black on its head and body is reduced to a three-lobed black cap and a dark spot on each side of its chest.

FEEDS *on marshes, lagoons, salt pans, estuaries, lakes, and reservoirs. Breeds on lakes and marshes. Winters mainly along coasts in Africa.*

greyish black head

dark smoky grey above

pale underwings

blackish bill

white under tail

blackish legs

dark chest spot

three-lobed dark cap

white forehead

browner body

dark chest spot

sharp wings

dark forewings

NOTE

Black Terns have a light, buoyant, rather erratic flight style, with frequent swoops and side-slips. When hunting, they often beat slowly into the wind, rising and falling over the water, their heads down, ready to dip down and snatch a small fish or insect from near the water surface.

VOICE *Usually a rather quiet bird, but may give short, low, squeaky, nasal flight calls, kik, or kik-keek.*
NESTING *Nest of stems and waterweed, often in shallow water or on mat of floating vegetation, in marsh or nearby drier land; 3 eggs; 1 brood; May–June.*
FEEDING *Dips to take insects, small fish, crustaceans, and amphibians such as frogs from the water.*
SIMILAR SPECIES *Little Gull (p.135).*

Guillemot

Uria aalge (Alcidae)

A slim, long-bodied auk with a slender, pointed bill, the Guillemot is one of the commonest breeding seabirds at cliff colonies. It often nests alongside the more thickset Razorbill (below), which has a deeper bill. Guillemots can often be seen flying low and fast off headlands, swimming in large groups below the cliffs, or diving, using their wings underwater.

BREEDS in colonies on narrow ledges on sea-cliffs and flat-topped stacks. Winters at sea, well offshore.

rounded head with tapered bill

pointed bill

white sides to rump

darker back on more northern birds

sharp bill

dark brown to black above

white below

black eye-stripe

white face

smudgy greyish streaks on flanks

VOICE Loud, whirring, growling chorus at colony, arrrr-rr-rr; juveniles make loud, musical whistle at sea.
NESTING On bare ledge on sheer cliff, in colony; 1 egg, broad at one end, pointed at the other, very variable in colour and pattern; 1 brood; May–June.
FEEDING Dives from surface to catch fish deep underwater, propelled by wings.
SIMILAR SPECIES Razorbill (below), Manx Shearwater (p.117).

Razorbill

Alca torda (Alcidae)

More heavily built than the very similar Guillemot (above), and not usually as numerous, the Razorbill has a pointed tail and a distinctive deep, flattened, blade-like black bill with a fine white line near the end. It breeds in company with Guillemots, but less conspicuously because it nests in cavities rather than open ledges.

LIVES on rocky coasts on cliffs with crevices, or among boulder scree, feeding at sea. Winters out at sea, usually far from land.

broader, longer white sides than Guillemot

black head

deep, white-lined bill

white throat and breast

black cap

pointed tail, often cocked

black upperparts

white below

VOICE Prolonged, tremulous growls and grunts at colony, deep urrr.
NESTING On sheltered cliff ledge, or cavity between boulders; 1 egg; 1 brood; May–June.
FEEDING Dives, often very deeply, from surface to pursue and catch fish, using its wings to "fly" underwater.
SIMILAR SPECIES Guillemot (above).

Black Guillemot

Cepphus grylle (Alcidae)

In summer, the unique, striking plumage of the Black Guillemot makes it easy to identify. It is less distinctive in winter, when it is barred black and white above, but adults retain the clean white patches above and below their wings. Less gregarious than other auks, it is usually seen in pairs or small groups.

FOUND on coasts, on fringes of rocky islets with boulders and rock cavities. Feeds at sea.

small, sharp, dagger-like bill

whitish head, smudged with black

smoky black body

bold white wing patch

oval white patch

black bars on wing patch

bright red legs

VOICE Shrill whistle, often extended into fast trill; quick, thin sip-sip-sip.
NESTING Crevice between boulders, or hole in harbour wall; 1 egg; 1 brood; May–June.
FEEDING Dives underwater to catch small fish and crustaceans.
SIMILAR SPECIES Guillemot (left), Puffin (below), Slavonian Grebe (p.116).

Puffin

Fratercula arctica (Alcidae)

Few seabirds are more instantly recognizable than the Puffin in summer, with its clown-like eye and huge, flamboyantly coloured bill. Even at a distance it is usually distinctive, bobbing on the water or whirring through the air like a clockwork toy. In winter, it is less striking, as the colourful eye ornaments and horny plates at the edges of its bill fall away; its face is also darker, although not as dark as that of a juvenile bird. In summer, Puffins are often to be seen bringing food to their nesting burrows on northern and western coasts, but Puffins in winter plumage are generally rare close inshore.

SEEN on coastal clifftops, mainly on islands, feeding in nearby waters. Winters well out to sea.

deep, triangular bill, striped bluish, orange, yellow, and red

dark eyes with bluish scale above

grey-white facial disc

black upperparts and neck

white below

grooves on bill increase with age

black back

dusky grey face

vivid orange legs

plain black wings

smaller, duller bill

NOTE

A breeding Puffin is hard to mistake for any other bird, but in winter, Puffins usually feed well offshore and may be confused with other auks at long range. One distinctive feature is the grey facial disc; a Puffin also has a dumpier, more front-heavy body than a Guillemot (left) or a Razorbill (left), and it has all-dark wings with no white trailing edge.

VOICE Loud, cooing growl at nest, aaarr, karr-oo-arr; generally silent outside breeding season.
NESTING Digs or occupies ready-made burrow at or near clifftop, often excavated by rabbit or Manx Shearwater, or finds suitable cavity between boulders; 1 egg; 1 brood; May–June.
FEEDING Dives from water surface to catch small fish such as sand eels; also takes small squid, crustaceans, and marine worms.
SIMILAR SPECIES Razorbill (left), Guillemot (left).

Rock Dove

Columba livia (Columbidae)

The wild ancestor of the town or feral pigeon, the Rock Dove is a bird of rocky coasts and crags. It is paler, with an ash-grey back, a green and purple gloss on its neck, two broad black wingbars, and a white rump. Feral pigeons have very varied plumage patterns, and interbreeding between the two forms has made the genuine wild Rock Dove a rarity.

BREEDS *on coastal cliffs and mountains. Feral birds widespread from coasts to cities, and on farmland.*

tiny white patch

pale grey back

larger white patch

glossy purple and green on neck

FERAL PIGEON

dark below

white rump

white underwing

two long, broad, black bars on wings

VOICE *Deep, rolling, moaning coo, oo-ooh-oorr, oo-roo-coo.*
NESTING *Loose, untidy, sparse nest on ledge or in cavity; 2 eggs; 3 broods; all year.*
FEEDING *Forages for seeds, buds, berries, and small invertebrates on ground.*
SIMILAR SPECIES *Woodpigeon (below), Stock Dove (below), Peregrine Falcon (p.126).*

Collared Dove

Streptopelia decaocto (Columbidae)

Identifiable by its pale, grey-brown body, its thin, black half-collar, and monotonous triple coo, the Collared Dove is common on farms and in suburbs. It prefers to nest and roost in tall conifers. The male has a dramatic display flight, rising steeply and gliding down in wide arcs on flat wings, with harsh nasal calls.

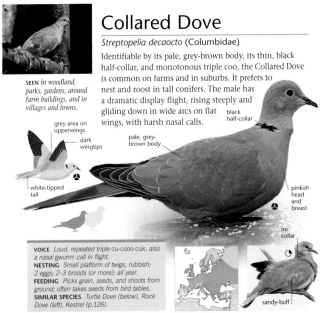

SEEN *in woodland, parks, gardens, around farm buildings, and in villages and towns.*

grey area on upperwings

dark wingtips

black half-collar

pale, grey-brown body

white-tipped tail

pinkish head and breast

no collar

sandy-buff

VOICE *Loud, repeated triple cu-cooo-cuk; also a nasal gwuurrr call in flight.*
NESTING *Small platform of twigs, rubbish; 2 eggs; 2–3 broods (or more); all year.*
FEEDING *Picks grain, seeds, and shoots from ground; often takes seeds from bird tables.*
SIMILAR SPECIES *Turtle Dove (below), Rock Dove (left), Kestrel (p.126).*

Stock Dove

Columba oenas (Columbidae)

A compact pigeon of farmland, parks, and uplands, the Stock Dove resembles a small Woodpigeon (below) but has a shorter tail, more bluish plumage, and no white markings. The two dark bars on its folded wing are a lot smaller and its head smaller and rounder than those of the similar Rock Dove (above).

FOUND *in a wide variety of places, from flooded fields and farmland with trees to rocky upland moors.*

glossy green neck patch

deep wine-pink breast

two short dark bars on wings

black trailing edge and wingtips

pale midwings

dark tail band

grey underwings

blue-grey body

VOICE *Rhythmic, booming coo, repeated with increased emphasis, ooo-woo ooo-woo.*
NESTING *Tree hole, ledge or cavity in cliff or building; 2 eggs; 2–3 broods; all year.*
FEEDING *Takes seeds, buds, shoots, roots, as well as berries from ground, but not in gardens.*
SIMILAR SPECIES *Rock Dove (above), Woodpigeon (below).*

Turtle Dove

Streptopelia turtur (Columbidae)

The purring song of the Turtle Dove used to be a common feature of high summer, but it is becoming less familiar as its woodland and hedgerow habitats are eliminated by intensive agriculture. Similar to the Collared Dove (above), it has a darker back, neatly chequered brown-black, and a striped bluish white and black neck patch.

LIVES *in wooded farmland, broadleaved woods with sunny clearings, and tall, dense, old hedgerows.*

barred black- and whitish neck patch

pink breast

blue-grey midwing

dark spots on orange-brown above

white belly

white tip to tail

no neck patch

duller body

VOICE *Deep, purring, crooning rooorrr rooorrr.*
NESTING *Small, flimsy platform of thin twigs in hedge or low branches of tree; 2 eggs; 2–3 broods; May–July.*
FEEDING *Takes seeds and shoots of arable weeds on ground.*
SIMILAR SPECIES *Collared Dove (above), Kestrel (p.126).*

Woodpigeon

Columba palumbus (Columbidae)

A large, common, boldly marked pigeon, often found in large flocks, the Woodpigeon is usually identifiable by its white neck patch, pink breast, white wingbar, and plump, small-headed look. Although tame in city parks, it is shy in rural areas where it is persecuted as a pest.

FEEDS *mainly on farmland; breeds in a variety of woodland and farmland with trees, also town parks and big gardens.*

bold white neck patch

grey back

rump paler than back

dark tail band

large white midwing patch

pink breast

dull red legs

white on wings

no white on neck

duller

broad dark band at end of tail

VOICE *Husky, muffled, repeated cooing, coo-coo-cu, cu-coo, cook; loud wing clatter in sudden take-off; wing claps in display flight.*
NESTING *Thin platform of twigs in tree or bush; 2 eggs; 1–2 broods; April–September.*
FEEDING *Eats buds, leaves, berries, and fruit in trees and on ground; visits bird tables.*
SIMILAR SPECIES *Stock Dove (above).*

Cuckoo

Cuculus canorus (Columbidae)

The Cuckoo's call is well known, but few people are familiar with the bird itself: a quite large, long-winged, long-tailed bird that resembles a small-headed hawk or falcon with barred under-parts. It often perches on trees or on overhead wires, its wings drooped and tail fanned.

PARASITIZES *nests of small birds in woods, reedbeds, on wooded farmland, bushy moorland, and heaths.*

pale band

yellow bill base and eyes

pale spot on nape

wedge shape

medium grey upperparts

grey bars on white underside

dark tail with white spots

yellow legs and feet

dark wingtips

barred above

VOICE *Familiar bright cuc-coo, sometimes cuc-cuc-oo; female has odd bubbling call.*
NESTING *Lays eggs in other birds' nests; 1–25 (usually 9) eggs, 1 per nest; May–June.*
FEEDING *Drops to ground to take large, hairy caterpillars; also eats small insects.*
SIMILAR SPECIES *Sparrowhawk (p.123), Kestrel (p.126), Stock Dove (left).*

Barn Owl

Tyto alba (Tytonidae)

Often seen by day, especially when it has young to feed, this is a strikingly pale owl with a heart-shaped face and black eyes. It often hunts in flight, flying low over the ground with quick, deep wingbeats. The buff-breasted European form is rare in the British Isles.

heart-shaped facial disc

black eyes

thin bars

pale buff upperparts

grey and black spots

white under-wings

buff below

T. a. guttata

white below

legs may dangle

BREEDS *and hunts in open country, from farmland to marshes and moorland, and young plantations.*

VOICE *Hissing, snoring calls from nest, nasal hi-wit, shrill, rolling shrieks and high squeals.*
NESTING *Big hole in tree, stack of hay bales, or building; 4–7 eggs; 1 brood; May–June.*
FEEDING *Hunts from perch or in low flight, for voles, mice, rats, and sometimes birds.*
SIMILAR SPECIES *Short-eared Owl (right), Tawny Owl (below).*

Little Owl

Athene noctua (Strigidae)

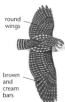

PERCHES *on posts and branches on farmland, open rocky slopes, and even semi-desert areas with rocks and cliffs.*

The small, chunky, flat-headed, short-tailed Little Owl frequently perches out in the open by day, when it often attracts the noisy attention of small birds. It can look very round and solid – although it may stretch upwards when alarmed and take off in a low, fast, bounding flight, like that of a thrush or woodpecker.

broad head with spotted crown

pale yellow eyes

round wings

brown and cream bars

brown back with cream-buff spots

wavy dark streaks

quite long legs

flattish white eyebrows

VOICE *Loud, musical, plaintive calls, rising keeeooo, sharper werro! short kip kip kip.*
NESTING *In long, narrow hole in tree, bank, or building; 2–5 eggs; 1 brood; May–July.*
FEEDING *Mostly takes small rodents, large insects, and worms from ground.*
SIMILAR SPECIES *Tawny Owl (below), Short-eared Owl (right).*

Tawny Owl

Strix aluco (Strigidae)

HUNTS *in all kinds of woodland, wooded farmland, and also in urban parks and large gardens with trees, even in big cities.*

A big-headed, bulky woodland owl that is generally strictly nocturnal, the Tawny Owl is responsible for the hooting and loud *ke-wick* notes often heard after dark. Beautifully camouflaged, it is hard to spot while roosting in the trees unless betrayed by the mobbing of small birds.

large black eyes

obvious facial disc

large, round head

brown back with row of white spots on each side

short wings and tail

pale spots and bars

VOICE *Loud, excited, yapping ke-wick!, long, quavering hoot, hoo hoo-hooo hoo-o-o.*
NESTING *Hole in tree or building, or old stick nest of crow; 2–5 eggs; 1 brood; April–June.*
FEEDING *Drops down to take rodents, frogs, beetles, and worms; also small roosting birds.*
SIMILAR SPECIES *Long-eared Owl (right).*

Long-eared Owl

Asio otus (Strigidae)

ROOSTS *in thorn and willow thickets, old hedgerows, and similar thick cover. Breeds mainly in conifer woods or shelter belts.*

A large, upright owl, with long ear tufts that it raises when alert, the Long-eared Owl is typically strictly nocturnal, with secretive habits that usually make it very hard to see. When relaxed, it can look rounded and bulky, but if alarmed it draws itself up into a slim, erect posture, its ear tufts upright, creating an unmistakable silhouette. Migrants can sometimes be seen by day, when they can be confused with Short-eared Owls (below), but the Long-eared Owl is slightly less buoyant in flight and never glides on raised wings. The pattern on its wings is less contrasted, with no white trailing edge.

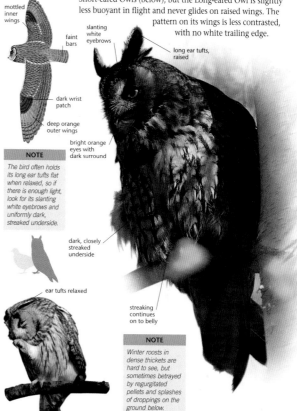

mottled inner wings

slanting white eyebrows

faint bars

long ear tufts, raised

dark wrist patch

deep orange outer wings

bright orange eyes with dark surround

dark, closely streaked underside

ear tufts relaxed

streaking continues on to belly

NOTE
The bird often holds its long ear tufts flat when relaxed, so if there is enough light, look for its slanting white eyebrows and uniformly dark, streaked underside.

NOTE
Winter roosts in dense thickets are hard to see, but sometimes betrayed by regurgitated pellets and splashes of droppings on the ground below.

VOICE *Song deep, moaning, short hoot, oo oo oo or uh uh; juvenile begs for food with incessant high, sharp "squeaky hinge" eee-ip calls.*
NESTING *Old nest of crow or hawk in tree, squirrel drey, or scrape on ground beneath bushes or thick growth of bracken or brambles; 3–5 eggs; 1 brood; March–June.*
FEEDING *Hunts from perch or in flight, catching small rodents on ground or (especially in winter) birds roosting in trees.*
SIMILAR SPECIES *Short-eared Owl (below), Tawny Owl (left).*

Short-eared Owl

Asio flammeus (Strigidae)

One of few owls that regularly appears in broad daylight, the Short-eared Owl has a buoyant flight and yellow eyes that give it a fierce expression, often visible at long range. It is very like the Long-eared Owl (above) in flight, but has a pale belly and bolder bars on the tail.

large round head with tiny ear tufts, usually hidden

PREYS *over grassland, plantations, marshes, heaths, and upland moors. Erratic breeder in south of range.*

whitish underwings

complex buff marbling on upperparts

blunt head

pale belly

scarcely streaked pale belly

narrow dark bar

black-rimmed, cold yellow eyes

orange-buff to yellowish outer wings

bold bars on tail

white trailing edge

dark wrist patch

VOICE *Nasal bark, kee-aw, or hoarse, whip-like ke-ow; male's song a deep, booming hoot, boo-boo-boo-boo, given in display flight.*
NESTING *Unlined scrape on the ground; 4–8 eggs; 1–2 broods; April–July.*
FEEDING *Rodents and other small mammals.*
SIMILAR SPECIES *Long-eared (above), Tawny (left), and Barn (left) Owls; female harriers.*

Nightjar

Caprimulgus europaeus (Caprimulgidae)

The strange, nocturnal Nightjar is best known for its song: a protracted mechanical trill that sounds wooden and rattling at close range. Invisible by day, thanks to its superb camouflage, it can be seen hawking for flying insects at twilight, in wonderfully light, buoyant, agile flight.

HUNTS *over heaths and open ground with low undergrowth, or in forest clearings.*

tiny bill

flat head

white line on cheek

elongated body and tail

long wings

♂

♀

white on tail corners

subtly barred, mottled, grey-brown body

white spots

♂

♀

VOICE *Frog-like, nasal gooik; song prolonged, mechanical churring, varying in pitch.*
NESTING *Unlined scrape on ground; 2 eggs; 1–2 broods; May–July.*
FEEDING *Catches insects, mainly moths, in flight, mostly at dusk and dawn.*
SIMILAR SPECIES *Song like Grasshopper Warbler's (p.151) but lower.*

Kingfisher

Alcedo atthis (Alcedinidae)

Usually glimpsed as a streak of electric blue as it flies over water, the Kingfisher can be surprisingly hard to see when perched in the dappled shade watching for prey. Its shape is unique: dumpy, almost tailless, with a long, heavy spike of a bill. It is often best located by its shrill whistled calls.

FOUND *along rivers and canals, on marshes, and flooded pits; also on coasts, especially in winter.*

vivid blue streak

white neck patch

red on base of bill

♂

♀

barred blue cap

dagger-like black bill

electric blue

white throat patch

rusty orange below

VOICE *Quite loud, sharp, high kit-cheeee or cheee; high, fast trill in spring.*
NESTING *Deep tubular tunnel, lined with fish bones, in earth bank over water; 5–7 eggs; 2 broods; May–July.*
FEEDING *Catches fish, frogs, and aquatic insects, in dive from perch or mid-air hover.*
SIMILAR SPECIES *None.*

Wryneck

Jynx torquilla (Picidae)

Looking more like a big warbler or a small, slim thrush, the Wryneck is a specialized woodpecker that feeds mainly on ants, either taking them from the ground or from bark crevices. It is elusive and hard to see, not least because of its beautiful and subtle camouflaging plumage, but its calls are distinctive. It is named for its habit of twisting its head round when alarmed, giving it a "wry-necked" look.

BREEDS *in farmed countryside with trees, copses, and more extensive pine or mixed forest; migrants often seen near coasts and on islands.*

barred tail

long, dark eye-stripe

pale grey crown

barred wings

large blackish back stripe

fine bars on buff throat

grey, brown, and blackish above

pale spots on wings

VOICE *Quick, nasal kwee-kee-kee-kee-kee, lower in pitch than similar calls of Lesser Spotted Woodpecker and Kestrel.*
NESTING *Existing hole in tree or wall; 7–10 eggs; 1–2 broods; May–June.*
FEEDING *Often on ground, taking ants, other insects, spiders, woodlice, and some berries.*
SIMILAR SPECIES *Barred Warbler (p.153).*

Green Woodpecker

Picus viridis (Picidae)

Easily detected, especially in spring, by its loud laughing calls, this big, pale woodpecker forages mainly on the ground. A wary feeder, it is often spotted as it flies up and into cover. Adults are mainly bright green with crimson crowns; young birds are mottled.

LIVES *in and around broadleaved and mixed woodland, and heaths with bushes and trees. Feeds on grassy areas with ants.*

red and black moustache; no red in female

black around whitish eye

♂

bright greenish yellow rump

vivid red cap (in both sexes)

♂

blackish spots and streaks

dark wingtips with pale bars

apple-green upperside

greenish yellow rump

VOICE *Loud, shrill, bouncing keu-keu-keuk; song a descending kleu-kleu-kleu-keu.*
NESTING *Bores nest hole in tree; 5–7 eggs; 1 brood; May–July.*
FEEDING *Eats ants, ants' eggs, and larvae, mainly on ground, using tongue to probe nests.*
SIMILAR SPECIES *Female Golden Oriole (Oriolus oriolus), which has a plain head.*

Great Spotted Woodpecker

Dendrocopos major (Picidae)

The rapid "drum roll" of this bird is a common sound of spring woodland. The woodpecker itself is often easy to locate, propped on its tail as it hammers at bark or timber. If disturbed, it swoops away in a deeply undulating flight.

FEEDS *in gardens and scrub as well as mature woodland; breeds in both deciduous and conifer woods.*

red patch on back of head

♂

bold black and white above

bright buff below

all-red crown; less on female

♂

big white shoulder patch

vivid red under tail

no red

♀

VOICE *Explosive tchik! fast rattle of alarm; loud, fast, very short drumming.*
NESTING *Bores nest hole in tree trunk or branch; 4–7 eggs; 1 brood; April–June.*
FEEDING *Digs insects and grubs from bark with strong bill; also eats seeds and berries.*
SIMILAR SPECIES *Lesser Spotted Woodpecker (below).*

Lesser Spotted Woodpecker

Dendrocopos minor (Picidae)

The size of a sparrow, this is the smallest of British woodpeckers and one of the most secretive. It forages high in the slender branches of trees, creeping over the bark and searching for insects with rapid pecks of its small, sharp bill. Its territorial drumming has a rattling quality.

LIVES *in woodland, copses, orchards, and tall hedges with old or diseased trees.*

red cap

black cheek patch

less red than male

barred back

♂

black cap

closely barred back

barred wings; no big white shoulder patches

♂

♀

variable streaks below

VOICE *Sharp, weak tchik; nasal, peevish pee-pee-pee-pee-pee-pee; weak drum.*
NESTING *Bores nest hole in tree; 4–6 eggs; 1 brood; May–June.*
FEEDING *Takes insects from under bark and also from woody stems of ground plants.*
SIMILAR SPECIES *Great Spotted Woodpecker (above); Wryneck (left); Kestrel (call) (p.126).*

Woodlark

Lullula arborea (Alaudidae)

One of the smallest and prettiest of the larks, the Woodlark is a bird of open woodland and sandy heaths. It has a distinct undulating flight with a curiously floppy wing action, and in spring, the males perform their beautiful song from trees or in a high, circling song-flight.

FOUND *in open woods, on bushy heaths, and in felled woodland, such as large conifer plantations with bare, sandy ground and short grass.*

- tan and black striped cap
- whitish stripe reaches back of neck
- white-black-white patch on broad wings
- dark-edged rufous cheek
- very short tail, white at corners
- very short crest
- black and white wing patch
- dark streaks
- whitish belly

VOICE Call three-syllable t'loo-i; song rich, slow tlootlootloo, twee twee twee, dyoo dyoo dyoo, dlui dlui dlui *in high song-flight.*
NESTING Hair- and grass-lined nest on bushy ground; 3–4 eggs; 2 broods; April–June.
FEEDING Picks insects and small seeds from the ground, often on bare, sandy patches.
SIMILAR SPECIES Skylark (below).

NOTE
Broad, rounded wings and a short tail give it a unique appearance in flight; lacks white rear edge to wings found in Skylark (below).

Shore Lark

Eremophila alpestris (Alaudidae)

A long, sleek lark with a unique head pattern that is boldest in summer, the Shore Lark breeds in the mountains of Scandinavia and southeast Europe. In winter, it appears on beaches and marshy spots around the Baltic and North Seas, where it often feeds on small animals alongside Snow Buntings (p.161).

FEEDS *on sandy beaches near the high-tide mark in winter, and nearby marshes and fields. Breeds on mountains.*

- duller yellow and black on face than summer
- broad black upper chest-band
- mid-brown upperparts
- plain wings
- dark tail with pale centre
- variable brown lower chest-band
- white underparts
- tiny "horns"
- primrose-yellow and black face

VOICE Call pipit-like, thin tseeeep or louder seep-seep; song prolonged, quiet warbling from perch or in flight.
NESTING Hair-lined grass cup, on ground; 4 eggs; 1–2 broods; May–July.
FEEDING Creeps over ground, taking seeds, insects, crustaceans, and tiny molluscs.
SIMILAR SPECIES Skylark (left).

Skylark

Alauda arvensis (Alaudidae)

The silvery song of the Skylark is a familiar sound over the farmlands and pastures of the British Isles, although the bird is becoming less common owing to intensive farming. Rising high in the air, it may hang stationary for several minutes as it pours out a stream of liquid warbles and trills. A typical streaky lark on the ground, it has a distinctive appearance in flight, with its angular, straight-edged wings and short, white-edged tail. It flies with erratic bursts of wingbeats alternating with swoops on almost closed wings. In winter, many gather to feed on farmland in large, loose flocks.

SINGS *over open fields, especially with cereal crops, moorland, heaths, and pastures. Feeds on arable land in winter.*

- raised crest blunt, streaked
- whitish over eye
- dark stripes on back
- narrow whitish trailing edge to wing
- pale-centred cheeks
- blackish tail with wide white sides
- buff breast
- closely streaked, pale to warm tan-brown above
- white belly
- long hind claw
- flattened crest
- dark under tail
- grey underwings

NOTE
During its song-flight, the Skylark rises vertically on constantly flickering wings, then hovers, singing all the while, before spiralling or parachuting to the ground with a final steep plunge.

VOICE Calls chirruping shrrup, trup, higher seee; song fast, rich, continuous outpouring from perch or in high, soaring flight, sounding thinner and higher-pitched at distance.
NESTING Grassy cup on ground, in crops or grass; 3–5 eggs; 2–3 broods; April–July.
FEEDING Forages on ground in grass or on bare earth, eating seeds, shoots, grain, and insects.
SIMILAR SPECIES Woodlark (above).

Sand Martin

Riparia riparia (Hirundinidae)

The smallest of the European swallows and martins, with the most fluttering flight, the Sand Martin is the first to appear on its northern breeding grounds in spring. At this time it usually hunts over water, where it can rely on a supply of flying insect prey. It feeds on the wing, swooping after flies with fast in-out flicks of its wings. Always gregarious, it roosts in noisy flocks.

BREEDS *in colonies in earth banks and sand quarries, often near water, excavating rows of nest holes.*

- brown breast-band
- all-brown above
- perches at nest hole
- white underparts
- angled-back wings
- tail with shallow fork

VOICE Low, dry, rasping or chattering chrrrp; song rambling, chattering, weak twitter.
NESTING Bores long hole into earth or soft sandstone; 4–5 eggs; 2 broods; April–July.
FEEDING Catches insects in flight, often over water; sometimes feeds on bare ground.
SIMILAR SPECIES Swift (p.144), House Martin (below).

House Martin

Delichon urbica (Hirundinidae)

Small, stocky, with pied plumage and a bold white rump, the House Martin is a common breeding bird in many towns and villages in northern Europe. It feeds entirely in the air on small flies and similar prey, circling high up over the rooftops or low over fresh waters. It comes down to the ground only to gather mud, which it uses to build its distinctive nest.

PERCHES *in flocks on wires before migration. Breeds on house walls, feeding over wetlands and open areas.*

- dark wings
- white rump
- nest on outside wall
- blue-black cap
- blue-black back
- forked tail
- white throat
- white underside

VOICE Hard, quick, chirping prrit or chrrit, tchirrup; twittering song of similar notes.
NESTING Enclosed mud nest with top entrance, under house eaves or (in south of range) cliff overhang; 4–5 eggs; 2–3 broods; April–September.
FEEDING Catches insects in flight, high up.
SIMILAR SPECIES Swallow (p.144).

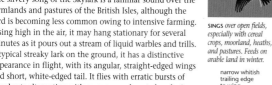

Swallow

Hirundo rustica (Hirundinidae)

The glossy, fork-tailed Swallow is a common sight around farmsteads in summer, since it prefers to nest in barns and sheds close to a steady supply of its favourite prey, large flies. It catches these on the wing, often swooping low among grazing cattle with a wonderfully fluent, graceful action, using its long tail to steer as it swerves and rolls from side to side through the air. Its tail streamers and deep red chin are usually conspicuous in flight, making it hard to confuse with any other species except the House Martin (p.143), which has a distinctive white rump if seen from above or behind. It often perches on wires, especially in autumn before migrating to Africa.

GATHERS in twittering flocks, perching in long rows on wires before migrating. Feeds over grassy or cultivated river valleys, open grassland, or farmland with hedgerows, and breeds in and around villages and farms.

long, slender wings

broad blue-black chest-band

deep rust-red chin

pale below

pale undertail coverts

dark rufous forehead

dark cap

deep, glossy blue upperparts

deeply forked tail with long streamers; longest on male

whitish to deep peach-buff underparts

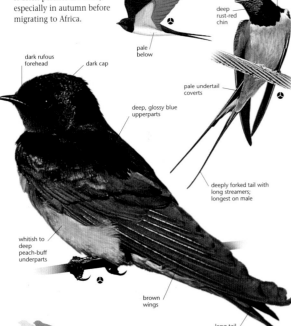

brown wings

long tail

VOICE Call liquid swit-swit-swit, nasal vit-vit-vit, tsee-tsee; song quick, chirruping warble.
NESTING Open cup of mud and straw, on beam or ledge in outbuilding; 4–6 eggs; 2–3 broods; April–August.
FEEDING Flies low to catch flying insects in its bill, mostly large flies.
SIMILAR SPECIES House Martin (p.143), Swift (below).

NOTE
Most Swallows nest in barns and similar buildings. They can be watched entering and leaving through open windows or doors as they bring food for their young.

Swift

Apus apus (Apodidae)

The only swift to occur over most of Europe, the common Swift is usually instantly identifiable by its scythe-like wings and loud, screaming calls. It spends most of its life in the air, only landing at the nest, and never perches like a swallow. In bad weather, it flies very low, giving good views.

BREEDS in holes in old buildings; rarely in cliffs nowadays; hunts over open country, villages, towns, and some large cities.

whitish edges

all-dark body; browner in late summer

whiter chin and forehead

hindwing slightly paler

pale throat, hard to see

scythe-shaped wings

looks all-black against sky

long, curved wings

forked tail

VOICE Loud, screeching, shrill screams from flocks, shrreeee, sirrr.
NESTING Feather-lined cavity in building, rarely in cliff; 2–3 eggs; 1 brood; May–June.
FEEDING Entirely aerial, taking flying insects and airborne spiders in its bill.
SIMILAR SPECIES Swallow (above).

Tree Pipit

Anthus trivialis (Motacillidae)

Very like a Meadow Pipit (below), but with a more confident air, the Tree Pipit is a bird of woodland edges rather than open grasslands. It has a superb song – rich and musical with Canary-like trills – delivered in a song flight that makes summer males relatively easy to identify. Autumn migrants are more confusing, although the call notes help.

BREEDS in open woods, woodland glades, edges of plantations, bushy heaths, and moors with scattered trees. Migrants are seen on coasts.

blackish tail with white sides

strong pale stripe over eye

browner in summer

thin, dark streaks

neat black stripes on pale back

dark spots across wings

buff-yellow below

often pumps tail

pale yellowish, unstreaked flanks

VOICE Call low teeess, sharp tzit; song loud series of sweet notes and trills, ending in slow sweee-sweee-sweee, from perch or song flight.
NESTING Grassy cup in thick grass; 4–6 eggs; 1–2 broods; April–July.
FEEDING Takes small insects from ground.
SIMILAR SPECIES Meadow Pipit (below), Rock Pipit (below), Skylark (p.143).

Meadow Pipit

Anthus pratensis (Motacillidae)

FOUND on grassland, heaths, dunes, and moors, from coasts to uplands; on farmland and marshes near coasts in winter.

The tinkling song of the Meadow Pipit is one of the evocative sounds of summer in the open hills. Often seen from a distance as it rises in a song flight, or flutters up jerkily with squeaky calls, the bird has a hesitant, nervous manner. A close look is needed to appreciate the subtle distinctions of its plumage.

slim dark bill

pale stripe

soft blackish streaks on brown back

streaked brown back

dark tail with white sides

evenly streaked flanks and chest

olive-buff or cream below

very long hind claw

VOICE Call sharp, weak pseeep, quiet pip, in winter flock; song long series of notes and trills in parachuting song flight.
NESTING Nest a cup of grass on ground; 4–5 eggs, 2 broods; May–July.
FEEDING Eats insects and some seeds.
SIMILAR SPECIES Tree Pipit (above), Rock Pipit (below), Skylark (p.143).

NOTE
Song-flight very like that of Tree Pipit (above), but it usually begins and ends it on ground, while Tree Pipit flies from perch to perch.

Rock Pipit

Anthus petrosus (Motacillidae)

SEEN on rocky coasts; on migration and in winter, some visit salt marshes and soft shores, fewer inland by water.

For much of the year, the habitat of the Rock Pipit helps to betray its identity, for it is truly a bird of rocky coasts and islands. Its song-flight and song are similar to those of the Meadow Pipit (above), but its loud, single call note is distinctive.

weak stripe over eye

grey-edged, dark tail

dark back

diffuse streaks on dusky olive back

blurry dark streaks

dull below

dark legs

dull white to yellowish underside

dark legs

VOICE Call slurred feest or pseeep; song like Meadow's but stronger, in similar song-flight.
NESTING Hair-lined nest on ground, in rock cavity; 4–5 eggs; 1–2 broods; April–July.
FEEDING Forages mainly on clifftops in summer, on stony/seaweedy shores in winter, for insects, sandhoppers, small molluscs.
SIMILAR SPECIES Meadow Pipit (above).

NOTE
A Rock Pipit can be distinguished from a Meadow Pipit (above) by its darker, duller, greyer plumage, dark legs, and longer, dark bill.

Water Pipit

Anthus spinoletta (Motacillidae)

In winter, Water Pipits retreat from their high mountain breeding grounds, mainly to inland marshes and mudflats. They look like migrant Scandinavian Rock Pipits (p.144) in spring plumage, though Water Pipits are paler, with bolder wingbars.

WINTERS *on marshes and lagoons with muddy edges; breeds on mountain pastures with scattered rocks.*

bold white stripe over eye

greyish head

warm brown back

pink flush below

dark tail with white edges

dark brown to reddish brown legs

two whitish wingbars

white stripe on brown head

dark brown

bold whitish wingbars

white below

VOICE Call quite strong, thin fist; song strong series of trills in high song-flight.
NESTING Grass-lined cup on ground among grass; 4–5 eggs; 2 broods; May–July.
FEEDING Takes small insects and spiders, and other invertebrates, from ground.
SIMILAR SPECIES Rock Pipit (p.144), Skylark (p.143), Wheatear (p.149).

NOTE
A Water Pipit is easy to confuse with a Rock Pipit (p.144), but if the bird is seen away from the coast it is less likely to be a Rock Pipit.

Yellow Wagtail

Motacilla flava (Motacillidae)

A male Yellow Wagtail in summer is elegant, colourful, and distinctive, but autumn birds, particularly juveniles, are easy to confuse with other species. Unlike other wagtails, it is never seen in Europe in winter, since it migrates to Africa to feed among the grazing herds on the tropical grasslands.

SNATCHES *prey from beneath feet of farm animals on wet fields; often near water.*

pale line

buff

white lines

grey-green

pale line

bright yellow stripe

green crown; blue-headed race occasional in spring

green back

two white wingbars

bright yellow below

white-sided black tail

VOICE Call full, flat or rising tsli, or tsweep; song repetiton of brief chirping phrases.
NESTING Grassy cup in vegetation on ground; 5–6 eggs; 2 broods; May–July.
FEEDING Takes insects from ground; skips and leaps after flies in short flycatching sallies.
SIMILAR SPECIES Grey Wagtail (below), juvenile Pied Wagtail (right).

Grey Wagtail

Motacilla cinerea (Motacillidae)

The extensive yellow in the Grey Wagtail's plumage can lead to confusion with the Yellow Wagtail (above), but its back is grey instead of green, and the summer male's black bib is distinctive. In winter, it often occurs near puddles, even in cities, when the Yellow Wagtail is far away in Africa.

BREEDS *along clean, often tree-lined rivers or open upland streams; widespread near water in winter, including briefly in urban areas.*

white stripe over eye

grey above

white edges

long black tail

brightest yellow under tail

yellow-green rump

black bib

broad white bar on dark wings

pale pinkish legs

yellow underparts

grey above

white or dusky throat

buffish below

paler

VOICE Sharp, explosive tchik, zi, or zi-zi; song penetrating, metallic trills and warbles.
NESTING Grassy cup in hole in bank, or under bridge; 4–6 eggs; 2 broods; April–August.
FEEDING Catches flies and other small insects on ground or in air.
SIMILAR SPECIES Yellow Wagtail (above), Pied Wagtail (right).

Pied Wagtail

Motacilla alba (Motacillidae)

Common throughout Europe, this boldly patterned wagtail occurs in two forms. The darker Pied Wagtail of Britain and Ireland has a black back, dark flanks and blackish wings. The mainland European form, the White Wagtail, is a scarce migrant in spring and autumn in the British Isles. It has a pale grey back and rump. Pied Wagtails are found in a wide variety of habitats, from farmland to urban areas. They chase insects with agile leaps and runs, constantly nodding their heads and bobbing their long tails.

ROOSTS *in trees in town centres; the birds feed in roadsides, car parks, and rooftops; also in fields, often by water.*

black cap, chin, and throat; white chin and throat in winter

whitish face

blackish rump

white streaks on wings

black back

white feather edges

black breast

sooty flanks

greyer back

white below

white belly

long black tail with white edges

♀ PIED

greyer above

buffish below

♂ ✿ PIED

♀♂ PIED

♂ **WHITE WAGTAIL** *M.a.alba*

pale grey back and rump

black tail, same as Pied form

NOTE
Outside the breeding season, Pied and White Wagtails form communal roosts, often with hundreds of birds. These roosts may occur in natural sites such as small trees or reedbeds, but in some areas wagtail roosts can be found on buildings, or even inside large commercial glasshouses, where the birds perch in long lines on the steel cross-beams below the roof.

VOICE Call loud, musical chirp, chuwee, chrruwee, grading into harder tissik or chiswik; song mixture of these calls and trills.
NESTING Grassy cup in cavity in bank, wall, cliff, or woodpile, in outbuilding or under bridge; 5–6 eggs; 2–3 broods; April–August.
FEEDING Feeds very actively on ground, roofs, or waterside mud or rocks, walking, running, leaping up or sideways, or flying in pursuit of flies; also takes other insects, molluscs, and some seeds.
SIMILAR SPECIES Grey Wagtail (left), juvenile Yellow Wagtail (left).

Waxwing

Bombycilla garrulus (Bombycillidae)

A winter visitor to the British Isles, the Waxwing appears in flocks when a poor berry crop in its far northern breeding grounds forces it south. Exotic-looking and very tame, it is easily identified by its pinkish plumage and bright wing markings, but in silhouette when flying it resembles the Starling (p.158).

BREEDS *in northern conifer forests, but flocks move south to feed on berries in rural and urban areas.*

large crest

yellow tip to black tail

white bars

fewer red spots or white edges

blurred lower edge to bib

♂

pinkish brown body

waxy red spots on wing

♀

yellow stripe and white edges to primary feathers

rusty under tail

VOICE Silvery, high, metallic trill on even pitch, trrreee or siirrrr.
NESTING Moss-lined twig nest in birch or conifer; 4–6 eggs; 1 brood; May–June.
FEEDING Eats insects in summer; eats some insects in winter, often caught in flight, but mostly berries such as rowan and hawthorn.
SIMILAR SPECIES Starling (p.158).

Robin
Robins remain in Britain all year round
and set up feeding territories, even in
winter. They are at their brightest, then,
and can look dull and faded by the end
of a busy summer rearing their families.

Dipper

Cinclus cinclus (Cinclidae)

The Dipper is quite unmistakable, thanks to its unique hunting technique. It feeds underwater, often by walking into a fast-flowing stream and foraging along the bottom. Out of the water it has a distinctive springy character, often bobbing and flicking its tail, and flies low and fast along watercourses.

HUNTS *aquatic prey in clean upland streams, moving to lowland rivers and even coasts in hard winters.*

- deep brown head
- blackish back
- greyer body
- plump body
- stout dark bill
- bold white chest
- chestnut band
- blackish tail
- stout black legs
- big feet

VOICE *Call sharp dzit or djink; song loud, rich warbling with explosive, grating notes.*
NESTING *Nest of moss and grass in hole or under overhang; 4–6 eggs; 2 broods; April–July.*
FEEDING *Forages for aquatic insect larvae, small fish, crustaceans, and molluscs by walking into water, swimming and diving.*
SIMILAR SPECIES *Ring Ouzel (p.150).*

Wren

Troglodytes troglodytes (Troglodytidae)

A tiny, plump, finely-barred bird with a surprisingly loud voice, the Wren has a habit of raising its very short tail vertically. It also has a distinctive flight: fast and direct, often plunging straight into dense cover. Wren populations decline in cold winters, but usually recover quite quickly.

SINGS *from exposed perches; seen foraging at low level in woods and thickets.*

- very slightly downcurved, fine bill
- pale stripe over eye
- dark barring
- short, rounded tail
- rusty-brown above with barred wings
- faint bars
- strong legs and feet

VOICE *Hard, rattling chit, chiti, tzerr; song amazingly loud, fast, warbling with low trill.*
NESTING *Small, loose ball of leaves and grass in bank; 5–6 eggs; 2 broods; April–July.*
FEEDING *Forages for insects under hedges, in ditches, and other dark, damp places.*
SIMILAR SPECIES *Dunnock (below), Robin (right).*

Dunnock

Prunella modularis (Prunellidae)

Although it is one of many small, streaky, sparrow-like birds, the Dunnock has a fine bill, grey head and breast, and forages on the ground with a distinctive, jerky, creeping shuffle. If disturbed, it generally flies at ground level into the nearest thick bush.

FORAGES *for food in low, dense scrub and bushes, on heaths and moors, and in forests, woods, parks, and gardens.*

- red-brown eyes
- fine, dark bill
- grey throat
- row of pale spots on wings
- browner head
- rich brown with black streaks
- orange-brown legs
- black-streaked brown wings and back

VOICE *Loud, high, penetrating pseep, vibrant teee; song high, fast warble.*
NESTING *Small grassy cup lined with moss, hair, in bush; 4–5 eggs; 2–3 broods; April–July.*
FEEDING *Picks small insects and seeds from ground, shuffling under and around bushes.*
SIMILAR SPECIES *Robin (right), Wren (above), House Sparrow (p.158).*

Robin

Erithacus rubecula (Turdidae)

The round-bodied, slim-tailed Robin is a shy, skulking woodland bird over most of its range. It is adapted to animals such as wild boar and pigs, taking small invertebrates that the animals disturb from the ground. In the British Isles, it follows gardeners in a similar way, taking worms and grubs turned up by their spades. It is perhaps the easiest of all birds to become hand-tame, given a regular diet of mealworms or other grubs, which it finds irresistible. Nevertheless, nesting Robins remain secretive and shy, quick to desert their eggs if disturbed.

LIVES *in open forests and woods, on bushy heaths, and in parks and gardens with hedges and shrubs.*

NOTE

Robins have developed the habit of singing at night under artificial lights, both in suburban areas and alongside car parks and industrial sites.

- warm brown above
- white breast spot
- big black eye
- bluish grey on sides of neck and chest
- orange-red breast
- mottled brown body

VOICE *Sharp tik, quick tik-ik-ik-ik, high, thin seep; song rich, sweet, musical, varied warble.*
NESTING *Domed nest of leaves and grass in bank or bush; 4–6 eggs; 2 broods; April–August.*
FEEDING *Takes spiders, insects, worms, berries, and seeds, mostly from ground.*
SIMILAR SPECIES *Dunnock (left), Nightingale (below), Redstart (p.149).*

Nightingale

Luscinia megarhynchos (Turdidae)

Famous for the male's rich and varied song, the Nightingale can be frustratingly difficult to see. It skulks in thick vegetation, often close to the ground. With its almost anonymous, brown plumage, it resembles a large juvenile Robin (above) or a Garden Warbler (p.150), but it has a longer rufous-brown tail, conspicuous in flight.

SINGS *in thickets in overgrown gardens, bushy gullies, heaths, and coppiced woodland.*

- pale ring around large, dark eyes
- grey neck side
- plain brown wings
- rusty rump and tail
- warm brown back
- grey-buff below
- rufous tail
- spotted above
- rufous tail
- tail often raised
- bright rump

VOICE *Calls include low, mechanical, grating kerrr, loud, bright hweet; song brilliant, varied.*
NESTING *Small cup of leaves, lined with grass and hair, built in low bush; 4–5 eggs; 1 brood; May–June.*
FEEDING *Eats worms, beetles, and berries.*
SIMILAR SPECIES *Juvenile Robin (above), Garden Warbler (p.152), Redstart (p.149).*

Black Redstart

Phoenicurus ochruros (Turdidae)

LIVES on mountains and rocky coasts with cliffs and gorges, in quarries, on derelict industrial sites, and in old towns.

A bird of rocky slopes with scree and crags, or deep gorges, the Black Redstart also breeds in run-down industrial areas and towns, in old buildings with plenty of holes suitable for nesting. This preference makes it relatively easy to distinguish it from the brighter Redstart (below), which nearly always lives in woodland.

grey cap

dark rusty tail with darker centre ♂

blackish and sooty grey body

white panel on wings ♂☀

pale grey body ☀✿

red-brown on tail

browner head

mousy grey body ♀

VOICE Call hard rattling, short tsip, tucc-tucc, tititic; song warble with crackling trills.
NESTING Grassy nest in hole in building, cliff or rocks; 4–6 eggs; 2 broods; May–July.
FEEDING Leaps and flies after insects; seizes worms on ground; some berries and seeds.
SIMILAR SPECIES Redstart (below), Dunnock (p.148).

Redstart

Phoenicurus phoenicurus (Turdidae)

SEEN in open woodland with sparse undergrowth. Migrants seen near coasts or lakes.

A male Redstart is an extremely handsome bird in spring and summer, best located in its breeding wood by its short, sweet song. The female, less distinctive, shares the male's habit of constantly flicking its rust-red tail up and down. They like old woods with open space beneath the canopy.

white forehead

rusty rump

orange-rufous below ♂☀

whitish mottling ♂✿

pale buff below ♀

bluish grey from crown to back ♂☀

pale rust-red tail with dark centre

VOICE Clear, rising wheet, sharp tac; song brief, musical warble, ending with weak trill.
NESTING Grassy nest lined with feathers or hair, in hole; 5–7 eggs; 1 brood; May–June.
FEEDING Forages in foliage or on ground for insects, spiders, small worms; some berries.
SIMILAR SPECIES Black Redstart (above), Robin (p.148), Nightingale (p.148).

Whinchat

Saxicola rubetra (Turdidae)

BREEDS in open places with heather, grass, and scattered taller stems of young trees; migrants are seen near coasts.

Although similar to the Stonechat (right) in appearance, the Whinchat has a pale stripe over its eye and is a summer visitor to Europe rather than a resident. It favours rough grassland, open heaths, and moors, and is declining in many areas as these habitats are eroded by intensive agriculture and urban development.

white stripe

white triangle on each side of tail ♀☀

dark streaked pale back

blackish cheeks

streaked cap ♂

pale throat

buff stripe

yellow-buff **1ST**✿

VOICE Loud, short tictic or wheet-tuc-tuc; song varied, sweet warble with hard notes.
NESTING Grassy nest low in tussock, bush, or on ground; 5–6 eggs; 1–2 broods; May–July.
FEEDING Drops to ground from perch for insects and worms; also seeds and berries.
SIMILAR SPECIES Wheatear (right), Stonechat (right), Sedge Warbler (p.151).

Stonechat

Saxicola torquata (Turdidae)

PERCHES prominently in open places with bushes and heather, on heaths, coasts, and moorland.

Small, chunky, and upright, the Stonechat is a bird of open, bushy terrain, such as gorse thickets above coastal cliffs. It likes to perch on the tops of bushes, where its scolding calls and the male's pied head-neck pattern make it conspicuous. It often darts down to snatch prey from the ground, flying back to its perch on whirring wings like a giant bumblebee.

white wing patch ♂☀

paler head

mottled chest ♀

black head and throat

paler head and throat

white neck patch

short dark tail

rust-red breast ♂☀

VOICE Hard, scolding tsak or tsak-tsak, sharp wheet; song rapid, chattery warble.
NESTING Grassy cup, often in grass with entrance tunnel; 5–6 eggs; 2 broods; May–July.
FEEDING Takes insects, spiders, worms and seeds from ground; also catches insects in air.
SIMILAR SPECIES Whinchat (left), Wheatear (below), Redstart (left).

Wheatear

Oenanthe oenanthe (Turdidae)

FOUND in mainly upland areas that combine boulders, scree, or cliffs with open grassland.

In summer, the Wheatear is a bird of open, rocky habitats, but it often turns up along coasts, on farmland, and even on golf courses while on migration. It has a distinctive habit of flying ahead of people, then perching before moving on again, flashing its white rump every time it moves. The Wheatear is less likely to be seen perched on a bush or tall stem than the Whinchat (left) or Stonechat (above), although it has a fondness for overhead wires. It avoids bushes and trees.

NOTE

The male and female Wheatear are easy to tell apart in spring, but in autumn, birds of both sexes, old and young, are much more alike.

bold black "T" ♀☀

small eye-patch

brownish above

white rump ♂☀

plumage like autumn adult ♀☀

white stripe above eye

pale grey crown

black patch through eye

buff below, fading to white

black legs ♂☀

VOICE Hard chak-chak, bright wheet-chak-chak; song rambling, scratchy warble, often given in fluttering songflight from ground or rock.
NESTING Grassy cup in hole in ground, stone wall, burrow; 5–6 eggs; 1–2 broods; April–July.
FEEDING Hops and runs after insects and spiders on open ground, especially on short grass; also leaps for flies.
SIMILAR SPECIES Whinchat (left), Stonechat (above).

Ring Ouzel

Turdus torquatus (Turdidae)

SEEN *mainly on high ground, on open moors with rocks, gullies, and eroded peat bogs. On coasts during migration.*

Typical of wild, open country, and declining where such places are invaded by weekend visitors, the Ring Ouzel resembles a slimmer, more upright Blackbird (below). It is often seen with its head up, tail cocked, and wings drooped, but it is a wary, elusive bird, quick to fly out of sight when disturbed.

dull breast-band
duller
white breast-band

♀

brown-black back
wings paler than body
pale wings ♂

sooty-black underside ♂

VOICE *Hard, rhythmic tak-tak-tak; song loud, wild repetition of short, musical, fluty phrases.*
NESTING *Loose cup of twigs and grass in hole or crevice; 5–6 eggs; 2 broods; April–June.*
FEEDING *Takes insects, worms, seeds, and fruit; eats many berries on migration.*
SIMILAR SPECIES *Blackbird (below). Dipper (p.148).*

Song Thrush

Turdus philomelos (Turdidae)

BREEDS *and feeds in broadleaved woodland, farmland with trees and hedges, parks and gardens with shrubs.*

Small, pale, and neatly spotted below, the Song Thrush is a familiar bird with a wonderfully vibrant, varied, full-throated song. Well known for its habit of smashing the shells of snails to extract their soft bodies, it also hauls many earthworms from their burrows. It is declining in many areas, particularly on farmland.

orange-buff underwings
pale eye-ring
plain olive-brown upperparts
plain wings

"V"-shaped brown spots

dark-spotted white belly

dark-spotted yellowish buff flanks

pale pinkish legs and feet

VOICE *Short, high stip; song exuberant repeated phrases of musical and harsh notes.*
NESTING *Grassy cup lined with mud in bush or tree; 3–5 eggs; 2–3 broods; March–July.*
FEEDING *Takes earthworms, snails, slugs, insects, berries, and fruit, mainly from ground.*
SIMILAR SPECIES *Mistle Thrush (below), Redwing (below), female Blackbird (left).*

Blackbird

Turdus merula (Turdidae)

LIVES *in woods with leaf litter, also parks and gardens, and farmland with tall hedges.*

A smart, plump thrush with a distinctive habit of raising its tail on landing, the Blackbird is a familiar garden bird. The glossy black male is easy to recognize, but the brown female can be confused with other thrushes despite her darker plumage. Males sing superbly, especially from high perches towards dusk.

yellow bill and eye-ring

paler wingtips

all-black body
dark bill
gingery body

dark brown legs

♂

dull black
♂ 1ST ❄

dark brown

mottled below

♀

VOICE *Low, soft chook, frequent pink-pink-pink, fast alarm rattle, high srreee; song superb, musical, varied, full-throated warbling.*
NESTING *Grass and mud cup in shrub or low in tree; 3–5 eggs; 2–4 broods; March–August.*
FEEDING *Finds worms, insects, and spiders on ground; fruit and berries in bushes.*
SIMILAR SPECIES *Ring Ouzel (above).*

Redwing

Turdus iliacus (Turdidae)

FOUND *on farmland with hedges and bushy heaths. Breeds in conifer and birch woods.*

A small, sociable thrush with a bold head pattern and well-defined streaks below, the Redwing is named for its distinctive rusty-red underwings and flanks. It is a winter visitor to much of Europe from the taiga forests of the far north, and typically forages in flocks for berries, often with Fieldfares (left). In hard winters, it often visits large gardens for food.

bold pale stripe over eye
dark cap
reddish underwing

dark brown back

pale stripe under dark cheeks
dull rust-red flanks

short, square tail

silvery white below, with dark streaks

NOTE

On calm, clear autumn nights, migrant Redwings can often be heard flying overhead, calling to each other to stay in contact.

VOICE *Flight call thin, high seeeh, also chuk, chittuk; song variable repetition of short phrases and chuckling notes.*
NESTING *Cup of grass and twigs, in low bush; 4–6 eggs; 2 broods; April–July.*
FEEDING *Worms, insects, and seeds taken from ground, berries in winter.*
SIMILAR SPECIES *Song Thrush (above).*

Fieldfare

Turdus pilaris (Turdidae)

FEEDS *on farmland, bushy heaths, shrubs, woods, orchards, and gardens in winter; breeds in woodland.*

A large, handsome thrush with a striking combination of plumage colours, the Fieldfare is usually identifiable by its blue-grey head and white underwing. It is a winter visitor to most of Europe, like the smaller Redwing (right), and the two often feed together in mixed flocks, stripping berries from fruiting trees and shrubs.

white underwings
blue-grey head with black mask
black and yellow bill

dark brown back

orange-buff breast with heavy black spots

pale grey rump

black tail

whiter flanks

dense black chevrons on white flanks

VOICE *Loud, chuckling chak-chak-chak, low, nasal weeip; song a rather unmusical mixture of squeaks, warbles, and whistles.*
NESTING *Cup of grass and twigs in bush or tree; 5–6 eggs; 1–2 broods; May–June.*
FEEDING *Mostly eats worms and insects on the ground; also fruit from trees and bushes.*
SIMILAR SPECIES *Mistle Thrush (right).*

Mistle Thrush

Turdus viscivorus (Turdidae)

LIVES *on farmland with tall trees, edges of moorland near forest, woodland clearings, orchards, and parks.*

Big, bold, and aggressive, the Mistle Thrush is the largest of the European thrushes. It has a tall, long-necked look compared to the Song Thrush (above), and often flies much higher when disturbed. Males often sing from the tops of tall trees in all weathers, and in winter single birds defend berry-laden trees against Fieldfares (left), Redwings (above), and other birds.

bold dark eye
slender neck
grey-brown back

white underwings
pale outer coverts
pale rump

whitish tail sides

bold black spots on creamy buff underside

pale head
pale spots

VOICE *Loud, rattling chatter, tsairrk-sairr-sairr-sairk; song repeated wild, fluty phrases.*
NESTING *Loose cup of twigs and grass high in tree; 3–5 eggs; 2 broods; March–June.*
FEEDING *Hops on ground, taking seeds and invertebrates; also eats berries and fruit.*
SIMILAR SPECIES *Song Thrush (above), Fieldfare (left), female Blackbird (left).*

Cetti's Warbler

Cettia cetti (Sylviidae)

Small, dark, and hard to see at any time, Cetti's Warbler usually stays well out of sight in thick cover. Yet it is often easy to detect because of its frequent, loud, abrupt outbursts of song. It often moves on between phrases, so actually locating the singer is no easy task – it seems to be always one step ahead.

SKULKS *in dense, damp thickets near rivers, ditches, and reedbeds, and often near extensive marshes.*

thin pale stripe

grey face

pale grey below

rounded tail

dark red-brown above

dark red-brown tail

short, round, rust-brown wings

VOICE *Explosive chich or plit; song loud chee! chewee! chewechewechewewe!*
NESTING *Deep cup of grass and leaves in dense cover; 3–5 eggs; 1–2 broods; April–June.*
FEEDING *Takes insects, spiders, snails, and some seeds from near ground in dense cover.*
SIMILAR SPECIES *Nightingale (p.148), Reed Warbler (right), Sedge Warbler (below).*

Marsh Warbler

Acrocephalus palustris (Sylviidae)

Although it has rather duller plumage than the Reed Warbler (below), and a more rounded form, the Marsh Warbler is very difficult to distinguish until it starts to sing. Then it produces a gloriously musical stream of sweet warbles, whistles, and trills, coupled with fluent mimicry of many European and African birds.

FAVOURS *thick wetland vegetation such as sedges, willowherb, umbellifers, nettles, and shrubs, with or without reeds.*

squarish, dark tail

plain back

yellowish white underside

whitish eye-ring

pale legs

VOICE *Call hard chek; song fluent, fast, with twangy, nasal notes, and much mimicry.*
NESTING *Grass cup suspended in cover by "jug handles"; 4–5 eggs; 1 brood; June–July.*
FEEDING *Forages in dense cover for insects and spiders; also takes some berries.*
SIMILAR SPECIES *Reed Warbler (below), Sedge Warbler (left).*

Grasshopper Warbler

Locustella naevia (Sylviidae)

This skulking, secretive warbler spends much of its time in thick undergrowth, creeping like a mouse in search of food. It is rarely seen more than briefly as it darts from a low bush and dives back into cover. But its strange song is unmistakable: a metallic ticking like a fishing reel, usually heard at dusk or on warm, sultry summer days.

finely streaked crown and cheek

CALLS *from perches in marshy, grassy areas, low thickets, heaths, and thorn scrub with tangled low growth.*

spotted or streaked olive-brown back

buff below

blunt wings

long, broad tail

rounded tail

VOICE *Call loud, piercing psit; song fast, mechanical, reeling sirrrrrrrrrrrrrrrrrrrrr.*
NESTING *Small nest of grass and leaves in low vegetation; 5–6 eggs; 2 broods; May–July.*
FEEDING *Small insects and spiders, taken from very low, thick vegetation.*
SIMILAR SPECIES *Sedge Warbler (below), Reed Warbler (right), Dunnock (p.148).*

Reed Warbler

Acrocephalus scirpaceus (Sylviidae)

Although it occasionally nests in willows growing over water, the Reed Warbler is basically a reedbed specialist, adept at grasping vertical stems and shuffling through the dense reeds in search of food. Very like the slightly plumper Marsh Warbler (above), it is best identified by its repetitive, conversational song.

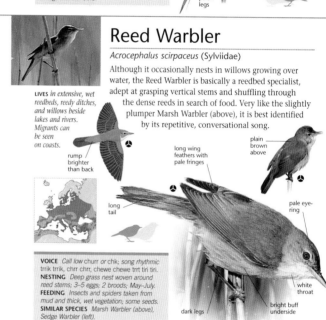

LIVES *in extensive, wet reedbeds, reedy ditches, and willows beside lakes and rivers. Migrants can be seen on coasts.*

rump brighter than back

long tail

long wing feathers with pale fringes

plain brown above

pale eye-ring

white throat

bright buff underside

dark legs

VOICE *Call low churr or chk; song rhythmic trrik trrik, chrr chrr, chewe chewe trrt tiri tiri.*
NESTING *Deep grass nest woven around reed stems; 3–5 eggs; 2 broods; May–July.*
FEEDING *Insects and spiders taken from mud and thick, wet vegetation; some seeds.*
SIMILAR SPECIES *Marsh Warbler (above), Sedge Warbler (left).*

Sedge Warbler

Acrocephalus schoenobaenus (Sylviidae)

A small, well-marked, active bird with a loud, fast, varied song, the Sedge Warbler is common in waterside and boggy habitats. It often occurs among reeds, but not always, for it prefers to forage among a variety of vegetation that may include willow and hawthorn scrub, and hedges beside wet ditches.

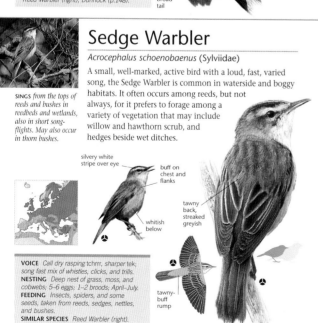

SINGS *from the tops of reeds and bushes in reedbeds and wetlands, also in short song-flights. May also occur in thorn bushes.*

silvery white stripe over eye

buff on chest and flanks

whitish below

tawny back, streaked greyish

tawny-buff rump

VOICE *Call dry rasping tchrrr, sharper tek; song fast mix of whistles, clicks, and trills.*
NESTING *Deep nest of grass, moss, and cobwebs; 5–6 eggs; 1–2 broods; April–July.*
FEEDING *Insects, spiders, and some seeds, taken from reeds, sedges, nettles, and bushes.*
SIMILAR SPECIES *Reed Warbler (right).*

Dartford Warbler

Sylvia undata (Sylviidae)

A skulking, secretive bird of warm heaths and sunny slopes, the Dartford Warbler is often hard to see clearly as it flicks from one bush to another and slips from sight. But in warm, still weather it may perch in full view, when it is easy to recognize. A year-round resident, it can suffer declines in hard winters.

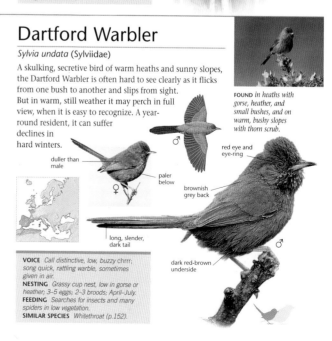

FOUND *in heaths with gorse, heather, and small bushes, and on warm, bushy slopes with thorn scrub.*

♂

duller than male

♀

paler below

red eye and eye-ring

brownish grey back

long, slender, dark tail

dark red-brown underside

♂

VOICE *Call distinctive, low, buzzy chrrr; song quick, rattling warble, sometimes given in air.*
NESTING *Grassy cup nest, low in gorse or heather; 3–5 eggs; 2–3 broods; April–July.*
FEEDING *Searches for insects and many spiders in low vegetation.*
SIMILAR SPECIES *Whitethroat (p.152).*

Lesser Whitethroat

Sylvia curruca (Sylviidae)

Smaller and neater than the Whitethroat (below), with a dark eye-patch and darker legs, the Lesser Whitethroat is a secretive warbler of woodland edges and hedgerows. Although easy to locate by its song, it often moves to a new perch. In autumn, it can be easy to find feeding on shrubs and trees with berries.

LIVES *in tall, dense thickets at the edges of woods, patches of scrub, and old, thick, overgrown hedgerows.*

grey cap

white eye-ring

slim tail, edged white

dark eye-patch

dull grey-brown back

plain brown wings

whitish underside, washed pink

dark grey legs

♂

white throat

head paler in spring

♀

VOICE *Sharp metallic tak, thin chi; song a rattling, wooden chikachikachikachikachika.*
NESTING *Cup of twigs or grass built in shrub; 4–6 eggs; 1 brood; May–June.*
FEEDING *Picks insects from foliage; also eats many berries in late summer.*
SIMILAR SPECIES *Whitethroat (below), Blackcap (right).*

Blackcap

Sylvia atricapilla (Sylviidae)

The Blackcap is a stocky warbler with a typical, hard, unmusical call. Its song, however, is beautiful, rich, and full-throated, less even than the similar song of the Garden Warbler (left). It may overwinter in northwest Europe, when it visits gardens to take seeds and scraps, often driving other birds away from feeders.

SINGS *brilliantly from perches in woods, parks, and large bushy gardens, with plenty of thick undergrowth.*

small, narrow black cap

grey-brown back

grey face and throat

pale grey below

♂

plain greyish wings and tail

brown cap

browner than male

♀

VOICE *Short, hard tac; song brilliant, fast, clear warbling, growing faster and louder.*
NESTING *Small cup of grass and stems in bush; 4–5 eggs; 2 broods; April–July.*
FEEDING *Takes insects from foliage; also eats soft, fleshy berries, especially elder.*
SIMILAR SPECIES *Marsh Tit (p.154), Garden Warbler (left).*

Whitethroat

Sylvia communis (Sylviidae)

Typically a bird of open spaces with low bushes and scrub, the Whitethroat often skulks in low, thick vegetation. It gives itself away by its irritable calls, and often emerges to scold intruders. It sings quite often, sometimes from a low perch or a high wire, but also during a short, bouncing song-flight.

SINGS *from perches in bushy, dry, and heathy places with low thorny scrub; also thickets, hedges, dense herbs.*

blue-grey head

broken whitish eye-ring

♂

long dark tail, edged white

pale below, washed pink

pale legs

orange-brown wing panel

♂

very bright wing panel

brown head

♀

VOICE *Harsh tcharr, scolding churr, musical wheet-a-wheet-a-whit; song a chattery warble.*
NESTING *Small, neat cup of stems low in thorny shrub; 4–5 eggs; 2 broods; April–July.*
FEEDING *Picks insects from foliage; takes many berries and some seeds in autumn.*
SIMILAR SPECIES *Lesser Whitethroat (above), Dartford Warbler (p.149).*

Wood Warbler

Phylloscopus sibilatrix (Sylviidae)

One of the biggest of the *Phylloscopus* warblers, the Wood Warbler is also the brightest, with areas of pure lemon-yellow and clear green in its plumage. It feeds quietly, high in the foliage of mature deciduous trees, and can be hard to spot. In early summer, the male is best located by his metallic, trilling song, delivered with such force that the bird's entire body vibrates with the effort.

TRILLS *ecstatically from branches in mature broadleaved woods with open ground beneath the canopy.*

long, broad yellow stripe over eye

clear green upperside

long wings

pale sulphur-yellow chin and upper breast

silky white underside

VOICE *Call loud song low, sweet sioo sioo sioo, or sharp ticking, accelerating into silvery trill, ti-ti-ti-ti-ti-tik-ik-ikrrrrrrrrrr.*
NESTING *Domed grassy nest in dead leaves on ground; 6–7 eggs; 1 brood; May–June.*
FEEDING *Insects and spiders, from foliage.*
SIMILAR SPECIES *Willow Warbler (p.153), Chiffchaff (below).*

Garden Warbler

Sylvia borin (Sylviidae)

This short-billed, round-faced warbler has no obvious patterning and few distinctive features apart from its song, which is a beautiful outpouring of mellow warbling notes. Normally solitary, it may join other warblers to feed on berries in late summer to fuel its migration. Despite its name, it rarely visits gardens unless they are large and overgrown, or to feed when on migration.

BREEDS *and feeds in open woods, wooded parkland, tall thickets, shrubs, and trees.*

dull, pale wings

grey neck patch

thin, pale eye-ring

large, dark eyes

pale buff-brown above

pale feather edges, sharper on juvenile

pale buff underside

VOICE *Call thick, soft tchak, churrr; song rich, throaty, musical, fast warbling.*
NESTING *Shallow, skimpy cup of grass and moss in bush; 4–5 eggs; 1 brood; May–July.*
FEEDING *Takes insects and spiders from foliage, berries and seeds in autumn.*
SIMILAR SPECIES *Blackcap (right), Reed Warbler (p.151), Spotted Flycatcher (p.154).*

Chiffchaff

Phylloscopus collybita (Sylviidae)

By sight the Chiffchaff is almost impossible to distinguish from the Willow Warbler (p.153), although the slightly plumper Chiffchaff's habit of dipping its tail downward is a useful clue. When it sings, it betrays its identity by repeating its name over and over again – and luckily it sings a lot, particularly in spring. Some Chiffchaffs spend the winter in western Europe, unlike Willow Warblers.

REPEATS *its name from perches in woodland, parks, bushy areas, and large gardens; favours taller trees in summer.*

short, round wings

rounder head than Willow Warbler's

white crescent under eye

dips tail while feeding

blackish legs

olive body

VOICE *Call slurred, sweet hweet; song easy, bright chip-chap-chip-chap-chip-chup-chip.*
NESTING *Domed grass nest, low in bush or undergrowth; 5–6 eggs; 1–2 broods; April–July.*
FEEDING *Takes insects and spiders from leaves, slipping easily through foliage.*
SIMILAR SPECIES *Willow Warbler (p.153), Wood Warbler (above).*

Willow Warbler

Phylloscopus trochilus (Sylviidae)

The most common and widespread of the leaf warblers, this small, slim bird closely resembles the Chiffchaff (p.150). It is most easily recognized by the simple, yet wonderfully evocative song that heralds its arrival in the north in spring. It usually feeds alone, slipping easily through foliage as it searches for insects and other prey.

SINGS *with beautiful fluid cadence in light woodland, scrub, and thickets, especially of birch and willow.*

pale stripe over eye

flatter head than Chiffchaff's

yellow stripe over eye

grey-green to olive above

greener back

buff-white to pale yellow underside

plain, round wings

pale yellow-brown legs

VOICE *Sweet, simple, double hoo-eet call; cascading, trilling song, fading with a flourish.*
NESTING *Domed nest of grass, near ground in thick cover; 6–7 eggs; 1 brood; April–May.*
FEEDING *Picks insects and spiders from foliage; catches some flies in air.*
SIMILAR SPECIES *Chiffchaff (p.152), Wood Warbler (p.152).*

Barred Warbler

Sylvia nisoria (Sylviidae)

One of the larger warblers, the Barred Warbler can resemble the quite unrelated Wryneck (p.142), with its heavily barred underside and rather severe expression. It has a clumsy, rather aggressive character, but tends to skulk in thick cover, where it is hard to watch.

BREEDS *in woodland clearings and bushy places. Rare migrants, mainly in autumn, visit coastal thickets.*

mid-grey above

dark eyes

bright yellow eyes

white below with close grey bars

dull whitish below

1ST❄

♂

white wing-bars

long tail with white corners

♀

VOICE *Loud, dry, hard rattle, trrr-r-r-rt; song long, bright, musical warble.*
NESTING *Substantial nest in thorny bush or scrub; 4–5 eggs; 1 brood; May–July.*
FEEDING *Takes insects and spiders from foliage; tugs at berries.*
SIMILAR SPECIES *Wryneck (p.142), Garden Warbler (p.152), female Blackcap (p.152).*

Melodious Warbler

Hippolais polyglotta (Sylviidae)

FOUND *in open woods, scrub, and orchards. Spring and autumn migrants feed on coasts.*

The western counterpart of the very similar, but more eastern, Icterine Warbler (below), the Melodious Warbler has a slightly rounder head, plainer wings, and weaker, more fluttering flight. More skulking in its habits, it also has a less melodious song, despite its name. Both species appear on Britain's coasts on migration, where they can be hard to tell apart.

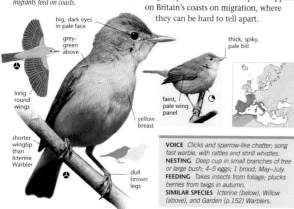

big, dark eyes in pale face

grey-green above

thick, spiky, pale bill

long round wings

faint, pale wing panel

yellow breast

shorter wingtip than Icterine Warbler

dull brown legs

VOICE *Clicks and sparrow-like chatter; song fast warble, with rattles and shrill whistles.*
NESTING *Deep cup in small branches of tree or large bush; 4–5 eggs; 1 brood; May–July.*
FEEDING *Takes insects from foliage; plucks berries from twigs in autumn.*
SIMILAR SPECIES *Icterine (below), Willow (above), and Garden (p.152) Warblers.*

Goldcrest

Regulus regulus (Sylviidae)

Britain's smallest bird, the agile, busy Goldcrest frequently forages very close to people, apparently oblivious of their presence. This needle-billed, round-bodied bird often gives its high-pitched calls as it searches restlessly for food. It has a plainer face than its close relative, the Firecrest (below).

FEEDS *in coniferous and mixed woodland, thickets, and large gardens, throughout the year.*

olive-green back

broad white "V"

blackish wings

yellow inner stripe on black crown

buff below

VOICE *High, sibilant see-see-see call; high, fast song, seedli-ee seedli-ee seedli-ee.*
NESTING *Cup of cobwebs and moss, slung from branch; 7–8 eggs; 2 broods; April–July.*
FEEDING *Picks tiny insects, spiders, and insect eggs from foliage, often hovering briefly.*
SIMILAR SPECIES *Firecrest (below), Willow Warbler (left), Chiffchaff (p.152).*

Icterine Warbler

Hippolais icterina (Sylviidae)

LIVES *in deciduous, coniferous, or mixed open woodland. Also coasts on spring and autumn migration.*

Larger than the confusingly similar Melodious Warbler (above), with which it often occurs during migration, the square-tailed, spike-billed Icterine Warbler has a flatter forehead, slightly peaked crown, longer wingtips, and a more obvious pale wing panel. Less secretive than the Melodious Warbler, it is much more likely to perch in full view.

flat forehead

long, square tail

pale grey-green above

orange-pink bill with dark ridge

long wingtips

whitish below; pale yellow in spring adult

pale wing panel

dull grey legs

VOICE *Call melodious dideroi, hard tik; song prolonged warbling incorporating dideroi call.*
NESTING *Deep cup suspended from forked tree branch; 4–5 eggs; 1 brood; May–August.*
FEEDING *Takes insects from foliage; pulls berries from twigs with tug of bill.*
SIMILAR SPECIES *Melodious Warbler (above), Willow Warbler (above), Reed Warbler (p.151).*

Firecrest

Regulus ignicapillus (Sylviidae)

Less widespread than the similar Goldcrest (above), but more common in mainland Europe, the Firecrest is brighter and more boldly patterned at close range. Its slightly stronger calls and less rhythmic song are useful identification features, especially when the bird is seen in silhouette at the top of a tall conifer tree.

NESTS *in conifer trees such as spruce, but also breeds in mixed and deciduous woods. Less tied to conifers than Goldcrest.*

orange crown stripe

white stripe

bright green above

dark wings with pale bars

"V" shaped white wingbar

bronze-yellow neck

whitish below

VOICE *High zeet call; song a sharp, quick, accelerating zi zi zi zezezeeeee.*
NESTING *Moss and lichen cup beneath branch; 7–11 eggs; 2 broods; April–July.*
FEEDING *Takes insects and spiders from foliage, often while hovering.*
SIMILAR SPECIES *Goldcrest (above), Chiffchaff (p.152).*

Spotted Flycatcher

Muscicapa striata (Muscicapidae)

Sharp-eyed and constantly alert, the Spotted Flycatcher specializes in targeting flying insects from a vantage point on an open perch. Launching itself with a burst of rapid wingbeats, it seizes its quarry in mid-air and usually returns to the same perch: a technique that makes it quite distinctive despite its unremarkable grey-brown plumage.

HUNTS *flying insects from perches in open woodland, parkland, and gardens with bushes and trees.*

streaked head

long, narrow wings

spotted crown

cream spots on back

soft brown streaks on breast

silvery white below

long brown tail held downwards

VOICE *Short, scratchy tzic or tzee, tzee-tsuk tsuk; song short, scratchy, weak warble.*
NESTING *Cup of grass, leaves, moss in vine or cavity; 3–5 eggs; 1–2 broods; June–August.*
FEEDING *Catches insects in air, sallying from perch and usually returning to same perch.*
SIMILAR SPECIES *Garden Warbler (p.152), female Pied Flycatcher (below).*

Long-tailed Tit

Aegithalos caudatus (Aegithalidae)

The tiny rounded body and slender tail of the Long-tailed Tit give it a ball-and-stick shape that is quite unique among British birds. In summer, family parties move noisily through bushes and undergrowth, but in winter they often travel through woodland in much larger groups, crossing gaps between the trees, one or two at a time.

LIVES *in deciduous or mixed woods with bushy undergrowth; also scrub. Increasingly visits garden feeders.*

pink shoulders

long, black, white-sided tail

black and pink back

black band on white head

black and white plumage

dark wings

dull white below

VOICE *High, thin, colourless seee seee seee; short, abrupt, low trrp or zerrp.*
NESTING *Rounded nest of lichen, moss, cobwebs, and feathers with side entrance, in low bush; 8–12 eggs; 1 brood; April–June.*
FEEDING *Tiny insects and spiders taken from twigs and foliage; some seeds.*
SIMILAR SPECIES *None.*

Pied Flycatcher

Ficedula hypoleuca (Muscicapidae)

A breeding male Pied Flycatcher is boldly pied and hard to mistake as he dashes out from a forest perch to seize flying insects on the wing. After the autumn moult, males resemble the browner females, but the white wing and tail patches are distinctive in both.

PREFERS *to breed in nest boxes, in mature broadleaved woodland, with clear air beneath canopy for hunting.*

one or two white spots on forehead

black tail with white sides

black and white plumage

♂☼

bold white patch

black wings

♂☼

white patch

dull brown and white

♀

VOICE *Sharp whit or whit-ic; song musical see, see, see sit, see-sit sitip-seweee.*
NESTING *Cup of leaves and moss in a hole or nest box; 5–9 eggs; 1 brood; April–May.*
FEEDING *Catches flies in air, picks insects from foliage and from ground; also eats seeds and berries.*
SIMILAR SPECIES *Spotted Flycatcher (above).*

Marsh Tit

Poecile palustris (Paridae)

Virtually identical to the Willow Tit (below) in its appearance, the slightly slimmer, neater Marsh Tit is most easily identified by its distinctive *pit-chew* call. Despite its name, it is not found in marshes, but prefers mature broadleaved woodland where it often feeds at low level among thick undergrowth.

FORAGES *among tall deciduous trees in woodland and parks, especially beech and oak; also in gardens.*

glossy black cap and back of neck

black bib, smaller than Willow Tit's

neck slimmer than Willow Tit's

pale grey-buff underside

neat, plain grey-brown upperparts

rounded grey-brown wings

VOICE *Bright pit-chew! and titi-zee-zee-zee; song rippling schip-schip-schip-schip.*
NESTING *Grass and moss cup in pre-existing tree hole; 6–8 eggs; 1 brood; April–June.*
FEEDING *Mostly insects and spiders in summer; seeds, berries, and nuts in winter.*
SIMILAR SPECIES *Willow Tit (below), Coal Tit (p.155), Blackcap (p.152).*

Bearded Tit

Panurus biarmicus (Timaliidae)

The tawny, long-tailed Bearded Tit lives almost exclusively in large reedbeds, although in winter it may briefly occupy tall grasses or reedmace when forced to move on by overcrowding. On windy days it stays out of sight, but in calm weather it can sometimes be located by its loud "pinging" call.

INHABITS *reedbeds, where it breeds and finds most of its food. Sometimes found in nearby tall vegetation.*

bright blue-grey head

tawny, cream, and black above

pale brown head

big black "moustache"

♂

round wings

♀

pale tawny underside

♂

black back

long tail

VOICE *Metallic psching, pink, or ping.*
NESTING *Deep cup of leaves, stems, and reed flowers, low down in reeds standing in water; 5–7 eggs; 2–3 broods; April–August.*
FEEDING *Caterpillars and reed seeds, taken from among reeds.*
SIMILAR SPECIES *Long-tailed Tit (right), Reed Warbler (p.151).*

Willow Tit

Poecile montana (Paridae)

More untidy-looking than the very similar Marsh Tit (above), with a bigger-headed, bull-necked appearance, the Willow Tit lives in a wider variety of habitats with fewer mature trees. It is not particularly attracted to willows, but may feed in damp willow woodland on peat bogs. Its frequent, low, harsh, buzzy calls are quite distinctive, and are the best way of distinguishing it from the Marsh Tit.

SEEN *in a wide variety of woodland, thickets, and hedgerows. Often visits gardens to raid hanging feeders.*

black bib, slightly larger than Marsh Tit's

big, dull black cap

bull-necked appearance

pale wing panel

plain brown rounded wings

orange-buff flanks

dull grey-buff below

VOICE *Thin zi zi and buzzing airr airr airr; song commonly full, piping tyoo tyoo tyoo.*
NESTING *Digs own hole in rotten tree stump; 6–9 eggs; 1 brood; April–June.*
FEEDING *Mainly insects and spiders in summer; seeds, berries, and nuts in winter.*
SIMILAR SPECIES *Marsh Tit (above), Coal Tit (p.155), Blackcap (p.152).*

Crested Tit

Lophophanes cristatus (Paridae)

The jaunty crest of this species makes it unique among British tits, aiding identification if one has a clear view of its head. But it often feeds high in pine trees, where it is best located by its stuttering call. In Britain it is restricted to northern Scotland, mainly in ancient forests of Scots pine.

FEEDS *and breeds in mature pine forests, but may occur in mixed or deciduous woods in parts of mainland Europe.*

mottled black and white crest

brown tail

warm brown back

brown wings

white face with black cheek edge

plain wings

black bib

VOICE *Quick, low, stuttering trill, b'd-rrr-rup; also thin, high zit or zee typical of tits.*
NESTING *Cup of moss and hair in decaying tree stump; 5–7 eggs; 1 brood, April–June.*
FEEDING *Small insects and spiders; seeds in winter, many from stores made in spring.*
SIMILAR SPECIES *Coal Tit (below), Marsh Tit (p.154), Willow Tit (p.154).*

Great Tit

Parus major (Paridae)

The bold, even aggressive Great Tit is one of the most familiar garden and woodland birds. Its calls can be confusing, but it is easily identified by the broad black stripe on its yellow breast. Less agile than the smaller tits, it feeds on the ground more often.

BREEDS *and feeds in wide variety of mixed woodland, as well as parks and gardens. Often uses nest boxes.*

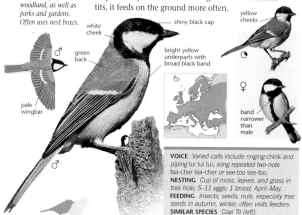

white cheek

green back

pale wingbar

shiny black cap

bright yellow underparts with broad black band

yellow cheeks

band narrower than male

VOICE *Varied calls include ringing chink and piping tui tui; song repeated two-note tea-cher tea-cher or see-too see-too.*
NESTING *Cup of moss, leaves, and grass in tree hole; 5–11 eggs; 1 brood; April–May.*
FEEDING *Insects, seeds, nuts, especially tree seeds in autumn, winter; often visits feeders.*
SIMILAR SPECIES *Coal Tit (left).*

Coal Tit

Periparus ater (Paridae)

Although often seen in gardens, the diminutive white-naped Coal Tit is typically a bird of conifer trees, where it makes the most of its minute weight by searching the thinnest twigs for food. Active and fearless, it often joins up with other species of tits in autumn and winter, roaming through woodlands and gardens in large, loose, mixed flocks.

FORAGES *among pines and other conifer trees, but also feeds in low shrubbery and visits garden bird feeders.*

yellower cheek

black head

white nape patch

greyish back

black bib

white cheek

dark wings with two white bars

bright buff underside

VOICE *Call high, sweet tseu, thin tsee, bright psuet; song quick wi-choo wi-choo wi-choo.*
NESTING *Cup of moss and leaves in hole in tree or wall; 7–11 eggs; 1 brood; April–June.*
FEEDING *Takes tiny insects and spiders from foliage; also seeds and nuts; visits feeders.*
SIMILAR SPECIES *Marsh Tit (p.154), Willow Tit (p.154), Great Tit (right).*

Nuthatch

Sitta europaea (Sittidae)

Identified by its blue-grey and buff plumage and oddly top-heavy look, the Nuthatch is an agile climber that (unlike other birds) often descends trees head-first, as well as climbing upwards. It wedges nuts and seeds in bark so it can crack them open, with loud blows of its long, grey, chisel-like bill.

FOUND *high in trees and on the ground in deciduous and mixed woodland, parkland, and large gardens, all year round.*

broad blue-grey wings

acrobatic pose

black stripe

dagger-like grey bill

buff below, with rusty flanks

strong feet for clinging to bark

short tail

VOICE *Loud, liquid whistles, pew pew pew, chwee chwee; fast ringing trills, loud chwit.*
NESTING *Typically plasters mud around old woodpecker hole lined with bark and leaves; 6–9 eggs; 1 brood; April–July.*
FEEDING *Variety of seeds, berries, and nuts, often wedged in bark for easy cracking.*
SIMILAR SPECIES *None.*

Blue Tit

Cyanistes caeruleus (Paridae)

Colourful, tame, and noisy, the Blue Tit is mainly yellow and greenish as well as blue. It is a common visitor to bird feeders where its acrobatic skills make it a favourite garden bird. Its black-and-white face pattern is distinctive. A thin, dark central streak often shows on its yellow underside.

VISITS *gardens to feed from nut baskets and other feeders. Lives in woods of all kinds, as well as parks, gardens, and bushy places.*

bright blue cap

white bars on blue wings

blue tail

yellow below

greenish cap

less blue

VOICE *Thin, quick tsee-tsee-tsee, scolding churrrr; song trilled tsee-tsee-tsee-tsisisisisisi.*
NESTING *Small cup of moss and hair in tree hole/nest box; 7–16 eggs; 1 brood; April–May.*
FEEDING *Mainly seeds, nuts, insects, and spiders; often visits garden feeders.*
SIMILAR SPECIES *Coal Tit (above), Great Tit (right), Goldcrest (p.153).*

Treecreeper

Certhia familiaris (Certhiidae)

The slender-billed Treecreeper searches for insect prey by shuffling up the trunks and branches of trees like a mouse, clinging to the bark with its strong toes and propped up on its stiff tail. It usually spirals up one tree, then flies down and lands near the bottom of another to start its next search. This habit makes it easy to identify, even in silhouette.

PROBES *bark of trees in mixed, deciduous, or coniferous woods. Also occurs in tall hedges, parks, and gardens with mature trees.*

fine, curved bill

white stripe over eye

silky white underside

rounded wings

mottled brown back

pale wingbars

pale feather shafts on notched brown tail

VOICE *Call thin, high seee and more vibrant sreee; song high, musical series of tsee notes ending in falling trill with final flourish.*
NESTING *Untidy nest behind loose bark or ivy; 5–6 eggs; 1 brood; April–June.*
FEEDING *Takes insects and spiders from bark, probing with bill while shuffling up trees.*
SIMILAR SPECIES *None.*

BIRDS

Red-backed Shrike

Lanius collurio (Laniidae)

A small, slim bird with a long tail and a sturdy bill, this Shrike hunts prey by scanning from a perch. Males are striking, with a grey top to the head, a black mask, and chestnut back; females are browner and duller. A casualty of intensive farming, it is now scarcer over much of its range.

black mask

grey crown and nape

white throat

dark patch behind eye

duller back

rusty brown back and forewings

grey rump

♀

rufous tail

black tail with white sides

greyish brown rump

♀ slight scaly barring

HUNTS and breeds on farmland and rough grassland with plenty of hedges, thorn bushes, and scrub.

pale pink below

♂

VOICE Call harsh hek, hard chek; song low, rambling, with jerky warbling and mimicry.
NESTING Untidy nest of grass, feathers, and moss in bush; 5–6 eggs; 1 brood; May–June.
FEEDING Drops from perch to seize insects and small lizards or rodents on ground.
SIMILAR SPECIES Nightingale (p.148), Linnet (p.160).

Great Grey Shrike

Lanius excubitor (Laniidae)

The largest of the European shrikes, the Great Grey Shrike is a powerful, long-tailed, relatively short-winged bird with a black "bandit" mask. It has a sturdy, sharply hooked bill that it uses to tear apart small animals, from beetles to lizards and small birds. It hunts in the classic shrike manner, watching from a high point and swooping down to seize its victims in its powerful feet. It then carries them back to its perch and may impale them on long thorns or barbed wire for easy dismemberment, a habit that earned it (and its relatives) the old name of "butcher bird". It also chases small birds in flight like a sparrowhawk (p.123), using ambush tactics to take them by surprise. During harsh winter weather, birds may form a large proportion of its diet.

PERCHES on high vantage points on bushy, heathy, or boggy ground in winter. Breeds in birch woods, wooded bogs, and arid Mediterranean scrub.

broad black band through eye

bold white bar on black wings

cold grey above; scaly barring on back and flanks of juvenile

long black tail with white sides

black wings with white patch

wingtips do not reach base of tail

dull white underside; faintly barred on juvenile

♂

long tail

slightly duller than male

slight barring on flanks

♀

NOTE
Some Great Grey Shrikes that breed in northern Europe migrate west in autumn to spend the winter in Britain. Here they occupy large feeding territories where they are often difficult to find, but can sometimes be seen at great distances as conspicuous white dots on bare bush tops. A closer view reveals the bird's black mask and its long tail, which it often flicks and sways to keep its balance.

VOICE Call dry trill and various short, hard notes; song composed of short, simple, squeaky notes.
NESTING Roughly-built grassy nest in thick bush; 5–7 eggs; 1 brood; May–July.
FEEDING Swoops onto small rodents, small birds, lizards, and large insects (especially beetles), after watching from vantage point such as a bush top.
SIMILAR SPECIES Magpie (right).

Jay

Garrulus glandarius (Corvidae)

Noisy but shy, the Jay often keeps to thick cover and beats a swift retreat if disturbed, flying off with a flash of its bold white rump. It has a curious habit of allowing ants to run over its plumage, probably to employ the ants' chemical defences against parasites. In town parks, it may become a little less elusive, and can be seen feeding on the ground, using long, bouncing or leaping hops. In gardens, it can even be bold enough to visit bird feeders, hanging on clumsily while taking peanuts, pieces of cheese, or lumps of fatball. However, it remains wary and unapproachable even here.

BREEDS in woodland and parks, especially with oak trees, and visits gardens.

moustache thick and black

pinkish grey body

barred blue wing panel

white rump

white patch on black wings

white under tail

black tail

pale legs

raised crest

"anting" posture

NOTE
The Jay's association with acorns is remarkable. With great industry, it gathers and buries hundreds of acorns every year in autumn. It remembers where most of them are and digs them out to eat late in the winter or spring, when other food is scarce. The Jay even feeds sprouting acorns to its chicks in spring if other food is in short supply.

VOICE Nasal, mewing pee-oo, short bark; loud, harsh, cloth-tearing skairk!
NESTING Bulky stick nest, low in dense bush; 4–5 eggs; 1 brood; April–June.
FEEDING Takes a variety of foods, ranging from caterpillars to small rodents; eats mainly insects in summer, with some eggs and nestlings; stores acorns in autumn for use in winter.
SIMILAR SPECIES Mistle Thrush (p.150), Jackdaw (p.157).

Magpie

Pica pica (Corvidae)

A handsome crow with boldly pied plumage and a long, tapered tail, the Magpie is unmistakable. In sunlight it has an iridescent sheen of blue, purple, and green. It has a reputation for wiping out songbirds, but research shows that its fondness for eating eggs and chicks has little overall effect on populations.

FOUND on farmland with hedges, woodland edges, and parks. Visits gardens to find food.

white shoulder

black breast

wedge-shaped tail

black head

black lines on white wingtips

black wings, glossed green-blue

white belly

long black tail, glossed green and bronze-purple

tail shorter than adult's

rather duller than adult

VOICE Hard, chattering, mechanical rattle, tcha-tcha-tcha-tcha or chak-ak-ak-ak.
NESTING Big domed nest of sticks and mud, high in tree; 5–8 eggs; 1 brood; April–June.
FEEDING Mostly takes insects, grain, and scraps from a wide range of places; eats eggs and chicks in summer.
SIMILAR SPECIES None.

Chough

Pyrrhocorax pyrrhocorax (Corvidae)

Sociable, noisy, exuberant, and spectacularly agile in the air, the Chough is a bird of wild rocky places with ancient grassland, where it gets most of its food by probing in the turf. Family parties and larger flocks soar and dive around cliffs, with total mastery of the turbulent air currents, their ringing calls echoing off the rocks.

longish red bill

square-ended wings with long "fingers"

LIVES *on rocky coasts, high-altitude pastures, gorges, crags, and quarries; also feeds on beaches in winter.*

glossy black body

square tail

paler, orange-red bill

red legs

VOICE *Explosive, ringing, pee-yaa or chia, also shorter chuk and kwarr calls.*
NESTING *Nest of sticks and hair in cavity in rock or ruin; 3–5 eggs; 1 brood; May–July.*
FEEDING *Eats ants on old pastures, insects dug from soil, and lichen prised from rocks.*
SIMILAR SPECIES *Rook (right), Carrion Crow (below).*

Jackdaw

Corvus monedula (Corvidae)

A small, short-billed crow with a black cap and a pale grey nape, the Jackdaw is a sociable bird that often flies in flocks, performing spectacular aerobatics with much calling. It also feeds in mixed flocks with Rooks (right), when its compact shape becomes obvious.

SEEN *around cliffs, quarries, old buildings, woods, farmland with mature trees, or towns and villages where there are old houses with chimneys.*

pale eyes

black cap

grey nape

grey-black body

rounded wings

short, thick bill

dark grey underwings

NOTE
Although similar to other black crows such as the Rook (right), the Jackdaw is distinctly smaller, with shorter legs and a shorter bill.

VOICE *Noisy kyak or tjak! with squeaky, bright quality; some longer calls like chee-ar.*
NESTING *Pile of sticks lined with mud, moss, and hair, in hole in tree, cliff, or building, or in chimney; 4–6 eggs; 1 brood; April–July.*
FEEDING *Takes worms, seeds, and scraps from ground; also caterpillars and berries.*
SIMILAR SPECIES *Rook (right).*

Rook

Corvus frugilegus (Corvidae)

Well known for its loud cawing calls, the Rook is a big, black, intensely social crow. It is slightly smaller than the similar Carrion Crow (below), and the adult is distinguished by the bare, parchment-white face that gives it a very long-billed look. The Rook – even the black-faced juvenile – has a peaked, rather than flat-topped crown. Ragged thigh feathers give it a "baggy trouser" effect. Rooks generally forage in groups, often with Jackdaws (left), probing the ground for insect grubs and other morsels which they store in a pouch beneath the bill to transport back to the nest. Flocks gather in noisy mass flights around the colony, often with soaring, diving, and swooping aerobatics.

BREEDS *in treetop colonies, typically in farmland, parks, and villages or small towns with scattered tall trees for nesting.*

wings more pointed than Carrion Crow's

narrow, rounded tail

peaked crown

bare white skin around base of long, pointed bill

glossy black body

body deeper, more angular, less sleek than Carrion Crow's

loose, ragged thigh feathers

rounded tail

bill thinner than Crow's

black bill base

looser feathers and slighter body than Crow

NOTE
Rooks are far more sociable than Carrion Crows (below). They normally nest in colonies, while Crows typically nest in pairs, but the distinction is not completely reliable. Occasionally a pair of Rooks will nest in isolation, and Crows and Ravens (p.158) may associate in loose flocks. So while a gathering of big black birds is likely to consist of Rooks, it is worth checking.

VOICE *Loud, raucous, but relaxed cawing, caaar, grah-gra-gra, plus variety of higher, strangled or metallic notes, especially around colony.*
NESTING *Big nest of sticks lined with grass, moss, and leaves, in treetop colony; 3–6 eggs; 1 brood; March–June.*
FEEDING *Eats worms, beetle larvae, seeds, grain, and roots from ground, especially ploughed fields or stubble, usually in flocks; also forages along roadsides for large insects and roadkill.*
SIMILAR SPECIES *Carrion Crow (left), Jackdaw (left), Raven (p.158).*

Carrion Crow

Corvus corone (Corvidae)

The all-black Carrion Crow is easy to confuse with other crows, particularly a juvenile Rook (right), but its head has a distinctly flatter crown and its body plumage is much tighter and neater-looking, with no "baggy trouser" effect. It is usually seen alone or in pairs, but may gather to feed and roost in flocks in autumn and winter, and often feeds alongside other crows.

INHABITS *all kinds of open areas, from farmland and upland moors to city centres; also feeds on coasts and estuaries.*

thick, arched bill

flat-topped head

neat, tight body feathering

glossy black body

squarer wingtips than Rook

square tail

VOICE *Loud, harsh, grating caw, krra krra krra, metallic konk, korr, and similar calls.*
NESTING *Big stick nest, in tree, bush, on cliff or building; 4–6 eggs; 1 brood; March–July.*
FEEDING *Feeds on ground, taking all kinds of invertebrates, eggs, grain, and various scraps; usually in pairs but sometimes flocks.*
SIMILAR SPECIES *Rook (right), Raven (p.158).*

Hooded Crow

Corvus cornix (Corvidae)

A close relative of the all-black Carrion Crow (left), and sometimes considered a subspecies of it, the Hooded Crow is a much more distinctive bird with a different range. Where the two meet, they interbreed to produce a range of hybrids, with varying amounts of grey plumage.

FOUND *in a wide range of open habitats; appears to prefer poorer land to Carrion Crow in breeding season.*

black hood

black wings and tail

black wings

pale body

black wings

grey body

black wings and tail

VOICE *Very like Carrion Crow's; often a more hard, rolling croak repeated 3–4 times.*
NESTING *Large stick nest, in tree or bush, some on cliffs, 4–6 eggs; 1 brood; March–July.*
FEEDING *Wide range of animal food, including carrion, grain, and food scraps.*
SIMILAR SPECIES *Jackdaw (left).*

Raven

Corvus corax (Corvidae)

LIVES *in large forests, mountain regions, open moorland, and hills with crags and isolated trees.*

The world's largest perching bird, bigger than a Buzzard (p.122), the Raven is a much heavier, more powerful bird than the Carrion Crow (p.157), which often shares its habitats and its taste for carrion. It has longer wings, a longer tail, and a big head with a much heavier bill. It often increases the apparent size of its head by bristling up its throat feathers, giving it a bearded appearance that is unmistakable. At a distance it is best identified by its shape and bold, strong flight, which often includes dramatic rolling and tumbling aerobatics, especially early in the breeding season. But the first clue to the presence of a Raven is usually its loud, deep, croaking call, which echoes from the surrounding peaks and crags. Usually seen alone, in pairs, or in family parties, it sometimes gathers in flocks at carcasses and communal roosts.

wedge-shaped tail

long, fingered wings

loose throat feathers may be expanded as a "beard"

protruding head

all-black plumage; metallic green and purplish gloss in strong light

tail diamond-shaped when spread

very large, deep, arched bill

long tail

NOTE
Ravens are usually to be seen flying over the wildest, craggiest country, and even on high, barren peaks, where they often call from prominent rock perches. But they also frequent softer, wooded landscapes and farmland, and they may even be seen flying over towns.

VOICE *Loud, abrupt, echoing crronk crronk crronk or prruk prruk, metallic tonk; various clicking, rattling or quiet musical notes, sometimes in rambling subsong audible only at close range.*
NESTING *Huge nest of sticks, wool, grass, and heather, used for many years, on cliff or in tall tree; 4–6 eggs; 1 brood; February–May.*
FEEDING *Catches small mammals and birds; eats carrion from dead sheep and roadkills; forages for scraps on shore; eats insects and grain.*
SIMILAR SPECIES *Carrion Crow (p.157), Rook (p.157).*

Starling

Sturnus vulgaris (Sturnidae)

GATHERS *in big winter flocks in forests, city centres, industrial sites, bridges, and piers. Breeds in woods, gardens, and towns.*

A common, active, noisy, sociable, but quarrelsome bird of urban and rural habitats, the Starling is instantly recognizable by its strong-legged walk and waddling run as it pokes and pries in the soil for insect grubs and seeds. Superficially black, its plumage is glossed with iridescent green and purple in summer, and spotted with buff in winter. Outside the breeding season it forms dense flocks that roost in trees, reedbeds, and on buildings, and swirl around the sky in perfectly co-ordinated aerobatic manoeuvres, particularly at dusk. These winter flocks can be so vast that they look like clouds of smoke at a distance, although declines in many areas have made such immense gatherings less common.

short, squarish tail

sharp yellow bill

NOTE
Starlings are skilled mimics and can even imitate noises such as telephones. A strange sound coming from an odd place often turns out to be a Starling.

blue-grey bill base; pale pink on female

glossy black body with green and purple sheen

long, strong, red-brown legs

silvery face with dark mask

body feathers tipped buff or whitish

dull head last to get adult colours

plain brown body

dark bill

feathers edged bright orange-buff

large spots near tail

MOULTING

VOICE *Loud, slightly grating cheer, musical, twangy, whistled tswee-oo, variety of clicks, gurgles, squawking notes; song fast mixture of rattles, trills, gurgles, and whistles, often with mimicry of other birds or sounds.*
NESTING *Loose, bulky nest of grass and stems, in tree hole, cavity in wall or building, or large nest box; 4–7 eggs; 1–2 broods; April–July.*
FEEDING *Forages for invertebrates, seeds, and berries on the ground, in small to large flocks; catches flying ants in mid-air.*
SIMILAR SPECIES *Blackbird (p.150).*

House Sparrow

Passer domesticus (Passeridae)

PREFERS *cities, towns, villages, farms, and on farmland; rarely found far from human habitation.*

This common, noisy sparrow is one of the most familiar small birds due to its habit of nesting in buildings. The male has a bold black bib and distinctive grey cap, but the female can be confused with a female finch. Although House Sparrow populations have declined, they are still widespread.

grey cap

big black bib

whitish wingbar

greyish rump

red-brown above, with dark streaks

unmarked grey below

pale stripe

plain plumage

VOICE *Lively chirrup, chilp, as loud chorus from flock; song a simple series of chirps.*
NESTING *Untidy nest of grass and feathers in cavity; 3–7 eggs; 1–4 broods; April–August.*
FEEDING *Takes seeds, nuts, and berries, mainly from ground, plus insects for young.*
SIMILAR SPECIES *Tree Sparrow (right), female Chaffinch (p.159).*

Tree Sparrow

Passer montanus (Passeridae)

INHABITS *farmland with scattered trees, in parks, woods, and woodland edges; also in towns and cities.*

Over much of its range the Tree Sparrow is a less suburban bird than the House Sparrow (left), preferring woods and farmland. The sexes are almost identical, both having the black mask, brown cap, black cheek patch, and white collar. This sparrow often feeds on the ground in company with finches and buntings.

rich brown cap

black mask and bib

white cheek with square black patch

buffish rump

black and brown streaked back

two whitish wingbars

plain grey-buff below

VOICE *Call loud chirruping and cheeping, plus a disyllabic tsu-wit, hard tek-tek in flight.*
NESTING *Domed nest of grass in holes in tree or building; 4–6 eggs; 2–3 broods; April–July.*
FEEDING *Picks seeds from ground, plus some insects and buds; visits bird feeders.*
SIMILAR SPECIES *House Sparrow (left).*

NOTE
Superficially similar to the male House Sparrow (left), this bird has a distinctive hard flight-call as well as a different head pattern.

Chaffinch

Fringilla coelebs (Fringillidae)

One of the least specialized of the finches, the Chaffinch is also one of the most successful and abundant. Unusually for finches, pairs breed in separate territories, proclaimed by males singing loudly from prominent perches. At other times they are social and often very tame.

BREEDS in coniferous and deciduous forests, woods, hedges, parks, and gardens; some winter in fields.

two bold white wingbars

greenish rump

♂❄

ochre-brown smudges on head

♂❄

olive head and back

♀

blue-grey head and bill

brownish pink cheeks and throat

brown back

dark wings

yellowish feather edges

dark tail with white sides

pink below, whiter on belly

♂❄

VOICE Soft chup, frequent pink! loud hweet; song chip-chip, chirichiri cheep-tcheweeoo.
NESTING Nest neat cup of grass, leaves, and moss, in tree; 4–5 eggs; 1 brood; April–May.
FEEDING Eats insects, mostly caterpillars, in summer; otherwise seeds, shoots, and berries.
SIMILAR SPECIES Brambling (below), Bullfinch (p.161), female House Sparrow (p.158).

Brambling

Fringilla montifringilla (Fringillidae)

Very like the Chaffinch (above), but with a white rump and a darker back, the Brambling is generally less common and absent from Britain in summer. In winter, Bramblings may gather in huge feeding flocks, especially in central Europe, but numbers fluctuate from year to year with the supply of beech-mast and other tree seeds.

SEEN in farmland and parks, in winter, especially areas with beech, birch, and spruce; breeds in northern forests.

white rump

big orange-buff upper wingbar ♂❄

"scaly" head

pale throat

black head and back ♂❄

bright yellow-orange breast and shoulder

dark back

duller ♀❄

white belly

dark spots on flanks ♂❄

VOICE Call hard chek, distinctive nasal tschair; song repeated nasal, buzzing dzeeee.
NESTING Cup of lichen, bark, and stems; in tree or bush; 5–7 eggs; 1 brood; May–June.
FEEDING Eats insects in summer, seeds at other times; takes beech-mast from ground.
SIMILAR SPECIES Chaffinch (above), female House Sparrow (p.158).

Greenfinch

Carduelis chloris (Fringillidae)

Males are easy to identify by their green plumage with bright yellow flashes, and a "frowning" look; the duller females and juveniles are also stocky and stout-billed, but trickier to distinguish. In spring, males sing during circling, stiff-winged display flights. Their songs are simple on the face of it, but actually quite varied in rhythm, pattern, and pitch, the best of them being surprisingly musical. If they choose to nest in tall evergreen hedges or mature conifers, Greenfinches add a lot to the atmosphere of a garden in spring and summer, especially in suburban housing areas.

FEEDS on sunflower seeds at garden feeders; breeds in open woods, hedges, large gardens.

yellow patches on tail ♂

flashes of yellow on outer part of grey wings

dark patch

yellow stripe

bright olive green

♂❄

NOTE

Male and female Greenfinches are very alike, but on average the male has broader yellow edges to the wing and tail feathers.

browner than adult ♀

streaked all over

greyer above

♂❄

duller than male ♀

VOICE Flight call fast, tinny chatter, tit-it-it-it, nasal dzoo-ee, hard jup-jup-jup; song series of rich trills, mixed with buzzy dzweee, often given from high perch but also in fluttering, bat-like song.
NESTING Bulky nest of grass and twigs in tree; 4–6 eggs; 1–2 broods; April–July.
FEEDING Takes seeds from trees, herbs, and ground; also berries and nuts; often visits bird feeders in gardens.
SIMILAR SPECIES Siskin (below).

Goldfinch

Carduelis carduelis (Fringillidae)

Flocks of colourful Goldfinches feed on waste ground, farmyards, and field edges, picking soft, milky seeds from thistles, tall daisies, and similar plants with their pointed bills. They are agile feeders, often swinging head-down from seedheads, and have a distinctive dancing flight and tinkling calls.

FORAGES in weedy places with tall seed-bearing flowers; also in alder and larch.

bold black, red, and white head

tawny back

tawny-chestnut patch

yellow on closed wing

black wings

pale underside

big yellow panels

grey head

duller wings

NOTE

At a distance the red face can be hard to see, but the yellow wing flashes and bouncy flight action usually make identification easy.

VOICE Call chattering, lilting skip-i-lip, rough tschair; song mix of call notes and liquid trills.
NESTING Neat nest of roots, grass, cobwebs in tree or bush; 5–6 eggs; 2 broods; May–July.
FEEDING Gathers soft, half-ripe seeds from thistles and similar plants, less often from ground; also eats seeds of alder and larch.
SIMILAR SPECIES Siskin (right).

Siskin

Carduelis spinus (Fringillidae)

A specialist at feeding on tree seeds, the neat, slender Siskin is particularly associated with conifers such as pines and spruces. It usually feeds high in the trees, displaying tit-like agility, and in spring the males often sing from treetops. In winter, Siskins forage in flocks, often with Redpolls (p.160).

VISITS gardens for peanuts, but breeds in spruce and pine forest. In winter, found in alder and larch along rivers.

black cap and chin

dark streaks on green back

yellow patch each side of black tail

♂

lime-green to yellowish breast

bold yellow wingbars

♂

greyer head than male

like greyer female ♀

VOICE Whistled tsy-zee; hoarse purr; song mixes calls with trills and hard twittering notes.
NESTING Tiny nest of twigs and stems, lined with down, high in tree; 4–5 eggs; 1–2 broods; May–July.
FEEDING Eats the seeds of pine, larch, alder, birch, and various other trees.
SIMILAR SPECIES Greenfinch (above).

Linnet

Carduelis cannabina (Fringillidae)

Lively and sociable, the Linnet is usually seen in tightly co-ordinated flocks that travel and feed together throughout much of the year. In winter, when the males lose much of their bright colour, the flocks usually feed on the ground. At such times they are easily disturbed, bursting up and dropping into cover at the slightest alarm. They are bolder in the breeding season, when smaller parties can be seen foraging for insects in bushes to feed their nestlings.

FLIES in tight, bounding flocks, which feed on heaths, commons, rough grassland, farmland, upland meadows, and coastal marshes. Breeds in gorse scrub, thickets, and hedges.

pale red forehead, brighter in spring

light grey head

pale cheek spot

plain orange-brown back

white panel on wings when closed

pink-red chest

dark tail with white side streaks

whitish streaks on dark wings

♂❄

blackish wings

forked tail

browner head

♂❄

less pink on chest

brown streaks on body ♀

tawny-buff chest

NOTE
Although typically shy, Linnets perch conspicuously on low bushes in the breeding season, when the male's plumage is at its most striking.

VOICE *Light, twittering, chattering flight call, tidit tidititit, nasal tseeoo; song quite rich, musical, varied warbling, mixed with chattering notes, often in chorus from flocks.*
NESTING *Small, neat nest of plant stems and roots, lined with hair, in bush near ground; 4–6 eggs; 2–3 broods; April–July.*
FEEDING *Takes seeds from ground, especially arable weeds, often feeding in groups; feeds young on insects.*
SIMILAR SPECIES *Twite (right), Common Redpoll (right).*

Twite

Carduelis flavirostris (Fringillidae)

Like the more colourful Linnet, the Twite is a ground feeder that moves around in flocks, which often rise into the air, circle, and then drop again as one. A good view reveals its pale buff wingbars, rich tawny-buff throat, and the deep pink rump of the breeding male, but from a distance a Twite is an unobtrusive, streaky brown. In winter, when the birds are at their least distinctive, they are best distinguished from Linnets (left) by the nasal *twa-eet* calls that gave the species its name. Unusually, Twites feed their young on small seeds, and the disappearance of flowery meadows from farmland has caused widespread declines.

DRINKS and bathes in shallow pools, and feeds on coastal salt marshes in winter. Breeds in weedy fields around upland farms, on mountains and moors, and on rocky ground near coasts.

narrow buff wingbar

♂❄

pink rump

unmarked, tawny-buff face and throat

white streaks

grey bill

rump less pink

yellow bill

♂❄

blackish streaks on tan-brown back

no pink on rump ♀

buff below with black streaks

pink rump

dark forked tail (longer than Linnet's), with white streaks ♂❄

NOTE
With its buff wingbars like the Common Redpoll's (below) and the white streaked wings and tail like the Linnet's (left), it is rather like a hybrid.

VOICE *Chattering flight call only slightly harder than Linnet's; distinctive main call twanging, nasal, rising twa-eet; song quick, twittering warble, with buzzing notes, hoarse jangling and chattering trills.*
NESTING *Deep cup of twigs, grass, and moss, lined with hair, in bush or bank; 4–6 eggs; 1–2 broods; May–June.*
FEEDING *Eats small seeds, particularly those of salt-marsh plants in winter; unlike most finches, feeds young on seeds.*
SIMILAR SPECIES *Linnet (left), Common Redpoll (below).*

Lesser Redpoll

Carduelis cabaret (Fringillidae)

The Lesser Redpoll breeds in Britain and is smaller and darker than the Common Redpoll (right). It is commonest in the north but numbers and range fluctuate – in the 1970s it was commoner as a nesting bird in southern Britain, where it is now known mostly as a winter visitor.

FEEDS on seeds in alders, larches, and birches, often seen with siskins and sometimes goldfinches.

buff wingbar ♀

red cap

black chin

pink chest (male in summer)

black legs ♂

streaked plumage

forked tail

VOICE *Metallic, abrupt chattering notes; longer trill in spring song; nasal tsoo-weee.*
NESTING *Small cup of twigs and leaves in bush; 4–6 eggs; 1–2 broods; April–June.*
FEEDING *Eats seeds of trees and shrubs, including birch seeds from ground; caterpillars in summer.*
SIMILAR SPECIES *Twite (right), Linnet (above).*

Common Redpoll

Carduelis flammea (Fringillidae)

The Common Redpoll is a very small, active, agile finch that typically feeds in the treetops in noisy, well co-ordinated flocks, often with Siskins (p.159). Usually quiet when feeding, it betrays itself by its staccato, chattering flight calls as the flocks move between the trees. It may gather fallen birch seeds from the ground, and even feed alongside Linnets (left) in weedy fields.

dark red forehead

FEEDS on the seeds of birch and larch, in woods and bushy heaths; also in large gardens and scrub.

tiny bill

small black chin

no pink ♀

short, forked tail

♂❄

pink breast

pale below with long, dark streaks

dark tail

streaked back

VOICE *Flight call hard chuchuchuchuch, twangy tsooeee; song combines flight call with fast, thin, reeling trill, treeeeee.*
NESTING *Cup of twigs and grasses in bush or tree; 4–6 eggs; 1–2 broods; May–July.*
FEEDING *Mostly tree seeds of birch, plus alder and larch; also takes seeds from ground.*
SIMILAR SPECIES *Twite (above), Linnet (left).*

Crossbill

Loxia curvirostra (Fringillidae)

This large, powerful finch is specialized for eating the seeds of spruces, pines, and other conifers, using its hooked, crossed bill to prise the cone scales apart so it can extract the seeds with its tongue. It feeds acrobatically and often noisily in the treetops, but has to drink frequently to moisten its diet of dry seeds.

LIVES *in extensive woods of spruce, larch, and pine, with easy access to water.*

dark wings

♂

orange-red to strawberry-red plumage

hooked bill with crossed mandibles

brightest red on rump

brownish wings

dark tail

♀

brown wings

green body

pale, streaked

VOICE *Loud, abrupt calls, jup-jup-jup, quiet conversational notes while feeding; song mixes buzzy notes, calls, warbles, and trills.*
NESTING *Small nest of twigs and moss high in conifer; 3–4 eggs; 1 brood; January–March.*
FEEDING *Eats seeds of conifers such as spruce and pine; also berries, buds, insects.*
SIMILAR SPECIES *Hawfinch (below).*

Bullfinch

Pyrrhula pyrrhula (Fringillidae)

Heavily built, rather sluggish, and often hard to see as it feeds quietly in dense cover, the Bullfinch is unmistakable when it emerges into the open. The male is a striking sight, with his bold red, grey, and black plumage and bright white rump. Generally shy, its caution may be warranted, because it is often treated as a pest due to its taste for soft buds of fruit trees. It is seriously declining in some regions.

RAIDS *flowering fruit trees in woodland, farmland with hedges, thickets, orchards, parks, and gardens.*

no dark cap

plumage like female

dull brownish back

♀

beige-grey below

thick, stubby bill

grey-white band on dark wing

red-pink below

♂

black cap, bill, and chin form distinct hood

pale grey back

white under tail

black tail

VOICE *Call low, clear whistles, peuuw or phiu; song infrequent, warble mixed with calls.*
NESTING *Cup of twigs, lined with moss and grass, in dense bush or tree; 4–5 eggs, 2 broods, April–June.*
FEEDING *Eats soft buds, seeds, berries, and shoots from bushes, shrubs, and fruit trees.*
SIMILAR SPECIES *Chaffinch (p.159).*

Hawfinch

Coccothraustes coccothraustes (Fringillidae)

The immensely powerful bill of the Hawfinch is adapted for cracking the toughest seeds, such as cherry stones and olive pits. It usually feeds in the treetops, where it can be elusive and difficult to see well, although its bulky silhouette is distinctive. In winter, it feeds on tree seeds on the ground, where it is more visible, although it flies up if disturbed.

FEEDS *and breeds in deciduous woodland, orchards, olive groves, and large gardens.*

♂☼

broad, diagonal, buff and white wingbars

scaly back

barred beneath

very deep, powerful bill

greyer wingbar

dark brown back

tawny cap on big head

grey nape

♀

blue-black wings

broad white tip to short tail

♂☼

VOICE *Call short, sharp, metallic tik or tzik, thin tzree, tikitik; weak scratchy song.*
NESTING *Nest of twigs, roots, and moss, in old tree; 4–5 eggs; 1 brood; April–May.*
FEEDING *Takes large tree seeds and berries from trees; picks seeds from ground in winter.*
SIMILAR SPECIES *Chaffinch (p.159), Crossbill (above), Bullfinch (above).*

Lapland Bunting

Calcarius lapponicus (Emberizidae)

Rarely seen in summer, when it breeds in remote, wild places, the Lapland Bunting appears on more southerly coasts in autumn and winter. It keeps a low profile, creeping among the grasses on dunes, salt marshes, and golf courses, and usually stays unnoticed until flushed from underfoot.

FEEDS *mainly on salt marshes and short, wet grassland near coasts in winter. Breeds on northern tundra.*

mainly rufous head

dark ear coverts

rufous wing panel between white wingbars

streaked back

dark tail with white sides

black cap, face, and breast

patchy head pattern

♂✳

bright rusty nape

♂☼

VOICE *Calls staccato rattle and clear whistle, t-r-r-r-r-ik teu; song like Skylark (p.143), but shorter.*
NESTING *Nest of moss and grass in tussock or among rocks; 5–6 eggs; 1 brood; May–June.*
FEEDING *Gathers seeds on the ground; eats insects in summer.*
SIMILAR SPECIES *Reed Bunting (p.162).*

Snow Bunting

Plectrophenax nivalis (Emberizidae)

The stark black and white of the breeding male Snow Bunting is well suited to its snowy northern breeding habitat, but in Britain it is seen only in its subdued winter plumage, when the sexes look very alike. Capable of thriving in the harshest climates, Snow Buntings often spend the winter on barren mountainsides, where they are regularly seen around ski resorts. Elsewhere they gather in flocks on sheltered beaches and gravelly marshes, where they feed on sandhoppers. They have a distinctive low-slung look on the ground, owing to their short legs, and the feeding flocks move forward by repeated leap-frogging flights as the birds at the back fly over those in front.

FEEDS *on shingle banks and muddy coastal marshes in winter, as well as on exposed mountain slopes. Breeds on northern tundra and mountains.*

small white wing patch

forked black tail with white sides

♂✳

long black and white wings

black tail with white sides

white wing panel

reddish or orange-brown cap

reddish or orange-brown cheeks

sandy brown back

red-brown on sides of breast

♂✳

white underside

dark grey head and back

stocky body

white head

black back and wingtips

♂☼

white below

brown cap

brown and black streaks

♀♀

VOICE *Call loud, deep, clear pyiew or tsioo, frequent lighter, trilling, rippling tiri-lil-il-il-il-il-ip; song short, clear, ringing, fluty phrase, turee-turee-turee-turitui.*
NESTING *Nest of moss, lichen, and grass stems in cavity among rocks; 4–6 eggs; 1–2 broods; May–July.*
FEEDING *Takes insects in summer, and mainly seeds and marine invertebrates picked from strandline in winter.*
SIMILAR SPECIES *Reed Bunting (p.162), Lapland Bunting (above).*

Yellowhammer

Emberiza citrinella (Emberizidae)

The repetitive song of the male of this species is a typical sound of warm summer days on farmland and bushy heaths. During colder months, Yellow-hammers form small groups, often with other buntings, to roam the fields in search of seeds.

GATHERS *to eat seeds in winter; breeds on pastures, heaths, and farmland with hedges.*

less yellow

more streaks

♀

rufous, buff, and black

yellow head with dusky stripes

black streaks on rufous back

♂☼

yellow below with fine dark streaks

black tail with white sides

rufous rump

♂☼

VOICE *Call sharp* tsik; *song thin trill, with longer notes at end,* ti-ti-ti-ti-ti-ti-teee-tyew.
NESTING *Nest of grass or straw in bank or below bush; 3–5 eggs; 2–3 broods; April–July.*
FEEDING *Takes seeds from ground, and also insects in summer.*
SIMILAR SPECIES *Cirl Bunting (below), female Reed Bunting (right).*

Reed Bunting

Emberiza schoeniclus (Emberizidae)

Easy to find and identify in summer, male Reed Buntings sing monotonously from low perches among reeds and other wetland vegetation. In winter, when the males are far less striking, they are harder to recognize – especially when feeding on farmland or even in gardens.

INHABITS *wet places with reeds, sedge, rushes; also willow thickets and heaths; gardens in winter.*

hint of pale collar

♀

cream and black streaks on back

black head

white collar and moustache

rufous forewing

♂☼

bold white tail sides

duller head pattern

brown back with black streaks

♂❄

long, notched tail

streaked, whitish underside

pale red-brown legs

black tail with broad white sides

VOICE *Call loud high* tseeu, *and high, thin, pure* sweee, zi zi; *song short, jangly phrase,* srip srip srip sea-sea-sea stitip-itip-itipip.
NESTING *Bulky nest of grass and sedge, on ground; 4–5 eggs; 2 broods; April–June.*
FEEDING *Eats seeds, plus insects in summer.*
SIMILAR SPECIES *Female House Sparrow (p.158).*

Cirl Bunting

Emberiza cirlus (Emberizidae)

Throughout much of its range in western and southern Europe, the Cirl Bunting is a common bird of open, bushy slopes, and farmland with plenty of trees, hedges, and thickets. It resembles a Yellowhammer (above), but is more compact and less yellow. The males have the same habit of singing from bush tops, but they also use inconspicuous perches in trees. Cirl Buntings rely on old grassland with plenty of grasshoppers, so they have suffered serious declines in countries such as the British Isles, where much of the ancient grassland has been destroyed by intensive farming methods.

LIVES *on warm, bushy, often stony slopes, around the edges of tall, leafy orchards, and in olive groves. Feeds on weedy or grassy fields in winter, and may visit gardens.*

streaked, dark greenish cap

bright yellow above and below eye

black eye-stripe

black chin

♂☼

olive-buff rump

olive-brown rump

♀

black tail with white sides

rusty patch on side of breast

pale yellow underside

♂☼

striped crown

strongly striped head

♀

striped crown

♂❄

fine streaks below

dark streaks

NOTE

A breeding male is distinguished from a Yellowhammer (above) by its head pattern. The head stripes and olive rump help to identify the Cirl Bunting.

VOICE *Call very simple, short, high, thin* sip; *song fast, rattling trill on one note, or slower, lighter, more bubbling variant,* t-r-r-r-r-r-r-r-r-r-r-r-r *or* ti-ti-ti-ti-ti-ti-ti-ti-ti-ti-ti-ti.
NESTING *Rough nest of grass and stalks, built low in shrub or hedge; 3–4 eggs; 2 broods; April–July.*
FEEDING *Needs to eat grasshoppers and similar insects in summer; otherwise takes seeds from ground.*
SIMILAR SPECIES *Yellowhammer (above), female Reed Bunting (right).*

Corn Bunting

Miliaria calandra (Emberizidae)

A big, pale bunting of wide open spaces, the Corn Bunting lives up to its name by favouring farmland with large cereal fields, as well as extensive grasslands. It shares this habitat with the Skylark (p.143), but has a quite different song: a unique, jangling rattle given by the male from a prominent exposed perch or in a display flight, with dangling legs. It feeds on insects and seeds on the ground, and the widespread use of weedkillers and insecticides on modern farmland has made it virtually extinct in many intensively farmed regions. Where it is still common, it can often be seen flying overhead in small groups towards dusk, heading for its communal roosts.

PERCHES *in hedges when disturbed while feeding on meadows, rough grassland, arable fields, and coastal scrub.*

dark stripes on crown

dark lower cheeks

row of dark spots on wing coverts

plain wings

streaked, pale brown back

stocky shape

dark streaks often merge into central smudge on chest

plain brown tail, with no white at sides

heavy, pale yellowish bill

upright posture when singing

pale, streaked breast

NOTE

Although it looks like a Skylark (p.143) and lives in the same places, the Corn Bunting tends to hop rather than walk, and has no white on its tail.

VOICE *Call short, abrupt, clicking* plip *or* quit; *song jangling, dry, fast, rattled phrase resembling rattling keys or broken glass.*
NESTING *Nest of grass and roots, lined with finer material, on ground; 3–5 eggs; 1–2 broods; April–June.*
FEEDING *Forages on ground, picking up insects and seeds in summer and only seeds in winter.*
SIMILAR SPECIES *Female Reed Bunting (above), female Yellowhammer (left), Skylark (p.143).*

Scottish Crossbill
A stocky bird, the Scottish Crossbill (*Loxia scotica*) is the only species of bird in Britain that is found nowhere else in the world. It occurs only in the Scots pine forests of the Scottish Highlands.

REPTILES & AMPHIBIANS

Cold-blooded and in need of warmth in order to remain active and develop, reptiles and amphibians are primarily tropical animals. A few species colonized the British Isles after the last ice age, before the continental land bridge flooded, and of around 200 European natives, only a tiny proportion are British. There are seven native amphibians (with another on the Channel Islands) and 11 native reptiles (again, with two more in the Channel Islands); five of the reptiles are sea-turtles that occasionally wash up on our shores. Six more species in each group have been introduced. Most reptiles are terrestrial, although some inhabit fresh or salt water; almost all amphibians favour damp habitats as they have a porous skin, prone to drying out.

SNAKES AND LIZARDS

Elongated, scale-clad animals, with or without legs, snakes and lizards are mostly diurnal predators of invertebrates and small vertebrates. Some, such as the Adder, use venom to kill or subdue their prey.

SHELLED REPTILES

Freshwater terrapins, tortoises, and sea-turtles are protected by a tough shell, only their scaly head, limbs, and tail exposed. With a hardened, beak-like mouth, they tackle both plant and animal food.

FROGS AND TOADS

Losing their tail during metamorphosis from aquatic, gilled larva to air-breathing adult, frogs and toads are well adapted for swimming and jumping. Their diet consists mainly of invertebrates.

NEWTS

As larvae, newts are similar to frogs and toads, but as adults they are more aquatic and retain their tail for swimming. The legs are equal in size, adults often leaving the water only for hibernation.

Identifying Reptiles

Reptiles were the first group of animals to evolve a wholly terrestrial way of life. Of the 8,000 or so species in the world today, few are dependent on wet habitats for their survival. All reptiles are "cold-blooded" (ectothermic). This means that they are unable to generate heat internally, and need to obtain sufficient heat from their environment to allow their bodily functions to operate normally. A consequence of cold-bloodedness is a low feeding requirement: many species are able to fast for extended periods of time.

Grass Snake with clutch

REPRODUCTION
Most reptiles produce soft-shelled eggs, which are incubated by warmth from the sun or rotting vegetation. Some, however, retain their eggs internally, producing live young.

SKIN
The texture of the scales that cover the surface of a reptile can impart a characteristic appearance. Detailed examination of the scales, however, is possible only on captive, torpid, or dead specimens.

GRANULAR   SMOOTH   KEELED

HORIZONTAL   VERTICAL   ROUND

EYES
The colour of the eyes and the shape and orientation (pictured left) of the pupil are important identification features if you can get close enough. Furthermore, the colour of the iris is often highly distinctive.

Behaviour

Reptiles bask to optimize their thermal balance, and this is a good time to observe them. If it is cold they slow down, becoming torpid, which may lead to full hibernation. Unless stated otherwise, species in this book hibernate and are diurnal.

DEFENCE
Defence may include behaviour like playing dead, biting, hissing, and tail shedding, as well as camouflage.

Grass Snake playing dead

Variations

There are several forms of variation possible within a reptile species: adaptive and geographic variations; sexual differences, in structure and pattern; age differences, the young often strikingly different in colour and pattern; and seasonal differences, with males assuming more vivid colours around the courtship period. There are also black, or melanic, forms among some species.

FEMALE ADDER

MALE ADDER

ADDERS
Both male and female adders have a distinctive zig-zag pattern along their backs, but the female is brown, with few marks along the side, while the male is black and grey.

Identifying Amphibians

Amphibians were the earliest animal group to exploit terrestrial habitats, but most still lay eggs in water, and the larvae possess external gills for breathing underwater. Being cold-blooded (ectothermic), they become inactive, and often hibernate, when it is cold. Conversely, in hot, dry conditions, they may also reduce their activity, a phenomenon called aestivation.

SKIN
Although toads, such as this Common Toad, tend to have dry, warty skin, most amphibians have smooth, moist skin and are thus found primarily in damp areas.

EYES
The form of the eyes, particularly the shape and orientation of the pupil, is a differentiating feature of many groups.

pupil

HORIZONTAL   ROUND   VERTICAL

SMOOTH   WARTY

SKIN
Usually smooth, lacking scales and with a mucus layer, some species may have a characteristic granular covering, which may vary seasonally.

Great Crested Newt

TAIL
Where present, the tail is used for swimming. In males, the tail may bear a distinctive crest in the breeding season.

Variations

The appearance of many species is often variable in colour, pattern, and structure. Such differences may be geographical, sexual, seasonal, or age-related, and can pose challenges to identification. Where such differences are apparent, it is invariably the adult males in breeding condition which have the brightest colours, and most flamboyant crests.

BREEDING MALE

SEX VARIATION
Variation between the sexes is often marked, especially in the breeding season, as seen here in the Smooth Newt.

FEMALE

Tracks and Signs

Amphibians leave rather little in the way of diagnostic tracks and signs. Apart from hearing the calls or finding the early developmental stages, the only realistic way of recording their presence is to locate the adults. This may require considerable time (some are very secretive; others dive for refuge as soon as they detect a threat and can remain submerged for hours).

eggs in long, double strings

SPAWN

TOAD SPAWN
The eggs (spawn) and larvae (tadpoles), of amphibians are distinctive within a group but cannot easily be identified to the species level.

Behaviour

Amphibians are active by day and night. Many newts have complex mating rituals, and the mating frenzies of some frogs and toads can be dramatic. Defensive behaviour includes threatening postures, display of warning colours, and the secretion of toxins.

Natterjack Toad

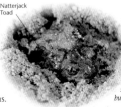

REFUGE
In unfavourably cold or dry conditions, many amphibians become inactive and take refuge in moist microhabitats, under stones and logs, or buried in mud or sand.

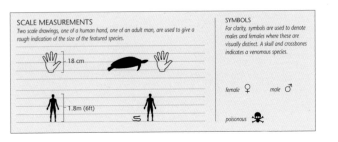

SCALE MEASUREMENTS
Two scale drawings, one of a human hand, one of an adult man, are used to give a rough indication of the size of the featured species.

18 cm

1.8m (6ft)

SYMBOLS
For clarity, symbols are used to denote males and females where these are visually distinct. A skull and crossbones indicates a venomous species.

female ♀   *male* ♂

poisonous ☠

Grass Snake

Natrix natrix (Squamata)

The only British snake that is associated with water and wetland habitats, the Grass Snake swims well, with its head and neck out of the water (the nostrils are not set at the top of the snout), and does much of its hunting in water. The eggs are brooded in rotting vegetation, enabling the Grass Snake to be the most northerly egg-laying snake. Dark olive, with variable darker spotting, most Grass Snakes have a distinctive yellow collar, with a blackish rear border. However, in the occasional dark specimens, which occur in all populations, and old, faded individuals, the collar may not be present. Hibernation takes place between October and March, often in traditional communal sites.

FAVOURS *damp areas, feeding in rivers, ponds, and marshes; also in meadows, heathland, and open woodland.*

rounded snout

STRIPED FORM

NOTE
If captured, Grass Snakes first wriggle violently. If this fails to secure release, they squirt an evil-smelling fluid from their anal glands, and finally feign death, with mouth open and tongue hanging out.

FEIGNING DEATH

variable back and flank spotting

dark olive-green ground colour

yellow collar, highlighted by black crescents

SIZE *70–150cm.*
YOUNG *Lays up to 100 eggs, hatching in August–September.*
DIET *Amphibians, fish, small mammals, birds, lizards, and invertebrates.*
STATUS *Common.*
SIMILAR SPECIES *Smooth Snake (Coronella austriaca), a rare snake of southern heathland, which has an indistinct head and lacks the yellow collar.*

Adder

Vipera berus (Squamata)

With a robust body (especially females), the Adder is a cold-tolerant species, found well into the Arctic Circle, and is the most northerly snake in the world. Its grey body, sometimes with yellow or reddish tones, is strongly marked with a dark stripe down the back, black in males and brown in females. Although it basks in sunshine, it tends to avoid the hottest conditions, and in the south hunts mostly at dusk. Some populations frequently produce dramatic melanic specimens: such animals are all black, with bright red eyes. The Adder is quite venomous and its bite requires medical attention.

PREFERS *heathland and moorland, open woods, meadows, and marshes; largely montane in the south.*

brown zig-zag stripe

♀

NOTE
Adders hibernate between September–October and February–March (according to location). Traditional hibernation sites may be used communally, and adults can navigate to them from distances of 2km or more.

red eyes with vertical pupils

HEAD

dark grey to black underside

dark V-mark on back of head

dark zig-zag stripe

♂

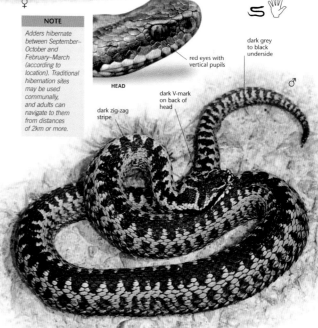

SIZE *50–65cm.*
YOUNG *Up to 20 live young in August, though not breeding every year.*
DIET *Small mammals (pursued in their burrows), lizards, newts, frogs, and nestling birds.*
STATUS *Common.*
SIMILAR SPECIES *The zig-zag stripe is unmistakeable; melanic animals could be confused with melanic Grass Snakes (left).*

Viviparous Lizard

Zootoca vivipara (Squamata)

Also called the Common Lizard, the Viviparous Lizard is the commonest lizard in Britain. The ground colour varies from grey-brown to reddish and olive green; there are variable stripes down the back, sometimes with black blotches or ocelli, often organized into rows down the back or flanks. It can be confused with the Sand Lizard (*Lacerta agilis*), a rare species of heaths and dunes, which is more robust and is often green in colour.

OCCUPIES *a wide range of habitats, lowland to montane, from open, dry sand dunes to damp, shady woodland; hibernates under logs or stones.*

white throat (may be blue in a breeding male)

variable black blotches

dark stripe down back

serrated collar edge

UNDERSIDE

yellow-orange below

SIZE *Body up to 6.5cm; tail 8–10cm.*
YOUNG *Up to 10 live young, born in damp areas, June–September.*
DIET *Insects, spiders, snails, earthworms, and other invertebrates.*
STATUS *Common.*
SIMILAR SPECIES *Sand Lizard (Lacerta agilis).*

Slow-worm

Anguis fragilis (Squamata)

Also (incorrectly) called the Blind Worm, the Slow-worm has a blunt head and its underparts are paler than the grey-brown upperparts. The females may have a dark stripe down the back, retained from the juveniles' colour, which has a deep bronze sheen.

FOUND *mostly in rather moist grassy areas, with scrub or hedgerows for refuge; also frequents large gardens and open woodland, up to montane levels.*

uniform bronze grey-brown upperparts

♂

males sometimes have blue spots

snake-like, limbless body

smooth scales

may have dark back stripe

round pupils

♀

SIZE *30–50cm.*
YOUNG *6–12 (sometimes more) live young, born August–September.*
DIET *Worms, slugs, and other invertebrates.*
STATUS *Common.*
SIMILAR SPECIES *Small individuals could be mistaken for large earthworms.*

REPTILES

Red-eared Terrapin

Trachemys scripta (Chelonia)

Introduced from North America, adult Red-eared Terrapins have a uniform dark grey-brown shell. The shell pattern of juveniles is more distinctive, with complex pale yellowish markings, making them much valued as pets. Their webbed feet aid them in swimming. The male is usually smaller than the female with a much longer, thicker tail.

FREQUENTS *lakes, ponds, canals, and slow-moving rivers; often close to human habitation.*

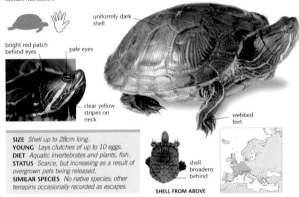

uniformly dark shell

bright red patch behind eyes

pale eyes

clear yellow stripes on neck

webbed feet

SIZE *Shell up to 28cm long.*
YOUNG *Lays clutches of up to 10 eggs.*
DIET *Aquatic invertebrates and plants, fish.*
STATUS *Scarce, but increasing as a result of overgrown pets being released.*
SIMILAR SPECIES *No native species; other terrapins occasionally recorded as escapes.*

shell broadens behind

SHELL FROM ABOVE

Common Frog

Rana temporaria (Anura)

The most widespread of the European frogs, the Common Frog is relatively robust, with a wide, blunt snout and two parallel ridges running down the back. Its colour is variable but the ground colour is usually yellowish to olive-brown, and the markings dark brown to almost black. The colour often intensifies during the breeding season, when the female develops a granular skin and the male's throat often turns bluish. Active during the day and the night, the northern populations hibernate under logs and stones, or in leaf mould or burrows.

ABUNDANT *in lowland meadows, marshes, and mountain pastures, with access to shallow ponds for breeding.*

smooth, variably coloured skin

dark blotches, especially on hind legs

gold-flecked brown iris

dark eye mask

large ear-drum

fully webbed hind feet

PALER FORM

HIND FOOT

SIZE *6–8cm.*
YOUNG *Lays 1,000 to 4,000 eggs.*
DIET *Slugs, snails, insects, worms, and other invertebrates.*
STATUS *Common.*
SIMILAR SPECIES *Marsh Frog (R. ridibunda), which is larger, and often greener.*

NOTE

When frogs gather at traditional breeding pools, the males utter a low, purring croak and grab anything that moves; if it happens to be a female, she can attract a whole host of suitors, and in the ensuing melée may even be drowned.

Common Toad

Bufo bufo (Anura)

A very widespread and robust species, the Common Toad is generally uniform brown in colour, and its skin covered in numerous warts. Rather constant in colour, Common Toads are more variable in size, with females growing to a size considerably larger than males. The parotid glands behind the eyes are prominent, and when viewed from above, are divergent rather than parallel as in the smaller Natterjack Toad (below). This gland exudes a secretion that repels predators. Common Toads are mainly nocturnal, except when breeding, and hibernate under logs, rocks, tree roots, or in leaf mould. Their normal gait is a lumbering walk, although they hop if alarmed.

FOUND *in a wide range of habitats, such as marshes, woodland, heathland, gardens, and mountain pastures, with access to pools and ponds for breeding.*

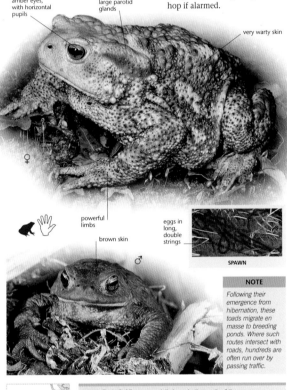

amber eyes, with horizontal pupils

large parotid glands

very warty skin

♀

powerful limbs

brown skin

♂

eggs in long, double strings

SPAWN

NOTE

Following their emergence from hibernation, these toads migrate en masse to breeding ponds. Where such routes intersect with roads, hundreds are often run over by passing traffic.

SIZE *Body 8–15cm, especially large in the south of the range.*
YOUNG *Lays 1,000–8,000 eggs, hatching in three weeks.*
DIET *Slugs, insects, spiders, and worms; large toads feed on other amphibians, small reptiles, and small mammals.*
STATUS *Common.*
SIMILAR SPECIES *Natterjack Toad (below), which is smaller and has a pale stripe down its back.*

Natterjack Toad

Bufo calamita (Anura)

A small but robust toad, the Natterjack Toad's characteristic marking is a yellow stripe down its spine, sometimes appearing very bright (although occasionally absent). It has parallel parotid glands that are often orange. Its gait is very distinctive – instead of walking like the Common Toad, the Natterjack has a scurrying run, rather like a mouse.

PREFERS *sandy heaths and dunes, with ponds, often temporary, for breeding; also marshes and salt marshes.*

golden iris, with horizontal pupils

pale to olive brown skin

darker brown marbling

short legs

SPAWN

yellow mid-line running down back

SIZE *Body 6–8cm.*
YOUNG *Lays 2,000–5,000 eggs, hatching rapidly; may develop quickly in shallow water. Tadpoles small and black, with bronze spots.*
DIET *Slugs, spiders, insects, and worms.*
STATUS *Scarce; locally abundant.*
SIMILAR SPECIES *Common Toad (above).*

Great Crested Newt

Triturus cristatus (Caudata)

OCCURS *in a wide range of weedy, deep, standing waters (larvae prefer depths of more than 30cm), and favours sites without predatory fish.*

Also known as the Warty Newt, on account of its granular skin, the Great Crested Newt has blackish skin, especially outside the breeding season. However, when breeding, its ground colour lightens, and black spots and blotches appear, along with white flecks on the head and flanks. The distinctive, jagged crest, with a gap at the base of the tail, and silvery tail flash feature only in males. Largely nocturnal, they also hibernate, sometimes buried in mud, but usually under logs and stones, up to 200m from the breeding site.

brown with black spots

JUVENILE

irregularly spotted orange belly

black throat, speckled white

UNDERSIDE

spiky crest

♂

BREEDING MALE

crest gap at base of tail

silvery tail stripe

NOTE

As with many newts, Great Crested Newts are most easily spotted during the breeding season by torchlight at night, when they may be seen rising to the surface; however, small populations are perhaps best located by searching water plants for their eggs.

orange lower tail margin

dark, almost black, skin

granular ("warty") skin

♀

SIZE Body up to 8cm; tail up to 7.5cm.
YOUNG Lays 200–400 eggs over many months, hatching in three weeks.
DIET Aquatic insects, worms, snails, and other invertebrates; small and larval amphibians.
STATUS Common, but declining.
SIMILAR SPECIES Breeding male Smooth Newt (right), which is smaller, has a smooth texture, and a large but continuous crest.

Smooth Newt

Triturus vulgaris (Caudata)

LIVES *on land in damp woodland, marshes, and gardens; breeds in ponds, ditches, lake margins, and slow-moving rivers.*

One of the most widespread and abundant amphibians in Britain, it is not surprising that an alternative name for the Smooth Newt is the Common Newt. It is much more terrestrial than many other newts, typically living in water as an adult only for breeding, between March and July. Non-breeding animals are olive-brown, with a black-spotted throat, and two ridges on the head which join near the snout. They have darker spots and a black-spotted, orange belly. Largely nocturnal, they shelter (as well as hibernate) under logs, stones, or leaf-litter. Breeding males, in contrast, are very showy, with a wavy crest up to 1cm high, and clear black face stripes.

NOTE

Sometimes mistaken for the Great Crested Newt (left) on account of its equally flamboyant crest, the most obvious point of distinction is that the crest of the breeding male Smooth Newt is continuous from the back onto the tail.

bright yellow-orange beneath

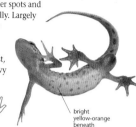

prominent black head stripes

large, wavy, continuous crest

black-spotted, olive brown upperparts

BREEDING MALE

silvery tail and flank flash

small crest on underside of tail

shiny, smooth skin

♀

SIZE Body up to 6cm; tail up to 5cm.
YOUNG Lays 200–500 eggs, hatching in 2–3 weeks.
DIET Insects, worms, and other invertebrates; tadpoles.
STATUS Common.
SIMILAR SPECIES Great Crested Newt (left); Palmate Newt (below), which has a whitish, unspotted throat, and a smooth crest in the breeding male, and tends to be found in more acidic waters.

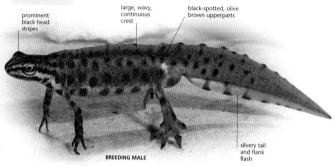

Palmate Newt

Triturus helveticus (Caudata)

FOUND *in shallow, still, often acidic, usually well vegetated, waterbodies in woodland, heathland, farmland, and mountains; can tolerate brackish conditions.*

The smallest of the native British newts, the Palmate Newt gets its name from the black webs which develop on the hind feet of the male during the breeding season; its breeding appearance is also characterized by a prominent crest on the tail, which terminates in a distinct filament. At all times, Palmate Newts have a blackish stripe through the eye, a pale yellow belly, and unspotted throat. Most adults leave the breeding pools in late summer and hibernate under rocks and logs. Hibernating individuals lose much of their colour, but the distinctive throat pattern usually remains.

dark line through the eye

smooth tail crest

terminal filament

BREEDING MALE

whitish throat

black webbing on hind feet

pale yellow, underparts

SIZE Body up to 4.5cm; tail up to 4.5cm.
YOUNG Lays 300–400 eggs.
DIET Invertebrates, worms, and tadpoles.
STATUS Common.
SIMILAR SPECIES Smooth Newt (above), which is more spotted below, especially in summer. In hibernation, the Palmate Newt usually retains a white or pinkish, unspotted throat.

NOTE

Although overlapping in range with other newts, the Palmate Newt is often the only species to be found in its preferred habitats. Acidic ponds, often associated with heathland, and pools within broad-leaved woodland are especially favoured by this species.

REPTILES

POOL FROG

The Pool Frog is one of a group of three species of green frog that occur widely across western Europe and that interbreed with one another in a complex way. Found in a number of places in southeast England, most populations were artificially introduced from southern mainland Europe. However, studies have established that Pool Frogs were in fact native to East Anglia until the 1990s, when they became extinct as a consequence of habitat loss resulting from intensive agriculture. It was also found that these frogs were part of a distinct group of northern Pool Frogs, and were closely related to Scandinavian Pool Frogs, rather than those from southern Europe. A protected site has been established near Thetford in Norfolk, where Pool Frogs from Sweden have been introduced. It is hoped that these frogs will breed successfully and that a viable population will become established. Pool Frogs vary in colour, with the adult female slightly larger than the male. During the spring breeding season, males call loudly from open water. The eggs are laid in clumps of 600 to 3,000 eggs. If a reasonable proportion of these survive to become tadpoles and, eventually, adults, the population can increase very quickly.

FISH

During the ice age, vast expanses of water around the British Isles were frozen, making them unsuitable for fish. As a result, British waters have relatively few fish species. More recently, human activity has had a significant influence. The number of species in our ponds and rivers has risen due to introductions from elsewhere, while most aquatic environments are experiencing problems with pollution or overfishing. Despite the low number of species, British fish fauna is diverse, including both sharks and a variety of bony fish – some of them occurring in great numbers. The species in the following pages are some of the most commonly encountered fish in Britain that may be seen while walking by a river or its estuary, a pond, or the seashore.

FRESHWATER

Britain has about 40 native freshwater species and about 13 introduced ones. A number of species, such as the Tench, belong to the cyprinid family; most of the others are solitary members of their group.

SALTWATER

The saltwater fish of Britain's shores vary from the small blennies of rock pools to the huge Basking Shark. Some fish live in shallow estuaries, where the salinity of the water varies considerably with the tide.

FRESH- AND SALTWATER

A few fish spend part of their lives in the sea and part in fresh water. The Eel matures in fresh water and spawns in the sea; while salmon move from the sea into freshwater to spawn.

Anatomy

Fish are adapted to live in all types of water, from rivers and ponds to seahore and estuary, as well as in man-made canals and reservoirs. They are unique in possessing fins which, along with a streamlined muscular body, allow them to move efficiently in water. They have paired pectoral and pelvic fins, and single dorsal, anal, and tail fins, which aid propulsion and steering and allow the fish to make very precise swimming movements. Most fish obtain their oxygen via structures called gills, which in bony fish are protected by a plate-like covering. These fish also tend to be covered in scales that are visible under a thin transparent outer layer – the epidermis. Fish have the same senses as terrestrial animals – sight, smell, taste, and hearing – but also possess a row of sensory organs that run along the sides of their bodies. This lateral line allows fish to assess its position. Most fish have bony skeletons but in a few, such as the sharks, it is made of cartilage.

LIFE CYCLE
Most fish, such as this Brown Trout, abandon their eggs after they have been fertilized. On hatching, the young trout, called alevin, remain hidden in the gravel, rising up as fry to feed once their yolk sacs have disappeared.

spherical eggs are layed in gravel

alevin remain close to the stream bottom

red and brown spots

parr mark

adult Brown Trout

yolk sacks provide nourishment

fry rapidly enter the next stage of development, and become parr

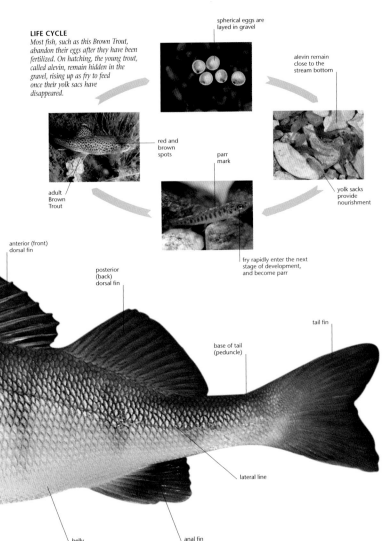

anterior (front) dorsal fin

scales

dark upper body

posterior (back) dorsal fin

eye

tail fin

base of tail (peduncle)

lateral line

mouth

gill covering (operculum)

paired pectoral fins

belly

anal fin

paired pelvic fins

AGE AND SIZE
Fish vary greatly in size from the 8cm Minnow to the 13m Basking Shark. Growth is dependent on a number of factors, including availability of food, and water temperature, so that size is not necessarily related to age. Some fish live for only a few years, but others, such as the Perch, may survive for well over a decade.

Identification

Some fish, such as the Pike, are easy to recognize because they are like no other – but closely related species, such as Dace and Chub, are more difficult to tell apart because the differences between them are more subtle. Colour and size are unreliable features to use for indentification purposes because they are highly variable between individual fish. There are, however, other characters which looked at either singly or together make a fish species unique. These features include scales, body shape, fin position, and behaviour.

Scales

Fish scales vary in size (see below), in shape, and in number. Bony fish have either oval ctenoid scales, which have edges that are rough to the touch, or round cycloid scales, which are smooth. Sometimes the number of scales present on the lateral line are counted and used to identify different fish.

LARGE SCALES
The individual scales are clearly visible, but their shape is obscured because the free edge of one scale covers the base of the one behind it.

SMALL SCALES
Sometimes visible on the surface, as here on a Tench, small scales are not easily counted. On some fish, such as the Pike, the scales are almost invisible.

MINUTE SCALES
Some fish, such as the Eel, either do not have scales or these are very small and embedded in the skin. Lacking reflective crystals, Eels have no metallic sheen.

Body shape

Fish have evolved into a variety of shapes that reflect their lifestyle. Slim streamlined fish tend to live in turbulent water or may need speed to catch their prey. Deep bodied fish, such as carp, prefer still water, while flat fish, such as the flounders, are often bottom-dwelling, estuarine species.

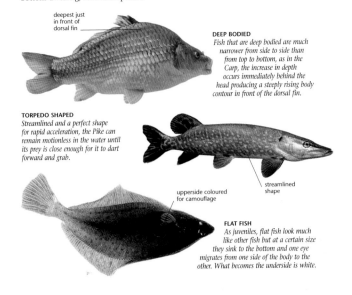

deepest just in front of dorsal fin

DEEP BODIED
Fish that are deep bodied are much narrower from side to side than from top to bottom, as in the Carp, the increase in depth occurs immediately behind the head producing a steeply rising body contour in front of the dorsal fin.

TORPEDO SHAPED
Streamlined and a perfect shape for rapid acceleration, the Pike can remain motionless in the water until its prey is close enough for it to dart forward and grab.

streamlined shape

upperside coloured for camouflage

FLAT FISH
As juveniles, flat fish look much like other fish but at a certain size they sink to the bottom and one eye migrates from one side of the body to the other. What becomes the underside is white.

Fins

Many fish can be recognized by the number, structure, and/or shape of their fins, and their arrangement relative to one another. Some fish, such as the Perch, have two dorsal fins while others, such as the Gudgeon, have only one. In other species the fins may be joined together. For example, in the Eel the dorsal, anal and tail fins form one continuous fin around the back part of the body.

FIN SHAPE

The free edge of the dorsal fin can be concave, straight, or convex. In some species, such as the Barbel, this fin also has a conspicuous spine on the leading edge. Dorsal spines are also seen in sticklebacks, which are named for the number of spines they possess.

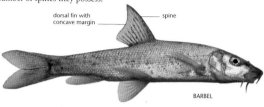

dorsal fin with concave margin — spine

BARBEL

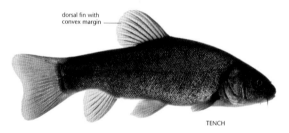

dorsal fin with straight margin

ROACH

dorsal fin with convex margin

TENCH

FIN POSITION

The position of the pelvic fins relative to the dorsal fin is an important diagnostic tool. The fin base may originate behind the front margin of the dorsal fin, at the same level, or in front of it. In some fish, the pelvic fins are so far forward that they are almost in line with the pectoral fins.

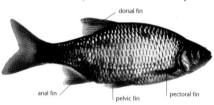

dorsal fin

anal fin / pelvic fin / pectoral fin

RUDD
Here the base of the pelvic fins is just in front of the dorsal fin and there is no overlap with the pectoral fins. The anal fin is relatively short-based.

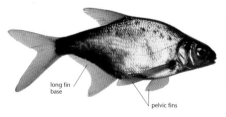

long fin base

pelvic fins

BREAM
In this fish the pelvic fins originate in advance of the dorsal fin and are much closer to the pectoral fins. The anal fin has a long fin base and concave margin.

FIN STRUCTURE

Fins can be spiny or soft rayed depending on species and/or position on the body. Spiny rays are much more rigid than the branching soft rays. Members of the salmon family have an additional fleshy adipose fin behind the dorsal fin that lacks either rays or spines.

spiny-rayed fin

soft-rayed fin

Mouths and Jaws

Fish have mouths of different sizes, some, like the Tench, are small, while others, like the Basking Shark, are huge. The mouth may be situated underneath for bottom feeding, level (pointing forwards), or point upwards. Barbels, fleshy outgrowths from the lips that have a sensory function, may also be present. Fish that are active predators of other fish, such as the Pike and Zander, often have large jaws lined with teeth.

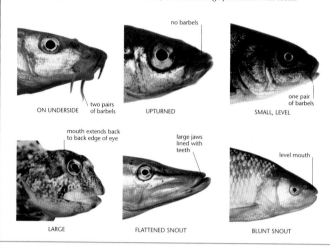

ON UNDERSIDE / two pairs of barbels

no barbels

UPTURNED

one pair of barbels

SMALL, LEVEL

mouth extends back to back edge of eye

LARGE

large jaws lined with teeth

FLATTENED SNOUT

level mouth

BLUNT SNOUT

Tails

Some fish have strongly forked tails while others have weakly forked, straight edged or convex margins to the fin. Because the tail is variable and easy to look at, it can help in identifying a fish in the wild. Look also at the base of the tail (peduncle) as it too may be characteristic; it can be broad or narrow, and long or short.

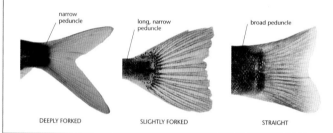

narrow peduncle

DEEPLY FORKED

long, narrow peduncle

SLIGHTLY FORKED

broad peduncle

STRAIGHT

Behaviour

Many fish have cryptic coloration for camouflage, and some, such as the plaice, can change colour depending on the surface they are resting on. Bottom-dwelling fish blend in very well with their surroundings especially if they remain still. During the spawning season some male fish, such as salmon and stickleback, develop bright colours to attract females; some others develop turbercles on their bodies.

▼ **CAMOUFLAGE** *Cryptic coloration as seen in this Sand Goby makes it difficult for predators to locate prey and prey to spot a predator.*

▲ **BREEDING COLOURS** *During the spawning season male sticklebacks develop a red belly and blue eyes and perform a courtship dance, to attract females into their nests.*

SCALE MEASUREMENTS
Two scale drawings. one of a human hand and one of an adult man, are used to convey a rough indication of the average size of the species being described. The hand represents an adult hand of 18cm in height. The man represents an average adult man 1.8m (6ft) tall.

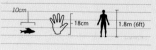

10cm

18cm

1.8m (6ft)

SYMBOLS
Male and female fish of some species sometimes look visually distinct. Not all instances are shown, but where they are, for clarity, symbols are used to denote males and females.

Female ♀   *Male* ♂

Common Carp

Cyprinus carpio (Cyprinidae)

FOUND *in stagnant water of lowland lakes and rivers that have a muddy substrate and abundant vegetation.*

The Common Carp has probably been farmed longer than any other fish. It can be recognized by its bronze-brown coloration and the two pairs of tiny barbels on its lips. The wild form has uniform-sized scales and is much slimmer than introduced fish, which have much deeper bodies and scales that vary in shape and number.

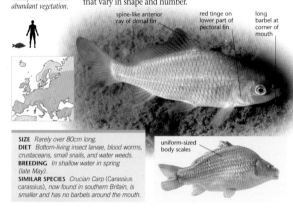

spine-like anterior ray of dorsal fin

red tinge on lower part of pectoral fin

long barbel at corner of mouth

uniform-sized body scales

SIZE *Rarely over 80cm long.*
DIET *Bottom-living insect larvae, blood worms, crustaceans, small snails, and water weeds.*
BREEDING *In shallow water in spring (late May).*
SIMILAR SPECIES *Crucian Carp (Carassius carassius), now found in southern Britain, is smaller and has no barbels around the mouth.*

Chub

Leuciscus cephalus (Cyprinidae)

SEEN *near the surface in the mid-reaches of rivers and in large lakes.*

The Chub is one of the most widespread freshwater fish. Slow to mature, it forms large schools near the water surface although larger adults tend to be more solitary. Coloured dark brown above and cream below, the Chub has a blunt-snouted head with a wide mouth. Its body is covered with large scales and the pelvic fin bases are situated anterior to the dorsal fin.

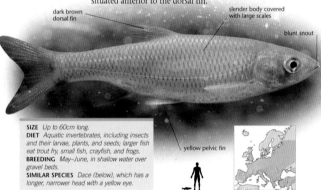

dark brown dorsal fin

slender body covered with large scales

blunt snout

yellow pelvic fin

SIZE *Up to 60cm long.*
DIET *Aquatic invertebrates, including insects and their larvae, plants, and seeds; larger fish eat trout fry, small fish, crayfish, and frogs.*
BREEDING *May–June, in shallow water over gravel beds.*
SIMILAR SPECIES *Dace (below), which has a longer, narrower head with a yellow eye.*

Barbel

Barbus barbus (Cyprinidae)

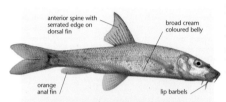

OCCURS *in mid- and lower reaches of clean rivers where the current is moderate to fast.*

A large, bottom-dwelling fish, the Barbel can be recognized by its ventrally situated mouth, the two pairs of barbels on its lips, and a broad, flattened belly. The anterior dorsal fin ray is long and modified into a serrated edged spine and the tail fin is deeply forked. Females are always bigger than males of an equivalent age. Barbels are most active at night when they disperse to feed. During daylight hours, they gather in small schools of similar sized fish and are found in the water current near areas of turbulence, such as waterfalls. During the spawning season, males develop rows of white tubercles along their heads and backs. They pursue the females until they release their eggs, which they then swim over and fertilize.

anterior spine with serrated edge on dorsal fin

broad cream coloured belly

orange anal fin

lip barbels

brown-green upper body

SIZE *Up to 50cm long (a few specimens of 90cm have been recorded).*
DIET *Bottom-living invertebrates such as water snails, Freshwater Shrimps, aquatic insect larvae, and plant debris.*
BREEDING *March–May.*
SIMILAR SPECIES *Gudgeon (below), which is much smaller and has only has one pair of barbels, one at each corner of the mouth. It lacks both the spiny fin ray with the serrated edge at the front of the dorsal fin and the broad flattened belly of this species.*

NOTE
During winter, when the water temperature drops below 3°C, Barbels cease feeding and activity levels drop. They move together into deeper water where they become torpid – a condition similar to mammal hibernation.

Dace

Leuciscus leuciscus (Cyprinidae)

In river habitats, shoals of Dace are so common that they often outnumber the other fish. The Dace has a slender body, with a small head and distinctive mottled yellow eyes; the outer edges of dorsal and anal fins are concave. Unlike many other cyprinids that fast over winter, the Dace feeds all year round. Its fry are eaten by birds such as the kingfisher.

THRIVES *in mid-reaches of rivers; sometimes in lakes and lowland rivers; occasionally in brackish water near river mouths.*

dorsal fin

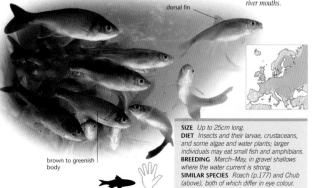

brown to greenish body

SIZE *Up to 25cm long.*
DIET *Insects and their larvae, crustaceans, and some algae and water plants; larger individuals may eat small fish and amphibians.*
BREEDING *March–May, in gravel shallows where the water current is strong.*
SIMILAR SPECIES *Roach (p.177) and Chub (above), both of which differ in eye colour.*

Gudgeon

Gobio gobio (Cyprinidae)

The elongated, round-bodied Gudgeon is a bottom-dwelling shoal fish that uses its fleshy lips and sensory barbels to locate food. Its scales are moderately sized and shaded silvery white below. There are a series of dark blotches running along its sides, following the course of the lateral line (a sensory structure).

FOUND *in lakes and rivers that are well oxygenated and clean, with sandy bottoms.*

dark blotches

scales coloured green-brown above

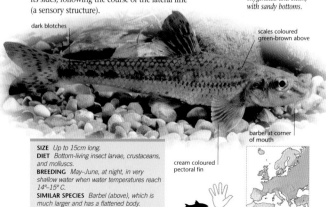

barbel at corner of mouth

cream coloured pectoral fin

SIZE *Up to 15cm long.*
DIET *Bottom-living insect larvae, crustaceans, and molluscs.*
BREEDING *May–June, at night, in very shallow water when water temperatures reach 14°–15° C.*
SIMILAR SPECIES *Barbel (above), which is much larger and has a flattened body.*

Bream

Abramis brama (Cyprinidae)

Nicknamed "skimmers" because juveniles trawl the surface waters in search of newly hatched midge larvae, the Bream can survive in water that is low in oxygen. It is a narrow, deep-bodied fish that skims over the bottom at an oblique angle when searching for food. It has a small head and in shallow water, its tail may break the surface as it moves.

OCCURS in slow-flowing rivers, lowland lakes, and ponds with stagnant water and muddy bottoms.

brown dorsal fin

terminal mouth

cream belly

anal fin with long base

pale pectoral fin

SIZE *Up to 80cm long.*
DIET *Insect larvae, worms, snails, bivalves, and crustaceans.*
BREEDING *May–July, where vegetation is dense; often occurs at night in shallow water.*
SIMILAR SPECIES *Silver Bream (Blicca bjoerka), which has a paler body; the eye and scales are relatively much larger.*

Roach

Rutilus rutilus (Cyprinidae)

The environment in which the Roach lives influences its shape and size – it is only in optimum conditions that it acquires any thickness or grows over 15cm in length. Its body is blue-grey dorsally, shading to silver on the sides and white below. The iris of the eye is reddish as are the pelvic and anal fins.

SEEN in lowland rivers and lakes, preferring areas with slower currents to faster ones; tolerant of low-level pollution.

conspicuous body scales

grey-brown dorsal fin

reddish anal fin

reddish pelvic fin

red iris

SIZE *Up to 35cm long.*
DIET *Insects and their larvae, crustaceans, and snails, as well as algae and plant matter.*
BREEDING *April–June, in dense vegetation in shallow water of at least 10° C.*
SIMILAR SPECIES *Rudd (Scardinius erythrophthalmus), which has a golden iris and a more upward-pointing mouth.*

Tench

Tinca tinca (Cyprinidae)

One of the few freshwater fish to show sexual dimorphism outside the breeding season, a male Tench is distinguishable from the female by the time it is two years of age. By then, its anal fin is longer than that of a female and the second fin ray of the anal fin also becomes greatly thickened.

FOUND in murky water of lakes and ponds with soft bottoms, sometimes in lower reaches of rivers; tolerant of low-oxygen conditions.

deep unforked tail

small scales

small red-orange eyes

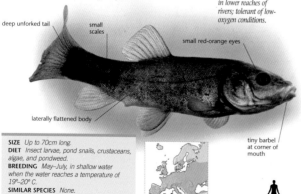

laterally flattened body

tiny barbel at corner of mouth

SIZE *Up to 70cm long.*
DIET *Insect larvae, pond snails, crustaceans, algae, and pondweed.*
BREEDING *May–July, in shallow water when the water reaches a temperature of 19°–20° C.*
SIMILAR SPECIES *None.*

Minnow

Phoxinus phoxinus (Cyprinidae)

This tiny fish forms an important part of the aquatic food chain because it is eaten by larger fish, such as trout and Pike (p.178), as well as being taken by birds, such as the Grey Heron (p.118). Usually seen in small schools, the Minnow has a blunt snout, short-based fins, and small, inconspicuous scales. During the breeding season, the belly of the male changes colour from white to red and both sexes may develop small tubercles on their heads. Minnows usually feed on bottom-dwelling invertebrates, but should an insect land on the surface of the water, they will swim up, take hold of its legs, and pull it under the water to eat it. Young minnows, called fry, gather in huge numbers in very shallow, warm water where they feed on algae and zooplankton.

FOUND typically in upland areas with gravel substrates in fast-flowing, well-oxygenated rivers and streams, or high-altitude lakes with cool, clean water.

NOTE

Minnow species have been used in laboratory experiments to determine how well fish can hear as sound travels better in water than in air.

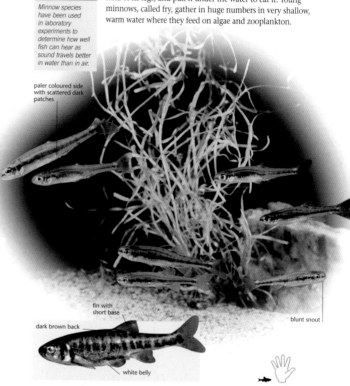

paler coloured side with scattered dark patches

fin with short base

dark brown back

blunt snout

white belly

SIZE *Rarely more than 8cm long.*
DIET *Insects and insect larvae, crustaceans, trout eggs, algae, and plants.*
BREEDING *May–mid-July, over gravel.*
SIMILAR SPECIES *Swamp Minnow (Phoxinus percnurus) is similar to the juvenile Minnow but has spots rather than scattered dark patches on the sides of the body. It is also found in a slightly different habitat, preferring well-vegetated ponds and lakes.*

Stone Loach

Barbatula barbatula (Balitoridae)

A nocturnal fish that hides by day under stones or in dense vegetation, the Stone Loach has a slender, rather elongated body and an unforked tail with rounded margins. It can be easily recognized by the six barbels around its mouth, four on the upper lip and one at each corner of the mouth. Its blotchy brown coloration provides excellent camouflage.

INHABITS lowland reaches of rivers and upland streams; lakes with gravel shores.

barbels in corner of mouth

posterior dorsal fin

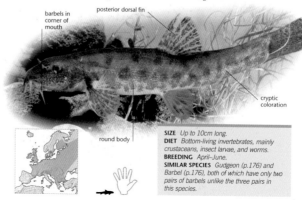

cryptic coloration

round body

SIZE *Up to 10cm long.*
DIET *Bottom-living invertebrates, mainly crustaceans, insect larvae, and worms.*
BREEDING *April–June.*
SIMILAR SPECIES *Gudgeon (p.176) and Barbel (p.176), both of which have only two pairs of barbels unlike the three pairs in this species.*

Pike

Esox lucius (Esocidae)

The Pike is an ambush predator that lies in wait for its prey among the weeds and strikes at great speed when it is close enough. It has a distinctive torpedo-shaped body with similarly shaped, opposing dorsal and anal fins far back on the body. The jaws are lined with sharp, backward-pointing teeth. Pike tend to be brown-green in colour, flecked with yellow on their sides, so as to blend into the pond vegetation.

INHABITS *varied habitats with slow currents – small ponds, large lakes, and rivers.*

broad, flattened snout

powerful tail

green-brown body flecked with yellow

dorsal fin

JUVENILE

SIZE *Up to 1.5m long.*
DIET *Fish, ducklings, and other small birds, frogs and newts, and even small mammals.*
BREEDING *March–late June, in daylight, depending on locality; spawning occurs later in the north of its range as the temperature rises more slowly in spring.*
SIMILAR SPECIES *None.*

Eel

Anguilla anguilla (Anguillidae)

A migratory fish, the Eel starts its life in the sea but moves into freshwater to grow and mature. The Eel is snake-like and has a continuous fin enveloping the hind part of the body, which is made up of fused dorsal, tail, and anal fins. Unusually for a fish, the Eel can survive short periods out of water and is capable of moving overland between different river systems.

OCCURS *in fresh and salt water depending on the stage of its life cycle.*

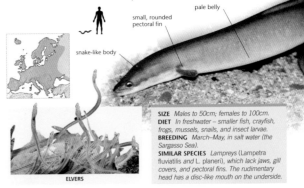

pale belly

small, rounded pectoral fin

snake-like body

ELVERS

SIZE *Males to 50cm; females to 100cm.*
DIET *In freshwater – smaller fish, crayfish, frogs, mussels, snails, and insect larvae.*
BREEDING *March–May, in salt water (the Sargasso Sea).*
SIMILAR SPECIES *Lampreys (Lampetra fluviatilis and L. planeri), which lack jaws, gill covers, and pectoral fins. The rudimentary head has a disc-like mouth on the underside.*

Bullhead

Cottus gobio (Cottidae)

Also referred to as the Miller's Thumb, this bottom-dwelling fish has a wide head, large eyes, and a tapering body that lacks scales. Its colour is variable and depends on the habitat but, like most fish, the upper body is dark and the belly pale. The dorsal fins are joined and form a continuous fin that extends along almost the entire length of the body. The Bullhead also has huge, rounded pectoral fins, and an anal fin with a long base. Unusually, the lateral line extends onto the tail fin. Males exhibit parental care, and like the sticklebacks, guard their eggs until they hatch in 21–28 days. It spends the day hidden under stones, only emerging at dusk to feed.

FOUND *in clean, clear, shallow water with strong to moderate currents in rivers, streams, and lakes with stony substrates.*

large eyes towards top of head

rounded pectoral fin

anterior dorsal fin

pale brown body with lighter mottling

SIZE *Exceptionally up to 18cm long – usually about 10cm.*
DIET *Crustaceans, especially freshwater shrimps, and bottom-dwelling insect larvae, such as the mayflies and caddisflies. It also feeds on eggs and fry of other fish, including Brown Trout (right) but not to an extent that is detrimental to fisheries.*
BREEDING *March–May, sometimes a second spawning occurs in July.*
SIMILAR SPECIES *None.*

NOTE

The lateral line system provides information about the distance between the Bullhead and its prey, allowing it to hunt in complete darkness.

Atlantic Salmon

Salmo salar (Salmonidae)

Like all salmonids, the Atlantic Salmon can be recognized by the small, fleshy adipose fin on its back, located between the dorsal fin and the tail. Males are red-brown in colour dorsally while females are silver-grey; both have white bellies. During the spawning season, the males develop a well-defined hook on the lower jaw. Salmon return to the rivers in which they hatched, to breed. Because they stop feeding at this time, they lose about 40 per cent of their body weight and most die of exhaustion after spawning.

SEEN *in freshwater (November–December) and in salt water; low tolerance to pollution.*

white belly

fleshy adipose fin

very slightly forked tail

head lacking in scales

JUVENILE

SIZE *Males to 1.5m; females to 1.2m.*
DIET *In freshwater – Bullhead (left), mayflies and their larvae, caddisfly larvae, and Freshwater Shrimps.*
BREEDING *November–December, in upper reaches of streams with gravel bottoms.*
SIMILAR SPECIES *Rainbow Trout (p.179), has a spotted tail and pink patches on its body.*

Brown Trout

Salmo trutta (Salmonidae)

There are two types of Brown Trout – one that is migratory and moves between river and sea, and one that is non-migratory and remains in freshwater, living in either lakes or rivers. The differences between them tend to be behavioural rather than genetic. The former is silver coloured with black spots while the latter is, as its name suggests, brown with both black and red spots on its back and on the sides.

INHABITS *cool, clean well-oxygenated water whether fresh or salty; small streams, rivers, lakes, and the sea; intolerant of pollution.*

black spots

upper jaw extends back beyond eye

ALEVINS

SIZE *Up to 1m long.*
DIET *Small crustaceans and insect larvae, small fish.*
BREEDING *October–January.*
SIMILAR SPECIES *Rainbow Trout (p.179), which is more colourful, has a blunter head, and no red spotting; Atlantic Salmon (above), which can be confused with the sea-going Brown Trout but is larger.*

Rainbow Trout

Oncorhynchus mykiss (Salmonidae)

The Rainbow Trout is now widespread in Britain and is important commercially, being farmed both for food and as a source for restocking rivers for anglers. It is easily recognized by the pink coloration along its sides and the dark spots that extend over the tail. It has a small head with a blunt snout; the body is covered in tiny scales.

FOUND *in streams, rivers, and lakes; more tolerant of pollution and high temperatures than the Brown Trout.*

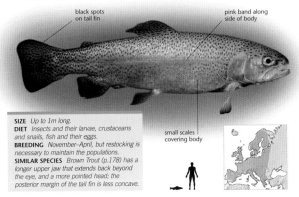

black spots on tail fin

pink band along side of body

small scales covering body

SIZE *Up to 1m long.*
DIET *Insects and their larvae, crustaceans and snails, fish and their eggs.*
BREEDING *November–April, but restocking is necessary to maintain the populations.*
SIMILAR SPECIES *Brown Trout (p.178) has a longer upper jaw that extends back beyond the eye, and a more pointed head; the posterior margin of the tail fin is less concave.*

Grayling

Thymallus thymallus (Salmonidae)

The distinctive appearance of the Grayling with its linear arrangement of body scales, elongated dorsal fin, and downward-directed mouth differentiates it not only from other salmonids, but also from all other freshwater fish. Grayling live in shoals in which all fish are of similar size, but larger individuals may be solitary.

INHABITS *fast-flowing, clear, well-oxygenated water in the upper reaches of rivers with sand or gravel.*

large dorsal fin

large scales arranged in distinct rows

pear-shaped iris in eye

SIZE *Up to 50cm long.*
DIET *Bottom-dwelling insect larvae, including stonefly nymphs, small worms, crustaceans, and molluscs. It also takes insects that land on the surface of the water. Larger individuals may consume small fish.*
BREEDING *March–May, in fast-flowing water in gravelly shallows.*
SIMILAR SPECIES *None.*

Perch

Perca fluviatilis (Percidae)

A deep-bodied fish, the Perch has a green-brown back and a white or cream belly. Its sides are more golden in colour with four to six vertical dark bands. The orange-red pelvic and anal fins add to its colourful appearance. The Perch feels rough to the touch because the body scales are covered in small tubercles. Not a particularly active fish, it lives in schools.

SEEN *in lowland lakes and ponds, and in slow-running rivers.*

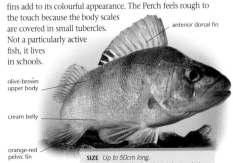

anterior dorsal fin

olive-brown upper body

cream belly

orange-red pelvic fin

EGGS

SIZE *Up to 50cm long.*
DIET *Juveniles feed on invertebrates, but as adults they also feed on fish such as smaller Perch, sticklebacks, and small cyprinids.*
BREEDING *March–June (peaking in April and May), in shallow water.*
SIMILAR SPECIES *Ruffe (Gymnocephalus cernuus), which has larger scales, and yellowish pelvic and anal fins.*

Zander

Sander lucioperca (Percidae)

Also called the "Pike-perch", the Zander has been introduced to Britain from eastern Europe. It is a predacious fish with a large head and powerful jaws, which extend beyond the anterior margin of the eye. There are several large fangs at the front of the mouth and many smaller teeth behind. The body is elongated and has two dorsal fins, the first of which is spiny. The green-brown colour of the back extends as barring onto its paler sides; the belly is cream or white. Like the Perch (left), the body scales are tuberculated. It feeds at dawn and dusk, resting close to the river bed at other times.

THRIVES *in murky, but well-oxygenated water in large lakes and lowland rivers with little vegetation.*

spiny dorsal fin

banding on sides

powerful jaws

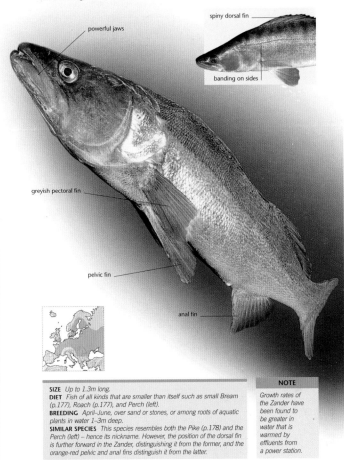

greyish pectoral fin

pelvic fin

anal fin

SIZE *Up to 1.3m long.*
DIET *Fish of all kinds that are smaller than itself such as small Bream (p.177), Roach (p.177), and Perch (left).*
BREEDING *April–June, over sand or stones, or among roots of aquatic plants in water 1–3m deep.*
SIMILAR SPECIES *This species resembles both the Pike (p.178) and the Perch (left) – hence its nickname. However, the position of the dorsal fin is further forward in the Zander, distinguishing it from the former, and the orange-red pelvic and anal fins distinguish it from the latter.*

NOTE

Growth rates of the Zander have been found to be greater in water that is warmed by effluents from a power station.

Thick-lipped Grey Mullet

Chelon labrosus (Mugilidae)

A sea fish that ventures into river estuaries to feed, the Thick-lipped Grey Mullet has a streamlined body covered with large grey-blue scales that become silvery on the sides and white on the belly. The fish has two dorsal fins, the first being small, with only four fin spines. As its name suggests, the upper lip is swollen and has two or three rows of tubercles on the lower half near the mouth.

FOUND *in coastal waters and in river estuaries.*

dark grey pectoral fin

large scales that extend onto head

deeply forked tail

streamlined body

SIZE *Up to 75cm long.*
DIET *Nematode worms, copepods, algae, and plant matter.*
BREEDING *Late June–early September, in shallow inshore waters.*
SIMILAR SPECIES *Thin-lipped Mullet (Liza ramada) is thinner and lacks tubercles on the upper lip; Golden-Grey Mullet (Liza aurata) has a gold spot behind each eye and gill.*

THE THAMES

B y the early 19th century the River Thames at London had become seriously polluted. Industrial discharges were partly to blame, but the main problem was raw sewage generated by the city's growing population. Bacteria growing on sewage use up a river's oxygen, suffocating fish and other life. New Victorian sewers stopped the stink in central London, but transferred the problem downstream to the estuary. By the 1950s, the tidal Thames was probably in the worst condition in its history – a consequence of further population growth and damage from two world wars. During the 1960s and 1970s, investment and better sewage treatment methods wrought a dramatic transformation, and many fish now thrive there. For conservationists, the "jewel in the crown" has been to re-establish a breeding population of salmon in the Thames. But for this to happen, every part of the species' complex life cycle has to be made possible again. Fish passes have been built beside locks and weirs, allowing the salmon to reach suitable breeding sites in the Thames's tributaries. Although results have varied so far – not helped by droughts and occasional sewage overflows – experts are hopeful that the salmon is now truly on its way back to the Thames.

Sea Bass

Dicentrarchus labrax (Moronidae)

A schooling fish of inshore waters, the Sea Bass can be recognized by the spines on its gill cover. On the lower edge, the spines point forwards, but the two spines on the back edge are flattened and point towards the tail. The two dorsal fins are separate, the first of them being spiny, as is the anal fin. The Sea Bass is slow to mature, but may live for 20 years.

FOUND *in inshore waters; juveniles especially enter estuaries to feed.*

spiny first dorsal fin

large head

second dorsal fin

large silver scales on sides

SIZE *Up to 1m.*
DIET *Wide range of fish – fish of the herring family, sand-eels, squids, and crustaceans.*
BREEDING *March–mid-June, in deep inshore seas.*
SIMILAR SPECIES *Large-mouthed Bass (Micropterus salmoides) has a continuous but notched dorsal fin, its jaw extends beyond the eye, and the gill covers lacks spines.*

Lesser Sand-eel

Ammodytes tobianus (Ammodytidae)

A shoaling, silvery fish, the Lesser Sand-eel is often abundant in the inshore zone. It has a thin, elongated body with a long dorsal fin that fits into a groove. It lacks pelvic fins and has a small forked tail. It forms the staple diet of many seabirds, including the Puffin (p.139) and terns. Unfortunately, many stocks have been over-fished on an industrial scale, and this has greatly reduced the numbers of birds that rely on Sand-eels as food for their chicks.

OCCURS *on sandy shores, from mid-tide level to the shallow sublittoral; often buried in sand, even at low tide.*

elongated body

pointed head

SIZE *Length to 10cm.*
DIET *Planktonic invertebrates.*
BREEDING *Two seasons: February–April and September–November.*
SIMILAR SPECIES *Greater Sand-Eel (Hyperoplus lanceolatus), which is longer, with a bluish appearance and a black spot in front of the eyes, and usually in the sublittoral. Many other similar species are found offshore.*

Shanny

Lipophyris pholis (Blenniidae)

Abundant in rock pools, the Shanny has a blunt head, large eyes, and an elongated, smooth scale-less body. The dorsal fin is long and has a dark red or black spot between the first and second fin rays. There is a small depression in the dorsal fin margin between the spiny and soft, rayed sections. The pelvic fins, situated just behind the head and anterior to the pectoral fins, are reduced and spine-like. The anal fin is as long as the soft, rayed section of the dorsal fin. The Shanny remains hidden under stones and seaweed while the tide is out, but at high water leaves its pool to forage on the shore for food.

INHABITS *coastal habitat; in rock pools from the high-water mark down to a water depth of 300m.*

tail fin with convex margin

cryptic coloration

blunt head

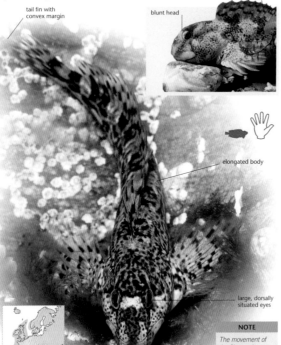

elongated body

large, dorsally situated eyes

SIZE *Up to 16cm.*
DIET *Barnacles, small crabs, and other crustaceans.*
BREEDING *April–August.*
SIMILAR SPECIES *Montagu's Blenny (Coryphoblennius galerita) and the Tompot Blenny (Parablennius gattorugine), both of which have a fleshy flap between their eyes that is not present in the Shanny.*

NOTE
The movement of the Shanny is dictated by the tides. If it is removed from its natural habitat, into a laboratory, this rhythmical behaviour vanishes. However, it is re-established very quickly when the fish is returned to its normal environment.

Ballan Wrasse

Labrus bergylta (Labridae)

A stout, laterally compressed wrasse, the Ballan Wrasse is very variable in colour. Most often, it is green or brown with pale spots, but reddish and purple colours often develop according to its habitat and the breeding stage. Like many related species, the fish starts its life as a female and then becomes male as it grows. Unusually among fish, the Ballan Wrasse sleeps on its side.

FAVOURS *rocky, seaweed-covered shores and rock pools, from the lower intertidal to the shallow sublittoral.*

rows of pale spots on fins

variable white or pale markings

SIZE *Length to 60cm.*
DIET *Molluscs and crustaceans, crushed in the strong jaws; juveniles clean parasites off other fish.*
BREEDING *April–August, eggs laid in a nest of seaweed, held together by mucus threads.*
SIMILAR SPECIES *Several other wrasse species have similar colours, including Brown Wrasse (L. merula).*

Sand Goby

Pomatoschistus minutus (Gobiidae)

A slender, sand-coloured fish, the Sand Goby has small scales on its body. It has two dorsal fins, rounded pectoral fins, and anteriorly positioned pelvic fins that have finger-like processes extending from the free edges. Males have a conspicuous dark patch, bordered with white, on the posterior edge of the first dorsal fin. The tail has a long base (peduncle) and a convex posterior margin.

INHABITS *marine habitats; inshore sandy areas from the mid-tide line down to 20m.*

prominent, dorsally positioned eye

pectoral fin

small body scales

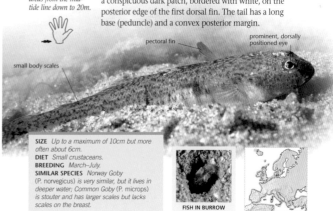

SIZE *Up to a maximum of 10cm but more often about 6cm.*
DIET *Small crustaceans.*
BREEDING *March–July.*
SIMILAR SPECIES *Norway Goby (P. norvegicus) is very similar, but it lives in deeper water; Common Goby (P. microps) is stouter and has larger scales but lacks scales on the breast.*

FISH IN BURROW

Three-spined Stickleback

Gasterosteus aculeatus (Gasterosteidae)

A small scale-less fish with a torpedo-shaped body, this Stickleback is named for the three spines on its back. The first two are longer than the third, which is considerably smaller and close to the base of the second dorsal fin. Usually brown-green in colour, males develop a bright red belly during the spawning season. They become very territorial, guarding their tubular nest and displaying to passing females.

three spines on back

large pectoral fin

large eye

SEEN *in rivers, lakes, estuaries, and coastal waters; common in marine habitats only in Scotland.*

SIZE *Up to 10cm but more usually 5–8cm.*
DIET *Larval insects, small crustaceans, worms, other fish eggs, and some plant material.*
BREEDING *April–late June, in spring and early summer.*
SIMILAR SPECIES *Nine-spined Stickleback (Pungitus pungitus), which has nine spines instead of three.*

Plaice

Pleuronectes platessa (Pleuronectidae)

The bottom-dwelling flatfish are divided into two groups according to whether their eyes are on the right or the left side of the fish. Plaice has its eyes on the upper, right side, the eyes moving into position in the juvenile stage. The upper parts are variable in colour, changing rapidly by the expansion and contraction of pigment cells; normally they are brown with orange blotches.

anal fin extending to whole length of body

both eyes on right side

eye looking up from sand

LIVES *on, or shallowly buried into, sandy sediments in intertidal pools and the sublittoral zone; extends a little into estuarine waters.*

BURIED IN SAND

SIZE *Length to 70cm, occasionally longer.*
DIET *Bottom-dwelling molluscs, crustaceans, and worms; small fish.*
BREEDING *December–April.*
SIMILAR SPECIES *Flounder (below), which is rough along the lateral line, less distinctly spotted, and extends well into estuaries; Dab (Limanda limanda), which has a rough texture overall, a sandy colour, and is often smaller.*

Fifteen-spined Stickleback

Spinachia spinachia (Gasterosteidae)

Also called the Sea Stickleback because it is the only wholly marine species of stickleback, the Fifteen-spined Stickleback has a very slender and elongated snout, head, and body. Males have larger pectoral fins than the females, and both are usually brown or green-brown in colour with a yellow belly. During the breeding season, females become yellower and males develop an attractive brown chequered pattern.

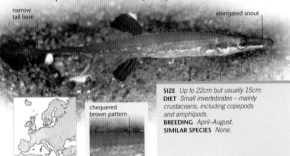

narrow tail base

elongated snout

chequered brown pattern

OCCURS *only in marine habitats, in shallow coastal waters to a depth of 10m.*

SIZE *Up to 22cm but usually 15cm.*
DIET *Small invertebrates – mainly crustaceans, including copepods and amphipods.*
BREEDING *April–August.*
SIMILAR SPECIES *None.*

Flounder

Platichthys flesus (Pleuronectidae)

Another right-eyed fish (though left-eyed specimens do occur), the Flounder is round in profile and has a row of tubercles running along the bases of the dorsal and anal fins. Feeding at night, it buries itself during the day, with its eyes showing above the substrate. It is the only flatfish that can survive in freshwater, the river Thames being one of the most important nursery areas.

anal fin

eyes usually on right side

dorsal fin

FOUND *in rivers that connect to the sea, on sandy or muddy substrate; has low tolerance to pollution.*

SIZE *Up to 51cm.*
DIET *Bottom-living invertebrates such as molluscs, worms, and crustaceans.*
BREEDING *March–May.*
SIMILAR SPECIES *Plaice (above); Dab (Limanda limanda), which lacks tubercles along the bases of the dorsal and anal fins; Lemon Sole (Microstomus kitt) has dorsal and anal fins that extend to the base of the tail fin.*

Shore Clingfish

Lepadogaster lepadogaster (Gobiesocidae)

Also known as the Cornish Sucker, the Shore Clingfish has a flattened body with a broad triangular head and "duck-billed" snout, accentuated by thick lips. The pelvic fins are modified into a thoracic sucking disc that allows it to adhere to rocks and other substrates. Usually a reddish brown colour with darker smudges, its most obvious markings are two deep blue spots behind the eyes.

"duck-billed" snout

broad head

dorsal and anal fins joined to tail fin

INHABITS *seaweed-covered rocky shores and rock pools, or clings to the underside of boulders at low tide.*

SIZE *Up to 8cm long.*
DIET *Small benthic invertebrates, including crustaceans and worms.*
BREEDING *May–August; eggs golden-yellow and flattened, guarded by parent.*
SIMILAR SPECIES *Connemara Clingfish (L. candollei), which has dorsal and anal fins separate from the tail, and often shows reddish markings.*

Basking Shark

Cetorhinus maximus (Cetorhinidae)

Despite its size (it is the second largest fish in the world) and fearsome gaping mouth, the Basking Shark is a harmless filter-feeder, trawling through inshore waters, collecting plankton. The first, and often only, sign of its presence is the large triangular dorsal fin, followed by the tip of its tail fin, moving from side to side as the shark slowly swims forward.

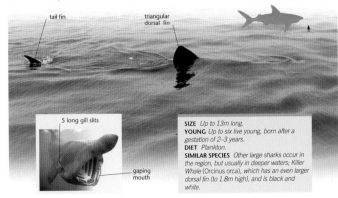

tail fin

triangular dorsal fin

5 long gill slits

gaping mouth

INHABITS *the open sea, moving into shallow coastal waters, especially during the summer months.*

SIZE *Up to 13m long.*
YOUNG *Up to six live young, born after a gestation of 2–3 years.*
DIET *Plankton.*
SIMILAR SPECIES *Other large sharks occur in the region, but usually in deeper waters; Killer Whale (Orcinus orca), which has an even larger dorsal fin (to 1.8m high), and is black and white.*

BUTTERFLIES & MOTHS

In Britain, we have a wealth of resident butterflies and moths, with over 2,000 moth species, and about 57 species of butterflies. Some species are migratory and, despite their fragile appearance, visit us from the continent. The first sign of a butterfly is often a flash of colour fluttering above the vegetation before it comes to rest on a flower. Moths are less frequently observed than butterflies, as many are nocturnal, but they are often no less colourful. In our wide range of landscapes these species have found ideal habitats. They are, however, very vulnerable to habitat loss. The ploughing up of old meadows and the use of pesticides and herbicides are a serious threat, and habitat conservation is vital for their survival.

BUTTERFLIES

Butterflies are day-flying and often brightly coloured. Apart from the 57 resident species, migrants arrive each summer. It is possible that these may now overwinter as a result of global warming.

MOTHS

Moths are far more varied in size than butterflies. Many have dull colours, but others, like Tiger Moths, are brightly coloured. Migrant moths, such as the Silver Y, add to the resident population.

Anatomy

Butterflies and moths are insects, forming the group – or order – Lepidoptera. A literal translation of Lepidoptera is "scale wings" and, indeed, the wings of almost all species in this group are entirely cloaked in scales, which give the wings their colours and patterns. Like other adult insects, the body of a butterfly or moth is divided into three sections: the head, on which are found the eyes, mouthparts, and antennae; the thorax, to which the wings and legs are attached by powerful internal muscles; and the abdomen, which contains many of the vital organs, including the digestive and reproductive systems.

antenna

eye

thorax

abdomen

basal area of wing

vein

leading edge

forewing

hindwing

eyespot

tail streamer

trailing edge

wing margin

Butterfly Upperside

When feeding or basking in sunshine, some butterflies rest with their wings held flat. From above, the hindwings are partially concealed by the forewings, but the degree to which they are hidden varies between species, and factors such as the intensity of the sun may also affect the basking position of individuals within a species. The wings are held rigid by a network of veins, often emphasized by bold markings. The upperwings of a butterfly are generally more colourful than the underwings.

FLIGHT TIME
Like all butterflies, the Swallowtail (pictured) is strictly diurnal. By contrast, the majority of moths are nocturnal, although some are day flying and others may be active at dawn or twilight.

Butterfly Underside

Almost all butterflies – some skipper species prove the exception – rest with their wings folded together above the abdomen, the upper surfaces lying face to face. In this position, the three pairs of legs characteristic of adult insects can be seen and the hindwings conceal the forewings to varying degrees, often depending upon the state of wariness or torpor of the individual. Some butterflies never reveal the upper surface of the wing except in flight; they feed, bask, and rest with wings folded.

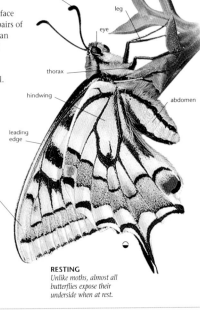

antenna

leg

eye

thorax

hindwing

abdomen

leading edge

forewing

RESTING
Unlike moths, almost all butterflies expose their underside when at rest.

CLUBBED OR TAPERED?
Moths' antennae taper to a point or, in males of some species, they are branched and feathery; a butterfly's antennae are clubbed or swollen toward the tip.

Moth

Most moths rest with their wings held in a tent-like manner, concealing the abdomen. From above, the hindwings are hidden by the forewings, only becoming visible when the insect is disturbed. A few moth species will spread their wings out flat when, for example, resting on tree bark: the upper surface of the moths' forewings is often beautifully patterned to afford the insect camouflage. Some moths resemble fallen leaves; others are a close match for lichen-covered tree bark.

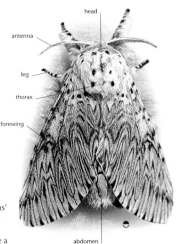

head

antenna

leg

thorax

forewing

abdomen

Identification

Some butterfly and moth species are easy to identify: think of the Peacock (p.203), whose unique upperwing colours and markings are unmistakable. Yet, within some groups – notably Browns, Blues, and Skippers – there are species that are bafflingly similar to one another. However, by observing physical features, such as colours, markings, and wing shape, along with habitat preferences and geographical range, almost all species can be identified by a persistent beginner.

Colour and Markings

The wings are generally the most striking part of a butterfly or moth, and their colour and markings offer vital clues to identification. Some features, such as eyespots or contrasting bands, are easy to discern in the field and to relate to images in this book; others, such as the relative size of small spots, are subtler and require close scrutiny and a degree of experience. Look carefully at the shape and position of markings and how these vary from upperside to underside and hindwing to forewing.

ROWS OF SPOTS

SPOTS

MARBLING

bluish-purple upperwings

bluish-grey underwings

LINES OR STREAKS

VEINING

DIFFERENT ABOVE AND BELOW

BAND OF COLOUR

SUFFUSION OF COLOUR

EYE SPOTS

IRIDESCENCE

camouflaged forewings

warning colours on the hindwings

CAMOUFLAGE AND WARNING

yellow hindwings

brown forewings

DIFFERENT HIND- AND FOREWINGS

Wing Shape

Butterfly and moth wing shape varies remarkably given that their primary role – flight – is purely functional. Some species have broad and rounded wings that permit extended gliding flight; others have narrow and rather angular wings, typically associated with a buzzing flight pattern. A peculiar wing outline may also enhance the camouflage of the underwing. For example, a resting Brimstone is a good match for a fresh ivy leaf, in outline shape as well as colour.

TAIL STREAMER JAGGED MARGIN ANGULAR MARGIN SCALLOPED HINDWING

BROAD AND NARROW ANGULAR FOREWING ROUNDED WINGS BROAD AND POINTED

long thin forewings

long thin forewings

long thin forewings

SQUARE-ENDED ROUND-ENDED FEATHERY PLUMES SMALL AND TRANSPARENT

Size

Size can be a useful way of distinguishing two superficially similar species. It may not always be possible to make precise measurements in the field, but size can be estimated for comparative purposes.

WINGSPAN 4.4–4.8cm

WINGSPAN 3cm

DUKE OF BURGUNDY FRITILLARY
This species looks like a Fritillary, but is much smaller and not a true member of the group.

HEATH FRITILLARY
Much larger and more active than the Duke of Burgundy, this species is representative of the Fritillary family.

Variations

Some species exhibit little variation: for example, almost all individual Peacocks appear identical. In other species, different broods appear entirely dissimilar, and strikingly different colour forms are found side by side.

first brood

second brood

fresh

faded

light non-banded

non-banded

banded

DIFFERENT BROODS
The upperwings of the first and second broods of the Map Butterfly differ greatly.

WEAR AND TEAR
Older specimens of the Light Emerald appear faded beside fresh individuals.

VARIABLE FORMS
The Riband Wave is notoriously variable and occurs in a wide range of forms.

Sex

In some species, obvious differences in colour or markings distinguish the sexes; in others, look for subtler identifying features. For example, males of some moth species, such as the Brindled Beauty, may vary in colour, but can always be identified by their feathery antennae; the females have non-feathered antennae.

violet-blue upperwings

just a hint of violet-blue

yellowish-buff

feathery antennae

feathery antennae

brown-black

COMMON BLUE BRINDLED BEAUTY

Resting Position

Considering how a species holds its wings while at rest can be a useful clue to identification. As a starting point, it is one of the simplest ways to distinguish a butterfly from a moth. Some butterflies, such as the Small Heath, never or very rarely reveal their upperwings at rest; some, such as the Silver-washed Fritillary, hold the wings out flat; others, like the Lulworth Skipper, may keep them angled. Moths typically hold the forewings angled or rolled, concealing the hindwings and abdomen, and revealing only the upperside of their forewings.

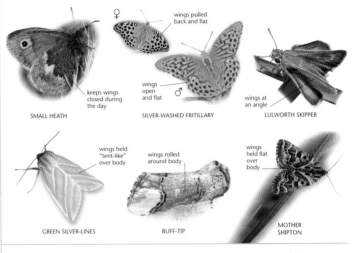

wings pulled back and flat

keeps wings closed during the day

wings open and flat

wings at an angle

SMALL HEATH SILVER-WASHED FRITILLARY LULWORTH SKIPPER

wings held "tent-like" over body

wings rolled around body

wings held flat over body

GREEN SILVER-LINES BUFF-TIP MOTHER SHIPTON

Habitat

Although a few butterfly and moth species will inhabit a broad range of habitats, most have very specific living requirements: habitat choice may be determined by the range of plant species eaten by the larva. This can be an important identification clue in cases where the species in question is extremely habitat-specific.

LOWLANDS
The Silver-studded Blue is associated with lowland heathland areas.

UPLANDS
The similar Zephyr Blue is more typically found in upland meadows.

yellow-white underside

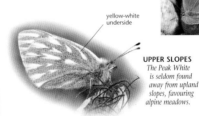

UPPER SLOPES
The Peak White is seldom found away from upland slopes, favouring alpine meadows.

FOOTHILLS
The Dappled White is found on lower mountain slopes, feeding on plants from the cabbage family.

Small Tortoiseshell

Peacock

Red Admiral

FLOWERS
Flower-rich habitats provide abundant nectar to feed on. Buddleja flowers are particularly effective at attracting butterflies.

SHELTER
Small Tortoiseshells often hibernate in attics and outhouses during winter, emerging again as soon as the weather is warm enough in spring.

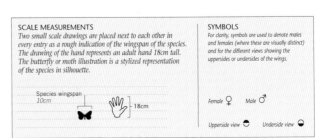

SCALE MEASUREMENTS
Two small scale drawings are placed next to each other in every entry as a rough indication of the wingspan of the species. The drawing of the hand represents an adult hand 18cm tall. The butterfly or moth illustration is a stylized representation of the species in silhouette.

Species wingspan 10cm

18cm

SYMBOLS
For clarity, symbols are used to denote males and females (where these are visually distinct) and for the different views showing the uppersides or undersides of the wings.

Female ♀ Male ♂

Upperside view Underside view

Lulworth Skipper

Thymelicus acteon (Hesperiidae)

This active little grassland butterfly basks with its forewings slightly raised at an angle. The ground colour of the wings is typically olive-brown and males in particular show a suffusion of yellowish scales and a black line on the forewing. A "paw-print" shape of yellowish spots on the forewing upperside is more obvious in females than males.

FOUND *on rough, grassy slopes and in meadows by the sea.*

yellow spots

suffusion of yellow

olive-brown ground colour

up to 2.5cm long

WINGSPAN *2.5cm.*
FLIGHT PERIOD *May–July.*
LARVAL FOODPLANT *Grasses (Poaceae) – False Brome (Brachypodium sylvaticum).*
SIMILAR SPECIES *Essex Skipper (right), Small Skipper (below).*
STATUS *Found only on a small area of the coast in Dorset and south Devon.*

Essex Skipper

Thymelicus lineola (Hesperiidae)

The bright orange-brown wings of the Essex Skipper catch the eye, both when it is resting and when in fast flight. The male has a small black line on its upper forewings. Very similar to the Small Skipper (left), it can be identified by its antennal club, which is black and not orange-brown as in its relative.

FAVOURS *inland meadows, roadside verges, and coastal grassland.*

antennal club black below

wings lack dark line

dark margin

orange-brown wings

up to 2.5cm long

WINGSPAN *2.5cm.*
FLIGHT PERIOD *May–August.*
LARVAL FOODPLANT *Various grasses (family Poaceae).*
SIMILAR SPECIES *Lulworth Skipper (left), Small Skipper (left).*
STATUS *Widespread and generally common throughout most of its range.*

Small Skipper

Thymelicus sylvestris (Hesperiidae)

One of the most widespread and numerous butterflies in the region, the Small Skipper's colourful and rather uniform orange-brown wings are a useful clue to its identity. However, it is easily confused with the very similar Essex Skipper (right), although in this species the antennal club is black underneath, whereas in the Small Skipper it is orange-brown. It usually sunbathes with its forewings slightly elevated and angled, the manner adopted by many other Skippers.

INHABITS *all kinds of grassy places, roadside verges, and grassy lowland meadows.*

antennal club orange-brown below

greenish grey tip to forewing

lacks the dark male sex-brand

up to 2.5cm long

black line or sex-brand

narrow dark margin

NOTE

The male Small Skipper has a longer and more striking black line on the upperside of its forewing (sex-brand) than the male Essex Skipper. However, to distinguish females, look for the orange-brown, and not black, underside of the antennal club.

WINGSPAN *2.5cm.*
FLIGHT PERIOD *May–September.*
LARVAL FOODPLANT *Various meadow species of grasses (family Poaceae).*
SIMILAR SPECIES *Lulworth Skipper (above), which has a "paw-print" of yellowish spots on its upper wings; Essex Skipper (right), females in particular.*
STATUS *Common, although absent from Cumbria, Scotland, and Ireland.*

Large Skipper

Ochlodes venata (Hesperiidae)

This familiar grassland butterfly has rich colours and markings on its upperwings. Like other members of the Skipper family, the male has a conspicuous sex-brand in the form of a dark line on the forewing. Generally, it has brighter colours than the otherwise similar female. The underwings of both sexes are yellowish with a variable suffusion of greenish scaling, and faint pale spots. Large Skippers visit flowers to feed on nectar and typically alight on them with their forewings swept back and elevated at an angle.

FAVOURS *a wide range of grassy habitats from meadows and open scrub to woodland and hedgerow margins; also hillsides up to 2,000m.*

rich ground colour

sex-brand on forewing

yellow-brown ground colour

dark veins

dark margin

pale yellow spots

dull ground colour

up to 3cm long

NOTE

This species has the buzzing, almost moth-like flight that is so characteristic of Skipper butterflies. At rest the wings are held open, and at an angle, in the manner of many other Skippers. This enables the observer to view both the upper and lower wing surfaces with ease.

WINGSPAN *2.8–3cm.*
FLIGHT PERIOD *May–September.*
LARVAL FOODPLANT *Various grasses (family Poaceae) including fescue (Festuca).*
SIMILAR SPECIES *Silver-spotted Skipper (p.189), which has silvery white spots on the underside hindwings.*
STATUS *Widespread and generally common throughout its range in Britain.*

Silver-spotted Skipper

Hesperia comma (Hesperiidae)

This species is easily recognized by the silvery white spots that adorn the greenish yellow underside of the hindwings. The orange-brown upperwings are also striking. Active on sunny days, it spends much of its time feeding on flowers or sunbathing, so close-up views are often possible.

RESTRICTED *to sparse chalk and limestone grassland, sand dunes at sea level, and downland.*

orange-brown ground colour

yellow spots

dark sex-brand

♂♂

forewings lack male sex-brand

♀♀

up to 3cm long

WINGSPAN *2.5–3cm.*
FLIGHT PERIOD *July–August.*
LARVAL FOODPLANT *A limited range of grass species, notably fescue (Festuca) and meadow grass (Poa).*
SIMILAR SPECIES *Large Skipper (p.188).*
STATUS *Isolated colonies in southern Britain.*

Dingy Skipper

Erynnis tages (Hesperiidae)

SEEN *in grassland with plenty of flowers, and also often on chalky soil.*

Although the Dingy Skipper may appear rather nondescript, its uniformly dark brown upperwings and pale brown underwings, when taken together, are unique and have diagnostic features: there are few butterflies with which it could be confused. However, observers should be aware that the buzzing flight and undeniably sombre appearance of this small butterfly do give it a distinctly moth-like appearance.

indistinct, pale and dark bands

pale brown ground colour

faint pale spots

small, faint marginal spots

up to 2cm long

WINGSPAN *2.5cm.*
FLIGHT PERIOD *May–August.*
LARVAL FOODPLANT *Trefoil (Lotus), Crown Vetch (Coronilla varia), and related plants in the pea family.*
SIMILAR SPECIES *None.*
STATUS *Widespread and locally common, although declining due to habitat loss.*

Grizzled Skipper

INHABITS *grassy heaths, woodland margins, and clearings; often found along tracks where foodplants flourish.*

Pyrgus malvae (Hesperiidae)

Although it is a small butterfly, the Grizzled Skipper makes up for what it lacks in terms of size with the beautiful patterning on its wings. The upper surfaces are a rich brown colour, adorned with an intricate pattern of squarish pale spots. Fortunately, the butterfly frequently sunbathes with its wings open and spread out, giving observers plenty of opportunity to study them. The underwing ground colour is yellowish brown with a pattern of whitish spots similar to that seen on the upper surfaces of the wings.

large, central white spot

yellow-brown ground colour

up to 2cm long

NOTE

The combination of its small size and the presence of squarish spots of rather uniform size and intensity across the upperwings are useful identification clues. Look also for the arc of pale spots on the upperside hindwing and the large central pale spot on the underside.

squarish pale spots

rich brown ground colour

crescent of pale spots

WINGSPAN *2cm.*
FLIGHT PERIOD *April–June, with a rare second brood in July–August in the south.*
LARVAL FOODPLANT *Wild Strawberry (Fragaria vesca), and Creeping Cinquefoil (Potentilla reptans).*
SIMILAR SPECIES *None.*
STATUS *Locally common, but under threat in many places from land development. However, new colonies have recently been discovered.*

Swallowtail

Papilio machaon (Papilionidae)

This large and spectacular species is almost unmistakable. Although Swallowtails seem rather restless, they often remain relatively still when feeding, allowing observers excellent views of their beautiful markings. The overall colour of both surfaces of the wings is yellow, and they are patterned with a network of black veins and bands. The upperwings also reveal a marginal band of blue scaling and a colourful eyespot. Lastly, there is the trademark tail streamer on the hindwing. This characteristic feature is found in many members of this butterfly family and lends it the name "Swallowtail".

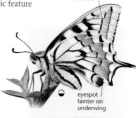

FOUND *once across wetlands in Britain, it is now confined to the damp fenland of the Norfolk Broads.*

similar upper and lower surface

NOTE

The Swallowtail's larvae are extremely colourful, a warning to birds that they are distasteful. They are quite easy to spot while feeding on the leaves of their foodplants.

eyespot fainter on underwing

up to 5cm long

network of black veins

yellow ground colour

band of blue scaling

tail streamer

colourful eyespot

♂♂

WINGSPAN *8–9cm.*
FLIGHT PERIOD *May–June, in favourable years a second brood may appear in August.*
LARVAL FOODPLANT *Fennel (Foeniculum vulgare), Milk Parsley (Peucedanum palustre), and other carrot family members.*
SIMILAR SPECIES *None.*
STATUS *Restricted to the Norfolk Broads, although some immigrants from Europe arrive in the far south each year.*

Wood White

Leptidea sinapis (Pieridae)

With its broad and rounded wings, the Wood White is relatively easy to identify by shape alone. Its delicate appearance is matched by its rather feeble flight – it may have difficulty flying at all on windy days. When it does take to the wing, its fluttery flight pattern is another good clue to its identity. The whitish upperwings are variably tipped with smoky grey, more pronounced in males than females. First broods are greyer overall than subsequent generations. The underwings of both sexes are variably flushed yellow and streaked with grey.

FAVOURS *grassy places, including woodland rides and meadows; however, it is always restricted to extremely sheltered sites.*

broad, rounded wings

yellowish white ground colour

grey streaks

dark smudge at wing tip

white wings ♂♀

up to 2cm long

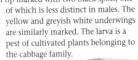

NOTE

The Wood White spends a lot of time sitting on sheltered plant stems. Even when it does fly on calm, sunny days, it keeps low to the ground, often flitting through, rather than over, vegetation.

WINGSPAN *4cm.*
FLIGHT PERIOD *Variable: May–June, as a single brood, in the north; April–September, with up to two broods, in the south.*
LARVAL FOODPLANT *Meadow Vetchling (Lathyrus pratensis) and other pea family members.*
SIMILAR SPECIES *Real's White (Leptidea reali), found only in Ireland.*
STATUS *Generally local, with a patchy distribution, but fairly common where it does occur.*

Orange-tip

Anthocharis cardamines (Pieridae)

The Orange-tip is one of the most distinctive spring butterflies in the region and can often be seen flitting along flowery verges and woodland rides. The male is particularly striking, with bright orange tips on its white upper forewings, which can also be seen on its underwings. The tips of the female's forewings are black rather than orange, making it quite subdued in appearance. The underside of the hindwing in both sexes is white with subtle greenish marbling.

FLIES *along flowery roadside verges, woodland rides, and meadows; sometimes appears in gardens.*

green marbling

♂♀

faint grey tip

dark spot

white ground colour

up to 2.5cm long ♀

NOTE

A female Orange-tip could be mistaken for a Bath White, so note the Orange-tip's paler appearance with fewer dark spots, and delicate flight.

bright orange wing tip

dark spot on forewing

white ground colour

♂♀

WINGSPAN *4cm.*
FLIGHT PERIOD *April–June.*
LARVAL FOODPLANT *Garlic Mustard (Alliaria petiolata), Cuckoo Flower (Cardamine pratensis), and other cabbage family members.*
SIMILAR SPECIES *Bath White (Pontia daplidice), which is a rare migrant.*
STATUS *Widespread and common.*

Small White

Pieris rapae (Pieridae)

This is a typical small white butterfly, with white upperwings that have a blackish tip marked with two black spots, one of which is less distinct in males. The yellow and greyish white underwings are similarly marked. The larva is a pest of cultivated plants belonging to the cabbage family.

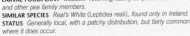

INHABITS *areas with cabbage family plants; particularly common in gardens and on farmland.*

hindwing yellow and grey

white ground colour ♀

twin black spots

dark tip to forewing

white ground colour ♂♀

up to 2.5cm long

dark spot on forewing

WINGSPAN *5cm.*
FLIGHT PERIOD *April–October.*
LARVAL FOODPLANT *Members of the cabbage family, especially the genus Brassica; Nasturtium (Tropaeolum majus).*
SIMILAR SPECIES *Large White (p.191), which is larger; Green-veined White (right).*
STATUS *Widespread and extremely common.*

Green-veined White

Pieris napi (Pieridae)

Once this butterfly's underwings have been seen clearly, there is usually no doubt about its identity. The well-defined network of greenish grey veins that criss-cross the yellow hindwings distinguishes it from related species. The females are marginally larger than males.

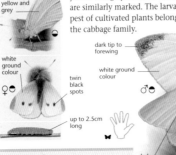

FOUND *in a wide range of flowery habitats, from roadside verges and gardens, to woodland rides and damp meadows.*

black forewing tip

green-grey veins

white ground colour ♂♀

yellow ground colour

twin spots

dark veins

white ground colour ♀

up to 2.5cm long

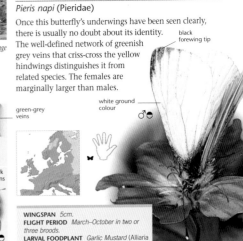

WINGSPAN *5cm.*
FLIGHT PERIOD *March–October in two or three broods.*
LARVAL FOODPLANT *Garlic Mustard (Alliaria petiolata) and other wild cabbage family members.*
SIMILAR SPECIES *Female Orange-tip (above).*
STATUS *Widespread and common.*

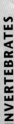
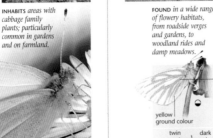

Large White

Pieris brassicae (Pieridae)

Although the adult Large White is a charming sight in the garden, the species has achieved notoriety thanks to its gregarious larvae. It is not uncommon to find hordes of them demolishing the leaves of cabbages and other related plants in cultivation. In both sexes, the upperwings are creamy white and show a dark tip to the forewing; in females, two dark spots can also be seen on the forewing. On the underside in both sexes, the hindwing is yellowish grey while the forewing is white with two dark spots.

OCCURS *in a range of flowery places, from meadows and roadside verges to farmland and town gardens.*

NOTE

As a bonus to gardeners, many Large White larvae are parasitized by a tiny wasp called Apanteles. It lays its eggs in the caterpillar's body, then having consumed the internal organs, the wasp larvae emerge and pupate in yellow cocoons around the dried larval skin.

yellow-grey ground colour

creamy ground colour

dark tip

twin dark spots on hindwing

grey tip on forewing

white forewing

dark spot on forewing

up to 4cm long

WINGSPAN *6cm.*
FLIGHT PERIOD *April–October, in successive broods.*
LARVAL FOODPLANT *Cabbage (Brassica oleracea) and other cultivated cabbage family members; also Nasturtium (Tropaeolum majus).*
SIMILAR SPECIES *Small White (p.190); in flight, male could be confused with female Brimstone (right).*
STATUS *Widespread and common; migrant visitor in the north of its range.*

Clouded Yellow

Colias crocea (Pieridae)

This colourful butterfly is active and fast-flying, qualities that enable it to undertake long migrations north each year from its stronghold in southern Europe. The extent of the species' travels varies from year to year but in most seasons the range extends northwards as far as southern Britain. Unfortunately, its life cycle is not completed here because of the cold, wet weather in autumn. In flight, the dominant orange-yellow wing colour catches the eye. The upperwings have a broad, dark brown margin. However, resting individuals rarely, if ever, open their wings fully.

FAVOURS *all sorts of flowery, grassy places. Given the species' migratory nature, it can appear in a variety of habitats within its range.*

NOTE

Some female Clouded Yellows occur in a pale form that looks confusingly similar to a Pale Clouded Yellow (left). Pay attention to the upperwing colour and wing shape.

orange-yellow ground colour

broad, dark brown margin

greenish margin

orange-yellow ground colour

dark spot on forewing

white forewing with yellow tip

pale yellow hindwing

PALE FORM

up to 3cm long

hindwing tinged green

WINGSPAN *5cm.*
FLIGHT PERIOD *May–October.*
LARVAL FOODPLANT *Clover (Trifolium), Lucerne (Medicago sativa), and other pea family members.*
SIMILAR SPECIES *Pale Clouded Yellow (left), which has a different wing shape and does not have dark brown upperwing margins.*
STATUS *An immigrant species, it is found in all parts of Britain in favourable years.*

Pale Clouded Yellow

Colias hyale (Pieridae)

This species may look like a variation of the Clouded Yellow (right) in the field, and be difficult to identify. However, the shape of its forewing, which is rather pointed, and the overall pale lemon yellow coloration, help to distinguish between it and other Clouded Yellows. The female is much paler in colour than the male.

FOUND *in a variety of flowery, grassy places, this migratory species can occur anywhere within its range.*

pointed forewing

single central black spot

red-ringed pale spot

whitish forewing

yellow tip

up to 3.5cm long

WINGSPAN *5cm.*
FLIGHT PERIOD *May–October, in successive broods.*
LARVAL FOODPLANT *Lucerne (Medicago sativa) and clover (Trifolium).*
SIMILAR SPECIES *Clouded Yellow (right), which has dark brown upperwing margins.*
STATUS *Widespread and common.*

Brimstone

Gonepteryx rhamni (Pieridae)

For many naturalists, the sight of a Brimstone in early spring is a sign that winter has finally ended. On sunny mornings as early as February, this species emerges from hibernation in search of nectar sources. The male Brimstone's bright yellow colour is sufficient to identify even flying individuals. The typical wing shape found in both sexes, can only be seen in resting butterflies and is the best way to identify a female.

SEEN *in areas of scrub, woodland rides, and gardens, the common factor being the presence of the larval foodplant.*

lemon yellow ground colour

greenish white ground colour

hook-tipped forewing

red spots

angular hindwing

up to 3cm long

WINGSPAN *6cm.*
FLIGHT PERIOD *July–October, and February–May after hibernation.*
LARVAL FOODPLANT *Buckthorn (Rhamnus) and Alder Buckthorn (Frangula alnus).*
SIMILAR SPECIES *None, it is the only resident yellow coloured butterfly in Britain.*
STATUS *Widespread and generally common.*

Small Blue

Cupido minimus (Lycaenidae)

This tiny butterfly is extremely active on sunny days. It can be difficult to follow on the wing because of its small size and buzzing flight. In both sexes, the ground colour of the upperwings is sooty brown, only the males showing a dusting of blue near the wing base. The pale grey underwings of both sexes are spotted with black. Both the slug-like larvae and the pupae are usually attended by ants. The larvae feed on the flowerheads of the foodplant.

FOUND *in flower-rich grassland, usually on areas of chalk and limestone. Typically favours warm and sunny slopes.*

wing base suffused blue

sooty brown ground colour

white-ringed black dots

pale grey ground colour

no blue at wing base

sooty brown wings

white fringe

up to 1cm long

NOTE
On warm and sunny days, the Small Blue can be found drinking from puddles on the ground. If water is in short supply, then a dozen or more will sometimes be found together. On occasions it is even attracted to human sweat, and can hover extremely close to the observer's face and neck.

WINGSPAN *2–2.5cm.*
FLIGHT PERIOD *May–August, in one or two broods.*
LARVAL FOODPLANT *Mainly Kidney-Vetch (Anthyllis vulneraria).*
SIMILAR SPECIES *Holly Blue (below), which has bluish white wings.*
STATUS *Widespread and locally common.*

Silver-studded Blue

Plebejus argus (Lycaenidae)

PREFERS *dry, open habitats including heathland, grassy hillsides, and coastal dunes.*

On sunny days, this beautiful little butterfly seems active all the time, flitting between flowerheads and resting on each only momentarily. Males have purplish blue upperwings. However, the extent of this colour, as well as the dark margin, varies across the species' geographical range. Females have mainly brown upperwings. Both sexes have pale grey-brown underwings (generally darker in females than males), and there are numerous spots and a submarginal orange band on both wings; the marginal black spots on the hindwing have shiny greenish centres.

purplish blue ground colour

orange band with black spots

greyish brown ground colour

shiny green or blue centres

rich brown ground colour

crescent of orange spots

pale fringe

dark margin, variable in extent

up to 1cm long

NOTE
The Silver-studded Blue usually suns itself in the early morning and late afternoon. These are the times of day when you will get the best and most prolonged views of this fast-flying butterfly. This butterfly is often seen resting on the very tips of clumps of heather (Calluna).

WINGSPAN *2.4–3cm.*
FLIGHT PERIOD *May–August, with a second brood extending the season to September in the south of its range.*
LARVAL FOODPLANT *Heather (Calluna) and gorse (Ulex) on heathland; elsewhere rock-rose (Helianthemum) and trefoil (Lotus).*
SIMILAR SPECIES *Adonis Blue (p.193), which has chequered wing borders.*
STATUS *Locally very common in southern Britain and North Wales.*

Holly Blue

Celastrina argiolus (Lycaenidae)

For many people, the Holly Blue is a familiar species as it is often found in gardens where holly and ivy are common. Both sexes have blue upperwings, although they are paler in females than males. The dark wing margins are more extensive in females.

INHABITS *diverse habitats such as woodland, inland cliffs, and gardens – the common factor being larval foodplants.*

narrow dark margin

violet-blue ground colour

faintly chequered pale fringe

small dark spots

bluish white wings

sky-blue base

variable dark margin

up to 1cm long

WINGSPAN *3cm.*
FLIGHT PERIOD *April–May and August– September, in two distinct broods.*
LARVAL FOODPLANT *Mainly holly (Ilex) for first brood larvae but ivy (Hedera) for second brood larvae.*
SIMILAR SPECIES *Small Blue (above).*
STATUS *Generally common and widespread.*

Common Blue

Polyommatus icarus (Lycaenidae)

One of the Britain's commonest butterflies, the male Common Blue has blue upperwings tinged with a hint of violet, while those of the female are brown with orange spots and violet-blue at the wing base. Underwings of both sexes are grey-brown with orange and black white-ringed spots.

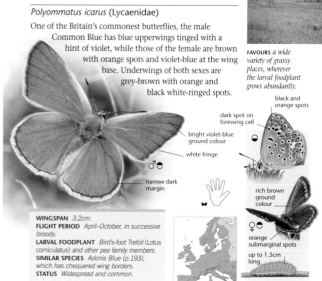

FAVOURS *a wide variety of grassy places, wherever the larval foodplant grows abundantly.*

black and orange spots

dark spot on forewing cell

bright violet-blue ground colour

white fringe

narrow dark margin

rich brown ground colour

orange submarginal spots

up to 1.5cm long

WINGSPAN *3.2cm.*
FLIGHT PERIOD *April–October, in successive broods.*
LARVAL FOODPLANT *Bird's-foot Trefoil (Lotus corniculatus) and other pea family members.*
SIMILAR SPECIES *Adonis Blue (p.193), which has chequered wing borders.*
STATUS *Widespread and common.*

Chalk-hill Blue

Polyommatus coridon (Lycaenidae)

A sun-loving butterfly that is characteristic of chalky grassland, the Chalk-hill Blue is a particularly attractive species. The male has bright sky-blue upperwings, which are often revealed when it is feeding or basking in the sunshine. The female is more subdued in appearance and has mainly dark brown upperwings; the hindwings are adorned with a submarginal row of orange, white, and black eyespots. In common with many other Blue butterflies, the larvae of the Chalk-hill Blue are attended by ants.

ASSOCIATED with flower-rich chalk and limestone grassland – habitats to which the larval foodplant is restricted.

pale-ringed dark spots

grey-brown ground colour

NOTE

The species is notoriously variable, particularly in the extent of the dark margin on the male upperwing. However, the sky-blue upperwing ground colour, and the favoured habitat are good clues to identity, of males at least.

brown ground colour

chequered fringe

orange spots

up to 1.5cm long

broad, dark brown margin

bright sky-blue ground colour

WINGSPAN *4cm.*
FLIGHT PERIOD *July–August.*
LARVAL FOODPLANT *Horseshoe Vetch (Hippocrepis comosa).*
SIMILAR SPECIES *None, no other "blue" in Britain has such silvery-blue wings, as the male Chalk-hill Blue. The female Adonis Blue (below) is similar to the female Chalk-hill Blue but is bluer.*
STATUS *Locally very common in the south. Declining due to habitat destruction.*

Large Blue

Glaucopsyche (Maculinea) arion (Lycaenidae)

This is one of the larger and more distinctive species among the Blue butterflies. It also has an intriguing life cycle – the larva resides in the nest of a red ant species for the latter part of its life, feeding on the grubs of its host. Both sexes have light blue upperwings. However, in females, the margins are broader, there are dark spots on both wings, and the hindwing spots are larger than in males. In both sexes, the underwings are grey-brown with dark spots that are fringed white, and have a blue suffusion at the base of the hindwing.

RESTRICTED to dry grassland, often on chalky soil, where Wild Thyme or marjoram and red ants are abundant.

pale grey-brown ground colour

bold dark spots

bluish suffusion at base of hindwing

up to 1.5cm long

NOTE

Changes in land use are adversely affecting this species' favoured habitat. A correct balance between too much and too little grazing is critical to ensure the survival of this fascinating butterfly. Following its extinction in Britain in the latter part of the 20th century, it has been re-introduced successfully.

dark spots on forewing

pale blue ground colour

white fringe

broad dark margin

WINGSPAN *4cm.*
FLIGHT PERIOD *July.*
LARVAL FOODPLANT *Wild Thyme (Thymus polytrichus) and marjoram (Origanum) in the larva's early stages; subsequently feeds on larvae of red ants (Myrmica).*
SIMILAR SPECIES *None.*
STATUS *Local and very rare, it is the subject of sustained conservation efforts in the British Isles (see pp.194–95).*

Adonis Blue

Polyommatus bellargus (Lycaenidae)

The male Adonis Blue has eye-catching electric blue upperwings offset by a chequered border. The female, however, has brown upperwings, with orange spots and a variable blue suffusion. Both sexes have grey-brown underwings with orange and black spots.

FOUND in flower-rich grassland on limestone or chalk, where grazing maintains relatively short turf.

wedge-shaped mark on hindwing

chequered border

electric blue upperwings

blue suffusion on brown wings

crescent-shaped orange spots

up to 1.5cm long

WINGSPAN *3.2cm.*
FLIGHT PERIOD *May–June and July–August.*
LARVAL FOODPLANT *Horseshoe Vetch (Hippocrepis comosa).*
SIMILAR SPECIES *Common Blue (p.192); Silver-studded Blue (p.192).*
STATUS *Locally common, but affected by changed land use and habitat loss.*

Green Hairstreak

Callophrys rubi (Lycaenidae)

In spite of its bright underside ground colour, this active butterfly can be very difficult to spot. At rest it looks exactly like a green leaf. In flight, its colours blend with the surroundings so well that it is almost impossible to follow its movements. It seldom exposes its brown upperwings when resting, showing only its underwings.

INHABITS a wide variety of scrubby habitats, such as heath, hedgerows, and rough grassland.

clear, broken white line on hindwing

faint, broken white line on forewing

bright green ground colour

brown ground colour

up to 1.5cm long

WINGSPAN *2.5cm.*
FLIGHT PERIOD *March–July in south of range, April–June in north of range; in a number of broods.*
LARVAL FOODPLANT *Gorse (Ulex), ling (Calluna), and other low-growing plants.*
SIMILAR SPECIES *None.*
STATUS *Widespread and locally common.*

INVERTEBRATES

LARGE BLUE

T he Large Blue, confined to the south-west of England, has never been a common British butterfly. First discovered in the late 18th century, it was much sought after by collectors. It thrived on areas of short, unfertilized turf that were traditionally grazed. As farming methods changed, land was ploughed, and in the 1950s rabbits, which had helped to keep the grass short, were decimated by myxomatosis. This was the beginning of the end for the Large Blue in Britain, and the hot, dry summer of 1976 reduced the remaining colony to just 16 individuals. By 1979 it was extinct. Scientists have found that the Large Blue's life cycle relies on a combination of short turf – where the caterpillar's food plant, Wild Thyme, grows – and on the presence of red ants. The caterpillar, which at first feeds on Wild Thyme, then drops from the plant and is found by an ant which feeds on a sweet, honey-like liquid from the caterpillar. The caterpillar is carried into the ant's nest, where it feeds on ant larvae and then hibernates. In 1983 the butterfly was re-introduced to a site in Devon, where it still flourishes. In 2004, the Large Blue was living at ten sites, from north Devon to the Cotswolds. By 2007, the British population approached 10,000.

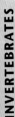

Small Copper

Lycaena phlaeas (Lycaenidae)

Despite its small size, the Small Copper catches the eye due to its bright markings. Although some of the upperwing surface is brown, this relatively sombre background serves to highlight the vivid orange markings. The underwings have more subdued colours than the upperwings although the pattern of markings is broadly similar. A subtle variation in wing markings exists across the species' range; in particular, the extent of the orange submarginal band on the hindwing shows considerable variation.

FLIES *over all kinds of flowery, grassy places, from roadside verges to meadows and cliffs.*

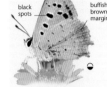

black spots

buffish brown margin

up to 1.5cm long

NOTE

Male Small Coppers are strongly territorial and it can be interesting to watch them defend their "home patch" against intruding rivals. They even attack male butterflies belonging to other species on occasion.

orange-red forewing

brown margin

brown spots

brown hindwing

pointed rear margin

submarginal orange band

WINGSPAN *3–3.8cm.*
FLIGHT PERIOD *April–October, in successive broods.*
LARVAL FOODPLANT *Sorrel and dock (both Rumex).*
SIMILAR SPECIES *None.*
STATUS *Widespread and one of the commonest butterflies in the British Isles.*

Brown Argus

Aricia agestis (Lycaenidae)

At first glance, the Brown Argus could be mistaken for a female Common Blue (p.192). However, the species is quite distinctive, the rich brown upperwings being adorned with bright orange crescent-shaped spots around the white-fringed margins. On the underwings, which are grey brown, there are orange spots arranged in a pattern similar to that seen on the upperwings. This species may be difficult, at times, to distinguish from the Northern Brown Argus (left), which also has orange spots, but they are smaller and are either absent or very faint on the forewing. There is still a debate as to whether there is an intermediate form between the two.

FAVOURS *free-draining, dry grassland areas, seeming equally at home on chalky or slightly acidic soil.*

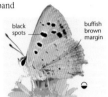

dark spots

white streak

up to 1.5cm long

submarginal row of orange spots

rich brown ground colour

dark central spot

white fringe

NOTE

The Brown Argus is found especially where its caterpillar foodplant, Helianthemum, grows. Since this plant thrives mainly on chalky soil, conservation of calcareous grassland areas is important for the continued well-being of this species.

WINGSPAN *2.5cm.*
FLIGHT PERIOD *May–August, in successive broods in the south.*
LARVAL FOODPLANT *Rock-rose (Helianthemum) and stork's bill (Erodium).*
SIMILAR SPECIES *Northern Brown Argus (left); female Common Blue (p.192).*
STATUS *Widespread and locally common. It has increased in some areas in recent years and in good summers its range has increased.*

Northern Brown Argus

Aricia artaxerxes (Lycaenidae)

To distinguish this species from the Brown Argus (right), look at the orange spots on the upperwings. Those of the Northern Brown Argus are small and are either absent or very faint on the forewing. Individuals from northern Britain often have a distinct white spot on the upper forewing.

ASSOCIATED *with flower-rich grassland, especially on limestone up to 300m.*

dark spots

up to 1.5cm long

dark brown ground colour

submarginal row of small orange spots

WINGSPAN *2.5cm.*
FLIGHT PERIOD *June–July.*
LARVAL FOODPLANT *Rock-rose (Helianthemum).*
SIMILAR SPECIES *Brown Argus (right); female Common Blue (p.192).*
STATUS *Locally common but widely scattered populations.*

Brown Hairstreak

Thecla betulae (Lycaenidae)

The underwings of the Brown Hairstreak are its most outstanding feature with their rich orange-brown ground colour and fine black and white lines. While the male has uniform dark brown upperwings, the female has an orange patch on the forewings. Both sexes have hindwing tail streamers.

INHABITS *areas of scrub, mature hedgerows, and woodland margins where larval foodplants grow.*

fine black and white lines

orange-brown ground colour

tail streamer on hindwings

uniform dark brown wings

orange patch

dark brown ground colour

up to 2cm long

WINGSPAN *4–5cm.*
FLIGHT PERIOD *July–August.*
LARVAL FOODPLANT *Mainly Blackthorn (Prunus spinosa) and related species, but also birch (Betula).*
SIMILAR SPECIES *None.*
STATUS *Widespread but distinctly local, forming discrete colonies.*

Purple Hairstreak

Favonius quercus (Lycaenidae)

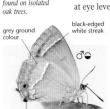

INHABITS *mature oak woodland but colonies are sometimes found on isolated oak trees.*

A familiar woodland species in many parts of Europe, the Purple Hairstreak is often seen flitting individually high among the treetops. Fortunately for observers, it often descends closer to ground level on dull days (particularly after rain) and at such times can be found resting on leaves at eye level. Unlike some of its Hairstreak relatives, it occasionally basks with its wings open, revealing the purple markings on its sooty brown upperwings. The Purple Hairstreak has small tail streamers at the tips of its hindwings. Its under surface is buffish grey with a white streak on both wings.

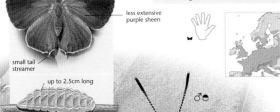

grey ground colour

black-edged white streak

♂♀

small orange spots

♀♂

less extensive purple sheen

small tail streamer

NOTE

There is no butterfly in the British Isles that looks like the Purple Hairstreak. However, in southwestern Europe, the Spanish Purple Hairstreak bears a strong resemblance to it but has an orange band with black arrowheads on its underwings and no tail streamers.

up to 2.5cm long

♂♀

purple or violet iridescence

WINGSPAN *4–5cm.*
FLIGHT PERIOD *July–August.*
LARVAL FOODPLANT *Mainly Blackthorn (Prunus spinosa) and related species, but also birch (Betula).*
SIMILAR SPECIES *None.*
STATUS *Widespread but distinctly local, forming discrete colonies.*

sooty-brown ground colour

small tail streamer

Black Hairstreak

Satyrium pruni (Lycaenidae)

FAVOURS *Blackthorn scrub, mature hedgerows, and woodland margins and clearings.*

A close view reveals the Black Hairstreak to be a most attractive and well-marked species, particularly when it displays its underwings. The rich brown ground colour is adorned with a white streak, and the orange submarginal band is studded with white-edged black spots. This rather sluggish species can sometimes be found crawling slowly over the leaves of hedgerow shrubs.

dark brown ground colour

white stripe

tail streamer

up to 1.5cm long

WINGSPAN *3.5cm.*
FLIGHT PERIOD *June–July.*
LARVAL FOODPLANT *Blackthorn (Prunus spinosa).*
SIMILAR SPECIES *White-letter Hairstreak (right), which has a W-shaped white line on the hindwing underside.*
STATUS *Distinctly local.*

White-letter Hairstreak

Satyrium w-album (Lycaenidae)

FOUND *invariably in the vicinity of elm trees and so occurs in mature hedgerows and along woodland margins and rides.*

As Hairstreak butterflies go, this is a rather distinctive species. Its best diagnostic feature is the white streak on the underside of the hindwing, shaped like the letter 'W'. The underwing ground colour is a rich brown and the hindwing is also marked with a fused row of submarginal, crescent-shaped orange spots. In addition to the tail streamer, a second, smaller projection can be seen on the margin.

W-shaped white streak

dark brown ground colour

crescent-shaped orange marking

tail streamer

faint orange spot

up to 1.5cm long

WINGSPAN *3.5cm.*
FLIGHT PERIOD *July.*
LARVAL FOODPLANT *Elm (Ulmus).*
SIMILAR SPECIES *Black Hairstreak (left), which has black spots along the orange band on the hindwing underside.*
STATUS *Widespread but local; affected by the impact of Dutch Elm disease on elms.*

Duke of Burgundy

Hamearis lucina (Riodinidae)

ASSOCIATED *with meadows and woodland margins, where the larval foodplants grow.*

The beautifully intricate wing patterns of this rather small species certainly merit close scrutiny. Fortunately, this is often possible because it tends to sunbathe just above the ground, allowing observers to get surprisingly close. The rich brown ground colour of the upperwings is studded with orange-buff spots while the tawny lower surface is adorned with dark spots on the forewing and white spots on the hindwing. The entire effect is offset by a uniformly chequered fringe. Broadly speaking, the sexes are similar, although the orange upperwing spots and white underwing spots are larger and brighter in females.

chequered fringe

orange-buff spots

rich brown ground colour

dark spots on forewing

rufous-brown ground colour

white spots on hindwing

up to 1.5cm long

NOTE

The Duke of Burgundy bears a superficial resemblance to the true Fritillary species (family Nymphalidae). However, all of these are much larger and generally more active butterflies.

WINGSPAN *3cm.*
FLIGHT PERIOD *May–June; sometimes a second brood in August–September in the south of its range.*
LARVAL FOODPLANT *Primrose (Primula vulgaris) and Cowslip (Primula veris).*
SIMILAR SPECIES *None.*
STATUS *Locally common, forming discrete colonies associated with an abundance of larval foodplants.*

Small Pearl-bordered Fritillary
As it rests with its wings held flat, the mosaic of orange, brown, black, and silvery white on this fritillary's wings is clearly visible, as are the seven pearl white spots along each hindwing.

Small Pearl-bordered Fritillary

Boloria selene (Nymphalidae)

FOUND *in a variety of habitats where larval foodplants grow, from open woodland, wet grassland, moors, and hillsides.*

It would be difficult to separate this species from some of its close relatives – notably the Pearl-bordered Fritillary (right) – by simply looking at its upperwings; they all appear confusingly similar. What distinguishes them are the markings on the underside of the hindwing. In addition to the seven white pearl-like spots along the margin, which are strongly defined by black lines along their inner edge, there are several silvery white spots at the centre and towards the base of the wing. In contrast, the Pearl-bordered Fritillary has just one central white spot, with another smaller one close to the wing base.

7 white spots on hindwing margin

several white spots

up to 2cm long

NOTE
To get the best views for identification, choose a partly sunny day when occasional clouds obscure the sun. During the brief, dull periods, the butterflies will stop flying and rest on flowerheads and stems with their wings shut.

orange ground colour

numerous black spots

WINGSPAN *4cm.*
FLIGHT PERIOD *June–July.*
LARVAL FOODPLANT *Violet (Viola).*
SIMILAR SPECIES *Pearl-bordered Fritillary (right), which has a single silvery spot at the centre of its hindwing undersides.*
STATUS *Widespread and locally common, although habitat loss is affecting its numbers.*

Heath Fritillary

Melitaea athalia (Nymphalidae)

Although a variable species across its range, most specimens of Heath Fritillary have a network of black markings on orange upperwings, creating a mosaic effect. The hindwings are darker, with a dark margin and at least two concentric rows of orange spots.

PREFERS *wooded heathland and along open woodland rides; the common factor being the presence of larval foodplants.*

orange ground colour ♂

network of black markings

concentric rows of orange spots

dark margin

orange-buff ground colour

pale central band

♂

up to 2.5cm long

WINGSPAN *4.4–4.8cm.*
FLIGHT PERIOD *June–July, in a single brood.*
LARVAL FOODPLANT *Common Cow Wheat (Melampyrum pratense) and Ribwort Plantain (Plantago lanceolata).*
SIMILAR SPECIES *Glanville Fritillary (M. cinxia).*
STATUS *Found only in a few sites in Britain.*

Pearl-bordered Fritillary

Boloria euphrosyne (Nymphalidae)

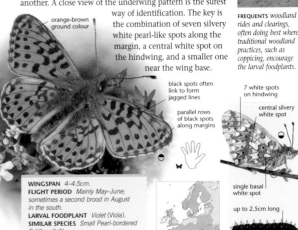

Many smaller Fritillary species look bafflingly similar to one another. A close view of the underwing pattern is the surest way of identification. The key is the combination of seven silvery white pearl-like spots along the margin, a central white spot on the hindwing, and a smaller one near the wing base.

orange-brown ground colour

FREQUENTS *woodland rides and clearings, often doing best where traditional woodland practices, such as coppicing, encourage the larval foodplants.*

black spots often link to form jagged lines

parallel rows of black spots along margins

7 white spots on hindwing

central silvery white spot

single basal white spot

up to 2.5cm long

WINGSPAN *4–4.5cm.*
FLIGHT PERIOD *Mainly May–June; sometimes a second brood in August in the south.*
LARVAL FOODPLANT *Violet (Viola).*
SIMILAR SPECIES *Small Pearl-bordered Fritillary (left).*
STATUS *Widespread and locally common.*

Small Tortoiseshell

Nymphalis urticae (Nymphalidae)

INHABITS *a variety of flowery wayside places, from fields, verges, and gardens in lowlands, to meadows on lower mountain slopes.*

The Small Tortoiseshell is one of Europe's most familiar and attractive butterflies. The colourful upperwings are mainly orange, but are boldly marked with black, yellow, and dark brown; discrete blue markings around the wing margins complete the mosaic effect. By contrast, the underwings are rather sombre and afford the butterfly a degree of camouflage when resting with its wings shut. Small Tortoiseshells appear in two or three successive broods each year; adults from the last generation of autumn hibernate over the winter months, often using attics and outhouses; they emerge again in early spring.

yellow and black markings on forewing

buffish yellow markings

orange ground colour

blue spots in margin

smoky brown ground colour

up to 2.5cm long

NOTE
If you want to attract Small Tortoiseshells to your garden, not only should you grow nectar-rich plants such as Buddleia (Buddleia) and Iceplant (Sedum spectabile) for the adults, but you must also include patches of nettle (Urtica) for the larvae.

WINGSPAN *4.2–4.5cm*
FLIGHT PERIOD *March–October, in a number of successive broods.*
LARVAL FOODPLANT *Nettle (Urtica dioica).*
SIMILAR SPECIES *None in the British Isles.*
STATUS *Widespread and common.*

Comma

Nymphalis c-album (Nymphalidae)

This is one of the most distinctive European butterflies. The colours and shape of its wings, with ragged margins, allow recognition even in silhouette. The sombre underwings, marked with a white comma-like shape, contrast with the orange upperwings.

FOUND in a wide range of flower-rich and wayside habitats, from verges and woodland to meadows and gardens.

marbled brown ground colour ♂⊖

small white "comma" mark

up to 3.5cm long

jagged wing margin

dark markings

♂⊖

bright orange ground colour

WINGSPAN 4.5cm.
FLIGHT PERIOD March–September, in two broods; second brood adults hibernate.
LARVAL FOODPLANT Nettle (Urtica), hop (Humulus), and elm (Ulmus).
SIMILAR SPECIES None.
STATUS Widespread and common in Britain.

Marsh Fritillary

Euphydryas aurinia (Nymphalidae)

Although this species is rather variable in appearance, its wings, which are comparatively narrow by Fritillary standards, are characterized by a beautiful mosaic of reddish orange, yellow-buff, and brown. The underwings have similar markings, which are equally attractive but in subdued colours. The Marsh Fritillary is a rather sluggish butterfly that spends time sitting on low vegetation and basking in the sunshine with its wings open, a trait that aids close-up observation. Females are usually larger than males.

FAVOURS grassy areas, often on marshy ground but also on dry slopes and moorland.

orange-buff ground colour

orange-buff ground colour ⊖

pale bands and spots

black spots in orange band

dark bands and lines

♂⊖

up to 3cm long

NOTE

This is the most widespread Euphydryas fritillary species in the region and one of the most common members of this rather narrow-winged group you are likely to encounter in grassy areas. The Marsh Fritillary can be surprisingly hard to find on dull days since it tends to hide away in the deep cover of foliage.

WINGSPAN 4.5–5.2cm.
FLIGHT PERIOD May–July.
LARVAL FOODPLANT Devil's-bit Scabious (Succisa pratensis), scabious (Scabiosa), and plantain (Plantago).
SIMILAR SPECIES None.
STATUS Scattered colonies, mainly in the west.

Silver-washed Fritillary

Argynnis paphia (Nymphalidae)

Across much of its range an experienced observer can identify a Silver-washed Fritillary, with a reasonable degree of confidence, by its size and flight pattern alone. It is a relatively large butterfly with a fast, gliding flight. A close view of a resting individual reveals the forewings to be rather angular while the hindwings are relatively large and rounded. In most specimens, the upperwings have a rich orange ground colour. By contrast, the buffish yellow and greenish underwings are marked with metallic, silvery bands – a feature that gives this butterfly its common name.

ASSOCIATED with wooded areas, favouring clearings, rides, and margins with brambles, which are a source of nectar for adult butterflies.

silvery bands

♀⊖

NOTE

The female Silver-washed Fritillary occurs in two colour forms. Typically, it resembles a duller, more heavily spotted version of the male, but in the form A. p. valesina the upperwings are greenish buff.

orange-buff ground colour

♀⊖

prominent black spots

up to 4cm long

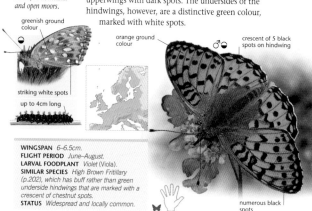

angular forewings

♂⊖

rich orange ground colour

rounded hindwings

WINGSPAN 6cm.
FLIGHT PERIOD June–August.
LARVAL FOODPLANT Violet (Viola).
SIMILAR SPECIES None.
STATUS Occurs locally in southern Britain and Ireland. Its numbers have been well-maintained over the last 30 years, and in Ireland its distribution has grown significantly.

Dark Green Fritillary

Argynnis aglaja (Nymphalidae)

This butterfly of open habitats is unaffected by strong winds and has a fast and direct flight. Fortunately, it frequently feeds on the flowers of thistle and knapweed, allowing for close-up views. Like most other Fritillaries, it has orange upperwings with dark spots. The undersides of the hindwings, however, are a distinctive green colour, marked with white spots.

INHABITS grassy habitats from coastal dunes, to downland and open moors.

greenish ground colour

orange ground colour

♂⊖

crescent of 5 black spots on hindwing

striking white spots

up to 4cm long

numerous black spots

WINGSPAN 6–6.5cm.
FLIGHT PERIOD June–August.
LARVAL FOODPLANT Violet (Viola).
SIMILAR SPECIES High Brown Fritillary (p.202), which has buff rather than green underside hindwings that are marked with a crescent of chestnut spots.
STATUS Widespread and locally common.

High Brown Fritillary

Argynnis adippe (Nymphalidae)

This well-marked butterfly is capable of fast and vigorous flight and, in sunny weather, it seldom seems to pause, except to feed on Bramble flowers. The upperwings are a rich orange-brown ground colour with striking black spots and streaks. On the underside, the forewings are orange-buff with dark spots while the hindwings are buff, often with a greenish tinge. Apart from bearing striking white spots, the hindwings also have a characteristic crescent of chestnut spots. The male High Brown Fritillary is typically smaller than the female. This is the most likely large and fast-flying Fritillary species to be encountered in upland grassland areas. In Britian and other areas on the margins of its range, this species has become decidedly scarce in recent decades.

FREQUENTS *sunny woodland and grassy scrub with plenty of open areas and sparse vegetation.*

orange-brown ground colour

black spots and markings

chequered fringe

crescent of chestnut spots

striking white spots

NOTE

Although the underwings vary in appearance, particularly in the extent of green suffusion, a crescent of chestnut dots on the hindwing is a constant feature and useful in identification; it is present in both the sexes.

up to 4cm long

WINGSPAN *6–6.5cm.*
FLIGHT PERIOD *July–August.*
LARVAL FOODPLANT *Violet (Viola).*
SIMILAR SPECIES *Dark Green Fritillary (p.201), which has green underside hindwings with white and no chestnut spots.*
STATUS *Rare in the British Isles; widespread but distinctly local on the continent.*

Painted Lady

Vanessa cardui (Nymphalidae)

With its distinctively patterned salmon-pink upperwings, the Painted Lady is one of the easiest British butterflies to recognize, even on the wing. Although duller in appearance, the underwing pattern is similar to that of the upperwings. The Painted Lady reaches Britain in early summer, having flown from Africa and bred a new generation in southern Europe. In some years they have occurred as early as February on the south coast. As they migrate through Britain they breed and may reach northern Scotland by late summer. They cannot hibernate in Britain's cold winters.

FOUND *in grassy places where flowers are in bloom, often visiting gardens on occasions.*

forewing has dark tip with white spots

salmon-pink and black pattern

salmon-pink forewing

submarginal eyespots

smoky brown wing base

hindwing marbled grey, buffish brown, and white

up to 3cm long

NOTE

When feeding on nectar from flowers such as thistle (Carduus/Cirsium) and knapweed (Centaurea), the Painted Lady is usually oblivious to the approach of an observer. This is the best time to get a close and rewarding view of the species.

WINGSPAN *6cm.*
FLIGHT PERIOD *April–October in the British Isles; March–November in southern Europe.*
LARVAL FOODPLANT *Thistle (Carduus/Cirsium) and Nettle (Urtica dioica).*
SIMILAR SPECIES *None.*
STATUS *Migratory species; numbers vary from year to year but it is usually common by late summer.*

Red Admiral

Vanessa atalanta (Nymphalidae)

The fact that it is a frequent visitor to gardens, along with its bright colours and distinctive markings, makes the Red Admiral one of the Britain's most familiar butterflies. Its jet-black upperwings are marked with bands of red and white spots, with a single blue spot at the base of each hindwing. The underside of the forewing has a similar pattern and colouring, along with a pinkish red patch. However, when resting, this is often concealed by the more cryptic undersurface of the hindwing, which is marbled smoky brown, bluish, and black. The antennae have alternate dark and light markings and a white tip.

OCCURS *in almost any flowery habitat, from grassy meadows, verges, and hedgerows to parks and gardens.*

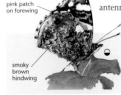

pink patch on forewing

smoky brown hindwing

up to 3.5cm long

white spots on wing tip

red band on forewing

red hindwing margin

blue spot on hindwing base

NOTE

Red Admirals are often found drinking fluid from rotting apples and other fallen fruit in autumn. At such times, they may even alight on the palm of a hand bearing fruit, in search of a meal.

WINGSPAN *6cm.*
FLIGHT PERIOD *May–October, and again in March and April after hibernation.*
LARVAL FOODPLANT *Nettle (Urtica).*
SIMILAR SPECIES *None.*
STATUS *Common; it arrives from Europe early in the spring to breed, spreading throughout Britain.*

Peacock

Nymphalis io (Nymphalidae)

Striking eyespots and gaudy colours make the Peacock an unmistakable butterfly. Like several of its colourful relatives, it is a frequent visitor to gardens, where it feeds on nectar; it is particularly fond of the flowers of buddleia and iceplant. When resting with its wings closed, the cryptic coloration of the undersides and the jagged wing margins make the species look like dead leaves or bark, affording it excellent camouflage. If startled, a resting Peacock will flash open its wings, the sudden revelation of the eyespots scaring off potential predators.

FREQUENTS *grassy and wayside habitats, from hedgerows and verges to meadows, gardens, and parks.*

yellow, maroon, and bluish purple eyespot

reddish maroon ground colour

blue and black eyespot on hindwing

marbled brown ground colour

jagged edge

up to 4cm long

NOTE

Peacock larvae live communally, constructing conspicuous silken tents on their foodplants, which are members of the nettle family. Look for these wispy structures among the clumps of nettles during summer months.

WINGSPAN *6cm.*
FLIGHT PERIOD *July–September, and after hibernation, March–May.*
LARVAL FOODPLANT *Nettle (Urtica).*
SIMILAR SPECIES *None.*
STATUS *Widespread and common. One of the commonest butterflies found in the garden.*

Purple Emperor

Apatura iris (Nymphalidae)

The large and impressive Purple Emperor is perhaps one of the most highly prized species for European butterfly-watchers. Not only is it beautifully marked, but it is also one of Britain's most elusive resident butterflies and so finally spotting one is a definite achievement. Purple Emperors spend much of their adult lives flying around the tops of tall oak trees. The wing patterns are essentially similar in both sexes but the upperwings of the male reveal a glorious purple iridescence when seen at certain angles.

OCCURS *in mature oak woodland with tall trees, which serve as territorial focal points for males.*

grey and brown wings

orange-ringed eyespot

up to 5.5cm long

NOTE

The Purple Emperor's rather unsavoury predilection for drinking fluids from carrion and fresh dung means that it occasionally visits the ground, rewarding observers with some excellent close-up views.

bright purple sheen

white spots

brown ground colour

white band

WINGSPAN *6–6.5cm.*
FLIGHT PERIOD *July–August.*
LARVAL FOODPLANT *Sallow, notably Goat Willow (Salix caprea).*
SIMILAR SPECIES *None.*
STATUS *Rare, being confined to woodlands in southern Britain. However, there is evidence that it is maintaining its numbers.*

White Admiral

Limenitis camilla (Nymphalidae)

A widespread and familiar woodland butterfly, the White Admiral is fast-flying and alert to danger. However, it also feeds on the flowers of Brambles and typically is reluctant to leave a good source of nectar. Consequently, it can often be observed at close range for extended periods if you approach it without making any sudden movements. The blackish brown upperwings are marked with distinctive white bands; the pattern of white is similar, but more extensive, on the underwings, which have a rich orange-brown ground colour.

FOUND *in mature woodland with sunny clearings and rides, and an abundance of larval foodplants.*

bold white markings

blackish brown ground colour

white markings

scalloped white edging

orange-brown ground colour

double row of black spots

up to 3cm long

NOTE

This woodland species has declined in numbers in the last forty years. Nevertheless, it has extended its range northward into Leicestershire, East Anglia, and Lincolnshire. In exceptional summers this species, which is usually single-brooded, can have a second generation.

WINGSPAN *5cm.*
FLIGHT PERIOD *June–August.*
LARVAL FOODPLANT *Honeysuckle (Lonicera), typically plants growing in gloomy, shady settings.*
SIMILAR SPECIES *Second-generation Map Butterflies (Araschnia levana), which have similar upperwings but strikingly different underwings.*
STATUS *Widespread and locally common.*

Gatekeeper

Maniola tithonius (Satyridae)

The emergence of this familiar wayside butterfly is perceived by many naturalists to be a sign that summer is at its height. The Gatekeeper is on the wing just as bramble flowers are at their best, and groups can be seen feeding on their nectar. Its upperwings are a rich orange colour with a brown margin and an eyespot bearing twin highlights on the forewing. The underwing coloration is rather similar, although the hindwing has a more marbled appearance. Male Gatekeepers are smaller than females, with more brightly coloured wings, and have a dark sex-brand on each forewing.

FREQUENTS *meadows, grassy hedgerows, and woodland margins, typically from sea level to around 750m.*

dark patch on forewing

highlights on twin eyespot

buffish yellow ground colour

buff-brown margin

broad brown margin with pale fringe

up to 2cm long

NOTE
Throughout most of its range, this is the most common small- to medium-sized orange member of the Brown family, and is the species most likely to be seen feeding in groups on the flowers of bramble and other meadow and hedgerow plants.

WINGSPAN 4cm.
FLIGHT PERIOD July–August.
LARVAL FOODPLANT Various grasses (family Poaceae), such as bents (Agrostis), meadow grasses (Poa), and fescues (Festuca).
SIMILAR SPECIES None.
STATUS Widespread and common.

Small Heath

Coenonympha pamphilus (Satyridae)

Although small and not especially colourful, the Small Heath is easy to spot in the field. It can be extremely common in habitats that suit its needs, so observers should not find it difficult to get good views. On dull days, it can sometimes be found sitting on grass leaves and stems, allowing close inspection of the marbled grey undersurface of its hindwings and orange-brown underside of the forewings. The forewing is marked with a small, but striking black eyespot on both surfaces.

INHABITS *a range of grassy habitats, from meadows and verges, to heaths; from lower levels up to altitudes of 2,000m.*

narrow brown margin ♂

orange-brown ground colour

up to 2cm long

NOTE
The Small Heath always rests and feeds with its wings closed, making it almost impossible to obtain a view of the upperwings. Fortunately, its small size and underwing markings allow identification of most individuals.

orange-brown forewing

black eyespot

greyish margin

jagged, creamy white band

marbled grey and brown hindwing

WINGSPAN 3cm.
FLIGHT PERIOD May–September, in successive broods.
LARVAL FOODPLANT Various grasses (family Poaceae), notably fescue (Festuca).
SIMILAR SPECIES Large Heath (left), which is much larger and has more eyespots on the forewing.
STATUS Found in many different habitats in Britain, from lowland grassland to moorland and mountain slopes.

Large Heath

Coenonympha tullia (Satyridae)

The Large Heath's upperwings are usually glimpsed only momentarily, because they are never revealed by individuals at rest. The underwings show orange-brown on the forewing and are greyish on the hindwing. Active in calm, sunny weather, at other times it hides among grassy tussocks. This is an extremely variable species with the forewing eyespots absent in some subspecies.

ASSOCIATED *with moors, bogs, and waterlogged grassland, from sea level to around 2,000m.*

dark eyespots

grey margin

jagged pale band

orange-brown forewing

orange-buff ground colour

up to 2.5cm long

WINGSPAN 3.8–4cm.
FLIGHT PERIOD June–July.
LARVAL FOODPLANT Cotton grass (Eriophorum) and White-beaked Sedge (Rhynchospora alba).
SIMILAR SPECIES Small Heath (right).
STATUS Widespread in upland areas but typically rather local.

Wall Brown

Pararge megera (Satyridae)

The boldly patterned upperwings of the Wall Brown make it a comparatively easy species to identify. It sunbathes frequently allowing excellent close-up views. The underside of the hindwings has a cryptic pattern that resembles tree bark or mottled stone, which helps the butterfly to camouflage.

FAVOURS *dry, grassy heaths, hillsides, and cliffs, typically with rocks and bare areas for sunbathing; from sea level to 2,000m.*

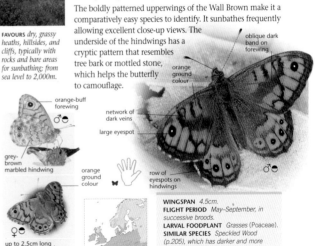

oblique dark band on forewing

orange ground colour

orange-buff forewing

network of dark veins

large eyespot

grey-brown marbled hindwing

orange ground colour

row of eyespots on hindwings

up to 2.5cm long

WINGSPAN 4.5cm.
FLIGHT PERIOD May–September, in successive broods.
LARVAL FOODPLANT Grasses (Poaceae).
SIMILAR SPECIES Speckled Wood (p.205), which has darker and more pointed upperwings.
STATUS Widespread but declining.

Speckled Wood

Pararge aegeria (Satyridae)

This butterfly is characterized by a dark upperwing surface, marked by large, marginal, yellowish blocks and spots. Some of these have small pale centres. The upperwing surface near the body is covered with a mass of hair-like scales. The underwings are browner with eyespots around the edges.

ASSOCIATED with woodland and typically found on the margins of sunny clearings and rides.

eyespot on forewing

single eyespot on forewing

dark brown ground colour

yellow-buff spots

marbled hindwing with pale spots

several eyespots on hindwing

orange and brown ground colour

SOUTHERN FORM

up to 2.5cm long

WINGSPAN *4.5cm.*
FLIGHT PERIOD *March–October, in successive broods.*
LARVAL FOODPLANT *Various woodland species of grasses (family Poaceae).*
SIMILAR SPECIES *None.*
STATUS *Widespread and locally common.*

Marbled White

Melanargia galathea (Satyridae)

An attractive and well-marked butterfly, the Marbled White exhibits some variation in its appearance. However, typically the upperwings are pale creamy white, with an extensive pattern of linked black veins and patches. Compared to other *Melanargia* species, the proportion of black to white is evenly balanced and distributed across the wings. The pattern on the underwings is similar but many of the black markings are replaced by grey, making the wings look much paler overall. While males and females are usually alike, females often have a yellowish suffusion on the underside of the hindwing.

FAVOURS flower-rich, grassy places such as meadows and verges; most common below 1,500m.

pale, creamy white ground colour

grey band with eyespots

grey patches

extensive black patches and veins

white scalloped margin

up to 2cm long

WINGSPAN *5cm.*
FLIGHT PERIOD *June–August.*
LARVAL FOODPLANT *Various grasses (family Poaceae), such as Red Fescue (Festuca rubra).*
SIMILAR SPECIES *None.*
STATUS *Widespread and locally common, typically forming discrete colonies.*

NOTE

The Marbled White is an easily recognized British species that lives mainly in the south and east of Britain, reaching as far north as Lincolnshire and east Yorkshire. Isolated colonies exist in Durham. It is thought to be colonizing new areas and extending its range.

Meadow Brown

Maniola jurtina (Satyridae)

This is probably the most numerous and widespread grassland butterfly species in the region. The underwings are most commonly seen: the forewing coloured orange and buff with a striking eyespot, and the brown hindwing with a paler band containing small black spots.

FOUND in a variety of grassy places, from meadows and roadside verges to woodland rides and hillsides up to 1,500m or more.

brown ground colour

orange forewings

buff band with black spots

eyespot on faint orange-buff patch

eyespot on orange band

up to 2.5cm long

WINGSPAN *5cm.*
FLIGHT PERIOD *June–October.*
LARVAL FOODPLANT *Various grasses (family Poaceae), such as fescues (Festuca), bents (Agrostis), and meadow grass (Poa).*
SIMILAR SPECIES *None.*
STATUS *Widespread and locally very common.*

Mountain Ringlet

Erebia epiphron (Satyridae)

Each upland region in which the Mountain Ringlet occurs may appear to have its own distinct form. However, in all cases, the ground colour of the wings is dark brown. Each wing has an orange band, varying in size and intensity, and it contains a variable number of small black spots. The upper and lower surfaces of the wings are rather similar.

INHABITS upland areas, notably grassy moorland, usually at altitudes from 500m to 2,500m.

black spots

dark brown ground colour

brown ground colour

orange band

up to 2cm long

variable number of black spots

WINGSPAN *3.2cm.*
FLIGHT PERIOD *July–August.*
LARVAL FOODPLANT *Various grasses (family Poaceae), such as Mat-grass (Nardus stricta).*
SIMILAR SPECIES *None.*
STATUS *Locally common in high mountains, in Cumbria and Scotland.*

Scotch Argus

Erebia aethiops (Satyridae)

This upland butterfly is easy to observe since it is slow-flying and often basks on vegetation. Its upperwing ground colour is rich dark brown and both wings are patterned with reddish orange bands containing eyespots with white highlights. The underside of the forewing resembles the upperside, but the hindwing is sooty brown with a lilac-grey submarginal band.

OCCURS in grassy places in open woodland and on moors, usually between 500m and 1,500m.

broad lilac-grey band

forewing underside resembles upper surface

sooty brown ground colour

eyespots with highlights

up to 2.5cm long

WINGSPAN *4-4.5cm.*
FLIGHT PERIOD *July–September.*
LARVAL FOODPLANT *Various grasses (family Poaceae), such as Blue Moor-grass (Sesleria caerulea) and Purple Moor-grass (Molinia caerulea).*
SIMILAR SPECIES *None.*
STATUS *Locally common.*

Diamond-back Moth

Plutella xylostella (Yponomeutidae)

This tiny moth occurs throughout the world and migrates long distances, sometimes moving northwards in such large numbers that the caterpillars become pests in cabbage fields. The adult Diamond-back Moth has a distinctive row of buff-coloured diamond-shaped marks along the edges of its folded wings. It flies by day and night and is attracted to light.

BREEDS *mainly in fields of cabbages and other brassicas, but as a migrant the adults may be found in almost any habitat.*

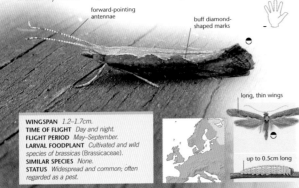

forward-pointing antennae

buff diamond-shaped marks

long, thin wings

up to 0.5cm long

WINGSPAN *1.2–1.7cm.*
TIME OF FLIGHT *Day and night.*
FLIGHT PERIOD *May–September.*
LARVAL FOODPLANT *Cultivated and wild species of brassicas (Brassicaceae).*
SIMILAR SPECIES *None.*
STATUS *Widespread and common; often regarded as a pest.*

Codling Moth

Cydia pomonella (Tortricidae)

The grey-brown wings of the Codling Moth are marked with black and gold on the tips. The larvae are sometimes found inside apples and other fruit, and can be a major pest in orchards. In commercial orchards, however, they are controlled either by pesticides or by pheromone traps, which catch the males in large numbers by attracting them to a synthetic version of the female's scent.

FOUND *wherever wild or cultivated fruit trees grow, especially in orchards and gardens.*

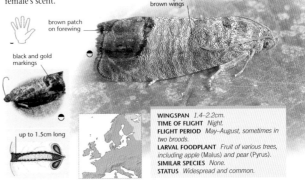

mottled grey and brown wings

brown patch on forewing

black and gold markings

up to 1.5cm long

WINGSPAN *1.4–2.2cm.*
TIME OF FLIGHT *Night.*
FLIGHT PERIOD *May–August, sometimes in two broods.*
LARVAL FOODPLANT *Fruit of various trees, including apple (Malus) and pear (Pyrus).*
SIMILAR SPECIES *None.*
STATUS *Widespread and common.*

White-shouldered House-moth

Endrosis sarcitrella (Oecophoridae)

The upperwings of this House-moth are grey-brown and heavily mottled, while its head and thorax are white. This is a common and distinctive species, often found in birds' nests, houses, and outbuildings where grain or other produce is stored. Adult moths may be seen indoors at any time of the year, and frequently come to light sources.

LIVES *in houses, barns, and outhouses; sometimes also found in old birds' nests.*

dark mottling

white head and thorax

up to 1cm long

grey-brown wings

WINGSPAN *1.3–2cm.*
TIME OF FLIGHT *Night.*
FLIGHT PERIOD *Throughout the year.*
LARVAL FOOD *Almost any vegetable matter, stored grain, wood, and birds' droppings and feathers.*
SIMILAR SPECIES *None.*
STATUS *Widespread and common.*

Light Brown Apple Moth

Epiphyas postvittana (Tortricidae)

Originally a native of Australia, the Light Brown Apple Moth was accidentally imported to Britain with apples. It was first recorded in Essex in 1911, but has since spread across most of the country, and is now very common in some areas. Adults may be found flying at almost any time of year, but are most abundant between April and November.

INHABITS *a wide variety of habitats, including gardens, orchards, hedgerows, and woodland.*

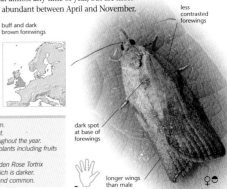

buff and dark brown forewings

less contrasted forewings

pointed wingtips

up to 2cm long

dark spot at base of forewings

longer wings than male

WINGSPAN *1.6–2.5cm.*
TIME OF FLIGHT *Night.*
FLIGHT PERIOD *Throughout the year.*
LARVAL FOOD *Many plants including fruits and vegetables.*
SIMILAR SPECIES *Garden Rose Tortrix (Acleris variegana), which is darker.*
STATUS *Widespread and common.*

Green Oak Tortrix

Tortrix viridana (Tortricidae)

This moth is a member of the large family of Micro-moths known as Leaf-rollers, from the larva's habit of rolling a leaf of the foodplant into a tube in which it lives. Entirely green forewings and greyish hindwings make this Tortrix one of the more easily recognized species. It can be abundant in oak woods, and the caterpillars sometimes defoliate entire trees.

FEEDS *on the leaves of oak trees, and is common in any deciduous wood where the foodplant grows.*

reddish-brown limbs and body

wing colour blends with oak leaves

green forewings

up to 1cm long

WINGSPAN *1.6–2.4cm.*
TIME OF FLIGHT *Mainly at night.*
FLIGHT PERIOD *June–August.*
LARVAL FOODPLANT *Oak (Quercus).*
SIMILAR SPECIES *Cream-bordered Green Pea (Earias clorana), which has white hindwings.*
STATUS *Widespread and common.*

Mint Moth

Pyrausta aurata (Pyralidae)

This attractive little moth is sometimes called the Mint Moth, reflecting its main foodplant. It is most frequently seen flying in bright sunshine, but also flies at night, when it is attracted to light. It is often confused with the very similar *P. purpuralis*, but that species is usually a brighter purple, and has three distinct yellow marks forming a band across each forewing.

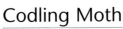

FOUND *wherever mint and other herbs grow: chalky downland, wetlands, wasteland, and woodland edges.*

dark purplish brown colour

 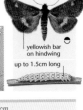

yellowish bar on hindwing

up to 1.5cm long

single yellow spot on forewing

WINGSPAN *1.5–2cm.*
FLIGHT PERIOD *May–August, in two broods.*
LARVAL FOOD *Mint (Mentha), marjoram (Origanum), and other herbs.*
SIMILAR SPECIES *P. purpuralis, which is a brighter purple and has more yellow markings on the forewings.*
STATUS *Widespread and locally common.*

Twenty-plume Moth

Alucita hexadactyla (Alucitidae)

This moth gets its name from the six linked feather-like "plumes" that make up each of its wings. At rest it often adopts a triangular posture, with the plumes held tightly together, and can look like an ordinary moth until its wings are spread, revealing the individual plumes. The adult hibernates, but may fly on mild nights in the winter.

FOUND *in gardens, woodland, and commons – wherever its larval foodplant, honeysuckle, grows.*

plumes spread out

up to 0.5cm long

dark double band on forewing

feathery plumes

WINGSPAN *1.4–1.6cm.*
TIME OF FLIGHT *Night.*
FLIGHT PERIOD *Adults occur at any time of the year.*
LARVAL FOODPLANT *Honeysuckle (Lonicera).*
SIMILAR SPECIES *None.*
STATUS *Common.*

Bee Moth

Aphomia sociella (Pyralidae)

The adult Bee Moth rolls, rather than folds, its pinkish brown wings when at rest. Its larvae live in the nests of bees and wasps, where they feed on honeycomb and bee or wasp larvae. An infested nest may contain hundreds of Bee Moth caterpillars, which make silk-lined tunnels, and later pupate in tough, papery cocoons.

OCCURS *in all habitats where bees or wasps nest, including woodland, gardens, and scrub.*

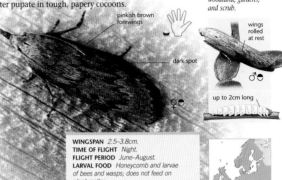

pinkish brown forewings

dark spot

wings rolled at rest

up to 2cm long

WINGSPAN *2.5–3.8cm.*
TIME OF FLIGHT *Night.*
FLIGHT PERIOD *June–August.*
LARVAL FOOD *Honeycomb and larvae of bees and wasps; does not feed on plant matter.*
SIMILAR SPECIES *None.*
STATUS *Widespread and common.*

Small Magpie

Eurrhypara hortulata (Pyralidae)

One of the most attractive and familiar of the Micro-moths, the Small Magpie is easily recognized by its black and white wings, and yellow and black body. The caterpillar feeds on Nettles, and the adult moth is easily disturbed from vegetation during the day. The moth's natural time of flight is from early evening onwards, and it is attracted to light.

FREQUENTS *any habitat where Nettles grow, favouring damper areas of woodland, commons, and gardens.*

yellow and black body

black margins

up to 2cm long

white wings with black spots

WINGSPAN *3.3–3.5cm.*
FLIGHT PERIOD *May–August.*
LARVAL FOODPLANT *Common Nettle (Urtica dioica), woundwort (Stachys), and mint (Mentha) species.*
SIMILAR SPECIES *Magpie Moth (p.213), which is much larger.*
STATUS *Widespread and common.*

White Plume-moth

Pterophorus pentadactyla (Pterophoridae)

This is the only completely white Plume moth. Although its wings are made up of feather-like plumes similar to those of the Twenty-plume Moth (left), the two are not closely related. Its forewings are divided into two plumes, and the hindwings into three. At rest it holds its wings outstretched. The moth flies mainly at dawn and dusk, and is often found sitting at lighted windows at night.

FOUND *in grassy places, gardens, commons, hedgerows, and wherever the foodplant grows.*

wings outstretched at rest

long legs

up to 2cm long

feathery wings

WINGSPAN *2.6–3.4cm.*
TIME OF FLIGHT *Night.*
FLIGHT PERIOD *June–August.*
LARVAL FOODPLANT *Bindweed (Convolvulus and Calystegia).*
SIMILAR SPECIES *Several other species of Plume moth, but none are all white.*
STATUS *Widespread and fairly common.*

Mother of Pearl

Pleuroptya ruralis (Pyralidae)

The Mother of Pearl is one of the larger Micro-moths, larger, in fact, than some of the Macro-moths. Its wings have an attractive pinkish pearly sheen, which resembles the inside of an oyster shell. Although it flies mainly at night, when it is attracted to light, it can be disturbed from Nettles during the day.

FAVOURS *areas where Nettles grow, such as gardens, wasteland, and damper woodland.*

pearly sheen

pale buff forewings

pointed wingtips

brownish markings

up to 2cm long

WINGSPAN *3.3–3.7cm.*
TIME OF FLIGHT *Night; but can be disturbed easily during the day.*
FLIGHT PERIOD *June–August.*
LARVAL FOODPLANT *Common Nettle (Urtica dioica).*
SIMILAR SPECIES *None.*
STATUS *Widespread and common.*

Chinese Character

Cilix glaucata (Drepanidae)

At rest, with its antennae, body, and legs all hidden under its folded wings, this moth bears a striking resemblance to a bird dropping. Its camouflage is obviously highly effective, as it may be found resting on the outside of a moth trap or on nearby foliage, when other more conspicuous species have been taken by birds.

INHABITS *hedgerows, gardens, commons, bushy places, waste ground, and open woodland.*

white ground colour

black and grey markings

smooth appearance

PALER FORM

up to 2cm long

WINGSPAN *2.2–2.7cm.*
TIME OF FLIGHT *Night.*
FLIGHT PERIOD *May–August, in two broods.*
LARVAL FOODPLANT *Hawthorn (Crataegus), Blackthorn (Prunus spinosa), and occasionally other trees and plants.*
SIMILAR SPECIES *None.*
STATUS *Widespread and common.*

Six-spot Burnet

Zygaena filipendulae (Zygaenidae)

INHABITS *downland, meadows, woodland rides, and other flower-rich places; also cliff tops and sand hills.*

This attractive day-flying species can be told apart from the similar Five-spot Burnet (*Z. trifolii*) by the presence of three pairs of red spots on an iridescent greenish black or bluish green background. The hindwings, revealed in flight, are the same bright crimson-red as the forewing spots. All species of burnet moth contain cyanide, and have bright colours warning predators they are toxic. However, despite this fact, they are occasionally eaten by birds. A rare colour variant of this moth has the red areas of the wings replaced by yellow instead. The papery cocoon may be found on the foodplant after the moth has emerged.

black head and body

papery cocoon

MOTH ON COCOON

up to 2.5cm long

NOTE

The extra red spot which separates this species from the Five-spot Burnet is at the tip of the forewing, making up three distinct pairs of spots.

thick, clubbed antennae

3 pairs of red spots on forewing

iridescent blue-green ground colour

WINGSPAN *2.5–4cm.*
FLIGHT PERIOD *June–August.*
LARVAL FOODPLANT *Bird's-foot Trefoil (Lotus corniculatus).*
SIMILAR SPECIES *Five-spot Burnet (Z. trifolii), which has fewer red spots on its forewing; Cinnabar (p.215).*
STATUS *Widespread and fairly common.*

Hornet Moth

Sesia apiformis (Sesiidae)

FAVOURS *areas where mature poplar trees grow, often near water or in damp habitats such as marshes and river valleys.*

With its transparent wings, yellow and black striped abdomen, and thickened antennae, the Hornet Moth bears a striking resemblance to a hornet or large wasp. All the Clearwing moths, of which this is one of the larger representatives, fly during the day, especially in sunshine, but are very rarely seen. The larva spends at least two years, sometimes three, in this stage before emerging as an adult. This is probably because of the low nutritional value of wood, on which it feeds.

thickened antennae

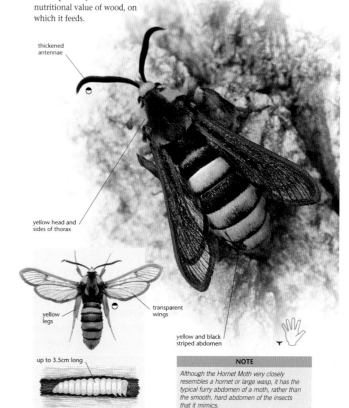

yellow head and sides of thorax

yellow legs

transparent wings

yellow and black striped abdomen

up to 3.5cm long

NOTE

Although the Hornet Moth very closely resembles a hornet or large wasp, it has the typical furry abdomen of a moth, rather than the smooth, hard abdomen of the insects that it mimics.

WINGSPAN *3.4–5cm.*
FLIGHT PERIOD *July–August.*
LARVAL FOODPLANT *Feeds on the trunks and roots of Black Poplar (Populus nigra); occasionally on other poplar (Populus) species.*
SIMILAR SPECIES *Lunar Hornet Moth (S. bembeciformis), which has no yellow on the sides of the thorax.*
STATUS *Widespread, but local in southern Britain.*

Pebble Hook-tip

Drepana falcataria (Drepanidae)

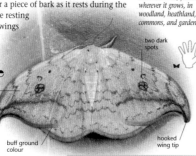

FEEDS *on birch; found wherever it grows, in woodland, heathland, commons, and gardens.*

One of several species of moths known as Hook-tips, from the distinctive shape of their wingtips, the Pebble Hook-tip has an intricate mottled pattern on its wings, making it look like a dead leaf or a piece of bark as it rests during the day. It has a distinctive resting posture, with the forewings partly concealing the hindwings, giving the moth an almost oval outline.

wing pattern resembles dead leaf

two dark spots

dark line on forewing

buff ground colour

hooked wing tip

up to 2.5cm long

WINGSPAN *3.6–4cm.*
TIME OF FLIGHT *Night.*
FLIGHT PERIOD *May–August, in two broods.*
LARVAL FOODPLANT *Birch (Betula), sometimes alder (Alnus).*
SIMILAR SPECIES *Dusky Hook-tip (D. curvatula) has a smaller spot on hindwing.*
STATUS *Locally common.*

Peach Blossom

Thyatira batis (Thyatiridae)

OCCURS *in woodland with bramble, but also in gardens, commons, and waste ground.*

A beautiful and unmistakable moth, the Peach Blossom has an unusual wing pattern made up of large pink, buff, and white spots on a brown background. The young caterpillar resembles a bird dropping, and rests exposed on the upperside of a bramble leaf during the day. As it grows, it becomes browner, and hides among leaf litter, coming out to feed only at night.

patterned forewings

plain brown hindwings

up to 3cm long

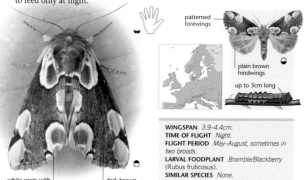

white spots with pinkish buff centres

dark brown ground colour

WINGSPAN *3.9–4.4cm.*
TIME OF FLIGHT *Night.*
FLIGHT PERIOD *May–August, sometimes in two broods.*
LARVAL FOODPLANT *Bramble/Blackberry (Rubus fruticosus).*
SIMILAR SPECIES *None.*
STATUS *Widespread and fairly common.*

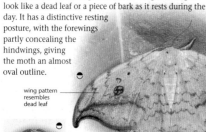

Double-striped Pug

Gymnoscelis rufifasciata (Geometridae)

The Pugs are a notoriously difficult group of moths to identify, being mostly small and dull brown, with few distinguishing features. The Double-striped Pug is one of the more distinctive species, however, with rather pointed wingtips and two dark wavy lines across the forewings. The adults feed at flowers, and are attracted to light.

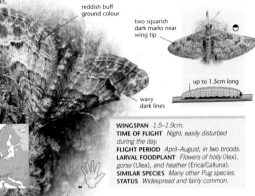

FREQUENTS *many habitats, including open woodland, gardens, commons, waste ground, and hedgerows.*

reddish buff ground colour

two squarish dark marks near wing tip

up to 1.5cm long

wavy dark lines

WINGSPAN *1.5–1.9cm.*
TIME OF FLIGHT *Night; easily disturbed during the day.*
FLIGHT PERIOD *April–August, in two broods.*
LARVAL FOODPLANT *Flowers of holly (Ilex), gorse (Ulex), and heather (Erica/Calluna).*
SIMILAR SPECIES *Many other Pug species.*
STATUS *Widespread and fairly common.*

Lime-speck Pug

Eupithecia centaureata (Geometridae)

This unmistakable Pug bears some resemblance to a bird dropping, being largely white with dark markings, which may help to reduce predation by birds. The moth rests with its slender wings stretched out at right angles to the body, the hindwings mostly concealed beneath the forewings.

OCCURS *in a variety of habitats, including parks, gardens, waste ground, commons, and open woodland.*

black spot on forewing

white thorax

grey-brown band near outer edge

white ground colour

up to 2cm long

blackish abdomen

WINGSPAN *2–2.4cm.*
TIME OF FLIGHT *Night.*
FLIGHT PERIOD *April–September, usually in two broods.*
LARVAL FOODPLANT *Various flowers, including ragwort (Senecio).*
SIMILAR SPECIES *None.*
STATUS *Widespread and generally common.*

Foxglove Pug

Eupithecia pulchellata (Geometridae)

One of the more distinctive Pugs, the Foxglove Pug usually has a strong reddish buff ground colour on its forewings, crossed by alternating dark and light brown bands. Some individuals are a paler buff, but even these have the light and dark bands. Like most of the Pugs, the Foxglove Pug is attracted to light.

FOUND *wherever foxgloves grow, in gardens, woodland, and on downland, moors, and shingle beaches.*

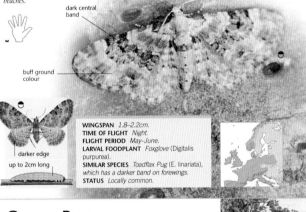

dark central band

buff ground colour

darker edge

up to 2cm long

WINGSPAN *1.8–2.2cm.*
TIME OF FLIGHT *Night.*
FLIGHT PERIOD *May–June.*
LARVAL FOODPLANT *Foxglove (Digitalis purpurea).*
SIMILAR SPECIES *Toadflax Pug (E. linariata), which has a darker band on forewings.*
STATUS *Locally common.*

Latticed Heath

Chiasmia clathrata (Geometridae)

On first sight, the Latticed Heath could be mistaken for a Skipper butterfly, particularly the Grizzled Skipper (p.189), which occurs in similar habitats. However, a close view will show that the moth is usually browner, while the Grizzled Skipper is more black and white. A rather variable moth – some specimens are darker or lighter than the typical form; the ground colour also varies from yellow-buff to whitish. The Latticed Heath flies by day in sunshine. However, it also flies at night, when it is attracted to light. The females are usually slightly smaller.

FAVOURS *a wide variety of habitats, including flowery meadows, downland, heathland, commons, and open woodland.*

wings often held closed

network of dark lines

buff or whitish background

pattern similar on upper and lower surfaces

up to 2.5cm long

NOTE

Although the Latticed Heath resembles the Grizzled Skipper, a close look will reveal that its wings are pale with a network of dark lines, whereas the butterfly's wings are black with small white rectangles.

WINGSPAN *2.6–3.2cm.*
FLIGHT PERIOD *May–September, in two broods.*
LARVAL FOODPLANT *Various clovers and trefoils (Trifolium/Lotus); also Lucerne (Medicago sativa).*
SIMILAR SPECIES *Grizzled Skipper (p.189), Dingy Skipper (p.189), Common Heath (Ematurga atomaria), which has a less sharply defined pattern of dark brown and buff on its wings.*
STATUS *Widespread and locally common.*

Green Pug

Pasiphila rectangulata (Geometridae)

When freshly emerged, the Green Pug usually lives up to its name, with a distinctly green coloration on its wings. However, this colour quickly fades. Some specimens may also be darker, occasionally almost black. The Green Pug is strongly attracted to light, and is often found at windows or in moth traps after dark.

INHABITS *orchards and other places where fruit trees grow, such as gardens, woodland, and commons.*

wavy lines on forewing

greenish ground colour

DARKER FORM

dark line at centre of forewing

up to 1.5cm long

WINGSPAN *1.7–2.1cm.*
TIME OF FLIGHT *Night.*
FLIGHT PERIOD *June–July.*
LARVAL FOODPLANT *Flowers of fruit trees.*
SIMILAR SPECIES *V-Pug (Chloroclystis v-ata), which has a black "V" on forewings; Sloe Pug (P. chloerata), which is less green.*
STATUS *Widespread and common.*

Barred Yellow

Cidaria fulvata (Geometridae)

A small, brightly coloured, and striking geometrid moth, the Barred Yellow rests with its wings swept back and its abdomen raised. Its natural flight time is at dusk, when it can be seen fluttering around vegetation, but some continue to fly throughout the night, when they are sometimes attracted to light.

FREQUENTS *gardens, hedges, and other bushy places; also found in commons and open woodland.*

bright yellow ground colour

buff hindwing up to 2cm long

brown "V"-shaped band on forewing

WINGSPAN *2.5–3cm.*
TIME OF FLIGHT *Night.*
FLIGHT PERIOD *June–August.*
LARVAL FOODPLANT *Wild and cultivated roses (Rosa).*
SIMILAR SPECIES *Yellow Shell (p.211), The Spinach (p.211), Brimstone Moth (p.211).*
STATUS *Locally common.*

Willow Beauty

Peribatodes rhomboidaria (Geometridae)

The Willow Beauty's wing pattern of dark wavy lines on a mottled grey background provides perfect camouflage when resting on a tree trunk. The ground colour varies from light grey-brown to a darker grey, with an almost black form occurring frequently in industrial areas. This moth can be very common at light traps in late summer, and occurs in a wide variety of habitats.

FOUND *wherever the larvae can feed, in woods, hedgerows, parks, and gardens.*

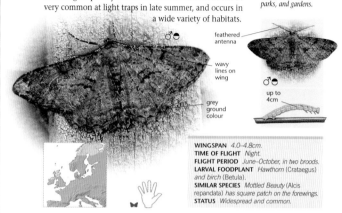

feathered antenna

wavy lines on wing

grey ground colour

up to 4cm

WINGSPAN *4.0–4.8cm.*
TIME OF FLIGHT *Night.*
FLIGHT PERIOD *June–October, in two broods.*
LARVAL FOODPLANT *Hawthorn (Crataegus) and birch (Betula).*
SIMILAR SPECIES *Mottled Beauty (Alcis repandata) has square patch on the forewings.*
STATUS *Widespread and common.*

Green Carpet

Colostygia pectinataria (Geometridae)

A freshly emerged Green Carpet is moss green, but fades to yellowish in a few days, older moths being almost white. Wavy lines extend across the wings from three dark triangles along the forewing leading edge. The moth rests with its forewings swept back, concealing the hindwings.

FOUND *in hedgerows, gardens, commons, heathland, downland, and open woodland.*

dark triangles on leading edge

FRESHLY EMERGED MOTH

dark wavy lines

OLDER MOTH

up to 2cm long

WINGSPAN *2.5–2.9cm.*
TIME OF FLIGHT *Night.*
FLIGHT PERIOD *May–July.*
LARVAL FOODPLANT *Bedstraws (Galium).*
SIMILAR SPECIES *None – this moth is unique in Britain.*
STATUS *Widespread and common throughout the region.*

Winter Moth

Operophtera brumata (Geometridae)

The Winter Moth, as its common name suggests, flies only during the winter months. As is the case with several other geometrids, only the male moth flies; the female is almost wingless, and rather spider-like in appearance. Both sexes may be found after dark sitting on tree trunks, and the male is often seen at lighted windows on mild nights.

FOUND *wherever there are deciduous trees and shrubs. This species can be a serious pest in orchards.*

plain underside

pale grey-brown ground colour

faintly darker bands

up to 2cm long

WINGSPAN *2.8–3.3cm.*
TIME OF FLIGHT *Night.*
FLIGHT PERIOD *November–February.*
LARVAL FOODPLANT *Oak (Quercus), birch (Betula), sallow (Salix), and apple (Malus).*
SIMILAR SPECIES *Northern Winter Moth (O. fagata), which is larger and paler.*
STATUS *Widespread and common.*

Garden Carpet

APPEARS *in various habitats with flowers, including gardens, commons, waste ground, and hedgerows.*

Xanthorhoe fluctuata (Geometridae)

The Garden Carpet may be distinguished from other small geometrid moths by the dark patch across the forewings, which extends only halfway across the wing. A common moth, even in suburban areas, it may be found during the day resting on walls, trees, or fences. It flies at dusk, and is attracted to light.

dark wing base

dark band on forewing

pale grey ground colour

grey hindwings

up to 2.5cm long

WINGSPAN *2.7–3.1cm.*
TIME OF FLIGHT *Night.*
FLIGHT PERIOD *April–October.*
LARVAL FOODPLANT *Various brassicas.*
SIMILAR SPECIES *Common Carpet (Epirrhoe alternata), which has a dark band right across the forewings.*
STATUS *Widespread and common.*

Chimney Sweeper

Odezia atrata (Geometridae)

At first glance the Chimney Sweeper's wings appear entirely sooty black, but a closer view reveals the narrow white borders to the tips of the forewings. Older specimens may fade to a dull brown. This day-flying moth is most active in sunny weather. It can sometimes be seen in large numbers in damp meadows.

OCCURS *in damp meadows, on chalk downland, and along woodland edges, where the foodplant grows.*

sooty black ground colour

dull brown wings

white border on wingtip

up to 2.5cm long

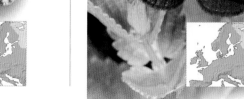

WINGSPAN *2.7–3cm.*
TIME OF FLIGHT *Day.*
FLIGHT PERIOD *June–July.*
LARVAL FOODPLANT *Flowers and seeds of Pignut (Conopodium majus), and other members of the carrot family.*
SIMILAR SPECIES *None.*
STATUS *Locally common.*

Yellow Shell

Camptogramma bilineata (Geometridae)

The Yellow Shell is rather variable in appearance. The typical form is mainly yellow, but darker varieties occur, particularly in the more northerly parts of its range. Its natural time of flight is from dusk onwards. However, it is easily disturbed from its resting place, and may be seen flying during the day.

INHABITS *a variety of habitats, including woodland, gardens, hedgerows, heathland, and commons.*

several dark and light wavy lines

plainer hindwings

up to 4.5cm long

yellow ground colour

WINGSPAN *2.8–3.2cm.*
FLIGHT PERIOD *June–August.*
LARVAL FOODPLANT *Dock (Rumex), chickweed (Stellaria), and grasses.*
SIMILAR SPECIES *The Spinach (below), Barred Yellow (p.210), and Brimstone Moth (right).*
STATUS *Widespread and common.*

Brimstone Moth

Opisthograptis luteolata (Geometridae)

This bright yellow geometrid moth sometimes flies by day, when it may be mistaken for a butterfly. More usually, it flies from dusk onwards, and is a common visitor to moth traps and lighted windows. This moth usually has several reddish brown marks along the leading edge of the wing, but occasional plain yellow specimens may also be found.

FOUND *in hedgerows, gardens, covered bushy places, as well as open woodland.*

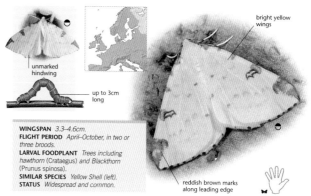

unmarked hindwing

up to 3cm long

bright yellow wings

reddish brown marks along leading edge

WINGSPAN *3.3–4.6cm.*
FLIGHT PERIOD *April–October, in two or three broods.*
LARVAL FOODPLANT *Trees including hawthorn (Crataegus) and Blackthorn (Prunus spinosa).*
SIMILAR SPECIES *Yellow Shell (left).*
STATUS *Widespread and common.*

Speckled Yellow

Pseudopanthera macularia (Geometridae)

An attractive, day-flying species, the Speckled Yellow typically lives up to its common name, although the ground colour is variable, and some individuals may be cream or almost white. It prefers warmer climates, and is commoner in the south of its European range, but may be found in mountainous areas.

OCCURS *in open woodland and scrubland, both in lowland and mountainous regions.*

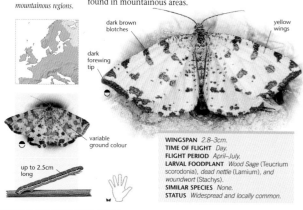

dark brown blotches

yellow wings

dark forewing tip

variable ground colour

up to 2.5cm long

WINGSPAN *2.8–3cm.*
TIME OF FLIGHT *Day.*
FLIGHT PERIOD *April–July.*
LARVAL FOODPLANT *Wood Sage (Teucrium scorodonia), dead nettle (Lamium), and woundwort (Stachys).*
SIMILAR SPECIES *None.*
STATUS *Widespread and locally common.*

Blood-vein

Timandra comai (Geometridae)

The Blood-vein is a rather delicate moth with pointed tips to both the forewings and hindwings. At rest, the reddish lines on each wing join up to form a continuous stripe. The sexes are similar, but the male can be distinguished by its feathered antennae.

FREQUENTS *a wide range of habitats, including wasteland, commons, gardens, field margins, and meadows.*

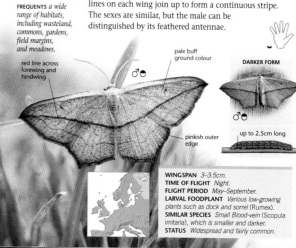

red line across forewing and hindwing

pale buff ground colour

♂♀

♂

DARKER FORM

pinkish outer edge

up to 2.5cm long

WINGSPAN *3–3.5cm.*
TIME OF FLIGHT *Night.*
FLIGHT PERIOD *May–September.*
LARVAL FOODPLANT *Various low-growing plants such as dock and sorrel (Rumex).*
SIMILAR SPECIES *Small Blood-vein (Scopula imitaria), which is smaller and darker.*
STATUS *Widespread and fairly common.*

The Spinach

Eulithis mellinata (Geometridae)

This geometrid moth has an unusual resting posture, sitting with its wings held at right angles to its body and the hindwings almost completely concealed beneath the forewings. Both the Barred Straw (*E. pyraliata*) and the Northern Spinach (*E. populata*) resemble this species and have a similar resting position, but both lack the chequered wing fringes of The Spinach.

FREQUENTS *any habitat where currants grow, in gardens, allotments, or open woodland.*

2 brown wavy lines across forewings

diagonal markings at tips

chequered fringes

up to 2.5cm long

WINGSPAN *3.3–3.8cm.*
TIME OF FLIGHT *Night.*
FLIGHT PERIOD *June–August.*
LARVAL FOODPLANT *Blackcurrant (Ribes nigrum) and Redcurrant (Ribes rubrum).*
SIMILAR SPECIES *Yellow Shell (above), Northern Spinach (E. populata).*
STATUS *Widespread and common.*

Riband Wave

Idaea aversata (Geometridae)

This moth occurs in two forms – one with a dark band across the wings and another non-banded form. Both are equally common. The Riband Wave is easily disturbed from its resting place during the day. However, the natural time of flight is at night, when it is attracted to light.

OCCURS *in gardens, commons, and wasteland with low-growing weeds.*

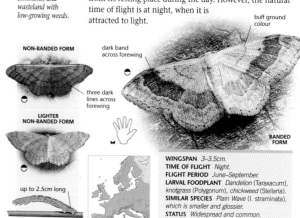

NON-BANDED FORM

dark band across forewing

buff ground colour

three dark lines across forewing

LIGHTER NON-BANDED FORM

BANDED FORM

up to 2.5cm long

WINGSPAN *3–3.5cm.*
TIME OF FLIGHT *Night.*
FLIGHT PERIOD *June–September.*
LARVAL FOODPLANT *Dandelion (Taraxacum), knotgrass (Polygonum), chickweed (Stellaria).*
SIMILAR SPECIES *Plain Wave (I. straminata), which is smaller and glossier.*
STATUS *Widespread and common.*

INVERTEBRATES

Scallop Shell

Rheumaptera undulata (Geometridae)

One of the most attractive geometrid moths, the Scallop Shell's wings are covered with an intricate pattern of light and dark zig-zag lines. Like many members of its family, it rests with its wings swept back, the forewings concealing the hindwings. Attracted to light, it flies at night, but rarely in large numbers.

FOUND *often in open woodland, especially with an undergrowth of bilberry. Also found in very damp places such as marshes.*

rounded wing

alternate light and dark zig-zag rows

forewings cover hindwings

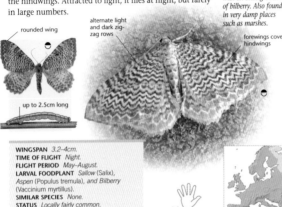

up to 2.5cm long

WINGSPAN *3.2–4cm.*
TIME OF FLIGHT *Night.*
FLIGHT PERIOD *May–August.*
LARVAL FOODPLANT *Sallow (Salix), Aspen (Populus tremula), and Bilberry (Vaccinium myrtillus).*
SIMILAR SPECIES *None.*
STATUS *Locally fairly common.*

Mottled Umber

Erannis defoliaria (Geometridae)

This highly variable species ranges from light buff with brown bands to wholly dark brown. The female, light brown with black spots on the abdomen, is completely wingless, and may be found sitting on tree trunks after dark. Adults emerge in late autumn, and continue to fly on mild nights until the end of the year.

INHABITS *deciduous woodland, hedgerows, and orchards, where the caterpillar may be a pest.*

DARK BROWN FORM

brown band across wing

variable buff to brown colour

wingless female

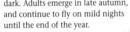

up to 3.5cm long

WINGSPAN *4–4.5cm.*
TIME OF FLIGHT *Night.*
FLIGHT PERIOD *October–January.*
LARVAL FOODPLANT *Oak (Quercus), birch (Betula), and hawthorn (Crataegus).*
SIMILAR SPECIES *Dotted Border (Agriopis marginaria) has dots along forewing edge.*
STATUS *Widespread and common.*

March Moth

Alsophila aescularia (Geometridae)

At rest, the March Moth does not look like a typical geometrid, as it holds its pointed wings tightly together, with one forewing overlapping the other. The wings have a subtle pattern of grey and brown, with a jagged whitish line across the centre of the forewings. The female is wingless and crawls around on tree trunks.

FEEDS *on many species of trees and shrubs, in woodland, hedgerows, gardens, and orchards, where the larvae may be a pest.*

white stripe

subtle grey and brown pattern

pointed wings

plain hindwings

up to 3cm long

WINGSPAN *3.4–4cm.*
TIME OF FLIGHT *Night.*
FLIGHT PERIOD *March–April.*
LARVAL FOODPLANT *Oak (Quercus), birch (Betula), hawthorn (Crataegus), and other deciduous trees.*
SIMILAR SPECIES *None.*
STATUS *Widespread and common.*

Orange Underwing

Archiearis parthenias (Geometridae)

An attractive day-flying species, the Orange Underwing can be found flying around birch trees on sunny days in early spring. It is a difficult moth to see well, as it spends most of its time high up around the treetops. However, it does occasionally descend to drink at patches of wet ground.

At rest, the bright orange hindwings are concealed below the mottled brown forewings. It should not be confused with any of the Yellow Underwings, as they are nocturnal, and fly much later in the year.

LIVES *in areas where birch grows, such as heathland and open woodland.*

NOTE

The Orange Underwing usually flies high up around the tops of birch trees. However, since it flies by day, it can be identified even at that height by its bright orange hindwings, which are visible in flight.

hindwings concealed at rest

dark markings on upperwing

up to 2.5cm long

light patches on dark brown forewing

orange hindwing

dark border

WINGSPAN *3.5–4cm.*
TIME OF FLIGHT *Day.*
FLIGHT PERIOD *March–April.*
LARVAL FOODPLANT *Birch (Betula).*
SIMILAR SPECIES *Light Orange Underwing (A. notha), which is slightly smaller and has less orange on its hindwings.*
STATUS *Widespread and locally common.*

Scorched Wing

Plagodis dolabraria (Geometridae)

This attractive moth's wings look as if they have been charred by fire. The pattern on the wings, in subtle shades of brown, provides very effective camouflage as the moth rests on a tree trunk or branch during the day. The Scorched Wing flies at night, and the male is attracted to light.

INHABITS *deciduous or mixed woodland, preferring open woods, rides, and clearings.*

dark forewing base

dark brown lines on forewing

pale buff ground colour

up to 4cm long

scorched look

WINGSPAN *3.4–4cm.*
TIME OF FLIGHT *Night.*
FLIGHT PERIOD *May–June.*
LARVAL FOODPLANT *Various deciduous trees, including oak (Quercus), birch (Betula), and sallow (Salix).*
SIMILAR SPECIES *None.*
STATUS *Fairly common.*

Bordered White

Bupalus piniaria (Geometridae)

Also known as the Pine Looper, this moth is often seeing flying by day in conifer plantations. At rest, it holds its wings closed over its back, in butterfly-like fashion, which makes it difficult to identify when comparing it to pinned specimens. However, there are no similar species, and it can be confidently identified from the underwing pattern alone. The ground colour of the males' forewings varies from yellowish in the south to white in the north, and the females are darker in the north. The larvae can cause damage in conifer plantations.

INHABITS both natural and planted conifer woods, usually pine, but may also be found on other conifers.

white ground colour

♂

NORTHERN FORM

♀

dark outer edge

up to 3.5cm long

NOTE
No other day-flying species that holds its wings over its back at rest has this pattern of white or yellowish blotches on the underside of the hindwings.

whitish patches

wings held back at rest

♂

WINGSPAN 3.5–4cm.
TIME OF FLIGHT Day and night.
FLIGHT PERIOD May–June.
LARVAL FOODPLANT Pine (Pinus).
SIMILAR SPECIES None – the pale patches on its underwings make it unique.
STATUS Widespread and common; often considered a pest in pine plantations.

Magpie Moth

Abraxas grossulariata (Geometridae)

This strikingly marked species is highly variable, with some forms showing very few black spots, and others being almost entirely black. However, these aberrations are usually the result of captive breeding, and are very rarely seen in the wild. The bold patterning suggests that the moth is distasteful, and serves as a warning to predators. Interestingly, the caterpillar has a similar pattern of black spots on a whitish body, and a reddish stripe along the sides. It may be a pest on currant and Gooseberry bushes.

FOUND in gardens and allotments where currant and Gooseberry are grown; also in hedgerows and open deciduous woodland.

yellow and black thorax and abdomen

yellow S-shaped line

DARKER FORM

large black patches

fewer black spots

LIGHTER FORM

white ground colour

black spots

up to 3.5cm long

NOTE
The caterpillar of the Magpie Moth is just as variable in its coloration as the adult moth. While most caterpillars are whitish with black spots, some are darker, or even completely black as in the case of the adult.

WINGSPAN 4.2–4.8cm.
TIME OF FLIGHT Night (occasionally day).
FLIGHT PERIOD July–August.
LARVAL FOODPLANT Currant (Ribes), Gooseberry (Ribes uva-crispa), Blackthorn (Prunus spinosa), and Hazel (Corylus avellana).
SIMILAR SPECIES Small Magpie (p.207), which is much smaller and belongs to the Micro-moth group.
STATUS Widespread and common.

Brindled Beauty

Lycia hirtaria (Geometridae)

The Brindled Beauty is a rather variable species, with a furry thorax and abdomen, and subtle coloration of buffs, browns, and greys. These patterns of colours provide excellent camouflage when the moth is at rest on a tree trunk. Some males, which can be told by their feathered antennae, may be almost black.

FEEDS on almost any deciduous tree, so may be found in a variety of habitats, including orchards, woods, parks, and gardens.

♂

feathered antennae

furry thorax and abdomen

LIGHTER FORM

brown and white pattern

mottled buff, grey, and brown wings

♂

♂

up to 5.5cm long

WINGSPAN 4.2–5.2cm.
TIME OF FLIGHT Night.
FLIGHT PERIOD March–May.
LARVAL FOODPLANT Various trees and shrubs, including sallow (Salix), birch (Betula), hawthorn (Crataegus), and alder (Alnus).
SIMILAR SPECIES Peppered Moth (p.214).
STATUS Widespread and common.

Purple Thorn

Selenia tetralunaria (Geometridae)

The group of geometrid moths known as Thorns rest with their wings raised. The Purple Thorn can be told from similar species by its habit of holding its wings half open over its back. The moth has two, sometimes three broods each year, the later generations usually being smaller and darker than the spring brood.

OCCURS in deciduous woodland; also in parks, gardens, and commons.

pale "half moon" mark

chestnut-tipped forewing

dark brown band

up to 4.5cm long

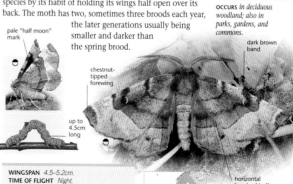

horizontal bands of buff and brown

WINGSPAN 4.5–5.2cm.
TIME OF FLIGHT Night.
FLIGHT PERIOD April–August.
LARVAL FOODPLANT Oak (Quercus), birch (Betula), and alder (Alnus).
SIMILAR SPECIES Early Thorn (Selenia dentaria), which is paler.
STATUS Widespread and fairly common.

Light Emerald

Campaea margaritata (Geometridae)

The Light Emerald's green coloration quickly fades almost to white. However, the pattern of two greenish brown lines bordered by white is usually visible, making this moth easy to identify, while a newly-emerged moth has small red-brown wing-tips. The females are larger than the males.

FOUND *in gardens, parks, woodland, hedgerows, and commons.*

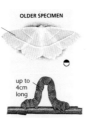

faded colours

OLDER SPECIMEN

greenish white ground colour

up to 4cm long

WINGSPAN *4–5.5cm.*
TIME OF FLIGHT *Night.*
FLIGHT PERIOD *July–September.*
LARVAL FOOD PLANT *Oak (Quercus), birch (Betula), beech (Fagus), and hawthorn (Crataegus).*
SIMILAR SPECIES *Large Emerald (right).*
STATUS *Widespread and common.*

Swallow-tailed Moth

Ourapteryx sambucaria (Geometridae)

This large, pale yellow moth has a very distinctive shape, and should not be confused with any other British species. The hindwings have projecting "tails" reminiscent of the Swallowtail Butterfly (p.189), and the forewings are also sharply pointed. This moth is strongly attracted to light, and is frequently found resting on lighted windows after dark.

OCCURS *in woodland, gardens, parks, hedgerows, and commons.*

brown lines across forewings

pointed tails on hindwings

pointed forewings

up to 5.5cm long

WINGSPAN *5–6.2cm.*
TIME OF FLIGHT *Night.*
FLIGHT PERIOD *June–July.*
LARVAL FOODPLANT *Various trees and plants, including hawthorn (Crataegus), ivy (Hedera), and privet (Ligustrum).*
SIMILAR SPECIES *None.*
STATUS *Fairly common.*

Peppered Moth

Biston betularia (Geometridae)

The Peppered Moth has three distinct forms – light, intermediate, and dark – and is often cited as an example of natural selection. In industrial areas, where tree trunks are blackened with soot, the lighter moths are highly visible to birds, and therefore eaten more often. The darker forms, however, are camouflaged, resulting in less predation; thus more dark moths survive to pass on their genes to their offspring. On the other hand, recent studies have shown how the darker form has become less common in areas formerly blighted by pollution, but where the situation has improved once clean air laws have taken effect. Both sexes fly at night and are strongly attracted to light.

FREQUENTS *woodland, gardens, parks, hedgerows, and commons, where there are trees for the caterpillar to feed on.*

DARK FORM

plain blackish wings

evenly mottled light and dark wings

INTERMEDIATE FORM

LIGHTER FORM

lightly mottled wings

NOTE
The three forms are genetically distinct from one another. The intermediate form cannot be reproduced by crossing the light form with the dark form. All three forms may occur in the same area, but one will usually predominate over the other two. The intermediate form is generally the least common.

dark mottling

up to 6cm long

whitish background

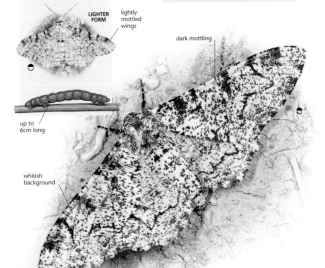

WINGSPAN *4.5–6cm.*
FLIGHT PERIOD *May–August.*
LARVAL FOODPLANT *Trees, including sallow (Salix), birch (Betula), lime (Tilia), and hawthorn (Crataegus).*
SIMILAR SPECIES *Brindled Beauty (p.213), which is more buff and brown.*
STATUS *Widespread and common.*

Large Emerald

Geometra papilionaria (Geometridae)

One of the larger and more robust members of its family, the Large Emerald's wings and body are a beautiful bright green when fresh, with delicate white markings. Like all green moths, this colour quickly fades, especially in museum specimens. This moth typically flies late at night, and is attracted to light.

SEEN *in areas where birch grows, such as heathland and open woodland.*

white scalloped line across forewing

bright green ground colour

faded specimen

up to 3.5cm long

WINGSPAN *5–6.5cm.*
FLIGHT PERIOD *June–August.*
LARVAL FOODPLANT *Birch (Betula), and occasionally on other trees.*
SIMILAR SPECIES *Light Emerald (left) has a delicate green coloration and two brownish lines across the wings.*
STATUS *Widespread and fairly common.*

Yellow-tail

Euproctis similis (Lymantriidae)

The Yellow-tail contains irritating chemicals at all stages of its life cycle, which can cause a severe allergic reaction in some people if they are touched. The adult moth has an unusual defensive posture: if disturbed, it lies on its side, with its yellow-tipped abdomen projecting beyond the trailing edge of the wings. The males have small dark marks on the forewings, while the females' wings are pure white.

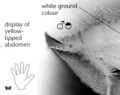

INHABITS *hedgerows, scrub, and other areas with bushy vegetation, where there is plenty of larval foodplant available.*

♂ furry body

display of yellow-tipped abdomen

small dark marks

white ground colour

♂♀

up to 4.5cm long

WINGSPAN *3.5–4.5cm.*
FLIGHT PERIOD *July–August.*
LARVAL FOODPLANT *Hawthorn (Crataegus), Blackthorn (Prunus spinosa), sallow (Salix), and other trees and shrubs.*
SIMILAR SPECIES *Brown-tail (Euproctis chrysorrhoea); White Satin (Leucoma salicis).*
STATUS *Widespread and generally common.*

Common Footman

Eilema lurideola (Arctiidae)

This moth rests with its long thin forewings folded flat over its back. However, if seen in flight, it appears much larger, owing to its broad yellowish hindwings. Flying from dusk onwards, it may be found feeding at thistle flowers (*Cirsium* and *Carduus*) or Traveller's Joy (*Clematis vitalba*). Like most members of the "Footman" family, the larvae feed on lichens.

FOUND *in hedgerows, gardens, and open woodland, wherever there are lichen-covered trees for the larvae to feed on.*

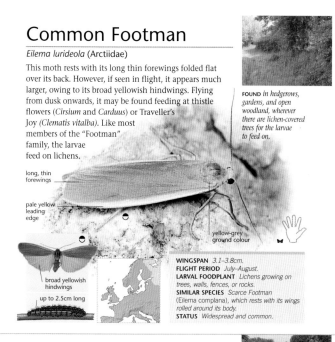

long, thin forewings

pale yellow leading edge

yellow-grey ground colour

broad yellowish hindwings

up to 2.5cm long

WINGSPAN *3.1–3.8cm.*
FLIGHT PERIOD *July–August.*
LARVAL FOODPLANT *Lichens growing on trees, walls, fences, or rocks.*
SIMILAR SPECIES *Scarce Footman (Eilema complana), which rests with its wings rolled around its body.*
STATUS *Widespread and common.*

The Cinnabar

Tyria jacobaeae (Arctiidae)

This distinctive and familiar species is sometimes seen flying by day, when the bright crimson hindwings draw attention to it. At rest, the crimson hindwings are concealed beneath the forewings, which are glossy dark grey, with red lines and spots. Unlike most members of its family, the caterpillars are gregarious, and can be found in large numbers on ragwort (*Senecio*) plants.

SEEN *wherever ragwort and groundsel grow; on waste ground, commons, and meadows.*

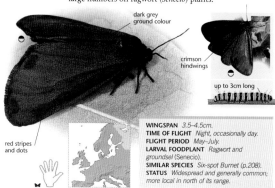

dark grey ground colour

crimson hindwings

up to 3cm long

red stripes and dots

WINGSPAN *3.5–4.5cm.*
TIME OF FLIGHT *Night, occasionally day.*
FLIGHT PERIOD *May–July.*
LARVAL FOODPLANT *Ragwort and groundsel (Senecio).*
SIMILAR SPECIES *Six-spot Burnet (p.208).*
STATUS *Widespread and generally common; more local in north of its range.*

Ruby Tiger

Phragmatobia fuliginosa (Arctiidae)

One of the smaller members of its family, the Ruby Tiger has plain reddish brown forewings with two small blackish dots. The hindwings vary from orange-red with dark markings to plain black. This moth flies mainly at night, when it often comes to light, but may sometimes be found flying on sunny days.

OCCURS *in waste ground, gardens, commons, heathland, and moorland.*

red-brown ground colour

furry head and thorax

red and black hindwings

blackish spots

plain forewings

up to 3.5cm long

WINGSPAN *2.8–3.8cm.*
FLIGHT PERIOD *April–September, in two broods.*
LARVAL FOODPLANT *Various plants, including dock (Rumex) and dandelion (Taraxacum).*
SIMILAR SPECIES *None.*
STATUS *Widespread and common.*

Garden Tiger

Arctia caja (Arctiidae)

The large and strikingly-marked Garden Tiger has declined dramatically in many parts of its range in recent years, possibly due to climatic change. The complex pattern of dark brown and cream on the forewings varies from moth to moth. The contrasting hindwings are a bright orange ground colour with prominent black spots. Also orange, the abdomen is marked with black bars. The caterpillar of the Garden Tiger is sometimes known as the "woolly bear" since it is covered with many long brown hairs. These contain an irritant poison and should never be handled.

INHABITS *gardens, parks, commons, waste ground, and any habitat where low plants grow.*

NOTE

The Garden Tiger is a very variable species, and individuals may sometimes be found with almost entirely brown forewings or, in contrast, with the brown markings much reduced. The hindwing colour also varies from the usual orange to yellow or dark brown.

exposed orange hindwings

DARKER FORM

cream ground colour

up to 6cm long

reddish brown head

variable brown patches

WINGSPAN *5–7.8cm.*
TIME OF FLIGHT *Night.*
FLIGHT PERIOD *July–August.*
LARVAL FOODPLANT *Various wild and cultivated plants.*
SIMILAR SPECIES *None.*
STATUS *Widespread, but not as common as it once was.*

White Ermine

Spilosoma lubricipeda (Arctiidae)

FREQUENTS *a wide variety of habitats, as the caterpillar is not at all fussy about what foodplants it feeds on.*

This attractive species is very variable – typical specimens have small black spots evenly scattered over the white forewings, but some may have larger or smaller spots. Occasionally, individuals may be seen with much more black, the spots being joined up to form bars. The ground colour also varies, some moths being more buff-coloured.

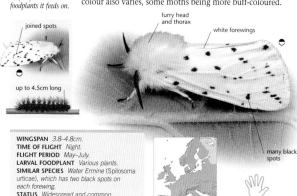

joined spots

up to 4.5cm long

furry head and thorax

white forewings

many black spots

WINGSPAN *3.8–4.8cm.*
TIME OF FLIGHT *Night.*
FLIGHT PERIOD *May–July.*
LARVAL FOODPLANT *Various plants.*
SIMILAR SPECIES *Water Ermine (Spilosoma urticae), which has two black spots on each forewing.*
STATUS *Widespread and common.*

Chocolate-tip

Clostera curtula (Notodontidae)

This attractive moth has an unusual resting position, sitting with its wings wrapped around its body and the tip of its abdomen raised. Its head and thorax are furry, with a well-defined dark brown stripe contrasting with the greyish background. It is often abundant in habitats where its larval foodplants grow.

FOUND *mainly in woodland, but also along rivers and in open country with scattered trees.*

overhead view with wings open

dark brown stripe on head and thorax

brown forewing tip

raised abdomen tip

buff ground colour

up to 3.5cm long

WINGSPAN *3.5–4cm.*
TIME OF FLIGHT *Night.*
FLIGHT PERIOD *April–September.*
LARVAL FOODPLANT *Poplar (Populus), Aspen (P. tremulus), and willow (Salix).*
SIMILAR SPECIES *Scarce Chocolate-tip (C. anachoreta) has a white line on wing tips.*
STATUS *Widespread and common.*

Pale Prominent

Pterostoma palpina (Notodontidae)

At rest during the day, the Pale Prominent relies on its excellent camouflage to avoid detection by predators, closely resembling a broken piece of wood. As with many highly camouflaged species, the moth contributes to the deception by remaining absolutely still; even if disturbed, it will often fall onto its side rather than fly off in alarm.

INHABITS *deciduous woodland, preferring damper areas; also occurs in gardens, parks, and on commons.*

very long mouth-parts

protruding abdomen tip

serrated forewing margin

up to 4cm long

WINGSPAN *4–6cm.*
TIME OF FLIGHT *Night.*
FLIGHT PERIOD *May–August, in two broods.*
LARVAL FOODPLANT *Poplar (Populus) and sallow (Salix).*
SIMILAR SPECIES *None.*
STATUS *Widespread and common.*

The Vapourer

Orgyia antiqua (Lymantriidae)

The red-brown male Vapourers are often seen flying rapidly in sunshine, but the females are wingless and rarely move far from the cocoon after hatching. Males also fly at night, and are attracted to light. The larvae have red and yellow tufts, and black and brown hairs, which can cause irritation if handled.

FREQUENTS *a wide variety of habitats, including gardens, woodland, commons, and urban areas.*

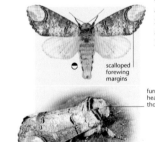

plain hindwings

WINGLESS FEMALE

white spots on forewing

fat, furry body

up to 4cm long

red-brown ground colour

WINGSPAN *3.5–4cm.*
TIME OF FLIGHT *Day and night.*
FLIGHT PERIOD *July–October, in two broods.*
LARVAL FOODPLANT *Many deciduous trees and shrubs.*
SIMILAR SPECIES *Scarce Vapourer (O. recens) has a white mark at forewing tip.*
STATUS *Widespread and common.*

Buff-tip

Phalera bucephala (Notodontidae)

A superbly camouflaged species, the Buff-tip almost perfectly resembles a broken-off birch twig. At rest, the moth's wings are rolled around its body in a tubular shape, with the pale hindwings concealed. Most of the forewing is an intricately mottled silvery grey, with delicate black and brown lines running across it; the wingtips are a contrasting pale buff, as are the fluffy head and thorax. Like all the members of this family, the adult moths have no proboscis, and so do not feed. The Buff-tip tends to fly late at night, when it is attracted to light.

OCCUPIES *hedgerows, gardens, and open woodland, wherever there are trees for the caterpillars to feed on.*

scalloped forewing margins

furry buff head and thorax

NOTE

The yellow and black Buff-tip caterpillars are gregarious at first, later becoming solitary before pupation. They often cause severe damage to trees by stripping the leaves off branches.

up to 7.5cm long

large buff tip to forewing

dark cross-lines

tubular shape resembles twig

WINGSPAN *5.5–7cm.*
TIME OF FLIGHT *Night.*
FLIGHT PERIOD *May–July.*
LARVAL FOODPLANT *Many deciduous trees and shrubs, including oak (Quercus), sallow (Salix), and lime (Tilia).*
SIMILAR SPECIES *None.*
STATUS *Widespread and common.*

Sallow Kitten

Furcula furcula (Notodontidae)

This is the commonest of three closely related species which differ in the shape of the central band on the strongly marked forewings. One of the smaller Prominent moths, it shares the family habit of resting with its wings raised over its body. Its head, thorax, and legs are furry.

OCCURS *in damp woodland, waterside habitats, and wherever sallows grow; also found in gardens, parks, and on commons.*

grey band across forewings

furry black thorax

black dots on wing margin

up to 3.5cm long

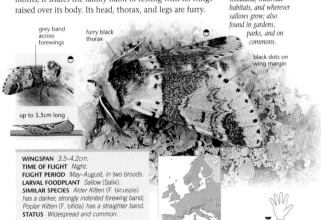

WINGSPAN *3.5–4.2cm.*
TIME OF FLIGHT *Night.*
FLIGHT PERIOD *May–August, in two broods.*
LARVAL FOODPLANT *Sallow (Salix).*
SIMILAR SPECIES *Alder Kitten (F. bicuspis) has a darker, strongly indented forewing band; Poplar Kitten (F. bifida) has a straighter band.*
STATUS *Widespread and common.*

Puss Moth

Cerura vinula (Notodontidae)

This large and attractive member of the Prominent family is tinged with a delicate green when freshly emerged. However, this colour quickly fades to a lighter shade. The white forewings of the adult moth are patterned with black lines. It does not seem to be strongly attracted to light, and is consequently not often seen. The caterpillar is one of the most extraordinary of the moth world. It has a large head, and two red-tipped "tails", which are actually modified hindlegs. If threatened, it waves these in the air, while rearing up its head to make itself look bigger.

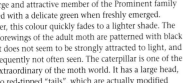

INHABITS *hedgerows, open woodland, parks, and gardens; also found at watersides, where poplar and sallow, the larval foodplants, grow.*

intricate pattern of black lines

buff veins

black spots on thorax

greyish white ground colour

furry head and thorax

FRESHLY EMERGED

greenish tinge to wings

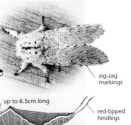

zig-zag markings

up to 6.5cm long

red-tipped hindlegs

NOTE

The bright green and brown caterpillar can squirt formic acid from special glands in the throat to deter predators. The young larvae are very similar to those of the Sallow Kitten (p.216) and can be found feeding in pairs.

WINGSPAN *6–8cm.*
TIME OF FLIGHT *Night.*
FLIGHT PERIOD *May–July.*
LARVAL FOODPLANT *Poplar (Populus) and sallow (Salix).*
SIMILAR SPECIES *None.*
STATUS *Widespread and fairly common throughout.*

Antler Moth

Cerapteryx graminis (Noctuidae)

This moth varies greatly in size, with females generally being larger than males. The wing pattern is also rather variable – in some individuals the white "antler" marks are much reduced or even lacking altogether. Adults may be seen flying and feeding at flowers during the day, but also fly at night, when they are attracted to light.

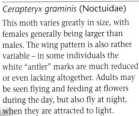

LIVES *in grassy areas such as meadows, moorland, downland, and commons.*

dark band on forewing

white "antler" pattern

REDDISH BROWN FORM

GREYISH FORM

up to 3.5cm long

WINGSPAN *2.5–4cm.*
TIME OF FLIGHT *Day and night.*
FLIGHT PERIOD *July–September.*
LARVAL FOODPLANT *Various grasses (family Poaceae), notably Sheep's Fescue (Festuca ovina) and Mat-Grass (Nardus stricta).*
SIMILAR SPECIES *None.*
STATUS *Locally common.*

Centre-barred Sallow

Atethmia centrago (Noctuidae)

The dark orange bar across the forewings, from which this species gets its common name, varies in intensity; on some specimens it hardly contrasts with the yellowish ground colour. The hindwings are whitish with an orange border. This moth flies at night and is attracted to light in small numbers.

FREQUENTS *woodland, parks, hedgerows, meadows, commons, and gardens; found wherever ash grows; the availability of ash is the common factor.*

darker central band on forewings

dark orange margin

yellow ground colour

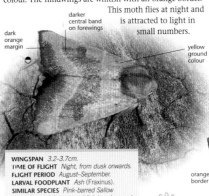

orange border

whitish hindwings

up to 3.5cm long

WINGSPAN *3.2–3.7cm.*
TIME OF FLIGHT *Night, from dusk onwards.*
FLIGHT PERIOD *August–September.*
LARVAL FOODPLANT *Ash (Fraxinus).*
SIMILAR SPECIES *Pink-barred Sallow (below), which is more reddish in colour and has a different larval foodplant.*
STATUS *Locally common.*

Marbled Beauty

Cryphia domestica (Noctuidae)

One of the smaller noctuids, the Marbled Beauty is attractively marked with black and grey on a cream background. As its scientific name implies, it is often found around houses and other buildings since the larvae feed on lichens that grow on walls. Some individuals are greenish, and can be confused with the Marbled Green (*C. muralis*).

FOUND *mainly in urban areas, but also on cliffs in open countryside.*

mottled forewings

cream ground colour

GREY-GREEN FORM

up to 2.5cm long

black and grey pattern

WINGSPAN *2.2–3cm.*
TIME OF FLIGHT *Night.*
FLIGHT PERIOD *July–August.*
LARVAL FOOD *Lichens, especially those growing on walls.*
SIMILAR SPECIES *Marbled Green (Cryphia muralis), which is larger and greener.*
STATUS *Widespread and common.*

Pink-barred Sallow

Xanthia togata (Noctuidae)

This moth's coloration, typical of many species that fly in autumn, is a camouflage against fallen leaves. The Pink-barred Sallow is attracted to light, and also feeds at flowers and ripe blackberries, rich in energy-providing sugar. The caterpillar, which feeds inside sallow or poplar catkins, is a rather dull brown colour.

OCCURS *in damp woodland, marshland, and riverbanks where sallows and poplars grow.*

yellow ground colour

red-brown head

pink band on forewings

brown blotches on forewings

up to 3.5cm long

WINGSPAN *2.8–3.7cm.*
TIME OF FLIGHT *Night.*
FLIGHT PERIOD *September–October.*
LARVAL FOODPLANT *Catkins of sallow (Salix) and poplar (Populus).*
SIMILAR SPECIES *Centre-barred Sallow (above); several other Sallow species.*
STATUS *Widespread and common.*

Common Rustic

Mesapamea secalis (Noctuidae)

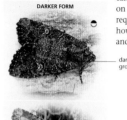

OCCURS *in a wide range of grassy habitats, such as meadows, commons, gardens, heathland, and moorland.*

Until recently, it was thought that there was just one species of Common Rustic in Britain. However, studies have shown that there are actually three very closely related species. These are the Common Rustic, the Lesser Common Rustic (*M. didyma*), and the very rare Remm's Rustic (*M. remmi*). All three species are so similar that they cannot be identified on wing pattern, but only on the structure of the genitalia, which requires dissection by experts. As a general rule, however, the Lesser Common Rustic is smaller and darker than the other two.

DARKER FORM

dark brown ground colour

whitish spot on forewing

PLAIN BROWN FORM

up to 3cm long

mottled ground colour

lacks white spot on forewing

NOTE

The Common Rustic is a variable moth, with many different forms; some are plain brown, while others are mottled light and dark brown. However, the same basic pattern can be found on most individuals.

MOTTLED LIGHT AND DARK BROWN FORM

WINGSPAN 2.8–3.6cm.
TIME OF FLIGHT Night.
FLIGHT PERIOD July–August.
LARVAL FOODPLANT Various grasses (family Poaceae).
SIMILAR SPECIES Lesser Common Rustic (M. didyma) and Remm's Rustic (M. remmi), which have different internal characteristics; several other brownish members of the noctuid family.
STATUS Widespread and often abundant.

The Spectacle

Abrostola tripartita (Noctuidae)

This moth has two distinctive, blackish circles on the front of the thorax, which resemble a pair of spectacles. In some urban industrial areas, a very dark form occurs, which has almost black wings. The Spectacle flies at night, and is a common visitor to moth traps. It may also be found feeding at flowers after dark.

OCCUPIES *damp woodland, gardens, river valleys, and wasteland, even in urban areas.*

FRONT VIEW

"spectacle" markings

brown ground colour

dark brown central patch

up to 4cm long

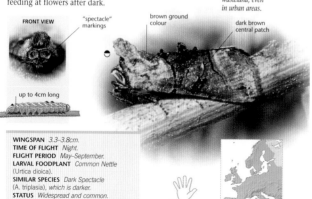

WINGSPAN 3.3–3.8cm.
TIME OF FLIGHT Night.
FLIGHT PERIOD May–September.
LARVAL FOODPLANT Common Nettle (Urtica dioica).
SIMILAR SPECIES Dark Spectacle (A. triplasia), which is darker.
STATUS Widespread and common.

Mother Shipton

Callistege mi (Noctuidae)

This day-flying species is often found in the same habitats as Dingy (p.189) and Grizzled Skipper (p.189) butterflies, and may be mistaken for them in flight. At rest, however, its wing patterns are quite different. The moth gets its common name, Mother Shipton, from a legendary witch whose profile, with its long, hooked nose and pointed chin, is said to be reflected in the markings.

INHABITS *grassy places such as downland, meadows and heaths; also open woodland and marshes.*

complex light and dark pattern

white-spotted hindwings

up to 4cm long

"chin of witch's profile"

WINGSPAN 3–3.5cm.
TIME OF FLIGHT Day.
FLIGHT PERIOD May–June.
LARVAL FOODPLANT Clover (Trifolium).
SIMILAR SPECIES Grizzled Skipper (p.189) and Dingy Skipper (p.189) butterflies are often mistaken for moths.
STATUS Locally common.

Pine Beauty

Panolis flammea (Noctuidae)

FOUND *in coniferous woodland and other places where pine trees grow.*

This orange and brown moth is extremely unpopular with foresters, as the caterpillars can be serious pests in conifer plantations, defoliating huge areas in the years when they are common. As with many spring-flying species, the adults feed at sallow blossom at night, and are drawn to light. The Pine Beauty is a variable moth, with three main colour forms: the mainly orange typical form, a darker, browner one, and a more heavily marked orange form; however, all forms have two pale spots on the forewings.

BROWNER FORM

ORANGE FORM

NOTE

The green and white striped caterpillars are very well camouflaged among pine needles, and difficult to find. They assist this resemblance by remaining rigid if disturbed or dislodged from the pine needles.

heavily marked forewings

up to 4cm long

2 pale spots on forewing

mottled orange and brown forewings

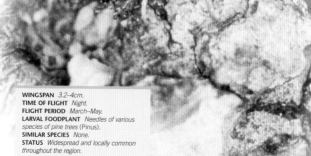

WINGSPAN 3.2–4cm.
TIME OF FLIGHT Night.
FLIGHT PERIOD March–May.
LARVAL FOODPLANT Needles of various species of pine trees (Pinus).
SIMILAR SPECIES None.
STATUS Widespread and locally common throughout the region.

Hebrew Character

Orthosia gothica (Noctuidae)

A very common moth, the Hebrew Character occurs in almost all habitats, including mountainous regions and within the Arctic Circle. Although it emerges to feed on sallow blossom after dark, it is also attracted to light. The black C-shaped mark is absent in some specimens, and the colour of the wings ranges from grey to red-brown.

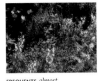

FREQUENTS *almost every possible habitat; particularly common in gardens.*

C-shaped mark on both wings

grey-brown ground colour

brown margin

PALER FORM

up to 4.5cm long

WINGSPAN *3–4cm.*
TIME OF FLIGHT *Night.*
FLIGHT PERIOD *March–May.*
LARVAL FOODPLANT *Trees and shrubs.*
SIMILAR SPECIES *Setaceous Hebrew Character (Xestia c-nigrum), which is larger, darker, and flies later in the year.*
STATUS *Widespread and common.*

Common Quaker

Orthosia cerasi (Noctuidae)

One of the commonest of the spring-flying species, this moth can be abundant in deciduous woodland. Like many species that emerge early in the year, it feeds at sallow blossom after dark, and is drawn to light. The colour of the forewings varies from light brown to dark reddish brown.

PREFERS *deciduous woodland, but also found in gardens, parks, and hedgerows.*

PALER FORM

DARKER FORM

up to 4cm long

2 pale rings on brown forewings

pale line at rear

diffused dark line

WINGSPAN *3.5–4cm.*
TIME OF FLIGHT *Night.*
FLIGHT PERIOD *March–April.*
LARVAL FOODPLANT *Trees, including oak (Quercus) and sallow (Salix).*
SIMILAR SPECIES *Powdered Quaker (O. gracilis); Small Quaker (O. cruda).*
STATUS *Widespread and common.*

Common Wainscot

Mythimna pallens (Noctuidae)

This is a rather plain species, with few distinguishing marks. The colour of the forewings varies from pale yellow to a darker orange-buff, on which the pale veins stand out more clearly. The hindwings are always white. It may be found resting on grass stems after dark, or feeding at flowers, and is strongly attracted to light.

OCCUPIES *grassy habitats, such as meadows, commons, heaths, marshes, and gardens.*

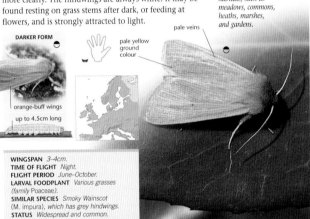

DARKER FORM

pale veins

pale yellow ground colour

orange-buff wings

up to 4.5cm long

WINGSPAN *3–4cm.*
TIME OF FLIGHT *Night.*
FLIGHT PERIOD *June–October.*
LARVAL FOODPLANT *Various grasses (family Poaceae).*
SIMILAR SPECIES *Smoky Wainscot (M. impura), which has grey hindwings.*
STATUS *Widespread and common.*

Bird's Wing

Dypterygia scabriuscula (Noctuidae)

This species gets its common name from the pattern on the forewings, which resembles a stylized bird's wing. These pale marks and the pale thorax break up the outline of the moth at rest, making it difficult for predators to spot. There is very little variation, enabling easy identification.

FOUND *in deciduous woodland and open habitats such as meadows, parkland, and gardens.*

broken outline for camouflage

pale centre of thorax

dark brown ground colour

up to 4cm long

"bird's wing" pattern

WINGSPAN *3.5–4cm.*
TIME OF FLIGHT *Night.*
FLIGHT PERIOD *May–September, in two broods.*
LARVAL FOODPLANT *Dock, sorrel (both Rumex), and other plants.*
SIMILAR SPECIES *None.*
STATUS *Locally common.*

Green Silver-lines

Pseudoips prasinana (Noctuidae)

This beautiful moth is aptly named, marked with silvery-white lines on a delicate green background. When freshly emerged, the wing fringes, legs, and antennae are tinged red. The slightly larger female is paler, with white hindwings, whereas those of the male are tinged with yellow.

LIVES *mainly in deciduous woodland; also hedgerows, parks, and gardens.*

reddish antennae

3 white diagonal lines

yellowish hindwings

pale green ground colour

up to 4cm long

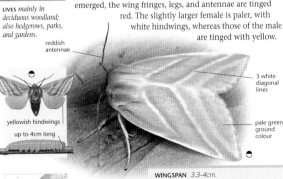

WINGSPAN *3.3–4cm.*
TIME OF FLIGHT *Night.*
FLIGHT PERIOD *May–July, with an occasional second brood in autumn.*
LARVAL FOODPLANT *Various trees.*
SIMILAR SPECIES *Scarce Silver-lines (Bena bicolorana), which is larger.*
STATUS *Widespread and common.*

Frosted Orange

Gortyna flavago (Noctuidae)

The mottled orange and brown forewings of this moth provide good camouflage against decaying autumn leaves. There is little variation, but northern specimens may be darker. At night it is attracted to light, but does not appear to feed at flowers. The rather maggot-like caterpillars live inside the stems and roots of the foodplants.

OCCURS *in fields, open countryside, commons, marshes, wasteland, and gardens.*

mottled orange and brown ground colour

brown band

2 pale spots on forewings

pale grey markings

up to 4cm long

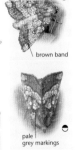

WINGSPAN *3.2–4.3cm.*
TIME OF FLIGHT *Night.*
FLIGHT PERIOD *August–October.*
LARVAL FOODPLANT *Thistle (Cirsium and Carduus), burdock (Arctium), Foxglove (Digitalis purpurea), and other plants.*
SIMILAR SPECIES *Golden Plusia (p.221).*
STATUS *Widespread and locally common.*

The Snout

Hypena proboscidalis (Noctuidae)

At rest, the Snout has a triangular outline, with long palps projecting from the front of its head like a snout. The forewings are dull brown, with two darker bands and a row of faint, pale dots. The Snout flies around nettles at dusk, and is also attracted to light later in the night.

FREQUENTS *gardens and waste ground, but also found in open woodland, and on marshland and commons.*

row of pale dots

up to 3cm long

dull brown ground colour

projecting palps

dark bands on forewings

triangular outline

WINGSPAN *3.4–4cm.*
TIME OF FLIGHT *Night.*
FLIGHT PERIOD *June–October, in two broods.*
LARVAL FOODPLANT *Common Nettle (Urtica dioica).*
SIMILAR SPECIES *None.*
STATUS *Widespread and common.*

Burnished Brass

Diachrysia chrysitis (Noctuidae)

The forewings of this moth have brassy scales that may form two patches, or are joined into a larger patch. It is found after dark feeding at Red Valerian and honeysuckle flowers, and is also attracted to light. The Slender Burnished Brass (*D. orichalcea*) is a rare visitor to Britain from southern Europe with slimmer wings, and a crescent-shaped, metallic patch.

INHABITS *gardens, waste ground, open woodland, marshland, and commons; or anywhere that nettles are found growing.*

brassy scales

reddish brown head

brown ground colour

single brassy patch

up to 4cm long

WINGSPAN *3.5–4.5cm.*
TIME OF FLIGHT *Night.*
FLIGHT PERIOD *June–September, in two broods.*
LARVAL FOODPLANT *Nettle (Urtica dioica).*
SIMILAR SPECIES *Slender Burnished Brass (D. orichalcea).*
STATUS *Widespread and common.*

Heart and Dart

Agrotis exclamationis (Noctuidae)

One of the commonest British moths, the Heart and Dart is found in a wide range of habitats. The ground colour of the forewings ranges from light brown to dark brown, but the markings, a blackish "heart" and "dart" on each wing are fairly constant. The hindwings are pure white in colour. It feeds at flowers after dark, and is a very frequent visitor to moth traps.

FOUND *in almost every possible habitat as the larvae feed on a wide variety of plants; a particularly common garden species.*

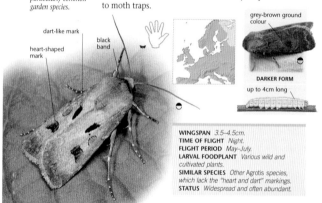

dart-like mark

heart-shaped mark

black band

grey-brown ground colour

DARKER FORM

up to 4cm long

WINGSPAN *3.5–4.5cm.*
TIME OF FLIGHT *Night.*
FLIGHT PERIOD *May–July.*
LARVAL FOODPLANT *Various wild and cultivated plants.*
SIMILAR SPECIES *Other Agrotis species, which lack the "heart and dart" markings.*
STATUS *Widespread and often abundant.*

Bright-line Brown-eye

Lacanobia oleracea (Noctuidae)

This species is also known as the Tomato Moth because of the caterpillar's fondness for feeding inside tomatoes, a habit that makes it unpopular with gardeners. The adult Bright-line Brown-eye has two main identifying features on the plain brown forewings, from which it gets its common name: a wavy white line along the trailing edge, and an orange-brown spot or "eye". The hindwings are light greyish brown.

FAVOURS *gardens and allotments where tomatoes are grown; also found in open countryside and in salt marshes.*

wavy white line

brown forewings

orange-brown spot

lighter hindwings

up to 4.5cm long

WINGSPAN *3.5–4.5cm.*
TIME OF FLIGHT *Night.*
FLIGHT PERIOD *May–July; occasionally a second brood in autumn.*
LARVAL FOODPLANT *Various plants, including tomato (Lycopersicon esculentum).*
SIMILAR SPECIES *None.*
STATUS *Widespread and common.*

Grey Dagger

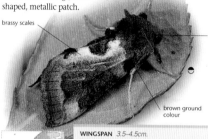

Acronicta psi (Noctuidae)

The Grey Dagger forms a species pair with the almost identical Dark Dagger (*A. tridens*). The two are so similar as adults that they can reliably be told apart only by examining the genitalia; however, the caterpillars are somewhat different (see Note). The hindwings may offer a clue to the moth's identity; those of the Dark Dagger are usually, but not always, pure white rather than off-white. The forewings of both species have a complex pattern of black markings on a grey background, resembling and old and cracked tree bark.

APPEARS *mainly in deciduous woodland; also hedgerows, parks, and gardens, and wherever there are trees for larvae to feed on.*

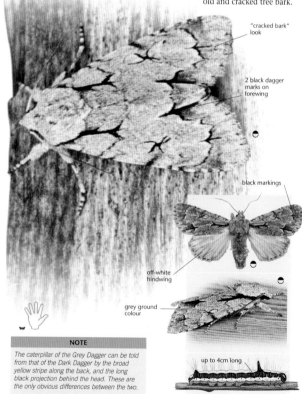

"cracked bark" look

2 black dagger marks on forewing

black markings

off-white hindwing

grey ground colour

up to 4cm long

NOTE

The caterpillar of the Grey Dagger can be told from that of the Dark Dagger by the broad yellow stripe along the back, and the long black projection behind the head. These are the only obvious differences between the two.

WINGSPAN *3.5–4.5cm.*
TIME OF FLIGHT *Night.*
FLIGHT PERIOD *June–August.*
LARVAL FOODPLANT *Various trees.*
SIMILAR SPECIES *Blair's Shoulder-knot (p.221); The Sycamore (p.221), which has grey, mottled wings; Dark Dagger (A. tridens), which is very similar and not really distinguishable as an adult.*
STATUS *Widespread and common.*

Blair's Shoulder-knot

Lithophane leautieri (Noctuidae)

This subtly marked species, at rest resembling a piece of dead wood, has recently undergone a dramatic range expansion in Europe. This is thought to have been aided by the popularity of its foodplants (various cypresses) as garden plants. From its original range in southwest France, it has spread north, reaching southern England in 1951.

FOUND *wherever cypresses grow, especially in gardens and parks.*

fine dark lines

pale grey forewings

brown ground colour

up to 4cm long

WINGSPAN *4–4.5cm.*
TIME OF FLIGHT *Night.*
FLIGHT PERIOD *September–November.*
LARVAL FOODPLANT *Cypress (Cupressus and Chamaecyparis).*
SIMILAR SPECIES *Grey Dagger (p.220), The Sycamore (right), The Shark (p.222).*
STATUS *Locally common.*

The Sycamore

Acronicta aceris (Noctuidae)

The Sycamore is more often noticed in the larval stage than as an adult, because of the caterpillar's extraordinary appearance, with brightly coloured hairs and black-ringed white spots along its back. The adult moth, by contrast, is well camouflaged in shades of grey with dark and light mottling. It flies after dark, and may be found feeding at flowers or on honeydew, and is also attracted to light.

APPEARS *wherever Sycamore grows; particularly common in urban areas where it has been planted.*

grey ground colour

LIGHTER FORM

dark and light mottling

wavy parallel lines

DARKER FORM

up to 4cm long

WINGSPAN *4–4.9cm.*
TIME OF FLIGHT *Night.*
FLIGHT PERIOD *June–August.*
LARVAL FOODPLANT *Sycamore and maple (Acer), Horse Chestnut (Aesculus hippocastanum), and oak (Quercus).*
SIMILAR SPECIES *Grey Dagger (p.220).*
STATUS *Locally common.*

The Satellite

Eupsilia transversa (Noctuidae)

This moth gets its common name from the markings on its forewings, which resemble a planet with two satellites. These markings may be white, yellow, or orange. The adults emerge in September, and may be seen on mild nights through the winter until April. They are attracted to light, and feed on ivy blossom and blackberries, as well as sallow blossom in spring.

INHABITS *deciduous woodland, parks, and gardens; also moors in the north of its range.*

pale "satellite" marks

yellowish brown ground colour

FORM WITHOUT PALE MARKINGS

up to 5cm long

WINGSPAN *4–4.7cm.*
TIME OF FLIGHT *Night.*
FLIGHT PERIOD *September–April.*
LARVAL FOODPLANT *Various trees such as oak (Quercus), elm (Ulmus), sallow (Salix), and birch (Betula).*
SIMILAR SPECIES *None.*
STATUS *Widespread and common.*

Golden Plusia

Polychrysia moneta (Noctuidae)

Originally from southern Europe, the Golden Plusia has spread over the last century to northern and western Europe, including Britain. By day the mottled ochre and brown adult is well camouflaged as it rests among withered leaves. After dark it feeds at flowers, and also comes to light in small numbers.

LIVES *in gardens, parks, and other places where foodplants grow.*

dark zig-zag line

light wing spot

pale wing tips

up to 4cm long

WINGSPAN *4–4.5cm.*
TIME OF FLIGHT *Night.*
FLIGHT PERIOD *June–September, in two broods.*
LARVAL FOODPLANT *Delphinium (Delphinium).*
SIMILAR SPECIES *Frosted Orange (p.219).*
STATUS *Locally common.*

Cabbage Moth

Mamestra brassicae (Noctuidae)

Despite its common name, the Cabbage Moth caterpillar feeds on many different plants, although it is partial to cabbages and other brassicas (and may be a pest in some areas). The adult moth is a rather nondescript brown, with darker mottling and pale marks on the forewings. It is attracted to light and may be found at night feeding at flowers such as Red Valerian.

OCCUPIES *almost every possible habitat, as the larvae feed on a wide variety of plants.*

white marks on forewings

pale margin

up to 5cm long

wavy light line on trailing edge

WINGSPAN *3.5–5cm.*
TIME OF FLIGHT *Night.*
FLIGHT PERIOD *May–September, but may be seen throughout the year.*
LARVAL FOODPLANT *Brassicas and many other wild and cultivated plants.*
SIMILAR SPECIES *Common Rustic (p.218).*
STATUS *Widespread and common.*

Merveille du Jour

Dichonia aprilina (Noctuidae)

This beautiful species varies greatly in the markings of the forewings: some individuals have a broad black band across the wings, while others may be almost completely black. The typical form has an intricate pattern of green, black, and white markings. This autumnal species feeds at ivy blossom, and is attracted to light.

OCCURS *mainly in mature oak woodland, also occasionally in gardens and parkland.*

black and white markings

green ground colour

dark hindwings

up to 5cm long

patterned legs

WINGSPAN *4.2–5.2cm.*
TIME OF FLIGHT *Night.*
FLIGHT PERIOD *September–October.*
LARVAL FOODPLANT *Oak (Quercus).*
SIMILAR SPECIES *Scarce Merveille du Jour (Moma alpium), which is smaller; Portland Moth (Ochropleura praecox) has thin wings.*
STATUS *Widespread and locally common.*

INVERTEBRATES

The Herald

Scoliopteryx libatrix (Noctuidae)

The brightly coloured Herald may be found hibernating in buildings such as sheds and barns, and in cellars during the winter months. In its natural habitat, its orange and brown coloration and the ragged outline of its forewings provide perfect camouflage against dead leaves. It is attracted to ivy blossom and blackberries, and also to sallow blossom in the spring, when it reappears after hibernation.

OCCURS *in damp woodland, waterside habitats, and wherever sallows grow. Also found in gardens, parks, and commons.*

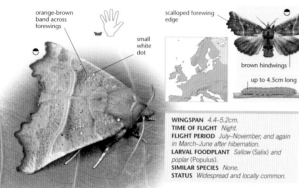

orange-brown band across forewings

small white dot

scalloped forewing edge

brown hindwings

up to 4.5cm long

WINGSPAN *4.4–5.2cm.*
TIME OF FLIGHT *Night.*
FLIGHT PERIOD *July–November, and again in March–June after hibernation.*
LARVAL FOODPLANT *Sallow (Salix) and poplar (Populus).*
SIMILAR SPECIES *None.*
STATUS *Widespread and locally common.*

The Shark

Cucullia umbratica (Noctuidae)

At rest, the Shark sits with its wings tightly folded around its body, its greyish coloration and subtle patterning providing good camouflage against tree trunks or fence posts. After dark, it feeds at the flowers of plants such as Honeysuckle, thistles, and Red Valerian, but is not often attracted to light. The very similar Chamomile Shark (*C. chamomillae*) is usually smaller and flies earlier in the year, between April and June.

PREFERS *gardens and weedy places such as downland, commons, waste ground, and shingle beaches.*

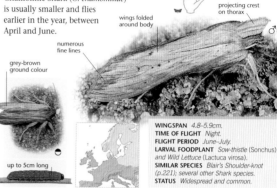

projecting crest on thorax

wings folded around body

numerous fine lines

grey-brown ground colour

up to 5cm long

WINGSPAN *4.8–5.9cm.*
TIME OF FLIGHT *Night.*
FLIGHT PERIOD *June–July.*
LARVAL FOODPLANT *Sow-thistle (Sonchus) and Wild Lettuce (Lactuca virosa).*
SIMILAR SPECIES *Blair's Shoulder-knot (p.221); several other Shark species.*
STATUS *Widespread and common.*

Angle Shades

Phlogophora meticulosa (Noctuidae)

The Angle Shades folds its wings in a unique way when at rest, giving it the appearance of a dried, dead leaf. The colour of the wings varies from olive-green to reddish brown, but the pattern is fairly constant. Some individuals migrate north each year, swelling the numbers of resident moths in northern Europe.

FOUND *in gardens, woodland, commons, and urban areas; not tied to any particular habitat as it feeds on a variety of plants.*

reddish brown markings

dark V-shaped markings

olive-brown ground colour

crumpled appearance

jagged edge

up to 4.5cm long

WINGSPAN *4.5–5.5cm.*
TIME OF FLIGHT *Night.*
FLIGHT PERIOD *May–October, in at least two broods, but may be found at any time of year.*
LARVAL FOODPLANT *Various wild and cultivated plants.*
SIMILAR SPECIES *None.*
STATUS *Widespread and often abundant.*

Silver Y

Autographa gamma (Noctuidae)

One of the great migrants of the insect world, the Silver Y sometimes arrives from warmer areas in vast numbers in spring and early summer to breed in northern Europe, including Britain. The species cannot survive the winter here, and caterpillars, pupae, and adults are all killed by the first frosts. The adult moth is active by day and night, and can be found feeding at the flowers of clover, teasel, heather, buddleia, and Red Valerian, especially at dusk; it is also attracted to light.

FOUND *in almost every possible habitat in temperate climates, as the larvae feed on a wide variety of plants.*

double crest on thorax

mottled grey and brown ground colour

silver Y marking on forewing

scalloped wing margin

dark outer edge

up to 4cm long

NOTE

Silver Y moths that emerge later in the year are often darker and browner than those that arrive as migrants in the spring. An uncommon variety is almost entirely black in colour, and very small specimens can occasionally be seen.

WINGSPAN *3.5–5cm.*
TIME OF FLIGHT *Night and day.*
FLIGHT PERIOD *May–October.*
LARVAL FOODPLANT *Feeds on a wide variety of wild and cultivated herbaceous plants.*
SIMILAR SPECIES *Beautiful Golden Y (A. pulchrina), which is browner; Scarce Silver Y (A. interrogationis), which is smaller and darker.*
STATUS *Widespread and often abundant.*

Dark Arches

Apamea monoglypha (Noctuidae)

This large brownish moth is very common throughout Britain and Europe, and is found in a wide variety of habitats. The forewings vary in colour from medium brown to almost black, the lighter forms having darker and lighter blotches and lines. Dark Arches is attracted to flowers such as Red Valerian, and is also attracted to light.

INHABITS *a variety of grassy areas such as meadows, moorland, downland, and commons.*

mottled wings

dark line at wing margin

blackish ground colour

DARKER FORM

up to 4.5cm long

WINGSPAN *4.6–5.4cm.*
TIME OF FLIGHT *Night.*
FLIGHT PERIOD *June–October, in two broods.*
LARVAL FOODPLANT *Various grasses (family Poaceae).*
SIMILAR SPECIES *Large Nutmeg (A. anceps), which is smaller.*
STATUS *Widespread and often abundant.*

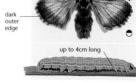

Copper Underwing

Amphipyra pyramidea (Noctuidae)

This moth forms a species pair with the very similar Svensson's Copper Underwing (*A. berbera*). The main difference is in the coloration of the underside of the hindwings, which is very difficult to see on a live moth. On the Copper Underwing, this area is pale yellow, while on Svensson's it is orange-brown. The colour of the forewings ranges from mottled brown to almost wholly black. The Copper Underwing is attracted to sweet substances such as ripe blackberries and rotting fruit, and is also drawn to light in small numbers.

FREQUENTS *deciduous woodland; also parks, gardens, hedgerows, and other areas where there are trees and shrubs for the caterpillars to feed on.*

NOTE

The Copper Underwing may be found resting by day, sometimes in small groups, in dark places such as sheds and hollow trees.

orange-brown hindwing

up to 4.5cm long

pale zig-zag line across forewing

pale oval mark with eyespot

yellow bars on legs

WINGSPAN *4.7–5.4cm.*
TIME OF FLIGHT *Night.*
FLIGHT PERIOD *August–October.*
LARVAL FOODPLANT *Various trees and shrubs, such as oak (Quercus), ash (Fraxinus), Hornbeam (Carpinus betulus), and privet (Ligustrum).*
SIMILAR SPECIES *Svensson's Copper Underwing (A. berbera), which is orange-brown on the underside of the hindwings.*
STATUS *Widespread and common.*

Large Yellow Underwing

Noctua pronuba (Noctuidae)

This is one of the commonest and most widespread moths in Europe, occurring in almost all habitats. In some years, numbers at light traps may run into hundreds, or even thousands. The forewing colour is variable, ranging from light brown with dark markings to a uniform dark brown, with males tending to have darker wings than females. Although most large moths have to warm up their wings by rapidly vibrating them before taking flight, the Large Yellow Underwing is able to take flight instantly without doing so. This sudden flight exposes the yellow and black hindwings, which scare off potential predators.

FOUND *in almost every possible habitat as the larvae feed on a wide variety of plants; a particularly common garden species.*

black border to hindwing

NOTE

The Large Yellow Underwing is the largest of several similar species with yellow and black hindwings. The Lesser Broad-bordered Yellow Underwing (p.224) has orange hindwings with broader black borders.

paler ground colour

up to 5.5cm long

yellow and black hindwing

black mark near forewing tip

dark patches on forewing

WINGSPAN *5–6cm.*
TIME OF FLIGHT *Night.*
FLIGHT PERIOD *June–September.*
LARVAL FOODPLANT *Various plants, including grasses.*
SIMILAR SPECIES *Lesser Yellow Underwing (below), which is smaller; Lesser Broad-bordered Yellow Underwing (p.224), which has orange hindwings; several other Yellow Underwing species.*
STATUS *Widespread and often abundant.*

Lesser Yellow Underwing

Noctua comes (Noctuidae)

Like its larger relative, the Large Yellow Underwing (above), the Lesser Yellow Underwing is a rather variable species. Most individuals are fairly plain yellowish brown with darker markings, but some have strong cross-lines on the forewings. Darker reddish brown or blackish forms may be found in the north of its range, and these are also usually smaller than moths from the south. The adult Lesser Yellow Underwing moths are attracted to light, and are frequent visitors to light traps in late summer and autumn. Like many other noctuids, they may also be found feeding at flowers, being particularly attracted to buddleia, heather, and ragwort.

INHABITS *a wide variety of habitats, including gardens, parks, deciduous woodland, waste ground, and commons.*

dark crescent on hindwing

strong cross-lines on forewings

up to 4.5cm

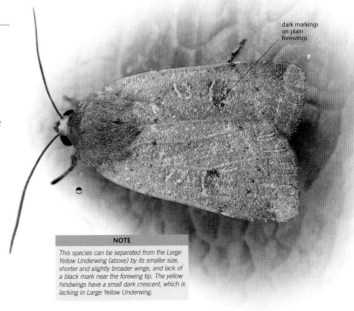

dark markings on plain forewings

NOTE

This species can be separated from the Large Yellow Underwing (above) by its smaller size, shorter and slightly broader wings, and lack of a black mark near the forewing tip. The yellow hindwings have a small dark crescent, which is lacking in Large Yellow Underwing.

WINGSPAN *3.8–4.8cm.*
TIME OF FLIGHT *Night.*
FLIGHT PERIOD *July–October.*
LARVAL FOODPLANT *Many trees and plants, including hawthorn (Crataegus), blackthorn (Prunus), sallow (Salix), and dock (Rumex).*
SIMILAR SPECIES *Large Yellow Underwing (above), Lesser Broad-bordered Yellow Underwing (p.224).*
STATUS *Widespread and common.*

Lesser Broad-bordered Yellow Underwing

Noctua janthe (Noctuidae)

OCCURS *in many different habitats, such as deciduous woodland, gardens, and hedgerows.*

This is one of the smaller yellow underwings, being slightly shorter-winged than the Lesser Yellow Underwing (p.223). The species is less variable than its relatives, although some individuals are more strongly tinged with purple than others. The area of yellow on the hindwings is smaller than in the other Yellow Underwing species, and the black border is broader. In 1991, the Lesser Broad-bordered Yellow Underwing was split into two species. The "new" species, named Langmaid's Yellow Underwing (*N. janthina*), is very difficult to identify, but usually has darker forewings and an even smaller area of yellow on the hindwings. It is also the rarer of the two species, only occuring as a migrant on the south coast of Britain.

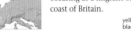

dark markings on forewing

banded legs

purple-brown bands across forewings

yellow area with black border

pale greenish leading edge to thorax

up to 4cm

WINGSPAN *3.5–4.5cm.*
TIME OF FLIGHT *Night.*
FLIGHT PERIOD *July–September.*
LARVAL FOODPLANT *Bramble (Rubus), sallow (Salix), dock (Rumex), birch (Betula), and many other plants and trees.*
SIMILAR SPECIES *Lesser Yellow Underwing (p.223); Langmaid's Yellow Underwing (N. janthina), which is very similar but rare in Britain.*
STATUS *Widespread and common.*

NOTE

This species is easily separated from its close relatives by its smaller size and dark purplish brown bands on the forewings. The pale greenish leading edge of the thorax gives it a neater appearance than the other Yellow Underwings.

Old Lady

Mormo maura (Noctuidae)

INHABITS *a wide variety of habitats, including open woodland, gardens, parks, commons, and open countryside.*

The upper wings of this large moth are banded in mottled greys and browns and have a serrated fringe. The Old Lady flies at night, when it feeds on tree sap and honeydew, and it can be recognized by its slow, lazy flight with deep flaps of its broad wings. By day, it hides in dark places, such as sheds and outbuildings, or in hollow trees, especially near water. The caterpillar starts life feeding on low-growing plants such as dock and chickweed, before hibernating. In the spring, it feeds on a wide variety of trees and shrubs.

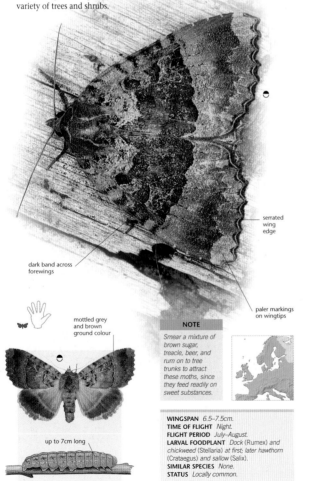

serrated wing edge

dark band across forewings

paler markings on wingtips

mottled grey and brown ground colour

up to 7cm long

NOTE

Smear a mixture of brown sugar, treacle, beer, and rum on to tree trunks to attract these moths, since they feed readily on sweet substances.

WINGSPAN *6.5–7.5cm.*
TIME OF FLIGHT *Night.*
FLIGHT PERIOD *July–August.*
LARVAL FOODPLANT *Dock (Rumex) and chickweed (Stellaria) at first; later hawthorn (Crataegus) and sallow (Salix).*
SIMILAR SPECIES *None.*
STATUS *Locally common.*

Red Underwing

Catocala nupta (Noctuidae)

FOUND *in damp woodland, waterside habitats, and wherever sallows and poplars grow; also in gardens, parks, and commons.*

At rest, the Red Underwing's mottled grey-brown forewings camouflage it perfectly against tree trunks and walls. If disturbed from its resting place during the day it may be seen in flight, when the vivid red and black hindwings are revealed. After dark it is found feeding on rotting fruit or tree sap, and also comes to sugar, but is only drawn to light in small numbers. There is considerable variation in the ground colour of both the forewings and the hindwings: some moths may have almost completely black forewings, while the normally red areas of the hindwings may be yellowish pink or even grey-brown.

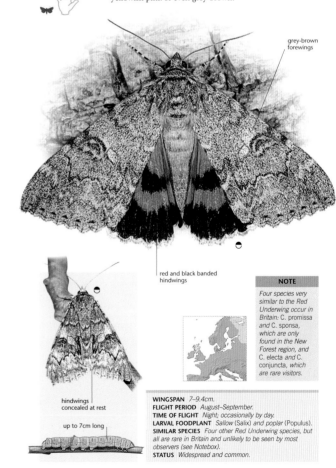

grey-brown forewings

red and black banded hindwings

hindwings concealed at rest

up to 7cm long

NOTE

Four species very similar to the Red Underwing occur in Britain: C. promissa and C. sponsa, which are only found in the New Forest region, and C. electa and C. conjuncta, which are rare visitors.

WINGSPAN *7–9.4cm.*
FLIGHT PERIOD *August–September.*
TIME OF FLIGHT *Night; occasionally by day.*
LARVAL FOODPLANT *Sallow (Salix) and poplar (Populus).*
SIMILAR SPECIES *Four other Red Underwing species, but all are rare in Britain and unlikely to be seen by most observers (see Notebox).*
STATUS *Widespread and common.*

Ghost Moth

Hepialus humuli (Hepialidae)

Also known as the Ghost Swift, this is a member of one of the most primitive groups of moths, characterized by long wings and very short antennae. The males, which are pure white, may be seen in large groups hovering in a ghostly fashion over vegetation at dusk. This is thought to be a display to attract females. The yellowish females are generally larger and have a distinctive pinkish brown pattern on the forewings. After mating, the female lays her eggs in flight, scattering them over the vegetation. The adults do not feed at flowers; they are attracted to light.

FREQUENTS *grassy places such as field margins, meadows, downland, commons, and gardens. Also found in arable fields.*

NOTE

The rather maggot-like caterpillar feeds inside the roots of the foodplants, often causing damage to crops. After feeding for about ten months, it pupates underground before emerging as an adult.

pinkish brown patterns

yellowish ground colour

up to 3.5cm long

silvery white wings

yellowish thorax

wing veins on forewing and hindwing

♂ ♀

WINGSPAN *4.5–5cm.*
TIME OF FLIGHT *Night.*
FLIGHT PERIOD *June–August.*
LARVAL FOODPLANT *Grasses (family Poaceae) and several other plants, including crops.*
SIMILAR SPECIES *None.*
STATUS *Widespread and generally common.*

Leopard Moth

Zeuzera pyrina (Cossidae)

This rather primitive-looking moth has white wings boldly spotted with black and a densely furred, almost woolly head and thorax. The female is much larger than the male, and has a long ovipositor (egg-laying tube) that could be mistaken for a sting. The adults can sometimes be found during the day, resting on trees, fences, or on the ground. The larvae feed inside the trunks and branches of trees for two or even three years, boring into the wood. This can occasionally cause severe damage to the tree, making the Leopard Moth an unpopular species with gardeners and fruit growers.

FOUND *in orchards, hedgerows, gardens, and open woodland, wherever there are trees for the caterpillars to feed on.*

black-spotted forewing

white ground colour

♀

up to 5.5–7cm long

NOTE

With its black-spotted, translucent white wings, the Leopard Moth is an unmistakable species. There is very little variation, but occasional specimens may be found with larger or smaller black spots.

furry head and thorax

6 black spots on thorax

black spots on white wings

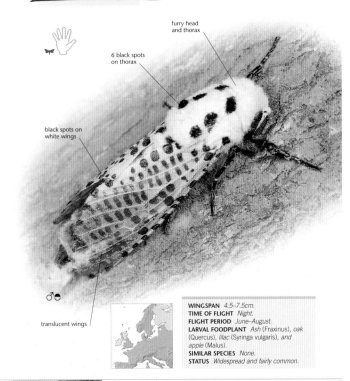

♂ ♀

translucent wings

WINGSPAN *4.5–7.5cm.*
TIME OF FLIGHT *Night.*
FLIGHT PERIOD *June–August.*
LARVAL FOODPLANT *Ash (Fraxinus), oak (Quercus), lilac (Syringa vulgaris), and apple (Malus).*
SIMILAR SPECIES *None.*
STATUS *Widespread and fairly common.*

The Drinker

Euthrix potatoria (Lasiocampidae)

The caterpillar of this large and attractive moth supposedly drinks more frequently than other species, and may be seen drinking from drops of water on leaves or other surfaces. The adult female is larger and paler than the male, and has more pointed wingtips. Both sexes fly at night, and are drawn to light, although the male is more frequently attracted than the female.

SEEN *in woodland, commons, moorland, fens, and other grassy habitats.*

large furry body

dark diagonal line across forewing

♂ ♀

pale spot

paler ground colour

pointed wingtip

♀

up to 7cm long

WINGSPAN *5–7cm.*
TIME OF FLIGHT *Night.*
FLIGHT PERIOD *July–August.*
LARVAL FOODPLANT *Grasses (family Poaceae) and reeds.*
SIMILAR SPECIES *Pine-tree Lappet (Dendrolimus pini); Oak Eggar (right).*
STATUS *Widespread and common.*

Oak Eggar

Lasiocampa quercus (Lasiocampidae)

This species is extremely variable in coloration, ranging from pale yellow-buff to a very dark brown or almost black. The female, which is more uniform in colour and much larger than the male, flies at night, and is sometimes attracted to light. The male flies with an erratic zig-zagging flight during the day in sunshine and is attracted to the female's scent.

FOUND *in a variety of habitats, including deciduous woodland, along hedgerows, and on commons and moorland.*

♀ ♂ **PALER FORM**

♂ ♀

feathery antennae

yellow-buff ground colour

dark and pale lines

♀

up to 8cm long

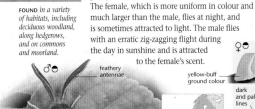

pale spot

lighter band across wings

WINGSPAN *5.5–10cm.*
TIME OF FLIGHT *Day (male); night (female).*
FLIGHT PERIOD *May–August.*
LARVAL FOODPLANT *Hawthorn (Crataegus), heather (Erica and Calluna), Bramble (Rubus fruticosus), and sallow (Salix).*
SIMILAR SPECIES *The Drinker (left).*
STATUS *Widespread and locally common.*

Emperor Moth
With its feathery antennae and startling black and yellow eye spots that resemble the eyes of an owl, the male Emperor Moth is an impressive insect of Britain's heaths and moorland.

Emperor Moth

Saturnia pavonia (Saturniidae)

The males of this spectacular moth may be seen flying in sunshine. The larger females fly at dusk, and are sometimes attracted to light. The males have feathery antennae and both sexes have large and conspicuous eyespots on all four wings. In the resting position, the hindwings of the Emperor Moth are concealed; the spots on the forewings, combined with the dark brown thorax, give the impression of the eyes and snout of a small mammal, which may deter birds from attacking it.

INHABITS *a variety of habitats such as heathland, moorland, and open woodland where the larval foodplants grow.*

feathery antennae
large furry body
large eyespots on all 4 wings
♂

DARKER FORM
♂
brown ground colour
red on forewing tip
lighter colouring than male
♀
up to 6.5cm long

NOTE
When ready to mate, the female releases a pheromone scent, which is detectable by the male, with its sensitive feathery antennae, from up to 2km away. Several males may be attracted to the same female – this behaviour is known as "assembling".

WINGSPAN *5.5–8.8cm.*
TIME OF FLIGHT *Day (male); night (female).*
FLIGHT PERIOD *May–August.*
LARVAL FOODPLANT *Mainly heather (Erica and Calluna), Bramble (Rubus fruticosus), hawthorn (Crataegus), sallow (Salix), but also several other plants.*
SIMILAR SPECIES *None.*
STATUS *Widespread and locally common.*

Elephant Hawk-moth

Deilephila elpenor (Sphingidae)

This species gets its common name from the caterpillar, which vaguely resembles an elephant's trunk. The adult moth has buff forewings, banded with pink, while the underside is mostly pink; the hindwings have white fringes. This attractive moth flies at dusk and through the night, often feeding at flowers such as honeysuckle or Red Valerian.

FOUND *in woodland clearings, river valleys, meadows, commons, and gardens; also found in wasteland.*

pink and buff forewing
pointed forewing tip
up to 8.5cm long
pink and buff striped body
pink wing margin

WINGSPAN *6.2–7cm.*
TIME OF FLIGHT *Night.*
FLIGHT PERIOD *May–June.*
LARVAL FOODPLANT *Willowherb (Epilobium) and bedstraw (Galium).*
SIMILAR SPECIES *Small Elephant Hawk-moth (D. porcellus), which is smaller.*
STATUS *Widespread and often common.*

Lime Hawk-moth

Mimas tiliae (Sphingidae)

The ground colour of the Lime Hawk-moth's forewings is variable, ranging from lime-green to a delicate salmon-pink. The dark markings on the wings also vary from dark green to brown. The adults have no proboscis, and so do not feed on nectar. The moth can be found even in urban areas, especially where lime trees are planted.

LIVES *in gardens, hedgerows, tree-lined streets, parks, and deciduous woodland.*

salmon-pink ground colour
dark blotches
BROWNER FORM
wavy margin
GREENER FORM
up to 6.5cm long

WINGSPAN *7–8cm.*
TIME OF FLIGHT *Night.*
FLIGHT PERIOD *May–June.*
LARVAL FOODPLANT *Lime (Tilia); also birch (Betula), elm (Ulmus), and alder (Alnus).*
SIMILAR SPECIES *Oleander Hawk-moth (Daphnis nerii) lacks wavy wing margin.*
STATUS *Widespread but locally common.*

Hummingbird Hawk-moth

Macroglossum stellatarum (Sphingidae)

This small, day-flying hawk-moth resembles a hummingbird as it hovers in front of flowers, feeding on nectar. It is particularly fond of fuchsia, jasmine, Red Valerian, and campion. A resident of southern Europe, it breeds all year round. Some migrate north in summer, and regularly turn up in Britain.

BREEDS *wherever bedstraws are present. Migrants found near flowers, in parks, gardens, meadows, and wasteland.*

brownish forewings
long proboscis
white marks on black abdomen
dark wavy bands
orange hindwing
up to 6.5cm long

WINGSPAN *5–5.8cm.*
TIME OF FLIGHT *Day.*
FLIGHT PERIOD *Adults may occur in any month of the year.*
LARVAL FOODPLANT *Bedstraw (Galium).*
SIMILAR SPECIES *None.*
STATUS *Irregular migrant to British Isles in summer, in varying numbers.*

Poplar Hawk-moth

Laothoe populi (Sphingidae)

Although quite closely related to the Eyed Hawk-moth (p.229), with which it can hybridize in captivity, the Poplar Hawk-moth has a very different resting position – it holds its hindwings at right angles to its body, projecting in front of the forewings. If disturbed, it flicks its hindwings forward, revealing a patch of orange-red.

FAVOURS *open woodland, waterside habitats, and wherever sallows and poplars grow. Also gardens, parks, and commons.*

large thorax and abdomen
hindwings project in front of forewings
short hindwings
red patch
grey-brown ground colour
up to 7cm long

WINGSPAN *7.2–9cm.*
TIME OF FLIGHT *Night.*
FLIGHT PERIOD *May–June.*
LARVAL FOODPLANT *Poplar (Populus), Aspen (Populus tremula), and sallow/willow (Salix).*
SIMILAR SPECIES *None.*
STATUS *Widespread and generally common.*

Eyed Hawk-moth

Smerinthus ocellata (Sphingidae)

INHABITS *open woodland, orchards, gardens, and waterside habitats where sallows grow.*

When it is at rest, with its hindwings concealed, the mottled brown Eyed Hawk-moth resembles the bark of a tree. If disturbed, however, it will suddenly open its wings to reveal a startling pair of blue and black eyespots on the pinkish hindwings. These, combined with the sharply defined, dark chocolate-brown centre of the thorax, which resembles the snout of a small mammal, have the effect of scaring off predators. Like the Lime Hawk-moth (p.228), this species does not feed at flowers as an adult. It is attracted to light in small numbers.

dark patch on thorax

pinkish hindwing

mottled brown forewing

prominent eyespots

NOTE

The caterpillar of the Eyed Hawk-moth has a blue tail "horn", which distinguishes it from that of the similar Poplar Hawk-moth (p.228). It feeds on the leaves of its foodplants from June to September, before spending the winter months as a pupa.

up to 7.5cm long

WINGSPAN *7.5–9.5 cm.*
TIME OF FLIGHT *Night.*
FLIGHT PERIOD *May–July.*
LARVAL FOODPLANT *Sallow (Salix), apple (Malus), and Aspen (Populus tremula).*
SIMILAR SPECIES *None.*
STATUS *Widespread and locally common.*

Death's-head Hawk-moth

Acherontia atropos (Sphingidae)

FOUND *in potato fields, where the adults and the larvae feed; migrant moths may turn up in any habitat.*

NOTE

The Death's-head Hawk-moth enters beehives to feed on honey. It uses its thick and strong tongue to pierce the wax and suck up its food.

This impressive species is the largest European hawk-moth. It gets its name from the markings on the thorax, which resemble a skull, and it was traditionally considered to be a harbinger of danger. At rest, the dark brown forewings are held over the abdomen, which is yellow with a broad central blue stripe. The hindwings are bright yellow with a faint brown edge. If disturbed or handled, the Death's-head Hawk-moth has the alarming habit of squeaking, which it does by forcing air through its short proboscis. It is a native of southern Europe, Africa, and the Middle East, but some moths migrate north each year; it is an annual visitor to Britain in small numbers.

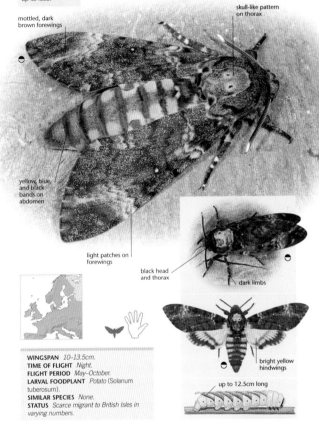

mottled, dark brown forewings

skull-like pattern on thorax

yellow, blue, and black bands on abdomen

light patches on forewings

black head and thorax

dark limbs

bright yellow hindwings

up to 12.5cm long

WINGSPAN *10–13.5cm.*
TIME OF FLIGHT *Night.*
FLIGHT PERIOD *May–October.*
LARVAL FOODPLANT *Potato (Solanum tuberosum).*
SIMILAR SPECIES *None.*
STATUS *Scarce migrant to British Isles in varying numbers.*

Privet Hawk-moth

Sphinx ligustri (Sphingidae)

FAVOURS *open countryside, gardens, woodland rides, hedgerows, and commons.*

This is the largest hawk-moth resident in Britain, on average just a little smaller than the migrant Convolvulus Hawk-moth (right) and Death's-head Hawk-moth (right). An impressive insect, it has a large blackish thorax and long, pointed forewings. The hindwings have pale pink bands, and the abdomen is striped pink and black. It flies at night, visiting flowers to feed, and is attracted to light.

black thorax

dark band across forewing

pink and black banded hindwing

up to 8.5cm long

WINGSPAN *10–12cm.*
TIME OF FLIGHT *Night.*
FLIGHT PERIOD *June–July.*
LARVAL FOODPLANT *Privet (Ligustrum), lilac (Syringa), and ash (Fraxinus).*
SIMILAR SPECIES *Convolvulus Hawk-moth (right), which lacks the black thorax.*
STATUS *Widespread and locally common.*

Convolvulus Hawk-moth

Agrius convolvuli (Sphingidae)

BREEDS *in fields, gardens, and waste ground. Migrants are most often seen in gardens or parks.*

This large hawk-moth is mostly seen at dusk, hovering in front of flowers, especially of the tobacco plant, from which it takes nectar with its long proboscis. It is a strong migrant, and moths from Africa and southern Europe regularly reach Britain. At rest, it resembles a piece of wood, but when it opens its wings, two bright red spots at the rear of the thorax are revealed.

black streaks

pink, black, and white bands

bright red spots

grey-brown wings

up to 10.5cm long

WINGSPAN *9.5–12cm.*
TIME OF FLIGHT *Dusk onwards.*
FLIGHT PERIOD *June–November.*
LARVAL FOODPLANT *Bindweed (Convolvulus).*
SIMILAR SPECIES *Privet Hawk-moth (left), which has pinkish bands on hindwings.*
STATUS *Migrant to British Isles.*

INVERTEBRATES

INSECTS & SPIDERS

As herbivores, predators, parasites, and pollinators, insects and spiders are essential to the functioning of any habitat. They are also a vital food source for countless other species. An average brood of nine Great Tit chicks will consume around 120,000 caterpillars while they are in the nest and a single Barn Swallow chick may consume upwards of 200,000 bugs, flies, and beetles before it fledges. Without the abundance of freshwater insect life, many fish could not survive. Unlike larger species of wildlife, you do not need to go very far to find them. Even an average-sized garden may be home to 200 species of fly (of which 50 or 60 might be hover flies), 200 to 300 species of beetles, almost 100 bugs, more than 300 species of moths, and hundreds of species of tiny wasps, ants, and bees.

INSECTS

Britain has a rich and varied insect fauna of around 20,000 species. Many are large and immediately recognizable, but many more are tiny and require detailed examination before they can be identified.

ARACHNIDS

In addition to 640 or so species of spider, Britain is home to 25 species of harvestmen, about the same number of pseudoscorpions and ticks, and a large number of species of mite.

Anatomy

Insects belong to a large group of animals called arthropods. Other arthropods include arachnids: (spiders and relatives), which are covered in this chapter; and myriapods (millipedes, centipedes, and relatives), and crustaceans (land-living woodlice and marine species such as shrimps and crabs), which are covered in the next chapter. Arthropods have a protective outer skeleton, or cuticle, made of a tough material called chitin and pairs of jointed legs. The body segments are arranged to form a number of functioning units.

Insects

Unlike other arthropods, insects possess only three pairs of legs and they usually have wings. The word "insect" is derived from the Latin for "cut into", and refers to the separate body sections that make up an insect: the head, thorax, and abdomen. The head carries the mouthparts, antennae, and eyes. The thorax has three segments, with legs and sometimes wings. The abdomen has up to 11 visible segments and may carry terminal "tails" known as cerci, as can be clearly seen in silverfish (p.234). Through the process of evolution, these basic insect body parts have become modified in various ways in different species giving rise to huge diversity in the insect world.

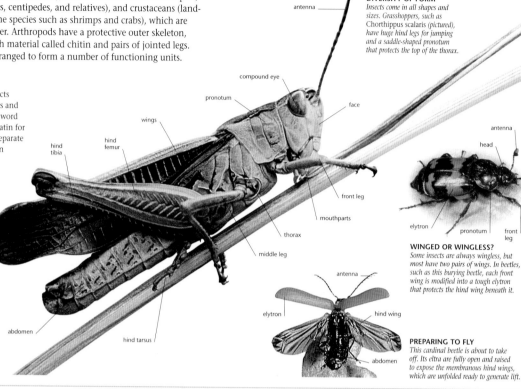

antenna

compound eye

pronotum

wings

hind tibia

hind femur

face

front leg

mouthparts

thorax

middle leg

abdomen

hind tarsus

DIVERSITY OF FORM
Insects come in all shapes and sizes. Grasshoppers, such as Chorthippus scalaris (pictured), have huge hind legs for jumping and a saddle-shaped pronotum that protects the top of the thorax.

antenna

head

elytron

pronotum

front leg

WINGED OR WINGLESS?
Some insects are always wingless, but most have two pairs of wings. In beetles, such as this burying beetle, each front wing is modified into a tough elytron that protects the hind wing beneath it.

antenna

elytron

hind wing

abdomen

PREPARING TO FLY
This cardinal beetle is about to take off. Its eltra are fully open and raised to expose the membranous hind wings, which are unfolded ready to generate lift.

Arachnids

The arachnids include spiders, scorpions, ticks, and mites. They differ from insects in that their bodies are divided into two, not three, segments. These are the cephalothorax, formed from the head and thorax fused together, and the abdomen. The cephalothorax bears six pairs of appendages. The first pair (chelicerae) may be pincer- or fang-like and are used mainly for feeding. The second pair (pedipalps) have several functions, including capturing prey and fertilizing the female. The other four pairs are walking legs.

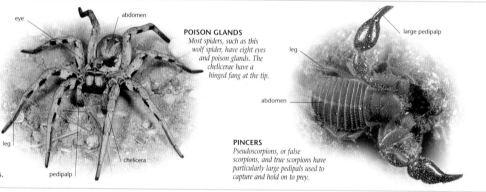

eye

abdomen

leg

chelicera

pedipalp

POISON GLANDS
Most spiders, such as this wolf spider, have eight eyes and poison glands. The chelicerae have a hinged fang at the tip.

large pedipalp

leg

abdomen

PINCERS
Pseudoscorpions, or false scorpions, and true scorpions have particularly large pedipals used to capture and hold on to prey.

Identification

When you find a land-living arthropod, start by deciding which group it belongs to. In general, if it has eight or more pairs of legs and a long body, it is a myriapod; if it has seven pairs of legs, it is a woodlouse. Both these groups are dealt with in Other Invertebrates in this book (pp.298–312). If it has four pairs, it must be an arachnid, and if it has three it is a hexapod. To narrow it down further, you will need to look more carefully and consider the factors outlined on these two pages. You will soon be able to determine the family an individual belongs to and start to identify a number of species.

Insect Life Cycle

All arthropods must shed their protective outer skeleton, or cuticle, at intervals to grow, but the development from egg to adult varies between the different groups. Nearly all insects change appearance in some way from the immature to the adult stage. Some groups of insect, such as bugs, grasshoppers, damselflies, and dragonflies, undergo a gradual change and their metamorphosis is described as incomplete. Other insect groups, such as beetles, ants, bees, and wasps, undergo a much more dramatic change, known as complete metamorphosis. During this process they go through a pupal stage, as represented here by the life cycle of one of Britain's most familiar insects, the ladybird.

COMPLETE METAMORPHOSIS
In this form of development, the immature stage, or larva, looks very different to the adult. It goes through a number of moults, then enters the pupal stage, in which it is transformed into an adult.

mature nymph crawls out of water

nymph moults several times

plant stem

emerging adult

unexpanded wings

mating pair of damselflies

adult damselfly

dried, fully expanded wing

empty nymphal skin

INCOMPLETE METAMORPHOSIS
In insects that undergo incomplete metamorphosis, the immature stages are called nymphs. They usually resemble adults but lack wings and reproductive structures. Wings develop gradually on the outside of the body.

eggs

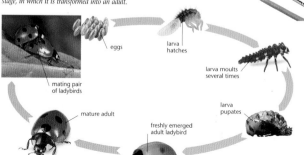

eggs

larva hatches

larva moults several times

larva pupates

mating pair of ladybirds

mature adult

freshly emerged adult ladybird

SYMBOLS
For clarity, the following symbols are used to denote males and females (where these are visually distinct).

Female ♀   Male ♂

Sex

In many arthropods, the sexes look the same, but in others the male and female differ. Sometimes, as in the case of crab spiders, the sexes are different in size or colour. In other groups, such as velvet ants, only one sex is winged. Often an appendage is unique to one sex, such as the ovipositor of female horntails or the impressively large jaws of male stag beetles.

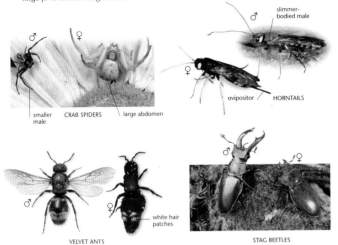

CRAB SPIDERS
smaller male
large abdomen

slimmer-bodied male
ovipositor   HORNTAILS

VELVET ANTS
white hair patches

STAG BEETLES

Camouflage and Warning

Many arthropods have dull or mottled coloration as camouflage or are a similar tone to their habitat. Usually, this is for defence, but sometimes it hides a predator from its prey. Other arthropods have bright warning colours that tell predators of their chemical defences. Some mimic other, more dangerous, species.

white coloration matches petals
CRAB SPIDER
drab colour
LARGE CADDISFLY
green camouflage
BUSH CRICKET
red warning coloration
bee-like appearance
mottled coloration
SEED BUG   ASSASSIN FLY   WEEVIL

Habitats

Arthropods are found in huge numbers almost everywhere. Their habitats can be grouped into broad types, such as woodland, grassland, or aquatic, each of which can be further subdivided. For example, woodland can be either deciduous, coniferous, or mixed. Each type of habitat has a different selection of species. Freshwater habitats are home to species such as mayflies, dragonflies, and damselflies; some members of other groups, such as flies, beetles, and bugs, also breed or live in fresh water. Insects such as ants occur in virtually every habitat on land, but many species are specialists found only in association with decaying wood or plant matter, dung, carcasses, or fungi. Some arthropods are parasites that live on or in the bodies of their animal hosts.

FRESH WATER
Freshwater habitats have a unique range of arthropods. Only about five per cent of insect species are aquatic, yet their abundance means they are vital parts of aquatic food chains.

GRASSLAND
Many insects and spiders live in meadows and other grasslands. Flower-rich grassland has most species; if it is heavily grazed or used for cultivation, the invertebrate diversity declines.

WOODLAND
Woods are home to many arthropod groups. Fertile soil, broad-leaved trees, deep leaf litter, and decaying wood all provide ideal conditions for arthropods.

DUNG
Several groups of insect are associated with the dung of mammals. Some, such as scarab beetles, eat only dung. Others, including dung beetles and many flies, use dung to rear their young.

DECAYING WOOD
The soft, rotting wood of dead or dying trees is a food resource for many insects, including both adults and, in particular, the larvae. A few attack only living or recently dead wood.

CARCASSES
Scavenging is a common lifestyle among arthropods and many species are attracted to carrion. Some feed on the flesh, and many lay their eggs on carcasses, which provide food for the young.

FUNGI
Some groups of arthropod are adapted for feeding on fungi, including springtails and the larvae of many flies and beetles. These can often be found inside the tissues of the fungal fruiting body.

SEASHORES
There are a surprising number of opportunities for insects and other arthropods among rocks, sand plants, and decaying seaweed along coasts. Beetles, flies, pill woodlice, and shore flies (pictured) are particularly abundant.

GARDENS
Arthropods thrive in gardens and even the smallest town garden can provide a refuge for a good variety of species. Some species enter greenhouses or buildings or are associated with rubbish.

Signs

Although you often cannot see arthropods, they may leave clear evidence of their activity. Things to look out for include holes and tunnels in wood, blotchy patches on leaves, yellowed or damaged vegetation, galls on leaves, spider webs, and frothy, saliva-like "cuckoo spit".

TUNNELS IN WOOD
Holes and tunnels in live or dead wood are a sign that arthropods have been at work.

CUCKOO SPIT
Some immature sap-sucking bugs use their watery excrement to protect themselves from drying out.

GALLS
Some insects induce abnormal growths called galls on their host plants.

LARVAL MINE
The larvae of some insects eat leaves on the inside, making a mine with a characteristic shape.

SPIDER WEB
The shape and location of a web can help in identifying a spider.

Collecting

It can be a good idea to catch an arthropod to permit closer study and identification, before letting it go unharmed. Equipment for catching arthropods includes butterfly nets, pond nets, and various beating trays. These can often be improvised at little cost.

BUTTERFLY NET
These nets should be made of fine mesh and are used to catch flying insects. Some have an extendible handle.

BEATING TRAY
A white tray placed under a tree is a good way to catch insects: shake the branch to dislodge them.

Handling

It is important to bear in mind that a few arthropods can inflict nasty bites or stings if handled without proper care. Bees and common wasps, for example, should never be handled. Never put your hand under a stone or into a crevice to see what is there – always look first. Some species can move quickly and may attack in self-defence.

DYSDERID SPIDER

COMMON WASP

HONEY BEE

The Water Springtail

Poduridae

This common, squat species is greyish blue to dark bluish black in colour. The water springtail spends its life on the surface of water in ditches, ponds, canals, boggy areas, and even rain-filled rock pools. It can be so abundant that the water surface appears dark. The spring under the body is long and flattened to ensure that it can jump effectively.

LIVE *on the surface of freshwater. It will even colonize large puddles in summer.*

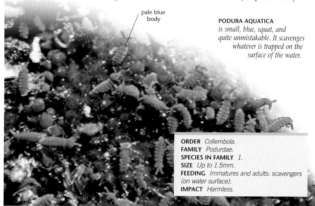

pale blue body

PODURA AQUATICA *is small, blue, squat, and quite unmistakable. It scavenges whatever is trapped on the surface of the water.*

ORDER *Collembola.*
FAMILY *Poduridae.*
SPECIES IN FAMILY *1.*
SIZE *Up to 1.5mm.*
FEEDING *Immatures and adults: scavengers (on water surface).*
IMPACT *Harmless.*

Entomobryid Springtails

Entomobryidae

These pale yellowish springtails are elongate with a small pronotum and often have dark bands or other markings. In many species, the fourth abdominal segment is larger than the third segment. The antennae, which have between four and six segments, can be longer than the body length. All stages of the life cycle eat single-celled algae, fungal threads, or decaying plant matter.

FOUND *mainly in leaf litter, soil, fungi, and caves.*

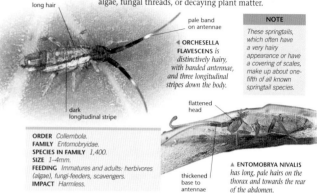

long hair

pale band on antennae

◀ **ORCHESELLA FLAVESCENS** *is distinctively hairy, with banded antennae, and three longitudinal stripes down the body.*

dark longitudinal stripe

NOTE

These springtails, which often have a very hairy appearance or have a covering of scales, make up about one-fifth of all known springtail species.

flattened head

thickened base to antenna

▲ **ENTOMOBRYA NIVALIS** *has long, pale hairs on the thorax and towards the rear of the abdomen.*

ORDER *Collembola.*
FAMILY *Entomobryidae.*
SPECIES IN FAMILY *1,400.*
SIZE *1–4mm.*
FEEDING *Immatures and adults: herbivores (algae), fungi-feeders, scavengers.*
IMPACT *Harmless.*

Globular Springtails

Sminthuridae

Also known as garden springtails, these species are pale to dark brown or green in colour with very rounded, almost spherical bodies. The segmentation of the abdomen is very indistinct, and the antennae are long and elbowed. Males often look different from females, and their antennae are often modfied for holding the antennae of the female during courtship.

COMMON *in a variety of habitats, including fields, pasture, leaf litter in woodland, and freshwater.*

NOTE

Sminthurus viridis, known as the Lucerne Flea, is a widespread pest of alfalfa, clover, and some vegetables. It nibbles holes in the stems and leaves.

globular abdomen

shortish, bent antennae

SMINTHURUS AQUATICUS *is widespread, but does not gather in such large numbers as the Water Springtail (above).*

ORDER *Collembola.*
FAMILY *Sminthuridae.*
SPECIES IN FAMILY *900.*
SIZE *1–3mm.*
FEEDING *Immatures and adults: herbivores.*
IMPACT *Several species can be pests of crop seedlings.*

Jumping Bristletails

Machilidae

These elongated, cylindrical, wingless insects are usually brownish in colour with a distinctive humped thorax. The body is covered with patterns of scales and the end of the abdomen has three slender "tails", the middle one being longer than the other two. The compound eyes are large and touch each other. Machilids run rapidly and jump when disturbed.

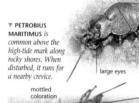

INHABIT *seashores, wooded areas, and grassland, usually under stones or among leaf litter.*

▼ **PETROBIUS MARITIMUS** *is common above the high-tide mark along rocky shores. When disturbed, it runs for a nearby crevice.*

central "tail" longest

▲ **DILTA LITTORALIS** *is one of many similar species found on the ground among low-growing vegetation, leaf litter, and mosses.*

large eyes

humped thorax

mottled coloration

ORDER *Archaeognatha.*
FAMILY *Machilidae.*
SPECIES IN FAMILY *250.*
SIZE *Up to 1.2cm.*
FEEDING *Nymphs and adults: herbivores (algae, mosses, lichens), scavengers.*
IMPACT *Harmless.*

Tomocerid Springtails

Tomoceridae

This family includes some very widespread and common species. Some species are darkly pigmented and smooth with a slightly shiny appearance, while others may be paler and rather hairy. The antennae are often longer than the body and the third segment is typically much longer than the fourth, allowing the antenna to curl up in a spiral. Adults continue to moult until they die.

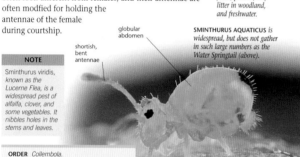

OCCUR *in leaf litter, woodland understorey, and decaying wood.*

long, tapering antennae

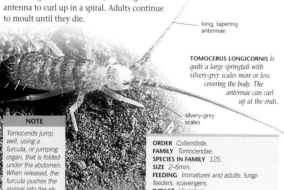

TOMOCERUS LONGICORNIS *is quite a large springtail with silvery-grey scales more or less covering the body. The antennae can curl up at the ends.*

silvery-grey scales

NOTE

Tomocerids jump well, using a furcula, or jumping organ, that is folded under the abdomen. When released, the furcula pushes the animal into the air.

ORDER *Collembola.*
FAMILY *Tomoceridae.*
SPECIES IN FAMILY *125.*
SIZE *2–6mm.*
FEEDING *Immatures and adults: fungi-feeders, scavengers.*
IMPACT *Harmless.*

Silverfish and Firebrats

Lepismatidae

These elongated and slightly flattened, wingless insects are brown or tan in colour and usually covered in greyish or silvery scales and hairs. The end of the abdomen has three slender "tails" of a similar length. The compound eyes are small and widely separated. Lepismatids run rapidly, but unlike jumping bristletails, do not jump.

OCCUPY *a range of habitats such as debris and vegetation, caves, bird nests, and warm places indoors.*

▶ **LEPISMA SACCHARINA,** *the Silverfish, prefers damp microhabitats in buildings. It is omnivorous.*

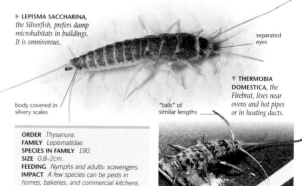

separated eyes

body covered in silvery scales

"tails" of similar lengths

▼ **THERMOBIA DOMESTICA,** *the Firebrat, lives near ovens and hot pipes or in heating ducts.*

ORDER *Thysanura.*
FAMILY *Lepismatidae.*
SPECIES IN FAMILY *190.*
SIZE *0.8–2cm.*
FEEDING *Nymphs and adults: scavengers.*
IMPACT *A few species can be pests in homes, bakeries, and commercial kitchens.*

Siphlonurid Mayflies

Siphlonuridae

These mayflies are typically pale reddish brown or yellowish brown in colour. The upper portions of the eyes have larger facets than the lower portions. The front wings are quite narrow rather than triangular, and have many veins running crosswise. The abdomen, which may have dark markings above and below, usually has two long tails.

COMMON in lakes, mountain streams, and drainage ditches.

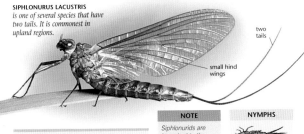

SIPHLONURUS LACUSTRIS is one of several species that have two tails. It is commonest in upland regions.

two tails

small hind wings

NOTE

Siphlonurids are important in the aquatic food chain as they form part of the diet of freshwater fish. They also rapidly colonize new habitats.

NYMPHS

The streamlined nymphs have short antennae, and gills on segments one to seven.

ORDER Ephemeroptera.
FAMILY Siphlonuridae.
SPECIES IN FAMILY 30.
SIZE 6–13mm.
FEEDING Nymphs: scavengers, predators. Adults: non-feeding.
IMPACT Harmless.

Burrowing Mayflies

Ephemeridae

The wings of these large mayflies are typically clear or brownish in colour, although they have dark spots in some species. The bodies are often pale yellowish or whitish cream with characteristic dark spots or other markings, especially towards the end of the abdomen, which has two or three very long tails.

FOUND in or near to streams, rivers, lakes, and ponds.

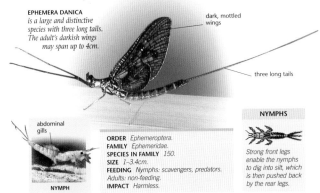

EPHEMERA DANICA is a large and distinctive species with three long tails. The adult's darkish wings may span up to 4cm.

dark, mottled wings

three long tails

abdominal gills

NYMPH

NYMPHS

Strong front legs enable the nymphs to dig into silt, which is then pushed back by the rear legs.

ORDER Ephemeroptera.
FAMILY Ephemeridae.
SPECIES IN FAMILY 150.
SIZE 1–3.4cm.
FEEDING Nymphs: scavengers, predators. Adults: non-feeding.
IMPACT Harmless.

Small Mayflies

Baetidae

Small mayflies are pale or dark brown or black with yellowish, grey, or white markings. The front wings are elongated and oval with a reduced number of veins. In some species the hind wings may be small or absent. The males have large eyes, divided into upper and lower portions. The abdomen has two very long, slender tails.

THRIVE in a wide range of aquatic habitats, such as ditches, pools, lakes, and streams.

NYMPHS

The small, slender nymphs are active swimmers and climb about on submerged plants.

▼ BAETIS RHODANI breeds in many types of water. The adults have very small hind wings and can be found all year.

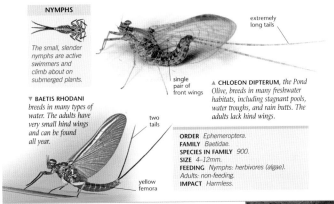

extremely long tails

single pair of front wings

two tails

yellow femora

▲ CHLOEON DIPTERUM, the Pond Olive, breeds in many freshwater habitats, including stagnant pools, water troughs, and rain butts. The adults lack hind wings.

ORDER Ephemeroptera.
FAMILY Baetidae.
SPECIES IN FAMILY 900.
SIZE 4–12mm.
FEEDING Nymphs: herbivores (algae). Adults: non-feeding.
IMPACT Harmless.

Crawling Mayflies

Ephemerellidae

The commonest species in this family are pale reddish in colour and often have small, dark abdominal markings. The hindwings are relatively large and can be up to one-third as long as the forewings. The end of the abdomen carries two or (usually) three long, slender tails. Females release their eggs in one clump that separates out on the water surface.

OCCUR in a wide variety of running water as well as ponds and margins of lakes.

NYMPHS

Nymphs crawl on submerged plants. Their legs are usually long and the abdomen has flap-like lateral gills.

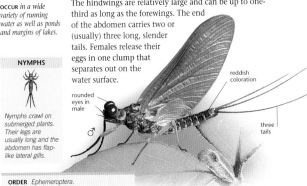

reddish coloration

rounded eyes in male

three tails

ORDER Ephemeroptera.
FAMILY Ephemerellidae.
SPECIES IN FAMILY 200.
SIZE 6–10mm.
FEEDING Nymphs: scavengers, predators. Adults: non-feeding.
IMPACT Harmless.

EPHEMERELLA IGNITA, known by anglers as the Blue-winged Olive, is a reddish species with three tails. It is common near fast-flowing streams and rivers. Males have partly rounded eyes.

Stream Mayflies

Heptageniidae

Also known as flat-headed mayflies, these insects usually are dark brown with clear wings, although some are yellow or reddish brown with black, white, or yellow markings. The wings are clear with distinctive (often dark brown) veins. The eyes of males are large but not divided into upper and lower portions. The abdomen has two long tails.

FOUND usually in fast-flowing water such as mountain streams, but also occur in ponds.

NYMPHS

Generally dark in colour, the nymphs are flattened, with antennae and eyes on the upper side.

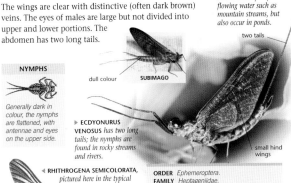
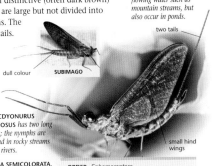

dull colour

SUBIMAGO

two tails

▶ ECDYONURUS VENOSUS has two long tails; the nymphs are found in rocky streams and rivers.

small hind wings

◀ RHITHROGENA SEMICOLORATA, pictured here in the typical resting position, lives in gravel-bottomed streams.

dark eyes

ORDER Ephemeroptera.
FAMILY Heptageniidae.
SPECIES IN FAMILY 500.
SIZE 4–15mm.
FEEDING Nymphs: herbivores (algae), scavengers, predators. Adults: non-feeding.
IMPACT Harmless.

Caenid Mayflies

Caenidae

The front wings of these small, delicate mayflies are very broad with highly distinctive dark longitudinal veins at the front margin and a very rounded hind margin. The hindwings are absent. The eyes in both sexes are small. The thorax is usually a little darker than the abdomen, which can be pale or greyish but always has three very long, slender tails.

OCCUPY a variety of waterbodies such as large lake margins, ponds, and slow-flowing rivers.

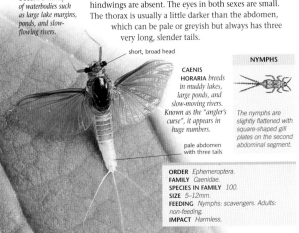

short, broad head

CAENIS HORARIA breeds in muddy lakes, large ponds, and slow-moving rivers. Known as the "angler's curse", it appears in huge numbers.

pale abdomen with three tails

NYMPHS

The nymphs are slightly flattened with square-shaped gill plates on the second abdominal segment.

ORDER Ephemeroptera.
FAMILY Caenidae.
SPECIES IN FAMILY 100.
SIZE 5–12mm.
FEEDING Nymphs: scavengers. Adults: non-feeding.
IMPACT Harmless.

Narrow-winged Damselflies

Coenagrionidae

Many of these slender damselflies are beautifully coloured in shades of light blue with dark markings. Others may have blue-green or red-brown coloration, also with dark markings. The adults are generally weak fliers and rest horizontally with their clear wings folded together over the body. Towards the tip at the front margin of both pairs of wings there is a short, diamond-shaped mark called the pterostigma. In most species, the males are more brightly coloured than the females, which tend to be greenish.

OCCURS *mainly along streams and rivers, but also around ponds, stagnant pools, and swampy areas.*

NYMPHS

The slender-bodied nymphs are variable in colour with three gill filaments arising from the end of the abdomen, the middle filament being the longest.

▶ **PYRRHOSOMA NYMPHULA**, *the Large Red Damselfly, is often one of the first species to be seen flying in spring.*

dark markings

black legs

greenish thorax

blue segment

red eyes

▶ **ERYTHROMMA NAJAS**, *the Red-eyed Damselfly, is an excellent flier. Females have browner eyes and lack the males' blue abdominal tip.*

◀ **ISCHNURA ELEGANS** *is known as the Blue-tailed Damselfly as the male has a blue abdominal segment.*

▼ **COENAGRION PUELLA**, *the Azure Damselfly, has blue and black males and brilliant green and black females.*

diamond-shaped pterostigma

one blue segment

black and green thorax

typical form

single black stripe on side of thorax

two blue segments

▲ **ENALLAGMA CYATHIGERUM**, *the Common Blue Damselfly, resembles Coenagrion males, but has a black club-shaped marking on the second abdominal segment. Females (left) vary from blue to brown.*

ORDER *Odonata.*
FAMILY *Coenagrionidae.*
SPECIES IN FAMILY *1,000.*
SIZE *Most species 2–5cm (wingspan).*
FEEDING *Nymphs and adults: predators.*
IMPACT *Harmless.*

Broad-winged Damselflies

Calopterygidae

Also called demoiselles, these fairly large, metallic-bodied damselflies have wings that narrow gradually towards their bases. The body is metallic green or blue. The male wings have a large dark patch or are entirely dark with a blue or purple sheen; females' wings are tinted green or brown.

INHABIT *both fast- and slow-flowing streams and rivers, as well as canals; adults also occur in woods far from water.*

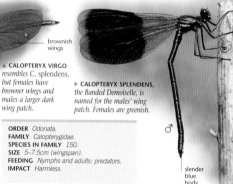

brownish wings

◀ **CALOPTERYX VIRGO** *resembles C. splendens, but females have browner wings and males a larger dark wing patch.*

▶ **CALOPTERYX SPLENDENS**, *the Banded Demoiselle, is named for the males' wing patch. Females are greenish.*

slender blue body

NYMPHS

A small head and three flap-like gill filaments are the nymphs' most distinctive features.

ORDER *Odonata.*
FAMILY *Calopterygidae.*
SPECIES IN FAMILY *150.*
SIZE *5–7.5cm (wingspan).*
FEEDING *Nymphs and adults: predators.*
IMPACT *Harmless.*

Stalk-winged Damselflies

Lestidae

Also known as spread-winged or emerald damselflies, these relatively sturdy species are usually metallic green or blue. At rest, they often perch vertically with the wings partly or fully open. The clear wings have narrow, stalk-like bases and a dark, elongated or rectangular pterostigma.

LIVE *around still water, swamps, bogs, drainage ditches, and acidic pools or lakes.*

◀ **SYMPECMA FUSCA** *is a relatively drab species that hibernates as an adult and can be seen very early in the year.*

▼ **LESTES SPONSA**, *the Emerald Damselfly, rests with its wings held out at an angle from the body.*

male has bluish thorax

metallic green abdomen

dull brown coloration

NYMPHS

The slender, long-bodied nymphs are light green to dark brown, with three long abdominal gills.

ORDER *Odonata.*
FAMILY *Lestidae.*
SPECIES IN FAMILY *160.*
SIZE *3.2–6.2cm (wingspan).*
FEEDING *Nymphs and adults: predators.*
IMPACT *Harmless.*

White-legged Damselflies

Platycnemididae

FOUND *in pastures and meadows, especially around slow, lowland rivers and canals with plenty of floating and waterside plants. Occasionally found in still waterbodies.*

Although hard to see, the feature that distinguishes these medium-sized damselflies from others is the shape of a cell at the wing bases. Known as the quadrilateral, it is roughly rectangular in this family, rather than diamond-shaped. Other features include a narrow head, fairly broad wings, and thickening of the tibiae of the middle and hind legs.

wings held over body

blue eyes

broad legs

NYMPHS

Variable in form, the nymphs have three very long and broad gills at the end of the abdomen.

PLATYCNEMIS PENNIPES *lives near lakes and slow-flowing watercourses with plenty of aquatic vegetation.*

ORDER *Odonata.*
FAMILY *Platycnemididae.*
SPECIES IN FAMILY *200.*
SIZE *2.4–3.1cm (wingspan).*
FEEDING *Nymphs and adults: predators.*
IMPACT *Harmless.*

Club-tailed Dragonflies

Gomphidae

These relatively big dragonflies are named for the swelling of the abdomen just before the apex, giving a club-like appearance; this is less noticeable in females and in both sexes of some species. Most species are brightly coloured in black, yellow, or green. The eyes are widely separated.

OCCUR *in or near to rivers, large streams, ponds, and lakes.*

NYMPHS

Either slender or squat, the nymphs have stout legs and rather short, flattened antennae.

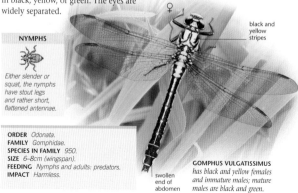

black and yellow stripes

swollen end of abdomen

GOMPHUS VULGATISSIMUS *has black and yellow females and immature males; mature males are black and green.*

ORDER *Odonata.*
FAMILY *Gomphidae.*
SPECIES IN FAMILY *950.*
SIZE *6–8cm (wingspan).*
FEEDING *Nymphs and adults: predators.*
IMPACT *Harmless.*

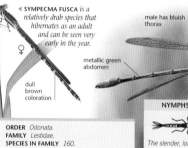

Hawkers

Aeshnidae

Also called darners, this family includes some of the largest and most powerful dragonflies. These robust insects are usually dark green, blue, or brown, with stripes on the thorax and spots or bands on the abdomen. The large eyes touch on top of the head. The wings, which are usually clear, sometimes have an amber or yellowish brown tint. Both pairs of wings have an elongated pterostigma. The end of the abdomen has a pair of claspers and, in males, a smaller appendage in between.

FOUND usually near still waters with plenty of aquatic vegetation, but may occur along hedgerows and paths and in urban areas.

▼ AESHNA MIXTA, the Migrant Hawker, is widespread in central and southern Europe. Females are yellow and brown.

eyes touch each other

hairy thorax

clear wings

paired blue spots on abdomen

blue eyes

alternate small white and larger blue marks

▶ AESHNA CYANEA has blue eyes and a blue abdominal tip in males; females are yellow and green with brownish eyes.

▲ BRACHYTRON PRATENSE, the Hairy Dragonfly, has a thick layer of hairs on the thorax. Females have yellow (not blue) spots.

blue tip to otherwise green-marked abdomen

apple-green thoracic markings

yellow stripes on thorax

▲ AESHNA GRANDIS, the Brown Hawker, has brownish wings and distinctive thoracic stripes.

mainly clear wings

NYMPHS

The cryptically coloured nymphs have strongly built, cylindrical bodies and large eyes. They live among weeds, crawling on the bottom in search of their prey.

black stripe down back

claspers

ORDER Odonata.
FAMILY Aeshnidae.
SPECIES IN FAMILY 420.
SIZE 6–14cm (wingspan).
FEEDING Nymphs and adults: predators.
IMPACT Harmless.

▲ ANAX IMPERATOR, the Emperor Dragonfly, is very large, with blue males and green females. It breeds in large ponds and even in weedy ditches.

Golden-ringed Dragonflies

Cordulegastridae

These large, sturdy dragonflies are brownish or black with yellow markings and are sometimes called biddies. In both sexes the eyes are large and touch each other at a single point on the top of the head. The wings are transparent, with a long, narrow pterostigma. The abdomen is usually elongated and has numerous distinctive rings.

TYPICALLY found along streams in upland regions, but also occur near woodland streams at lower levels.

eyes meet at one point

CORDULEGASTER BOLTONI, the Golden-ringed Dragonfly, lives in uplands and moorland. The sexes are quite similar in appearance.

NYMPHS

The nymphs are quite elongated and strong, with a noticeably broad head and big eyes.

golden yellow rings

ORDER Odonata.
FAMILY Cordulegastridae.
SPECIES IN FAMILY 50.
SIZE 8–10.5cm (wingspan).
FEEDING Nymphs and adults: predators.
IMPACT Harmless.

Green-eyed Skimmers

Corduliidae

These insects – also known as emerald dragonflies – are often quite hairy in appearance, with a distinctive metallic green or bronze coloration. The wings may have a yellow tint, especially at the base. The head and eyes are green in common species; the latter are large and touch each other, and there is a noticeable indentation on their rear margins.

COMMON around stagnant water, and sometimes found near streams.

◀ SOMATOCHLORA METALLICA, the Brilliant Emerald, is scarce and localized in Britain, but fairly common in central and northern Europe.

metallic green

yellowish tint to wing

NYMPHS

Usually flat with long legs, the nymphs may be either short and stout or elongated.

bronze sheen

▶ CORDULIA AENEA, the Downy Emerald, frequents shaded ponds in wooded areas, flying close to the water surface.

ORDER Odonata.
FAMILY Corduliidae.
SPECIES IN FAMILY 400.
SIZE 5–8cm (wingspan).
FEEDING Nymphs and adults: predators.
IMPACT Harmless.

Common Skimmers

Libellulidae

These dragonflies, which represent a large proportion of the order Odonata, are also called darters or chasers due to their fast, unpredictable flight interspersed with short periods of hovering. They are colourful and males often differ from females, their bodies sometimes having a pale blue, powdery appearance. The wingspan is typically longer than the body length and the wings sometimes have dark bands or other markings, especially at their bases. In many species the abdomen is broad and flattened. The large eyes always touch on top of the head.

OCCUR over still or slow-moving water in a variety of habitats, from mountains and moors to forests.

NYMPHS

Fiercely predatory and aquatic, the nymphs are short, stocky, and slightly flattened, often with spines projecting from the abdomen. Their facial masks are hollow and large.

NOTE

Adult males are very territorial and command their patch from a perch on an exposed plant stem or twig. They dart away to chase off rival males.

clear wings

blue abdomen

black tip

◀ ORTHETRUM CANCELLATUM is also known as the Black-tailed Skimmer; the female is yellowish with two black stripes along the length of the abdomen.

wings take on a yellow tinge with age

blood red colouring

▲ SYMPETRUM SANGUINEUM, the Ruddy Darter, can be found around shallow ponds, ditches, and lakes. The male is bright red while the female is yellowish. Both have a yellow mark at the base of their wings.

brown wing bases

clear wings

▶ LIBELLULA DEPRESSA, the Broad-bodied Chaser, breeds in ponds. The abdomen in females is broader than in males and is brown with yellow lateral patches.

two dark marks on each wing

brown hindwing base

small dark spot

▶ LIBELLULA QUADRIMACULATA is known as the Four-spotted Chaser on account of the small dark spot in the middle of the front margin of each wing. The sexes are quite similar.

yellow at sides

ORDER Odonata.
FAMILY Libellulidae.
SPECIES IN FAMILY 1,250.
SIZE 4–8cm (wingspan).
FEEDING Nymphs and adults: predators.
IMPACT Harmless.

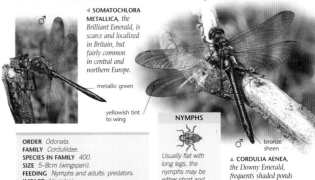
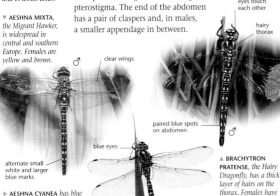

Emperor Dragonfly
Britain's largest dragonfly, this insect is a
powerful and incredibly agile flier,
swooping and darting over water as it
hunts for other insects. The broad wings
are strongly veined and transparent.

Common Stoneflies

Perlidae

Yellowish brown to dark brown in colour, these often quite stout and flat-bodied stoneflies have minute remains of the nymphal gill tufts on the underside of the thorax near the bases of the legs. The front wings have a distinctive "double ladder" made up of numerous cross veins in the basal half. Males can be much smaller than the females. The abdomen has a pair of longish tails, called cerci, which are made up of many segments. The nymphs can be patterned but always have branched gills on the thoracic segments.

FOUND *in a variety of flowing water bodies, such as rivers and streams with stony beds.*

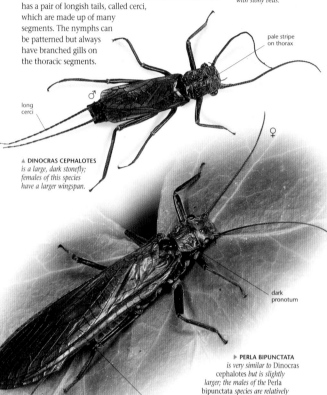

pale stripe on thorax

long cerci

♂

♀

▲ DINOCRAS CEPHALOTES *is a large, dark stonefly; females of this species have a larger wingspan.*

dark pronotum

fully winged

▶ PERLA BIPUNCTATA *is very similar to Dinocras cephalotes but is slightly larger; the males of the Perla bipunctata species are relatively short-winged.*

ORDER *Plecoptera.*
FAMILY *Perlidae.*
SPECIES IN FAMILY *400.*
SIZE *2–5cm.*
FEEDING *Nymphs: predators. Adults: non-feeding.*
IMPACT *Harmless.*

NYMPHS

The nymphs may take up to five years to become adult, and moult as many as thirty times.

Predatory Stoneflies

Perlodidae

The commonest species in this family have yellowish or olive-green bodies and green wings, while others are dark brown or nearly black. The pronotum is rectangular in shape; the cerci are long. The rear, or anal, region of the hindwings is often enlarged with only a few lengthwise veins. Males of some species have short wings. The flattened, elongate nymphs of this family are distinctive in that they typically have contrasting patterns of light and dark coloration, giving rise to an alternative common family – Patterned Stoneflies. Nymphs vary in the sort of prey they eat and the time of the day that they are active.

LIVE *near shallow streams with gravel or stone beds, often on chalky ground.*

NYMPHS

The long-legged nymphs appear to have a waxy texture and many lack gills.

yellowish body

▲ ISOPERLA GRAMMATICA, *or Yellow Sally, is a popular bait to catch trout. It is a very common and widespread species in gravelly or rocky bottomed streams.*

yellow-orange rear of head

♂

ORDER *Plecoptera.*
FAMILY *Perlodidae.*
SPECIES IN FAMILY *250.*
SIZE *1–3.2cm.*
FEEDING *Nymphs: predators, scavengers. Adults: non-feeding.*
IMPACT *Harmless.*

▲ DIURA BICAUDATA *is a slender-legged stonefly mainly found in mountain streams. The nymphs eat the larvae of black flies and other sedentary or slow-moving prey.*

Willowflies

Taeniopterygidae

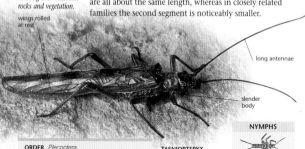

OCCUR *in streams of all kinds, where adults can be seen flying and running over waterside rocks and vegetation.*

These dark brown or black stoneflies have very long, slender antennae. The front wings may have a darkish broad band across them and the abdomen has a pair of very short tails. Although difficult to see, a good identification feature of these stoneflies is that the segments of the tarsi are all about the same length, whereas in closely related families the second segment is noticeably smaller.

wings rolled at rest

long antennae

slender body

ORDER *Plecoptera.*
FAMILY *Taeniopterygidae.*
SPECIES IN FAMILY *75.*
SIZE *0.7–1.4cm.*
FEEDING *Nymphs: scavengers (plant fragments). Adults: mainly non-feeding.*
IMPACT *Harmless.*

TAENIOPTERYX NEBULOSA *is a dark, slender species with long antennae. The wings are rolled around the body while at rest.*

NYMPHS

The nymphal abdominal cerci and antennae of these stoneflies are quite long.

Spring Stoneflies

Nemouridae

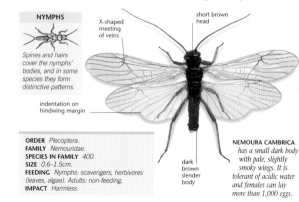

SEEN *around rocky, fast-flowing streams or springs and lakes.*

Also called brown stoneflies because of their typical body colour, these stoneflies are often stout-bodied and hold their wings rolled loosely around the body at rest. Several veins meet towards the tip of the front wings, giving the impression of an "X". The wings of some species are mottled and the abdomen has a pair of very short cerci.

NYMPHS

Spines and hairs cover the nymphs' bodies, and in some species they form distinctive patterns.

X-shaped meeting of veins

short brown head

indentation on hindwing margin

ORDER *Plecoptera.*
FAMILY *Nemouridae.*
SPECIES IN FAMILY *400.*
SIZE *0.6–1.5cm.*
FEEDING *Nymphs: scavengers, herbivores (leaves, algae). Adults: non-feeding.*
IMPACT *Harmless.*

dark brown slender body

NEMOURA CAMBRICA *has a small dark body with pale, slightly smoky wings. It is tolerant of acidic water and females can lay more than 1,000 eggs.*

True Crickets

Gryllidae

The insects of this family are slightly flattened in body shape, with distinctive rounded heads and long, thin antennae, which are as long as or longer than the body. Crickets are rather drably coloured black or shades of brown. In winged species the front wings are held flat over the body at rest; males rub them together to produce songs. The end of the abdomen bears a pair of noticeable, often bristly, unsegmented cerci. In females the conspicuous ovipositor is cylindrical or needle-like. In Britain, the Field Cricket and the Wood Cricket are very rare and confined to the far south.

FOUND *in all manner of herbage in woods, hedgerows, grassland, and scrub.*

short wings

▶ **GRYLLUS CAMPESTRIS,** *the Field Cricket, is a stocky insect with a big head and large hind legs. It makes burrows in grassland.*

dark, shiny head

◀ **NEMOBIUS SYLVESTRIS,** *known as Wood Cricket, has short front wings and no hind wings.*

folded hind wings

spines

dull brown coloration

pale wing base

▲ **ACHETA DOMESTICA** *is a nocturnally active species. It is dull brown in colour and both sexes are fully winged.*

ovipositor

NOTE

Males sing mostly at night, by using their front wings, a series of small teeth on one wing rubbing over a scraper on the other.

ORDER *Orthoptera.*
FAMILY *Gryllidae.*
SPECIES IN FAMILY *1,800.*
SIZE *0.5–2.5cm.*
FEEDING *Nymphs and adults: herbivores, scavengers, predators.*
IMPACT *Some species can be crop pests.*

Bush Crickets

Tettigoniidae

Highly distinctive due to their long, thread-like antennae and saddle-shaped pronotum, these brownish or greenish insects are sometimes known as long-horned grasshoppers. The wings are short in some species, but in fully-winged species the folded wings extend well beyond the end of the abdomen. Females have a conspicuous, laterally flattened ovipositor, which may be short and curved like a sickle or long like a sabre, depending on where the female lays her eggs. The hind legs are enlarged for jumping. Males make a species-specific song by rubbing the front wings together. Songs can take the form of soft drumming or ticking.

OCCUR *in a variety of habitats, both lush and sparsely vegetated, from ground level up to the treetops.*

NOTE

Bush cricket songs have been likened, among other things, to high-speed drills, watch winding, knife grinding, buzzing, and sliding a comb over a ruler's edge.

small, brownish red spots all over body

large, sword-like ovipositor

▲ **LEPTOPHYES PUCTATISSIMA,** *the Speckled Bush Cricket, is common and widespread in well-vegetated areas such as woodland margins, hedgerows, and gardens. The wings are always very short.*

▶ **DECTICUS VERRUCIVORUS** *is known as the Wart Biter due to its use as a cure for warts in folk medicine. It eats insects and some plants and sings in open, sunny locations.*

slightly curved ovipositor

wings extend past abdomen

▶ **MECONEMA THALASSINUM,** *the Oak Bush Cricket, is a pale green species that lives in trees, typically oaks, where it feeds on small insects after dark. Males sing by drumming on a leaf.*

◀ **TETTIGONIA VIRIDISSIMA,** *the Great Green Bush Cricket, is a large but very well-camouflaged species. It is fairly common in the southern half of Britain. The female lays eggs in the soil or leaf litter.*

brown stripe

▼ **METRIOPTERA BRACHYPTERA** *is known as the Bog Bush Cricket, but also inhabits drier places such as heathland. Its song is a train of chirps that sound like "zrit".*

short wings

▼ **PHOLIDOPTERA GRISEOAPTERA,** *the Dark Bush Cricket, varies from brown to almost black. It lives in a variety of habitats, especially woodland rides and margins, where it feeds on both plants and insects.*

saddle-shaped pronotum

greenish yellow underside

long wings

sloping face

short wings

◀ **CONOCEPHALUS DORSALIS,** *the Short-winged Conehead, is a slender species that favours moist habitats such as damp grassland, river edges, and the margins of salt marshes.*

slender body

ORDER *Orthoptera.*
FAMILY *Tettigoniidae.*
SPECIES IN FAMILY *5,000.*
SIZE *1.6–6cm.*
FEEDING *Nymphs and adults: herbivores, scavengers, predators.*
IMPACT *A few species can be plant pests.*

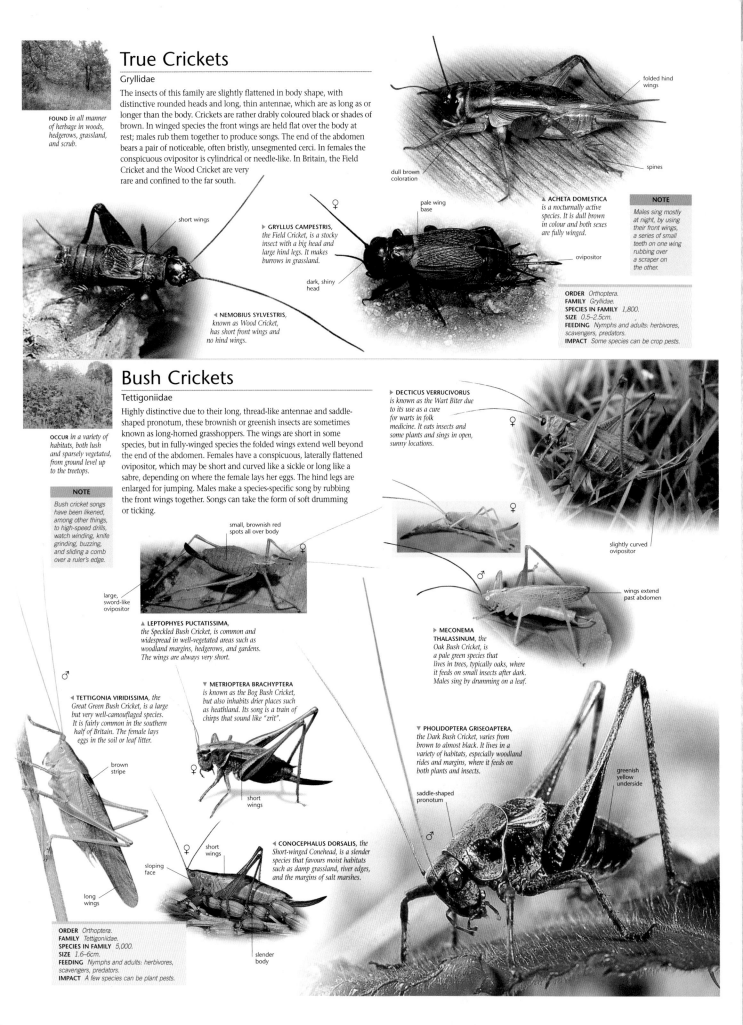

Great Green Bush Cricket
The slightly turned down, sabre-like ovipositor projecting from the end of the abdomen of this bush cricket marks it out as a female. She will use this to lay her eggs in the soil or in crevices.

Grasshoppers and Locusts

Acrididae

NOTE

Females lay their eggs on the ground and surround them with a sticky secretion which dries and hardens to form a protective egg pod.

These insects are active during the day and prefer hot, sunny conditions. Most species are brownish or greenish with markings and patterns of all kinds. Two distinctive characteristics are the short antennae and the large saddle-shaped pronotum. The hind legs are greatly enlarged for jumping. The jump is an escape response, but if trapped, grasshoppers can use their hind legs to kick out at enemies. The large hindwings are folded beneath the narrower and tougher front wings, but some species are short-winged. Many species have brightly coloured hindwings, which they can flash to startle enemies. Females are mostly larger than males, which sing by rubbing a row of small pegs on the inside of their hind femora against a hard, thickened vein on the edge of the front wings.

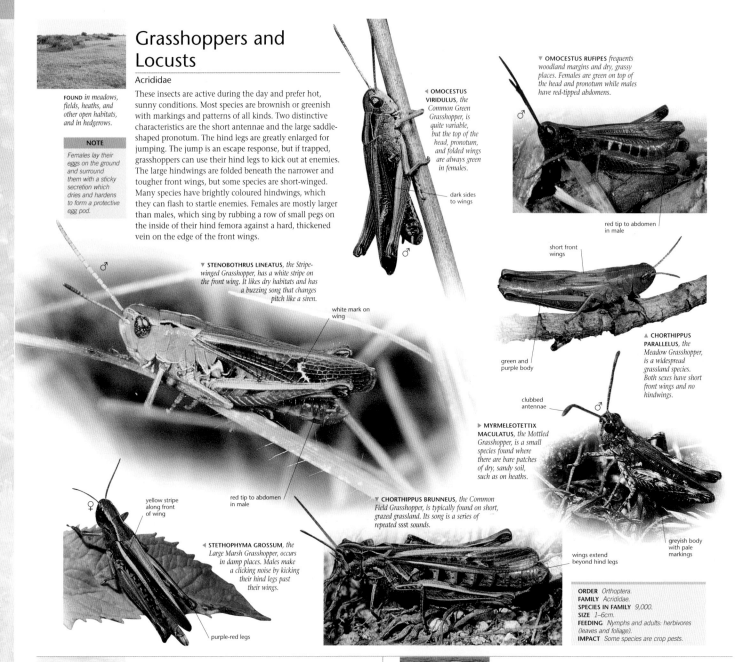

◄ **OMOCESTUS VIRIDULUS**, the Common Green Grasshopper, is quite variable, but the top of the head, pronotum, and folded wings are always green in females.

dark sides to wings

▼ **OMOCESTUS RUFIPES** frequents woodland margins and dry, grassy places. Females are green on top of the head and pronotum while males have red-tipped abdomens.

red tip to abdomen in male

short front wings

green and purple body

▲ **CHORTHIPPUS PARALLELUS**, the Meadow Grasshopper, is a widespread grassland species. Both sexes have short front wings and no hindwings.

clubbed antennae

▶ **MYRMELEOTETTIX MACULATUS**, the Mottled Grasshopper, is a small species found where there are bare patches of dry, sandy soil, such as on heaths.

▼ **STENOBOTHRUS LINEATUS**, the Stripe-winged Grasshopper, has a white stripe on the front wing. It likes dry habitats and has a buzzing song that changes pitch like a siren.

white mark on wing

yellow stripe along front of wing

red tip to abdomen in male

◄ **STETHOPHYMA GROSSUM**, the Large Marsh Grasshopper, occurs in damp places. Males make a clicking noise by kicking their hind legs past their wings.

purple-red legs

▼ **CHORTHIPPUS BRUNNEUS**, the Common Field Grasshopper, is typically found on short, grazed grassland. Its song is a series of repeated ssst sounds.

wings extend beyond hind legs

greyish body with pale markings

ORDER Orthoptera.
FAMILY Acrididae.
SPECIES IN FAMILY 9,000.
SIZE 1–6cm.
FEEDING Nymphs and adults: herbivores (leaves and foliage).
IMPACT Some species are crop pests.

Mole Crickets

Gryllotalpidae

It would be very hard to confuse these brownish insects with anything else. Resembling miniature moles, they spend most of their life underground. Their body is very robust, cylindrical, and covered with short, velvety hairs. The legs are short and strong and the front legs are broad with strong teeth for digging. The head is narrower than the thorax, with short antennae and small eyes.

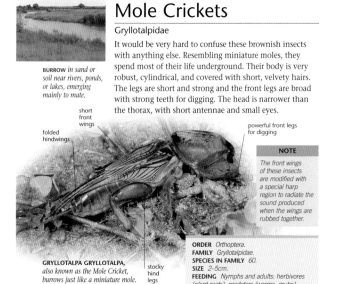

short front wings

folded hindwings

powerful front legs for digging

NOTE

The front wings of these insects are modified with a special harp region to radiate the sound produced when the wings are rubbed together.

GRYLLOTALPA GRYLLOTALPA, also known as the Mole Cricket, burrows just like a miniature mole. This insect is found especially where the soil is damp and sandy.

stocky hind legs

ORDER Orthoptera.
FAMILY Gryllotalpidae.
SPECIES IN FAMILY 60.
SIZE 2–5cm.
FEEDING Nymphs and adults: herbivores (plant roots), predators (worms, grubs).
IMPACT Some species can be crop pests.

Pygmy Locusts

Tetrigidae

These poorly known insects look like small grasshoppers, but the pronotum extends backwards over the whole of the abdomen and tapers to a point. Most species are drably coloured greyish or brownish to match mossy or stony ground. The front wings are reduced to small, scale-like structures or are absent, while the hindwings are fully developed. The males do not sing.

elongated pronotum

pale mottling on sides

TETRIX UNDULATA, the Common Groundhopper, varies in colour from pale brown to almost black. It is found in a variety of habitats.

NOTE

As these insects do not sing to attract mates and are cryptically coloured to blend in with their background, it is not surprising that they are overlooked.

ORDER Orthoptera.
FAMILY Tetrigidae.
SPECIES IN FAMILY 1,200.
SIZE 1–1.5cm.
FEEDING Nymphs and adults: scavengers, herbivores (decaying plants, algae, mosses).
IMPACT Harmless.

Little Earwigs

Labiidae

These small, secretive earwigs are light yellowish brown or dull dark brown in colour, with pale legs; many species are covered with shortish golden hairs. The antennae have 11 to 15 segments and the second tarsal segment of each leg is cylindrical, not expanded as in common earwigs (right). Most species of little earwigs are fully winged; some are good fliers and are attracted to lights at night.

dark head

reddish brown front wings ♀

short forceps

LABIA MINOR, the Lesser Earwig, at less than 7mm long, is the smallest earwig in Britain. It is commonly found in compost heaps and rotting vegetation.

ORDER Dermaptera.
FAMILY Labiidae.
SPECIES IN FAMILY 500.
SIZE Up to 1.2cm (most species).
FEEDING Nymphs and adults: scavengers.
IMPACT Harmless.

NOTE
The commonest Lesser Earwig, Labia minor, has been introduced to the USA from Europe. It is a good flier and is attracted to house lights after dark.

Common Earwigs

Forficulidae

These nocturnal insects are reddish brown to dark brown with paler legs and thread-like antennae. The front wings are small and toughened, covering the folded, fan-shaped hindwings. The second tarsal segment of each leg is expanded sideways. The body is flattened and the abdomen has a pair of forceps at the tip. Those of males are very curved and – as with all earwigs – used for courtship and defence; those of females are much straighter.

▶ FORFICULA AURICULARIA is a very common earwig. It is reddish brown in colour and the folded ends of the hindwings stick out from under the front wing.

pale margins to pronotum

reddish brown, flattened abdomen

teeth on inner edge of forceps

long, curved forceps

♂

thread-like antennae

NOTE
Common earwigs rarely fly, perhaps due to the difficulty of folding their hindwings, but more likely because their lifestyle does not require flight often.

ORDER Dermaptera.
FAMILY Forficulidae.
SPECIES IN FAMILY 470.
SIZE 1–1.5cm.
FEEDING Nymphs and adults: scavengers, predators, herbivores.
IMPACT Some species can be pests of crops.

Blattellid Cockroaches

Blattellidae

Most of these smallish cockroaches are light to dark brown in colour with yellowish or reddish markings on the pronotum and wings. Most species are fully winged and the wings, when folded, reach the end of the abdomen. In some species and the females of others, the wings are short. However, all species show a marked reluctance to fly. Females of *Blattella germanica* produce an average of five egg cases containing about 40 eggs each. Rather than sticking the egg cases to objects, the female carries them around, protruding from her body, until they hatch.

▶ ECTOBIUS PANZERI, small pale to dark brown, this cockroach lives in sandy coastal regions and is not a pest. Females have pale legs with dark markings.

egg case

black cerci

short, speckled wings ♀

▼ ECTOBIUS LAPPONICUS is known as the Dusky Cockroach. This species lives in a variety of habitats among leaf litter, sometimes moving up into bushes.

♀

reddish head

wings just shorter than abdomen

black cerci

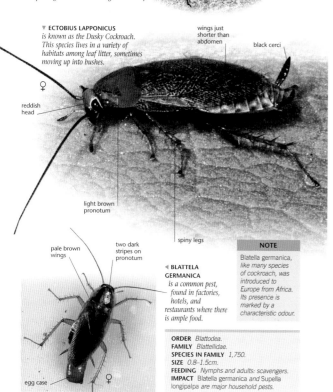

light brown pronotum

spiny legs

pale brown wings

two dark stripes on pronotum

◀ BLATTELA GERMANICA is a common pest, found in factories, hotels, and restaurants where there is ample food.

egg case

♀

NOTE
Blatella germanica, like many species of cockroach, was introduced to Europe from Africa. Its presence is marked by a characteristic odour.

ORDER Blattodea.
FAMILY Blattellidae.
SPECIES IN FAMILY 1,750.
SIZE 0.8–1.5cm.
FEEDING Nymphs and adults: scavengers.
IMPACT Blatella germanica and Supella longipalpa are major household pests.

Blattids

Blattidae

These cockroaches are broadly oval, with flattened bodies. In general, they are brown, reddish brown, or blackish brown in colour with darker or paler markings. Many species have a glossy or shiny appearance. The slender antennae are as long as the body and the underside of the middle and hind legs are spiny. Many species favour places such as houses, restaurants, bakeries, warehouses, sewers, and rubbish dumps; some species are common around ports and on ships.

NOTE
By day these insects hide in cracks and crevices, behind skirting boards, and under floors. They are very active and fast-running but fly only if very warm.

yellow "ring" around pronotum

pale marks on sides of elytra

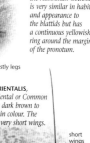

▲ PERIPLANETA AUSTRALASIAE, the Australian Cockroach, is very similar in habits and appearance to the blattids but has a continuous yellowish ring around the margin of the pronotum.

▼ PERIPLANETA AMERICANA is found on ships and in food warehouses; females glue their egg cases to hidden surfaces.

pronotum hides head

yellow patches at rear of pronotum

bristly legs

flattened body

♀

egg case

▼ BLATTA ORIENTALIS, known as Oriental or Common Cockroach, is dark brown to almost black in colour. The females have very short wings.

short wings

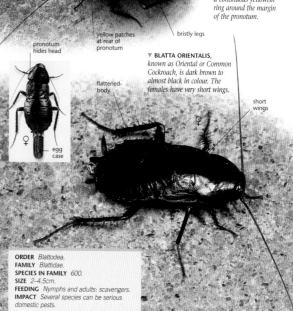

ORDER Blattodea.
FAMILY Blattidae.
SPECIES IN FAMILY 600.
SIZE 2–4.5cm.
FEEDING Nymphs and adults: scavengers.
IMPACT Several species can be serious domestic pests.

Booklice

Liposcelidae

These small, light to yellowish brown insects have squat, slightly flattened bodies and are quite difficult to see. The hind legs are larger than the first two pairs and the hind femora are very enlarged, allowing the insects to make small jumps. The tarsi have three segments. The head, which is large in comparison to the rest of the body and appears to bulge at the front, carries a pair of small compound eyes, chewing mouthparts, and shortish, thread-like antennae. Most species are wingless; when present, the wings have rounded ends.

INFEST *houses and collections of stored plants and insects; also found in scrub and woods under bark and among leaf litter.*

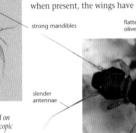

▲ LIPOSCELIS SP. *are prepared and mounted on glass slides for microscopic examination due to their small size and similarity.*

strong mandibles

flattened, yellowish olive body

slender antennae

stout hind legs

pale antennae

NOTE

Some species are pests of stored food that has become damp, including pasta, cereals, and flour. Outbreaks occur due to high humidity levels.

▲ LIPOSCELIS TERRICOLIS *is a widespread domestic pest that eats a wide range of damp or starchy foodstuffs and gnaws damp papers and books.*

▼ LIPOSCELIS LIPARUS *is a common pest species in libraries and archives where conditions are dark and damp.*

small, dark eyes

swollen front to head

narrow prothorax

ORDER *Psocoptera.*
FAMILY *Liposcelidae.*
SPECIES IN FAMILY *150.*
SIZE *0.5–1.5mm.*
FEEDING *Nymphs and adults: scavengers, fungi-feeders.*
IMPACT *May be pests of stored produce.*

Bird Lice

Menoponidae

These small, wingless ectoparasites are pale brown in colour. The head is triangular and expanded behind the eyes. It has biting mandibles and short, slightly clubbed antennae that can be concealed in grooves on the underside of the head. The abdomen is oval and the legs are short and stout, each with claws for gripping their host's feathers. All species feed on skin and feather fragments, supplemented with blood.

OCCUR *only on the plumage and skin of a variety of birds.*

broad head

stout legs

two claws on each leg

pale body hairs

oval abdomen

NOTE

Bird lice attach their eggs singly to their host's feathers with a water-insoluble glue-like substance. Most have specific hosts; some attack several bird species.

ORDER *Phthiraptera.*
FAMILY *Menoponidae.*
SPECIES IN FAMILY *650.*
SIZE *1–6mm.*
FEEDING *Nymphs and adults: parasites (skin, feathers, blood).*
IMPACT *Some species are pests of poultry.*

MENACANTHUS STRAMINEUS, *the Chicken Body Louse, infests poultry, often leading to feather loss and infections.*

Bird-chewing Lice

Philopteridae

These pale, yellowish brown lice have a relatively large head with prominent mandibles. The antennae have five segments. The thorax is short with the middle and hind thorax segments fused together. The legs are short and similarly sized, and each has a pair of claws. The abdomen is slightly flattened and may be pear-shaped in species that live on the short feathers of birds' heads and necks; species found on the wing feathers are more elongated.

REMAIN *permanently on their bird hosts and are never free-living.*

NOTE

These insects are difficult to observe in the wild. One way to see them is to examine the wings of freshly dead birds under a hand lens.

COLUMBICOLA CLAVIFORMIS, *the Pigeon Louse, is found on feathers, often in small groups, and usually aligned with the direction of the feather barbs.*

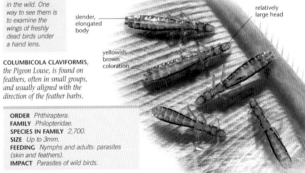

relatively large head

slender, elongated body

yellowish brown coloration

ORDER *Phthiraptera.*
FAMILY *Philopteridae.*
SPECIES IN FAMILY *2,700.*
SIZE *Up to 3mm.*
FEEDING *Nymphs and adults: parasites (skin and feathers).*
IMPACT *Parasites of wild birds.*

Common Barklice

Psocidae

Most common barklice have dull brown, grey, or blackish coloration and many have pale markings. The antennae have 13 segments. The wings, which are hairless, may be mottled with brown or have rows of smoky spots or irregular patches. The thorax is humped in side view and often shiny. These insects may occur in "herds" of many hundreds or even thousands.

INHABIT *the bark, twigs, and branches of various trees and shrubs, and on the foliage of conifers.*

PSOCOCERASTIS GIBBOSA *lives on a number of trees and is the largest member of its genus in Britain.*

transparent wings with dark veins

large, bulging eyes

NOTE

Some species have specialized feeding preferences; for example, eating only a few species of lichen. Others scavenge all types of organic detritus.

ORDER *Psocoptera.*
FAMILY *Psocidae.*
SPECIES IN FAMILY *500.*
SIZE *1–6mm.*
FEEDING *Nymphs and adults: scavengers, fungi-feeders, herbivores (pollen, algae).*
IMPACT *Harmless.*

Mammal-chewing Lice

Trichodectidae

Generally pale brown in colour, these lice have large, squarish heads with distinctive mandibles. The antennae are conspicuous, short, and have three segments. The legs are short, each with a single tarsal claw. Females have oval, blunt-ended abdomens, while those of males are more pointed towards the rear and carry prominent genitalia.

FOUND *on mammalian hosts in a variety of habitats, including fields and farms.*

shortish legs

short antennae

jaws

oval abdomen

squarish head

NOTE

Some species are pests of domestic animals. They can cause severe irritation and loss of hair and fur by inducing prolonged scratching.

ORDER *Phthiraptera.*
FAMILY *Trichodectidae.*
SPECIES IN FAMILY *360.*
SIZE *1–3mm.*
FEEDING *Nymphs and adults: parasites (skin, hair, secretions, blood).*
IMPACT *Infest wild and domestic animals.*

TRICHODECTES CANIS *feeds on bits of skin and fur. The louse looks blue here as it has been stained and mounted on a glass slide to enable detailed examination.*

Human Lice

Pediculidae

These lice are small and pale with narrow heads and pear-shaped, flattened bodies. The mouthparts are modified for piercing and sucking. The legs are short, strong, and inwardly curved. Each has a large claw for grasping and climbing through hair. Human head and body lice appear to differ only in the area of the body they occupy.

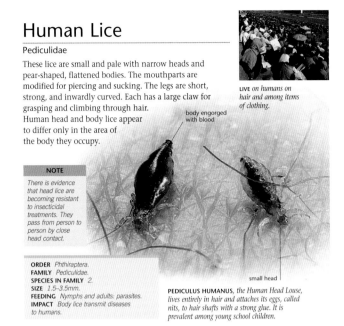

LIVE on humans on hair and among items of clothing.

body engorged with blood

NOTE

There is evidence that head lice are becoming resistant to insecticidal treatments. They pass from person to person by close head contact.

small head

PEDICULUS HUMANUS, the Human Head Louse, lives entirely in hair and attaches its eggs, called nits, to hair shafts with a strong glue. It is prevalent among young school children.

ORDER Phthiraptera.
FAMILY Pediculidae.
SPECIES IN FAMILY 2.
SIZE 1.5–3.5mm.
FEEDING Nymphs and adults: parasites.
IMPACT Body lice transmit diseases to humans.

Acanthosomatids

Acanthosomatidae

Typically greenish or reddish brown with dark markings, acanthosomatids have broad bodies that taper slightly to the rear, behind the broad pronotum. The relatively small head has antennae with five segments, and can appear sunk into the front margin of the pronotum. The scutellum is large and triangular. The tarsi have two segments.

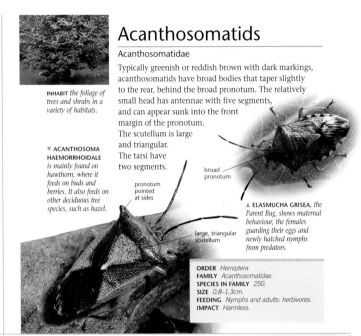

INHABIT the foliage of trees and shrubs in a variety of habitats.

▼ ACANTHOSOMA HAEMORRHOIDALE is mainly found on hawthorn, where it feeds on buds and berries. It also feeds on other deciduous tree species, such as hazel.

pronotum pointed at sides

broad pronotum

▲ ELASMUCHA GRISEA, the Parent Bug, shows maternal behaviour, the females guarding their eggs and newly hatched nymphs from predators.

large, triangular scutellum

ORDER Hemiptera.
FAMILY Acanthosomatidae.
SPECIES IN FAMILY 250.
SIZE 0.8–1.3cm.
FEEDING Nymphs and adults: herbivores.
IMPACT Harmless.

Pubic Lice

Pthiridae

Also called the Crab Louse, this pale to translucent louse has a squat, flat body and a head that is much narrower than the thorax. The middle and hind legs are especially stout with strong curved claws for gripping pubic hair shafts. The family includes the Human Pubic Louse, Pthirus pubis, and the Gorilla Pubic Louse, P. gorillae.

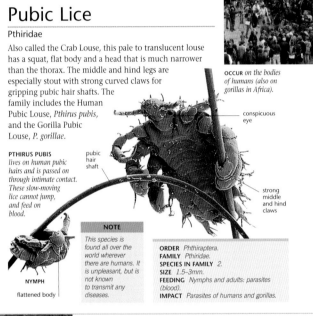

OCCUR on the bodies of humans (also on gorillas in Africa).

PTHIRUS PUBIS lives on human pubic hairs and is passed on through intimate contact. These slow-moving lice cannot jump, and feed on blood.

conspicuous eye

pubic hair shaft

strong middle and hind claws

NYMPH

flattened body

NOTE

This species is found all over the world wherever there are humans. It is unpleasant, but is not known to transmit any diseases.

ORDER Phthiraptera.
FAMILY Pthiridae.
SPECIES IN FAMILY 2.
SIZE 1.5–3mm.
FEEDING Nymphs and adults: parasites (blood).
IMPACT Parasites of humans and gorillas.

Burrowing Bugs

Cydnidae

These small bugs are broadly oval and slightly convex in shape. They are generally shiny black or dark reddish brown, often with blue tinges and white markings. The head can appear sunk into the pronotum. The antennae have five segments. The front tibiae are flattened, and the tibia of all legs are distinctively spiny.

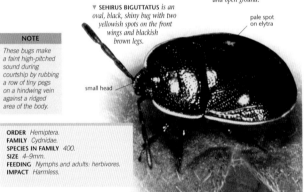

FOUND on foliage or among roots near the base of susceptible host plants, mainly in woodland, hedgerows, and open ground.

▼ SEHIRUS BIGUTTATUS is an oval, black, shiny bug with two yellowish spots on the front wings and blackish brown legs.

pale spot on elytra

NOTE

These bugs make a faint high-pitched sound during courtship by rubbing a row of tiny pegs on a hindwing vein against a ridged area of the body.

small head

ORDER Hemiptera.
FAMILY Cydnidae.
SPECIES IN FAMILY 400.
SIZE 4–9mm.
FEEDING Nymphs and adults: herbivores.
IMPACT Harmless.

Bark Bugs

Aradidae

Also known as flat bugs, these insects have a very flat, oval shape and are reddish brown or dark in colour. The surface of the body looks roughened due to the presence of many small dimples and bumps. The distinctive head narrows behind the eyes; it has short, stout antennae with four segments and a very short rostrum, also with four segments. Bark bugs have short legs and many species are wingless.

FOUND in woodland under bark, in fungi, and in leaf litter.

stout antennae

dimpled surface

flattened body

ARADUS DEPRESSUS feeds on fungal threads and fruiting bodies. It lives under the bark of birch, oak, beech, and some other deciduous trees.

NOTE

Most bark bugs live on trees, but some live in leaf litter on forest floors. One species is found on old Scots Pine trees, where it feeds on sap.

ORDER Hemiptera.
FAMILY Aradidae.
SPECIES IN FAMILY 1,800.
SIZE 3–6mm.
FEEDING Nymphs and adults: scavengers, fungi-feeders.
IMPACT Harmless.

Scutellerids

Scutelleridae

These rounded, almost beetle-like bugs are convex in side view and are yellowish to black with pale to dark brown markings. They are similar to shield bugs, but have a much larger scutellum that covers the abdomen and completely covers the membranous wings. The head is triangular or broad, and the antennae have five segments. All scutellerids are plant suckers. Some have attained pest status by the damage they cause to grain crops, and cotton in particular.

LIVE in damp, marshy habitats and coastal areas; some on arable farmland.

very large, parallel-sided scutellum

triangular head

NOTE

When the European Tortoise Bug takes off, the wings are folded out from under the large, shield-like scutellum, from which it gets its common name.

EURYGASTER MAURA, the European Tortoise Bug, is a generalist feeder on many grasses and sometimes attacks cereal crops. It is not as serious a pest as some other scutellerids.

ORDER Hemiptera.
FAMILY Scutelleridae.
SPECIES IN FAMILY 400.
SIZE 5–12mm.
FEEDING Nymphs and adults: herbivores.
IMPACT A few species can be pests; Eurygaster maura damages cereal crops.

INVERTEBRATES

Stink Bugs

Pentatomidae

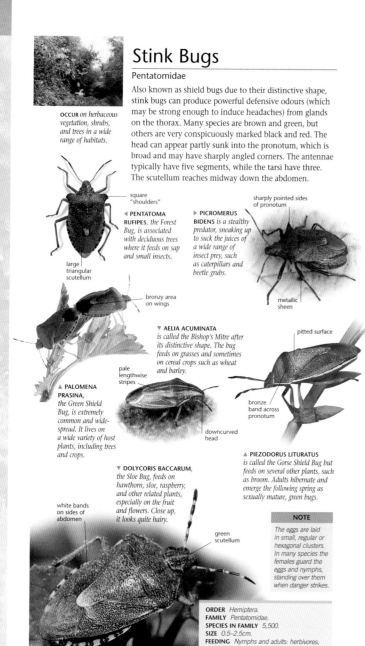

OCCUR on herbaceous vegetation, shrubs, and trees in a wide range of habitats.

Also known as shield bugs due to their distinctive shape, stink bugs can produce powerful defensive odours (which may be strong enough to induce headaches) from glands on the thorax. Many species are brown and green, but others are very conspicuously marked black and red. The head can appear partly sunk into the pronotum, which is broad and may have sharply angled corners. The antennae typically have five segments, while the tarsi have three. The scutellum reaches midway down the abdomen.

square "shoulders"

◄ PENTATOMA RUFIPES, the Forest Bug, is associated with deciduous trees where it feeds on sap and small insects.

large triangular scutellum

► PICROMERUS BIDENS is a stealthy predator, sneaking up to suck the juices of a wide range of insect prey, such as caterpillars and beetle grubs.

sharply pointed sides of pronotum

metallic sheen

bronzy area on wings

▼ AELIA ACUMINATA is called the Bishop's Mitre after its distinctive shape. The bug feeds on grasses and sometimes on cereal crops such as wheat and barley.

pitted surface

pale lengthwise stripes

downcurved head

◄ PALOMENA PRASINA, the Green Shield Bug, is extremely common and wide-spread. It lives on a wide variety of host plants, including trees and crops.

bronze band across pronotum

▲ PIEZODORUS LITURATUS is called the Gorse Shield Bug but feeds on several other plants, such as broom. Adults hibernate and emerge the following spring as sexually mature, green bugs.

▼ DOLYCORIS BACCARUM, the Sloe Bug, feeds on hawthorn, sloe, raspberry, and other related plants, especially on the fruit and flowers. Close up, it looks quite hairy.

white bands on sides of abdomen

green scutellum

NOTE

The eggs are laid in small, regular or hexagonal clusters. In many species the females guard the eggs and nymphs, standing over them when danger strikes.

ORDER Hemiptera.
FAMILY Pentatomidae.
SPECIES IN FAMILY 5,500.
SIZE 0.5–2.5cm.
FEEDING Nymphs and adults: herbivores, predators.
IMPACT Some species are crop pests.

Squash Bugs

Coreidae

DISTRIBUTED wherever their host plants grow, especially in grassland, heathland, and light woodland.

Squash bugs are so named because some species feed on squash plants. Most are roughly oval in shape and dull brown. In some species, the abdomen is flattened, projects sideways, and may be lobed and angular. The head is very much narrower and shorter than the pronotum. The antennae have four segments. The hind part of the front wings has a distinctive pattern of parallel veins. All squash bugs are herbivorous as adults and nymphs, eating shoots, buds, fruits, and unripe seeds of their food plants.

white tubercles

NOTE

When threatened, some large species of squash bug produce unpleasant or fruity-smelling secretions from special glands in the thorax.

▼ SYROMASTUS RHOMBEUS inhabits dry, sandy places. The lack of wings and presence of dorsal gland openings show that this specimen is a nymph.

► CORIOMERIS DENTICULATUS is a relatively slender squash bug with many short spines. It feeds on leguminous plants on well-drained soils.

scent gland opening

NYMPH

thickened antennae

distinctive veins on wing membrane

broad abdomen

pronotum broad at front

centre of antenna is orange

forward-pointing spines

◄ COREUS MARGINATUS has a noticeably broad abdomen. Nymphs feed on dock plants; adults feast on fruit prior to hibernating.

ORDER Hemiptera.
FAMILY Coreidae.
SPECIES IN FAMILY 2,000.
SIZE 1–1.8cm.
FEEDING Nymphs and adults: herbivores.
IMPACT Mainly harmless, although a few species are pests of crops and vegetables.

Scentless Plant Bugs

Rhopalidae

These pale, light brown or greenish bugs are similar to squash bugs (right). The head is quite broad but narrower than the hind margin of the pronotum, and the antennae have four segments. The body can be covered with punctures or tiny pits and may be quite hairy.

USUALLY found among weeds and rough vegetation in old fields, by roadsides, and in other disturbed areas.

▼ RHOPALUS SUBRUFUS browses on low-growing plants in light woodland, rides, and clearings. It has distinctive bulging eyes.

► MYRMUS MIRIFORMIS feeds on grasses, especially the unripe seeds. Males may be green or brown.

short wings

bulging eyes

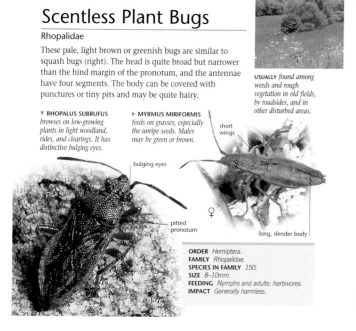

pitted pronotum

♀

long, slender body

ORDER Hemiptera.
FAMILY Rhopalidae.
SPECIES IN FAMILY 150.
SIZE 8–10mm.
FEEDING Nymphs and adults: herbivores.
IMPACT Generally harmless.

Assassin Bugs

Reduviidae

Most of these bugs are yellowish brown, grey, or blackish, but some are reddish orange. The body shape varies from robust and oval to very elongated and slender with thread-like legs. The head has a transverse groove between the eyes and the antennae; the latter are often bent after the long, first segment, have four main segments, and many subsegments. The rostrum has three segments and is distinctively short and curved. The front legs are often enlarged.

OCCUR on vegetation of all kinds and sometimes in houses where their prey is present.

▼ EMPICORIS VAGABUNDUS, a small thread-legged assassin bug, lives mainly in trees where it preys on small soft-bodied insects.

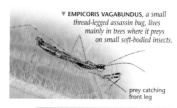

prey catching front leg

brownish body

▲ REDUVIUS PERSONATUS, the Masked Hunter, is named for the nymphs, which cover themselves with dust and debris as camouflage.

NYMPH

ORDER Hemiptera.
FAMILY Reduviidae.
SPECIES IN FAMILY 6,000.
SIZE 0.6–1.6cm.
FEEDING Nymphs and adults: predators.
IMPACT If handled roughly, larger species may bite, piercing human skin.

Seed Bugs

Lygaeidae

FOUND *close to the ground in leaf litter, under stones, or among low-growing vegetation.*

Also known as ground bugs, these bugs are dull-coloured, being mainly pale yellow, brown, or black, although a few species are bright red and black. The body is quite tough and flattened and is either elongate or oval. The head is typically triangular but can be very broad in some species. The antennae arise from well down the sides of the head, below the prominent eyes. Many of the ground-living species may be short-winged or wingless. The femora of the front legs may be swollen, with stout spines. As their name suggests, seed bugs are mostly seed-feeders, using the strong, toothed or spined front legs to grasp their food.

NOTE

Sound production by stridulation plays an important part in the mating of some species. Males may use lengthy matings to ensure paternity of the offspring.

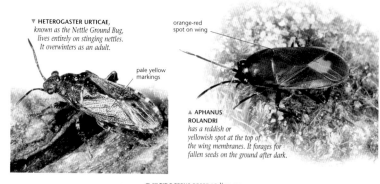

▼ **HETEROGASTER URTICAE,** *known as the Nettle Ground Bug, lives entirely on stinging nettles. It overwinters as an adult.*

pale yellow markings

orange-red spot on wing

▲ **APHANUS ROLANDRI** *has a reddish or yellowish spot at the top of the wing membranes. It forages for fallen seeds on the ground after dark.*

▼ **KLEIDOCERYS RESEDAE** *lives on birch, alder, and some other trees. Both sexes make characteristic calls before mating commences.*

unusually clear, transparent wings

▼ **ISCHNODEMA SABULETI,** *the European Chinch Bug, occurs in long- and short-winged forms. It feeds on grasses and reeds.*

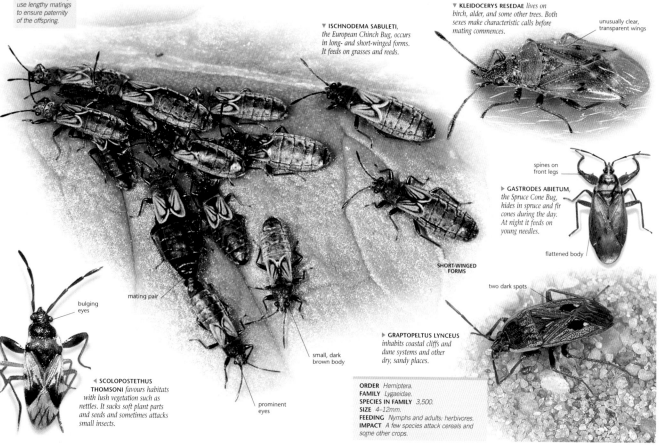

mating pair

small, dark brown body

prominent eyes

bulging eyes

◄ **SCOLOPOSTETHUS THOMSONI** *favours habitats with lush vegetation such as nettles. It sucks soft plant parts and seeds and sometimes attacks small insects.*

spines on front legs

▶ **GASTRODES ABIETUM,** *the Spruce Cone Bug, hides in spruce and fir cones during the day. At night it feeds on young needles.*

flattened body

SHORT-WINGED FORMS

two dark spots

▶ **GRAPTOPELTUS LYNCEUS** *inhabits coastal cliffs and dune systems and other dry, sandy places.*

ORDER *Hemiptera.*
FAMILY *Lygaeidae.*
SPECIES IN FAMILY *3,500.*
SIZE *4–12mm.*
FEEDING *Nymphs and adults: herbivores.*
IMPACT *A few species attack cereals and some other crops.*

Flower Bugs

Anthocoridae

Also known as minute pirate bugs, these tiny, flattened insects are blackish or brownish in colour, with paler markings. The body may be elongated or oval and shiny or dull. The head is pointed, the antennae have four segments, and the rostrum has three segments. Most species are fully winged; the rear part of the front wings has no closed cells and few or no veins.

OCCUR *on flowers, as the name suggests, but often in leaf litter, foliage, and fungi or under bark in woods.*

NOTE

These bugs feed on tiny insects, eggs, and larvae. A few species may be found in bird nests, bat caves, mammal burrows, grain stores, and houses.

pale wing pads

antennae have four segments

sharp rostrum

NYMPH

▲ **ANTHOCORIS NEMORUM,** *the Common Flower Bug, has fiercely predatory, reddish brown nymphs (here, on human skin).*

shiny black head

black pronotum

◄ **ANTHOCORIS NEMORUM** *lives on lush vegetation and trees throughout Britain, especially on nettles. The adults hunt aphids and soft insect prey.*

ORDER *Hemiptera.*
FAMILY *Anthocoridae.*
SPECIES IN FAMILY *500.*
SIZE *2–5mm.*
FEEDING *Nymphs and adults: predators.*
IMPACT *If handled roughly, some species, such as Anthocoris nemorum, will try to bite.*

Damsel Bugs

Nabidae

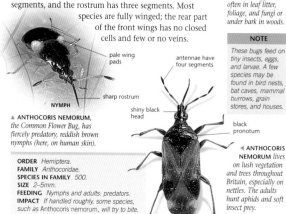

LIVE *on the ground or among vegetation, wherever small insect prey is plentiful.*

Damsel bugs are usually dull brown or straw-coloured with a variety of markings, but a few are black and red. The head is elongated and the antennae has four or five segments; the rostrum has four segments. The front femora are thickened and armed with short spines.

dark central stripe

curved rostrum

ant-like body outline

▶ **NABIS RUGOSUS** *is a widespread and common bug of all manner of grassy habitats. It feeds on soft-bodied prey.*

NYMPH

▲ **HIMACERUS MIRMICOIDES** *is named the Ant Damsel Bug after the shape of its nymphs. This species is a ground-active predator.*

broad abdomen

slender antennae

short wings

rostrum

▲ **HIMACERUS APTERUS,** *the Tree Damsel Bug, lives in a range of deciduous trees, where it feeds on small insects such as aphids.*

NOTE

Damsel bugs suck the juices of aphids, caterpillars, and a range of soft-bodied insects. Nymphs seek their first, very small meal straight after hatching.

ORDER *Hemiptera.*
FAMILY *Nabidae.*
SPECIES IN FAMILY *400.*
SIZE *3–11mm.*
FEEDING *Nymphs and adults: predators.*
IMPACT *Larger species can deliver a painful bite that may pierce human skin.*

INVERTEBRATES

Stilt Bugs

Berytidae

These pale, reddish or yellowish brown to grey bugs have elongated, slender bodies, and are named for their long, thin, spindly legs and the way in which they appear to "stilt-walk" with their bodies held high. The first of the four antennal segments is long, while the last segment is short and swollen at the tip. The rostrum has four segments. They are generally slow-moving, often "freezing" when disturbed.

FOUND *among weeds and tall grass in meadows and woods, and around the margins of ponds.*

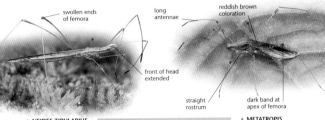

swollen ends of femora

long antennae

reddish brown coloration

front of head extended

straight rostrum

dark band at apex of femora

▲ **NEIDES TIPULARIUS** *is found in heathland and dry, weedy fields where it feeds on a variety of plants. Adults find dry places to overwinter and emerge in spring.*

ORDER *Hemiptera.*
FAMILY *Berytidae.*
SPECIES IN FAMILY *180.*
SIZE *6–10mm.*
FEEDING *Nymphs and adults: herbivores, predators.*
IMPACT *Harmless.*

▲ **METATROPIS RUFESCENS** *may be confused with the thread-legged Empicoris (p.248) but the front legs are not modified for prey capture and the rostrum is not short and curved.*

Bed Bugs

Cimicidae

Unlike lice, these blood-sucking bugs do not keep in permanent contact with their hosts. They are oval and flattened in shape, with vestigial (very reduced) front wings and no hindwings. Generally orange or reddish brown in colour, they have a sparse covering of pale hairs. The head is not very large and carries the sharp rostrum, or beak, which lies in a groove along the underside of the body when not in use. The antennae have four segments.

FEED *on their mammal and bird hosts at night; during the day, they hide in crevices, in and under wallpaper and skirting floorboards.*

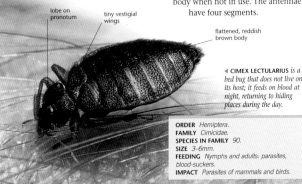

lobe on pronotum

tiny vestigial wings

flattened, reddish brown body

◄ **CIMEX LECTULARIUS** *is a bed bug that does not live on its host; it feeds on blood at night, returning to hiding places during the day.*

ORDER *Hemiptera.*
FAMILY *Cimicidae.*
SPECIES IN FAMILY *90.*
SIZE *3–6mm.*
FEEDING *Nymphs and adults: parasites, blood-suckers.*
IMPACT *Parasites of mammals and birds.*

Plant Bugs

Miridae

LIVE *in almost every habitat from ground level to the treetops.*

This family is the largest group of true bugs in the world. Plant bugs have a delicate structure and are variously coloured green, brown, red, and black, with a great diversity of markings. The rostrum and the antennae have four segments and the hind part of the front wings, or membrane, has one or two distinctive closed cells. Most species are fully winged, although short-winged and wingless forms occur. Diverse in their biology, plant bugs are mostly herbivores, eating seeds, fruits, leaves, and plant juices. Others are scavengers or are predators of aphids, mealy bugs, mites, and soft-bodied prey.

mainly green

brown membrane

◄ **LYGOCORIS PABULINUS,** *the Common Green Plant Bug, is a serious pest of a wide range of plants, including fruits such as raspberries, pears, and apples.*

orange-yellow patch on scutellum

◄ **CAMPLYONEURA VIRGULA** *is a tree-living predator that hunts bark lice, aphids, and other soft-bodied prey. Despite its fragile appearance, it can bite if handled.*

shiny red upperside

▶ **HETEROTOMA MERIOPTERA** *is recognizable by its antennae, the first two segments of which are swollen. It lives among nettles and other rank vegetation.*

swollen and hairy segments

pale green legs

▲ **PANTILIUS TUNICATUS** *feeds on hazel, birch, and alder trees. Adults are yellowish green when they first appear, becoming reddish and darker as they get older.*

pink veins

▼ **NOTOSTIRA ELONGATA** *is a common grass bug, found on rough, grassy verges. Females are green with a swollen abdomen; males are darker and more slender.*

swollen abdomen

slender body

♀

◄ **STENODEMA LAEVIGATUM** *has a slender, elongated body and can be found on a variety of grasses, where the nymphs and adults feed on the flower-heads and unripe seeds.*

ORDER *Hemiptera.*
FAMILY *Miridae.*
SPECIES IN FAMILY *7,000.*
SIZE *2–12mm.*
FEEDING *Nymphs and adults: herbivores, predators, scavengers.*
IMPACT *Several species attack crops.*

◄ **MIRIS STRIATUS** *is a relatively large and well-marked bug. It lives on a variety of trees such as oak, hazel, and elm, feeding on soft-bodied insects.*

striped wing

♂

▶ **LEPTOPTERNA DOLABRATA,** *the Meadow Plant Bug, is abundant in damp, grassy places. The males are fully winged, while females are short-winged.*

banded pronotum

pinkish bands

pale markings on wings

▲ **LIOCORIS TRIPUSTULATUS** *can often be found in large numbers on nettles where the adults and nymphs feed on nettle buds and flowers.*

▶ **CALOCORIS ROSEOMACULATUS** *is well named for its rose-coloured markings. It feeds on the fruit and flowers of a wide range of plants.*

white stripes across wings

ant-like head

▼ **DERAEOCORIS OLIVACEUS** *is a large bug with red leg banding and front wing patches. Mainly predatory, it also feeds on hawthorn berries.*

banded tibia

▲ **PILOPHORUS PERPLEXUS** *is very ant-like at first glance. It lives on oaks and other deciduous trees and feeds on aphids, insect eggs, and young moth caterpillars.*

shiny black thorax

red head

NOTE

The eggs of plant bugs are laid inside plant tissues and normally overwinter before hatching in spring. In some species, the adult or nymph hibernates.

Water Measurers

Hydrometridae

Also called marsh-treaders, these delicate, reddish to dark brown bugs are very slender, with thread-like legs. The eyes are fairly large and bulge out from the sides of the elongated head. The antennae and rostrum have four segments. Most species are wingless, but short-winged or fully-winged forms occur in some species. Water measurers are slow-moving and take small prey.

FOUND *in quiet pools, marshes, and swamps, including stagnant and brackish water. Stay at the water's edge or on floating plants.*

very slender body

elongated head

thread-like legs

ORDER *Hemiptera.*
FAMILY *Hydrometridae.*
SPECIES IN FAMILY *120.*
SIZE *8–12mm.*
FEEDING *Nymphs and adults: predators (mainly small aquatic insects).*
IMPACT *Harmless.*

HYDROMETRA STAGNORUM *is very slow-moving and feeds on small insects and crustaceans such as water fleas.*

Water Crickets

Veliidae

These bugs are also called small water striders and resemble pond skaters (left), but are generally much smaller, more robust, and have shorter, stouter legs. Most are brownish with orange undersides and orange or silver markings. The antennae and rostrum have four segments. Some species are fully winged; others can be short-winged or wingless.

LIVE *among vegetation or on the surface of still or slow-moving water in ponds, lakes, and damp forests.*

parallel-sided abdomen

wings held flat over body

◀ **VELIA CAPRAI,** *the Water Cricket, can be found on the surface of ponds or slow streams. It detects ripples that are made by drowning insects.*

wings absent

pale bases to legs

▲ **MICROVELIA RETICULATA,** *the Minute Water Cricket, less than 2mm long, lives among the aquatic plants growing at the margins of ponds and lakes.*

white spots on pronotum

ORDER *Hemiptera.*
FAMILY *Veliidae.*
SPECIES IN FAMILY *500.*
SIZE *2–8mm.*
FEEDING *Nymphs and adults: predators (small floating organisms, eggs, larvae).*
IMPACT *Harmless.*

Pond Skaters

Gerridae

Also known as water striders, these fast-moving and often wingless bugs are adapted to living on the surface of water. They are dark brown or blackish, with a covering of velvety hairs. The antennae and rostrum have four segments. The front legs are short for grasping prey, while the middle and hind legs are more elongated. Ripple-sensitive hairs on the legs locate struggling prey.

WALK *on the surface film of any available freshwater, including ditches and ponds, even water troughs.*

splayed legs

bulging eyes

▼ **GERRIS LACUSTRIS,** *the Common Pondskater, is found in almost any sort of water body. It is easily recognizable as it darts about on the surface film.*

◀ **AQUARIUS NAJAS,** *a greyish black bug, is usually wingless and is found near the banks of rivers and large streams.*

short front legs

ORDER *Hemiptera.*
FAMILY *Gerridae.*
SPECIES IN FAMILY *500.*
SIZE *0.8–1.8cm.*
FEEDING *Nymphs and adults: predators (dead or dying insects).*
IMPACT *Harmless.*

Water Scorpions

Nepidae

These brownish bugs are also known as water stick insects due to their shape. They may be oval, flattened with short legs, or cylindrical and elongated with relatively long legs. The head has rounded eyes and a short, curved rostrum. The front legs are modified for catching prey. There is a distinctive breathing siphon at the rear that may be as long as the body.

OCCURS *in either still or slow-moving water, with some species in muddy shallows and others in deeper water.*

breathing siphon

enlarged femur

▼ **RANATRA LINEARIS,** *the yellowish brown Water Stick Insect, is a predator and attacks even small vertebrates.*

wings folded over broad body

narrow body

▲ **NEPA CINEREA,** *or the Water Scorpion, has a long breathing siphon at its rear end. It also has powerful front legs.*

front legs gripping prey

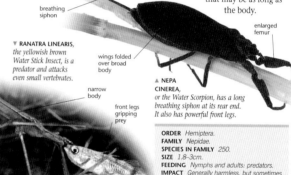

ORDER *Hemiptera.*
FAMILY *Nepidae.*
SPECIES IN FAMILY *250.*
SIZE *1.8–3cm.*
FEEDING *Nymphs and adults: predators.*
IMPACT *Generally harmless, but sometimes bite if handled.*

Saucer Bugs

Naucoridae

Also known as creeping water bugs, these flat, streamlined insects have a smooth, rounded or oval body. Most species are dark greyish green or brown. The front legs are adapted for capturing prey, with curved, sickle-like tibiae that fold back like a jack-knife on to the enlarged femora. The hind legs have rows of specialized swimming hairs.

MOVE *slowly on the bottom of static or moving water bodies, or climb about on submerged vegetation.*

head appears sunk into prothorax

NOTE

Saucer bugs lack a breathing siphon: supplies of oxygen are obtained at the water surface and retained in the space under the wings.

broad, flat body

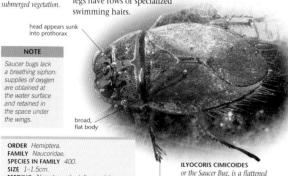

hairs on legs

ORDER *Hemiptera.*
FAMILY *Naucoridae.*
SPECIES IN FAMILY *400.*
SIZE *1–1.5cm.*
FEEDING *Nymphs and adults: predators (mainly larvae, crustaceans, snails).*
IMPACT *Occasionally bite if handled.*

ILYOCORIS CIMICOIDES *or the Saucer Bug, is a flattened greyish green insect that has wings, but cannot fly. Instead, it uses the space beneath the wings to store air.*

Backswimmers

Notonectidae

These compact, wedge-shaped bugs swim upside-down in water, and when resting at the surface they hang from the end of their abdomen. The surface of their back is typically pale-coloured and convex, with a ridge or keel running down the middle. Their underside is dark brown to black. The stout rostrum and the very short antennae have four segments. Used for propulsion, the oar-like hind legs are fringed with hairs.

FAVOUR *still, open stretches of water such as lake margins, pools, and stream edges.*

hair fringes

oar-like hind leg

▼ **NOTONECTA MACULATA** *is found in the northern hemisphere and feeds on prey trapped by the surface film in temporary habitats.*

mottled reddish wings

pale upper surface

▲ **NOTONECTA GLAUCA,** *the Common Backswimmer, is widespread and can be found in ponds, lakes, and even canals or ditches.*

pale pronotum

dark, shiny eyes

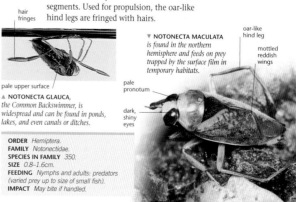

ORDER *Hemiptera.*
FAMILY *Notonectidae.*
SPECIES IN FAMILY *350.*
SIZE *0.8–1.6cm.*
FEEDING *Nymphs and adults: predators (varied prey up to size of small fish).*
IMPACT *May bite if handled.*

INVERTEBRATES

Water Boatmen

Corixidae

FOUND *in still and slow-moving water in ponds, lakes, and occasionally streams.*

Superficially similar to backswimmers (p.251), these streamlined bugs are generally dark reddish- or yellowish brown, often with fine transverse markings. The upper body surface is flattened without a central keel and the under body is pale. Corixids do not swim upside-down. The short head has large dark eyes, short antennae, and a short, stout rostrum. The front legs have scoop-shaped ends for feeding; the middle legs are used for holding plants; and the clawless back legs are fringed with hairs.

NOTE

While underwater, corixids carry bubbles of air under their wings where the concave, dorsal surface of the abdomen acts as a reservoir.

▼ CORIXA PUNCTATA *is common and has a wide distribution. Typically, the back is patterned and dark, while the underside is pale. This species flies and is attracted to lights at night.*

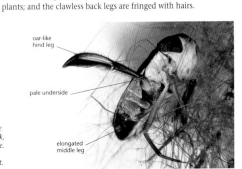

oar-like hind leg

pale underside

elongated middle leg

swimming hairs on hind leg

▲ CORIXA SP. *feed on algae, diatoms, and plant debris at the bottom of well-vegetated ponds, using their hair-fringed front legs to filter through the debris.*

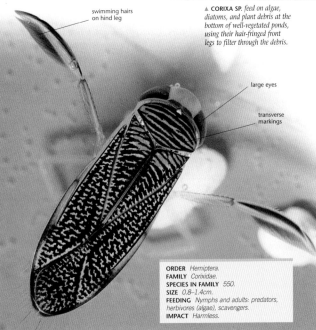

large eyes

transverse markings

ORDER *Hemiptera.*
FAMILY *Corixidae.*
SPECIES IN FAMILY *550.*
SIZE *0.8–1.4cm.*
FEEDING *Nymphs and adults: predators, herbivores (algae), scavengers.*
IMPACT *Harmless.*

Froghoppers

Cercopidae

INHABIT *well-vegetated areas such as woods, meadows, and scrub, occurring on a variety of shrubs, trees, and herbaceous plants.*

These squat, round-eyed bugs are good jumpers and very similar to spittle bugs (right). Most species are brown, grey, or drab, but some are black with vivid red or orange markings. The head has rounded eyes and is narrower than the thorax, which can look hexagonal or angular. Like spittle bugs, the nymphs produce frothy excrement to reduce evaporation and provide protection from predators.

NOTE

This species is quite common in the south of Britain. The nymphs live underground, feeding on the root sap of host plants.

rounded eyes

▶ CERCOPIS VULNERATA *is a very conspicuous species, with bright warning coloration to deter potential predators.*

bold red markings

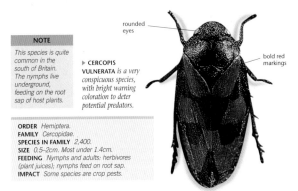

ORDER *Hemiptera.*
FAMILY *Cercopidae.*
SPECIES IN FAMILY *2,400.*
SIZE *0.5–2cm. Most under 1.4cm.*
FEEDING *Nymphs and adults: herbivores (plant juices); nymphs feed on root sap.*
IMPACT *Some species are crop pests.*

Spittle Bugs

Aphrophoridae

COMMON *in nearly all habitats on a wide range of woody and herbaceous plants.*

Spittle bugs vary from pale to dark brown with lighter mottling and markings. Some species have many colour forms. The head is almost as wide as the pronotum, the front of which is arched or curved forwards. The hind tibiae have one or two strong spines and a circle of smaller spines at their ends. These bugs are good jumpers.

variable colour and pattern

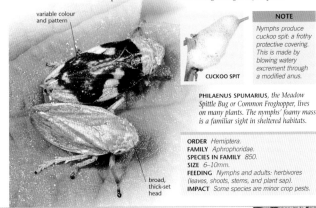

NOTE

Nymphs produce cuckoo spit: a frothy protective covering. This is made by blowing watery excrement through a modified anus.

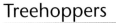

CUCKOO SPIT

PHILAENUS SPUMARIUS, *the Meadow Spittle Bug or Common Froghopper, lives on many plants. The nymphs' foamy mass is a familiar sight in sheltered habitats.*

broad, thick-set head

ORDER *Hemiptera.*
FAMILY *Aphrophoridae.*
SPECIES IN FAMILY *850.*
SIZE *6–10mm.*
FEEDING *Nymphs and adults: herbivores (leaves, shoots, stems, and plant sap).*
IMPACT *Some species are minor crop pests.*

Treehoppers

Membracidae

Treehoppers, or thorn bugs, are mainly green or brown to blackish. They are easily recognized by the large pronotum, which extends sideways and backwards to cover part of the abdomen. The head, with hair-like antennae, is blunt, downward-facing, and much smaller than the pronotum. The enlarged hind legs allow these insects to make short jumps.

OCCUR *on all kinds of shrubs, trees, and other vegetation. Most are specific to a host plant.*

lateral extension

extended pronotum

head tucked under

NOTE

Two species are found in Britain: the Horned Treehopper, which lives on oak trees and Gargara genistae, which lives on broom in the south.

▲ CENTROTUS CORNUTUS, *the Horned Treehopper, has a very long projection on its pronotum that extends backwards.*

ORDER *Hemiptera.*
FAMILY *Membracidae.*
SPECIES IN FAMILY *2,500.*
SIZE *6–10mm.*
FEEDING *Nymphs and adults: herbivores.*
IMPACT *Can damage host plants.*

Planthoppers

Delphacidae

These small bugs are mostly brown or greenish. Their bodies are elongated and almost parallel-sided. The antennae are short and often arise from a small indentation on the lower edge of the eyes. A distinctive feature of these insects is a flat, moveable spur at the end of the hind tibiae. Most species have short-winged and fully-winged forms.

ABUNDANT *at or near ground level in grassy areas, meadows, and woodland margins, especially near water.*

thickened antennal segments

▼ DELPHAX PULCHELLUS *feeds on reeds in wetlands. The female (shown here) has short wings that reach only halfway along the abdomen.*

▼ ASIRACA CLAVICORNIS *occurs in damp meadows. It has broad front legs.*

♀

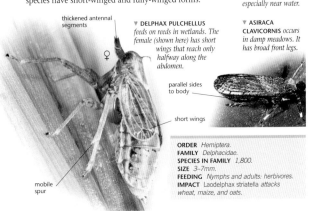

parallel sides to body

short wings

mobile spur

ORDER *Hemiptera.*
FAMILY *Delphacidae.*
SPECIES IN FAMILY *1,800.*
SIZE *3–7mm.*
FEEDING *Nymphs and adults: herbivores.*
IMPACT *Laodelphax striatella attacks wheat, maize, and oats.*

Leafhoppers

Cicadellidae

Leafhoppers are generally slender with broad or triangular heads and large eyes. Many species are green or brown in colour and may have brightly striped markings. The body has parallel sides or tapers towards the rear end. One of the most characteristic features of these bugs is their excellent jumping ability. The hind legs are enlarged and the hind tibiae are slightly flattened and distinctive in having three or four regular rows of very conspicuous spines arranged along their length. All leafhoppers are herbivores: most species suck the juices of plants' phloem vessels (the main transport vessels in plants), while others suck the contents of individual plant cells.

ABUNDANT *virtually everywhere, especially in lush, well-vegetated habitats.*

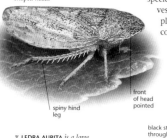

▼ **EUPELIX CUSPIDATA** *occurs in dry, grassy areas and is recognized by its large, shovel-shaped head.*

spiny hind leg

front of head pointed

▼ **LEDRA AURITA** *is a large, flat-bodied species with distinctive horns on the sides of the pronotum. It is well camouflaged against the lichen-covered bark of the oak trees on which it lives.*

broad head

♂ distinctive white bands

pale underside

pale streaks on abdomen

◀ **IDIOCERUS VITREUS** *is widespread in central and southern Britain, where it may be locally common on poplar trees and willows.*

▲ **APHRODES BIFASCIATUS** *feeds in grassy areas and bogs. Males have black and white bands; females are more brownish.*

▼ **GRAPHOCEPHALA FENNAHI**, *the Candy-Striped Leafhopper, is native to the USA but is now widespread in central and southern Britain on rhododendrons.*

black stripe through eye

▶ **IASSUS LANIO** *is a distinctive species found on oak trees. The head and thorax are broad and brownish, while the wings are greenish.*

greenish wings

broad, brownish head

net-like pattern of veins

camouflaged coloration

horns on pronotum

two dark spots on head

◀ **CICADELLA VIRIDIS** *is widespread in very wet grassland, boggy areas, and marshes. The front wings of the female are green, while those of the male are dark purple-brown.*

contrasting veins on wings

spiny hind leg

▼ **EUPTERYX AURATA** *can be found on nettles and related plants, but it is also a pest of potatoes, causing wilting and yellowing of the leaves.*

yellow and black markings

whitish spots at end of wings

> **NOTE**
> *Leafhoppers make large quantities of sweet excrement called honeydew, which can be expelled rapidly by species known as sharpshooters.*

ORDER *Hemiptera.*
FAMILY *Cicadellidae.*
SPECIES IN FAMILY *21,000.*
SIZE *0.3–2cm.*
FEEDING *Nymphs and adults: herbivores.*
IMPACT *Many species are pests, attacking a wide range of crops.*

Adelgids

Adelgidae

These very small, pale brown insects are closely related to aphids (p.254), with fully-winged and wingless forms. The front wings have a darkened pterostigma and very few veins. The blunt-ended abdomen has no abdominal projections, or cornicles. Wingless females have a covering of powdery wax.

FOUND *on coniferous trees such as larch, spruce, and fir.*

> **NOTE**
> *The galls induced by adelgids damage and deform young conifers, and can ruin the shape of those grown as a crop for Christmas.*

ADELGES ABIETIS *lays its eggs at the base of needles near the ends of branches, inducing the growth of a gall.*

creamy, yellowish white coloration

pineapple-shaped gall

GALLS

very dry, tough old gall

ORDER *Hemiptera.*
FAMILY *Adelgidae.*
SPECIES IN FAMILY *60.*
SIZE *Up to 1.4mm.*
FEEDING *Nymphs and adults: herbivores.*
IMPACT *Some species can damage conifers and may be a pest in plantations.*

Jumping Plant Lice

Psyllidae

These variously coloured bugs look superficially like small leafhoppers (above), but have longer antennae with ten segments. The mouthparts take the form of a beak in three segments. Both sexes have two pairs of broadly oval wings held together roof-like over the body. The front wings may be clear or clouded with smoky patterns. The hind legs are slightly enlarged, enabling psyllids to jump.

OCCUR *in a variety of habitats wherever their host plants occur.*

wings held together, roof-like, over body

striped thorax

red eyes

dark marks at wingtips

> **NOTE**
> *Psyllids lay stalked eggs on or inside plants, where some may induce the formation of galls or deform the leaves. The nymphs live in aggregations.*

PSYLLOPSIS FRAXINI *is a boldly marked plant louse that lives on ash trees. The feeding activities of its woolly larvae cause the edges of leaves to become reddish and swollen.*

ORDER *Hemiptera.*
FAMILY *Psyllidae.*
SPECIES IN FAMILY *1,500.*
SIZE *2–4mm.*
FEEDING *Nymphs and adults: herbivores.*
IMPACT *Some species are pests of pear and apple trees; others attack carrots and onions.*

Plant Lice, Greenfly, or Aphids

Aphididae

FOUND *on almost all plant types, including the roots, in most habitats.*

▼ **THECABIUS AFFINIS** *is a woolly aphid which causes distortion and folding of the leaves of poplar and also the leaves of some buttercups.*

These small, slow-moving, soft-bodied insects make up one of the most destructive insect families. They reproduce with phenomenal speed and cause immense damage to plants, weakening them, feeding on their sap, and infecting them with plant viral diseases. Aphid life cycles can be complex, involving sexual and asexual generations on different host plants. Most species are green, but some may be pink, black, or brown. The antennae have between four and six segments. The pear-shaped abdomen ends in a short, pointed tail – the cauda – and usually has a pair of projecting tubes, or cornicles, from which a defensive secretion can be produced. In some species the entire body may be coated with a white waxy secretion. When present, the wings are held tent-like over the body and are either clear or have darkish markings; the hind wings are smaller than the front wings.

two or three spirals

▲ **PEMPHIGUS SPIROTHECAE** *lives inside elongated, spiral galls, which it induces on the leaf stalks of Black Poplar.*

▶ **MACROSIPHUM ROSAE**, *the Rose Aphid, may be pink or green. This common garden pest feeds on roses in spring; later, a winged generation flies to teasels or scabious.*

pear-shaped abdomen

green individual

long cornicles

long hind legs

NOTE

Aphid excrement (honeydew) is rich in sugar, attracting ants which feed on it. In return the ants protect the aphids from enemies such as parasitic wasps.

short dark cornicle

mass of eggs

▼ **TUBEROLACHNUS SALIGNUS** *is a large and widespread aphid occurring on willow. The back of the fourth abdominal segment has a single projection called a tubercle.*

aggregation of aphids

▲ **LACHNUS ROBORIS** *lays eggs in clusters on oak branches. The aphids live in colonies and are attended by ants, which feed on their honeydew.*

▼ **PERIPHYLLUS ACERICOLA** *lives on the leaves of sycamore trees. The nymphs have a resting period in the height of summer.*

winged adult

▼ **TUBERCULOIDES ANNULATUS** *is a small yellow, greenish, or pinkish aphid that lives underneath oak leaves.*

drop of honeydew

soft body

▼ **APHIS FABAE**, *the Black Bean Aphid or Blackfly, attacks beans and other plants during the summer.*

black body with short cornicles

ORDER *Hemiptera.*
FAMILY *Aphididae.*
SPECIES IN FAMILY *2,250.*
SIZE *2–5mm.*
FEEDING *Nymphs and adults: herbivores.*
IMPACT *Many species are pests of crops and garden plants.*

Phylloxerans

Phylloxeridae

Phylloxerans are minute, greenish or pale brown, aphid-like insects. Females may be winged or wingless, although the former are rare in Britain. When present, the white wings are held flat over the body at rest. The head has a pair of small dark eyes and the antennae have three segments. The abdomen has no "tails" (cauda) or projections (cornicles).

LIVE *on the roots and leaves of susceptible plants, such as oak trees and vines.*

small yellowish eggs

adult female

NOTE

Vine Phylloxerans, Viteus vitifoliae, were introduced from North America in 1858–1862, causing immense damage to Europe's vineyards.

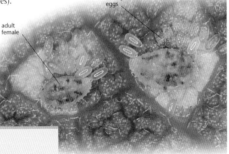

ORDER *Hemiptera.*
FAMILY *Phylloxeridae.*
SPECIES IN FAMILY *55.*
SIZE *0.8–1.6mm.*
FEEDING *Nymphs and adults: herbivores.*
IMPACT *Viteus vitifoliae is an extremely serious pest of cultivated vines.*

PHYLLOXERA QUERCUS *is one of several similar species found on oak tree foliage. Early in the year, the wingless females can be seen on the undersides of leaves, surrounded by eggs.*

Whiteflies

Aleyrodidae

Whiteflies are very small, white, moth-like insects with two pairs of relatively broad wings that are usually white with a distinctive dusting of white, powdery wax. The hind and front wings are of the same size and, when resting, are held horizontally over the body. The head has a pair of antennae with seven segments. Females lay their eggs on tiny stalks on the undersides of leaves.

THRIVE *on both wild and cultivated plants in a range of habitats, including greenhouses.*

▼ **ALEYRODES PROLETELLA** *attacks brassica species such as cabbages. It can be found at almost any time of year.*

empty skin

freshly emerged adult

white wings covered in powdery wax

dark spots on wings

▼ **TRIALEURODES VAPORARIORUM**, *the Glasshouse Whitefly, is a pest of glasshouse crops such as tomatoes.*

white legs and antennae

ORDER *Hemiptera.*
FAMILY *Aleyrodidae.*
SPECIES IN FAMILY *1,200.*
SIZE *1–3mm.*
FEEDING *Nymphs and adults: herbivores.*
IMPACT *May be pests of glasshouse crops and plants in the cabbage family.*

Soft, Wax, and Tortoise Scales

Coccidae

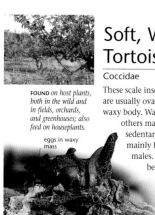

FOUND *on host plants, both in the wild and in fields, orchards, and greenhouses; also feed on houseplants.*

These scale insects are very variable in form, but females are usually oval and flattened with a hard, smooth, or waxy body. Wax-covered species appear white, while others may be brownish. Females are almost always sedentary on their host plant. They reproduce mainly by parthenogenesis, without the need for males. Males, which are rarely seen, may be winged or wingless and are short-lived.

eggs in waxy mass

mature scale

◀ **PULVINARIA REGALIS** *is known as the Horse Chestnut Scale; females reproduce without males and lay as many as 3,000 eggs.*

mature scale insect

reddish brown body

▶ **PARTHENOLECANIUM CORNI**, *the Brown Scale, is a pest of some fruit trees and around 300 ornamental plant species.*

ORDER *Hemiptera.*
FAMILY *Coccidae.*
SPECIES IN FAMILY *1,250.*
SIZE *2–6mm.*
FEEDING *Nymphs and adults: herbivores.*
IMPACT *Many species are pests of crops, gardenplants, and houseplants.*

Mealy Bugs

Pseudococcidae

OCCUR *wherever their host plant grows, in the wild or in glasshouses.*

Unlike related families of scale insects, mealy bugs have functional legs at all stages of their life history (in others, there is a sedentary stage). The sexes are very different. Females are elongated, wingless, covered with a wax coating, and possess sucking mouthparts. Males have a pair of wings, so look like typical insects, but lack developed mouthparts.

NOTE

Mealy bugs are sap-suckers and infest all parts of their host plant. Some species lay eggs in a mass of downy wax; others give birth to live nymphs.

long tail filaments

soft, waxy body

PSEUDOCOCCUS ADONIUM, *the Long-tailed Mealy Bug, is a pest of apple, pear, and citrus trees and attacks crops and garden and house plants.*

ORDER *Hemiptera.*
FAMILY *Pseudococcidae.*
SPECIES IN FAMILY *2,000.*
SIZE *1.5–4mm.*
FEEDING *Nymphs and adults: herbivores.*
IMPACT *Some species are pests of crops, gardenplants, and houseplants.*

Common Thrips

Thripidae

The wings of these pale yellow, brown, or blackish thrips are narrower than in banded thrips and their ends are more pointed. The body appears flattened and the antennae usually have seven or eight segments. The front wings may have one or two longitudinal veins. In females the ovipositor curves downwards, not upwards.

FAVOUR *the leaves and flowers of a vast range of plants, often including crops.*

▼ **TAENIOTHRIPS SIMPLEX** *can be a serious pest on Gladiolus and related flowers, leaving pale speckled marks on the flowers.*

pale wings

▶ **LIMOTHRIPS CEREALIUM**, *or the Grain Thrips, is a cosmopolitan species that attacks grasses and cereals.*

wings not overlapped at rest

flattened body

ORDER *Thysanoptera.*
FAMILY *Thripidae.*
SPECIES IN FAMILY *1,500.*
SIZE *0.7–2mm.*
FEEDING *Nymphs and adults: herbivores.*
IMPACT *Some species cause serious damage to field crops by feeding.*

Alderflies

Sialidae

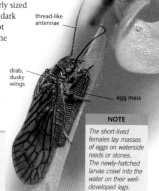

SPEND *long periods resting on alders and similar vegetation beside slow-moving streams, canals, and mud-bottomed pools.*

Alderflies are day-flying insects with stout, dark brown to blackish grey bodies and a brownish or greyish tint to the wings, which are held together, tent-like, over the body. The head is blunt with large eyes and long, thread-like antennae. The pronotum is squarish. The front and hind wings are similarly sized with prominent dark veins that are not forked close to the wing margins.

thread-like antennae

LARVAE

The aquatic larvae have powerful jaws and seven pairs of feathery abdominal gills on each side.

SIALIS LUTARIA, *the Alderfly, is often seen in late spring and early summer, perching on trees and other plants near to or overhanging water.*

drab, dusky wings

egg mass

NOTE

The short-lived females lay masses of eggs on waterside reeds or stones. The newly-hatched larvae crawl into the water on their well-developed legs.

ORDER *Megaloptera.*
FAMILY *Sialidae.*
SPECIES IN FAMILY *75.*
SIZE *1.8–2.2cm.*
FEEDING *Larvae: predators (small aquatic insects and worms). Adults: non-feeding.*
IMPACT *Harmless.*

Snakeflies

Raphidiidae

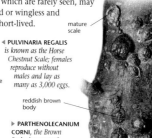

OCCUPY *lush, low-growing vegetation in wooded areas.*

These shiny, dark brown insects have an elongated prothorax on which the head can be raised. The head is broadest across the eyes and tapers behind. The clear wings have a pterostigma and a prominent network of veins, which fork close to the wing margins. Females are a little larger than males, with a long ovipositor.

▼ **RAPHIDIA NOTATA** *inhabits deciduous woodland, especially with oak trees. The larvae are often found in rotting stumps.*

clear wings with dark veins

▶ **RAPHIDIA XANTHOSTIGMA** *lives in woodland, where the larvae hunt small insects under bark. The sexes are identical, except for the female's ovipositor.*

elongated prothorax

head narrows to rear

LARVAE

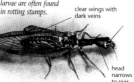

The slender larvae lack abdominal gills and have short, curved mandibles like those of adults.

long ovipositor

ORDER *Raphidioptera.*
FAMILY *Raphidiidae.*
SPECIES IN FAMILY *85.*
SIZE *1.4–2cm.*
FEEDING *Larvae and adults: predators (mainly aphids and soft-bodied insects).*
IMPACT *Harmless.*

Osmylids

Osmylidae

Sometimes called giant lacewings, these brownish insects are scavengers that also feed on nectar. They are relatively slender-bodied and have distinctively broad wings with dark spots and blotches and many cross veins; despite their large wings, they are weak fliers. The reddish head has prominent eyes and slender, thread-like antennae. The prothorax is slightly elongated. The legs are yellowish brown.

CONFINED *to the margins of streams in woodland.*

LARVAE

The semiaquatic larvae are predators and are armed with straight, needle-like mouthparts.

dark blotches on wings

reddish head

pale yellow legs

▲ **OSMYLUS FULVICEPHALUS** *flies after dark near slow-flowing streams, and rests near the water on foliage during the day.*

ORDER *Neuroptera.*
FAMILY *Osmylidae.*
SPECIES IN FAMILY *150.*
SIZE *3.8–5.2cm (wingspan).*
FEEDING *Larvae: predators. Adults: liquid-feeders (nectar), scavengers.*
IMPACT *Harmless.*

Brown Lacewings

Hemerobiidae

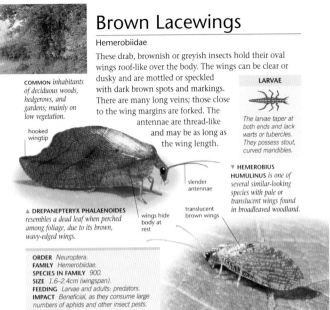

COMMON *inhabitants of deciduous woods, hedgerows, and gardens; mainly on low vegetation.*

These drab, brownish or greyish insects hold their oval wings roof-like over the body. The wings can be clear or dusky and are mottled or speckled with dark brown spots and markings. There are many long veins; those close to the wing margins are forked. The antennae are thread-like and may be as long as the wing length.

LARVAE

The larvae taper at both ends and lack warts or tubercles. They possess stout, curved mandibles.

hooked wingtip

slender antennae

▲ DREPANEPTERYX PHALAENOIDES *resembles a dead leaf when perched among foliage, due to its brown, wavy-edged wings.*

wings hide body at rest

translucent brown wings

▼ HEMEROBIUS HUMULINUS *is one of several similar-looking species with pale or translucent wings found in broadleaved woodland.*

ORDER *Neuroptera.*
FAMILY *Hemerobiidae.*
SPECIES IN FAMILY *900.*
SIZE *1.6–2.4cm (wingspan).*
FEEDING *Larvae and adults: predators.*
IMPACT *Beneficial, as they consume large numbers of aphids and other insect pests.*

Common Lacewings

Chrysopidae

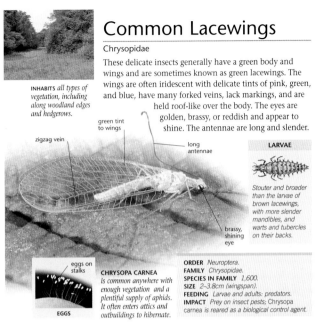

INHABITS *all types of vegetation, including along woodland edges and hedgerows.*

These delicate insects generally have a green body and wings and are sometimes known as green lacewings. The wings are often iridescent with delicate tints of pink, green, and blue, have many forked veins, lack markings, and are held roof-like over the body. The eyes are golden, brassy, or reddish and appear to shine. The antennae are long and slender.

green tint to wings

zigzag vein

long antennae

LARVAE

Stouter and broader than the larvae of brown lacewings, with more slender mandibles, and warts and tubercles on their backs.

brassy, shining eye

eggs on stalks

CHRYSOPA CARNEA *is common anywhere with enough vegetation and a plentiful supply of aphids. It often enters attics and outbuildings to hibernate.*

EGGS

ORDER *Neuroptera.*
FAMILY *Chrysopidae.*
SPECIES IN FAMILY *1,600.*
SIZE *2–3.8cm (wingspan).*
FEEDING *Larvae and adults: predators.*
IMPACT *Prey on insect pests; Chrysopa carnea is reared as a biological control agent.*

Ground Beetles

Carabidae

FOUND *on the ground in a wide variety of habitats, including under wood, stones, leaf litter, and debris.*

These beetles are active hunters with long, slender legs and powerful jaws; most species are nocturnal. They may be dull or shiny. The majority are brown or black, often with a metallic sheen, although a few species are green, red, and black or have yellow or green markings. The body is long, parallel-sided, and slightly flattened, usually with striations running along the elytra. The head has thread-like antennae, conspicuous eyes, and toothed jaws. The head, thorax, and abdomen tend to be clearly differentiated.

LARVAE

Most larvae live in soil or debris and are black or dark brown with long bodies that taper at both ends. They use enzymes to digest prey, then suck in the resulting liquid.

4 pale spots

▲ DROMIUS QUADRIMACULATUS *is easily recognized by its dark elytra with four yellowish brown spots. It hides under tree bark.*

reddish legs

▶ HARPALUS RUFIPES *occurs in cultivated land, waste ground, and gardens. It forages after dark for seeds, sometimes attacking strawberries.*

▼ BRACHINUS CREPITANS *hides under stones in dry locations. Like all bombardier beetles, it can fire hot chemicals from its rear end in defence.*

bluish or greenish elytra

reddish brown head, thorax, and legs

flattened body

▲ NEBRIA BREVICOLLIS *is found in many habitats, most commonly under stones and logs in woodland and hedgerows.*

metallic violet sheen

▼ CARABUS VIOLACEUS, *better known as the Violet Ground Beetle, is a large, widespread species that feeds on a range of invertebrates, including slugs. It is commonest in woodland.*

faint yellowish spot at rear of elytra

narrow head

▲ BEMBIDION LUNATUM *is common and widespread near water, especially on riverbanks. There are many similar species.*

yellow legs

▲ CYCHRUS CARABOIDES *crawls under moss and bark on old tree stumps in woodland. It emerges after dark to hunt snails.*

pale spot

◀ CICINDELLA CAMPESTRIS, *the Green Tiger Beetle, is an active flier and very fast runner. It likes hot, sunny, open areas.*

large jaws

pale, circular spots

bronze sheen to elytra

large eyes

▲ ELAPHRUS RIPARIUS *is unmistakable due to its rows of pale spots. It forages on bare ground near ponds and streams.*

▲ NOTIOPHILUS BIGUTTATUS *is a squat species with very large eyes. It is a specialist predator of springtails, which it catches in its strong jaws.*

long, thin antennae

broad body

bronze sheen

▲ CALOSOMA INQUISITOR *inhabits deciduous woodland. Like other Calosoma species, it hunts caterpillars among foliage.*

prominent striations

◀ PTEROSTICHUS NIGER *is one of numerous similar nocturnal species that forage on the ground for prey or carrion.*

shiny black body

NOTE

The larvae of Tiger beetles live in vertical burrows in sandy or gravel soil. They seize any passing insects and drag them down to eat them.

ORDER *Coleoptera.*
FAMILY *Carabidae.*
SPECIES IN FAMILY *29,000.*
SIZE *0.2–2.8cm.*
FEEDING *Immatures and adults: predators, scavengers; some species partly herbivores.*
IMPACT *Many species help to control pests.*

Predatory Diving Beetles

Dytiscidae

INHABIT *streams, ditches, canals, lakes, and ponds, usually in shallower water.*

LARVAE

Due to their highly predatory nature, the larvae are often called water tigers. They are elongated with hairy legs and large, curved jaws and obtain air at the water surface.

These voracious predators have smooth, streamlined, shiny bodies. Many species are reddish to dark brown or black, but some have extensive yellowish or reddish bands, spots, and other markings. The head appears to be partly sunk into the pronotum and the antennae are thread-like. The hind legs, which are flattened and paddle-like with fringes of long hairs, are used for swimming; they are often longer than the other legs. The front legs are used for holding prey and the middle legs for clinging to vegetation. The males of some species have swollen structures on the front tarsi, used to hold the females' smooth backs during mating.

▶ **GRAPHODERUS ZONATUS** *is recognized by the black bands at the front and rear of the pronotum, as well as the extensive mottling on the elytra.*

black and yellow pronotum

"sunken" head

smooth elytra in male

modified front tarsus

hairy fringes to legs

♂

▽ **DYTISCUS MARGINALIS**, *the Great Diving Beetle, is a pond-dweller big enough to catch vertebrates such as newts, frogs, and fish.*

♀

pale grooves on elytra in female

NOTE

Adults and larvae alike feed on many kinds of aquatic animal, from snails to tadpoles, frogs, newts, and fish, attacking prey larger than themselves.

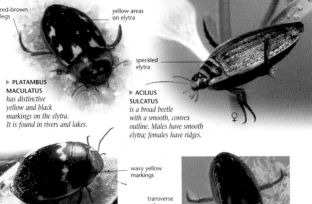

red-brown legs

yellow areas on elytra

speckled elytra

▶ **PLATAMBUS MACULATUS** *has distinctive yellow and black markings on the elytra. It is found in rivers and lakes.*

▶ **ACILIUS SULCATUS** *is a broad beetle with a smooth, convex outline. Males have smooth elytra; females have ridges.*

♀

wavy yellow markings

transverse pale marking

▲ **AGABUS UNDULATUS** *has a smooth, oval outline. It lives among aquatic vegetation in ponds and small lakes.*

yellow edges to elytra

▲ **HYDATICUS TRANSVERSALIS** *frequents ditches and ponds. Its elytra have a transverse pale mark at the front and dark stripes at the sides to the rear.*

▶ **COLYMBETES FUSCUS** *has a dark brown or black head and its pronotum is black with yellowish margins. The elytra also have a thin yellowish border.*

narrow body

streamlined body

green tinge

orange head with black markings

▶ **LACCOPHILUS MINUTUS** *is quite flattened and can be tinged green with very indistinct pale patches. It is widespread and common in ponds.*

mottled or speckled elytra

▲ **RHANTUS EXSOLETUS** *is brownish yellow above and paler yellow below. It occurs in ponds and drainage ditches and at lake margins.*

yellow and brown markings

relatively slender hind legs

ORDER Coleoptera.
FAMILY Dytiscidae.
SPECIES IN FAMILY 3,500.
SIZE 0.2–3.8cm.
FEEDING Larvae and adults: predators.
IMPACT Larger species may eat small fish in ornamental ponds. Can bite if handled.

▲ **HYDROPORUS FERRUGINEUS** *is a small, reddish brown and yellow beetle. There are more than 30 very similar species with variable coloration.*

Screech Beetles

Hygrobiidae

OCCUR *in ponds and other waterbodies with muddy bottoms.*

Screech beetles are reddish brown with dark markings, smooth, and broadly oval. The upperside of the body is convex, the underside even more so. The head is fairly broad, with bulging eyes. The legs have special swimming hairs on the tibiae, femora, and tarsi; when swimming, the legs are used alternately. When disturbed, adults make a distinctive squeaking noise by rubbing the end of the abdomen against a ridged structure on the wing cases.

HYGROBIA HERRMANNI *is deep reddish brown and has a covering of short hairs on its underside.*

convex surface

dark band at front of pronotum

large eyes

LARVAE

The larvae have a broad head and thorax with three pairs of strong legs.

ORDER Coleoptera.
FAMILY Hygrobiidae.
SPECIES IN FAMILY 5.
SIZE 8–10mm.
FEEDING Larvae and adults: predators.
IMPACT Harmless.

Whirligig Beetles

Gyrinidae

These oval, streamlined beetles are typically black, with a bronze or steel-blue sheen in some species. The head has short antennae and the eyes are divided into upper and lower portions for vision above and below water. The long front legs are adapted for grasping prey, while the middle and hind legs are short, flat, and paddle-like.

FOUND *on the surface of ponds, pools, slow-moving streams, and sluggish rivers.*

hairy upper surface

grasping front leg

LARVAE

The yellowish or greenish larvae are elongated with sharp mouthparts and narrow heads.

▲ **ORECTOCHILUS VILLOSUS**, *the Hairy Whirligig, has short, pale hairs on its dorsal surface. It is narrower and more elongated than other whirligig beetles.*

▶ **GYRINUS SP.** *are dark, shiny beetles that swim rapidly in circles on the water.*

smooth, dark elytra

ORDER Coleoptera.
FAMILY Gyrinidae.
SPECIES IN FAMILY 750.
SIZE 4–8mm.
FEEDING Larvae and adults: predators, scavengers.
IMPACT Harmless.

Water Scavenger Beetles

Hydrophilidae

FAVOUR *freshwater habitats; also occur in dung, soil, and decaying vegetation.*

Most of these beetles live in water, carrying air under their wing cases and on their body surface. Oval in shape, they are black, brown, or yellowish. The upperside of the body is convex and smooth; the underside is flat with a covering of short, velvety hairs that looks silvery underwater. The maxillary palps (a pair of sensory mouthparts) are typically longer than the short, club-ended antennae.

LARVAE

Surface-breathing or equipped with gills, the predatory larvae may have warty or hairy backs.

▶ **HYDROPHILUS PICEUS,** *the Great Silver Diving Beetle, is up to 5cm long. A sharp spine on its underside can pierce human skin.*

faint striations

long palp

smooth, rounded outline

◀ **HYDROCHARA CARABOIDES** *is quite a good swimmer and, like Hydrophilus piceus (above), it lays its eggs in floating cocoons. It is found in weedy, still water.*

ORDER *Coleoptera.*
FAMILY *Hydrophilidae.*
SPECIES IN FAMILY *2,000.*
SIZE *0.4–4.8cm.*
FEEDING *Larvae: predators. Adults: mainly scavengers, also predators.*
IMPACT *Harmless.*

Hister Beetles

Histeridae

LIVE *in dung, carrion, and leaf litter, under bark, and in tunnels of wood-boring insects.*

These tough-bodied beetles are oval or rounded, with a convex profile; some are flattened for living under bark. Many are shiny black or have reddish markings. The head is sunk into the prothorax. The antennae are elbowed; the front tibiae have teeth for digging.

LARVAE

The square-headed larvae are extremely long, with roughly parallel body sides.

▼ **HISTER QUADRIMACULATUS** *is compact and slightly flattened, with short elytra. It lives in horse and cow manure.*

elytra do not cover abdomen

red markings join at side of elytra

▶ **HISTER UNICOLOR** *feeds on dung and preys on insect larvae developing in carcasses.*

shiny black elytra

ORDER *Coleoptera.*
FAMILY *Histeridae.*
SPECIES IN FAMILY *3,000.*
SIZE *1–16mm.*
FEEDING *Larvae and adults: predators (mostly fly maggots and beetle grubs).*
IMPACT *Harmless.*

Carrion Beetles

Silphidae

Many of these slightly flattened, soft-bodied beetles are black or brown, often with yellow, red, or orange markings. The body surface may be dull or shiny and some have a roughened texture or ridges. The head, which is much narrower than the thorax, has round, slightly bulging eyes, strong, curved mandibles, and short, club-ended antennae. The legs of most species are strong and spiny.

OCCUR *on the ground close to carcasses; also under dung and in rotting fungi in damp, shady woodland.*

narrow head

ridged elytra

LARVAE

The larvae are long and flattened, with a small head and broad pronotum. In some species, they are fed on regurgitated carrion by the parents.

▶ **SILPHA ATRATA** *has a narrow, elongated head to allow it to feed on snails inside their shells. This dark, shiny species lives in dense woodland and other damp places.*

red pronotum

NOTE

Carrion beetles have an excellent sense of smell for locating corpses. Two adults are strong enough to move an animal as large as a rat in order to bury it.

▶ **OICEOPTOMA THORACICUM,** *which is identifiable by its black, ridged elytra and reddish pronotum, occurs in dung, carrion, and rotting fungi.*

wavy orange-red bands across elytra

clubbed antennae

short elytra

▲ **NICROPHORUS INVESTIGATOR** *is one of several species of burying beetle with distinctive reddish orange to yellowish bands on the elytra. It is very quickly attracted to the smell of decaying animals.*

orange, clubbed antennae

▼ **NICROPHORUS HUMATOR** *retains the characteristic shape of a burying beetle, despite its all-black elytra.*

ORDER *Coleoptera.*
FAMILY *Silphidae.*
SPECIES IN FAMILY *250.*
SIZE *0.9–3.2cm.*
FEEDING *Larvae and adults: scavengers, predators, herbivores.*
IMPACT *Major recyclers of animal corpses.*

Rove Beetles

Staphylinidae

Most rove beetles are small and smooth with elongated, parallel-sided bodies and black or brown coloration. Some species have bright colours, a sculptured surface, or dense body hairs. The head is squarish with long, sharp jaws that cross over each other; the antennae are short and thread-like. All species have distinctively short elytra that expose five or six of the abdominal segments. The full-sized hind wings are folded under the elytra when not in use. The flexible abdomen may be raised in a defensive posture.

FOUND *in dung and carrion, and also in soil, fungi, leaf litter, decaying plant matter, and ant nests.*

raised abdomen

matt black all over

◀ **STAPHYLINUS OLENS,** *the Devil's Coach Horse, displays alarm by raising its abdomen and opening its jaws.*

red-orange spot

broad head

▶ **TACHYPORUS HYPNORUM** *is one of many similar small species with tapering bodies and red elytra.*

tapering abdomen

▲ **STENUS BIMACULATUS** *lives in marshy places. It secretes a surface tension-reducing chemical from its rear end to move over water.*

short red elytra

▼ **EMUS HIRTUS,** *the Hairy Rove Beetle, is restricted to southern Britain where it eats insects found in animal dung.*

hind wings folded beneath short elytra

orange-red prothorax

large jaws

bluish green sheen to elytra

▼ **PHILONTHUS FIMETARIUS** *eats fly maggots and beetle larvae. There are numerous very similar species.*

flexible abdomen

black end to femur

LARVAE

The larvae are dark and elongated, with short antennae and cerci. Some larvae produce odours to trick ants into taking them into their nests and feeding them.

▶ **PAEDERUS LITTORALIS** *is a flightless, orange and black species found in riverine habitats.*

NOTE

Most rove beetles can fly well. Smaller species tend to be diurnal, whereas large species are generally nocturnal. A few species are associated with ants.

ORDER *Coleoptera.*
FAMILY *Staphylinidae.*
SPECIES IN FAMILY *27,000.*
SIZE *0.8–2.6cm.*
FEEDING *Larvae: predators, scavengers. Adults: predators, scavengers, herbivores.*
IMPACT *Harmless.*

Stag Beetles

Lucanidae

These beetles are typically large, shiny, robust insects with black or reddish brown coloration, although some species are smaller or have a bluish sheen. The males of most species have greatly enlarged, toothed mandibles; females are often smaller and have proportionately smaller mandibles. The antennae are elbowed or bent in the middle with a terminal club of three or four expanded, flattened segments. The elytra are smooth and shiny with faint striations. Stag beetles are attracted to lights at night, when they may wander far from woodland.

OCCUR in deciduous woodland, especially with mature trees and decaying timber.

horn on head

▲ SINODENDRON CYLINDRICUM has a very rounded shape. The male has a horn on its head and the front of its pronotum is toothed.

large prothorax

▲ DORCUS PARALLELIPIPEDUS, the Lesser Stag Beetle, has a relatively large head and prothorax. The male's jaws are curved but not enlarged.

▼ LUCANUS CERVUS, the Stag Beetle, is unmistakable. It has declined in recent years due to the loss of rotten wood as a breeding site for its larvae.

massive mandibles

large head

elbowed antennae

smooth brown elytra

LARVAE

The C-shaped larvae have strong legs on the thorax. They feed on decaying logs and tree stumps and may take several years to develop.

NOTE
During courtship, male stag beetles fight pitched battles with rivals. Their jaws have teeth that lock onto a rival's pronotum to try to flip it upside down.

ORDER Coleoptera.
FAMILY Lucanidae.
SPECIES IN FAMILY 1,300.
SIZE 1.4–6.4cm.
FEEDING Larvae: wood-feeders (decaying timber). Adults: liquid-feeders.
IMPACT May try to bite if handled.

Dor Beetles

Geotrupidae

These stout insects are broadly oval and rounded. They are brown or black, shiny, and often have a metallic greenish, blue, or purplish sheen. In many species, males have tooth-like projections and horns on the head and thorax. The jaws are large and clearly visible; the club-ended antennae have 11 segments but are not elbowed. The elytra have obvious lengthwise grooves, while the tibiae of the broad front legs are armed with strong teeth for digging.

FOUND beneath dung of all kinds and in carrion, decaying wood, and fungi.

convex body

slender horn

▲ ODONTAEUS ARMIGER is a small, dark, convex-bodied beetle. The male has upturned lobes while the female is reddish brown without lobes.

three horns on thorax

spines for digging

▲ TYPHAEUS TYPHOEUS, the Minotaur Beetle, digs deep into sandy soil beneath piles of sheep and rabbit droppings.

very faint grooves

iridescent body

▲ GEOTRUPES VERNALIS generally has an iridescent bluish sheen and has less noticeable striations on the elytra than Geotrupes stercorarius.

▼ GEOTRUPES STERCORARIUS is often infested with parasitic mites. It is black, often with a shiny metallic blue or purplish sheen underneath.

clubbed antennae

LARVAE

The pale C-shaped larvae is found under animal dung in burrows. Larval development can take many months. They make noises by rubbing their legs on their body.

NOTE
Adult dor beetles dig tunnels many centimetres deep below dung and carry pieces of it down to provide a food source for their larvae.

ORDER Coleoptera.
FAMILY Geotrupidae.
SPECIES IN FAMILY 600.
SIZE 1–2.5cm.
FEEDING Larvae and adults: scavengers, dung-feeders.
IMPACT Harmless, beneficial.

Click Beetles or Skip Jacks

Elateridae

LIVE on foliage, under bark, and in leaf litter, rotting wood, and soil.

The most remarkable feature of these elongated, narrow-bodied beetles is their ability, when lying on their backs, to click loudly as they throw themselves into the air. Most are brownish or black, although a few are greenish. The antennae are quite long and slender, but may have a comb-like appearance. The rear angles of the pronotum are sharp and often extend backwards to form an acute point that meets the rounded shoulders of the elytra.

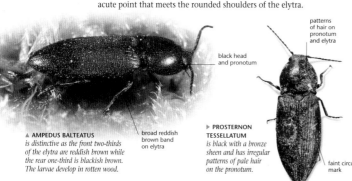

black head and pronotum

▲ AMPEDUS BALTEATUS is distinctive as the front two-thirds of the elytra are reddish brown while the rear one-third is blackish brown. The larvae develop in rotten wood.

broad reddish brown band on elytra

patterns of hair on pronotum and elytra

▶ PROSTERNON TESSELLATUM is black with a bronze sheen and has irregular patterns of pale hair on the pronotum.

faint circular mark

◀ SERICUS BRUNNEUS is reddish brown with a central dark stripe running down the pronotum. The larvae live in the soil in cooler regions.

dark central stripe

▼ ATHOUS HAEMORRHOIDALIS is one of the commonest European click beetle species and is found in a wide range of habitats. The larvae are herbivorous.

broad head

yellow-brown hairs on elytra

LARVAE

Often known as wireworms for their slender, elongated, cylindrical shape, and tough bodies, click beetle larvae are commonly found in rotten wood, under bark, or soil.

NOTE
The beetles can "flick" themselves upwards at an amazing 300 times the acceleration of gravity. The loud click and movement frightens predators.

ORDER Coleoptera.
FAMILY Elateridae.
SPECIES IN FAMILY 8,500.
SIZE 0.2–3cm.
FEEDING Larvae: scavengers, herbivores, predators. Adults: herbivores.
IMPACT May be pests of crops and pasture.

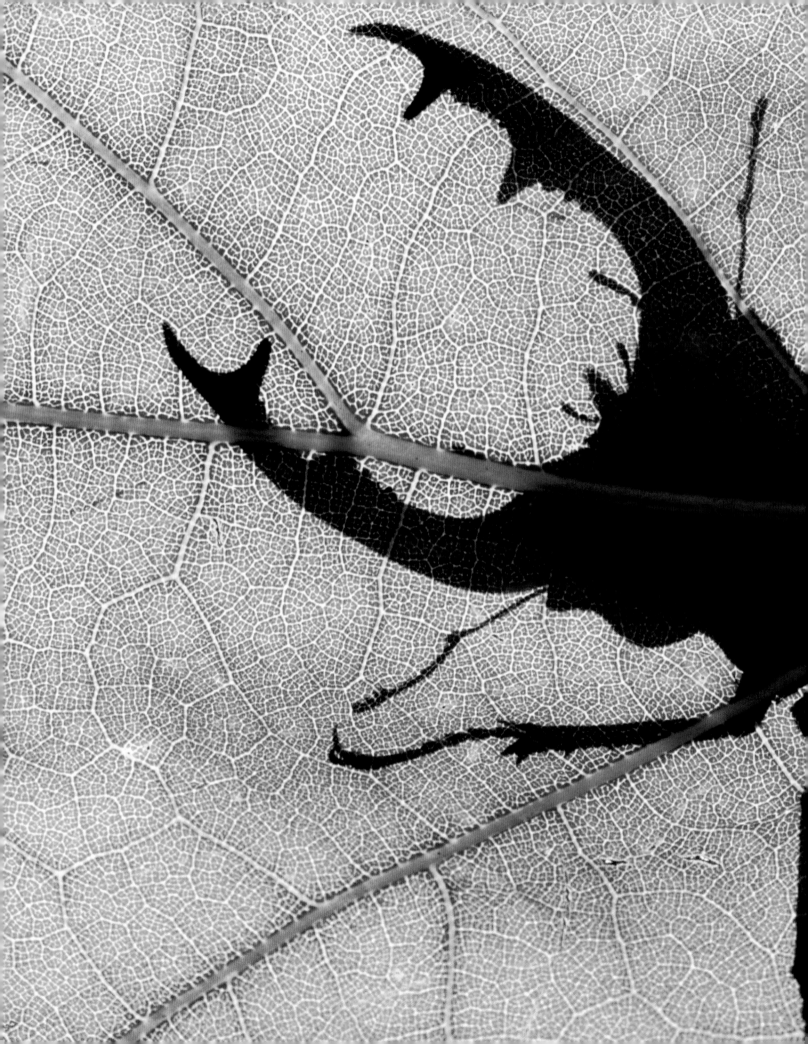

Stag Beetle
The imposing silhouette of a male Stag Beetle contrasts sharply with the delicate veining of a leaf as the sun shines from above. The males use the huge mandibles in sexual combat for access to females.

Scarab Beetles and Chafers

Scarabaeidae

OCCUR *in a huge range of places, including decaying wood, fungi, carrion, dung, flowers, vegetation, bark, and the nests of mammals and social insects.*

Scarabs and chafers comprise a very large group of beetles and there is enormous variation in shape and size between species. The body colour varies from dull brown and black through red, yellow, and orange to metallic blues and greens. Despite this variety, a single character can identify these beetles: the antennae, which have between eight and ten segments and end in a distinctive club. The club is made up of three to seven flat, moveable, plate-like flaps, which can be separated or folded together. In many species the males have horns, used to fight for mates.

LARVAE

The larvae are white grubs with strong mandibles and a C-shaped body. Many live in the soil and feed on roots; others are found in dung, rotten wood, and decaying matter.

shiny green

▶ **CETONIA AURATA,** *the Rose Chafer, is a broad and somewhat flattened beetle that is often shiny green with white markings.*

yellowish brown elytra

thin white markings

head rounded at front

dark brown overall

▲ **APHODIUS RUFIPES** *is one of many similar-looking beetles attracted to fresh cow, sheep, and horse dung. These species do not burrow or bury, but simply lay their eggs in the dung.*

◀ **AMPHIMALLON SOLSTITIALIS** *is called the Summer Chafer as it can be seen flying in swarms around the tops of trees on June evenings.*

white hairs on thorax

reddish brown elytra

◀ **PHYLLOPERTHA HORTICOLA,** *the Garden Chafer, can damage the leaves and buds of apple and pear trees by chewing them; its larvae eat the roots of grasses, including cereals.*

black convex shape

curved horn

♂

white hairs on elytra

♂

5 to 7 segments in antennal club

long hairs on head and thorax

bee-like markings on abdomen

▶ **TRICHIUS FASCIATUS,** *the Bee Beetle, can be yellow or orange, but always has black markings and a very hairy body. Its larvae develop in rotting wood.*

▲ **COPRIS LUNARIS,** *the Horned Dung Beetle, has a distinctive horn on the head and a large, flat-fronted pronotum. Both sexes dig brood chambers in sandy soil.*

NOTE

Dung beetles are extremely important recyclers in many regions. They clear away and bury vast amounts of dung, returning valuable nutrients to the soil.

ORDER *Coleoptera.*
FAMILY *Scarabaeidae.*
SPECIES IN FAMILY *20,000.*
SIZE *0.2–15cm.*
FEEDING *Larvae: scavengers, fungi-feeders. Adults: liquid-feeders (nectar).*
IMPACT *A few species are serious pests.*

▲ **MELOLONTHA MELOLONTHA,** *the Common Cockchafer, is also known as the May Bug since the adult emerges around this time. It flies around tree tops and is attracted to lights.*

Jewel Beetles

Buprestidae

FOUND *in deciduous and coniferous woods, especially with dead trees or fallen timber, in which the larvae often develop.*

Jewel beetles are among the most beautiful of all insects and fly rapidly on sunny days. Many species are brightly coloured metallic green, blue, and red with attractive markings in the form of stripes, bands, and spots, although a few species are dull brown, or black. Jewel beetles are tough-bodied and bullet-shaped, tapering towards the rear end. The head appears sunken into the thorax and bent downwards, the eyes are large, and the short antennae are slender or slightly toothed. Jewel beetles look rather like broad-bodied click beetles, but unlike that family they cannot jump. Adults fly very rapidly in sunshine and are very difficult to catch. At the least disturbance, jewel beetles will take to flight or feign death.

▶ **TRACHYS MINUTUS** *mines inside the leaves of birch, willow, lime, and elm as a larva. The larva makes an irregular blotch mine and leaves dark threads of excrement inside as it grows.*

marks left by larvae feeding under bark

LARVAL TUNNELS

black elytra with pale markings

LARVAE

Known as flathead borers due to their clubbed body shape, the larvae have small heads sunk into a very broad, expanded prothorax. Their legs are short or absent.

NOTE

Jewel beetles lay their eggs in wood and the larvae chew tunnels with an oval cross section in tree roots and trunks. Weak or dying trees are usually chosen.

▼ **AGRILUS PANNONICUS** *tapers strongly towards the end of the abdomen. It has a greenish sheen near the front, becoming bluish at the rear.*

white spots on elytra and abdomen sides

brassy green sheen to upperside

▲ **AGRILUS ANGUSTULUS** *is a slender beetle with the pronotum broadest at the front. The larvae develop under the bark of twigs of deciduous trees.*

ORDER *Coleoptera.*
FAMILY *Buprestidae.*
SPECIES IN FAMILY *14,000.*
SIZE *0.2–3.5cm.*
FEEDING *Larvae: wood-feeders, herbivores. Adults: herbivores, nectar-feeders.*
IMPACT *Many species are pests of orchards.*

Net-winged Beetles

Lycidae

These soft-bodied, black and red or reddish brown beetles, derive their common name from the net-like pattern of cells on the wing cases of many species. They appear typically elongated and parallel-sided or slightly expanded towards the rear. The head, with conspicuous, rounded eyes, is usually hidden from above by the pronotum, which may have shallow depressed areas bounded by ridges.

INHABIT *woodland and well-vegetated habitats, often in sunny areas with umbelliferous flowers.*

DICTYOPTERA AURORA *has bright red elytra and segmented pronotum, which almost covers the head.*

head hidden by pronotum

sunken pits

soft, ribbed elytra

LARVAE

The larvae live under the bark of trees and eat beetle larvae and small grubs.

ORDER *Coleoptera.*
FAMILY *Lycidae.*
SPECIES IN FAMILY *3,500.*
SIZE *0.5–1.5cm.*
FEEDING *Larvae: scavengers, predators. Adults: non-feeders, liquid-feeders (nectar).*
IMPACT *Harmless.*

Spider Beetles

Ptinidae

The common name of these small brownish beetles refers to the rounded, spider-like appearance of the females of many species. The head and prothorax are narrower than the elytra and this clear division gives them what resembles a "waist". The legs are long and quite slender. Males are more elongated and beetle-like.

FOUND *in a variety of habitats, especially woodland and inside buildings.*

NOTE

A few species in this family can cause damage in houses as they attack dry materials such as leather and textiles while some can be pests of stored grain.

long antennae

hood-like pronotum

patterns of white scales on elytra

LARVAE

The larvae feed on seeds and other dry plant parts. Fully grown larvae burrow into wood to pupate.

ORDER *Coleoptera.*
FAMILY *Ptinidae.*
SPECIES IN FAMILY *500.*
SIZE *3–5mm.*
FEEDING *Larvae and adults: scavengers.*
IMPACT *A few species are pests in houses, and of stored products.*

PTINUS SEXPUNCTATUS *has dark elytra with six irregular white spots, although some of the spots are fused together.*

Fireflies and Glow-worms

Lampyridae

Once seen, the sight of fireflies emitting pulses of eerie greenish light as they fly through the night air is never forgotten. These slightly flattened, parallel-sided beetles are generally drab brown, but may have paler markings of red or yellow. The head, which is small with slender antennae, is concealed by the large, hood-like pronotum. Males are fully winged and the wing cases are soft and rather hairy. The females of some species look like the flattened larvae and lack wings. Only two species are found in Britain – the Glow-worm, seen mostly in southern Britain, and a smaller and very rare species called *Phosphaenus hemipterus*, which is confined to localities in one or two southern counties.

FAVOUR *woods, hedgerows, meadows, and damp grassland; also chalk grassland.*

NOTE

These insects produce light by a chemical reaction in luminous organs. The flashing is used to attract a mate and is specific to each species.

LARVAE

The broad, flattened larvae are predatory and attack snails, using their narrow head and elongate, flattened body, to push inside as they feed.

wings absent ♀

light-emitting organs

flattened body

▼ LAMPYRIS NOCTILUCA, *the Glow-worm, is mainly found in southern Britain on chalk grassland. The female, which can resemble a woodlouse, glows to attract males.*

LARVA

dull brown elytra

pale at pronotum margins

ORDER *Coleoptera.*
FAMILY *Lampyridae.*
SPECIES IN FAMILY *2,000.*
SIZE *0.8–1.8cm.*
FEEDING *Larvae: predators. Adults: non-feeding, predators.*
IMPACT *Harmless.*

Soldier Beetles

Cantharidae

These beetles may have been named after the black and red coloration and contrasting markings of the commonest species, reminiscent of 18th- and 19th-century military uniforms. Soldier beetles are elongate, nearly parallel-sided, and have soft bodies. The head has curved, sharp jaws and relatively long, slender antennae. The pronotum is relatively short and squarish; the wing cases of some species are short and do not reach the abdomen's tip.

OCCUR *on flowers and other vegetation in grassland, woodland edges, and hedgerows.*

LARVAE

The larvae appear similar to those of ground beetles (p.256), with flattened bodies and a fine, velvety covering of short hair.

dark elytra

black spot on pronotum

red base to antennae

◄ CANTHARIS FUSCA *is largely black but for the reddish pronotum with a black patch at the front.*

reddish femora

reddish orange pronotum

yellow tips to elytra

black area at back of head

◄ CANTHARIS PELLUCIDA, *is similar to other species of Cantharis with its reddish orange, unmarked pronotum and red femora.*

▲ MALTHINUS FLAVEOLUS *is a distinctive small beetle with a broad head that narrows behind the eyes, and shortened elytra.*

▼ RHAGONYCHA FULVA, *a common species in Britain, is usually seen on the flowers of umbellifers, where they mate.*

dark tip to elytra

shiny, reddish orange pronotum

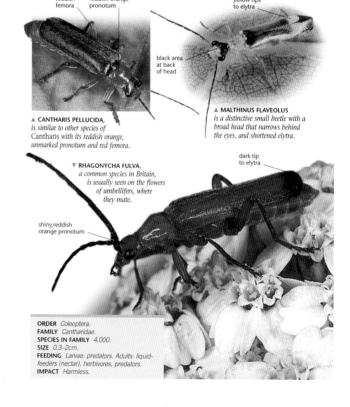

ORDER *Coleoptera.*
FAMILY *Cantharidae.*
SPECIES IN FAMILY *4,000.*
SIZE *0.3–2cm.*
FEEDING *Larvae: predators. Adults: liquid-feeders (nectar), herbivores, predators.*
IMPACT *Harmless.*

Skin, Larder, and Museum Beetles

Dermestidae

Beetles in this family are small and typically broadly oval and rounded in side view. Most species are dull brown or black in colour, but others may appear variegated. They are often thickly covered with white, yellow, brown, or red scales or hair that form spots or delicate patterns. The head is mostly concealed by the pronotum, into which it fits neatly. The short, club-ended antennae can be concealed in grooves on the underside of the thorax and are often hard to see.

SCAVENGE in all kinds of places, such as bird nests, rodent burrows, fur, stored food, and museum collections.

LARVAE

The larvae are very hairy and the long hair tufts of many species produce nettle-like rashes in sensitive people. Anthrenus larvae are commonly called woolly bears.

◀ **ANTHENUS VERBASCI** is also known as the Varied Carpet Beetle. It is a small rounded beetle with distinctive patterns of white, yellow, and black scales.

variegated pattern of scales

rounded, convex body

sombre scale patterns

◀ **ANTHRENUS FUSCUS** lives mainly in sheds, outbuildings, and stone walls where the females lay eggs on dead insects.

rounded body outline

pale front half of elytra

dark rear half of abdomen

▶ **DERMESTES LARDARIUS,** the Bacon or Larder Beetle, is a dry carrion feeder but will also eat dried meat, fish, skins, and a large range of other stored produce.

white patches on rear of pronotum

NOTE

The larvae feed on a range of organic materials, including spices and carpets. They may destroy entire museum collections of biological material.

▶ **ATTAGENUS PELLIO,** known as the Two-spotted Carpet Beetle or Fur Beetle, can be a serious domestic pest; it is also found outdoors.

white spots on elytra

ORDER *Coleoptera.*
FAMILY *Dermestidae.*
SPECIES IN FAMILY *800.*
SIZE *2–10mm.*
FEEDING *Larvae: scavengers. Adults: liquid-feeders (nectar), herbivores (pollen).*
IMPACT *Pests of stored items and textiles.*

Furniture and Drugstore Beetles

Anobiidae

NATIVE to woodland, but thrive in all kinds of artificial wooden structures, both outside and in buildings.

These small, hairy, light brown to black beetles are better known to many people as woodworm, although this name strictly refers to the grub-like larvae of the wood-boring species. The adults are typically elongated and cylindrical in shape, and, from the side, the head appears partly hooded by the pronotum. The antennae have eight to eleven segments, with the last three lengthened or expanded. The legs are short and can be pulled into special grooves on the underside of the body.

▼ **ANOBIUM PUNCTATUM** is very common in trees and structural timbers alike. Its larvae are called woodworm.

branched antennae

NOTE

Feeding larvae bore circular tunnels into dry or dead wood. The adults tend to emerge in May and June, leaving small exit holes and neat piles of wood dust.

fine hairs on upper surface

exit holes

DAMAGED WOOD

▶ **PTILINUS PECTINICORNIS** is fairly common throughout Britain and sometimes attacks furniture. Antennae are branched in males and more saw-like in females.

humped pronotum

pattern of white hairs

▶ **PTINOMORPHUS IMPERIALIS** feeds as a larva on hardwoods such as beech and oak. Adults feed at flowers from May onwards.

▼ **XESTOBIUM RUFOVILLOSUM,** the Deathwatch Beetle, attacks oak as a larva. Adults make tapping noises to attract a mate.

hood-like pronotum extends over head

LARVAE

The white, soft-bodied, grub-like larvae have very small legs and antennae.

ORDER *Coleoptera.*
FAMILY *Anobiidae.*
SPECIES IN FAMILY *1,500.*
SIZE *2–8mm.*
FEEDING *Larvae: scavengers, wood-feeders. Adults: scavengers, non-feeding.*
IMPACT *May damage furniture and timbers.*

Powder-post Beetles

Lyctidae

These beetles are small and slender in shape and brown in colour. The head has rounded, prominent eyes and antennae with eleven segments, of which the last two form a small club. The family's common name refers to the fine, powdery material that is all that is left after the larvae have burrowed into the sapwood of certain hardwoods.

SEEN in dead and dying trees in woodland, and seasoned wood indoors.

LARVAE

The larvae are white, quite hairless, and slightly curved. They bear three pairs of short legs.

LYCTUS BRUNNEUS is very widespread. Females have long ovipositors to lay their eggs in cracks and fissures.

NOTE

Larvae bore in the sapwood of hardwoods such as oak or elm with high starch content and leave their tunnels packed with very fine powdery dust.

elongated body

antennal club made of two segments

ORDER *Coleoptera.*
FAMILY *Lyctidae.*
SPECIES IN FAMILY *100.*
SIZE *3–7mm.*
FEEDING *Larvae and adults: wood-feeders.*
IMPACT *A few species are serious pests of wood.*

Ship-timber Beetles

Lymexylidae

These soft-bodied beetles are characteristically elongated, with parallel sides. The wing cases are shorter than the body, usually leaving the last two or three abdominal segments exposed. Males differ from the slightly larger females in that their eyes are larger and sometimes touch each other and the last segment of the maxillary palps may be enlarged and feathery.

COMMON in parkland and old woodland, on dead wood which has usually lost its bark.

black head and thorax

reddish brown overall

HYLECOETUS DERMESTOIDES has a localized distribution in Britain. The head and thorax are brown in females and shiny black in males.

darker end to elytra

LARVAE

The slender larvae have a prominent prothorax and a highly distinctive, toughened spiny appendage on the last segment of the abdomen.

ORDER *Coleoptera.*
FAMILY *Lymexylidae.*
SPECIES IN FAMILY *60.*
SIZE *0.8–1.6cm.*
FEEDING *Larvae: wood-feeders, fungi-feeders. Adults: non-feeding.*
IMPACT *Lymexylon navale damages oak.*

264

INVERTEBRATES

Soft-winged Flower Beetles

Melyridae

These beetles are narrow and elongated with a soft and flattened body. Many are brightly coloured in green and red and can be quite hairy. The head is typically short and broad with conspicuous eyes and slender antennae that have less than 11 segments. When disturbed, red sac-like swellings appear at the sides of the thorax and abdomen.

THRIVE *in woodland, meadows, grassland, and hedgerows.*

LARVAE

The larvae are long and slender, and may be slightly flattened or broader in the middle.

red margins and rear to elytra

◄ **MALACHIUS AENEUS** *has iridescent coloration and can often be seen feeding on flowers, especially buttercups.*

◄ **MALACHIUS BIPUSTULATUS** *is a common beetle of flower-rich grassland and meadows, where it hunts for small, soft-bodied prey.*

reddish orange tips to elytra

metallic green coloration

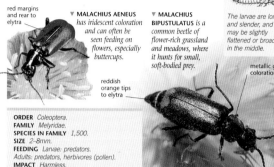

ORDER *Coleoptera.*
FAMILY *Melyridae.*
SPECIES IN FAMILY *1,500.*
SIZE *2–8mm.*
FEEDING *Larvae: predators. Adults: predators, herbivores (pollen).*
IMPACT *Harmless.*

Pollen or Sap Beetles

Nitidulidae

These small beetles are often oval, squarish, or rectangular in outline. The majority are smooth, shiny and either dark or black, and are often marked with reddish or yellowish irregular spots. In some species, the elytra are a little shorter than the abdomen, exposing the last two segments. The short antennae have swollen or clubbed ends. The legs are short.

FOUND *on flowers, fungi, carrion, oozing sap on trees, and decaying fruit.*

clubbed antennae

◄ **GLISCHROCHILUS HORTENSIS,** *an oval black beetle with four reddish orange spots on the elytra, can be found feeding at tree sap and the juices of ripe fruit.*

small, compact body

▼ **MELIGETHES AENEUS** *is often seen in large numbers in flowers where there is a good pollen supply.*

four orange spots on elytra

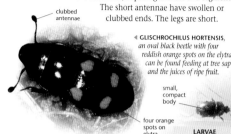

LARVAE

The larvae, which are long, pale, and slightly curved, may be pests of mustard and oilseed rape.

ORDER *Coleoptera.*
FAMILY *Nitidulidae.*
SPECIES IN FAMILY *2,800.*
SIZE *1–14mm.*
FEEDING *Larvae and adults: liquid-feeders, herbivores (pollen), predators, scavengers.*
IMPACT *Pests of crops and stored foods.*

Ladybirds or Ladybugs

Coccinellidae

OCCUR *in coniferous and deciduous woodland, heather, gardens, and parks; wherever there is prey.*

These brightly marked, oval or round, sometimes almost hemispherical beetles are immediately recognizable. Ladybirds are shiny, and have a ground colour of black, red, yellow, or orange. The elytra have contrasting spots or regular markings in similar colours. The bright colouring and marking of adults warns predators of their poisonous or distasteful nature. Confusingly, many species have several colour forms. The head is nearly completely concealed from view by the pronotum, and has antennae with three to six segments, and a short, terminal club. The legs are short, and can be drawn tightly into grooves on the underside of the body. Most adults and larvae are highly predacious on soft-bodied insects. There are, however, some herbivorous species (*Epilachna*) that can be a pest on plants, such as beans and squashes. The adults of many species hibernate in sheltered microhabitats and are often found in attics, and in cooler areas inside houses.

LARVAE

Often warty or spiny with dark bodies and red or white spots, larvae moult four times before pupating. Pupae are dark coloured or look like bird droppings.

NOTE

Adult ladybirds show what is known as reflex bleeding. If attacked, they can cause toxic body fluids to ooze out from the leg joints.

► **APHIDECTA OBLITERATA,** *the Larch Ladybird, has four, dark longitudinal marks on the pronotum. The species is associated with larch and some other coniferous trees.*

black and white markings on head

brown elytra

▼ **CALVIA 14-GUTTATA,** *the Cream-spot Ladybird, is quite small, and has no black markings. Common on trees such as alder, hazel, and whitethorn, it has also been found on flowers of Scots Pine.*

whitish yellow spots

orangish brown background

yellowish orange background

rectangular dark patches

► **PROPYLEA 14-PUNCTATA** *is very variable in colour. Some are all yellow or all black where all the spots seem to have joined up. This species eats aphids on shrubs and trees.*

► **PSYLLOBORA 22-PUNCTATA** *is small with a very round outline. It lives on low vegetation, shrubs, and trees, where it feeds on mildews and moulds.*

warty bumps

pale-ringed dark spots

small black spots

yellow background

PUPA

▲ **ANATIS OCELLATA,** *the Eyed Ladybird, is quite a large predatory species, which is associated with coniferous trees.*

red elytra with seven black spots

white patches on pronotum

antennae

▼ **COCCINELLA SEPTEMPUNCTATA** *is more commonly known as the Seven-spot Ladybird. It is a common species in a wide variety of habitats throughout Britain.*

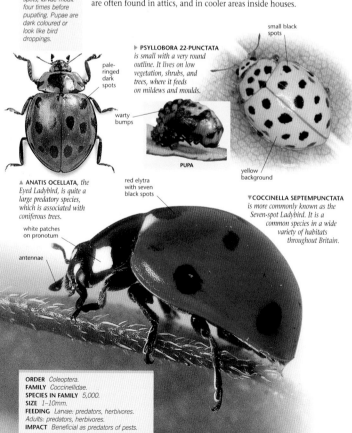

one dark spot on each elytron

► **ADALIA BIPUNCTATA,** *the Two-spot Ladybird, is a variable species, ranging from mainly black to mainly red with a large number of varieties in between.*

white patches on sides of pronotum

elytra predominantly red

ADALIA BIPUNCTATA VARIANT

dark markings predominate

ADALIA BIPUNCTATA VARIANT

predominant dark markings

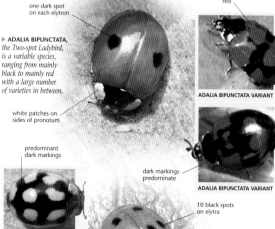

VARIANT

10 black spots on elytra

◄ **ADALIA DECEMPUNCTATA,** *the Ten-spot Ladybird, is another variable species. Some (not pictured) are all black with two pale spots and others are black with ten yellowish orange spots.*

ORDER *Coleoptera.*
FAMILY *Coccinellidae.*
SPECIES IN FAMILY *5,000.*
SIZE *1–10mm.*
FEEDING *Larvae: predators, herbivores. Adults: predators, herbivores.*
IMPACT *Beneficial as predators of pests.*

Chequered Beetles

Cleridae

Although some species can be drab brown or yellowish brown, most chequered beetles are brightly coloured and patterned in red, yellow, blue, and black. The elongated, parallel-sided, and slightly flattened body is typically soft and very hairy. The head is large and quite elongated with prominent eyes and antennae that can be clubbed or slightly comb-like. The legs are very hairy and the second, third, and fourth segments of the tarsi are distinctly heart-shaped. Most species are predators as adults, although some feed on pollen. Species whose larvae feed on pest bark beetles (p.269) are of obvious benefit, but they probably do not have a significant impact.

SEEN *on the foliage of trees and woody plants; some live on carrion and stored animal products.*

LARVAE

Typically cylindrical and slender, the larvae may have bright coloration and be quite hairy. Many species prey on the larvae of jewel, bark, and longhorn beetles.

▼ **OPILO MOLLIS** *is a brownish beetle found in woodland, where it and its larvae eat the grubs of bark beetles and various other wood-boring insects.*

hairy legs

pale spots on elytra

▼ **TILLUS ELONGATUS** *is found on the trunks of broad-leaved trees. The female has a red pronotum; the male is all-black. The larvae prey on beetle grubs.*

black, elongated elytra

red pronotum ♀

downturned head

▼ **THANASIMUS FORMICARIUS** *has very distinctive markings. It can sometimes be found on the trunks of conifers, especially pine.*

black head

pale, wavy bands

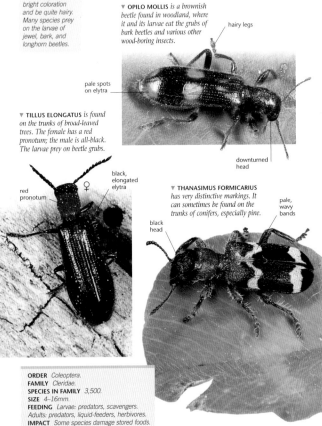

ORDER *Coleoptera.*
FAMILY *Cleridae.*
SPECIES IN FAMILY *3,500.*
SIZE *4–16mm.*
FEEDING *Larvae: predators, scavengers. Adults: predators, liquid-feeders, herbivores.*
IMPACT *Some species damage stored foods.*

Darkling Beetles

Tenebrionidae

Darkling beetles are mostly black or very dark brown, but some species have reddish markings. The body shape ranges from small and parallel-sided to large and broadly oval, and may be smooth and shiny or dull and roughened. The antennae usually have 11 segments and can be relatively long and slender, or short with clubbed ends. The eyes do not have a circular or oval outline. In many species, the hind wings are very small.

INHABIT *virtually all terrestrial habitats, including those with very dry conditions.*

LARVAE

The larvae, known as mealworms, are elongated and cylindrical, usually with very tough bodies and short legs. Some species are reared as bird and reptile food.

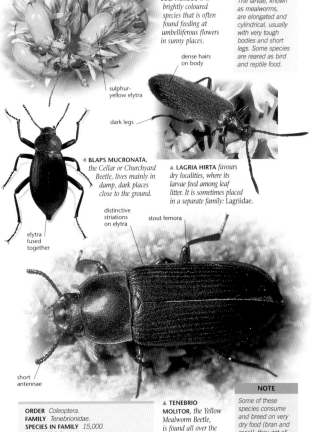

◄ **CTENOPIUS SULPHUREUS** *is a brightly coloured species that is often found feeding at umbelliferous flowers in sunny places.*

dense hairs on body

sulphur-yellow elytra

dark legs

◄ **BLAPS MUCRONATA,** *the Cellar or Churchyard Beetle, lives mainly in damp, dark places close to the ground.*

▲ **LAGRIA HIRTA** *favours dry localities, where its larvae feed among leaf litter. It is sometimes placed in a separate family: Lagriidae.*

elytra fused together

distinctive striations on elytra

stout femora

short antennae

▲ **TENEBRIO MOLITOR,** *the Yellow Mealworm Beetle, is found all over the world. It can be a pest of stored grain, meal, and flour.*

ORDER *Coleoptera.*
FAMILY *Tenebrionidae.*
SPECIES IN FAMILY *15,000.*
SIZE *0.2–2.5cm.*
FEEDING *Larvae and adults: scavengers.*
IMPACT *Some species are pests of stored grain, flour, meal, and dried fruit.*

NOTE

Some of these species consume and breed on very dry food (bran and meal); they get all the water they need from digesting what they eat.

False Oil Beetles

Oedemeridae

These beetles are soft-bodied, elongated, and parallel-sided, like soldier beetles (p.263). Many are brownish, but some are a shiny, iridescent green. The head is small and almost as wide as the pronotum, which is itself widest towards the front. The antennae are long and slender. The margins of the eyes have a small notch.

COMMON *in meadows and flower-rich grassland; the adults feed at flowers.*

swollen hind femora

narrow pronotum

OEDEMERA NOBILIS *is a metallic green meadow beetle that feeds on pollen. Males have greatly swollen hind femora, which are normal in females.*

♂

LARVAE

Grow in certain plant stems and decaying stumps of some deciduous and coniferous trees.

ORDER *Coleoptera.*
FAMILY *Oedemeridae.*
SPECIES IN FAMILY *1,000.*
SIZE *5–14mm.*
FEEDING *Larvae: wood- and fungi-feeders. Adults: liquid-feeders (nectar), herbivores.*
IMPACT *Harmless.*

Ant-like Beetles

Anthicidae

Named for their vaguely ant-like appearance, these small, very active beetles are brownish yellow to brownish black in colour, with reddish markings. The body is narrow and elongated and may be hairy. The head is constricted at the rear to form a neck where it joins the pronotum, which itself may be constricted near the rear. The antennae are slender, often with the last three segments expanded.

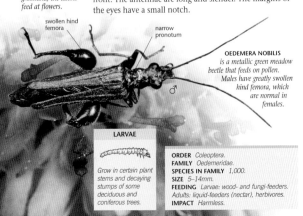

FOUND *often in flowers, while the larvae are to be seen in compost and manure heaps.*

LARVAE

The slender larvae are scavengers, feeding on dead insects and other rotting matter.

▼ **NOTOXUS MONOCERUS** *is unmistakable due to the forward-pointing horn extending over its head.*

swollen tips to antennae

narrow pronotum

▶ **ANTHICUS ANTHERINUS** *often lives among rotting vegetation and can look entirely dark, but usually has reddish brown elytral markings.*

rounded head

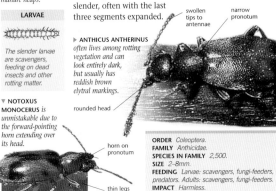

horn on pronotum

thin legs

ORDER *Coleoptera.*
FAMILY *Anthicidae.*
SPECIES IN FAMILY *2,500.*
SIZE *2–8mm.*
FEEDING *Larvae: scavengers, fungi-feeders, predators. Adults: scavengers, fungi-feeders.*
IMPACT *Harmless.*

Oil or Blister Beetles

Meloidae

The name "blister beetle" comes from the fact that the members of this family can produce oily defensive fluids capable of blistering skin. These beetles have a soft, leathery texture and are often bluish black, bright green, or red and black. The head is large, broadly triangular, and bent downwards, while the pronotum is often squarish and narrower than the back of the head. The elytra of ground-living species can be very short and gape to expose a large part of the swollen abdomen. In many species, the adults are herbivorous and, when present in large numbers, may completely defoliate plants.

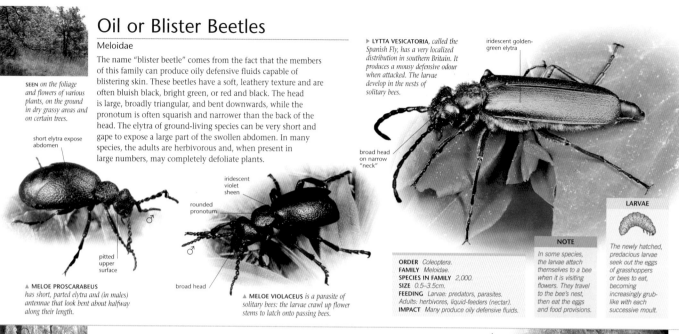

▶ **LYTTA VESICATORIA**, called the Spanish Fly, has a very localized distribution in southern Britain. It produces a mousy defensive odour when attacked. The larvae develop in the nests of solitary bees.

iridescent golden-green elytra

broad head on narrow "neck"

short elytra expose abdomen

pitted upper surface

▲ **MELOE PROSCARABEUS** has short, parted elytra and (in males) antennae that look bent about halfway along their length.

iridescent violet sheen

rounded pronotum

broad head

▲ **MELOE VIOLACEUS** is a parasite of solitary bees: the larvae crawl up flower stems to latch onto passing bees.

LARVAE

NOTE
In some species, the larvae attach themselves to a bee when it is visiting flowers. They travel to the bee's nest, then eat the eggs and food provisions.

The newly hatched, predacious larvae seek out the eggs of grasshoppers or bees to eat, becoming increasingly grub-like with each successive moult.

ORDER Coleoptera.
FAMILY Meloidae.
SPECIES IN FAMILY 2,000.
SIZE 0.5–3.5cm.
FEEDING Larvae: predators, parasites. Adults: herbivores, liquid-feeders (nectar).
IMPACT Many produce oily defensive fluids.

Longhorn Beetles

Cerambycidae

Named for their most distinctive feature, these beetles have antennae that are always at least two-thirds as long as the body, and sometimes up to four times as long. Coloration varies from shades of brown to very brightly marked black and yellow or orange, while some species are even bluish or violet. Often large, the beetles have long bodies with parallel sides. The eyes are notched or occasionally completely divided and the antennae are usually raised on conspicuous tubercles (swellings). Adults of many species are non-feeding, but others may feed on pollen, nectar, leaves, or roots.

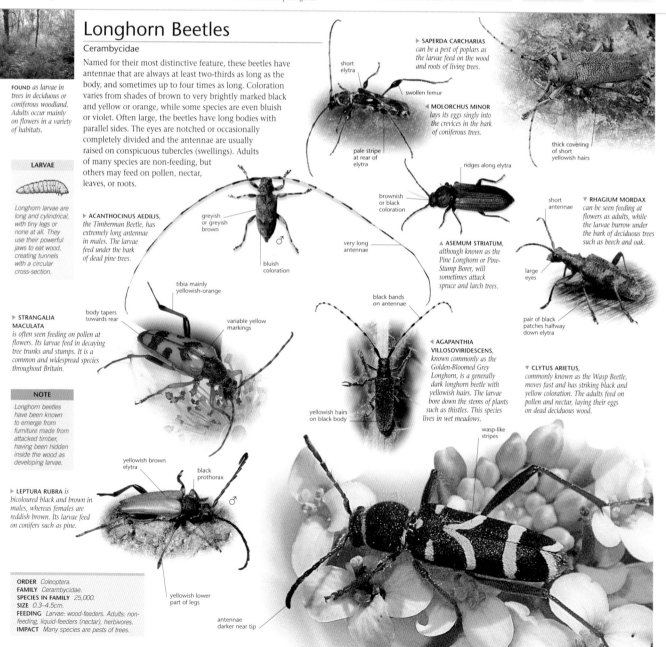

LARVAE

Longhorn larvae are long and cylindrical, with tiny legs or none at all. They use their powerful jaws to eat wood, creating tunnels with a circular cross-section.

▶ **ACANTHOCINUS AEDILIS**, the Timberman Beetle, has extremely long antennae in males. The larvae feed under the bark of dead pine trees.

▶ **STRANGALIA MACULATA** is often seen feeding on pollen at flowers. Its larvae feed in decaying tree trunks and stumps. It is a common and widespread species throughout Britain.

NOTE
Longhorn beetles have been known to emerge from furniture made from attacked timber, having been hidden inside the wood as developing larvae.

▶ **LEPTURA RUBRA** is bicoloured black and brown in males, whereas females are reddish brown. Its larvae feed on conifers such as pine.

ORDER Coleoptera.
FAMILY Cerambycidae.
SPECIES IN FAMILY 25,000.
SIZE 0.3–4.5cm.
FEEDING Larvae: wood-feeders. Adults: non-feeding, liquid-feeders (nectar), herbivores.
IMPACT Many species are pests of trees.

▶ **SAPERDA CARCHARIAS** can be a pest of poplars as the larvae feed on the wood and roots of living trees.

short elytra

swollen femur

◀ **MOLORCHUS MINOR** lays its eggs singly into the crevices in the bark of coniferous trees.

pale stripe at rear of elytra

thick covering of short yellowish hairs

greyish or greyish brown

bluish coloration

ridges along elytra

brownish or black coloration

very long antennae

▲ **ASEMUM STRIATUM**, although known as the Pine Longhorn or Pine-Stump Borer, will sometimes attack spruce and larch trees.

short antennae

▼ **RHAGIUM MORDAX** can be seen feeding at flowers as adults, while the larvae burrow under the bark of deciduous trees such as beech and oak.

large eyes

pair of black patches halfway down elytra

body tapers towards rear

tibia mainly yellowish-orange

variable yellow markings

black bands on antennae

▲ **AGAPANTHIA VILLOSOVIRIDESCENS**, known commonly as the Golden-Bloomed Grey Longhorn, is a generally dark longhorn beetle with yellowish hairs. The larvae bore down the stems of plants such as thistles. This species lives in wet meadows.

yellowish hairs on black body

▼ **CLYTUS ARIETUS**, commonly known as the Wasp Beetle, moves fast and has striking black and yellow coloration. The adults feed on pollen and nectar, laying their eggs on dead deciduous wood.

wasp-like stripes

yellowish brown elytra

black prothorax

antennae darker near tip

yellowish lower part of legs

Cardinal Beetles

Pyrochroidae

Also called fire-coloured beetles, these insects are usually flattened and soft-bodied. The head narrows at the rear, giving the appearance of a broad neck, and the antennae are slender or comb-like (those of males may be feathery). The elytra broaden noticeably towards the rear of the body.

OCCUPY *deciduous woodland, where adults are found crawling on fallen trees and stumps.*

▲ **SCHIZOTUS PECTINICORNIS**, *the Black-headed or Scarce Cardinal Beetle, can be found in upland areas across Britain, but is uncommon.*

- dark spot on pronotum
- branched antennae
- black legs
- body tapers towards rear
- red head

LARVAE

The slightly flattened larvae live under bark and feed on fungal threads or smaller insects.

ORDER Coleoptera.
FAMILY Pyrochroidae.
SPECIES IN FAMILY 150.
SIZE 0.6–1.8cm.
FEEDING Larvae: predators, scavengers, fungi-feeders. Adults: herbivores, predators.
IMPACT Harmless.

▲ **PYROCHROA SERRATICORNIS** *can be told from the very similar but slightly larger species Pyrochroa coccinea by the latter's black head.*

Pea and Bean Weevils

Bruchidae

These dull brownish, oval or egg-shaped beetles – which are not true weevils (p.269) – are often mottled with patches of white or pale brown hairs or scales. The small head has a short snout and shortish antennae, which are comb-like or club-ended. The hind legs are often thicker than the other legs and have strong tooth-like projections. The elytra are typically shortened, exposing the end of the abdomen.

FOUND *mainly near leguminous plants or on stored pulses, but also on other foliage.*

- mottled pattern of hairs on elytra
- head narrows behind eyes

LARVAE

The whitish, small-headed grubs spend their entire larval development inside seeds.

BRUCHUS RUFIMANUS, *the Bean Beetle, can be a serious pest of broad beans and cultivated peas, but also attacks vetches and other wild leguminous plants.*

ORDER Coleoptera.
FAMILY Bruchidae.
SPECIES IN FAMILY 1,300.
SIZE 3–6mm.
FEEDING Larvae: herbivores (in seeds). Adults: herbivores (pollen), liquid-feeders.
IMPACT Pests of stored peas and beans.

Leaf Beetles

Chrysomelidae

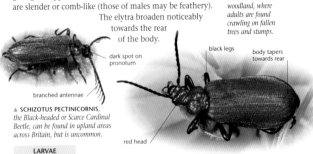

OCCUR *on almost every type of plant in most terrestrial habitats.*

Typical leaf beetles are hairless, broadly oval when seen from above, and rounded when seen from the side. Many are brightly coloured and patterned or have a metallic sheen (such conspicuous coloration often serves to warn predators that the beetles are unpalatable). Although related to longhorn beetles (p.267), leaf beetles never have long antennae; these are usually less than half the body length. Some species look rather like ladybirds (p.265), but can be distinguished by the fact that the latter have three clearly visible tarsal segments on each leg, while leaf beetles have four.

LIFE CYCLE

Long and grub-like, leaf beetle larvae bore through plant tissues and also feed on the surface of plants. Species in the subfamily Donaciinae have aquatic larvae.

◄ **DONACIA VULGARIS** *lives on reeds and other vegetation in swampy places. Its larvae feed on the roots of aquatic plants and obtain air from inside the plants using a pair of spines at their rear end.*

- greenish bronze sheen
- swollen abdomen
- metallic green

PREGNANT FEMALE

◄ **GASTROPHYSA VIRIDULA** *occurs in damp locations such as meadows near to ponds, where the larvae feed on dock leaves. Adult females become greatly distended with eggs.*

- unmarked red elytra

▲ **CHRYSOMELA POPULI**, *the Poplar Leaf Beetle, feeds on the leaves of poplar and, occasionally, willow, as larvae, sometimes reducing entire leaves to skeletons.*

- brilliant green coloration

▲ **CHRYSOLINA MENTHASTRI** *favours hedgerows and damp waterside meadows, where it feeds on mint and related plants. Its body is extremely rounded.*

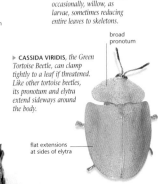

- broad pronotum

▶ **CASSIDA VIRIDIS**, *the Green Tortoise Beetle, can clamp tightly to a leaf if threatened. Like other tortoise beetles, its pronotum and elytra extend sideways around the body.*

- flat extensions at sides of elytra

- elytra have six pale, squarish spots
- head broadest across eyes
- elongated prothorax

▲ **CRIOCERIS ASPARAGI**, *the Asparagus Beetle, feeds on the foliage of asparagus. Its larvae can defoliate a plant, leaving behind liquid black droppings.*

- black ladybird-like spots

▶ **CLYTRA QUADRIPUNCTATA** *lays its eggs near to or on colonies of wood ants. The larvae, which construct a protective case of soil and excrement, scavenge inside the nests.*

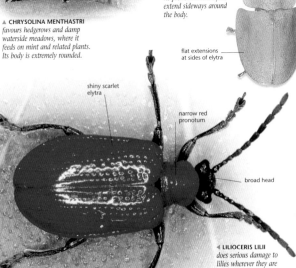

- shiny scarlet elytra
- narrow red pronotum
- broad head

▲ **LILIOCERIS LILII** *does serious damage to lilies wherever they are grown. Adult females lay clumps of orange eggs at the bottom of lily stems; larvae can strip entire plants bare.*

- reddish brown elytra

▲ **LOCHMAEA CAPREA** *can be found on the foliage of birch and willow trees. The adults and larvae chew holes in the leaves, but leave the veins intact.*

- reddish pronotum
- shiny blackish blue elytra

▶ **OULEMA MELANOPUS**, *known as the Cereal Leaf Beetle, can be a serious pest of wheat, oats, and barley, but it also feeds on other grasses. The larvae graze the upper surface of leaf blades in long strips.*

NOTE

Some leaf beetles can defeat chemical plant defences. Before feeding, these species cut trenches in leaves to isolate them from the rest of the plant.

ORDER Coleoptera.
FAMILY Chrysomelidae.
SPECIES IN FAMILY 30,000.
SIZE 0.2–2cm.
FEEDING Larvae: herbivores (leaves, stems, roots). Adults: herbivores (flowers, leaves).
IMPACT Many species are serious pests.

Weevils

Curculionidae

WIDELY distributed in all land habitats and associated with almost every species of plant.

Weevils form the largest family in the animal world. Also known as snout beetles, they possess a snout, or rostrum, which is a prolongation of the head. It carries the jaws at its end and it may be short and broad or slender and as long as the body. The antennae, which arise from the rostrum, are normally "elbowed" and have clubbed ends. Most weevil species are covered by small scales and are cryptically coloured, although some are bright green or pinkish. This family also includes the bark beetles, which live on coniferous and deciduous trees. They are compact, either brown or black, and lack a conspicuous rostrum. Their head is usually almost hidden from view by a hood-like shield covering the thorax.

◄ **POLYDRUSUS MOLLIS** occurs on a wide variety of deciduous trees, including birch, beech, and willow. The larvae feed on roots in the soil.

clubbed antennae

shiny scales

broad larval tunnels

BARK

▶ **POLYDRUSUS SERICEUS** is found mainly on birch, hazel, and oak trees. The adults browse on the edges of the leaves.

▼ **OTIORHYNCHUS SULCATUS**, the Black Vine Weevil, is a widespread pest of many plants. Adults notch the edges of leaves, while larvae eat the roots of crops such as vines and strawberries.

abdomen appears swollen

▶ **IPS TYPOGRAPHUS** is one of several species called engraver beetles. It attacks spruce trees and can be a serious pest in plantations.

relatively short snout

dark, compact body

metallic gold or bronze scales

◄ **PHYLLOBIUS ARGENTATUS**, the Silver-green Leaf Weevil, chews the young leaves of hazel, beech, and other trees as an adult. Its larvae feed on the roots of grasses.

radiating larval burrows

tufts of dark and light hairs cover body

hood-like pronotum conceals head

BARK

▲ **SCOLYTUS SCOLYTUS**, the Large Elm Bark Beetle, carries and spreads a fungus that causes Dutch elm disease. Females tunnel under the bark to lay their eggs.

▲ **CRYPTORHYNCHUS LAPATHI**, commonly known as the Poplar and Willow Borer, has effective camouflage. The larvae burrow under the bark of alders and sometimes birch.

very long, curved snout

▶ **CURCULIO VENOSUS**, the Acorn Nut Weevil, lays its eggs inside acorns. Larvae leave the acorn after it has fallen and then crawl into the soil to pupate.

covering of fine hairs

surface covered with long scales

long snout, curved at tip

♀

▲ **CURCULIO NUCUM** feeds on pollen and nectar. The snout is very long and curved in females, which use it to make holes in hazelnuts before they lay their eggs.

ORDER Coleoptera.
FAMILY Curculionidae.
SPECIES IN FAMILY 50,000.
SIZE 0.3–2.4cm.
FEEDING Larvae: fungi- and wood-feeders, herbivores. Adults: fungi-feeders, herbivores.
IMPACT Many species are pests of plants.

Leaf-rolling Weevils

Attelabidae

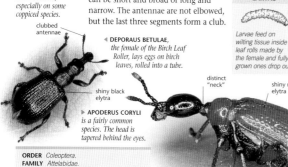

OCCUR on host species in scrubland, hedgerow, and woodland, especially on some coppiced species.

These beetles are closely related to weevils (above). They vary from oval to moderately elongated and are often bright reddish and black. The head is sometimes "pinched" at the rear to form a neck; its rostrum can be short and broad or long and narrow. The antennae are not elbowed, but the last three segments form a club.

LARVAE

Larvae feed on wilting tissue inside leaf rolls made by the female and fully grown ones drop out.

clubbed antennae

▼ **DEPORAUS BETULAE**, the female of the Birch Leaf Roller, lays eggs on birch leaves, rolled into a tube.

distinct "neck"

shiny black elytra

shiny red elytra

▶ **APODERUS CORYLI** is a fairly common species. The head is tapered behind the eyes.

red femora

ORDER Coleoptera.
FAMILY Attelabidae.
SPECIES IN FAMILY 1,800.
SIZE 3–7mm.
FEEDING Larvae and adults: herbivores.
IMPACT A few species can be serious pests of fruit trees and soft fruit.

Apionid Weevils

Apionidae

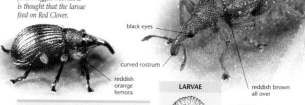

ABUNDANT on a wide variety of habitats from wasteland to woodland margins and coasts to gardens.

These small or very small pear-shaped weevils are usually matt black in colour but can be greenish or reddish. The head is rounded and, unlike leaf-rolling weevils (left), is not constricted behind the eyes. There is a long, narrow, curved rostrum. The antennae are usually not elbowed and end in an elongated club with three segments.

▼ **PROTAPION RYEI** is one of several, small, yellow-legged weevils. It is thought that the larvae feed on Red Clover.

black eyes

curved rostrum

reddish orange femora

LARVAE

Larvae bore into the stems, seed pods, and other parts of plants. Some are pests of field crops.

reddish brown all over

▲ **APION FRUMENTARIUM** is a small weevil with a narrow, pointed front end and broad rear end.

ORDER Coleoptera.
FAMILY Apionidae.
SPECIES IN FAMILY 2,000.
SIZE 2–5mm.
FEEDING Larvae and adults: herbivores (seeds, stems, and other plant parts).
IMPACT Many species can damage crops.

Snow Scorpionflies

Boreidae

These small insects are very dark brown or bronze to black in colour, so contrast strongly against a snowy background. The head, as in all scorpionflies, is extended downwards, forming an obvious beak that bears the jaws. The antennae are quite long, but the wings are very much reduced, resembling small hooks in the males or scales in females.

NOTE

Superbly adapted for life in the cold, these scorpionflies die if held in a warm hand for too long. They walk rapidly across the ground and can also jump.

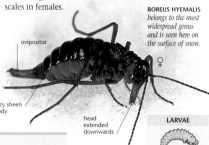

ovipositor

BOREUS HYEMALIS *belongs to the most widespread genus and is seen here on the surface of snow.*

♀

bronzy sheen to body

head extended downwards

fairly long antennae

LARVAE

The larvae hatch from eggs laid in moss. They look like small, curved caterpillars.

ORDER *Mecoptera.*
FAMILY *Boreidae.*
SPECIES IN FAMILY *30.*
SIZE *3–5mm.*
FEEDING *Larvae and adults: herbivores (mainly mosses and lichens), scavengers.*
IMPACT *Harmless.*

Common Scorpionflies

Panorpidae

FOUND *in low-growing vegetation, usually in shady places such as groves and woodland.*

The head of these brownish yellow and black insects is elongated downwards to form a beak that carries biting mouthparts. The wings often have dark markings. Males have an upturned abdomen with bulbous genitalia; the abdomen of females tapers towards the rear.

♂

▶ PANORPA COMMUNIS *lives in cool, moist places and feeds on dead or dying insects. The enlarged genitalia of this male are clearly visible.*

spotted wings

LARVAE

The larvae look like caterpillars, with eight pairs of short abdominal feet and (often) spines.

elongated head

♀

pointed abdomen

ORDER *Mecoptera.*
FAMILY *Panorpidae.*
SPECIES IN FAMILY *360.*
SIZE *0.9–2.5cm.*
FEEDING *Larvae: scavengers. Adults: liquid-feeders (nectar, honeydew), scavengers.*
IMPACT *Harmless.*

Common Fleas

Pulicidae

Fleas are immediately recognizable by their small size, dark brown or black coloration, winglessness, laterally flattened bodies, and – above all – remarkable jumping ability. The head is fused to a small thorax and carries short antennae concealed in grooves at the side. The simple lateral eyes are quite well developed and the mouthparts are modified for piercing skin and sucking blood. On many fleas, there is a comb of stout bristles at the back of the pronotum and at the sides of the head. Fleas are prolific breeders; owners of untreated pets risk having flea eggs and larvae in their home.

PARASITES *on a range of mammals, such as dogs, cats, hedgehogs, rabbits, and humans.*

NOTE

In general, fleas avoid light and are attracted to a variety of hosts. Hungry fleas may jump hundreds of times an hour for several days to find a host.

◀ PULEX IRRITANS *is called the Human Flea but is more often found attacking pigs and goats. People are more likely to be bitten by cat and dog fleas.*

▶ SPILOPSYLLUS CUNICULI, *the Rabbit Flea, is a major vector of the rabbit disease myxomatosis.*

piercing mouthparts

"comb" on pronotum

"comb" on pronotum

long, spiny hind legs

flat, shiny abdomen

▼ CTENOCEPHALIDES FELIS, *the Cat Flea, is capable of a high jump of 34cm at up to 130 times the acceleration of gravity.*

◀ CTENOCEPHALIDES CANIS, *the Dog Flea, also lives on wolves. It is the intermediate host for the tapeworm Dipylidium caninum, which also infects cats.*

LARVAE

Flea larvae are tiny and elongated. They feed on detritus in the host's nest, the faeces of adult fleas, and dried blood. When fully grown, they each spin a silken cocoon.

ORDER *Siphonaptera.*
FAMILY *Pulicidae.*
SPECIES IN FAMILY *200.*
SIZE *1–8mm.*
FEEDING *Larvae: scavengers (dried blood and faeces). Adults: blood-feeders.*
IMPACT *Bites may cause allergic reactions.*

Crane Flies

Tipulidae

LIVE *near water and lush vegetation; larvae occur in diverse places such as rotting wood, soil, and water.*

Also known as "daddy-long-legs", crane flies are easy to identify due to their slender, fragile bodies, elongated wings, and long, thread-like legs. A highly characteristic feature of these flies is that their legs are shed very easily if they are trapped or handled. The body is brown, black, or grey, often with yellow, orange, or pale brown markings, and there is a distinctive V-shaped groove on top of the thorax.

♀

dark marks on wings

yellow bands on abdomen

♀

▲ NEPHROTOMA CROCATA *is a black crane fly with three bright yellow bands on the abdomen.*

▶ CTENOPHORA ORNATA *males have a swollen abdominal tip, while the females are slender with a reddish abdomen.*

feathery antennae

▲ TIPULA MAXIMA *is a very large species with clear dark marks all over the wings. The thorax is greyish and abdomen reddish brown.*

♂

dark spot on wings

NOTE

Large species of crane fly rest with their wings fully outstretched, while smaller species tend to fold their wings back along the body.

LARVAE

The brown or grey larvae are long and cylindrical and are called leatherjackets due to their texture. They may be partly aquatic, aquatic, or terrestrial in habit.

wings held open at rest

brown front edge to wing

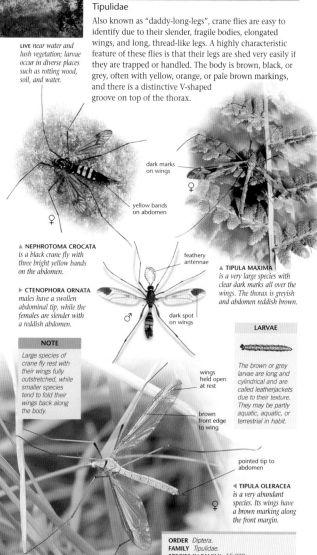

pointed tip to abdomen

◀ TIPULA OLERACEA *is a very abundant species. Its wings have a brown marking along the front margin.*

♀

ORDER *Diptera.*
FAMILY *Tipulidae.*
SPECIES IN FAMILY *15,000.*
SIZE *1–6cm (wingspan).*
FEEDING *Larvae: scavengers. Adults: liquid-feeders (plant sap, nectar).*
IMPACT *Pests of grasses and some crops.*

Mosquitoes

Culicidae

REMAIN *near to the larval breeding grounds in a range of aquatic habitats, from puddles to ponds and lakes.*

It might not be easy to spot these very slender, delicate flies, but they produce a high-pitched whine in flight that is a sure sign of their presence. The head is small and rounded with very long and slender, forward-facing sucking mouthparts. The body and legs are covered with tiny scales and appear pale brown to reddish brown, although some species have bright markings. The wings are long and narrow with scales along the veins and margins. The antennae are feathery in males and slightly hairy in females. Females suck blood from vertebrate hosts; males feed on nectar or honeydew.

LARVAE

The larvae, known as "wrigglers" after the way in which they thrash about in water, are mainly scavengers, but a few are predators. Most obtain air at the surface.

biting mouthparts

▲ CULEX PIPIENS *is a very common greyish brown mosquito with pale bands on the abdomen. It rarely bites humans.*

wings longer than abdomen

banded abdomen

rounded head

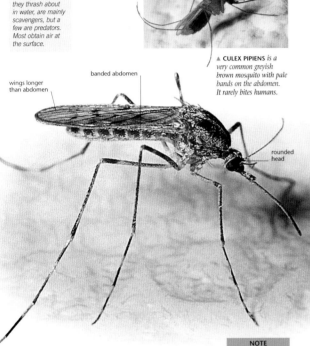

▲ CULISETA ANNULATA, *a large species, has spotted wings and banded legs. It can breed in quite polluted water and often enters houses.*

ORDER *Diptera.*
FAMILY *Culicidae.*
SPECIES IN FAMILY *3,100.*
SIZE *3–9mm.*
FEEDING *Larvae: scavengers. Adults: blood-feeders (females), liquid-feeders (males).*
IMPACT *Bites are painful; transmit diseases.*

NOTE
The eggs are laid in almost any standing water. Although they tend to remain near water, the adults may be common in shady woodland and forest at dusk.

Biting Midges

Ceratopogonidae

These small flies are similar to but somewhat smaller than non-biting midges (left), with shorter front legs. They often have dark patterns on their wings. The rounded head is not concealed from above by the thorax and the antennae of males are feathery. The mouthparts, especially those of the females, are short and piercing for sucking up fluids.

PLENTIFUL *near the margins of ponds, lakes, and rivers, and in boggy areas.*

humped thorax

wings folded flat over body

shortish front legs

LARVAE

The minute, slender, worm-like larvae can be aquatic or may live in damp soil or under tree bark.

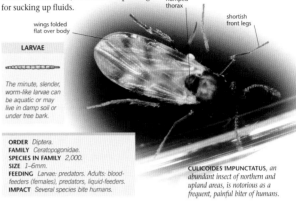

ORDER *Diptera.*
FAMILY *Ceratopogonidae.*
SPECIES IN FAMILY *2,000.*
SIZE *1–6mm.*
FEEDING *Larvae: predators. Adults: blood-feeders (females), predators, liquid-feeders.*
IMPACT *Several species bite humans.*

CULICOIDES IMPUNCTATUS, *an abundant insect of northern and upland areas, is notorious as a frequent, painful biter of humans.*

Black Flies

Simuliidae

THRIVE *around rivers and other fast-flowing bodies of water.*

Black flies have stout bodies, short legs, and a distinctively humped thorax. The head is relatively large and rounded with short, thick mouthparts, which, in the females of most species, are used for cutting skin and sucking blood. The antennae are short with no more than nine segments. The wings are broad at the base and narrow towards the end with distinct veins at the leading edge.

SIMULIUM SP. *appear at certain times of the year in swarms and attack humans and domesticated animals. Their bites are very painful, itchy, and can cause serious allergic reactions.*

humped thorax

wings become narrow at rear

prominent veins at front of wings

LARVAE

The aquatic larvae use hooks or a "sucker" on the rear of the abdomen to hold on to objects.

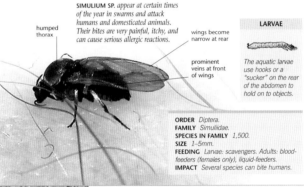

ORDER *Diptera.*
FAMILY *Simuliidae.*
SPECIES IN FAMILY *1,500.*
SIZE *1–5mm.*
FEEDING *Larvae: scavengers. Adults: blood-feeders (females only), liquid-feeders.*
IMPACT *Several species can bite humans.*

Non-biting Midges

Chironomidae

These pale green, brown, or grey flies are delicate and look a bit like mosquitoes (above), but lack scales on the wings and their mouthparts are very short or absent. Males have very feathery antennae and a slender body, while females have hairy antennae and a stoutish body.

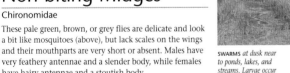

SWARMS *at dusk near to ponds, lakes, and streams. Larvae occur in all aquatic habitats.*

humped thorax ♂

LARVAE

The long, slender larvae occasionally have gills at the rear of the body. Their coloration varies.

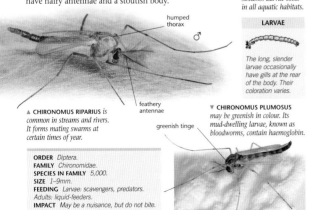

▲ CHIRONOMUS RIPARIUS *is common in streams and rivers. It forms mating swarms at certain times of year.*

feathery antennae

greenish tinge

▼ CHIRONOMUS PLUMOSUS *may be greenish in colour. Its mud-dwelling larvae, known as bloodworms, contain haemoglobin.*

ORDER *Diptera.*
FAMILY *Chironomidae.*
SPECIES IN FAMILY *5,000.*
SIZE *1–9mm.*
FEEDING *Larvae: scavengers, predators. Adults: liquid-feeders.*
IMPACT *May be a nuisance, but do not bite.*

Owl Midges

Psychodidae

FOUND *in damp and shady places such as woods and bogs; often rest in cracks, crevices, or burrows by day.*

Also called moth flies due to the long hairs or scales covering their bodies, wings, and legs, these small flies are greyish or brownish. The eyes are large and the antennae are made up of 10 to 14 bead-like segments. The wings are usually broad with pointed tips and have few, if any, cross-veins. Like night-flying moths, owl midges are largely nocturnal and are often attracted to lights after dark.

LARVAE

Owl midge larvae are elongated and cylindrical. They live in decaying matter, often in sewers.

PERICOMA FULIGINOSA *is found wherever its semi-aquatic larvae breed in mud; also often found in outbuildings and at windows after dark.*

moth-like overall shape

patterns of long hairs

ORDER *Diptera.*
FAMILY *Psychodidae.*
SPECIES IN FAMILY *1,500.*
SIZE *1.5–5mm.*
FEEDING *Larvae: scavengers. Adults: liquid-feeders.*
IMPACT *Harmless.*

Wood Gnats

Anisopodidae

Wood gnats are small to medium-sized, gnat-like flies with long legs and a slightly flattened head. The eyes are quite large and may touch in males; the antennae are about as long as the head and thorax together. The wings are large and lie flat on the abdomen at rest. Some species are known as window flies because they are common inside houses and can often be seen at windows.

OCCUR *in damp or wooded areas, often near larval habitats of sewage and decaying organic matter.*

slightly flattened head

long legs

relatively large wings

LARVAE

The larvae are slender and elongate with a smooth body and a small head.

SYLVICOLA SP. *often form mating swarms in the late afternoon or around dusk. Some species are known as window flies and are sometimes confused with mosquitoes.*

ORDER *Diptera.*
FAMILY *Anisopodidae.*
SPECIES IN FAMILY *100.*
SIZE *2–10mm.*
FEEDING *Larvae: scavengers. Adults: liquid-feeders.*
IMPACT *Harmless.*

March Flies

Bibionidae

These flies are stout-bodied, black or dark brown insects, often with very hairy bodies and shortish legs. The heads of males and females are differently shaped: the former are larger and have large compound eyes that meet on top of the head; females have narrower heads, and eyes which do not meet. March flies are common in spring, when males can swarm in large numbers.

PLENTIFUL *on flowers in pastures, meadows, gardens, and other similar habitats.*

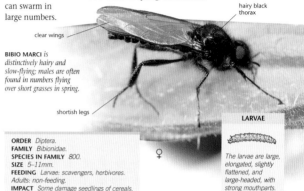

clear wings

hairy black thorax

BIBIO MARCI *is distinctively hairy and slow-flying; males are often found in numbers flying over short grasses in spring.*

shortish legs

♀

LARVAE

The larvae are large, elongated, slightly flattened, and large-headed, with strong mouthparts.

ORDER *Diptera.*
FAMILY *Bibionidae.*
SPECIES IN FAMILY *800.*
SIZE *5–11mm.*
FEEDING *Larvae: scavengers, herbivores. Adults: non-feeding.*
IMPACT *Some damage seedlings of cereals.*

Gall Midges

Cecidomyiidae

THRIVE *in almost all habitats, around fungi, the larval host plants, and decaying organic matter.*

Gall midges are tiny, delicate, pale or sombre flies with slender legs. The antennae are long and slender, with each bead-like segment bearing a whorl of fine hairs. The wings can be hairy and, characteristically, have only a few unbranched veins. The eyes of both sexes touch or nearly touch on top of the head and in some species are divided in two. Most species induce galls on plants; a few are free-living.

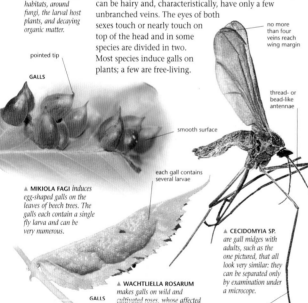

pointed tip

GALLS

no more than four veins reach wing margin

thread- or bead-like antennae

smooth surface

each gall contains several larvae

▲ MIKIOLA FAGI *induces egg-shaped galls on the leaves of beech trees. The galls each contain a single fly larva and can be very numerous.*

◀ CECIDOMYIA SP. *are gall midges with adults, such as the one pictured, that all look very similar: they can be separated only by examination under a microscope.*

▲ WACHTLIELLA ROSARUM *makes galls on wild and cultivated roses, whose affected leaves thicken and fold into a pouch-like gall.*

GALLS

long, slender legs

▼ JAAPIELLA VERONICAE *lays eggs in the buds of Germander Speedwell, causing hairy galls.*

white, hairy gall

LARVAE

The larvae are red, yellow, or orangish and they lack any clear distinguishing feature, except for a structure called the sternal spatula, or breast plate.

▼ DIDYMOMYIA TILIACEA *galls are commonly clustered on lime leaves. The pale, yellowish green galls stick out on both sides of the leaf.*

pale greenish coloration

GALLS

galls packed together

ORDER *Diptera.*
FAMILY *Cecidomyiidae.*
SPECIES IN FAMILY *4,600.*
SIZE *1–5mm.*
FEEDING *Larvae: herbivores, fungi-feeders, predators. Adults: liquid-feeders.*
IMPACT *Damage plants, including crops.*

Fungus Gnats

Mycetophilidae

The best recognition features for these mosquito-like flies are the thorax, which is very humped in side view, and the long legs, which have two strong spurs at the end of the bristly tibiae. Most species of fungus gnat are dull black, brown, or yellow, but some have brighter markings. The head is flattened from front to back and the antennae are generally long, although the females of some species may have short antennae. In many species, the larvae live gregariously in fungi and can be serious pests of cultivated mushroom beds; pupation occurs inside the host fungus or in a loose cocoon made of soil particles and silk. Other larvae damage the roots of wheat seedlings, cucumber, and potted plants.

ATTRACTED *to moist, dark places, often in woodland, where found on fungi, under bark, and in dead wood, and bird nests.*

minute hairs on wings

very elongated antennae

LARVAE

The thin, cylindrical larvae are soft and white, with a dark head. They mostly eat fungal matter, but some species prey on tiny insects and worms.

elongated first leg segment

◀ MACROCERA STIGMA *is sometimes found feeding at umbelliferous flowers and, more rarely, occurs in caves. Its antennae are up to three times as long as the body.*

NOTE

One way to see fungus gnats, is to put attacked fruiting bodies of fungi into a plastic container with a fine mesh top. Eventually adult flies will appear. Fungus gnats attack wild fungi as soon as they appear.

▼ MYCETOPHILA ORNATA *is a fairly common species throughout Great Britain and Ireland. The larvae are found in fruiting bodies of various fungi.*

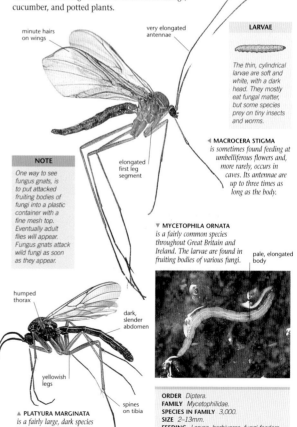

pale, elongated body

humped thorax

dark, slender abdomen

yellowish legs

spines on tibia

▲ PLATYURA MARGINATA *is a fairly large, dark species widespread in Britain and Wales. Its larvae live under rotting wood and prey on insects.*

ORDER *Diptera.*
FAMILY *Mycetophilidae.*
SPECIES IN FAMILY *3,000.*
SIZE *2–13mm.*
FEEDING *Larvae: herbivores, fungi-feeders, scavengers, predators. Adults: liquid-feeders.*
IMPACT *Pests of mushrooms.*

Horse Flies

Tabanidae

Also called deer flies, clegs, or gad flies, these insects are stout-bodied, hairless, and fast-flying. They are black, grey, or brown and often have bright yellow or orange bands or other markings. The head is large, hemispherical, and flattened; the short antennae are the most typical feature. The large eyes, which occupy most of the head, are green or purple with iridescent bands and spots. The females' mouthparts are adapted to cut skin and lap blood.

SEEN *near mammals, often far from larval breeding grounds in marshy areas or near water.*

NOTE

Female horse flies approach victims with great stealth and feed in hard-to-reach places. Their bites are painful and may cause allergic reactions.

mottled wings

bands on legs

▲ HAEMATOPOTA PULVIALIS, *known as the Cleg, is a silent and notorious biter of humans. It is found close to water in woodland.*

hairy, striped thorax

iridescent, "spotty" eyes

LARVAE

The larvae are predacious on small worms, crustaceans, and insect larvae and may be aquatic or live in very damp soil, litter, or rotting wood.

▶ CHRYSOPS RELICTUS *has broad brown marks on its wings and shiny green eyes. It is very common near water, especially in upland areas and on heathland.*

blade-like mouthparts

▶ TABANUS SUDETICUS *is a large horse fly with a bee-like abdomen with distinctive pale, triangular marks in a line down the middle.*

pale tibiae

▼ TABANUS BOVINUS *is found in meadows and light woodland near flowing water. Females attack cattle and horses. The larvae develop in wet soil.*

stripes on abdomen

pale triangle on each abdominal segment

hairy thorax

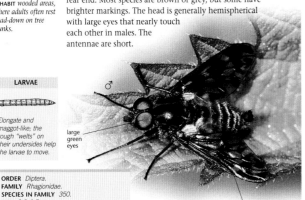

ORDER *Diptera.*
FAMILY *Tabanidae.*
SPECIES IN FAMILY *4,100.*
SIZE *0.6–2.8cm.*
FEEDING *Larvae: predators. Adults: blood-feeders (females), liquid-feeders (males).*
IMPACT *Severe nuisance with painful bite.*

Soldier Flies

Stratiomyidae

These robust, rather flattened flies sometimes have yellow, green, or pale abdominal markings. Some large species resemble wasps, while others are smaller, and coloured brown, green, or metallic bluish black. The eyes cover a large area of the broad, hemispherical or very rounded head, especially in males. The short antennae are distinctive, with the third segment bent outwards from the basal segments. The wings are folded flat over the body at rest. Although they are not particularly strong fliers, some can hover.

FOUND *mainly in damp areas on the flowers of willow, hawthorn, irises, and umbellifers.*

green thorax

LARVAE

◀ CHLOROMYIA FORMOSA *has a rather blunt-ended, broad abdomen. It is bronze coloured in males and bluish in females.*

The larvae of the soldier flies are elongate and flattened; their tough and leathery bodies are impregnated with calcareous deposits.

smoky-tinged wings

yellow scutellum

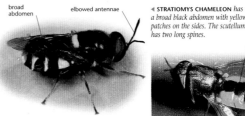

yellow stripes on head

◀ OXYCERA RARA *is a stout-bodied species with strong yellow on black markings. It favours sunny clearings in wet areas, such as fenland.*

pale tibia

broad abdomen

elbowed antennae

◀ STRATIOMYS CHAMELEON *has a broad black abdomen with yellow patches on the sides. The scutellum has two long spines.*

black central stripe

▲ ODONTOMYIA VIRIDULA *has a black, hairy thorax and a broad, flattened abdomen. It is found in wet meadows.*

lime green sides to abdomen

ORDER *Diptera.*
FAMILY *Stratiomyidae.*
SPECIES IN FAMILY *1,800.*
SIZE *2–17mm.*
FEEDING *Larvae: scavengers, predators, herbivores. Adults: liquid-feeders (nectar).*
IMPACT *Harmless.*

Snipe Flies

Rhagionidae

Snipe flies are small to medium-sized and quite slender, with longish legs and a long abdomen that tapers to the rear end. Most species are brown or grey, but some have brighter markings. The head is generally hemispherical with large eyes that nearly touch each other in males. The antennae are short.

INHABIT *wooded areas, where adults often rest head-down on tree trunks.*

LARVAE

Elongate and maggot-like; the rough "welts" on their undersides help the larvae to move.

♂

large green eyes

ORDER *Diptera.*
FAMILY *Rhagionidae.*
SPECIES IN FAMILY *350.*
SIZE *0.6–1.5cm.*
FEEDING *Larvae and adults: predators.*
IMPACT *Harmless.*

ATHERIX IBIS, *known as the Water Snipe Fly, is found near fresh water. Females are grey with more prominent stripes.*

smoky patches on wings

Small-headed Flies

Acroceridae

There is no mistaking these oddly-shaped flies. The large thorax can appear very humped in side view and the abdomen is typically rounded and swollen. The head is small but covered almost entirely by the eyes, which touch each other in both sexes, unlike snipe flies (above). The short antennae sometimes look as if they have only two segments because the basal segment is concealed.

LIVE *in grassland and flower-rich meadows where their spider hosts occur.*

small head hidden by thorax

very rounded thorax

LARVAE

CYRTUS PUSSILUS *is a small fly with a large rounded thorax and a globular abdomen, which is distinctively marked black and yellow.*

Inside a spider, the larvae wait until it is about to moult for the last time, before emerging to pupate.

ORDER *Diptera.*
FAMILY *Acroceridae.*
SPECIES IN FAMILY *500.*
SIZE *4–8mm.*
FEEDING *Larvae: parasites (spiders). Adults: liquid-feeders (nectar).*
IMPACT *Harmless.*

Stiletto Flies

Therevidae

Elongate, yellowish brown to black, and often very hairy flies, therevids are similar in shape to small robber flies (below), but lack the groove between the eyes and tuft of facial hair. The large eyes touch each other in males. The antennae have three segments, and the proboscis is short, soft, and fleshy.

OCCUR *mainly in well-vegetated habitats; also in coastal sand dunes.*

pointed abdomen

slender legs

hairy thorax

♂

LARVAE

The larvae are white and slender with a dark head. They usually feed on small insects.

▲ **THEREVA NOBILITATA**
is a dark brown species with a thick covering of yellowish hairs, especially at the front of the head, around the thorax, and at the sides of the abdomen.

♂

▲ **ACROSATHE ANNULATA** *is a hairy species. The males are silver in appearance, whereas the females have greyish silver abdomens with light brown markings.*

ORDER *Diptera.*
FAMILY *Therevidae.*
SPECIES IN FAMILY *550.*
SIZE *4–15mm.*
FEEDING *Larvae: predacious. Adults: liquid-feeders.*
IMPACT *Harmless.*

Bee Flies

Bombyliidae

As the name implies, bee flies can look very similar to bees. Some are stout-bodied and very hairy. Their body colour is usually brown, red, and yellow. The wings may be clear or have dark bands or patterned markings, particularly at the leading edge. The head is often rounded, and the proboscis can be very long for sucking nectar from deep flowers.

SEEN *feeding or flying in open, sunny locations or resting on bare sandy ground.*

hairy, bee-like body

▶ **VILLA MODESTA** *looks quite bee-like. It has a rounded head, short proboscis, and a furry body.*

head pale at sides

clear wings

dark area on front of clear wing

▲ **BOMBYLIUS MAJOR**
looks like a bee and hovers like a hover fly. It has a long proboscis that projects in front of the head.

ORDER *Diptera.*
FAMILY *Bombyliidae.*
SPECIES IN FAMILY *5,000.*
SIZE *2–18mm.*
FEEDING *Larvae: parasitic, predators. Adults: liquid-feeders (nectar).*
IMPACT *Harmless.*

LARVAE

Most larvae are parasitic on other insect larvae. Some eat eggs of grass-hoppers in the soil.

Robber or Assassin Flies

Asilidae

Robber flies are aerial or ambush hunters with excellent eyesight. Most are brownish or black with reddish orange or yellow markings and the body varies from slender and relatively hairless to stout and hairy. The head has a groove between the separated, bulging eyes and the face has a tuft of long hairs, called the beard. The forward-pointing proboscis is stiff and sharp for stabbing and sucking. The legs are strong and bristly for catching insect prey in flight.

FOUND *in a variety of habitats, but prefer sunny sites in open or lightly wooded areas.*

LARVAE

The ground-living larvae are cryptically coloured, elongated, and tapered at both ends. They are scavengers or prey on the eggs, larvae, and pupae of other insects.

◀ **PHILONICUS ALBICEPS**
inhabits sandy areas, including coastal sand dunes. It is pale yellowish grey, with a "dusty" appearance.

long, cylindrical abdomen

yellowish bristles on abdomen sides

widely separated eyes

dusky wings

▲ **LEPTOGASTER CYLINDRICA**
flies holding its front and middle legs forward, ready to catch prey. It hunts aphids, small flies, and bugs.

four yellow abdomen segments

▲ **ASILUS CRABRONIFORMIS**
is a very large, wasp-like fly that makes short, darting flights to seize large prey such as crane flies (as here).

bee-like abdomen

facial tuft

NOTE

Most species perch on an exposed twig or stone to spot passing prey, then give chase. They quickly stab victims and inject a protein-dissolving saliva.

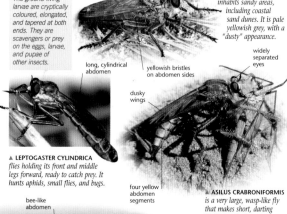

▼ **DIOCTRIA BAUMHAUERI**
has a less-developed facial hair tuft than other genera of robber flies. It occurs in cool, deciduous woodland.

very hairy legs

◀ **LAPHRIA SP.** *can seem very bee-like due to their large size and hairy bodies. Their larvae burrow inside wood and eat wood-boring beetle larvae.*

dark, slender wasp-like body

ORDER *Diptera.*
FAMILY *Asilidae.*
SPECIES IN FAMILY *5,000.*
SIZE *0.3–2.8cm.*
FEEDING *Larvae: predators, scavengers. Adults: predators.*
IMPACT *Harmless.*

Long-legged Flies

Dolichopodidae

These flies are small or very small, bristly-bodied, and have very shiny green or yellow coloration. The head is rounded and bears a short, fleshy proboscis. The wings are oval and about as long as the body. In males, the genitalia are large and held curved forward under the abdomen; in females the abdomen ends in a sharp point. Males may have hairy tufts on the tarsi, antennae, and other parts of the body, used as sexual signals to females during mating.

COMMON *in damp habitats such as hedgerows, woodland, meadows, and lake and stream margins.*

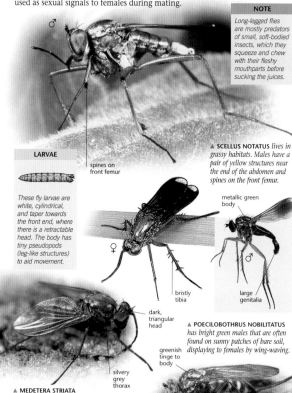

♂

NOTE

Long-legged flies are mostly predators of small, soft-bodied insects, which they squeeze and chew with their fleshy mouthparts before sucking the juices.

spines on front femur

LARVAE

These fly larvae are white, cylindrical, and taper towards the front end, where there is a retractable head. The body has tiny pseudopods (leg-like structures) to aid movement.

♀

bristly tibia

▲ **SCELLUS NOTATUS** *lives in grassy habitats. Males have a pair of yellow structures near the end of the abdomen and spines on the front femur.*

metallic green body

♂

large genitalia

dark, triangular head

▲ **POECILOBOTHRUS NOBILITATUS**
has bright green males that are often found on sunny patches of bare soil, displaying to females by wing-waving.

greenish tinge to body

silvery grey thorax

▲ **MEDETERA STRIATA**
runs in all directions to catch prey and walks about on tree trunks. The larvae of this genus are beneficial as they eat bark beetle larvae.

pale bands on abdomen

▲ **LIANCALUS VIRENS**
is commonly found near small streams, where freshwater runs down rock surfaces.

ORDER *Diptera.*
FAMILY *Dolichopodidae.*
SPECIES IN FAMILY *5,500.*
SIZE *1–7mm.*
FEEDING *Larvae: predators. Adults: mostly predators, also liquid-feeders (nectar).*
IMPACT *Harmless.*

Dance Flies

Empididae

FOUND on vegetation in moist locations, often resting on tree trunks or branches and sometimes on water.

These flies' common name refers to the mating swarms in which the males fly up and down as if dancing. Most are small with a stout thorax and a slender, tapering abdomen. The coloration varies from dark brown and black to yellow or light brown. The rounded head has large eyes, antennae with three segments, and a long, downward-pointing proboscis. Dance flies are all predators, but may drink nectar as well.

LARVAE

The spindle-shaped larvae can retract their head and live in leaf litter, humus, wood, and water.

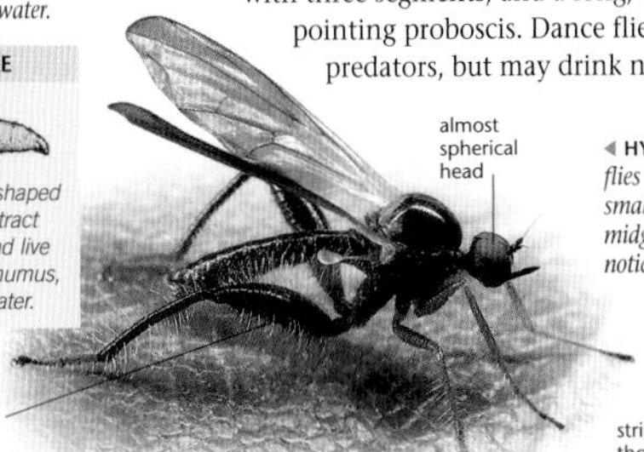

almost spherical head

◄ **HYBOS FEMORATUS** flies slowly, hunting small flies such as midges. Its thorax is noticeably humped.

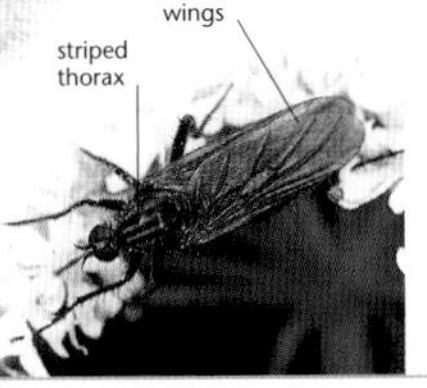

brownish wings

enlarged hind femora

striped thorax

ORDER Diptera.
FAMILY Empididae.
SPECIES IN FAMILY 3,500.
SIZE 2–11mm (body length).
FEEDING Larvae: predators. Adults: mainly predators; also nectar-feeders.
IMPACT Harmless.

► **EMPIS TESSELLATA** preys on other small flies, but can also be seen feeding on nectar at flowers such as hawthorn.

Scuttle Flies

Phoridae

Scuttle flies are named for the adults' fast, jerky running movements. Their alternative name of hump-backed flies refers to their distinctive, well-developed thorax. They are small in size and dark brown, black, or yellowish. The fairly large wings are clear or light brown, and only have obvious veins near the front edge. The hind legs are often enlarged and flattened.

ATTRACTED to rotting fungi, compost heaps, and carcasses in many habitats. Also seen at flowers, dung, and the nests of social insects.

LARVAE

The larvae are fattest in the middle and feed on a wide variety of plant and animal foods.

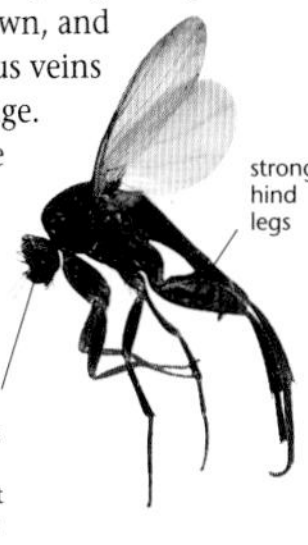

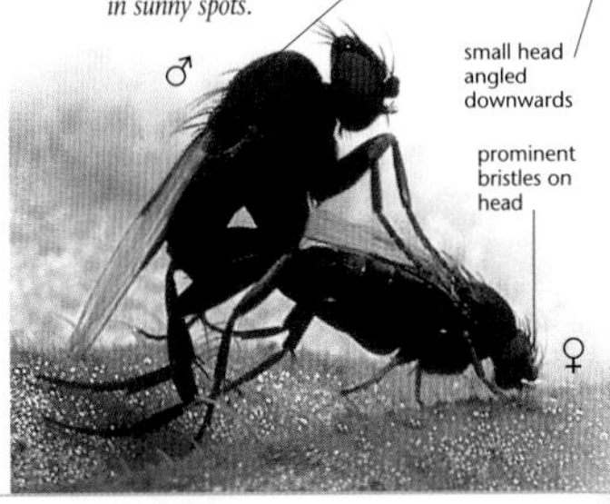

▼ **PHORA ATRA**, shown here mating, feeds on flowers and honeydew. Males often form mating swarms in sunny spots.

humped thorax

small head angled downwards

prominent bristles on head

strong hind legs

◄ **ANEVRINA THORACICA** is a widespread species whose larvae live in soil, in the corpses of small mammals, and the nests of moles.

ORDER Diptera.
FAMILY Phoridae.
SPECIES IN FAMILY 2,800.
SIZE 0.5–5mm (body length).
FEEDING Larvae: scavengers, predators. Adults: predators, liquid-feeders.
IMPACT May feed on cultivated mushrooms.

Hover Flies or Flower Flies

Syrphidae

INHABIT a range of habitats, particularly localities with plenty of umbelliferous (flat-topped) flowers.

NOTE

Most hover flies are important as plant pollinators and pest controllers. Often it is possible to find four or five different species feeding on a single flowerhead.

Hover flies are the most easily recognizable of all the flies due to their often wasp-like or bee-like appearance and their ability to hover. These superb aerial acrobats can move in all directions, including backwards, and can hold a fixed position in the air even in gusty conditions. The adults are typically slender-bodied with black and yellow or white stripes; some are stout and hairy. The eyes are large and in males meet on top of the head. The wings have a characteristic false vein running down the middle (a simple thickening of the wing membrane) and a false margin at the edge (the joining together of the outer wing veins). Despite the warning, wasp-like markings, and the bee-like appearance of many species, hover flies are harmless nectar feeders. The larvae of a few species can be pests of cultivated bulbs.

◄ **VOLUCELLA BOMBYLANS** may have a reddish or a whitish tail and mimics the red- and buff-tailed bumble bees, but can be distinguished by its large eyes and single pair of wings.

DARK FORM

large, stout, hairy body

separated eyes

black posterior of abdomen

▲ **VOLUCELLA PELLUCENS** is often to be seen feeding at bramble blossom. Its larvae live inside the nests of wasps and bees, where they are scavengers.

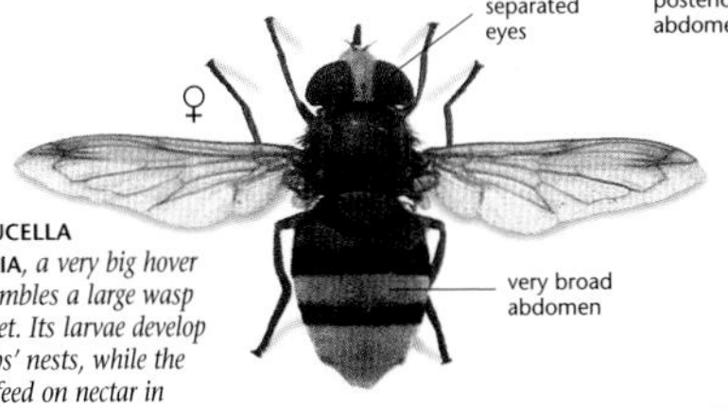

► **VOLUCELLA ZONARIA**, a very big hover fly, resembles a large wasp or hornet. Its larvae develop in wasps' nests, while the adults feed on nectar in sheltered habitats.

very broad abdomen

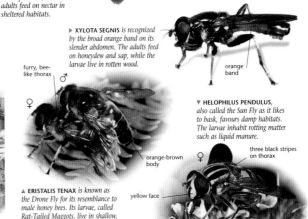

► **XYLOTA SEGNIS** is recognized by the broad orange band on its slender abdomen. The adults feed on honeydew and sap, while the larvae live in rotten wood.

orange band

false wing margin

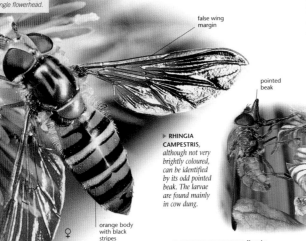

furry, bee-like thorax

▼ **HELOPHILUS PENDULUS**, also called the Sun Fly as it likes to bask, favours damp habitats. The larvae inhabit rotting matter such as liquid manure.

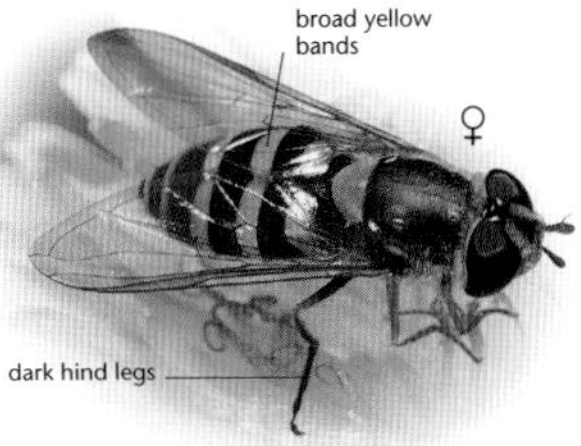

pointed beak

► **RHINGIA CAMPESTRIS**, although not very brightly coloured, can be identified by its odd pointed beak. The larvae are found mainly in cow dung.

three black stripes on thorax

orange-brown body

yellow face

orange body with black stripes

◄ **EPISYRPHUS BALTEATUS** is common in any habitat with suitable nectar-rich flowers. The larvae prey on aphids; the adults often migrate south in swarms.

► **SYRPHUS VITRIPENNIS** lives in a wide variety of habitats, preferring woodland. It is very hard to distinguish from S. ribesii (below), but the female's hind femora are dark.

broad yellow bands

white patches

shiny black thorax

brownish veins on wings

▲ **ERISTALIS TENAX** is known as the Drone Fly for its resemblance to male honey bees. Its larvae, called Rat-Tailed Maggots, live in shallow, nutrient-rich or stagnant water.

▼ **MYATHROPA FLOREA** looks like a paler version of the Drone Fly (above left). Like Rat-Tailed Maggots, the larvae have a breathing siphon at their rear end, but live in water-filled tree holes.

◄ **SERICOMYIA SILENTIS** occurs on acid heathland. The larvae of this species live in boggy pools, such as those that form after cutting peat.

LARVAE

Some larvae are aquatic or live in liquid manure, and possess a breathing tube (above). Many others are slug-like and fierce predators of aphids and other soft-bodied pests.

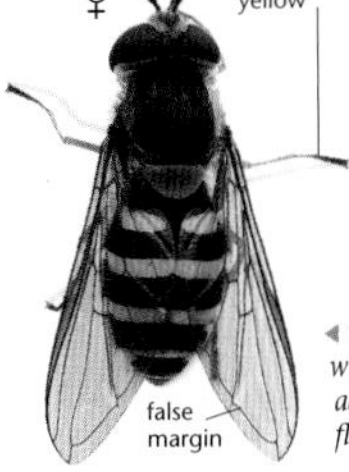

all legs yellow

dark hind legs

false margin

◄ **SYRPHUS RIBESII** commonly occurs in gardens, where its larvae are major predators. The adults feed on nectar, so planting suitable flowers will improve pest control.

ORDER Diptera.
FAMILY Syrphidae.
SPECIES IN FAMILY 6,000.
SIZE 0.4–2.8cm (body length).
FEEDING Larvae: predators and scavengers. Adults: liquid-feeders, herbivores.
IMPACT Beneficial as predators of aphids.

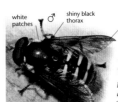

orange hairs

Thick-headed Flies

Conopidae

Many of these species resemble bees or wasps, some having yellow and black stripes on the abdomen and others being reddish brown or black. The head is often the broadest part of these flies and carries short, erect antennae with three segments and (usually) a long proboscis. The abdomen is narrow where it joins the thorax and is swollen and bent down at the rear. Females lay eggs on a variety of hosts.

OCCUR *in a variety of mainly open habitats, usually feeding at flowers.*

constricted abdomen

broad head

wasp-like markings

long proboscis

▲ PHYSOCEPHALA RUFIPES *is a parasite of bumble bees and honey bees. It closely resembles some digger wasps (Sphecidae).*

LARVAE

▲ CONOPS QUADRIFASCIATA *grabs wasps and bees in flight and lays an egg on them. Its larvae are internal parasites, finally killing the host.*

Much narrower at the front, the larvae suck the body fluids of wasps, bees, and other hosts.

ORDER *Diptera.*
FAMILY *Conopidae.*
SPECIES IN FAMILY *1,000.*
SIZE *0.4–2cm (body length).*
FEEDING *Larvae: parasites. Adults: liquid-feeders (nectar).*
IMPACT *Harmless.*

Leaf-mining Flies

Agromyzidae

These small to medium-sized grey, black, or greenish yellow flies have moderately hairy heads and thoraxes. The wings are relatively large and usually clear. The abdomen is distinctly tapered, and females have a rigid, pointed ovipositor for laying eggs. The distinct feeding trails or mines made in leaves by the larvae are easy to see.

FOUND *in a variety of habitats wherever their host trees, shrubs, or herbaceous plants grow.*

clear wings

◀ PHYTOMYZA ILICIS *lays its eggs on holly leaves. The feeding larva makes a mine between the upper and lower leaf surfaces.*

irregular blotch mine

▶ LIRIOMYZA SP. *are typically black, but some species have yellow markings. The genus has more than 40 species in Britain.*

yellow scutellum

mine

LARVAE

Larvae pupate inside their mine or gall, or drop to the ground and pupate in the soil.

ORDER *Diptera.*
FAMILY *Agromyzidae.*
SPECIES IN FAMILY *2,500.*
SIZE *1–6mm.*
FEEDING *Larvae: herbivores. Adults: liquid-feeders.*
IMPACT *Many species are pests.*

▶ AGROMYZA ALNIBETULAE *lays eggs on birch or alder leaves. As the larvae feeds, the width of the mine becomes larger.*

Black Scavenger or Ensign Flies

Sepsidae

In summer these slender flies may form large swarms on plants. They have a shiny black, purplish, or reddish body, narrow wings, a rounded head, and slender legs. The wings of most species are clear, with a noticeable, dark spot at the ends. Adult males gather on vegetation and display their wing tips by walking back and forth, flicking their wings.

LIVE *in many different types of habitat, on dung and decaying matter or at flowers.*

LARVAE

The somewhat slim and tapering larvae may occur in huge numbers in ideal conditions.

▶ SEPSIS FULGENS *can be seen in groups on plants and cow dung. The base of the abdomen often has an orange tinge.*

black shiny body

rounded head

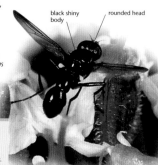

ORDER *Diptera.*
FAMILY *Sepsidae.*
SPECIES IN FAMILY *250.*
SIZE *2–6mm (body length).*
FEEDING *Larvae: scavengers, dung-feeders. Adults: liquid-feeders (nectar).*
IMPACT *Harmless.*

Fruit Flies

Tephritidae

Sometimes called picture-winged flies, these small to medium-sized species are immediately recognizable by their wing markings. The patterning, which can be present in the form of transverse bands, patches, zigzag stripes, or spotting, can help to identify species. The females' abdomen tapers and ends in a pointed, rigid ovipositor, while in males, it is blunt or round-ended and does not taper. The larvae often feed inside galls that develop on the host plants. During courtship, the males of many species show a high degree of territoriality. They display by walking about slowly, waving one patterned wing while holding the other upright.

FOUND *in many habitats, wherever their host plants are found.*

NOTE

The Mediterranean Fruit Fly, Ceratitis capitata, damages citrus and soft fruit. Other species are pests of walnuts, cherries, apples, and blueberries.

patterned wings

yellow head

clear area at apex of wings

greenish eyes

▲ PLATYPAREA DISCOIDEA *larvae are thought to bore into the stems of the Giant Bellflower, (Campanula latifolia). A very similar species infests asparagus.*

▲ PHAGOCARPUS PURMUNDUS *has very distinctively patterned wings. The larvae of this fly species develop inside the berries of Hawthorn trees.*

mottled wings

pale hair on thorax

yellowish orange head

LARVAE

The yellowish, pale brown, or whitish larvae live inside soft fruit, and in the flowerheads of daisies and related plants, either as stem or leaf miners or as gall formers.

▲ OXYNA PARIETINA *has wings with dark areas, large clear patches, and smaller semi-clear spots. The larvae bore into the stems of Mugwort (Artemisia vulgaris).*

swollen gall

▶ UROPHORA CARDUI *lays eggs on stems of Creeping Thistle (Cirsium arvense). This causes the growth of a gall inside which several larvae develop.*

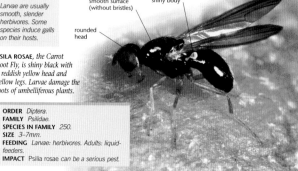
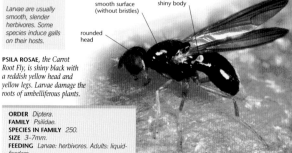

ORDER *Diptera.*
FAMILY *Tephritidae.*
SPECIES IN FAMILY *4,500.*
SIZE *4–14mm.*
FEEDING *Larvae: herbivores. Adults: liquid-feeders (nectar, sap).*
IMPACT *Several species are serious pests.*

Rust Flies

Psilidae

Rust flies are slender or moderately robust, and reddish brown to black in colour. The body does not have strong bristles and may be virtually bare. The head is rounded or slightly triangular in outline, and the antennae may be relatively long. The wings are generally clear, but may be smoky or yellowish in some species. Some species induce galls on their host plants.

INHABIT *damp or moist areas near their host plants.*

LARVAE

Larvae are usually smooth, slender herbivores. Some species induce galls on their hosts.

smooth surface (without bristles)

shiny body

rounded head

PSILA ROSAE, *the Carrot Root Fly, is shiny black with a reddish yellow head and yellow legs. Larvae damage the roots of umbelliferous plants.*

ORDER *Diptera.*
FAMILY *Psilidae.*
SPECIES IN FAMILY *250.*
SIZE *3–7mm.*
FEEDING *Larvae: herbivores. Adults: liquid-feeders.*
IMPACT *Psilia rosae can be a serious pest.*

Shore Flies

Ephydridae

OCCUR *in ditches, bogs, marshes, and seashores; also found around stagnant water, cesspits, and drains.*

Many shore flies are dark grey, brownish, or black, without any clear identification features. The wings are usually clear but can be patterned in some species. The face can appear somewhat bulging, with reddish eyes. Some species swarm in large numbers over salt marshes. The larvae generally feed by filtering micro-organisms from the water; others feed on decaying plant matter or are predators.

LARVAE

The larvae are pointed towards the front, with many small hairs all over their surface.

large red eyes

clear wings

enlarged front legs

insect prey

OCHTHERA MANTIS *preys on small insects, while its aquatic larvae eat the larvae of chironomid midges (p.271) and other flies.*

ORDER *Diptera.*
FAMILY *Ephydridae.*
SPECIES IN FAMILY *1,400.*
SIZE *2–9mm.*
FEEDING *Larvae and adults: scavengers, herbivores (algae only in adults), predators.*
IMPACT *Some are pests of cereals.*

Dung Flies

Scathophagidae

Dung flies are black, yellow, grey, or brown and sometimes show two of these colours in striking contrast. These flies may look superficially like house flies (p.278), but the commonest species are very hairy or bristly, some looking almost furry. The wings are usually clear but may have darkish tinges or spots. The abdomen is slender, but, in males, is enlarged at the rear end.

FOUND *in a variety of habitats, often on dung or in boggy areas.*

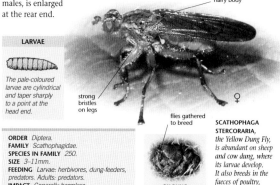

hairy body

LARVAE

The pale-coloured larvae are cylindrical and taper sharply to a point at the head end.

strong bristles on legs

♀

flies gathered to breed

ON DUNG

SCATHOPHAGA STERCORARIA, *the Yellow Dung Fly, is abundant on sheep and cow dung, where its larvae develop. It also breeds in the faeces of poultry, horses, and humans.*

ORDER *Diptera.*
FAMILY *Scathophagidae.*
SPECIES IN FAMILY *250.*
SIZE *3–11mm.*
FEEDING *Larvae: herbivores, dung-feeders, predators. Adults: predators.*
IMPACT *Generally harmless.*

Lesser Fruit Flies

Drosophilidae

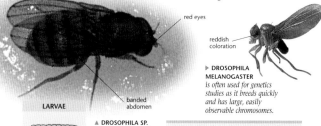

OCCUPY *a variety of habitats and buildings where there is a supply of rotting plant matter.*

If you want to see these small flies, which are also known as vinegar flies, simply leave out some wine, cider, or rotting fruit. Most species are light yellow or brown with clear or lightly marked wings and pale or bright red eyes. The thorax (and sometimes the abdomen) has spots or stripes. These insects are often used as laboratory insects in studies of genetics.

red eyes

reddish coloration

▶ **DROSOPHILA MELANOGASTER** *is often used for genetics studies as it breeds quickly and has large, easily observable chromosomes.*

LARVAE

banded abdomen

The pale, maggot-like larvae, which can develop rapidly, have hooked spines on each segment.

▲ **DROSOPHILA SP.** *are quickly attracted to rotting fruit of all kinds and to the smell of cider or vinegar, both in buildings and outdoors. One species breeds in leftover milk.*

ORDER *Diptera.*
FAMILY *Drosophilidae.*
SPECIES IN FAMILY *2,900.*
SIZE *1–6mm.*
FEEDING *Larvae: scavengers, herbivores. Adults: liquid-feeders.*
IMPACT *May be pests in orchards.*

Anthomyiid Flies

Anthomyiidae

INHABIT *a very wide range of habitats from cultivated land and grassland to woodland and gardens; widespread and ubiquitous.*

These rather ordinary-looking flies are very similar in general appearance to house flies (p.278), although some may be larger or smaller. The body colour may be dull yellowish brown, grey, brown, or black, and the slender, bristly legs are yellowish brown or black. The wings may be clear or have a light smoky tinge. The adults of many species feed on pollen and nectar at umbelliferous and other flowers, while some species are predators of small insects. The larvae can be terrestrial or semiaquatic and show a wide range of feeding types.

LARVAE

The herbivorous white larvae are found as stem borers, gall formers, and leaf miners in the roots, stems, flower heads, and leaves of a huge range of host plants.

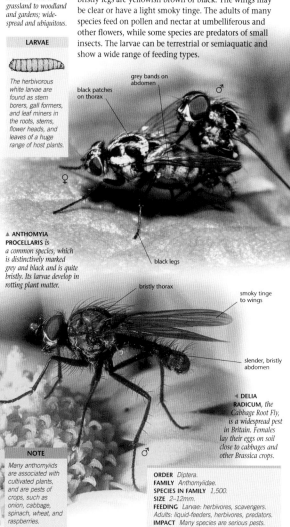

grey bands on abdomen

black patches on thorax

♂

♀

black legs

▲ **ANTHOMYIA PROCELLARIS** *is a common species, which is distinctively marked grey and black and is quite bristly. Its larvae develop in rotting plant matter.*

bristly thorax

smoky tinge to wings

slender, bristly abdomen

♂

◀ **DELIA RADICUM,** *the Cabbage Root Fly, is a widespread pest in Britain. Females lay their eggs on soil close to cabbages and other Brassica crops.*

NOTE

Many anthomyiids are associated with cultivated plants, and are pests of crops, such as onion, cabbage, spinach, wheat, and raspberries.

ORDER *Diptera.*
FAMILY *Anthomyiidae.*
SPECIES IN FAMILY *1,500.*
SIZE *2–12mm.*
FEEDING *Larvae: herbivores, scavengers. Adults: liquid-feeders, herbivores, predators.*
IMPACT *Many species are serious pests.*

Stem, Grass, or Fruit Flies

Chloropidae

Species in this large and common group of flies are grey, green, or black with bright yellow markings, especially on the thorax. The body has very few obvious hairs or bristles, but a good recognition feature is a clear, shiny triangular mark on top of the head between the eyes. The abdomen is usually broad and tapers towards the rear.

LARVAE

LIVE *in cereal crops, grassland, reedbeds, and hedgerows.*

Usually the larvae are slender and cylindrical, tapering at the head and with a blunt rear.

elongated abdomen

MEROMYZA PRATORUM *occurs in coastal sand dunes, where its larvae burrow and feed inside the stems of Marram grasses.*

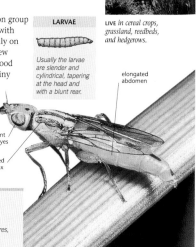

iridescent green eyes

striped thorax

ORDER *Diptera.*
FAMILY *Chloropidae.*
SPECIES IN FAMILY *2,000.*
SIZE *2–7mm.*
FEEDING *Larvae: scavengers, herbivores, predators. Adults: liquid-feeders.*
IMPACT *Some are pests of cereals.*

INVERTEBRATES

Lesser House Flies

Fanniidae

Like smaller and more slender house flies (below), these flies are generally dark, although the legs or abdomen may be wholly or partly yellowish. The eyes of the males can be large and may even touch each other, while those of the females are smaller and separated. Males swarm in the shade of branches or overhangs and will fly indoors, where they dart about and land on the underside of ceiling lights.

COMMON *near decaying matter, in sheltered, well-vegetated locations, and under trees at woodland margins, parkland, or gardens.*

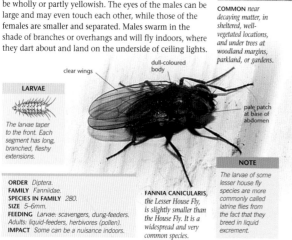

clear wings
dull-coloured body
pale patch at base of abdomen

LARVAE

The larvae taper to the front. Each segment has long, branched, fleshy extensions.

ORDER *Diptera.*
FAMILY *Fanniidae.*
SPECIES IN FAMILY *280.*
SIZE *5–6mm.*
FEEDING *Larvae: scavengers, dung-feeders. Adults: liquid-feeders, herbivores (pollen).*
IMPACT *Some can be a nuisance indoors.*

FANNIA CANICULARIS, *the Lesser House Fly, is slightly smaller than the House Fly. It is a widespread and very common species.*

NOTE

The larvae of some lesser house fly species are more commonly called latrine flies from the fact that they breed in liquid excrement.

Flesh Flies

Sarcophagidae

These stout-bodied, non-metallic flies are mostly dull grey or black with yellowish body hair. The most distinctive features are the longitudinally striped thorax, and the chequered or marbled abdominal patterns, which change from light to dark depending on the viewing angle. Adults are frequently seen feeding on nectar, sap, and honeydew. The females lay larvae, not eggs, often in carrion.

FOUND *in a variety of habitats, wherever there is decaying matter or carrion. Often associated with human habitations.*

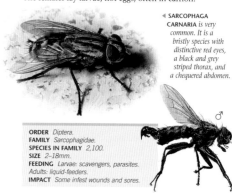

◄ **SARCOPHAGA CARNARIA** *is very common. It is a bristly species with distinctive red eyes, a black and grey striped thorax, and a chequered abdomen.*

LARVAE

The larvae taper to the front and hatch inside the female, which lays them in a suitable place.

◄ **SARCOPHAGA MELANEURA** *is very difficult to identify as there are numerous similar species; however, males have distinctive genitalia.*

ORDER *Diptera.*
FAMILY *Sarcophagidae.*
SPECIES IN FAMILY *2,100.*
SIZE *2–18mm.*
FEEDING *Larvae: scavengers, parasites. Adults: liquid-feeders.*
IMPACT *Some infest wounds and sores.*

♂

House Flies and their relatives

Muscidae

LIVE *wherever there is excrement, carcasses, and rotting matter; ubiquitous in all habitats.*

The House Fly is a typical member of this family. These flies can be slender or stoutish, dull black, grey, or yellowish in colour, with clear wings. All parts of the body usually have strong, dark bristles. The legs are slender and quite long. The mouthparts act like a sponge and draw in liquid foods, except in blood-feeding species, which have piercing mouthparts. Identification of species relies on bristle patterns and structure of the genitalia. Muscids are found on flowers, excrement, and decaying organic matter. Blood-feeding species are associated with their hosts.

LARVAE

The larvae are typically maggot-shaped, tapering towards the front and blunt at the rear. They develop quickly in rotting material, and pupate in just over a week.

▼ **STOMOXYS CALCITRANS**, *the Stable Fly, looks like a House Fly with a striped thorax, and lightly chequered abdomen.*

yellowish orange at base of wings

sharp proboscis

▲ **MESEMBRINA MERIDIANA** *is an unmistakable large, shiny, dark fly, identified by the yellowish orange patches at the wing bases.*

grey patches on abdomen

abdomen with orange patches

▼ **POLIETES LARDARIUS** *is grey with a bluish tinge, a longitudinally striped thorax, and a dark-marked abdomen.*

clear wings

▲ **MUSCA DOMESTICA**, *the House Fly, is dark grey with lighter, longitudinal stripes down its thorax.*

silvery stripes on thorax
reddish eyes

NOTE

Many of these flies transmit harmful micro-organisms via their mouthparts and feet, which cause diseases such as dysentery and typhoid.

ORDER *Diptera.*
FAMILY *Muscidae.*
SPECIES IN FAMILY *3,000.*
SIZE *2–12mm.*
FEEDING *Larvae: scavengers, herbivores. Adults: predators, scavengers, herbivores.*
IMPACT *Some bite, others transfer disease.*

Blow Flies

Calliphoridae

Typical species, often called "bluebottles" or "greenbottles", are stout-bodied, medium to large, metallic green or blue flies that are attracted to carrion, as well as fresh and cooked meat and fish. Some species are shiny black or drab coloured. Most are usually the same size or bigger than a house fly. The tips of the antennae are distinctively feathered, and the proboscis is short. In some species, the sexes are different colours.

OCCUR *on all habitats, with the larvae on soil, dung, and carcasses.*

► **LUCILIA CAESAR** *is a cosmopolitan, shiny, metallic green species that breeds on rotting carcasses and dung.*

metallic green coloration

LARVAE

The larvae are typical white maggots that taper at the front end and are blunt ended at the rear. The head is narrow with dark, hook-like mouthparts.

shiny blue abdomen

◄ **CALLIPHORA VOMITORIA** *is a common "bluebottle". The dark thorax has faint longitudinal stripes and the abdomen has a metallic blue sheen.*

yellowish hairs

► **POLLENIA RUDIS**, *also known as the Cluster Fly, has distinctive, golden-yellow hair on its thorax.*

bristly rear of abdomen

dark red eyes

◄ **CALLIPHORA VICINA** *is very similar to C. vomitoria, but can be separated from it by the "cheeks" of the head below the eyes, which are red, not black, in colour.*

NOTE

Many species in this family are of medical and veterinary importance. Besides flesh-eating larvae, some calliphorids carry diseases such as dysentery.

ORDER *Diptera.*
FAMILY *Calliphoridae.*
SPECIES IN FAMILY *1,200.*
SIZE *4–16mm.*
FEEDING *Larvae: scavengers, parasites. Adults: scavengers, liquid-feeders, herbivores.*
IMPACT *Can infest livestock and humans.*

hair
wings

CALLIPHORA VICINA

Parasitic Flies

Tachinidae

Although parasitic flies show a wide range of body colour and patterns, most of them are dark-coloured, and stout-bodied. Some are like very bristly house flies, others are much larger, very hairy, and almost bee-like. The abdomen is well provided with stout, erect bristles, particularly on the rear half and around the margins. The wings are usually clear, but some species have dark markings. The larvae of this family are parasitic on other insects and very rarely on arthropods.

OCCUPY *a wide variety of habitats, often at flowers or sap oozing from plants.*

mottled, angular wings ♂

◄ **ALOPHORA HEMIPTERA** *males are slightly larger than the females, and have dark wing markings.*

LARVAE

Larvae are white or yellowish and may have spines or hairs. As they are within their hosts, they are rarely seen.

▶ **TACHINA GROSSA** *looks like a bumble bee. The front margins of the wings are yellowish towards the base. This species parasitizes large hairy caterpillars.*

large, dark bristly body

wings yellowish at base

▶ **TACHINA FERA** *has a distinct dark stripe on the abdomen. Widely distributed across Britain, it parasitizes the caterpillars of noctuid moths.*

ORDER *Diptera.*
FAMILY *Tachinidae.*
SPECIES IN FAMILY *7,800.*
SIZE *0.5–2cm.*
FEEDING *Larvae: parasites. Adults: liquid-feeders.*
IMPACT *Beneficial control agents of pests.*

Horse Bot Flies

Gasterophilidae

These flies, which are stout-bodied, resemble honey bees in colour and hairiness. They have strong legs, and non-functional mouthparts. Typically, the females lay their eggs on the shoulders and legs of horses. When licked off, the larvae burrow into the gums and tongue of the horse before completing their development in the stomach or intestines. When mature, the larvae pass out with the excrement, and pupate in the soil.

FOUND *in association with horses, wherever they are found.*

dark patches on wings

LARVAE

Larvae are stout with distinct bands of backward-pointing spines encircling the body. The spines help the larvae to burrow through the host's tissues.

broad head

short antennae

hairy bee-like body

GASTEROPHILUS INTESTINALIS *is short-lived and does not feed. Adults survive long enough to lay their eggs.*

ORDER *Diptera.*
FAMILY *Gasterophilidae.*
SPECIES IN FAMILY *50.*
SIZE *1–2cm.*
FEEDING *Larvae: parasites. Adults: non-feeding.*
IMPACT *Serious veterinary pest species.*

Bot Flies and Warble Flies

Oestridae

These hairy flies often resemble honey or bumble bees. The head is large, broad, and flattened from front to back, the antennae are small, and mouthparts are small or absent. The males of some species congregate on hilltops for mating purposes. Females are rarely encountered. Species are host-specific.

OCCUR *anywhere that their host animals are found, often on fields and pasture.*

antenna hidden in groove

wrinkled surface

mottled abdomen

▲ **HYPODERMA BOVIS,** *the Ox Warble Fly, is a widespread bee-like fly that attacks cattle.*

LARVAE

Larvae are broad, stout-bodied, and circled with bands of backward-pointing spines.

▲ **OESTRUS OVIS,** *the Sheep Nostril Fly, has a characteristically wrinkled-looking body surface, and a broad blunt head.*

ORDER *Diptera.*
FAMILY *Oestridae.*
SPECIES IN FAMILY *80.*
SIZE *0.8–1.8cm.*
FEEDING *Larvae: parasites. Adults: non-feeding.*
IMPACT *Serious veterinary pest.*

Louse Flies or Flat Flies

Hippoboscidae

There can be no mistaking these odd, flattened, parasitic flies. The head has a short, piercing proboscis, short antennae, and rounded or oval eyes. Many species have reduced wings or are wingless. The fully-winged species lose their wings once a bird or mammalian host is found. They have strong claws to hold onto feathers or hair. The females do not lay eggs but instead, produce mature larvae. In most cases, only one larva is produced per year. The adults are all blood-suckers and mostly host-specific, although some species can attack a small range of related hosts.

LIVE *mainly in wooded areas where their host animals occur.*

LARVAE

Females produce fat, rounded larvae, which pupate almost immediately on the host.

broad head

▲ **LIPOPTENA CERVI,** *the reddish brown Deer Fly, has a short, broad head that appears to be partly sunk into the thorax.*

small abdomen

strong legs

NOTE

The female produces mature larvae, which have developed inside its uterus and have been nourished on the secretions of special milk glands.

broad, flat thorax

ORDER *Diptera.*
FAMILY *Hippoboscidae.*
SPECIES IN FAMILY *200.*
SIZE *2–8mm.*
FEEDING *Larvae: parasites. Adults: blood-feeders.*
IMPACT *Some species are considered pests.*

▲ **HIPPOBOSCA EQUINA** *is known as the Forest Fly. It is reddish brown with dark markings on the head and thorax. This species is now only common in the New Forest.*

fully winged in both sexes

Net-spinning Caddisflies

Hydropsychidae

COMMON *along streams, rivers, and other watercourses.*

These insects are named after the cup-shaped nets spun by their aquatic larvae to gather floating organisms and debris to eat. The drab adults have hairy or clear wings. The antennae are shorter or longer than the wings; the basal segment is short and bulbous. The middle and hind tibiae usually have four spurs; the front tibiae may have two.

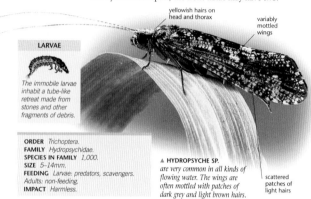

yellowish hairs on head and thorax

variably mottled wings

LARVAE

The immobile larvae inhabit a tube-like retreat made from stones and other fragments of debris.

ORDER *Trichoptera.*
FAMILY *Hydropsychidae.*
SPECIES IN FAMILY *1,000.*
SIZE *5–14mm.*
FEEDING *Larvae: predators, scavengers. Adults: non-feeding.*
IMPACT *Harmless.*

▲ HYDROPSYCHE SP. *are very common in all kinds of flowing water. The wings are often mottled with patches of dark grey and light brown hairs.*

scattered patches of light hairs

Northern Caddisflies

Limnephilidae

WIDESPREAD *around pools, lakes, streams, ditches, rivers, and marshes of all sizes.*

Abundant at northern latitudes and in hills or mountains, these caddisflies are quite large with a pale reddish, yellowish, or dark brownish coloration, often with dark wing markings. The front wings are fairly narrow, paper-like, and have few hairs. The antennae have a bulbous basal segment and are as long as the front wings.

LARVAE

The larvae make a diverse variety of elegant cases from sand, stones, sticks, shells, or plants.

mottled front wings

▷ ANABOLIA NERVOSA *varies in size as an adult. Its larvae attach sticks to their cases as defence against fish.*

▽ GLYPHOTAELIUS PELLUCIDUS *has a distinctive notch at the end of its wings. It is grey or brown and mottled all over.*

yellowish brown wings

notch on wing margin

ORDER *Trichoptera.*
FAMILY *Limnephilidae.*
SPECIES IN FAMILY *1,500.*
SIZE *0.8–3cm.*
FEEDING *Larvae: scavengers, herbivores, predators. Adults: non-feeding.*
IMPACT *Harmless.*

Finger-net Caddisflies

Philopotamidae

Named after the tube-like silk nets that their larvae make on the underside of rocks, these caddisflies are often dull greyish brown, although some species have distinctly mottled front wings in shades of yellow and brown. Usually, the antennae are shorter than the body length. The front tibiae have two spurs; there are four on the middle and hind tibiae. Some species are characteristic of streams in upland and mountainous areas.

FOUND *near moderate to fast-flowing streams and springs.*

shortish, dark antennae

long palps

pattern of yellowish spots and bands

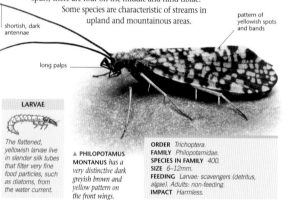

LARVAE

The flattened, yellowish larvae live in slender silk tubes that filter very fine food particles, such as diatoms, from the water current.

▲ PHILOPOTAMUS MONTANUS *has a very distinctive dark greyish brown and yellow pattern on the front wings.*

ORDER *Trichoptera.*
FAMILY *Philopotamidae.*
SPECIES IN FAMILY *400.*
SIZE *6–12mm.*
FEEDING *Larvae: scavengers (detritus, algae). Adults: non-feeding.*
IMPACT *Harmless.*

Goerid Caddisflies

Goeridae

The wings of these caddisflies are blackish, brownish, or yellowish in colour and are typically short, broad, and very hairy. The basal segment of the antennae is stout, hairy, and about twice the length of the head. The front tibiae have two spurs, while the middle and hind tibiae have four. In some species, sexes are different: males are black while females are brown.

OCCUR *around lakes as well as moderately fast-flowing streams and rivers.*

SILO NIGRICORNIS *has very dark, almost black, males and light brown females.*

short hairy fringe

dark wings

swollen base to antennae

LARVAE

The larvae make a central tube of sand or pebbles weighted down at the sides by angular stones.

pale legs

ORDER *Trichoptera.*
FAMILY *Goeridae.*
SPECIES IN FAMILY *100.*
SIZE *6–12mm.*
FEEDING *Larvae: scavengers. Adults: non-feeding.*
IMPACT *Harmless.*

NOTE

The larva of a species of parasitic wasp develops in the cases of goerid larvae. The larva of this wasp breathes through a worm-like gill structure.

Giant Casemakers or Large Caddisflies

Phryganeidae

These insects are light brown or grey, often mottled, and their wings can be quite brightly marked with black and yellow-orange or have dark margins and stripes. The antennae are quite short: in some cases about as long as the front wings. The front, middle, and hind tibiae bear two, four, and four spurs respectively.

LIVE *near slow-moving rivers and streams and around ponds, lakes, and marshes.*

LARVAE

The larvae move around in beautifully regular cases made of plant fibres and lined with silk.

▽ PHRYGANIA GRANDIS, *a common species, lays its eggs in jelly-like masses on aquatic plants.*

smoky brown wings

shortish antennae

▽ PHRYGANEA VARIA *is attractively mottled and well camouflaged at rest. It flies at dusk.*

mottled upperside

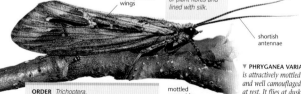

ORDER *Trichoptera.*
FAMILY *Phryganeidae.*
SPECIES IN FAMILY *500.*
SIZE *1–2.8cm.*
FEEDING *Larvae: predators, scavengers. Adults: non-feeding.*
IMPACT *Harmless.*

Long-horned Caddisflies

Leptoceridae

As their common name implies, these caddisflies have slender antennae that are typically two to three times longer than the front wings. The basal segment of the antenna is bulbous and about as long as the head. The front wings are long, narrow, and very hairy, often with dark cross bands. The front tibiae may have one or two spurs or none; the middle and hind tibiae always have two spurs.

ABUNDANT *around lakes, large ponds, and medium to large rivers.*

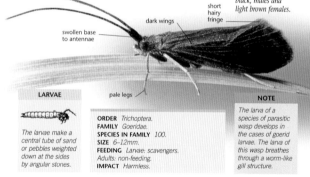

LARVAE

The larval cases are mostly made of sand grains, small stones, and plant material.

extremely long antennae

OECETIS OCHRACEA *is widely distributed and has very long antennae typical of its family.*

ORDER *Trichoptera.*
FAMILY *Leptoceridae.*
SPECIES IN FAMILY *850.*
SIZE *0.6–1.6cm.*
FEEDING *Larvae: scavengers, herbivores, predators. Adults: non-feeding.*
IMPACT *Harmless.*

Leaf-rolling Sawflies

Pamphilidae

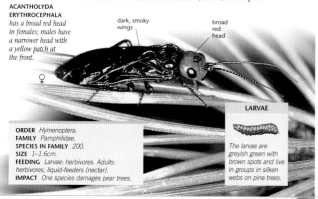

FAVOUR *woodland scrub and hedgegrow where host trees grow, in a variety of habitats.*

Also known as web-spinning sawflies, these robust, fast-flying insects have a broad head and are flattened from top to bottom. Most species are black or dark with yellow markings. The antennae are slender and tapered. The larvae, which do not have prolegs on the abdomen, feed in groups under silken webs or in the rolled up foliage of deciduous trees such as hawthorn, birch, and aspen.

ACANTHOLYDA ERYTHROCEPHALA *has a broad red head in females; males have a narrower head with a yellow patch at the front.*

dark, smoky wings

broad red head

♀

LARVAE

The larvae are greyish green with brown spots and live in groups in silken webs on pine trees.

ORDER *Hymenoptera.*
FAMILY *Pamphilidae.*
SPECIES IN FAMILY *200.*
SIZE *1–1.6cm.*
FEEDING *Larvae: herbivores. Adults: herbivores, liquid-feeders (nectar).*
IMPACT *One species damages pear trees.*

Stem Sawflies

Cephidae

FOUND *among cereal crops and in meadows and grassland; adults often at yellow flowers.*

Stem sawflies are cylindrical, slender-bodied, slow-flying insects with a large prothorax, clear or smoky-tinged wings, and a slightly flattened abdomen. Although the basic coloration is dark, many species have yellow thorax markings and abdominal bands. The antennae are quite long and slender and may be slightly clubbed at the ends. Species in the genera *Cephus* and *Trachelus* attack a variety of cereals.

slightly clubbed antennae

CEPHUS NIGRINUS *is an all-black sawfly with a slim body. There are two very similar species both with yellow markings.*

very slender body

LARVAE

The slender larvae have vestigial legs; they bore into stems of plants such as grasses and willows.

ORDER *Hymenoptera.*
FAMILY *Cephidae.*
SPECIES IN FAMILY *100.*
SIZE *4–12mm.*
FEEDING *Larvae: herbivores. Adults: herbivores, liquid-feeders (nectar).*
IMPACT *Some species attack cereal crops.*

Horntails or Woodwasps

Siricidae

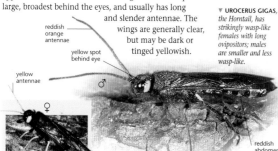

OCCUR *in coniferous or deciduous forests, where females attack diseased, weakened, or fallen trees.*

The common names for these large, stout-bodied sawflies refer to a spine-like structure at the end of their abdomen, which is short and triangular in males and long and spear-like in females. In addition, females have an even longer ovipositor, with which they drill into wood to lay a single egg. Despite their large size and (sometimes) wasp-like appearance, these insects do not sting. The head is quite large, broadest behind the eyes, and usually has long and slender antennae. The wings are generally clear, but may be dark or tinged yellowish.

▼ **UROCERUS GIGAS**, *the Horntail, has strikingly wasp-like females with long ovipositors; males are smaller and less wasp-like.*

reddish orange antennae

yellow spot behind eye

yellow antennae

♂

♀

reddish abdomen

long ovipositor

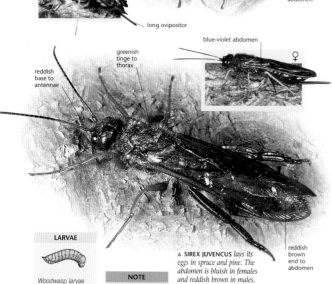

greenish tinge to thorax

blue-violet abdomen

♀

reddish base to antennae

reddish brown end to abdomen

LARVAE

Woodwasp larvae have a stout spine at their rear end, with which they push themselves through tunnels in heartwood. Their development takes up to two years.

NOTE

Despite their large size and alarmingly long ovipositors, which are often mistaken for stings, these insects are entirely harmless to humans.

▲ **SIREX JUVENCUS** *lays its eggs in spruce and pine. The abdomen is bluish in females and reddish brown in males.*

ORDER *Hymenoptera.*
FAMILY *Siricidae.*
SPECIES IN FAMILY *100.*
SIZE *2–4cm.*
FEEDING *Larvae: wood-feeders, fungi-feeders. Adults: liquid-feeders.*
IMPACT *Many species are pests of trees.*

Common Sawflies

Tenthredinidae

LIVE *in nearly all land habitats, especially gardens, pastures, and woodland, as far north as the Arctic.*

Common sawflies vary a great deal and may be quite narrow-bodied and wasp-like or broader and more robust. The body colour is typically brown, black, or green but many are brightly marked with yellow or red. The slender antennae can be made up of anything between 7 and 13 segments, but usually have 9 segments. The tibiae of the front legs have two apical (near the tip) spurs, and in many species the sexes have different coloration.

vivid red swelling

GALL

◀ **PONTANIA VESICATOR** *is one of several similar sawflies in its genus that make bright red galls on willow leaves.*

wasp-like markings

thorax black with yellow markings

thick yellow antennae

▶ **TENTHREDO SCROPHULARIAE**, *is called the Figwort Sawfly because its larvae feed on this plant (Scrophularia) in boggy habitats, woodland, and hedgerows.*

distinctive black markings

black wing veins

broad head

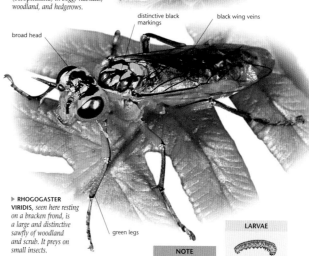

▶ **RHOGOGASTER VIRIDIS**, *seen here resting on a bracken frond, is a large and distinctive sawfly of woodland and scrub. It preys on small insects.*

green legs

ORDER *Hymenoptera.*
FAMILY *Tenthredinidae.*
SPECIES IN FAMILY *4,000.*
SIZE *4–15mm (body length).*
FEEDING *Larvae: herbivores (leaves). Adults: predators, liquid-feeders.*
IMPACT *Many species are pests of crops.*

NOTE

Females use their ovipositor to cut egg-laying slits in the leaves, twigs, and shoots of host plants. Most larvae browse on foliage; some produce galls.

LARVAE

The caterpillar-like larvae may have warning coloration or be cryptically coloured. Some are smooth, while others have spines, hairs, and bumps.

Cimbicid Sawflies

Cimbicidae

Many of these large, broad-bodied sawflies can look superficially like hairless bees and even make a buzzing noise when they fly. Most species are black or yellowish and black, but some are metallic green. The antennae have less than seven segments, with the last one or two segments greatly swollen to form a club. The larvae eat the foliage of specific hosts, such as birch and hawthorn trees.

FOUND *wherever their host plants – usually trees – grow.*

club

metallic
green
sheen

▲ **ABIA SERICEA** *has a fat body. Its larvae feed on Devil's Bit Scabious (Succisa pratensis), and Field Scabious (Knautia arvensis).*

▼ **CIMBEX LUTEUS** *feeds on willow and sometimes poplar foliage as a larva. The adult has a largely yellow abdomen.*

clouded brown wings

yellow abdomen

bronze sheen

▶ **ZARAEA LONICERA** *feeds on Dwarf or Fly Honeysuckle (Lonicera xylosteum), during its larval stage.*

stout body

brownish wings

▼ **TRICHIOSOMA LUCORUM** *is a stout-bodied sawfly whose larvae feed on hawthorn foliage in scrub and hedgerows. When fully grown, the larvae pupate inside a tough cocoon attached to twigs.*

very hairy

LARVAE

Slightly curved in shape, the larvae have several legs on the thorax and numerous prolegs (unsegmented legs) on the abdomen. They pupate inside a tough cocoon.

NOTE

The population of some of these species are declining due to the disappearance of hedgerows, and efficient methods of hedge trimming.

ORDER *Hymenoptera.*
FAMILY *Cimbicidae.*
SPECIES IN FAMILY *150.*
SIZE *2–2.6cm (body length).*
FEEDING *Larvae: herbivores (leaves). Adults: liquid-feeders.*
IMPACT *Harmless.*

Ichneumon Wasps

Ichneumonidae

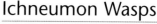

Ichneumons are generally slender-bodied with antennae at least half as long as the body and composed of a minimum of 16 segments. Many species are uniformly coloured pale yellowish- or reddish brown to black, while others are brightly patterned with yellow and black. The slender, sometimes laterally flattened abdomen is joined to the thorax by a slender stalk of variable length. Most species are fully winged with a prominent pterostigma on the leading edge of the front wings.

COMMON *almost everywhere, above all in damp habitats. Strongly attracted to umbelliferous (flat-topped) flowers and lights.*

yellowish brown all over

▲ **NETELIA SP.** *parasitize the caterpillars of moths. If handled, females will try to "sting" fingers with their ovipositors.*

♀

ovipositor sheath

ovipositor in use

red legs

▶ **LISSONOTA SP.** *parasitize wood-feeding moth larvae, which females drill down to reach.*

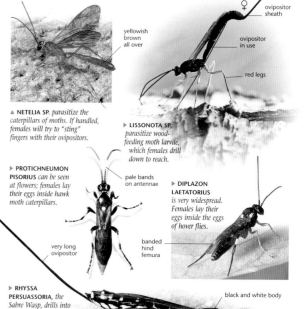

▶ **PROTICHNEUMON PISORIUS** *can be seen at flowers; females lay their eggs inside hawk moth caterpillars.*

pale bands on antennae

▶ **DIPLAZON LAETATORIUS** *is very widespread. Females lay their eggs inside the eggs of hover flies.*

banded hind femura

very long ovipositor

▶ **RHYSSA PERSUASSORIA,** *the Sabre Wasp, drills into the trunks of pine trees to locate the larvae of wood wasps deep within the wood.*

black and white body

♀

LARVAE

Pale and maggot-like, the larvae may have a tail that gets shorter with age. Most are internal parasites that eventually kill the host organism.

reddish legs

ORDER *Hymenoptera.*
FAMILY *Ichneumonidae.*
SPECIES IN FAMILY *20,000.*
SIZE *0.3–4.2cm (body length).*
FEEDING *Larvae: parasites. Adults: liquid-feeders.*
IMPACT *Many species control other pests.*

NOTE

Females use their long ovipositors to lay eggs on or inside the larvae or pupae of insects such as beetles, flies, moths, butterflies, sawflies, and other wasps.

Conifer Sawflies

Diprionidae

CONFINED *to areas of coniferous woodland, including plantations.*

These very stout-bodied, slow-flying sawflies are mainly dull brown or black in colour, although some may have yellowish or reddish thorax markings and abdominal bands. The antennae of males are very broad and feathery; those of females are narrow and slightly toothed. The abdomen is widest across the middle and slightly flattened.

♀

orange head and body

black body

reddish underside

large feathery antennae

♂

LARVAE

The larvae are either solitary with cryptic coloration or social and vividly coloured.

▲ **NEODIPRION SERTIFER,** *the Pine Sawfly, can be a major pest in plantations of pine and occasionally spruce. The males are active, but the larger females rarely fly.*

ORDER *Hymenoptera.*
FAMILY *Diprionidae.*
SPECIES IN FAMILY *100.*
SIZE *6–12mm (body length).*
FEEDING *Larvae: herbivores (pine needles). Adults: liquid-feeders.*
IMPACT *Some species damage host trees.*

Braconid Wasps

Braconidae

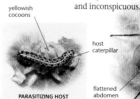

FOUND *almost everywhere there are insect pests to parasitize.*

The majority of braconid wasps are brownish, reddish brown, or black, and none are brightly coloured. Nearly all are small and inconspicuous, and the slender antennae may have anything from 10 to more than 50 segments. The abdomen – which is never particularly long – is slender, laterally flattened, or stalked. The ovipositor may be long and thin, or short and inconspicuous.

yellowish cocoons

host caterpillar

flattened abdomen

PARASITIZING HOST

▲ **APANTELES GLOMERATUS** *is a small, dark wasp and is an internal parasite of certain white butterflies, such as the Cabbage White.*

ORDER *Hymenoptera.*
FAMILY *Scelionidae.*
SPECIES IN FAMILY *15,000.*
SIZE *2–8mm.*
FEEDING *Larvae: parasites. Adults: liquid-feeders.*
IMPACT *Many help to control insect pests.*

LARVAE

The pale larvae live inside host insects. Minute differences in the mouthparts distinguish species.

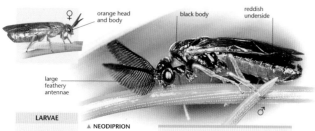

Scelionid Wasps

Scelionidae

These very small, black or rarely brownish wasps vary in body shape from quite slender to stout with a flattened abdomen. The antennae normally have 11 or 12 segments and in females may have a distinct terminal club. The antennae, which are elbowed, arise from low on the head. When not in use, the ovipositor is concealed within the female's body.

OCCUR *in a wide variety of habitats in association with their hosts.*

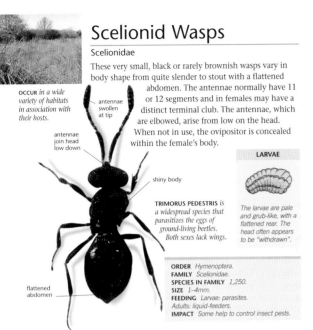

antennae swollen at tip

antennae join head low down

shiny body

TRIMORUS PEDESTRIS *is a widespread species that parasitizes the eggs of ground-living beetles. Both sexes lack wings.*

flattened abdomen

LARVAE

The larvae are pale and grub-like, with a flattened rear. The head often appears to be "withdrawn".

ORDER *Hymenoptera.*
FAMILY *Scelionidae.*
SPECIES IN FAMILY *1,250.*
SIZE *1–4mm.*
FEEDING *Larvae: parasites. Adults: liquid-feeders.*
IMPACT *Some help to control insect pests.*

Chalcid Wasps

Chalcididae

Most species of chalcid wasp are dark brown, black, red, or yellow. Although the tough body may have pitting or sculpturing, it never has a metallic sheen. A distinguishing feature of these tiny insects is that the first two segments of each hind leg – the coxa and femur – are greatly enlarged. The hind femora are also toothed underneath. Females have a short, inconspicuous ovipositor.

FOUND *in a variety of well-vegetated habitats wherever there are host insects.*

▼ **BRACHYMERIA MINUTA** *parasitizes moth pupae and fly puparia. Adults vary considerably in size and can be up to 6mm long.*

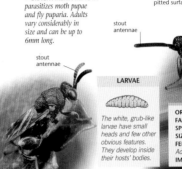

pitted surface

stout antennae

stout antennae

▼ **CHALCIS SISPES** *is a parasite of soldier fly larvae in coastal marshes and fenland.*

LARVAE

The white, grub-like larvae have small heads and few other obvious features. They develop inside their hosts' bodies.

ORDER *Hymenoptera.*
FAMILY *Chalcididae.*
SPECIES IN FAMILY *1,500.*
SIZE *2–8mm.*
FEEDING *Larvae: parasites. Adults: liquid-feeders.*
IMPACT *Many help to control insect pests.*

Gall Wasps

Cynipidae

Gall wasps are tiny and have shiny black or blackish brown bodies. The thorax has a characteristic humped appearance in side view. Most species are fully winged, with much reduced vein patterns; some are short-winged or wingless. Males are typically smaller than females, which have an oval abdomen flattened from side to side. The galls that these wasps induce on their host plants are unique to each species and much easier to identify than the wasps themselves as they vary greatly in size, colour, texture, and location. Gall wasps have complex life cycles, often involving sexual and asexual (no males involved) generations that occur at different times of year.

THRIVE *in a range of habitats, wherever suitable host trees or plants grow.*

hairy surface

GALLS

▲ **LIPOSTHENES GLECHOMAE** *makes small, globular, hairy galls on ground ivy (Glechoma species). Inside each gall is a single developing larva.*

GALL · hard and knobbly gall

spherical, woody galls

green first, then brown when mature

GALLS

▲ **ANDRICUS QUERCUSCALICIS** *induces knobbly galls to grow from the base of acorns of the English Oak. Each houses a larva of the asexual generation.*

▲ **ANDRICUS KOLLARI** *causes Marble Galls on oak trees. These were once collected as their high tannin content was important in ink-making.*

hard, scaly orange galls

▲ **DIPLOLEPIS EGLANTERIAE** *causes rounded, green or red galls on the underside of wild and cultivated roses. A single larva feeds inside each gall.*

GALLS

pea-like shape

irregular, elongated form

GALL

◄ **DIASTROPHUS RUBI** *induces swollen galls on the shoots and young stems of Rubus species such as raspberry, dewberry, and bramble. Each contains many larvae.*

GALL

extensive "mossy" growth

▲ **DIPLOLEPIS ROSAE** *causes the Rose Bedeguar Gall, or Robin's Pincushion, on wild roses and sometimes on cultivated varieties. The gall contains many larvae.*

▲ **NEUROTERUS QUERCUSBACCARUM** *is one of several species to produce Spangle Galls on the underside of oak leaves. Some leaves may be completely covered with galls.*

GALLS

green at first, then turn red

▼ **CYNIPS QUERCUSFOLII** *has two generations. The second, bisexual generation lays eggs on the lower surface of oak leaves, creating Cherry Galls (left).*

GALLS

▶ **BIORHIZA PALLIDA** *has a unisexual generation (shown right) that develops in galls on oak tree roots. This emerges to lay eggs on oak buds, producing Oak Apple Galls (below). These in turn give rise to a bisexual generation.*

smooth, shiny abdomen ♀

large thorax

reddish and spongy

GALL

♀

humped thorax

shiny abdomen

ORDER *Hymenoptera.*
FAMILY *Cynipidae.*
SPECIES IN FAMILY *1,250.*
SIZE *1–8mm.*
FEEDING *Larvae: herbivores, parasites. Adults: liquid-feeders.*
IMPACT *High infestations weaken host plants.*

NOTE

Some gall wasps do not form galls, instead share those of other species; some are parasitic on the larvae of dipteran flies or parasitic wasps.

LARVAE

The pale, smooth, grub-like larvae hatch from eggs laid inside plant tissues, inducing the plant to produce galls that both protect and nourish the developing larvae.

Eurytomids

Eurytomidae

These wasps are yellow, reddish, or dull black. A few have a metallic sheen, while others can be shiny and dimpled. Eurytomids look similar to chalcid wasps (p.283), but the hind coxae are never very enlarged and the femora do not have tooth-like projections. The antennae, which are elbowed low down, have 6 to 13 segments. The larvae of many species develop inside seeds and are called seed chalcids.

LIVE *in habitats where there are suitable seeds and stem-mining or other insect larvae or galls to attack.*

LARVAE

The tiny larvae are white and grub-like, with a few long hairs. Many develop inside seeds; others parasitize insect larvae or eggs.

EURYTOMA BRUNNIVENTRIS *is a parasite of the larvae of gall-forming wasps. This adult is visiting a gall.*

dimpled thorax · elbowed antennae · shiny black abdomen

ORDER *Hymenoptera.*
FAMILY *Eurytomidae.*
SPECIES IN FAMILY *1,400.*
SIZE *3–6mm.*
FEEDING *Larvae: parasites, herbivores. Adults: liquid-feeders.*
IMPACT *Many help to control insect pests.*

Ruby-tailed Wasps or Jewel Wasps

Chrysididae

FOUND *in a range of habitats, wherever their hosts occur.*

These shiny, metallic insects can be blue, green, red, or combinations of these colours. The armour-like body surface is sculpted with coarse pits and dimples. The eyes are large and the antennae normally have 13 segments. The underside of the abdomen is nearly always flattened or concave, enabling the wasps to curl into a ball if attacked.

LARVAE

The larvae are stout, smooth, and the middle of their body is the broadest part. Most species eat the larval food supply of solitary bees and wasps; others target butterflies or moths.

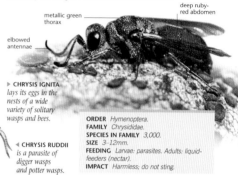

metallic green thorax · deep ruby-red abdomen · elbowed antennae

▶ **CHRYSIS IGNITA** *lays its eggs in the nests of a wide variety of solitary wasps and bees.*

◀ **CHRYSIS RUDDII** *is a parasite of digger wasps and potter wasps.*

purplish red abdomen · strong jaws

ORDER *Hymenoptera.*
FAMILY *Chrysididae.*
SPECIES IN FAMILY *3,000.*
SIZE *3–12mm.*
FEEDING *Larvae: parasites. Adults: liquid-feeders (nectar).*
IMPACT *Harmless; do not sting.*

Torymid Wasps

Torymidae

OCCUR *in a range of habitats, wherever suitable host insects can be found.*

The body of these small wasps is typically elongated and usually metallic blue or green. The thorax is sculptured with dimples and the abdomen is normally smooth, with a very long ovipositor in females. The first segment (coxa) of the hind legs is much larger than the coxa of the front legs and the femora of the hind legs may have one or more tooth-like projections.

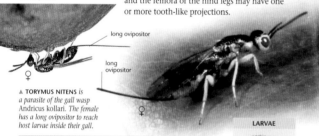

long ovipositor · long ovipositor ♀ ♀

▲ **TORYMUS NITENS** *is a parasite of the gall wasp Andricus kollari. The female has a long ovipositor to reach host larvae inside their gall.*

ORDER *Hymenoptera.*
FAMILY *Torymidae.*
SPECIES IN FAMILY *1,500.*
SIZE *1–6mm.*
FEEDING *Larvae: parasites, herbivores. Adults: liquid-feeders.*
IMPACT *Some species help to control pests.*

◀ **MEGASTIGMUS DORSALIS** *has a long ovipositor and is able to drill deep into oak galls such as the oak apple to parasitize the occupant. It also attacks marble galls.*

LARVAE

The larvae are pale, grub-like, and often hairy, with indistinct segments on the abdomen.

Spider-hunting Wasps

Pompilidae

These slender-bodied wasps are generally dark in colour with yellowish or orange bands or other markings on the abdomen and yellowish or smoky wings. The pronotum is quite large and extends back towards the wing bases. The legs, especially the hind legs, are long and spiny. Pompilids rarely fly but are highly active: they can be seen running quickly, flicking and jerking their wings, as they look for spiders. When found, the spider is swiftly paralysed and the female then digs a burrow. She buries the spider and lays an egg on it before sealing the burrow.

SEEN *at flowers or on the ground, often in open, sandy habitats.*

LARVAE

The larvae are pale and grub-like, and widest in the middle like those of ruby-tailed or jewel wasps (above). They are rarely seen as they live in burrows dug by the females.

overall dark coloration · strong front legs

◀ **ANOPLIUS VIATICUS** *is a dark species with distinctive reddish orange patches on the abdomen.*

orange patches on abdomen

NOTE

The venom of these wasps is strong enough to overcome even the largest spiders. Before a wasp stings, it must grapple with its prey and avoid its fangs.

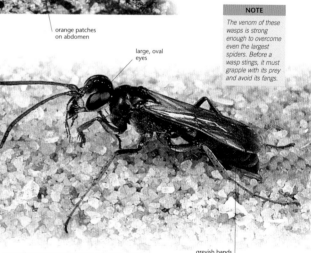

large, oval eyes

greyish bands of hairs

▲ **POMPILIUS CINEREUS** *has a grey appearance, with bands of hairs across the abdomen. Females have strong combs on their front legs for digging in sandy soil and hunting for wolf spiders.*

ORDER *Hymenoptera.*
FAMILY *Pompilidae.*
SPECIES IN FAMILY *4,200.*
SIZE *0.5–2.5cm.*
FEEDING *Larvae: parasites. Adults: liquid-feeders (nectar).*
IMPACT *The stings can be extremely painful.*

Trichogrammatid Wasps

Trichogrammatidae

Due to their small size, these wasps are often overlooked. Nevertheless, most species are stout-bodied and have fully developed wings with characteristic lines of small hairs in radiating patterns. The front wings are fairly broad with a single vein, while the hind wings are much smaller and narrower with a fringe of hairs. Unlike other wasps, the tarsi have only three segments.

INHABIT *a wide variety of habitats where there are insect eggs (usually exposed on foliage) to parasitize.*

NOTE

Females lay their eggs inside those of other insects, so the best way to see these tiny wasps is to collect insect eggs and wait to see what emerges.

TRICHOGRAMMA SEMBLIDIS *is widespread but rarely seen due to its small size, and has been used in the biological control of certain species of moth pests.*

broad head ♀

LARVAE

The pale, minute larvae have few obvious features and live inside the eggs of host insects.

fine hairs at wing margin · veinless wings

ORDER *Hymenoptera.*
FAMILY *Trichogrammatidae.*
SPECIES IN FAMILY *530.*
SIZE *0.3–1.2mm.*
FEEDING *Larvae: parasites. Adults: liquid-feeders.*
IMPACT *Many species help to control pests.*

Common Wasps, Paper Wasps, and Potter Wasps

Vespidae

The commonest species in this family are yellow-jackets, which live in colonies inside rounded paper nests and catch insects, often caterpillars, to feed to their larvae. Most species are black or brown with yellow or white markings. Vespid's eyes are notched on the internal margins and may look crescent-shaped. At rest, the wings are folded in longitudinal pleats along the sides of the body. Paper wasps, which are occasionally found in Britain, make nests of combs that are never enclosed by an outer carton. The solitary potter wasps make small mud nests on stems and in natural cavities. Nests of common wasps are not reused and only the queen wasps survive the winter to start a new colony in the spring.

LARVAE

The wrinkled body is broadest about a third of the way from the head. The larvae are fed by workers which live in colonies inside individual nest cells.

NOTE

Nest shape, colour, and location help to identify social wasps, which may look very similar. Wasps remove many garden pests to feed their larvae.

▼ **DOLICHOVESPULA MEDIA,** *the Median Wasp, has a small black spot or bar on the face, and a slim "7"-shaped line at the sides of the thorax. It builds nests in bushes and shrubs.*

antennae

variable markings on abdomen

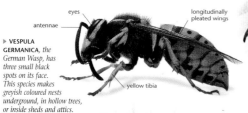

▶ **VESPULA GERMANICA,** *the German Wasp, has three small black spots on its face. This species makes greyish coloured nests underground, in hollow trees, or inside sheds and attics.*

eyes
antennae
longitudinally pleated wings
yellow tibia

▶ **VESPULA VULGARIS,** *the Common Wasp, has a small anchor-shaped mark on its face. This worker (right) is scraping wood fibres from a tree to make paper for its nest.*

antennae
yellow stripes on thorax

chestnut brown thorax
yellow head

◀ **VESPA CRABRO,** *the Hornet, is a very large species. The front of the abdomen is largely chestnut brown; the posterior part is dull yellow with dark markings.*

large nest on roof timbers

NEST

▼ **EUMENES COARCTATUS** *is the Potter Wasp. Common on heathland, females gather mud with their mandibles to construct the elegant vase-shaped nests.*

very slender first abdominal segment
stout thorax
vase-shaped mud nest

NEST

ORDER *Hymenoptera.*
FAMILY *Vespidae.*
SPECIES IN FAMILY *4,000.*
SIZE *8–26mm.*
FEEDING *Larvae: carnivorous. Adults: predators, liquid-feeders (nectar).*
IMPACT *Very beneficial but can sting.*

Solitary Hunting, Digger, and Sand Wasps

Sphecidae

These wasps paralyse insects as food for their larvae. Some species are stocky; in others the abdomen is elongated and thread-like where it joins the thorax. The body is typically black with yellow or reddish markings. The head is fairly broad and the pronotum is narrow, collar-like, and does not extend back towards the wing bases. Both sexes are fully winged. Females often have a comb-like, digging structure on their front legs.

LARVAE

The carnivorous larvae are pale creamy white and have dark mouthparts. The body is tapered slightly at both ends and is usually slightly curved.

yellow spots on head

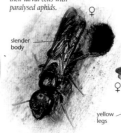

▶ **CERCERIS ARENARIA** *is shown here stinging a weevil, with which to stock her nest. The female pushes soil out of her burrow backwards, using her abdomen.*

▼ **PEMPHREDON LUGUBRIS** *is a small wasp that nests in rotting wood. Females stock their larval cells with paralysed aphids.*

slender body
♀
♀

▼ **AMMOPHILA SABULOSA** *is a species of sand wasp that hunts for large caterpillars to stock its nests with. Females deposit one paralysed victim in each nest, sealing it with sand before feeding on it.*

slender abdomen, narrow at front

♀

large jaws for carrying prey

broad head

◀ **PHILANTHUS TRIANGULUM,** *the Bee Killer or Bee Wolf, fills its nests with paralysed honey bees, with up to six bees in each larval cell.*

yellow legs

ORDER *Hymenoptera.*
FAMILY *Sphecidae.*
SPECIES IN FAMILY *8,000.*
SIZE *0.6–2.4cm.*
FEEDING *Larvae: carnivorous (paralysed prey provided by adults). Adults: liquid-feeders.*
IMPACT *Help to control certain pests.*

Ants

Formicidae

FOUND *in virtually every habitat across the region.*

Ants are familiar and ubiquitous social insects, and may be pale yellow, reddish to brown, or black. The individuals commonly seen are the wingless workers, but the reproductive males and females that appear from time to time are fully winged. The second, or second and third segments of the abdomen are constricted to form a waist, called the pedicel, which may have bumps or spine-like processes. The head carries strong jaws, and the antennae are elbowed immediately after the long first segment.

▶ **MYRMICA RUBRA** *is a common reddish brown species (males are darker) that is found in many habitats, including gardens. The pedicel is made up of two segments.*

ant larva

pedicel

reddish brown workers

▼ **FORMICA RUFA**, *the Wood Ant, is an active predator, but also likes honeydew. The ants shown below are tending a colony of aphids.*

reddish thorax of worker

worker tending aphid

black abdomen

LARVAE

The white larvae are grub-like, slightly curved, and may have fine body hairs. They are fed by worker ants and moved to a new site if the nest is disturbed.

black workers

yellowish brown thorax

dark head

▶ **LASIUS BRUNNEUS** *nests in old trees. The abdomen is darker than the petiole or the thorax, unlike L. niger, which is uniformly brown.*

nest mound

▼ **LASIUS FLAVUS**, *the Yellow Meadow Ant, is similar in all but colour to L. niger. It nests in meadows and rough grassland.*

pupa inside cocoon

yellowish brown workers

ANT NEST

ORDER *Hymenoptera.*
FAMILY *Formicidae.*
SPECIES IN FAMILY *8,800.*
SIZE *1–12mm.*
FEEDING *Larvae and adults: predators, herbivores, liquid-feeders.*
IMPACT *May sting, bite, or spray formic acid.*

▲ **LASIUS NIGER**, *the common Black Garden Ant, occurs in soil under stones and pavements. In late summer, large mating swarms of winged ants are produced.*

Velvet Ants

Mutillidae

FEMALES *run over the ground in dry, shady or open locations; males often visit flowers.*

Velvet ants are stout-bodied and black or reddish brown in colour, with abdominal spots or bands of red, yellow, or silver hairs. The sexes often have different markings, but the body is always sculptured with coarse dimples. The males are fully winged; the wingless females are more strongly built, with a powerful sting.

LARVAE

Females lay their eggs in the larval cells of bees or wasps. Their larvae eat the host grubs.

yellow-tinged wings

♂

MUTILLA EUROPEA
females have pale abdominal hair patches and parasitize bumble bees. Males have two yellow abdominal bands.

pale patches ♀

ORDER *Hymenoptera.*
FAMILY *Mutillidae.*
SPECIES IN FAMILY *5,000.*
SIZE *3–15mm.*
FEEDING *Larvae: parasites (bee and wasp larvae and pupae). Adults: liquid-feeders.*
IMPACT *Females have very powerful stings.*

Tiphiid Wasps

Tiphiidae

OCCUR *in open, sunny, flower-rich habitats; females often run over the bare ground.*

These wasps are quite slender, shiny, and either black or reddish brown and black. The body is slightly hairy, the legs are short and spiny, and the waist may be very strongly constricted. The males of all species are fully winged and usually have a short upturned spine at the end of the abdomen. Females can be fully winged or wingless. The larvae are parasitic on the larvae of various beetles, bees, and wasps.

shiny black abdomen

rounded black head ♀

LARVAE

Elongate, smooth, and white, the larvae attack beetle larvae in soil or decayed wood.

red thorax

METHOCHA ICHNEUMONIDES *has sexes of different sizes: males are larger to be able to carry females during the nuptial flight. The wingless females lay their eggs on tiger beetle larvae.*

ORDER *Hymenoptera.*
FAMILY *Tiphiidae.*
SPECIES IN FAMILY *1,500.*
SIZE *0.4–3cm.*
FEEDING *Larvae: parasites (larvae of beetles, bees, and wasps). Adults: liquid-feeders.*
IMPACT *Help to control certain pests.*

Fairyflies

Mymaridae

This family includes the world's smallest flying insects. Fairyflies are very small or minute wasps with non-metallic yellow, dark brown, or black coloration broken with pale or dark markings. The narrow front wings have no obvious venation and are fringed with fine hairs, while the hindwings – which are very narrow or even stalk-like – are fringed with long hairs. Fairyflies are mostly parasites of the eggs of leaf hoppers and various bugs.

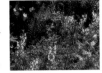

OCCUPY *any well-vegetated location with insect eggs to parasitize.*

LARVAE

During their early development, the larvae are tiny and have tails; later, they are more grub-like.

ANAGRUS SP. *are small, delicate wasps, which are usually parasites of leafhopper eggs.*

thick base to antennae

stalk-like wing bases

♀

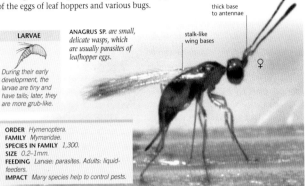

ORDER *Hymenoptera.*
FAMILY *Mymaridae.*
SPECIES IN FAMILY *1,300.*
SIZE *0.2–1mm.*
FEEDING *Larvae: parasites. Adults: liquid-feeders.*
IMPACT *Many species help to control pests.*

Mining or Andrenid Bees

Andrenidae

Superficially resembling honey bees, mining bees can be reddish brown, brown, or brownish black, although some species are yellow and a few are white. The thorax may be covered with white, yellow, or golden hairs and the abdomen, which is often rather flattened, may have crosswise bands of hairs.

INHABIT *virtually every flower-rich habitat; particularly common at flowers in spring.*

reddish front to abdomen

◄ ANDRENA FLOREA *has variable reddish brown coloration. The males are paler.*

LARVAE

The larvae can be slender or relatively stout. There are small swellings on the abdomen.

reddish brown hairs on thorax

dark bands on abdomen

◄ ANDRENA FULVA, *the Tawny Mining Bee, appears in early spring and nests in the soil of lawns and short turf.*

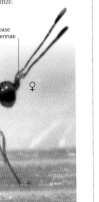

ORDER *Hymenoptera.*
FAMILY *Andrenidae.*
SPECIES IN FAMILY *4,000.*
SIZE *0.4–2cm.*
FEEDING *Larvae and adults: herbivores (pollen), liquid-feeders (nectar).*
IMPACT *Essential plant pollinators.*

Plasterer and Yellow-faced Bees

Colletidae

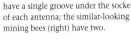

FOUND *at flowers in many habitats, nesting in areas of sandy, well-drained soil.*

Generally slender to moderately robust, these solitary bees are very dark or black with no distinct markings, and have sparse light golden or whitish body hairs (those on the abdomen are often arranged in conspicuous bands). Some species also have yellow facial markings. The mouthparts are short and broad.

reddish hairs on thorax

bands of pale hair

► HYLAEUS COMMUNIS *is rather wasp-like and can often be found foraging at bramble flowers.*

hairless body

◄ COLLETES SUCCINTUS *digs nesting tunnels in dry, sandy soil. It sometimes nests in quite dense groups.*

LARVAE

The larvae are curved, maggot-like, and feed on a runny mixture of pollen and honey.

ORDER *Hymenoptera.*
FAMILY *Colletidae.*
SPECIES IN FAMILY *3,000.*
SIZE *3–13mm.*
FEEDING *Larvae and adults: herbivores (pollen), liquid-feeders (nectar).*
IMPACT *Essential plant pollinators.*

Sweat Bees

Halictidae

Most of these small to medium-sized, ground-nesting bees are brownish or black, but some have a metallic blue or green appearance or are entirely shiny, bluish green. The surface of the body is not generally very hairy and may have sculpturing in the form of pits or dimples. Sweat bees have a single groove under the socket of each antenna; the similar-looking mining bees (right) have two.

WIDELY *distributed, mainly in flower-rich meadows, woodland edges, and areas of waste ground.*

bands of pale hair

single groove under socket of antenna

LARVAE

The larvae may have bumps on the upper surface, as well as a covering of tiny spines.

LASIOGLOSSUM MALACHURUS *makes vertical nests in the ground, with clusters of cells.*

ORDER *Hymenoptera.*
FAMILY *Halictidae.*
SPECIES IN FAMILY *5,000.*
SIZE *4–10mm.*
FEEDING *Larvae and adults: herbivores (pollen), liquid-feeders (nectar).*
IMPACT *Essential plant pollinators.*

Leaf-cutter and Mason Bees

Megachilidae

OCCURS *especially where dead wood and pithy plant stems provide nest sites.*

Most of these bees are solitary. Leaf-cutter bees cut circular pieces of leaves to line their nests' brood cells, while mason bees make mud cells under stones and in burrows. The former are typically stout-bodied and many species are dark brown to black, often with yellow or pale markings. Mason bees are short, broad, and metallic blue or green. The mouthparts are long and pointed and the wings may be clear or smoky.

LARVAE

The larvae of these bees are rather fat, especially near the rear of the body. Most feed on pollen or honey provided by the female, but a few are parasites in other bees' nests.

► ANTHIDIUM MANICATUM, *known as the Common Carder Bee, nests in old beetle or moth larvae burrows.*

yellow edging to black abdomen

densely hairy abdomen

bright yellow hairs

clypeal horns

♀

◄ HOPLITIS SPINULOSA *nests inside empty snail shells and uses sheep or rabbit dung to make the walls between adjacent cells.*

▲ OSMIA RUFA, *the Red Mason Bee, nests in natural cavities and holes in walls. It can be encouraged to nest using bundles of dry bamboo.*

pollen carried in a brush of hairs below abdomen

stout body

NOTE

A group of species known as carder bees use their jaws to strip the hairs from woolly-leaved plants, which they then tease out to make cell linings.

◄ MEGACHILE CENTUNCULARIS *is a common leaf-cutter bee. Leaves with semicircular holes along the edges are evidence that a nest is nearby.*

pieces cut by female leaf-cutter

DAMAGED LEAF

ORDER *Hymenoptera.*
FAMILY *Megachilidae.*
SPECIES IN FAMILY *3,000.*
SIZE *0.7–2.1cm.*
FEEDING *Larvae: pollen- and honey-feeders. Adults: pollen- and nectar-feeders.*
IMPACT *Essential plant pollinators.*

Cuckoo, Digger, and Carpenter Bees

Anthophoridae

THRIVE *in a variety of flower-rich habitats, especially in sunny, open localities.*

Cuckoo bees are black and yellow or brown and white, lack pollen baskets on their hind legs, are relatively hairless, and can look extremely wasp-like. Digger bees are typically bumble bee-like and hairy. Carpenter bees can be divided into two main groups: very large, hairy, blackish or bluish species; and small, relatively bare, dark bluish green species. Female digger and carpenter bees have densely hairy pollen baskets on their hind legs.

long antennae in male

golden, hairy body

◀ **EUCERA LONGICORNIS** *nests on the ground, often in groups. Males are attracted to the Bee Orchid and attempt to mate with it, thus serving as the flower's pollinators.*

pinched "wasp-like" waist

short, straight antennae

black and yellow markings

▲ **NOMADA FLAVA,** *a very wasp-like cuckoo bee, does not make a nest of its own but is a parasite of various mining bees, in whose nests it lays its eggs.*

NOTE

Also known as the long-tongued bees, this family is notable for its members' long tongues, which in some cases may exceed the length of the body itself.

purplish blue wings

huge, robust body

▶ **XYLOCOPA VIOLACEA,** *the Violet Carpenter Bee, is a very large, noisy-flying species that has been breeding sporadically in Britain in recent years. It nests in old wood.*

resembles small bumble bee

entirely black

♀ ♂

▲ **ANTHOPHORA PLUMIPES** *has distinct sexes: males are yellowish brown, while females are blackish. Nests are excavated in soil or the soft mortar of old walls.*

LARVAE

These bees' larvae may be fat-bodied or slender and pale or yellow. Cuckoo bee larvae develop in the nests of other bees, killing the resident larvae and eating their food.

ORDER *Hymenoptera.*
FAMILY *Anthophoridae.*
SPECIES IN FAMILY *4,200.*
SIZE *0.5–2.2cm.*
FEEDING *Larvae: pollen- and honey-feeders. Adults: pollen- and nectar-feeders.*
IMPACT *Essential plant pollinators.*

Bumble Bees and Honey Bees

Apidae

SEEN *in almost any flower-rich habitat. Bumble bees are particularly common in northern regions and in mountains.*

These familiar social bees live in complex and often very large colonies with a queen, males, and sterile worker females. Bumble bees are very hairy, stout-bodied, and brownish or orange to black with yellow markings. Their body hairs are typically yellow, orange, or black. Honey bees are smaller, more slender, and golden brown with pale hairs. The females of most species have a specialized pollen-carrying structure called the corbiculum on the outer surface of the hind tibiae.

white tail

yellow scutellum

♂

▲ **PSITHYRUS BARBUTELLUS** *does not collect pollen and is a "cuckoo" that lays its eggs in the nests of Bombus hortorum (right), which it resembles.*

▼ **APIS MELLIFERA,** *the Western Honey Bee, nests in cavities in trees. Widely domesticated, it also lives in artificial hives, providing honey, wax, and other products.*

enlarged abdomen

QUEEN

WORKER

DRONE

thousands of workers

SWARM

♀

▲ **BOMBUS LAPIDARIUS,** *the Red-tailed Bumble Bee, is common in open habitats and nests in the ground under stones. The male has a yellow collar.*

yellow collar

yellow front of abdomen

red tail

▶ **BOMBUS HORTORUM,** *the Large Garden Bumble Bee, has a yellow collar, yellow at the rear of the thorax and the first abdominal segment, and a white tail.*

yellow collar

▲ **BOMBUS PRATORUM** *inhabits light woodland and gardens. Workers have a yellow collar, a yellowish second abdominal segment, and a red "tail".*

yellowish abdominal segment

orange collar

▲ **BOMBUS TERRESTRIS,** *the Buff-tailed Bumble Bee, is an abundant species. It makes nests underground and can find its way back after foraging trips to 13km.*

orange-yellow second abdominal segment

LARVAE

The pale, grub-like larvae are fed pollen and honey in brood cells made of wax. At first, the larvae produce female workers to build up the colony; males appear later.

▼ **BOMBUS LUCORUM** *is a very common species which rests underground and sometimes in grass tussocks.*

pollen on leg

yellow collar

NOTE

Western Honey bees have been spread all over the world by commerce. The value of the crops that they pollinate exceeds that of their honey and wax.

ORDER *Hymenoptera.*
FAMILY *Apidae.*
SPECIES IN FAMILY *1,000.*
SIZE *0.3–2.7cm (body length).*
FEEDING *Larvae: herbivores (pollen), honey-feeders. Adults: herbivores, honey-feeders.*
IMPACT *Essential plant pollinators.*

Neobisiids

Neobisiidae

The back of the thorax of these widely distributed pseudoscorpions is quite angular or square and the chelicerae are quite large. In all the pairs of walking legs, the tarsi are made up of two segments. There are usually four eyes, although there may be fewer or none at all in cave-living species. Overall coloration varies from olive to brown and the legs are often slightly green in colour.

FOUND *mainly in leaf litter and soil, with some species in caves.*

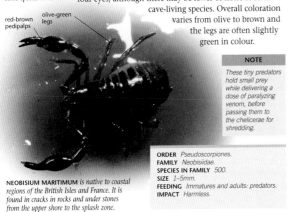

red-brown pedipalps / olive-green legs

NOTE
These tiny predators hold small prey while delivering a dose of paralyzing venom, before passing them to the chelicerae for shredding.

ORDER *Pseudoscorpiones.*
FAMILY *Neobisiidae.*
SPECIES IN FAMILY 500.
SIZE *1–5mm.*
FEEDING *Immatures and adults: predators.*
IMPACT *Harmless.*

NEOBISIUM MARITIMUM *is native to coastal regions of the British Isles and France. It is found in cracks in rocks and under stones from the upper shore to the splash zone.*

Chernetids

Chernetidae

In these brown or greenish brown pseudoscorpions, the abdomen is typically much longer than the thorax and often has parallel sides. Most species have four eyes and the tarsi of the first two pairs of legs have a single segment, while those of the third and fourth pair have two segments.

OCCUR *under the bark of dead or very old deciduous trees, and in soil and leaf litter.*

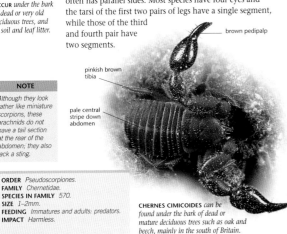

brown pedipalp / pinkish brown tibia / pale central stripe down abdomen

NOTE
Although they look rather like miniature scorpions, these arachnids do not have a tail section at the rear of the abdomen; they also lack a sting.

ORDER *Pseudoscorpiones.*
FAMILY *Chernetidae.*
SPECIES IN FAMILY 570.
SIZE *1–2mm.*
FEEDING *Immatures and adults: predators.*
IMPACT *Harmless.*

CHERNES CIMICOIDES *can be found under the bark of dead or mature deciduous trees such as oak and beech, mainly in the south of Britain.*

Phalangiids

Phalangiidae

These harvestmen usually have soft bodies and may have many spiny projections. Typical species are brownish or greyish with a dark area on the upper surface known as the saddle. On the front edge of the carapace there is often a cluster of three closely grouped spines, called the trident. Leg segments may have longitudinal ridges, which are sometimes spined. Males and females can look different, especially in the shape of the chelicerae, which are enlarged in males.

LIVE *under stones and among leaf litter in wooded and grassy areas; some also found in buildings.*

NOTE
Harvestmen in this family are mainly nocturnal: look for them after dark, when they wander about searching for food or mates. Some species are active during the day as well, and a few are adapted to life in buildings.

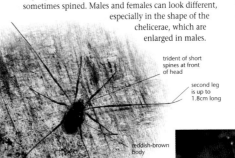

trident of short spines at front of head / second leg is up to 1.8cm long / reddish-brown body

▲ **OLIGOLOPHUS TRIDENS** *has a brown body with a black central mark, which is broad at the front and more parallel-sided towards the rear.*

► **PHALANGIUM OPILIO** *is one of the few day-active species in gardens. Males (shown here) have horn-like extensions on the chelicerae.*

horned chelicerae in male

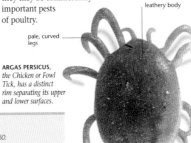

ORDER *Opiliones.*
FAMILY *Phalangiidae.*
SPECIES IN FAMILY 200.
SIZE *1–12mm.*
FEEDING *Immatures and adults: predators, scavengers.*
IMPACT *Harmless.*

pale sides / second leg up to 4cm long

▲ **MITOPUS MORIO** *is variable in general body colour, but always has a very broad, saddle-shaped dark band running down its back. It lives among low-growing vegetation and bushes.*

Hard Ticks

Ixodidae

These flattened, yellowish red to dark brown or almost black ticks have a very tough (sometimes patterned) plate on the back of the body. In males, this plate covers the whole body, but in females and immatures it covers only the front half. Some species are distinctively marked. The abdomen is soft and flexible to allow large blood meals to be taken from the animal hosts on which these ticks are found. Hard ticks transmit disease and may carry viral diseases that affect humans, such as encephalitis.

OCCUPY *grassland, scrub, or woodland, in association with their bird or mammal hosts.*

flattened abdomen / tough dorsal shield / sucking mouthparts

IXODES RICINUS, *the Sheep Tick, actually sucks blood from a wide range of hosts. It is greyish to reddish brown with a dark dorsal plate and head.*

NOTE
Females gorge on blood after mating, then drop off to lay their eggs. There are two immature stages: a six-legged larva and an eight-legged nymph.

ORDER *Acari.*
FAMILY *Ixodidae.*
SPECIES IN FAMILY 650.
SIZE *2–10mm.*
FEEDING *Immatures and adults: blood-feeders (mammals and birds).*
IMPACT *Serious pests of domestic animals.*

Soft Ticks

Argasidae

Soft ticks generally have a rounded, berry-like body, although some species can be flattened. The body surface, which is tough and leathery, may appear wrinkled or roughened. The strong mouthparts are adapted for cutting through the skin of their hosts, including mammals such as bats, birds, and snakes. Feeding mostly takes place at night. Many species are significant vectors of disease and they may be commercially important pests of poultry.

OCCUR *in association with a wide range of mammals and birds, mainly in warm, dry regions.*

NOTE
Female soft ticks usually lay their eggs in the nests of birds or the burrows of mammals. Argas persicus transmits a disease known as fowl relapsing fever.

leathery body / pale, curved legs

ARGAS PERSICUS, *the Chicken or Fowl Tick, has a distinct rim separating its upper and lower surfaces.*

ORDER *Acari.*
FAMILY *Argasidae.*
SPECIES IN FAMILY 150.
SIZE *2–10mm.*
FEEDING *Immatures and adults: blood-feeders (mammals and birds).*
IMPACT *Serious pests of domestic animals.*

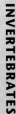

INVERTEBRATES

Buff-tailed Bumble bee
The buff-tailed is the largest British bumble bee and among the first to emerge after winter. Having hibernated in a hole or under moss, each new fertilized queen then starts her own colony.

Gall Mites

Eriophyidae

FOUND *in woodland, parkland, gardens, hedgerows, and wherever their host species grow.*

It is extremely difficult indeed to see these tiny mites, but very easy to recognize the galls that they make on the leaves of their host plants and inside which they develop. Each species of mite produces a uniquely shaped gall, often on a specific host plant. Gall mites range from white to yellowish, pinkish, or transparent and are widest just behind the head, giving them a distinctive, carrot-like shape. The thorax and abdomen are completely fused and, unlike any other mites, which have four pairs of legs, gall mites have only two pairs of legs. Many species are parthenogenetic.

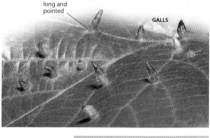

▷ **ACERIA PSEUDOPLATANI** *grows on Sycamores forming a bulge on the leaf's upper surface, which eventually turns brown and withered looking.*

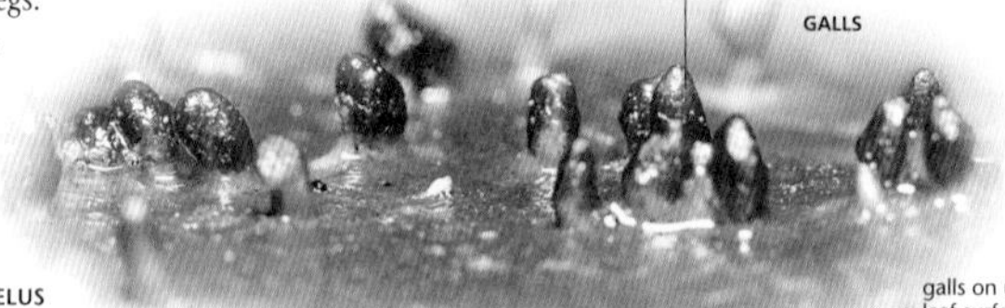

brown bulge on upper surface

GALLS

shiny red gall

GALLS

◁ **ARTACRIS MACRORHYNCHUS** *forms numerous and crowded elongate pimple-like galls up to 2mm long. Each gall has a minute opening on the underside of the leaf.*

GALLS

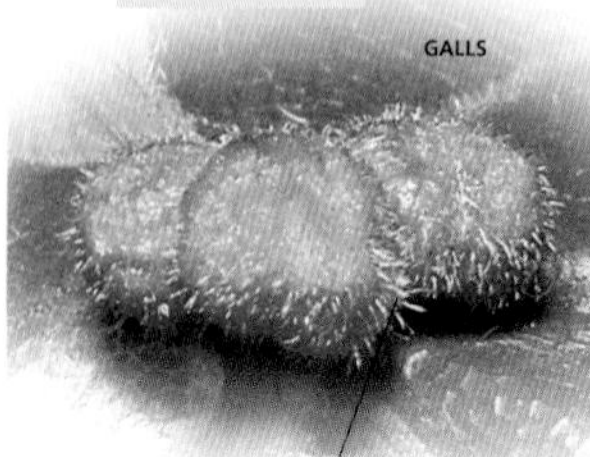

◁ **ERIOPHYES MACROCHELUS** *galls found on the surface of Field Maple leaves, are green and hairy. They grow up to 5mm across, and occur in groups of up to 4.*

silver-white hair

galls on upper leaf surface

▷ **ACERIA BREVIPUNCTATUS** *makes pale, pimple-like galls up to 2mm in diameter. They have a small opening on the underside of the leaf surface guarded by fine hair.*

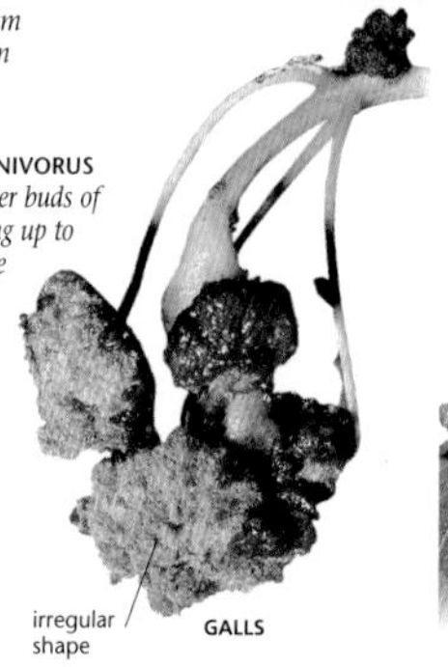

▷ **ACERIA FRAXINIVORUS** *inhabits the flower buds of ash trees. Growing up to 2cm, the galls are green but darken as they mature.*

tiny growth on leaves

GALLS

▷ **PHYTOPUS AVELLANAE** *occurs on the buds of Hazel. This causes the buds to swell and open, making them more conspicuous than normal buds.*

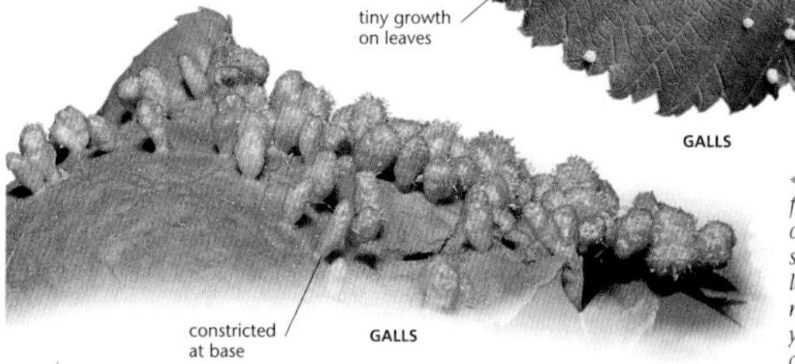

GALLS

swollen Hazel bud

irregular shape

GALLS

constricted at base

GALLS

◁ **ERIOPHYES PADI** *forms dense clusters of galls on the upper surface of cherry leaves, often near the midrib. These are yellowish brown and constricted at the base.*

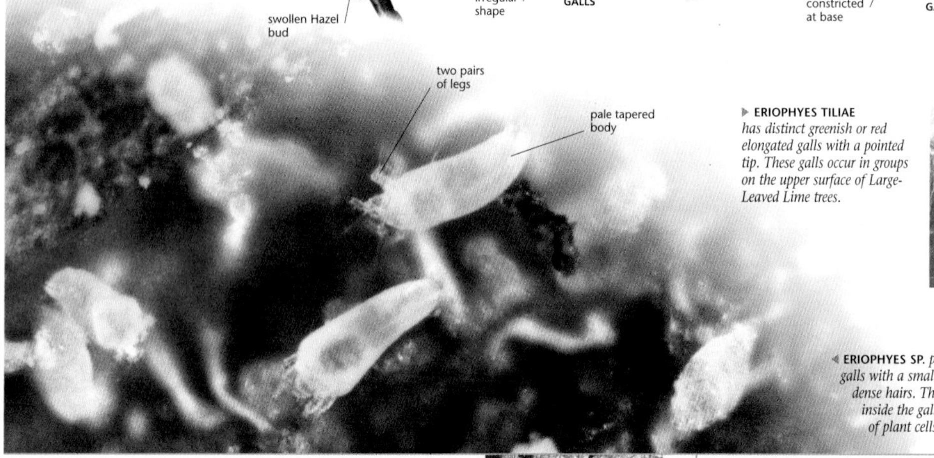

two pairs of legs

pale tapered body

long and pointed

▷ **ERIOPHYES TILIAE** *has distinct greenish or red elongated galls with a pointed tip. These galls occur in groups on the upper surface of Large-Leaved Lime trees.*

GALLS

◁ **ERIOPHYES SP.** *produce pouch-like galls with a small opening guarded by dense hairs. The mites live and feed inside the gall, sucking the contents of plant cells.*

Spider Mites

Tetranychidae

OCCUR *in a variety of habitats on shrubs, trees, and herbaceous plants.*

These tiny, soft-bodied mites are orange, red, greenish, or yellow in colour and have a spider-like appearance. Large numbers infest and feed on plants, which may then develop pale blotches and wither or die. Spider mites produce silk from glands in the front part of the body and often cover affected plant parts with a fine webbing. The plants attacked include a number of commercially important crops such as wheat, citrus and other fruit trees, cotton, and coffee; yields may suffer dramatically.

orange-red coloration

▽ **TETRANYCHUS URTICAE** *feeds on a wide range of host plants. It hibernates deep in leaf litter in winter.*

pale, fine body hairs

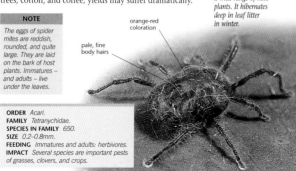

Varroa Mites

Varroidae

LIVE *in association with both wild and domesticated honey bees.*

Typically, varroa mites are tan in colour, broader than they are long, and have smooth, convex bodies. These mites are parasites of bees. Their eggs are laid inside bees' nests in the brood cells and the varroa mite nymphs feed on the bee larvae. The adult mites attach themselves to adult bees both to feed off them and as an efficient means of dispersal.

▷ **VARROA SP.** *larvae feed on bee pupae; the pupae in this image have been removed from their brood cells to show this.*

smooth, oval outline

mite nymph feeding on bee pupa

◁ **VARROA PERSICUS** *attaches itself to the body of a honey bee to suck its body fluids.*

sucking mouthparts

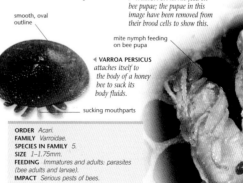

Velvet Mites

Trombidiidae

Many of these soft-bodied mites have bright red or orange bodies that are extremely hairy, giving them a dense, velvety appearance. The legs are relatively long and the body, which does not appear pinched in the middle, is often broader towards the front than the rear. At certain times of year, usually after rain, adults emerge from the soil to mate and lay eggs.

FOUND in a range of habitats, mainly in or on the soil.

▼ **TROMBIDIUM HOLOSERICEUM** is a fairly large, red mite. It can be seen crawling about on tree trunks in early spring.

dense covering of hairs

long front legs

wrinkled surface

▶ **EUTROMBIDIUM ROSTRATUS** feeds as an immature by attaching itself to an insect, sucking its blood for 1–2 days. It then detaches and burrows into soil.

ORDER Acari.
FAMILY Trombidiidae.
SPECIES IN FAMILY 250.
SIZE 2–5mm (body length).
FEEDING Immatures and adults: parasites, predators, scavengers.
IMPACT Harmless.

Parasitid Mites

Parasitidae

Most of these mites are slightly pear-shaped and yellowish brown with one or two visible plates on the upper surface of the body. In the male, the second pair of legs may be stouter than the others in order to grasp the female during mating. Female parasitid mites lay their eggs in organic debris. The immatures are often found on the bodies of insects and many feed on small insects, their larvae, and other mites.

COMMONLY found in leaf litter and decaying wood in wooded areas.

cluster of mites

underside of host insect

PARASITUS SP. feed on haemolymph as immatures. Their mouthparts penetrate the soft parts of the host.

ORDER Acari.
FAMILY Parasitidae.
SPECIES IN FAMILY 375.
SIZE 0.75–2mm (body length).
FEEDING Immatures and adults: parasites.
IMPACT Harmless. Some species may actually be bad for the health of pest species.

Orb Web Spiders

Araneidae

The most distinctive feature of these spiders is their vertical and circular webs, which have a central hub with radiating lines and spirals of sticky and non-sticky silk. The structure of the web is often species specific. The spider usually sits at the hub of the web, awaiting the arrival of prey. These species often have very large, egg-shaped abdomens, which can be brightly coloured and patterned with all manner of bands, spots, and irregular markings. There are eight eyes, the middle four often forming a square, with two pairs further out towards the side of the head. The legs of most orb web spiders have numerous bristles and spines.

OCCUR in a wide variety of habitats, from heathland to woodland and gardens to meadows.

▼ **AGALENATEA REDII** is a variably marked, reddish brown spider with a very broad abdomen. It spins webs with close-woven silk at the hub on shrubs and low vegetation.

▶ **ARGIOPE BRUENNICHI** has distinctive yellow or cream and black bands on the abdomen. Males are much smaller than females.

extra silk, called the stabilimentum, may protect the web

striped abdomen

grey hairs

white patches on abdomen

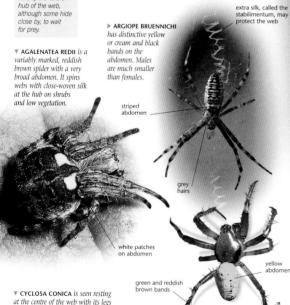

▼ **CYCLOSA CONICA** is seen resting at the centre of the web with its legs drawn up over the cephalothorax. It has a mottled abdomen.

pointed abdomen

green and reddish brown bands

prey

yellow abdomen

♂

▲ **ARANIELLA CUCURBITINA** is very small and has a small red patch just above the spinners. Females have a bright green abdomen and are larger than males.

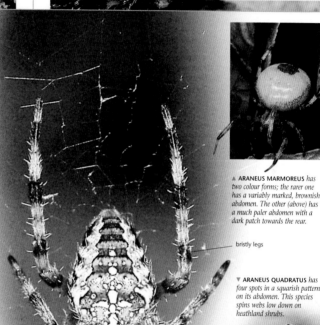

▲ **ARANEUS MARMOREUS** has two colour forms; the rarer one has a variably marked, brownish abdomen. The other (above) has a much paler abdomen with a dark patch towards the rear.

bristly legs

▼ **ARANEUS QUADRATUS** has four spots in a squarish pattern on its abdomen. This species spins webs low down on heathland shrubs.

cross-shaped markings

▲ **ARANEUS DIADEMATUS**, the Garden Cross Spider, is extremely common. It is very variable in colour, but always seems to have a cross-shaped mark on its abdomen.

▶ **LARINIOIDES CORNUTUS** makes its webs between grass stems and other plants, often near freshwater or in coastal areas. The female has a less distinct abdominal pattern.

four pale spots on the abdomen

♂

patterning on the abdomen

dark, flattened body

▲ **NUCTENEA UMBRATICA**, common and widespread in Britain, hides under the bark of dead trees and other crevices during the day, and spins a web to trap nocturnal flying insects.

ORDER Araneae.
FAMILY Araneidae.
SPECIES IN FAMILY 4,000.
SIZE 3–16mm.
FEEDING Immatures and adults: predatory.
IMPACT Beneficial and harmless, although some larger species may bite in defence.

Fishing Spider
Also know as the Raft Spider, this arachnid can walk on water and, if threatened, will submerge, remaining underwater for up to an hour. The female carries its large egg sac under its body.

Purse-web Spiders

Atypidae

These unmistakable reddish brown spiders make distinctive silk tube nests in burrows, with part of the silk extending outwards over the ground. They have massive, forward-facing chelicerae that look almost as large as the cephalothorax. Unlike most spiders, in which the fangs act like a pair of pincers, the fangs are parallel and stab downwards. There are eight, closely grouped eyes: two middle eyes with two groups of three either side.

FANGS
downward-stabbing fangs

LIVE *inside silk-lined burrows in sandy or chalky soil in south-facing spots with low vegetation.*

ATYPUS AFFINIS *makes very distinctive finger-like silk tubes. Prey walking over the silk is impaled from below and dragged inside.*

huge chelicerae

large, broad cephalothorax

ORDER *Araneae.*
FAMILY *Atypidae.*
SPECIES IN FAMILY *30.*
SIZE *0.7–1.8cm (body length).*
FEEDING *Immatures and adults: predators.*
IMPACT *Beneficial and harmless.*

Lace-webbed Spiders

Amaurobiidae

Named for their distinctive webs, these small spiders make irregular or tangled webs with a tube-shaped retreat in dark or concealed places. The silk produced by these spiders has a bluish appearance when fresh. The spiders have a dark reddish brown cephalothorax with eight eyes in two rows at the front. The abdomen is dark or greyish brown with lighter, sometimes chevron-shaped, markings.

WEB

WEBS *of these spiders can be found in holes in walls and bark, underneath stones, and in leaf litter.*

funnel-like retreat

abdominal pattern similar in both sexes

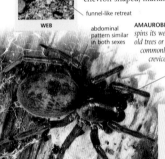

dark head

AMAUROBIUS FENESTRALIS *spins its webs under the bark of old trees or stumps but is most commonly found in the crevices of stone walls.*

NOTE

A vibrating tuning fork held to the web of a lace-webbed spider will lure it out of its retreat. The webs are produced at night under the cover of darkness.

ORDER *Araneae.*
FAMILY *Amaurobiidae.*
SPECIES IN FAMILY *350.*
SIZE *4–14mm (body length).*
FEEDING *Immatures and adults: predators.*
IMPACT *Beneficial and harmless.*

Nursery-web Spiders

Pisauridae

These large, long-legged hunting spiders are very similar in habit and appearance to wolf spiders (right), but differ in the size of their eyes. Viewed from the front, the two eyes forming the second row of eyes are quite small. The carapace is oval, with longitudinal markings. They do not make webs, but run and hunt on the ground, on the surface of still water, and on aquatic plants.

WIDESPREAD *on grassland, heathland, woodland rides and margins, and also in marshy areas.*

pale lateral stripe

white stripe

long, stout legs

egg sac carried on fangs

▲ **PISAURA MIRABILIS** *is seen here with an egg sac. Females make tent-like nursery webs just before the spiderlings emerge.*

▼ **DOLOMEDES FIMBRIATUS,** *the Fishing Spider, lives in wet habitats and hunts for prey on the surface of water.*

ORDER *Araneae.*
FAMILY *Pisauridae.*
SPECIES IN FAMILY *550.*
SIZE *1–2.2cm.*
FEEDING *Immatures and adults: predators.*
IMPACT *Beneficial and harmless. Dolomedes fimbriatus is protected by law in the UK.*

The Water Spider

Argyronetidae

This unique spider lives permanently underwater, and makes a dome-shaped, silk diving bell attached to submerged plants. Prey items are dragged back to the bell for eating. The water spider has a reddish brown cephalothorax and a dark brown abdomen with a distinctive dense pile of short hair. The third and fourth pairs of legs are much hairier than the first two pairs.

FOUND *in very slow-flowing and still water with plenty of aquatic vegetation.*

diving bell

ARGYRONETA AQUATICA *carries bubbles of air from the surface on the abdomen (left), and on the hind legs.*

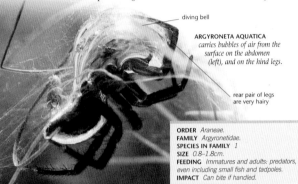

rear pair of legs are very hairy

ORDER *Araneae.*
FAMILY *Argyronetidae.*
SPECIES IN FAMILY *1.*
SIZE *0.8–1.8cm.*
FEEDING *Immatures and adults: predators, even including small fish and tadpoles.*
IMPACT *Can bite if handled.*

Wolf Spiders

Lycosidae

Drably coloured, the bodies of wolf spiders are densely covered with light and dark hairs that form patterns. These spiders have very good eyesight for hunting prey. The head has eight eyes: four small eyes in a row at the front, and above this a much larger pair of forward-facing eyes; another pair, further back, point sideways. Females often carry their egg sacs around with them, attached to their spinnerets. When the young spiderlings hatch, the mother may carry them on her back for a week or so. Most species live on the ground among leaf litter or on low-growing vegetation. Wolf spiders are fast runners.

OCCUR *everywhere from grassland to marshes and mudflats, on low vegetation.*

NOTE

Although wolf spiders look similar to nursery-web spiders, their middle forward-facing eyes are much larger than the other eyes.

light margins

yellow mark

♂

light brown to black coloration

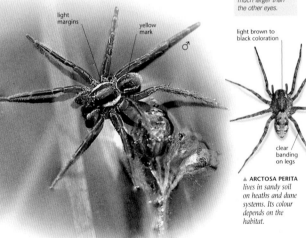

clear banding on legs

▲ **ARCTOSA PERITA** *lives in sandy soil on heaths and dune systems. Its colour depends on the habitat.*

▲ **PIRATA PIRATICUS** *is common and widespread throughout Britain in marshes and boggy places. It moves quickly over water and plants and can make small jumps.*

▶ **TROCHOSA RURICOLA** *hunts after dark. It lives under stones or among leaf litter in damp areas.*

dark brown

striped legs

▶ **PARDOSA LUGUBRIS** *lives in wooded areas. Females are not as dark as the males, and have less distinct stripes.*

light median stripe

distinct, light, central stripe

ORDER *Araneae.*
FAMILY *Lycosidae.*
SPECIES IN FAMILY *3,000.*
SIZE *4–20mm.*
FEEDING *Immatures and adults: predators.*
IMPACT *Beneficial and harmless, but large species may bite.*

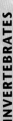

Jumping Spiders

Salticidae

Despite the fact that most of these short-legged, compact spiders are small, they are immediately recognizable. Four eyes form a row at the front of the square-fronted head, and the middle pair are very much larger than any of the others. Further back there are another two small eyes, and behind those, another pair of slightly larger eyes. These active hunters use their excellent eyesight to help stalk their prey, before leaping on top of victims at close range. Many species are attractively patterned and some have iridescent hair on the body.

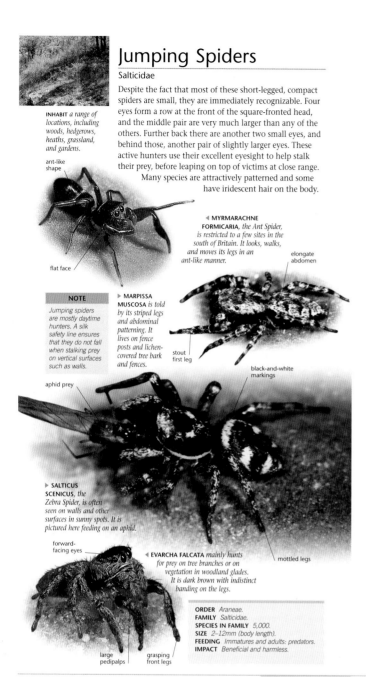

INHABIT *a range of locations, including woods, hedgerows, heaths, grassland, and gardens.*

ant-like shape

flat face

NOTE

Jumping spiders are mostly daytime hunters. A silk safety line ensures that they do not fall when stalking prey on vertical surfaces such as walls.

◀ **MYRMARACHNE FORMICARIA**, *the Ant Spider, is restricted to a few sites in the south of Britain. It looks, walks, and moves its legs in an ant-like manner.*

elongate abdomen

▶ **MARPISSA MUSCOSA** *is told by its striped legs and abdominal patterning. It lives on fence posts and lichen-covered tree bark and fences.*

stout first leg

black-and-white markings

aphid prey

▶ **SALTICUS SCENICUS**, *the Zebra Spider, is often seen on walls and other surfaces in sunny spots. It is pictured here feeding on an aphid.*

forward-facing eyes

mottled legs

◀ **EVARCHA FALCATA** *mainly hunts for prey on tree branches or on vegetation in woodland glades. It is dark brown with indistinct banding on the legs.*

large pedipalps

grasping front legs

ORDER *Araneae.*
FAMILY *Salticidae.*
SPECIES IN FAMILY *5,000.*
SIZE *2–12mm (body length).*
FEEDING *Immatures and adults: predators.*
IMPACT *Beneficial and harmless.*

Spitting Spiders

Scytodidae

Spitting spiders do not spin webs but instead employ a unique hunting technique in which prey is pinned down with zigzag strands of sticky glue shot from the chelicerae. The large carapace of these spiders is very domed towards the rear and is cream or yellow-brown and black. The front of the carapace is narrowed and has only six eyes: a close-set pair pointing forwards and a similar pair at each side.

FOUND *mainly in buildings and among rocks, especially in warmer regions.*

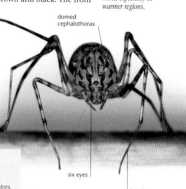

domed cephalothorax

SCYTODES THORACICA *has a distinctively domed cephalothorax and unique colour pattern. It is a slow-moving, nocturnal, indoor species.*

six eyes

banded legs

ORDER *Araneae.*
FAMILY *Scytodidae.*
SPECIES IN FAMILY *180.*
SIZE *3–7mm (body length).*
FEEDING *Immatures and adults: predators.*
IMPACT *Beneficial and harmless.*

Oonopids

Oonopidae

These small spiders are pinkish, reddish, or sometimes yellowish, with a distinctive style of movement that alternates between a slow walk and a fast sprint. The head has six characteristically oval eyes, which are grouped very closely together. Oonopids do not spin webs but move about on the ground after dark to find prey.

OCCUR *mainly in forested regions, often in leaf litter.*

brownish red cephalothorax

light brown abdomen

OONOPS DOMESTICUS *is a small, red-brown or pinkish spider that lives indoors. It hunts small prey after dark.*

NOTE

Sometimes these spiders scavenge the remains of prey trapped in the sheet or funnel webs of other spiders. They also eat food scraps on the ground.

ORDER *Araneae.*
FAMILY *Oonopidae.*
SPECIES IN FAMILY *250.*
SIZE *1–3mm.*
FEEDING *Immatures and adults: predators.*
IMPACT *Harmless.*

Cobweb Spiders

Agelenidae

These spiders are also called funnel-weavers due to their web – a flat, tangled silk sheet with a funnel-shaped tube at one side. They are often long-legged and the front of the cephalothorax is narrowed, with eight smallish eyes grouped together. The abdomen is quite slender, oval, and may be patterned.

chevron markings

long legs

oval abdomen

LIVE *in grassland, meadows, gardens, and similar habitats, often entering houses.*

funnel-shaped tube

▶ **AGELENA LABYRINTHICA** *spins a sheet web among grasses, low-growing vegetation, or bushes, resting in the funnel-shaped retreat.*

▲ **TEGENARIA DUELLICA** *is common in houses and gardens. The large specimens seen moving around indoors are usually males looking for mates.*

ORDER *Araneae.*
FAMILY *Agelenidae.*
SPECIES IN FAMILY *700.*
SIZE *4–16mm (body length).*
FEEDING *Immatures and adults: predators.*
IMPACT *Entirely harmless, but responsible for frightening arachnophobic householders.*

Dysderids

Dysderidae

These nocturnal, ground-living spiders have six eyes arranged roughly in a circle on the head. The carapace is reddish brown or dark brown to black. The chelicerae can be large and the fangs are long and sharp to pierce the cuticle of their prey. The abdomen is pinkish grey or dark grey. *Dysdera* species are known as woodlice-eating spiders after their main prey.

FOUND *in damp locations under stone, rotting wood, debris, or tree bark.*

NOTE

The jaws of Dysdera crocata are wide and strong enough to penetrate human skin; a few people may have a serious allergic reaction to the venom.

◀ **HARPACTEA HOMBERGI** *is a small, elongate species with a greyish brown abdomen and a dark, shiny cephalothorax.*

▼ **DYSDERA CROCATA** *lives wherever woodlice, its prey, occur. Its fangs open sideways to impale victims.*

ORDER *Araneae.*
FAMILY *Dysderidae.*
SPECIES IN FAMILY *250.*
SIZE *0.5–1.6cm.*
FEEDING *Immatures and adults: predators.*
IMPACT *Beneficial by controlling pests. Dysdera crocata can bite if handled roughly.*

Six-eyed Spiders

Segestriidae

Despite their common name of six-eyed spiders, segestriids are not the only family of spiders with six eyes. The eyes are arranged in three groups of two – a close-set pair in the middle, facing forward, and one pair on each side. A good recognition feature for these spiders is that the first three pairs of legs are held forwards. They also lay threads like trip wires radiating from the nest entrance.

LIVE in tubular nests in holes in walls, and sometimes in bark.

silk tube

dark cephalothorax

SEGESTRIA SENOCULATA inhabits a funnel-shaped retreat in walls and bark, surrounded by radiating signal threads that alert it to suitable-sized prey.

ORDER Araneae.
FAMILY Segestriidae.
SPECIES IN FAMILY 100.
SIZE 0.7–2.1cm.
FEEDING Immatures and adults: predators.
IMPACT Harmless.

Daddy-Long-Legs Spiders

Pholcidae

FOUND in caves and buildings, especially near ceilings and in dark corners.

Also known as cellar spiders, these small spiders make irregular, tangled webs of criss-cross threads. They quickly wrap prey in silk before biting it. The carapace is rounded in outline and the legs are much longer than the body, giving a spindly appearance similar to crane flies (p.270). The head has a pair of small eyes flanked by two groups of three closely-set eyes.

NOTE

The males look very similar to females but have a slender abdomen and are slightly smaller. The mating of these spiders can last for hours.

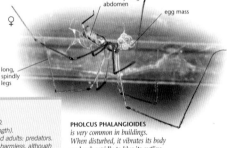

relatively long abdomen

egg mass

long, spindly legs

ORDER Araneae.
FAMILY Pholcidae.
SPECIES IN FAMILY 350.
SIZE 3–14mm (body length).
FEEDING Immatures and adults: predators.
IMPACT Beneficial and harmless, although sometimes regarded a nuisance in houses.

PHOLCUS PHALANGIOIDES is very common in buildings. When disturbed, it vibrates its body and web rapidly to blur its outline, confusing potential predators.

Crab Spiders

Thomisidae

These spiders are named for their typically squat shape and characteristic sideways, scuttling movement. The carapace is nearly circular and the abdomen is short and often blunt-ended. The first two pairs of legs, which are used to seize prey, are larger and more spiny than the other two pairs and are turned to face forwards. The head has eight small, dark and beady, equally-sized eyes arranged in two rows.

OCCUR on a variety of plants, especially the flowerheads, and on the bark of trees.

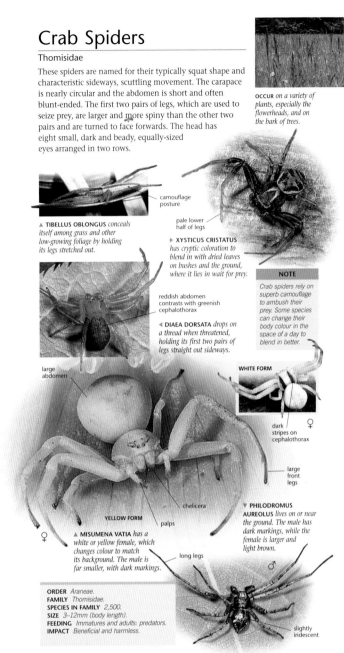

camouflage posture

TIBELLUS OBLONGUS conceals itself among grass and other low-growing foliage by holding its legs stretched out.

pale lower half of legs

XYSTICUS CRISTATUS has cryptic coloration to blend in with dried leaves on bushes and the ground, where it lies in wait for prey.

reddish abdomen contrasts with greenish cephalothorax

NOTE

Crab spiders rely on superb camouflage to ambush their prey. Some species can change their body colour in the space of a day to blend in better.

DIAEA DORSATA drops on a thread when threatened, holding its first two pairs of legs straight out sideways.

WHITE FORM

large abdomen

dark stripes on cephalothorax

large front legs

chelicera

YELLOW FORM

palps

PHILODROMUS AUREOLUS lives on or near the ground. The male has dark markings, while the female is larger and light brown.

MISUMENA VATIA has a white or yellow female, which changes colour to match its background. The male is far smaller, with dark markings.

long legs

slightly iridescent

ORDER Araneae.
FAMILY Thomisidae.
SPECIES IN FAMILY 2,500.
SIZE 3–12mm (body length).
FEEDING Immatures and adults: predators.
IMPACT Beneficial and harmless.

Ground Spiders

Gnaphosidae

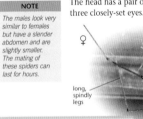

INHABIT a variety of habitats from grassland, heathland, and wooded areas to parks and gardens.

Most ground spiders are greyish brown to black with no clear patterning on the abdomen, although some have patches or bands of white hairs. The head has eight eyes arranged in two rows. The two middle eyes of the second row have a distinctively oval or elongated shape. Most species hide in a silk nest under stones and logs during the day and hunt at night.

black cephalothorax

ZELOTES SP. spend the day hiding under stones, where females attach their egg sacs.

sleek black abdomen

spinnerets

ORDER Araneae.
FAMILY Gnaphosidae.
SPECIES IN FAMILY 2,000.
SIZE 0.3–1.8cm (body length).
FEEDING Immatures and adults: predators.
IMPACT Beneficial and harmless.

Foliage Spiders

Clubionidae

OCCUPY a wide range of habitats, well vegetated with bushes or trees and places to hide; some in coastal areas or marshes.

Similar in habits to ground spiders (left), these nocturnal hunters spend the day in a silken cell, in vegetation or under stones. Most species have relatively elongate bodies and are generally yellowish, reddish grey, or darkish brown in colour. The arrangement of the eight eyes is the same as in ground spiders, but the middle pair in the back row have a circular outline.

CHEIRACANTHIUM ERRATICUM is common on low-growing plants and grasses. It hunts at night, hiding during the day in a silk retreat.

first pair of legs are longest

yellow band with dark central stripe

drab, reddish brown coloration

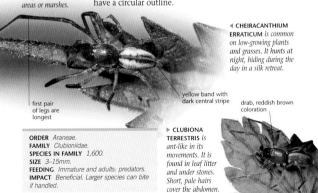

CLUBIONA TERRESTRIS is ant-like in its movements. It is found in leaf litter and under stones. Short, pale hairs cover the abdomen.

ORDER Araneae.
FAMILY Clubionidae.
SPECIES IN FAMILY 1,600.
SIZE 3–15mm.
FEEDING Immature and adults: predators.
IMPACT Beneficial. Larger species can bite if handled.

Comb-footed Spiders

Theridiidae

Also called cobweb spiders on account of their tangled, irregular webs, these nocturnal species can be greyish or brown to black. Many have intricate patterning on the rounded, almost spherical abdomen. The legs are typically banded. The hind pair have a comb-like row of stout bristles, but these are actually very difficult to see even under magnification. The head has eight eyes, arranged in two rows, with the outer eyes of each row set very close together.

SEEN *in a variety of habitats on shrubs, gorse, trees, low vegetation; some in human habitation.*

large globular abdomen

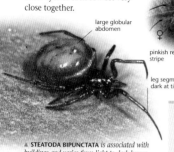

pinkish red stripe

row of black spots

leg segments dark at tips

▲ ENOPLOGNATHA OVATA *females are small with globular abdomens that have pinkish red stripes. In both sexes there are two rows of black spots.*

▲ STEATODA BIPUNCTATA *is associated with buildings and varies from light to dark brown. Females are large and may live for several years.*

ORDER *Araneae.*
FAMILY *Theridiidae.*
SPECIES IN FAMILY *2,200.*
SIZE *2–10mm.*
FEEDING *Immatures and adults: predators.*
IMPACT *Beneficial; however, Steatoda nobilis can bite if handled.*

Ladybird Spiders

Eresidae

INHABIT *south-facing heathland and low vegetation.*

These are robust, fairly hairy spiders with a distinctively large, square-fronted head and eight small eyes, four of which are placed at each "corner" of the head. Females are long-lived, black, and velvety; they usually live inside silk-lined tubular burrows covered by a silk roof. The short-lived males resemble ladybirds due to their red abdomen with four black spots.

white bands on legs

black head

ERESUS CINNABERINUS *lives in silk-lined tubes in the ground and spins a small sheet of "fuzzy" silk above to catch prey.*

black spots on abdomen

ORDER *Araneae.*
FAMILY *Eresidae.*
SPECIES IN FAMILY *120.*
SIZE *0.6–1.6cm.*
FEEDING *Immatures and adults: predators.*
IMPACT *May bite if handled; beneficial in controlling pest species.*

NOTE

Eresus cinnaberinus is one of the most colourful European spiders and is protected due to its rarity. It has been recorded on heathland in Dorset.

Pirate Spiders

Mimetidae

LIVE *in a variety of habitats on trees and bushes, as well as woodland, heathland, scrub, and gardens.*

Spider-eating spiders might be a better name as these small species invade the webs of other spiders and eat them. They pluck the threads of a web gently to attract the spider, and then bite it. This paralyses the prey so they can suck the internal contents through a small hole. They do not spin webs themselves. The abdomen is roughly spherical with one or two pairs of small, blunt conical bumps.

tubercle on abdomen

dark and light bands on legs

ERO ARPHANA *has clearly banded legs, and two pairs of small conical bumps (tubercle) on its abdomen. It lives among low heath vegetation.*

NOTE

Females do not carry their eggs around with them. Instead they hang the egg sac from a plant by a thin silk thread, and cover it with a tangle of silk.

ORDER *Araneae.*
FAMILY *Mimetidae.*
SPECIES IN FAMILY *150.*
SIZE *2–4mm.*
FEEDING *Immatures and adults: predators.*
IMPACT *Beneficial and harmless; attack other species.*

Long-jawed Orb Web Spiders

Tetragnathidae

OCCUPY *grassy places such as meadows, low vegetation, damp woodland, and dark places such as caves.*

In common with orb web spiders, most of these spiders spin an orb web; however, they differ in that the webs are not vertical but usually at an angle and the hub of the web is open with no silk spirals at the centre. Many species are elongated with long legs and very large diverging chelicerae; others are more oval-bodied with a rounded abdomen.

long abdomen

large jaws

pale triangular marks

pale brown, ringed legs

▲ TETRAGNATHA EXTENSA *has long, curved chelicerae and fangs. At rest, it holds its legs parallel to grass blades.*

long legs

olive cephalothorax

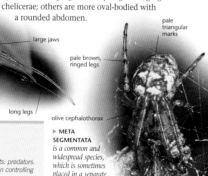

◄ META SEGMENTATA *is a common and widespread species, which is sometimes placed in a separate family, the Metidae.*

ORDER *Araneae.*
FAMILY *Tetragnathidae.*
SPECIES IN FAMILY *800.*
SIZE *3–15mm.*
FEEDING *Immatures and adults: predators.*
IMPACT *Harmless; beneficial in controlling pest species.*

Dwarf Spiders

Linyphiidae

FOUND *among lush vegetation; some species in leaf litter.*

As this family's common name implies, many of these species are small. They vary widely in colour and pattern and many have bristly legs. The head has eight eyes arranged in two rows, but the heads of some males may have strange extensions on top, sometimes bearing the eyes. Dwarf spiders, also called money spiders, are common and travel great distances by "ballooning" on long silk threads.

black abdomen

humped cephalothorax

palps

▲ HYPOMMA BITUBERCULATUM *has an orangish cephalothorax and black abdomen. It inhabits damp habitats such as streamsides.*

▲ ERIGONE ATRA *is a small, shiny black spider with yellowish brown legs in females and reddish brown legs in males. This and related species are often extremely common.*

◄ LINYPHIA TRIANGULARIS *is a very common species. It has a pale, speckled, quite elongated abdomen with a row of darkish marks.*

distinctive dark markings

NOTE

Some species spin horizontal sheet webs, which can be up to 30cm wide and are supported by a random network of threads leading upwards.

shiny black abdomen

orangish red legs

► GONGYLIDIUM RUFIPES *is widespread all across Britain. The cephalothorax is dark shiny brown at the front and orangish to the rear. It has pale, reddish brown legs.*

ORDER *Araneae.*
FAMILY *Linyphiidae.*
SPECIES IN FAMILY *4,200.*
SIZE *1–7mm.*
FEEDING *Immatures and adults: predators.*
IMPACT *Harmless; beneficial in controlling pest species.*

INVERTEBRATES

OTHER INVERTEBRATES

The sea is home to a greater diversity of life forms than is found anywhere else and the varied nature of Britain's coastline means that an impressive number of invertebrate species can be found there. Crustaceans are the dominant arthropods in the marine environment, but some, the woodlice, have made a successful transition to life on land. Similarly, a few of the molluscs, a predominantly marine group of animals, have adapted well to the terrestrial environment. On land, decaying vegetation, rotting wood, leaf litter, and soil provide a vast resource for many hundreds of invertebrate species. And freshwater habitats of all kinds, from tiny rain-filled tree holes to lakes, and from small streams to rivers, harbour a remarkable variety of invertebrates.

OTHER ARTHROPODS

Crustaceans are a mainly marine group of arthropods with around 5,000 species, ranging in size from a few millimetres to 50cm in length. Millipedes and centipedes are exclusively terrestrial.

MOLLUSCS

This group includes squids and octopuses as well as bivalves and gastropods. The most characteristic feature of molluscs is their shell, which in some species may be internal or even absent.

SPONGES

Sponges are simple, multi-cellular animals with no muscles, nervous system, or internal organs. They live in water, attached to the substrate, and feed on minute suspended particles of food.

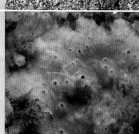

SEA ANENOMES

These exclusively marine, sedentary animals belong to the same class as corals. Both sea anemones and corals catch their food by the use of specialized stinging cells called nematocysts.

STAR FISH AND SEA URCHINS

Sea urchins and starfish are marine animals that have a five-rayed body symmetry and an external skeleton made up of calcareous plates, which are called ossicles.

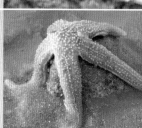

WORMS

The annelids, or segmented worms, are a large group of animals that can be found in terrestrial, freshwater, and marine habitats. Leeches and earthworms are the annelids that are the most well-known.

Geophilids

Geophilidae

The name of these rather slow-moving centipedes means "earth-loving" and is an apt description of their habitat preferences. The body is straw-coloured to brown and is very long, slender, and made up of at least 35 segments. The head is relatively small but usually wider than long and at least as big as the first segment of the trunk. The antennae are slender and the legs are short.

FOUND in leaf litter, soil, rotting wood, and debris in a variety of habitats; sometimes inside buildings.

small head

straw coloration

thread-like body

NOTE

Some geophilids produce a secretion that is luminescent. If one is held in the hand in complete darkness, a faint afterglow can often be seen behind it.

GEOPHILUS CARPOPHAGUS is a slender centipede with a pale reddish brown body. It is nocturnal and creeps slowly through soil and damp leaf litter.

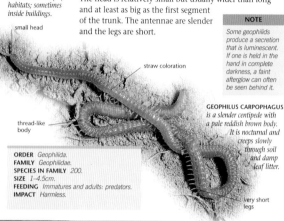

very short legs

ORDER Geophilida.
FAMILY Geophilidae.
SPECIES IN FAMILY 200.
SIZE 1–4.5cm.
FEEDING Immatures and adults: predators.
IMPACT Harmless.

Himantariids

Himantariidae

These pale yellowish to brown, slender centipedes have a slightly flattened, ribbon-like appearance. The trunk segments are broadest in the middle of the body and become narrow towards either end, especially towards the head. The head is broader than long and always much narrower than the first trunk segment. The antennae are quite short and compressed.

INHABIT soil, leaf litter, and debris in woods and grassland.

short antennae

slim, flexible body

HAPLOPHILUS SUBTERRANEUS is a pale yellowish species with as many as 80 pairs of short legs. It feeds in soil and leaf mould.

short legs

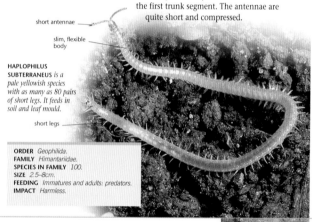

ORDER Geophilida.
FAMILY Himantariidae.
SPECIES IN FAMILY 100.
SIZE 2.5–8cm.
FEEDING Immatures and adults: predators.
IMPACT Harmless.

Lithobiids

Lithobiidae

Most lithobiids are reddish brown and the body is tough and quite flattened. The plates that cover the upper surface of the body segments are alternately large and small. There are 15 pairs of legs, with the last two pairs being longer than the others. The antennae are slender and tapering.

LITHOBIUS VARIEGATUS is common among the leaf litter of deciduous woods. It climbs trees in search of food.

poison claw

LIVE in cracks and crevices, mainly in woodland but also in grassland, upland, and coastal areas.

light and dark bands on legs (sometimes hard to see)

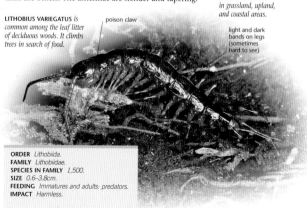

ORDER Lithobiida.
FAMILY Lithobiidae.
SPECIES IN FAMILY 1,500.
SIZE 0.6–3.8cm.
FEEDING Immatures and adults: predators.
IMPACT Harmless.

Blaniulids

Blaniulidae

These are small, slender-bodied species of less than 1mm in width. Blaniulids vary from creamy white to dark brown in colour and they often have red or very dark brown spots on most segments. Some species may have as many as 60 body segments. The legs and the antennae are short. Several species are common garden pests.

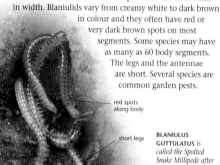

OCCUPY gardens, open land, and woodland, usually in fallen logs, tree stumps, leaf litter, and soil.

red spots along body

short legs

BLANIULUS GUTTULATUS is called the Spotted Snake Millipede after its elongated body and very short legs.

NOTE

Young of Blaniulus guttulatus have only a few segments and three pairs of legs when they hatch. It takes about a year for them to reach adult size.

ORDER Julida.
FAMILY Blaniulidae.
SPECIES IN FAMILY 120.
SIZE 0.5–1.8cm.
FEEDING Immatures and adults: scavengers, herbivores.
IMPACT A few species damage seedlings.

Pill Millipedes

Glomeridae

Pill millipedes are small. Their trunk has 13 segments, and the shape of the body plates allows them to roll into a tight ball with the head tucked in. This species should not be confused with pill woodlice (p.303), which can also roll up for protection. Millipedes have many more legs, and two pairs of legs for each body segment. The young have only three pairs of legs when they hatch. They reach the full complement of 15 pairs at adulthood.

OCCUR in many habitats, but especially in woodland, rough pasture, and farmland.

tough, shiny body

saddle-shaped segment behind head

GLOMERIS MARGINATA is very widespread and common. It has a shinier body than the pill woodlouse.

rolled-up position

ORDER Glomerida.
FAMILY Glomeridae.
SPECIES IN FAMILY 200.
SIZE 0.2–2cm.
FEEDING Immatures and adults: scavengers, herbivores.
IMPACT Harmless.

Flat-backed Millipedes

Polydesmidae

The 20 or so body segments of these flattened species have lateral expansions, which stick out sideways giving them an almost centipede-like appearance. However, each segment has two pairs of legs, and the upper surface has characteristic pitted sculpturing. Some species are reddish brown, while others are dark with pale lateral margins.

FOUND in woodland, gardens, farmland, and grassland, under stones and in leaf litter; some species occur in caves.

sculpturing on dorsal plate

two pairs of legs per segment

POLYDESMUS ANGUSTUS is a brownish, flat-backed millipede. Males are generally slightly larger than females, and have stouter legs.

NOTE

These millipedes sometimes occur in large numbers. In most species, many body segments have glands that produce toxic chemicals to deter predators.

ORDER Polydesmida.
FAMILY Polydesmidae.
SPECIES IN FAMILY 200.
SIZE 0.5–3cm.
FEEDING Immatures and adults: scavengers, herbivores.
IMPACT May be pests of seedlings.

Cylinder Millipedes

Julidae

Cylinder millipedes vary from shortish, pale-coloured species to longer dark or black species with reddish stripes. The antennae are fairly long and slender. Most species are tough-bodied and relatively broad. As the common name implies, they have a circular cross-section. These are slow-moving species, which are good at pushing through soil and leaf litter. Like most millipedes, the species in this family have a pair of defence glands located on each of the body segments that are able to produce a range of chemicals to deter enemies.

LIVE in a wide variety of habitats including grassland, heaths, and woodland, in soil and leaf litter and under stones and rotting wood.

NOTE

This family is the largest in Britain, comprising 18 of the 52 species present. The millipedes are important in decomposition and nutrient recycling.

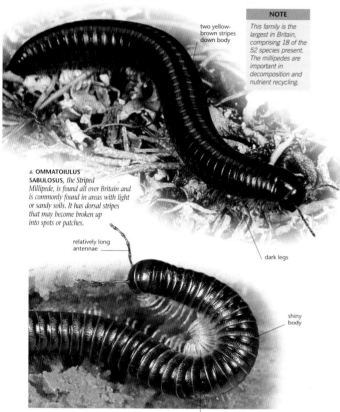

two yellow-brown stripes down body

▲ OMMATOIULUS SABULOSUS, the Striped Millipede, is found all over Britain and is commonly found in areas with light or sandy soils. It has dorsal stripes that may become broken up into spots or patches.

relatively long antennae

dark legs

shiny body

pale legs

ORDER Julida.
FAMILY Julidae.
SPECIES IN FAMILY 450.
SIZE 0.8–5cm.
FEEDING Immatures and adults: scavengers, herbivores.
IMPACT Harmless.

▲ TACHYPODOIULUS NIGER, the White-legged Snake Millipede, is a common species in Britain except for the very far north. It is a shiny back-bodied species with contrasting white legs.

Oniscid Woodlice

Oniscidae

The common, shiny woodlouse, *Oniscus asellus*, is the only member of this family you are likely to encounter very often. The last part of the antennae, after the longer fifth segment, is called the flagellum, and in this family, is made up of three segments. There are distinctive lobes on either side of the head. This species varies from greyish with paler markings to yellowish or orangish.

OCCUPY leaf litter, compost heaps, under stones and in rotting wood.

ONISCUS ASELLUS is found in damp areas with plenty of decaying plant material. Known also as the Common Shiny Woodlouse, juveniles are less shiny than adults.

flagellum with three segments

lobe at side of head

light patches

ORDER Isopoda.
FAMILY Oniscidae.
SPECIES IN FAMILY 1,100.
SIZE 1–1.8cm.
FEEDING Immatures and adults: scavengers.
IMPACT Harmless but an important part of the nutrient recycling process.

NOTE

These woodlice can live up to four years and females may carry as many as 80 eggs in their brood pouch which they keep moist, like a portable aquarium.

Pill Woodlice

Armadillidiidae

Light brown to black with yellow patches, these woodlice have a convex cross-section and a rounded hind margin. They are also known as pill bugs. When threatened, many can roll up into a ball to protect themselves. Some species, such as *Armadillidium vulgare* and *A. pictum*, make a more perfect ball than other species.

OCCUR in many habitats from shoreline to mountains; in leaf litter and debris in woodland and gardens.

rolled up for defence

convex body

flagellum with two segments

ORDER Isopoda.
FAMILY Armadillidiidae.
SPECIES IN FAMILY 250.
SIZE 5–20mm.
FEEDING Immatures and adults: scavengers, herbivores, dung.
IMPACT Harmless.

ARMADILLIDIUM VULGARE, the Pill Woodlouse, occurs with other species but can tolerate drier conditions than them.

NOTE

Pill woodlice have several narrow tail segments, whereas pill millipedes have a single, broad tail segment. They also roll into a looser ball than pill millipedes.

Porcellionid Woodlice

Porcellionidae

The body surface of these woodlice can be smooth and slightly glossy or warty, but is usually grey or greyish brown with other markings. The last section of the antennae, called the flagellum, is composed of two segments. The body of some species is narrow, and these species can run quickly. Woodlice excrete ammonia gas and this gives large colonies a characteristic smell.

WIDESPREAD where there is a humid microhabitat provided by rotting plant matter.

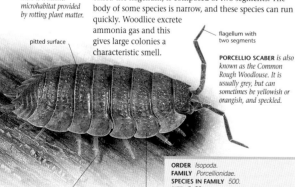

pitted surface

flagellum with two segments

PORCELLIO SCABER is also known as the Common Rough Woodlouse. It is usually grey, but can sometimes be yellowish or orangish, and speckled.

seven pairs of walking legs

greyish body segments

ORDER Isopoda.
FAMILY Porcellionidae.
SPECIES IN FAMILY 500.
SIZE 9–20mm.
FEEDING Immatures and adults: scavengers, dung.
IMPACT Harmless.

Sea Slaters

Ligiidae

Greyish green or light brown in colour, sea slaters have large, dark eyes at the sides of the head resembling the compound eyes of insects. The flagellum of the antennae has ten or more small segments. Most species run very fast when disturbed. *Ligia oceanica* is a large species, common on shores where it grazes on seaweed during the day, and hides in rock crevices at night. It can change colour to suit its background. *L. hypnorum* is smaller and is found in woodland litter.

FOUND on seashores, among rocks and seaweeds up to the high tide mark and in the splash zone.

flagellum with many segments

forked tail

greyish green mottled body

LIGIA OCEANICA lives on rocky shores. It has a pair of forked tails at the rear, and specialized dermal cells that allow it to change colour.

ORDER Isopoda.
FAMILY Ligiidae.
SPECIES IN FAMILY 100.
SIZE 8–30mm.
FEEDING Immatures and adults: scavengers, herbivores (algae).
IMPACT Harmless.

Swimming Crabs

Portunidae

This family includes the swimming crabs and the common shore crabs. The carapace has clear symmetrical patterns and is typically trapezoidal in outline, being broad at the front and narrow at the rear. The edge of the carapace has three blunt teeth between the eyes and five sharp teeth on either side of the eyes. The colour of the carapace is greenish grey to brownish or reddish in adults. Portunids are generally nocturnal and eat bivalve molluscs such as clams, oysters, and mussels.

THRIVES *in a very wide range of marine and estuarine habitats.*

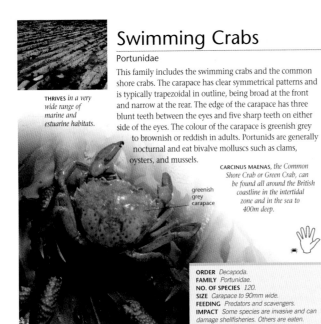

CARCINUS MAENAS, *the Common Shore Crab or Green Crab, can be found all around the British coastline in the intertidal zone and in the sea to 400m deep.*

greenish grey carapace

ORDER	*Decapoda.*
FAMILY	*Portunidae.*
NO. OF SPECIES	*120.*
SIZE	*Carapace to 90mm wide.*
FEEDING	*Predators and scavengers.*
IMPACT	*Some species are invasive and can damage shellfisheries. Others are eaten.*

Prawns

Palaemonidae

Also known as shrimps, these crustaceans have an elongated body with a cylindrical carapace and an abdomen composed of six segments. The carapace is extended forwards in the form of a rostrum, which may be straight or curved, and bears a number of sharp tooth-like projections along the upper and lower edges.

INHABIT *rock pools and sea grass beds down to depths of 50m.*

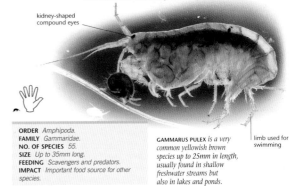

eye stalks

brown, yellow, and blue spots

PALAEMON ELEGANS, *the Rock Pool Prawn, grows to 60mm in length and inhabits intertidal pools on rocky shores all around Britain.*

ORDER	*Decapoda.*
FAMILY	*Palaemonidae.*
NO. OF SPECIES	*425.*
SIZE	*Up to 15cm long.*
FEEDING	*Predators and scavengers.*
IMPACT	*Some species are caught commercially.*

Rock Crabs

Cancridae

These crabs are generally heavily built with an oval-shaped body. The carapace of the best-known species, the Edible Crab, has distinctive crimped edges like that on a piecrust. The claws of males are typically larger than those of females. The abdomens of females are wider than that of males. Rock crabs are nocturnal to avoid predators such as seals and wolf fish, and hide in deep cracks or lie buried in the substrate during the day. They feed on molluscs, small fish, other crustaceans, and echinoderms.

FOUND *on British coasts from the intertidal zone to 100m deep.*

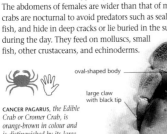

abdomen folded under carapace

oval-shaped body

large claw with black tip

CANCER PAGURUS, *the Edible Crab or Cromer Crab, is orange-brown in colour and is distinguished by its large size and black-tipped claws.*

ORDER	*Decapoda.*
FAMILY	*Cancridae.*
NO. OF SPECIES	*15.*
SIZE	*Carapace to 25cm wide.*
FEEDING	*Predators and scavengers.*
IMPACT	*Some species are commercially important.*

Gammarids

Gammaridae

The slender body of these small crustaceans is smooth, distinctively flattened from side to side, and typically curved towards the lower body surface. The head carries a pair of kidney-shaped compound eyes and two pairs of longish antennae. The thorax contains the gills and has seven pairs of jointed limbs, two of which are used for grasping and the others for swimming, crawling, and jumping.

PREFERS *in freshwater habitats; others are marine, living in the intertidal zone or at depths to 30m.*

kidney-shaped compound eyes

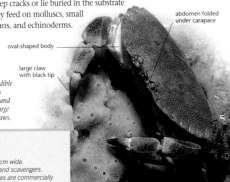

ORDER	*Amphipoda.*
FAMILY	*Gammaridae.*
NO. OF SPECIES	*55.*
SIZE	*Up to 35mm long.*
FEEDING	*Scavengers and predators.*
IMPACT	*Important food source for other species.*

GAMMARUS PULEX *is a very common yellowish brown species up to 25mm in length, usually found in shallow freshwater streams but also in lakes and ponds.*

limb used for swimming

Hermit Crabs

Paguridae

Hermit crabs have a carapace that is roughly cylindrical and longer than it is wide, although in some species it can be slightly flattened from top to bottom. As the right claw is always bigger than the left one, pagurids are sometimes known as right-handed hermit crabs. The fourth and fifth pairs of walking legs are very reduced in size. The abdomen is soft, long, and twisted, with the end modified to grip the inside of the shell.

ABUNDANT *and widely distributed on all British coasts and can eat anything it catches.*

occupied gastropod shell

PAGURUS BERNHARDUS, *the Common Hermit Crab uses empty gastropod shells as a home – commonly using winkle shells when young, moving on to Dog Whelks when they are older and have outgrown their original shells.*

large right claw

ORDER	*Decapoda.*
FAMILY	*Paguridae.*
NO. OF SPECIES	*135.*
SIZE	*Carapace to 45mm long, whole body to 140mm.*
FEEDING	*Predators and scavengers.*
IMPACT	*None.*

Landhoppers and Sand Fleas

Talitridae

Similar in general appearance to gammarids (above), these crustaceans have a smooth and very flexible body, which is not very flattened from side to side. The eyes are conspicuous and the first pair of antennae is much smaller than the second pair, which may also be thicker, and enlarged in males.

LIVES *on sandy shores, though some species may also be found inland.*

greyish brown body

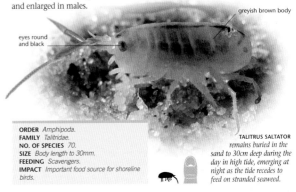

eyes round and black

ORDER	*Amphipoda.*
FAMILY	*Talitridae.*
NO. OF SPECIES	*70.*
SIZE	*Body length to 30mm.*
FEEDING	*Scavengers.*
IMPACT	*Important food source for shoreline birds.*

TALITRUS SALTATOR *remains buried in the sand to 30cm deep during the day in high tide, emerging at night as the tide recedes to feed on stranded seaweed.*

Water Fleas

Daphniidae

The bodies of these tiny transparent crustaceans can be bluish grey, greenish, yellowish brown, or even reddish. The head, which has a distinctive pointed rostrum, is covered by a hood-like shell and the thorax and abdomen by a bivalved carapace or shell that ends in a terminal spine. The head is bent downwards and has a prominent pair of compound eyes.

FOUND in all types of freshwater, except in fast-flowing rivers, and can be an indicator of ecosystem health.

laterally compressed body

DAPHNIA SP has males that are much smaller than the females, which carry one or more young inside a brood pouch within the carapace.

ORDER Cladocera.
FAMILY Daphniidae.
NO. OF SPECIES 65.
SIZE Under 6mm in length.
FEEDING Suspension feeders; some species are predatory.
IMPACT Food source for many species.

Periwinkles

Littornidae

Periwinkles have strong conical or globular shells, typically with a pointed apex. Some species can be a brightly coloured yellow, orange, or red with contrasting bands, but most are greyish brown. The whorls are often finely grooved and the lip of the aperture is thin.

OCCUPIES rocky shores with a good covering of seaweeds; also in brackish estuaries.

globular shell

short, pointed spire

usually greyish brown in colour

LITTORINA LITTOREA, the Common or Edible Periwinkle, is very common and widespread on rocky shores all around the British coastline. Its colour varies from blackish to greyish brown.

ORDER Mesogastropoda.
FAMILY Littorinidae.
NO. OF SPECIES 75.
SIZE Shell to 4cm tall.
FEEDING Algal grazers.
IMPACT Some species are collected as human food.

Barnacles

Balanidae

Barnacles are sedentary crustaceans that live permanently cemented to the substrate and are surrounded by a calcareous shell, which they add to as they grow. These barnacles have a shell composed of 4–6 heavily ridged plates, which together have an irregular outline. They feed by waving a pair of specially modified feathery limbs called "cirri" in the water. The flow of water that is generated carries tiny suspended planktonic food particles towards the mouth.

ATTACHES permanently to rocks in the intertidal zone; can colonize low-salinity estuarine waters.

conical profile

more columnar growth when crowded

SEMIBALANUS BALANOIDES, the Northern Acorn Barnacle, is the most widespread species in the north, and has a membranous shell-base, unlike other species that have calcified bases.

ORDER Thoracica.
FAMILY Balanidae.
NO. OF SPECIES 45.
SIZE Up to 15cm in diameter and height; British species are much smaller.
FEEDING Omnivorous suspension feeders.
IMPACT Can foul ships' hulls and pilings.

True Whelks

Buccinidae

True whelks have large and strongly built shells, which are pale cream or yellowish brown in colour. The whorls have a number of fine lines and ribs, which together give the appearance of squarish, raised patterning. The aperture is oval in shape and tapers to a short siphonal canal, which can be curved in some true whelks. The aperture edges can be folded outwards and the operculum is thick and brown with clearly visible concentric rings.

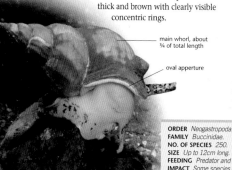

INHABITS a range of shoreline types, from rocky to deposits of gravel, sand, or mud; sometimes in estuaries.

main whorl, about ¾ of total length

oval apperture

BUCCINUM UNDATUM, the Common or Edible Whelk or Buckie, is common around the British coast and can be found on sandy, muddy, or rocky shores.

ORDER Neogastropoda.
FAMILY Buccinidae.
NO. OF SPECIES 250.
SIZE Up to 12cm long.
FEEDING Predator and scavenger.
IMPACT Some species are a long-standing human food source.

Muricids

Muricidae

The shells of these marine snails are characteristically tall and sharply pointed. The elongated shell is made up of a number of ridged and grooved whorls, typically 5–8. At the bottom of the shell aperture, there is a groove called the siphonal canal, which supports the siphon, a tube-like extension of the mantle that is used to suck water into the mantle cavity. This water flow contains chemical cues that alert the snail to the presence of prey.

FAVOURS all manner of rocky shores, except the most sheltered, seaweed-covered locations.

NUCELLA LAPILLUS, the Dog Whelk, is found on rocky shores all around Britain. It has a heavy shell and is usually pale cream, grey, or whitish in colour.

broadly conical, thick shell

shell usually pale coloured

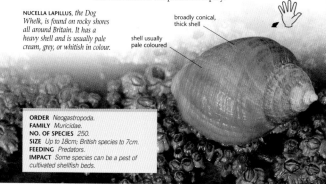

ORDER Neogastropoda.
FAMILY Muricidae.
NO. OF SPECIES 250.
SIZE Up to 18cm; British species to 7cm.
FEEDING Predators.
IMPACT Some species can be a pest of cultivated shellfish beds.

Top Shells

Trochidae

These shells are known as Top Shells because their conical profile resembles an old-fashioned children's spinning top. The apex of the shell varies in shape; it can be very sharply pointed, or blunt or flattened. The whorls of the shell are finely lined and can be attractively patterned with regular flecks and patches of contrasting colours. Chipped or damaged shells reveal an internal mother-of-pearl appearance. The operculum is horny and circular.

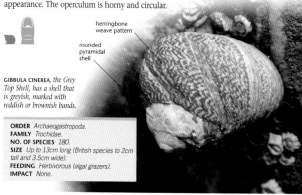

PREFERS sheltered rocky shores, under stones and seaweed on the lower shore, and in upper shore rock pools.

herringbone weave pattern

rounded pyramidal shell

GIBBULA CINEREA, the Grey Top Shell, has a shell that is greyish, marked with reddish or brownish bands.

ORDER Archaeogastropoda.
FAMILY Trochidae.
NO. OF SPECIES 180.
SIZE Up to 13cm long (British species to 2cm tall and 3.5cm wide).
FEEDING Herbivorous (algal grazers).
IMPACT None.

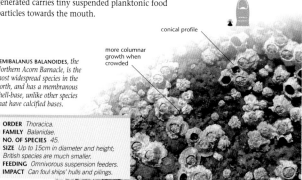

OTHER INVERTEBRATES

Limpets

Patellidae

With unmistakable conical, uncoiled shells and no operculum, or bony plate, limpets cling tightly to rocks to avoid the effects of desiccation when they are exposed at low tide. The shells of some species are tall while others are more flattened and many have radiating ribs or ridges and distinctive growth rings. Larger specimens may become encrusted with barnacles. The keyhole limpet has a small hole at the apex and its shells are lined with mother-of-pearl.

STICKS *"like a limpet" on intertidal rocks, especially on exposed rocky shores; not common where there is lots of seaweed.*

conical shell

muscular foot

PATELLA VULGATA, *the Common Limpet, has a home scar, a shallow depression in the rock made by abrasion, to which it returns after grazing.*

ORDER *Archaeogastropoda.*
FAMILY *Patellidae.*
NO. OF SPECIES *8.*
SIZE *Typically less than 6cm in diameter.*
FEEDING *Herbivorous (algal grazer).*
IMPACT *Can foul ships' hulls and other structures; sometimes eaten.*

Ram's-horn Shells

Planorbidae

As the common name implies, these gastropods have flattened, disc-like, coiled shells that resemble curled ram's horns. Subtle differences exist between species in coloration – ranging from brown to greyish green, texture, aperture shape, and the cross-section of the coils. There is no operculum to close the aperture.

FOUND *commonly in well-vegetated ponds, lakes, and sluggish streams; also often found in garden ponds.*

red-brown colour

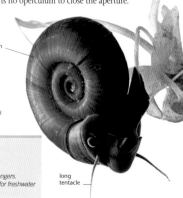

PLANORBIS CORNEUS, *the Great Ram's-horn Snail, is olive-brown to red with fine, irregular striations along its whorls.*

long tentacle

ORDER *Pulmonata.*
FAMILY *Planorbidae.*
NO. OF SPECIES *50.*
SIZE *Up to 4cm wide.*
FEEDING *Herbivores and scavengers.*
IMPACT *Important food source for freshwater fish and birds.*

Pond Snails

Lymnaeidae

The pond snails generally have a large last whorl and a number of smaller whorls forming a tall slender spire. The aperture is quite large and not closed by an operculum. Most species are shiny but drably coloured in shades of brown, yellow, and cream. The surface of the shell has fine lines and striations running parallel to the lip.

FOUND *very commonly in well-vegetated ponds and lakes, often near the surface.*

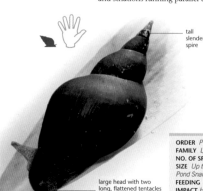

tall slender spire

LYMNAEA STAGNALIS, *the Great Pond Snail, is the largest pond snail in Britain. It grazes plants and carrion, but has been known to attack other snails, insect larvae, and even small fish and newts.*

large head with two long, flattened tentacles

ORDER *Pulmonata.*
FAMILY *Lymnaeidae.*
NO. OF SPECIES *100.*
SIZE *Up to 8cm long; the shell of the Great Pond Snail can reach up to 6cm long.*
FEEDING *Omnivorous.*
IMPACT *Harmless.*

Land Snails

Helicidae

Land snails are air-breathing gastropods. The large muscular foot produces mucus to aid locomotion. Many are medium- to large-sized and their shells can be flattened, conical, or globular, depending on the species. The shells of many can be quite thick and flecked, mottled, or otherwise patterned although some are thin and translucent or even hairy. The head has four tentacles, the larger upper pair carrying the eyes. The mouth is situated under the tentacles and houses the radula, a file-like structure for grasping food.

FAVOURS *a wide range of habitats from sand dunes and mountains to meadows and woodland.*

brownish shell marked with yellow

hard thin shell

NOTE
The family includes Helix pomatia, the well-known Roman Snail. This species, which is locally distributed in the south of Britain, and Helix aspersa are the two commonly eaten species in Europe.

brownish tentacle

ORDER *Pulmonata.*
FAMILY *Helicidae.*
NO. OF SPECIES *230.*
SIZE *Up to 5cm in height.*
FEEDING *Herbivores and scavengers.*
IMPACT *Important food source for other species; some species are horticultural pests.*

HELIX ASPERSA, *the Garden Snail, is widely distributed in Britain, except in the far north where it is confined to the coastal regions.*

Limacid Slugs

Limacidae

These slugs have a small, chalky shell, which is typically enclosed completely by the mantle and a keel, or raised ridge, that runs down the middle of the body from behind the mantle to the tail. The pneumostome, the opening to the lung cavity, is situated on the right of the body and well towards the rear of the mantle.

OCCUPIES *gardens, grassland, hedgerows, and agricultural land.*

pneumostome

DEROCERAS RETICULATUM, *the Netted Slug, is probably the commonest slug found all over Britain. It grows up to 5cm in length. The skin of the mantle has a pattern that resembles a fingerprint.*

ORDER *Pulmonata.*
FAMILY *Limacidae.*
NO. OF SPECIES *15.*
SIZE *Up to 30cm long.*
FEEDING *Herbivores and scavengers.*
IMPACT *Some are significant agricultural and horticultural pests.*

Arionid Slugs

Arionidae

FOUND *in all kinds of terrestrial habitats – gardens, parks, meadows, and lawns throughout Britain.*

These slugs have a very small internal shell, sometimes just chalky fragments, enclosed by the mantle. There is no raised keel running from behind the mantle to the tail and the opening to the respiratory cavity, the pneumostome, is situated in front of the midline of the mantle. The head has two pairs of tentacles, the upper pair carrying the eyes. When disturbed, arionids can contract themselves into a tight hemispherical ball and may sway from side to side. Like all slugs, they are only active at night or in wet weather as they are very sensitive to desiccation.

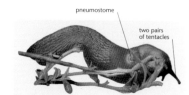

pneumostome

two pairs of tentacles

ARION ATER, *the Black Slug, can also be reddish, pale orange, or grey, is found all over Britain in all kinds of terrestrial habitats. The young are pale, whitish, or greenish with yellow flecks, becoming darker as they age.*

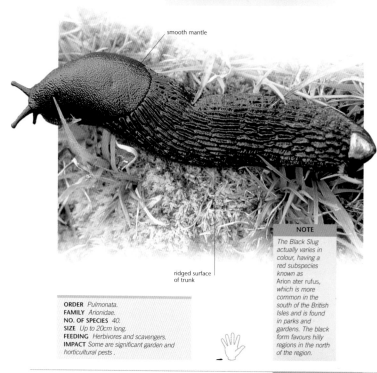

smooth mantle

ridged surface of trunk

NOTE
The Black Slug actually varies in colour, having a red subspecies known as Arion ater rufus, which is more common in the south of the British Isles and is found in parks and gardens. The black form favours hilly regions in the north of the region.

ORDER *Pulmonata.*
FAMILY *Arionidae.*
NO. OF SPECIES *40.*
SIZE *Up to 20cm long.*
FEEDING *Herbivores and scavengers.*
IMPACT *Some are significant garden and horticultural pests .*

Marine Mussels

Mytilidae

Mussels are bivalve molluscs that typically attach themselves to the substrate by tough golden-coloured byssus threads, which are secreted by a gland in the foot. Some mussel species are found in burrows. The shell is roughly triangular to pear-shaped, and smooth-edged with clear concentric growth lines. A layer known as the periostracum, which may be thin or tough and horny, and with whiskers or spines, covers the outside of the shell. Mussels feed by extracting bacteria, plankton, and dissolved organic matter from the seawater.

ATTACHED *to rocks and other hard substrates on rocky coasts, often forming dense beds.*

deep blue to purple in colour

shell sculptured with concentric lines

MYTILIS EDULIS, *the Common or Edible Mussel, is an important food source for many marine species and birds such as Eider (p.110) and Oystercatcher (p.127).*

ORDER *Mytiloida.*
FAMILY *Mytilidae.*
NO. OF SPECIES *90.*
SIZE *Up to 24cm long.*
FEEDING *Suspension feeder.*
IMPACT *Some commercial species; can foul submerged structures and pipes.*

Scallops

Pectiniidae

OCCUPIES *coasts all around Britain, on lower shores and to depths of 100m.*

Scallops are marine bivalve molluscs with symmetrical fan-shaped shells or valves, which are typically strongly ridged or corrugated. Most species live freely and swim by opening and closing their shells, but some remain attached to the substrate by byssus threads and have a reduced foot. The mantle has a row of small eyes along its edge that allow the scallop to detect changes in light intensity and alert it to nearby objects.

prominent ribs

oval and convex shell

CHLAMYS VARIA, *the Variegated Scallop, is variably patterned and ranges in colour from white to yellow, red, pinkish, orange, and even purplish.*

ORDER *Ostreoida.*
FAMILY *Pectinidae.*
NO. OF SPECIES *250.*
SIZE *Up to 18cm long.*
FEEDING *Suspension feeders.*
IMPACT *Some very important commercial species.*

True Oysters

Ostreidae

FORMS *beds around low water mark of estuaries and open shores, often attached to small rocks or other shells.*

Oysters are marine bivalve molluscs with rounded, ribbed, corrugated, and roughly sculptured shells. The wrinkle-edged shells are of unequal sizes; the lower shell being larger, slightly hollowed, and stuck to the substrate, while the upper shell is smaller and flat. Similar to the scallops, there is an adductor muscle that draws the two valves tightly together.

pale brownish in colour

OSTREA EDULIS, *the Common, Native, or Edible Oyster, is rounded or pear-shaped, and roughly sculptured.*

ORDER *Ostreoida.*
FAMILY *Ostreidae.*
NO. OF SPECIES *22.*
SIZE *Up to 30cm long.*
FEEDING *Suspension feeder.*
IMPACT *Some very important commercial species.*

Cockles

Cardiidae

Cockles have heart-shaped shells and the two valves are similar in shape and size. The shells are strong and typically have a number of radiating ridges and furrows. In some species, the ridges bear blunt projections or strong sharp spines. Two adductor muscles hold the halves of the shell together, the wavy or serrated margins fitting tightly against each other. Cockles have a large foot.

BURROWS *in the upper 5cm of sand, muddy, and fine gravel shores, all around the British coastline.*

shell rounded and humped

opened cockle

CERASTODERMA EDULIS, *the Common Cockle, can tolerate the low salinity of estuaries where they can be harvested in huge numbers.*

shell with radiating ribs

ORDER *Veneroida.*
FAMILY *Cardiidae.*
NO. OF SPECIES *180.*
SIZE *Up to 12cm long.*
FEEDING *Suspension feeders.*
IMPACT *Some important commercial species; important food source for wading birds.*

Tellins

Tellinidae

Typically, these marine bivalves have narrow, thin, oval shells although some can be more broadly oval and strong-shelled. The surface is generally smooth with distinctive concentric growth rings and the colour varies from white to yellow, orange, pale brown, or pinkish. Tellins have long siphons, which extend above the level of the sand when they are feeding and although fish can nibble these off, the lost portion can be regenerated. They have a wide muscular foot.

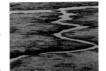

OCCURS *in very high densities, in the muddy sediments of tidal flats and estuaries.*

concentric bands

flattened shell

MACOMA BALTHICA, *the Baltic Tellin, has stronger shells and is more broadly oval than the Thin Tellin (Angulus tenuis).*

ORDER *Veneroida.*
FAMILY *Tellinidae.*
NO. OF SPECIES *130.*
SIZE *Up to 10cm long.*
FEEDING *Suspension feeders.*
IMPACT *Tellins are an important food source for many marine species and shoreline birds.*

Razor Clams

Solenidae

These marine bivalve molluscs are instantly recognizable by their very long, narrow and equally sized shells, which look like a cut-throat razor. The shells may be straight or slightly curved. The muscular foot is long and powerful and protrudes from one end, enabling these molluscs to burrow very quickly into the bottom sediment. The glossy perisotracum peels away from the surface quite readily.

LIVES *in permanent burrows in firm sand at lower shore levels; may be very abundant in sheltered locations.*

ENSIS ENSIS, *the Common Razor Shell, is common in shallow waters all around the coast of Britain wherever the bottom is made of fine sand or mud.*

pale shell with brown patches

muscular foot

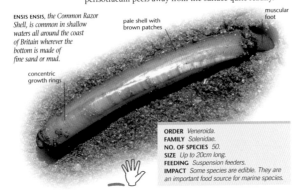

concentric growth rings

ORDER *Veneroida.*
FAMILY *Solenidae.*
NO. OF SPECIES *50.*
SIZE *Up to 20cm long.*
FEEDING *Suspension feeders.*
IMPACT *Some species are edible. They are an important food source for marine species.*

Freshwater Mussels

Unionidae

These flattened bivalves lie buried in the sediment of ponds and rivers with their siphons sticking out. Water, bringing particles of food and oxygen, is sucked in one siphon and expelled from the other. Larvae are ejected through the female mussel's exhalant siphon. They then become parasitic and encysted on the skin or gills of fish. After a few weeks, they drop to the bottom and become free-living.

FOUND *in the muddy bottoms of sluggish rivers and lakes throughout Britain.*

clear, concentric rings

ANODONTA CYGNEA, *the Swan Mussel, is a large and common bivalve species found throughout the British Isles. It can move forward over the bottom using its muscular foot.*

brownish shell

ORDER *Unionoida.*
FAMILY *Unionidae.*
NO. OF SPECIES *300.*
SIZE *Up to 25cm long.*
FEEDING *Suspension feeders.*
IMPACT *Edible, used as fishing bait; some yield pearls.*

Halichondriid Sponges

Halichondriidae

Many of these marine sponges can be brightly coloured and form encrustations on the surface of rocks, in crevices on overhangs, on seaweeds, on the shells of molluscs and crabs and the tubes of marine worms. Some species have finger-like projections or branched lobes. The spicules of these sponges typically form a jumbled net-like arrangement.

FORMS *encrustations on rocks, seaweed, in crevices on overhangs, and on the shells of molluscs and crabs.*

irregular shaped growth pattern

HALICHONDRIA PANICEA, *the Breadcrumb Sponge, has a strong seaweed odour. It can be reddish orange in shady localities or green in sunlit spots.*

pores on small bumps

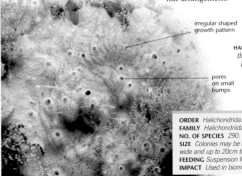

ORDER *Halichondrida.*
FAMILY *Halichondriidae.*
NO. OF SPECIES *290.*
SIZE *Colonies may be up to several metres wide and up to 20cm thick.*
FEEDING *Suspension feeders.*
IMPACT *Used in biomedical research.*

Sea Anemones

Actiniidae

Anemones are solitary organisms that attach themselves to a solid substrate by means of an adhesive foot or disc. The smooth or warty stalk (column) of the anemone, which is capable of contraction, terminates in an oral disc in the centre of which is the mouth. Elongate tentacles, armed with stinging cells called nematocysts, surround the oral disc. When touched by prey or a predator, the nematocysts explode, releasing a tiny harpoon-like dart loaded with paralysing toxins. Prey caught by the tentacles is then passed to the mouth for digestion inside the gastrovascular cavity.

INHABITS *all rocky shore habitats, from exposed to sheltered, and tolerant of temperature and salinity fluctuations; favours rock pools.*

ACTINIA EQUINA, *the Beadlet Anemone, is common on rocky shores all around the British coast and can be found fastened to rocks from the middle of the shore to depths of 10m.*

retracts tentacles out of water

5–6 rows of tentacles

ring of warts at top of stalk

ORDER *Actiniaria.*
FAMILY *Actiniidae.*
NO. OF SPECIES *300.*
SIZE *Up to 35cm diameter and 10cm high.*
FEEDING *Carnivorous.*
IMPACT *Some species used in genetic and biomedical research.*

NOTE

The Beadlet Anemone ranges in colour from red to brown or green. A row of blue beadlike warts is always present at the top of the stalk. Anemones will sting each other with their tentacles if they get too close.

Starfish

Asteriidae

Starfish are echinoderms typically with five arms radiating from a central disc. They have a skeleton made up of calcified elements called ossicles. The upper surface is covered with tubercles, spines, and tiny tweezer-like structures called pedicellaira, which nip off anything that settles on the arms. The lower surfaces of the arms are covered with numerous tube-feet with which they move around and hold their prey.

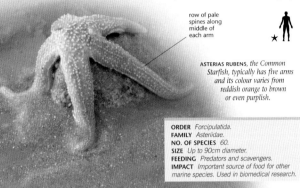

FOUND *on rocky shores all around the British coast, especially in mussel beds where it can be a pest.*

row of pale spines along middle of each arm

ASTERIAS RUBENS, *the Common Starfish, typically has five arms and its colour varies from reddish orange to brown or even purplish.*

ORDER *Forcipulatida.*
FAMILY *Asteriidae.*
NO. OF SPECIES *60.*
SIZE *Up to 90cm diameter.*
FEEDING *Predators and scavengers.*
IMPACT *Important source of food for other marine species. Used in biomedical research.*

Lug Worms

Arenicolidae

The body of these annelid worms comprises three main parts made up of many segments. The small head has a proboscis. The segments of the thoracic region are swollen and have a pair of fleshy, bilobed parapodia – most have branched gills. The rest of the body has slender segments with no appendages. The worms live in a U-shaped burrows.

OCCUPIES *tubes in clean or muddy sand flats, at middle to lower beach levels and in estuaries.*

ARENICOLA MARINA, *the Common Lug Worm or Blow Lug, can be found burrowing in sand all around the coast in large numbers.*

sand cast, one end of the burrow

"blow hole", other end of the burrow

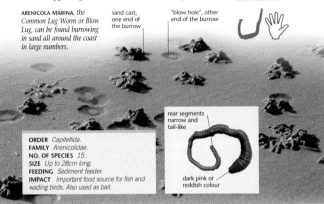

rear segments narrow and tail-like

dark pink or reddish colour

ORDER *Capitellida.*
FAMILY *Arenicolidae.*
NO. OF SPECIES *15.*
SIZE *Up to 28cm long.*
FEEDING *Sediment feeder.*
IMPACT *Important food source for fish and wading birds. Also used as bait.*

Sea Urchins

Echinidae

Sea urchins are echinoderms with skeletal plates that are fused together to form a rounded hard shell or test. Around the test are five bands with holes through which the tube feet project. Between these bands are five more bands through which moveable spines project. The mouth is located in the middle of the underside of the test and has a unique five-jaw chewing structure known as Aristotle's lantern.

FAVOURS *rocky shores to areas with a coarse, sandy bottom, often among seagrass beds.*

short, violet spines

PSAMMECHINUS MILIARIS, *the Green Sea Urchin, which grows up to 4–5cm in diameter, is common on rocky shores all around the British coastline.*

ORDER *Echinoida.*
FAMILY *Echinidae.*
NO. OF SPECIES *9.*
SIZE *Up to 18cm in diameter.*
FEEDING *Algal grazers and scavengers .*
IMPACT *Some species are edible.*

Freshwater Leeches

Erpobdellidae

These leeches, which do not feed on blood, are also known as swallowing leeches as they consume prey items such as worms, insect larvae, and crustaceans whole. Freshwater leeches have a cylindrical or slightly flattened body and are brownish or yellowish in colour. The head has a small sucker and lacks the powerful jaws present in other leech families.

INHABITS *rivers, ponds, lakes, and fens throughout Britain and does well in water polluted with organic matter.*

slender body

ERPOBDELLA OCTOCULATA *is up to 4cm long with a slightly flattened body that has variable patterns of dark marks. The head of this species has 8 tiny eyes in two rows. It eats the larvae of non-biting midges (Chironomidae) and small worms.*

rounded head

ORDER *Arhynchobdellida.*
FAMILY *Erpobdellidae.*
NO. OF SPECIES *50.*
SIZE *Up to 6cm long.*
FEEDING *Predators and scavengers.*
IMPACT *Used in freshwater toxicology research.*

Honeycomb Worms

Sabellariidae

These segmented worms form dense colonies, each worm making a curved tusk-shaped tube from large sand grains, which it sticks together with mucus. The head has three concentric circles of spines, which can be used to block the opening of the tube. Most of the body segments have finger-like gills on the back and a pair of fleshy appendages called parapodia. The body ends in a smooth tail.

FOUND *encrusting rocks from the lower shore to shallow water around the British coastline to southern Scotland.*

honeycomb-like colony

tubes of cemented sand grains

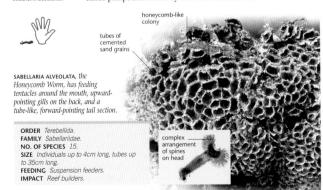

SABELLARIA ALVEOLATA, *the Honeycomb Worm, has feeding tentacles around the mouth, upward-pointing gills on the back, and a tube-like, forward-pointing tail section.*

complex arrangement of spines on head

ORDER *Terebellida.*
FAMILY *Sabellariidae.*
NO. OF SPECIES *15.*
SIZE *Individuals up to 4cm long, tubes up to 35cm long.*
FEEDING *Suspension feeders.*
IMPACT *Reef builders.*

Earthworms

Lumbricidae

Earthworms have segmented bodies with eight short, stiff bristles on each segment to assist with locomotion. Sexually mature individuals have a swollen band around the body called the clitellum. This structure is used in the mating process and its secretions form a cocoon around the eggs that are produced. Earthworms make permanent vertical burrows in the soil and come to the surface to mate and feed.

COMMON *and abundant in soil in most British terrestrial habitats.*

swollen clitellum

flattened tail end

ORDER *Haplotaxida.*
FAMILY *Lumbricidae.*
NO. OF SPECIES *350.*
SIZE *Up to 30cm long.*
FEEDING *Herbivore and decomposer.*
IMPACT *Play a key role in soil formation and fertility. Important food source for vertebrates.*

LUMBRICUS TERRESTRIS, *the Common Earthworm or Lob Worm, flattens the tail end of its body to anchor itself in its burrow. Abundantly found, in lawns these worms can reach densities of 40 worms per square metre.*

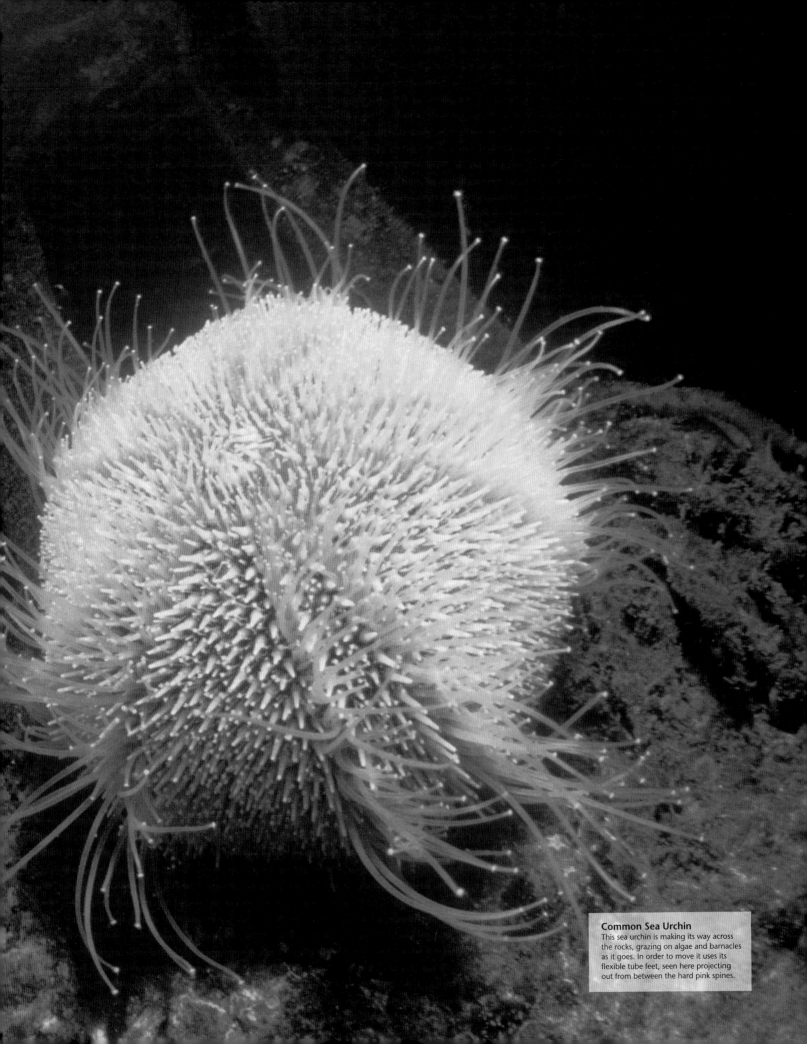

Common Sea Urchin
This sea urchin is making its way across
the rocks, grazing on algae and barnacles
as it goes. In order to move it uses its
flexible tube feet, seen here projecting
out from between the hard pink spines.

TREES

Britain boasts around 60 native species that can be classed as trees. This relatively small number is due the short time available for trees to recolonize the country between the end of the last ice age and the formation of the English Channel. In spite of this, many British trees are well known and make a major contribution to the landscape. They include large forest-forming species such as the English Oak, the Common Beech, and the Scots Pine, as well as others such as the Rowan and Silver Birch; some 18 species are found nowhere else and are usually rare, with a restricted distribution. Many exotic species are cultivated in gardens or plantations, and some, such as Horse Chestnut, Spanish Chestnut, and Turkey Oak, have become naturalized.

CONIFERS WITH NEEDLES

Some conifers have needle-like leaves, which may be blunt or sharp pointed. The most familiar conifers such as pines, firs, and spruces belong to this group.

CONIFERS WITH SCALES

These conifers have tiny, scale-like leaves closely covering the shoots, which often makes them similar in appearance. They include the cypresses, such as Leyland Cypress, and many junipers.

BROADLEAVED COMPOUND

Broad-leaved (non-coniferous) trees with compound leaves have the leaves divided into individual leaflets, either palmately as in Horse Chestnut or pinnately as in Rowan.

BROADLEAVED SIMPLE

Broad-leaved trees with simple leaves have leaves that range from untoothed to toothed or deeply lobed, but are never divided into leaflets. They include Common Beech.

Identification

Trees have many characters that can be used to identify them, some obvious, some less so. Note the shape of the tree and where and when it is growing, but also study closely the leaves, flowers, fruit, and bark. Remember that most plants are variable and features such as leaves can differ in size and shape, even on the same tree.

Leaf Shape

Tree leaves are extremely diverse. Check if the leaf is simple (one individual blade) or compound (divided into leaflets) and how any leaflets are arranged (pinnately or palmately, for example). Assess the shape and size of all its elements.

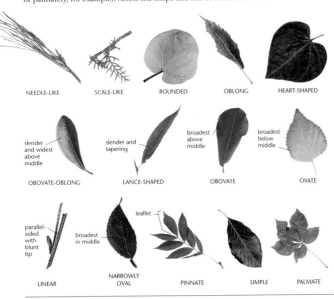

NEEDLE-LIKE SCALE-LIKE ROUNDED OBLONG HEART-SHAPED

OBOVATE-OBLONG (slender and widest above middle) LANCE-SHAPED (slender and tapering) OBOVATE (broadest above middle) OVATE (broadest below middle)

LINEAR (parallel-sided with blunt tip) NARROWLY OVAL (broadest in middle, leaflet) PINNATE SIMPLE PALMATE

Leaf Colour and Markings

Leaf colour and markings vary both between and within species. Some leaves change colour as they mature, or just before they fall in autumn; some leaves are marked with prominent veins or are variegated, consisting of patches of colour.

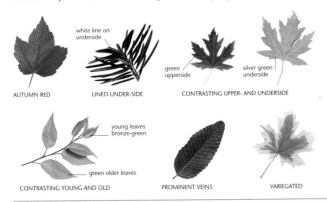

AUTUMN RED LINED UNDER-SIDE (white line on underside) CONTRASTING UPPER- AND UNDERSIDE (green upperside, silver green underside)

CONTRASTING YOUNG AND OLD (young leaves bronze-green, green older leaves) PROMINENT VEINS VARIEGATED

Leaf Margin and Texture

The leaf margin can vary from untoothed to wavy, toothed, spiny, or variously lobed, depending on the species. Look at them, but also touch and smell the leaves. Plant parts can be characteristically rough, hairy, or scented. For example, evergreens usually have rather leathery leaves while some species of poplar may be hairy or downy on one or both sides.

TOOTHED WAVY MARGINED SPINY

LOBED GLOSSY MATT HAIRY

Leaf Arrangement

Leaf arrangement can provide clues to a tree's identity. All maples and ashes, for example, have leaves that grow opposite one another on the shoots, while oak leaves are alternate and sometimes in a cluster towards the ends of the shoots. The leaves of some conifers, such as the Juniper, are arranged in whorls, the number of needles in the whorl often offering a clue to identity.

ALTERNATE OPPOSITE CLUSTERED

FLATTENED SPRAYS IRREGULAR SPRAYS WHORLS

Flowers

Note their size, colour, and form, but also consider how and where flowers are borne on the plant. Some trees may have separate male and female flowers, on the same or on different plants.

female flower / male flower — SEPARATE MALE AND FEMALE PLANTS

female opens red / male opens yellow — SEPARATE MALE AND FEMALE FLOWERS ON SAME PLANT

FLOWERS AT END OF SHOOTS FLOWERS IN LEAF AXIL FLOWERS IN CLUSTER FLOWERS BORNE SINGLY

Fruit

Fruits protect the tree's seeds and facilitate seed distribution. Their attractiveness to birds and mammals often ensure their transportation to new sites where they can germinate; some fruits have wings to aid wind-borne dispersal. While different types of cone help to distinguish conifers, other trees bear very different forms of fruit, including fleshy, characteristically coloured berries, hard-shelled nuts, and flattened pods. Even fruits that have fallen to the ground can help identification.

EGG-SHAPED CONES SINGLE UPRIGHT CONE

CONTAINING MULTIPLE SEEDS CONTAINING A SINGLE SEED

ACORN IN CUP GREEN HUSK HARD SHELL ENCLOSED IN BRACTS

WOODY HUSK CYLINDRICAL PODS SMALL AND WOODY BROAD WINGS

Habit

Observing a tree's shape, or habit, can help species identification, but be aware that shape can vary greatly: a tree growing in the open will differ in shape to one of the same species growing in a dense forest. Age can also affect the shape of a tree. Take note of all external factors.

SPREADING
Many evergreen trees have open branches, giving them a spreading habit.

CONICAL
Most coniferous trees, especially young ones, have a distinctly conical shape.

COLUMNAR
Some trees are naturally much taller than they are wide.

SHRUB-LIKE
In this exposed location this Juniper grows as a shrub.

Seasons

Flowering time and leaf persistence can be defining features for a tree. Deciduous trees lose their leaves in autumn but evergreens retain them, at least until the following season's leaves open. A tree may produce its flowers before its leaves open; another similar-looking tree may flower only after the young leaves are produced.

HOLM OAK

SEASONALITY
The Holm Oak is evergreen while its cousin the Turkey Oak is deciduous.

TURKEY OAK

FLOWERING
The Norway Maple flowers before its leaves appear; the Sycamore flowers open later.

SYCAMORE

NORWAY MAPLE

Bark

Bark is the distinctive protective outer covering of a tree. Without it the tissues within the wood that conduct water and nutrients to the leaves, and sugars to all parts of the tree would be vulnerable to attack by the elements and invasion by insects, other animals, and disease. As a tree grows, its trunk lays on new layers of wood each season and expands, causing the exterior layers of dead bark to peel or crack. This expansion creates various bark patterns, which are characteristic to each species; it also produces colour and textural differences between young and old specimens. Some trees, such as White Poplar, have very distinctive bark colour.

SMOOTH

RIDGED AND FISSURED

PEELING (VERTICAL)

PEELING (HORIZONTAL)

FLAKING (PLATES)

SQUARES

PATCHY

GLOSSY RED-BROWN

young

old

DIFFERENT YOUNG AND OLD

SCALE MEASUREMENTS
Two small scale drawings are placed next to each other in every entry as a rough indication of tree size. The figure represents a 6-ft human. The tree illustration represents the tree at maturity in the wild. Bare branches on one side mean the tree is deciduous; full foliage means the tree is evergreen.

Tree height 20m | Human figure represents a height of 1.8m (6ft)

Habitat

Some trees are naturally widespread but others, due to their preference for specific environmental conditions, may be confined to certain habitats and particular geographical regions. Tree species found in a lowland valley are likely to be very different to those found high in the mountains.

RIVER BANKS
The Alder tree is likely to be found by rivers and in other wet areas.

WOODLAND
The Holm Oak finds its natural habitat in upland woods.

HEATHLAND
The Scots Pine favours sandy soils in heaths and mountains.

Field Maple

Acer campestre (Aceraceae)

Also known as Hedge Maple, this deciduous tree sometimes appears shrubby. The opposite leaves are dark green above, paler and hairy beneath, and turn yellow in autumn. They are heart-shaped at the base and deeply cut into five lobes, which are usually untoothed and pointed. Clusters of green flowers open with the young leaves. When cut, the leaf stalk exudes a milky sap.

HANGING *in clusters, each fruit has two spreading wings; ripens from green to reddish.*

round crown

spreading habit

leaf to 10cm wide

fruit to 2.5cm long, 5cm wide

HEIGHT *15m.* **SPREAD** *10m.*
BARK *Pale brown, with orange fissures, and somewhat corky.*
FLOWERING TIME *Mid- to late spring.*
OCCURRENCE *Woods and hedgerows throughout Britain, particularly on alkaline soils; less common in Scotland.*
SIMILAR SPECIES *None.*

Norway Maple

Acer platanoides (Aceraceae)

YELLOW *or red in autumn, the broad, bright green leaves each have five lobes, ending in teeth with long, slender points.*

A large, vigorous, deciduous tree with a broadly columnar crown, the Norway Maple has shoots ending in red buds. The large, opposite leaves are divided into five lobes, each with several tapered teeth; bright green above, they are paler and glossy beneath, and turn yellow, orange, or red in autumn. The leaf stalk exudes a milky sap when cut. Clusters of small, bright yellow flowers open before the young leaves emerge, followed by fruit with large wings. Several forms are grown in gardens, such as 'Crimson King', with purple foliage, and 'Drummondii', which has leaves broadly edged creamy white.

autumn foliage

leaf to 18cm long

fruit to 5cm long

bright yellow flowers

NOTE
This tree is often confused in winter with the Sycamore (right). Both are common trees, but they are easily distinguished by the buds – red in the Norway Maple and green in the Sycamore.

HEIGHT *25m.*
SPREAD *15m.*
BARK *Grey and smooth.*
FLOWERING TIME *Early spring.*
OCCURRENCE *Woods and hedgerows; introduced and naturalized in many areas; commonly planted.*
SIMILAR SPECIES *Sycamore (right), which has pendulous flower clusters after the leaves emerge and leaves that are blue-grey beneath.*

Sycamore

Acer pseudoplatanus (Aceraceae)

The broad crown of this large, deciduous tree spreads with age. Its shoots end in green buds and the opposite leaves are divided into five sharp-toothed lobes. The leaves are dark green above and blue-grey beneath, turning yellow in autumn. Small yellow-green flowers are borne in dense, drooping panicles, followed by fruit with green or red-flushed wings. Several selections are grown in gardens, such as 'Atropurpureum', which has leaves with purple undersides, 'Brilliantissimum', a small tree with bright pink young foliage, and 'Erythrocarpum', which has red fruit wings.

YELLOW-GREEN *flowers hang in pendulous clusters from slender shoots; leaves are heart-shaped at base and palmately lobed.*

dense foliage

broad, columnar head

leaf to 15cm wide

5-lobed leaf

flower cluster to 12cm long

NOTE
This species is known as a plane tree in Scotland but has no connection with the true planes. The leaves are very often infected by tar spot fungus, which causes conspicuous black blotches.

fruit wing to 3cm long

'ERYTHROCARPUM'

HEIGHT *30m.* **SPREAD** *20m.*
BARK *Pinkish to yellow-grey, flaking in irregular plates when old.*
FLOWERING TIME *Mid-spring.*
OCCURRENCE *Woods, hedgerows, and roadsides; introduced and widely naturalized throughout Britain and Ireland. It is commonly cultivated.*
SIMILAR SPECIES *Norway Maple (left), which has flowers in upright clusters before or with the young leaves, and leaves that are glossy green beneath.*

Common Holly

Ilex aquifolium (Aquifoliaceae)

This evergreen tree is sometimes shrubby, with green or purple shoots. Glossy, dark green, alternate leaves range from oval to oblong. Spiny leaves generally occur on younger trees and lower shoots, while smooth leaves occur on older trees and higher shoots. White or purple-flushed flowers grow in clusters, with males and females on separate trees.

SHINY, *usually bright red berries are densely clustered on the branches of female trees. The 1cm-wide berries are yellow or orange.*

columnar to conical habit

white male flowers

green ovary of female flower

leaf to 10cm long

HEIGHT *20m.*
SPREAD *15m.*
BARK *Pale grey and smooth.*
FLOWERING TIME *Late spring.*
OCCURRENCE *Throughout Britain and Ireland, woods and hedgerows; commonly planted.*
SIMILAR SPECIES *None – it is a distinct tree.*

Alder

Alnus glutinosa (Betulaceae)

The Alder is a deciduous tree of conical habit, whose young green shoots and alternate leaves are slightly sticky to the touch. The dark green, mature leaves, paler beneath, are up to 10cm long; they are widest at the tip, which may be indented, and have a tapering base. The tiny flowers are borne in separate male and female catkins formed during the summer. The males are pendulous and yellow, up to 10cm long; the upright females are red and much smaller, only about 5mm long.

SMALL *green unripe fruit are borne in clusters and mature to woody, dark brown cones that remain on the tree during winter.*

conical habit

green unripe fruit

ripe fruit 2cm long

NOTE

This is the only British native alder. 'Imperialis', a garden selection, is a smaller tree with leaves that are deeply cut into pointed lobes. The Alder is often grown in gardens and parks as an ornamental tree.

HEIGHT *25m.*
SPREAD *12m.*
BARK *Dark grey; cracks into square plates on old trees.*
FLOWERING TIME *Early spring.*
OCCURRENCE *Riverbanks and other wet places throughout Britain and Ireland.*
SIMILAR SPECIES *None – the leaves, broadest at the end with a notched tip, are distinct in shape from other species of Alnus.*

Hornbeam

Carpinus betulus (Betulaceae)

Conical when young, the deciduous Hornbeam develops a more rounded outline, the slender shoots often drooping at the tips. The oval to oblong leaves have prominent veins and are sharply double-toothed at the margins. They are dark green above, paler beneath, and turn yellow in autumn. The tiny flowers are borne in pendulous catkins as the young leaves emerge; males are yellow-brown, females are green and shorter. Small fruit, in hanging clusters, ripen from green to yellow-brown, each hidden at the base of a conspicuous bract with three untoothed lobes.

PENDULOUS *fruiting clusters, which are made conspicuous by their three-lobed green bracts, are borne in summer.*

broadly spreading habit

leaf to 10cm long

male catkin to 5cm long

female catkin

fruit cluster to 7.5cm long

NOTE

A Hornbeam without fruit can be identified by its fluted trunk. When used in hedges, this species can be recognized by its sharply double-toothed leaves which are folded along the veins.

HEIGHT *30m.*
SPREAD *25m.*
BARK *Pale grey and smooth, fluted on old trees.*
FLOWERING TIME *Early spring.*
OCCURRENCE *Woods and hedgerows mainly in S.E. Britain. It is commonly cultivated, particularly forms with upright branches such as 'Fastigiata'. Elsewhere, it is less common, or only planted.*
SIMILAR SPECIES *None – the fruit is distinct among British trees.*

Downy Birch

Betula pubescens (Betulaceae)

Softly hairy young shoots and leaves give this conical, deciduous tree its name. Its broadly oval, dark green leaves, edged with single teeth, turn smooth and yellow in autumn. Tiny flowers are borne in catkins, the males drooping and yellow, the females smaller, upright, and green. The upright, cylindrical clusters of small brown fruit, up to 3cm long, break up when ripe.

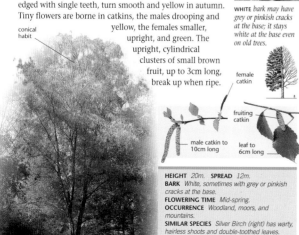

conical habit

WHITE *bark may have grey or pinkish cracks at the base; it stays white at the base even on old trees.*

female catkin

fruiting catkin

male catkin to 10cm long

leaf to 6cm long

HEIGHT *20m.* **SPREAD** *12m.*
BARK *White, sometimes with grey or pinkish cracks at the base.*
FLOWERING TIME *Mid-spring.*
OCCURRENCE *Woodland, moors, and mountains.*
SIMILAR SPECIES *Silver Birch (right) has warty, hairless shoots and double-toothed leaves.*

Silver Birch

Betula pendula (Betulaceae)

The young shoots of this deciduous tree are rough to the touch, with numerous small warts. The glossy and dark green leaves are oval to triangular, edged with double teeth, and turn yellow in autumn. Tiny flowers are borne in catkins, the males drooping, and the females upright, and later drooping. The brown fruit clusters break up when ripe.

WHITE *bark of mature trees is prominently marked with dark scars, and has deep cracks and knobbly bumps towards the base.*

fruit cluster to 3cm long

leaf to 6cm long

green female catkin

narrow, weeping habit

yellow male catkin to 6cm long

HEIGHT *30m.* **SPREAD** *20m.*
BARK *White, often developing diamond-shaped, black markings at the base of mature trees.*
FLOWERING TIME *Mid-spring.*
OCCURRENCE *Woods, heaths, and mountains, except on chalky soil.*
SIMILAR SPECIES *Downy Birch (left).*

PLANTS

Common Hazel

Corylus avellana (Betulaceae)

Frequently shrubby and forming thickets, this spreading tree has several stems from the base and is often coppiced for its shoots. The alternate, heart-shaped, hairy, dark green leaves turn yellow in autumn. Male flowers appear before the leaves open and female flowers are tiny, with only the red stigmas showing. Partially enclosed in a deeply lobed pale green husk, the edible nuts (cobnuts) are carried in clusters of up to four.

PALE *yellow, pendulous catkins hang from bare shoots, and contain the male flowers.*

multiple stems

edible nuts

leaf to 10cm long

HEIGHT *10m.* **SPREAD** *10m.*
BARK *Grey-brown, glossy, peeling in strips.*
FLOWERING TIME *Late winter to early spring.*
OCCURRENCE *Woods, hedgerows, and thickets throughout Britain.*
SIMILAR SPECIES *This is the only species native to Britain although others are cultivated and sometimes escape from gardens.*

Common Box

Buxus sempervirens (Buxaceae)

This evergreen plant is more often a shrub than a tree. Its opposite, dark green leaves are often blue-green when young. The flowers of both sexes are separate but in the same cluster, the males with conspicuous yellow anthers. The small green fruit are topped with three horns, which are much shorter than the fruit.

OFTEN *a shrub, particularly in exposed positions, but can become a tree in sheltered woodland.*

conical to columnar or spreading habit

leaf to 3cm long

male flowers

fruit to 8mm long

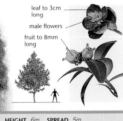

HEIGHT *6m.* **SPREAD** *5m.*
BARK *Grey and smooth, cracking into small squares on older trees.*
FLOWERING TIME *Early spring.*
OCCURRENCE *Beechwoods on alkaline soil. A scarce native of S. Britain; widely planted and naturalized elsewhere.*
SIMILAR SPECIES *None.*

Elder

Sambucus nigra (Caprifoliaceae)

With a broadly columnar to rounded head, a rather twisted growth, and arching branches, the deciduous Elder tree is often shrubby, with several stems sprouting from the base. The leaves, borne in opposite pairs on stout grey-brown shoots, are pinnate, with 5–7 sharply toothed, oval, elliptical, and pointed leaflets, each up to 20cm long; they have a rather unpleasant smell. The flat heads of white flowers, each about 6–10mm wide, are followed by glossy black, edible berries, which are green when unripe, and have red stalks.

TINY, *creamy white, fragrant flowers are borne in broad, flattened heads up to 25cm wide.*

broadly columnar to rounded head

creamy white flowers

leaflet to 12cm long

leaf to 30cm long

berry about 6mm wide

NOTE

Both the flowers and fruit are used to make wine. Many selections are grown in gardens, including the purple-leaved, variegated, and cut-leaved forms. The ripe fruit are occasionally green.

HEIGHT *10m.*
SPREAD *8m.*
BARK *Grey-brown, deeply furrowed, and corky.*
FLOWERING TIME *Summer.*
OCCURRENCE *Woods, scrub, hedgerows, and waste places throughout Britain.*
SIMILAR SPECIES *Danewort (S. ebulus), which is herbaceous.*

Wayfaring Tree

Viburnum lantana (Caprifoliaceae)

This upright, deciduous shrub has stout, scurfy-hairy shoots. The opposite, oval, dark green leaves are up to 10cm long and 8cm wide, with hair beneath. Small, creamy white flowers are borne in domed heads to 10cm wide. These are followed by flattened, oval berries, each up to 8mm long that turn from red to black as they ripen. Each berry contains a single seed.

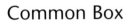

SMALL, *white, five-lobed flowers with projecting stamens are borne in dense, domed clusters.*

unlobed leaf

domed heads of flowers

fruits turn from red to black

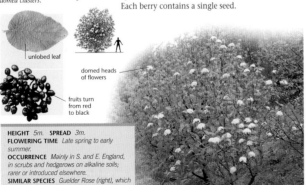

HEIGHT *5m.* **SPREAD** *3m.*
FLOWERING TIME *Late spring to early summer.*
OCCURRENCE *Mainly in S. and E. England, in scrubs and hedgerows on alkaline soils; rarer or introduced elsewhere.*
SIMILAR SPECIES *Guelder Rose (right), which has lobed leaves.*

Guelder Rose

Viburnum opulus (Caprifoliaceae)

A large deciduous shrub, the Guelder Rose is upright when young, and later rounded. The smooth shoots bear opposite leaves with 3–5 toothed lobes that often turn red in autumn. Small white flowers in broad flowerheads up to 10cm wide are surrounded by a ring of sterile flowers. The bright red, spherical berries contain a single seed and ripen in autumn.

JUICY *red fruits ripen as the leaves start to colour in autumn and are edible if cooked.*

maple-like leaf

smooth shoot

flattened flowerhead

large sterile flowers

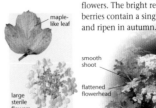

HEIGHT *5m.*
SPREAD *5m.*
FLOWERING TIME *Early summer.*
OCCURRENCE *Scrubs, hedgerows, and woods, also commonly planted; widely distributed but less common in the far north.*
SIMILAR SPECIES *Wayfaring Tree (left), which lacks the large, sterile flowers.*

Spindle Tree

Euonymus europaeus (Celastraceae)

This often low-branching or shrubby, spreading, deciduous tree has green shoots ending in small leaf buds, up to 5mm long. The dark green, opposite leaves are oval to lance-shaped and edged with fine teeth. They turn orange-red or purple in autumn. The tiny, greenish white flowers, each with four petals, open in small clusters, males and females separately, sometimes on different plants.

FOUR-LOBED, bright pink fruit, up to 1.2cm wide, open to reveal orange seeds.

orange autumn foliage

leaf to 10cm long

small greenish flowers

HEIGHT *6m.* **SPREAD** *8m.*
BARK *Grey and smooth, fissured with age.*
FLOWERING TIME *Late spring to early summer.*
OCCURRENCE *Woods and hedgerows usually on alkaline soil; widely distributed but less common in Scotland.*
SIMILAR SPECIES *None.*

Common Juniper

Juniperus communis (Cupressaceae)

This evergreen conifer is of variable habit, from bushy and spreading, to upright and tree-like. Its sharp-pointed needles are glossy green on both surfaces, marked with a broad white band on the upper surface, and arranged in whorls of three on the shoots. The flowers are very small; males are yellow and females green, growing in clusters on separate plants. Female plants bear fleshy, blue-black berry-like cones up to 6mm long, covered at first with a white bloom. Many selections are grown in gardens and the creeping *J. communis* var. *montana* is common in mountainous regions.

PROSTRATE *and creeping, or a bushy shrub, or sometimes a tree, this species is of very variable habit.*

glossy green needles

bushy, spreading habit

cone to 6mm long

leaf to 1.2cm long

HEIGHT *6m.*
SPREAD *1–3m.*
BARK *Red-brown with longitudinal ridges; peeling in vertical strips.*
FLOWERING TIME *Spring.*
OCCURRENCE *In scrub on heathland, chalk, and limestone; widely but often locally distributed.*
SIMILAR SPECIES *None.*

NOTE
This is the only juniper native to northern Europe. The fruit takes two years to ripen, and is found at any time of the year.

Monterey Cypress

Cupressus macrocarpa (Cupressaceae)

A large, vigorous evergreen tree of usually dense, columnar habit, the Monterey Cypress spreads with age. Its aromatic, bright green foliage is composed of tiny, scale-like leaves with pointed tips, densely arranged in sprays all around the shoots. Male flower clusters are yellow, while females are green, both borne at the tips of the shoots. The rounded purple-brown cones have scales with small, blunt points. They ripen in the second autumn and usually remain on the tree for several years. Although a rare species in the wild, the Monterey Cypress is commonly cultivated in Britain.

FOLIAGE *is arranged around the shoots as in all Cupressus species, and not in flattened sprays as in Chamaecyparis.*

bright green foliage

dense, columnar habit

cone to 4cm wide

spray of leaves around shoot

pointed tips

NOTE
Several garden selections of the Monterey Cypress are frequently seen, particularly those with yellow foliage, such as 'Goldcrest'.

HEIGHT *30m.*
SPREAD *15m.*
BARK *Red-brown with shallow ridges.*
FLOWERING TIME *Early spring.*
OCCURRENCE *Introduced, commonly planted particularly in western and coastal regions; native to California.*
SIMILAR SPECIES *Other cypresses are grown in gardens.*

Leyland Cypress

x *Cupressocyparis leylandii* (Cupressaceae)

A very fast-growing, evergreen tree, the Leyland Cypress has a dense, narrow, columnar habit, tapering towards the top. The tiny, scale-like, dark green leaves have pointed tips. They are borne in small, flattened sprays densely arranged all around the shoots. While male flower clusters are yellow, females are green.

SPHERICAL *green young cones, when produced, ripen to brown the second year after flowering and so appear clustered on the old shoots.*

narrow, columnar habit

yellow male flowers

densely arranged leaves

cone 2cm wide

HEIGHT *30m or more.* **SPREAD** *10m.*
BARK *Red-brown and smooth, ridged and flaking with age.*
FLOWERING TIME *Spring.*
OCCURRENCE *Known only in cultivation (several forms are grown, with various foliage colours, especially yellow).*
SIMILAR SPECIES *None.*

PLANTS

Western Red Cedar

Thuja plicata (Cupressaceae)

Fast-growing and conical, the evergreen Western Red Cedar has pleasantly aromatic foliage and its dark green leaves are borne in flattened sprays. While male flower clusters are blackish red, turning yellow when open, the females are yellow-green; both are borne at the ends of the shoots. The upright, egg-shaped cones ripen the same year from yellow-green to brown. Each cone has 10–12 leathery scales.

TINY, *scale-like leaves are dark green above, and have white markings beneath.*

dark green leaves

cone to 1.2cm long

narrowly conical habit

HEIGHT *35m or more.*
SPREAD *15m.*
BARK *Purple-brown, peeling in vertical strips.*
FLOWERING TIME *Early spring.*
OCCURRENCE *Commonly planted for timber and as an ornamental; native to W. North America.*
SIMILAR SPECIES *None. The cones and large size distinguish it from similar species such as Thuja occidentalis, which is grown in gardens.*

NOTE
A popular garden tree making an effective large screen. There are several selections, including 'Zebrina' that have yellow-striped foliage.

Strawberry Tree

Arbutus unedo (Ericaceae)

A spreading, evergreen tree, the Strawberry Tree has sticky hairs on the young shoots. The alternate, oval leaves are glossy, dark green, with toothed margins. Small, urn-shaped white or, more rarely, pink flowers are borne in drooping clusters at the ends of the shoots as the fruit from the previous year's flowers are ripening. The very characteristic, strawberry-like fruit, which give the tree its name, ripen from green through yellow to red. Unlike many members of its family, this tree can often be found growing on alkaline soil. Some forms have untoothed leaves. There are famous stands of this tree in western Ireland (Cork, Killarney, and Sligo).

PENDULOUS *and roughly warty on the surface, the fruit resemble small strawberries.*

broadly spreading habit

glossy green foliage

flower cluster about 5cm long

leaf to 10cm wide

red-brown bark

HEIGHT *10m.* **SPREAD** *10m.*
BARK *Red-brown, rough, and flaking but not peeling.*
FLOWERING TIME *Autumn.*
OCCURRENCE *Cliffs and woodland in S.W. Ireland; widely planted in gardens as an ornamental.*
SIMILAR SPECIES *A. x andrachnoides, a hybrid between A. unedo and A. andrachne (the Grecian Strawberry Tree), is cultivated in gardens. It differs in its peeling bark.*

NOTE
"Unedo" means literally "I eat one", referring to the fact that the fruit is edible, although it is not exactly delicious.

Sea Buckthorn

Hippophae rhamnoides (Elaeagnaceae)

This deciduous, thicket-forming shrub or small tree, with spiny shoots, spreads by suckers from the base. Its alternate, slender, linear, untoothed leaves are covered in silver scales on both sides. Tiny yellowish flowers open in small clusters before or as the leaves emerge, with males and females on separate plants. It is frequently planted as an ornamental tree and to stabilize sand dunes.

ROUNDED, *fleshy, bright orange fruit are densely clustered along the shoots.*

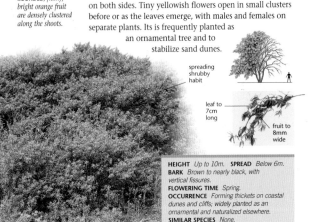

spreading shrubby habit

leaf to 7cm long

fruit to 8mm wide

HEIGHT *Up to 10m.* **SPREAD** *Below 6m.*
BARK *Brown to nearly black, with vertical fissures.*
FLOWERING TIME *Spring.*
OCCURRENCE *Forming thickets on coastal dunes and cliffs; widely planted as an ornamental and naturalized elsewhere.*
SIMILAR SPECIES *None.*

Rhododendron

Rhododendron ponticum (Ericaceae)

The stout shoots of this large, rounded, and evergreen shrub bear alternate, oblong, glossy dark green, untoothed leaves up to 20cm long and 6cm wide. The purple-pink flowers have brownish spots inside. The fruit is a small capsule that splits to release numerous tiny seeds. Rhododendron is an invasive alien, taking over British woodland.

ATTRACTIVE *bell-shaped flowers, to 5cm wide, open in rounded clusters at the end of the shoots.*

brownish spots on upper petal

glossy dark green leaf

5-lobed flower

purple-pink flower

prominent stamens

HEIGHT *3m.* **SPREAD** *5m.*
FLOWERING TIME *Late spring to early summer.*
OCCURRENCE *Introduced; native of extreme S.W. and S.E. Europe, and S.W. Asia; hybrids are naturalized in woods throughout most of Britain on sandy or peaty soils.*
SIMILAR SPECIES *Other hybrids in gardens.*

Common Laburnum

Laburnum anagyroides (Leguminosae/Fabaceae)

PEA-LIKE, *fragrant, golden yellow flowers are borne in slender, pendulous clusters up to 25cm long.*

Also known as the Golden Rain Tree, this deciduous, spreading tree has alternate leaves with three leaflets, each rounded at the tip. They are deep green above, grey-green and whitish beneath, and covered with silky white hair when young. Golden yellow flowers are borne in dense and showy leafless clusters. The fruit is a slightly rounded, hairy, pale brown pod, up to 8cm long, with black seeds, and hangs in clusters. Although known as Common Laburnum, in gardens this species has largely been replaced by Voss's Laburnum (*L.* x *watereri*).

NOTE

All parts of this tree and of other Laburnums are poisonous.

broadly spreading habit

leaflet to 9cm long

flower to 2.5cm long

HEIGHT *7m.* **SPREAD** *3m.*
BARK *Smooth and dark grey, fissured with age.*
FLOWERING TIME *Late spring to early summer.*
OCCURRENCE *Introduced and mainly grown in gardens, occasionally naturalized; native to S. and C. Europe.*
SIMILAR SPECIES *Voss's Laburnum (L. x watereri), which is common in gardens, has longer flower clusters, and rarely sets seed. L. alpinum is also cultivated and has flowers in very long, slender racemes.*

Spanish Chestnut

Castanea sativa (Fagaceae)

SLENDER, *creamy white flower spikes cover the tree in summer, making for a spectacular sight in parks and gardens.*

Also known as the Sweet Chestnut, this deciduous tree was widely introduced outside its native region of southern Europe by the Romans. Large and vigorous, it has stout shoots and a broadly columnar head. Its alternate, oblong leaves taper to a point and are edged with numerous slender-pointed teeth. They are glossy, dark green and turn yellow-brown in autumn. The flowers are borne in long, slender, upright to spreading catkins. The pale green fruit husk, densely covered with slender, sharp spines, encloses up to three glossy brown, edible nuts.

catkin to 25cm long

leaf to 20cm long

nuts in spiny husk

broadly columnar habit

NOTE

Ornamental selections of this tree include 'Albomarginata', which has leaves edged creamy white; other varieties are generally grown for their particularly tasty fruit.

HEIGHT *30m.* **SPREAD** *20m.*
BARK *Grey and smooth; brown with spiralling ridges on older specimens.*
FLOWERING TIME *Midsummer.*
OCCURRENCE *Introduced, commonly planted, and often naturalized; native to S. Europe across to S.W. Asia.*
SIMILAR SPECIES *Horse Chestnut (p.325), which has superficially similar fruit, but larger flower clusters and opposite leaves.*

Black Locust

Robinia pseudoacacia (Leguminosae/Fabaceae)

Often spreading widely by means of suckers, this is a vigorous, deciduous tree with a broadly columnar head. The alternate, pinnate leaves on red-brown shoots have up to 21 leaflets, usually with a pair of spines at the base. Pea-like, fragrant white flowers hang in clusters to 20cm long, with dark brown pods up to 10cm long.

DARK *blue-green leaves have many elliptical untoothed leaflets, up to 5cm long, that are grey-green beneath.*

leaf to 30cm long

flower to 2cm long

columnar habit

HEIGHT *25m.* **SPREAD** *15m.*
BARK *Grey-brown with deep furrows.*
FLOWERING TIME *Early summer.*
OCCURRENCE *Cultivated, and widely naturalized; native to S.E. USA.*
SIMILAR SPECIES *The cultivated species, Honey Locust (Gleditsia triacanthos) has pink flowers, spiny shoots, and bipinnate leaves.*

Common Beech

Fagus sylvatica (Fagaceae)

Zig-zag shoots ending in long, slender-pointed buds characterize this spreading, deciduous tree. It has alternate, dark green, wavy-edged leaves, widest above the middle, with up to ten pairs of veins. Its tiny flowers open with the young leaves, males and females in separate clusters. The more conspicuous males are borne in drooping, rounded, pale yellow heads. The fruit is a woody husk, up to 2.5cm long, and contains one or two edible nuts.

SILKY *and hairy when young, the dark green leaves turn bright yellow in autumn.*

spreading habit

yellow autumn foliage

leaf to 10cm long

HEIGHT *30m.*
SPREAD *20m.*
BARK *Pale grey and smooth.*
FLOWERING TIME *Mid-spring.*
OCCURRENCE *Woods in S. England and S. Wales, commonly planted and naturalized further north.*
SIMILAR SPECIES *None.*

PLANTS

Oak Woods
Wistmans Wood, in Devon, is one of the few remnants of ancient oak woodland in the British Isles, dating back to prehistoric times. The gnarled, moss- and lichen-covered trees give the wood an eerie feel.

Turkey Oak

Quercus cerris (Fagaceae)

The hairy shoots of this large, vigorous, deciduous tree are tipped with leaf buds surrounded by characteristic long whisker-like stipules. Its alternate leaves are variable in shape, toothed, and deeply lobed, on stalks up to 2cm long. They are dark green above, slightly rough, blue-green beneath, and hairy, at least when young. The flowers are borne in catkins, the males yellow-green and drooping, up to 6cm long; the females inconspicuous and borne separately.

DENSELY *covered in narrow, bristle-like scales, the acorn cup encloses half the acorn, which ripens in the second year.*

spreading habit

leaf to 12cm long

acorn to 2.5cm long

HEIGHT *35m.* **SPREAD** *25m.*
BARK *Grey brown and deeply ridged.*
FLOWERING TIME *Early summer.*
OCCURRENCE *Introduced; commonly planted and naturalized mainly in the south and central British Isles.*
SIMILAR SPECIES *English Oak (p.325) and Sessile Oak (right), which have smooth leaves.*

Holm Oak

Quercus ilex (Fagaceae)

The young shoots of this large, evergreen tree are densely covered with grey-white hairs. The elliptic to narrowly ovate, leathery and rigid leaves are glossy, dark green above, closely covered with grey hairs beneath, and may be toothed or untoothed. They are very variable in shape on young plants, with a spiny margin. Young trees and shoots from the base of old trees often have sharply toothed leaves, like those of holly (*Ilex*), which are green beneath. The flowers are borne in catkins: the males, blooming on young shoots, are drooping, yellow-green and pendulous; the females, borne separately on the same plant, are small and inconspicuous. The acorns are held in cups up to one-third their length and they ripen in the first year.

PENDULOUS *catkins appear along with the grey young leaves – a showy sight in early summer.*

leaf to 10cm long

pointed acorn

acorn to 2cm long

spreading habit

dense, rounded head

HEIGHT *30m.*
SPREAD *30m.*
BARK *Nearly black, cracking into small, scaly squares with age.*
FLOWERING TIME *Early summer.*
OCCURRENCE *Introduced; commonly planted and naturalized mainly in the south of the British Isles. Native to the Mediterranean region and Turkey.*
SIMILAR SPECIES *None – it is the only commonly seen evergreen oak.*

NOTE
In most regions, this is the most commonly cultivated evergreen oak tree. Often seen in coastal areas in its native regions, the Holm Oak has become widely naturalized in similar situations in southern Britain.

Sessile Oak

Quercus petraea (Fagaceae)

This is a large, deciduous tree with a spreading head and smooth young shoots. The alternate leaves are borne on stalks up to 1cm or more long and are edged with rounded, untoothed lobes. Dark, slightly glossy green above, they have a thin layer of hair beneath. Male and female flowers are borne separately in catkins: the males yellow-green and drooping, up to 8cm long; the females inconspicuous. Unstalked or very short-stalked, about one-third of the acorn is enclosed in a cup. A variable and widely distributed species, the Sessile Oak has many garden selections varying in leaf shape.

PROMINENT *and deep vertical ridges develop on the grey bark of mature trees.*

broadly spreading habit

leaf to 12cm long

acorn to 3cm long

HEIGHT *40m.*
SPREAD *25m.*
BARK *Grey; vertically ridged in mature trees.*
FLOWERING TIME *Late spring.*
OCCURRENCE *Widespread in woods on acidic soil.*
SIMILAR SPECIES *English Oak (p.325), which has leaves with very short stalks but long-stalked acorns; Turkey Oak (left), which has long scales on the acorn cups and rough leaves.*

NOTE
Where this species grows alongside English Oak (p.325), it hybridizes to form Q. x rosacea, with intermediate characters.

Red Oak

Quercus rubra (Fagaceae)

This is a deciduous, spreading tree with smooth reddish shoots. Blue-green beneath, matt dark green above, the alternate leaves are shallowly cut into bristle-tipped lobes and have stalks that are red at the base. The flowers are borne in catkins, the males yellow-green and pendulous, the females inconspicuous. Ripening the second year, only the base of the 3cm-long acorn is enclosed in a shallow cup.

DESPITE *the tree's name, the leaves often colour yellow or brown in autumn.*

broadly spreading habit

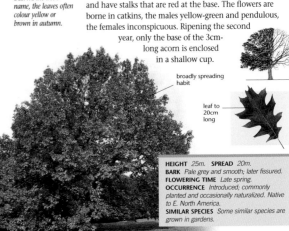

leaf to 20cm long

HEIGHT *25m.* **SPREAD** *20m.*
BARK *Pale grey and smooth; later fissured.*
FLOWERING TIME *Late spring.*
OCCURRENCE *Introduced; commonly planted and occasionally naturalized. Native to E. North America.*
SIMILAR SPECIES *Some similar species are grown in gardens.*

English Oak

Quercus robur (Fagaceae)

This oak is a deciduous, spreading tree with smooth shoots. The alternate, widest above the middle, very short-stalked leaves have 5–7 lobes on each side, and are dark green above and blue-green beneath. Flowers are borne in catkins: the males yellow-green and drooping; the females inconspicuous.

LONG-STALKED acorns are enclosed in a scaly cup, turning brown and developing dark stripes.

rounded head

spreading habit

yellow-green male flowers

leaf to 12cm long

acorn to 4cm long

HEIGHT 35m. **SPREAD** 30m.
BARK Grey with vertical fissures.
FLOWERING TIME Late spring.
OCCURRENCE Woods throughout British Isles.
SIMILAR SPECIES Sessile Oak (p.324), which has long-stalked leaves and unstalked acorns; Turkey Oak (p.324), which has long scales on the acorn cups and rough leaves.

Walnut

Juglans regia (Juglandaceae)

A deciduous tree, the Walnut has pinnate, dark green leaves with 5–9 leaflets, which are bronze when young. They are borne on stout, smooth shoots and are aromatic when crushed. The yellow-green flowers are small and without petals; males hang in conspicuous catkins up to 10cm long from the ends of old shoots, while the shorter female catkins form at the tips of new shoots as the leaves are expanding. The fruit of the Walnut is the familiar creamy white walnut, enclosed in a rounded green husk that ripens to brown. There are many garden selections grown for their fruit.

MALE and female flowers are clustered in separate pendulous catkins on the same tree, the females shorter than the males.

dark green leaves

broadly spreading habit

leaf to 45cm long

green husk

fruit to 5cm long

HEIGHT 25m.
SPREAD 20m.
BARK Pale grey, smooth on young trees, becoming fissured with age.
FLOWERING TIME Late spring to early summer.
OCCURRENCE Introduced; commonly grown for its fruits and occasionally naturalized, particularly in the south of the British Isles. Native from S.E. Europe to China.
SIMILAR SPECIES None – no other walnuts are commonly seen.

NOTE
Walnuts can be distinguished from the related hickories (Carya) by the chambered pith, which can be seen if shoots are cut lengthways.

Horse Chestnut

Aesculus hippocastanum (Hippocastanaceae)

The familiar Horse Chestnut is characterized by the large, glossy brown and very sticky buds that appear in winter. Its flowers are white with a yellow blotch that turns red. They are borne in large, upright, conical clusters and are followed by distinctive green fruit that contain up to three glossy brown seeds or conkers. A deciduous tree with a broadly columnar to spreading habit, it has palmate, dark green leaves each with 5–7 large, sharply toothed leaflets with short stalks. The leaves turn orange-red in autumn. 'Baumannii', a selection of this species, has double flowers and no fruit.

LARGE, creamy white flower clusters – a spectacular sight in spring, in parks, streets, and gardens, where the tree is common.

columnar to spreading shape

vigorous habit

leaf to 30cm long

flower cluster to 30cm long

HEIGHT 30m.
SPREAD 20m.
BARK Red-brown to grey; flaking in scales on large trees.
FLOWERING TIME Late spring.
OCCURRENCE Introduced; commonly planted and naturalized. Native to Greece and Albania.
SIMILAR SPECIES The commonly planted Red Horse Chestnut (A. x carnea) is a hybrid of this species.

NOTE
Although commonly planted in parks and large gardens, the origin of this tree was unknown for many years, until it was discovered in the wild in the mountains of N. Greece. The seeds are used in the game of conkers.

Common Ash

Fraxinus excelsior (Oleaceae)

A large, deciduous tree, the Common Ash has stout, smooth shoots and prominent black buds. The opposite, pinnate leaves have up to 13 sharply toothed, dark green leaflets, with a slender, tapered point at the tip. Vigorous shoots from the base may be produced in summer and these often have purple foliage.

TINY purple flowers in dense clusters have no petals; glossy green, winged fruit are produced in clusters.

broadly columnar habit

leaf to 30cm long

fruit to 4cm long

HEIGHT 30m or more. **SPREAD** 20m.
BARK Smooth and pale grey when young, developing deep fissures with age.
FLOWERING TIME Spring.
OCCURRENCE Moist woods and river banks; often on alkaline soils throughout the British Isles.
SIMILAR SPECIES None – this is the only ash native to Britain; others are grown in gardens.

PLANTS

Giant Fir

Abies grandis (Pinaceae)

The slender leaves of this fast-growing, large, evergreen tree are bright green above, with two white bands beneath. The leaves are arranged neatly on each side of the shoots. Hanging beneath the shoots are the male flower clusters, which are yellow, or red before they open. The upright, green female flower clusters mature into erect, cylindrical cones. These are green when young, ripening to brown.

SLENDER leaves spread out in two ranks on either side of the shoots.

conical habit

2 white bands below leaf

HEIGHT 50m or more. **SPREAD** 15m.
BARK Grey-brown and smooth on young trees; cracks with age.
FLOWERING TIME Spring.
OCCURRENCE Cultivated (in gardens and for forestry); native to W. North America.
SIMILAR SPECIES None – the leaf arrangement is quite distinct.

Atlas Cedar

Cedrus atlantica (Pinaceae)

This evergreen has dark to blue-green leaves that are slender, needle-like, and up to 2cm long. They are borne singly on long shoots, and in whorls on the short side shoots. The shoots have upcurved tips. The male flower clusters are yellow-brown and upright. Clusters of tiny female flowers mature in one year to barrel-shaped cones, green at first, ripening to brown over two to three years.

BARREL-SHAPED cones break up on the tree once they ripen, before falling off.

broadly conical habit

male flower cluster to 5cm long

cone to 8cm long

HEIGHT 30m. **SPREAD** 20m.
BARK Dark grey, cracking into scaly plates on old trees.
FLOWERING TIME Autumn.
OCCURRENCE Cultivated; native to the Atlas Mountains in Algeria and Morocco.
SIMILAR SPECIES European Larch (left); Japanese Larch (below).

European Larch

Larix decidua (Pinaceae)

This fast-growing species is deciduous. Its slender, soft, bright green leaves, each up to 4cm long, open in early spring, turning yellow in autumn. They are arranged singly on distinctive, long yellow shoots but are borne in dense whorls on short side shoots. Male flower clusters, on the underside of the shoots, are yellow, while the upright female clusters are red or yellow. The egg-shaped cones have upward-pointing scales and ripen in the first autumn after flowering.

OVAL red young cones with upright scales are clearly visible on the slender, drooping branches, interspersed with needle-like leaves in clusters.

conical habit

NOTE

It is the deciduous leaves, upright cone scales, and yellow shoots that distinguish this species from the other larches.

thin, drooping branches

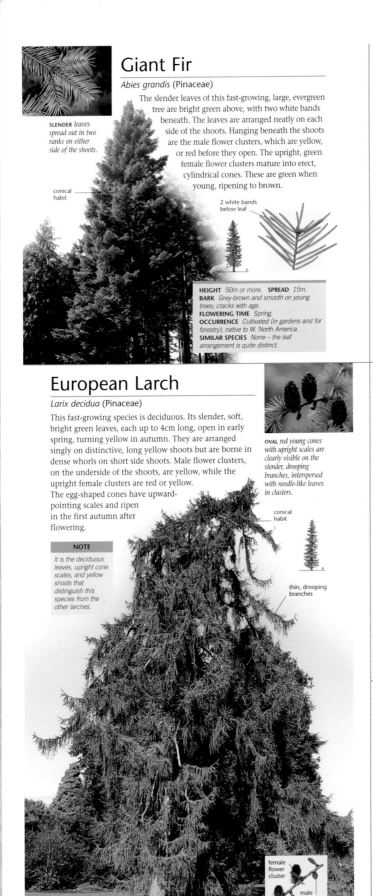

female flower cluster

male flower cluster

cone to 4cm long

HEIGHT 30–40m. **SPREAD** 15m.
BARK Grey and smooth; becoming red-brown and cracking into scaly plates with age.
FLOWERING TIME Spring.
OCCURRENCE Introduced; commonly planted for timber and often naturalized. Native to C. Europe.
SIMILAR SPECIES Japanese Larch (right), which has cones with the scales curved outwards.

Japanese Larch

Larix kaempferi (Pinaceae)

This deciduous tree is characterized by slender and soft, blue- to grey-green leaves that open in early spring, turning yellow in autumn. They are arranged singly on long shoots, but are borne in dense whorls on short side shoots. Male flower clusters are yellow, borne on the undersides of the shoots, while upright, creamy to pink female flowers are borne in larger clusters on top of the shoots.

CONE scales curve backwards, making the cones look like rosettes.

cone to 3cm long

leaf to 4cm long

male flowers

female flowers

conical habit

HEIGHT 30m. **SPREAD** 15m.
BARK Red-brown, cracking into scaly plates with age.
FLOWERING TIME Spring.
OCCURRENCE Cultivated (particularly for timber); native to Japan.
SIMILAR SPECIES European Larch (left) has upright cone scales and bright green leaves.

Sitka Spruce

Picea sitchensis (Pinaceae)

Vigorous and large, this evergreen tree with a conical habit has smooth shoots that are white to pale brown. Its slender, glossy, dark green leaves are flattened, with a pointed tip and two white bands beneath. The clusters of male flowers are red, while the female clusters are green, maturing into pendulous, pale brown cones.

CYLINDRICAL, hanging, and pale brown, the mature cones fall from the tree intact.

cone to 10cm long

leaf to 3cm long

conical habit

HEIGHT 50m. **SPREAD** 15m.
BARK Purple-grey, flaking in large plates.
FLOWERING TIME Late spring.
OCCURRENCE Cultivated (particularly as a forestry tree); native to W. North America.
SIMILAR SPECIES Norway Spruce (p.327), which has 4-sided leaves without white lines beneath.

Norway Spruce

Picea abies (Pinaceae)

A vigorous, upright evergreen, the Norway Spruce grows very large and has many cultivars and varieties. Its slender, four-sided, dark green leaves, with pointed tips, are arranged on stout orange-brown shoots. Flowers of both sexes bloom separately on the same tree. The male flower clusters are upright, reddish at first, becoming yellow when ripe and releasing pollen; the female flower clusters are also upright and red, developing into pendulous green cones that turn brown when ripe.

CYLINDRICAL, *hanging brown cones have scales that are notched at the tips, and fall intact from the tree when ripe.*

conical tip

leaf to 2cm long

cone to 15cm long

female flowers

male flowers

large, upright tree

NOTE

The Norway Spruce is the common spruce of Europe and frequently used as a Christmas tree. Many garden selections are grown, particularly dwarf forms.

HEIGHT *50m.*
SPREAD *15m.*
BARK *Purple, developing scaly plates when mature.*
FLOWERING TIME *Late spring.*
OCCURRENCE *Introduced; widely planted for timber and as an ornamental tree. Native to mainland Europe.*
SIMILAR SPECIES *Sitka Spruce (p.326), which has flattened leaves with white lines beneath.*

Beach Pine

Pinus contorta (Pinaceae)

The evergreen Beach Pine is usually bushy and spreading when small, later becoming conical. The short, twisted, dark green leaves are densely borne in pairs on the shoots. Male flower clusters are yellow; the red female flowers mature in the second autumn into brown cones, up to 5cm long. These often persist, open, for some time on the tree.

EGG-SHAPED, *pale brown cones point backward along the shoot; the cone scales end in a sharp point.*

leaf to 5cm long

male flower clusters

young green cone

broadly conical habit

HEIGHT *25m.*
SPREAD *10m.*
BARK *Red-brown, cracking into squares.*
FLOWERING TIME *Late spring.*
OCCURRENCE *Introduced; frequently planted for timber. Native to W. North America.*
SIMILAR SPECIES *Austrian Pine (right), which has longer leaves and cones.*

Austrian Pine

Pinus nigra (Pinaceae)

A stoutly branched, large, evergreen tree, the Austrian Pine is conical when young, becoming broadly columnar with age. It is often seen with several stems emerging from a trunk that is sometimes short. The rigid, dark green leaves have a sharp pointed tip and are borne in pairs. While male flower clusters are yellow, females are red, maturing to egg-shaped brown cones in the second autumn, that fall intact from the tree when ripe.

DENSE *stands of Austrian Pine can be found in the European mountains.*

cone to 8cm long

broadly columnar habit

leaf to 15cm long

HEIGHT *40m or more.*
SPREAD *15m.*
BARK *Dark grey to nearly black, ridged.*
FLOWERING TIME *Early summer.*
OCCURRENCE *Introduced; commonly planted. Native to C. Europe.*
SIMILAR SPECIES *Scots Pine (below), which has blue-green leaves.*

Scots Pine

Pinus sylvestris (Pinaceae)

An evergreen tree, with branches that grow in whorls, the Scots Pine is conical when young, developing a rounded, spreading head on a tall trunk with age. The stout, needle-like leaves are blue-green to blue-grey. Male flower clusters are cylindrical and yellow, and found at the base of young shoots. Female clusters are upright and red, and are scattered in ones or twos at the tips of the young shoots. They mature in the second autumn to egg-shaped, woody green cones that are brown when ripe.

YELLOW *male flowers nestle among the rigid and twisted blue-green leaves that are borne in pairs on the shoots; sometimes they have a silvery tinge.*

rounded, spreading head

orange to pink bark on upper trunk

NOTE

Many selections, particularly dwarf forms, are cultivated in gardens. Of those that grow into trees, P. sylvestris 'Aurea' has bright yellow leaves in winter, while P. sylvestris 'Fastigiata' is narrowly columnar in habit.

female flower

leaf to 7cm long

male flower

cone to 8cm long

HEIGHT *30m or more.*   **SPREAD** *15m.*
BARK *Purple-grey, orange to pink towards top of trunk; deeply cracked, and fissured, flaking into small plates with age.*
FLOWERING TIME *Early summer.*
OCCURRENCE *Scottish highlands; commonly planted and naturalized elsewhere.*
SIMILAR SPECIES *None – its blue-green foliage and coloured upper bark make it easy to recognize.*

Scots Pine
The largest and longest-lived tree in the Caledonian Forest, the Scots Pine can be straight-trunked with few branches, as here, to spreading. In Britain it is native only in the Scottish Highlands.

Douglas Fir

Pseudotsuga menziesii (Pinaceae)

A fast-growing, large, evergreen tree, the Douglas Fir is conical when young, taking on an irregular and flat-topped shape with age. Its slender, dark green leaves have two white bands beneath and are arranged radially, all around the shoots. Male flower clusters are yellow and found on the underside of the shoots. Clusters of female flowers are green or flushed with pink and borne at the ends of shoots. They later form long and pendulous cones with three-pronged bracts. Green at first, they become red-brown, and fall intact when ripe.

GREY- to purple-brown, the bark is thick, developing deep red-brown cracks with age.

narrow-tipped branches

irregular habit

leaf to 3cm long

male flower cluster

female flower cluster

cone to 10cm long

NOTE
The three-pronged bracts on the cones make identification of Douglas Fir easy. The bracts, or their remains, can usually be found under the tree at any time of year.

HEIGHT *40m or more.* **SPREAD** *15m.*
BARK *Grey-brown to purple-brown, deeply fissured with age.*
FLOWERING TIME *Late spring.*
OCCURRENCE *Cultivated (very commonly for forestry), occasionally naturalized. Native to W. North America, with a variety extending to Mexico.*
SIMILAR SPECIES *None – the three-pronged bracts on the cones make it distinct and easy to recognize.*

Dunkeld Larch

Larix x *marschlinsii* (Pinaceae)

This deciduous tree is a hybrid between the European Larch (p.326) and Japanese Larch (p.326), hence its alternative common name Hybrid Larch. Its slender, soft grey-green to green leaves, which turn yellow in autumn, are arranged singly on long shoots, but are borne in dense whorls on short side shoots. Male flowers are drooping and yellow, while the upright female flowers are cream to pink or red.

UPRIGHT, egg-shaped cones have scales curved slightly outwards.

green to grey-green foliage

cone to 3cm long

conical habit

leaves in dense whorls

female flower cluster

HEIGHT *30m.* **SPREAD** *15m.*
BARK *Red-brown, growing scaly with age.*
FLOWERING TIME *Spring.*
OCCURRENCE *Cultivated; often occurs when seed is collected from Japanese Larch (p.326) growing near European Larch (p.326).*
SIMILAR SPECIES *None – it is intermediate between its parent species.*

London Plane

Platanus x *hispanica* (Platanaceae)

This vigorous, large, deciduous tree with a spreading to broadly columnar head has alternate, maple-like leaves with five toothed lobes. Glossy bright green above, the leaves are paler beneath, with brown hair when young. Tiny flowers are borne in pendulous, rounded clusters – male clusters yellow, females red. Dense, rounded fruit clusters persist on the tree over winter, in groups of up to six.

broadly columnar

GREY, brown, and cream, the bark begins to flake conspicuously in large patches with age.

leaf to 20cm long

HEIGHT *35m.* **SPREAD** *25m.*
BARK *Grey, brown, and cream.*
FLOWERING TIME *Late spring.*
OCCURRENCE *Known only in cultivation; origin uncertain.*
SIMILAR SPECIES *None – this is the most commonly grown Plane, particularly common in cities.*

Eastern Hemlock

Tsuga canadensis (Pinaceae)

The leading shoot at the top of this conical, evergreen tree is distinctly drooping. Arranged flatly on either side of the shoots, the leaves taper slightly from the base and have a blunt tip. On top of the shoot, the upturned dark green leaves point forwards, exposing their blue-green undersides with two white bands. Male flower clusters are yellow, while females are green, maturing to small, light brown cones.

PENDULOUS, egg-shaped cones persist on the tree after shedding their seeds in autumn.

leaf to 1.2cm long

drooping leading shoot

broadly conical habit

cone to 2cm long

HEIGHT *30m.* **SPREAD** *15m.*
BARK *Purple-grey, flaking in scaly patches.*
FLOWERING TIME *Late spring.*
OCCURRENCE *Cultivated (with many dwarf forms); native to E. North America.*
SIMILAR SPECIES *Western Hemlock (T. heterophylla), which lacks the overturned leaves and has parallel-sided leaves.*

Buckthorn

Rhamnus cathartica (Rhamnaceae)

Deciduous, spreading, and often shrubby, this tree has slender, rigid shoots that are frequently spine-tipped. Its opposite, oval, glossy green leaves have a finely toothed margin and turn yellow in autumn. Tiny, fragrant flowers are followed by fleshy, round berries, which ripen from green to black.

CLUSTERS of tiny, four-lobed green flowers are borne in the axils of the leaves.

spreading habit

leaf to 6cm long

dense fruit clusters

HEIGHT *5m.* **SPREAD** *6m.*
BARK *Orange-brown, scaly.*
FLOWERING TIME *Summer.*
OCCURRENCE *Woods, thickets, and hedgerows, often on alkaline soils, but rare in the north and west.*
SIMILAR SPECIES *Alder Buckthorn (p.331), which has untoothed, alternate leaves.*

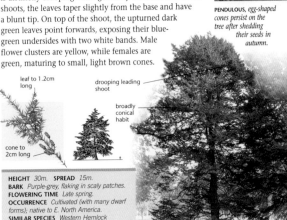

Alder Buckthorn

Rhamnus frangula (Rhamnaceae)

This is a deciduous, spreading or shrubby tree, often with several main stems. The alternate, untoothed leaves are widest towards the end, where there is a short point. They are glossy, dark green above, paler beneath, and turn yellow or red in autumn. The fleshy, rounded fruit are green becoming red and then ripening to black.

TINY *flowers are green tinged with pink and borne in dense clusters in the leaf axils.*

tiny flowers

leaf to 7cm long

fruit to 1cm wide

broadly spreading habit

HEIGHT *5m.* **SPREAD** *6m.*
BARK *Grey and smooth, with vertical fissures.*
FLOWERING TIME *Summer.*
OCCURRENCE *Woods, thickets, and hedgerows, often on wet soil; rare in the north.*
SIMILAR SPECIES *Buckthorn (p.330) has opposite leaves, and fruit that are never red.*

Midland Hawthorn

Crataegus laevigata (Rosaceae)

The alternate leaves of this deciduous, spreading tree are shallowly divided into blunt lobes and are usually broadest above the middle. They are glossy, dark green above and paler beneath. Shoots are smooth and glossy. Rounded to oval, inedible, bright red fruit, with two seeds, follow the white flowers. 'Paul's Scarlet' is a commonly planted hybrid with deep pink, double flowers.

WHITE *flowers, to 2cm wide, have red anthers, and are borne in small clusters.*

spreading habit

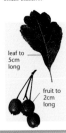

leaf to 5cm long

fruit to 2cm long

HEIGHT *10m.* **SPREAD** *10m.*
BARK *Grey and smooth, cracking with age.*
FLOWERING TIME *Late spring.*
OCCURRENCE *Woods, usually with clay soils, mainly in central and S.E. England.*
SIMILAR SPECIES *Hawthorn (left), which has more deeply lobed leaves and fruit with a single stone.*

Hawthorn

Crataegus monogyna (Rosaceae)

The smooth, thorny shoots of this deciduous species are often somewhat pendulous on old trees. The alternate leaves are oval to diamond-shaped in outline, with a broadly tapered base. They are deeply cut into three or five sharply toothed lobes and are glossy, dark green above and paler beneath. The fragrant white flowers have pink anthers and are borne in dense clusters. These are followed by bright red oval fruit up to 1.2cm wide, each containing a single stone. The Hawthorn is a variable and widely distributed species, often used for hedging.

SHINY, *bright red fruit or hips ripen in attractive clusters at the end of branches from September to October.*

broadly spreading habit

white blossom

flower to 1.5cm wide

leaf to 5cm long

NOTE

The garden selection 'Biflora', known as the Glastonbury Thorn, flowers twice: once in winter or early spring, depending on the weather, and again at the normal time of late spring. It was said to have grown from the staff of Joseph of Arimathea, which he plunged into the ground at Glastonbury when he came to England from the Holy Land.

HEIGHT *10m.* **SPREAD** *10m.*
BARK *Orange-brown; cracked and scaly in old trees.*
FLOWERING TIME *Late spring.*
OCCURRENCE *Woods, scrub, and hedgerows; widely distributed throughout the British Isles.*
SIMILAR SPECIES *Midland Hawthorn (right), which has less deeply cut leaves with three to five more or less blunt lobes and fruit containing two stones.*

Wild Apple

Malus sylvestris (Rosaceae)

This deciduous, spreading tree or shrub sometimes has spiny shoots. The oval to nearly rounded leaves have finely toothed margins and short-pointed tips; they are dark green above, paler below, and smooth or nearly so on both sides when mature. White or pink-tinged flowers, up to 4cm wide, are borne in clusters, followed by small, yellow-green or red-flushed fruit.

WHITE, *often pink-tinged flowers appear in clusters in April and May.*

spreading habit

leaf to 8cm long

fruit to 4cm wide

HEIGHT *10m.* **SPREAD** *10m.*
BARK *Brown, cracked, and fissured with age.*
FLOWERING TIME *Late spring.*
OCCURRENCE *Woods, thickets, and hedgerows almost throughout the British Isles.*
SIMILAR SPECIES *Other species of Apple are grown in gardens and may be locally naturalized.*

Wild Cherry

Prunus avium (Rosaceae)

A deciduous tree, the Wild Cherry or Gean is conical when young becoming broadly columnar to spreading with age. Elliptic to oblong, the alternate, sharply toothed leaves are up to 15cm long and taper to a short point at the tip. They are bronze when young, maturing to matt dark green, and turn yellow or red in autumn.

FIVE-PETALLED *white flowers, 3cm wide, are borne in clusters just before or as the young leaves emerge.*

spreading habit

profusion of white flowers

fruit to 1cm wide

pink-tinged buds

flower to 3cm wide

HEIGHT *25m.* **SPREAD** *15m.*
BARK *Red-brown, smooth, and glossy at first; peeling horizontally in strips.*
FLOWERING TIME *Spring.*
OCCURRENCE *Woods and hedgerows throughout the British Isles.*
SIMILAR SPECIES *It is distinct among native trees due to its large flowers and large size.*

Cherry Plum

Prunus cerasifera (Rosaceae)

FIVE-PETALLED, *white flowers, 2.5cm wide, open singly or in clusters.*

A deciduous, thicket-forming shrub or a small, spreading tree, the Cherry Plum has hairy, sometimes spiny shoots. The alternate, oval, sharply toothed leaves are glossy, dark green and smooth above, downy on the veins beneath. White flowers open along the shoot before the leaves emerge. The rounded, plum-like red fruit, 3cm wide, are sweet and edible. Purple-leaved forms of this tree are commonly grown: *P. cerasifera* 'Nigra' has pink flowers, while *P. cerasifera* 'Pissardii' has white flowers.

broadly spreading habit

leaf to 6cm long

HEIGHT *8m.*
SPREAD *10m.*
BARK *Purple-brown, scaly, flaking with age.*
FLOWERING TIME *Early spring.*
OCCURRENCE *Introduced; widely planted, and sometimes naturalized. Native to S.W. Asia.*
SIMILAR SPECIES *Blackthorn (right), which is more shrubby with blue-black, bitter fruit; it flowers several weeks later.*

NOTE

The purple-leaved forms of the Cherry Plum are popular trees, and are often seen planted in parks, gardens, and streets.

Blackthorn

Prunus spinosa (Rosaceae)

ROUNDED *blue-black berries are covered with a white bloom; inedible and bitter.*

More a deciduous, thicket-forming shrub than a spreading tree, the Blackthorn has spiny shoots. The small, alternate leaves are broadest at the end, with a toothed margin. They are dark green above; hairy beneath when young. Small white flowers, about 1.5cm wide, are usually borne singly and open on the bare shoots before the leaves emerge.

white flowers clothe shoots in spring

leaf to 4cm long

blue-black fruit

HEIGHT *5m.* **SPREAD** *6m.*
BARK *Dark grey-black.*
FLOWERING TIME *Spring.*
OCCURRENCE *Thickets, wood margins, and hedgerows throughout the British Isles.*
SIMILAR SPECIES *Cherry Plum (left), which flowers earlier, and has edible, plum-like fruit.*

Snowy Mespilus

Amelanchier lamarckii (Rosaceae)

ROUNDED *and purple-black, the fruit are up to 1cm wide and very juicy.*

Often shrubby, this deciduous, spreading tree usually has several stems starting from the base. The oval, pointed, alternate leaves have a finely toothed margin. Bronze and covered in silky hairs when young, they mature to dark green and turn red in autumn. The white flowers are borne in clusters opening with the young foliage and have five slender petals.

red autumn foliage

leaf to 8cm long

5-petalled flowers

HEIGHT *12m.* **SPREAD** *15m.*
BARK *Smooth and grey, cracking with age.*
FLOWERING TIME *Spring.*
OCCURRENCE *Introduced; naturalized in Britain; mainly on sandy soils. Native to Europe, but probably of North American origin.*
SIMILAR SPECIES *Can be confused only with rarer Amelanchier species seen in gardens.*

Bird Cherry

Prunus padus (Rosaceae)

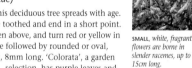

SMALL, *white, fragrant flowers are borne in slender racemes, up to 15cm long.*

Conical when young, this deciduous tree spreads with age. The alternate leaves are toothed and end in a short point. They are matt, dark green above, and turn red or yellow in autumn. The flowers are followed by rounded or oval, bitter, glossy black fruit, 8mm long. 'Colorata', a garden selection, has purple leaves and pink flowers.

spreading habit

leaf to 10cm long

flower to 1cm wide

HEIGHT *15m.* **SPREAD** *15m.*
BARK *Dark grey and smooth, rather unpleasantly scented.*
FLOWERING TIME *Spring.*
OCCURRENCE *Woodlands and river banks in the north; commonly planted elsewhere.*
SIMILAR SPECIES *Cherry Laurel (P. laurocerasus) is shrubby and evergreen.*

Rowan

Sorbus aucuparia (Rosaceae)

HEAVY *clusters of rounded orange-red berries, attractive to birds, often weigh down the branches.*

Spreading with age, this deciduous, conical tree has shoots that end in purple buds covered in grey hairs. Alternate, pinnate leaves have up to 15 sharply toothed, taper-pointed, dark green leaflets, which are blue-green beneath. The small white flowers, each with five petals and conspicuous stamens, open in broad heads and develop into berries, which are poisonous when raw.

broadly conical habit

flowerhead to 15cm wide

leaf to 20cm long

fruit to 8mm wide

HEIGHT *15m.* **SPREAD** *10m.*
BARK *Glossy grey and smooth, becoming ridged with age.*
FLOWERING TIME *Late spring.*
OCCURRENCE *Widely distributed, except on chalk soils; often planted.*
SIMILAR SPECIES *Service Tree (p.333), which has similar leaves but much larger fruits.*

Wild Service Tree

Sorbus torminalis (Rosaceae)

This deciduous tree has a broadly columnar head and glossy brown shoots that are hairy when young. The alternate, maple-like leaves are deeply cut into sharply toothed, triangular lobes. Glossy dark green above, they turn yellow, red, or purple in autumn. Small white flowers, 1.5cm wide, open in flattened heads and are followed by rounded to egg-shaped, russet-brown fruit.

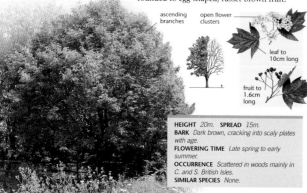

DARK brown, the bark begins to crack into scaly plates as the tree ages.

ascending branches

open flower clusters

leaf to 10cm long

fruit to 1.6cm long

HEIGHT *20m.* **SPREAD** *15m.*
BARK *Dark brown, cracking into scaly plates with age.*
FLOWERING TIME *Late spring to early summer.*
OCCURRENCE *Scattered in woods mainly in C. and S. British Isles.*
SIMILAR SPECIES *None.*

Whitebeam

Sorbus aria (Rosaceae)

A rounded, deciduous tree, the Whitebeam is conical when young. The shoots are covered with white hairs at first but become smooth with age. Arranged alternately, the oval leaves have sharply pointed teeth; they are white with hairs on both sides when young, becoming smooth and glossy, dark green above. The white flowers, up to 1.5cm wide, are followed by rounded, bright red fruit dotted with pale lenticels. *S. aria* 'Lutescens' is a commonly planted form with silvery young foliage. Some cultivated selections such as 'Majestica', have leaves 10–15cm long.

FIVE-PETALLED *flowers, with numerous white stamens, open in flattened clusters, 10cm wide.*

leaf to 12cm long

fruit to 1.5cm wide

broadly columnar habit

HEIGHT *20m.*
SPREAD *20m.*
BARK *Grey and smooth; cracking and shallowly ridged with age.*
FLOWERING TIME *Late spring to early summer.*
OCCURRENCE *In woods and open areas, mainly on chalk in southern Britain; widely planted and often naturalized elsewhere.*
SIMILAR SPECIES *Several other very locally distributed species occur in parts of Britain.*

NOTE

In most areas, this is the commonest whitebeam with unlobed leaves. The attractive foliage and fruit has made this tree popular.

Service Tree

Sorbus domestica (Rosaceae)

The green shoots of this deciduous, broadly columnar to spreading tree end in sticky green buds. The alternate, pinnate yellow-green leaves have up to 21 oblong, toothed leaflets which are smooth above and hairy beneath when young, turning red or purple in autumn. Small white flowers, up to 1.5cm wide, each with five petals, are borne in rounded to conical clusters.

GREEN or flushed with red, the large, apple- or pear-shaped fruit have a gritty texture.

broadly columnar habit

leaf to 22cm long

flower cluster to 10cm wide

fruit to 3cm long

HEIGHT *20m.*
SPREAD *15m.*
BARK *Dark brown, cracking into scales with age.*
FLOWERING TIME *Late spring.*
OCCURRENCE *Probably only native in S. Wales; cultivated elsewhere and sometimes naturalized in a few localities in the south of the British Isles.*
SIMILAR SPECIES *Rowan (p.332), which has smoother bark, and smaller, orange-red fruit that are poisonous when raw.*

NOTE

Mainly confined to the European mainland, a small native population was found in S. Wales in 1983. The relatively large apple- or pear-shaped fruit are sometimes eaten when slightly rotted.

Grey Poplar

Populus x canescens (Salicaceae)

This vigorous, deciduous tree spreads by suckers from the base. Its young shoots are covered in white hairs. The oval to nearly rounded leaves are toothed or only shallowly lobed. They are hairy on both sides when young, becoming smooth and dark green above, and nearly smooth beneath. Most Grey Poplars are male, bearing flowers with red anthers in pendulous catkins. This species is thought to be a hybrid between White Poplar and Aspen (p.336).

PALE grey with dark, diamond-shaped marks, the bark is dark brown and furrowed on older trees.

columnar habit

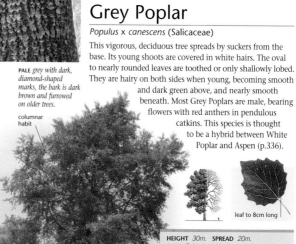

leaf to 8cm long

HEIGHT *30m.* **SPREAD** *20m.*
BARK *Pale grey with diamond-shaped marks*
FLOWERING TIME *Late spring.*
OCCURRENCE *Damp woods in C. and S. Britain; planted and naturalized elsewhere.*
SIMILAR SPECIES *White Poplar (p.336), which has maple-like leaves; Aspen (p.336), which has smooth leaves.*

PLANTS

MILLENNIUM SEED BANK

B ased in the beautiful grounds of Wakehurst Place, West Sussex, the Millennium Seed Bank Project (MSBP) is the world's largest off-site conservation project of wild plants. Working with around 50 countries across five continents, the MSBP collects and stores seed from the most vulnerable plant species. Seeds are stored at Wakehurst and at partner seed banks in the country of origin, offering insurance against the extinction of plant species in the wild. Storage involves drying and freezing, with relatively few species, the acorns pictured being among them, not surviving this process. In Britain, the MSBP has collected seed from at least 90 per cent of seed-plant species, including the same proportion of threatened species. This impressive result is in no small part thanks to the efforts of volunteer collectors, who collected over half of the seeds. One such endangered species is the grass Interrupted Brome (*Bromus interruptus*), last seen in the wild in 1972. It was saved from total extinction by botanist Phillip Smith, who had taken seeds from one of the last wild plants, and grown them on in pots. He passed seed from these plants to the MSBP and in 2004 seeds were sown in the wild, where the plants produced seed in 2005.

White Poplar

Populus alba (Salicaceae)

A deciduous tree, the White Poplar is broadly columnar, spreading with age, and has young shoots that are densely covered in white hair. The alternate leaves have rounded stalks. They have a dense layer of white hair on both surfaces when young, but later become dark green and smooth above. On vigorous shoots, they are maple-like and deeply lobed, the larger lobes toothed, while elsewhere on the tree they have very shallow lobes. Male and female flowers are borne in drooping catkins on separate plants, the males grey with red anthers, the females green. The small green fruit capsules open to release tiny cottony seeds.

DENSE *white hair cover the underside of leaves, which are hairy on both sides when young; they have three to five deep lobes when on vigorous shoots.*

spreading habit

leaf to 10cm long

white, hairy young leaves

NOTE
This tree, also known as Abele, produces many suckers, often at some distance from the parent. These show the lobed, maple-like leaves particularly well.

HEIGHT *30m.* **SPREAD** *20m.*
BARK *Pale grey, dark, and fissured at the base of the tree.*
FLOWERING TIME *Early spring.*
OCCURRENCE *Introduced and commonly planted; native to mainland Europe, N. Africa, and W. Asia.*
SIMILAR SPECIES *Aspen (right), which has unlobed leaves that are smooth beneath when mature, and flattened leaf stalks; Grey Poplar (p.333), which has shallowly lobed leaves.*

Aspen

Populus tremula (Salicaceae)

The deciduous Aspen is conical when young, but spreads with age. Often found on poor soils, this species forms large colonies in woods, spreading by means of suckers produced by the roots. Carried on long, flattened stalks, the rounded to broadly oval leaves are edged with rounded teeth, the largest leaves borne on vigorous shoots. Bronze and hairy when young, the leaves become grey-green above, paler beneath, usually smooth on both sides, and turn yellow in autumn. The flowers are borne in drooping catkins up to 8cm long, males and females on separate trees. The male catkins are grey, while the female catkins are green. Small green fruit open to release tiny seeds that are contained within cottony white hair.

PENDULOUS *grey male catkins, with red anthers, hang from the bare shoots in early spring.*

conical to spreading habit

leaf to 8cm long

rounded leaf

NOTE
The long, slender, flattened leaf stalks make the leaves tremble in the slightest breeze, making a rattling sound distinctive to the Aspen.

HEIGHT *20m.*
SPREAD *15m.*
BARK *Smooth and grey, darker and ridged at the base of old trees.*
FLOWERING TIME *Early spring.*
OCCURRENCE *Moist woods throughout Britain, more common in the north.*
SIMILAR SPECIES *White Poplar (left), which has lobed leaves that are white beneath.*

Black Poplar

Populus nigra (Salicaceae)

The trunk of this fast growing, deciduous tree often develops large burrs. The broadly oval to triangular, finely toothed leaves have a tapered tip, and no hairs at the margin. They are bronze when young becoming glossy dark green. The flowers are in drooping catkins, the males with red anthers, the females green, on separate trees. Subsp. *betulifolia* has hairy young shoots. The selection 'Italica' is narrowly columnar with upright branches.

SMALL *green fruit, borne in catkins, open to release tiny, cottony seeds.*

broadly spreading habit

leaf to 10cm long

HEIGHT *30m.* **SPREAD** *25m.*
BARK *Dark grey and deeply fissured.*
FLOWERING TIME *Early spring.*
OCCURRENCE *The native tree, subsp. betulifolia, is scattered in lowland areas of Britain; subsp. nigra is planted and is native to mainland Europe.*
SIMILAR SPECIES *Hybrid Black Poplar (right).*

Hybrid Black Poplar

Populus x canadensis (Salicaceae)

Several selections of this very vigorous, deciduous tree with a broadly columnar head, such as 'Robusta', are commonly grown. The broadly oval to nearly triangular, alternate leaves are longer on very vigorous shoots. They are often bronzy red and hairy margined when young, becoming glossy, dark green above. Tiny cottony seeds are released by small green fruit capsules.

DROOPING *catkins of male flowers with red anthers, and green female catkins, are borne on separate trees.*

leaf to 10cm long

pale grey bark

broadly columnar habit

HEIGHT *30m.* **SPREAD** *20m.*
BARK *Pale grey and deeply furrowed.*
FLOWERING TIME *Early spring.*
OCCURRENCE *Known only in cultivation; a hybrid between Cottonwood (P. deltoides) and Black Poplar (left).*
SIMILAR SPECIES *Black Poplar (left), which lacks hair on the leaf margins.*

White Willow

Salix alba (Salicaceae)

The common large waterside willow of Europe, White Willow is a vigorous, spreading, deciduous tree, often with drooping shoots. The slender, lance-shaped, finely toothed leaves end in long, tapered points. They are silky and hairy when young, becoming dark green above and blue-green below. The tiny flowers are borne in small catkins as the leaves emerge; the males are yellow, while the females are green and are borne on separate trees. Small green fruit open to release cottony seeds. The Scarlet Willow (*Salix alba* 'Britzensis') has orange-red winter shoots.

LONG, narrow leaves show their blue-green underside with the slightest breeze blowing along the river bank.

spreading habit

drooping branches

leaf to 10cm long

leaves taper to fine point

green female catkin

yellow male catkin

NOTE

The White Willow is pollarded to encourage the growth of young shoots; the wood of Salix alba var. caerulea is highly valued as it is used for making cricket bats.

HEIGHT *25m.* **SPREAD** *20m.*
BARK *Grey-brown, deeply fissured with age.*
FLOWERING TIME *Spring.*
OCCURRENCE *Riversides and other wet places almost throughout Britain; also commonly planted.*
SIMILAR SPECIES *Crack Willow (right), which has fragile shoots and dark green leaves that are smooth below; Common Osier (right), which is smaller with usually untoothed leaves.*

Crack Willow

Salix fragilis (Salicaceae)

The twigs of this deciduous tree snap off easily from its branches giving rise to the common name. Its alternate leaves are silky-hairy when young, soon becoming smooth. The small flowers lack petals and are borne in catkins on separate trees; the males have yellow anthers, while the females are green. Small green fruit open to release fluffy white seeds.

SLENDER, toothed leaves end in a finely tapered point and are dark green above and blue-green below.

broadly spreading habit

leaf to 15cm long

HEIGHT *15m or more.* **SPREAD** *15m.*
BARK *Dark grey and deeply fissured.*
FLOWERING TIME *Spring.*
OCCURRENCE *Riverbanks, meadows, and other wet places; frequently planted and widely distributed except in N. Scotland.*
SIMILAR SPECIES *White Willow (left), which has silky leaves and lacks the fragile shoots.*

Common Osier

Salix viminalis (Salicaceae)

A large vigorous shrub, the Common Osier has long, flexible shoots that are hairy when young. The alternate, narrow, lance-shaped leaves are usually untoothed, dark green above, and silky hairy beneath. Male and female upright catkins are borne on separate plants.

LONG and flexible, the shoots of this species are traditionally used for making baskets.

long shoots

leaf to 25cm long

male catkin with yellow anthers

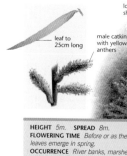

HEIGHT *5m.* **SPREAD** *8m.*
FLOWERING TIME *Before or as the young leaves emerge in spring.*
OCCURRENCE *River banks, marshes, and other wet places throughout most of Britain, commonly planted.*
SIMILAR SPECIES *White Willow (left), which is a large tree with smaller, toothed leaves.*

Goat Willow

Salix caprea (Salicaceae)

This deciduous shrub, sometimes a small tree, is upright when young, later spreading and often branching low down or with several stems, the shoots not ridged beneath the bark. The oval, toothed, alternate leaves are hairy on both sides when young, though the grey-green uppersides becomes smooth in older trees. The flowers are borne in tiny catkins, up to 4cm long, on separate trees. Small green fruit open to release cottony seeds.

FLOWERS are in catkins; the males are silvery with yellow anthers, the females are green.

multiple stems

leaf to 10cm long

HEIGHT *10m.* **SPREAD** *8m.*
BARK *Grey and smooth; fissured on old trees.*
FLOWERING TIME *Early spring.*
OCCURRENCE *Woods and hedgerows; widely distributed and common.*
SIMILAR SPECIES *None, the size of the broad leaves, hairy beneath, make it distinct.*

Weeping Willow

Salix x sepulcralis 'Chrysocoma' (Salicaceae)

This deciduous, spreading tree has a rounded crown and long, pendulous yellow shoots. The alternate, finely toothed leaves end in tapered points. The flowers are borne in catkins and are mostly male with yellow anthers. The fruit is a small green capsule.

PALE grey-brown, the bark is marked with shallow fissures as the tree ages.

weeping habit

leaf to 12cm long

catkin to 7.5cm long

HEIGHT *20m.*
SPREAD *25m.*
BARK *Pale grey-brown and fissured.*
FLOWERING TIME *Spring.*
OCCURRENCE *Known only in cultivation.*
SIMILAR SPECIES *The species is a hybrid of White Willow (left) and S. babylonica, which was at one time grown in Europe.*

PLANTS

Bay Willow

Salix pentandra (Salicaceae)

The alternate, elliptic to narrowly ovate, slightly aromatic dark green leaves of this deciduous, spreading tree distinguish it from other species. They are paler beneath, finely toothed, and end in a short point. The flowers are borne in cylindrical catkins after the leaves emerge, the males dense and showy, with bright yellow anthers, the females green, on separate plants. Cottony seeds emerge from the small green fruit capsules.

CYLINDRICAL, *showy, bright yellow male catkins appear after the leaves.*

leaf to 12cm long

slender female catkin

spreading habit

HEIGHT *15m.*
SPREAD *15m.*
BARK *Grey-brown, with shallow fissures.*
FLOWERING TIME *Early summer.*
OCCURRENCE *Wet places mainly in the north; planted and often naturalized elsewhere.*
SIMILAR SPECIES *None – the leaves of this tree are distinctive.*

Tree of Heaven

Ailanthus altissima (Simaroubaceae)

This fast-growing, large, deciduous tree has a broadly columnar crown. The alternate, pinnate, dark green leaves have 15 or more pairs of leaflets. Flowers are small, with five or six yellow-green petals and are borne in large panicles at the end of the shoots. Male and female flowers usually grow on separate trees, and the females are followed by winged fruit, up to 4cm long, similar to those of ash (*Fraxinus*). The fruit are green at first, becoming yellow-brown flushed with red.

PINNATE, *dark green leaves have many pairs of leaflets, which are tapered at the tip and untoothed except for 1–3 notches near the base.*

leaf to 60cm or longer

notch at leaflet base

columnar crown

dark green pinnate leaves

HEIGHT *20m or more.* **SPREAD** *15m.*
BARK *Grey-brown with fine streaks, becoming darker and rougher with age.*
FLOWERING TIME *Late summer.*
OCCURRENCE *Introduced; naturalized mainly in the south of the British Isles, often cultivated; native to China.*
SIMILAR SPECIES *Ash (Fraxinus excelsior), which has opposite leaves without notches.*

NOTE

This vigorous tree thrives in warm cities where it is much planted, and often naturalized. In cooler areas, it may not flower or fruit well.

Yew

Taxus baccata (Taxaceae)

A broadly conical, evergreen tree, the Yew is often many-trunked. Linear and pointed at the tip, the leaves are dark green above, with two pale bands below, mainly spread in two rows on either side of the shoots. Male flowers grow beneath the shoots, while the tiny green female flowers are borne singly at the ends of the shoots on separate plants. The fruit is a single seed, held in a fleshy, usually red aril. It is open at the top, exposing the green seed, ripening the first autumn. All parts (except the arils) are poisonous. 'Fastigiata', or Irish Yew, is a selection with upright branches and leaves growing all around the shoots.

ROUNDED, *pale yellow male flower clusters, about 3–4mm wide, are found in the leaf axils beneath the shoots.*

conical habit

upright branches

yellow aril

leaf to 3cm long

fleshy red aril with seed

'LUTEA'

NOTE

The Yew is often seen in gardens as hedges or topiary. Many selections have been made, including several with variegated foliage. 'Lutea' is an unusual form with yellow fruit.

HEIGHT *20m.*
SPREAD *10m.*
BARK *Purple-brown, smooth, and flaking.*
FLOWERING TIME *Early spring.*
OCCURRENCE *In woods and thickets, mainly on chalk or limestone; also commonly cultivated.*
SIMILAR SPECIES *None – it is not easily confused with other species, especially when bearing fruit.*

Broad-leaved Lime

Tilia platyphyllos (Tiliaceae)

One of the parents of Common Lime (p.339), this large, deciduous tree, with a broadly columnar head, may sometimes have many suckers at the base. Its young shoots are usually covered with soft white hair. The alternate leaves are dark green above, paler beneath, and usually softly hairy on both sides. The fragrant flowers and fruit are similar to those of Small-leaved Lime (p.339).

ROUNDED *to broadly oval, the leaves are sharply toothed and end in a short point.*

leaf to 12cm long

leaves turn yellow in autumn

flower to 2cm wide

HEIGHT *30m.* **SPREAD** *20m.*
BARK *Grey, shallowly fissured with age.*
FLOWERING TIME *Summer.*
OCCURRENCE *In woods on alkaline soils.*
SIMILAR SPECIES *Common Lime (p.339), and Small-leaved Lime (p.339), both of which have leaves with smoother undersides, except for the tufts of hair in the axils.*

Common Lime

Tilia x europaea (Tiliaceae)

A hybrid between Small-leaved Lime (below) and Broad-leaved Lime (p.338), this vigorous and large deciduous tree is broadly columnar in habit, and is often seen with numerous suckers at the base. The rounded to broadly oval, alternate leaves are sharply toothed and end in a short point. They are dark green above, green and smooth beneath except for tufts of hairs in the axils of the veins.

EGG-SHAPED *grey-green fruit is 1.2cm long, and similar to those of the Small-leaved Lime.*

broadly columnar habit

leaf to 10cm long

flower to 2cm wide

HEIGHT *40m.* **SPREAD** *20m.*
BARK *Grey-brown, shallow fissures with age.*
FLOWERING TIME *Early spring.*
OCCURRENCE *Introduced; widely planted, and sometimes naturalized. Native to Europe.*
SIMILAR SPECIES *Small-leaved Lime (below), has blue-green leaf undersides; Broad-leaved Lime (p.338) has hairy leaf undersides.*

Small-leaved Lime

Tilia cordata (Tiliaceae)

FRAGRANT *pale yellow flowers, 2cm wide, open in small, hanging clusters at the base of which are single, conspicuous yellow-green bracts.*

The Small-leaved Lime is a large, deciduous tree with a broadly columnar head. The rounded, alternate leaves have a sharply toothed margin, are heart-shaped at the base, and end in a short, abruptly tapered point. They are dark green above and blue-green beneath, turning yellow in autumn. The leaves are smooth below with conspicuous tufts of brown hairs in the leaf axils. The rounded, grey-green fruit are about 1.2cm long. Unlike other limes, this tree is usually without or with few suckers at the base.

broadly columnar habit

leaf to 8cm long

HEIGHT *30m.* **SPREAD** *20m.*
BARK *Smooth and grey; furrowed with age.*
FLOWERING TIME *Summer.*
OCCURRENCE *In woods on alkaline soils and limestone cliffs in England and Wales; commonly planted elsewhere.*
SIMILAR SPECIES *Common Lime (above), which has leaves with green undersides; Broad-leaved Lime (p.338), which has leaves covered with soft hairs beneath.*

NOTE
This species is one of the parents of the Common Lime (above). Several selections of narrow or conical habit are grown in gardens.

Wych Elm

Ulmus glabra (Ulmaceae)

SMALL *flowers with red anthers open on the bare shoots in late winter before the leaves emerge.*

Conical when young, this large, deciduous tree develops a rounded head with age and has rough young shoots. The alternate, oval leaves have unequal halves, with sharp teeth that are larger towards the tip. They are dark green and very rough above, with a short stalk. The flowers are followed by winged green fruit. Dutch Elm (*U. x hollandica*) is a hybrid between Wych Elm and Field Elm (below).

rounded head

fruit to 2cm long

leaf to 15cm long

HEIGHT *30m.*
SPREAD *25m.*
BARK *Grey and smooth, becoming ridged in old trees.*
FLOWERING TIME *Late winter.*
OCCURRENCE *Woods and hedgerows, particularly in the north.*
SIMILAR SPECIES *None.*

Field Elm

Ulmus minor (Ulmaceae)

Like other elms, the alternate, oval leaves of the Field Elm are very unequal at the base and have sharply toothed margins. They are glossy green and smooth above, paler beneath with hairs only on the veins. The tree is deciduous, with a columnar head and has smooth young shoots. The fruit, to 1.5cm long, are green-winged with the seed positioned above the middle.

TINY *flower clusters with red anthers; open on bare shoots.*

columnar habit

unequal leaf base

leaf to 12cm long

HEIGHT *30m.* **SPREAD** *20m.*
BARK *Pale grey and smooth when young, becoming fissured with age.*
FLOWERING TIME *Late winter.*
OCCURRENCE *Hedgerows and thickets mainly in the south; often reduced to suckers.*
SIMILAR SPECIES *English Elm (below), which has hairs covering the leaf underside.*

English Elm

Ulmus procera (Ulmaceae)

This deciduous tree with a broadly columnar head usually has suckers at the base, and shoots which can become corky when a few years old. The broadly oval to rounded alternate leaves are sharply toothed with a very unequal base. They are dark green and rough to the touch above and hairy beneath. Winged, green fruit, 1.5cm long, have seeds positioned above the middle.

DENSE *clusters of tiny flowers with red anthers open on the bare shoots.*

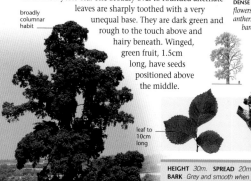

broadly columnar habit

flowers open on bare shoots

leaf to 10cm long

HEIGHT *30m.* **SPREAD** *20m.*
BARK *Grey and smooth when young, becoming furrowed with age.*
FLOWERING TIME *Late winter.*
OCCURRENCE *Woods and hedgerows mainly in the south; often reduced to suckers.*
SIMILAR SPECIES *Field Elm (above), which has leaves smooth on the upper side.*

PLANTS

WILD FLOWERS

Britain is in an enviable position for the study of wild flowers. It is the most botanically studied place on Earth with a wealth of information available, as well as many local and national societies to offer help and advice. Britain's mild climate and extremely varied geology have contributed to a huge diversity of habitats available for plants to colonize. Furthermore, its 1,500 native plant species have been augmented over the centuries with at least the same number again of introductions from further afield, including some deliberately brought over by the Romans, some that have been imported accidentally in ships' cargoes, and those that have simply "escaped" from gardens. Britain's favourite flower, however, remains the native Bluebell.

WETLAND

Wetlands are rich habitats, providing excellent growing conditions for a wide variety of specially adapted plants. Types of wetland found in Britain include ditches, marshes, fens, and bogs.

COAST

Coasts provide a harsh environment, where salt, wind, and lack of fresh water create conditions suitable only for specialized plants that can grow in places such as cliffs, shingle beaches, and dunes.

GRASSLAND

The comparatively poor soil of grasslands support the greatest variety of wild flowers because strongly competitive plant species are unable to dominate. They include hay meadows and chalk downs.

HEATHLAND

Heathlands are largely man-made habitats dominated by low, shrubby plants such as heathers and gorse growing on acidic soils. Plant diversity is low but specialization to the acid conditions is high.

WOODLAND

Woodlands have fertile soils, but light levels are very low for most of the growing season, so many plants flower in the spring before the tree canopy has closed. Some species grow around the margins instead.

WASTE GROUND

Waste grounds have a rich but recently disturbed soil, and so provide ideal conditions for pioneer plant species. They are also the most likely place to find alien species or garden escapees.

Anatomy

Flowering plants have evolved in different ways to cope with a wide variety of local conditions, adopting different lifestyles and developing different physical characteristics in order to compete for resources. Some plants, for example, are annuals, others perennials or biennials; most get their energy from photosynthesis, but some parasitize other plants or adopt a carnivorous lifestyle; some use tendrils to climb up towards the light, others develop tall stems to rise above surrounding vegetation. Each plant part has a specific function. For the vast majority, the leaves are the food factories that enable the plant to store energy; the roots provide anchorage and absorb water and essential minerals; and the flowers are the plant's reproductive parts. Using the correct terms will add precision to your descriptions and help identification.

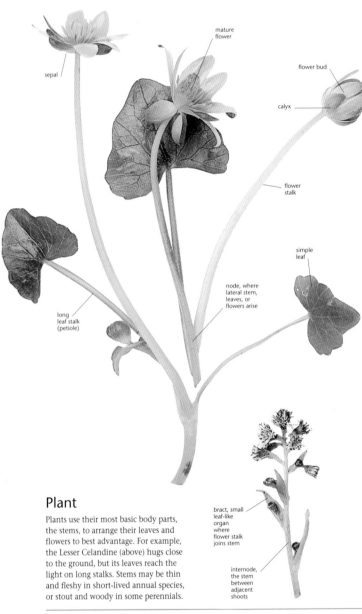

sepal

mature flower

flower bud

calyx

flower stalk

simple leaf

node, where lateral stem, leaves, or flowers arise

long leaf stalk (petiole)

Plant

Plants use their most basic body parts, the stems, to arrange their leaves and flowers to best advantage. For example, the Lesser Celandine (above) hugs close to the ground, but its leaves reach the light on long stalks. Stems may be thin and fleshy in short-lived annual species, or stout and woody in some perennials.

bract, small leaf-like organ where flower stalk joins stem

internode, the stem between adjacent shoots

Leaf

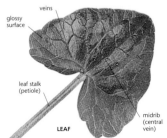

veins

glossy surface

leaf stalk (petiole)

midrib (central vein)

LEAF

Green chlorophyll present in the leaves harnesses the sun's energy to manufacture sugars and sustain growth. Leaf shape and stem arrangement evolve to maximize available light, and reduce water loss. For example, lower leaves often have a long stalk, while leaves higher up the plant may be smaller and stalkless, so as not to shade those below.

Flower

All parts of the flower work together to promote fertilization. The female ovary, found at the base of the style and stigma, is fertilized by the pollen, which is produced by the male anthers. Insects pick up pollen and distribute it to the stigmas of other flowers. The sepals, collectively known as the calyx, and petals surround and protect the reproductive parts. Flowerheads are made up of small flowers called florets.

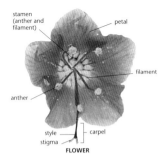

stamen (anther and filament)

petal

filament

anther

style

stigma

carpel

FLOWER

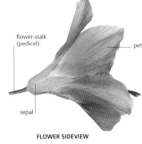

flower-stalk (pedicel)

petal

sepal

FLOWER SIDEVIEW

ray floret

disc floret

FLOWERHEAD

Fruit and Seed

Once the ovary has been fertilized, a fruit forms around one or many of the developing seeds. The purpose of the fruit covering is to protect the seed as it develops, and it also often plays a role in its effective dispersal. For instance, an achene may have feathered hairs to aid wind dispersal, pods and capsules split open when the seeds are ripe, and fleshy fruits such as berries attract animals to eat them as a dispersal strategy.

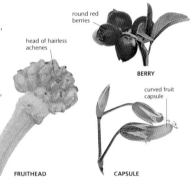

round red berries

head of hairless achenes

BERRY

curved fruit capsule

FRUITHEAD

CAPSULE

Identification

Occasionally, the flower form or the leaf type alone may be enough to pinpoint a species but, generally, this kind of identification comes with the experience of observing the plant many times in the field. As a beginner, it is important to note all features, including habitat or flowering season, before finally deciding upon a precise identification.

Flowers

Flowers are an obvious plant feature, and their colour can assist identification, but be aware of those species that exist in several colour forms. Also note how the individual flowers are clustered together and where, on the plant, they are borne, as well as the number and form of the petals and sepals.

FLOWER ARRANGEMENT

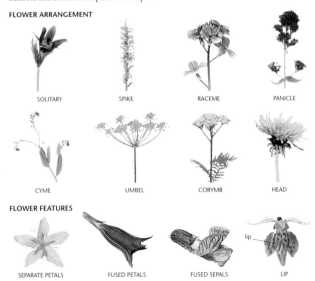

SOLITARY

SPIKE

RACEME

PANICLE

CYME

UMBEL

CORYMB

HEAD

FLOWER FEATURES

SEPARATE PETALS

FUSED PETALS

FUSED SEPALS

lip

LIP

Leaves

Assess the colour, texture, and shape of the leaves, how they are divided, whether they have toothed margins, and how they are arranged on the stem. Remember that lower leaves may differ from those above.

LEAF SHAPES

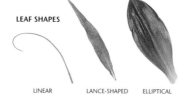

LINEAR   LANCE-SHAPED   ELLIPTICAL

OBLONG   OVAL   SPOON-SHAPED   KIDNEY-SHAPED

HEART-SHAPED   ARROW-SHAPED   TRIFOLIATE   DIGITATE

pinnate

leaflet

tendril

PALMATE   PINNATE   PINNATELY LOBED   PINNATE WITH TENDRIL

BIPINNATE   3- TO 4-PINNATE   FINELY TOOTHED   COARSELY TOOTHED

LEAF ARRANGEMENT

ALTERNATE   OPPOSITE   WHORLS

Fruit

Fruit occur in a huge variety of forms. Closely-related species often develop fruit of a similar type, thus the slight differences between them may be key identification characters. For example, Rape and Charlock (p.362), appear rather similar, but for the longer length of the siliqua growing on the Rape plant. Fruits may also be a useful diagnostic feature if the plant is discovered after the flowers have faded and disappeared.

NUTLETS   POINTED ACHENES   FEATHERY ACHENES   HOOKED ACHENES

ACHENES IN CLOCK   MERICAP   POD   SILIQUA

SILICULA   FOLLICLE   CAPSULE   BERRIES

Seasons

Even though the green parts of the plant are visible for a much longer period than the flowers, the time of flowering can still provide major clues to a species' identity. In general, plants will flower earlier in warm, sheltered locations, and at more southerly latitudes.

SIMILAR FLOWERS
Cat's-ear (left) flowers earlier than Autumn Hawkbit (right), but their seasons can overlap.

Habitat

Habitat categories can be defined by: geography, such as northerly or southerly latitudes; land-forms, such as mountains or the coast; vegetation, such as grassland or woodland; and human management, such as grazed and farmed land. Plant species have adapted to specific habitats, thus the habitats themselves are identifying features. However, watch out for plants on the margins of different habitats; also, some of the most successful species, such as Bramble (*Rubus fruticosus*), exploit several different habitats.

COASTAL
Sea Holly occurs on coastal sand dunes and shingle. Other coastal habitats include salt marshes and cliffs.

WETLANDS
White Water-lily prefers open water; other wetlands include marshes, fens, bogs, and ditches.

UPLAND
Yellow Saxifrage grows in damp, rocky places, such as along mountain streams and cliffs.

GRASSLAND
Red Clover likes meadows and pastures maintained by regular mowing and grazing.

HEATHS
Heather likes the grazed, burned, or cleared habitat of heaths on acid soils.

WOODLAND
Wood Anemone grows in the shady areas of long-established woods with rich soils.

WASTE GROUND
Coltsfoot colonizes bare soils of disturbed ground. It also grows on arable land.

Soil

Soil types are crucial in determining which plant species can grow where. Basic – lime-rich or chalky – soils generally support a greater diversity of species than other soils: their alkaline chemistry provides nutrients more readily for more species.

WELL-DRAINED
Hare's-foot Clover is one of the plant species that has adapted to dry, sandy soils with poor water-retention.

POORLY DRAINED
Marsh Cinquefoil is able to tolerate the waterlogged, airless soils of marshes and flooded grassland.

ACID
Sundew supplements the low-nutrient levels of acid soil conditions by growing leaves adapted to digest insects.

NEUTRAL
Snake's-head Fritillary prefers neutral pH soil conditions that are neither too acidic nor too alkaline.

BASIC
Wild Marjoram is one of the many flowers that grow abundantly on calcium-rich chalk or limestone soils.

SCALE MEASUREMENTS
Two small scale drawings are placed next to each other in every entry as a rough indication of plant size. The drawing of the hand represents a height of 18cm. The plant illustration is an accurate drawing of the species featured in the entry. The scale represents average height.

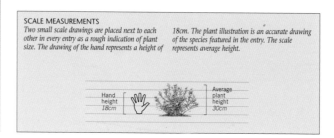

Hand height 18cm   Average plant height 30cm

Bog Myrtle

Myrica gale (Myricaceae)

A small shrub of wet, generally acidic places, the Bog Myrtle spreads to form large thickets by suckering. Its most distinguishing feature is the powerful, pleasantly balsamic scent that comes from the crushed leaves. These make an excellent moth-repellent to protect clothes, and are used to make tea, though this should be avoided by pregnant women as this plant contains a substance that induces abortion.

FORMS *colonies on bogs, wet heaths, moorland, and light woodland on damp, acid sites.*

leaf toothed at tip

female catkin on stemless branch

fruits clustered together

male catkin

PERENNIAL

PLANT HEIGHT *Up to 2m though usually much less.*
FLOWER SIZE *Catkins up to 10mm long.*
FLOWERING TIME *April–May.*
LEAVES *Elliptical, toothed at the apex, aromatic.*
FRUIT *Dry, flattened nut.*
SIMILAR SPECIES *None.*

Hop

Humulus lupulus (Cannabaceae)

The deeply lobed leaves of the Hop are noticeable round the year as stems scramble on twisting stems over bushes and hedges. Male flowers form loose panicles; female flowers, borne on separate plants, form leafy, cone-like catkins that develop into the fruit used to flavour beer.

SCRAMBLES *over or through hedgerows, bushes, and woodland trees, on walls, and up telegraph poles.*

drooping flower panicles

rough, toothed leaf

green male flowers

PERENNIAL

twining stems

cone-like fruit

PLANT HEIGHT *Up to 6m.*
FLOWER SIZE *Male 4–5mm long.*
FLOWERING TIME *July–September.*
LEAVES *Opposite, divided into 3–5 lobes.*
FRUIT *Cone, 2.5–3cm long, with overlapping bracts; pale brown when ripe.*
SIMILAR SPECIES *White Bryony (p.382), which has red berries.*

Mistletoe

Viscum album (Loranthaceae)

This evergreen plant, long associated with Christmas, is easily spotted in winter, as its almost spherical form is clearly visible in the bare branches of trees. It is semi-parasitic on its host tree. The small green flowers are less noticeable than the round white berries, whose seeds are distributed by birds.

FORMS *a spherical mass on the branches of deciduous trees, notably poplars, limes, and apples.*

PERENNIAL

forked branches

yellowish green leaves

paired leaves

shiny white berries

PLANT HEIGHT *Up to 2m wide.*
FLOWER SIZE *Inconspicuous.*
FLOWERING TIME *February–April.*
LEAVES *Opposite and paired, resembling rabbits' ears, leathery, with smooth margins.*
FRUIT *Berries, 6–10mm wide, borne at the fork of stems.*
SIMILAR SPECIES *None.*

Common Nettle

Urtica dioica (Urticaceae)

Also known as Stinging Nettle, this plant is well known to all walkers in the countryside, for the leaves and stems are clothed in stiff, needle-like, hollow hairs which break at the slightest touch, releasing an intensely irritating fluid. There are also many non-stinging hairs, the number varying from plant to plant. The tiny flowers are green, sometimes with a reddish tinge, and have yellow stamens. Males and females are on separate plants; male flowers are borne on long, pendent branches, while the female flowers are in tighter clusters. The plant spreads by rhizomes to form large patches, which may persist for many years.

FORMS *colonies on cultivated and waste ground, hedgerows, roadsides, and scrub; on rich, disturbed soil, especially close to manure heaps.*

male flowers in long spikes

coarsely toothed leaves

PERENNIAL

female flower cluster

stiff, erect stem

NOTE

Abundant in chlorophyll, the leaves of the Common Nettle were collected in vast quantities for dyeing camouflage nets during the Second World War; the fibrous stems may be used to make textiles.

PLANT HEIGHT *50–150cm.*
FLOWER SIZE *1–2mm wide.*
FLOWERING TIME *May–September.*
LEAVES *Opposite, heart-shaped, toothed, strongly veined, and hairy.*
FRUIT *Small, rounded achene.*
SIMILAR SPECIES *Small Nettle (U. urens), which is an annual, smaller, and has a less potent sting.*

Japanese Knotweed

Fallopia japonica (Polygonaceae)

Introduced into European gardens in the 19th century, this weed has become widely naturalized and is now a serious pest in some areas. It is easily recognized by its robust and upright habit, broad, triangular leaves on either side of the zig-zag stem, and short spikes of creamy white flowers at the leaf bases.

INVADES *wasteland, roadsides, river banks, and railway embankments.*

pointed tip

short flower spikes

PERENNIAL

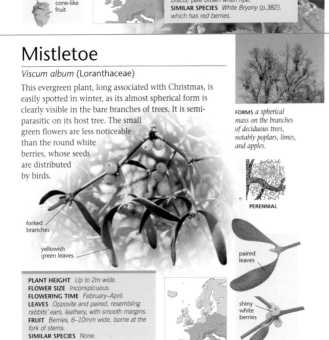

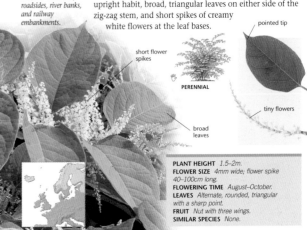

tiny flowers

broad leaves

PLANT HEIGHT *1.5–2m.*
FLOWER SIZE *4mm wide; flower spike 40–100cm long.*
FLOWERING TIME *August–October.*
LEAVES *Alternate, rounded, triangular with a sharp point.*
FRUIT *Nut with three wings.*
SIMILAR SPECIES *None.*

Sheep's Sorrel

Rumex acetosella (Polygonaceae)

The loosely branched flowering spikes of this plant are of varying height and have many whorls of tiny greenish or reddish wind-pollinated flowers. Although male and female flowers are on separate plants, they look identical. Each oblong, stalked leaf has two lobes at the base which point forwards, so the leaf looks like an arrowhead. The leaves have a sharp, acid taste.

GROWS *abundantly in dry meadows, grassy pastures, bare places and heaths, usually on sandy, acid soil.*

arrow-shaped leaf

forward-pointing lobe

reddish flowers

tiny flowers in branched spikes

slender stems

PERENNIAL

PLANT HEIGHT *5–30cm.*
FLOWER SIZE *2mm wide.*
FLOWERING TIME *May–August.*
LEAVES *Basal, alternate, and arrow-shaped.*
FRUIT *Triangular achene, 1.5mm long.*
SIMILAR SPECIES *Common Sorrel (R. acetosa), which is larger with bigger leaves, often turning red in summer.*

Bistort

Persicaria bistorta (Polygonaceae)

One of the most attractive members of the dock family, this plant is recognizable by its dense, terminal clusters of pink flowers on long, slender stems, often seen en masse. Each individual flower has five pink petals and eight protruding stamens.

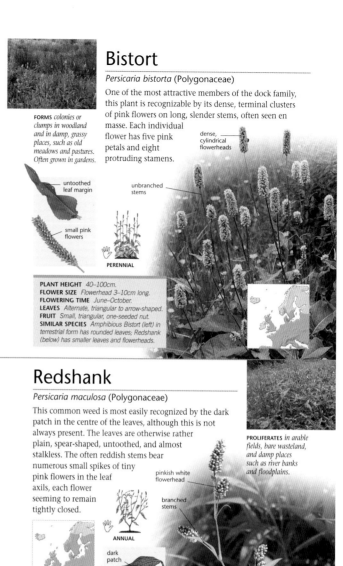

FORMS *colonies or clumps in woodland and in damp, grassy places, such as old meadows and pastures. Often grown in gardens.*

dense, cylindrical flowerheads

untoothed leaf margin

unbranched stems

small pink flowers

PERENNIAL

PLANT HEIGHT *40–100cm.*
FLOWER SIZE *Flowerhead 3–10cm long.*
FLOWERING TIME *June–October.*
LEAVES *Alternate, triangular to arrow-shaped.*
FRUIT *Small, triangular, one-seeded nut.*
SIMILAR SPECIES *Amphibious Bistort (left) in terrestrial form has rounded leaves; Redshank (below) has smaller leaves and flowerheads.*

Curled Dock

Rumex crispus (Polygonaceae)

This common species may be identified by its leaves. They are long-stalked and rather narrow, with distinctly wavy or crimped edges and strong midribs. The three-parted greenish flowers are arranged in dense whorls along the branched upper stems. The fruit is a rounded achene with three swollen wings or valves, without lobes or teeth.

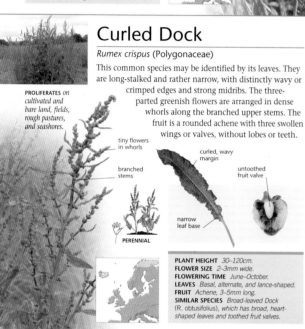

PROLIFERATES *on cultivated and bare land, fields, rough pastures, and seashores.*

tiny flowers in whorls

branched stems

curled, wavy margin

untoothed fruit valve

narrow leaf base

PERENNIAL

PLANT HEIGHT *30–120cm.*
FLOWER SIZE *2–3mm wide.*
FLOWERING TIME *June–October.*
LEAVES *Basal, alternate, and lance-shaped.*
FRUIT *Achene, 3–5mm long.*
SIMILAR SPECIES *Broad-leaved Dock (R. obtusifolius), which has broad, heart-shaped leaves and toothed fruit valves.*

Redshank

Persicaria maculosa (Polygonaceae)

This common weed is most easily recognized by the dark patch in the centre of the leaves, although this is not always present. The leaves are otherwise rather plain, spear-shaped, untoothed, and almost stalkless. The often reddish stems bear numerous small spikes of tiny pink flowers in the leaf axils, each flower seeming to remain tightly closed.

PROLIFERATES *in arable fields, bare wasteland, and damp places such as river banks and floodplains.*

pinkish white flowerhead

branched stems

ANNUAL

dark patch

PLANT HEIGHT *30–80cm.*
FLOWER SIZE *Flowerhead 2–4cm long.*
FLOWERING TIME *June–October.*
LEAVES *Alternate, spear-shaped.*
FRUIT *Shiny black nut, 2–3mm wide.*
SIMILAR SPECIES *Bistort (above); Pale Persicaria (P. lapathifolia), which has unblotched leaves.*

Amphibious Bistort

Persicaria amphibium (Polygonaceae)

This plant may be found growing in mud alongside bodies of water, but is more usually aquatic with its elliptical, pointed leaves floating on the surface of water, and dense spikes of bright pink flowers held upright on short stems just above it. The terrestrial form has hairy leaves that are more rounded at the base.

FOUND *in slow-moving water, such as lakes, ditches, dykes, and ponds, and along water edges.*

PERENNIAL

blunt leaf base

flowers in terminal spike

leaves float on surface

pointed tip

PLANT HEIGHT *Water surface, or up to 75cm on land.*
FLOWER SIZE *Flowerhead 2–6cm long.*
FLOWERING TIME *June–September.*
LEAVES *Alternate, lance-shaped.*
FRUIT *Small nut, but rarely formed.*
SIMILAR SPECIES *Bistort (right), which has thicker flowerheads; Redshank (right).*

Water Pepper

Persicaria hydropiper (Polygonaceae)

This plant forms extensive patches of upright stems bearing spear-shaped leaves, often with slightly wavy edges. At the base of each leaf is a small, fringed brown sheath (ochrea). The tiny, pink or greenish white flowers are arranged close to the stem in long, drooping spikes.

THRIVES *in damp meadows, pastures, and marshes; also in shallow water and semi-shaded places.*

narrow, stalkless leaves

pointed leaf

flowers in slender spikes

papery sheath

branched stems

ANNUAL

PLANT HEIGHT *30–75cm.*
FLOWER SIZE *3–4mm wide.*
FLOWERING TIME *June–September.*
LEAVES *Alternate, lance-shaped, and untoothed, with a very hot, peppery taste.*
FRUIT *Small brown nutlet.*
SIMILAR SPECIES *Redshank (above), which has slightly wider, blotched leaves.*

Sea Beet

Beta vulgaris (Chenopodiaceae)

There is little in the appearance of this plant to show that it is the forerunner to the modern beetroot, except that the glossy, fleshy leaves and stems are often red-tinged. It has a very prostrate habit, with long, trailing, flowering stems. The tiny greenish flowers are borne in clusters of three on leafy spikes.

slender flower spike

untoothed margin

flowers in small clusters

long leaf stalk

SPRAWLS *over shingle beaches, margins of salt marshes, old sea walls, and grassy embankments. Often close to the tide line.*

ANNUAL/PERENNIAL

long flower stems

PLANT HEIGHT *20–100cm.*
FLOWER SIZE *2–4mm wide.*
FLOWERING TIME *June–September.*
LEAVES *Alternate, fleshy, untoothed, often red-tinged.*
FRUIT *Corky, swollen segments.*
SIMILAR SPECIES *Fat Hen (below), which has diamond-shaped lower leaves.*

Glasswort

Salicornia europaea (Chenopodiaceae)

This plant is a familiar sight in estuaries, appearing as huge blue-green to red drifts of succulent, upward-pointing fingers protruding from the mud at low tide. The whole plant is edible, although it can be rather woody when mature. The stems are jointed, and the leaves reduced to scales fused to the stem. The flowers are insignificantly tiny, with two barely visible stamens, on fleshy, branched spikes.

PROLIFERATES *in drifts on estuaries, coastal mudflats, and salt marshes.*

scale-like leaves fused to stem

ascending branches

often red-tinged

ANNUAL

PLANT HEIGHT *10–30cm.*
FLOWER SIZE *Spike 1–5cm long.*
FLOWERING TIME *August–September.*
LEAVES *Triangular scales fused to stem.*
FRUIT *Tiny achene.*
SIMILAR SPECIES *Annual Seablite (Suaeda maritima), which has narrow grey-green leaves, and often grows alongside Glasswort.*

Fat Hen

Chenopodium album (Chenopodiaceae)

The lower leaves of this common weed of arable fields are diamond-shaped, lobed, and toothed, while the smaller, lance-shaped upper leaves are usually unlobed and untoothed. The tiny greenish grey flowers are clustered in spikes along the upper branches. Once cultivated as a food source, the plant is now regarded as a pest on farms.

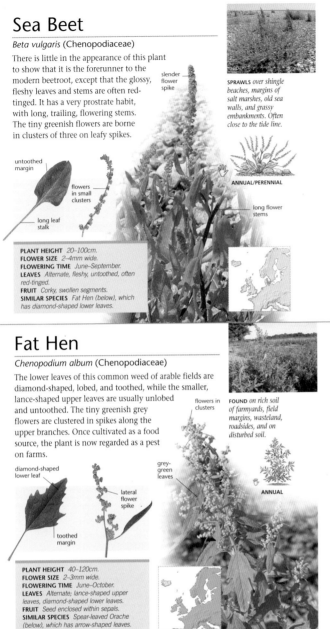

FOUND *on rich soil of farmyards, field margins, wasteland, roadsides, and on disturbed soil.*

ANNUAL

flowers in clusters

grey-green leaves

diamond-shaped lower leaf

lateral flower spike

toothed margin

PLANT HEIGHT *40–120cm.*
FLOWER SIZE *2–3mm wide.*
FLOWERING TIME *June–October.*
LEAVES *Alternate; lance-shaped upper leaves, diamond-shaped lower leaves.*
FRUIT *Seed enclosed within sepals.*
SIMILAR SPECIES *Spear-leaved Orache (below), which has arrow-shaped leaves.*

Prickly Saltwort

Salsola kali (Chenopodiaceae)

This plant is recognizable by the sharp spine on the tip of each leaf, unusual for a plant that is out of reach of grazing animals. The plant is succulent, much branched, and bluish green. The tiny flowers, hidden at the base of the fleshy leaves, may have a pinkish tinge.

OCCURS *on sandy coastal beaches, or in shingle, often close to the tide line.*

ANNUAL

flowers at base of upper leaves

stiff, sharp spines

narrow leaves

5-parted flower

ridged stems

PLANT HEIGHT *20–80cm.*
FLOWER SIZE *2–3mm wide.*
FLOWERING TIME *July–October.*
LEAVES *Alternate, linear to oval, succulent, spine-tipped.*
FRUIT *Achene covered by flower parts.*
SIMILAR SPECIES *Butcher's Broom (p.427), which has dull green flowers.*

Spear-leaved Orache

Atriplex prostrata (Chenopodiaceae)

The oraches are characterized by their weedy appearance and the mealy covering of scales on the leaves, which rubs off as the plant ages. In this species, the upper leaves are narrower than the spear-shaped lower leaves. The clusters of knobbly fruit are more noticeable than the tiny flowers, as they are surrounded by fleshy, triangular bracts.

GROWS *as a weed on cultivated or waste land, or as a prostrate plant on the coast.*

branched flower spike

3-pointed leaf lobes

tight clusters of flowers

narrow upper leaves

ANNUAL

PLANT HEIGHT *10–20cm when prostrate, otherwise 50–100cm.*
FLOWER SIZE *1–2mm wide.*
FLOWERING TIME *July–October.*
LEAVES *Mostly alternate, spear-shaped.*
FRUIT *Achene, 2–6mm long, within bracts.*
SIMILAR SPECIES *Fat Hen (above), which has toothed leaves and less knobbly fruit.*

Sea Sandwort

Honkenya peploides (Caryophyllaceae)

This unusual member of the pink family survives on windswept coasts by hugging the ground in mats and by conserving moisture in its succulent leaves. The tiny green flowers, with five sepals and five shorter petals, are insignificant compared to the spherical fruit.

FORMS *mats or large patches on coastal shingles, dunes, and rocks; tolerates salt spray and may grow close to the tide line.*

criss-cross leaf arrangement

oval, stalkless leaves

PERENNIAL

tiny green flower

5 petals

round, yellow fruit capsule

PLANT HEIGHT *4–12cm.*
FLOWER SIZE *6–10mm wide.*
FLOWERING TIME *May–August.*
LEAVES *Opposite pairs, in two rows at right angles, oval and stalkless.*
FRUIT *Many-seeded capsule.*
SIMILAR SPECIES *Biting Stonecrop (p.363), which has star-shaped flowers.*

Greater Stitchwort

Stellaria holostea (Caryophyllaceae)

This familiar plant brightens its woodland habitat in spring. Its pure white flowers, in loose clusters, have five deeply notched petals and yellow stamens, with the sepals much shorter than the petals. The rough, oppositely paired leaves persist for many weeks after flowering. The weak stems are often partially supported by other plants.

GROWS *in grassy places, such as woodland, shady field margins, roadsides, and hedgerows.*

PERENNIAL

loosely branched flower stalks

linear leaf

deeply notched petals

large white flowers

yellow centres

NOTE
There are many local names for this plant: "Shirt Buttons", "Milkmaids", "Poorman's-Buttonhole", and "Poppers", which refer to the seed capsules that explode noisily, scattering the seeds some distance away.

PLANT HEIGHT *30–60cm.*
FLOWER SIZE *1.8–3cm wide.*
FLOWERING TIME *April–June.*
LEAVES *Opposite, linear to lance-shaped, untoothed, with long, tapered points, and mostly unstalked.*
FRUIT *Capsule split by six teeth.*
SIMILAR SPECIES *Chickweed (below), which is smaller, with longer sepals; Common Mouse-ear (right), which has hairy leaves.*

Common Mouse-ear

Cerastium fontanum (Caryophyllaceae)

The most distinctive feature of this plant is the covering of fine hairs on the oval leaves, each looking like a mouse's ear. Like Chickweed (left), its flowers each have five deeply notched white petals, but these are the same length as the white-margined green sepals beneath. The fruit capsule is slightly curved and sits within the sepals, looking like a tiny, half-peeled banana.

THRIVES *in moist areas in grassland, sandy places, and shingle banks, usually on neutral or chalky soils.*

PERENNIAL

sepals as long as petals

opposite, unstalked leaves

oval, hairy leaf

curved fruit capsule

PLANT HEIGHT *5–30cm.*
FLOWER SIZE *6–10mm wide.*
FLOWERING TIME *April–October.*
LEAVES *Opposite, oval, and finely hairy.*
FRUIT *Oblong, curved capsule.*
SIMILAR SPECIES *Greater Stitchwort (left) has large flowers with yellow stamens; Chickweed (left), which has sepals longer than petals.*

Corn Spurrey

Spergula arvensis (Caryophyllaceae)

The leaves of this plant are unusual for a member of the pink family, in that they are fleshy and linear, and form whorls at the swollen joints of the stems. The plant is branched at the base, the stems bending upwards. The flowers, with five white unnotched petals and five green sepals beneath, open in the afternoon.

FOUND *in sandy, arable and cultivated land; also on waste and bare ground where soil has been disturbed.*

fleshy leaves

linear leaves

5 white petals

ANNUAL

5–10 stamens

leaf whorls at stem joints

PLANT HEIGHT *5–40cm.*
FLOWER SIZE *4–8mm wide.*
FLOWERING TIME *May–August.*
LEAVES *Whorled, linear, fleshy, and grooved underneath.*
FRUIT *Pendent capsule, split into five valves.*
SIMILAR SPECIES *None.*

Chickweed

Stellaria media (Caryophyllaceae)

This sprawling plant with weak, straggly stems has star-like flowers with five deeply notched white petals, slightly smaller than the green sepals that surround them. The small, oval leaves are hairless, but there is a single line of hairs running along the stem. Chickweed is a ubiquitous weed throughout Britain, with some medicinal properties, and is often fed to poultry as a tonic.

PROLIFERATES *on cultivated land, road verges, and rubbish tips; in pastures and bare places. Tolerates nutrient-rich soils.*

deep cleft in petal

starry white flowers

ANNUAL

sepals longer than petals

untoothed leaf

PLANT HEIGHT *5–35cm.*
FLOWER SIZE *8–10mm wide.*
FLOWERING TIME *Year round.*
LEAVES *Opposite, oval with untoothed margins.*
FRUIT *Capsule splitting into six segments.*
SIMILAR SPECIES *Greater Stitchwort (above); Common Mouse-ear (right).*

Greater Sand-spurrey

Spergularia media (Caryophyllaceae)

Even from a distance, the often extensive mats of this plant brighten salt marshes and coasts with their flowers. The five pink petals are whitish at the base, and interspersed with shorter green sepals. The whorled leaves are linear, fleshy, and flattened on the upper surface; they are rounded below, with a small sheath at the base.

FORMS *small or extensive colonies on drier salt marshes and coastal sands, away from other plants.*

petals longer than sepals

fleshy leaves

papery sheath

5-parted flower

starry petals

PERENNIAL

PLANT HEIGHT *8–20cm.*
FLOWER SIZE *7–12mm wide.*
FLOWERING TIME *May–September.*
LEAVES *Whorled, slightly fleshy.*
FRUIT *Pendent capsule, with three valves.*
SIMILAR SPECIES *Lesser Sand-spurrey (S. marina) and Sand Spurrey (S. rubra), which have petals shorter than the sepals.*

Red Campion
Seen close up, the soft white hairs covering the stems, upper leaves, and sepals of the Red Campion are obvious. The long flower tubes contain nectar, which attracts moths as well as bees.

Bladder Campion

Silene vulgaris (Caryophyllaceae)

The conspicuous, inflated sepal tubes of Bladder Campion give its flowers the appearance of bladders or old-fashioned bloomers, making it instantly recognizable. The sepal tubes may be greenish, yellowish, or pinkish, with a fine network of veins, and the five deeply notched petals are white. The flowers become fragrant in the evening. The leaves are oval, pointed, and rather wavy-edged.

INHABITS *rough ground at the edge of fields and roads, and grassy places; often on dry, chalky soil.*

branched flower stalks

unstalked upper leaves

deeply cleft white petals

PERENNIAL

inflated sepal tube

prominent midrib

PLANT HEIGHT 40–90cm.
FLOWER SIZE 1.6–1.8cm wide.
FLOWERING TIME May–August.
LEAVES Opposite, oval, untoothed, with wavy margins; only the lowermost stalked.
FRUIT Many-seeded capsule with six teeth.
SIMILAR SPECIES White Campion (S. alba), which does not have an inflated calyx.

Corncockle

Agrostemma githago (Caryophyllaceae)

With modern farming practices, this plant has gone from being a familiar cornfield weed to a rare wildflower, both in farmland and in the wild. However, it is still much used in wildflower seed mixes. The five broadly overlapping petals are deep pink, paler towards the centre, and open into a shallow saucer-shape. The long, hairy sepals taper to a fine point, projecting beyond the petals like a star. The hairy leaves are exceptionally long and narrow, and somewhat greyish. The large, round black seeds are finely sculpted, resembling a drill-bit.

OCCURS *sporadically in "unimproved" cornfields or other cultivated land where cereal crops grow, sometimes escaping.*

long, narrow sepals

narrow leaf

untoothed margin

sepals joined below

pale flower centre

long, slender stems

overlapping petals

ANNUAL

PLANT HEIGHT 60–100cm.
FLOWER SIZE 3–5cm wide.
FLOWERING TIME May–August.
LEAVES Opposite, linear to narrowly lance-shaped, hairy, and well-spaced along the stem.
FRUIT Capsule 1–2.2cm long, containing large black seeds.
SIMILAR SPECIES Red Campion (left).

Red Campion

Silene dioica (Caryophyllaceae)

In early spring, this plant's tufts of oblong, hairy leaves may be recognizable along woodland paths, but borne later, the profusion of bright, pinkish red flowers on the reddish stems is unmistakable. Male and female flowers are on separate plants; and the fruit capsule enlarges into a flask shape with turned back teeth.

GROWS *in field margins, woodland, and hedgerows; on roadsides and wasteland; in ditches and on rocky slopes.*

notched petals

oblong leaf

fruit splits at top

tall stem

BIENNIAL/ PERENNIAL

stalkless stem leaves

PLANT HEIGHT 50–100cm.
FLOWER SIZE 1.8–2.5cm wide.
FLOWERING TIME May–August.
LEAVES Opposite, unstalked, hairy; oval to oblong stem leaves.
FRUIT Capsule with ten turned back teeth.
SIMILAR SPECIES Corncockle (right); White Campion (S. alba) has white flowers.

Soapwort

Saponaria officinalis (Caryophyllaceae)

A robust plant found in semi-shaded places, Soapwort has fleshy, veined leaves, which were once gathered and boiled to make a soapy lather for washing. The flowers are in tight clusters, each of the petals broadening towards the tip like an aeroplane propeller, and are notable for their very long, pale green sepal tubes.

FOUND *in grassy places, woodland margins, hedgerows, and roadsides; on waste, fallow, and cultivated land.*

5 narrow, unnotched petals

oval to elliptic leaves

pale pink flowers

long sepal tube

leafy stem

PERENNIAL

PLANT HEIGHT 60–90cm.
FLOWER SIZE 2.5–2.8cm wide.
FLOWERING TIME June–September.
LEAVES Opposite, oval to elliptic, veined.
FRUIT Many-seeded capsule with four teeth.
SIMILAR SPECIES Hybrids of Red Campion (left) and White Campion (Silene alba) have notched petals and striped calyces.

Ragged Robin

Lychnis flos-cuculi (Caryophyllaceae)

This distinctive marsh-loving plant is easily recognized by the ragged appearance of its bright pink or red flowers. However, each of the five petals is actually rather neatly divided into four finger-like lobes. Below the petals are red-striped sepals that are fused into a tube. The opposite leaves are usually hairy; the basal leaves are almost linear, but the stem leaves are wider or spoon-shaped.

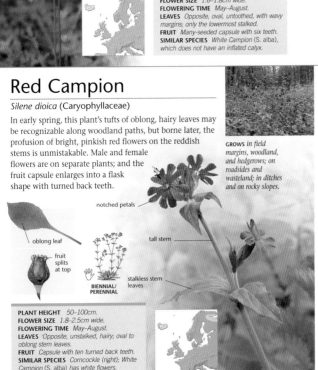

THRIVES *in moist grassland, fens, wet woodland, marshes, and streamsides.*

loose, spreading petals

petal cut into 4 narrow lobes

linear leaves

slender stems

PERENNIAL

PLANT HEIGHT 30–70cm.
FLOWER SIZE 3–4cm wide.
FLOWERING TIME May–August.
LEAVES Opposite, linear or spoon-shaped.
FRUIT Capsule, splitting at the tip into five teeth.
SIMILAR SPECIES None with such finely divided petals.

Maiden Pink

Dianthus deltoides (Caryophyllaceae)

The deep pink petals of this plant have a row of darker spots near the base, forming a ring on the open flower. They are daintily spotted with white, like a dusting of icing sugar. The thin stems are branched, so the flowers are very loosely clustered, mingling with non-flowering shoots.

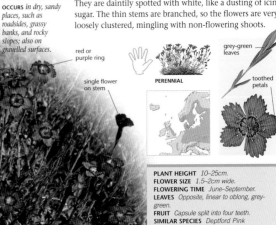

OCCURS *in dry, sandy places, such as roadsides, grassy banks, and rocky slopes; also on gravelled surfaces.*

red or purple ring

grey-green leaves

PERENNIAL

single flower on stem

toothed petals

PLANT HEIGHT 10–25cm.
FLOWER SIZE 1.5–2cm wide.
FLOWERING TIME June–September.
LEAVES Opposite, linear to oblong, grey-green.
FRUIT Capsule split into four teeth.
SIMILAR SPECIES Deptford Pink (D. armeria) has tightly clustered flowers.

White Water-lily

Nymphaea alba (Nymphaeaceae)

This unmistakable aquatic plant has often been hybridized to produce many garden varieties and cultivars. The leaves are rounded and dark green, often with a bronze sheen, and are cleft where they join the stem. They either float on or rise above the water surface. The white flowers, which open only in bright sunshine, are held just at the water surface, each with 20 or more fleshy, oval petals and 4–6 green-backed sepals underneath. There are numerous yellow fertile stamens and infertile stamens (staminodes) in the centre, which attract pollinating insects.

COVERS *the surface of still or slow-flowing freshwater in ponds, lakes, ditches, dykes, and streams.*

PERENNIAL

large white solitary flower

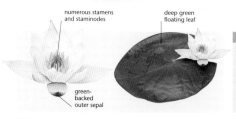

numerous stamens and staminodes

deep green floating leaf

green-backed outer sepal

NOTE

After pollination, the flower sinks below the water surface to develop into a large spongy, warty capsule, which contains many seeds.

PLANT HEIGHT 10cm above the water surface.
FLOWER SIZE 10–20cm wide.
FLOWERING TIME June–September.
LEAVES Basal, rounded with cleft, split to the stalk, 10–30cm wide.
FRUIT Spongy capsule, containing many seeds, that ripens under the water surface.
SIMILAR SPECIES Yellow Water-lily (right), which has larger, oval leaves, and smaller yellow flowers.

Yellow Water-lily

Nuphar lutea (Nymphaeaceae)

A robust, aquatic plant, Yellow Water-lily has the largest leaves of any water-lily in the region, and can cover large expanses of water. The solitary, spherical, deep yellow flowers are small in comparison, and are always held slightly above the water on thick stalks. Each flower has five or six large, overlapping, concave sepals and several smaller, narrower yellow petals, which never open fully to reveal the numerous curved stamens. They go on to form green fruit, shaped like a flask, each with a flat cap marked by prominent stigma rays. The leaves are of two kinds. The thick, leathery floating leaves are oval, deeply cleft, and more pointed than those of other water-lilies, while the submerged leaves are thin and translucent, rounded, and short-stalked. Both arise from thick, woody rhizomes buried in underwater mud.

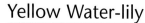

GROWS *abundantly in freshwater lakes, ponds, dykes, and slow-moving streams and rivers, often in water to 5m in depth.*

flask-shaped green seed capsule

PERENNIAL

NOTE

The flowers of Yellow Water-lily attract pollinating flies by producing a strong scent of stale alcohol. The green fruit capsule, coincidentally, has a shape that bears a resemblance to a brandy bottle.

curved stamens

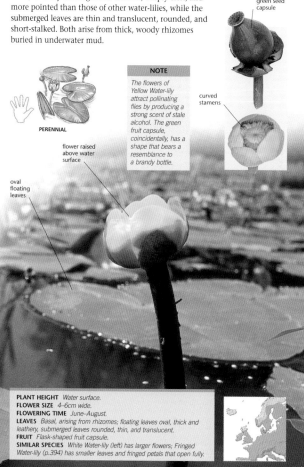

flower raised above water surface

oval floating leaves

PLANT HEIGHT Water surface.
FLOWER SIZE 4–6cm wide.
FLOWERING TIME June–August.
LEAVES Basal, arising from rhizomes; floating leaves oval, thick and leathery, submerged leaves rounded, thin, and translucent.
FRUIT Flask-shaped fruit capsule.
SIMILAR SPECIES White Water-lily (left) has larger flowers; Fringed Water-lily (p.394) has smaller leaves and fringed petals that open fully.

Stinking Hellebore

Helleborus foetidus (Ranunculaceae)

This unpleasant smelling plant is distinctive for its bell-like green flowers, which hang in clusters in spring. The large sepals are bright yellow-green and rimmed with purple. The deep green leaves are palmately lobed, with up to 12 finger-like lobes. The plant is poisonous.

FOUND *in the light shade of open woodland and scrub, on stony, chalky soil; also grown in gardens.*

PERENNIAL

nodding, bell-like flowers

deep green leaves

palmate leaves

purple sepal rim

narrow leaf lobes

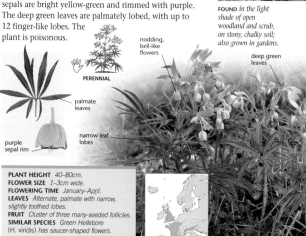

PLANT HEIGHT 40–80cm.
FLOWER SIZE 1–3cm wide.
FLOWERING TIME January–April.
LEAVES Alternate, palmate with narrow, slightly toothed lobes.
FRUIT Cluster of three many-seeded follicles.
SIMILAR SPECIES Green Hellebore (H. viridis) has saucer-shaped flowers.

Wood Anemone

Anemone nemorosa (Ranunculaceae)

An early spring flower, Wood Anemone occurs in great sweeps in mature woodland. The white petals, often flushed with pink underneath, open fully only in good light, and follow the direction of the sun. The long-stalked, deeply lobed leaves increase in number after flowering.

FORMS *spectacular drifts in deciduous woodland, coppices, meadows, hedgerows, and mountain ledges.*

PERENNIAL

stem leaves in whorls of 3

solitary flower

3-lobed leaves

6–12 white petals

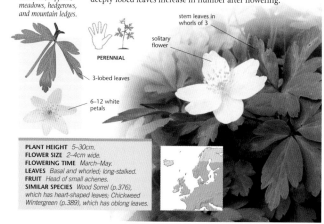

PLANT HEIGHT 5–30cm.
FLOWER SIZE 2–4cm wide.
FLOWERING TIME March–May.
LEAVES Basal and whorled; long-stalked.
FRUIT Head of small achenes.
SIMILAR SPECIES Wood Sorrel (p.376), which has heart-shaped leaves; Chickweed Wintergreen (p.389), which has oblong leaves.

PLANTS

Pasque-flower

Pulsatilla vulgaris (Ranunculaceae)

The clue to the identity of this member of the buttercup family are the numerous yellow stamens, surrounded by deep violet-purple sepals. Flowers open from within downy, leaf-like bracts, and are upright at first, but nodding later. The basal leaves are pinnately divided into fine, linear segments.

OCCURS *in open meadows and short turf, preferring well-drained, chalky soil.*

whorl of leaf-like bracts

numerous stamens

feathery achenes

PERENNIAL

sepals look like petals

finely divided leaves

PLANT HEIGHT *15–30cm.*
FLOWER SIZE *5.5–8cm wide.*
FLOWERING TIME *April–May.*
LEAVES *Basal, pinnately divided into linear segments, long-stalked.*
FRUIT *Showy, dense head of feathery achenes.*
SIMILAR SPECIES *None.*

Traveller's Joy

Clematis vitalba (Ranunculaceae)

This scrambling plant produces masses of creamy white flowers in late summer and persistent fruitheads lasting well into winter. These silky, feathery, pompom-like clusters of silvery achenes trail over hedges and trees on long stems that become woody with age, resembling thick rope. The leaves are pinnately divided, with slightly toothed leaflets.

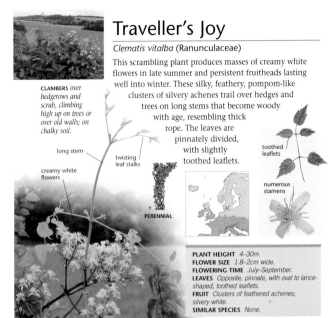
CLAMBERS *over hedgerows and scrub, climbing high up on trees or over old walls; on chalky soil.*

long stem

twisting leaf stalks

toothed leaflets

creamy white flowers

numerous stamens

PERENNIAL

PLANT HEIGHT *4–30m.*
FLOWER SIZE *1.8–2cm wide.*
FLOWERING TIME *July–September.*
LEAVES *Opposite, pinnate, with oval to lance-shaped, toothed leaflets.*
FRUIT *Clusters of feathered achenes; silvery white.*
SIMILAR SPECIES *None.*

Marsh Marigold

Caltha palustris (Ranunculaceae)

The bright golden yellow flowers of this huge buttercup are a striking and unmistakable feature of damp places in early spring. Each flower is composed of five brightly coloured sepals, opening at daybreak to expose up to a hundred stamens. The glossy green leaves are heart-shaped with toothed margins, mostly arising from the base but occasionally rooting at the nodes to form a new clump. The stem leaves are smaller and almost stalkless. In common with many other members of the buttercup family, the whole plant is poisonous.

THRIVES *in damp places in the open or in shade, forming clumps and small colonies in marshes, bogs, stream margins, and wet woodland.*

dark green kidney-shaped leaf

PERENNIAL

long leaf stalk

large, bright yellow flowers

numerous stamens

5 yellow sepals

NOTE

The scientific name – Caltha palustris – of Marsh Marigold comes from the Greek calathos, which means "cup-shaped", referring to the appearance of the flowers. Palustris is from the Latin palus, which means "marsh". Double-flowered forms of this plant are often grown in gardens.

PLANT HEIGHT *30–60cm.*
FLOWER SIZE *2.5–5cm wide.*
FLOWERING TIME *March–June.*
LEAVES *Mostly basal, heart- or kidney-shaped, with finely toothed margins; glossy green; stem leaves almost stalkless.*
FRUIT *Cluster of pod-like follicles, each containing several seeds.*
SIMILAR SPECIES *Globeflower (right), which has spherical flowers and divided leaves. Other buttercups have smaller flowers.*

Globeflower

Trollius europaeus (Ranunculaceae)

A member of the buttercup family, Globeflower owes its distinctive spherical shape to the incurved form of its many lemon-yellow sepals, which enclose the small nectar-secreting petals. The whole plant is robust and hairless, the flower stems rising above the long-stalked basal leaves, which are lobed into five or seven coarsely toothed segments. Smaller in size, the stem leaves may be short-stalked or stalkless. The whole plant is poisonous.

FORMS *colonies in damp open grassland, often among rocks or close to streams.*

palmately divided leaves

curved sepals

PERENNIAL

single flower on long stalk

rounded flowers

NOTE

In order to protect the pollen from being washed away by rain, the sepals of Globeflower overlap to form a "roof" over the anthers, shedding raindrops but allowing pollinating insects to enter.

PLANT HEIGHT *40–70cm.*
FLOWER SIZE *3–5cm wide.*
FLOWERING TIME *May–August.*
LEAVES *Mostly basal, palmately lobed, coarsely toothed; smaller stem leaves.*
FRUIT *Many-seeded follicles.*
SIMILAR SPECIES *Marsh Marigold (left), which has open flowers and kidney-shaped leaves.*

Creeping Buttercup

Ranunculus repens (Ranunculaceae)

The creeping surface runners of this plant enable it to rapidly colonize entire fields, which may appear entirely yellow in early summer. Each flower has five bright yellow petals. The leaves of Creeping Buttercup are triangular in outline and divided into three coarsely toothed lobes; the middle lobe usually has a short stalk.

THRIVES *in meadows, and other grassy places; on damp soil, forming large colonies.*

numerous stamens

bright yellow flowers

triangular leaf

rounded fruit cluster

PERENNIAL

PLANT HEIGHT *10–50cm.*
FLOWER SIZE *1.5–2.5cm wide.*
FLOWERING TIME *May–September.*
LEAVES *Basal, alternate, three toothed lobes.*
FRUIT *Spherical cluster of hooked achenes.*
SIMILAR SPECIES *Lesser Celandine (right), Meadow Buttercup (R. acris), and Bulbous Buttercup (R. bulbosus).*

Lesser Celandine

Ranunculus ficaria (Ranunculaceae)

This is the first of the buttercups to appear in spring, and its flowers are easy to recognize with their three green sepals and up to 12 golden yellow petals, which open fully only in bright sunshine. Sometimes, the petals fade to white as they age. The leaves are heart-shaped, deeply cleft, and with blunt tips. Dark glossy green, they are often mottled with purplish or pale markings.

GROWS *in moderately damp, open places, preferring the partial shade of deciduous woodland and hedgerows.*

PERENNIAL

glossy surface

green fruiting head

8–12 narrow petals

blunt leaf tip

PLANT HEIGHT *7–20cm.*
FLOWER SIZE *2–3cm wide.*
FLOWERING TIME *March–May.*
LEAVES *Mostly basal, heart-shaped.*
FRUIT *Rounded head of achenes.*
SIMILAR SPECIES *Creeping Buttercup (left) and other members of the buttercup family, which have divided leaves.*

Celery-leaved Buttercup

Ranunculus sceleratus (Ranunculaceae)

The small flowers of this plant are distinctive, as the oblong fruiting head of green achenes is already formed when the well-separated yellow petals open. The entire plant has a succulent appearance, with thick, grooved stems often growing out of water. Its lower leaves have rounded lobes with rounded teeth, while the upper leaves are much narrower and untoothed.

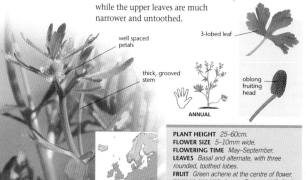

INHABITS *marshes, ditches, pond and lake margins, wet tracks, and woodland rides.*

well spaced petals

3-lobed leaf

thick, grooved stem

oblong fruiting head

ANNUAL

PLANT HEIGHT *25–60cm.*
FLOWER SIZE *5–10mm wide.*
FLOWERING TIME *May–September.*
LEAVES *Basal and alternate, with three rounded, toothed lobes.*
FRUIT *Green achene at the centre of flower.*
SIMILAR SPECIES *Lesser Spearwort (below), which has yellow centres to flowers.*

Greater Spearwort

Ranunculus lingua (Ranunculaceae)

Although this member of the buttercup family shares many characteristics with Lesser Spearwort (left), it is quite distinct. Its tall, fleshy stems are erect and the spear-shaped leaves, much broader than those of its relative, are often thick and leathery. The flowers have five broad, rounded yellow petals. It often grows among taller plants emerging from shallow water and is a favourite plant for garden ponds.

FOUND *in streams, ditches, marshes, fens, and pond margins. Often in shallow water among taller plants, on neutral or chalky soils.*

large flowers

spear-shaped grey-green leaf

thick, fleshy stems

5-petalled flower

PERENNIAL

PLANT HEIGHT *80–150cm.*
FLOWER SIZE *3–5cm wide.*
FLOWERING TIME *June–September.*
LEAVES *Alternate, broadly lance-shaped, untoothed, leathery; grey-green.*
FRUIT *Spherical cluster of achenes.*
SIMILAR SPECIES *Lesser Spearwort (left), which is smaller and has reddish stems.*

Lesser Spearwort

Ranunculus flammula (Ranunculaceae)

This common buttercup has narrow, spear-shaped leaves in twos or threes. The long-stemmed basal leaves may be broader. Its flowers are in loosely branched clusters, and its stems, which run along the ground and root at intervals, are often reddish.

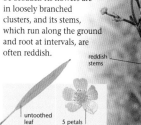

loose clusters of flowers

FORMS *colonies in wet meadows, marshes, or pond margins, often in mountainous areas in the south of its range.*

reddish stems

PERENNIAL

untoothed leaf

5 petals

PLANT HEIGHT *10–50cm.*
FLOWER SIZE *1–2cm wide.*
FLOWERING TIME *May–September.*
LEAVES *Alternate, spear-shaped, untoothed.*
FRUIT *Spherical achene.*
SIMILAR SPECIES *Celery-leaved Buttercup (above); Greater Spearwort (right), which has larger flowers and fleshier leaves and stems.*

Pond Water-crowfoot

Ranunculus peltatus (Ranunculaceae)

Essentially an aquatic white buttercup, this plant has two kinds of leaves. Those under the water surface are divided into feathery threads, while the leaves that float on the water are rounded, with shallow lobes. The white flowers rise above the water surface on short stems. There are many similar species, but with different leaves.

APPEARS *on the surface of shallow ponds, lakes, ditches, and slow-moving streams, or in mud at the water's edge.*

5 white petals

numerous yellow anthers

shallow-lobed upper leaf

ANNUAL/PERENNIAL

thread-like lower leaves

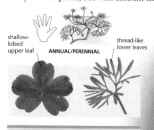

PLANT HEIGHT *Water surface.*
FLOWER SIZE *1.5–2cm wide.*
FLOWERING TIME *May–August.*
LEAVES *Alternate; rounded and lobed upper leaves, thread-like lower leaves.*
FRUIT *Collection of achenes.*
SIMILAR SPECIES *Frogbit (p.424), which has three-petalled flowers.*

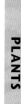

PLANTS

Buttercups
Seen here in lush pasture, buttercups are common on lawns and playing fields, and so, along with dandelions and daisies, are among the first wild flowers that children learn to recognize.

Columbine

Aquilegia vulgaris (Ranunculaceae)

The rounded, broadly lobed leaves of this member of the buttercup family are a good aid to identification, and the deep blue to purple flowers are unmistakable. The five narrow sepals are the same colour as the broader petals, each of which has a long, hooked spur containing nectar to attract long-tongued bees. Columbine is widely grown in gardens.

FORMS *loose colonies in damp meadows, fens, and scrub, and alongside hedgerows and woodland margins; generally on chalky soil.*

petals end in hooked spurs

nodding flowers

3–9 main leaflets

rounded lobes

fruit of clustered follicles

sepals same colour as petals

unstalked stem leaves

erect, branched stems

PERENNIAL

> **PLANT HEIGHT** 50–90cm.
> **FLOWER SIZE** 3–5cm wide.
> **FLOWERING TIME** May–July.
> **LEAVES** Mostly basal, with two- to three-lobed leaflets; dull green but paler beneath.
> **FRUIT** Collection of five pod-like follicles.
> **SIMILAR SPECIES** Garden varieties in a range of colours may occur in the wild.

Welsh Poppy

Meconopsis cambrica (Papaveraceae)

The four rounded, tissue-thin petals of this plant's poppy-like flowers open orange-yellow but soon fade to bright lemon-yellow. Each bloom is borne on a slender stem with two hairy sepals that fall when the flower opens, and goes on to form a ribbed fruit capsule. The leaves are often pale yellow-green and pinnately divided into five toothed lobes.

FOUND *in moist, semi-shaded, rocky places, old walls, and upland woods. Commonly cultivated in gardens, from which it frequently escapes.*

BIENNIAL/PERENNIAL

pale green leaves

four orange-yellow petals

numerous stamens

> **PLANT HEIGHT** 40–60cm.
> **FLOWER SIZE** 4–8cm wide.
> **FLOWERING TIME** June–August.
> **LEAVES** Alternate, pinnately divided; pale yellow-green.
> **FRUIT** Erect capsule with many seeds.
> **SIMILAR SPECIES** Greater Celandine (left), which has similar leaves but smaller flowers.

Common Meadow-rue

Thalictrum flavum (Ranunculaceae)

The flowers of this plant appear to consist almost entirely of numerous creamy yellow stamens, although there are four tiny sepals. The leaves are divided into distinctive, dark greyish green leaflets, each one usually bearing three points. The leaves are difficult to spot among vegetation but the tall, bright flowerheads are very noticeable.

THRIVES *in damp meadows, fens, and flooded areas, usually among other tall vegetation in lowland.*

fluffy flowerhead

flowers on tall stems

3-pointed leaflets

long stamens

PERENNIAL

> **PLANT HEIGHT** 0.6–1.5m.
> **FLOWER SIZE** 1–1.5cm wide.
> **FLOWERING TIME** June–August.
> **LEAVES** Alternate, pinnately divided.
> **FRUIT** Achenes twisted together.
> **SIMILAR SPECIES** Meadowsweet (p.366), which has coarser leaves; Baneberry (Actaea spicata) is smaller and occurs on limestone.

Yellow Horned Poppy

Glaucium flavum (Papaveraceae)

This distinctive and colourful beach flower is easily recognized by its fleshy, grey-green leaves, which are pinnately divided into coarse, toothed segments with an undulating surface. The large, bright yellow flowers have four tissue-like petals and the very unusual fruit is a narrow, elongated capsule.

OCCURS *on shingle or sandy beaches, dunes, sea-cliffs, and very occasionally on waste ground inland.*

overlapping petals

grey-green leaves

large yellow flowers

long, slender capsule

> **PLANT HEIGHT** 50–90cm.
> **FLOWER SIZE** 6–9cm wide.
> **LEAVES** Alternate, pinnately divided.
> **FRUIT** Elongated capsule, up to 30cm long.
> **FLOWERING TIME** June–September.
> **SIMILAR SPECIES** None (its large flowers and coastal habitat prevent confusion with other species).

BIENNIAL/PERENNIAL

Greater Celandine

Chelidonium majus (Papaveraceae)

An unusual member of the poppy family, this plant has small flowers with four well-separated yellow petals, numerous yellow stamens, and a prominent style in the centre. The same plant may produce flowers for several months and flowering is said to coincide with the presence of swallows (*chelidon* is Greek for swallow). The leaves are pale green, with rounded lobes. Ants are attracted to the oily seeds and often unwittingly carry them off stuck to their bodies.

GROWS *in semi-shaded places such as hedgerows, alongside walls, rocky places, and wasteland, often close to habitation.*

4 separated petals

numerous stamens

pinnate leaves

PERENNIAL

slender fruit capsule

> **PLANT HEIGHT** 40–90cm.
> **FLOWER SIZE** 1.5–2.5cm long.
> **FLOWERING TIME** April–October.
> **LEAVES** Alternate; pinnate with rounded lobes.
> **FRUIT** Linear-oblong, hairless capsule, splitting to release seeds.
> **SIMILAR SPECIES** Welsh Poppy (right), which has larger flowers.

Common Poppy

Papaver rhoeas (Papaveraceae)

Poppies often appear in great profusion in fields or land that has been disturbed after a long period of neglect, as the seeds can lie dormant in the ground for many years, then germinate when brought close to the surface. The deep green leaves are deeply lobed, with toothed margins. The nodding flower buds are hairy; the flowers have four huge, overlapping scarlet petals, each with a small black blotch at the base. The stamens are also black.

FLOURISHES *in arable fields and field margins, and disturbed and waste ground, on roadsides; often colours whole fields scarlet.*

ANNUAL

brilliant red petals

black centre of flower

oval fruit capsule

pinnately divided leaves

slender stem

> **PLANT HEIGHT** 30–60cm.
> **FLOWER SIZE** 7.5–10cm wide.
> **FLOWERING TIME** June–September.
> **LEAVES** Alternate, pinnately divided, toothed.
> **FRUIT** Oval, smooth capsule with holes near the top, filled with numerous tiny black seeds.
> **SIMILAR SPECIES** Other poppy species, which have differently shaped or hairy fruit capsules.

Climbing Corydalis

Ceratocapnos claviculata (Fumariaceae)

This delicate, climbing plant is easily missed as it scrambles over other vegetation. Borne on thin, twining red stems, the small, almost lace-like leaves are divided into three or more oval leaflets and end in branched tendrils. The tiny, two-lipped flowers, have a complex tubular shape.

CLIMBS *over other vegetation or on the ground in the shade, on acid or peaty soils.*

ANNUAL

flowers in tight clusters of 4–8

oval leaflets

short spur

creamy yellow flower

PLANT HEIGHT *30–75cm.*
FLOWER SIZE *4–6mm long.*
FLOWERING TIME *May–September.*
LEAVES *Alternate, oval leaflets, with tendrils.*
FRUIT *Brown capsule, 9–10mm long.*
SIMILAR SPECIES *Common Ramping Fumitory (Fumaria muralis), which has larger, pinker flowers and is more robust.*

Garlic Mustard

Alliaria petiolata (Brassicaceae)

The large, triangular leaves of this plant appear in early spring. The four-petalled white flowers are borne at the stem tips, in clusters that seem small for the size of the plant. The flowering stem elongates as the long seed pods develop. When crushed, the leaves have a distinct smell of garlic, which is unusual outside the onion family.

FLOURISHES *along hedgerows and roads, in woodland margins and among scrub, in the open or semi-shade, on neutral or chalky soils.*

BIENNIAL

smaller leaves on upper stem

small flower clusters

small white flowers

long, thin seed pods

triangular, toothed leaves

PLANT HEIGHT *40–120cm.*
FLOWER SIZE *3–5mm wide.*
FLOWERING TIME *April–June.*
LEAVES *Alternate, triangular to heart-shaped, toothed and stalked.*
FRUIT *Seed pods (siliquas), 2–7cm long, splitting lengthwise when dry.*
SIMILAR SPECIES *Dame's-violet (below).*

Yellow Corydalis

Pseudofumaria lutea (Fumariaceae)

Although originally from the Alps, this plant is now naturalized throughout much of Europe. The golden yellow flowers with two outer lips are borne in one-sided spikes, and the whole plant may continue to flower for many months. The delicate leaves are pinnately divided, each leaflet with three rounded lobes.

OCCURS *on limestone rocks in native habitat. Also found on moist, shady old walls in towns and gardens.*

pinnate leaves

up to 16 flowers in spike

bright yellow flowers

PERENNIAL

pendent capsule

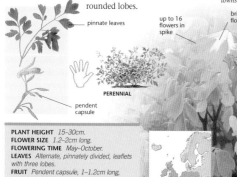

PLANT HEIGHT *15–30cm.*
FLOWER SIZE *1.2–2cm long.*
FLOWERING TIME *May–October.*
LEAVES *Alternate, pinnately divided, leaflets with three lobes.*
FRUIT *Pendent capsule, 1–1.2cm long, containing black seeds.*
SIMILAR SPECIES *None.*

Dame's-violet

Hesperis matronalis (Brassicaceae)

The bold clusters of four-petalled white, violet, or pink flowers of this stately plant are easily noticed. The flowers are fragrant only in the evening. The finely toothed, short-stalked leaves are narrow at the base. A native of southern Europe, Dame's-violet is now naturalized in the British Isles.

FOUND *in damp, semi-shaded places such as woodland margins, riversides, hedgerows, and road verges; often near settlements.*

BIENNIAL/PERENNIAL

4 petals

narrow leaf

stalked flowers

branched stems

PLANT HEIGHT *70–120cm.*
FLOWER SIZE *1.5–2cm wide.*
FLOWERING TIME *May–August.*
LEAVES *Alternate, lance-shaped, toothed.*
FRUIT *Siliquas, 2.5–10cm long, containing many seeds.*
SIMILAR SPECIES *Garlic Mustard (above); Cuckooflower (p.360) has pinnate leaves.*

Common Fumitory

Fumaria officinalis (Fumariaceae)

This widespread weed has racemes of upright flowers, each flower with a pouched spur at the back, and two crimson-tipped lips at the front. The weak, straggly stems bear finely divided leaves, each leaflet on its own stalk. The feathery greyish green leaves look almost like smoke, hence the plant's scientific name.

SPRAWLS *over bare ground or grassy places in cultivated fields, wasteland, or pastures, and along roadsides.*

dark-tipped flowers

flowers in racemes

ANNUAL

feathery, divided leaves

thin leaf stalk

pouched spur

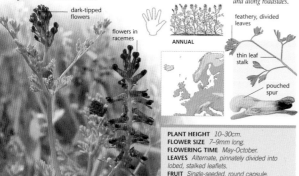

PLANT HEIGHT *10–30cm.*
FLOWER SIZE *7–9mm long.*
FLOWERING TIME *May–October.*
LEAVES *Alternate, pinnately divided into lobed, stalked leaflets.*
FRUIT *Single-seeded, round capsule.*
SIMILAR SPECIES *Common Ramping-fumitory (F. muralis) has fewer flowers.*

Wallflower

Erysimum cheiri (Brassicaceae)

Originally from southeast Europe, the Wallflower is now frequently used as a garden plant throughout the British Isles. It has tufts of narrowly lance-shaped, hairy leaves on branched stems that often become woody near the bases. The large and fragrant flowers range from orange-yellow to golden brown. Some garden escapes have white or purple flowers.

CLINGS *to cliffs, old walls, monuments, and rocky places, often close to the sea.*

golden yellow flowers

narrow, hairy leaves

4-petalled flowers

long, slender seed pod

PERENNIAL

PLANT HEIGHT *30–60cm.*
FLOWER SIZE *2–2.5cm wide.*
FLOWERING TIME *March–June.*
LEAVES *Alternate, lance-shaped, hairy, with a short stalk.*
FRUIT *Siliqua, 7.5cm long.*
SIMILAR SPECIES *Wild Cabbage (p.362), which has a woody stem and larger leaves.*

PLANTS

Long-headed Poppies
Poppies provide some of the boldest, most intense splashes of natural colour in the British landscape. The Long-headed Poppy (*Papaver dubium*) has unblotched, pinkish-red blooms that last just one day.

Wintercress

Barbarea vulgaris (Brassicaceae)

The four-petalled yellow flowers of Wintercress brighten the banks of streams and damp ditches in spring. They are clustered at the top of the stems, which elongate as the long seed pods develop beneath. The lower leaves, which are a rich source of vitamin C, have a large terminal lobe each, while the unlobed upper leaves clasp the stem.

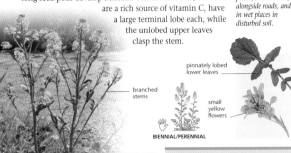

GROWS *close to ditches, ponds, and streams, alongside roads, and in wet places in disturbed soil.*

pinnately lobed lower leaves

branched stems

small yellow flowers

BIENNIAL/PERENNIAL

PLANT HEIGHT *30–90cm.*
FLOWER SIZE *7–9mm wide.*
FLOWERING TIME *May–August.*
LEAVES *Basal leaves, lobed and stalked; alternate stem leaves, unstalked, toothed.*
FRUIT *Narrow siliqua, 1.5–3cm long.*
SIMILAR SPECIES *Hedge Mustard (p.362); Charlock (p.362), which has broader leaves.*

Hairy Bittercress

Cardamine hirsuta (Brassicaceae)

This common weed of towns and gardens has very small flowers that are easily overlooked. They are in tight clusters at the tips of the gradually lengthening stems, but are usually topped by the long seed pods sprouting from beneath. The narrow, hairy leaves are comprised of well-separated, rounded leaflets in pairs.

THRIVES *on wasteland, cultivated and rocky ground, old walls, and in gardens and pavement cracks.*

long seed pods

ANNUAL/BIENNIAL

large terminal leaflet

tiny flower clusters

four petals

PLANT HEIGHT *5–30cm.*
FLOWER SIZE *3–4mm wide.*
FLOWERING TIME *February–November.*
LEAVES *Mostly basal, upper alternate, with paired leaflets.*
FRUIT *Siliqua, 2–2.5cm long.*
SIMILAR SPECIES *Cuckooflower (below), which has larger, pinkish flowers.*

Horse-radish

Armoracia rusticana (Brassicaceae)

This robust and erect plant, whose root is used as a condiment, is mostly without flowers. However, it is easily identified by its stout, shiny leaves, with wavy margins and pale midribs, which have a faint but distinct horse-radish scent. When flowers do occur, they are white with four petals and borne in dense panicles.

FORMS *patches on roadsides, wasteland, and river banks, and along farmland edges.*

oblong, toothed leaves

crinkled leaf surface

panicle of white flowers

PERENNIAL

PLANT HEIGHT *30–90cm.*
FLOWER SIZE *8–10mm wide.*
FLOWERING TIME *May–July.*
LEAVES *Basal, alternate on flowering stem.*
FRUIT *Silicula, 4–6mm wide, but rare.*
SIMILAR SPECIES *Broad-leaved Dock (Rumex obtusifolius), which has similar leaves and habit before it flowers.*

Cuckooflower

Cardamine pratensis (Brassicaceae)

Widespread in damp meadows and pastures, this member of the cabbage family is identifiable by its flowers, each with four broad, oval petals ranging from white to lilac or deep pink. The basal leaves have rounded lobes, similar to those of Water-cress (left), and the stem leaves are divided into narrow, well-separated lobes that resemble a ladder.

FAVOURS *damp areas such as verges, river banks, and wet pastures.*

clusters of flowers at stem tips

PERENNIAL

yellow anthers

rounded leaflets

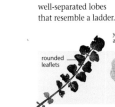

PLANT HEIGHT *Up to 60cm.*
FLOWER SIZE *1.2–1.8cm wide.*
FLOWERING TIME *April–June.*
LEAVES *Loose rosette of pinnately divided leaves; stem leaves with narrower leaflets.*
FRUIT *Slender pod, up to 4cm long.*
SIMILAR SPECIES *Coralroot Bittercress (C. bulbifera) has larger and elliptic leaflets.*

Water-cress

Rorippa nasturtium-aquaticum (Brassicaceae)

The glossy, succulent, edible leaves of Water-cress have a characteristic shape, and grow like a ladder up its fleshy stems. Creeping along freshwater habitats, the plant roots into the mud at intervals or floats on the water surface. It may flower for many weeks, forming rows of long, curved seed pods.

SPRAWLS *along ditches, ponds, streams, and wet flushes, sometimes forming colonies.*

tight clusters of flowers

oval leaflets

PERENNIAL

4-petalled white flower

curved seed pod

PLANT HEIGHT *30–70cm.*
FLOWER SIZE *4–6mm wide.*
FLOWERING TIME *May–October.*
LEAVES *Alternate, pinnately divided into oval leaflets.*
FRUIT *Slender, curved seed pods.*
SIMILAR SPECIES *Fool's-water-cress (p.387), which has toothed leaves.*

Honesty

Lunaria annua (Brassicaceae)

Introduced from southeast Europe as a garden plant, Honesty is now naturalized in the British countryside. The large purple or white flowers, the heart-shaped leaves, and particularly the fruit, are distinctive. The fruit splits to reveal a persistent silvery membrane, to which the seeds are attached.

OCCURS *on roadsides, banks, wasteland, rubbish tips, and cultivated land.*

deep green foliage

coarsely toothed leaf

flowers in clusters

BIENNIAL

4-petalled flowers

rounded fruit

PLANT HEIGHT *50–100cm.*
FLOWER SIZE *2.5–3cm wide.*
FLOWERING TIME *April–June.*
LEAVES *Alternate, heart-shaped, coarsely toothed.*
FRUIT *Round, flat silicula, 3–5cm wide.*
SIMILAR SPECIES *Dame's Violet (p.357), which is taller with narrower leaves.*

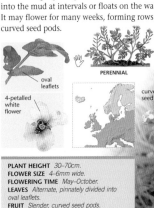

Common Scurvy-grass

Cochlearia offinalis (Brassicaceae)

A variable plant, Common Scurvy-grass has a succulent nature and often prostrate habit, typical of many coastal plants. The long-stalked basal leaves are rounded, while the upper leaves clasp the stem and may be lobed. The four-parted white flowers are in tight clusters above stems that lengthen as the fruit develop.

GROWS *on coastal rocks, salt marshes, sea walls, and motorway verges.*

tight flower clusters

round, fleshy leaves

BIENNIAL/PERENNIAL

heart-shaped base

round seed pod

> **PLANT HEIGHT** *10–40cm.*
> **FLOWER SIZE** *8–10mm wide.*
> **FLOWERING TIME** *April–August.*
> **LEAVES** *Mostly basal, rounded and fleshy.*
> **FRUIT** *Spherical siliculas, with cork-like texture.*
> **SIMILAR SPECIES** *Danish Scurvy-grass (C. danica), which has lilac flowers.*

Field Pepperwort

Lepidium campestre (Brassicaceae)

This widespread weed of cultivated land is more noticeable when the fruit appear, forming long columns of seed pods (siliculas). The stems of the plant, on which the seed pods are held horizontally, elongate as the fruit develops. Each fruit is flat on one side, curved on the other, and faintly winged with a notch at the tip. The tiny, four-petalled white flowers are in tight clusters at the tops of the stems. The upper leaves, clasping the stem, are narrow and toothed, while the lower leaves are oval.

INHABITS *cultivated, waste; and disturbed ground, dry, open places, and roadsides.*

tight flower cluster

narrow upper leaves clasp stem

ANNUAL/BIENNIAL

small white flowers

notched fruit

> **PLANT HEIGHT** *30–60cm.*
> **FLOWER SIZE** *2mm wide.*
> **FLOWERING TIME** *May–August.*
> **LEAVES** *Alternate, narrow, toothed upper leaves; basal leaves wither by flowering time.*
> **FRUIT** *Oval silicula, 5–6mm long.*
> **SIMILAR SPECIES** *Shepherd's Purse (left), which has heart-shaped fruit.*

Shepherd's Purse

Capsella bursa-pastoris (Brassicaceae)

This familiar, ubiquitous plant is variable in size, with tiny, four-petalled white flowers. Below them, rows of heart-shaped seed cases develop along the stem, resembling an old-fashioned leather purse. The leaves are mostly basal in a loose rosette. If Shepherd's Purse is fed to chickens, the egg yolks become darker.

FLOURISHES *even in poor soil, in fields, gardens, cultivated or waste ground, along walls, and in pavement cracks.*

rows of seed cases

tiny white flowers above seeds

ANNUAL/BIENNIAL

lance-shaped leaf

upper leaves clasp stem

heart-shaped fruit

> **PLANT HEIGHT** *8–50cm.*
> **FLOWER SIZE** *2–3mm wide.*
> **FLOWERING TIME** *Year round.*
> **LEAVES** *Basal leaves pinnately lobed; stem leaves alternate, lance-shaped, toothed.*
> **FRUIT** *Heart-shaped capsules in racemes.*
> **SIMILAR SPECIES** *Field Penny-cress (below); Field Pepperwort (right) has oval fruit.*

Hoary Cress

Cardaria draba (Brassicaceae)

Long associated with coastal areas, often in dry, stony places, this plant is now common along salted roadways. It is easily spotted by the foaming mass of tiny creamy white flowers on its many-branched stems, forming attractive drifts. Each flower has four petals, and develops into a rounded fruit. The toothed, greyish leaves are oblong.

OCCURS *in drifts along roadsides, trackways, and on cultivated and disturbed ground, by the coast.*

flowers in clusters

white petals

heart-shaped fruit

unstalked stem leaves

PERENNIAL

> **PLANT HEIGHT** *30–80cm.*
> **FLOWER SIZE** *5–6mm wide.*
> **FLOWERING TIME** *May–June.*
> **LEAVES** *Alternate, oval and coarsely toothed; basal leaves may be untoothed.*
> **FRUIT** *Heart-shaped silicula, 3–4mm long.*
> **SIMILAR SPECIES** *Sea Kale (below), which has similar characteristics but is more robust.*

Field Penny-cress

Thlaspi arvense (Brassicaceae)

The seed pods of this cabbage family member form papery discs with broad, rounded wings that resemble notched coins. When the sun catches the papery discs, they appear to glow yellow. The white flowers are at the top of the branched stems.

FOUND *in disturbed areas such as margins of arable land where the soil is rich, and in wasteland.*

toothed leaves

stem elongates in fruit

tiny flowers in tight clusters

coin-like fruit

ANNUAL

> **PLANT HEIGHT** *20–60cm.*
> **FLOWER SIZE** *4–6mm wide.*
> **FLOWERING TIME** *May–July.*
> **LEAVES** *Alternate, narrow, and roughly toothed.*
> **FRUIT** *Papery, disc-like wings in clusters.*
> **SIMILAR SPECIES** *Shepherd's Purse (above), which has heart-shaped seed capsules.*

Sea Kale

Crambe maritima (Brassicaceae)

The great clumps of grey-green, waxy leaves of this plant are difficult to miss in the barren expanse of a shingle beach or coastal sands. They are succulent, lobed, and with wavy margins, like those of a cabbage. Large, domed clusters of four-petalled white flowers are produced in profusion.

FORMS *clumps, often close to the shoreline, on shingle beaches and coastal sands, sometimes on cliffs and sea walls.*

dense clusters of white flowers

spherical fruit

plant forms large clumps

PERENNIAL

thick, fleshy leaves

thick, branched stem

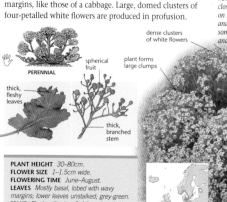

> **PLANT HEIGHT** *30–80cm.*
> **FLOWER SIZE** *1–1.5cm wide.*
> **FLOWERING TIME** *June–August.*
> **LEAVES** *Mostly basal, lobed with wavy margins; lower leaves unstalked; grey-green.*
> **FRUIT** *Fleshy siliculas, 8–14mm long.*
> **SIMILAR SPECIES** *Hoary Cress (above), which is less robust; Wild Cabbage (p.362).*

PLANTS

Hedge Mustard

Sisymbrium officinale (Brassicaceae)

A common and coarse-looking weed of wasteland, Hedge Mustard is notable for its clusters of tiny yellow flowers at the end of long, branched stems that elongate further as the fruit develop. The fruit is pressed close to the stem. The lower leaves are divided into jagged lobes, the points of which turn back towards the stem; the upper leaves are narrower.

PROLIFERATES *on bare ground, wasteland, in margins of arable fields, and on roadsides, often with poppies.*

ANNUAL/BIENNIAL

clusters of yellow flowers

jagged leaves

triangular leaf lobe

unnotched petals

slender seed pods

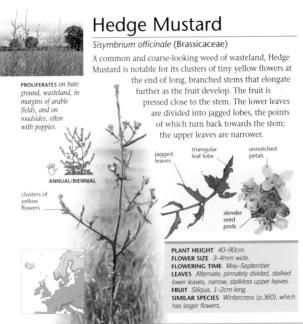

PLANT HEIGHT *40–90cm.*
FLOWER SIZE *3–4mm wide.*
FLOWERING TIME *May–September.*
LEAVES *Alternate; pinnately divided, stalked lower leaves, narrow, stalkless upper leaves.*
FRUIT *Siliqua, 1–2cm long.*
SIMILAR SPECIES *Wintercress (p.360), which has larger flowers.*

Rape

Brassica napus (Brassicaceae)

Frequently grown as a crop for its oil, this is a tall plant. Its large yellow flowers are usually overtopped slightly by unopened buds, with long seed pods on the elongated stems beneath. The leaves are greyish green with very wavy margins and a pale midrib, the lower ones stalked and lobed, the upper unstalked and clasping the stem.

NATURALIZES *on cultivated land, field margins, roadsides, bare and waste ground, usually close to farmland.*

4-petalled yellow flowers

rounded lobes

slender seed pod

elongated stems

ANNUAL/BIENNIAL

PLANT HEIGHT *50–150cm.*
FLOWER SIZE *1.5–2.5cm wide.*
FLOWERING TIME *May–August.*
LEAVES *Basal leaves stalked and lobed, stem leaves alternate and unstalked.*
FRUIT *Cylindrical siliqua, 5–10cm long.*
SIMILAR SPECIES *Wild Cabbage (left); Charlock (below) has less lobed leaves.*

Wild Cabbage

Brassica oleracea (Brassicaceae)

A large number of cultivated vegetables are derived from this rather rare, robust, and hairless plant of coastal cliffs. Wild Cabbage leaves are indeed cabbage-like – thick, fleshy, and grey-green in colour, with a thick midrib, the basal leaves somewhat pinnate with small lobes. The stout woody stem base bears the scars of former leaf attachments, and the large four-petalled, yellow flowers are borne in long branched spikes. Shaped like a long, cylindrical pod, the fruit is rather fleshy.

GROWS *at the top of sea-cliffs and rocky maritime places, particularly on thin, chalky soil.*

BIENNIAL/PERENNIAL

prominent upright flower stems

long-branched flower spikes

thick, fleshy leaf

4-petalled flowers

NOTE

Wild Cabbage often grows close to colonies of cliff-nesting sea birds, which help to disperse the seeds to other areas of its restricted habitat.

PLANT HEIGHT *60–120cm.*
FLOWER SIZE *3–4cm wide.*
FLOWERING TIME *May–September.*
LEAVES *Basal leaves fleshy and lobed, upper leaves unlobed and clasping the stem; grey-green.*
FRUIT *Long, fleshy siliqua, 5–7cm long.*
SIMILAR SPECIES *Rape (right) has less fleshy leaves; Sea Kale (p.361), which has white flowers; Wallflower (p.357), which has smaller leaves.*

Charlock

Sinapis arvensis (Brassicaceae)

One of the commonest yellow crucifers, which used to be a serious arable pest, this plant is rather bristly, with coarsely toothed, lyre-shaped basal leaves that have a wrinkled surface. Its upper leaves are narrower, without lobes, and do not clasp the stem. The flowers have four yellow petals, widely separated to reveal the narrow sepals underneath.

APPEARS *on disturbed ground, roadsides, and rubbish tips, often on chalky soil.*

4-petalled yellow flowers

narrow sepals

hairy leaves

reddish midrib

beaked seed pod

ANNUAL

PLANT HEIGHT *40–80cm.*
FLOWER SIZE *1.5–2cm wide.*
FLOWERING TIME *May–October.*
LEAVES *Basal, stalked, coarsely toothed; upper leaves alternate, unstalked, unlobed.*
FRUIT *Siliqua, 2.5–4.5cm long.*
SIMILAR SPECIES *Rape (above) has less hairy leaves; Wintercress (p.360).*

Sea Rocket

Cakile maritima (Brassicaceae)

In common with many coastal plants living in dry soil, the Sea Rocket has fleshy leaves that retain moisture. They are oblong, bright green, and deeply lobed into rounded "fingers". The pale pink flowers are clustered at the top of the stems, and the fleshy, bullet-shaped fruit has two shoulder-like projections at the base.

FOUND *in open, sandy areas, dunes, and shingle beaches on coastal sites.*

ANNUAL

long, rounded segments

pale midrib

clusters of flowers

4 petals

PLANT HEIGHT *Up to 30cm.*
FLOWER SIZE *6–12mm wide.*
FLOWERING TIME *June–September.*
LEAVES *Alternate, pinnately lobed, fleshy.*
FRUIT *Siliqua, 2cm long, with two segments, the lower one with two projections.*
SIMILAR SPECIES *Cuckooflower (p.360), which has less fleshy leaves.*

Weld

Reseda luteola (Resedaceae)

An easy plant to identify even at a distance, Weld has tall, thin flowering spikes. These are often branched towards the top, and are clothed in hundreds of tiny flowers with deeply cut petals, held very close to the stem. The untoothed leaves, simple but with wavy edges, form a rosette in the first year.

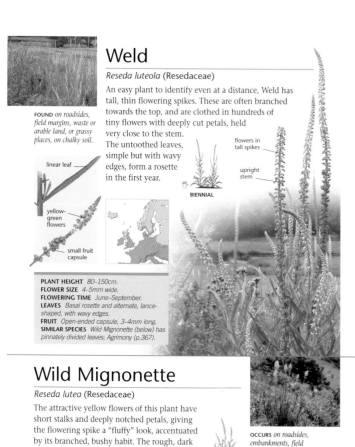

FOUND on roadsides, field margins, waste or arable land, or grassy places, on chalky soil.

linear leaf

yellow-green flowers

small fruit capsule

flowers in tall spikes

upright stem

BIENNIAL

PLANT HEIGHT 80–150cm.
FLOWER SIZE 4–5mm wide.
FLOWERING TIME June–September.
LEAVES Basal rosette and alternate, lance-shaped, with wavy edges.
FRUIT Open-ended capsule, 3–4mm long.
SIMILAR SPECIES Wild Mignonette (below) has pinnately divided leaves; Agrimony (p.367).

Wild Mignonette

Reseda lutea (Resedaceae)

The attractive yellow flowers of this plant have short stalks and deeply notched petals, giving the flowering spike a "fluffy" look, accentuated by its branched, bushy habit. The rough, dark green leaves are pinnately divided into long thin lobes, each with a wavy margin, folding around the midrib. The fruit is an elongated capsule.

OCCURS on roadsides, embankments, field margins, and dry grassland.

BIENNIAL/PERENNIAL

flowers in loose spikes

long, narrow leaf lobe

tiny flowers

PLANT HEIGHT 40–80cm.
FLOWER SIZE 7–9mm wide.
FLOWERING TIME May–September.
LEAVES Alternate, pinnately and thinly lobed.
FRUIT Open-ended, elongated capsule, 7–12mm long.
SIMILAR SPECIES Weld (above), which is taller and more upright, with unlobed leaves.

White Stonecrop

Sedum album (Crassulaceae)

The fleshy, cylindrical leaves of this plant, like little waxy fingers, help it to conserve moisture in the dry conditions in which it lives. The leafy stems are branched at the top, where they bear a mass of starry white flowers. English Stonecrop (*S. anglicum*) is a shorter plant with fewer flowers to each cluster.

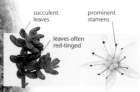

APPEARS on rocks, walls, and dunes, in shingle or on gravel paths, in very dry, exposed places.

PERENNIAL

broad, terminal cluster of flowers

succulent leaves

prominent stamens

leaves often red-tinged

5-petalled flowers

PLANT HEIGHT 8–20cm.
FLOWER SIZE 6–9mm wide.
FLOWERING TIME June–August.
LEAVES Alternate, small, cylindrical, and succulent.
FRUIT Cluster of small follicles.
SIMILAR SPECIES Biting Stonecrop (right), English Stonecrop (S. anglicum).

Round-leaved Sundew

Drosera rotundifolia (Droseraceae)

The Round-leaved Sundew is usually seen nestling in moss, and its curiously adapted leaves are unmistakable. They are clothed in long, red glandular hairs, each tipped with a drop of sticky liquid. These ensnare an insect hoping to find nectar, whereupon the leaf rolls up and digests the insect inside. The small white flowers of this plant are borne in a loose spike at the top of a leafless stalk, high above the leaves. Each flower has 5–8 sepals and petals.

GROWS among sphagnum moss and other plants, on bare peat in acid bogs, in moist conditions, and in wet heaths and moors.

PERENNIAL

rounded leaf blade

long stalk

leaves with sticky, red hairs

white flower

NOTE

Sundews live in wet, acidic soils, which are very low in nutrients such as nitrates. Capturing and digesting insects provides the plant with nitrates and phosphates so that it can survive in harsh conditions.

PLANT HEIGHT 5–15cm.
FLOWER SIZE 5mm wide.
FLOWERING TIME June–August.
LEAVES Basal, rounded leaf blade, with sticky, red glandular hairs.
FRUIT Small, many-seeded capsule.
SIMILAR SPECIES Great Sundew (D. longifolia), which has narrow, oblong leaves covered in sticky glands.

Biting Stonecrop

Sedum acre (Crassulaceae)

The brilliant yellow flowers of this mat-forming, creeping plant, each with five petals and ten stamens, make a bold impact when seen in its dry, bare habitat. The short, blunt leaves, adapted to hold moisture, are succulent and overlap each other close to the tip, often turning partially or wholly red.

FORMS mats in dry, stony or sandy places such as old walls, embankments, shingle beaches, and rooftops.

star-shaped flowers

PERENNIAL

red-tinged leaves

flowers in small clusters

PLANT HEIGHT 4–10cm.
FLOWER SIZE 1–1.2cm wide.
FLOWERING TIME May–July.
LEAVES Alternate, succulent, 3–6mm.
FRUIT Five follicles in star shape, 4mm long.
SIMILAR SPECIES Sea Sandwort (p.346) and White Stonecrop (left) have similar leaves; Yellow Saxifrage (p.365) is bushier.

Navelwort

Umbilicus rupestris (Crassulaceae)

The coin-shaped leaves of this plant of dry walls are very characteristic, being fleshy and circular, with a dimple in the centre of each leaf (which gives them their name), where the stem joins underneath. The tall, flowering spikes are also distinctive, with many drooping flowers, each with a five-parted tube, like a miniature Foxglove (p.406). The colour of the flowers varies from cream or green to deep pink. The Navelwort is able to grow in places where there is almost no soil.

RESIDES *on cliffs, rocky outcrops, old walls, and stony banks, from sea-level up to 2,500m.*

long, tapered spike

shallowly lobed leaf margin

PERENNIAL

bell-like flowers

dimple in centre

NOTE

Like all members of the Sedum family, the Navelwort has fleshy leaves which are used to store water during wet periods, enabling the plant to survive in growing conditions that are generally very dry.

PLANT HEIGHT *15–40cm.*
FLOWER SIZE *8–10mm long.*
FLOWERING TIME *June–August.*
LEAVES *Basal rosettes, circular, fleshy, with the stem attached to the centre.*
FRUIT *Group of follicles with tiny seeds.*
SIMILAR SPECIES *Marsh Pennywort (p.384), which has similar leaves, but tiny flowers.*

Orpine

Sedum telephium (Crassulaceae)

An attractive member of the stonecrop family, Orpine has fairly large, succulent, pale green leaves, elliptical in shape with slightly toothed margins. The tight, domed clusters of flowers remain in bud for some weeks, but eventually open to reveal starry, five-petalled pink blooms, with purple-pink blotches on the petal tips and in the centres. The stamens are red.

OCCURS *along woodland margins and road verges, and in grassy, rocky places; on light, sandy soil.*

tight clusters of red-pink flowers

pale green leaf

toothed margin

PERENNIAL

red stamens

leafy stems

pointed petals

PLANT HEIGHT *30–60cm.*
FLOWER SIZE *8–10mm wide.*
FLOWERING TIME *July–September.*
LEAVES *Alternate, elliptical, and toothed.*
FRUIT *Cluster of carpels.*
SIMILAR SPECIES *Roseroot (p.365), which has similar leaves but yellow flowers and a more bushy habit; generally grows on cliffs.*

Rue-leaved Saxifrage

Saxifraga tridactylites (Saxifragaceae)

This is a diminutive plant but one that is clearly visible in the dry, bare places it inhabits. It is red-tinged, or entirely red in colour, with tiny but characteristic three- or five-lobed leaves, the lower ones often withered. The minute five-petalled white flowers are on long stalks, and each sits in a red calyx, which inflates as the fruit is formed.

INHABITS *dry, rocky, and bare places such as old walls and sandy heaths, on chalky soil.*

tiny white flowers

reddish stems

ANNUAL

flower stalks longer than flowers

lobed lower leaves

PLANT HEIGHT *4–15cm.*
FLOWER SIZE *3–5mm wide.*
FLOWERING TIME *June–September.*
LEAVES *Alternate, fleshy, three- or five-lobed, reddish.*
FRUIT *Two-parted capsule inside the calyx.*
SIMILAR SPECIES *None; this plant is unique with its reddish foliage.*

Meadow Saxifrage

Saxifraga granulata (Saxifragaceae)

The white flowers of this delicate plant stand out among the grasses of old meadows. The flowers are borne in loosely branched clusters of up to 12, on a single, leafless stem arising from a basal rosette of leaves. Bulbils, which are able to form new plants, usually form just below the soil surface, at the base of the lowest leaves. A species of unimproved pastures and hay meadows, Meadow Saxifrage has declined in recent decades due to changes in agricultural practices, especially in the south of England, but sometimes it may still be found growing in old churchyards.

FOUND *in meadows, pastures, on road verges and rocky places; on chalky soil.*

bluntly lobed leaves

NOTE

Most species of Saxifraga come from arctic or Alpine regions, and are grown as ornamental garden plants. Some, such as the familiar London Pride (S. x urbium) may become naturalized in the countryside.

5-petalled flowers

PERENNIAL

rounded petals

PLANT HEIGHT *20–50cm.*
FLOWER SIZE *1.5–3cm wide.*
FLOWERING TIME *April–June.*
LEAVES *Mostly basal rosettes, rounded or kidney-shaped, and bluntly toothed.*
FRUIT *Small, two-parted capsule.*
SIMILAR SPECIES *Grass of Parnassus (p.365), which has stalked, heart-shaped leaves.*

Yellow Saxifrage

Saxifraga aizoides (Saxifragaceae)

Creating bold splashes of colour in its rocky habitat, this saxifrage has numerous hairy, slightly toothed leaves. Not all stems bear flowers but those that do, bear branched clusters of flowers, each with five bright yellow, sometimes red-spotted petals, with clearly visible sepals in between. The name *aizoides* refers to its slight resemblance to *Sedum aizoon*, a stonecrop from Asia, sometimes grown in gardens.

FOUND in rocky places and marshes, and along mountain streams, from sea level to 3,000m.

narrow, unstalked leaves

green sepals

orange anthers

PERENNIAL

loose, bright yellow flower clusters

NOTE

The name Saxifraga comes from the Latin saxum (stone) and a modification of frango (to break), and refers to their habit of growing among cracks and crevices in rocks, appearing to have broken them.

PLANT HEIGHT 10–25cm.
FLOWER SIZE 5–10mm wide.
FLOWERING TIME June–September.
LEAVES Alternate, narrowly linear, fleshy and hairy, slightly toothed.
FRUIT Two-parted capsule.
SIMILAR SPECIES Biting Stonecrop (p.363), which has smaller, succulent leaves; Yellow Marsh Saxifrage (S. hirculus), which has more delicate, untoothed leaves.

Roseroot

Rhodiola rosea (Crassulaceae)

Often found on cliffs, Roseroot forms mounded tufts, like giant pincushions of yellow-headed pins. The thick, erect stems arise from a common base, each with many fleshy, reddish-tinged leaves. At the apex of each stem is a cluster of rose-scented, greenish yellow flowers with four petals, many yellow stamens, and purple anthers.

FORMS cushions on inland and coastal cliffs, mountain slopes, and rocky places.

fruit in clusters

leaves spiral up the stem

tight terminal flower cluster

PERENNIAL

fleshy oval leaves

PLANT HEIGHT 20–35cm.
FLOWER SIZE 5–8mm wide.
FLOWERING TIME May–July.
LEAVES Alternate, fleshy, oval, and toothed.
FRUIT Cluster of orange-red follicles.
SIMILAR SPECIES Orpine (p.364), which is similar when not in flower, but without the clustered habit.

Opposite-leaved Golden-saxifrage

Chrysosplenium oppositifolium (Saxifragaceae)

Forming golden-green mats in wet woodland, this short plant hugs the ground, spreading by creeping shoots that root at intervals. It has yellow-green leaves and tiny flowers, with bright yellow stamens, in the upper leaf axils.

GROWS on damp patches or streamsides, in wet woodland and rocks, in shady places.

small, round leaves

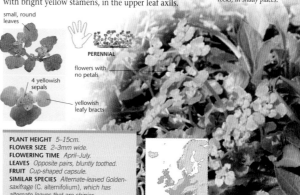

PERENNIAL

flowers with no petals

4 yellowish sepals

yellowish leafy bracts

PLANT HEIGHT 5–15cm.
FLOWER SIZE 2–3mm wide.
FLOWERING TIME April–July.
LEAVES Opposite pairs, bluntly toothed.
FRUIT Cup-shaped capsule.
SIMILAR SPECIES Alternate-leaved Golden-saxifrage (C. alternifolium), which has alternate leaves that are shinier.

Grass of Parnassus

Parnassia palustris (Parnassiaceae)

The solitary flowers of this meadow plant have five white petals with greenish veins and a characteristic and unusual arrangement of branched staminodes surrounding the true stamens. Most of the rather waxy leaves are basal and heart-shaped, on long stalks, but there is also a single, centrally placed leaf that clasps the flower stem. The fruit is a single capsule, which contains many seeds. This species has been lost from most of southern Britain due to land drainage.

FAVOURS damp, grassy places, marshes, fens, and meadows; on neutral or chalky soil, also in mountains.

heart-shaped leaf

feathery yellow staminodes

PERENNIAL

long stalk

5-petalled white flower

solitary flower

NOTE

The staminodes at the base of each petal are modified infertile stamens, each branched like the strings of a harp, and serve to attract pollinating insects to the true stamens by secreting a drop of nectar.

PLANT HEIGHT 10–30cm.
FLOWER SIZE 1.5–3cm wide.
FLOWERING TIME June–September.
LEAVES Basal, heart-shaped, and long-stalked, having a somewhat waxy appearance, with a single clasping stem leaf.
FRUIT Capsule that splits into four.
SIMILAR SPECIES Meadow Saxifrage (p.364), which has lobed, toothed leaves and branched flowerheads.

Dropwort

Filipendula vulgaris (Rosaceae)

This plant is most easily identified by the small, round, pink-flushed flower buds, which look like beads, borne at the tops of the long, upright stems. The flowers each have six white petals and numerous long stamens; when they open they give the plant a fluffy appearance. The leaves are finely divided into many pairs of leaflets.

THRIVES *in meadows and dry grassland, and on roadsides, especially on chalky soil. Prefers open, sunny situations.*

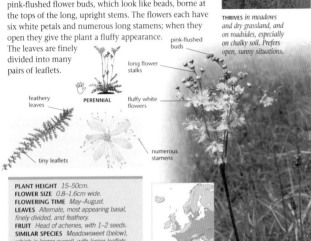

pink-flushed buds

long flower stalks

feathery leaves

PERENNIAL

fluffy white flowers

tiny leaflets

numerous stamens

PLANT HEIGHT *15–50cm.*
FLOWER SIZE *0.8–1.6cm wide.*
FLOWERING TIME *May–August.*
LEAVES *Alternate, most appearing basal, finely divided, and feathery.*
FRUIT *Head of achenes, with 1–2 seeds.*
SIMILAR SPECIES *Meadowsweet (below), which is larger overall, with larger leaflets.*

Meadowsweet

FLOURISHES *in wet meadows, fens, and tall herb communities, and along river banks, stream margins, and damp road verges.*

Filipendula ulmaria (Rosaceae)

This member of the rose family is most attractive when its creamy white flowerheads are seen in great masses along a river bank. The fragrant flowers, each with many stamens, open from the spherical buds at the top of branched stems, which stand tall above other vegetation. The seeds are coiled together like tiny snail shells. The deep green foliage has a rough texture similar to that of elm leaves.

spherical flower buds

PERENNIAL

tall, rigid stems

flowers in loose clusters

toothed leaflets

deep green leaves

NOTE
This fragrant herb was once strewn on the floors of houses to impart its scent; it was also used to flavour mead or honey wine.

spirally twisted seeds

PLANT HEIGHT *60–120cm.*
FLOWER SIZE *4–8mm wide.*
FLOWERING TIME *June–August.*
LEAVES *Alternate, pinnately divided, small leaflets between bigger ones.*
FRUIT *Small collection of achenes, individual fruit tightly coiled.*
SIMILAR SPECIES *Dropwort (above), which has long fern-like leaves; Common Meadow-rue (p.356), which has three-lobed leaves and flowers with tiny petals.*

Bramble

Rubus fruticosus (Rosaceae)

Also known as Blackberry, this species is divided by some botanists into hundreds of microspecies, but they all look very similar. The tenacious scrambling stems are covered with vicious thorns and, arching down to the ground, take root to form new plants. Rose-like flowers, present throughout summer, may be any shade from white to deep pink or purple. The edible fruit is a cluster of segments called drupelets that ripen from green to red to blue-black and may be seen at the same time as the flowers.

OCCURS *in almost any habitat on many types of soil, but favours woodland, hedges, and scrub, where it may form thickets.*

PERENNIAL

5-petalled flowers

prickly, arching stems

3 leaflets

NOTE
Crawling under a Bramble bush was once thought to be an effective charm against rheumatism and boils.

numerous stamens

toothed margin

cluster of drupelets

PLANT HEIGHT *0.5–2.5m.*
FLOWER SIZE *2–3cm wide.*
FLOWERING TIME *May–September.*
LEAVES *Alternate; divided into three toothed leaflets with prickly surface.*
FRUIT *Cluster of segments or drupelets.*
SIMILAR SPECIES *Dewberry (R. caesius) has fewer druplets; Raspberry (below) has tiny petals and five-lobed leaves; Field Rose (p.367) and Dog Rose (p.367), which have larger flowers and scarlet hips.*

Raspberry

PREFERS *shady areas in woodland and scrub, and on heaths, wasteland, and embankments.*

Rubus idaeus (Rosaceae)

Clusters of nodding flowers are borne on this tall, bushy plant, each flower having five tiny white petals, which are bent backwards and are smaller than the green sepals between them. The leaves, on prickly stems, are divided into finely toothed leaflets, pale green above with whitish down beneath. The slightly hairy fruit is a cluster of bright red drupelets.

pale green leaves

nodding white flowers

PERENNIAL

green sepals

cluster of red drupelets

oval leaflets

PLANT HEIGHT *80–150cm.*
FLOWER SIZE *9–11mm wide.*
FLOWERING TIME *May–August.*
LEAVES *Alternate, pinnately divided into 5–7 leaflets.*
FRUIT *Collection of red drupelets.*
SIMILAR SPECIES *Bramble (above), which has larger prickles and flowers, and black fruit.*

Dog Rose

Rosa canina (Rosaceae)

Perhaps one of the prettiest wildflowers to grace the countryside in early summer, the Dog Rose has long, arching, thorn-covered stems that clamber over bushes and hedges or occasionally form free-standing bushes. The stems and leaves are free from any hair or glands, and the thorns are hooked at the end like an eagle's beak. The scentless flowers have five white petals that are usually flushed with pale pink, setting off the numerous yellow stamens. The styles form a small dome, rather than a column, in the centre of the flower.

SCRAMBLES *over hedges and bushes, along woodland margins, and in rough, scrubby, grassy places.*

PERENNIAL

coarsely toothed margins
numerous yellow stamens
pink-flushed petals
5–7 leaflets
oval red rosehip

NOTE

The hips have long been used in commercial preparations to ease coughs and sore throats; they may also be fermented to make wine.

PLANT HEIGHT *1–2.5m.*
FLOWER SIZE *4–5cm wide.*
FLOWERING TIME *June–July.*
LEAVES *Alternate, pinnately divided into 5–7 toothed leaflets, with long stipules attached to the leaf stalk.*
FRUIT *Oval to round red hips.*
SIMILAR SPECIES *Bramble (p.366); Field Rose (below) has flowers with styles forming a column; other Rosa species with hairy flower stalks.*

Field Rose

Rosa arvensis (Rosaceae)

This climbing, straggling rose has white flowers, with the styles forming short columns, protruding about 5mm. Its leaves, borne on sparsely prickled stems, are divided into two or three pairs of small, neat, oval leaflets. The fruit is an oval, bright red hip, emerging from the flower sepals, which fall off when the fruit ripens.

CLAMBERS *over other vegetation in scrub, hedgerows, and woodland margins. May form low bushes.*

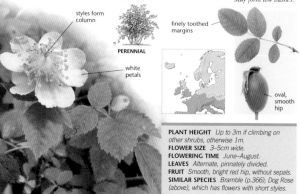
styles form column
PERENNIAL
finely toothed margins
white petals
oval, smooth hip

PLANT HEIGHT *Up to 3m if climbing on other shrubs, otherwise 1m.*
FLOWER SIZE *3–5cm wide.*
FLOWERING TIME *June–August.*
LEAVES *Alternate, pinnately divided.*
FRUIT *Smooth, bright red hip, without sepals.*
SIMILAR SPECIES *Bramble (p.366); Dog Rose (above), which has flowers with short styles.*

Burnet Rose

Rosa pimpinellifolia (Rosaceae)

Perhaps the easiest of the native roses to identify, Burnet Rose rarely grows to more than knee-height and usually much shorter. The leaflets are small, and the stems are very densely covered with long straight spines and bristles. The flowers are pale lemon in bud, opening to purest white, but produce a distinctive black, rounded hip in the autumn.

GROWS *on sand dunes and sea cliffs, or among scrub and rough grassland.*

PERENNIAL

numerous yellow stamens
pure white flowers
toothed leaflets
rounded black hip
unripe fruit

PLANT HEIGHT *Up to 1m, though usually 50cm or less.*
FLOWER SIZE *20–40mm wide.*
FLOWERING TIME *May–July.*
LEAVES *Alternate, dull green, with 5–11 small, toothed leaflets.*
FRUIT *Rounded black hip, 10mm wide.*
SIMILAR SPECIES *Field Rose (left), which is taller; Bramble (p.366) has bigger leaves.*

FLOURISHES *in tall grassland, meadows, scrub, and woodland margins, and along hedgerows and road verges.*

Agrimony

Agrimonia eupatoria (Rosaceae)

The long, narrow spires of yellow flowers are highly distinctive in this unusual member of the rose family, and particularly conspicuous as they rise above the surrounding vegetation. The leaves are divided into 3–6 toothed leaflets, with smaller leaflets in between. The hooked spines of the calyx that surrounds the fruit readily attach themselves to animal fur, and to trousers and bootlaces, helping to disperse the seeds to new locations. Fragrant Agrimony (*A. procera*), a related plant, has scented flowers and sticky leaf undersides. It has a similar distribution but prefers acid soil.

NOTE

Extracts of this plant were used in the 15th century to help heal wounds. Modern research indicates that Agrimony does have anti-viral properties.

PERENNIAL

flowers in long, slender spikes
erect stems
divided leaves
tiny leaflets between main leaflets
5 separate petals
up to 20 stamens

PLANT HEIGHT *50–100cm.*
FLOWER SIZE *5–8mm wide.*
FLOWERING TIME *June–August.*
LEAVES *Alternate, pinnate, with 3–6 pairs of toothed leaflets, and smaller intermediate leaflets.*
FRUIT *Cup-shaped and grooved, covered with hooked bristles.*
SIMILAR SPECIES *Weld (p.363), which has smaller, yellowish green flowers; Dark Mullein (p.404), which has much larger flowers.*

Salad Burnet

Sanguisorba minor (Rosaceae)

The distinctive leaves of this plant are pinnately divided into pairs of tiny, oval leaflets, well separated on the leaf stalk, like a row of little bird's wings. They smell like cucumber when crushed, and may be eaten in salads. The flowerheads open first with the crimson female styles, followed by drooping male stamens with fluffy yellow anthers.

male flowers

FORMS *large colonies in dry grassland and rocky places, and on roadsides; on slopes and on chalky soil.*

rounded flowerheads

long stem

crimson female flowers

slender, pinnate leaves

PERENNIAL

PLANT HEIGHT *20–50cm.*
FLOWER SIZE *Flowerheads 1–2cm wide.*
FLOWERING TIME *May–July.*
LEAVES *Alternate, pinnately divided with small, toothed leaflets, smelling of cucumber.*
FRUIT *One or two achenes within the calyx.*
SIMILAR SPECIES *Great Burnet (below), which is much larger and has bigger leaves.*

Herb Bennet

Geum urbanum (Rosaceae)

Although this leafy member of the rose family has branched flower stems, there is never a mass of flowers on display at the same time. Each five-petalled, pale yellow flower is often partnered by the fruithead, with its characteristic hooked spines. The toothed leaves are deeply lobed or divided into leaflets, the stem leaves with a pair of large leaf-like stipules at the base.

PROLIFERATES *in woodland, along hedgerows, roadsides, paths, and other shady places.*

PERENNIAL

hooked styles of fruithead

rounded petals

numerous stamens

coarsely toothed leaflets

cluster of achenes

PLANT HEIGHT *40–70cm.*
FLOWER SIZE *1–1.5cm wide.*
FLOWERING TIME *May–September.*
LEAVES *Basal with pairs of lobed leaflets; stem leaves with three lobes or leaflets.*
FRUIT *Rounded cluster of hairy achenes.*
SIMILAR SPECIES *Water Avens (left), which has pendent flowers.*

Great Burnet

Sanguisorba officinalis (Rosaceae)

This damp-loving plant is intolerant of grazing or drying out of its habitat. The tall, slender, branched stems bear oval flowerheads with densely packed crimson flowers, often visible above surrounding tall grasses. There are no petals, but deep red sepals and prominent stamens form the flowerheads. The alternate leaves are pinnately divided into about seven pairs of stalked and oval leaflets, dark green above but greyish beneath.

INHABITS *damp meadows and open, grassy places on chalky or rich soil.*

dark green and greyish leaves

toothed margin

oblong heads of crimson flowers

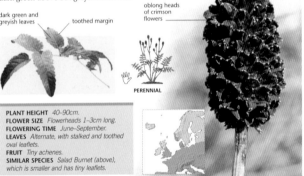

PERENNIAL

PLANT HEIGHT *40–90cm.*
FLOWER SIZE *Flowerheads 1–3cm long.*
FLOWERING TIME *June–September.*
LEAVES *Alternate, with stalked and toothed oval leaflets.*
FRUIT *Tiny achenes.*
SIMILAR SPECIES *Salad Burnet (above), which is smaller and has tiny leaflets.*

Mountain Avens

Dryas octopetala (Rosaceae)

A plant of often inaccessible places, Mountain Avens has flowers that identify it as a rose family member, with eight white petals and many yellow stamens, each flower on a single stem. The leathery leaves, shaped like miniature oak leaves (*drys* is ancient Greek for oak), can form extensive mats or carpets. The seeds have long, feathery "beards", twisted together at first but unfurling as the seedhead opens.

FOUND *in rock crevices and on ledges, cliffs, mountain heaths, and sand dunes; on neutral or chalky soil.*

NOTE

Mountain Avens was widespread over Britain after the last Ice Age, but is now confined to Snowdonia, the Lake District and the western Highlands of Scotland, as well as the Burren in western Ireland.

bluntly toothed leaf

silvery underside

PERENNIAL

numerous stamens

glossy green leaves

feathery fruit

PLANT HEIGHT *10–25cm.*
FLOWER SIZE *2–4cm wide.*
FLOWERING TIME *May–July.*
LEAVES *Alternate, oblong; glossy above, silvery below.*
FRUIT *Collection of achenes.*
SIMILAR SPECIES *Cloudberry (Rubus chamaemorus) has orange blackberry-like fruit and rough, rounded, or kidney-shaped leaves with large lobes; Burnet Rose (p.367) has pinnate leaves and thorny stems.*

Water Avens

Geum rivale (Rosaceae)

GROWS *in colonies in marshy grassland, ditches, meadows, and wet woodland. Prefers chalky soil.*

This graceful plant often hybridizes with the closely related Herb Bennet (right), resulting in flowers that have features of both plants. The flowers of Water Avens have pinkish cream petals and purplish brown sepals that become upright when the feathery fruit is formed. The leaves are divided into lobed leaflets; the stem leaves are smaller.

large terminal leaflet

toothed margin

arched flower stalks

PERENNIAL

pendent flowers

achenes with hooked styles

PLANT HEIGHT *30–50cm.*
FLOWER SIZE *8–15mm wide.*
FLOWERING TIME *April–September.*
LEAVES *Basal pinnate leaves, with 3–6 pairs of oval to round leaflets; stem leaves trifoliate.*
FRUIT *Collection of achenes.*
SIMILAR SPECIES *Herb Bennet (right); hybrids, which have pendent yellow flowers.*

Marsh Cinquefoil

Potentilla palustris (Rosaceae)

The short-stalked leaves of this plant are pinnately divided into 5–7 serrated leaflets. The distinctive flower has prominent, deep maroon or purplish sepals; the crimson petals are much smaller. The central core of immature achenes is surrounded by dark stamens.

SEEN *in marshland, fens, bogs, and wet meadows, on acid soil.*

serrated leaflet margin

strawberry-like flower centre

5 large sepals

PERENNIAL

PLANT HEIGHT *30–50cm.*
FLOWER SIZE *2–3cm wide.*
FLOWERING TIME *May–July.*
LEAVES *Alternate, 5–7 oblong, serrated leaflets with papery stipules at leaf stalk base.*
FRUIT *Head of achenes surrounded by persistent calyx.*
SIMILAR SPECIES *None.*

Wild Strawberry

Fragaria vesca (Rosaceae)

The fruit of this plant has an excellent flavour, but is much smaller than that of the cultivated variety. The plant creeps by runners, which root to form new plants. Its conspicuous flowers have five rounded white petals, backed with ten green sepals. The leaves have three coarsely toothed leaflets, like a giant clover leaf.

CREEPS *along the ground in woods, scrub, rocky places, and hedgerows, and along walls; on chalky soil.*

yellow stamens

veined leaf
green sepals
fleshy red fruit

PERENNIAL

PLANT HEIGHT *10–25cm.*
FLOWER SIZE *1.2–1.8cm wide.*
FLOWERING TIME *April–July.*
LEAVES *Mostly basal, with three leaflets.*
FRUIT *Strawberry with seeds on the outside.*
SIMILAR SPECIES *Barren Strawberry (Potentilla sterilis), which has a smaller terminal tooth to each leaflet.*

Silverweed

Potentilla anserina (Rosaceae)

This creeping plant spreads by means of rooting runners. Its leaves are easily recognized by their ladder-like rows of 15–25 serrated leaflets, grey-green above and covered with fine silvery hair below. The solitary flowers, which may not grow in some damp habitats, have rounded yellow petals, with an epicalyx behind each solitary flower.

PROLIFERATES *in open places such as farm tracks, grassy verges, waste, and cultivated ground.*

bright yellow flower

sharply toothed leaflets

5–6 large petals

PERENNIAL

PLANT HEIGHT *5–20cm.*
FLOWER SIZE *1.5–2cm wide.*
FLOWERING TIME *May–August.*
LEAVES *Basal rosettes, pinnate.*
FRUIT *Tight head of achenes.*
SIMILAR SPECIES *Creeping Cinquefoil (P. reptans) has palmately lobed leaves; Tormentil (below) has four-petalled flowers.*

Lady's-mantle

Alchemilla vulgaris (Rosaceae)

There are many similar varieties of Lady's-mantle that are difficult to differentiate. *Alchemilla vulgaris* represents an aggregate of several species including *A. xanthochlora* and *A. filicaulis*. They all exhibit the same silky, lobed, grey-green leaves which are covered with downy hairs that repel water so that dewdrops collect on them. The yellow-green flowers are in rounded clusters, and each tiny flower has four sepals but no petals.

FOUND *in grassy and rocky places, meadows, woodland margins, and streamsides, at high and low altitudes.*

PERENNIAL

palmately lobed leaf

4 stamens

grey-green leaves

tiny green flowers

flowers in loose clusters

NOTE
The dew that collects on the leaves was highly prized by alchemists as very pure water for turning base metals into gold. The plant is an effective treatment for wounds and menstrual problems.

PLANT HEIGHT *30–60cm.*
FLOWER SIZE *3–4mm wide.*
FLOWERING TIME *May–August.*
LEAVES *Mostly basal with clasping stem leaves; palmately lobed, soft, and hairy.*
FRUIT *Small solitary achene.*
SIMILAR SPECIES *Alpine Lady's-mantle (A. alpina), which is much smaller, with leaves divided into 5 or 7 separate finger-like leaflets.*

Tormentil

Potentilla erecta (Rosaceae)

A slender, delicate plant that trails through grassland, Tormentil has long, non-rooting flower stems held up by other vegetation. Its bright lemon-yellow flowers have four petals, notched at the tip, in the shape of a cross. The leaves are three-lobed with bluntly toothed, oval segments; there are two smaller stipules at the base.

FORMS *patches in lawns, meadows, heaths, woodland, and on roadsides, preferring acid soil.*

solitary lemon-yellow flower

slender flower stalk

PERENNIAL

3-lobed leaf

4 petals

PLANT HEIGHT *4–12cm.*
FLOWER SIZE *7–11mm wide.*
FLOWERING TIME *May–September.*
LEAVES *Alternate, three-lobed, toothed.*
FRUIT *Tiny achenes.*
SIMILAR SPECIES *Silverweed (above), which has ladder-like leaves; Creeping Cinquefoil (P. reptans), which has 5 petals.*

PLANTS

Broom

Cytisus scoparius (Fabaceae)

This deciduous shrub has had a long association with people, especially, as its name suggests, in the use of its branches as brooms. The many slender green branches are ridged and angled, producing surprisingly small, virtually stalkless, oval leaves which may be single or in threes. The strongly scented pealike flowers, borne in leafy spikes, are large and brilliant golden yellow, the upper and lower petals opening wide to reveal the curled stamens.

small stalkless leaflets

slender stems

wide open yellow peaflowers

oval leaf

oblong seed pod

PERENNIAL

NOTE
The branches of this shrub were used for making brooms, the buds used as capers, the leaves for flavouring beer, the fibre for making cloth, the bark for tanning leather, and the plant has had a host of medicinal uses. Its fibrous root system is excellent for stabilizing sandy banks, and it is often planted on new motorway embankments.

PLANT HEIGHT *1–2m.*
FLOWER SIZE *1.6–1.8cm long.*
FLOWERING TIME *April–June.*
LEAVES *Alternate, single or trifoliate, mostly stalkless, very small.*
FRUIT *Hairy, oblong pod, black when ripe.*
SIMILAR SPECIES *Gorse (right), which has spiny stems; Dyer's Greenweed (below), which is much smaller overall and has smaller flowers.*

Gorse

Ulex europaeus (Fabaceae)

Although viciously spiked on mature plants, when young, the branches of Gorse are soft and palatable – so much so that, in rabbit-infested areas, this normally large shrub may grow no more than a few centimetres high. The ridged stems bear tiny, three-lobed, scale-like leaves when the plant is young, but these are soon replaced by a dense covering of grooved spines. The yellow peaflowers may be seen all through the year and are coconut-scented, with an arrangement of stamens that shoot out pollen onto visiting bees. The brown pods expel the seeds explosively when ripe, and may be heard popping open in bright sunshine.

NOTE
Peasants with no available grazing land used to soak and pulp the spiny shoots of Gorse to provide their cattle nutritious fodder during winter.

PERENNIAL

covering of spines

brown pod

hairy sepals

sharp spines

PLANT HEIGHT *Up to 2m.*
FLOWER SIZE *1.5–2cm long.*
FLOWERING TIME *January–April, but may flower throughout the year.*
LEAVES *Tiny, three-lobed, scale-like when young, soon replaced by alternate, branched spines.*
FRUIT *Hairy brown pod, 1.2–2cm long.*
SIMILAR SPECIES *Broom (left) has smaller, oval leaves and no spines on the stems; Dwarf Gorse (U. minor), which is shorter with smaller flowers.*

Dyer's Greenweed

Genista tinctoria (Fabaceae)

This subshrub forms small, compact bushes, resembling miniature versions of Broom (above). Its non-spiny branches are sparsely covered with oblong leaves, each with a pair of tiny stipules at the base. The yellow peaflowers, borne on the tops of the stems, open out wide so that the two lower wing petals droop downwards.

flowers in stalked spikes

drooping lower petals

narrow seed pod

hairless surface

small, simple leaves

PERENNIAL

PLANT HEIGHT *30–60cm.*
FLOWER SIZE *8–15mm long.*
FLOWERING TIME *May–July.*
LEAVES *Alternate, oblong, and untoothed.*
FRUIT *Pod, hairless, oblong, brown.*
SIMILAR SPECIES *Broom (above), which is larger; Petty Whin (G. anglica), which has small spines on its woody stems.*

Garden Lupin

Lupinus polyphyllus (Fabaceae)

Introduced from North America, this plant has become widely naturalized. Blue, pink, white, yellow, or bicoloured peaflowers are borne in tight spirals up the stem. The long-stalked, finger-like leaves, covered with tiny hair, radiate from a single point.

tall, pyramidal flower spikes

digitate leaves

PERENNIAL

long leaf stalk

whorls of flowers

PLANT HEIGHT *70–120cm.*
FLOWER SIZE *1.2–1.4cm long.*
FLOWERING TIME *June–August.*
LEAVES *Mostly basal with some stem leaves; digitate with 9–17 lance-shaped leaflets.*
FRUIT *Black, hairy pod, 2.5–4cm long.*
SIMILAR SPECIES *Tree Lupin (L. arboreus), which is a shrub with yellow flowers.*

Bush Vetch

Vicia sepium (Fabaceae)

This plant uses its long tendrils to scramble over other vegetation. It produces small, tight clusters of peaflowers that vary in colour from a greyish blue to a purplish pink, the standard petal veined with streaks of dark purple. The flowers turn brown once pollinated. The leaves have neat rows of oblong leaflets.

CLAMBERS *over other plants in woodland, scrub, meadows, and hedgerows, avoiding acid soil.*

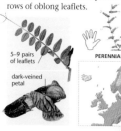

5–9 pairs of leaflets

PERENNIAL

short-stalked flower clusters

dark-veined petal

PLANT HEIGHT *20–60cm.*
FLOWER SIZE *1.2–1.5cm wide.*
FLOWERING TIME *May–October.*
LEAVES *Alternate, pinnate, toothed stipules.*
FRUIT *Black, hairless pod, 2–3.5cm long.*
SIMILAR SPECIES *Common Vetch (below), which has narrower leaflets; Wood Vetch (V. sylvatica), which has larger, paler flowers.*

Common Vetch

Vicia sativa (Fabaceae)

SCRAMBLES *among grasses and other vegetation in cultivated fields, wasteland, roadsides, banks, and scrub.*

Introduced from southern Europe as a fodder crop for cattle, Common Vetch is now established throughout the British Isles. The ladder-like leaves are pinnately divided, each leaflet with a "needle" at the tip. Each leaf terminates in a long, branched tendril, and at the base are a pair of small, coarsely toothed stipules, each with a black spot. The flowers, usually paired but occasionally solitary, are vivid red to purple, the wing and keel petals usually being a shade darker than the standard petal.

narrow, sharply tipped leaflets

ANNUAL

NOTE
The spots on the stipules secrete a sugary substance that attracts ants, which, in turn, help to defend the plant against attack by other insects.

flowers usually in pairs

terminal branched tendril

3–8 pairs of leaflets

red to purple peaflower

slender seed pod

PLANT HEIGHT *50–120cm.*
FLOWER SIZE *1.8–2.5cm long.*
FLOWERING TIME *April–September.*
LEAVES *Alternate, pinnately divided, with 3–8 pairs of oval to lance-shaped leaflets.*
FRUIT *Hairy pod, green, ripening to brown or black, 2.5–7cm long.*
SIMILAR SPECIES *Bush Vetch (above), which has broader leaflets; Bitter Vetch (p.372), which has larger leaves and no tendrils.*

Tufted Vetch

Vicia cracca (Fabaceae)

The deep violet-blue flowers of Tufted Vetch are produced in such profusion that they can be seen from some distance, often alongside roads and motorways. Up to 40 bluish violet flowers are clustered into long racemes, with each flower on a tiny stalk, arranged on one side of the stem. The leaves are divided into many pairs of narrow leaflets, sometimes with a fine covering of downy hairs. Each leaf terminates in a long, branching tendril, which can support the plant to a considerable height when it would otherwise flop on to the ground.

PROLIFERATES *among tall grasses in meadows, hedgerows, woodland margins, scrub, roadsides, and over coastal rocks and shingle.*

NOTE
Plants with tendrils exploit other plants by climbing up them to reach better light, without committing any food resources into building robust stems.

flowers in one-sided racemes

slender stems

PERENNIAL

twining tendrils

paired leaflets

bluish violet petals

PLANT HEIGHT *0.8–1.8m.*
FLOWER SIZE *8–12mm wide.*
FLOWERING TIME *June–August.*
LEAVES *Alternate, pinnate, with 6–15 pairs of linear-oblong leaflets.*
FRUIT *Three-lobed capsule, splitting to the base.*
SIMILAR SPECIES *Lucerne (p.373), which has smaller flower clusters; Wood Vetch (V. sylvatica), which has purple-veined white flowers; Fodder Vetch (V. villosa), which is a casual that has paler wing petals.*

Smooth Tare

Vicia tetrasperma (Fabaceae)

This plant is so fine and dainty that it gives a misty look to grasses and other vegetation over which it clambers by means of its long leaf tendrils. The tiny peaflowers are veined with purple or pale blue, and develop into small seed pods that contain four seeds.

SPRAWLS *over grasses in old meadows and along hedgerows and arable fields.*

veined petals

long, narrow leaflets

fine, slender stems

paired peaflowers

oblong seed pods

ANNUAL

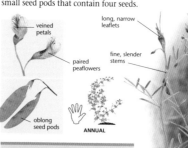

PLANT HEIGHT *20–60cm.*
FLOWER SIZE *4–8mm long.*
FLOWERING TIME *May–August.*
LEAVES *Alternate, pinnate with 3–6 pairs of linear leaflets, ending in tendrils.*
FRUIT *Green or brown four-seeded pod.*
SIMILAR SPECIES *Hairy Tare (V. hirsuta), which has whitish flowers and hairy pods.*

Bitter Vetch

Lathyrus linifolius (Fabaceae)

Rather similar to Bush Vetch (p.371), Bitter Vetch is a more delicate plant, with narrower, spear-shaped leaflets. The clearest distinguishing feature is that the stems are winged. The flowers turn from pink-purple to blue as they mature, and the leaves end in tiny points, rather than tendrils.

OCCURS *on heaths, road verges, grassy banks, woodland margins, and scrub, on neutral to acid soil.*

PERENNIAL

narrow, untoothed leaflets

pink-purple peaflower

loose clusters of 2–3 flowers

long flower stalk

PLANT HEIGHT 20–40cm.
FLOWER SIZE 1–1.6cm long.
FLOWERING TIME April–July.
LEAVES Alternate, pinnate with 2–4 pairs of elliptical or narrow leaflets.
FRUIT Hairless brown pod, 2.5–4.5cm long.
SIMILAR SPECIES Bush Vetch (p.371), which has tendrils and oval leaflets.

Narrow-leaved Everlasting-pea

Lathyrus sylvestris (Fabaceae)

TWINES *over other plants in hedgerows and woodland, and on shady roadsides and sea-cliffs; prefers chalky soil.*

This straggly pea has distinctive, strongly winged stems, up to 1cm wide, which climb over other plants. The leaves are reduced to just one pair of veined, grey-green leaflets, and a long, branched, twining tendril. The flowers, in very loose clusters, are creamy yellow in bud before turning reddish purple later.

single pair of leaflets

creamy yellow flower bud

long-stalked flower clusters

branched tendril

PERENNIAL

PLANT HEIGHT 1–2m.
FLOWER SIZE 1.4–2cm long.
FLOWERING TIME June–August.
LEAVES Alternate, pinnate with one pair of leaflets, ending in tendrils.
FRUIT Brown hairless pod, 4–6cm long.
SIMILAR SPECIES Broad-leaved Everlasting-pea (below), which has larger flowers.

Broad-leaved Everlasting Pea

Lathyrus latifolius (Fabaceae)

CLIMBS *over vegetation on rough grassy and bushy sites, roadsides, wasteland, and woodland margins.*

A vigorous climber, this plant has been introduced throughout Europe where cultivated forms have become naturalized and flower even more freely. The stems and leaf stalks have very broad wings. The leaflets are prominently veined with a pair of stipules at the base.

long branching tendril

lance-shaped leaflets

slender fruit pod

PERENNIAL

flower clusters on erect stalks

PLANT HEIGHT 1–3m.
FLOWER SIZE 2–3cm long.
FLOWERING TIME May–July.
LEAVES Broad leaflets with branching tendril.
FRUIT Pod, 5–10cm long, ripening to brown.
SIMILAR SPECIES Narrow-leaved Everlasting Pea (above), which has narrower leaflets and shorter pods.

Meadow Vetchling

Lathyrus pratensis (Fabaceae)

A member of the pea family, Meadow Vetchling clambers and twines its way through tall, grassy vegetation. Its thin stems are slightly winged, and bear a pair of spear-shaped leaflets with a twisting tendril between them. At the base of each leaf-stalk are a pair of large, characteristically arrow-shaped stipules. A tight cluster of bright yellow flowers blooms at the end of a long stem, but each cluster is widely scattered throughout the supporting vegetation. The plant produces only a small amount of seed, propagation often occurring directly from the roots.

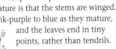

CLAMBERS *through meadow grasses and other vegetation, on roadsides, and in scrub and woodland.*

NOTE

The tendrils of climbing plants are actually modified leaves, and enable the plant to quickly devote more of its energy into flower production as there is no need to develop stout supporting stems.

5–12 flowers in a cluster

PERENNIAL

erect stem

tendril between leaflets

single pair of leaflets

yellow flowers

PLANT HEIGHT 50–100cm.
FLOWER SIZE 1–1.6cm long.
FLOWERING TIME May–August.
LEAVES Alternate, pairs of spear-shaped leaflets, with tendril between.
FRUIT Black pod, 2–4cm long.
SIMILAR SPECIES Common Bird's-foot Trefoil (p.375) and Greater Bird's-foot Trefoil (Lotus uliginosus), which have flowers clustered in a "crown" and trifoliate leaves with large, oval stipules at the base.

Grass Vetchling

Lathyrus nissolia (Fabaceae)

It takes sharp eyes and a little luck to find this plant, even if it is in flower. The leaves look like the grasses it grows among, each reduced to a long, flat, tapering blade. The solitary peaflowers are small, delicate, and brilliant scarlet. The long, narrow seed pod is pale brown.

GROWS *in meadows, fields, woodland margins, and hedgerows.*

ANNUAL

tapering leaf blade

grass-like leaf

scarlet peaflower

long, slender flower stalk

PLANT HEIGHT 20–50cm.
FLOWER SIZE 1–1.5cm long.
FLOWERING TIME May–July.
LEAVES Alternate, long, tapering, grass-like.
FRUIT Slender, tapering pod, 3–5cm long.
SIMILAR SPECIES Common Vetch (p.371), which has similarly coloured flowers but leaves that are quite different.

Purple Milk-vetch

Astragalus danicus (Fabaceae)

The peaflowers clustered on the long, erect stalks of this plant are worth a close look. The violet or purple standard petal and the central white keel petal are flushed pink. The blunt, neatly divided leaves are ladder-like and covered in dense hairs, with a pair of small stipules joined at the bases.

INHABITS *meadows and other grassy places, on chalky soil, as well as on coastal sand dunes.*

PERENNIAL

6–13 pairs of oblong leaflets

flowers in tight clusters

dark veins on purple petals

PLANT HEIGHT *10–35cm.*
FLOWER SIZE *1.5–1.8cm long.*
FLOWERING TIME *May–July.*
LEAVES *Alternate, pinnate.*
FRUIT *Dark brown swollen pods, 7–8mm long, covered with white hairs.*
SIMILAR SPECIES *Red Clover (p.374), which has 3-lobed leaves.*

Ribbed Melilot

Melilotus officinalis (Fabaceae)

As with many other members of the pea family, this plant has leaves divided into three leaflets. Unlike the rest, however, the margins of each oval leaflet are gently toothed as though nibbled away. The tiny peaflowers are arranged in long, branching spikes, giving the plant an untidy look; the seed pods turn brown when ripe.

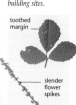

GROWS *in clumps along roadsides and field edges, on waste or disturbed ground, and building sites.*

alternate leaves

flowers droop from stems

toothed margin

slender flower spikes

BIENNIAL/ PERENNIAL

PLANT HEIGHT *80–150cm.*
FLOWER SIZE *3–4mm wide.*
FLOWERING TIME *July–September.*
LEAVES *Alternate with three oval leaflets, sharply toothed.*
FRUIT *Rounded pod with transverse ridges.*
SIMILAR SPECIES *Tall Melilot (M. altissima), which has hairy black pods.*

Wild Liquorice

Astragalus glycyphyllos (Fabaceae)

This straggling plant is not the source of the liquorice used in medicine and confectionery, which comes from *Glycyrrhiza glabra*, but its leaves are similar to those of true liquorice. They are pinnately divided with oval leaflets, including a terminal leaflet rather than a tendril. The tight cluster of peaflowers on a long stalk is greenish cream with green streaks on the upper or standard petal.

STRAGGLES *among vegetation on road verges, and in open woodland, scrub, and other rough places; prefers chalky soil.*

long flower stalk

cluster of creamy flowers

blunt, oval leaflets

PERENNIAL

green streaks on standard petal

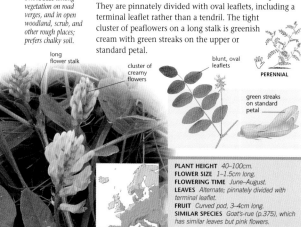

PLANT HEIGHT *40–100cm.*
FLOWER SIZE *1–1.5cm long.*
FLOWERING TIME *June–August.*
LEAVES *Alternate; pinnately divided with terminal leaflet.*
FRUIT *Curved pod, 3–4cm long.*
SIMILAR SPECIES *Goat's-rue (p.375), which has similar leaves but pink flowers.*

Black Medick

Medicago lupulina (Fabaceae)

There are several small, trailing, clover-like species, but Black Medick may easily be identified by its yellow peaflowers and clusters of tiny, coiled seed pods, which become jet-black when ripe. The small yellow flowers are in a crowded, spherical cluster on a long stalk, while the trifoliate leaves have a minute terminal tooth on each leaflet.

SPRAWLS *over grassy places, wasteland, and recently cultivated or disturbed land.*

3 oval leaflets

cluster of 10–20 tiny flowers

ANNUAL

small teeth

coiled black pods

PLANT HEIGHT *10–50cm.*
FLOWER SIZE *Flowerheads 6–10mm wide.*
FLOWERING TIME *May–August.*
LEAVES *Alternate, with three oval leaflets.*
FRUIT *Black pods, 2–3mm long, in clusters.*
SIMILAR SPECIES *Lesser Trefoil (Trifolium dubium), which has tiny fruit; Spotted Medick (M. arabica), which has spotted leaves.*

Common Restharrow

Ononis repens (Fabaceae)

The tough roots and creeping habit of this plant caused problems for farmers before the days of mechanized ploughs. It is a low, bushy plant with woody, hairy stems and rough, trifoliate leaves, each leaflet with oval stipules at the base. The flowers, larger than the leaves, consist of a huge pink standard petal, and white and pink wing and keel petals.

OCCURS *in clumps in meadows, pastures, and grassland, on chalky soil.*

oval, toothed leaflet

pink keel petal

PERENNIAL

flowers in leafy spikes

small trifoliate leaves

white wing petal

large standard petal

PLANT HEIGHT *15–50cm.*
FLOWER SIZE *1.5–2cm long.*
FLOWERING TIME *June–September.*
LEAVES *Alternate, three oval, toothed leaflets.*
FRUIT *Hairy pod, 5–8mm long, containing one or two seeds.*
SIMILAR SPECIES *Spiny Restharrow (O. spinosa), which has stiff spines.*

Lucerne

Medicago sativa (Fabaceae)

Also known as Alfalfa, this plant was introduced throughout Europe as a fodder crop for cattle. Its trifoliate leaves are divided into long, slender leaflets, each toothed at the tip. The flowers, in loose clusters, vary in colour from pale pink to deep violet.

FORMS *colonies on cultivated and waste ground, roadsides, and disturbed, rough, grassy areas.*

pink to violet flowers

toothed leaflet tip

flowers in clusters

PERENNIAL

long, narrow leaflets

coiled seed pod

PLANT HEIGHT *40–90cm.*
FLOWER SIZE *7–11mm long.*
FLOWERING TIME *June–July.*
LEAVES *Alternate, trifoliate, elliptical leaflets.*
FRUIT *Spiralled pod, 5–6mm wide, with a hole in the centre.*
SIMILAR SPECIES *Tufted Vetch (p.371), which has pinnate leaves and longer flower clusters.*

PLANTS

White Clover

Trifolium repens (Fabaceae)

A familiar grassland plant, White Clover spreads by means of rooting runners. Its three-parted leaves usually have a white band on each leaflet. Rounded heads of white or cream peaflowers may become pinkish brown as they mature, the lower flowers drooping like a wide skirt. The flowers are sweet-scented and a rich source of nectar.

PROLIFERATES *in pastures, commons, lawns, roadsides, heaths, and other grassy places.*

3 oval leaflets

V-shaped, whitish band on leaflet

rounded, cream to white flowerhead

drooping lower flowers

ball-shaped flower cluster

PERENNIAL

PLANT HEIGHT *5–20cm.*
FLOWER SIZE *7–10mm long.*
FLOWERING TIME *June–September.*
LEAVES *Alternate with three oval leaflets.*
FRUIT *Narrow pod with 3–4 seeds.*
SIMILAR SPECIES *Red Clover (below), which has darker red flowers; Strawberry Clover (right), which has smaller flowerheads.*

Strawberry Clover

Trifolium fragiferum (Fabaceae)

Similar to the pink-tinged forms of White Clover (left), this plant is more delicate, with smaller flowerheads. The three-parted leaves are in the characteristic cloverleaf shape, but without white marks. The hairy sepals of each flower swell up, forming the fruit. The hairs then rub off so that the fruit looks like a pinkish brown strawberry.

FORMS *loose colonies in damp meadows and pastures, often where floods occur, or close to the sea.*

small pink flowerheads

oval leaflets

PERENNIAL

swollen fruiting head

PLANT HEIGHT *5–15cm.*
FLOWER SIZE *6–7mm long.*
FLOWERING TIME *July–September.*
LEAVES *Alternate, trifoliate with oval leaflets.*
FRUIT *Collection of inflated, downy calyces, strawberry-like, contains the small seed pod.*
SIMILAR SPECIES *White Clover (left), which has drooping flowers.*

Red Clover

Trifolium pratense (Fabaceae)

Whole fields become crimson with the flowers of this prolific plant, which nourishes the soil with nitrogen, and is excellent fodder for livestock. The round or oblong heads of tightly clustered, pink to red flowers have a leaf directly below them. The leaves are made up of three oval leaflets, often with a V-shaped white mark. The flowers are pollinated by bumblebees. Varieties which have been sown as fodder crops occasionally naturalize and are usually more robust, with paler flowerheads than the truly wild form.

GROWS *in grassy places, old meadows, and wasteland, from lowland up to 3,000m.*

3 oval leaflets

pink petals

PERENNIAL

dense, rounded flowerheads

leaf directly below flowerhead

erect stems

NOTE

Red Clover is an important source of nectar for long-tongued bumble bees, but a decline in old clover meadows has consequently led to a fall in the bumble bee population.

PLANT HEIGHT *20–50cm.*
FLOWER SIZE *Flowerhead 1.5–3cm wide.*
FLOWERING TIME *May–September.*
LEAVES *Alternate, with three oval leaflets.*
FRUIT *Small pod hidden in the calyx.*
SIMILAR SPECIES *White Clover (above); Zigzag Clover (T. medium), has stalked flowerheads, and no leaf directly below; Crimson Clover (T. incarnatum) has longer flowerheads of deep crimson flowers.*

Hop Trefoil

Trifolium campestre (Fabaceae)

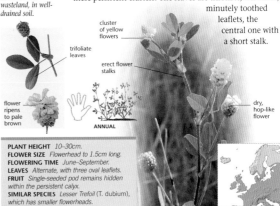

A sprawling, clover-like plant, Hop Trefoil has erect stems bearing tight clusters of untidy peaflowers, which ripen from yellow to pale brown, looking like miniature Hop fruit. The single seed of each flower remains hidden within these persistent clusters. The leaves are trifoliate, with oval, minutely toothed leaflets, the central one with a short stalk.

FLOURISHES *in dry, grassy places and on roadsides and wasteland, in well-drained soil.*

cluster of yellow flowers

trifoliate leaves

erect flower stalks

flower ripens to pale brown

ANNUAL

dry, hop-like flower

PLANT HEIGHT *10–30cm.*
FLOWER SIZE *Flowerhead to 1.5cm long.*
FLOWERING TIME *June–September.*
LEAVES *Alternate, with three oval leaflets.*
FRUIT *Single-seeded pod remains hidden within the persistent calyx.*
SIMILAR SPECIES *Lesser Trefoil (T. dubium), which has smaller flowerheads.*

Hare's-foot Clover

Trifolium arvense (Fabaceae)

The dense, fluffy flowerheads are almost like those of grass, but close examination shows that each tiny pink flower is surrounded by a calyx of long, silky hair, which gives the flowerhead the appearance of a hare's foot. The trifoliate leaves are more slender than those of other clovers.

FORMS *mats in dry, grassy areas, scrub, and woodland margins, on sandy soil.*

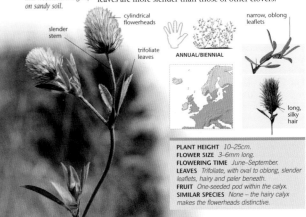

slender stem

cylindrical flowerheads

trifoliate leaves

ANNUAL/BIENNIAL

narrow, oblong leaflets

long, silky hair

PLANT HEIGHT *10–25cm.*
FLOWER SIZE *3–6mm long.*
FLOWERING TIME *June–September.*
LEAVES *Trifoliate, with oval to oblong, slender leaflets, hairy and paler beneath.*
FRUIT *One-seeded pod within the calyx.*
SIMILAR SPECIES *None – the hairy calyx makes the flowerheads distinctive.*

PLANTS

Common Bird's-foot Trefoil

Lotus corniculatus (Fabaceae)

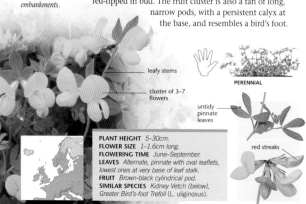

THRIVES *in grassy fields, pastures, and scrub, and along roadsides and embankments.*

This common member of the pea family produces erect stems topped with fan-shaped clusters of brightly coloured yellow or orange peaflowers with red streaks, which are red-tipped in bud. The fruit cluster is also a fan of long, narrow pods, with a persistent calyx at the base, and resembles a bird's foot.

leafy stems

cluster of 3–7 flowers

untidy pinnate leaves

PERENNIAL

red streaks

PLANT HEIGHT *5–30cm.*
FLOWER SIZE *1–1.6cm long.*
FLOWERING TIME *June–September.*
LEAVES *Alternate, pinnate with oval leaflets, lowest ones at very base of leaf stalk.*
FRUIT *Brown-black cylindrical pod.*
SIMILAR SPECIES *Kidney Vetch (below), Greater Bird's-foot Trefoil (L. uliginosus).*

Bird's-foot

Ornithopus perpusillus (Fabaceae)

A diminutive member of the pea family, with a prostrate habit, this plant is worth looking at close up. It bears 3–8 tiny peaflowers, which are predominantly white, each with a yellow blotch and delicate pink veins. The leaves are ladder-like and pinnately divided, with many pairs of leaflets, ending in a terminal leaflet. The curved, segmented seed pods resemble the claws of a bird's foot.

GROWS *in patches in open places such as sandy grassland and heaths, or among short turf; prefers acid soil.*

terminal leaflet

tiny, pink-veined peaflowers

ANNUAL

ladder-like leaf

PLANT HEIGHT *5–30cm.*
FLOWER SIZE *3–5mm wide.*
FLOWERING TIME *May–August.*
LEAVES *Alternate, pinnate with 5–12 pairs of leaflets and terminal leaflet.*
FRUIT *Many-seeded pod.*
SIMILAR SPECIES *Horseshoe Vetch (left), which has bright yellow flowers.*

Kidney Vetch

Anthyllis vulneraria (Fabaceae)

The colour of the flowers in this unusual member of the pea family varies widely from cream to red, even within the same flowerhead. Each flowerhead is surrounded at the base by thick, downy sepals, which give the plant a woolly and rather robust appearance. The leaves are pinnately divided, like a ladder, each with a large terminal leaflet.

FORMS *patches in dry grassland, on cliff-tops, and rocky ledges, often on slopes. Prefers chalky soil, especially near the sea.*

variable colours for individual flowers

large terminal leaflet

leaf-like bracts below flowerhead

PERENNIAL

whitish calyx

PLANT HEIGHT *20–50cm.*
FLOWER SIZE *Flowerhead 2–4cm wide.*
FLOWERING TIME *June–September.*
LEAVES *Alternate, pinnately divided.*
FRUIT *Seed pod enclosed within calyx.*
SIMILAR SPECIES *Common Bird's-foot Trefoil (above) and Horseshoe Vetch (below), which have yellow peaflowers.*

Goat's-rue

Galega officinalis (Fabaceae)

This robust, bushy pea family member has pink or white, but often bicoloured, flowers. Each large leaf, divided into well-separated, untoothed leaflets, ends in a terminal leaflet, and has a three-pointed green stipule at the base. Native to southern Europe and naturalized in Britain, Goat's-rue is known for its fever-reducing properties.

OCCURS *on river or stream banks, in ditches, and on damp, grassy road verges.*

flowers in long-stalked spikes

large, oblong leaflets

bristly calyx

PERENNIAL

PLANT HEIGHT *80–150cm.*
FLOWER SIZE *1–1.5cm long.*
FLOWERING TIME *July–September.*
LEAVES *Alternate, pinnate.*
FRUIT *Cylindrical seed pod, 2–5cm long.*
SIMILAR SPECIES *Wild Liquorice (p.373), which has greenish flowers; Sainfoin (below), which has narrower leaflets.*

Horseshoe Vetch

Hippocrepis comosa (Fabaceae)

This plant is an important foodplant for some of the Blue butterfly larvae. The yellow peaflowers with faint reddish veins are arranged like an open fan on a long flower stalk, while the fruithead is an extraordinary collection of twisted pods, each divided into several horseshoe-shaped segments.

SEEN *in patches on sunny grassland, often on slopes or cliff-tops, always on chalky soil.*

fan-shaped flower cluster

PERENNIAL

neat, pinnate leaves

crimped fruit

long flower stalk

PLANT HEIGHT *15–30cm.*
FLOWER SIZE *6–10mm long.*
FLOWERING TIME *May–July.*
LEAVES *Alternate, 4–7 pairs of oval leaflets.*
FRUIT *Pod divided into wavy, horseshoe-shaped segments that separate when ripe.*
SIMILAR SPECIES *Common Bird's-foot Trefoil (above), Kidney Vetch (above).*

Sainfoin

Onobrychis viciifolia (Fabaceae)

A tall, attractive plant, Sainfoin was once grown for cattle fodder. The long-stalked flowers are clustered in spikes, each petal striped with crimson on a pink background. The leaves are pinnately divided, with very slender, ladder-like leaflets; and the unusual, rounded seed pods have coarse, toothed ridges.

FOUND *in clumps or small colonies in short grassland and pastures, and close to cultivated land, on chalky soil.*

pyramidal spikes of flowers

crimson-striped peaflowers

narrow leaflets

ridged fruit

PERENNIAL

PLANT HEIGHT *20–70cm.*
FLOWER SIZE *1–1.4cm long.*
FLOWERING TIME *June–September.*
LEAVES *Alternate and pinnately lobed with a slender, terminal leaflet.*
FRUIT *Seed pod, 5–8mm long.*
SIMILAR SPECIES *Goat's-rue (above), which has broader leaflets and unstriped flowers.*

PLANTS

Wood Sorrel

Oxalis acetosella (Oxalidaceae)

This dainty, creeping plant has bell-like white flowers veined pink or white. Its leaves are distinctive, divided into three drooping, folded, heart-shaped leaflets, which close up in strong sunshine and at night. Bright green above and purplish beneath, they contain a mild acid which gives them a sharp, lemony flavour.

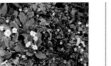

FORMS *patches in scrub, woodland, hedgerows, and rocky places, in shade; on humus-rich soils.*

leaf folded in centre

bell-like flowers

PERENNIAL

solitary flowers

drooping leaflets

5-petalled flower

PLANT HEIGHT *4–10cm.*
FLOWER SIZE *0.8–1.5cm wide.*
FLOWERING TIME *April–June.*
LEAVES *Basal, with three leaflets.*
FRUIT *Capsule 3–4mm long, that explodes, expelling seeds over a distance.*
SIMILAR SPECIES *Wood Anemone (p.351) has six-petalled flowers and divided leaves.*

Bloody Crane's-bill

Geranium sanguineum (Geraniaceae)

This crane's-bill has flowers with astonishing colours, more akin to a garden cultivar than a wild plant. They are deep purplish pink or cerise and have almost overlapping petals, with a pair of tiny bracts beneath. The distinctive, stalked leaves are almost circular in outline and are deeply divided into finger-like lobes.

PREFERS *shaded places in rocky habitats, open woodland, and glades, on well-drained soil.*

solitary flower on long stem

rounded, slightly notched petals

narrow lobes

PERENNIAL

stalked leaf

PLANT HEIGHT *10–30cm.*
FLOWER SIZE *2.5–3cm wide.*
FLOWERING TIME *July–August.*
LEAVES *Alternate, palmately lobed.*
FRUIT *Five mericarps, joined by their styles.*
SIMILAR SPECIES *Wood Crane's-bill (left); French Crane's-bill (G. endressii), which has 5 broad leaf lobes and silky pink flowers.*

Wood Crane's-bill

Geranium sylvaticum (Geraniaceae)

The flowers of this species range from pink to violet to purple and are usually arranged in pairs. The petals are paler at the flower centre and do not overlap. The palmate leaves are divided down to the base into broad, coarsely toothed segments, and the entire plant is covered with fine hair. The flower stalks remain erect after flowering, when the characteristic beaked fruit is formed. The beak, formed from the long styles which remain attached to the seeds, resembles the long bill of a crane or heron.

PROLIFERATES *along woodland margins, hedgerows, and streams, in mountain pastures, damp meadows, and rocky places, generally on rich soil.*

flowers in pairs

PERENNIAL

NOTE

The (male) anthers of the flower of this species ripen and wither away before the (female) stigma opens, a process called protandry. This prevents self-pollination, which would reduce the species' ability to adapt.

unstalked stem leaf

whitish flower centre

5–9 lobed leaves

barely notched petals

PLANT HEIGHT *30–70cm.*
FLOWER SIZE *2.2–2.6cm wide.*
FLOWERING TIME *June–July.*
LEAVES *Mostly basal, palmately lobed leaves.*
FRUIT *Five mericarps, joined by persistent styles into a long beak.*
SIMILAR SPECIES *Bloody Crane's-bill (right), which has more narrowly lobed leaves; Meadow Crane's-bill (right), which is a taller plant, with slightly larger flowers.*

Meadow Crane's-bill

Geranium pratense (Geraniaceae)

Distinctive among the geraniums, this plant has violet-blue flowers rather than the more usual pink. The petals are large, and often veined with white or crimson, and make an attractive sight along the verges of country lanes. Also large, the leaves are more or less rounded in outline but very deeply cut, almost to the base, into slender segments, giving them a rather tattered look and differentiating them from many garden cultivars.

GROWS *in meadows, pastures, hedgebanks, and road verges on rich or chalky soil. Garden cultivars of this species sometimes escape into the countryside.*

toothed leaf segments

PERENNIAL

beaked fruit

hairy stems

petals rounded at tip

lighter veins on petals

NOTE

The beak of geranium fruit is formed from the elongated styles of the flowers. As they dry, they pull on the seeds, which are suddenly released and catapulted away from the plant.

PLANT HEIGHT *60–100cm.*
FLOWER SIZE *2.5–3cm wide.*
FLOWERING TIME *June–September.*
LEAVES *Basal and alternate, palmately lobed into many slender, deeply cut segments.*
FRUIT *Beaked fruit, splitting into five one-seeded portions.*
SIMILAR SPECIES *Wood Crane's-bill (left), which has pinker flowers and less deeply cut leaves.*

Hedgerow Crane's-bill

Geranium pyrenaicum (Geraniaceae)

This species has long stems topped with medium-sized flowers – unlike most other pale pink crane's-bills, which have smaller flowers. The pale to mid-pink petals overlap, giving a starry effect. As with other crane's-bills, the fruit is beaked and is usually in pairs.

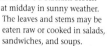

STRAGGLES *among tall vegetation along hedgerows and woodland margins, and in meadows.*

deeply notched petals

PERENNIAL

blunt-toothed leaf lobes

beaked fruit

flowers in pairs

PLANT HEIGHT *40–60cm.*
FLOWER SIZE *1.4–1.8cm wide.*
FLOWERING TIME *June–August.*
LEAVES *Alternate, palmately lobed.*
FRUIT *Five mericarps with a long beak, hairy, on long, downturned stalk.*
SIMILAR SPECIES *Dove's-foot Crane's-bill (G. molle), which has smaller flowers.*

Herb Robert

Geranium robertianum (Geraniaceae)

The often red-tinged leaves of Herb Robert help it to stand out among other vegetation. The scented leaves are characteristically deeply lobed and toothed down to the midrib. The small flowers are bright pink, fading to white at the centre, with two red stripes along their length, and bright orange anthers. As with all geraniums, the fruit bears a very long beak formed by the persistent styles attached to the seeds. As the ripe fruit dries out, they spring back, helping to disperse the seeds.

INHABITS *semi-shaded places along old walls, in woodland glades, and banks; also well-drained, rocky or gravelly sites.*

NOTE

The scent of the Herb Robert leaves recalls that of the garden geranium, which belongs to the Pelargonium genus, native to Africa.

ANNUAL/BIENNIAL

5 rounded petals

flowers in pairs

deeply lobed leaves

thin stalk

long beak on fruit

paired fruit

PLANT HEIGHT *10–50cm.*
FLOWER SIZE *1.4–1.8cm wide.*
FLOWERING TIME *May–September.*
LEAVES *Alternate, deeply palmately divided, stalked, with 3–4 lobes; often flushed red.*
FRUIT *Five mericarps, joined by their persistent styles into a long beak.*
SIMILAR SPECIES *Shiny Crane's-bill (G. lucidum), which has smaller flowers and glossy, less deeply divided leaves.*

Common Stork's-bill

Erodium cicutarium (Geraniaceae)

Stork's-bills have even longer beaks on the fruit than the related crane's-bills, and they are often clustered tightly together like a bunch of upright fingers. The feathery leaves are pinnately, rather than palmately, divided. The slightly unequal petals sometimes have a blackish blotch at the base, and begin to fall at midday in sunny weather. The leaves and stems may be eaten raw or cooked in salads, sandwiches, and soups.

FOUND *in dry, sandy places such as heathy grassland, disturbed and bare ground, often near the coast.*

fine-toothed leaflets

ANNUAL/BIENNIAL

petals of unequal length

pink flowers

long-beaked fruit

NOTE

An unusual characteristic of the fruit is that the persistent style twists like a corkscrew as it dries, then drills the seeds into the ground as it uncoils on rehydration.

PLANT HEIGHT *10–40cm.*
FLOWER SIZE *0.8–1.8cm wide.*
FLOWERING TIME *June–September.*
LEAVES *Basal and alternate, pinnate.*
FRUIT *Five mericarps joined into a hairy beak, 1–4cm long.*
SIMILAR SPECIES *Musk Stork's-bill (E. moschatum), which has larger flowers (1.6–2.4cm wide) that smell of musk, and much broader, toothed leaflets.*

Pale Flax

Linum bienne (Linaceae)

Although the flowers of Pale Flax have five petals, they are often seen with fewer in the afternoon, for after midday these begin to fall off. They are a delicate lilac shade with violet veins, and form a flat or saucer-shaped flower. The slender, erect stems bear just a few stalkless, linear leaves, which have one or three veins.

GROWS *in dry grassy places such as cliff slopes, field margins, old quarries; near the sea on neutral to chalky soil.*

BIENNIAL/PERENNIAL

slender stem

saucer-shaped flower

narrow leaf

rounded petals

PLANT HEIGHT *30–60cm.*
FLOWER SIZE *1.6–2.4cm wide.*
FLOWERING TIME *May–September.*
LEAVES *Alternate, linear, untoothed.*
FRUIT *Rounded capsule, 4–6mm wide, with a small beak at the top.*
SIMILAR SPECIES *Flax (L. usitatissimum), which has deep blue flowers.*

PLANTS

Dog's Mercury

Mercurialis perennis (Euphorbiaceae)

This plant may form extensive carpets of green on woodland floors early in the year, before the trees come into leaf. The green male flowers are on long, erect spikes, while the rather insignificant female flowers are formed on separate plants. Like many members of the spurge family, Dog's Mercury is very poisonous.

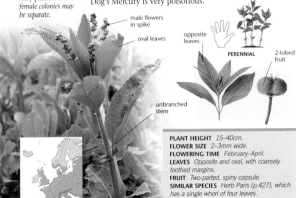

COVERS *the floors of woodland, coppices, hedgerows, and shady, rocky places. Male and female colonies may be separate.*

male flowers in spike
oval leaves
opposite leaves
PERENNIAL
2-lobed fruit
unbranched stem

PLANT HEIGHT 15–40cm.
FLOWER SIZE 2–3mm wide.
FLOWERING TIME February–April.
LEAVES Opposite and oval, with coarsely toothed margins.
FRUIT Two-parted, spiny capsule.
SIMILAR SPECIES Herb Paris (p.427), which has a single whorl of four leaves.

Sun Spurge

Euphorbia helioscopa (Euphorbiaceae)

This spurge produces a clock-like arrangement of yellow-green saucers facing towards the sky, each one made up of whorls of leaf-like bracts that surround the flowers. The flowers themselves are a complex assembly of crescent-shaped glands surrounding the stamens. The smooth, rounded fruit capsule is attached to one side by a small stalk. As with other spurges, the milky juice is very poisonous.

OCCURS *on field edges, cultivated or disturbed land, and exposed, dry, or sandy wastelands.*

saucer-like bracts in whorls
oval leaves
fleshy stem
flowers borne in umbels
ANNUAL
round fruit capsule

PLANT HEIGHT 20–50cm.
FLOWER SIZE 1.5–3cm wide, with bracts.
FLOWERING TIME May–August.
LEAVES Rounded bracts in whorls at top; alternate, oval leaves lower down.
FRUIT Round capsule on one side of umbel.
SIMILAR SPECIES Petty Spurge (E. peplus), which has smaller flowers.

Cypress Spurge

Euphorbia cyparissias (Euphorbiaceae)

This plant looks like a miniature fir tree with its linear leaves. On slender stems, the flower umbels are encircled by pale yellow-green bracts, which often turn a fiery red in summer. The flower is made up of kidney-shaped glands, surrounded by tiny horns.

GROWS *on arable field margins and wasteland, often as a garden escape.*

soft, needle-like leaves
PERENNIAL
yellow-green bracts
9–18 flowers in umbel
red bracts

PLANT HEIGHT 20–50cm.
FLOWER SIZE 8–15mm wide, with bracts.
FLOWERING TIME April–July.
LEAVES Alternate, linear, and dense.
FRUIT Three-lobed capsule with grainy surface.
SIMILAR SPECIES Dwarf Spurge (E. exigua), which has much smaller flowers.

Wood Spurge

Euphorbia amygdaloides (Euphorbiaceae)

The spurge family consists of around 7,000 species worldwide. The flowers of Wood Spurge, borne in umbels at the end of an unbranched stem, have no petals. Instead, the ovary is surrounded by curious horned glands and cupped by conspicuous yellow-green bracts. The stems may be red-tinged, while the leaves are deep green and untoothed. When the stems and leaves are broken, this spurge like many others, exudes a poisonous milky latex that can be irritating to the skin. Varieties of this plant are grown in gardens.

FORMS *large patches in woodland clearings or coppices, especially among oak or beech. Prefers neutral or mildly acid soils.*

yellow-green bracts
PERENNIAL
oblong, untoothed leaf
bracts form a disc

NOTE
The milky juice of Wood Spurge can aggressively corrode human flesh, and has been used (rather unwisely) in the past to treat warts. Do not try.

PLANT HEIGHT 30–80cm.
FLOWER SIZE 1.5–2.5cm wide, including bracts.
FLOWERING TIME April–June.
LEAVES Alternate, oblong and untoothed, tapered towards the base; deep green.
FRUIT Capsule, 3–4mm wide.
SIMILAR SPECIES Sun Spurge (left), which has whorls of leaves; Caper Spurge (below), which has opposite leaves.

Caper Spurge

Euphorbia lathyrus (Euphorbiaceae)

This spurge has an upright, neat form that makes it recognizable even when young. The grey-green leaves are arranged oppositely up the stem in a criss-cross fashion, and the inconspicuous flowers have leaf-like bracts below. The fruit capsule, which explodes to expel seeds when dry, is very poisonous.

BIENNIAL

CROPS *up by roadsides, field margins, and in gardens where soil is disturbed, usually near human habitation, in semi-shade.*

long, narrow leaf
caper-like capsule
leaf-like bracts

PLANT HEIGHT 80–150cm.
FLOWER SIZE 3–4mm wide, without bracts.
FLOWERING TIME June–July.
LEAVES Opposite, lance-shaped, criss-cross up the stem; grey-green.
FRUIT Caper-like capsule, 1–1.8cm wide.
SIMILAR SPECIES Wood Spurge (above), which has alternate leaves.

Common Milkwort

Polygala vulgaris (Polygalaceae)

The dainty blue flowers of Common Milkwort are the easiest to spot in the grass of its habitat, although it often has magenta or even white flowers. The coloured parts are actually three of the five sepals forming two wings and a hood, while the true petals are tiny, forming a frilly white tuft in the centre.

OCCURS *on short, often grazed grassland, on heaths, commons, and sand dunes.*

narrow leaf

fringed white petals

sepals form hood

PERENNIAL

wing-like sepals

deep green leaves

PLANT HEIGHT *10–30cm.*
FLOWER SIZE *5–8mm long.*
FLOWERING TIME *May–September.*
LEAVES *Alternate, oval-elliptic, untoothed.*
FRUIT *Small, two-lobed capsule.*
SIMILAR SPECIES *Heath Milkwort (P. serpyllifolia), which has opposite lower leaves, and is found on acid soil.*

Common Mallow

Malva sylvestris (Malvaceae)

A robust, hairy-stemmed plant frequently found in wasteland, the Common Mallow has flowers with five notched, pink to purple petals, with darker veins along their length, and a long column of pale pink stamens. Behind the petals, the calyx of sepals is backed by three narrow segments – the epicalyx. The felty leaves are rounded, with blunt-toothed margins.

GROWS *in wasteland and along field margins, hedgerows, and road verges.*

thin dark veins on petals

PERENNIAL

shallow toothed lobes

ring of nutlets

PLANT HEIGHT *50–100cm.*
FLOWER SIZE *2–5cm wide.*
FLOWERING TIME *June–September.*
LEAVES *Alternate, shallowly palmately lobed, and toothed, covered in felty hair.*
FRUIT *Ring of nutlets within persistent calyx.*
SIMILAR SPECIES *Musk Mallow (left); Dwarf Mallow (M. neglecta), which is smaller.*

Himalayan Balsam

Impatiens glandulifera (Balsaminaceae)

Introduced to the British Isles in the 19th century from the Himalayas, this plant has now become an invasive pest in many areas. The succulent, red-tinged stems grow quickly, bearing whorls of pointed leaves with a whitish midrib. Numerous branches produce two-lipped, pendent flowers at the top, each with a pair of almost opalescent sepals that form a sac.

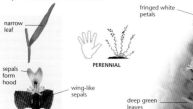

PROLIFERATES *along ditches, river banks, and streamsides, and in damp wasteland and woodland, usually in sheltered situations.*

leaves in whorls

white to dark pink flowers

serrated leaf margin

helmet-like upper petal

ANNUAL

flowers in loosely branched clusters

2 petals form lower lip

PLANT HEIGHT *1–2.5m.*
FLOWER SIZE *2.5–4cm long.*
FLOWERING TIME *July–October.*
LEAVES *Opposite or in whorls of 3–5, lance-shaped, finely toothed with pale midrib.*
FRUIT *Spindle-shaped capsule.*
SIMILAR SPECIES *Orange Balsam (I. capensis) is smaller with orange flowers.*

Marsh Mallow

Althaea officinalis (Malvaceae)

The tall Marsh Mallow produces spires of delicately pink-flushed flowers clustered together towards the stem tops, often standing out among reeds or other tall waterside plants. The petals are broader than in other mallows, more deeply coloured towards the middle, and have a column of purplish red anthers in the centre.

FOUND *in salt marshes and damp meadows, by brackish ditches, and on the banks of tidal rivers, usually by the sea.*

coarsely toothed margin

triangular leaf

PERENNIAL

flowers in tight clusters

purplish red anthers

downy leaf underside

calyx enclosing young fruit

5 broad, slightly notched petals

PLANT HEIGHT *80–150cm.*
FLOWER SIZE *2.5–4cm wide.*
FLOWERING TIME *August–September.*
LEAVES *Alternate, triangular, 3–5 lobes, and long-stalked; softly hairy; greyish.*
FRUIT *Hairy mericarps in a ring, surrounded by the calyx.*
SIMILAR SPECIES *Hollyhock (A. rosea).*

Musk Mallow

Malva moschata (Malvaceae)

The pale powder-pink flowers of this plant are a common sight along roadsides in late summer. They have five distinctly notched petals, with a central column of white to pink stamens, and a sweet, musky scent. The lower leaves are kidney-shaped and toothed, while the upper leaves are deeply divided into narrow segments.

FORMS *clumps along roadsides, hedgerows, and field margins, in meadows and other grassy places.*

PERENNIAL

deeply notched petals

ring of nutlets

lobed lower leaf

segmented upper leaf

PLANT HEIGHT *50–80cm.*
FLOWER SIZE *3–6cm wide.*
FLOWERING TIME *July–August.*
LEAVES *Alternate, palmately lobed, upper leaves more deeply cut into narrow segments.*
FRUIT *Nutlets, surrounded by sepals.*
SIMILAR SPECIES *Common Mallow (right), which has felty, slightly toothed leaves.*

Tree Mallow

Lavatera arborea (Malvaceae)

Impossible to miss in its coastal habitat, this is a robust, tall plant with a woody stem. The large leaves are rounded, with 5–7 lobes that are wrinkled or wavy – an adaptation that helps the plant to conserve moisture in a dry environment. The cup-shaped flowers are a deep magenta-pink, with dark lines radiating out from the centre, and have pale pink anthers.

GROWS *on coasts, on shingle beaches, cliffs, wasteland, rocks, and sand dunes.*

BIENNIAL

wavy lobes

dark flower centre

dark-veined petals

stout stem

PLANT HEIGHT *1–2.5m.*
FLOWER SIZE *3–4cm wide.*
FLOWERING TIME *June–September.*
LEAVES *Alternate, palmate, lobed, downy when young, with pale undersides.*
FRUIT *Cluster of nutlets in a ring.*
SIMILAR SPECIES *Common Mallow (above), which has pink-centred flowers.*

PLANTS

Spurge Laurel

Daphne laureola (Thymelaeaceae)

This small shrub is quite unrelated to the spurges and may easily be mistaken for a small rhododendron bush. In deep shade, it takes on a rather weedy appearance and has only one woody stem. However, it may look more bushy in better light. Its leathery leaves are glossy green and the inconspicuous, four-petalled green flowers are found within the upper leaves. The berries ripen from green to black.

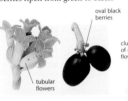

OCCUPIES *shady places, deep within woodland, on dry, chalky soil; also found in rocky places or hedgerows.*

PERENNIAL

oval black berries

clusters of green flowers

leathery leaves

tubular flowers

PLANT HEIGHT 50–120cm.
FLOWER SIZE 8–12mm long.
FLOWERING TIME January–April.
LEAVES Alternate; lance-shaped, leathery, clustered towards the top of plant.
FRUIT Oval berry.
SIMILAR SPECIES None, but can be easily mistaken for a rhododendron.

Mezereon

Daphne mezereum (Thymelaeaceae)

Although cultivated in gardens for its showy appearance, the wild form of this shrub first appears as a few meagre stems. These are transformed in early spring by the almost stalkless, bright pink flowers. The leaves appear after the flowers, in tufts at first on the stem tip.

GROWS *in woods and scrub, or in mountain pastures to 2,500m; prefers chalky soil.*

4-petalled flowers

PERENNIAL

long, narrow leaves

shiny red berries

small flower clusters

PLANT HEIGHT 0.5–1.8m.
FLOWER SIZE 8–12mm wide.
FLOWERING TIME February–April.
LEAVES Alternate, simple, lance-shaped, untoothed; pale to bright green.
FRUIT Highly poisonous, glossy red berries, in tight clusters on stem.
SIMILAR SPECIES None.

Tutsan

Hypericum androsaemum (Clusiaceae)

FOUND *in shady corners of deciduous woodland or by walls and hedgerows.*

This small shrub of shady corners has clusters of five-petalled, bright yellow flowers, each studded with a pincushion of long, straight stamens. The leaves are large and oblong and feel rather soft. The fruits are inedible egg-shaped berries which ripen from red to black, to which the reflexed sepals remain attached for some time.

large, opposite leaves

pin-like stamens

PERENNIAL

reflexed sepals

shiny berries

oblong leaf

PLANT HEIGHT 50–80cm.
FLOWER SIZE 1.8–2.2cm wide.
FLOWERING TIME June–August.
LEAVES Opposite, oval, and unstalked.
FRUIT Oval berries, 7–10mm long.
SIMILAR SPECIES Rose of Sharon (H. calycinum), a garden plant that naturalizes, has larger flowers, and is leafier.

Marsh St John's-wort

Hypericum elodes (Clusiaceae)

FORMS *creeping mats in wet areas of acid bogs, heaths, marshes, and in ponds.*

A lover of damp habitats, this St John's-wort forms extensive mats of greyish green leaves. These are small, oval, and stalkless, and are covered in fine down, as are the upright stems. The yellow flowers form terminal clusters, but there is usually only one flower open at a time, and the petals unfurl fully only in strong sunlight.

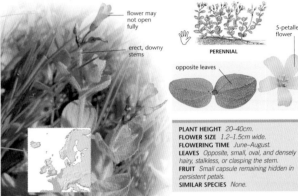

flower may not open fully

erect, downy stems

opposite leaves

PERENNIAL

5-petalled flower

PLANT HEIGHT 20–40cm.
FLOWER SIZE 1.2–1.5cm wide.
FLOWERING TIME June–August.
LEAVES Opposite, small, oval, and densely hairy, stalkless, or clasping the stem.
FRUIT Small capsule remaining hidden in persistent petals.
SIMILAR SPECIES None.

Perforate St John's-wort

Hypericum perforatum (Clusiaceae)

OCCURS *singly or in loose clumps in woodland margins, hedgerows, grassy places, on roadsides and banks, in open or semi-shaded places.*

There are many similar St John's-worts, but this one may be identified by its round stems, which have two opposite ridges or wings that are more easily felt than seen. The plant has an upright branched habit. Its oval, unstalked leaves are peppered with tiny, translucent dots, which are visible only when the leaf is held up to the light. They also have a few tiny black glands on the underside, as do the margins of the petals. The flowers are yellow, with five petals and numerous stamens, and are borne in clusters. The fruit is a capsule, containing many seeds.

PERENNIAL

terminal flower cluster

NOTE

This plant was placed over religious images as it was believed to ward off evil spirits; in Greek, "Hypericum" means "over an apparition".

hairy surface

tiny black dots

5 petals

many stamens

PLANT HEIGHT 40–80cm.
FLOWER SIZE 1.8–2.2cm wide.
FLOWERING TIME May–September.
LEAVES Opposite, oval, and stalkless, with translucent black dots underneath.
FRUIT Small, many-seeded capsule.
SIMILAR SPECIES Imperforate St John's-wort (H. maculatum), which has square stems and no translucent leaf dots.

Field Pansy

Viola arvensis (Violaceae)

This small plant has long and toothed leaves. More obvious are the deeply pinnately divided stipules at the base of the leaf stalks, like little ladders. The flowers are variable, cream to white with a small or large yellow blotch on the lower petal, and varying degrees of purple streaks. They open fully only in strong sunshine, and are otherwise hidden within the long green sepals.

solitary flower

long green sepals

FOUND *in arable fields, or bare ground, spreading over an entire field; on chalky or neutral soils.*

ANNUAL

shallowly toothed margin

oblong leaf

5 petals

yellow blotch

pinnately divided stipules

PLANT HEIGHT *8–20cm.*
FLOWER SIZE *4–8mm wide.*
FLOWERING TIME *May–October.*
LEAVES *Alternate, oblong, toothed.*
FRUIT *Rounded, green-yellow capsule.*
SIMILAR SPECIES *Eyebright (p.406) has jagged leaves; Wild Pansy (p.382) has larger flowers; other Viola flowers may be white.*

Common Dog-violet

Viola riviniana (Violaceae)

This is the one of the commonest violets, and may be identified by the distinctly heart-shaped leaves, each ending in a blunt point. The petals are generally spread widely, and there is a stout, gently curved spur at the back, paler in colour than the petals and slightly grooved at the tip. There is a pair of tiny bracts about one third of the way down the flower stem. This is usually the last of the woodland violet species to flower in spring, though also perhaps the most beautiful.

INHABITS *deciduous woodland, grassy heaths, and old pastures, on a variety of soils.*

NOTE
The leaves of this and other violets persist for many months after the flowers have faded, and are an important food source for the caterpillars of certain butterflies, especially the Fritillaries.

heart-shaped leaf

PERENNIAL

darker veins in centre of flower

widely spread petals

PLANT HEIGHT *8–20cm.*
FLOWER SIZE *1.4–2.5cm wide.*
FLOWERING TIME *April–June.*
LEAVES *Basal, alternate, and long-stalked.*
FRUIT *Three-parted capsule.*
SIMILAR SPECIES *Sweet Violet (right); Heath Dog-violet (right); Early Dog-violet (V. reichenbachiana), which has narrower petals and a dark purple spur; Heath Violet (V. hirta), which has bracts lower down.*

Sweet Violet

Viola odorata (Violaceae)

One of the clues to identifying this tuft-forming species is its early flowering time, when the flowers add a splash of colour to the arrival of spring. They may be deep violet with a spur of the same shade or white with a pink spur, and are sweetly scented. Another important clue to identification are the two tiny, triangular bracts more than halfway down the stem. The kidney-shaped, bright green leaves are much more rounded than those of Common Dog-violet (left), but sometimes taper to a slight point.

GROWS *in patches in hedgerows, woods, coppices, plantations, and scrub on chalky or neutral soils.*

NOTE
Since the flowers appear so early in the year and insects often fail to pollinate them, the plant forms cleistogamous (closed) flowers that self-pollinate.

deep violet spur

solitary flower

rounded leaf

kidney-shaped

separate petals

bluntly toothed margin

PERENNIAL

PLANT HEIGHT *8–15cm.*
FLOWER SIZE *1.3–1.5cm wide.*
FLOWERING TIME *February–May.*
LEAVES *Basal tufts, kidney-shaped with blunt teeth.*
FRUIT *Three-valved, hairy capsule.*
SIMILAR SPECIES *Common Dog-violet (left) has more pointed leaves; Marsh Violet (p.382) has darker flowers; Early Dog-violet (V. reicenbachiana) has more pointed leaves and narrow upper petals.*

Heath Dog-violet

Viola canina (Violaceae)

Very similar to Common Dog-violet (left), this plant is more likely to be found on acid soil and in open places, away from shade. The delicate, pale slate-blue (occasionally violet) flower has dark veins on the lower petal. The flower spur is usually straight and has a greenish tinge. The heart-shaped leaves are bluntly toothed.

FORMS *small patches on grassy heaths, fens, commons, woodland, and coastal dunes, on acid soil.*

dark-veined lower petal

PERENNIAL

bluntly toothed leaf

5-petalled flower

PLANT HEIGHT *5–20cm.*
FLOWER SIZE *1–1.8cm wide.*
FLOWERING TIME *April–July.*
LEAVES *Alternate, heart-shaped, toothed.*
FRUIT *Three-valved, hairless capsule.*
SIMILAR SPECIES *Common Dog-violet (left), which has broader leaves and usually deeper violet flowers.*

Wild Pansy

Viola tricolor (Violaceae)

Also known as Heartsease, this plant's flowers are highly variable in colour and form, appearing in combinations of yellow, purple, and white, but always with a few dark veins pointing to the centre of the flower, and with petals larger than the sepals. This natural ability of the Wild Pansy to produce "sports" of different kinds and to hybridize easily with other species has led to the many varieties of garden pansy available. It has declined substantially in recent years, particularly in south-east England.

FOUND *in rough grassland, neglected and cultivated arable fields, on neutral or acid soils.*

ANNUAL/PERENNIAL

NOTE

As its alternative name Heartsease suggests, this plant was once used for cardiac complaints, but is now an effective treatment for both respiratory disorders and skin problems, especially eczema.

5-petalled flower

narrow, toothed leaf

dark veins on petals

PLANT HEIGHT *10–30cm.*
FLOWER SIZE *1–2.5cm wide.*
FLOWERING TIME *April–October.*
LEAVES *Alternate, oval to elliptical; large, pinnately lobed stipules at the base.*
FRUIT *Three-parted capsule.*
SIMILAR SPECIES *Field Pansy (p.381); Mountain Pansy (V. lutea), which has yellow flowers.*

White Bryony

Bryonia dioica (Cucurbitaceae)

Unrelated to Black Bryony (p.430), this plant climbs by means of tendrils borne near the base of the fig-like leaves. Male and female flowers, both greenish white, are borne on separate plants, the male in longer-stalked clusters than the female, which have the developing berries beneath them. The poisonous berries are bright red when ripe.

CLIMBS *over hedges and bushes in scrub, and at woodland margins, on lime-rich soil at low altitudes.*

PERENNIAL

5-lobed leaves

5-petalled flowers

coiled tendrils

small red berries

PLANT HEIGHT *2–3m.*
FLOWER SIZE *1–1.8cm wide.*
FLOWERING TIME *May–September.*
LEAVES *Alternate; divided into five deep lobes.*
FRUIT *Poisonous, bright red berries.*
SIMILAR SPECIES *Hop (p.344), which has three-lobed leaves and pale brown fruit.*

Common Rock Rose

Helianthemum nummularium (Cistaceae)

Thin, crumpled yellow petals like tissue paper distinguish this plant of grassy, rocky places. The five petals are backed by three large, striped sepals and two tiny ones. Drooping buds and developing fruit also display these characteristic stripes. The small, oblong, and rather stiff leaves are in opposite pairs, and the stems are woody.

INHABITS *dry areas, with short turf and thin soil over chalky rock, up to 2,500m.*

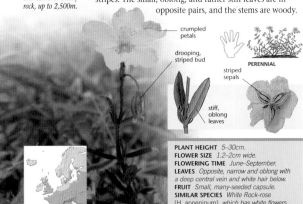

crumpled petals

drooping, striped bud

striped sepals

stiff, oblong leaves

PERENNIAL

PLANT HEIGHT *5–30cm.*
FLOWER SIZE *1.2–2cm wide.*
FLOWERING TIME *June–September.*
LEAVES *Opposite, narrow and oblong with a deep central vein and white hair below.*
FRUIT *Small, many-seeded capsule.*
SIMILAR SPECIES *White Rock-rose (H. appeninum), which has white flowers.*

Marsh Violet

Viola palustris (Violaceae)

Although easily missed among the lush vegetation of marshes, this violet is, once seen, simple to identify. The small flowers are a distinctive pinkish violet colour, with dark purple veins that guide insects to the pollen. The leaves, persisting for many weeks after flowering time, are kidney-shaped, with tiny stipules at the base.

CREEPS *low along the ground among wetland vegetation, in marshes, bogs, and woodland, on acid soil.*

PERENNIAL

solitary flower

pale green leaves

heart-shaped base

dark veins on petal

PLANT HEIGHT *4–8cm.*
FLOWER SIZE *1–1.5cm wide.*
FLOWERING TIME *April–July.*
LEAVES *Basal, heart- to kidney-shaped, long-stalked, toothed margins.*
FRUIT *Three-parted capsule.*
SIMILAR SPECIES *Sweet Violet (p.381), which has similar leaves but darker flowers.*

Purple Loosestrife

Lythrum salicaria (Lythraceae)

Purple spires of this plant can be seen towering over other vegetation in damp areas. The erect, square, ridged stems bear stalkless leaves in whorls of three below but in opposite pairs above. They branch towards the top, bearing tiered ranks of flowers in tight whorls, each flower with five purple petals that are wrinkled and tissue-like. It often grows with the unrelated Yellow Loosestrife (p.392).

FORMS *clumps in damp sites such as marshes and wet meadows, alongside rivers, ponds, and ditches; also at the edges of reedbeds.*

tall flower spikes

lance-shaped, stalkless leaf

bright purple flowers

12 stamens

5 narrow petals

PERENNIAL

PLANT HEIGHT *70–150cm.*
FLOWER SIZE *1–1.5cm wide.*
FLOWERING TIME *June–August.*
LEAVES *Whorled below, opposite above, lance-shaped, untoothed, and stalkless.*
FRUIT *Capsule containing many seeds.*
SIMILAR SPECIES *Rosebay Willowherb (p.383) has alternate leaves and larger flowers.*

Enchanter's-nightshade

Circaea lutetiana (Onagraceae)

The tiny white flowers of this plant are easily spotted in the gloom of its preferred habitat. The petals are deeply notched; the sepals and anthers are rosy-pink. Several flowers are arranged loosely along the leafless, upright stems, often above rows of drooping club-shaped, bristly fruits that attach themselves to clothing. The leaves are elliptical, with a barely toothed margin, and are noticeably veined.

OCCUPIES *dark and shaded corners of woodland, gardens, and pathways, under hedges or bushes.*

leafless stem

PERENNIAL

white flowers

rosy-pink anthers

pink sepals

elliptical leaf

PLANT HEIGHT *20–60cm.*
FLOWER SIZE *4–7mm wide.*
FLOWERING TIME *June–August.*
LEAVES *Opposite, elliptical.*
FRUIT *Semi-pendent achene with bristles.*
SIMILAR SPECIES *Upland Enchanter's Nightshade (C. x intermedia), which is almost identical but rarely sets fruit.*

Rosebay Willowherb

Chamerion angustifolium (Onagraceae)

Spreading by means of underground rhizomes, this plant can form an extensive patch or colony, which may really be a single plant. Flowers are borne on tall, narrow, pyramidal spikes; each has four broad, rounded rose-pink petals and eight drooping stamens. The flowers at the tip may still be in tight bud when the lower ones have formed fruit. The leaves are narrow and pointed, with finely toothed, often rather wrinkled margins.

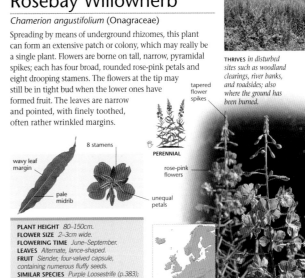

THRIVES *in disturbed sites such as woodland clearings, river banks, and roadsides; also where the ground has been burned.*

tapered flower spikes

PERENNIAL

wavy leaf margin

pale midrib

8 stamens

rose-pink flowers

unequal petals

PLANT HEIGHT *80–150cm.*
FLOWER SIZE *2–3cm wide.*
FLOWERING TIME *June–September.*
LEAVES *Alternate, lance-shaped.*
FRUIT *Slender, four-valved capsule, containing numerous fluffy seeds.*
SIMILAR SPECIES *Purple Loosestrife (p.383); Great Willowherb (below).*

Large-flowered Evening-primrose

Oenothera erythrosepala (Onagraceae)

As the name indicates, the flowers of the Evening-primrose open just before sunset. It takes just a few minutes for the sepals to curl back and the four pale primrose-yellow petals to unfurl into an almost luminous disc, but by noon the next day, this begins to wilt. The plant produces flowers every day for several weeks. These are pollinated by night-flying moths in their native North America, but in Europe they often self-pollinate. The sepals and stems of this species are covered in tiny hairs with red swollen bases; the leaves are lance-shaped, with crinkled margins and a pale midrib.

OCCURS *on waste and disturbed ground, embankments, roadsides, rubbish tips, and sand dunes, on well-drained soil.*

BIENNIAL

NOTE

Evening Primrose is an excellent source of gamma-linolenic acid, which is used for balancing hormone levels, especially in women.

tight bud cluster

very large yellow flowers

lance-shaped leaf

sepals covered with red hair

crinkled leaf margin

PLANT HEIGHT *80–150cm.*
FLOWER SIZE *5–8cm wide.*
FLOWERING TIME *June–September.*
LEAVES *Alternate, lance-shaped, with crinkled margins and a pale midrib.*
FRUIT *Four-valved capsule.*
SIMILAR SPECIES *Common Evening-primrose (O. biennis), which has smaller flowers and no red hairs on sepals or stems.*

Great Willowherb

Epilobium hirsutum (Onagraceae)

This tall, hairy plant forms large patches at the edges of wet areas. Born in racemes, the saucer-shaped flowers are deep pink with four-lobed creamy white stigmas. They give rise to long, downy fruit capsules that peel back to reveal many light, hairy seeds. The narrow leaves are stalkless or clasp the stem.

PROLIFERATES *in damp, open sites, such as river banks, reedbeds, lake margins, and marshes.*

saucer-like flowers

PERENNIAL

shallowly notched petals

lance-shaped leaf

capsules split lengthwise

PLANT HEIGHT *1–1.8m.*
FLOWER SIZE *1.5–2.5cm wide.*
FLOWERING TIME *June–September.*
LEAVES *Mostly opposite, occasionally whorled, lance-shaped, coarsely toothed.*
FRUIT *Capsule with four segments.*
SIMILAR SPECIES *Rosebay Willowherb (above), which has flowers in distinct spikes.*

Broad-leaved Willowherb

Epilobium montanum (Onagraceae)

A slender plant of semi-shaded places, this willowherb usually just has a few pale pink flowers with four deeply notched petals arranged in a cross. Despite the plant's name, the oval leaves are not particularly wide, but are broader than those of similar species. The rounded, slender stems are reddish.

INHABITS *sheltered spots on woodland margins, along ditches, hedgerows, and old walls; also in gardens.*

PERENNIAL

oval leaves

few flowers in loose clusters

toothed margin

4-lobed stigma

notched petals

strongly veined leaf

PLANT HEIGHT *30–75cm.*
FLOWER SIZE *6–12mm wide.*
FLOWERING TIME *May–August.*
LEAVES *Opposite, oval, toothed, and veined.*
FRUIT *Long, slender capsule, with purplish tinge, producing fluffy seeds.*
SIMILAR SPECIES *American Willowherb (E. ciliatum), which has narrower leaves.*

Dogwood

Cornus sanguinea (Cornaceae)

Dogwood is easily recognized at any time of year, for the bare red shoots are very conspicuous, even in winter. The leaves have a distinctive wavy margin and deep-set veins. They turn a deep crimson in early autumn, before the leaves of other trees have begun to turn colour. The 4-petalled flowers are produced in an umbel-like, cream or greenish white cluster.

OCCURS *in woodland margins, hedgerows, and scrub on limestone soil.*

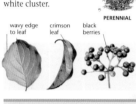

PERENNIAL

rounded clusters of flowers

wavy edge to leaf

crimson leaf

black berries

prominent leaf veins

PLANT HEIGHT *1–4m.*
FLOWER SIZE *8–10mm wide.*
FLOWERING TIME *June–July.*
LEAVES *Opposite, elliptical, green becoming gold then crimson, wavy edged, deep-veined.*
FRUIT *Rounded black berry, 5–8mm wide.*
SIMILAR SPECIES *C. sericea, which has brighter red twigs and white berries.*

Ivy

CLIMBS *deciduous and coniferous trees, even in dense shade. Trails over walls, buildings, rocks, and hedgerows.*

Hedera helix (Araliaceae)

An evergreen, woody climber, Ivy is a familiar sight in woodland, as it scrambles up trees and carpets the ground. The leaves are a shiny deep green but it is only the young leaves that have the classic three- or five-lobed triangular shape. The mature leaves on the flowering stems are quite different, being oval, without lobes. The flowers, in spherical yellow-green clusters, are some of the latest to bloom in the year, providing valuable nectar for bees. These later form persistent, round black fruit.

PERENNIAL

yellow flowers

rounded flower cluster

oval leaves on flowering stem

rounded fruit cluster

triangular young leaf

pale veins

ripe black fruit

NOTE

The Ivy, often wrongly accused of parasitizing and damaging healthy trees, uses trees only for support, but its weight may bring down weaker limbs.

PLANT HEIGHT *Up to 30m.*
FLOWER SIZE *7–9mm wide.*
FLOWERING TIME *September–November.*
LEAVES *Alternate; three- or five-lobed when young; oval, unlobed when mature, stalked and untoothed, pale veins; deep green.*
FRUIT *Green berries that turn brown, then black when ripe.*
SIMILAR SPECIES *Black Bryony (p.430), which has longer twining stems and smaller flowers; Ivy-leaved Toadflax (p.404).*

Marsh Pennywort

Hydrocotyle vulgaris (Apiaceae)

This plant is recognizable by its perfectly round leaves, which form small carpets like scattered coins, although they may be on long stems if growing among taller vegetation. The inconspicuous flowers, formed beneath the leaves, are in tiny umbels, one of the few features Marsh Pennywort shares with other members of the carrot family. It is often obscured by the leaves of other plants growing with it.

FORMS *small carpets in damp grassy places, on muddy edges of freshwater, or slightly brackish, pools.*

coin-like leaves

broadly toothed margin

PERENNIAL

stem joins leaf at centre

PLANT HEIGHT *5–15cm.*
FLOWER SIZE *2–3mm wide.*
FLOWERING TIME *June–August.*
LEAVES *Basal, rounded with broad, blunt teeth, may be long-stalked; deep green.*
FRUIT *Two-parted mericarp, 2mm wide.*
SIMILAR SPECIES *Floating Pennywort (H. ranunculoides), which is larger, highly invasive, and completely covers waterways; Navelwort (p.364).*

NOTE

The related Floating Pennywort (H. ranunculoides), is a North American species introduced to Britain by water garden nurseries. It deoxygenates water, killing fish and aquatic invertebrates.

Sanicle

Sanicula europaea (Apiaceae)

This plant bears small umbels of white flowers at the end of the long, branched stalks. The outer flowers of each umbel are male and have protruding stamens. Mostly basal, the leaves are broadly rounded but with three or five deep-cut lobes, each with a few bristly teeth.

INHABITS *shady places in ancient deciduous woodland, edges of old fields, and meadows.*

small white umbels

deeply lobed leaf

coarsely toothed margin

protruding stamens

long, branched stalks

PERENNIAL

PLANT HEIGHT *20–50cm.*
FLOWER SIZE *Umbels 5–10mm wide.*
FLOWERING TIME *May–July.*
LEAVES *Basal, three- or five-lobed, toothed.*
FRUIT *Oval, bristly mericarp, 4–5mm long.*
SIMILAR SPECIES *Upright Hedge-parsley (p.385) has larger umbels and finely divided leaves; Pignut (p.386) has thread-like leaves.*

Cow Parsley

Anthriscus sylvestris (Apiaceae)

GROWS *in masses along roadsides, woodland margins, and hedgerows, and in meadows and pastures. Prefers moist soil.*

One of the first members of the carrot family to bloom in spring, Cow Parsley is also one of the most familiar, often forming crowds of frothy white flowerheads along roadsides. Occasional plants may flower as early as February, but the spectacular display does not begin until April – still earlier than any similar species. The deeply divided leaves may appear during winter. They are slightly hairy, and each has a small sheath at the base of the leaf stalk. The ridged and hollow stems are unspotted.

BIENNIAL/ PERENNIAL

white flowers in frothy heads

broad umbels with 4–15 spokes

toothed leaf segments

sheath at base of leaf stalk

beak-like tip

2-parted fruit

NOTE
The leaves may be eaten as a substitute for the herb, Garden Chervil (A. cerefolium).

PLANT HEIGHT 60–150cm.
FLOWER SIZE Umbels 6–12mm wide.
FLOWERING TIME April–June.
LEAVES Alternate, deeply divided with toothed segments; hairy surface.
FRUIT Two-parted, narrow mericarp, 7–10mm long.
SIMILAR SPECIES Upright Hedge-parsley (below); Fool's Parsley (right), which has long bracteoles; Sweet Cicely (p.386), which is more robust; Rough Chervil (Chaerophyllum temulum), which has red-spotted stems.

Wild Carrot

Daucus carota (Apiaceae)

PREFERS *grassy and waste places, roadsides, dry cliffs, and field margins. Prefers dry, open situations, often near the coast.*

This is one of the easiest members of the carrot family to identify. The umbels of flowers are domed and often pink at first and then flatten out, turning white. Very close examination often reveals a purple flower in the centre of the mass of flowers in each umbel. There is a spreading ruff of bracts beneath the umbel, which turns brown and contracts as the fruit develops. The fruit and the bracts that enclose it resemble a tight bird's nest. The leaves are pinnately divided with many narrow segments.

lace-like umbels fan out

outer florets larger than inner ones

long flower stems

BIENNIAL

finely divided leaves

dense fruit clusters

NOTE
An ancestor of the cultivated carrot, Wild Carrot has many applications. Among these is the use of the seeds in liqueurs, in perfumery, and also as a cure for hangovers.

PLANT HEIGHT 30–100cm.
FLOWER SIZE Umbels 5–10cm wide.
FLOWERING TIME June–August.
LEAVES Alternate, finely divided.
FRUIT Two-parted mericarp, 2–4mm long, in a cluster that contracts to look like a bird's nest.
SIMILAR SPECIES Fool's Parsley (below), which has smaller umbels and long bracteoles instead of bracts; Yarrow (p.414).

Upright Hedge-parsley

Torilis japonica (Apiaceae)

This plant resembles a smaller version of Cow Parsley (above), but appears much later in the year. The umbels of tiny white, pink, or pale purplish flowers are relatively small and spaced out on widely branching slender stems, showing up clearly against the dark background of hedges. The leaves are like small, neat fern fronds.

FOUND *on the edges of hedgerows and grassy woodland, and on roadsides.*

slender, branched stems

small, neat umbels

small, fern-like leaves

coarsely toothed leaflets

flowers may be pink in bud

tiny flowers

ANNUAL/BIENNIAL

PLANT HEIGHT 50–120cm.
FLOWER SIZE Umbels 3–4cm wide.
FLOWERING TIME July–September.
LEAVES Alternate and pinnately divided.
FRUIT Egg-shaped mericarp, 3–4mm long, and covered in tiny spines.
SIMILAR SPECIES Cow Parsley (above), Sanicle (p.384); Sweet Cicely (p.386).

Fool's Parsley

Aethusa cynapium (Apiaceae)

The most distinguishing feature of this delicate plant is the long bracteoles that hang beneath the flowers; these form smaller umbels than in the similar Wild Carrot (above). The stems are ridged and leaves are finely divided. Fool's Parsley is poisonous so care should be taken if found growing near salad vegetables.

INHABITS *cultivated land at edges of crops, wasteland, gardens, and roadsides.*

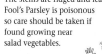

finely divided leaves

ANNUAL

flowers in umbels

long, pendent bracteoles

PLANT HEIGHT 50–90cm.
FLOWER SIZE 3–6cm wide.
FLOWERING TIME June–October.
LEAVES Alternate, finely divided.
FRUIT Two-parted mericarp, 3–4mm long, divided into two parts.
SIMILAR SPECIES Cow Parsley (left); Wild Carrot (above); Sweet Cicely (p.386).

PLANTS

Sweet Cicely

Myrrhis odorata (Apiaceae)

A member of the carrot family, Sweet Cicely is highly aromatic and has often been used for flavouring food. The hollow, unspotted stems smell strongly of aniseed when crushed. The plant often grows tall and bushy, and has large, finely divided, fern-like leaves. The white flowers each have five petals, and are borne in tightly packed umbels, the petals on the outer flowers being uneven. However, it is the two-parted fruit that is the plant's most distinctive feature. Strongly ridged and beaked at the tip, it is very long and slender, and also tastes of aniseed.

GROWS *in semi-shade in damp meadows, woodland margins, pastures, and streamsides, and on roadsides, mainly in mountains.*

PERENNIAL

NOTE

The seeds of this plant were once used to polish and scent wooden floors; a decoction made from the roots was used to treat dog and snake bites.

pale green leaves

densely packed flower umbels

finely divided leaves

long, narrow fruit

ridged surface

PLANT HEIGHT 0.8–1.8m.
FLOWER SIZE *Umbels 5cm wide.*
FLOWERING TIME *May–July.*
LEAVES *Alternate, finely pinnate and fern-like; pale green, occasionally with white spots.*
FRUIT *Two-parted, elliptical, ridged mericarp, 2.5cm long.*
SIMILAR SPECIES *Cow Parsley (p.385), which is less robust and has small fruit; Hemlock (p.387) has finer leaves and red-spotted stems.*

Pignut

Conopodium majus (Apiaceae)

A small, delicate plant of grassland and woods, Pignut has feathery leaves, the upper ones almost hair-like, the lowest leaves having withered by flowering time. It bears white flowers in loose umbels, each with spokes that have tiny bracts beneath. The plant has small, edible brown tubers with a pleasant nutty taste, which used to be gathered in quantity by children.

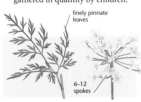

INHABITS *meadows, woodland edges and clearings, road verges, and hedgerows.*

white flowers in loose umbels

PERENNIAL

finely pinnate leaves

slender, erect stems

6–12 spokes

PLANT HEIGHT 20–50cm.
FLOWER SIZE *Umbels 3–7cm wide.*
FLOWERING TIME *May–July.*
LEAVES *Alternate, finely divided and feathery; hair-like upper leaves.*
FRUIT *Ridged mericarp, 3–4mm long.*
SIMILAR SPECIES *Burnet-saxifrage (right), Sanicle (p.384), Fennel (p.388).*

Burnet-saxifrage

Pimpinella saxifraga (Apiaceae)

THRIVES *in dry, grassy places with little or no shade, also in rocky places, on chalky soil. Usually spreads out in loose colonies.*

Flowering later in the year than Pignut (left), this plant has more compact umbels of 10–20 spokes. The lower leaves, divided into oval, veined leaflets, are like those of Salad Burnet (p.368). The word "saxifraga" means "stone-breaker", as this plant was once thought to dissolve stones in the kidneys or bladder.

PERENNIAL

10–20 spokes with no bracts

slender, upright stems

finely divided leaves

compact umbels

PLANT HEIGHT 30–90cm.
FLOWER SIZE *Umbels 4–8cm wide.*
FLOWERING TIME *July–September.*
LEAVES *Alternate; pinnate basal leaves with narrow leaflets, feathery.*
FRUIT *Ridged mericarp, 2–3mm long.*
SIMILAR SPECIES *Pignut (left) has more feathery leaves and flowers earlier in the year.*

Ground-elder

Aegopodium podagraria (Apiaceae)

An invasive plant that creeps to cover large areas by means of its underground stolons, Ground-elder may be a persistent weed in gardens. The soft leaves resemble those of the Elder tree (p.318). Introduced to Britain by the Romans, the leaves were cooked and eaten as spinach. The delicate white flowerheads show up well in shade.

FORMS *colonies on shaded wasteland and roadsides, in open woodland, and close to human habitation.*

small, delicate flowers

branched umbels

PERENNIAL

broad, toothed leaflets

flowers in umbels

PLANT HEIGHT 30–80cm.
FLOWER SIZE *Flowerhead 4–7cm wide.*
FLOWERING TIME *May–July.*
LEAVES *Basal and alternate, divided into three broad, toothed leaflets.*
FRUIT *Mericarp, oval and finely ridged.*
SIMILAR SPECIES *Cow Parsley (p.385), which has more finely divided leaves.*

Hemlock Water-dropwort

Oenanthe crocata (Apiaceae)

This robust member of the carrot family is one of the most poisonous plants in Europe, responsible for the deaths of many cattle. It has large white flowerheads and triangular leaves divided into leaflets of the same shape. Its damp habitat is a key to identification.

FLOURISHES *in damp sites by fresh water, in ditches, and along rivers and streams.*

large white umbels

toothed leaflets

fruithead

PERENNIAL

stout, rigid stem

PLANT HEIGHT 60–150cm.
FLOWER SIZE *Umbels 5–10cm wide.*
FLOWERING TIME *June–July.*
LEAVES *Alternate, pinnate.*
FRUIT *Cylindrical fruithead, 4–6mm long.*
SIMILAR SPECIES *Fine-leaved Water-dropwort (p.387), which has finer leaves; Wild Angelica (p.387), which has purple stems.*

Fine-leaved Water-dropwort

Oenanthe aquatica (Apiaceae)

GROWS *in shallow, freshwater habitats such as ditches and river and stream margins; often on floodplains.*

The leaves of this plant are very finely divided, resembling the filigree foliage of a fern or of Hemlock (below). It always grows in shallow water, with its thread-like leaves under the surface. The hollow, plain green stems are thick and grooved, especially at the base. The flowerheads appear rather small for what is often quite a large plant.

feathery leaves

petals of equal size

stout stem

flowers in small white umbels

PLANT HEIGHT *1–1.5m.*
FLOWER SIZE *Umbels 3–5cm wide.*
FLOWERING TIME *June–September.*
LEAVES *Alternate, finely pinnate.*
FRUIT *Oblong mericarp, 3–4mm long, with very short styles.*
SIMILAR SPECIES *Hemlock Water-dropwort (p.386); Hemlock (below).*

PERENNIAL

Wild Angelica

Angelica sylvestris (Apiaceae)

GROWS *among tall herb communities, in damp meadows and wet woodland; also along river banks.*

The stout purplish stems and round, pink- to brown-tinged flowerheads make this tall member of the carrot family easy to identify. The neatly divided leaves are quite different from those of Hogweed (below) with which it may grow. Wild Angelica is often seen towering above other vegetation.

large, rounded flowerheads

inflated sheath base of upper leaves

purple stems

PERENNIAL

neat leaf segments

PLANT HEIGHT *1–2m.*
FLOWER SIZE *Umbels 8–20cm wide.*
FLOWERING TIME *July–September.*
LEAVES *Alternate, pinnately divided into neat, oval segments.*
FRUIT *Two-parted mericarp, 4–5mm long.*
SIMILAR SPECIES *Hogweed (below), Giant Hogweed (below).*

Fool's-water-cress

Apium nodiflorum (Apiaceae)

SPRAWLS *along ditches, slow streams, marshes, and lake and river margins. May clamber on long stems among other vegetation.*

This water-loving member of the carrot family is unusual in that its flowers arise midway along the stems, opposite leaf junctions, rather than at the end. There are 3–12 widely separated spokes to each umbel, the tiny flowers in small clusters. The leaves are divided into oval leaflets in a ladder-like fashion.

alternate leaves

PERENNIAL

off-white flowers in rounded clusters

toothed leaflets

small umbels

PLANT HEIGHT *30–90cm.*
FLOWER SIZE *Umbels 3–6cm wide.*
FLOWERING TIME *June–August.*
LEAVES *Alternate, pinnately divided.*
FRUIT *Two-parted mericarp, 1–2mm long.*
SIMILAR SPECIES *Water-cress (p.360), which has different flowers; Lesser Water-parsnip (Berula erecta), which has terminal umbels.*

Hogweed

Heracleum sphondylium (Apiaceae)

DOMINATES *rough areas such as hedgerows, roadsides, woodland margins, and embankments.*

This familiar, coarse weed lacks the grace of its relatives in the carrot family. The unpleasant-smelling flowerheads are dirty white, broad, and flat-topped, the outer petals of each umbel having clearly larger petals. Each leaf has an inflated sheath where it joins the stem.

grey-white flowers

large, flat umbels

coarsely divided leaves

BIENNIAL

flattened fruit

PLANT HEIGHT *0.6–2m.*
FLOWER SIZE *Umbels 10–20cm wide.*
FLOWERING TIME *June–September.*
LEAVES *Alternate, pinnately divided into big, toothed lobes with rough surface; dark green.*
FRUIT *Two-parted mericarp, 7–10mm long.*
SIMILAR SPECIES *Wild Angelica (above) has more finely divided leaves; Hemlock (left).*

Hemlock

Conium maculatum (Apiaceae)

FOUND *at the margins of damp places such as ditches, rivers, and streams; also grows on wasteland and roadsides.*

All parts of the Hemlock plant are poisonous, but the seeds contain the greatest amount of coniine, which is fatal. Hemlock is extremely tall and robust and one of the easiest of the carrot family to identify. The ridged, hollow stems are clearly blotched with purple, and the leaves are divided like those of a fern.

fern-like leaves

purple-spotted stems

small, white umbels

oval fruit

BIENNIAL/ANNUAL

PLANT HEIGHT *1–2m.*
FLOWER SIZE *Umbels 2–5cm wide.*
FLOWERING TIME *June–July.*
LEAVES *Alternate, finely pinnate, lower ones large and triangular, upper ones smaller.*
FRUIT *Two-parted mericarp, 2.5–3.5mm long, with wavy ridges.*
SIMILAR SPECIES *Sweet Cicely (p.386).*

Giant Hogweed

Heracleum mantegazzianum (Apiaceae)

FLOURISHES *on damp ground along river banks or roadside ditches. May dominate areas where it has become established.*

Exceptionally large specimens of Hogweed (above) are sometimes misidentified as this plant, but Giant Hogweed itself is unmistakable. Everything about it is bigger – the huge umbels of flowers, the purple-spotted stems, which may be up to 10cm wide, and the rough leaves that are up to a metre long. The whole plant may be twice as tall as a human.

fruiting head with over 50 rays

sharply jagged edges

large, domed or flat umbels

BIENNIAL/PERENNIAL

PLANT HEIGHT *1.5–5m.*
FLOWER SIZE *Umbels up to 50cm wide.*
FLOWERING TIME *June–July.*
LEAVES *Alternate, deeply lobed with sharply jagged margins; to 1m long.*
FRUIT *Two-parted mericarp, 10mm long.*
SIMILAR SPECIES *Hogweed (above), which is smaller and has less jagged leaves.*

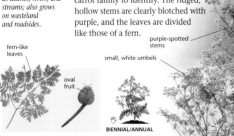
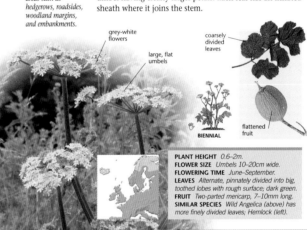

Wild Parsnip

Pastinaca sativa (Apiaceae)

A member of the carrot family, Wild Parsnip is the parent of cultivated parsnip, but the sap from the leaves and stems can cause intense skin irritation, especially in sunlight. Its leaves are divided into large, flat leaflets, the lower ones long-stalked, the upper ones much smaller and almost stalkless. The ochre-yellow flowers are borne in broad, flat-topped umbels.

OCCURS *in grassland on roadsides, on scrub, wasteland, and embankments, on dry, chalky soil.*

flat leaflets

coarsely toothed margin

yellow-ochre flowers

ridged stems

BIENNIAL

broad umbels

PLANT HEIGHT *60–100cm.*
FLOWER SIZE *Umbels 4–10cm wide.*
FLOWERING TIME *July–August.*
LEAVES *Alternate, pinnately divided.*
FRUIT *Two-parted mericarp, 6mm long, elliptical with ringed ridges.*
SIMILAR SPECIES *Fennel (below) has hair-like leaves; Alexanders (below) is more leafy.*

Rock Samphire

Crithmum maritimum (Apiaceae)

Like many seaside plants, Rock Samphire has thickened succulent leaves that conserve moisture. The stems and leaves branch to form tight clumps and smell of polish when crushed. The tight, fairly rounded umbels are made up of small flowers that form oval, corky fruit.

INHABITS *coastal rocks, sea-cliffs, sand, and shingle, always very close to the sea.*

greenish yellow flower umbels

finger-like leaves

PERENNIAL

tiny flowers

PLANT HEIGHT *20–50cm.*
FLOWER SIZE *Umbels 3–6cm wide.*
FLOWERING TIME *June–August.*
LEAVES *Alternate, triangular, divided into cylindrical, fleshy, upward-pointing segments.*
FRUIT *Oval mericarp, ripening yellow to purple.*
SIMILAR SPECIES *None.*

Fennel

Foeniculum vulgare (Apiaceae)

Cultivated since ancient times as a culinary and medicinal herb, this tall and elegant plant is recognizable even at a distance. It has very fine and hair-like leaves, and loose clusters of bright yellow-green flowers. Its tough, ridged stems are shiny and hollow with inflated leaf bases.

FOUND *singly or in small patches on roadsides, in rocky places, and wasteland, on chalky soil or limestone, often near the sea.*

many-branched umbels

flowers in loose cluster

tiny yellow flower

oblong fruit

hair-like leaves

PERENNIAL

PLANT HEIGHT *1.5–2.2m.*
FLOWER SIZE *Umbels 4–8cm wide.*
FLOWERING TIME *July–October.*
LEAVES *Alternate, very finely divided and hair-like; grey-green or bronze-green.*
FRUIT *Oblong, ridged mericarp, 4–8mm long, sweet and aromatic.*
SIMILAR SPECIES *Wild Parsnip (above).*

Sea Holly

Eryngium maritimum (Apiaceae)

This member of the carrot family is unmistakable for many reasons. Most distinctive are its bluish or greenish grey leaves. They are stiff and waxy, undulating like dried leather, and are coarsely toothed, with each tooth ending in a sharp spine. The upper leaves are unstalked while the lower leaves are long-stalked. A tight ruff of bracts below the flowerhead is similarly spined, but may have a blue-violet tint, reflecting the colour of the blue flowers. The final clue to identity is the habitat, for the plant is restricted to sandy coasts.

GROWS *in small patches or extensive colonies along the coast, chiefly on sand dunes and sometimes on shingle.*

PERENNIAL

waxy, grey-green leaves

tiny blue flowers

spiny bracts below flowerhead

whitish leaf veins

NOTE
The root of this plant was popular in the 17th century as a candied sweetmeat; the candied root was also used as an expectorant.

rounded flowerhead

PLANT HEIGHT *30–60cm.*
FLOWER SIZE *Flowerhead 1.5–3cm wide.*
FLOWERING TIME *June–September.*
LEAVES *Basal and alternate, roughly rounded, lobed and toothed into spines; bluish or greenish grey.*
FRUIT *Mericarp with overlapping scales.*
SIMILAR SPECIES *Milk Thistle (Silybum marianum), which has green rosette leaves with white veins, but pink flowers.*

Alexanders

Smyrnium olusatrum (Apiaceae)

One of the earliest members of the carrot family to flower, this is a robust, clump-forming, very leafy plant. The leaves are divided into three groups of three flat leaflets, the upper ones arranged oppositely on the stem and often yellowish in colour. The five-petalled yellow or greenish yellow flowers are borne in tight, domed umbels without bracts.

FORMS *clumps or patches by the sea, along estuaries and coastal cliffs, or along salted roads inland.*

rounded flower umbels

broad, flat leaflets

long leaf stalk

yellow flowers

BIENNIAL

PLANT HEIGHT *80–150cm.*
FLOWER SIZE *Umbels 4–8cm wide.*
FLOWERING TIME *April–June.*
LEAVES *Alternate at base, opposite at top, divided into three groups of three leaflets.*
FRUIT *Oval mericarp, black when ripe.*
SIMILAR SPECIES *Wild Parsnip (above), which is less leafy, with flat umbels.*

PLANTS

Common Wintergreen

Pyrola minor (Pyrolaceae)

The tiny flowers of this plant resemble those of Lily-of-the-Valley (p.427) but are arranged on all sides of the straight, upright stem. They have five, bell-like petals that are white or tinged with pink, and an enclosed, straight style which does not protrude. The leaves, from which wintergreen oil is extracted, are oval, rather leathery and mostly arranged in loose rosettes.

FOUND *in damp places, woodland, moors, marshes, and mountains.*

bell-like flowers

oval leaves

PERENNIAL

finely toothed margin

PLANT HEIGHT *10–25cm.*
FLOWER SIZE *6mm wide.*
FLOWERING TIME *June–August.*
LEAVES *Mostly basal in loose rosette.*
FRUIT *Round capsule, splitting into five segments.*
SIMILAR SPECIES *Lily-of-the-Valley (p.427), which has flowers only on one side.*

Bilberry

Vaccinium myrtillus (Ericaceae)

This compact, deciduous shrub appears in clumps. The ridged, angled stems bear soft, oval leaves with short stalks. Tiny flowers, green or flushed with red, hang in loose clusters, going on to form small black berries covered in a whitish bloom. The berries are edible, but being sparsely distributed on the plant, take time to gather.

OCCURS *on moors and heaths, in deciduous or coniferous woodland, on dry, acid soil.*

PERENNIAL

pale green leaves

bell-shaped flowers

bluish black berry

PLANT HEIGHT *20–50cm.*
FLOWER SIZE *4–6mm wide.*
FLOWERING TIME *April–June.*
LEAVES *Alternate, oval, toothed.*
FRUIT *Fleshy black berry, 5–8mm wide.*
SIMILAR SPECIES *Cowberry (left); Bearberry (below); Bog Bilberry (V. uliginosum), which has blue-green leaves.*

Common Dodder

Cuscuta epithymum (Convolvulaceae)

This leafless plant obtains its nutrients by parasitizing other plants, such as heather. It is instantly recognizable by the mass of twining, hair-like, red stems, which attach themselves to the host by tiny suckers. The pale pink flowers, each with five tiny petals and protruding red stamens, appear at intervals along the stems.

TWINES *among the stems of its host plants, particularly heather, clover, and gorse; found in dry sites such as heaths.*

pale pink flowers

thread-like red stems

red stamens

ANNUAL

spherical clusters of flowers

PLANT HEIGHT *Up to 60cm.*
FLOWER SIZE *3–4mm wide.*
FLOWERING TIME *June–October.*
LEAVES *Tiny, inconspicuous scales.*
FRUIT *Small capsule, split transversely.*
SIMILAR SPECIES *Greater Dodder (C. europea), is larger, with thicker stems, and is parasitic on nettles and thistles.*

Cranberry

Vaccinium oxycoccus (Ericaceae)

A straggling plant that can be easily missed, Cranberry has slender, creeping stems and small, oval leaves with whitish undersides. The curious shape of the pink flowers, with their recurved petals and columns of purple and yellow anthers, recall that of the unrelated Bittersweet (p.403). The large berries are orange-red with brown speckles.

CREEPS *over sphagnum and other mosses in bogs, moors, heaths, and damp woodland.*

wiry reddish stems

long-stalked, pink flowers

recurved petal

PERENNIAL

anthers in spike

orange-red berries

tiny leaves

PLANT HEIGHT *3–7cm.*
FLOWER SIZE *6–10mm wide.*
FLOWERING TIME *June–August.*
LEAVES *Alternate, oval, 3–6mm wide; deep green above, whitish underneath.*
FRUIT *Orange-red berry, 8–10mm wide.*
SIMILAR SPECIES *Small Cranberry (V. microcarpa), which has smaller leaves.*

Cowberry

Vaccinium vitis-idaea (Ericaceae)

This small, neat shrubby plant is a member of the heather family. The five-petalled, bell-shaped flowers are in tight clusters. They are white with a pinkish tinge and the pointed tip of each petal is turned slightly outwards. The leathery leaves have downturned margins. The berries have a bitter taste.

GROWS *in coniferous woodland, moors, mountains, and heaths, on acid soil; forms colonies.*

oblong leaves

notched leaf tip

PERENNIAL

upturned petal tip

round red berries

PLANT HEIGHT *30–70cm.*
FLOWER SIZE *5–8mm wide.*
FLOWERING TIME *May–August.*
LEAVES *Alternate, oblong.*
FRUIT *Rounded red berry, 5–10mm wide.*
SIMILAR SPECIES *Bilberry (right), which has black berries; Bearberry (right), which has darker pink flowers.*

Bearberry

Arctostaphylos uva-ursi (Ericaceae)

This short, evergreen shrub, with its sprawling, rooting branches, has oval leaves that are broadest near the tip and have a finely stippled surface like leather. The small, pale pink flowers are borne in clusters, and are formed of petals fused together. The fruit is a shiny red berry.

FORMS *mats on acid peaty soil of moors, heaths, mountains, open woodland, scrub, and rocky places.*

fused petals

glossy, dark green leaves

PERENNIAL

flat leaf margin

urn-shaped flowers

woody stems

shiny red berries

PLANT HEIGHT *10–30cm.*
FLOWER SIZE *5–6mm long.*
FLOWERING TIME *July–September.*
LEAVES *Alternate, oval and leathery.*
FRUIT *Glossy red berry, 6–8mm wide.*
SIMILAR SPECIES *Cowberry (left), which is taller; Black Bearberry (A. alpina), which has black berries.*

PLANTS

Bog Rosemary

Andromeda polifolia (Ericaceae)

A small, evergreen, shrubby plant of upland areas, Bog Rosemary has narrow leaves that are dark green above but silvery white below, with the margins rolled under. The flowers are borne at the tips of the stems in small clusters, each on a long, curved stalk. The fruit is a dry capsule, unlike the fleshy berry of related plants.

OCCURS *in moist, acid habitats such as bogs and moors; associated with sphagnum moss.*

narrow leaves

PERENNIAL

nodding, bell-like flowers

pink flowers

spear-shaped leaf

PLANT HEIGHT *15–40cm.*
FLOWER SIZE *8–10mm long.*
FLOWERING TIME *May–September.*
LEAVES *Alternate; spear-shaped with in-rolled margins, whitish underneath.*
FRUIT *Erect, greyish capsule.*
SIMILAR SPECIES *Cowberry (p.389) and Bearberry (p.389), which have oval leaves.*

Heather

Calluna vulgaris (Ericaceae)

With its woody stems and scale-like leaves, Heather is well adapted to habitats with low-nutrient soil; it may grow slowly, but it lives for a long time. The tiny leaves, in pairs on small branches, overlap each other almost like the shoots on moss. They are somewhat leathery, becoming rough to the touch as they mature, but are surprisingly soft when young and provide an important food source for caterpillars and gamebirds such as grouse. For this reason, the plant is cut or burnt on grouse moors to stimulate further young growth. Each flower has prominent sepals and a protruding style, with eight hidden anthers.

FORMS *carpets on heaths, moors, bogs, acid soil, and dry, sandy banks, and in pine or birch woods.*

PERENNIAL

NOTE

Heather was an invaluable resource for peasant communities; the stiff, woody branches were used for thatching roofs, strengthening wattle-and-daub clay walls, and in household articles.

numerous flowers

very dense flowerheads

pale pink to purple flowers

leaves crowded on stem

PLANT HEIGHT *20–80cm.*
FLOWER SIZE *3–4mm long.*
FLOWERING TIME *July–September.*
LEAVES *Opposite, closely pressed on short branches, tiny and scale-like.*
FRUIT *Small, many-seeded capsule.*
SIMILAR SPECIES *Bell Heather (right), which has larger, darker flowers, and linear leaves in whorls.*

Bell Heather

Erica cinerea (Ericaceae)

This evergreen shrub often grows scattered among other plants in the same family, such as Heather (left), but also forms large expanses on its own. An entire landscape of hills and low mountains may be coloured with the rich magenta-purple of these flowers, which usually open one or two weeks earlier than the paler pink flowers of Heather. The bell-shaped flowers are slightly flared at the mouth and are borne in whorls or clusters on short stems. The tiny, leathery leaves are in whorls of three on very short stems, so they appear bunched together.

GROWS *in small or extensive colonies on the dry, acid, sandy soil of heaths and moors, or in clearings in open pine woodland.*

magenta-purple flowers

flowers in whorls

PERENNIAL

NOTE

The stamens are hidden within the petals, but if insect pollination does not take place, then they protrude, so that wind pollination may occur.

tiny, linear leaves

short leaf stems

bell-shaped flowers

woody stems

PLANT HEIGHT *20–60cm.*
FLOWER SIZE *5–7mm long.*
FLOWERING TIME *July–September.*
LEAVES *Whorled, tough, needle-like, and hairless, on very short stems; green to bronze.*
FRUIT *Small, dry, hairless capsule.*
SIMILAR SPECIES *Heather (left); Cross-leaved Heath (below), which has pale pink flowers and hairy leaves in whorls of four.*

Cross-leaved Health

Erica tetralix (Ericaceae)

Although often found growing with both Heather (left) and Bell Heather (above), this plant is easily recognized as its flowers are tightly gathered in a globular cluster at the ends of the stems, and are a much paler pink than those of Bell Heather. The tiny, upward-pointing leaves are in whorls of four, each whorl well spaced so that the stem is visible between them.

FOUND *in wetter parts of heaths, bogs and moors; occasionally on drier ground in S.W. Britain.*

greyish leaves

PERENNIAL

tight clusters of flowers

pink petals form a tube

PLANT HEIGHT *20–70cm.*
FLOWER SIZE *6–9mm long.*
FLOWERING TIME *June–October.*
LEAVES *Linear, 2–3mm long, in whorls of 4, hairy when young.*
FRUIT *Small dry, downy capsule.*
SIMILAR SPECIES *Bell Heather (above), which has darker flowers in loose spikes.*

Yellow Bird's-nest

Monotropa hypopitys (Monotropaceae)

This extraordinary plant is a saprophyte, drawing its nutrients from a tangled root system (said to resemble a bird's nest) that feeds on decaying vegetable matter in the soil. The leaves are scales lying close to the stem, and the flowers are a cluster of tubular bells, each with four or five petals. The stems become upright when the fruit develops.

INHABITS *dark corners of deciduous and coniferous woods of beech, pine, or hazel, or under hedgerows.*

PERENNIAL

calyx enclosing fruit

flowers in clusters

creamy yellow plant

drooping, bell-like flowers

tiny, scale-like leaf

PLANT HEIGHT *8–20cm.*
FLOWER SIZE *9–12mm long.*
FLOWERING TIME *June–August.*
LEAVES *Alternate; oval scales; yellow or ivory.*
FRUIT *Rounded capsule, held in calyx that becomes upright as it develops.*
SIMILAR SPECIES *Toothwort (p.407), which has flowers in a one-sided spike.*

Chickweed Wintergreen

Trientalis europaea (Primulaceae)

The starry white flowers of this plant brighten its coniferous woodland habitat, forming carpets in spring. The flowers are usually solitary, but are sometimes in pairs, on long stalks. The large, oblong leaves are in whorls beneath the flowers, and below them on the single, slender stem are a few tiny leaves.

OCCURS *in coniferous woodland, moors, and heaths, and on acid soil.*

5–9 pointed petals

untoothed leaf margin

yellow anthers

whorl of leaves

unbranched stem

PERENNIAL

PLANT HEIGHT *10–25cm.*
FLOWER SIZE *1.2–1.8cm wide.*
FLOWERING TIME *May–July.*
LEAVES *Whorled, oblong.*
FRUIT *Capsule splitting into five parts.*
SIMILAR SPECIES *Wood Anemone (p.351), Meadow Saxifrage (p.364), and Grass of Parnassus (p.365): all have different leaves.*

Primrose

Primula vulgaris (Primulaceae)

The pale yellow flowers of Primrose signal the arrival of spring. Each flower is on a solitary stalk and has a long, tubular calyx and broad yellow petals, often with orange markings in the centre (although other colours occur in garden cultivars). As distinctive as the flowers, the oblong, toothed leaves are in basal rosettes.

PROLIFERATES *in deciduous woodland, along embankments, in meadows, and on grassy roadside verges.*

pale midrib

pale yellow flowers

bright green leaves

PERENNIAL

5 notched petals

PLANT HEIGHT *10–15cm.*
FLOWER SIZE *2–4cm wide.*
FLOWERING TIME *February–May, or earlier.*
LEAVES *Basal, oblong, with wrinkled surface and margin, pale midrib.*
FRUIT *Many-seeded capsule.*
SIMILAR SPECIES *Oxlip (P. elatior), which has one-sided clusters of flowers.*

Cowslip

Primula veris (Primulaceae)

Entire meadows are often coloured in spring by the abundant yellow flowers of Cowslip. Borne in tight clusters on each stem, or scape, they are fragrant, with a long, yellow-green calyx and five petals that form a tube, opening slightly to reveal an orange mark on each petal. The leaves form a rosette close to the ground, and have a surface texture very similar to that of Primrose (left), but are usually darker, smaller, and more rounded. In long grass or semi-shade, the leaves may grow longer, when they may be the caterpillar foodplant of the rare Duke of Burgundy butterfly.

GROWS *in meadows and dry, grassy places; also on embankments, usually on chalky soil; prefers open situations.*

PERENNIAL

nodding flowers

one-sided clusters of flowers

NOTE

The nectar-rich flowers have been used as a sedative, an antihistamine, and to reduce spasms and inflammation, but they have an even longer history as the major ingredient in cowslip wine.

flower tube

oblong leaf

pale midrib

neatly toothed edge

5 notched petals

PLANT HEIGHT *10–25cm.*
FLOWER SIZE *7–14mm wide.*
FLOWERING TIME *April–May.*
LEAVES *Basal rosette, oblong; with wrinkled surface; dark green.*
FRUIT *Many-seeded capsule.*
SIMILAR SPECIES *False Oxlip (P. veris x vulgaris), which has fewer one-sided umbels; Oxlip (P. elatior), which has larger, primrose-like flowers in a one-sided umbel and is found in East Anglia.*

Bird's-eye Primrose

Primula farinosa (Primulaceae)

The delicate flowers of the Bird's-eye Primrose are borne in an umbel on top of a single, slender stem. The stalked flowers have five, bright pink petals, purple-tinged sepals, and a yellow centre or "eye". The leaves are in a tight rosette at the base. Each leaf has a green, wrinkled surface but a white underside with a floury "meal" that can be rubbed off.

FOUND *in tufts in short, usually grazed grassland, on peaty or stony ground, in damp habitats; may be abundant.*

5 notched, bright pink petals

flower centre or "eye"

PERENNIAL

spoon-shaped leaf

PLANT HEIGHT *7–15cm.*
FLOWER SIZE *0.8–1.6cm wide.*
FLOWERING TIME *May–August.*
LEAVES *Basal rosette, spoon-shaped.*
FRUIT *Small green capsule.*
SIMILAR SPECIES *Scottish Primrose (P. scotica) is much shorter with smaller, darker flowers; restricted to north coast of Scotland.*

PLANTS

Yellow Loosestrife

Lysimachia vulgaris (Primulaceae)

This tall plant punctuates the landscape of marshes and fens with its golden yellow flowers. These have five oval petals with an orange centre, and are grouped in panicles produced from the upper leaf axils. The oval to lance-shaped leaves are sometimes dotted with black or orange glands and have bluish green undersides. They are arranged in opposite pairs at the top of the stem, then in whorls of 3–4 leaves lower down. The fruit is a spherical capsule, and often occurs in the same cluster as the buds or open flowers.

INHABITS *tall vegetation in moist habitats such as streamsides, wet meadows, fens, and marshes, on neutral or chalky soil.*

PERENNIAL

tightly clustered yellow flowers

5-petalled flower

NOTE

Yellow Loosestrife used to be burned in houses to clear the rooms of flies and gnats; it was also tied to cattle and horses to keep biting insects away.

whorl of 3–4 lower leaves

spherical fruit capsule

oval leaf

PLANT HEIGHT *60–150cm.*
FLOWER SIZE *1.5–2cm wide.*
FLOWERING TIME *July–August.*
LEAVES *Opposite on upper stem, whorls of 3–4 below, oval to lance-shaped.*
FRUIT *Spherical, five-parted capsule.*
SIMILAR SPECIES *Dotted Loosestrife (L. punctata), which has narrow spikes of tightly clustered flowers.*

Scarlet Pimpernel

Anagallis arvensis (Primulaceae)

The brilliant red petals of this diminutive plant are easily spotted when the flowers open in bright sunshine. Occasionally, blue-flowered forms occur. The oval, shiny leaves have tiny black dots underneath, while the fruit is a tiny, rounded capsule that splits around the middle.

GROWS *on wasteland, in fields and field margins, and coastland; on dry, well-drained soil.*

opposite, oval leaves

shiny leaves

yellow anthers

ANNUAL

5-petalled flowers

toothed margin

PLANT HEIGHT *5–15cm.*
FLOWER SIZE *4–7mm wide.*
FLOWERING TIME *May–September.*
LEAVES *Opposite, oval, and unstalked.*
FRUIT *Small, rounded capsule.*
SIMILAR SPECIES *Sea Milkwort (below), which has short-stalked flowers; Pheasant's Eye (Adonis annua), has feathery leaves.*

Water Violet

Hottonia palustris (Primulaceae)

This aquatic plant may go unnoticed before flowering time, as its leaves do not show above the water surface. However, dense whorls of fern-like, bright green fronds may be seen floating below. In summer, a single stem rises above the water surface, bearing several whorls of five-petalled, pale-pink to lilac flowers, each with a yellow centre.

FOUND *in colonies, in still, shallow water of lowland ditches, lakes, and ponds; prefers neutral soil.*

yellow centre of flower

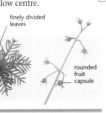

PERENNIAL

finely divided leaves

rounded fruit capsule

flowers in whorls

leafless stem

PLANT HEIGHT *15–30cm above water.*
FLOWER SIZE *2–2.5cm wide.*
FLOWERING TIME *May–July.*
LEAVES *Whorled, submerged or floating, finely pinnately divided, fern-like.*
FRUIT *Rounded, pendent capsule within persistent calyx.*
SIMILAR SPECIES *Bogbean (p.394).*

Creeping-Jenny

Lysimachia nummularia (Primulaceae)

This creeping plant can be easily missed among taller vegetation. Once discovered, however, there is no mistaking its cup-shaped yellow flowers nestling along the twining stem. The leaves, arranged in opposite pairs like a ladder, are rounded to oval, decreasing in size along the stem. When produced, the fruit capsule is on a long stalk.

CREEPS *along in damp habitats, in woodland, pond and stream margins, and ditches.*

cup-shaped flowers

oval leaves

smaller leaves at top of stem

broad sepals

PLANT HEIGHT *3–6cm.*
FLOWER SIZE *1.2–1.8cm wide.*
FLOWERING TIME *May–July.*
LEAVES *Opposite, rounded to oval.*
FRUIT *Five-parted capsule, rarely produced.*
SIMILAR SPECIES *Yellow Pimpernel (L. nemorum), which has less ladder-like leaves and narrow sepals.*

PERENNIAL

Sea Milkwort

Glaux maritima (Primulaceae)

A plant that has adapted well to the dry conditions of a coastal habitat, Sea Milkwort keeps low, hugging the ground, and has small, fleshy leaves on succulent stems that help to conserve moisture. The numerous tiny, short-stalked flowers are tucked in close to the leaf bases. Each flower consists of five pink to red sepals only, the petals being absent.

OCCURS *in mats in rocky places, on salt marshes, coastal sands, and shingle.*

PERENNIAL

solitary flowers in leaf axils

unstalked, fleshy leaf

5-lobed flower

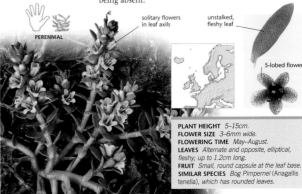

PLANT HEIGHT *5–15cm.*
FLOWER SIZE *3–6mm wide.*
FLOWERING TIME *May–August.*
LEAVES *Alternate and opposite, elliptical, fleshy; up to 1.2cm long.*
FRUIT *Small, round capsule at the leaf base.*
SIMILAR SPECIES *Bog Pimpernel (Anagallis tenella), which has rounded leaves.*

Thrift

Armeria maritima (Plumbaginaceae)

This plant forms cushions of narrow grey-green leaves that persist throughout the year. In summer, it produces long-stalked, bright pink flowerheads, each with papery scales surrounding the base, transforming the coastal scenery with extensive patches of colour. The plant is variable in height, with taller forms on inland sites.

FORMS *mats on cliffs, coastal rocks, and salt marshes, and inland on sandy grassland.*

grass-like leaves

spherical flowerheads

sheath below flowerhead

pink flowers

PERENNIAL

PLANT HEIGHT *5–30cm.*
FLOWER SIZE *Flowerhead 1.5–3cm wide.*
FLOWERING TIME *April–August.*
LEAVES *Basal, linear.*
FRUIT *Small, one-seeded capsule, with a papery wall.*
SIMILAR SPECIES *Common Sea-lavender (below), which has oblong to elliptical leaves.*

Common Centaury

Centaurium erythraea (Gentianaceae)

The pink flowers of Common Centaury stand out among the grasses of the plant's natural habitat. They each have five elliptical petals, which are fused below into a tube about twice as long as the narrow sepals, and are borne in flat-topped clusters. The waxy, pale green leaves are arranged in a basal rosette, and in opposite pairs on the branching stems.

FLOURISHES *in grassy habitats on chalky or sandy soil, such as pastures, heaths, and among scrub.*

flowers in clusters

petals fused into long tube

untoothed leaf margin

yellow-orange anthers

BIENNIAL

PLANT HEIGHT *10–40cm.*
FLOWER SIZE *1–1.5cm wide.*
FLOWERING TIME *June–September.*
LEAVES *Basal rosette and opposite, elliptical, three-veined stem leaves.*
FRUIT *Two-parted capsule, with waxy seeds.*
SIMILAR SPECIES *Lesser Centaury (C. pulchellum), which has no basal rosette.*

Common Sea-lavender

Limonium vulgare (Plumbaginaceae)

The wiry stems of this plant branch at the top and bear tight heads of pink to lilac flowers, each flower surrounded by papery bracts. The cut flowers retain their colour well and are commonly used in dried flower arrangements. The narrow, basal leaves, each with a single prominent vein, taper to a stalk about half the length of the leaf blade.

FOUND *in extensive carpets on the mud of salt marshes, colouring large areas with its flowers.*

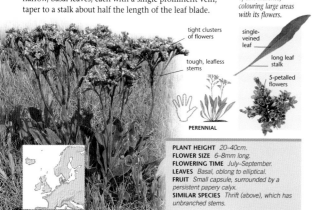

tight clusters of flowers

single-veined leaf

long leaf stalk

tough, leafless stems

5-petalled flowers

PERENNIAL

PLANT HEIGHT *20–40cm.*
FLOWER SIZE *6–8mm long.*
FLOWERING TIME *July–September.*
LEAVES *Basal, oblong to elliptical.*
FRUIT *Small capsule, surrounded by a persistent papery calyx.*
SIMILAR SPECIES *Thrift (above), which has unbranched stems.*

Marsh Gentian

Gentiana pneumonanthe (Gentianaceae)

Sometimes partly concealed among the grasses of peaty bogs, the violet-blue petals of this plant are flushed with olive green on the outside, and spotted greyish white on the in side. The flowers are trumpet-shaped and large in comparison to the leaves, which are exceptionally narrow for a gentian.

OCCURS *in loose colonies in marshy areas, bogs, and wet heaths, on thin peaty acid soil; avoids shade.*

5-lobed flowers

linear, unstalked leaves

whitish spots

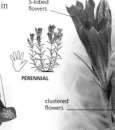

PERENNIAL

clustered flowers

PLANT HEIGHT *20–50cm.*
FLOWER SIZE *2.5–4.5cm long.*
FLOWERING TIME *July–October.*
LEAVES *Opposite, lance-shaped.*
FRUIT *Capsule that splits to release seeds.*
SIMILAR SPECIES *Clustered Bellflower (p.411), which has blue-violet flowers and hairy stems and leaves.*

Yellow-wort

Blackstonia perfoliata (Gentianaceae)

This plant has a distinctive arrangement of leaves in that each pair is fused together around the stem – the upper pairs occurring where the stems branch. Unusually for a member of the gentian family, the flowers have up to eight starry petals, which open almost flat.

GROWS *sporadically on grassland and other rocky, open places on dry, well-drained chalky soil.*

slender calyx lobes

leaves encircle stem

ANNUAL

8 starry petals

fused, paired leaves

PLANT HEIGHT *15–40cm.*
FLOWER SIZE *1–1.5cm wide.*
FLOWERING TIME *June–September.*
LEAVES *Basal rosette and opposite, oval, waxy; grey-green.*
FRUIT *Two-parted, many-seeded capsule.*
SIMILAR SPECIES *None; the number of petals and leaf arrangement are distinctive.*

Autumn Gentian

Gentianella amarella (Gentianaceae)

Flowers of this small gentian usually have five short petal lobes which form a long tube at the base, but occasionally there are only four. Usually bluish violet, they may also be dull purple or magenta. The calyx also has four or five lobes of equal width.

GROWS *in short turf in pastures and other dry, grassy areas, and on dunes; on chalky soil and slopes.*

clustered flowers

clearly veined leaves

5 petal lobes

BIENNIAL

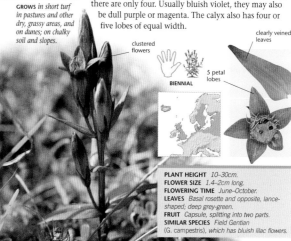

PLANT HEIGHT *10–30cm.*
FLOWER SIZE *1.4–2cm long.*
FLOWERING TIME *June–October.*
LEAVES *Basal rosette and opposite, lance-shaped; deep grey-green.*
FRUIT *Capsule, splitting into two parts.*
SIMILAR SPECIES *Field Gentian (G. campestris), which has bluish lilac flowers.*

Privet

Ligustrum vulgare (Oleaceae)

Privet is a looser, more open-growing shrub than the familiar Garden Privet (*L. ovalifolium*). It is nevertheless densely branched, with smooth greyish bark, and freely forms small panicles of white flowers when growing in a sunny position, followed by small, mildly poisonous black berries. The leaves are usually evergreen, being dark, glossy, and clearly veined.

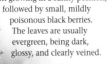

OCCURS *in woodland margins, hedgerows, and embankments.*

PERENNIAL

panicles of small white flowers

4-petalled flower

shiny black berries

glossy leaves

PLANT HEIGHT 1–3m.
FLOWER SIZE 4–6mm wide.
FLOWERING TIME May–June.
LEAVES Evergreen, opposite, lance-shaped, with glossy surface.
FRUIT Shiny black berry, 6-8mm wide.
SIMILAR SPECIES Garden Privet (L. ovalifolium), which has broader leaves.

Bogbean

Menyanthes trifoliata (Menyanthaceae)

This plant is unmistakable when seen en masse, with its white blossoms dotted over the surface of acid bog pools. The flowers appear in a loose cluster on a single stem. Rosy-pink in bud, the fully open flowers are white, each petal with an extraordinary fringe of long white hair that give the flower a fluffy appearance. Rising up out of the water, the rather fleshy, trifoliate leaves have elliptical leaflets and are reminiscent of those of a garden bean.

RISES *up out of pools of water in bogs, fens, mountains, and lake margins; often forming large colonies.*

NOTE

Bogbean was once valued as a cure for scurvy, with the leaves dried and made into tea, and was also used as a substitute for hops in beer-making.

pink buds

flowers in loose clusters

PERENNIAL

trifoliate leaves

fleshy, elliptical leaflets

petals fringed with white hair

PLANT HEIGHT 10–35cm.
FLOWER SIZE 1.4–1.6cm wide.
FLOWERING TIME April–June.
LEAVES Basal, in three elliptical leaflets rising above water surface, fleshy and bean-like.
FRUIT Egg-shaped capsule that splits into two halves when ripe.
SIMILAR SPECIES Water Violet (p.392), which has no aerial leaves and has pinkish lilac flowers.

Fringed Water-lily

Nymphoides peltata (Menyanthaceae)

Like its close relative, the Bogbean (left), this aquatic plant has petals with a delicately fringed margin of tiny hairs; they may also appear creased or slightly folded. The long-stemmed, bright yellow flowers are held just above the water surface. Rounded, dark green leaves, sometimes purple blotched, have a slit to the centre where the stalk joins the leaf. They are much smaller than those of other water-lilies.

FORMS *large patches on the surface of slow-moving rivers and streams, ponds, lakes, and in ditches.*

PERENNIAL

bright yellow flower

creased petals

long stem

deep leaf cleft

5 petals

PLANT HEIGHT Up to 10cm above water surface.
FLOWER SIZE 3–4cm wide.
FLOWERING TIME June–September.
LEAVES Whorled, on long stems, rounded.
FRUIT Egg-shaped capsule.
SIMILAR SPECIES Yellow Water-lily (p.351), which has spherical flowers.

Lesser Periwinkle

Vinca minor (Apocynaceae)

The shiny, deep green leaves and trailing stems of this plant may carpet large areas of woodland in spring – only a few flowers may occur in such shaded places. The flowers are violet-purple, occasionally white, with each petal twisted and blunt-ended, resembling a ship's propeller. The calyx at the base of the long petal tube has tiny, triangular teeth.

FORMS *extensive mats in woodland, coppices, hedgerows, banks, and rocky ground, often in deep shade.*

glossy, deep green leaves

violet-purple flower

PERENNIAL

oval leaf

blunt-edged petals

slightly twisted petals

tiny sepals

PLANT HEIGHT 15–40cm.
FLOWER SIZE 2.5–3cm wide.
FLOWERING TIME March–May.
LEAVES Opposite, oval to elliptic, short-stalked.
FRUIT Forked capsule, 2.5cm wide, but rare.
SIMILAR SPECIES Greater Periwinkle (V. major) has larger flowers with long sepals.

Squinancywort

Asperula cynanchica (Rubiaceae)

This small, ground-hugging plant forms masses of pink blooms. The tiny flowers, at the ends of slender, many-branched stems, are white or pink, with four petals fused at the base to form a tube. Like other members of the bedstraw family, the leaves are in whorls, but they are very small and narrow.

SEEN *as cushions of flowers on short, dry chalk grassland or sand dunes.*

pink or white flowers

small linear leaves

branched flower stems

four petals

PERENNIAL

PLANT HEIGHT 5–30cm.
FLOWER SIZE 3mm wide.
FLOWERING TIME June–September.
LEAVES Whorled, linear or lance-shaped.
FRUIT Tiny, two-parted mericarp, finely warty.
SIMILAR SPECIES Field Madder (p.396) and other bedstraws, which generally have broader leaves.

Sweet Woodruff

Galium odoratum (Rubiaceae)

This neat, attractive plant has whorls of 6–9 elliptical leaves up the stem, each with tiny prickles along the margin. The white flowers form small, branched clusters, set off by the leaf whorl beneath them. The leaves contain an aromatic substance called coumarin, which is used to flavour liqueurs.

PERENNIAL

GROWS *in the shade of deciduous woodland and hedgerows, sometimes forming extensive patches, usually on chalky soil.*

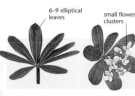

4-petalled flowers

6–9 elliptical leaves

small flower clusters

PLANT HEIGHT *10–30cm.*
FLOWER SIZE *4–7mm wide.*
FLOWERING TIME *May–June.*
LEAVES *Whorls, elliptical.*
FRUIT *Nutlet, 2–3mm wide, with bristles.*
SIMILAR SPECIES *Cleavers (below), which is a scrambling plant; Hedge Bedstraw (right) which has smaller leaves.*

Hedge Bedstraw

Galium mollugo (Rubiaceae)

Masses of creamy white flowers are produced by this scrambling plant along hedgerows and roadsides. Each tiny flower has four petals in the form of a cross, and is borne in loose, many-branched clusters. The leaves are small with rough prickly margins, and the stem is smooth and square. Hedge Bedstraw does not grow on acid soil, unlike the similar Heath Bedstraw.

CLAMBERS *over hedgerows, scrub, dry grassland, meadows, and along roadsides.*

whorls of 6–8 leaves

many-branched flower clusters

pairs of fused nutlets

creamy white flowers

PERENNIAL

PLANT HEIGHT *40–150cm.*
FLOWER SIZE *2–3mm wide.*
FLOWERING TIME *June–September.*
LEAVES *Whorls, oblong.*
FRUIT *Fused nutlets, black when ripe.*
SIMILAR SPECIES *Sweet Woodruff (left); Lady's Bedstraw (below) has yellow flowers; Heath Bedstraw (G. saxatile) is shorter.*

Cleavers

Galium aparine (Rubiaceae)

A common hedgerow plant, Cleavers is especially well known to walkers and dog-owners because the entire plant is covered in hooked hair that help it to clamber over other vegetation, but it may also stick (cleave) to clothing or fur. The paired, rounded fruit are also studded with hooked spines to facilitate their distribution. The white flowers are very small and have four petals; they are borne in sparse clusters at the leaf-bases.

SCRAMBLES *over and through vegetation in scrub or on hedgerows, wasteland, and also cultivated sites. May form extensive patches.*

ANNUAL

flowers in small clusters

whorls of narrow leaves

sharp-pointed leaves

hooked hair

NOTE

The hooked spines of this plant have given rise to many local names for it: Goosegrass, Sticky Willy, Stickleback, Kisses, Bobby Buttons, and others. The plant is often fed to geese and other poultry.

4 petals

bristly, paired fruit

PLANT HEIGHT *30–150cm.*
FLOWER SIZE *2mm wide.*
FLOWERING TIME *May–August.*
LEAVES *Whorls of 4–6, narrow and elliptical.*
FRUIT *Mericarps with hooked bristles.*
SIMILAR SPECIES *Hedge Bedstraw (right) and Sweet Woodruff (above); Heath Bedstraw (G. saxatile) and Marsh Bedstraw (G. palustre), which are less robust with more flowers and hairless fruit.*

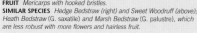

Lady's Bedstraw

Galium verum (Rubiaceae)

The tiny flowers of Lady's Bedstraw seem, at a distance, like candyfloss. Each flower has four well-separated petals and is grouped into a branched, greenish yellow panicle, which is highly fragrant. The leaves are borne in whorls of 8–12 tiny, linear, shiny dark green leaflets arranged around the thin, wiry stems. The tiny fruits turn black when ripe. The growth-form may be anything from a bushy mass to small spikes hidden in the grass, depending on the level of grazing.

INHABITS *dry, open grassy places, banks, and roadsides; also sand dunes and other places near the sea.*

dense, branched panicles of flowers

PERENNIAL

greenish yellow flowers

whorl of tiny leaves

NOTE

The leaves contain coumarin, and have an attractive smell of new-mown hay on drying. The plant was used to stuff mattresses (hence bedstraw) and for "strewing" around the house to control insect pests.

PLANT HEIGHT *20–80cm.*
FLOWER SIZE *2–3mm wide.*
FLOWERING TIME *June–September.*
LEAVES *Whorls of 8–12 small, linear leaves; dark green.*
FRUIT *Fused black nutlets.*
SIMILAR SPECIES *Hedge Bedstraw (above), which has creamy white flowers. Hybrids of this species and Hedge Bedstraw have characteristics of both, with very pale yellow flowers.*

PLANTS

Crosswort

Cruciata laevipes (Rubiaceae)

This member of the bedstraw family is recognizable by its neat, tufted habit and yellowish green colour. The softly hairy leaves are arranged in whorls of four. The short-stalked, four-petalled flowers are borne in tight clusters at the base of each leaf whorl.

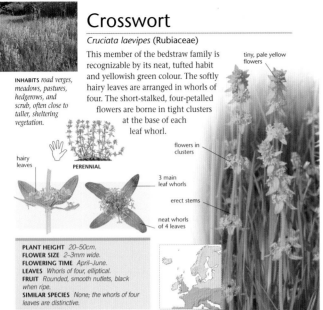

tiny, pale yellow flowers

INHABITS *road verges, meadows, pastures, hedgerows, and scrub, often close to taller, sheltering vegetation.*

PERENNIAL

hairy leaves

flowers in clusters

3 main leaf whorls

erect stems

neat whorls of 4 leaves

PLANT HEIGHT *20–50cm.*
FLOWER SIZE *2–3mm wide.*
FLOWERING TIME *April–June.*
LEAVES *Whorls of four, elliptical.*
FRUIT *Rounded, smooth nutlets, black when ripe.*
SIMILAR SPECIES *None; the whorls of four leaves are distinctive.*

Field Madder

Sherardia arvensis (Rubiaceae)

This low, bristly plant often goes unnoticed among taller vegetation. The pointed, oval leaves have prickly margins, and, as in other bedstraws, are borne in distinct whorls around square stems. The stems have downward-pointing bristles, and the pink flowers are borne in small clusters at the tip, with a ruff of green bracts below each cluster.

SPRAWLS *close to the ground in grassy places and on bare ground, preferring chalky soil.*

whorl of 4–6 leaves

tiny, 4-petalled flowers

leaf-like bracts

ANNUAL

PLANT HEIGHT *5–30cm.*
FLOWER SIZE *3mm wide.*
FLOWERING TIME *May–September.*
LEAVES *Whorled, oval to elliptical, with prickly margins.*
FRUIT *Bristly nutlets, in pairs.*
SIMILAR SPECIES *Squinancywort (p.394), which has narrow leaves.*

Jacob's-ladder

Polemonium caeruleum (Polemoniaceae)

This is a neat-looking plant, with characteristically ladder-like leaves. The flowers are clustered towards the top of the stems, each with five separate, pale blue-violet petals forming a cup shape. There are five long stamens with bright orange anthers, and an even longer purple style. The whole plant forms an erect tuft, but rarely forms colonies.

OCCURS *in rocky places, limestone screes, damp meadows, hedgerows, scrub, and roadsides.*

PERENNIAL

up to 12 pairs of leaflets

orange anthers

erect stem

PLANT HEIGHT *50–100cm.*
FLOWER SIZE *2–3cm wide.*
FLOWERING TIME *May–August.*
LEAVES *Alternate, pinnate, with many pairs of lance-shaped leaflets.*
FRUIT *Small capsule containing many seeds.*
SIMILAR SPECIES *Peach-leaved Bellflower (p.411); Harebell (p.411).*

Hedge Bindweed

Calystegia sepium (Convolvulaceae)

This familiar weed may completely cover hedges and fences with its white flowers in late summer, often becoming a serious garden pest. The tough, sinuous stems twist and wind themselves around other plant stems or any other object in their path, and produce heart-shaped leaves at intervals. The trumpet-shaped, bold white flower unfurls like an umbrella, and has two green sepals at the base, partially hidden by two bracts which do not quite overlap.

CLIMBS *over hedges, other tall plants, scrub, woodland margins, fences, and poles. Prefers damp soil.*

PERENNIAL

trumpet-shaped white flowers

NOTE

The flowers have no scent but are rich in nectar, and are attractive to long-tongued moths, such as the Convolvulus Hawk-moth, at night.

heart-shaped leaf

bracts do not overlap

PLANT HEIGHT *1–3m.*
FLOWER SIZE *3–3.5cm wide.*
FLOWERING TIME *July–September.*
LEAVES *Alternate, arrow- or heart-shaped.*
FRUIT *Rounded green capsule.*
SIMILAR SPECIES *Black Bryony (p.430), which has smaller flowers; Field Bindweed (below), which usually has pink flowers; Large Bindweed (C. sylvatica), which has larger flowers and bracts that do overlap.*

Field Bindweed

Convolvulus arvensis (Convolvulaceae)

A fast-growing plant, this bindweed twines itself around other plants in an anti-clockwise direction, or sprawls along the ground. The leaves are either arrow-shaped with sharp, backward-pointing lobes at the base, or oblong. The trumpet-shaped flowers are usually pink with white stripes, but may be pure white or dark pink.

TWINES *around stems of other plants, fences, and other objects, and along hedgerows; on waste or arable land.*

PERENNIAL

striped petals

rounded or arrow-shaped leaves

untoothed leaf

yellow centre

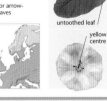

PLANT HEIGHT *Up to 1.5m.*
FLOWER SIZE *2–2.5cm wide.*
FLOWERING TIME *June–September.*
LEAVES *Alternate; arrow-shaped or oblong.*
FRUIT *Rounded, many-seeded capsule.*
SIMILAR SPECIES *Hedge Bindweed (above); Sea Bindweed (Calystegia soldanella), which has fleshy leaves.*

Common Comfrey

Symphytum officinale (Boraginaceae)

This robust and bushy, damp-loving plant has bristly, spear-shaped leaves that are generally stalkless, the leaf base continuing down the stem to the next leaf joint, forming a pair of wings. The tubular or bell-shaped flowers appear in a coiled spray like a scorpion's tail, opening in sequence, and are creamy white, pink, or violet. Common Comfrey was once grown in cottage gardens for its efficacy in helping to heal wounds and mend broken bones.

FLOURISHES *in damp places such as river and stream margins, marshes, fens, wet woodland, and damp meadows.*

PERENNIAL

spear-shaped leaves

untoothed leaf margin

bushy habit

tubular flowers

stalkless leaf

flowers may be pink

coiled spray

NOTE

Steeped in water and left to decay, comfrey leaves make an excellent liquid garden manure.

PLANT HEIGHT *80–150cm.*
FLOWER SIZE *1.2–1.8cm long.*
FLOWERING TIME *May–July.*
LEAVES *Alternate and basal; stalkless, untoothed, coarsely hairy, running down the stem to the next leaf joint.*
FRUIT *Four shiny nutlets.*
SIMILAR SPECIES *Russian Comfrey (S. x uplandicum), which has shorter wings down the stem and blue flowers.*

Common Gromwell

Lithospermum officinale (Boraginaceae)

This tufted, rather erect plant is more noticeable for its mass of lance-shaped leaves than for its tiny white or creamy yellow flowers; these are borne in spiralled clusters that are tucked tightly into the stem. The fruit consists of hard, shiny white nutlets, which look like little beads of porcelain and persist even after the foliage dies down.

flowers tucked into stem

PERENNIAL

5-petalled flower

narrow leaf

very leafy stems

GROWS *in semi-shaded woodland margins, hedgerows, and scrub, always on chalky soil.*

PLANT HEIGHT *40–80cm.*
FLOWER SIZE *3–6mm long.*
FLOWERING TIME *May–August.*
LEAVES *Alternate, lance-shaped, untoothed.*
FRUIT *Four shiny, white or greyish nutlets.*
SIMILAR SPECIES *Corn Gromwell (L. arvense), which is less leafy and grows in arable fields.*

Viper's-bugloss

Echium vulgare (Boraginaceae)

The long, bristly stems of this plant arise from a rosette of leaves formed in the first year, and are clothed in masses of five-petalled, deep purple flowers. Each cluster or cyme of flowers unfurls along the stem like a scorpion's tail, the buds gradually changing from pink to violet as they mature. The leaves and bracts are rough and hairy.

FLOURISHES *in dry, open places, road verges, cliffs, shingle, sand dunes, heaths, and grassy banks, often on disturbed soil.*

scarlet protruding stamens

narrow, stalkless leaves

funnel-shaped flowers

coiled flower buds

BIENNIAL

PLANT HEIGHT *50–100cm.*
FLOWER SIZE *1.5–2cm wide.*
FLOWERING TIME *June–September.*
LEAVES *Basal rosette and alternate, narrow-elliptical to lance-shaped, unstalked; bristly stem leaves.*
FRUIT *Four nutlets at base of persistent calyx.*
SIMILAR SPECIES *None.*

Common Lungwort

Pulmonaria officinalis (Boraginaceae)

This plant can be instantly recognized by its oval, heavily spotted leaves, which were once thought to resemble lungs and therefore to act as a cure for lung diseases. The flowers are borne in dense, branched clusters, pink in bud but maturing to a range of colours from reddish violet to blue. Each flower has five rounded, tissue-like petals fused into a tube at the base.

FORMS *clumps in damp woodland and hedgebanks, in semi-shade on humus-rich soil; dislikes acid soil.*

flowers in clusters

PERENNIAL

slender flower tube

5 petals

white-spotted leaf

PLANT HEIGHT *18–30cm.*
FLOWER SIZE *1.3–1.8cm long.*
FLOWERING TIME *March–May.*
LEAVES *Lower, basal and stalked; upper, alternate, oval with white or pale blotches.*
FRUIT *Four small nutlets.*
SIMILAR SPECIES *Narrow-leaved Lungwort (P. longifolia) in the New Forest area.*

Bugloss

Anchusa arvensis (Boraginaceae)

This erect, extremely bristly plant has rough, alternate leaves with undulating and slightly toothed margins. The lower leaves are stalked, but the smaller upper leaves are unstalked and clasp the stem with heart-shaped bases. The tiny, five-petalled blue flowers are borne in clusters, each with a white centre and a curved tube at the base. A common plant in farmland, it may grow hidden among rows of cereal crops.

GROWS *on arable fields, field margins, waste and bare land, and sandy heaths, especially near the sea.*

5-petalled blue flower

fine bristles

unstalked upper leaf

white centre

ANNUAL

PLANT HEIGHT *15–60cm.*
FLOWER SIZE *4–6mm wide.*
FLOWERING TIME *May–September.*
LEAVES *Alternate, rough and bristly.*
FRUIT *Four nutlets at the base of the calyx.*
SIMILAR SPECIES *Green Alkanet (p.398), which has larger flowers; Forget-me-nots (p.398), which have untoothed leaves.*

Borage

Borago officinalis (Boraginaceae)

Borne in loose, branched clusters, the nodding, ultramarine blue flowers of this plant have a curious appearance as the black stamens form a cone inside the white centre of the flower. The whole plant is bristly and hairy, giving it a frosted appearance. It originates from the Mediterranean but is widely naturalized.

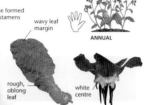

OCCURS *in arable fields, wasteland, and disturbed soil; favours dry, sunny places.*

bristly flower stems

cone formed by stamens

wavy leaf margin

ANNUAL

rough, oblong leaf

white centre

PLANT HEIGHT *30–60cm.*
FLOWER SIZE *2–2.5cm wide.*
FLOWERING TIME *May–September.*
LEAVES *Alternate, basal, oval to oblong, untoothed, stalked.*
FRUIT *Four nutlets at the base of the calyx.*
SIMILAR SPECIES *Green Alkanet (below), which lacks prominent black stamens.*

Wood Forget-me-not

Myosotis sylvatica (Boraginaceae)

There are several species of forget-me-nots in Europe, all of which have the same basic flower structure of sky-blue petals with a yellow centre, as well as hairy leaves (the name Myosotis means "mouse's ear"). The chief differences are the size of the flowers and the preferred habitat. The Wood Forget-me-not has the largest flowers and is found in woodland.

GROWS *in semi-shaded situations in woodland rides and clearings, road verges, and damp meadows.*

flat, 5-petalled flowers

yellow centre

untoothed margin

PERENNIAL

flowers borne in clusters

lance-shaped leaf

PLANT HEIGHT *20–50cm.*
FLOWER SIZE *6–10mm wide.*
FLOWERING TIME *April–July.*
LEAVES *Basal and alternate, lance-shaped, hairy; stem leaves stalkless.*
FRUIT *Small, shiny nutlets in the calyx.*
SIMILAR SPECIES *Field Forget-me-not (M. arvensis), which has smaller flowers.*

Green Alkanet

Pentaglottis sempervirens (Boraginaceae)

PROLIFERATES *in damp, semi-shaded sites along woodland margins, hedgebanks, and roadsides, often close to habitation.*

The large, slightly bristly, basal leaves of Green Alkanet are formed early in the year and may be mistaken for those of Foxglove (p.406) at first. Covered with fine hair, they are somewhat wrinkled, and paler beneath. The flowering shoots are distinctive, bearing coiled clusters of blue flowers, darker than those of the related forget-me-nots (right), each with a pure white throat and spreading, rounded petals. The plant was introduced from southwestern Europe, but has naturalized in many parts of Britain as a result of its escape from gardens.

PERENNIAL

flowers in small clusters

5 well-separated petals

NOTE

The fine, bristly hair on the stems and leaves of this and other members of the borage family can cause skin irritation if handled without protection.

long, leafy stem

untoothed leaves

oval basal leaf

long stalk of basal leaf

white centre

PLANT HEIGHT *40–80cm.*
FLOWER SIZE *8–10mm wide.*
FLOWERING TIME *April–July.*
LEAVES *Basal leaves, oval to oblong, long-stalked and hairy; alternate stem leaves, unstalked.*
FRUIT *Four nutlets, rough, netted on surface.*
SIMILAR SPECIES *Bugloss (p.397) is shorter and more bristly, with smaller flowers; Borage (above) has prominent, black stamens.*

Water Forget-me-not

Myosotis scorpioides (Boraginaceae)

This species appears less hairy than most forget-me-nots, as the hairs lie very flat on the stems and leaves. The stems look fleshy, befitting its moist habitat. The flower cluster, a cyme, is coiled in bud and resembles a scorpion's tail when it uncoils. Pink in bud, the flowers open sky-blue.

FORMS *colonies in wet places along rivers and streams, in marshes, ditches, and meadows, on neutral soil.*

flowers in cymes

yellow centre

PERENNIAL

oblong leaf

5 spreading, rounded petals

fleshy leaves

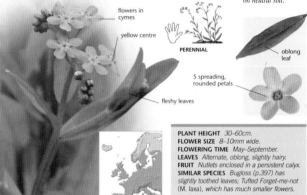

PLANT HEIGHT *30–60cm.*
FLOWER SIZE *8–10mm wide.*
FLOWERING TIME *May–September.*
LEAVES *Alternate, oblong, slightly hairy.*
FRUIT *Nutlets enclosed in a persistent calyx.*
SIMILAR SPECIES *Bugloss (p.397) has slightly toothed leaves; Tufted Forget-me-not (M. laxa), which has much smaller flowers.*

Hound's-tongue

Cynoglossum officinale (Boraginaceae)

This is a roughly hairy plant, with soft, hairy, greyish green leaves with a coarse texture. It forms a distinct tuft, sending up long branching cymes that uncoil to reveal a row of five-petalled, very dark crimson or dull purplish flowers, which have a characteristic smell of mice. Four large, bristly nutlets are squeezed tightly into the outspread calyx.

OCCURS *in rough grassland, among scrub, or alongside hedgerows, on chalky soil.*

funnel-shaped flowers

hooked bristles

5 petals

4 nutlets

dark centre

BIENNIAL

untoothed leaves

PLANT HEIGHT *40–70cm.*
FLOWER SIZE *6–10mm wide.*
FLOWERING TIME *May–August.*
LEAVES *Alternate, lance-shaped.*
FRUIT *Four nutlets, with hooked bristles.*
SIMILAR SPECIES *Green Hound's-tongue (C. germanicum), which has hair only on the undersides of its leaves.*

Vervain

Verbena officinalis (Verbenaceae)

A wiry, hairy, and rather rough plant, Vervain has long, square, branching stems that spread out like a candelabra, bearing tall leafless spikes of surprisingly small flowers. Only a few flowers in a spike are open at any one time. These are pink with white centres, and each have five asymmetric lobes, appearing almost two-lipped. The opposite leaves are strongly pinnately lobed, and coarsely toothed, but nevertheless rather delicate. Vervain, once used as a charm against snake bites, has a long history of medicinal and sacred uses. It is now chiefly used as a remedy for hyperactivity.

GROWS in bare, rocky places, on wasteland and roadsides, avoiding acid soil.

PERENNIAL

narrow flower spikes

pink flowers

NOTE

The name Vervain is thought to derive from the Celtic ferfaen, meaning to drive away (fer) stones (faen), as the plant was once used to treat kidney and bladder stones. It is still used for many other ailments.

tough, wiry stems

deeply lobed leaf

PLANT HEIGHT 50–75cm.
FLOWER SIZE 4–5mm wide.
FLOWERING TIME June–September.
LEAVES Opposite; pinnately lobed and coarsely toothed, the lower leaves more strongly lobed than the upper.
FRUIT Four ribbed nutlets.
SIMILAR SPECIES Gipsywort (p.402) and other small-flowered members of the mint family, which have leafy flower spikes.

Bugle

Ajuga reptans (Lamiaceae)

Bugle only produces fertile seed in small quantities, and spreads chiefly by long runners, which form roots and new shoots at intervals. These runners die off in winter, but the following spring the dormant, newly-rooted plants spring into life to produce taller, densely-flowered spikes. The flowers are blue, each with a reduced upper lip, and are surrounded with oval leaves which are often flushed with purple or bronze, especially towards the top. The square stems are hairy on two opposite sides only, with a dark purple line on the corners.

FOUND in mats in damp areas of woodland rides and shady grassland, or along hedgerows.

PERENNIAL

flowers in whorls

oval leaf

dense flower spike

prominent flower lobes

flower appears one-lipped

violet-flushed leaves

square stem

NOTE

The name Ajuga is a corruption of the Latin word abigo, meaning to drive away – a reference to the belief that it could drive away disease. It may however be used externally to treat bruises.

PLANT HEIGHT 10–25cm.
FLOWER SIZE 1.4–1.7cm long.
FLOWERING TIME April–June.
LEAVES Opposite, oval, flushed purple towards the top.
FRUIT Four small nutlets.
SIMILAR SPECIES Self-heal (p.401) has more tightly clustered 2-lipped flowers; Ground Ivy (p.401) has toothed leaves and 2-lipped flowers; Pyramidal Bugle (A. pyramidalis), which is larger and leafier.

Wood Sage

Teucrium scorodonia (Lamiaceae)

One-sided spikes of yellow-green flowers and wrinkled leaves, similar in appearance to the leaves of the culinary sage, make this plant distinctive. Close examination of the flowers shows that they have only one lip, which is slightly lobed, so that the brown stamens are exposed. The leaves are in opposite pairs and the stems are square, as in other members of the mint family.

FORMS tufts in dry and often sandy, open woods, grassland and hedgerows, and on heaths and dunes; prefers acid soil.

flowers in leafless spikes

wrinkled, toothed leaf

maroon anthers

square stems

PERENNIAL

one-lipped flower

PLANT HEIGHT 30–50cm.
FLOWER SIZE 8–9mm long.
FLOWERING TIME July–September.
LEAVES Opposite pairs, oval, toothed, with heart-shaped bases.
FRUIT Four nutlets within the calyx.
SIMILAR SPECIES None; the leafless flower spikes are distinctive within the mint family.

Skullcap

Scutellaria galericulata (Lamiaceae)

Not easy to spot among the taller vegetation of its marshland habitat, this member of the mint family produces just a few flowers, always in pairs, often quite low down on the square stem, at the base of the leaves. The bright violet-blue flowers have a distinctive shape, especially in bud, when they look like a pair of tiny, downy boxing gloves. The bluntly toothed leaves are oval to lance-shaped.

OCCURS in damp places, wet meadows, marshes, margins of rivers, streams, and ditches, often among taller vegetation.

leafy stems

violet-blue flowers

opposite leaves

toothed leaf margin

2-lipped flowers in pairs

PERENNIAL

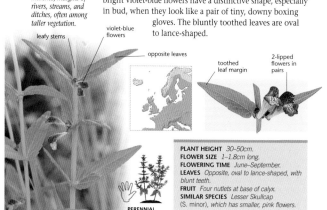

PLANT HEIGHT 30–50cm.
FLOWER SIZE 1–1.8cm long.
FLOWERING TIME June–September.
LEAVES Opposite, oval to lance-shaped, with blunt teeth.
FRUIT Four nutlets at base of calyx.
SIMILAR SPECIES Lesser Skullcap (S. minor), which has smaller, pink flowers.

PLANTS

Common Hemp-nettle

Galeopsis tetrahit (Lamiaceae)

This member of the mint family has pairs of leaves neatly arranged on opposite sides of the square, very hairy stems. The pink flowers are in whorls around the base of the leaves; each has white and purple markings on the lower lip, and a very bristly calyx with pointed teeth.

OCCURS *in woodland margins and glades, heaths, and sides of ditches and marshes.*

2-lipped pink flowers

leafy upper stems

ANNUAL

purple markings

oval leaf

pointed calyx

PLANT HEIGHT *30–70cm.*
FLOWER SIZE *1.5–2cm long.*
FLOWERING TIME *June–September.*
LEAVES *Opposite, oval to spear-shaped.*
FRUIT *Four nutlets held within calyx.*
SIMILAR SPECIES *Black Horehound (right), Red Dead-nettle (below), Marsh Woundwort (Stachys palustris), which is less leafy.*

White Dead-nettle

Lamium album (Lamiaceae)

The leaves of this plant resemble those of common nettles, but do not have stinging hairs. Like other members of the mint family, this plant has a square stem and leaves on opposite sides. Two-lipped white flowers emerge in tight whorls, and bloom for many months.

INHABITS *grassy roadsides, wasteland, and hedgerows; on rich soil, particularly where disturbed.*

coarsely toothed leaf margin

large, pure white flowers

hairy upper lip

black anthers

alternate leaves

PERENNIAL

PLANT HEIGHT *20–50cm.*
FLOWER SIZE *1.8–2.5cm long.*
FLOWERING TIME *April–November.*
LEAVES *Opposite; oval to heart-shaped, stalked, with toothed margins.*
FRUIT *Four small nutlets.*
SIMILAR SPECIES *None with such large white flowers.*

Red Dead-nettle

Lamium purpureum (Lamiaceae)

One of the earliest plants to flower in the year, this plant is a member of the mint family. It does not sting as it is not related to common nettles. The smaller, upper leaves, bunched together at the top of the plant, are flushed with purple, while the two-lipped flowers are pink to red.

INVADES *cultivated, disturbed, and waste ground, roadsides, and gardens; also alongside walls.*

coarsely toothed leaves

ANNUAL

purple-flushed upper leaves

flowers in whorls

upper lip

straight tube

PLANT HEIGHT *8–25cm.*
FLOWER SIZE *1–1.8cm long.*
FLOWERING TIME *March–December.*
LEAVES *Opposite, oval, and toothed.*
FRUIT *Four tiny nutlets at the base of calyx.*
SIMILAR SPECIES *Black Horehound (right), Common Hemp-nettle (above), Wild Basil (p.402), Hedge Woundwort (p.401).*

Yellow Archangel

Lamiastrum galeobdolon (Lamiaceae)

A plant that brightens the landscape with its striking colour in spring, Yellow Archangel has unusually large flowers for a member of the mint family. Each two-lipped flower is bright butter-yellow in colour, with red markings on the lower lip. The stalked, paired leaves are almost triangular in outline, with coarse teeth. A form with silver markings on the leaves, subsp. *argentatum* is a garden variety frequently occurring in the wild. The fruit is in the form of four nutlets that are found at the base of the calyx.

GROWS *in shady woodland, hedgerows, and coppices, on heavy clay or chalky soil.*

stalked leaves

jagged leaf margin

PERENNIAL

2-lipped flower

red streaks on lower lip

flowers in tight whorls

large, pointed leaves

NOTE

The form most frequently seen in the wild is subsp. montanum, and is a good indicator of ancient woodland where it occurs. Subsp. galeobdolon has smaller flowers (1.7–2.1cm long) and is very rare.

PLANT HEIGHT *20–50cm.*
FLOWER SIZE *1.8–2.5cm long.*
FLOWERING TIME *April–June.*
LEAVES *Opposite, almost triangular, coarsely toothed.*
FRUIT *Four nutlets at base of calyx.*
SIMILAR SPECIES *Yellow Rattle (p.406); Large-flowered Hemp-nettle (Galeopsis speciosa) has flowers with a deep violet blotch; Yellow Bartsia (Parentucellia viscosa) has a 3-lobed lower lip and smaller leaves.*

Black Horehound

Ballota nigra (Lamiaceae)

This hairy, scruffy-looking plant has an unpleasant smell when the leaves are crushed. It has two-lipped, reddish mauve flowers, in compact whorls along the upper stem, with distinctive, sharply pointed calyces; these turn brown or black, giving the plant a dirty appearance.

FOUND *in hedgerows and woodland edges; on rich, neutral or chalky soil.*

toothed leaves

whorls of flowers

erect stems

PERENNIAL

pointed calyx

2-lipped flower

PLANT HEIGHT *50–100cm.*
FLOWER SIZE *1.2–1.5cm long.*
FLOWERING TIME *June–September.*
LEAVES *Opposite, narrow and toothed.*
FRUIT *Four nutlets at the base of the calyx.*
SIMILAR SPECIES *Red Dead-nettle (left); Common Hemp-nettle (left); Hedge Woundwort (p.401).*

Betony

Stachys officinalis (Lamiaceae)

The bright magenta flowerheads of Betony, with leaf-like bracts drooping below them, are hard to miss among the grasses with which it grows. The plant has a neater appearance than many of its relatives in the mint family, with square stems bearing 2–4 pairs of narrowly oval, deep green leaves, with rounded teeth. Betony was used medicinally for centuries and as a protective charm by the Anglo-Saxons.

GROWS *in dry, grassy places, in heaths, woodland, and hedgerows.*

tapered flower spike

whorls of magenta flowers

PERENNIAL

rounded teeth

2-lipped flower

PLANT HEIGHT *20–75cm.*
FLOWER SIZE *1.2–1.8cm long.*
FLOWERING TIME *June–October.*
LEAVES *Opposite, narrowly oval, toothed.*
FRUIT *Four small nutlets within the calyx.*
SIMILAR SPECIES *Common Hemp-nettle (p.400); Wild Basil (p.402); Hedge Woundwort (below).*

Ground Ivy

Glechoma hederacea (Lamiaceae)

Although this plant may flower throughout summer, it is in early spring that extensive mats bloom with bluish mauve, sometimes pink, two-lipped flowers that have pink spots on the lower lip. In summer, Ground Ivy spreads by sending long, leafy runners over the ground, much like Ivy (p.384).

GROWS *in mats on bare ground, field margins, woodland rides and clearings, and along hedgerows; prefers damp places.*

long leaf stalk

large, blunt teeth

PERENNIAL

red-tinged upper leaves

flowers in whorls

2-lipped flower

PLANT HEIGHT *10–25cm.*
FLOWER SIZE *1.5–2.2cm long.*
FLOWERING TIME *March–September.*
LEAVES *Opposite, kidney-shaped or rounded, long-stalked, coarsely toothed.*
FRUIT *Four nutlets in persistent calyx.*
SIMILAR SPECIES *Bugle (p.399), which has untoothed leaves and one-lipped flowers.*

Hedge Woundwort

Stachys sylvatica (Lamiaceae)

The dark claret or dull purple flowers of Hedge Woundwort do not seem bright enough to attract insects in their shady woodland habitat, but they do have some white markings that guide bees and flies to the throat of the flower to help pollination. The leaves give off a strong, foetid smell that may also entice insects. They are distinctly heart-shaped, with a wrinkled surface and toothed margin. The square stems have crimson ridges on the corners and are clothed in glandular hair.

FOUND *in woodland margins, cultivated or wasteland, and along hedgerows and footpaths, in semi-shaded situations.*

NOTE
The Hedge Woundwort and other Stachys species have a long medicinal history. They have been used since the time of the ancient Greeks in poultices for wounds and to help staunch bleeding.

flowers in whorled spike

dull purple petals

calyx with equal teeth

square stems

PERENNIAL

toothed margin

heart-shaped base

pale markings on lower lip

2-lipped flower

PLANT HEIGHT *60–100cm.*
FLOWER SIZE *1.3–1.8cm long.*
FLOWERING TIME *June–September.*
LEAVES *Opposite, heart-shaped, with toothed margins; short-stalked upper leaves, long-stalked lower leaves.*
FRUIT *Four nutlets at the base of the calyx.*
SIMILAR SPECIES *Black Horehound (p.400); Betony (above); Marsh Woundwort (S. palustris), which has pink flowers and grows in marshes.*

Self-heal

Prunella vulgaris (Lamiaceae)

This plant forms distinctive oblong flowerheads, tightly packed with often purplish calyces. A pair of sharp bracts and rounded, dark-margined leaves below each flower, make the whole flowerhead look like a fir-cone. The flowers, each with a long, hooded upper lip, are usually deep blue, but colonies of pure pink flowers are often seen.

FORMS *patches in grassy places, lawns wasteland, and woodland clearings, or among scrub.*

dark bracts below each flower

finely pointed teeth on calyx

dark lines on square stems

PERENNIAL

oval leaf

hooded upper lip

PLANT HEIGHT *15–30cm.*
FLOWER SIZE *1.3–1.5cm long.*
FLOWERING TIME *June–November.*
LEAVES *Opposite, oval to lance-shaped, very slightly toothed.*
FRUIT *Four nutlets at base of calyx.*
SIMILAR SPECIES *Bugle (p.399), which has one-lipped flowers in leafy spikes.*

Balm

Melissa officinalis (Lamiaceae)

A native of southern Europe, Balm has long been grown in gardens in Britain, frequently escaping into the countryside. The leaves are small and diamond-shaped with coarse, rounded teeth, but the most distinctive feature is the strong scent of lemon when they are crushed. The small two-lipped flowers, in loose whorls at the base of the leaves, are mostly white, with a pinkish tinge.

FORMS *tufts on wasteland, dry banks, scrub, and along hedgerows, often near human habitation.*

opposite leaves

small white flowers

rounded teeth

pink tinge

2-lipped flower

PERENNIAL

PLANT HEIGHT *40–70cm.*
FLOWER SIZE *8–15mm long.*
FLOWERING TIME *July–September.*
LEAVES *Opposite, diamond-shaped, slightly pointed with rounded teeth.*
FRUIT *Four nutlets.*
SIMILAR SPECIES *White Dead-nettle (p.400), which has larger flowers.*

PLANTS

Wild Basil

Clinopodium vulgare (Lamiaceae)

Although Wild Basil is not the culinary herb, it is faintly aromatic, with a scent similar to thyme. A rather weak and straggly plant, it has dense whorls of deep pink flowers clustered around the upper leaf bases. The lower sepals of the calyx are slightly longer and more slender than the upper ones. The hairy leaves are oval and gently toothed.

GROWS *in dry, grassy places along woodland margins, hedgerows, and on embankments; prefers chalky soil.*

flowers in dense whorls

oval leaves

bluntly toothed margin

2-lipped flower

PERENNIAL

spiky calyx

PLANT HEIGHT *40–75cm.*
FLOWER SIZE *1.2–2cm long.*
FLOWERING TIME *July–September.*
LEAVES *Opposite, toothed, and hairy.*
FRUIT *Four nutlets at the base of calyx.*
SIMILAR SPECIES *Red Dead-nettle (p.400), which has purple-flushed leaves; Betony (p.401) has darker leaves with larger teeth.*

Gipsywort

Lycopus europaeus (Lamiaceae)

Instantly recognizable in its habitat, this plant has very distinctive leaves. They are oval to elliptical, with large, jagged, forward-pointing teeth, and are arranged in opposite pairs at well-spaced intervals along the stem. The whorls of tiny white flowers, patterned with minute purple dots, are clustered very tightly on the stem, and each has a rather spiny calyx of sepals.

THRIVES *in wet areas such as pond margins, boggy woodland, and edges of reedbeds, often growing among taller vegetation.*

evenly spaced leaves

jagged teeth

tiny dots on petals

tight whorl of flowers

PERENNIAL

spiny calyx

PLANT HEIGHT *30–80cm.*
FLOWER SIZE *3–4mm long.*
FLOWERING TIME *July–September.*
LEAVES *Opposite, oval to elliptical.*
FRUIT *Four nutlets.*
SIMILAR SPECIES *Corn Mint (Mentha arvensis), which has pinker flowers, more rounded leaves, and a sickly smell.*

Wild Thyme

Thymus polytrichus (Lamiaceae)

The scent of thyme is released when the leaves of this plant are crushed, although it is not the species grown for culinary use. The slender, hairy, square stems bear tiny, oval leaves, and dense clusters of pink flowers with red sepals at their tips. In the Brecklands of Norfolk, this species is replaced by *T. serpyllum*, which is almost identical but with rounded stems.

FORMS *creeping mats, often in the short, grazed turf of chalk grassland; also heaths, banks, and dunes.*

oval leaf

2-lipped flower

red sepals

pink flowers in dense heads

PERENNIAL

PLANT HEIGHT *4–10cm.*
FLOWER SIZE *5–6mm long.*
FLOWERING TIME *May–September.*
LEAVES *Opposite, oval, up to 8mm long.*
FRUIT *Four nutlets in the persistent calyx.*
SIMILAR SPECIES *Wild Marjoram (right); Large Thyme (T. pulegioides), which has hairs only on the angles of the square stems.*

Wild Marjoram

Origanum vulgare (Lamiaceae)

Commonly cultivated as the herb oregano, this hairy, bushy plant often grows in large colonies, filling the air with its strong scent. The culinary herb marjoram comes from two similar, related plants of the Mediterranean, *O. majorana* and *O. onites*. The leaves are a simple oval shape, untoothed and short-stalked, and covered with tiny glands. Numerous flowers, with protruding stamens, are borne in dense clusters on the much-branched reddish stems. The two-lipped, pink petals are surrounded by prominent crimson sepals and bracts.

FOUND *in rough, dry grassland, woodland, and scrub; also along roadsides, hedgerows, and embankments, and often on slopes; prefers chalky soil.*

tough red-purple stems

flat-topped clusters of flowers

PERENNIAL

NOTE

The scientific name of this plant comes from the Greek oros *(mountain) and* ganos *(joy). It was used by Greeks and Romans to crown brides and grooms.*

untoothed leaf margin

red-flushed bracts

PLANT HEIGHT *30–50cm.*
FLOWER SIZE *4–7mm long.*
FLOWERING TIME *July–September.*
LEAVES *Opposite, untoothed, strongly aromatic; bright green.*
FRUIT *Four nutlets within the calyx.*
SIMILAR SPECIES *Wild Thyme (left) and Large Thyme (Thymus pulegioides), which are smaller and have a distinctly different scent.*

Water Mint

Mentha aquatica (Lamiaceae)

The strong, sickly sweet scent of this plant is noticeable even without bruising the leaves. Its large flowerheads are bunched on top of one another, the flowers having two-lipped lilac-pink petals and crimson sepals, the prominent, protruding stamens giving them a fluffy appearance. The leaves are oval and toothed, the lower ones short-stalked, and often tinged with red.

FLOURISHES *at the edges of ponds, ditches, and lakes, often in the water, or in the damp parts of freshwater marshes and swamps.*

fluffy flowerhead

toothed leaf margin

red-tinged leaf

long stamens

PERENNIAL

2-lipped flower

PLANT HEIGHT *4–8m.*
FLOWER SIZE *4–6mm long.*
FLOWERING TIME *July–September.*
LEAVES *Opposite, oval, coarsely toothed.*
FRUIT *Four nutlets at the base of the calyx.*
SIMILAR SPECIES *Corn Mint (M. arvensis), which has stems ending in leaves, not flowers; hybrids also occur frequently.*

Deadly Nightshade

Atropa belladonna (Solanaceae)

A medium-sized, shrub-like plant, Deadly Nightshade looks innocuous, but is highly poisonous. Shiny black and slightly flattened, the berries look a little like cherries. They are said to taste sweet, but are fatally poisonous and can be identified by the persistent, five-sepalled calyx at the base of the fruit. The flowers are short greenish tubes flushed with brownish violet, with five spreading, triangular lobes at the mouth. Each flower is solitary in the upper leaf base. Slightly reminiscent of those of the related potato, the leaves are oval and pointed.

INHABITS *semi-shaded places in old quarries, near ruins, woodland, banks, and pathways, usually among other scrubby vegetation, on chalky soil.*

PERENNIAL

thick green stem

large, oval leaves

5 triangular flower lobes

bell-shaped flower

NOTE
The poisonous juice of the berry of this plant was used by women to dilate the pupils as a beauty treatment (bella donna); nowadays eye-surgeons use a refined form.

5 sepals | black ripe berry

PLANT HEIGHT *1–1.8m.*
FLOWER SIZE *2.5–3cm long.*
FLOWERING TIME *June–September.*
LEAVES *Alternate, oval, pointed and untoothed, on short stalks.*
FRUIT *Black berry, 1.5–2cm wide, with persistent five-sepalled calyx, highly poisonous.*
SIMILAR SPECIES *None; the unique combination of flower shape and black berry minimizes the chance of dangerous confusion.*

Thorn-apple

Datura stramonium (Solanaceae)

A poisonous plant, Thorn-apple has jaggedly toothed, oval leaves with an unpleasant smell. The long white flowers, similar to Hedge Bindweed (p.396), may be flushed with purple and are generally produced singly. The egg-shaped green fruit splits open to reveal the highly toxic black seeds. The plant may be absent in some years and prolific in others.

GROWS *on wasteland, cultivated or disturbed sites, and in farmyards and field margins; on rich soil.*

trumpet-shaped flower

ANNUAL

sharp-toothed margin | fruit covered with spines | bushy habit

PLANT HEIGHT *70–150cm.*
FLOWER SIZE *5–10cm long.*
FLOWERING TIME *July–October.*
LEAVES *Alternate, oval, jaggedly toothed.*
FRUIT *Egg-shaped, spiny green capsule.*
SIMILAR SPECIES *Hedge Bindweed (p.396), which is a climbing plant and has arrow-shaped leaves.*

Black Nightshade

Solanum nigrum (Solanaceae)

This common bushy weed has similar flowers to those of the potato plant, with which it often grows. Each consists of a yellow cone of anthers surrounded by five white petals. These later form clusters of poisonous, round berries, which ripen from green to black. The stems are blackish, and the variable leaves are slightly toothed or lobed.

pointed, oval leaves

PREFERS *wasteland, bare soil, and rich cultivated ground, often with crops.*

starry, white and yellow flowers

ANNUAL

reflexed petals | shiny fruit | short anthers

PLANT HEIGHT *10–50cm.*
FLOWER SIZE *1–1.4cm wide.*
FLOWERING TIME *July–October.*
LEAVES *Alternate, oval to broadly triangular.*
FRUIT *Clusters of round berries, ripening from green to black.*
SIMILAR SPECIES *Bittersweet (below); Green Nightshade (S. physalifolium) has green stems.*

Henbane

Hyoscyamus niger (Solanaceae)

This poisonous, foetid-smelling plant is related to Deadly Nightshade (above), but looks different. The pale-veined stem leaves are unstalked and clasp the stem. Small, trumpet-shaped, five-petalled flowers are creamy yellow, with a lacy network of purple lines. The plant is very short as an annual but more vigorous as a biennial.

OCCURS *on disturbed ground, field edges, farmyards, and on coastal shingles, usually on rich soil.*

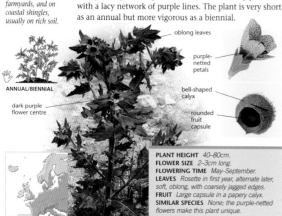

oblong leaves

purple-netted petals

bell-shaped calyx

rounded fruit capsule

ANNUAL/BIENNIAL

dark purple flower centre

PLANT HEIGHT *40–80cm.*
FLOWER SIZE *2–3cm long.*
FLOWERING TIME *May–September.*
LEAVES *Rosette in first year, alternate later, soft, oblong, with coarsely jagged edges.*
FRUIT *Large capsule in a papery calyx.*
SIMILAR SPECIES *None; the purple-netted flowers make this plant unique.*

Bittersweet

Solanum dulcamara (Solanaceae)

The flowers of this poisonous woody climber are instantly recognizable as they are similar to those of the related tomato and potato. The five slender petals surround cone-shaped bright yellow anthers. These form clusters of green fruit that later ripen to orange and finally to red, persisting long after the leaves have withered. The leaves have deeply cut lobes.

CLAMBERS *over hedges and other vegetation in scrub, marsh, and fens; also sprawls over shingle beaches.*

cone of yellow stamens

large terminal lobe

PERENNIAL

egg-shaped berries

swept-back purple petals

PLANT HEIGHT *1–2.5m (20cm on shingle).*
FLOWER SIZE *1–1.5cm wide.*
FLOWERING TIME *May–September.*
LEAVES *Alternate, arrow-shaped, untoothed, 3–5 lobes, short stalks.*
FRUIT *Red, egg-shaped berry.*
SIMILAR SPECIES *Potato (S. tuberosum), which grows as a short bushy plant.*

PLANTS

Great Mullein

Verbascum thapsus (Scrophulariaceae)

Usually much taller than Dark Mullein (below), this plant has characteristic dense spires of bright yellow flowers. The first flowers to open are at the base of the spike, but as this elongates and branches, flowers open at intervals along it. Each flower has five spreading, rounded lobes, and stamens that have white filaments. The leaves of this plant are soft, thick, and felty. Grey-green in colour, they are covered with fine, branched hairs, and are easily identifiable in the plant's first year, when this biennial does not flower.

FOUND *on wasteland and banks, rough, dry grassland, along roadsides, and in stony places; often on disturbed soil.*

tall spires of yellow flowers

NOTE

The tiny hairs, which give the leaves of this plant a velvety look, ignite easily and were once used to make lamp wicks.

BIENNIAL

grey-green leaf

untoothed margin

rounded flower lobes

PLANT HEIGHT *0.5–2m.*
FLOWER SIZE *1.2–3.5cm wide.*
FLOWERING TIME *June–August.*
LEAVES *Alternate, densely packed together, oblong to elliptical, thick and velvety.*
FRUIT *Small, many-seeded capsule.*
SIMILAR SPECIES *Dark Mullein (below); White Mullein (V. lychnitis) has white flowers; Hoary Mullein (V. pulverulentum) has very woolly leaves.*

Common Toadflax

Linaria vulgaris (Scrophulariaceae)

The tufted spikes of Common Toadflax flower late into the autumn. Each lemon-yellow flower is composed of two closed lips, the lower with two orange bosses (palette), and a slender, tapering spur which hangs downward. Only large bees are able to push the lips apart to reach the nectar. The narrow leaves grow spirally up the stem.

GROWS *in clumps on roadsides, meadows, embankments, field margins, and other open, grassy places.*

PERENNIAL

2-lipped flower

orange boss

alternate leaves

linear leaf

tapering spur

PLANT HEIGHT *30–70cm.*
FLOWER SIZE *2–3.5cm long.*
FLOWERING TIME *July–October.*
LEAVES *Alternate, linear, untoothed.*
FRUIT *Large, oval capsule, split near apex.*
SIMILAR SPECIES *Garden snapdragons (Antirrhinums), which sometimes become naturalized, and occur in a range of colours.*

Purple Toadflax

Linaria purpurea (Scrophulariaceae)

A robust plant originating from southern Italy, Purple Toadflax is becoming increasingly naturalized in wasteland close to human habitation. The long, slender, almost wiry spikes are composed of whorls of two-lipped, purple flowers, each with a slender spur at the back, reminiscent of a snapdragon. The grey-green leaves are linear, whorled at the bottom, but alternate at the top.

SEEN *on cultivated and waste ground, on or along old walls and pavements, close to human habitation.*

slender flower spikes

PERENNIAL

deep purple flowers

dark-veined flower

linear leaf

slender spur

PLANT HEIGHT *60–100cm.*
FLOWER SIZE *0.9–1.5cm long.*
FLOWERING TIME *June–August.*
LEAVES *Whorls at bottom, alternate higher up, linear.*
FRUIT *Small, rounded capsule.*
SIMILAR SPECIES *Pale Toadflax (L. repens), which has pale lilac flowers with darker veins.*

Dark Mullein

Verbascum nigrum (Scrophulariaceae)

The upright yellow flower spikes of this robust plant make it easy to spot. Each flower has prominent purple hairs on the stamens, which contrast with the five yellow petals. Unlike Great Mullein (above), which has soft, velvety leaves, it has glossy, dark green leaves that are paler beneath, with gently toothed margins. The basal leaves are in tufts.

OCCURS *on roadsides, embankments, dry grassland, and along hedgerows, often in semi-shade.*

PERENNIAL

oval petals

purple stamens

tall, narrow flower spike

oblong leaf

PLANT HEIGHT *50–100cm.*
FLOWER SIZE *1.8–2.5cm wide.*
FLOWERING TIME *June–September.*
LEAVES *Alternate, oblong, long-stalked.*
FRUIT *Small, many-seeded capsule.*
SIMILAR SPECIES *Agrimony (p.367), which has lobed leaves; Great Mullein (above) is larger, with velvety leaves and white stamens.*

Ivy-leaved Toadflax

Cymbalaria muralis (Scrophulariaceae)

Originally from southern Europe, this plant is now found further afield. The long, trailing stems are reddish, with fleshy, lobed leaves similar in shape to those of Ivy (p.384). The long-stemmed flowers have two lilac or violet lips, with two central yellow patches and a short spur.

LIVES *in nooks and crannies, old walls, pavements, and rocky places, generally on vertical surfaces, in full or partial shade.*

5–9 broad lobes

PERENNIAL

slender reddish stems

yellow patch

lilac or violet petals

short spur

PLANT HEIGHT *10–25cm.*
FLOWER SIZE *9–15mm long.*
FLOWERING TIME *May–September.*
LEAVES *Alternate, palmately lobed, fleshy.*
FRUIT *Small capsule, opens by irregular slits.*
SIMILAR SPECIES *Ivy (p.384), which has similar leaves; Round-leaved Fluellen (p.405), which has oval leaves.*

Common Figwort

Scrophularia nodosa (Scrophulariaceae)

A tall, robust plant, Common Figwort has surprisingly small flowers, which in bud look like beads on stalks. They are borne on square stems, usually opening one at a time within a cluster. Each flower has a notched, purplish brown upper lip, which forms a little hood over the pouched lower lip, with two of the four stamens protruding.

GROWS *in damp places, along stream and river banks, in meadows and open woodland.*

PERENNIAL

oval leaf

yellow stamens

bead-like flower buds

hooded upper lip

branching stems

PLANT HEIGHT *60–100cm.*
FLOWER SIZE *7–9mm long.*
FLOWERING TIME *June–September.*
LEAVES *Opposite, oval, with finely toothed margins and wrinkled surface.*
FRUIT *Two-parted, rounded capsule.*
SIMILAR SPECIES *Water Figwort (S. auriculata), which has winged stems.*

Brooklime

Veronica beccabunga (Scrophulariaceae)

Brooklime is a distinctive plant, with its fat, succulent stems flushed red around the leaf-joints. The flowers form loose clusters on long stalks that arise from the leaf bases. Each flower is a rich blue, with a small white "eye" ringed with scarlet. The hairless leaves are also a little succulent and have a wavy margin.

INHABITS *margins of ponds, ditches, rivers, and permanently damp parts of marshes and wet meadows.*

wavy-edged leaf

red-tinged succulent stems

red ring around white centre

deep blue flowers

PERENNIAL

PLANT HEIGHT *20–60cm.*
FLOWER SIZE *5–8mm wide.*
FLOWERING TIME *May–September.*
LEAVES *Opposite, oval to elliptical, slightly fleshy, toothed; deep green.*
FRUIT *Small, round capsule.*
SIMILAR SPECIES *Blue Water-speedwell (V. anagallis-aquatica) has longer leaves.*

Round-leaved Fluellen

Kickxia spuria (Scrophulariaceae)

This low-growing, creeping plant has short-stalked, alternate leaves along the trailing stems. Lying close to the ground, the small, long-stalked flowers may be partially hidden by the leaves. Each flower has a three-lobed, lemon-yellow lower lip, a deep purple upper lip, and a slender curved spur at the back.

TRAILS *usually on bare ground in cultivated fields and in waste or disturbed places.*

oval leaf

ANNUAL

small flowers

hairy leaves

2-lipped flower

curved spur

PLANT HEIGHT *5–10cm.*
FLOWER SIZE *1–1.5cm long.*
FLOWERING TIME *July–October.*
LEAVES *Alternate, oval and hairy.*
FRUIT *Round capsule, opening near apex.*
SIMILAR SPECIES *Ivy-leaved Toadflax (p.404); Sharp-leaved Fluellen (K. elatine), which has arrow-shaped leaves.*

Germander Speedwell

Veronica chamaedrys (Scrophulariaceae)

The flowers of this plant are an exceptionally deep and vivid blue, with a contrasting white "eye" in the centre and two divergent protruding stamens. The flower stalks are produced from the base of hairy, stalkless leaves. Close examination of the hairy stems reveals that the hairs are in two neat, opposite rows.

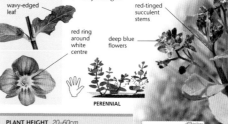

PROLIFERATES *in shady grassy areas, alongside woodland, hedgerows, among scrub, and on embankments.*

PERENNIAL

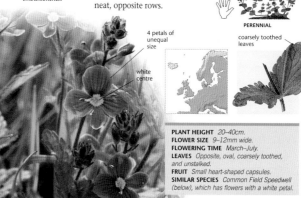

4 petals of unequal size

white centre

coarsely toothed leaves

PLANT HEIGHT *20–40cm.*
FLOWER SIZE *9–12mm wide.*
FLOWERING TIME *March–July.*
LEAVES *Opposite, oval, coarsely toothed, and unstalked.*
FRUIT *Small heart-shaped capsules.*
SIMILAR SPECIES *Common Field Speedwell (below), which has flowers with a white petal.*

Heath Speedwell

Veronica officinalis (Scrophulariaceae)

This speedwell may be recognized by its small spikes of lilac flowers. The plant sends out runners which root at intervals, so the flowering stems arch upwards from the ground. The opposite, deep green leaves are neater in appearance than those of most speedwells.

CREEPS *over the ground on heaths, open woods, and grassy places; on well-drained, acid soil.*

serrated leaf margin

flowers in short spike

deep green leaves

PERENNIAL

dark veins on petals

hairy stem

PLANT HEIGHT *10–40cm.*
FLOWER SIZE *5–9mm wide.*
FLOWERING TIME *May–August.*
LEAVES *Opposite, oblong, with neatly serrated margin.*
FRUIT *Hairy, heart-shaped capsule.*
SIMILAR SPECIES *Wood Speedwell (V. montana), has flowers in loose clusters.*

Common Field Speedwell

Veronica persica (Scrophulariaceae)

Introduced into Europe in the early 19th century, this species has become a common sight on farmland in many places. The lowest of the four petals is smaller than the others and is usually white, the others being violet with dark radiating veins. The oval, hairy leaves are very short-stalked, with just a few coarse teeth.

FLOURISHES *on disturbed soil such as wasteland, and among farmland crops.*

coarsely toothed leaves

dark-veined flower

ANNUAL

lower petal usually white

oval leaf

PLANT HEIGHT *5–20cm.*
FLOWER SIZE *8–12mm wide.*
FLOWERING TIME *Year round.*
LEAVES *Mostly alternate, lower ones opposite.*
FRUIT *Heart-shaped capsule.*
SIMILAR SPECIES *Germander Speedwell (above); Green Field Speedwell (V. agrestis) has white flowers with a blue upper petal.*

PLANTS

Foxglove

Digitalis purpurea (Scrophulariaceae)

Recognizable even in its first year, by the rosettes of large, wrinkled, hairy leaves, Foxglove is unmistakable in the following year when the tall flower stems are formed. As many as 60 or more pink to purple flowers droop in one-sided spikes. The whole plant is poisonous.

PROLIFERATES *on heaths, in woodland clearings and margins, and along road verges, hedgerows, and banks; mostly on acid soil.*

tapered flower spikes

wrinkled leaf surface

BIENNIAL/ PERENNIAL

tubular flowers

many-seeded fruit capsule

blunt, hairy leaf

PLANT HEIGHT *1–2m.*
FLOWER SIZE *4–5.5cm long.*
FLOWERING TIME *June–September.*
LEAVES *Basal rosette at first, followed by alternate stem leaves; oval, densely hairy.*
FRUIT *Capsule expelling numerous seeds through three slits at the tip.*
SIMILAR SPECIES *Great Mullein (p.404).*

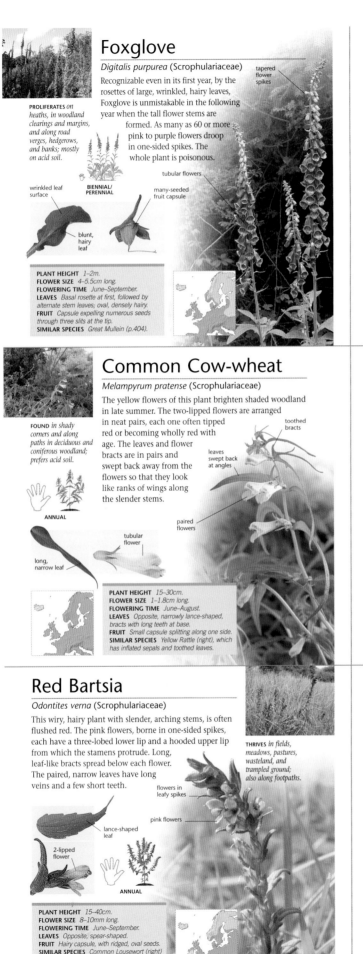

Eyebright

Euphrasia species (Scrophulariaceae)

There are about 20 *Euphrasia* species in Britain, but they are extremely difficult to tell apart. All have the same basic structure of small, two-lipped flowers, the lower lip being three-lobed. The flowers are usually white or lilac with a yellow blotch and purple streaks. The leaves, sometimes purple-flushed, are small and stalkless, with jagged teeth. The plant is semi-parasitic on the grasses with which it grows.

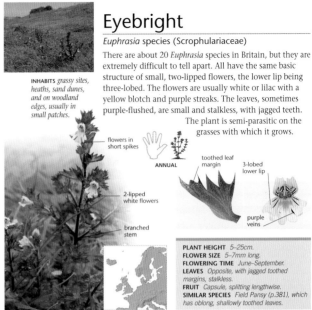

INHABITS *grassy sites, heaths, sand dunes, and on woodland edges, usually in small patches.*

flowers in short spikes

ANNUAL

toothed leaf margin

3-lobed lower lip

2-lipped white flowers

purple veins

branched stem

PLANT HEIGHT *5–25cm.*
FLOWER SIZE *5–7mm long.*
FLOWERING TIME *June–September.*
LEAVES *Opposite, with jagged toothed margins, stalkless.*
FRUIT *Capsule, splitting lengthwise.*
SIMILAR SPECIES *Field Pansy (p.381), which has oblong, shallowly toothed leaves.*

Common Cow-wheat

Melampyrum pratense (Scrophulariaceae)

The yellow flowers of this plant brighten shaded woodland in late summer. The two-lipped flowers are arranged in neat pairs, each one often tipped red or becoming wholly red with age. The leaves and flower bracts are in pairs and swept back away from the flowers so that they look like ranks of wings along the slender stems.

FOUND *in shady corners and along paths in deciduous and coniferous woodland; prefers acid soil.*

ANNUAL

toothed bracts

leaves swept back at angles

paired flowers

long, narrow leaf

tubular flower

PLANT HEIGHT *15–30cm.*
FLOWER SIZE *1–1.8cm long.*
FLOWERING TIME *June–August.*
LEAVES *Opposite, narrowly lance-shaped, bracts with long teeth at base.*
FRUIT *Small capsule splitting along one side.*
SIMILAR SPECIES *Yellow Rattle (right), which has inflated sepals and toothed leaves.*

Common Lousewort

Pedicularis sylvatica (Scrophulariaceae)

This tufted, compact plant has densely crowded leaves and flowers. The flowers are pale pink, each with a three-lobed lower lip and a hooded upper lip, emerging from a papery calyx that expands in fruit. The leaves are divided into small, "frilly" leaflets with crisped edges.

GROWS *in clumps in damp areas of heaths, bogs, moors, grassy places, and woodland.*

elongated upper lip

wavy leaf margins

BIENNIAL/ PERENNIAL

3-lobed lower lip

red-veined calyx

PLANT HEIGHT *10–25cm.*
FLOWER SIZE *2–2.5cm long.*
FLOWERING TIME *April–July.*
LEAVES *Alternate, pinnately lobed, fern-like.*
FRUIT *Capsule in the inflated, hairless calyx.*
SIMILAR SPECIES *Red Bartsia (left); Marsh Lousewort (P. palustris), which has longer leaves.*

Red Bartsia

Odontites verna (Scrophulariaceae)

This wiry, hairy plant with slender, arching stems, is often flushed red. The pink flowers, borne in one-sided spikes, each have a three-lobed lower lip and a hooded upper lip from which the stamens protrude. Long, leaf-like bracts spread below each flower. The paired, narrow leaves have long veins and a few short teeth.

THRIVES *in fields, meadows, pastures, wasteland, and trampled ground; also along footpaths.*

flowers in leafy spikes

pink flowers

lance-shaped leaf

2-lipped flower

ANNUAL

PLANT HEIGHT *15–40cm.*
FLOWER SIZE *8–10mm long.*
FLOWERING TIME *June–September.*
LEAVES *Opposite, spear-shaped.*
FRUIT *Hairy capsule, with ridged, oval seeds.*
SIMILAR SPECIES *Common Lousewort (right) has pinnate leaves; Subsp. serotina of S. Britain has shorter bracts.*

Yellow Rattle

Rhinanthus minor (Scrophulariaceae)

This partially parasitic plant derives water and minerals from the adjoining root systems of grasses. The small, rather squat, yellow flowers have two lips, with tiny violet teeth on the upper lip. The calyx is extremely inflated and, when ripe and dry, the enclosed capsule and its seeds rattle when moved by the wind. The narrow leaves are dark green.

GROWS *in open, grassy places on roadsides, banks, pastures, and meadows; prefers chalky soil.*

leaves clasp stem

toothed upper lip

inflated, dry calyx

serrated leaf margins

ANNUAL

PLANT HEIGHT *20–40cm.*
FLOWER SIZE *1.3–1.5cm long.*
FLOWERING TIME *May–August.*
LEAVES *Opposite, lance-shaped, unstalked.*
FRUIT *Round capsule, with a short beak, enclosing winged seeds.*
SIMILAR SPECIES *Yellow Archangel (p.400); Common Cow-wheat (left).*

Toothwort

Lathraea squamaria (Fabaceae)

FOUND *in shady parts of damp deciduous woods and hedges, where it is parasitic on roots of trees such as hazels or elms.*

This unusual plant has no green parts or leaves as it is parasitic, deriving its nutrients from the roots of trees, usually hazels. The upright, unbranched stems have one-sided rows of ivory or pink two-lipped flowers, interspersed with scale-like bracts that look like teeth. The bracts are pressed close to the stem.

two-lipped flower

one-sided rows of flowers

ivory or pink flowers

PERENNIAL

PLANT HEIGHT *10–20cm.*
FLOWER SIZE *1.4–1.7cm long.*
FLOWERING TIME *April–May.*
LEAVES *Cream-coloured scale-like bracts.*
FRUIT *Capsule that splits along the middle.*
SIMILAR SPECIES *Common Broomrape (below), which is parasitic on herbs; Bird's-nest Orchid (p.433), which has brown flowers.*

Common Broomrape

Orobanche minor (Orobanchaceae)

PARASITIZES *other plants in meadows, hedgerows, scrub, and grassy fields.*

Broomrapes are plants without the green pigment chlorophyll, which live parasitically on the roots of other plants, such as White Clover (p.374) and members of the daisy family, the host being the best clue to their identification. Common Broomrape is brown and dead-looking. The flowers, in spikes with tiny bracts in between, are two-lipped tubes, each with a three-lobed lower lip. The plant has no need of leaves, instead having a few brown scales scattered along the stem.

PERENNIAL

pointed tip

scale-like bract

2-lipped flower

flowers in simple spikes

purplish yellow flowers

NOTE
This is the most frequent Broomrape species in Britain. Other species are associated with Greater Knapweed, Ivy, and Gorse or Broom; and rarer species with Thyme; Yarrow, Bedstraws, and Thistles.

PLANT HEIGHT *20–50cm.*
FLOWER SIZE *1–1.8cm long.*
FLOWERING TIME *June–September.*
LEAVES *Alternate, tiny, scale-like bracts.*
FRUIT *Capsule containing small seeds.*
SIMILAR SPECIES *Toothwort (above), which has a one-sided spike of pale flowers; Bird's-nest Orchid (p.433), which has a more complex arrangement of petals with a longer lower lip.*

Greater Bladderwort

Utricularia vulgaris (Lentibulariaceae)

INHABITS *fresh, still water of ponds, lakes, ditches, and canals. It is intolerant of pollution.*

This extraordinary insectivorous aquatic plant has numerous thread-like leaves that float in the water. Minute sacs are attached to these, each with a microscopic "trap-door" operated by a hair-like trigger. Tiny crustacea and other pondlife that touch the trigger hairs are inadvertently sucked into the sacs as the "trap-doors" open, where they are digested by the plant. The two-lipped flowers are bright yellow, with red markings, and are borne on long stalks held above the water surface. The plant may exist for many years without flowering.

flowers on stalks above water surface

bright yellow flowers

single, erect stalk

thread-like leaves

sacs to trap pondlife

two lipped flower

PERENNIAL

NOTE
This plant may suddenly come into bloom after a major disturbance in its habitat, such as cleaning out of ditches or ponds.

PLANT HEIGHT *Flowerstalk 10cm.*
FLOWER SIZE *1.2–1.8cm wide.*
FLOWERING TIME *July–August.*
LEAVES *Mass of threads.*
FRUIT *Rounded capsule.*
SIMILAR SPECIES *Lesser Bladderwort (U. minor), which has much smaller flowers. There are other Utricularia species that may only be identified by microscopic examination.*

Common Butterwort

Pinguicula vulgaris (Lentibulariaceae)

FORMS *small colonies in wet, acid locations such as bogs, moors, heaths, and damp rocks, often along streams.*

The pale yellow-green leaves of Common Butterwort have a very sticky surface that attracts small insects. These become trapped when they alight and are digested by the plant, as the leaf margins roll in slightly. The solitary purple flowers have a whitish centre and a spur at the back.

flower spur

leafless stem

PERENNIAL

rounded petals

pale yellow-green leaf

PLANT HEIGHT *8–18cm.*
FLOWER SIZE *1.5–2cm wide.*
FLOWERING TIME *May–July.*
LEAVES *Basal rosette, elliptical with in-rolled margin, fleshy and sticky; yellow-green.*
FRUIT *Small, erect, many-seeded capsule.*
SIMILAR SPECIES *Pale Butterwort (P. lusitanica), which has pale lilac flowers.*

PLANTS

Greater Plantain

Plantago major (Plantaginaceae)

This common weed of wasteland has distinctive thick, dark green leaves that form a flat rosette close to the ground. The plant becomes even more conspicuous when the long, upright flower spikes develop. Varying in length, these bear many tiny green flowers, which for a short while produce purple to yellowish or brown anthers.

FOUND *in bare areas in wasteland, on field margins, and on paths. Also in grassy places that are mown regularly, such as lawns.*

spikes of tiny green flowers

large, rounded leaf

long stalk

basal leaf rosettes

PERENNIAL

PLANT HEIGHT *10–45cm.*
FLOWER SIZE *1–2mm wide.*
FLOWERING TIME *June–October.*
LEAVES *Basal rosette, rounded, thick with long stalks, and veined; dark green.*
FRUIT *Small capsule enclosing several tiny seeds.*
SIMILAR SPECIES *None.*

Ribwort Plantain

Plantago lanceolata (Plantaginaceae)

This common grassland weed can be easily overlooked until its most noticeable feature – the anthers – are mature. These are large and white, forming a conspicuous ring around the flowerhead, whose tiny brown sepals give it a rusty look. The leaves, clustered in a tuft at the base, are long, erect, and tapering, with raised, longitudinal veins on their undersides. The extremely tough and fibrous flower stems are also furrowed. Ribwort Plantain was once used to improve the forage in pastures.

FORMS *extensive patches in meadows, roadsides, pastures, and untended lawns; on neutral soils with little shade.*

tapering, rusty flowerheads

PERENNIAL

NOTE

The seeds of this and other plantains absorb up to 25 times their own weight in water, producing a mucilage or gel used in cosmetics.

ring of white anthers

leafless flower stalks

parallel veins on leaf

tiny flowers

narrow leaf

PLANT HEIGHT *20–50cm.*
FLOWER SIZE *4mm wide.*
FLOWERING TIME *April–October.*
LEAVES *Basal, linear to almost elliptical, with toothed or entire margins, and veined undersides.*
FRUIT *Capsule containing two boat-shaped seeds.*
SIMILAR SPECIES *Spiked Rampion (Phyteuma spicatum), which has oval, bluntly toothed leaves.*

Dwarf Elder

Sambucus ebulus (Caprifoliaceae)

A strong-smelling plant, often growing in a large patch, Dwarf Elder is hard to miss. It resembles the elder tree, but does not have woody stems. It has branched clusters of white flowers with purple stamens, which later produce poisonous purple-black berries on reddened stems. The leaves are divided into narrow, finely toothed leaflets.

FORMS *large patches or colonies on disturbed ground, roadsides, woodland margins, and hedgerows. Dislikes acid soil.*

many clusters of white flowers

large, neat leaves

PERENNIAL

5-petalled flower

purple-black berries

PLANT HEIGHT *80–150cm.*
FLOWER SIZE *Clusters 7–14cm wide.*
FLOWERING TIME *July–August.*
LEAVES *Opposite, pinnate, finely toothed.*
FRUIT *Small, fleshy berries.*
SIMILAR SPECIES *Common Valerian (p.409), which is less leafy and does not have berries.*

Honeysuckle

Lonicera periclymenum (Caprifoliaceae)

The delightful fragrance of Honeysuckle flowers, most noticeable on warm summer evenings, is designed to attract pollinating moths. The plant trails over the ground or climbs high into trees, bearing oblong leaves. In clusters of up to 12, the two-lipped flowers may be white or cream to dark peach, darkening as they mature, followed by a cluster of berries.

CLIMBS *over hedges, fences, or high up a tree to form a "bush" midway; trails on ground in woodland.*

whorl of flowers

protruding stamens

PERENNIAL

bright red berries

long flower tube

PLANT HEIGHT *1–6m.*
FLOWER SIZE *3.5–5cm long.*
FLOWERING TIME *June–October.*
LEAVES *Opposite, oblong to elliptical, untoothed.*
FRUIT *Red berries.*
SIMILAR SPECIES *Fly Honeysuckle (L. xylosteum), which has flowers in pairs.*

Moschatel

Adoxa moschatellina (Adoxaceae)

A dainty, unusual looking plant, Moschatel is the only species in its family. The tiny flowerhead is quite distinctive with four five-petalled flowers facing each point of the compass and a four-petalled flower on top, facing up. It frequently grows with Wood Anemone (p.351), with which its leaves may be confused.

FORMS *carpets in shade in coppices, damp woodland, rocky places, and among scrub.*

small, terminal flower cluster

PERENNIAL

4 flowers on each side, 1 on top

rounded leaf lobes

4-petalled upper flower

PLANT HEIGHT *6–15cm.*
FLOWER SIZE *6–8mm wide.*
FLOWERING TIME *April–May.*
LEAVES *Basal and opposite, divided into lobes; soft; bright green.*
FRUIT *Small green drupe, rarely produced.*
SIMILAR SPECIES *Wood Anemone (p.351), which has solitary flowers.*

Common Valerian

Valeriana officinalis (Valerianaceae)

This plant of damp places has white flowerheads that may be flushed with pink. Each flower is five-lobed, narrowing to a tube with a pouched base. The leaves comprise long, narrow leaflets giving a ladder-like appearance, although the upper leaves are much smaller.

OCCURS *along river and stream margins, in wet meadows, ditches, pastures, and damp woodland.*

slender leaflets

ladder-like leaves

5-lobed flower

dense, branched flowerheads

pinkish white flowers

PERENNIAL

PLANT HEIGHT *1–1.8m.*
FLOWER SIZE *3–5mm long.*
FLOWERING TIME *June–August.*
LEAVES *Opposite, pinnately divided into lance-shaped, toothed leaflets.*
FRUIT *Achene with a pappus of hairs.*
SIMILAR SPECIES *Dwarf Elder (p.408), which has larger leaves.*

Small Teasel

Dipsacus pilosus (Dipsacaceae)

Just as tall and robust as Teasel (below), this plant has much smaller, almost spherical flowerheads with a ruff of small spines beneath them. The individual flowers are white, with prominent purple stamens. The leaves are more oval than those of Teasel, without spines under the midrib, and often have a pair of leaflets at their base. The whole plant is prickly, including the stems.

GROWS *in damp places with partial shade such as stream- and riversides, open woodland, and scrub.*

spherical white flowerhead

BIENNIAL

protruding purple stamens

prickly leaf

PLANT HEIGHT *1–2m.*
FLOWER SIZE *Flowerhead 1.5–2cm wide.*
FLOWERING TIME *August–September.*
LEAVES *Opposite, oval to elliptical, hairy; often with a pair of basal leaflets.*
FRUIT *Small achene.*
SIMILAR SPECIES *Teasel (below), which is taller and has violet flowerheads.*

Common Cornsalad

Valerianella locusta (Valerianaceae)

The flowers of Common Cornsalad are so tiny and profuse that they give the impression, at a distance, of a bluish mist. They are borne in dense clusters, with a little ruff of bracts below each cluster, at the top of the many branched stems. Also known as Lamb's Lettuce, the plant is often cultivated as a salad crop.

GROWS *in colonies on rocky outcrops, old walls, cultivated or waste ground, shingle, and sandy places, often near the sea.*

ANNUAL

tiny blue flowers

ruff of bracts

flowers in clusters

pale green leaf

PLANT HEIGHT *5–20cm.*
FLOWER SIZE *1–2mm wide.*
FLOWERING TIME *April–June.*
LEAVES *Opposite, elliptical or spoon-shaped, slightly toothed; pale green.*
FRUIT *Tiny one-seeded nutlet.*
SIMILAR SPECIES *Other species occur, but are different only in the shape of the fruit.*

Teasel

Dipsacus fullonum (Dipsacaeae)

Shaped like the blade of a spear, the leaves of Teasel are unmistakable, with a bold white midrib armed with long prickles underneath, and many lateral veins creating a rather wavy margin. The opposite leaves are joined together around the stem, and may collect pools of rainwater in wet weather. The flowerhead is a dense collection of stiff, straight spines, between which the lilac-blue flowers emerge. They open in a concentric ring about one third of the way up the head, and then spread upwards and downwards simultaneously.

FLOURISHES *in rough, grassy places and along embankments, roadsides, river and stream banks, hedgerows, and woodland margins.*

NOTE

Fuller's Teasel (D. sativus) is a variety cultivated (mostly in Somerset) for its flowerheads, which have flexible hooked spines used for "fleecing" or raising the knap of woollen cloth.

stiff spines

whorl of long bracts below flowerhead

BIENNIAL

white midrib

florets open in concentric rings

dried, bristly fruithead

Red Valerian

Centranthus ruber (Valerianaceae)

A distinctive plant when in full flower through the summer months, this native of the Mediterranean is now a popular garden plant and naturalized throughout Britain. The waxy leaves, in opposite pairs, clasp thick, erect stems. Flowers are usually deep red, but pink and white forms are also common.

broad clusters of flowers

CLINGS *to coastal rocks and cliff faces, old walls and monuments, usually near the sea, on shingle beaches and sandy places.*

thick, erect stems

oval, grey-green leaf

long, slender flower tube

spur at flower base

lobed, unequal petals

PERENNIAL

PLANT HEIGHT *50–80cm.*
FLOWER SIZE *8–12mm long.*
FLOWERING TIME *July–September.*
LEAVES *Opposite, oval, fleshy, and usually untoothed, clasping the stem; grey-green.*
FRUIT *One-seeded nut with a feathery pappus.*
SIMILAR SPECIES *Common Valerian (above).*

PLANT HEIGHT *1–2m.*
FLOWER SIZE *Flowerhead 4–8cm long.*
FLOWERING TIME *July–October.*
LEAVES *Basal rosette in first year; opposite stem leaves, lance-shaped with spines on lower midrib, fused around stem.*
FRUIT *Small achene.*
SIMILAR SPECIES *Small Teasel (above), which has white flowerheads; Fuller's Teasel (D. sativus), which has recurved spines in the flowerhead.*

PLANTS

Small Scabious

Scabiosa columbaria (Dipsacaceae)

The flowerhead of this pretty grassland plant is a cluster of lilac-blue tubular florets, each with five tiny petals. The outer florets have an enlarged petal which gives the flowerhead a lacy appearance. The upper leaves are very finely divided into linear segments; the lower leaves are long-stalked, with fine teeth.

OCCURS *on dry, chalky soil on embankments, roadsides, downland and coastal areas.*

PERENNIAL

lilac-blue flowerhead

lance-shaped leaf

tubular florets

enlarged petal

fine teeth

PLANT HEIGHT	*10–70cm.*
FLOWER SIZE	*2–4cm wide.*
FLOWERING TIME	*July–August.*
LEAVES	*Basal leaves oval to lance-shaped, upper leaves finely pinnately divided.*
FRUIT	*Achene with a feathery calyx.*
SIMILAR SPECIES	*Field Scabious (right), which is taller with larger pinnate leaves.*

Devil's-bit Scabious

Succisa pratensis (Dipsacaceae)

Entire meadows may be coloured purple by swathes of this plant in late summer. The flowers are generally darker than other scabious species, and form a rounded rather than flat-topped head. Each tubular floret is the same in shape and size, without larger petals on the outside. When in bud, the flowerhead is like a collection of green or purple beads but later, when the flowers open and the stamens protrude, it comes to resemble a pincushion.

FLOURISHES *in meadows and heaths, in dry or moist conditions, in the open or in light shade of scrub, on chalky to slightly acid soils.*

PERENNIAL

florets of equal size

small linear bracts below flowers

rounded flowerhead in bud

prominent pale midrib

protruding stamens

NOTE

The long root of this plant formed in the first year, was thought to have been bitten off by the devil, as it later withers away when the side-roots are formed.

PLANT HEIGHT	*50–100cm.*
FLOWER SIZE	*Flowerhead 1.5–2cm wide.*
FLOWERING TIME	*July–October.*
LEAVES	*Basal leaves, lance-shaped with prominent white midrib; stem leaves opposite and toothed.*
FRUIT	*One-seeded achene.*
SIMILAR SPECIES	*Sheep's-bit (right), which does not have protruding stamens; Round-headed Rampion (p.411), which has curved florets.*

Field Scabious

Knautia arvensis (Dipsacaceae)

This is the largest and most robust of the scabious family flowers and may be recognized by its large leaves dissected into narrow, pointed lobes, though the basal ones are usually undivided. The flowerhead is a collection of tubular florets, in some ways similar to a dandelion-type member of the daisy family. Each of the pinkish lilac florets has four petals fused at the base, with an enlarged petal on the the outer florets contributing to its rather untidy appearance. The narrow bracts below the flowerhead are about the same length as the florets.

GROWS *in meadows, pastures, open woodland, hedgerows, and roadside verges; generally on chalky soil.*

PERENNIAL

tubular florets

long, slender flower stem

pinnately lobed leaf

ruff of bracts below flowerhead

enlarged outer petals

NOTE

This species was called Scabious arvensis, but has been renamed after the 17th-century Saxon botanist, Dr Knaut. The juice and roots of Field Scabious and related plants were once used to treat scabies and other skin disorders.

PLANT HEIGHT	*50–100cm.*
FLOWER SIZE	*Flowerhead 2–4cm wide.*
FLOWERING TIME	*July–September.*
LEAVES	*Basal rosettes; upper leaves opposite and pinnately lobed.*
FRUIT	*Achene with a feathery calyx attached.*
SIMILAR SPECIES	*Small Scabious (left), which has finely divided leaves; Devil's-bit Scabious (left), which has simpler leaves and is usually much darker in colour.*

Sheep's-bit

Jasione montana (Campanulaceae)

There are no obvious clues that this is a member of the bellflower family, but the small, alternate, hairy leaves show that it is not scabious, although apparently similar. The flowerhead is made up of tiny florets with five narrow petals, usually deep blue though sometimes pink or white, with a prominent pink style. There is a neat ruff of oval or triangular bracts below.

FORMS *on heaths, hills, meadows, dry, rough grassland, coastal rocks, and sand-cliffs, on light sandy soil.*

PERENNIAL

very compact flowerhead

small, wavy-edged leaves

oval bracts below flowerhead

PLANT HEIGHT	*20–50cm.*
FLOWER SIZE	*Flowerhead 1–2.5cm wide.*
FLOWERING TIME	*July–October.*
LEAVES	*Alternate, lance-shaped, hairy, with wavy margins; grey-green.*
FRUIT	*Capsule opens by two valves at apex.*
SIMILAR SPECIES	*Devil's-bit Scabious (left), which is taller with protruding stamens.*

Harebell

Campanula rotundifolia (Campanulaceae)

The scientific name *rotundifolia* refers to the round basal leaves, which have almost always withered away by flowering time. By contrast, the stem leaves are linear, the lowest ones lance-shaped. It is the dainty nodding bells, however, that are the noticeable feature of the plant: a rich sky-blue with five pointed lobes, usually in a very loose cluster.

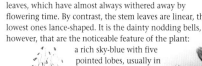

PERENNIAL

5-lobed corolla

tiny calyx

nodding bells

linear stem leaf

SEEN *in dry, grassy places, such as commons, heaths, banks and hills; on rocky ground and sand dunes.*

PLANT HEIGHT *20–50cm.*
FLOWER SIZE *1.2–2cm long.*
FLOWERING TIME *July–September.*
LEAVES *Basal leaves rounded, usually withered by flowering time; stem leaves alternate, narrow, and untoothed.*
FRUIT *Pendent capsule.*
SIMILAR SPECIES *None.*

Clustered Bellflower

Campanula glomerata (Campanulaceae)

This plant is easily identified by the close grouping of the flowers at the top of the stems, giving it a rather top-heavy look. Each upright flower is deep blue-violet in colour, the five petals fused into a long bell shape but with pointed lobes at the mouth and a fold along the length of each. The slightly toothed stems and leaves are roughly hairy.

INHABITS *dry, rough grassland, pastures, and meadows; also along roadsides and among scrub, on chalky soil.*

5 narrow lobes

flowers clustered at top of stem

bell-shaped flowers

PERENNIAL

PLANT HEIGHT *15–30cm.*
FLOWER SIZE *1.5–2cm long.*
FLOWERING TIME *July–September.*
LEAVES *Basal leaves oval to lance-shaped, stem leaves narrower and clasping the stem.*
FRUIT *Capsule containing many seeds.*
SIMILAR SPECIES *Nettle-leaved Bellflower (right) is taller, with loose racemes of flowers.*

Nettle-leaved Bellflower

Campanula trachelium (Campanulaceae)

Coarsely toothed, very hairy, triangular, and sometimes with a heart-shaped base, the leaves of this plant resemble those of a stinging nettle, though they carry no stinging hairs. When the sun catches them, the deep violet-blue flowers show up brightly against the shady gloom of dense woodland, the edges of which are its favoured habitat. The flowers are upright or horizontal, which prevents pollen falling from the short stamens onto the style, but when the fruit begins to ripen the calyx droops down. The flowers have a considerable amount of nectar, and make a sweet and very attractive addition to salads.

FOUND *on the margins of woodland, tracks, hedgerows, and scrub, sometimes in the shade, preferring chalky soil.*

PERENNIAL

prominent white style

horizontal or upright flowers

coarsely toothed leaf

petals spreading at tip

PLANT HEIGHT *40–80cm.*
FLOWER SIZE *2.5–5cm long.*
FLOWERING TIME *July–September.*
LEAVES *Basal and alternate, triangular to heart-shaped; deep green above, paler beneath.*
FRUIT *Pendent capsule.*
SIMILAR SPECIES *Giant Bellflower (C. latifolia), which is taller with larger, more profuse flowers.*

NOTE

This and other bellflowers have a protruding style, which is longer than the stamens, to prevent self-pollination as a bee enters. Hairs inside the bell afford extra grip for the bee.

Peach-leaved Bellflower

Campanula persicifolia (Campanulaceae)

This familiar garden plant sometimes forms extensive loose colonies. It produces widely open bell-shaped flowers with broad petals, which open upright but mature to a horizontal position, though not drooping. The calyx has rather narrow, pointed sepals. The basal leaves are lance-shaped to oval and stalked, while the stem leaves are almost linear and more finely toothed.

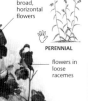

OCCURS *in meadows, woodland edges, rough grassland, and along road verges.*

broad, horizontal flowers

PERENNIAL

flowers in loose racemes

flower bud

linear bract

PLANT HEIGHT *40–80cm.*
FLOWER SIZE *3–4cm long.*
FLOWERING TIME *June–August.*
LEAVES *Basal leaves lance-shaped and stalked, upper leaves linear and toothed.*
FRUIT *Capsule splitting lengthwise.*
SIMILAR SPECIES *Creeping Bellflower (C. rapunculoides) has narrow, drooping bells.*

Round-headed Rampion

Phyteuma orbiculare (Campanulaceae)

The spherical heads of Round-headed Rampion are a collection of strongly incurved, narrow, deep violet florets, the petals of which split down to the base when they open to reveal the styles. They may be hidden by tall grasses as the stems are quite short. Most of the leaves are basal, the stem leaves being reduced to very narrow bract-like scales.

GROWS *in rough pastures and meadows, on embankments and on grazed slopes, on chalky soil.*

lance-shaped leaf

rounded flowerhead

tiny, narrow stem leaves

incurved florets

PERENNIAL

PLANT HEIGHT *20–40cm.*
FLOWER SIZE *Flowerhead 1–2cm wide.*
FLOWERING TIME *June–August.*
LEAVES *Lance-shaped, and slightly toothed.*
FRUIT *Capsule splitting into two or three pores.*
SIMILAR SPECIES *Devil's-bit Scabious (p.410); Sheep's-bit (p.410).*

PLANTS

Hemp Agrimony

Eupatorium cannabinum (Asteraceae)

Tall and robust, Hemp Agrimony has characteristic lobed leaves and red stems, which begin growing long before the flowerheads open. The short-stalked and hairy leaves are palmately lobed into three or five spear-shaped, toothed leaflets that droop down from the stems. The flowers are easily spotted when they do eventually open: distinctive, flat-topped, fluffy heads are composed of tubular pink florets with long, protruding stamens. Each group of five to six florets is enclosed by crimson-tipped bracts. Rich in nectar, the flowers attract numerous bees and butterflies.

FORMS *clumps on road verges, in spaces left by tree clearance, and in damp areas such as margins of rivers, streams, and ditches.*

protruding stamens

many-branched flower clusters

PERENNIAL

stout red stems

spear-shaped leaflet

3-lobed upper leaves

broad, flat flowerhead

PLANT HEIGHT *90–150cm.*
FLOWER SIZE *2–5mm wide.*
FLOWERING TIME *July–September.*
LEAVES *Opposite, palmately lobed into lance-shaped, toothed leaflets – lower leaves with five lobes and upper leaves with three lobes or undivided.*
FRUIT *Achene with a hairy pappus.*
SIMILAR SPECIES *None.*

Goldenrod

Solidago virgaurea (Asteraceae)

INHABITS *dry, grassy places, open woods, heaths, meadows, and rocky sites.*

The stiff, erect stems of Goldenrod may produce a single spike of yellow flowers or many branches bearing golden bunches of flowers. Each flower is actually a mass of tiny florets, the outer ones with a single petal or ray. The leaves are narrow and slightly toothed, the lower leaves are long-stalked and broader.

branched flower spikes

PERENNIAL

yellow ray florets

wavy, toothed margin

PLANT HEIGHT *10–60cm.*
FLOWER SIZE *Flowerhead 1.5–1.8cm wide.*
FLOWERING TIME *July–September.*
LEAVES *Alternate, variable but narrow.*
FRUIT *Achene with a brown pappus, forming a clock.*
SIMILAR SPECIES *Common Ragwort (p.416), which is more bushy and has divided leaves.*

Canadian Goldenrod

Solidago canadensis (Asteraceae)

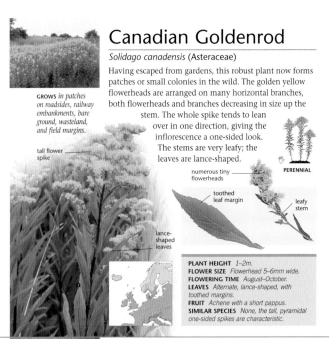

GROWS *in patches on roadsides, railway embankments, bare ground, wasteland, and field margins.*

Having escaped from gardens, this robust plant now forms patches or small colonies in the wild. The golden yellow flowerheads are arranged on many horizontal branches, both flowerheads and branches decreasing in size up the stem. The whole spike tends to lean over in one direction, giving the inflorescence a one-sided look. The stems are very leafy; the leaves are lance-shaped.

tall flower spike

numerous tiny flowerheads

PERENNIAL

toothed leaf margin

leafy stem

lance-shaped leaves

PLANT HEIGHT *1–2m.*
FLOWER SIZE *Flowerhead 5–6mm wide.*
FLOWERING TIME *August–October.*
LEAVES *Alternate, lance-shaped, with toothed margins.*
FRUIT *Achene with a short pappus.*
SIMILAR SPECIES *None, the tall, pyramidal one-sided spikes are characteristic.*

Daisy

Bellis perennis (Asteraceae)

ASSOCIATED *with old grassland, this plant is now ubiquitous on railway embankments, lawns, roadsides, and short turf by the sea.*

A familiar plant, Daisy is easily recognized. The small, central yellow disc of the solitary flower is surrounded by numerous white rays which are tinged pink on the undersides, visible when the flower closes in the evening or when in bud. The hairy leaves are often bluntly toothed, and crowded into a tight rosette. The leaves and flowers of this plant may be added to salads, though the leaves have a mildly sour flavour.

PERENNIAL

NOTE

Daisies have a long history of medicinal use, particularly for treating wounds, and to ease throat infections. Recently, they have been under investigation as a potential treatment for HIV infection.

spoon-shaped leaf

white rays tinged pink below

solitary flower

central yellow disc florets

PLANT HEIGHT *5–10cm.*
FLOWER SIZE *Flowerhead 1.5–2.5cm wide.*
FLOWERING TIME *Year round.*
LEAVES *Basal, spoon-shaped with short stalk.*
FRUIT *Simple achene, with no feathery attachment.*
SIMILAR SPECIES *Oxeye Daisy (p.415), which has larger flowers, but can be very short; Scentless Mayweed (p.414) and other mayweeds all have divided, feathery leaves.*

Sea Aster

Aster tripolium (Asteraceae)

Most easily observed at low tide, this plant may be almost engulfed by the incoming sea over salt marshes. The daisy-like flowers have narrow, rather untidy, pale lilac or purple ray florets, though sometimes these are missing altogether, leaving only the bright yellow disc florets on the short column of bracts. The leaves are fleshy and rounded in cross-section.

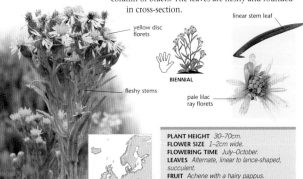

FORMS *large colonies in salt marshes and estuaries, often inundated by high tide.*

yellow disc florets

linear stem leaf

BIENNIAL

fleshy stems

pale lilac ray florets

PLANT HEIGHT	*30–70cm.*
FLOWER SIZE	*1–2cm wide.*
FLOWERING TIME	*July–October.*
LEAVES	*Alternate, linear to lance-shaped, succulent.*
FRUIT	*Achene with a hairy pappus.*
SIMILAR SPECIES	*Michaelmas-daisy (below), which grows inland.*

Marsh Cudweed

Gnaphalium uliginosum (Asteraceae)

A small, weedy plant, Marsh Cudweed is often overlooked. The stems and leaves are covered in a fine white down so that the whole plant has a pale, silvery grey appearance. The lance-shaped leaves are slightly greener on the upper surface. The tiny flowers have no rays; they are yellow only when freshly opened, and soon fade to brown.

GROWS *in damp places on bare ground or turf, in marshes, on paths, and pavement cracks.*

flowers partially concealed by leaves

ANNUAL

alternate leaves

narrow leaves

tiny flowers

silvery grey stalks

PLANT HEIGHT	*5–20cm.*
FLOWER SIZE	*Flowerhead 3–4mm long.*
FLOWERING TIME	*July–September.*
LEAVES	*Alternate, lance-shaped, downy.*
FRUIT	*Tiny achene.*
SIMILAR SPECIES	*Small Cudweed (Filago minima) has smaller flowers; Common Cudweed (Filago vulgaris) has larger flowers.*

Michaelmas-daisy

Aster novi-belgii (Asteraceae)

This garden plant was introduced into Britain from North America along with several other *Aster* species which have since hybridized, making identification difficult. However, they are all robust plants with white to blue or purple ray florets and yellow centres, and small leaves that clasp the wiry stems.

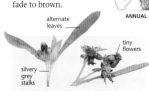

PROLIFERATES *on fens, wasteland, commons, roadsides, and river or stream banks.*

branched clusters of flowers

PERENNIAL

red-tinged stems

ray florets around yellow centre

unstalked stem leaf

PLANT HEIGHT	*80–150cm.*
FLOWER SIZE	*2.5–4cm wide.*
FLOWERING TIME	*September–October.*
LEAVES	*Alternate, oval to lance-shaped, hairy.*
FRUIT	*Achene with a hairy pappus*
SIMILAR SPECIES	*Sea Aster (above) grows near the sea; there are several hybrids of Michaelmas-daisy which are common.*

Ploughman's Spikenard

Inula conyza (Asteraceae)

This erect and wiry-looking plant has long, slender red stems. The flowers themselves consist of a tight bunch of yellow disc florets surrounded by an eye-catching cylinder of pointed, orange-red bracts, and a few short green bracts below. The leaves are spear-shaped and toothed.

OCCURS *in open grassy and rocky places, among scrub or open woodland, preferring dry, chalky soil.*

finely toothed leaf

orange-red bracts

PERENNIAL

yellow disc florets

branched flower clusters

wiry, reddish stems

PLANT HEIGHT	*60–120cm.*
FLOWER SIZE	*9–11mm wide.*
FLOWERING TIME	*July–September.*
LEAVES	*Alternate, spear-shaped, toothed, upper leaves unstalked, lowermost long-stalked, with reddish veins.*
FRUIT	*Achene with a feathery top.*
SIMILAR SPECIES	*None.*

Blue Fleabane

Erigeron acer (Asteraceae)

Rather spindly and modest, this little daisy is easily missed among other vegetation, as it may grow very short if conditions are dry. The flowers are at the branched tops of erect, wiry stems. The ray florets are a pale bluish lilac, but instead of spreading outwards they remain upright, and are barely longer than the straw-coloured disc florets.

INHABITS *dry places such as embankments, rough grassland, field margins, and old walls.*

short, erect ray florets

narrow, hairy leaves

stiff, red-spotted stems

dark-tipped bracts

ANNUAL/BIENNIAL

PLANT HEIGHT	*10–40cm.*
FLOWER SIZE	*1–1.5cm wide.*
FLOWERING TIME	*July–August.*
LEAVES	*Basal, elliptical, and stalked; stem leaves alternate and lance-shaped, very hairy.*
FRUIT	*Achenes with a yellowish pappus.*
SIMILAR SPECIES	*Canadian Fleabane (Conyza canadensis) is taller with white flowers.*

Fleabane

Pulicaria dysenterica (Asteraceae)

This member of the daisy family may be differentiated from its relatives by the flat-topped disc in the centre of its flower, and numerous very narrow or linear rays, which are often somewhat ragged. The stems are grey with woolly hairs, and the leaves, which clasp the stem, have a finely wrinkled surface, wavy edges, and are greyish beneath.

OCCURS *in extensive colonies in damp grassland, meadows, and marshes, and by ditches and canals.*

PERENNIAL

flat disc

daisy-like flowerhead

many narrow rays

leaf clasps stem

clock of achenes

PLANT HEIGHT	*40–60cm.*
FLOWER SIZE	*1.5–3cm wide.*
FLOWERING TIME	*July–September.*
LEAVES	*Alternate, arrow-shaped, wrinkled surface with wavy edges, clasping the stem.*
FRUIT	*Clock of hairy, brown achenes.*
SIMILAR SPECIES	*Common Ragwort (p.416) is more bushy and has divided leaves.*

Nodding Bur-marigold

Bidens cernua (Asteraceae)

The nodding golden brown flowerheads of this plant, without rays and surrounded by a ring of long, leaf-like bracts, are rather like miniature sunflowers. Very occasionally, a few short, broad yellow rays emerge, which transform the look of the flowers. The opposite leaves have large teeth.

OCCUPIES *damp, open places such as river and lake margins, ditches, and floodplains.*

long, spear-shaped leaf

leaf-like bracts

golden brown disc florets

nodding flowerhead

ANNUAL

PLANT HEIGHT *30–60cm.*
FLOWER SIZE *1.5–2.5cm wide.*
FLOWERING TIME *July–September.*
LEAVES *Opposite, spear-shaped, toothed.*
FRUIT *Achene with bristles.*
SIMILAR SPECIES *Trifid Bur-marigold (B. tripartita), which has upright flowers, and leaves with a pair of lobes at the base.*

Sneezewort

Achillea ptarmica (Asteraceae)

Closely related to Yarrow (right), Sneezewort inhabits damp sites and often grows among taller vegetation. It has daisy-like flowerheads, each with a distinct, pale greenish white disc surrounded by white rays, and borne in loose clusters. The scentless leaves are small, narrow, and undivided, but finely toothed.

FOUND *in damp, grassy places, marshes, and meadows, on heavy, acid soil.*

white flowerheads

linear, deep green leaves

PERENNIAL

disc of tubular florets

PLANT HEIGHT *20–50cm.*
FLOWER SIZE *Flowerhead 1.2–1.8cm wide.*
FLOWERING TIME *July–September.*
LEAVES *Alternate, lance-shaped to linear.*
FRUIT *Achene, no pappus, 1.2–1.8cm wide.*
SIMILAR SPECIES *Yarrow (right), which has smaller flowerheads and feathery leaves with a pungent aroma.*

Yarrow

Achillea millefolium (Asteraceae)

This plant may form large drifts of white flowers among the dry grasses of late summer. The erect stems are very tough and hairy. Numerous small flowers are borne in flat-topped clusters, and are usually white but may be tinged with pink. The yellow anthers soon turn brown, making the flowers look rather dirty. The dark green leaves are very finely divided and have a strong and pungent aroma. In the past, they were traditionally used to flavour liqueurs.

FORMS *patches in dry grassland and meadows, and on embankments and roadsides; commonly found in untended lawns and wasteland.*

PERENNIAL

flat-topped flowerheads

hairy, erect stems

stiff, green leaves

fine leaf segments

flowers may be tinged pink

NOTE

Yarrow is drought resistant and may look green and fresh even in dried-up grassland in the heat of summer.

PLANT HEIGHT *40–80cm.*
FLOWER SIZE *4–6mm wide.*
FLOWERING TIME *July–October.*
LEAVES *Alternate, feathery, divided into many fine segments; aromatic when crushed.*
FRUIT *Achenes with no pappus.*
SIMILAR SPECIES *Wild Carrot (p.385), which has umbels of numerous flowers; Sneezewort (left), which has narrow, toothed leaves.*

Scentless Mayweed

Tripleurospermum inodorum (Asteraceae)

This attractive plant forms bushy masses, and bears larger flowers than other mayweeds, each with a solid, dome-shaped, central yellow disc. The leaves are fleshy, very finely divided and feathery, and have no scent. In Scented Mayweed, the disc is hollow and the plant has a looser habit and a chamomile scent.

FLOURISHES *on disturbed soil of arable fields, and on wasteland, roadsides, and bare ground.*

large, daisy-like white flowerheads

thread-like leaves

PERENNIAL/BIENNIAL

domed centre

robust, bushy habit

PLANT HEIGHT *20–60cm.*
FLOWER SIZE *2–4cm wide.*
FLOWERING TIME *June–October.*
LEAVES *Alternate, finely divided, and fleshy.*
FRUIT *Simple achene without hair.*
SIMILAR SPECIES *Scented Mayweed (Chamomilla recutita); Sea Mayweed (Matricaria maritime), which is coastal.*

Pineappleweed

Matricaria discoidea (Asteraceae)

This delicate plant has daisy-like green flowers, with only the central disc and no ray florets. Not only do the flowers look similar to a pineapple but the plant smells like one too. Although well established in Britain, this is probably a 19th-century introduction from northeast Asia.

PROLIFERATES *on bare paths, in wasteland, and cultivated fields; withstands trampling.*

domed, bud-like flowerhead

thread-like foliage

finely divided leaves

central disc

ANNUAL

PLANT HEIGHT *10–30cm.*
FLOWER SIZE *5–9mm wide.*
FLOWERING TIME *May–November.*
LEAVES *Alternate, pinnately divided into narrow segments.*
FRUIT *Achenes with a pappus of hair.*
SIMILAR SPECIES *Scentless Mayweed (left), when not in flower.*

Oxeye Daisy

Leucanthemum vulgare (Asteraceae)

Although very variable in height, there is no mistaking the Oxeye Daisy for the common Daisy (p.412), as its flowerheads are much larger. These comprise a bright yellow disc surrounded by a ring of pure white ray florets and they are borne singly on branched or unbranched stems. The leaves are bright green and spoon-shaped, becoming small and clasping the stem towards the top of the plant. Oxeye Daisy is being used increasingly in wildflower seed mixes, particularly on the embankments of new motorways, although the seed used is often not native to the region.

GROWS *profusely in grassy meadows and on wasteland; also along embankments and road verges.*

PERENNIAL

large flowerhead

prominent yellow central disc

rigid, upright stem

small leaves on upper stem

NOTE

The bracts beneath the flowerhead contain an acrid juice distasteful to insects, which deters them from biting through to the nectaries.

coarsely toothed margin

spoon-shaped leaf

broad, spreading ray florets

PLANT HEIGHT *20–70cm.*
FLOWER SIZE *Flowerhead 2.5–5cm wide.*
FLOWERING TIME *May–September.*
LEAVES *Alternate and basal; spoon-shaped.*
FRUIT *Small single-seeded achenes.*
SIMILAR SPECIES *Daisy (p.412), which has smaller flowers; Scentless Mayweed (p.414), which has finer leaves; Corn Marigold (right); Shasta Daisy (L. x superbum), which has larger flowers.*

Corn Marigold

Chrysanthemum segetum (Asteraceae)

Although this medium to tall plant appears quite robust, it soon flops over if not supported by neighbouring vegetation in its favoured cornfield habitat. The fleshy leaves are deeply lobed and toothed; the upper leaves clasp the stem at their base. The golden yellow flowerheads, however, are the most striking feature of this plant. They have broad, overlapping rays, slightly toothed at the ends, rather like those of the Oxeye Daisy (left). They can appear in thousands where the plant is able to take hold.

APPEARS *among cereal crops and in fields where herbicides are not used; escapes into the wider countryside.*

daisy-like yellow flowerhead

broad ray florets

ANNUAL

NOTE

Corn Marigold used to be considered a serious pest for cereal crops, but due to modern use of herbicides, has now become much more scarce.

long flower stalk

greyish green leaves

toothed ray florets

PLANT HEIGHT *30–70cm.*
FLOWER SIZE *3–5cm wide.*
FLOWERING TIME *June–August.*
LEAVES *Alternate, oblong, clasping the stem, rather fleshy; pinnately lobed, unstalked lower leaves.*
FRUIT *Simple achene with no pappus.*
SIMILAR SPECIES *Oxeye Daisy (left); Yellow Chamomile (Anthemis tinctoria), which has narrow-toothed, pinnate leaves.*

Tansy

Tanacetum vulgare (Asteraceae)

This tall, aromatic plant is recognizable by its tight clusters of rayless flowerheads. These are often flat-topped on much-branched stems, and look like a collection of yellow buttons. The deeply divided leaves, with many tiny, regular teeth, are distinctive too. The whole plant is robust yet graceful, forming small patches where it grows.

FORMS *small patches in waste or cultivated land, on roadsides, and riverbeds, on a variety of soils.*

tight clusters of flowerheads

fern-like leaves

PERENNIAL

button-like yellow flowerheads

PLANT HEIGHT *80–120cm.*
FLOWER SIZE *8–12mm wide.*
FLOWERING TIME *July–September.*
LEAVES *Alternate, pinnately divided, small toothed, fern-like.*
FRUIT *Simple achene with no pappus.*
SIMILAR SPECIES *None; the fern-like leaves and button-like flowers make it distinctive.*

Mugwort

Artemisia vulgaris (Asteraceae)

A common wasteland plant with insignificant flowers, Mugwort can be distinguished from similar plants by its lower leaves. They are delicate and finely lobed, very dark green above, but bright silvery below, with distinct veins. The margins remain green, giving the leaf an "outlined" look. The flowerheads, with pale grey bracts, open golden yellow but quickly turn reddish brown.

FLOURISHES *on wasteland, disturbed ground, and rubbish tips, and in farmyards, in bare, rich soil.*

finger-like leaf lobes

numerous tiny flowerheads in clusters

reddish brown florets

erect stems

PERENNIAL

PLANT HEIGHT *80–150cm.*
FLOWER SIZE *Flowerhead 3–4mm wide.*
FLOWERING TIME *June–September.*
LEAVES *Alternate, oval in outline, lobed.*
FRUIT *Tiny, hairless achene.*
SIMILAR SPECIES *Wormwood (A. absinthium), which has yellower flowers, and more rounded leaf lobes.*

PLANTS

Coltsfoot

Tussilago farfara (Asteraceae)

This plant flowers early and is one of the first of the daisy family to dot the February landscape with its flowerheads. Each is a small disc encircled by narrow rays, on a stem with overlapping scales like an asparagus tip. The leaves, with tiny, black-tipped teeth, grow large in summer.

FOUND *in damp places, cultivated land, roadsides, spoil-heaps, gravel car-parks, embankments, and woodland edges.*

PERENNIAL

leafless stems

hair-like yellow rays

angled leaf

long stalk

cluster of achenes

PLANT HEIGHT *10–25cm.*
FLOWER SIZE *1.5–2.5cm wide.*
FLOWERING TIME *February–April.*
LEAVES *Basal, horse hoof-shaped, downy, white and hairy beneath; appear after flowers.*
FRUIT *Clock of feathered achenes.*
SIMILAR SPECIES *Winter Heliotrope (below), which has vanilla-scented flowers.*

Groundsel

Senecio vulgaris (Asteraceae)

A common, ubiquitous weed, Groundsel is found in flower at almost any time of year. It has many-branched stems topped with small yellow flowerheads, which soon become tufts of white pappus hairs, although occasionally there is a form with a few short, yellow rays. The leaves are pinnately and untidily lobed.

FLOURISHES *in gardens, wasteland, cultivated land, road verges, and open habitats.*

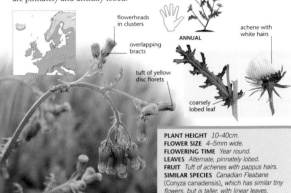

ANNUAL

flowerheads in clusters

overlapping bracts

tuft of yellow disc florets

coarsely lobed leaf

achene with white hairs

PLANT HEIGHT *10–40cm.*
FLOWER SIZE *4–5mm wide.*
FLOWERING TIME *Year round.*
LEAVES *Alternate, pinnately lobed.*
FRUIT *Tuft of achenes with pappus hairs.*
SIMILAR SPECIES *Canadian Fleabane (Conyza canadensis), which has similar tiny flowers, but is taller, with linear leaves.*

Butterbur

Petasites hybridus (Asteraceae)

The leaves of this plant, although small at flowering time, grow up to a metre wide, and were once used for wrapping butter. The white or pink flowerheads are borne in dense, cone-like spikes, female and male flowers on separate plants; male flowers have short stalks.

OCCURS *in colonies alongside streams, rivers, ditches, and in damp woodland and meadows.*

PERENNIAL

kidney-shaped leaf

irregular toothed margin

tight flowerheads

conical spike of flowers

PLANT HEIGHT *70–150cm.*
FLOWER SIZE *Female flowerhead 3–6mm wide; male flowerhead 7–12mm wide.*
FLOWERING TIME *March–May.*
LEAVES *Basal, kidney-shaped, felty beneath.*
FRUIT *Clock of achenes with a hairy pappus.*
SIMILAR SPECIES *White Butterbur (P. albus), which has white flowers and smaller leaves.*

Common Ragwort

Senecio jacobaea (Asteraceae)

A widespread weed of cultivation, Common Ragwort forms extensive colonies. It proliferates in pastures for horses, where the seeds germinate easily in bare soil kicked up by the horses' hooves. It is poisonous to livestock, especially when dried and palatable, and has earned a bad reputation in areas where horses are kept. It produces loose clusters of bright yellow daisy-like flowerheads, each with 12–20 spreading rays above linear, black-tipped bracts. The stems are ridged and the leaves are pinnately divided.

THRIVES *in disturbed soil of pastures, wasteland, rubbish tips, roadsides, and rabbit-infested areas, usually on dry soil.*

BIENNIAL/
PERENNIAL

long, spreading rays

flowerheads in large, flat-topped clusters

bright yellow flowerheads

branched stems

deeply lobed leaves

black-tipped bracts

NOTE

This is the sole foodplant of the Cinnabar Moth (Tyria jacobaeae) caterpillar, which absorbs its poisons as a defence against birds.

PLANT HEIGHT *80–150cm.*
FLOWER SIZE *Flowerhead 1.5–2.5cm wide.*
FLOWERING TIME *June–October.*
LEAVES *Alternate, deeply divided, curling up at edges.*
FRUIT *Achene with pappus of long white hairs.*
SIMILAR SPECIES *Goldenrod (p.412) has narrow leaves; Fleabane (p.413) has arrow-shaped leaves; Oxford Ragwort (S. squalidus), found on wasteland near towns has lemon-yellow flowers and tidier leaves.*

Winter Heliotrope

Petasites fragrans (Asteraceae)

This winter-flowering plant produces small clusters of pinkish white flowers that smell pleasantly of vanilla. Small, rounded leaves appear at the base on short stalks, which grow throughout the following summer, long after the flowers have faded. Lance-shaped bracts grow along the flowering stem.

SPREADS *by means of underground runners, to form large clumps on road verges, footpaths, stream margins, and disturbed ground; in damp, semi-shaded sites.*

lilac-pink flowers

loosely clustered flowerheads

long stalk

branched flowerhead

PERENNIAL

PLANT HEIGHT *15–40cm.*
FLOWER SIZE *Spikes up to 25cm long.*
FLOWERING TIME *November–February.*
LEAVES *Basal, rounded with toothed margin; green above, paler below.*
FRUIT *A clock of feathery achenes.*
SIMILAR SPECIES *Coltsfoot (above), which has similar leaves; Butterbur (above).*

Carline Thistle

Carlina vulgaris (Asteraceae)

This plant appears in its first year as an easily overlooked basal rosette of leaves. However, if touched or sat upon, its spiky, needle-like spines soon make their presence felt. The flowerheads are composed of tubular, yellow-brown disc florets, surrounded by stiff, curved, straw-coloured bracts. The fruiting head persists for many months.

GROWS *in meadows and dry grassland, usually among short turf on chalky soil.*

ray-like bracts

densely leafy stems

fruiting head

feathered seeds

BIENNIAL

wavy, spiny leaf

PLANT HEIGHT *15–50cm.*
FLOWER SIZE *2–4cm wide.*
FLOWERING TIME *July–September.*
LEAVES *Basal rosette at first, alternate, narrow, stiff, spiny, cottony on underside.*
FRUIT *Achene with pappus of yellow hairs.*
SIMILAR SPECIES *Dwarf Thistle (p.418), which has pink flowers without spiny bracts.*

Greater Burdock

Arctium lappa (Asteraceae)

This robust plant, with thick, branched stems, has large, rough leaves that appear longer than the flowers. Resembling those of thistles, the flowers themselves are reddish purple or pink and are surrounded by numerous hooked green spines or bracts, which form a much larger, spiny ball. These readily attach themselves to fur or clothing thereby helping to distribute the seed. The fruit is an achene with a pappus of rough yellowish hairs. The similar Lesser Burdock (*A. minor*) is a generally smaller plant that has a purple flowerhead of roughly the same size as the ball of spiny bracts beneath it.

FORMS *large clumps in woodland clearings and wasteland, and alongside roads and hedgerows; dislikes deep shade.*

hooked bracts surround flowerhead

rounded flowerhead

BIENNIAL

NOTE

The scientific name Arctium is derived from the Greek word arktos, which means "a bear", and refers to the roughness of the spiny burs.

large, stalked leaves

slightly toothed margin

spiny bracts

PLANT HEIGHT *80–160cm.*
FLOWER SIZE *Flowerhead 2–2.5cm wide.*
FLOWERING TIME *July–September.*
LEAVES *Basal and alternate, oval to heart-shaped, with a rough surface.*
FRUIT *Achene with a pappus of hairs.*
SIMILAR SPECIES *Spear Thistle (p.418), which has bristly leaves; Lesser Burdock (A. minor), which is smaller, with purple flowerheads and hollow leaf stalks.*

Musk Thistle

Carduus nutans (Asteraceae)

One of the most attractive thistles, Musk Thistle has large, rounded, rather regal flowerheads nodding outwards, each with a ruff of spiny bracts curving back. The flowerheads, solitary or in clusters, are made up of deep crimson-red, five-lobed, tubular florets. All the stems are covered with small wings armed with stiff spines, except for a tiny section just below each flowerhead. Narrow in outline, the deep green leaves are pinnately lobed into viciously spiny segments, and covered with a white down on the veins beneath.

INHABITS *grassy, open places, including meadows, pastures, abandoned farmland, embankments, and road verges, on rich, chalky soil.*

BIENNIAL

large, nodding flowerhead

spine-tipped leaves

spiny bracts

spiny, winged stems

NOTE

The flowers have a faint but sweet, musky scent; take care when handling the flowerheads as they are surrounded by very sharp, stiff spines.

PLANT HEIGHT *70–120cm.*
FLOWER SIZE *3–5cm wide.*
FLOWERING TIME *May–September.*
LEAVES *Alternate, narrow, pinnately divided, with sharp spines on the margins.*
FRUIT *Achene with a pappus of simple hairs.*
SIMILAR SPECIES *Spear Thistle (p.418), which has flowerheads that remain erect.*

Marsh Thistle

Cirsium palustre (Asteraceae)

Easily identified even at a distance by its very tall, slender stature, this thistle has spiny wings along the length of its stems. The narrow leaves are pinnately lobed and, as well as being spiny, are covered in dark purplish hairs, especially when young. The small and pinkish red flowers are crowded in clusters at the top of the stems.

INHABITS *damp areas in pastures, meadows, marshy ground, and wet woods, in less disturbed places than many other thistles.*

small, dark flowerhead

flowerheads in tight clusters

spiny leaf

pinkish red flowers

BIENNIAL

spiny stems

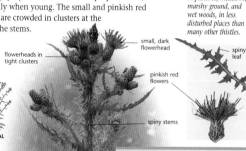

PLANT HEIGHT *1–2m.*
FLOWER SIZE *Flowerhead 1–2cm wide.*
FLOWERING TIME *July–September.*
LEAVES *Alternate, pinnately lobed, spiny margins, dark purplish hairs when young.*
FRUIT *Achene; brownish feathery pappus.*
SIMILAR SPECIES *Slender Thistle (Carduus tenuiflorus), which is shorter, with pink flowers.*

PLANTS

Spear Thistle

Cirsium vulgare (Asteraceae)

One of the most imposing and prickly of thistles, Spear Thistle has deep green leaves, which are paler beneath. They are shaped rather like a spearhead, with long, pinnate lobes, each ending in a very sharp, stiff spine. The stems are also covered in little irregular, triangular wings that are armed with spines. Part of the flowerhead is enclosed by green bracts and shaped like a vase, each bract tapering to a sharp point. The flowers themselves are reddish purple and fan out from the top, so that the whole flowerhead is shaped like a fat mushroom. The whole plant appears quite tall, with a particularly fearsome appearance.

PROLIFERATES *on wasteland, dry, grassy sites, embankments, scrub, and roadsides on chalky soil. A persistent weed on rich, cultivated soil.*

spear-shaped leaf

lobes terminate in spine

BIENNIAL

large, feathery pappus

short, spiny bracts

mushroom-shaped flowerhead

uneven spiny wings on upper stems

NOTE
The feathery seeds of Spear Thistle are carried considerable distances by the wind, so some landowners destroy the plants before they fruit.

PLANT HEIGHT *80–150cm.*
FLOWER SIZE *Flowerhead 2–4cm wide.*
FLOWERING TIME *July–October.*
LEAVES *Alternate, spear-shaped leaves with deeply cut triangular, spine-tipped lobes.*
FRUIT *Achenes with large, feathery yellowish pappus.*
SIMILAR SPECIES *Welted Thistle (Carduus crispus), which has smaller flowerheads and more numerous spines; Musk Thistle (p.417).*

Creeping Thistle

Cirsium arvense (Asteraceae)

The stems of this spreading, persistent plant are hairy but, unlike many other thistles, have no spines or wings. Its narrow, toothed leaves, although spiny, are slightly softer too. The flowers are pale red to pink, or sometimes lilac. They are borne above narrow bracts, which are softly spiny. This untidy plant produces prodigious quantities of feathery yellow-brown seeds. Regarded as a serious pest by farmers, it quickly invades recently turned soil and spreads freely through its aggressive root system. Like Spear Thistle (left), the plants are usually "topped" to remove their flowers to prevent further infestation.

ABOUNDS *in pastures, wasteland, and farmland; may form large colonies.*

PERENNIAL

NOTE
The young roots of Creeping Thistle may be cooked and eaten. The dry feathery pappus of brown hair attached to the seeds make an excellent tinder for starting fires, as it is easy to collect large quantities.

small pinkish flowerheads

spineless, hairy stems

narrow, wavy leaf

feathery pappus

PLANT HEIGHT *60–100cm.*
FLOWER SIZE *Flowerhead 1.5–2.5cm wide.*
FLOWERING TIME *June–September.*
LEAVES *Alternate, thin-spined, hairy beneath.*
FRUIT *Achene, brownish feathery pappus.*
SIMILAR SPECIES *Saw-wort (below), which has spineless, pinnate leaves with finely toothed margins; Welted Thistle (Carduus crispus) and Slender Thistle (Carduus tenuiflorus) both have spiny-winged stems.*

Dwarf Thistle

Cirsium acaule (Asteraceae)

This plant is stemless, making it the easiest of the thistles to identify, and the very large flowerhead is stalkless, or on a very short stalk. The leaves are in a tight rosette held flat to the ground. They have sharp spines on the margins and hairs on the surface, as a defence against being grazed.

GROWS *in the short turf of chalk grassland, in pastures, and rabbit-infested areas.*

PERENNIAL

single purple flowerhead

overlapping spineless bracts

leaf rosette

spiny leaf margin

narrow leaf

linear florets

PLANT HEIGHT *5–12cm.*
FLOWER SIZE *Flowerhead 2.5–4cm wide.*
FLOWERING TIME *June–September.*
LEAVES *Basal rosette, pinnately lobed.*
FRUIT *Achene with a white feathery pappus.*
SIMILAR SPECIES *Carline Thistle (p.417), which may be short-stemmed, and has similar leaves but yellowish flowers.*

Saw-wort

Serratula tinctoria (Asteraceae)

Saw-wort is an exceptionally variable plant in stature, degree of branching, and leaf shape. The leaves may be deeply pinnately lobed, or spear-shaped and quite unlobed, but the margins are regularly fine-toothed. It is in effect a thistle without spines, and its chief diagnostic feature is the neat arrangement of overlapping, finely pointed, purple-tipped bracts below each small head of tubular florets.

GROWS *in rough grassland, meadows, open woodland, heaths, and bogs, on a range of soil.*

PERENNIAL

cluster of flowerheads

finely toothed leaf

reddish purple florets

slender stems

PLANT HEIGHT *10–70cm.*
FLOWER SIZE *1.5–2cm wide.*
FLOWERING TIME *July–August.*
LEAVES *Alternate, with finely serrated teeth.*
FRUIT *Achene with a pappus of hairs.*
SIMILAR SPECIES *Thistles (pp.417–18), which have spiny leaves; Common Knapweed (p.419), which has feathery bracts.*

Common Knapweed

Centaurea nigra (Asteraceae)

The stems of this common, colourful plant have many branches, each topped with a tight, neat head of reddish purple florets, all of equal length. Below this are overlapping dark or black bracts, each with a fringe of untidy hairs. The narrow leaves are pointed, sometimes with a few large teeth lower down.

THRIVES *in meadows, among scrub, and on road verges and embankments; absent from grazed areas.*

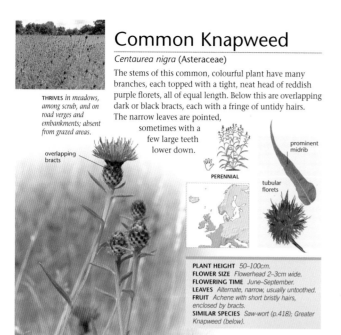

overlapping bracts

PERENNIAL

prominent midrib

tubular florets

PLANT HEIGHT *50–100cm.*
FLOWER SIZE *Flowerhead 2–3cm wide.*
FLOWERING TIME *June–September.*
LEAVES *Alternate, narrow, usually untoothed.*
FRUIT *Achene with short bristly hairs, enclosed by bracts.*
SIMILAR SPECIES *Saw-wort (p.418); Greater Knapweed (below).*

Greater Knapweed

Centaurea scabiosa (Asteraceae)

More imposing than Common Knapweed (above), this bristly plant has stiff, slender stems. The large flowerhead has branched outer florets, which spread out in a ring. They are sterile and serve to attract bees to the flower. The bracts at the base of the flowerhead are also distinctive: green with a horseshoe-shaped fringe of black or brown hairs, and neatly overlapping like tiles on a roof. The soft, delicate, grey-green leaves are pinnately lobed, the upper leaves much smaller and unlobed. When the fruit has been dispersed, the bracts open out to form a shiny, pale brown saucer.

FOUND *in rough grassland and meadows, on road verges, among scrub, on embankments and cliff tops.*

PERENNIAL

large, solitary flowerhead

overlapping bracts

NOTE
The roots and seeds of this plant are known for their diuretic properties. Combined with pepper, they were once used as a remedy for loss of appetite. Do not attempt.

lobed lower leaves

spreading outer florets

inner florets

PLANT HEIGHT *80–120cm.*
FLOWER SIZE *Flowerhead 3.5–5cm wide.*
FLOWERING TIME *July–October.*
LEAVES *Alternate, pinnately divided into narrow lobes – somewhat ladder-like.*
FRUIT *Achene topped with bristly hair.*
SIMILAR SPECIES *Cornflower (right); Perennial Cornflower (C. montana), which has blue florets and oblong, unlobed leaves.*

Cornflower

Centaurea cyanus (Asteraceae)

What used to be a common and beautiful flower of the farmed countryside has now, sadly, become scarce. The resilient, tough, and wiry stems would resist the reaper's sickle in cornfields, and it grew in such profusion that it drained valuable nutrients from the soil. The use of powerful herbicides has now eradicated it from many areas. Cornflower is rather like a blue form of Greater Knapweed (left), with broad and finely cut, spreading ray florets. The disc florets are blackish pink, and the overlapping bracts have a short fringe of brown hair.

GROWS *on the cultivated soil of arable fields, but only where herbicides are not used. Grown in gardens and sometimes escapes to wasteland.*

NOTE
The juice from the petals is a brilliant blue and was once used as ink, as a watercolour, and to dye linen, although the colour is not permanent.

solitary flowerhead

ANNUAL

brown-edged flower bracts

linear leaf

large, spreading ray florets

blackish pink disc florets

PLANT HEIGHT *30–70cm.*
FLOWER SIZE *Flowerhead 2–4cm wide.*
FLOWERING TIME *June–August.*
LEAVES *Alternate, linear to lance-shaped, becoming toothed and lobed towards base of plant.*
FRUIT *Achene with short hair.*
SIMILAR SPECIES *Greater Knapweed (left); Perennial Cornflower (C. montana), which has larger flowerheads and broader leaves.*

Cat's-ear

Hypochaeris radicata (Asteraceae)

This plant can be difficult to distinguish from other dandelion-like plants. Its hairy leaves have very broad teeth and are in a loose, untidy rosette. The leafless flower stems are sometimes branched and have tiny, scale-like, dark-tipped bracts resembling miniature cats' ears. The outer ray florets of the yellow flowerheads are tinged green beneath.

OCCURS *in meadows, lawns, on roadsides, and other grassy places; prefers slightly acid or sandy soils.*

PERENNIAL

yellow ray florets

yellow flowerhead

leafless stem

broadly toothed margin

oblong leaf

greenish tinge on underside

PLANT HEIGHT *20–60cm.*
FLOWER SIZE *Flowerhead 2–3cm wide.*
FLOWERING TIME *June–September.*
LEAVES *Basal rosette, oblong, lobed, hairy.*
FRUIT *Cluster of hairy achenes.*
SIMILAR SPECIES *Hawkweed (p.421), which has unlobed leaves; Autumn Hawkbit (p.420), which has deeper lobed leaves.*

Chicory

Cichorium intybus (Asteraceae)

The tall, flowering spikes of Chicory are an unmistakable sight among the grass on road verges and wasteland. Each flower is made up of broad, strap-like ray florets that are sky-blue, an unusual colour for the daisy family. It is cultivated as a salad vegetable; the roots and young shoots are also roasted, ground, and then blended with coffee.

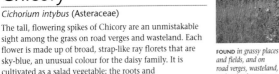

FOUND *in grassy places and fields, and on road verges, wasteland, and embankments, on chalky soil.*

PERENNIAL

lobed lower leaf

green flower bracts

spreading ray florets

flowers in tall spikes

stiff, upright stem

PLANT HEIGHT *60–100cm.*
FLOWER SIZE *2.5–4cm wide.*
FLOWERING TIME *July–October.*
LEAVES *Alternate; upper leaves spear-shaped and toothed, lower leaves pinnately lobed.*
FRUIT *Achene without a pappus.*
SIMILAR SPECIES *None.*

Autumn Hawkbit

Leontodon autumnalis (Asteraceae)

This small, neat plant comes into its own in late summer, when many similar-looking species have had their main flowering period. The stems are slightly branched, with a few tiny bracts, and are topped by yellow-rayed flowerheads. The leaves are in a basal rosette and are very narrow, with long lobes that are thinner than those of Dandelion (p.421).

INHABITS *grassy places, roadsides, short-turf pasture, and rocky habitats, preferring chalky soil.*

PERENNIAL

yellow rays

tiny bracts

red stripes underneath rays

long, thin leaf

PLANT HEIGHT *5–40cm.*
FLOWER SIZE *Flowerhead 2–3cm wide.*
FLOWERING TIME *June–October.*
LEAVES *Basal rosette, hairless, lobed.*
FRUIT *Achene with pappus of white hairs.*
SIMILAR SPECIES *Cat's-ear (p.419), which has hairy leaves; Mouse-ear Hawkweed (p.421), which has unlobed leaves.*

Bristly Oxtongue

Picris echioides (Asteraceae)

Easily recognized by the white pimples on the leaves, each one with a hooked bristle in the centre, this rough plant is covered with bristly hair. The upper leaves clasp the stem and the lower ones are stalked. The flowerheads are made up of pale yellow rays, with curved bracts curling up at the base.

GROWS *in rough grassy places, abandoned fields, roadsides, and wasteland.*

ANNUAL/BIENNIAL

branched stems

broad bracts

wavy edge

red-striped yellow rays

long, narrow leaf

PLANT HEIGHT *40–90cm.*
FLOWER SIZE *Flowerhead 2–2.5cm wide.*
FLOWERING TIME *June–October.*
LEAVES *Alternate, oblong, with bristles.*
FRUIT *Clock of hairy achenes.*
SIMILAR SPECIES *Perennial Sow-thistle (right), which has larger flowerheads and more pointed leaves, without bristles.*

Goat's-beard

Tragopogon pratensis (Asteraceae)

This stately member of the daisy family stands robust and erect. It has few branches, its stems are ridged, and the unusual leaves are linear, tapered to fine tips. In Britain and western France, there is a form whose flowerheads have very short ray florets, inside a ring of lance-like bracts that stand proud like a monarch's crown. The continental form has long ray florets, but both forms are folded tightly shut by midday. The bracts elongate and swell as the fruit develops, eventually opening out to reveal an enormous fluffy "clock".

OCCURS *among tall grasses in meadows, on road verges and embankments, and alongside paths.*

NOTE

The roots of this plant were once stored over the winter and eaten as a vegetable, and the young flowering shoots boiled and eaten as asparagus.

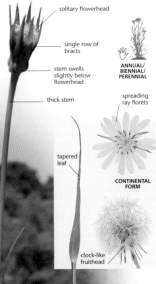

solitary flowerhead

single row of bracts

stem swells slightly below flowerhead

thick stem

ANNUAL/BIENNIAL/PERENNIAL

spreading ray florets

tapered leaf

CONTINENTAL FORM

clock-like fruithead

PLANT HEIGHT *40–75cm.*
FLOWER SIZE *Flowerhead 1.8–4cm wide, depending on length of rays.*
FLOWERING TIME *June–July.*
LEAVES *Alternate, linear to lance-shaped, grass-like.*
FRUIT *"Clock" of white feathery achenes forming a whitish ball, up to 12cm wide.*
SIMILAR SPECIES *None, its large size and linear leaves make it distinctive.*

Perennial Sow-thistle

Sonchus arvensis (Asteraceae)

Although superficially similar to other sow-thistles and dandelion-like plants, this bristly plant is distinctive. Its very large flowerheads, commonly seen in late summer and early autumn, sit on a base of sticky, hairy bracts. The whole plant is tall and stiff with greyish leaves, and produces milky latex when cut.

GROWS *on disturbed and cultivated ground, wasteland, abandoned fields, and along streams and rivers.*

large flowerhead

lobed, toothed leaf

slender stems

upper leaf clasps stem

PERENNIAL

yellow ray florets

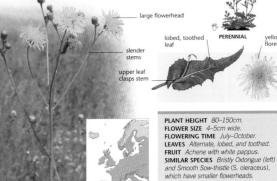

PLANT HEIGHT *80–150cm.*
FLOWER SIZE *4–5cm wide.*
FLOWERING TIME *July–October.*
LEAVES *Alternate, lobed, and toothed.*
FRUIT *Achene with white pappus.*
SIMILAR SPECIES *Bristly Oxtongue (left) and Smooth Sow-thistle (S. oleraceus), which have smaller flowerheads.*

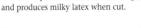

Prickly Lettuce

Lactuca serriola (Asteraceae)

Although related, this plant has little in common with the edible garden lettuce. It has ranks of waxy, grey-green leaves up the dark stem, with stiff prickles along the midrib under each leaf. The top branches of the stem bear numerous, tiny yellow flowerheads with scaly, dark-tipped bracts beneath.

GROWS *singly or in clumps on disturbed and waste ground, and along roadsides.*

widely branched stems

tall, upright plant

prickly midrib

tiny flowerheads

leaf clasps stem vertically

wavy leaf margin

ANNUAL/BIENNIAL

PLANT HEIGHT *1–1.8m.*
FLOWER SIZE *Flowerhead 1.1–1.3cm wide.*
FLOWERING TIME *July–September.*
LEAVES *Alternate, held vertically on the stem, oblong, prickly margins and midrib.*
FRUIT *Fluffy tuft of white-haired achenes.*
SIMILAR SPECIES *Great Lettuce (L. virosa), which has horizontal stem leaves.*

Smooth Hawk's-beard

Crepis capillaris (Asteraceae)

A dandelion-like plant with many branched flowering stems, Smooth Hawk's-beard has small flowerheads, with the outer ray florets tinged red underneath. Below the rays are two sets of green bracts, one long, and the other shorter at the base. The upper leaves clasp the stem; the lower leaves are lobed.

FORMS *small colonies in grassy places, such as pastures, wasteland, and cultivated land.*

tapered point

clasping base of upper leaf

yellow ray florets

flowerheads in clusters

green bracts

ANNUAL/BIENNIAL

PLANT HEIGHT *30–80cm.*
FLOWER SIZE *Flowerhead 1–1.5cm wide.*
FLOWERING TIME *June–September.*
LEAVES *Alternate, narrow upper leaves; basal rosette of lobed, toothed lower leaves.*
FRUIT *Small achene with white hairs.*
SIMILAR SPECIES *Cat's-ear (p.419), which has larger flowers and hairy leaves.*

Dandelion

Taraxacum officinale (Asteraceae)

Dandelions create a swathe of yellow during spring. Their flowerheads are made up of about 200 ray florets and have a ruff formed by the lower bracts. They are borne on unbranched, hollow, shiny, reddish flower stems, which exude milky-white juice if broken. The leaves have backward-pointing terminal lobes and are on winged stalks.

PROLIFERATES *in bare and grassy places, lawns, pastures, road verges, open woodland, and alongside paths.*

arrow-shaped leaf lobe

solitary flowerhead

clock of white hairs

PLANT HEIGHT *5–30cm.*
FLOWER SIZE *Flowerhead 2.5–4.5cm wide.*
FLOWERING TIME *March–October.*
LEAVES *Basal rosette, deeply lobed and toothed, pale midrib.*
FRUIT *Clock of achenes with a hairy pappus.*
SIMILAR SPECIES *Many similar Taraxacum species, all with solitary, shiny, hollow stems.*

PERENNIAL

Mouse-ear Hawkweed

Pilosella officinarum (Asteraceae)

This plant spreads by overground runners or stolons that occasionally take root. The leaves, in basal rosettes, are densely white-felted beneath, with a few long, bristly white hairs on the surface. The lemon-yellow flowerheads are on leafless stalks, the rays striped red beneath.

FOUND *in dry grassy sites such as pastures, roadsides, and lawns, on acid or chalky soils.*

solitary flowerhead

PERENNIAL

oblong leaf

red-striped rays

slender runners

PLANT HEIGHT *5–20cm.*
FLOWER SIZE *Flowerhead 1.8–2.5cm wide.*
FLOWERING TIME *June–September.*
LEAVES *Basal rosette, oblong, untoothed with long hairs above, white-felted below.*
FRUIT *Small achene with brownish pappus.*
SIMILAR SPECIES *Autumn Hawkbit (p.420) has lobed leaves and no runners.*

Nipplewort

Lapsana communis (Asteraceae)

This common plant is easily recognized by its branched, slender stems bearing slim, neat buds and many small dandelion-like flowerheads. The leaves are broad, dark-tipped, slightly toothed, and are unlobed, except for the basal leaves, which are stalked and have two or more lobes.

INHABITS *semi-shaded sites alongside paths, open woodland, waste and disturbed land, old walls, and gardens.*

lemon-yellow flowerheads

loosely branched stems

broad, toothed leaf

yellow ray florets

ANNUAL

PLANT HEIGHT *30–80cm.*
FLOWER SIZE *Flowerhead 1–2cm wide.*
FLOWERING TIME *May–September.*
LEAVES *Alternate, lower leaves broad with basal lobes, uppermost leaves lance-shaped.*
FRUIT *Simple achene without pappus.*
SIMILAR SPECIES *Smooth Hawk's-beard (right), which has arrow-shaped leaves.*

Common Hawkweed

Hieracium vulgatum (Asteraceae)

The hawkweeds are a complex group of species, divided further to include hundreds of "microspecies", which are difficult to differentiate. Common Hawkweed represents a group of these, recognizable by the loose rosette of mostly basal leaves that are oval to lance-shaped. They are toothed, but never lobed, and are crowded towards the base. The slender stems are branched at the top and the yellow ray florets have hairy bracts beneath them.

OCCURS *in rocky and grassy habitats, open woodland, heaths, cliff-tops, and other dry places.*

bright yellow flowerhead

leafless stem

toothed margin

ray florets

PERENNIAL

PLANT HEIGHT *30–80cm.*
FLOWER SIZE *2–3cm wide.*
FLOWERING TIME *June–September.*
LEAVES *Mostly basal, oval to lance-shaped with short stalk.*
FRUIT *Achene with brittle brown pappus.*
SIMILAR SPECIES *Cat's-ear (p.419), which has lobed leaves and a white pappus.*

PLANTS

Snakeshead Fritillary
Although not a tall plant, the distinctive lantern-like blooms of this wild flower make it hard to miss, or confuse with any other plant. The chequered pattern of its petals are reminiscent of a snake's scales.

Arrowhead

Sagittaria sagittifolia (Alismataceae)

A semi-aquatic plant, Arrowhead has large, arrow-shaped leaves that rise up on long stalks out of the water. It also has smaller, elliptical leaves that float on the surface, and these are the first to appear in spring. The three-petalled flowers, in whorls of three, are white with dark purple centres; male flowers sit above the females.

INHABITS *margins of shallow, freshwater lakes, slow-moving rivers and streams, and ditches.*

PERENNIAL

long-lobed leaf

white flowers with purple anthers

unbranched stem

3 petals

PLANT HEIGHT *60–100cm.*
FLOWER SIZE *2–2.5cm wide.*
FLOWERING TIME *July–August.*
LEAVES *Basal, arrow-shaped; smaller, elliptical leaves on water surface.*
FRUIT *Round, knobbly, bur-like achene.*
SIMILAR SPECIES *Water-plantain (below), which has smaller flowers.*

Water-plantain

Alisma plantago-aquatica (Alismataceae)

This plant forms a large tuft of spear-shaped leaves at the edges of standing water, and these are often more obvious than the small flowers borne on the tall, widely branching stems. Each flower has three white petals, which may have a pinkish tinge, and numerous yellow anthers. Each flower lasts for a day and only opens in the afternoon.

FOUND *in ponds, streams, lakes, marshes, and rivers, in the water or in mud at the water's edge.*

PERENNIAL

untoothed margin

long-stalked flowers

white or pinkish petals

flowers in whorls

PLANT HEIGHT *30–100cm.*
FLOWER SIZE *6–10mm wide.*
FLOWERING TIME *June–August.*
LEAVES *Basal and elliptical to oval, long-stalked, with a pointed tip.*
FRUIT *Tight cluster of in-curved achenes.*
SIMILAR SPECIES *Arrowhead (above); Flowering Rush (right).*

Frogbit

Hydrocharis morsus-ranae (Hydrocharitaceae)

Floating on the water surface, this pretty plant looks like a miniature water-lily (p.351). Each leaf is rounded, with a heart-shaped base, often with a bronze tinge. The flowers have three white petals and a yellow centre and the male and female flowers are borne on separate plants. Frogbit spreads by means of long runners under the water, rooting at intervals.

OCCURS *in unpolluted, slow-moving water of ditches, ponds, lakes, and canals.*

PERENNIAL

rounded leaves

curved veins on leaf

wrinkled petals

white flowers with yellow centres

PLANT HEIGHT *Water surface.*
FLOWER SIZE *1.8–2cm wide.*
FLOWERING TIME *June–August.*
LEAVES *In whorls from runners, rounded with heart-shaped base; often tinged bronze.*
FRUIT *Small capsule.*
SIMILAR SPECIES *Marsh Pennywort (p.384), which has similar leaves, but is not aquatic.*

Flowering Rush

Butomus umbellatus (Butomaceae)

Although the narrow leaves of this aquatic plant are superficially similar to those of a rush or sedge, the Flowering Rush is quite unrelated and, unlike them, it produces elegant umbels of reddish flower stalks. Each umbel looks like an upturned umbrella, with a pink flower at the tip of each spoke. The flowers have three petals, red-striped beneath, with three smaller sepals in between, and several dark-tipped stamens. In cross-section, the leaves are triangular at the bottom, thinning out to a flat blade at the top.

GROWS *in shallow water at the edges of rivers, streams, ditches, and ponds; prefers recently cleared areas and dislikes acid soil.*

PERENNIAL

crimson flower bud

cup-shaped flower

umbrella-like flowerhead

leaf tapers to a point

blade-like leaf

dark-tipped stamens

NOTE

The seeds of the Flowering Rush contain air-filled tissue. This means that they will float when they fall into the water and may be carried along by the current to a suitable germination site away from the main plant.

PLANT HEIGHT *80–150cm.*
FLOWER SIZE *1.6–2.6cm wide.*
FLOWERING TIME *July–August.*
LEAVES *Basal, linear, triangular in cross-section in the lower half, with a broad sheath at the base.*
FRUIT *Six follicles, fused together, red to purple.*
SIMILAR SPECIES *Water-plantain (left), which has smaller flowers and broad leaves.*

Broad-leaved Pondweed

Potamogeton natans (Potamogetonaceae)

The broad leaves of this aquatic plant appear to be hinged at the base, enabling them to float flat on the water surface, while longer, narrower leaves are submerged. The tiny green flowers, which have no petals, are borne in short spikes held above the water. Unusually for a water plant, they are wind-pollinated – contact with water sterilizes the pollen.

COVERS *the surface of nutrient-rich, freshwater ponds, ditches, and slow rivers. May colonize cleaned-out ponds.*

PERENNIAL

flower spike held above water

leathery surface

green fruiting spike

PLANT HEIGHT *Water surface, to 1m deep.*
FLOWER SIZE *3–4mm wide.*
FLOWERING TIME *May–September.*
LEAVES *Opposite, broad above water; long and narrow underwater.*
FRUIT *Four small nutlets, each 3–4mm long.*
SIMILAR SPECIES *Frogbit (left), which has white flowers; Amphibious Bistort (p.345).*

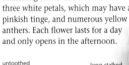

Bog Asphodel

Narthecium ossifragum (Liliaceae)

This colourful plant forms large colonies within its very specific habitat. Greenish to orange stems rise from a clump of strap-shaped leaves, and buds in a neat spike open from the base upwards to produce yellow flowers, each with six furry stamens. As the fruit develops, the stems and dry sepals become fiery orange.

FOUND only in acid bogs, moors, and heaths in damp areas, particularly on hills and mountains.

yellow-green flower buds

orange-red fruit capsules

starry, bright yellow flower

6 petals

PERENNIAL

PLANT HEIGHT 15–40cm.
FLOWER SIZE 1–1.6cm wide.
FLOWERING TIME July–September.
LEAVES Basal, strap-shaped, short, often orange-flushed; small, bract-like stem leaves.
FRUIT Narrow, oblong, three-parted capsule, orange-red.
SIMILAR SPECIES None.

Martagon Lily

Lilium martagon (Liliaceae)

This is a robust plant with tall, red-streaked stems. Ranks of alternate, drooping flower buds persist for some weeks before finally opening, with the dark-spotted pink petals curving right back on themselves, revealing orange anthers and a long stigma that seem to hang like a pendent carousel.

OCCURS in mountain meadows and pastures, and among scrub or open woodland, often on slopes, preferring chalky soil.

bract at leaf stalk base

drooping flower buds

leaves in whorls

flowers at bottom open first

pendent orange anthers

recurved petals

PERENNIAL

PLANT HEIGHT 1–1.8m.
FLOWER SIZE 3–4cm wide.
FLOWERING TIME June–July.
LEAVES Whorled, broadly oval to elliptical, ridged, with 7–9 veins; deep green.
FRUIT Three-lobed capsule.
SIMILAR SPECIES Pyrenean Lily (L. pyrenaicum), which has yellow flowers.

Meadow Saffron

Colchicum autumnale (Liliaceae)

The flowers and leaves of this poisonous plant are never seen together. In autumn, large, crocus-like flowers appear from a single papery spathe at ground level, the six petals often flopping open. The flowers have six stamens, unlike true crocuses, which have three. In spring, the large, shiny green leaves are pushed up along with the fruit capsule.

APPEARS in damp, grassy meadows and on roadsides; often planted in gardens from where it spreads.

bright green leaf

large, crocus-like flowers

dark to light pink flower

PERENNIAL

PLANT HEIGHT 10–40cm.
FLOWER SIZE 4–6cm wide.
FLOWERING TIME August–October.
LEAVES Basal, elliptical or lance-shaped.
FRUIT Fleshy, three-parted capsule.
SIMILAR SPECIES Autumn Crocus (Crocus nudiflorus), which is occasionally naturalized and has purple flowers and three stamens.

Snakeshead Fritillary

Fritillaria meleagris (Liliaceae)

The extraordinary pattern on the nodding flowers of this plant, neatly chequered like a chessboard, is distinctive. The six overlapping petals are usually reddish crimson but may also be white, with greenish markings. The flowerheads become upright as the papery fruit develops. The grey-green leaves are grass-like and slightly channelled.

FORMS colonies in damp grassland, riverside meadows, pastures, and gardens.

curved stalk

petals may be white

3-parted papery capsule

crimson, chequered flowers

PERENNIAL

linear leaves

PLANT HEIGHT 25–40cm.
FLOWER SIZE 3–4.5cm long.
FLOWERING TIME April–May.
LEAVES Alternate, linear, fleshy, channelled; grey-green.
FRUIT Three-valved capsule on erect stalk.
SIMILAR SPECIES None; the distinctive chequered flowers make this plant unique.

Yellow Star-of-Bethlehem

Gagea lutea (Liliaceae)

Found in semi-shade, this member of the lily family produces seven flowers in an umbel, which arises from the centre of a pair of opposite leaves on the main stem. Each flower has six petals with a broad green stripe on the back and orange anthers. Below the flowers is a solitary, flat, yellowish green basal leaf.

GROWS in damp grassland, woodland, and among scrub, on neutral to chalky soil.

PERENNIAL

strap-shaped basal leaf

starry, lemon-yellow flowers

6 petals

PLANT HEIGHT 15–25cm.
FLOWER SIZE 1.5–2.5cm wide.
FLOWERING TIME March–May.
LEAVES One strap-shaped basal leaf; two opposite stem leaves with hairy margins.
FRUIT Small capsule.
SIMILAR SPECIES Lesser Celandine (p.353), which has rounded or kidney-shaped leaves.

Star-of-Bethlehem

Ornithogalum umbellatum (Liliaceae)

This plant has loose clusters of starry white flowers. The petals have a green stripe on the outside that is clearly visible, except in sunshine when the flowers open fully. Each flower, with its six prominent anthers, appears flat-topped, like an umbel. The leaves have a pale central stripe.

INHABITS grassy places, woodland glades, meadows, roadsides, scrub, and wasteland.

grass-like leaf

yellow anthers

long, narrow leaves

PERENNIAL

green stripe on petal

6-petalled flower

PLANT HEIGHT 15–30cm.
FLOWER SIZE 3–4cm wide.
FLOWERING TIME April–June.
LEAVES Basal, linear, with pale stripe, limp and floppy.
FRUIT Three-parted capsule.
SIMILAR SPECIES Wood Anemone (p.351), which has broader, lobed, and toothed leaves.

PLANTS

Bluebell

Scilla non-scripta (Liliaceae)

An easily recognizable plant, the Bluebell forms dense carpets of blue over the woodland floor, where it blooms just as the trees are coming into leaf. The fragrant, nodding, violet-blue (rarely white or pink) flowers have creamy white anthers. They are clustered on one side in groups of five to fifteen, each flower ending with two blue membranous bracts on its base. The narrow, dark green leaves, which rise from the base may persist for some weeks after flowering.

FORMS *carpets in woodland and scrub; found on hedgebanks and sea-cliffs in the far west of its range.*

PERENNIAL

NOTE

The "bluebell woods" of Britain and Ireland, often written about over the centuries, are considered to be some of the most spectacular floral displays in Europe.

blue bracts

fleshy, leafless flower stalks

strap-shaped, dark green leaf

bell-shaped flowers

6-parted flower forms a tube

PLANT HEIGHT *25–50cm.*
FLOWER SIZE *1.5–2cm long.*
FLOWERING TIME *April–June.*
LEAVES *Basal, linear to lance-shaped.*
FRUIT *Small, three-parted capsule.*
SIMILAR SPECIES *Spanish Bluebell (S. hispanica), which is a more robust plant with broader bells and blue anthers; frequently escapes gardens.*

Ramsons

Allium ursinum (Liliaceae)

Woodland floors can be entirely carpeted with this vigorous plant in spring, to the exclusion of all other plants, and the scent of garlic may be overpowering when a colony of Ramsons is in full bloom. There are two or three bright green leaves, each broadly elliptical and rising directly from the bulb below the ground. They have a mild taste of garlic and may be used in salads. Each cluster of up to 25 six-petalled, starry flowers is enclosed within two papery spathes before it opens out.

GROWS *in extensive colonies in deciduous woodland, scrub, coppices, shaded banks, and hedgerows; prefers damp sites on rich soil.*

PERENNIAL

umbels of 6-petalled white flowers

widely spreading petals

NOTE

The juice from the onion-like bulb has been used to treat rheumatic pain and as a slimming aid.

pointed tip

bright green leaf

2 spathes enclose buds

broadly elliptical leaves

PLANT HEIGHT *30–45cm.*
FLOWER SIZE *1.2–2cm wide.*
FLOWERING TIME *April–June.*
LEAVES *Basal, growing directly from the underground bulb; broadly elliptical; bright green.*
FRUIT *Small, three-parted capsule, containing numerous black seeds.*
SIMILAR SPECIES *Lily-of-the-Valley (p.427), which has diminutive flowers borne in racemes.*

Crow Garlic

Allium vineale (Alliaceae)

This slender plant may go unnoticed among tall summer grasses. The long, cylindrical, garlic-scented leaves disappear by flowering time, when a papery spathe encloses the developing flowerhead on its long stem. The flowerhead may consist of greenish bulbils, which give rise to new plants, or of small tubular flowers on long stems – or both.

INHABITS *dry, grassy places, commons, dunes, often close to the sea. May be hidden among tall grasses.*

papery spathe

clusters of bulbils

violet flowers

PERENNIAL

long stem

PLANT HEIGHT *60–100cm.*
FLOWER SIZE *Flowerhead 2–3cm wide.*
FLOWERING TIME *June–August.*
LEAVES *Alternate, narrow, and cylindrical.*
FRUIT *Small capsule.*
SIMILAR SPECIES *Field Garlic (A. oleraceum), which has white flowers and two long spathes enclosing the flowerhead.*

Three-cornered Leek

Allium triquetrum (Liliaceae)

One of the most distinctive of the *Allium* species, this plant is easily recognized by its nodding head of bell-like flowers all facing in one direction. The petals of each flower overlap for much of their length, never opening out fully, and each has a narrow green stripe, visible on both the inside and the outside of the flower. The stems are markedly triangular in cross-section, with sharp edges. The leaves have a prominent keel so they too are somewhat triangular in cross-section. When crushed, they produce a strong garlic smell.

SEEN *in damp, semi-shaded spots such as woodland clearings, grassy places, and road verges; often cultivated.*

spathe encloses young flowers

narrow green stripe

drooping head of flowers

strongly angled stem

PERENNIAL

PLANT HEIGHT *20–45cm*
FLOWER SIZE *1.8cm long.*
FLOWERING TIME *March–May.*
LEAVES *Narrow, tapering, with keel on back.*
FRUIT *Three-parted capsule with many seeds.*
SIMILAR SPECIES *White forms of Bluebell (left); Drooping Star-of-Bethlehem (Ornithogalum nutans) has round stems.*

Lily-of-the-Valley

Convallaria majalis (Liliaceae)

Although the leaves of this plant are simple in shape, they are distinctive when seen in pairs along the woodland floor. The small, fragrant white flowers are like little bells, borne in a loose raceme on one side of the stalk, and develop into poisonous red berries. The plant spreads by means of underground runners.

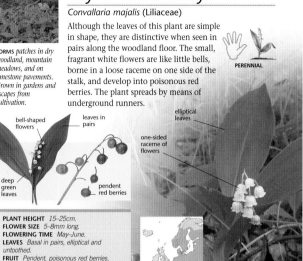

FORMS *patches in dry woodland, mountain meadows, and on limestone pavements. Grown in gardens and escapes from cultivation.*

PERENNIAL

bell-shaped flowers

leaves in pairs

elliptical leaves

one-sided raceme of flowers

deep green leaves

pendent red berries

PLANT HEIGHT *15–25cm.*
FLOWER SIZE *5–8mm long.*
FLOWERING TIME *May–June.*
LEAVES *Basal in pairs, elliptical and untoothed.*
FRUIT *Pendent, poisonous red berries.*
SIMILAR SPECIES *Ramsons (p.426) has similar leaves; Common Wintergreen (p.389).*

Butcher's Broom

Ruscus aculeatus (Liliaceae)

The leaf-like structures of this extraordinarily spiky, evergreen plant are in fact flattened extensions of the stems called cladodes. The stems themselves are upright, and branched on the upper part of the plant. The small green flowers appear directly on the surface of the cladodes and each has three petals and three sepals, the male flowers with purple anthers. Not all the female flowers are successfully pollinated but when one is, a large red berry develops. The whole plant resembles a small holly bush and may grow alongside it.

OCCURS *in ancient woodland, scrub, and hedgerows, even in deep shade. Also in rocky places by the sea. Prefers dry conditions.*

PERENNIAL

tough, spine-tipped cladodes

flowers with 3 petals and 3 sepals

NOTE

So tough and spiky is the foliage of this plant that it was once used to sweep butcher's blocks – hence its name.

bright red berry

finely grooved stem

PLANT HEIGHT *25–80cm.*
FLOWER SIZE *3–5mm wide.*
FLOWERING TIME *January–April.*
LEAVES *Alternate, leaf-like structures (cladodes), rigid, elliptical with pointed tips; dark green.*
FRUIT *Bright red berry, 1–1.5cm wide, borne singly.*
SIMILAR SPECIES *None, but may be mistaken for a small Holly (Ilex aquifolium) bush at a glance.*

Herb Paris

Paris quadrifolia (Liliaceae)

This unusual member of the lily family bears a whorl of just four leaves halfway up the stem. Above these it produces a single flower, which has four very slender green petals and sepals, and eight yellowish stamens. The most notable feature is the large blackish fruit capsule in the centre, which splits to reveal red seeds. A low-growing plant, it may also spread by means of underground rhizomes. The plant can be very difficult to spot among other vegetation.

FOUND *in patches in ancient woodland and other shady habitats on chalky soil.*

8 prominent stamens

PERENNIAL

round blackish capsule

4 petals and sepals

whorl of 4 oval leaves

NOTE

The small, green flowers are not visually attractive to bees and produce no nectar, but are pollinated by small flies that the plant attracts with its strong foetid smell, which is similar to that of rotting meat.

PLANT HEIGHT *20–40cm.*
FLOWER SIZE *3–5cm wide.*
FLOWERING TIME *May–June.*
LEAVES *Whorled, oval, pointed.*
FRUIT *A rounded black capsule to 1cm wide, which splits to reveal small red seeds.*
SIMILAR SPECIES *Dog's Mercury (p.378), which is leafier and has small green flowers in spikes.*

Solomon's-seal

Polygonatum multiflorum (Liliaceae)

This plant has leaves arranged alternately, in two rows on either side of the long, arvching, round stems. Each leaf is oval and pointed, with distinct parallel veins, and the margin is untoothed. Hanging in small clusters of 1–6 from the leaf axils, the nodding, unscented, green-tipped white flowers are like elongated bells. The fruit persists on the plant into autumn.

GROWS *in shady places in ancient woodland and along hedgerows, on chalky soil.*

PERENNIAL

alternate leaves in two rows

narrow, bell-shaped flowers

round black berries

long stem

PLANT HEIGHT *40–70cm.*
FLOWER SIZE *1–2cm long.*
FLOWERING TIME *May–June.*
LEAVES *Alternate, oval, pointed.*
FRUIT *Black berry with bluish bloom, 1cm wide.*
SIMILAR SPECIES *Angular Solomon's-seal (P. odoratum) has larger, scented flowers.*

PLANTS

Bluebells
Once seen never forgotten, the azure haze created by the bell-shaped flowers of bluebells in a wood is a spectacular sight, and one closely tied to the traditional image of the British countryside.

Summer Snowflake

Leucojum aestivum (Amaryllidaceae)

The daffodil-like leaves of Summer Snowflake are tall, strap-shaped, and dark green. The flower stalk (scape) unfurls to reveal 3–6 bell-shaped flowers, each having six white petals with a green spot at the tip. Spring Snowflake is similar but has solitary or paired flowers that open in early spring.

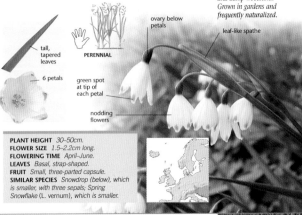

INHABITS *moist places close to rivers and streams, marshes, wet meadows, and damp woodland. Grown in gardens and frequently naturalized.*

PERENNIAL

tall, tapered leaves

6 petals

green spot at tip of each petal

ovary below petals

leaf-like spathe

nodding flowers

PLANT HEIGHT *30–50cm.*
FLOWER SIZE *1.5–2.2cm long.*
FLOWERING TIME *April–June.*
LEAVES *Basal, strap-shaped.*
FRUIT *Small, three-parted capsule.*
SIMILAR SPECIES *Snowdrop (below), which is smaller, with three sepals; Spring Snowflake (L. vernum), which is smaller.*

Snowdrop

Galanthus nivalis (Amaryllidaceae)

Among the earliest of plants to flower, the Snowdrop first pushes its two slender grey-green leaves up through the bare earth, and these are closely followed by the flower stalks. Each bears a solitary white flower with three spreading sepals, and three much shorter notched petals streaked green on the inside. Leaves continue to grow from the bulbs after flowering. Double-flowered forms frequently escape from gardens.

FORMS *patches in scrub, woodland, and shady meadows, and on banks. Cultivated and naturalized.*

3 white sepals

3 shorter petals

double flower

green streaks

PERENNIAL

nodding flower

strap-shaped leaves

clump-forming habit

NOTE

Snowdrops are probably only native in the south and west of Britain, but have spread widely along watercourses or through planting. For centuries, they have been planted in churchyards as a symbol of purity.

PLANT HEIGHT *10–20cm.*
FLOWER SIZE *1.5–2cm long.*
FLOWERING TIME *January–March.*
LEAVES *Basal, strap-shaped.*
FRUIT *Small, three-parted capsule, though rarely formed as the plant most often spreads by division of the bulbs.*
SIMILAR SPECIES *Summer Snowflake (above); Spring Snowflake (Leucojum vernum), which has six green-tipped petals.*

Wild Daffodil

Narcissus pseudonarcissus (Amaryllidaceae)

This tuft-forming plant has leafless stems (scapes). The solitary flowers are made up of six outer, pale primrose yellow tepals (petal-like sepals and petals), and a central trumpet (corona), which is a darker, more opaque yellow. Each flower has a green or brown papery spathe at the base. The grey-green basal leaves are flat, linear, and fleshy. The fruit capsule contains many seeds, helping extensive colonies to develop. The Wild Daffodil is smaller than the many hundreds of cultivated varieties grown in gardens, which are sometimes naturalized in the wider countryside.

FORMS *colonies in ancient deciduous woodland and meadows, on river banks, and along hedgerows.*

PERENNIAL

triangular, slightly twisted tepals

trumpet-shaped, deep yellow corona

solitary flower

papery spathe

long, narrow leaf

6 pale yellow tepals

yellow stamens

NOTE

The bulbs resemble onions but are highly poisonous, and, if eaten, can cause the fatal collapse of the nervous system.

PLANT HEIGHT *30–50cm.*
FLOWER SIZE *2.5–4cm long.*
FLOWERING TIME *March–May.*
LEAVES *Basal, linear, 6–12mm wide, 2–5 in number, fleshy; grey-green.*
FRUIT *Three-parted capsule, with many seeds.*
SIMILAR SPECIES *Many cultivated varieties of this plant, which have flowers in a wide range of sizes, colours, and shapes.*

Black Bryony

Tamus communis (Dioscoreaceae)

CLAMBERS *over hedges, woodland trees, and scrub; also twines over wire fences; usually at low altitudes.*

The glossy, heart-shaped leaves of this climbing plant are unmistakable. The greenish yellow flowers are borne on long, trailing stems; the male flowers in slender spikes and the female flowers in shorter clusters on separate plants. The shiny red berries are long-lasting but poisonous; although the plant is related to yams, its black tuber is poisonous too.

PERENNIAL

6-lobed flowers

twining stems

male flowers in drooping spikes

cluster of red berries

PLANT HEIGHT *Up to 4m.*
FLOWER SIZE *3–6mm wide.*
FLOWERING TIME *May–July.*
LEAVES *Alternate, heart-shaped; dark green.*
FRUIT *Red, fleshy berries.*
SIMILAR SPECIES *Ivy (p.384), which has flowers in umbels; Hedge Bindweed (p.396), which has trumpet-shaped white flowers.*

Yellow Flag

Iris pseudacorus (Iridaceae)

A marsh-loving iris, Yellow Flag often grows among other plant species with similar tall, strap-shaped leaves. It may be identified by its base, where the flat leaves grow one inside another, layered to form a chevron pattern. The leaves are sword-shaped and bright grey-green, each with a slightly raised midrib. There is no mistaking the showy, brilliant yellow iris flowers. Each is composed of three fall petals with faint brown markings, supported by a green leaf-like spathe, and three erect standard petals that are smaller, narrower, and unmarked. The large, oblong, drooping fruit capsule dries and splits to reveal neat ranks of orange-brown seeds, a little like niblets of maize.

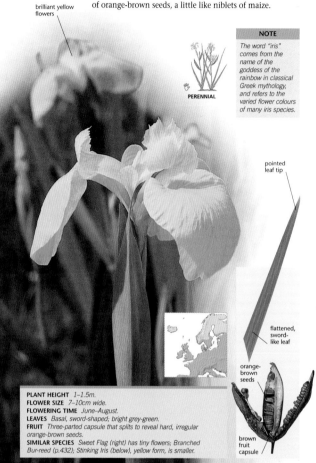

brilliant yellow flowers

NOTE
The word "iris" comes from the name of the goddess of the rainbow in classical Greek mythology, and refers to the varied flower colours of many iris species.

PERENNIAL

pointed leaf tip

flattened, sword-like leaf

orange-brown seeds

brown fruit capsule

PLANT HEIGHT 1–1.5m.
FLOWER SIZE 7–10cm wide.
FLOWERING TIME June–August.
LEAVES Basal, sword-shaped; bright grey-green.
FRUIT Three-parted capsule that splits to reveal hard, irregular orange-brown seeds.
SIMILAR SPECIES Sweet Flag (right) has tiny flowers; Branched Bur-reed (p.432); Stinking Iris (below), yellow form, is smaller.

Stinking Iris

Iris foetidissima (Iridaceae)

The tufts of strap-like leaves of the Stinking Iris are evergreen, and most easily seen in winter. They give off a strong smell like that of roast meat and a more offensive odour if crushed. Yellow and purple petals of the flowers sometimes occur as dull violet-brown. The inner petals are actually modified styles. Berries remain until early winter.

GROWS in shady corners of woodland, alongside hedgerows, embankments, and paths, in dampish areas; dislikes acid soil.

purple outer petals
notched, yellowish inner "petals"
dark-veined purple petals
numerous bright red berries
3-parted fruit capsule
PERENNIAL

PLANT HEIGHT 40–70cm.
FLOWER SIZE 5.5–8cm wide.
FLOWERING TIME May–July.
LEAVES Basal and alternate, sword-shaped, up to 2.5cm wide, strong-smelling.
FRUIT Three-parted capsule, with red berries.
SIMILAR SPECIES A form with yellow flowers, (var. citrina) is a frequent garden escape.

Sweet Flag

Acorus calamus (Araceae)

The leaves strongly resemble those of other waterside plants, but are wrinkled on one side and smell of tangerines when crushed. The rarely produced flower spike is borne halfway up the plant. It is cylindrical, appearing at an angle to the flattened stems, and consists of a tightly packed cone of very tiny yellow flowers, each with six stamens.

INHABITS the muddy margins of reedbeds, ponds, and slow-flowing streams, often among other similar-looking plants.

section of narrow, stiff leaf
wrinkled on one side
PERENNIAL
tapered point
yellow flower spike

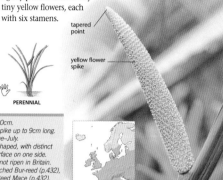

PLANT HEIGHT 80–120cm.
FLOWER SIZE Flower spike up to 9cm long.
FLOWERING TIME June–July.
LEAVES Basal, sword-shaped, with distinct midrib and wrinkled surface on one side.
FRUIT Berry, but does not ripen in Britain.
SIMILAR SPECIES Branched Bur-reed (p.432), Yellow Flag (left), and Reed Mace (p.432).

Lords and Ladies

Arum maculatum (Araceae)

The arrow-shaped leaves of this plant are a deep green colour. They are often, though not always, spotted with dark blotches, and have a wrinkled surface. A large yellow-green bract (spathe) pushes up from the base of the plant and unfurls to reveal the club-shaped, brown flower spike (spadix). This is warm and scented to attract flies down to the true flowers, which are hidden in the bulge below. The green parts of the plant die off but the flowers remain to form berries in late summer, which brighten from green to orange-red.

FOUND in shade in woodland or scrub, alongside hedgerows, particularly close to paths and tracks, or on dry banks.

PERENNIAL

large yellow-green spathe
club-shaped brown spadix
wrinkled, arrow-shaped leaves
deep green leaf

NOTE
Flies visiting the flowers are trapped within the spathe, often overnight, by downward-pointing hairs, to ensure pollination of the flowers.

green to orange-red fruit
occasional black blotches
berries borne on short stalk

PLANT HEIGHT 15–35cm.
FLOWER SIZE Spathe 10–20cm long.
FLOWERING TIME April–May.
LEAVES Basal, arrow-shaped and wrinkled; dark green, often with dark blotches.
FRUIT Red berries.
SIMILAR SPECIES Large Cuckoo Pint (A. italicum), which has white-veined leaves, a yellow spadix, and a larger spike of berries.

PLANTS

Branched Bur-reed

Sparganium erectum (Sparganiceae)

The leaves of this plant are similar to those of iris and bulrush. The flowers, however, are distinctive. The branched flowering stem has a number of female flowerheads ranged along it, with the male flowerheads at the top. As the fruit is formed, the female flowerheads swell to become a spiky ball or bur. The plant spreads with the aid of rhizomes.

male flowerheads in spikes

FOUND *on the edges of freshwater ponds, ditches, lakes, slow-moving rivers, and streams; may grow among other plants with similar leaves.*

strap-shaped leaf

round female flowerheads in clusters

PERENNIAL

white anthers

PLANT HEIGHT *80–150cm.*
FLOWER SIZE *1–2cm wide.*
FLOWERING TIME *June–August.*
LEAVES *Basal, strap-shaped, stiff, and erect.*
FRUIT *Single-seeded drupe, borne on the female bur.*
SIMILAR SPECIES *Unbranched Bur-reed (S. emersum), is smaller with floating leaves.*

Marsh Helleborine

Epipactis palustris (Orchidaceae)

The subtle colouring of this orchid's flowers is best appreciated when seen close-up, each flower having three white petals, flushed and striped with pink. The lower petal is longer than the other petals, and shaped with a constricted waist. The three erect sepals are green but often tinted strongly with red. The 3–8 alternate leaves decrease in size up the stem.

GROWS *in colonies in wet places such as marshes, fens, and dune slacks. Prefers chalky soil.*

frilly-edged petals

flowers in loose spike

spear-shaped leaf

glossy, pale green surface

spreading sepals

yellow blotch

PERENNIAL

PLANT HEIGHT *30–50cm.*
FLOWER SIZE *Lower lip 1–2cm long.*
FLOWERING TIME *July–August.*
LEAVES *Alternate, spear- or lance-shaped.*
FRUIT *Three-parted, pendent capsule.*
SIMILAR SPECIES *Violet Helleborine (E. purpurata), which has green-violet leaves; Broad-leaved Helleborine (below).*

Reed Mace

Typha latifolia (Typhaceae)

This robust, often invasive plant is also known as Bulrush. It has stout stems and grows from rhizomes in shallow water or mud. Its erect, flat, sword-like leaves are difficult to distinguish from those of other similar plants, except that they are often the tallest. However, there is no mistaking the highly distinctive flowers, borne in two dense spikes, one above the other. The dark brown, felty "cigar" is actually a collection of female flowers. The yellow male flowers appear in a narrower spike immediately above this, producing copious amounts of pollen, usually before the female section is fully ripe. In winter or the following spring, the seedhead bursts, expelling thousands of light, fluffy seeds that are carried away by the wind.

PROLIFERATES *in wetland habitats such as pond and river margins, marshes, and ditches, always with its base in water.*

dense, cylindrical spikes of flowers

NOTE

The light fluffy seeds resemble cotton wool and have been used to stuff mattresses. They may also be used as a source of dry tinder in wet habitats.

PERENNIAL

tall, sword-like leaves

yellow male flowering spike

cigar-like female spike

fruiting spike

PLANT HEIGHT *1.5–2.8m.*
FLOWER SIZE *Female spike up to 15cm long.*
FLOWERING TIME *July–August.*
LEAVES *Mostly basal; flat, sword-like, and erect; up to 2cm wide; greyish green.*
FRUIT *Capsule containing light, fluffy seeds.*
SIMILAR SPECIES *Branched Bur-reed (above) has yellow-green flowerheads; Lesser Reed Mace (T. angustifolia) has narrower leaves.*

Broad-leaved Helleborine

Epipactis helleborine (Orchidaceae)

This *Epipactis* species is unusual in that it grows and flowers at the darkest, shadiest time of year, when most other woodland plants are dormant. These orchids are able to do this with the help of a fungus around their roots that provides them with extra nourishment, a partnership from which the fungus appears to derive no benefit. Up to 50 flowers are borne in long spikes, each a complex shape of greenish sepals and petals, with a large pink or crimson, occasionally white, lower lip, recurved at the tip. Found mainly near the bottom of the stem, the strongly veined leaves are broadly oval.

OCCURS *in shady areas of deciduous woodland, scrub, roadsides, and banks, preferring chalky soil. Sometimes found on sand dunes.*

narrow bract under flower

greenish sepals

winged side petals

recurved lower lip

PERENNIAL

NOTE

The pollen of orchids forms in two waxy masses called pollinia, which stick to visiting insects to be deposited on the flowers of other plants.

broad, veined leaf

smooth fruit capsule

PLANT HEIGHT *50–80cm.*
FLOWER SIZE *Lower lip 1cm long.*
FLOWERING TIME *July–August.*
LEAVES *Spirally arranged, oval to elliptical, strongly veined.*
FRUIT *Pendent, many-seeded capsule.*
SIMILAR SPECIES *Marsh Helleborine (above) has narrower leaves; Violet Helleborine (E. purpurata) has violet-grey stems and leaves; Green-flowered Helleborine (E. phylanthes) has greenish flowers.*

Bird's-nest Orchid

Neottia nidus-avis (Orchidaceae)

FOUND *in shady areas of deciduous woodland, particularly beech but also hazel. Blends into leaf-litter so is difficult to spot.*

Lacking chlorophyll, this orchid instead derives its nutrients from a fungus within its root system that breaks down dead organic material. The whole plant is yellowish brown. There are numerous flowers, each with brown petals, a long lower lip, and small, papery bracts at the base. The leaves are reduced to papery, overlapping scales on the stem and the mass of tangled roots resembles a bird's nest.

brown petals

lobed lower lip

PERENNIAL

many-flowered spike

yellowish brown stem

PLANT HEIGHT *20–40cm.*
FLOWER SIZE *Lower lip 8–12mm long.*
FLOWERING TIME *May–July.*
LEAVES *Alternate, papery scales.*
FRUIT *Capsule, containing many seeds.*
SIMILAR SPECIES *Toothwort (p.407); Common Broomrape (p.407); other broomrapes, which have tubular, two-lipped flowers.*

Common Twayblade

Listera ovata (Orchidaceae)

This common and widespread orchid bears only two prominently veined, broad, oval leaves near the base of the plant and produces a single flowering stem, at the top of which is a spike of numerous yellow-green flowers. Each flower has a long, grooved, and deeply forked lower lip. The leaves are more noticeable than the flower stem, but may quickly be devoured by insects.

OCCURS *in semi-shaded woods, scrub, meadows, marshy ground, and dunes, on a variety of soils.*

unbranched veins

numerous flowers on upper stem

PERENNIAL

tall, erect stem

forked lower lip of flower

PLANT HEIGHT *20–60cm.*
FLOWER SIZE *Lip 7–15mm long.*
FLOWERING TIME *May–July.*
LEAVES *Basal, simple, two broad, oval leaves on each plant.*
FRUIT *Capsule, containing many tiny seeds.*
SIMILAR SPECIES *Man Orchid (p.437), which has long, narrow leaves.*

Autumn Lady's-tresses

Spiranthes spiralis (Orchidaceae)

This small orchid is difficult to spot even in short grassland, but once seen is easily recognized. Numerous tiny flowers, each with a frilly-margined lower lip, are borne in a spiral up the spike. The greyish green leaves, in a basal rosette, wither by flowering time, but the following year's rosette is often present next to the flowering spike.

THRIVES *in some years, absent in others, on dry grassland, lawns, and dunes, preferring chalky soil.*

white flowers

flower spike

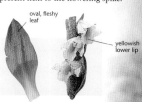

oval, fleshy leaf

yellowish lower lip

PERENNIAL

PLANT HEIGHT *8–15cm.*
FLOWER SIZE *4–6mm long.*
FLOWERING TIME *August–September.*
LEAVES *Basal rosette, scale leaves on stem.*
FRUIT *Capsule containing many tiny seeds.*
SIMILAR SPECIES *Creeping Lady's-tresses (Goodyera repens), of N. Scotland, which has fewer flowers in a less obvious spiral.*

Lesser Butterfly Orchid

Platanthera bifolia (Orchidaceae)

GROWS *in various habitats such as bogs, heaths, pastures, woodland margins and clearings; on a variety of soils.*

This attractive orchid has just two oblong, shiny leaves arising from the base. It produces a stout spike, with a few scale-like leaves, bearing vanilla-scented, creamy or greenish white flowers. The outer sepals are thinly triangular, but most noticeable is the very long, thin, unlobed lower lip, increasingly green towards the tip, with a very long, slender spur behind. The two small yellow anthers are parallel to each other. The Greater Butterfly Orchid (*P. chlorantha*) is larger, more strongly vanilla-scented, and has anthers that diverge.

butterfly-like flower

slender, unlobed lip

PERENNIAL

narrow basal leaf

small anthers

NOTE

Many orchids, such as Lesser Butterfly Orchid, have a vanilla-like fragrance. The seed pod of a tropical orchid, carefully cured to intensify the flavour, is the vanilla pod used in cooking. The scent attracts night-flying moths, which pollinate the flowers.

PLANT HEIGHT *30–45cm.*
FLOWER SIZE *Lower lip 6–12mm long; spur 2.5–3cm.*
FLOWERING TIME *May–July.*
LEAVES *Basal, oblong.*
FRUIT *Capsule containing many tiny seeds.*
SIMILAR SPECIES *Greater Butterfly Orchid (P. chlorantha), which is larger in all parts and the flowers have a stronger, richer fragrance. It occurs mostly on alkaline soils.*

Fragrant Orchid

Gymnadenia conopsea (Orchidaceae)

This orchid's densely packed flowering spikes vary in size, but always have a delicate vanilla scent. Each pink, sometimes lilac, flower has a lower lip with three small, round lobes, wing-like sepals at either side, and a long, slender curving spur drooping down behind. The linear leaves are bright green, without any spots or markings, and are grooved along the middle.

SEEN *singly or in large, loose colonies on dry grassland and scrub, preferring slopes on chalky soil; also in undisturbed fens.*

small flowers in dense spikes

long, narrow leaf

3-lobed lower lip

long spur

erect stem

PERENNIAL

PLANT HEIGHT *20–40cm*
FLOWER SIZE *Lower lip 4–6mm long.*
FLOWERING TIME *June–July.*
LEAVES *Alternate, simple, and linear.*
FRUIT *Capsule containing many tiny seeds*
SIMILAR SPECIES *Pyramidal Orchid (p.437), which has shorter, more conical flower spikes of a darker colour.*

LADY'S SLIPPER ORCHID

W ith some justification the Lady's Slipper Orchid may be said to be Britain's rarest flower. For decades the plant, which was widespread across northern England, was taken from the wild by Victorian plant collectors – a craze that was termed "orchidelirium" at the time. By 1917 the plant was declared extinct in Britain. However, in 1930, a single specimen was found by a botanist in North Yorkshire, who informed a few trusted friends and the Cypripedium Committee (named after the genus of the orchid family that the Lady's Slipper belongs to) was created. Since then the committee has kept the location of that plant a closely guarded secret, known only by a handful of botanists who watch over it round-the-clock during the flowering season. This precarious situation was addressed in 1983 when the Sainsbury Orchid Conservation Project began at the Royal Botanic Gardens, Kew. It took some years to perfect techniques to germinate the seeds, but now hundreds of British gene-stock Lady's Slipper Orchid seedlings have been planted out in several secret locations in northern England, with flowers now beginning to appear. It is hoped that one day this exquisite plant will be widespread enough for the general public to be able to enjoy it in the wild again.

Common Spotted Orchid

Dactylorhiza fuchsii (Orchidaceae)

Even before the flowering spike has developed, this orchid is identifiable by the dark, rounded blotches on its shiny, deep green leaves. Borne in spikes, the flowers have wing-like sepals set high up, and a lower lip deeply lobed into three and patterned with looping lines and dots. The colour of the petals ranges from white and pink to reddish purple, but always with the dots on the lower lip.

OCCURS *in colonies in open woods, meadows, fens, and marshes, on road verges and among scrub, on chalky soil.*

flowers in dense spikes

solitary stem

narrow leaf
rounded blotches

pattern on lip

PERENNIAL

PLANT HEIGHT 20–45cm.
FLOWER SIZE Lower lip 1–1.2cm long.
FLOWERING TIME June–July.
LEAVES Basal rosette at first, then alternate.
FRUIT Capsule containing many tiny seeds.
SIMILAR SPECIES Heath Spotted Orchid (D. maculata), which has circular, brown leaf spots and a shallow-lobed lip.

Lady Orchid

Orchis purpurea (Orchidaceae)

Largely restricted to Kent, Lady Orchid has flowers with a dark brownish purple hood formed by the upper petals and sepals. The pale pink lower lip is said to resemble a lady, with arms on either side and a wide skirt. It is lobed with a tiny, central tooth, and spotted with purple. The broad, shiny leaves are basal, with one or two small narrow leaves on the long stem.

FOUND *among grasses in woodland margins and glades, on road verges and hill slopes; prefers chalky soil.*

broad flower spike

PERENNIAL

dark purple-brown hood

broad leaf
purple spots on lip

solitary stem

PLANT HEIGHT 40–70cm.
FLOWER SIZE Lower lip 1–1.5cm long.
FLOWERING TIME May–June.
LEAVES Basal, oval to elliptical, shiny green.
FRUIT Capsule containing many tiny seeds.
SIMILAR SPECIES Burnt Orchid (O. ustulata), which is shorter, with very dark flower buds, giving it a scorched look.

Broad-leaved Marsh Orchid

Dactylorhiza majalis (Orchidaceae)

FORMS *loose, but sometimes extensive, colonies in damp meadows and marshes on chalky soil.*

This orchid is largely restricted to Ireland, but belongs to a group of closely related species, including Early Marsh Orchid (*D. incarnata*), Lapland Marsh Orchid (*D. lapponica*), Northern Marsh Orchid (*D. purpurella*), and Southern Marsh Orchid (*D. praetermissa*). These are usually separated by their range, but hybridize freely where ranges overlap, making identification difficult. This plant has a leafy stem, with broad, bluish green leaves, sometimes covered with dark brown spots. The flowers have upward-spreading sepals, and long bracts between the flowers. The lower lip of each has toothed side-lobes with dark markings, and a short, unmarked central lobe.

PERENNIAL

dense flowerhead

magenta or reddish purple flowers

NOTE

The Dactylorhiza species of orchid have finger-like tubers, while the Orchis species have two rounded tubers (orchis means testicle in Greek).

brick-red flower

folded lip

D. incarnata

barely lobed lip
D. lapponica

spotted leaf

D. lapponica

PLANT HEIGHT 30–75cm.
FLOWER SIZE Lower lip 9–10mm long.
FLOWERING TIME May–July.
LEAVES Alternate, oval to elliptical, bluish green and deeply spotted.
FRUIT Capsule containing many tiny seeds.
SIMILAR SPECIES Common Spotted Orchid (above); Early Purple Orchid (right); Northern (D. purpurella), Southern (D. praetermissa), and Early (D. incarnata) Marsh Orchids are shorter and have unspotted leaves.

Early Purple Orchid

Orchis mascula (Orchidaceae)

GROWS *singly or in loose colonies in semi-shady, grassy places such as woodland, scrub, and road verges, and sometimes out in open grassland.*

Often the first orchid to appear in spring, this plant may also be identified by the long, dark purple blotches on the dark green leaves. The lower lip of the flower appears narrow, as it is folded back, and it has a pale patch towards the base, with a variable amount of darker spots. The sepals, with a long spur behind them, are swept upwards like wings. Their fragrance is pleasant at first but soon degenerates to an animal-like odour. They often grow among Bluebells (p.426), flowering at the same time, but may also be seen in more open situations.

PERENNIAL

long, narrow spike of flowers

erect stem

long dark blotches

dark green leaf

upward-pointing spur

paler patch on lip

NOTE

The round tubers of the Early Purple Orchid contain a great deal of starch; traditionally, this was ground and mixed with milk, honey, and spices to make a nutritious drink called "salep".

PLANT HEIGHT 20–50cm.
FLOWER SIZE Lower lip 7–9mm long.
FLOWERING TIME April–May.
LEAVES Basal, lance-shaped.
FRUIT Capsule containing many tiny seeds.
SIMILAR SPECIES Green-winged Orchid (O. morio), which has green-tinged sepals with purple veins; Common Spotted (left), Broad-leaved (left), and Lapland Marsh (D. lapponica) Orchids all have spotted leaves.

Man Orchid

Aceras anthropophorum (Orchidaceae)

This orchid is not easy to spot as it tends to be hidden among other vegetation. Its flowers are greenish with red tinges and borne in a long spike. When seen close up, the individual flower is highly distinctive – the elongated lobes of the lower lip look like narrow arms and legs, while the upper sepals and petals appear to form a hood.

GROWS *in fairly open, dry, grassy places such as roadsides, downs, dunes, scrub, and woodland margins, on chalky soil.*

sepals and petals form hood

greenish flowers tinged red

crowded spike

unspotted, shiny green leaf

lip lobes resemble human limbs

long lower lip

PERENNIAL

PLANT HEIGHT *20–40cm.*
FLOWER SIZE *Lip 1.2–1.5cm long.*
FLOWERING TIME *May–June.*
LEAVES *Mostly basal, narrow and oblong.*
FRUIT *Many-seeded capsule.*
SIMILAR SPECIES *Common Twayblade (p.433) has a two-lobed green lip; Fly Orchid (below) has a dark lip and three green petals.*

Pyramidal Orchid

Anacamptis pyramidalis (Orchidaceae)

The triangular shape of the newly formed flower spike gives this plant its name. The small, neat flowers are pale pink or, more often, deep pink, or cerise. They have no veins or spots but each has a long, slender spur at the back, from which butterflies and moths sip nectar.

PROLIFERATES *in open, grassy places, lightly grazed pastures, dunes, downland, scrub, and on roadsides. Prefers well-drained, chalky soil.*

dense, conical flowerhead

tapered point

unspotted leaf

deep pink flower

PERENNIAL

sheath-like upper leaf

3-lobed lip

PLANT HEIGHT *20–40cm.*
FLOWER SIZE *Lip 6–8mm long.*
FLOWERING TIME *June–August.*
LEAVES *Alternate, lance-shaped, pale green.*
FRUIT *Capsule containing many tiny seeds.*
SIMILAR SPECIES *Fragrant Orchid (p.433), which has longer, cylindrical flower spikes that are lighter in colour.*

Fly Orchid

Ophrys insectifera (Orchidaceae)

Often hidden in shady undergrowth, this slender orchid can be difficult to spot. It has narrow, pale green leaves and a single long flower stalk bearing a loose spire of 2–12 narrow flowers that look like flies. They have green sepals and a long, three-lobed chocolate-brown lip with a violet patch (speculum).

FOUND *in semi-shaded grasses in woodland, coppices, road verges, and scrub; on chalky soil.*

green sepals

widely spaced flowers

violet patch

lobed lip resembles a fly

PERENNIAL

slender flower stalk

PLANT HEIGHT *30–60cm.*
FLOWER SIZE *Lip 9–13mm long.*
FLOWERING TIME *May–June.*
LEAVES *Alternate, simple, thin and narrow.*
FRUIT *Capsule containing many tiny seeds.*
SIMILAR SPECIES *Man Orchid (above); Bee Orchid (right); Early Spider Orchid (O. sphegodes) has a much larger lower lip.*

Bee Orchid

Ophrys apifera (Orchidaceae)

The *Ophrys* species of orchids have an unusual flower shape, which mimics the form of a bee or wasp. In most species, the flower is pollinated by male insects in search of a mate, but in the Bee Orchid – unusually – the flowers are almost always self-pollinated. The stem is slender with just a few flowers, borne in a loose spike. Each flower has three prominent pink sepals, a narrow green hood, and a large lip which is bulbous, slightly velvety, and dark chocolate brown. There is a distinctive shiny patch (speculum) on the lip of the flower, with a yellow U-shaped margin and two yellow dots.

INHABITS *woodland margins, meadows, embankments, and road verges, singly or in very loose colonies; prefers chalky soil.*

PERENNIAL

flowers in loose spikes

pale, leaf-like bracts

green hood

furry, dark brown lip

shiny, pale green leaf

leaf edges turned inwards

3 prominent pink sepals

yellow markings on lip

NOTE

A pallid, faintly coloured form occasionally occurs, with a yellowish lip and greenish yellow sepals, giving the flower a bleached appearance.

PLANT HEIGHT *25–45cm.*
FLOWER SIZE *Lower lip 1–1.3cm long.*
FLOWERING TIME *May–June.*
LEAVES *Mostly basal, forming loose rosettes, oval to lance-shaped; pale green.*
FRUIT *Capsule containing many tiny seeds.*
SIMILAR SPECIES *Fly Orchid (left); Late Spider Orchid (below), which has a broader lip with a small, central tooth.*

Late Spider Orchid

Ophrys fuciflora (Orchidaceae)

Similar in general appearance to the Bee Orchid (above), the flowers of this species have a much broader lower lip, often with a small, central, forward-pointing tooth. The central area of the lip (speculum) may be in the shape of an H or X; it has a dark, metallic blue sheen and is outlined with yellow. The narrow leaves are pale green.

OCCURS *in grassy places, such as road verges, woodland margins, meadows, pastures, and scrub, on chalky soil.*

uppermost bract

pink sepals

dark brown lower lip

flowers in loose clusters

PERENNIAL

PLANT HEIGHT *20–40cm.*
FLOWER SIZE *Lower lip 9–13mm long.*
FLOWERING TIME *June–July.*
LEAVES *Mainly basal, lance-shaped.*
FRUIT *Capsule containing many tiny seeds.*
SIMILAR SPECIES *Bee Orchid (above), which has a narrower lip; Early Spider Orchid (O. sphegodes), which has green sepals.*

PLANTS

OTHER PLANTS

There are several important groups of plants that often go unnoticed, not needing sweetly scented or brightly coloured flowers to attract insects in order to reproduce. The wind-pollinated grasses, sedges, rushes, and woodrushes are classed as flowering plants; ferns, clubmosses, horsetails, mosses, liverworts, and algae have no flowers. Grasses are among the most important plants, cultivated to provide grain, a staple food for mankind, and also fodder for livestock. Tall reeds shelter many animals and are used for water purification. Clubmosses, mosses, and liverworts are low-growing; ferns and horsetails are usually taller. The algae are an extremely varied group, of marine and freshwater plants, ranging from tiny single-celled organisms to huge seaweeds.

ALGAE

There are three main groups of seaweeds, green, brown, and red. Usually, these plants are attached at the base by a structure called a holdfast, which anchors them down.

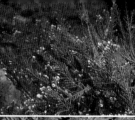

MOSSES

Often cushion-forming plants, mosses produce spores in capsules, requiring water to complete their reproductive cycle. The tiny leaves are usually only one cell thick. There are no true roots.

LIVERWORTS

The structure of liverworts is very variable and different groups are recognized. Some are very simple, without stems or leaves; others are more complex. The location of the reproductive organs varies.

FERNS

Ferns produce spores, contained in sporangia that are grouped together as sori, often covered by a flap, the indusium. Sori may be borne on normal fronds or on separate fertile fronds.

HORSETAILS

Some horsetails carry spore-bearing cones at the top of normal green stems, others produce separate unbranched, pinkish brown fertile stems. Green stems usually carry whorls of branches.

CLUBMOSSES

These creeping or epiphytic plants have small, scale-like leaves arranged spirally on the stem. They reproduce by means of spores, either clustered into small cones or borne in the leaf axils.

GRASSES

Grass flowers have small scales instead of petals. The flowers are usually grouped together in spikelets, which form the inflorescences. The base of each leaf blade usually has a small outgrowth, the ligule.

SEDGES

In sedges, a small scale, the glume, encloses a spikelet of petal-less flowers. The spikelet is often a single male or female flower. The spikelets are frequently grouped together in spikes.

RUSHES

The flowers of woodrushes and rushes consist of male and female parts surrounded by six brown or green segments. Rush leaves are cylindrical or flat; those of woodrushes are flat, with long white hairs.

Toothed Wrack

Fucus serratus (Phaeophyceae)

INHABITS *sheltered rocky shores; dominant below the Bladder Wrack zone.*

This seaweed is distinctive, flattened, and olive-green. The reproducing male plants, however, assume a golden colour from the swollen reproductive frond tips. After reproduction the fertile fronds are shed, and this, along with damage from storms, leads to a lower dominance of this species. The fronds are often covered by the white spiral tubes of the worm *Spirorbis spirorbis*.

frond split into two

PERENNIAL

serrated frond edge

SIZE *Length to 70cm, or up to 2m in very sheltered conditions; frond about 2cm wide.*
REPRODUCTION *May–October, peaking in late summer.*
DISTRIBUTION *All British and Irish coasts.*
SIMILAR SPECIES *None – the serrated frond margins distinguish it from the bladderless Horned Wrack (F. ceranoides), and Spiral Wrack (F. spiralis).*

Furbelows

Saccorhiza polyschides (Phaeophyceae)

FOUND *attached firmly to rocks at the low-water mark, and well into the sublittoral.*

Despite its considerable size, Furbelows is an annual plant. It has a very high growth rate in favourable conditions – growing 15cm a day at the peak. Its broad, flat, golden-brown fronds are divided into numerous strap-like lobes. It has a short, wavy-edged stem, and its hemispherical holdfast is covered in warty protuberances.

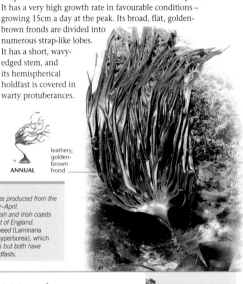

stem attached to holdfast

ANNUAL

leathery, golden-brown frond

SIZE *Length to 4.5m.*
REPRODUCTION *Spores produced from the stem and base, October–April.*
DISTRIBUTION *All British and Irish coasts except for the east coast of England.*
SIMILAR SPECIES *Oarweed (Laminaria digitata) and Cuvie (L. hyperborea), which also have digitate fronds but both have branching, root-like holdfasts.*

Bladder Wrack

Fucus vesiculosus (Phaeophyceae)

OCCURS *in the middle intertidal zone of rocky shores; also in estuaries and brackish water.*

A common mid-shore seaweed, the Bladder Wrack has distinctive pairs of gas-filled bladders on its fronds, on either side of the midrib. The bladders help the frond to reach sunlight at high tide, when light penetration is limited by sediment stirred up by waves. In season, the tips of the fronds develop swollen, warty, forked reproductive bodies.

almost spherical, paired gas bladders

dark olive-brown fronds

PERENNIAL

prominent midrib on frond

SIZE *Length to 1.5m; shorter with increased exposure.*
REPRODUCTION *Mid-winter to late summer.*
DISTRIBUTION *All British and Irish coasts.*
SIMILAR SPECIES *On exposed shores, a short, bladderless form occurs, which is similar to Horned Wrack (F. ceranoides), but the latter is found only in sheltered, low-salinity water.*

Knotted Wrack

Ascophyllum nodosum (Phaeophyceae)

OCCURS *on rocky shores, sometimes extending into estuaries.*

Sometimes known as Egg Wrack, the single, egg-shaped, gas-filled flotation bladders of the Knotted Wrack are found at intervals along the strap-like frond. It is often found on the mid-shore, brown seaweed zone, especially where it is sheltered. In exposed conditions, it still survives, but is reduced to a tattered tuft of stem bases.

older bladder

raisin-like reproductive bodies

PERENNIAL

young bladder

branched frond

SIZE *To 2m long, although can be longer in favoured areas.*
REPRODUCTION *April–June.*
DISTRIBUTION *All British and Irish coasts.*
SIMILAR SPECIES *None, although small, battered examples could be mistaken for Channelled Wrack (P. canaliculata), but the stalked reproductive bodies of Knotted Wrack are distinctive.*

Oarweed

Laminaria digitata (Laminariaceae)

ATTACHES *to rocks on the lower shore down to a depth of 20m in clear waters.*

Also known as Tangle or Sea Girdle, this familiar kelp attaches to rocks by means of a domed, claw-like holdfast, often home to colonies of barnacles and algae. The smooth, flexible stalk, or stipe, is oval in cross-section and gives rise to broad, glossy dark brown fronds that are divided into finger-like segments and lack a midrib.

glossy brown fronds

PERENNIAL

frond variably divided

frond battered by wave action

SIZE *Length to 2m.*
REPRODUCTION *By spores, year round.*
DISTRIBUTION *Common on all coasts of Britain and Ireland except Yorkshire to Kent.*
SIMILAR SPECIES *Young L. hyperborea, which has a brittle stipe that is circular in cross-section and lighter brown fronds; L. saccharina, which has unlobed fronds with ruffled edges.*

Channelled Wrack

Pelvetia canaliculata (Phaeophyceae)

FOUND *on upper rocky shores, from above the Fucus species up to the splash zone.*

An upper-shore brown seaweed, Channelled Wrack has tough fronds that lack a midrib and are curled over lengthwise to create a channel, perhaps to help conserve water. The colour is brown-black when dry, which the plant often is at its usual location on the shore. It is highly resistant to desiccation, capable of tolerating 65 per cent water loss. In fact, permanent immersion is sufficient to kill it.

tufted growth form

curled frond edges

reproductive body on frond tip

PERENNIAL

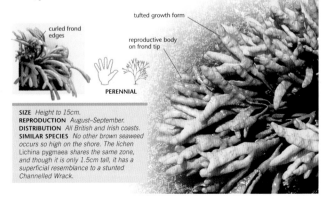

SIZE *Height to 15cm.*
REPRODUCTION *August–September.*
DISTRIBUTION *All British and Irish coasts.*
SIMILAR SPECIES *No other brown seaweed occurs so high on the shore. The lichen Lichina pygmaea shares the same zone, and though it is only 1.5cm tall, it has a superficial resemblance to a stunted Channelled Wrack.*

Carragheen

Chondrus crispus (Rhodophyceae)

With flat fronds, dividing into two up to five times, Carragheen, or Irish Moss, is fan-shaped. However, its shape, size, and colour vary according to habitat conditions: smaller plants with narrower lobes are found in more exposed conditions. It turns green in strong sunlight. Underwater, the tips of the fronds are often iridescent.

OCCURS *on rocky shores, at lower intertidal levels, in rock pools, and estuaries.*

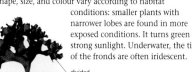

narrow stalk

divided fronds

rounded frond tips

flat fronds

fronds usually purplish red

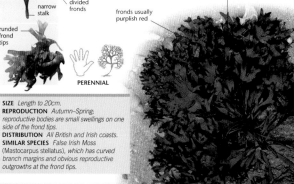

PERENNIAL

SIZE *Length to 20cm.*
REPRODUCTION *Autumn–Spring; reproductive bodies are small swellings on one side of the frond tips.*
DISTRIBUTION *All British and Irish coasts.*
SIMILAR SPECIES *False Irish Moss (Mastocarpus stellatus), which has curved branch margins and obvious reproductive outgrowths at the frond tips.*

Coral Weed

Corallina officinalis (Corallinaceae)

GROWS *on rocky shores, attached to rocks in rock pools on middle and lower shore.*

Usually purple-pink in colour, but paler when growing in strong light, Coral Weed is a small, tufted, calcareous alga, common in mid- and lower-shore rock pools. The rigid fronds bear opposite pairs of branches, growing in a flat plane, and these in turn produce opposite branchlets, also in a flat plane. The plant consists of many tiny, calcified, cylindrical segments, joined together like strings of beads, with uncalcified joints linking the segments. Its branches are too hard for most marine grazers and it is generally left alone.

tiny segments

BLEACHED BY LIGHT

whiter growing tips

PERENNIAL

NOTE

While it may not be valuable as food for most other marine life, the nooks and crannies and accumulation of sediments that build up around this alga provide valuable shelter for crustaceans and other animals.

SIZE *Length to 12cm long, usually less.*
REPRODUCTION *Urn-shaped reproductive bodies produced near the tips of the fronds; November–March.*
DISTRIBUTION *All British and Irish coasts.*
SIMILAR SPECIES *C. elongata, which is more densely tufted and found only in the south-west; Lomentaria articulata, which is segmented, but not calcified; Jania rubens, which is less branched.*

Gut Weed

Enteromorpha intestinalis (Ulvophyceae)

Previously and perhaps more commonly known as *Enteromorpha intestinalis*, Gut Weed forms an inflated, irregularly constricted, tube-like frond, resembling an intestine. Its holdfast is small and disc-like, and may become detached from the rock allowing this seaweed to rise to the water surface, where it continues to grow in floating masses. It requires high nutrient levels, and so is very well developed near sewage outfalls or other nutrient-rich discharges from the land. This seaweed blankets estuarine mudflats, especially in late summer, and is a favoured food of grazing ducks and geese.

ATTACHES *to rocks and stones on sandy or muddy shores; abundant in low-salinity areas.*

ANNUAL

pale to bright green fronds

irregular constrictions

unbranched fronds

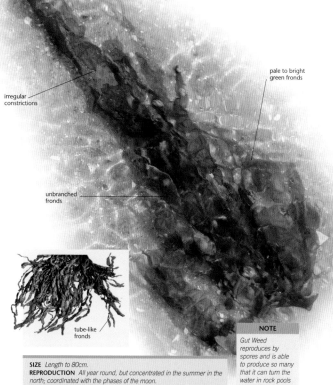

tube-like fronds

SIZE *Length to 80cm.*
REPRODUCTION *All year round, but concentrated in the summer in the north; coordinated with the phases of the moon.*
DISTRIBUTION *All British and Irish coasts.*
SIMILAR SPECIES *Other members of the genus Enteromorpha can be very similar and difficult to tell apart. E. compressa and E. linza are both common and widespread around the British coast; E. linza has flattened, crinkly fronds; E. compressa, is also flat, often with branched fronds.*

NOTE

Gut Weed reproduces by spores and is able to produce so many that it can turn the water in rock pools green. As an annual, it decays at the end of its lifecycle forming bleached masses along the high-tide line.

Sea-lettuce

Ulva lactuca (Ulvophyceae)

TOLERATES *brackish water; found in estuaries and on rocky shores; also free-floating.*

A widespread green seaweed, tolerant of most conditions except extreme exposure, Sea-lettuce is found throughout the intertidal zone. It thrives especially in brackish water, but is also found in shallow inshore waters. Its flat frond is often split or divided, and has a wavy edge. Fertile plants are sometimes recognizable by changes to the marginal colour of the frond, becoming yellowish green in male plants and dark green in the female.

translucent green frond

wavy edge

dark green female plant

PERENNIAL

SIZE *Length to 40cm.*
REPRODUCTION *Vegetative and sexual; all year round.*
DISTRIBUTION *Ubiquitous on all British and Irish coasts.*
SIMILAR SPECIES *Monostroma grevillei, which is smaller, funnel-shaped; Udotea petiolata, which has long-stalked fronds.*

Bog Moss

Sphagnum palustre (Sphagnaceae)

One of the commonest mosses, occurring throughout the British Isles, Bog Moss, one of several closely related sphagnum mosses, can tolerate a wide range of dampness. The unique character of these mosses is that the individual stems continue growing upwards while the lowest parts die back to form peat. They can hold up to 20 times their own weight in water – each tiny leaf contains some empty cells and acts like a sponge. Bog Moss has robust, branched stems, crowded with concave leaves.

OCCURS *in wet places such as bogs, fens, damp hollows, and flushes in woods on wet heaths.*

whitish green leaves

SIZE *Stems to 25cm high.*
REPRODUCTION *Small black spore-producing capsules in summer.*
DISTRIBUTION *Throughout the British Isles; internationally important populations found in Britain and Ireland.*
SIMILAR SPECIES *Distinguishing Sphagnum species often needs microscopic examination.*

Mnium hornum

Mnium hornum (Mniaceae)

This very common woodland moss can be seen in most woods in the British Isles. In spring, the pale green young leaves contrast strongly with the rather dull, darker older leaves. Individual plants are either male or female, the females, producing spore-bearing cylindrical capsules borne on reddish stalks.

FOUND *on soil, rocks, and tree bases, in all types of woodland with acidic conditions.*

leaves taper at tip

toothed leaves

pendulous capsule

SIZE *Individual stems to 4cm high, leaves 4–5mm long.*
REPRODUCTION *Cylindrical fruiting capsules borne on 2–6-cm long reddish stalks.*
DISTRIBUTION *Throughout the British Isles.*
SIMILAR SPECIES *Catherine's Moss (Atrichum undulatum), which has narrow, wavy-edged leaves and curved capsules.*

Common Hair Cap

Polytrichum commune (Polytrichaceae)

Easily recognized, no other moss forms such tall tussocks as the Common Hair Cap. It has strong, erect stems and toothed leaves, each with a transparent sheathing base. The fruiting capsules, with their golden pointed caps, are a common sight in summer, young capsules being particularly conspicuous as they are covered by a golden-haired cover or calyptra.

FORMS *tussocks in bogs, damp heath, moorland, and in damp acid flushes in woodland.*

box-shaped capsule

stalk up to 12cm

narrow leaves

SIZE *Erect stems to 50cm high.*
REPRODUCTION *Spores in beaked, box-shaped, long-stalked fruiting capsules.*
DISTRIBUTION *Throughout the British Isles.*
SIMILAR SPECIES *Polytrichum formosum, which is similar in appearance when it is in luxuriant growth, but has shorter stems and capsule stalks.*

Tortula muralis

Tortula muralis (Pottiaceae)

An extremely common moss, even in urban areas, *Tortula muralis* has narrow, tongue-shaped leaves with a long, white hairpoint at the leaf tip. When dry, the hairpoints of the curled and twisted leaves make the moss cushions appear grey. Abundant narrowly cylindrical, erect capsules are borne on a stalk 1–2cm long, which is yellowish at first but turns purple brown with age.

FORMS *cushions on walls; common in towns and favours manmade habitats.*

white hairpoint

erect capsules

cushion-like growth

curved leaves

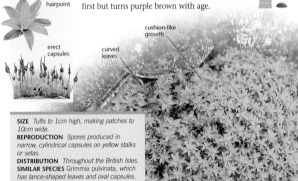

SIZE *Tufts to 1cm high, making patches to 10cm wide.*
REPRODUCTION *Spores produced in narrow, cylindrical capsules on yellow stalks or setas.*
DISTRIBUTION *Throughout the British Isles.*
SIMILAR SPECIES *Grimmia pulvinata, which has lance-shaped leaves and oval capsules.*

Large White-moss

Leucobryum glaucum (Leucobryaceae)

The Large White-moss can be easily recognized, even from a distance. The individual stems support lance-shaped leaves that taper from a broad base to a pointed tip. The tightly packed, greyish green cushions, which form patches, are only very loosely attached to the soil and occasionally become detached. They can continue to survive and if the cushions overturn, they can form "moss balls".

INHABITS *woodland floors, under beech, oak, and conifers, and bare peaty slopes and bogs in moorland.*

moss ball

dense cushion

SIZE *Patches varying from a few centimetres to 1m wide.*
REPRODUCTION *Fruiting capsules are rarely produced, in autumn.*
DISTRIBUTION *Throughout the British Isles, especially associated with beech woods.*
SIMILAR SPECIES *None.*

Grimmia pulvinata

Grimmia pulvinata (Grimmiaceae)

The greyish, hedgehog-like cushions of *Grimmia pulvinata* are one of the most common and distinctive mosses on wall tops or rocks. The closely crowded oblong, lance-shaped leaves have a long silvery hairpoint at the tip, which is often as long as the leaf itself. At an early stage, the long curved stalks appear to bury the fruiting capsules among the leaves, but these gradually straighten with age.

FOUND *in limestone areas, but will tolerate more acidic habitats such as brick walls.*

capsules buried among leaves

silvery hairpoints

SIZE *Individual stems to 1cm tall.*
REPRODUCTION *Spores in beaked, oval, grooved capsules produced on long, very curved stalks in spring.*
DISTRIBUTION *Lowland areas of the British Isles, scarce in the north and west.*
SIMILAR SPECIES *Schistidium apocarpum, which forms looser green-brown cushions.*

Cord Moss

Funaria hygrometrica (Funariaceae)

A common, tufted species, Cord Moss has sharp-tipped leaves, the upper ones being larger. Its favoured habitat is bonfire sites, where it forms pale green carpets with a profusion of pear-shaped capsules on yellow stalks. The capsules are green at first, changing to yellow-brown, and becoming strongly furrowed and brown when fully mature.

COLONIZES *bare soil in woods, moorland, heaths, greenhouses, and gardens; cracks on roadsides, and bonfire sites.*

immature green capsule

mature brown capsules

yellow stalk

SIZE *Tufts 2–15mm high.*
REPRODUCTION *Spores produced in pear-shaped capsules on long stalk or seta to 3–5cm tall.*
DISTRIBUTION *Throughout the British Isles.*
SIMILAR SPECIES *Leptobryum pyriforme, which is less common and has extremely narrow leaves and glossy red-brown capsules.*

Eurhynchium praelongum

Eurhynchium praelongum (Brachytheciaceae)

This feathery moss grows in untidy, widely spreading, dull green patches and is often the only moss in heavily shaded places. Its stems are pinnately branched. The leaves have toothed margins; those growing on the main stem are heart-shaped, while those on the branches are narrower and lance-shaped.

ABUNDANT *in shady places, on ground under shrubs and trees, tree bases, and streamsides.*

pinnate stems

pointed leaves

SIZE *To 4cm high, branches to 12cm long.*
REPRODUCTION *Long-beaked fruiting capsules on reddish stalks; very rare.*
DISTRIBUTION *Throughout the British Isles.*
SIMILAR SPECIES *E. swartzii, which is brighter yellowish green and less regularly branched; the branch leaves are similar in shape to the stem leaves.*

Hypnum cupressiforme

Hypnum cupressiforme (Hypnaceae)

There are several common species of *Hypnum*, all of which are regularly branched, with closely overlapping, downcurved leaves. A good guide to identification, this arrangement resembles the branchlets of cypress trees. The finely tipped, oval leaves are particularly conspicuous at the ends of the branches. *Hypnum cupressiforme* has slightly curved, short, cylindrical fruiting capsules on red stalks, which are often seen in autumn and winter.

FORMS *dark green mats on lower parts of broadleaved trees and rocks in woodland.*

overlapping leaves

cylindrical capsule

red stalk

SIZE *Stems up to 10cm.*
REPRODUCTION *Slightly curved, spore-producing capsules on red stalks.*
DISTRIBUTION *Throughout the British Isles.*
SIMILAR SPECIES *H. jutlandicum, which is more slender, with erect stems, and has strongly downcurved leaves that give a hooked appearance to the silky shoot tips.*

Common Tamasisk Moss

Thuidium tamariscinum (Thuidiaceae)

The stems of this species are regularly branched into three divisions, giving it a very fern-like appearance. The bright green or golden "fronds" are roughly triangular in outline. The main stems are dark green or almost black, with broadly triangular or heart-shaped leaves; the leaves on the branches are narrower, tapering to a long point. All the leaves are toothed towards the tip.

GROWS *in shady places on the ground in woodland, particularly on heavy clay soil.*

fern-like appearance

SIZE *To 2–3cm high, branches to 20cm long.*
REPRODUCTION *Fruit capsules are extremely rare.*
DISTRIBUTION *Throughout the British Isles.*
SIMILAR SPECIES *Hylocomnium splendens, which has distinctive red stems and is particularly common in upland woods in the north and west of the British Isles.*

Brachythecium rutabulum

Brachythecium rutabulum (Brachytheciaceae)

Robust and extremely common, this moss is abundant, particularly in lowland habitats. Its glossy, golden, or pale green leaves are oval, sharply pointed, and very finely toothed along the edges. The leafy, branching shoots of this tuft-forming or straggling moss taper to a fine point. Beak-shaped fruit capsules are produced on rough, slender, reddish stalks above the leaves.

GROWS *on rocks and wood, cliffs, and trees, in woodland, lawns, and bogs.*

downcurved capsule

long stalks

glossy leaves

SIZE *Leaves 2–3mm long.*
REPRODUCTION *Spore-producing capsules appear in spring, autumn, and winter.*
DISTRIBUTION *Throughout the British Isles.*
SIMILAR SPECIES *B. rivale, which is similar in structure but is a glossy golden-green in colour and prefers damper places and fruiting capsules are rare.*

Pseudoscleropodium purum

Pseudoscleropodium purum (Brachytheciaceae)

Nicknamed "Juicy Lucy" for its extremely glossy yellow-green shoots, this plant has robust, pinnately branched, pale stems and crowded concave leaves that make large wefts within grassland.

ABUNDANT *in open grassland and woods; common on acid heaths and chalk downland.*

glossy stems

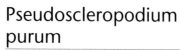

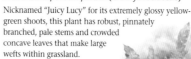

tiny crowded leaves

SIZE *Stems to 15cm long, leaves to 2mm.*
REPRODUCTION *Fruiting capsules are rarely produced; it is probably spread by pieces being dispersed by birds and mammals.*
DISTRIBUTION *Throughout the British Isles.*
SIMILAR SPECIES *Pleurozium schreberi, which has distinctly red stems and only grows in acid heaths.*

Marchantia polymorpha

Marchantia polymorpha (Marchantiaceae)

One of Britain's commonest liverworts, this shiny green, ribbon-like plant grows in a wide range of damp habitats. Its stems are anchored by root-like hairs, and they repeatedly divide in two as they grow. This way of growing – shared by many liverworts – produces a plant that gradually spreads in all directions. Throughout the year, the plant reproduces asexually by forming objects called gemmae, which look like tiny green eggs. However, in spring and summer, it sprouts male and female reproductive structures with stalks. The female ones have ribs, which look like the struts of tiny parasols.

FOUND *in marshy ground and wet streamsides, on soil in flowerpots, outside or under glass.*

NOTE

Gemmae form in cups on the surface of the plant. If a raindrop lands in a cup, its gemmae are dislodged, and thrown clear of the parent plant. They start growing, and produce new plants.

spores released from underside

female structure

female reproductive structure with spreading rays

cup containing gemmae

SIZE *Width of stem (thallus) 1–3cm.*
STEM *Glossy dark to light green, with a central midrib. Surface has a hexagonal pattern, created by internal air chambers.*
REPRODUCTIVE STRUCTURES *Male: stalked, with a terminal disc that has scalloped edges; female: stalked with 8–10 terminal rays. Both are 3–4cm high.*
DISTRIBUTION *Throughout the British Isles.*
SIMILAR SPECIES *Crescent-cup Liverwort (below) has narrower ribbons.*

Crescent-cup Liverwort

Lunularia cruciata (Lunulariaceae)

A familiar sight in greenhouses and damp corners in gardens, this bright green liverwort is thought to have arrived in Britain in Roman times. It gets its name from its crescent-shaped gemmae cups – reproductive structures that look like minute fingernails. Like other ribbon-shaped liverworts, it grows by repeatedly dividing in two, but it rarely forms spores.

GROWS *along shady stream-banks, but is more often found in flowerpots and under glass.*

densely-branched stems often overlap

Gemmae produced in cups

SIZE *Width of stem (thallus) 0.5–1cm; spread 5–15cm.*
STEM *Bright green, except when dry, without a pronounced midrib.*
REPRODUCTIVE STRUCTURES *Crescent-shaped gemma cups.*
DISTRIBUTION *Throughout the British Isles.*
SIMILAR SPECIES *None.*

Pellia epiphylla

Pellia epiphylla (Pelliaceae)

In early spring, this shade-loving liverwort is often covered with black spore capsules, which grow on translucent hair-like stalks. The plant itself is a deep glossy green. Given enough space, its stems lie flat, but when crowded the plant often becomes cushion-like, as the stems arch upwards to catch the light. The capsules split open when the spores are ripe, revealing a tuft of brownish hairs.

FREQUENTLY *seen on damp, acidic ground close to streams, and in waterlogged soil in upland areas. Absent from limestone regions.*

lobes often overlap

spore capsule

slender translucent stalk

SIZE *Width of stem (thallus) 0.5–1cm.*
STEM *Deep green without any conspicuous surface markings.*
REPRODUCTIVE STRUCTURES *Female spore-producing structures are stalked; male structures are on surface of plant.*
DISTRIBUTION *Throughout the British Isles.*
SIMILAR SPECIES *P. endiviifolia.*

Leafy Liverwort

Lophocolea cuspidata (Geocalycaceae)

Often mistaken for a moss, this liverwort is a common inhabitant of damp woodland and grassy areas. Like other leafy liverworts, it has trailing stems with tiny leaves, each made of a single layer of cells. In this species, the leaves are arranged in two main ranks, and each one has a pair of teeth. The plant divides as it grows, and if it has sufficient space it eventually forms a springy tuft. It reproduces in two ways – by breaking off fragments, or by releasing spores. The spores are formed in black capsules, which develop on slender translucent stalks.

GROWS *in damp grass, on rotting logs, and in many other places that are open but frequently wet or waterlogged.*

spore capsule

slender supporting stalk

each leaf has two points

leaves overlap

NOTE

Most leafy liverworts have their main leaves arranged in two opposite rows, with a third row of smaller leaves on their underside. Mosses usually have a spiral of leaves winding around the central stem.

SIZE *Leaves 2–4mm long, with two teeth, individual stems to 3cm.*
REPRODUCTIVE STRUCTURES *Spores are produced in black capsules which split open when ripe. Stalks up to 3cm long.*
DISTRIBUTION *Throughout the British Isles.*
SIMILAR SPECIES *A number of similar species live in damp grassland, on fallen logs, and on shaded tree-trunks. Lophocolea bidentata – is the commonest leafy liverwort of lawns. Some leafy liverworts are more flattened, and cling firmly to rocks or bark.*

Bracken

Pteridium aquilinum (Dennstaedtiaceae)

Often covering entire hillsides, Bracken is difficult to eradicate and is regarded as a pest. It grows from widely creeping, branching rhizomes, which produce numerous tall, sturdy fronds. The young, pale green, tri-pinnate fronds first appear as "shepherds' crooks", unfurling as they grow. The undersides of the blades are hairy; the upper sides darker, leathery, and hairless. Pinnule margins are untoothed and inrolled, covering the sori. The dead brown fronds remain on the plant throughout winter.

GROWS *abundantly on open hillsides, moors, and heaths, in neglected pastures and open woods, usually on acid soil.*

NOTE

Bracken is the only fern that grows in closed communities. It can carpet the whole forest floor in open woodland or cover dry heathland.

sturdy frond

unfurling pinnae

autumn colour

sori covered by inrolled edge

PLANT HEIGHT *Up to 4m.*
FROND DIVISION *Tripinnate.*
SORI *Continuous around, and covered by inrolled pinnule margins.*
SPORES RIPE *August–October.*
DISTRIBUTION *Throughout the British Isles. Bracken is a truly cosmopolitan plant and is found on every continent apart from Antarctica. It can tolerate an incredibly wide range of climates.*
SIMILAR SPECIES *None.*

Broad Buckler-fern

Dryopteris dilatata

The distinctive, pointed scales on the frond stalks of Broad Buckler-fern are dark brown in the centre and pale brown on the margins. Overwintering, dark green fronds grow from the rootstock in a shuttlecock-shaped tuft, which spread out later. The lowest pinnae are longest, giving the blade a triangular outline. Sori occur on either side of the pinnule midrib.

GROWS *in woods, hedgebanks, and rock crevices on moors and heaths.*

two rows of sori

scale with dark centre and pale edges

pointed frond

PLANT HEIGHT *Up to 1.5m.*
FROND DIVISION *Usually tri-pinnate.*
SORI *In two rows on either side of pinnule margin, covered by a kidney-shaped indusium.*
SPORES RIPE *July–September.*
DISTRIBUTION *Throughout British Isles.*
SIMILAR SPECIES *Narrow Buckler-fern (D. carthusiana).*

Lady Fern

Athyrium filix-femina (Woodsiaceae)

An elegant species, Lady Fern has pointed, deeply divided pinnules, and is pale green in colour. The drooping fronds grow in tufts, dying in autumn. There are brownish scales on the frond stalks. Sori are borne in two rows on either side of the pinnule midrib, and have a distinctive long and curved shape. Each sorus is covered by an indusium with the same crescent-like shape.

FAVOURS *acid soils, growing in damp woods, rocky places, and marshes.*

frond drooping at tip

long, curved sori

PLANT HEIGHT *Frond length to 1m, sometimes to 1.5m.*
FROND DIVISION *Usually bi-pinnate.*
SORI *Curved, on either side of the pinnule midrib, with a crescent-shaped indusium.*
DISTRIBUTION *Throughout the British Isles.*
SIMILAR SPECIES *Alpine Lady Fern (A. distentifolium).*

Male Fern

Dryopteris filix-mas (Dryopteridaceae)

One of Britain's commonest ferns, the Male Fern has a tuft of fronds, shaped like a large shuttlecock, arising from its rootstock. Pointed, pale brown scales grow on the stalks. The bi-pinnate frond blade tapers at both ends and is mid-green in colour. Individual pinnules have broad bases, blunt tips, and toothed margins.

FLOURISHES *in woods, hedgebanks, and screes, and among rocks.*

fronds arranged like a shuttlecock

large sori close to midrib

unfurled young frond

PLANT HEIGHT *Up to 1.2m.*
FROND DIVISION *Bipinnate.*
SORI *On veins on the underside of pinnule, covered by a kidney-shaped indusium.*
SPORES RIPE *August–November.*
DISTRIBUTION *Throughout the British Isles.*
SIMILAR SPECIES *Several Dryopteris species, especially Golden-scaled Male Fern (D. affinis).*

Soft Shield-fern

Polystichum setiferum (Dryopteridaceae)

The fronds of Soft Shield-fern grow in a drooping circle around the top of the rootstock. Large, pale brown, sharply pointed scales clothe the stalk. The bi-pinnate frond blade is soft, coloured mid-green above and paler beneath, especially when fresh. The pinnules have short stalks and a blunt angle at the base, with a much enlarged lobe on one side. The pinnule teeth end in fine hair-like points.

PREFERS *wetter areas, growing in woods, hedge banks, and rocky places.*

pinnule teeth with hair-like points

dopping frond tip

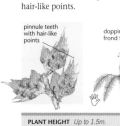

PLANT HEIGHT *Up to 1.5m.*
FROND DIVISION *Bipinnate.*
SORI *On either side of pinnule midrib; covered by a round indusium.*
SPORES RIPE *July–September.*
DISTRIBUTION *England, Wales, southern Scotland and Ireland.*
SIMILAR SPECIES *P. aculeatum.*

OTHER PLANTS

Young Ferns
Tightly curled as they first emerge, fern fronds unfurl as they mature. Superficially similar to the Male Fern, the leaves of this Lemon-scented Fern (*Oreopteris limbosperma*) smell of lemons if crushed.

Hard Fern

Blechnum spicant (Blechnaceae)

Hard Fern is a distinctive, tufted species with two types of frond. Bright green, shiny, sterile fronds spread out over the ground, forming rosettes, and surround erect, narrow, fertile fronds. Both types of blade are pinnate and hairless, the fertile fronds bearing linear sori, extending from the pinna base to its tip and covered by linear indusia. The sterile fronds are evergreen, while the fertile ones die in autumn.

FAVOURS *acid soils, on heaths and moors and in woods, especially in upland areas.*

tufted growth

SIZE *Sterile fronds to 15cm, fertile fronds to 75cm.*
FROND DIVISION *Pinnate.*
SORI *Linear, extending the length of the pinna, with a linear indusium.*
SPORES RIPE *August–November.*
DISTRIBUTION *Throughout the British Isles.*
SIMILAR SPECIES *None.*

Wall-rue

Asplenium ruta-muraria (Aspleniaceae)

The dark-based stalks of Wall-rue are often longer than the leaves. Persisting through the winter, the fronds grow in dense tufts and are dark green and tough. The leaflets are fan-shaped, their pinnules varying in shape, with wedge-shaped bases and rounded teeth on the edges. Linear sori are situated on the veins on the lower surface of the pinnules.

LIVES *in calcareous areas, on walls, rocks, and limestone pavements; on cracks in walls in acid soil.*

sori on veins of pinnules

dark green fronds

fan-shaped pinna

SIZE *Frond height to 15cm, usually less than 10cm.*
FROND DIVISION *Usually bipinnate.*
SORI *On veins on lower surface of pinnules.*
SPORES RIPE *June–October.*
DISTRIBUTION *Throughout; absent from much of Scotland.*
SIMILAR SPECIES *None.*

Common Polypody

Polypodium vulgare (Polypodiaceae)

Common Polypody is seen in small groups of evergreen fronds. The pinnae are straight-sided, shallowly toothed and almost joined at the base, often with blunt tips. Most of the pinnae are of equal length, tapering gradually along the final quarter or so of the blade to the tip. Round sori are borne on either side of the midrib, with no indusia.

PREFERS *acid soils, and is found growing on tree trunks, walls, rocks, and banks.*

pinnae almost joined at base

round sori

SIZE *Frond length to 25cm.*
FROND DIVISION *Pinnate.*
SORI *Round, on either side of the midrib, without an indusium.*
SPORES RIPE *July–September.*
DISTRIBUTION *Throughout the British Isles.*
SIMILAR SPECIES: *Western (P. interjectum) and Southern Polypody (P. cambricum).*

Maidenhair Spleenwort

Asplenium trichomanes (Aspleniaceae)

This attractive, evergreen fern bears tufts of pinnate fronds. The short stalk is purplish black or brownish, hairless, and shiny, and the midrib has the same characteristics. Small, rounded, slightly toothed pinnae grow from each side of the midrib, giving the frond a long, linear outline. Linear sori lie between the midrib and the pinna margin, each covered by a linear indusium.

GROWS *in walls, on ledges, or in crevices between rocks or stones.*

rounded pinnae

linear sori

dark stalk

SIZE *Frond length to 20cm.*
FROND DIVISION *Pinnate.*
SORI *Linear, between midrib and pinna edge.*
SPORES RIPE *August–November.*
DISTRIBUTION *Throughout the British Isles.*
SIMILAR SPECIES *Green Spleenwort (A. viride), which has a green midrib and stalk.*

Hart's-tongue

Phyllitis scolopendrium (Aspleniaceae)

Even in the depths of winter, the glossy, bright green fronds of Hart's-tongue brighten up dark corners in woods and rocky places, growing in dense tufts. The stalk is clothed with sharply pointed brown scales, and both stalk and midrib are dark purple-brown, becoming green towards the tip. The blade is strap-shaped and undivided, usually with wavy margins.

GROWS *in woods, hedgebanks, rocky places, and on damp walls.*

wavy margin on blade

sporangia in parallel rows

SIZE *Frond length to 50cm.*
FROND DIVISION *Undivided, strap-shaped.*
SORI *Linear, in pairs along the underside of veins, each covered by a linear indusium.*
SPORES RIPE *July–November.*
DISTRIBUTION *Throughout; absent from most of northern Scotland.*
SIMILAR SPECIES *None.*

Adder's-tongue

Ophioglossum vulgatum (Ophioglossaceae)

An unusual looking plant, the fertile fronds of Adder's-tongue consist of two blades, one fertile and the other sterile. Barren fronds, lacking a fertile blade, are also produced. The fronds are commonly solitary. The sterile blade is undivided, hairless, and fleshy. Sporangia are borne on either side of the axis of the narrow, fertile blade, which ends in a sterile tip.

FAVOURS *damp, grassy places, old meadows and dune slacks.*

undivided sterile blade

sporangia on fertile blade

spike-like fertile blade

SIZE *Frond length to 30cm, usually less.*
FROND DIVISION *One sterile blade and one fertile blade to each fertile frond.*
SPORANGIA *In two rows on the fertile blade.*
SPORES RIPE *June–August.*
DISTRIBUTION *Throughout, except for most of northern Scotland.*
SIMILAR SPECIES *O. azoricum.*

Common Horsetail

Equisetum arvense (Equisetaceae)

In spring, the pale, pinkish brown, fertile stems of Common Horsetail, also called Field Horsetail, appear above ground. As they wither, the plant produces green, sterile stems. The fertile stems are unbranched and fleshy, with toothed sheaths covering the stem joints. Each fertile stem has at its tip a long, blunt-ended reproductive cone that bears the sporangia.

FLOURISHES *in damp, grassy and waste places and cultivated ground.*

branched sterile stem

fleshy fertile stem

round-tipped cone

SIZE *Fertile stems to 25cm, sterile to 80cm.*
BRANCHES *Simple, rigid.*
CONES *On fertile stems, which appear before the sterile stems.*
SPORES RIPE *April–May.*
DISTRIBUTION *Throughout the British Isles.*
SIMILAR SPECIES *Other horsetails, especially Great Horsetail (below).*

Great Horsetail

Equisetum telmateia (Equisetaceae)

A robust, patch-forming perennial of damp places, the Great Horsetail is the largest British species of this prehistoric group of plants, which once dominated the Earth. It has distinctive fertile and sterile shoots. The unbranched, white fertile shoots, topped with a spore cone, usually emerge in spring before the more persistent, "bottlebrush-like" sterile summer shoots.

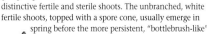

THRIVES *in damp areas with soft soil, such as clay.*

slender cone at top of fertile stem

tall sterile stem

green branches in dense whorls

stout whitish stem

SIZE *Sterile stems to 1.5m, occasionally more; fertile stems to 50cm tall.*
BRANCHES *In whorls at each stem joint.*
CONES *Narrowly conical, to 8cm long, on end of fertile stems.*
SPORES RIPE *March–April.*
DISTRIBUTION *Throughout, except for most of Scotland.*
SIMILAR SPECIES *Common Horsetail (above).*

Marsh Horsetail

Equisetum palustre (Equisetaceae)

The fertile stems of Marsh Horsetail are similar to the sterile stems in appearance, but have a reproductive cone at their tip. Both types of stem are green, with rounded ridges, and whorls of erect branches. The sheaths covering the joints on the stem are green and toothed, the teeth having black centres and pale margins. The sheaths on the branches have black teeth.

GROWS *in bogs, marshes, ditches, and wet grassland.*

dark teeth on sheaths

toothed sheath on fertile stem

pointed cone tip

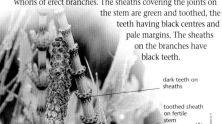

SIZE *Stem height to 60cm.*
BRANCHES *In whorls up the stem.*
CONES *On fertile stems.*
SPORES RIPE *June–September.*
DISTRIBUTION *Throughout the British Isles.*
SIMILAR SPECIES *Common Horsetail (above), which has similar sterile stems but the teeth of the stem sheaths are green.*

Stag's-horn Clubmoss

Lycopodium clavatum (Lycopodiaceae)

Long, branching stems of Stag's-horn Clubmoss trail along the ground and root at intervals. Fertile branches are erect, and each bears at its end 1–3 cigar-shaped cones on a long stalk. The cones are made up of specialized leaves and at the base of each of these leaves, is a sporangium.

GROWS *on mountain grassland, heaths, and moors.*

slender stalk with few leaves

erect fertile branches

cigar-shaped cone

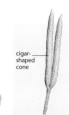

SIZE *Stem length to 1m.*
LEAVES *Spirally arranged, incurving, with toothed margins and white, hair-like tips.*
CONES *1–3, on long stalks of fertile stems.*
SPORES RIPE *July–August.*
DISTRIBUTION *Widespread in Scotland and Wales, rare in England.*
SIMILAR SPECIES *None.*

Common Couch

Elytrigia repens (Poaceae)

Also known as Twitch, Common Couch is a pernicious weed, which spreads by rhizomes, or underground stems. The fertile stems are erect and the unbranched inflorescence consists of unstalked spikelets alternately arranged on opposite sides of the axis. The flowers are usually unawned.

FLOURISHES *on cultivated and waste ground, rough grassland, roadsides, and field margins.*

spikelets on each side of axis

PERENNIAL

spike-like inflorescence

creeping rhizome

spikelets unawned

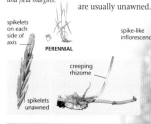

SIZE *Up to 1.2m high.*
LEAVES *Dull green, flat, usually hairless.*
INFLORESCENCE *Spike-like; spikelets unstalked, consisting of several flowers, and alternately arranged on opposite sides of the axis; June–August.*
DISTRIBUTION *Throughout the British Isles.*
SIMILAR SPECIES *Perennial Rye-grass (below).*

Perennial Rye-grass

Lolium perenne (Poaceae)

Tolerating trampling, and re-growing strongly after cutting, Perennial Rye-grass has been widely cultivated in Britain for over 300 years. Several flowering stems grow together, giving it a tufted appearance. The inflorescence is long, narrow, and flattened, with green or purplish, flat spikelets. They are unstalked, and the flowers lack awns.

FLOURISHES *in pastures, sports grounds, and lawns, where it is often sown, and on roadsides and waste ground.*

greenish, sometimes purple, flat spikelet

narrow edge of spikelet pressed against axis

blunt ligule

PERENNIAL

SIZE *Up to 60cm or more.*
LEAVES *Hairless, flat (folded when young), with narrow projections at the base.*
INFLORESCENCE *Long, narrow, flattened; spikelets flattened, alternate. May–August.*
DISTRIBUTION *Throughout the British Isles.*
SIMILAR SPECIES *Italian Rye-grass (L. multiflorum).*

Great Horsetail
Belonging to an ancient group of plants, horsetails have kept that oddly primeval look about them. The bottle-brush-like infertile stems are less conspicuous than the cone-topped fertile stems seen here.

Wall Barley

Hordeum murinum (Poaceae)

The smooth stems of Wall Barley may be tufted or solitary, erect or spreading. The dense, spike-like inflorescence is composed of many groups of three spikelets, each spikelet consisting of a single long-awned flower. The middle spikelet of each group is unstalked, with both male and female reproductive organs, while the other two are male or barren. There are no sterile shoots.

GROWS *on waste ground and roadsides, particularly at the foot of walls.*

flowers with long awns

spike-like inflorescence

pale green leaves

tightly packed spikelets

ANNUAL

PLANT HEIGHT *Up to 60cm.*
LEAVES *Pale green with short ligule.*
INFLORESCENCE *Spike-like; spikelets single-flowered, with long awns; May–October.*
DISTRIBUTION *Throughout, but rare in Scotland and Ireland.*
SIMILAR SPECIES *Sea Barley (H. marinum), which has blue-green leaves.*

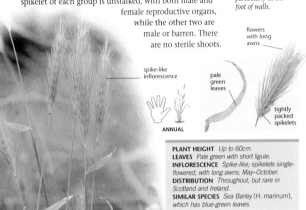

Meadow Foxtail

Alopecurus pratensis (Poaceae)

One of the earliest flowering grasses, coming into flower in April, Meadow Foxtail is an attractive, tufted species with smooth flowering and non-flowering stems. The leaves are flat and hairless, with blunt ligules. Numerous spikelets, each containing a single flower, form a dense, soft, narrowly cylindrical inflorescence with a blunt top. The flowers are awned and softly hairy, with purple or yellow anthers.

FLOURISHES *in grassy places, especially on rich, damp soil.*

purple anthers

softly hairy inflorescence

tufted growth

PERENNIAL

PLANT HEIGHT *Up to 1.2m.*
LEAVES *Flat, hairless, with blunt ligules.*
INFLORESCENCE *Narrow, cylindrical, dense and soft; spikelets with a single awned flower produced April–June.*
DISTRIBUTION *Throughout the British Isles.*
SIMILAR SPECIES *Marsh Foxtail (A. geniculatus) has stems bent near the base.*

False Brome

Brachypodium sylvaticum (Poaceae)

The leaves of False Brome are a distinctive bright yellowish green, often hairy, and have blunt ligules. Its growth is tufted, with sterile and fertile stems. The inflorescence is a nodding spike, with stalked spikelets arranged alternately on opposite sides of the axis. Each spikelet is made up of several green, awned flowers. Although it is a plant of shady places, it often persists in the open when trees and bushes are removed.

INHABITS *woods and hedgerows, persists on roadsides and grassland after the clearing of trees and bushes.*

yellow-green leaves

spikelet of awned flowers

nodding flowerheads

PERENNIAL

PLANT HEIGHT *Up to 1m.*
LEAVES *Often hairy, with blunt ligules.*
INFLORESCENCE *Spike-like; spikelets stalked, composed of several awned flowers; flowers July–August.*
DISTRIBUTION *Throughout the British Isles.*
SIMILAR SPECIES: *Tor-grass (B. pinnatum), which has erect inflorescences.*

Sweet Vernal Grass

Anthoxanthum odoratum (Poaceae)

Flowering as early as April, Sweet Vernal Grass is a variable, tufted species, producing both flowering and non-flowering shoots, the former erect, unbranched, and smooth. The narrow, yellow-green flower spikes are composed of many short-stalked, three-flowered spikelets.

OCCURS *in meadows, pastures, moors, and heaths, flourishing in a wide range of soils and situations.*

flowers have 2 anthers

narrow flower spike

PERENNIAL

finely pointed leaves

spikelet with awned flowers

PLANT HEIGHT *Up to 50cm.*
LEAVES *Variable, fringed with hairs at the base, with a blunt, toothed ligule.*
INFLORESCENCE *Spike; spikelets short-stalked, three-flowered; flowers with one bent and one straight awn; April–July.*
DISTRIBUTION *Throughout the British Isles.*
SIMILAR SPECIES *None.*

Timothy

Phleum pratense (Poaceae)

The tall flowering stems of this grass are smooth and usually swollen at the base. The leaves are flat with pointed tips and blunt ligules. At the top of each flowering stem is a dense flower spike, made up of many green or purple-tinged, one-flowered spikelets, each flower with two short awns. Non-flowering shoots are also produced.

GROWS *on grassland, roadsides, and waste ground, often cultivated for hay and grazing.*

cylindrical spike

flat, hairless leaves

spike of short-stalked spikelets

tufted growth

PERENNIAL

PLANT HEIGHT *Up to 1.5m.*
LEAVES *Hairless, flat, with blunt ligules.*
INFLORESCENCE *Cylindrical to 20cm long; spikelets numerous, with awned flowers; flowers June–August.*
DISTRIBUTION *Throughout the British Isles.*
SIMILAR SPECIES *Smaller Cat's-tail (P. bertolonii) has pointed ligules and is smaller.*

Crested Dog's-tail

Cynosurus cristatus (Poaceae)

Crested Dog's-tail is a tufted grass with erect, smooth stems and usually hairless leaves, which are rough towards the pointed tip. The ligules are short and blunt. All the spikelets grow on one side of the axis, forming a dense, stiff, spike-like inflorescence. The spikelets are of two kinds – fertile ones, consisting of several awned flowers and flattened sterile ones.

GROWS *abundantly in meadows and pastures and on roadsides, on a wide range of soils.*

flattened spikelets

stiff, one-sided inflorescence

leaf rough towards tip

awned flowers

PERENNIAL

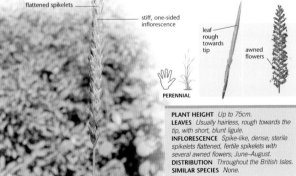

PLANT HEIGHT *Up to 75cm.*
LEAVES *Usually hairless, rough towards the tip, with short, blunt ligule.*
INFLORESCENCE *Spike-like, dense; sterile spikelets flattened, fertile spikelets with several awned flowers; June–August.*
DISTRIBUTION *Throughout the British Isles.*
SIMILAR SPECIES *None.*

Common Bent

Agrostis capillaris (Poaceae)

A tufted grass with a creeping rootstock, Common Bent produces erect flowering and non-flowering stems. The flowering stems are slender with an open, branching inflorescence; the hair-like branches grow in whorls, each dividing again and bearing spikelets at the tips. Awns are usually absent but the flower sometimes has a short one.

FLOURISHES *on heaths, moors, and pastures, especially on poor, acid soil.*

PERENNIAL

slender stems

flat, hairless leaf

branching inflorescence

PLANT HEIGHT *Up to 70cm high.*
LEAVES *Smooth, with short, blunt ligules.*
INFLORESCENCE *Open, branched, and spreading; flowers usually without awns; June–August.*
DISTRIBUTION *Throughout the British Isles.*
SIMILAR SPECIES *Creeping Bent (A. stolonifera), which has long, pointed ligules.*

Marram

Ammophila arenaria (Poaceae)

Spreading widely from extensive, branching rhizomes, Marram grows in large tufts, its tough rhizomes binding the loose sand of coastal dunes. The rigid, greyish green leaves are sharply pointed and inrolled, ribbed on the upper surface and smooth beneath, with long ligules. The spike-like, cylindrical inflorescence is made up of many overlapping, one-flowered spikelets. There are no awns on the flowers.

BINDS *the loose sand of dunes with its tough, spreading rhizomes; often planted to control erosion.*

overlapping spikelets

tapering spike

sharply pointed leaf

straw-coloured spikelets

greyish green leaves

PERENNIAL

PLANT HEIGHT *Up to 1.2m.*
LEAVES *Greyish green, with sharp points, inrolled margins, and long ligules.*
INFLORESCENCE *Spike-like and cylindrical, straw coloured, tapering towards the tip; spikelets containing a single awnless flower; June–August.*
DISTRIBUTION *Throughout, on coasts.*
SIMILAR SPECIES *None.*

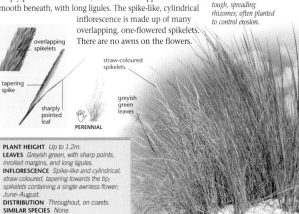

Common Reed

Phragmites australis (Poaceae)

THRIVES *in fresh to brackish water, to one-third the salinity of sea water, in upper salt marshes, lagoons, and grazing marsh ditches, often in large stands.*

Extensively creeping rhizomes mean that Common Reed often forms dense reedbeds, an important habitat for a wide range of other plants and animals. The nodding, purplish flowers contain silky hairs, which are especially obvious when fruiting: caught by low autumn sunlight, they create a beautiful golden glow over vast areas of wetland.

silky-hairy inflorescence

dark purple inflorescence

greyish green leaf

PERENNIAL

PLANT HEIGHT *Up to 3m or more.*
LEAVES *Greyish green, blades flat, tapering to long slender points, spreading, with a fringe of short hairs as the ligule.*
INFLORESCENCE *Long, soft, purple, branched; spikelets with long silky hairs and unawned flowers; August–October.*
DISTRIBUTION *Throughout the British Isles.*
SIMILAR SPECIES *None.*

Tufted Hair-grass

Deschampsia caespitosa (Poaceae)

As its name suggests Tufted Hair-grass is a tufted species that forms large tussocks. The leaves are ribbed on their upper surface and smooth beneath. Smooth, erect flowering stems carry a delicate inflorescence. The spikelets are two-flowered and silvery, green, or purple in colour. Each flower has a straight awn.

FLOURISHES *in damp, rough grassland, wet woods, ditches, and marshes.*

much-branched inflorescence

hair-like branches

rough-edged leaves

PERENNIAL

PLANT HEIGHT *Up to 2m.*
LEAVES *Hairless, ribbed above, with rough ribs and margins and long, pointed ligules.*
INFLORESCENCE *Branched; spikelets with two awned flowers; June–August.*
DISTRIBUTION *Throughout the British Isles.*
SIMILAR SPECIES *Wavy Hair-grass (D. flexuosa), has short, blunt ligules.*

Yorkshire Fog

Holcus lanatus (Poaceae)

GROWS *in pastures, meadows, and open woods, tolerating a wide range of soils, wet or dry.*

Softly downy all over and velvety to the touch, Yorkshire Fog is a very common grass of pastures and meadows. The erect flowering and non-flowering stems are bent at the base and grow in tufts. The leaves have a fairly short ligule. The inflorescence can be spreading or fairly compact, erect or nodding, and is branched, with short-stalked spikelets which may be pale green or whitish, but are often pinkish or purple. It is similar to Creeping Soft-grass (*Holcus mollis*) which has densely hairy stem joints and prefers woodland to open grassland.

erect, or drooping, inflorescence

branched inflorescence

PERENNIAL

softly downy leaf

pinkish spikelets

softly downy stem

stalked spikelets

PLANT HEIGHT *Up to 1m.*
LEAVES *Softly downy, with a fairly short ligule.*
INFLORESCENCE *Spreading or compact, erect or nodding, branched; spikelets pinkish, purple, whitish, or green, flowers with inconspicuous hooked awns; May–August.*
DISTRIBUTION *Throughout the British Isles.*
SIMILAR SPECIES *Creeping Soft-grass (H. mollis), which has a creeping rootstock and densely hairy joints.*

NOTE

Yorkshire Fog is a foodplant of the larvae of the Marbled White (p.405) and Skipper butterflies (pp.188–89).

Cock's-foot

Dactylis glomerata (Poaceae)

A very common grassland plant, Cock's-foot is a distinctive, tufted perennial, with compressed non-flowering shoots and sturdy flowering stems. The rather greyish green leaves are folded at first and later open out flat. They are rough, with pointed tips and long ligules. The one-sided inflorescence consists of stalked, oval clusters of densely grouped spikelets, the clusters growing on rough, spreading branches. The flowers have short awns.

FLOURISHES *in meadows and pastures and on roadsides.*

PERENNIAL

pointed leaf tip

lowest inflorescence branch spreading

greyish green leaf

densely clustered spikelets

short awns

PLANT HEIGHT *Up to 1.4m.*
LEAVES *Folded at first, later flat, greyish green, rough, with long ligules.*
INFLORESCENCE *One-sided, consisting of dense, oval clusters of spikelets; spikelets with several shortly awned flowers; May–November.*
DISTRIBUTION *Throughout the British Isles.*
SIMILAR SPECIES *None.*

NOTE
Cock's-foot is a foodplant for the caterpillars of several British butterflies, including the Essex Skipper and the Large Skipper (p.188).

Red Fescue

Festuca rubra (Poaceae)

Because it is so variable, Red Fescue is often divided into several subspecies. Its growth can be tufted or creeping. The leaves are extremely narrow and may be flat or folded, green, greyish green, or bluish green, their sheaths completely enfolding the stem. The ligules are very short. Small green, bluish, or purple spikelets are borne on the inflorescence branches and the flowers usually have short awns. Non-flowering shoots are also produced.

GROWS *in grassy places, on sand dunes and salt marshes.*

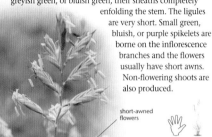

short-awned flowers

PERENNIAL

purplish spikelets

branched inflorescence

PLANT HEIGHT *Up to 75cm.*
LEAVES *Very narrow, flat or folded; sheaths tightly closed; ligules very short.*
INFLORESCENCE *Spikelets green, bluish green, or purple; May–July.*
DISTRIBUTION *Throughout the British Isles.*
SIMILAR SPECIES *Sheep's Fescue (F. ovina), another very variable species.*

Soft Brome

Bromus hordeaceus (Poaceae)

Notable for its variability, Soft Brome is a common species, divided into several subspecies. This plant is clothed with soft hairs. Its stems are erect or spreading, slender or sturdy. The inflorescence is usually branched and bears plump spikelets with awned flowers, but may be unbranched, with a single spikelet.

INHABITS *meadow and other grassy places, roadsides, waste ground, dunes, and sea cliffs.*

awned flowers

branched inflorescence

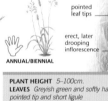

plump spikelets

pointed leaf tips

erect, later drooping inflorescence

ANNUAL/BIENNIAL

PLANT HEIGHT *5–100cm.*
LEAVES *Greyish green and softly hairy, with pointed tip and short ligule*
INFLORESCENCE *Initially erect, later drooping to one side; spikelets plump, usually hairy, greyish green; May–July.*
DISTRIBUTION *Throughout the British Isles.*
SIMILAR SPECIES *Several other bromes.*

Annual Meadow-grass

Poa annua (Poaceae)

Flowering throughout the year, Annual Meadow-grass is one of Britain's commonest grasses. Its name is not always accurate, as it is sometimes a short-lived perennial. The tufted stems are usually spreading, quite often horizontal at the base and rooting at the lowest joints. Inflorescence branches are borne singly or in pairs.

GROWS *on cultivated and waste ground, paths and roadsides; on a wide range of soils.*

triangular inflorescence

spikelet of unawned flowers

protruding anthers

hairless leaf

ANNUAL/PERENNIAL

PLANT HEIGHT *Up to 25cm.*
LEAVES *Hairless, fresh pale green, often crinkled when young; ligule pointed.*
INFLORESCENCE *Branched; spikelets with several unawned flowers; January–December.*
DISTRIBUTION *Throughout the British Isles.*
SIMILAR SPECIES *Rough Meadow-grass (P. trivialis), which is usually much taller.*

False Oat-grass

Arrhenatherum elatius (Poaceae)

Also known as Tall Oat-grass, False Oat-grass is a commonly found loosely tufted perennial. It has erect, shiny flowering stems. The flat leaves have pointed tips and short ligules, and are usually hairless. Whorls of branches form a long, somewhat spreading inflorescence. Each of the shiny spikelets comprise two flowers with long, straight awns.

FLOURISHES *in grassland and on roadsides, hedgebanks, and waste ground, on most types of soil.*

inflorescence with whorls of branches

two-flowered spikelets

long, straight awn

PERENNIAL

PLANT HEIGHT *Up to 1.8m.*
LEAVES *Flat, usually hairless, with pointed tips and short, blunt ligules.*
INFLORESCENCE *Somewhat spreading; spikelets shiny; May–September.*
DISTRIBUTION *Throughout the British Isles.*
SIMILAR SPECIES *Downy Oat-grass (Helictotrichon pubescens) has pointed ligules.*

Common Club-rush

Schoenoplectus lacustris (Cyperaceae)

Also known as Bulrush, a name which was wrongly given, but is now accepted, for Reedmace (*Typha latifolia*), Common Club-rush has tall, rounded stems. The strap-like leaves grow from below the water-line. The inflorescence is branched and made up of stalked clusters of unstalked spikelets with smooth, reddish brown glumes. Each egg-shaped spikelet contains several bisexual flowers, each with three stigmas.

GROWS *in still water, in lakes, ponds, canals, and ditches, and also in slow-moving rivers.*

spikelets in stalked clusters

tiny flowers

unstalked spikelets

PERENNIAL

PLANT HEIGHT *Up to 3m.*
LEAVES *Strap-like.*
INFLORESCENCE *Branching; spikelets with smooth, reddish brown glumes; June–August.*
DISTRIBUTION *Widespread, in most of the British Isles.*
SIMILAR SPECIES *Grey Club-rush (S. tabernaemontani) has red-dotted glumes.*

False Fox-sedge

Carex otrubae (Cyperaceae)

With densely tufted growth, False Fox-sedge has three-sided stems that are smooth towards the base but rough above. The erect, bright green leaves are keeled, with a pointed tip, rough margins, basal projections, and a pointed ligule. The inflorescence consists of numerous overlapping flower spikes growing all around the axis. Each flower has a pale orange-brown glume with a green midrib. The fruit is smooth and glossy.

GROWS *in damp grassland, marshes and ditches; prefers clay soil.*

fruiting spikes look prickly

overlapping flower spikes

dense inflorescence

PERENNIAL

PLANT HEIGHT *Up to 1m.*
LEAVES *Bright green, with rough margins.*
INFLORESCENCE *Composed of numerous flower spikes; fruits July–September.*
DISTRIBUTION *Mainly southern and eastern Britain and in Ireland.*
SIMILAR SPECIES *True Fox-sedge (C. vulpina) has wings on the stem angles.*

Common Cottongrass

Eriophorum angustifolium (Cyperaceae)

Also known as Bog Cotton, Common Cottongrass is more conspicuous in fruit than in flower. Long, creeping rhizomes produce scattered, erect stems which are three-sided at the top. The leaves are dark green in summer, turning deep red in autumn. Several spikelets with smooth stalks grow together in drooping clusters. The brown fruit have long, white, unbranched hairs, brightening wet ground with their snowy tassels.

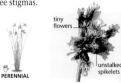
FLOURISHES *in bogs and wet places on acid soil.*

cottony white hairs on fruit

drooping clusters of fruiting spikelets

three-sided stem

PERENNIAL

PLANT HEIGHT *Up to 70cm.*
LEAVES *Three-sided at tip; short ligule.*
INFLORESCENCE *Drooping clusters; spikelets smooth stalked; flowers with yellow anthers; flowers April–May; fruits May–July.*
DISTRIBUTION *Mainly in west and north.*
SIMILAR SPECIES *Hare's-tail Cottongrass (E. vaginatum) has a single, erect spikelet.*

Common Sedge

Carex nigra (Cyperaceae)

The stems of Common Sedge may be solitary or tufted. The leaves are greyish green on both sides, with rounded ligules. There are one or two male flower spikes at the top of the stem, with one to four female spikes below. The female spikes are usually overlapping, the upper ones erect, with a few male flowers at the top, the lower nodding, all having purple-black glumes with a broad, pale midrib. The female flowers have two stigmas, and the fruit has a tiny beak.

FLOURISHES *in bogs and dune slacks and wet, grassy places, on acid, neutral, or calcareous soil.*

male flower spike

female flower spike

PERENNIAL

PLANT HEIGHT *Up to 70cm.*
LEAVES *Greyish green, with a rounded ligule.*
INFLORESCENCE *1–2 male flower spikes above 1–4 female; fruits June–August.*
DISTRIBUTION *Throughout the British Isles.*
SIMILAR SPECIES *Glaucous Sedge (p.456) has leaves that are green on their upper surface, and the flowers have three stigmas.*

Deergrass

Trichophorum cespitosum (Cyperaceae)

Low tussocks of Deergrass are a common sight on heaths and bogs. Most of the narrow leaves grow in dense tufts from the base of the plant. The smooth, rounded stems bear a single, strap-shaped leaf near the base. There is a solitary yellowish or red-brown spikelet at the top of each stem. The flowers are bisexual, with three stamens and three stigmas.

ABUNDANT *on wet moors, heaths, and in bogs; favours acid, peaty soil.*

slender, rounded stems

PERENNIAL

several flowers

densely tufted growth

solitary spikelet

PLANT HEIGHT *Up to 35cm.*
LEAVES *Hairless, mostly basal.*
INFLORESCENCE *Single spikelet at top of stem, composed of several flowers; May–June.*
DISTRIBUTION *Common in northern and western British Isles, rarer elsewhere.*
SIMILAR SPECIES *Spike-rushes (Eleocharis species), which have leafless stems.*

Remote Sedge

Carex remota (Cyperaceae)

Stems of Remote Sedge form dense tufts with drooping leaves. Flower spikes at the top of the inflorescence are closely grouped, lower down they are widely spaced. Upper flower spikes are male at the top and female below; the lower ones are entirely female. The glumes are pale brown with a green midrib. The leaf-like bract below the lowest spike is longer than the inflorescence.

INHABITS *woods, hedgerows, shady banks, sides of ditches, and other damp places.*

pale brown glumes

upper spikes

female flower spike

PERENNIAL

PLANT HEIGHT *Up to 75cm.*
LEAVES *Narrow and drooping, with a rounded or blunt ligule.*
INFLORESCENCE *Long; upper flower spikes closely grouped; glumes pale brown with a green midrib; fruits July–August.*
DISTRIBUTION *Throughout the British Isles.*
SIMILAR SPECIES *None.*

Hairy Sedge

Carex hirta (Cyperaceae)

Some sedges are difficult to identify, but Hairy Sedge is a very distinctive species, its hairy leaves with short, hair-fringed ligules making it easily recognizable. It has a creeping rootstock, which gives rise to tufts of stems. There are two or three male flower spikes above two or three female spikes. The male glumes are brownish and hairy, the female greenish with the midrib extending well beyond the top of the glume. The fruit is green and hairy and produced June to September.

FAVOURS *damp, grassy places on various types of soil.*

extended midrib

green female glumes

female flower spike

PERENNIAL

PLANT HEIGHT *Up to 70cm.*
LEAVES *Hairy, with a short hair-fringed ligule.*
INFLORESCENCE *2–3 male spikes above 2–3 female, spaced along stem; male glumes brownish and hairy, females greenish.*
DISTRIBUTION *Throughout; rare in northern Scotland and southern and western Ireland.*
SIMILAR SPECIES *None.*

Glaucous Sedge

THRIVES *in calcareous grassland, on dunes, and in estuarine marshes, sometimes on boulder clay.*

Carex flacca (Cyperaceae)

Loose tufts of stems grow from the creeping rootstock of Glaucous Sedge. The leaves are greyish green beneath, dull green on the upper surface. Bluntly three-sided, the rigid stem bears an inflorescence of male and female spikes, the lowest bract about equalling the inflorescence in length. The female flowers have three stigmas. The rough fruit is yellow-green or purple-black.

male spike

fruit with short beak

purple glumes

PERENNIAL

PLANT HEIGHT *Up to 60cm.*
LEAVES *Flat, fine-pointed; ligule rounded.*
INFLORESCENCE *2 or 3 male spikes above, 1–5 females; glumes purplish, with colourless margins, pale midrib; fruits June–September.*
DISTRIBUTION *Throughout the British Isles.*
SIMILAR SPECIES *Carnation Sedge (C. panicea) has a single male spike.*

Pendulous Sedge

FLOURISHES *in damp woods and on streamsides, especially on clay soils.*

Carex pendula (Cyperaceae)

The stems of this distinctive sedge are smooth and bluntly three-sided and bear one or two male spikes above four or five elegantly drooping, long female spikes. The male glumes are brownish, narrow and pointed, the shorter female glumes red-brown, with a pale midrib. There three-sided fruit is short-beaked. The leaves are long and strap-shaped.

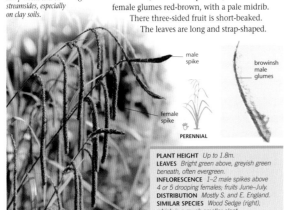

male spike

female spike

browinsh male glumes

PERENNIAL

PLANT HEIGHT *Up to 1.8m.*
LEAVES *Bright green above, greyish green beneath, often evergreen.*
INFLORESCENCE *1–2 male spikes above 4 or 5 drooping females; fruits June–July.*
DISTRIBUTION *Mostly S. and E. England.*
SIMILAR SPECIES *Wood Sedge (right), which is a much smaller plant.*

Greater Pond Sedge

Carex riparia (Cyperaceae)

Growing in tufts, the stems of Greater Pond Sedge are sharply three-sided and rough. The erect, rigid leaves are broad and greyish green in colour, when young. There are three to six overlapping male flower spikes, their sharply pointed glumes dark brown with a paler midrib and margins. Below them are one to five overlapping female spikes, the upper stalkless the lower stalked. The female glumes are sharply pointed and purplish brown, with a paler or green midrib. Produced June to September, the fruit tapers gradually to a beak.

FORMS *large patches on riversides and pond margins, also in marshes and ditches.*

dark brown glumes

PERENNIAL

yellow stamens

overlapping male spikes

female spike

broad, erect leaves

NOTE

Cultivars of Greater Pond Sedge are often grown as ornamental plants. There are many cultivars, such as C. riparia 'Variegata', which has boldly white-striped, arching leaves.

PLANT HEIGHT *Up to 1.3m.*
LEAVES *Broad, erect, greyish green, with a blunt or rounded ligule.*
INFLORESCENCE *3–6 male spikes above 1–5 females; female flowers with three stigmas; male glumes dark brown, females purplish brown; fruits June–September.*
DISTRIBUTION *Mainly south-east England, scattered elsewhere.*
SIMILAR SPECIES *Lesser Pond Sedge (C. acutiformis) has arching leaves, blunt-pointed male glumes, and fruit abruptly narrowing to a beak.*

Wood Sedge

Carex sylvatica (Cyperaceae)

The leaves of Wood Sedge are mid-green or yellow-green, with a short, blunt ligule. There is usually only a single male flower spike at the top of the stem, with three to five drooping female spikes spread out along the stem on long, thread-like stalks. The male glumes are brownish, the female straw coloured or brownish with a green midrib.

GROWS *mainly in woods, sometimes in hedgerows and scrub, favouring damp, heavy soil.*

brownish male spike

long female spike

green fruit

PERENNIAL

PLANT HEIGHT *Up to 60cm.*
LEAVES *Soft, drooping.*
INFLORESCENCE *Single male spike above 3–5 females.*
DISTRIBUTION *Throughout, except for much of Scotland.*
SIMILAR SPECIES *Thin-spiked Wood Sedge (C. strigosa) has erect female spikes.*

Soft Rush

Juncus effusus (Juncaceae)

Widespread and common in a variety of damp habitats, Soft Rush often forms extensive patches, becoming a pest in pastures. It is a deceptive plant, for what look like leaves are, in fact, barren stems, and although the flower clusters seem to emerge part-way up the fertile stems, they are actually on the end, the green part above the cluster being a bract, not a continuation of the stem. The brown, egg-shaped fruit is normally shorter than the flowers.

GROWS *in damp, often grassy places, in overgrazed, poorly drained fields; also in ditches and bogs.*

smooth bright green stems

loosely clustered flowers

PERENNIAL

PLANT HEIGHT *Up to 1.2m, usually less.*
LEAVES *None; stems glossy bright green.*
INFLORESCENCE *Loose flower clusters; June–July.*
DISTRIBUTION *Throughout the British Isles.*
SIMILAR SPECIES *Compact Rush (J. conglomeratus) has stems which are dull and distinctly ridged, and compact flower clusters.*

Toad Rush

Juncus bufonius (Juncaceae)

Toad Rush has erect, spreading or trailing stems. Narrow leaves are produced at the base and on the stems. The inflorescence is made up of spreading branches bearing clusters of greenish white flowers with pointed segments. The brown, egg-shaped fruit is usually pointed and is the same length as, or shorter than, the inner flower segments.

GROWS *in bare damp places, widely distributed, and common.*

branched inflorescence

clusters of greenish white flowers

pointed flower segments

ANNUAL

PLANT HEIGHT *Up to 50cm, usually less.*
LEAVES *Narrow, at base and on stems.*
INFLORESCENCE *Branching, with clusters of greenish white flowers; June–September.*
DISTRIBUTION *Throughout the British Isles.*
SIMILAR SPECIES *Leafy Rush (J. foliosus) has erect stems, broader leaves, and dark lines on the flower segments.*

Hard Rush

Juncus inflexus (Juncaceae)

Tufts of hard, bluish green, strongly ridged stems are characteristic of Hard Rush. The flower clusters arise at the base of a long bract, which looks like a continuation of the slender stem. They are rather loose, with brown flowers borne on more or less erect stalks of unequal length. The brown fruit are egg-shaped, with a tiny point at the top.

FAVOURS *neutral or calcareous soil, inhabiting damp grassland, marshes, ditches, and other wet habitats.*

brown flowers

stalks of unequal length

egg-shaped fruit

PERENNIAL

PLANT HEIGHT *Up to 1.2m.*
LEAVES *None.*
INFLORESCENCE *Loose cluster of more or less erect stalks, with brown flowers; May–July.*
DISTRIBUTION *Throughout, except for most of Scotland.*
SIMILAR SPECIES *Compact Rush (J. conglomeratus) has compact flower clusters.*

Field Wood-rush

Luzula campestris (Juncaceae)

Producing short runners, Field Wood-rush forms extensive colonies. The leaves are narrow and grass-like, tapering to a fine point, and fringed with long white hairs. The chestnut brown flowers have very conspicuous yellow anthers. The globular brown fruit is shorter than the flower segments.

FLOURISHES *in short grassland, preferring calcareous or neutral soil.*

chestnut brown flowers

pointed flower segments

one flower cluster unstalked

PERENNIAL

PLANT HEIGHT *to 25cm, but usually less.*
LEAVES *Grass-like with hairy margins.*
INFLORESCENCE *Several flower clusters, one unstalked, the others stalked; April–May.*
DISTRIBUTION *Throughout the British Isles.*
SIMILAR SPECIES: *Heath Wood-rush (L. multiflora) favours acid soil, lacks runners, and flowers May–June.*

Jointed Rush

Juncus articulatus (Juncaceae)

A very common and widely distributed species, Jointed Rush grows from a creeping rootstock. The leaves have internal cross-partitions, hence the name "Jointed". At the top of the stem is a branching inflorescence comprising small clusters of dark brown flowers with pointed segments. The brown, egg-shaped fruit is abruptly narrowed to end in a small point.

FLOURISHES *in damp grassland, marshes, on wet moorland, pond edges, and riversides.*

PERENNIAL

pointed flower segments

clusters of flowers

branching inflorescence

PLANT HEIGHT *Up to 60cm.*
LEAVES *Curved and flattened, with internal cross-partitions.*
INFLORESCENCE *Branched, with small clusters of dark brown flowers; July–August.*
DISTRIBUTION *Throughout the British Isles.*
SIMILAR SPECIES *Sharp-flowered Rush (J. acutiflorus) has rounded, unflattened leaves.*

Great Wood-rush

Luzula sylvatica (Juncaceae)

The tallest and sturdiest of the wood-rushes, Great Wood-rush is an attractive plant, with large tufts of glossy, bright green leaves fringed with long white hairs. It forms extensive patches, the rhizomes producing creeping runners. The leafy stem ends in a widely branching inflorescence with clusters of brown flowers, brightened by yellow anthers. The fruit is brown and egg-shaped.

INHABITS *inhabits woods and rocky places, mainly on acid soil.*

widely branching inflorescence

brown flowers in clusters

PERENNIAL

PLANT HEIGHT *Up to 80cm.*
LEAVES *Broad, glossy, bright green, fringed with long, white hairs.*
INFLORESCENCE *Widely branching, with clusters of brown flowers; April–June.*
DISTRIBUTION *Throughout the British Isles, except for parts of eastern England.*
SIMILAR SPECIES *None.*

OTHER PLANTS

FUNGI

The most recent catalogue of the larger fungi of the British Isles lists over 4,000 species; when you add in all of the microscopic rusts, smuts, mildews, and so on this total rises dramatically to some tens of thousands. The British Isles, despite their relatively small size, encompass almost every type of temperate habitat, from the high mountains of Scotland, to the dry sand dunes of our coasts, the steep beechwoods of our southern downs to the bogs of Ireland. It is this diversity of habitat that allows such large numbers of fungal species to flourish. This means that almost any walk in search of fungi has a high chance of seeing some unusual or even rare examples, and sometimes even undiscovered species, making it an exciting hobby for both amateur and professional alike.

CAP AND STEM
Including the Cultivated Mushroom and the classic "toadstool", these fungi produce spores on gills, tubes, or spines on the underside of a cap that sits on a more or less central stem.

SHELF AND BRACKET
Growing mainly on standing trees or dead wood stumps these fungi can have tubes, spines, or a smooth undersurface. They range from a few centimetres to nearly a metre across.

BALL, CLUB, AND OTHER
Those fungi that do not fit into the shelf, bracket, or cap and stem categories occur in an almost bewildering range of shapes and structures, including Puffballs, Club Fungi, and Birds Nest Fungi.

LICHEN
A lichen forms when two organisms – a fungus and an algae – live together symbiotically to form a new structure. These unusual life forms are adapted to often harsh environments.

Anatomy

From familiar toadstools with cap and stem to stranger fungal forms with spines, tubes, or wrinkles, the structure and the anatomical details of all fungi reflect the main function of dispersing their single-celled reproductive spores. The different fruitbodies – the visible, fertile part of the fungus – represent varying methods of overcoming the common problem of releasing spores into an often-harsh environment. All fruitbodies have an area of spore-producing tissue, known as the hymenium, which may be spread over thin gills, spines, tubes, wrinkles, the entire fungus, or even enclosed inside the fruitbody. These varied structures help us to initially divide and classify the fungi. The finer details will help you to identify the fungus species.

cap flesh

cap

cap scales (remains of veil)

stem

FLY AGARIC

swollen stem base

universal veil

emerging fruitbody

GRISETTE

volva (remains of veil at base)

Cap and Stem

The typical fungus has a variably shaped cap lifted up on a central stem. On the underside of the cap are thin gills, spines, tubes, or fleshy wrinkles, where spores are produced and discharged. The cap and stem shape, any surface structures, and the colour are all diagnostic features.

Universal veil

Many fungi are covered by a cobweb-like or fleshy protective tissue. As the fungus grows, this "veil" ruptures, leaving patches on the cap, stem, or base.

Section

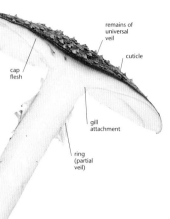

Cutting a fungus in half reveals many identifying features. For example, the way in which the gills, tubes, or other spore-producing structures attach to the stem, the shape of the stem, and whether the stem is solid or hollow. Also, the remains of a partial veil – in the form of a ring on the upper stem – may be revealed more readily in section.

remains of universal veil

cuticle

cap flesh

gill attachment

ring (partial veil)

cobweb veil

WEBCAP

Gills

Observing the shape of the gills, their thickness and spacing, and how they attach to the stem will help in identification. Shorter, intermediate gills may also be present. Gill colour is often – but not always – a guide to spore colour.

hymenium (covers gills)

gills

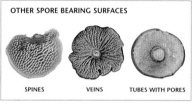

OTHER SPORE BEARING SURFACES

SPINES   VEINS   TUBES WITH PORES

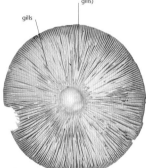

Identification

To accurately identify fungi, you need to take detailed notes in the field, while the specimens are still fresh and untouched. Take great care when handling, so as not to damage the often delicate surface, or any other diagnostic character. Use a hand lens to study fungi in detail and, if possible, always examine a range of specimens.

Fruitbody shapes

Identifying the shape of the fruitbody is often the first step in identifying the species. The broad classification of fungal groups in this book is based in part on the extraordinary shapes and structures of the fruitbody. Every possible variation may be encountered, many of which are pictured here, from the typical cap, stem, and gills, to fungi with animal-like arms or tentacles.

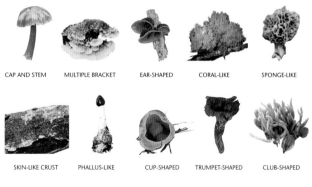

CAP AND STEM   MULTIPLE BRACKET   EAR-SHAPED   CORAL-LIKE   SPONGE-LIKE

SKIN-LIKE CRUST   PHALLUS-LIKE   CUP-SHAPED   TRUMPET-SHAPED   CLUB-SHAPED

STAR-SHAPED    CAGE-LIKE    BALL-SHAPED    BRAIN-LIKE    ANTLER-SHAPED

Spores

The colour, size, and shape of spores can assist in the correct identification of a species. To assess the spore colour, collect a thick spore deposit (see opposite). You need a good-quality microscope to measure and assess the spores accurately: most are less than 0.02mm long or wide.

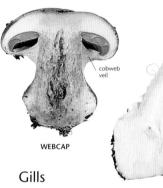

SPORES OF GLISTENING INKCAP

Cap shape

It is very important to make a record of the shape of the cap. In many species, cap shape is consistent and diagnostic; in others, it is more variable, changing as it matures.

CONVEX    CONICAL

FUNNEL-SHAPED   UMBONATE    SADDLE-SHAPED    HONEYCOMBED   DEPRESSED

FOLDED    LINED    PLEATED    INROLLED MARGIN    GROOVED

Texture

Cap textures include many variations, ranging from smooth and sticky to dry, fibrous to scaly. Some species will have an external veil of tissue, which may be thick and skin-like, fine and cobweb-like, or even sticky.

LOOSE SCALES    FIXED SCALES    FIBROUS    SHAGGY-WOOLY    STICKY

Colour

The colour of the different parts of the fungus is one of the most important characters to record, but is also one of the most variable and difficult to define. Try to examine a range of specimens and look at every part of the fungus – the underside of the cap, for example, is often very different to the upper surface. Colour may change with age or if you bruise the fungus.

CONCENTRIC ZONES OF COLOUR

DARKER CENTRE

Stem

In fungi that have a stem, the proportion of stem length compared to cap width, and the shape, girth, and flesh of the stem are diagnostic features. Viewing the base of the stem is often crucial since there may be special shapes or structures here; the presence or absence of a stem ring can also be diagnostic.

SWOLLEN

SLENDER

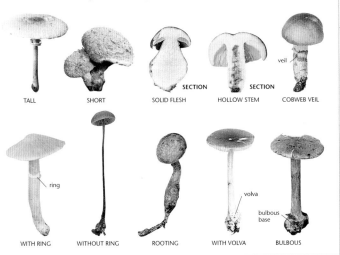

TALL

SHORT

SOLID FLESH

HOLLOW STEM

veil

COBWEB VEIL

ring

WITH RING

WITHOUT RING

ROOTING

volva

bulbous base

WITH VOLVA

BULBOUS

Flesh

Cutting through a specimen with a sharp knife will provide useful information. The texture and solidity of the flesh varies from species to species; some being very solid and fleshy, others fragile and crumbly. When cut or bruised, the flesh may also change colour or exude a "milk", or latex.

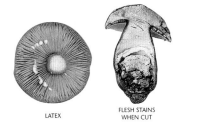

LATEX

FLESH STAINS WHEN CUT

Gills

With gilled mushrooms, you should make a note of the gill colour, their general spacing (crowded or widely spaced), and whether they are flexible or brittle. Examine how the gills are attached to the stem; they may be attached narrowly, broadly, or with an indent or notch, or the gills may run down the stem slightly or markedly. Also check whether the gills exude a latex when broken. Gill characteristics are usually constant within a species.

GILL SPACING

GILL ATTACHMENTS

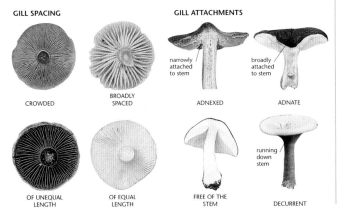

CROWDED

BROADLY SPACED

narrowly attached to stem

ADNEXED

broadly attached to stem

ADNATE

OF UNEQUAL LENGTH

OF EQUAL LENGTH

FREE OF THE STEM

running down stem

DECURRENT

Spore Colour

The colour of fungal spores is easily determined. Remove the cap, lay it gills downward on white paper, cover, and leave it, for several hours, to deposit its spores. When the spores are dry, scrape together to assess the colour. You need a high-magnification microscope to see the structure.

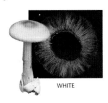

WHITE

DEEP OCHRE

Odour

The smell of fungi can be quite peculiar, but it is often subtle and difficult to define: different people may have different opinions on an odour. With gilled fungi, try smelling the gills and the cut flesh. Enclosing the specimen in a box can help to concentrate the odour.

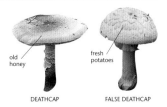

old honey

fresh potatoes

DEATHCAP

FALSE DEATHCAP

Variations

Individual fungi can vary extraordinarily, particularly young and old specimens. You need to see as many examples within a species as possible to become experienced with all of their forms and variety.

older fungus

young fungus

SNOWY WAXCAP

Occurrence

The occurence of a species may distinguish it from similar-looking species. The manner in which it grows – singly, in clusters, in rings etc – can be diagnostic. Also, not all species are common or widespread; some are very rare and exciting to find, and some are also restricted to certain times of the year.

IN CLUSTERS

IN TROOPS

SINGLY

FALSE PARASOLS IN A FAIRY RING

Chicken of the Wood

Oak Polypore

Livid Pinkgill

St. George's Mushroom

COMMON

RARE

LATE SUMMER TO AUTUMN

SPRING TO EARLY SUMMER

Habitats

Fungi are often very specific about where they grow. Many grow with particular tree species; others grow on decaying leaves and debris or even other fungi.

DECIDUOUS WOODLAND

Bitter Poisionpie

CONIFEROUS WOODLAND

Larch Bolete

BROADLEAF LEAF LITTER

Blackedge Bonnet

SAND DUNES

Winter Stalkball

DEAD WOOD

Smokey Bracket

SCALE MEASUREMENTS
Two small scale drawings are placed next to each other in every entry as an indication of the typical height of the fungus (cap or fruitbody diameter is provided in the annotation). The drawing of the hands represents a height of 18cm. The silhouette is a stylized representation of the species.

Fungi Height 15cm

18cm

POISONOUS FUNGI
The toxic effect of fungi can range from stomach upset through to organ failure and death. Even some fungi classed as edible can cause stomach upsets. If in any doubt about the identification of the species, do not eat it. It is a good idea to keep a sample of the species. If poisoning is suspected, seek medical advice and take the sample of the fungus for identification. Two symbols are used in this guide for species that are poisonous or potentially so.

Poisonous ☠ Poisonous but edible after cooking

FUNGI

Panthercap ☠

Amanita pantherina (Amanitaceae)

This extremely poisonous species has high concentrations of muscarin and other toxins. Its smooth, rounded cap flattens out with age, has a finely grooved margin, and varies from light to dark brown with numerous rounded or pointed white veil scales on the surface. The gills are free and white. The stem has a bulbous base that has a gutter-like margin and a series of narrow girdles on the upper edge. There is a pendent ring about half way up the stem, and the upper surface is smooth and ungrooved – important features to note.

FRUITS *in leaf litter in woodland, both broadleaf and coniferous, usually on alkaline soil.*

NOTE

The guttered margin at the stem base and the structure of the ring are vital signs for accurate identification of the Panthercap; another typical feature is the grooved cap margin.

cap 5–12cm wide

white veil scales on cap

stem 5–10cm high

radial grooves along cap margin

ring half way up stem

young cap rounded

bulbous stem base with gutter

light to deep brown cap

flattened mature cap

SPORES *White.*
FRUITING *Summer to autumn.*
OCCURENCE *Rare to locally frequent.*
EDIBILITY *Highly poisonous.*
SIMILAR SPECIES *Grey Spotted Amanita (right), which has a grey-brown cap with greyish veil scales, no margin or girdles on the stem bulb, and a ring that is high on the stem and grooved above.*

Fly Agaric ☠

Amanita muscaria (Amanitaceae)

The striking red cap with white spots makes this species the classic "toadstool" of children's storybooks. Depending on age and weathering, the colour of the fungus varies, tending to wash out with rain. The cap – domed when young, flattened later – can vary in colour from vivid red to orange or even a very pale orange-yellow. Its margin is grooved and the surface covered in wart-like white veil scales which wash off in the rain. The gills, stem, and drooping stem ring are all white; the stem has a scaly surface and a volval swelling at the base. Extremely toxic, the Fly Agaric can cause severe symptoms if eaten.

FOUND *in troops and rings on the ground in woods, growing with birch and spruce, more rarely with beech.*

red to orange-red cap

cap to 15cm wide

wart-like cap scales

crowded gills

white gills free from stem

volval swelling at stem base

SECTION

scaly stem base

SPORES *Off-white.*
FRUITING *Summer to late autumn.*
OCCURENCE *Common throughout.*
EDIBILITY *Highly poisonous.*
SIMILAR SPECIES *Orange Grisette (A. crocea), which is more golden orange and without a ring; red species of Russula, which have no ring or volva.*

NOTE

Collect the fungus carefully so that the volval swelling on the stem base is visible. Without it, rain-washed specimens, which do not have any white spots or ring, could be mistaken for red species of Russula.

The Blusher ☠

Amanita rubescens (Amanitaceae)

The pinkish brown cap of The Blusher can be mottled with lighter, pale pink areas with age, after heavy rain, or even if the weather has been particularly hot. The grey to pink cap scales can be dense and warty or more fleecy and sparse, making it difficult to identify at first. White to pinkish grey, the stem is often stout with a broad swollen base that has remains of volval bands.

GROWS *singly and in groups, in woodland – both broadleaf (such as birch, beech, and oak) and conifer (such as pine and spruce).*

crowded off-white gills

swollen stem base

scaly, pinkish brown cap

cap 6–18 cm wide

white to pinkish grey stem

SECTION

large floppy, furrowed ring on stem

SPORES *White.*
FRUITING *Early summer to late autumn.*
OCCURENCE *Common and widespread.*
EDIBILITY *Poisonous when raw, edible on being cooked.*
SIMILAR SPECIES *Panthercap (above), which is poisonous, has a grooved cap margin, white veil scales, and a distinctly rimmed bulb.*

Grey-spotted Amanita

Amanita spissa (Amanitaceae)

The fleshy, rounded cap of this species soon flattens and varies from dull grey to grey-brown or almost silvery-grey. Its surface is covered in flattened patches and warts of greyish veil remnants. The white gills are free and quite crowded. It has a stout stem that may be short and squat to tall with a swollen base – greyish warts on its upper edge and a white grooved ring that hangs from the top of the stem.

FOUND *in mixed woodland on acid soils.*

white gills

grey veil flakes on cap

ring with grooves

rounded cap

cap 4–12 cm wide

SPORES *White.*
FRUITING *Summer to late autumn.*
OCCURENCE *Common throughout.*
EDIBILITY *Edible.*
SIMILAR SPECIES *Panthercap (left), which has pure white veil scales on the cap, a smooth ring low down on the stem, and ridged "hoops" just above stem bulb.*

Death Cap ☠

Amanita phalloides (Amanitaceae)

Variability in colour makes this poisonous fungus tricky to identify at first, and has led to its confusion with edible species. The cap can vary from yellowish green to bronze, greyish, and even, though rarely, white. It is always radially streaked with a smooth cap margin, and can be slightly greasy. The gills and stem are white, though the stem is sometimes flushed with the cap colour and banded with faint zig-zag marks. The stem has a white, drooping, slightly grooved ring, which may fall off, and the base has a white membranous volval bag which may be greenish inside. The Death Cap has a sweet sickly smell, strongest with age. It is highly poisonous – if consumed it will cause vomiting, then slow liver and kidney failure.

GROWS *in woodland of all types, including grassy fringes or parks; associated with broadleaf trees, such as beech, oak, and hazel, on rich soils.*

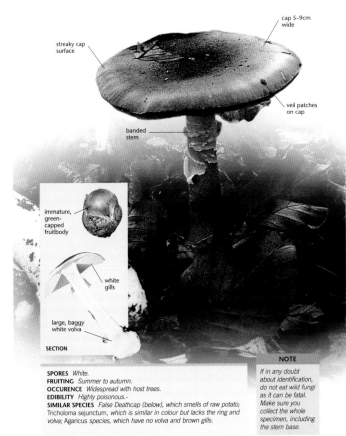

cap 5–9cm wide

streaky cap surface

veil patches on cap

banded stem

immature, green-capped fruitbody

white gills

large, baggy white volva

SECTION

SPORES *White.*
FRUITING *Summer to autumn.*
OCCURENCE *Widespread with host trees.*
EDIBILITY *Highly poisonous.*
SIMILAR SPECIES *False Deathcap (below), which smells of raw potato; Tricholoma sejunctum, which is similar in colour but lacks the ring and volva; Agaricus species, which have no volva and brown gills.*

NOTE
If in any doubt about identification, do not eat wild fungi as it can be fatal. Make sure you collect the whole specimen, including the stem base.

Destroying Angel ☠

Amanita virosa (Amanitaceae)

Fatally poisonous, as the common name suggests, this species is pure white all over. The often sticky cap is pointed and egg-shaped when immature and later flattens out. The slender, shaggy stem has a floppy ring at the top, which is often torn, and an egg-like volva enclosing the base. This fungus develops a sickly sweet odour with age.

FOUND *in damp woodland on acidic soils, especially with birch or conifers.*

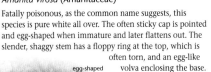

egg-shaped cap

cap 5–10cm wide

volva encloses base

white gills

white flesh

SECTION

SPORES *White.*
FRUITING *Summer to late autumn.*
OCCURENCE *Rare to occasional, mostly found in the northern region.*
EDIBILITY *Highly poisonous.*
SIMILAR SPECIES *White Agaricus species, which can look very similar but lack a volva and develop pink then brown gills and spores.*

Tawny Grisette ☠

Amanita fulva (Amanitaceae)

This species has a conical to umbonate, smooth, dull tawny-brown cap with few, if any, scaly patches and a grooved margin. Its smooth, pale to light brown stem is ringless and at its base, which is often buried in soil, has a thick persistent off-white and tan-brown volva. The Tawny Grisette has white to cream gills, which are crowded and free from the stem.

GROWS *singly or in small troops, in broadleaf woods but occasionally with conifers.*

cap up to 8cm wide

crowded free gills

white to cream gills

hollow stem

pale to light brown stem

dull tawny-brown cap

off-white and brown volva

SECTION

SPORES *White.*
FRUITING *Summer to autumn.*
OCCURENCE *Common and widespread throughout.*
EDIBILITY *Edible only when cooked.*
SIMILAR SPECIES *Orange Grisette (A. crocea), which is bright orange; A. vaginata, which is pale grey.*

False Deathcap

Amanita citrina (Amanitaceae)

The smooth-edged cap of this fungus can either be lemon-yellow or pure white, and when young is covered in a map-like mosaic of detachable white or beige scales. The crowded gills are whitish yellow. There is a drooping ring at the top of the stem and a rounded bulb with a distinct rim at the base. The flesh smells strongly of raw potatoes, especially when rubbed.

FOUND *singly or in troops in woodland, on acidic soil; grows with conifers or broadleaf trees (beech, oak, and birch).*

off-white to yellow gills

beige scales on cap

cap 5–10cm wide

bulbous stem base

drooping ring

SECTION

SPORES *Off-white.*
FRUITING *Late summer to autumn.*
OCCURENCE *Common and widespread.*
EDIBILITY *Inedible.*
SIMILAR SPECIES *Destroying Angel (right) has an irregular cap; Death Cap (above) has a sickly smell; A. gemmata is buff-yellow – all three species are poisonous.*

Deer Shield

Pluteus cervinus (Pluteaceae)

The pale fawn to buff or dark brown cap of the Deer Shield is variable in size as well as colour. It has a felty centre and becomes greasy when wet. The gills are cream, later deep pinkish brown. The club-shaped stem is white with blackish brown fibres. The flesh is white and thick, with a musty, radish-like smell.

FOUND *on dead stumps, logs, branches, and fallen timber, also on sawdust; in woods, parks, and gardens.*

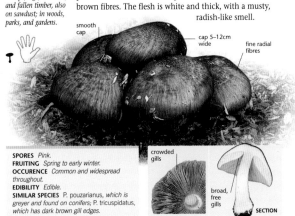

smooth cap

cap 5–12cm wide

fine radial fibres

crowded gills

broad, free gills

SECTION

SPORES *Pink.*
FRUITING *Spring to early winter.*
OCCURENCE *Common and widespread throughout.*
EDIBILITY *Edible.*
SIMILAR SPECIES *P. pouzarianus, which is greyer and found on conifers; P. tricuspidatus, which has dark brown gill edges.*

FUNGI

Fly Agaric
This striking troop of Fly Agarics is growing among the spruce and pine of Hafren Forest, Powys, Wales. While attractive and intriguing to look at, this species is poisonous and not to be eaten.

Parasol

Macrolepiota procera (Agaricaceae)

This is a well-known, edible species that often grows very large. The egg-shaped young cap soon expands and flattens with a large central umbo. It has a pale buff-brown surface with very dark, flattened scales radiating out from the centre. The free gills are broad and pale cream, while the tall, club-shaped stem is very firm and pale buff with numerous bands of dark brown scales in a pattern resembling snakeskin. There is a large, double ring on the stem which can be moved up and down when it gets old. The flesh is whitish in colour and bruises to dull yellowish red.

FOUND *in small troops in meadows, fields, and woodland clearings, as well as in dune grassland and on roadsides.*

dark scales radiate out from centre

cap 10–30cm wide

white to cream gills

large stem ring

dark scales on tall stem

dark umbo

bulbous stem base

SPORES *White.*
FRUITING *Summer to late autumn.*
OCCURENCE *Common and widespread throughout the region.*
EDIBILITY *Edible and tasty.*
SIMILAR SPECIES *M. fuliginosa, which has a grey-brown cap with dark brown scales; M. permixta, which often has pinkish gills and its flesh stains a deeper red-brown; The Blusher (p.463).*

NOTE
The Parasol can be easily distinguished by its banded stem. The toxic Blusher (p.463), with which it may be confused, has detachable cap scales.

Stinking Dapperling ☠

Lepiota cristata (Agaricaceae)

The small, domed cap of the Stinking Dapperling is white with red-brown scales concentrated at the centre and radiating out to the margin, growing paler as they spread out. The free gills are white to pale cream and crowded. Slender and cylindrical, the white stem becomes dull brown lower down and has a silky surface. At the top of the stem is a thin, easily detached white ring. The gills and white flesh strongly smell of fresh rubber or chemicals; the flesh is poisonous, but not fatal.

SEEN *in small groups, usually in grass along woodland paths, field edges, on lawns and meadows, or sometimes near nettle beds; prefers rich soil.*

NOTE
The white cap of this fungus always has the dark central spot of scales, and its flesh has a strong, chemical smell. The tiny ring on the stem is another identifying feature, although it may slip off from older specimens.

free cream gills

dark spot at centre of cap

cap 2–4cm wide

scales radiate outwards from centre

paler scales near outer margin

tough, thin stem

SPORES *White.*
FRUITING *Summer to late autumn.*
OCCURENCE *Common and widespread everywhere.*
EDIBILITY *Poisonous.*
SIMILAR SPECIES *Other small species of Lepiota, which differ in colour of scales or lack the strong smell; several are fatally poisonous, including Star Dapperling (L. josserandii), which has pinkish brown scales and is occasionally found in gardens and parks.*

Shaggy Parasol ☠

Macrolepiota rhacodes (Agaricaceae)

Reaching large sizes, the fleshy cap of the Shaggy Parasol has a dark umbo with recurved brown scales on a whitish background. The free gills are white, and the stout, smooth stem is whitish to dull brown, with a bulbous base and thick, double ring. While the gills bruise dark brown, the flesh bruises deep red, then brown.

EMERGES *singly, or in clumps or rings, in gardens and mixed woods, and on compost heaps and roadsides.*

free, pale cream gills

white flesh bruises red

cap 5–20cm wide

drumstick shaped fruitbody

pale buff-brown stem

dark scales

SPORES *White.*
FRUITING *Summer to late autumn.*
OCCURENCE *Frequent to common everywhere.*
EDIBILITY *Edible, but toxic in some cases.*
SIMILAR SPECIES *M. olivieri, which is dark brown overall, less robust, and grows mostly in coniferous woodland.*

The Prince

Agaricus augustus (Agaricaeae)

A large, beautiful species with a finely scaly, tawny-brown cap, The Prince has a tall stem with a woolly-scaly surface below a floppy ring. The cap scales may vary from straw-yellow to gold or reddish brown over a much paler, almost white background. When cut, the flesh turns a pale yellow to orange-brown and smells pleasantly of aniseed.

GROWS *on roadsides, woodland edges, and gardens, on sandy or clayey soils.*

cap 9–22cm wide

flattened, yellow-brown scales

large, floppy, delicate ring

pinkish grey gills

woolly scales below stem ring

SECTION

SPORES *Dark brown.*
FRUITING *Summer to late autumn.*
OCCURENCE *Occasional to frequent everywhere.*
EDIBILITY *Edible.*
SIMILAR SPECIES *Blushing Wood Mushroom (p.467), which is smaller with pointed, brown scales. Its flesh stains bright red when cut.*

Horse Mushroom

Agaricus arvensis (Agaricaceae)

This is a well-known edible species formerly cultivated in rural districts. Often quite large, the fungus has a mainly smooth, rounded white cap, becoming dull bronze-yellow with age. The cap may crack into fibres when exposed to hot sun. Its similarly coloured stem is cylindrical to slightly club-shaped, thickening towards the base. It is smooth below a large, soft floppy ring that hangs down from the top. The underside of the ring has thick flakes of veil arranged rather like a cogwheel. The crowded gills are pinkish to brown in colour and free from the stem. The thick white flesh slowly bruises to a dull yellow and smells of aniseed.

OCCURS *in grass meadows, parks, or near broadleaf woods. Also in gardens on manured soil.*

gills age from pale pink to brown

ring with "cogwheel" on underside

SECTION

cap 6–10cm wide

white cap ageing to dull yellow

cylindrical to club-shaped stem

flattened, thimble-shaped young caps

NOTE

The pleasant anise smell of the cut flesh distinguishes this popular edible species. You can also identify this fungus by its pink gills that turn brown.

SPORES *Dark brown.*
FRUITING *Summer to late autumn.*
OCCURENCE *Occasional to frequent everywhere.*
EDIBILITY *Edible and tasty.*
SIMILAR SPECIES A. macrocarpus, *which is more robust, with a woolly stem below the ring, and prefers woodlands;* A. osecanus, *which is whiter, woolier on the stem, and prefers chalky soil.*

Field Mushroom

Agaricus campestris (Agaricaceae)

The edible Field Mushroom has a flattened white cap with bright pink gills when young. Later the cap may turn pinkish grey, while the gills become chocolate brown. It has a short, tapering or cylindrical stem with a very fragile ring that is often visible as just a faint zone at the top of the stem.

FOUND *often in large numbers, forming fairy rings in grassy meadows and field and grass verges.*

cap 4–10cm wide

finely scaled white cap

small, fragile ring

white flesh

young pink gills

short, stout stem

SECTION

SPORES *Dark brown.*
FRUITING *Summer to late autumn.*
OCCURENCE *Common and widespread.*
EDIBILITY *Edible.*
SIMILAR SPECIES Agaricus lutosus, *which is smaller with purplish scales in the cap centre, and stains dull yellow.*

Blushing Wood Mushroom

Agaricus sylvaticus (Agaricaceae)

The white flesh of this mushroom stains deep red when cut. Initially rounded, the pale brown cap soon flattens, and has finely pointed, dark brown scales at the centre. The greyish pink, free gills turn dark brown, and the smooth stem is cream to pale brown, with a large, floppy ring.

SEEN *in small troops in both broadleaf and coniferous woods, also along roadsides and in parks and gardens.*

convex cap

dark brown centre

grey-pink gills

small, pointed scales

deep red staining

SECTION

floppy, fragile ring

cap 5–10cm wide

SPORES *Brown.*
FRUITING *Summer to late autumn.*
OCCURENCE *Frequent to common everywhere.*
EDIBILITY *Edible and tasty.*
SIMILAR SPECIES Scaly Wood Mushroom (A. langei), *which is more robust, has broader scales, larger spores, and stains deeper red.*

Cultivated Mushroom

Agaricus bisporus (Agaricaceae)

The ancestor of our common cultivated mushroom, this wild form has a darker, more scaly cap. The Cultivated Mushroom is short and stout. Its flesh is white with a mushroomy smell and turns faint pinkish brown when bruised. The spore-producing cells have only two spores. This species has given rise to many commercial varieties, from smooth and white to brown and scaly.

ABUNDANT *in disturbed soil – often where manured or composted – on roadsides, woodland edges, and in gardens; usually not meadows.*

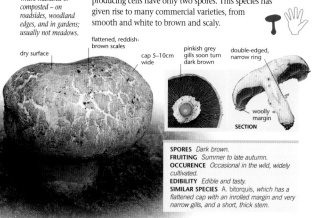

dry surface

flattened, reddish-brown scales

cap 5–10cm wide

pinkish grey gills soon turn dark brown

double-edged, narrow ring

woolly margin

SECTION

SPORES *Dark brown.*
FRUITING *Summer to late autumn.*
OCCURENCE *Occasional in the wild, widely cultivated.*
EDIBILITY *Edible and tasty.*
SIMILAR SPECIES A. bitorquis, *which has a flattened cap with an inrolled margin and very narrow gills, and a short, thick stem.*

Yellow Stainer ☠

Agaricus xanthodermus (Agaricaceae)

A toxic species easily confused with other field mushrooms, the Yellow Stainer is bright white throughout when young, becoming a dirty orange-brown in patches when older. When young, the whole mushroom very easily bruises a bright chrome-yellow, especially in the stem base; this is less obvious when it is older. The gills change from grey to pink to brown as it ages, and the fungus has a strong, unpleasant, chemical smell, like that of ink.

SEEN *in grassland or woodland edges, in bare soil, grass, or bark mulch, especially in man-made habitats like parks and cemeteries.*

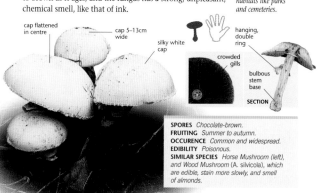

cap flattened in centre

cap 5–13cm wide

silky white cap

hanging, double ring

crowded gills

bulbous stem base

SECTION

SPORES *Chocolate-brown.*
FRUITING *Summer to autumn.*
OCCURENCE *Common and widespread.*
EDIBILITY *Poisonous.*
SIMILAR SPECIES Horse Mushroom (left), *and* Wood Mushroom (A. silvicola), *which are edible, stain more slowly, and smell of almonds.*

Shaggy Inkcap

Coprinus comatus (Coprinaceae)

Also known as the Lawyer's Wig, this fungus has an egg-shaped or elongated cap covered in shaggy scales when young – hence the common name. A narrow ring around the middle of the stem elongates as the fungus matures, lifting the cap upwards. The cap and white gills gradually blacken to release the spores – until the cap dissolves entirely and only the stem remains.

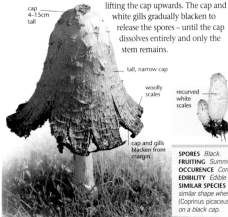

GROWS *in small troops in grassy areas and lawns, and on roadsides, often where soil has been disturbed and turfed over.*

cap 4–15cm tall

tall, narrow cap

woolly scales

recurved white scales

tall, hollow stem

SECTION

cap and gills blacken from margin

SPORES *Black.*
FRUITING *Summer to late autumn.*
OCCURENCE *Common and widespread.*
EDIBILITY *Edible and tasty when young.*
SIMILAR SPECIES *Several species are a similar shape when young; Magpie Inkcap (Coprinus picaceus), which has white patches on a black cap.*

Ringed-blue Roundhead

Stropharia aeruginosa (Strophariaceae)

The distinctive blue-green domed cap of this species has fleecy white scales at the margin when young, which fade to ochre-yellow. The gills are brownish violet with a frosted white edge. There is a prominent though fragile ring on the stem, which is whitish above the ring and pale blue-green below, with fleecy scales.

GROWS *singly or in small groups on debris in broadleaf and coniferous woods, or among moss in pasture or on roadsides.*

white edge on dark gills

glutinous cap

cap to 7cm wide

white scales at margin

grey-brown gills

SECTION

SPORES *Dark brown.*
FRUITING *Autumn.*
OCCURENCE *Common to very common.*
EDIBILITY *Inedible.*
SIMILAR SPECIES *Blue Roundhead (S. caerulea), which lacks the white gill edge; Peppery Roundhead (S. pseudocyanea), which smells of pepper.*

Glistening Inkcap

Coprinus micaceus (Coprinaceae)

An egg-shaped, bright tan to brown, clustering, inedible fungus, the Glistening Inkcap is often found in large groups. The caps appear pleated, and are darker in the centre with a pale cream line at the edge. They are covered in fine, powdery granules which make the cap surface glisten, though these can rub off with age. The brittle stems are pale by contrast, and the gills turn inky black with age.

OCCURS *often in dense clusters on and around the base of rotting trees and fallen broadleaf wood of all kinds.*

brown gills edged white

silvery stem

SECTION

'pleated' egg-shaped caps

cap to 4cm wide

SPORES *Black.*
FRUITING *Late spring to early winter.*
OCCURENCE *Common and widespread.*
EDIBILITY *Inedible.*
SIMILAR SPECIES *C. domesticus, which has a yellow mat around the base; Psathyrella clusters, which have no granules or pleats on the cap.*

Sulphur Tuft ☠

Hypholoma fasciculare (Strophariaceae)

Domed when young, the yellow-edged caps are more orange at the centre, becoming funnel-shaped and undulating when older. The stem is yellow and fibrous, its ring-zone becoming brownish purple with fallen spores. The gills are a garish yellow-green when young, darkening to a purplish black with age. The flesh of the Sulphur Tuft is very bitter and can cause severe stomach upsets.

SEEN *in tufts, often in large numbers, growing on the rotting wood of both conifers and broadleaf trees.*

cap to 7cm wide

sulphur-yellow cap

darker centre on caps

green and purplish black gills

stem yellow at top

darker stem base

SPORES *Purple-brown.*
FRUITING *Summer to autumn.*
OCCURENCE *Common and widespread.*
EDIBILITY *Poisonous.*
SIMILAR SPECIES *Brick Tuft (H. lateritium) and Snakeskin Brownie (H. marginatum), which have whitish gills and a silky white stem layer when young.*

Common Inkcap ☠

Coprinus atramentarius (Coprinaceae)

This species is edible except when mixed with alcohol in any form. It causes palpitations and sickness even when alcohol is consumed days after the fungus is eaten. The egg-shaped cap has a red-brown centre and a smooth surface that is ridged. The cap expands slightly and gradually becomes inky black, liquifying from the margin, which can be lobed. Its stem has a ring-zone.

SEEN *in clusters in humus-rich places, often on buried wood of broadleaf trees, in woods and gardens.*

grey to grey-brown cap

cap to 7cm wide

reddish brown fibres

free gills

hollow white stem

SECTION

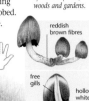

SPORES *Black.*
FRUITING *Spring to autumn.*
OCCURENCE *Common and widespread.*
EDIBILITY *Potentially poisonous; edible with extreme caution.*
SIMILAR SPECIES *C. acuminatus has a pointed umbo on the cap; C. romagnesianus has cap with reddish orange flattened scales.*

Shaggy Scalycap

Pholiota squarrosa (Strophariaceae)

An easily recognizable species, the Shaggy Scalycap has dense, dark brown scales on its light yellow cap and stem. The upturned, pointed scales cover both the rounded cap and the lower part of the tough stem below the ring-zone. Its crowded gills are straw-yellow when young, later becoming brown, and the pale yellow flesh smells of radishes.

FOUND *clustered at the base of broadleaf trees, especially beech and ash.*

yellow gills turn brown

rounded, scaly cap

scaly stem

cap to 15cm wide

upturned brown scales

SPORES *Brown.*
FRUITING *Late summer to early winter.*
OCCURENCE *Common and widespread.*
EDIBILITY *Inedible.*
SIMILAR SPECIES *Golden Scalycap (P. aurivella), which is golden-yellow with flat scales; Spectacular Rustgill (p.472), which lacks cap scales.*

Deadly Fibrecap ☠

Inocybe erubescens (Cortinariaceae)

Dangerously poisonous due to high levels of the toxin muscarine, this species is entirely ivory-white with a rounded to strongly umbonate cap, splitting into radial fibres. Its gills, grey-buff then deep brown, are almost free from the stem. The solid, cylindrical stem is fibrous. All parts of the fungus stain deep pinkish red when scratched. This early fruiting species has a pleasant odour and can be easily mistaken for some edible fungi.

GROWS *with broadleaf trees, particularly beech, on warm calcareous soil, especially southern slopes.*

cap 3–6cm wide

basal bulb with rim

greyish gills turn brown

reddish bruising on ivory cap

SECTION

SPORES *Brown.*
FRUITING *Spring to late summer.*
OCCURENCE *Rare to occasional.*
EDIBILITY *Highly poisonous.*
SIMILAR SPECIES *Silky Fibrecap (I. fibrosa), which is larger, whitish, and does not stain red; I. godeyi, which has a distinct basal bulb with a rim.*

Dappled Webcap ☠

Cortinarius bolaris (Cortinariaceae)

This striking species has a rounded then flattened cap, covered in flattened red scales on a cream background. The gills are cinnamon- to rust-brown and the cylindrical stem is speckled with red scales and girdles. There is a fine, cobwebby zone at the top of the stem. This species is poisonous.

SEEN *often in small groups in leaf litter, especially under oaks and birch, on acid soil.*

reddish scales on cap

cap 4–6cm wide

SECTION

flattened cap

yellowish orange flesh

cylindrical stem

SPORES *Brown.*
FRUITING *Summer to late autumn.*
OCCURENCE *Locally frequent and widespread.*
EDIBILITY *Poisonous.*
SIMILAR SPECIES *C. rubicundulus, which has reddish fibres but no scales, and slowly stains red to orange.*

Split Fibrecap ☠

Inocybe rimosa (Cortinariaceae)

Members of the genus *Inocybe* are notoriously difficult to identify. A good clue to this species is its distinctly pointed cap which often has an upturned margin that splits easily, giving it a torn appearance. The cap surface is covered by coarse radial fibres; the stem is off-white to yellow and often scurfy looking. The gills have a spermatic smell.

APPEARS *singly or in small troops associated with broadleaf trees, often in disturbed soil of woodland edges, paths, and banks.*

cap to 7cm wide

margin flared upwards

yellow-grey gills

off-white stem

SECTION

SPORES *Tobacco-brown.*
FRUITING *Summer to autumn.*
OCCURENCE *Common and widespread.*
EDIBILITY *Poisonous.*
SIMILAR SPECIES *Frosty Fibrecap (I. maculata), which is a darker chestnut-brown, sometimes with a bulb at the base of the stem.*

Wrinkled Webcap

Cortinarius elatior (Cortinariaceae)

This species has a large, conical, slimy cap, which is dark honey-brown with a strongly wrinkled and violet-tinged margin. Its dark brown gills are broad and either very wavy or wrinkled. The deeply rooting, pointed stem is slimy and violet below the ring-zone and smells of honey at the base.

INHABITS *mature broadleaf woodland, especially with beech; more rarely under conifers, usually on acid soil.*

large, central umbo

cap 3–12cm wide

dark brown gills

orange-buff flesh at base of stem

thin ring-zone

SECTION

SPORES *Rust-brown.*
FRUITING *Summer to late autumn.*
OCCURENCE *Occasional to frequent and widespread.*
EDIBILITY *Inedible.*
SIMILAR SPECIES *Purple Stocking Webcap (C. stillatitius), which has a less wrinkled cap and a thick, slimy violet veil on stem.*

Pearly Webcap

Cortinarius alboviolaceus (Cortinariaceae)

Both the cap and stem of this pretty species are pale silvery lavender to almost white. The cap is rounded then expanded with a broad umbo; while the gills are initially grey-blue, later becoming deep rust-brown. The club-shaped stem is thick-fleshed and fibrous, darkening to deep violet at the top.

FOUND *in small troops in broadleaf woods especially on acid soil; rarely with conifers.*

silky, bell-shaped cap

gills notched where they join stem

deep violet flesh in stem apex

cap whiter when dry

SECTION

club-shaped stem

cap 3–8cm wide

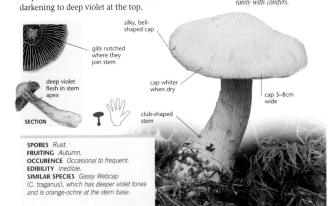

SPORES *Rust.*
FRUITING *Autumn.*
OCCURENCE *Occasional to frequent.*
EDIBILITY *Inedible.*
SIMILAR SPECIES *Gassy Webcap (C. traganus), which has deeper violet tones and is orange-ochre at the stem base.*

Violet Webcap

Cortinarius violaceus (Cortinariaceae)

This fungus is intensely dark to blackish violet in colour. The convex to umbonate cap has a fibrous surface. The cylindrical stem has a web-like veil at the top that joins the stem to the cap margin. The flesh has a smell that is reminiscent of cedar wood or leather. The form that grows in broadleaf woods is usually larger and has smaller spores than subsp. *hercynicus*, which is found in coniferous woodland.

OCCURS *usually in small groups in both broadleaf and coniferous woods, especially birch and pine.*

violet to dark purple cap

cap 5–15cm wide

dry, scaly surface

club-shaped stem

fibrous violet flesh

SECTION

SPORES *Rust-brown.*
FRUITING *Summer to late autumn.*
OCCURENCE *Rare to locally common.*
EDIBILITY *Edible.*
SIMILAR SPECIES *Bruising Webcap (C. purpurascens), which is brown with violet darkening flesh and gills; all other violet Cortinarius species.*

FUNGI

Sheathed Woodtuft
Looking here like a pile of syrup-covered mini pancakes, this golden yellow fungus is indeed a tasty edible species, although the stems are too tough to eat. It grows in clumps on dead logs and tree stumps.

Funeral Bell ☠

Galerina marginata (Strophariaceae)

This is a seriously poisonous or even deadly fungus with toxins similar to those of the poisonous *Amanita* species, and its characteristics should be carefully noted to avoid confusion with similar edible fungi. Its small to medium cap is initially convex and then flattened. Rather thin-fleshed, it is rich reddish brown to honey-coloured when dry, and often has a wavy margin. When moist, the cap margin tends to be lined (striate). The narrow, crowded, pale ochre-yellow gills run down the stem slightly. Although similar to the cap in colour, the stem is paler towards the top. It has lengthwise fibres and a delicate ring at the top, which frequently tears and may not be complete. The ring is often stained brown from deposited spores.

FOUND *in small to large clumps on rotten logs and stumps of conifers and broadleaf trees; increasingly common on bark mulch in gardens.*

NOTE

Always examine stems carefully for any signs of a ring. On this, and other species, it is fragile, and may collapse or even be rubbed off with age. Be sure to check all the specimens that you collect.

pale yellow-ochre gills

stem paler on top

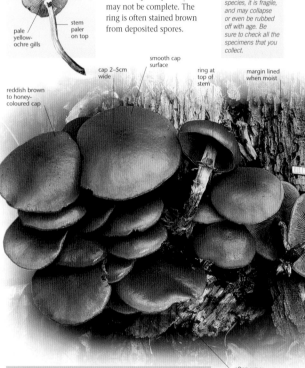

reddish brown to honey-coloured cap

cap 2–5cm wide

smooth cap surface

ring at top of stem

margin lined when moist

often wavy cap margin

SPORES *Brown.*
FRUITING *Spring to early winter.*
OCCURENCE *Occasional to frequent and widespread.*
EDIBILITY *Highly poisonous – all small Galerina species should be treated as poisonous.*
SIMILAR SPECIES *Sheathed Woodtuft (right), which has scales below the ring and a two-toned cap as it dries; Honey Fungus (p.477), which has white spores.*

Poisonpie ☠

Hebeloma crustuliniforme (Cortinariaceae)

The common name reflects the appearance of this species – it has a pale cream to buff colour like that of uncooked pastry, but is poisonous. Its cap is round to flattened with a central dome, the margin is inrolled, and the surface is smooth and quite sticky when wet. Extremely crowded, the gills are pale brown and exude numerous tiny droplets of clear liquid in damp weather. As they dry around the gill edge, these droplets turn dark brown and trap mature spores within them. The cylindrical stem is white to cream with a very fleecy and granular surface. The flesh is white with a bitter taste and the whole fungus smells strongly of radish.

GROWS *often in small troops, among grass in mixed woods, along woodland paths, parks, and gardens; grows with broadleaf trees and conifers.*

pale brown gills

brown spots

sticky, rounded young cap

NOTE

Use a hand lens to see both the tiny drops of liquid on the gill margin and the woolly-granular stem surface – features specific to this fungus. The sticky cap and smell of radish or cocoa distinguish the Hebeloma species in general.

buff cap surface

white cap margin

cap 5–10cm wide

SPORES *Dull brown.*
FRUITING *Summer to late autumn.*
OCCURENCE *Common to widespread.*
EDIBILITY *Poisonous, although rarely fatal.*
SIMILAR SPECIES *A number of similar species differ only in microscopic characteristics, although their taste may be less bitter and the smell more akin to cocoa than radish. All Hebeloma species are regarded as poisonous.*

Spectacular Rustgill ☠

Gymnopilus junonius (Cortinariaceae)

A large, spectacular orange-brown fungus, the cap of this species is domed and dry, sometimes with a central umbo, covered in radial fibres, and may have a tattered margin of veil fragments. The gills become progressively more rust-brown with age as does the large, floppy ring on the stem. This bitter-tasting fungus is sometimes reported as being hallucinogenic.

CLUSTERED, *often in large numbers, at base of trees and on fallen wood – especially broadleaf but occasionally coniferous.*

orange-brown fibrous cap

floppy stem ring

yellow flesh

SECTION

cap to 20cm wide

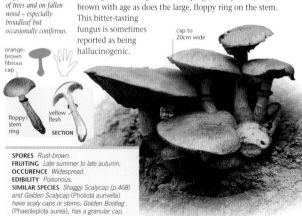

SPORES *Rust-brown.*
FRUITING *Late summer to late autumn.*
OCCURENCE *Widespread.*
EDIBILITY *Poisonous.*
SIMILAR SPECIES *Shaggy Scalycap (p.468) and Golden Scalycap (Pholiota aurivella) have scaly caps or stems; Golden Bootleg (Phaeolepiota aurea), has a granular cap.*

Sheathed Woodtuft

Kuehneromyces mutabilis (Strophariaceae)

The convex, leathery, date-brown to yellow cap of this popular, edible species soon expands to become umbonate and is fairly thick-fleshed and aromatic. When wet, the surface is smooth or even sticky. The most distinctive characteristic is that the cap becomes much paler ochre from the centre outwards as it dries. The gills are ochre-brown, joined to the stem with a slight tooth, and run a little way down the stem.

OCCURS *in small or large clumps on dead or rotten logs and stumps of broadleaf trees, rarely on conifers.*

broad gills

centre turns pale on drying

pale brown flesh

SECTION

cap 2–6cm wide

small ring

smooth, 2-tone cap

dark, scaly stem

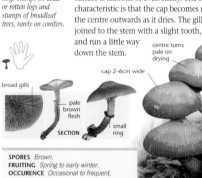

SPORES *Brown.*
FRUITING *Spring to early winter.*
OCCURENCE *Occasional to frequent, and widespread.*
EDIBILITY *Edible.*
SIMILAR SPECIES *Funeral Bell (left) is poisonous, has fibres and no scales below the ring; Honey Fungus (p.477) has white spores.*

Livid Pinkgill ☠

Entoloma sinuatum (Entolomataceae)

Responsible for a number of accidental poisionings, this species generally has a large cap which is pale silvery grey to greyish ochre, often with a domed centre. The medium to widely spaced gills are initially pale grey but rapidly mature to deep salmon-pink. They are notched or curved where they join the stem. White to pale greyish cream in colour, the stem is tough and cylindrical to pointed. The fungus has a strong mealy, sometimes unpleasant smell. Because of its similarity to some edible fungi, it is often eaten by mistake, causing severe stomach upsets and at times proving to be fatal.

SEEN *often in groups, usually on clay soils, especially with beech and oak, in clearings and margins, in broadleaf woodland.*

silvery grey to greyish ochre cap

dry, smooth cap

cap 15–20cm wide

domed cap

gills turn deep pink

notched gills

tough, fleshy stem

SECTION

NOTE

Check for habitat near trees, pink gills, leaden grey cap, and an unpleasant mealy smell to distinguish from similar edible species. Very similar to this is St. George's Mushroom (Calocybe gambosa), which is a spring to late summer species with cream spores.

SPORES *Pink.*
FRUITING *Summer to late autumn.*
OCCURENCE *Rare to occasional.*
EDIBILITY *Highly poisonous.*
SIMILAR SPECIES *Flowery Blewit (Lepista irina), which has a fibrous stem; Clouded Funnel (p.474), which has grey-white gills that never turn pink, and white spores. Neither species has a mealy odour.*

The Miller

Clitopilus prunulus (Entolomataceae)

Very variable in shape, the white to greyish cap of The Miller can be domed to quite flat, or even funnel-shaped. The gills are crowded and run down the stem, white at first, but turning pink when mature. Similarly coloured, the stem may be shorter than the cap diameter. This fungus has a floury smell and tastes of fresh meal.

FOUND *along woodland paths, in gardens, and parks; in groups in broadleaf and coniferous woods.*

crowded gills

greyish white cap

cap 3–10cm wide

gills run down stem

off-white stem

inrolled cap margin when young

SECTION

SPORES *Pink.*
FRUITING *Summer to late autumn.*
OCCURENCE *Common and widespread.*
EDIBILITY *Edible.*
SIMILAR SPECIES *Some white Clitocybe species such as C. dealbata; these species have white gills and spores, and are poisonous.*

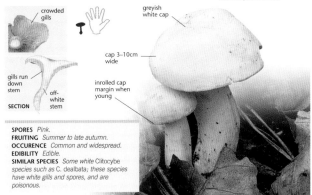

Yellow Knight

Tricholoma equestre (Tricholomataceae)

The cap of this species is bronze- to orange-yellow, sometimes with scales, especially at the centre. It has bright yellow gills, even when young. The stem, which is also yellow, has a slightly fibrous texture and the whitish yellow flesh has a mealy smell. The Yellow Knight varies considerably in stature from slender to robust.

OCCURS *singly or in troops on the ground with conifers, especially pine; also broadleafs such as beech.*

scales on cap

yellow-brown cap

cap to 14cm wide

SPORES *White.*
FRUITING *Autumn to early winter.*
OCCURENCE *Rare to occasional.*
EDIBILITY *Edible and tasty.*
SIMILAR SPECIES *Plums and Custard (Tricholomopsis rutilans); Soapy Knight (T. saponaceum) has a soapy smell; T. bufonium has a gassy smell.*

Ashen Knight

Tricholoma virgatum (Tricholomataceae)

This species tends to remain conical for some time, and even when expanded, is umbonate. The cap has a distinctive silky grey appearance, with a dry, fibrous texture, and often has a splitting margin. The gills are greyish white with a plain edge, and the fibrous stem is white. The flesh is hot and burning to taste.

FOUND *in small numbers or singly, usually below broadleaf trees or sometimes conifers, in the mountains.*

dry, silky surface

white fibres on cap

greyish white gills

cap to 8cm wide

conical cap

white stem

SECTION

SPORES *White.*
FRUITING *Late summer to late autumn.*
OCCURENCE *Common and widespread.*
EDIBILITY *Inedible.*
SIMILAR SPECIES *T. sciodes, which has pinkish gills with a dark or flecked edge; Reddening Knight (T. orirubens), the flesh of which turns pinkish with age.*

Wood Blewit

Lepista nuda (Tricholomataceae)

Wood Blewit's cap is violet- to grey-brown or pinkish lavender. Smooth and rounded, it soon expands, and has a slightly inrolled margin. The gills are pale bluish lilac when young, becoming pinker with age. The stout, fleshy stem becomes browner when old, and has a white, scurfy appearance towards the top. Pleasantly scented, the flesh is marbled with buff-ochre.

FOUND *often in large groups or in circles in broadleaf woods, gardens, roadsides, or rich composted areas.*

smooth violet- to grey-brown cap

cap 4–15cm wide

fibrous blue-violet stem

central umbo on cap

crowded gills

pale lilac-blue flesh

SECTION

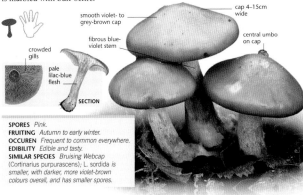

SPORES *Pink.*
FRUITING *Autumn to early winter.*
OCCUREN *Frequent to common everywhere.*
EDIBILITY *Edible and tasty.*
SIMILAR SPECIES *Bruising Webcap (Cortinarius purpurascens); L. sordida is smaller, with darker, more violet-brown colours overall, and has smaller spores.*

FUNGI

Ivory Funnel

Clitocybe dealbata (Tricholomataceae)

This small to medium fungus, commonly found in grassy places, is extremely poisonous. Symptoms caused by eating it are serious, and include a lowered heart rate, sweating, tears, and gastric upset. However, these are all reversible if treated with atropine. The cap is funnel-shaped or flat, and cream to pinkish beige with a white bloom that makes it look frosted. It can be zoned or blotched and sometimes cracks when old. White to greyish cream gills run slightly down the creamy beige stem. Ivory Funnel can smell mealy when young and can easily be mistaken for several edible species. It is not uncommon to find Ivory Funnel growing in fairy rings along with the common, edible Fairy Ring Champignon (p.476). Great care must be taken to distinguish between this poisonous species and its edible counterparts.

GROWS *in grassy places including lawns, parks, gardens, cemeteries, fields, meadows, wood edges, and coastal dunes.*

cream gills

frosted white bloom on cap

cap 2–6cm wide

cap cracks in older fungi

gills run slightly down stem

SPORES *White.*
FRUITING *Early summer to late autumn.*
OCCURRENCE *Very common and widespread throughout.*
EDIBILITY *Poisonous.*
SIMILAR SPECIES *Other species that grow in grass, but which are edible, such as Fairy Ring Champignon (p.476), which is brownish with a bump in its cap, and The Miller (p.473), which has a mealy smell but pink gills and spores.*

NOTE

Since this species can be confused with edible species, confirm its identity by its white gills and spores, concentric zones or blotches on the cap, and gills running slightly down the stem.

Trooping Funnel

Clitocybe geotropa (Tricholomataceae)

A very large, edible species, the Trooping Funnel has a funnel-shaped cap, usually with a raised centre. White to pale cream or beige, the cap is dry and smooth. The white gills are crowded and run down the very tall stem, which is club-shaped and fibrous. Its large size and distinctive shape, and its habit of growing in large circles, make this fungus easy to identify. It also has a distinctive, almost rancid smell.

SEEN *in large groups, often in circles, in mixed woods, usually on alkaline soils.*

cap 6–20cm wide

crowded white gills

funnelled cap with central umbo

tall, club-shaped stem

gills run down stem

SECTION

SPORES *White.*
FRUITING *Summer to late autumn.*
OCCURRENCE *Occasional to frequent on alkaline soils.*
EDIBILITY *Edible.*
SIMILAR SPECIES *Common Funnel (right), which is smaller, pale pinkish buff; Clitocybe inversa, which is yellow-orange.*

Common Funnel

Clitocybe gibba (Tricholomataceae)

The funnel-shaped cap and stem of this delicate, edible species are pale buff-brown to pinkish beige. The cap often has a small umbo at the centre and its surface is dry and felty. The thin, crowded gills run down the stem, which is slender and fibrous. Faintly smelling of bitter almonds, the flesh has a mild taste.

APPEARS *in small groups, usually in leaf or needle litter in mixed woods, often along paths.*

funnel-shaped cap

cap 4–8cm wide

crowded pale gills

SECTION

gills run down stem

tall, slender stem

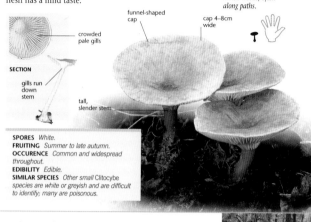

SPORES *White.*
FRUITING *Summer to late autumn.*
OCCURRENCE *Common and widespread throughout.*
EDIBILITY *Edible.*
SIMILAR SPECIES *Other small Clitocybe species are white or greyish and are difficult to identify; many are poisonous.*

Clouded Funnel

Clitocybe nebularis (Tricholomataceae)

A rather variable, mid-grey species, the Clouded Funnel has a felty grey cap, domed when young, later becoming largely flattened to deeply funnel-shaped, with a wavy margin. The margin is often paler and inrolled, and the entire cap surface becomes increasingly dusted with a white bloom. The cap is blue-grey to brown-grey or even yellowish, and may be slightly sticky. Creamy yellow to greyish gills run part way down the club-shaped stem, which has a strong, distinctive, and slightly unpleasant smell. The Clouded Funnel causes severe gastric upsets in some people, possibly as an allergic reaction, although many find it a tasty edible species. However, it is best eaten only when young.

APPEARS *in troops and rings – often in large numbers late in the year – or occasionally singly, in leaf litter in woods of all types.*

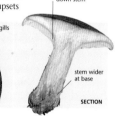

gills run down stem

creamy yellow gills

stem wider at base

SECTION

cap to 25cm wide

domed blue-grey cap

whitish dust on cap surface

paler margin

SPORES *Cream.*
FRUITING *Late summer to winter.*
OCCURRENCE *Very common and widespread, especially in northern regions.*
EDIBILITY *Edible when young but may cause gastric upset.*
SIMILAR SPECIES *Livid Pinkgill (p.473), which is poisonous, has a similar wavy, inrolled grey cap, but the gills become pinkish and the spores are pink.*

NOTE

In older specimens, a whitish bloom may develop on the cap. There is also a tendency for the already pungent smell to become stronger and more unpleasant as the fruitbody ages.

Aniseed Funnel

Clitocybe odora (Tricholomataceae)

Not many fungi are blue-green and this unusual colour, along with a strong smell of aniseed, distinguishes this edible fungus. The rounded cap is often inrolled at the margin and becomes flat to slightly depressed with age. It also fades to grey-green and rarely, white. The creamy yellow gills run slightly down the stem.

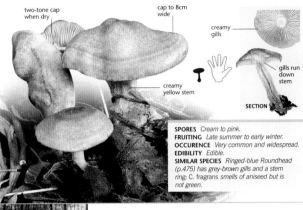

APPEARS *singly but often in troops or rings, sometimes in large numbers in leaf litter.*

two-tone cap when dry

cap to 8cm wide

creamy gills

gills run down stem

creamy yellow stem

SECTION

SPORES *Cream to pink.*
FRUITING *Late summer to early winter.*
OCCURRENCE *Very common and widespread.*
EDIBILITY *Edible.*
SIMILAR SPECIES *Ringed-blue Roundhead (p.475) has grey-brown gills and a stem ring; C. fragrans smells of aniseed but is not green.*

Deceiver

Laccaria laccata (Tricholomataceae)

The small, rounded cap of the Deceiver soon flattens, varying from pale pinkish brown to orange-ochre, with a smooth to slightly scurfy surface. The gills are thick, widely spaced, and pale pink, and are often dusted with white, powdery spores. Its stem is slender, pinkish brown, and fibrous. This species lacks a distinctive smell or taste.

FOUND *in mixed woods and heaths, as well as in sphagnum bogs; common everywhere.*

cap 2–4 cm wide

thick gills

scurfy scale at cap centre

SPORES *White.*
FRUITING *Almost throughout the year.*
OCCURRENCE *Very common throughout.*
EDIBILITY *Edible.*
SIMILAR SPECIES *Scurfy Deceiver (L. proxima), which is larger (5–7 cm wide) and taller, with a very scurfy cap and fibrous stem; it smells like a radish.*

Amethyst Deceiver

Laccaria amethystina (Hydnangiaceae)

When fresh and moist, the Amethyst Deceiver's cap, stem, and gills are an intense, almost luminous, a violet-amethyst, making it one of the most attractive woodland fungi. The cap is dry to felty, with a central navel, and paler marginal stripes. As the fungus dries, it turns a drab greyish violet and is difficult to recognize. The gills are thick and widely spaced, while the stem is slender, tough, and very fibrous. The stem usually has a white, cottony-felty base. This edible species does not have a distinctive taste or smell.

OCCURS *usually in small troops in both broadleaf and coniferous woods, especially in wet areas.*

violet-amethyst in all parts

cap 2-5cm wide

thick, widely spaced gills

hollow stem centre

SECTION

slender, fibrous stem

SPORES *White.*
FRUITING *Summer to late autumn.*
OCCURRENCE *Common to very common throughout.*
EDIBILITY *Edible.*
SIMILAR SPECIES *Bicoloured Deceiver (L. bicolor), which has a brownish cap with lavender-blue gills and a brownish stem with a violet base.*

NOTE

At first sight, you might think this species has violet spores, but as the gills mature they are clearly dusted with white spores.

Woolly Milkcap

Lactarius torminosus (Russulaceae)

An extremely woolly-hairy cap makes this a striking species. Broadly depressed in the centre, the cap is pinkish white to flesh-pink with darker pink zones and an inrolled, very hairy margin. The gills are very crowded, narrow, white to pale pink, and run a little way down the stem. Rather short and hollow, the stem is smooth and paler than the cap, with brittle white flesh. When broken, the gills and flesh exude a white milk which is very hot to taste. Although often considered poisonous, this species is widely eaten in Scandinavia, cooked or pickled.

ASSOCIATED *with birch trees, often in open, grassy areas, along roads and paths.*

crowded, pale pink gills

hollow stem

SECTION

NOTE

To distinguish between Lactarius species, note whether the milk is thick or watery, and if it changes colour on a white handkerchief or like this species, stays the same.

pale pink cap with darker pink zones

depressed cap

cap 5–12cm wide

short, smooth stem

hairy, inrolled margin

SPORES *White.*
FRUITING *Summer to late autumn.*
OCCURENCE *Frequent to common and widespread throughout.*
EDIBILITY *Poisonous raw; edible when correctly cooked.*
SIMILAR SPECIES *Bearded Milkcap (L. pubescens), which also grows under birch, is smaller, and much paler in colour, varying from very pale pinkish yellow to almost white.*

FUNGI

Clustered Toughshank

Collybia confluens (Tricholomataceae)

The dense clumps of fruitbodies and an aromatic smell help to identify this inedible species. The cap is pale tan to greyish buff, thin, tough, and domed to flattened. Narrow and crowded, the gills are white to cream. The buff to deep brown stem is hollow, tough, and hairy with a dry surface. Several stems are fused together at the base.

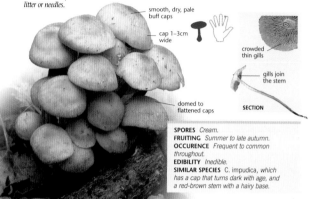

OCCURS *in dense clusters both in broadleaf and coniferous woods, also in thick leaf litter or needles.*

smooth, dry, pale buff caps

cap 1–3cm wide

crowded thin gills

gills join the stem

domed to flattened caps

SECTION

SPORES *Cream.*
FRUITING *Summer to late autumn.*
OCCURENCE *Frequent to common throughout.*
EDIBILITY *Inedible.*
SIMILAR SPECIES *C. impudica, which has a cap that turns dark with age, and a red-brown stem with a hairy base.*

Spindle Toughshank

Collybia fusipes (Tricholomataceae)

The greasy cap of this distinctive, clustered fungus is varied in shape from umbonate to irregular. Often with dark brown spots, the reddish brown cap is paler at the edges and dries out to a lighter colour. The beige gills spot reddish brown with age. Contorted and fibrous, the stem tapers to the clustered base, which is often deeply rooted in the ground. The fruitbodies usually push up from below the root buttresses of trees, and may last for many days or weeks, the old blackened caps persisting longer.

GROWS *usually in fused clusters around the base of broadleaf trees, mainly oak and sometimes beech.*

widely spaced beige gills

mottled, reddish brown cap

fused clusters

cap to 8cm wide

twisted, tough stem

SECTION

SPORES *White.*
FRUITING *Early summer to autumn.*
OCCURENCE *Rare in north, very common in south.*
EDIBILITY *Inedible.*
SIMILAR SPECIES *Spectacular Rustgill (p.472), which is more orange with a stem ring; other clustered Collybia species.*

Fairy Ring Champignon

Marasmius oreades (Tricholomataceae)

A popular edible species, this Fairy Ring Champignon has very tough, fleshy fruitbodies. The entire fungus is more or less pale buff-tan, darker when wet, much paler when dry and sun-baked. The rounded or domed cap soon expands, becoming flatter with a broad umbo with age, and is smooth. The broad, widely spaced gills are almost free of the stem, and are pale cream to buff. The tough, solid stem is dry, slightly powdery to touch, and off-white to pale buff. The mushroom has a pleasant taste and smells faintly of bitter almonds. While the caps are used in cooking, the tough stems are usually discarded.

FORMS *circles or arcs in short turf in meadows, parks, gardens, and near roadsides.*

rounded or smooth domed cap

pale buff cap

cap 2–5cm wide

tough, dry stem

broad, widely spaced gills

gills free of stem

white to buff flesh

SECTION

SPORES *White.*
FRUITING *Spring to late autumn.*
OCCURENCE *Common throughout.*
EDIBILITY *Edible and tasty.*
SIMILAR SPECIES *Ivory Funnel (p.474), which also grows in circles, but is highly poisonous – it has a white, frosted-looking cap, and gills that run very slightly down a stem that is not as tough.*

NOTE

To be certain you have this species, look for the almost free, broadly spaced gills, very tough stem (try bending it), combined with a buff cap.

Velvet Shank

Flammulina velutipes (Tricholomataceae)

This widely eaten species grows clustered on wood. It has a smooth, sticky, orange-brown cap, which is domed and inrolled at the margin. Very rarely, a white form of this species also occurs. The gills are yellowish and moderately spaced, producing white spores. Tapering to the base, the stem is smooth and yellow at the top and distinctly velvety and black towards the base. The flesh is pale yellow with an indistinct mushroomy smell. Velvet Shank has a good flavour and is cultivated and marketed under various Japanese names, including Inotake. It is stimulated to fruit by cold and even frosty weather.

FOUND *clustered in tufts on a variety of broadleaf trees, especially elm and willow. Prefers decaying wood or old, standing trees.*

orange-brown cap

cap to 6cm wide

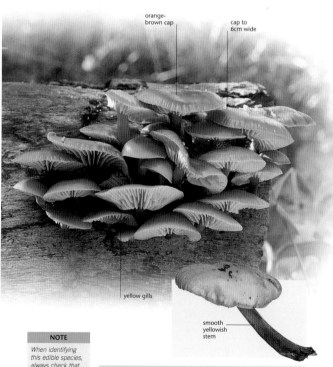

yellow gills

smooth yellowish stem

NOTE

When identifying this edible species, always check that the spore print is white. The poisonous orange-yellow species that grow in clusters on wood have brownish to rusty brown spores.

SPORES *White.*
FRUITING *Late autumn to early spring.*
OCCURENCE *Occasional to widespread throughout.*
EDIBILITY *Edible.*
SIMILAR SPECIES *Sulphur Tuft (p.468), which has purplish green gills and purple spores, and is poisonous; Common Rustgill (Gymnopilus penetrans) and Spectacular Rustgill (p.472), which have spotted orange-brown gills and brown spores.*

Honey Fungus

Armillaria mellea (Tricholomataceae)

This common, edible fungus is one of the most confusing for the beginner to identify as it has such a variable appearance. It is now reclassified as a group of closely related separate species. Growing in clusters, the fruitbodies are firmly joined together at the base. The cap can be domed, flattened, or funnel-shaped and wavy, and varies in colour from honey-brown, to yellowish or olive, with a darker brown centre covered in sparse brownish scales. The gills are white, becoming spotted brown. Often tapering, the brownish stem is darker towards the base, sometimes with lighter fibres. It has a thick, woolly, cream or yellow-tinged ring. The young, fresh caps should be cooked well.

FORMS *large, dense clusters in woods, parks, and gardens. Parasitic mainly on broadleaf trees, especially beech and oak. Also known to attack garden shrubs.*

well-spaced gills

darker stem base

cap 3–15cm wide

tapering stems

NOTE

Look out for black "bootlaces", or rhizomorphs, on the ground or along logs and a dusting of white spores on the fruitbodies from the caps above. Eat only young, fresh caps and cook well.

SPORES *White.*
FRUITING *Autumn.*
OCCURENCE *Very common and widespread.*
EDIBILITY *Edible but can cause gastric upset.*
SIMILAR SPECIES *A. ostoyae, which has more scales, a brown-tinged ring, and is most likely to cause stomach upsets; A. cepistipes, which has darker greyish scales with a more fragile ring; A. gallica, which is less clustered with a bulbous stem base.*

Common Bonnet

Mycena galericulata (Tricholomataceae)

This common but inedible fungus differs from other species of *Mycena* in its tough stem and gills that turn pinkish with age. The bell-shaped cap is grey-brown; the pale grey gills are broad, medium-spaced, and have connecting veins. The smooth, shiny stems are tough, and often have a long rooting base.

APPEARS *in tufts or dense clumps, on or around the stumps of broadleaf trees.*

bell-shaped to convex cap

cap 1–6cm wide

pale to pinkish grey gills

smooth, tough stem

grey-brown cap

SECTION

SPORES *White.*
FRUITING *Summer to early winter.*
OCCURENCE *Common and widespread throughout.*
EDIBILITY *Inedible.*
SIMILAR SPECIES *Clustered Bonnet (below), which has a rancid smell, and a stem that is deep reddish brown lower down.*

Clustered Bonnet

Mycena inclinata (Tricholomataceae)

Growing in dense clumps, the smooth, bell-shaped caps of this pretty species are whitish grey, becoming browner with age, and often have a toothed margin. The white to cream gills are narrow, joined to the stem, and smell of soap or candles. Smooth and shiny, the stems are cream above and deep reddish brown below, often woolly-white at the base.

FOUND *in clumps on dead stumps and logs of broadleaf trees, occasionally on standing trees.*

toothed margin

older fungi turn brown

cap 2–4cm wide

SECTION

red-brown below

gills join stem

stem bases fuse together

SPORES *White.*
FRUITING *Summer to late autumn.*
OCCURENCE *Frequent to common throughout.*
EDIBILITY *Inedible.*
SIMILAR SPECIES *M. maculata, which has a smooth cap margin, purplish brown stem, and red-brown spots on the cap and gills.*

Ringless Honey Fungus

Armillaria tabescens (Tricholomataceae)

Particularly common in hot, dry summers, this species grows in dense clusters. The rounded caps, which soon flatten, are pale honey-brown with minute blackish scales at the centre. Moderately crowded, the tawny-buff gills join and run slightly down the slender, fibrous stem, which does not have a ring. Many stems are fused together at the base. The off-white flesh is edible only after cooking.

GROWS *parasitically in dense clumps on broadleaf trees, especially oak, usually around the roots.*

gills run down stem

flattened cap

cap 3–6cm wide

stems fused at base

SPORES *Cream.*
FRUITING *Late summer to early autumn.*
OCCURENCE *Rare to locally common, especially in the south.*
EDIBILITY *Edible.*
SIMILAR SPECIES *More common Armillaria species (see above) have a distinct ring or cobwebby ring-zone at the top of the stem.*

Porcelain Fungus

Oudemansiella mucida (Tricholomataceae)

The Porcelain Fungus has a slimy, pure white to pale grey cap that resembles glistening porcelain, and is difficult to grip. The stem has a narrow ring that is white above and grey on the underside. The base of the stem is often dark brown and the broad, widely spaced gills are white and attached to the stem.

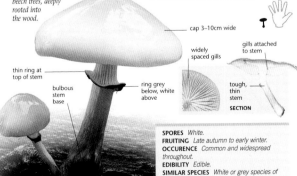

OCCURS *in large numbers on fallen dead wood or on the trunks of standing beech trees, deeply rooted into the wood.*

wrinkled at centre

cap 3–10cm wide

gills attached to stem

widely spaced gills

thin ring at top of stem

bulbous stem base

ring grey below, white above

tough, thin stem

SECTION

SPORES *White.*
FRUITING *Late autumn to early winter.*
OCCURENCE *Common and widespread throughout.*
EDIBILITY *Edible.*
SIMILAR SPECIES *White or grey species of Mycena, which also grow on wood but are not slimy and do not have a ring on the stem.*

FUNGI

Oyster Mushroom

Pleurotus ostreatus (Polyporaceae)

The rounded, oyster-shaped caps of this species grow in large clumps, often with several fruitbodies overlapping each other. The caps vary from pale brown to deep blue-grey, and may often have a whitish woolly coating at the centre in wet and cold weather. Crowded and narrow, the white gills run down the very short, or almost absent stem, and are often home to small insects. The white flesh of this fungus has a pleasant smell and taste, and a firm, meaty texture. Very easy to cultivate, the edible Oyster Mushroom is now grown around the world for sale as a popular food item. It is available in most supermarkets and even in kits for growing at home.

INHABITS *dead or dying hardwood trees, rarely on conifers, often found on the side of standing trees at a great height.*

very crowded gills

many overlapping fruitbodies

smooth cap surface

SPORES *Pale lavender.*
FRUITING *Autumn to early winter.*
OCCURRENCE *Common and widespread throughout.*
EDIBILITY *Edible.*
SIMILAR SPECIES *Branching Oyster (P. cornucopiae), which forms dense trumpet-shaped clusters with distinct stems; P. pulmonarius, which is paler and appears in early summer and autumn.*

NOTE
Since small beetles are often found in the gills of Oyster Mushroom, gently shake the caps to make them drop out; wash and dry the fungi before cooking them.

Blackening Waxcap

Hygrocybe conica (Hygrophoraceae)

One of the most common waxcaps, this species occurs in a variable range of colours, combining yellow, orange, tomato-red, and even olive-green tones with grey and black. The one constant feature that enables easy recognition of this poisonous species is the slow blackening of the entire fruitbody with age and after collection. The sticky cap of the fungus is conical and the greasy stem is finely fibrous. Although a similar colour to the cap, the gills tend to be more yellowish. Some of the more distinctive forms have been classified as separate species by certain scientists.

GROWS *singly and in small groups in grassland, including lawns, parks, and churchyards, and occasionally in woods.*

NOTE
Carefully check waxcap specimens a while after collection for signs of blackening. This process of dramatic colour change may take several hours, until the entire fungus is pitch black as if burnt.

sticky, fibrous cap

gills narrowly attached to stem

fruitbody turns black

finely fibrous stem

SECTION

conical cap

cap to 5cm wide

cap colour variable

SPORES *White.*
FRUITING *Late summer to early winter.*
OCCURRENCE *Occasional to very common, widespread.*
EDIBILITY *Poisonous.*
SIMILAR SPECIES *Date Waxcap (H. spadicea), which is very rare and has a date-brown cap and pure yellow gills; Dune Waxcap (H. conicoides), which occurs in sand dunes; Persistent Waxcap (H. persistens), which is also conical, mostly yellow, and does not blacken.*

NOTE
The Blackening Waxcap is one of a small number of Hygrocybe species which can grow in woodlands as well as open fields and dunes.

Pink Waxcap

Hygrocybe calyptriformis (Hygrophoraceae)

The presence of this species is a good indication of the quality of grasslands and meadows, as it never grows in soil treated with fertilizers. Its pointed, waxy caps often split as they expand. The broad, almost free white to very pale pink gills are fleshy and waxy. The fragile, waxy stem is pale pink above, whitish below, and extremely smooth.

OCCURS *in grasslands where fertilizers have not been applied, meadows, parks, old churchyards; especially on alkaline soil.*

sharply pointed top

pale to bright rose-pink cap

cap 4–7cm wide

thick, waxy gills

almost free gills

SECTION

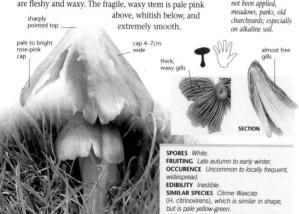

SPORES *White.*
FRUITING *Late autumn to early winter.*
OCCURRENCE *Uncommon to locally frequent, widespread.*
EDIBILITY *Inedible.*
SIMILAR SPECIES *Citrine Waxcap (H. citrinovirens), which is similar in shape, but is pale yellow-green.*

Golden Waxcap

Hygrocybe chlorophana (Hygrophoraceae)

This small yellow waxcap has pale whitish to lemon-coloured gills. It is waxy to the touch and so slimy on the cap that when wet, it is often difficult to hold. The compressed yellow stem may have a groove along its length. The stem base is whitish while the upper portion, near the gills, is often finely powdery.

FOUND *singly or often in some numbers, in grassland, especially short mossy patches free from chemical fertilizers.*

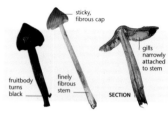

flattened, lemon-yellow cap

cap to 7cm wide

whitish yellow gills

flattened, yellow stem

yellow flesh

SECTION

SPORES *White.*
FRUITING *Late summer to early winter.*
OCCURRENCE *Occasional to common, widespread.*
EDIBILITY *Edible.*
SIMILAR SPECIES *H. ceracea has a dry stem and gills; H. glutinipes has a sticky cap and stem; H. persistens has a dry cap.*

Snowy Waxcap

Hygrocybe virginea (Hygrophoraceae)

The slippery cap of this small to medium-sized fungus is domed at first, but later expands and flattens with a small central umbo or occasionally a central dip. It is cream to ivory with translucent bands at the cap edge. The waxy white gills are arched when young and run down the tapering stem.

SEEN *in grassland, including lawns, dunes, and cemeteries; occasionally in woods and mossy scrub.*

well-spaced gills

cap to 5cm wide

waxy gills

cream to ivory cap

dry, solid stem

SECTION

SPORES *White.*
FRUITING *Autumn to winter.*
OCCURENCE *Common and widespread throughout.*
EDIBILITY *Edible.*
SIMILAR SPECIES *Ivory Funnel (p.474) is poisonous with a blotchy cap; Cedarwood Waxcap (H. russocoriacea) smells of cedar.*

Beech Milkcap

Lactarius blennius (Russulaceae)

This milkcap has a depressed and very sticky cap which is a combination of greyish brown, olive, and dark reddish brown. It has indistinct darker zones and more conspicuous dark spots at the cap margin. The gills are white becoming pale cream, and the milk is white drying to pale olive-grey on the gills. Often hollow, the stem is smooth and sticky.

FOUND *singly or in groups on the ground; associated with beech.*

cap to 9cm wide

white to cream gills

grey acrid flesh

slightly funnel-shaped cap

SECTION

SPORES *Pale yellow.*
FRUITING *Late summer to late autumn.*
OCCURENCE *Very common to common, widespread with beech.*
EDIBILITY *Inedible.*
SIMILAR SPECIES *Hornbeam Milkcap (L. circellatus) has pinkish buff gills; Abundant Milkcap (L. fluens) has a white cap margin.*

False Saffron Milkcap

Lactarius deterrimus (Russulaceae)

One of the most brightly coloured milkcap species, the cap, gills, and stem of this fungus are all a rich salmon-orange, becoming mottled green with age, frost, or bruising. Its gills exude orange milk which may slowly darken. Sticky when moist, the cap may be funnel-shaped with faint, darker concentric zones. The smooth stem easily bruises green. The False Saffron Milkcap is a good edible species, although it has the alarming but harmless side-effect of turning the urine red.

NOTE

Species within this group are not always easy to separate unless habitat is clear. However, all milkcaps with orange milk are thought to be edible, although some, like the False Saffron Milkcap, are tastier than others.

GROWS *usually in rings or troops; associated solely with spruce in all types of locations, including parks and roadsides.*

gills produce bright orange milk

fruitbody bruises green

cap to 12cm wide

funnel-shaped, sticky cap

smooth stem

SPORES *Off-white.*
FRUITING *Late summer to autumn.*
OCCURENCE *Common to very common, widespread.*
EDIBILITY *Edible and tasty.*
SIMILAR SPECIES *L. quieticolor has buff, cinnamon, and greenish blue tones; L. salmonicolor is entirely bright orange and does not stain green but wine red; L. deliciosus has similar colours but its stem has small pock marks and its flesh is much slower to change colour.*

Peppery Milkcap

Lactarius piperatus (Russulaceae)

This white to cream-coloured species has a firm, funnel-shaped cap with extraordinarily crowded gills that run a little way down the stem. The texture of the cap is dry to slightly velvety, while the stem has crumbly, brittle flesh. The stem is usually as tall as the cap is wide. All parts of this fungus, but especially the gills, bleed white latex or milk, which tastes very peppery and dries to a dull olive-green colour. The whole fungus frequently becomes spotted with olive-brown stains when old. It is tasty if well cooked but can cause gastric irritation.

ABUNDANT *in small troops in broadleaf woods, occasionally under conifers, in leaf litter, often pushing up through soil.*

extremely crowded gills

tall stem

latex dries to olive-green

gills run slightly down stem

SECTION

depressed, funnel-shaped cap

cap 5–15cm wide

creamy white cap

NOTE

No other white milkcap has this combination of extremely crowded gills with white latex. To best observe the latex, try running a fingernail across the gills. It will ooze out and dry to small olive-green spots.

brown spots appear with age

SPORES *White.*
FRUITING *Summer to late autumn.*
OCCURENCE *Occasional to common throughout.*
EDIBILITY *Edible, but may cause stomach upset or gastric irritation.*
SIMILAR SPECIES *Willow Milkcap (L. controversus), which has a buff-coloured cap, more widely-spaced pinkish gills, and grows under poplar and willow.*

Oakbug Milkcap

Lactarius quietus (Russulaceae)

The smell of engine or bed bugs is the clue to identifying the Oakbug Milkcap. Rounded to slightly depressed, the cap is a reddish- to grey-brown with faint but distinct darker zones. The gills are pale brown while the smooth stem is usually darker than the cap and club-shaped. When scratched, the fungus bleeds an unchanging white milk.

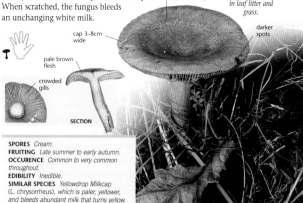

ASSOCIATED *with oaks, often in partial fairy-rings around a tree, in leaf litter and grass.*

depressed cap

cap 3–8cm wide

darker spots

pale brown flesh

crowded gills

SECTION

SPORES *Cream.*
FRUITING *Late summer to early autumn.*
OCCURENCE *Common to very common throughout.*
EDIBILITY *Inedible.*
SIMILAR SPECIES *Yellowdrop Milkcap (L. chrysorrheus), which is paler, yellower, and bleeds abundant milk that turns yellow.*

Geranium Brittlegill

Russula fellea (Russulaceae)

The Geranium Brittlegill can be identified by the overall honey colour of all its parts. The rounded, smooth cap soon expands and flattens and the margin may become slightly grooved. Moderately spaced, the gills join the cylindrical and smooth stem. The flesh of the fungus has the distinct smell of pelargoniums.

GROWS *under beech trees only and blends well with fallen leaves.*

cap 3–8cm wide

pale honey-yellow gills

smooth stem 4–8cm high

stem hollow and brittle

SECTION

SPORES *Cream.*
FRUITING *Summer to late autumn.*
OCCURENCE *Common to very common throughout.*
EDIBILITY *Edible.*
SIMILAR SPECIES *Ochre Brittlegill (R. ochroleuca) has a white to greyish stem, a more greenish yellow cap, and no smell.*

Charcoal Burner

Russula cyanoxantha (Russulaceae)

The cap of this very variable species is usually shades of purple, lavender, or violet; however, it may also be partly or entirely green. The cap surface is dry, smooth, and tough. Rounded at first, it becomes flattened when mature. The crowded white gills are very flexible and feel greasy or oily when touched, unlike the brittle and dry gills of most *Russula* species. The sturdy stem is white to dull cream in colour. Quite tough, it turns brittle when old. The flesh of the edible Charcoal Burner is mild to slightly hot to taste and has a crunchy texture.

OCCURS *singly, or in small groups, in broadleaf woods, especially beech but also under conifers, on acid soil.*

crowded white gills

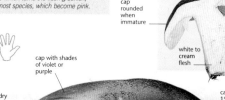

SECTION

cap rounded when immature

white to cream flesh

NOTE

Only two or three Russula species have gills that are flexible – the Charcoal Burner being one of them. To confirm identity, test with iron sulphate which turns the flesh greenish, unlike most species, which become pink.

cap with shades of violet or purple

smooth, dry cap surface

cap 5–15cm wide

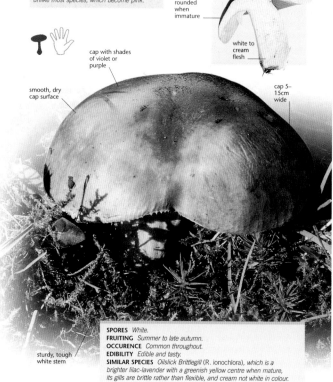

sturdy, tough white stem

SPORES *White.*
FRUITING *Summer to late autumn.*
OCCURENCE *Common throughout.*
EDIBILITY *Edible and tasty.*
SIMILAR SPECIES *Oilslick Brittlegill (R. ionochlora), which is a brighter lilac-lavender with a greenish yellow centre when mature, its gills are brittle rather than flexible, and cream not white in colour.*

The Sickener ☠

Russula emetica (Russulaceae)

This striking and common species has a bright scarlet-red cap contrasting with pure white stem and pale gills. The stem is often tall and cylindrical while the cap is smooth, domed to flattened, and depressed when old. White to pale cream in colour, the gills are medium-spaced. The mildly poisonous, crumbly white flesh tastes extremely hot but has no particular smell and does not stain. One of a number of bright red species, this poisonous mushroom stands apart by its pure red cap without any trace of purple or black; the skin of the cap also peels off almost completely.

APPEARS *usually in wet, mossy, or even boggy areas in conifer woods, singly but often in small troops.*

medium-spaced gills

scarlet-red cap

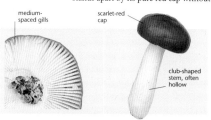

club-shaped stem, often hollow

cap to 10cm wide

smooth, glossy surface

domed to flattened cap

slightly furrowed margin

SPORES *White.*
FRUITING *Summer to late autumn.*
OCCURENCE *Common and widespread.*
EDIBILITY *Poisonous.*
SIMILAR SPECIES *R. silvestris, which is more pinkish red, and grows with oaks or pines on dry sandy soils; R. mairei, which looks and tastes very similar but grows with beech.*

NOTE

There are many species with red caps. However, The Sickener is among a few that have unique features, which make them easily identifiable.

Oak Bolete

Boletus appendiculatus (Boletaceae)

The cap of this large species is a rich reddish ochre to red-brown or bay. Smooth and slightly fibrous, it often cracks with age. Its tubes and pores are bright golden yellow, ageing to brownish yellow, and bruising to a bluish shade. The stout, tapering stem of the Oak Bolete is pale yellow with a fine, raised network of the same colour on its surface. The flesh of this edible fungus is yellow, staining blue when bruised, and has a pungent odour.

FOUND *growing under oak on warm, rich soils, especially in the south.*

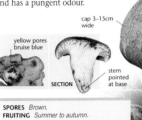

yellow pores bruise blue

SECTION

stem pointed at base

cap 3–15cm wide

stout, pale yellow stem

SPORES *Brown.*
FRUITING *Summer to autumn.*
OCCURENCE *Uncommon but widespread in the southern British Isles.*
EDIBILITY *Edible.*
SIMILAR SPECIES *Rooting Bolete (B. radicans) is pale buff white; Pale Bolete (B. fechtneri) is pale greyish buff to pinkish grey.*

Bitter Beech Bolete

Boletus calopus (Boletaceae)

This very large and colourful bolete has a domed cream cap with a felty texture, which may crack in dry weather and can also be tinged with ochre-brown or olive-green. The pores are bright yellow, becoming more olive with age. They bruise blue, as does the bitter, cream-coloured flesh. The bright crimson stem is yellow at the top and covered in a fine, contrasting yellow network of veins that darkens towards the base.

GROWS *singly or in small groups, in acid soil, especially in beech woodland.*

cap up to 14cm wide

pale cream or ochre cap

yellow pores

crimson stem

SECTION

SPORES *Olive-brown.*
FRUITING *Summer to autumn.*
OCCURENCE *Uncommon but widespread.*
EDIBILITY *Inedible.*
SIMILAR SPECIES *Rooting Bolete (B. radicans), which has a yellow stem and Pale Bolete (B. fechtneri), which has mild-tasting flesh.*

Penny Bun

Boletus edulis (Boletaceae)

Among the most famous edible fungi, the Penny Bun, also known as Cep Steinpilz and Porcini, grows in both deciduous and coniferous woodland. It can be a very large, robust fungus and has a yellow-brown to dark brown cap that appears toasted on the outer surface. The usually swollen, pale brown stem has a fine network of white veins over the upper half, while the pores are white turning yellowish to olive when old. Widely sought-after for its white flesh that does not stain on being cut, the Penny Bun has a pleasant smell and mild taste.

FOUND *in leaf litter or moss of deciduous and coniferous woods, associated with a large variety of different trees.*

bun-shaped brown cap

cap to 25cm wide

network of veins

pores start white then turn yellowish olive

white flesh

SECTION

swollen, pale brown stem

SPORES *Olive-brown.*
FRUITING *Summer to late autumn.*
OCCURENCE *Common to very common, and widespread.*
EDIBILITY *Edible and tasty.*
SIMILAR SPECIES *B. aereus, which has a darker, black-brown cap and a dark brown network on the stem; B. aestivalis, which has a pale biscuit-brown cap and stem, and a dry, roughened cap surface. Both are edible.*

NOTE

Before cooking, check the flesh for maggot holes, and for yellowish stains, which may be caused by parasites. These affected portions can be cut out, but if badly damaged, discard the entire fruitbody.

Scarletina Bolete

Boletus luridiformis (Boletaceae)

A stout fungus, Scarletina Bolete, like several other *Boletus* species, turns blue rapidly when bruised or cut. The bun-shaped cap is velvety dark brown when young, becoming paler with age. However, it nearly always has a distinct yellow-orange edge. The stem is yellow but appears orange-red since it is covered with red dots, which can be seen only through a hand lens. Although the flesh and tubes are bright yellow to olive, they turn bright blue within seconds of being cut, then fade to a dull shade. The pores are bright blood-red, becoming orange with age. Its popularity as an edible species varies across Europe as it is poisonous when raw, and may cause gastric upsets if not well-cooked.

GROWS *in woods, especially broadleaf, and along woodland edges; mycorrhizal with oak, beech, and sometimes conifers.*

yellow tubes

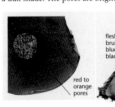

flesh bruises blue-black

red to orange pores

SECTION

cap 5–20cm wide

velvety brown cap

yellow cap edge

reddish tinge on yellow stem

SPORES *Olive-brown.*
FRUITING *Summer to autumn.*
OCCURENCE *Common and widespread throughout.*
EDIBILITY *Poisonous when raw, edible when cooked.*
SIMILAR SPECIES *Inkstain Bolete (B. pulverulentus), which has yellow pores and turns inky blue more rapidly; Lurid Bolete (p.482), which has a net pattern on the stem and is orange above the tubes; Deceiving Bolete (B. queletii), which has dots only at the stem base and more orange pores.*

NOTE

To identify this mushroom, cut it in half to see whether the flesh turns blue; also use a hand lens to check that there is no orange line above the tubes or fine network on the stem.

Lurid Bolete

Boletus luridus (Boletaceae)

This is a beautiful and highly variable species. The cap can be yellow-orange, olive-yellow, or darker brown, often mixed with pink or apricot. The pores are orange to red and bruise deep blue when touched. The club-shaped stem is yellow to apricot-orange, with a fine, raised red network. The flesh is yellowish, except for the purplish stem base, and stains deep blue when cut.

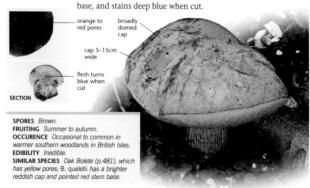

SEEN *in broadleaf woods, especially with oaks and beech, in grassy areas, often on alkaline soils.*

orange to red pores

broadly domed cap

cap 5–15cm wide

flesh turns blue when cut

SECTION

SPORES *Brown.*
FRUITING *Summer to autumn.*
OCCURENCE *Occasional to common in warmer southern woodlands in British Isles.*
EDIBILITY *Inedible.*
SIMILAR SPECIES *Oak Bolete (p.481), which has yellow pores; B. queletii has a brighter reddish cap and pointed red stem base.*

Devil's Bolete

Boletus satanas (Boletaceae)

This spectacular, poisonous bolete can cause severe stomach upsets. It has a large, bun-shaped, suede-like cap that is sometimes sticky; pale cream to grey, this may also have grey-green tones. When very young, the pores start yellow but rapidly become a distinctive blood-red, remaining orange-yellow only at the margin. The stem is usually very stout and swollen, yellow at the top, reddish towards the middle and base, and covered in a fine blood-red network. The thick cream to straw-coloured flesh bruises pale blue, as do the pores. The Devil's Bolete smells spicy when young but with age develops an unpleasant odour, which is said to be reminiscent of rotting meat. Fruitbodies may persist for some time during dry conditions.

OCCURS *singly or in small numbers in warm, south-facing, chalky sites with broadleaf trees such as beech and oak.*

bun-shaped cap

domed, cream to grey cap

cap to 25cm wide

yellow and red stem with blood-red network

NOTE
Check that the network colour on the stem is red by using a hand lens or magnifying glass. Also, cut the fungus in half to observe changes in flesh colour – this may take longer in dry conditions.

SPORES *Olive-brown.*
FRUITING *Summer to early autumn.*
OCCURENCE *Locally widespread, especially in southern British Isles.*
EDIBILITY *Poisonous.*
SIMILAR SPECIES *B. radicans, which has a yellow stem and yellow pores; B. legalliae, which has a cap flushed with pinkish brown. These and other such large, blue-staining boletes could be poisonous and should be avoided.*

Bay Bolete

Boletus badius (Boletaceae)

A popular edible species, this bolete has a rounded cap that soon expands and flattens. It is deep bay brown to reddish brown, or even pale orange-brown in colour in some forms. When dry, the cap is finely felty or velvety to smooth, but when wet it may be quite sticky. The tubes and pores start pale cream and age to greenish yellow. Often cylindrical, the stem is coloured like the cap but is slightly paler and finely streaked with darker brown, and with no raised network. The whitish flesh, and the tubes and pores bruise blue when cut.

SEEN *in small groups in needle or leaf litter in both broadleaf and coniferous woods, on acid soils.*

cap 5–15cm wide

bay brown cap

slightly streaked stem surface

cylindrical, pale reddish brown stem

pores bruise blue

yellow-olive pores

whitish flesh

SECTION

SPORES *Brown.*
FRUITING *Summer to autumn.*
OCCURENCE *Common and widespread in mixed woods throughout.*
EDIBILITY *Edible and tasty.*
SIMILAR SPECIES *Penny Bun (p.481), which is similar but has a white network on the stem and does not bruise blue.*

NOTE
The presence or absence of a network on the stem is a diagnostic feature of species in this genus. Use a magnifying glass and closely examine the top of the stem, where the markings are most prominent.

Ruby Bolete

Boletus rubellus (Boletaceae)

The cap of this small bolete is velvety, rounded, and blood-red to scarlet when young. It slowly flattens out, becoming smooth, then cracked, and dull red-brown. The red stem may have darker streaks. The yellow flesh stains deep blue and may be carrot-orange in colour at the stem base.

GROWS *under oaks, usually in damp grassy areas along paths and woodland edges.*

bright yellow tubes and pores

broadly rounded cap

cap 2–6cm wide

yellow flesh

blood-red stem

SECTION

SPORES *Olive.*
FRUITING *Summer to autumn.*
OCCURENCE *Occasional to common under oaks in southern British Isles.*
EDIBILITY *Edible.*
SIMILAR SPECIES *Red Cracking Bolete (p.483) and Matt Bolete (B. pruinatus), which do not have orange flesh at the stem base.*

Red Cracking Bolete

Boletus chrysenteron (Boletaceae)

Fine cracks appear on the older, olive-brown caps, revealing the dull reddish flesh beneath, which give this species its name. The angular pores are yellow to dull olive and the flesh is white to pale yellow. Yellowish and streaked red below, the slender stem has fine red dots and fibrous lines. The stem, pores, and flesh stain slightly blue.

OCCURS *in woodland, on a wide range of soil types, although prefers acid soils.*

olive-brown cap

cap 3–10cm wide

yellow to olive pores

slightly notched tubes

SECTION

red flesh in cracks

SPORES *Brown.*
FRUITING *Summer to autumn.*
OCCURENCE *Occasional to common and widespread in the British Isles.*
EDIBILITY *Edible.*
SIMILAR SPECIES *Sepia Bolete (B. porosporus), which has a dull sepia brown cap without red in the cracks.*

Suede Bolete

Boletus subtomentosus (Boletaceae)

As its common name suggests, the cap of this species is velvety and suede-like in texture, and varies in colour from yellow or yellow-brown to olive or reddish brown. Its tubes and pores are bright yellow. The usually slender stem is yellowish, often with brown dots or ridges at the top. The flesh is pale whitish yellow and does not stain when cut or bruised. Although it is edible, it tastes quite bland.

OCCURS *in woodland, on a wide range of soil types, although prefers acid soils.*

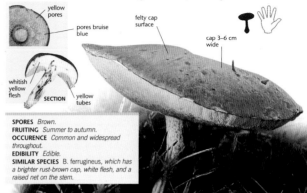

yellow pores

felty cap surface

cap 3–6 cm wide

pores bruise blue

whitish yellow flesh

SECTION

yellow tubes

SPORES *Brown.*
FRUITING *Summer to autumn.*
OCCURENCE *Common and widespread throughout.*
EDIBILITY *Edible.*
SIMILAR SPECIES *B. ferrugineus, which has a brighter rust-brown cap, white flesh, and a raised net on the stem.*

Peppery Bolete

Chalciporus piperatus (Boletaceae)

This small species of bolete has a bright yellow-brown to tawny or ochre cap that becomes smooth and sticky when wet. The rounded to flattened cap may be quite felty to smooth when dry. Its pores are a bright cinnamon-orange to rust or copper-red. Rather large and angular, they run down the stem to some extent. The tubes are the same colour when cut. The short stem is often tapered and coloured similar to the cap but the base is bright chrome yellow. The flesh is pale yellowish cream and pinkish in the cap, and bright chrome yellow at the stem base. This fungus tastes hot and peppery. There seems to be a close association with the Fly Agaric (p.462) and the two species are usually found in close proximity.

FOUND *under birch and occasionally, conifers or even beech, usually on acid soils.*

cap 3–5 cm wide

tubes run slightly down the stem

cinnamon-copper pores

bright yellow flesh at stem base

NOTE

An easy way to spot this species is by first finding the distinctive bright red and white spotted Fly Agaric (p.462). Once you have located this species, look in the immediate vicinity, where the Peppery Bolete will almost always be found.

SPORES *Dull brown.*
FRUITING *Late summer to autumn.*
OCCURENCE *Widespread throughout.*
EDIBILITY *Inedible.*
SIMILAR SPECIES *Suede Bolete (p.483), which has pale yellow pores and lacks yellow flesh in base of stem; Boletus parasiticus, which has similar coloured pores but grows attached to the Common Earthball (p.490); it has a mild taste.*

Orange Birch Bolete

Leccinum versipelle (Boletaceae)

A popular edible species, the Orange Birch Bolete often grows to a very large size. Bright yellow-orange to orange, its cap is rounded and felty when young, but later expands broadly. A ragged, overhanging margin is visible on the "buttons" or young fruitbodies. The tubes of the fungus are up to 3cm long and pale buff in colour. Very young pores are almost black, but they soon become pale ochre-buff and bruise to a darker brown. The stout, often quite tall stem is off-white and densely covered in small black scales. When cut, the thick white flesh rapidly turns lavender-grey, and later becomes grey-black.

ASSOCIATED *with birch in wet woodland, sometimes found in large numbers.*

NOTE

Since young pores may be a different colour from those of mature fruitbodies in the Bolete family, try to collect specimens in a range of different sizes.

bright yellow-orange cap

cap 8–20cm wide

grey scales on stem

pale buff tubes

flesh stains lavender-grey

SECTION

stout stem

SPORES *Brown.*
FRUITING *Summer to autumn.*
OCCURENCE *Common and widespread throughout.*
EDIBILITY *Edible and tasty.*
SIMILAR SPECIES *Orange Oak Bolete (L. quercinum), which has a dark fox-red cap and stem scales and grows with oaks and poplars; Poplar Bolete (L. aurantiacum), which has a bright orange cap and white stem scales and grows only with aspen.*

FUNGI

Brown Birch Bolete

Leccinum scabrum (Boletaceae)

Reaching large sizes, this common species has a dark to medium- or buff-brown cap, which is smooth and sticky when wet. The off-white tubes and pores turn pale brown with age. Often tall, the cylindrical or club-shaped stem is cream with tiny blackish brown scales. The cream flesh hardly changes colour when cut or bruised.

ASSOCIATED with birch, singly or in small clumps, often in damper areas.

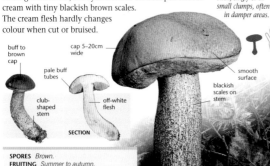

buff to brown cap

cap 5–20cm wide

pale buff tubes

smooth surface

blackish scales on stem

club-shaped stem

off-white flesh

SECTION

SPORES Brown.
FRUITING Summer to autumn.
OCCURENCE Common and widespread throughout.
EDIBILITY Edible.
SIMILAR SPECIES Mottled Bolete (L. variicolor), which has a mottled grey-brown cap.

Larch Bolete

Suillus grevillei (Gomphidiaceae)

Very common wherever larch grows, this edible species has a convex, slimy, bright yellow-orange to deep orange-brown cap. The fine tubes and pores are lemon-yellow. The stem is orange-brown with a slimy, yellow-white ring at the top and the firm, thick, deep yellow flesh does not change colour when cut.

FOUND in woodland, only under larch, often abundant in plantations.

broadly rounded cap

cap 5–12cm wide

tiny pores

yellow flesh

yellow ring

SECTION

SPORES Olive.
FRUITING Summer to autumn.
OCCURENCE Common and widespread throughout.
EDIBILITY Edible.
SIMILAR SPECIES S. flavidus, which is smaller, pale yellow with darker streaks, and grows under pines.

Slippery Jack

Suillus luteus (Gomphidiaceae)

Like all *Suillus* species, Slippery Jack is associated with conifers, in this case pines. It has a slimy, convex, purple-brown cap whose skin is easily peeled. The stout off-white stem has a large, floppy ring at the top, which covers the pores when young; it has dark dots above the ring, while the stem below and the underside of the ring are purple. Slippery Jack has pale yellow pores and tubes that are rather short. Its flesh is pale yellowish white and does not stain when cut.

FOUND in large groups, in coniferous forests, only under two-needled pine trees.

cap 5–10cm wide

large, floppy ring

slimy purple-brown cap

pale yellow pores

pale yellowish-white flesh

SECTION

SPORES Brown.
FRUITING Summer to autumn.
OCCURENCE Common and widespread throughout.
EDIBILITY Edible with caution – it is essential to remove the slimy cap skin which may be toxic.
SIMILAR SPECIES Suillus collinitus, which is ochre-brown, lacks a ring, and has bright pink mycelium at the very bottom of the stem.

NOTE

Suillus species, although widely eaten, can cause stomach upsets in some people. As with all fungi, you should eat only a small portion at first to make sure that it does not disagree with your system.

Brown Rollrim

Paxillus involutus (Paxillaceae)

Although widely eaten in some areas, this controversial species has been implicated in a number of serious poisonings. It has a variable or cumulative toxin, whose effect is poorly understood, so it should definitely not be eaten. The yellow-brown cap, with a strongly inrolled, woolly margin, is slightly domed when young but expands with age and sinks in the centre. It can be very slimy when wet. Yellowish gills run down the short brown stem and bruise deep brown on handling; they are soft, thick, and easily separated from the flesh.

GROWS in small troops, associated with a number of trees, mostly broadleaf but conifers also; often in wet, boggy places.

pale yellow-brown flesh

cap 5–15cm wide

broad, depressed cap

inrolled margin

soft, thick gills

thick, usually short stem

deep brown bruising

woolly margin

SECTION

SPORES Brown.
FRUITING Spring to late autumn.
OCCURENCE Common throughout.
EDIBILITY Poisonous.
SIMILAR SPECIES Alder Rollrim (P. rubicundulus), which grows only under alders, is usually smaller with a few, flattened, reddish brown scales on the cap, and brighter ochre-yellow gills that bruise red-brown.

NOTE

When unsure of the identity of a fungus, always try bruising the gills and cutting the flesh. Any colour change can be a helpful pointer in identification. In the case of Brown Rollrim, the gills and stem bruise to deep brown.

Coral Tooth

Hericium coralloides (Hericiaceae)

An important and rare species of conservation interest, this fungus forms a large shelf-like clump of numerous branching stems emerging from a fleshy base. Each branch has several pendant white spines on the underside, often with a longer group of spines hanging down at the end. The white flesh is soft and brittle and tastes of radish when raw. Although edible, Coral Tooth should be conserved because of its rarity. One of the most beautiful of the larger fungi, it looks very much like an exotic undersea coral.

GROWS *high up on standing broadleaf trees, but also on fallen logs, especially beech and birch.*

drooping white spines

fruitbody 10–20cm wide

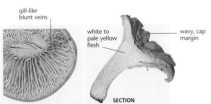

yellow mature fungus

SPORES *White.*
FRUITING *Summer to autumn.*
OCCURRENCE *Rare to occasional throughout.*
EDIBILITY *Edible, but too rare to eat.*
SIMILAR SPECIES *Bearded Tooth (H. erinaceum), which forms a single, rounded ball or mass of long, pendant white spines; H. cirrhatum, which forms large white brackets with small pendant spines.*

NOTE
This, and other similar species, are now being cultivated on a wide scale for food, reducing the pressure on wild fungi.

Wood Hedgehog

Hydnum repandum (Hydnaceae)

This common, highly prized edible species has soft but brittle ochre spines below the cap, which are easily rubbed off. The cap has a depressed centre, inrolled margins, and is often lobed and irregularly shaped. It is dry to felty in texture, and pale cream to pinkish ochre in colour. The stem, which is paler than the cap and fairly smooth, is sometimes off-centre. It has very solid whitish flesh that usually discolours pinkish. Older specimens of Wood Hedgehog tend to become bitter, so if it is to be eaten, it is best collected when young. There is no particular smell to this species.

GROWS *in rings, troops, or clusters in conifer as well as broadleaf woodland, especially with spruce, pine, beech, oak, and birch.*

spines 4–6mm long

tapering stem

SECTION

yellow-ochre spines

CAP UNDERSIDE

NOTE
Hydnum species are distinguished from the tooth fungi (Phellodon, Bankera, Sarcodon, and Hydnellum species) by their fleshy fruitbodies and brittle, not tough flesh. Cutting through with a knife will help to confirm this. Also check that the specimen lacks any smell, and for colour changes to the flesh.

lobed, bumpy cap

inrolled margin

cap to 15cm wide

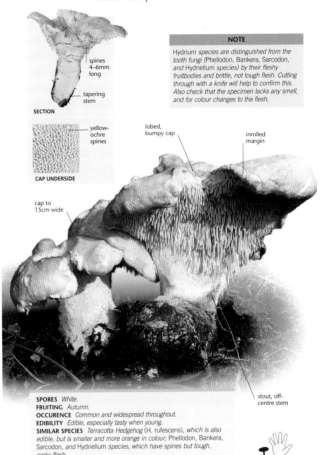

stout, off-centre stem

SPORES *White.*
FRUITING *Autumn.*
OCCURRENCE *Common and widespread throughout.*
EDIBILITY *Edible, especially tasty when young.*
SIMILAR SPECIES *Terracotta Hedgehog (H. rufescens), which is also edible, but is smaller and more orange in colour; Phellodon, Bankera, Sarcodon, and Hydnellum species, which have spines but tough, corky flesh.*

Chanterelle

Cantharellus cibarius (Cantharellaceae)

The smooth golden cap of this edible species forms a broad, flattened trumpet, often slightly depressed in the middle, with a wavy margin. The pale apricot-yellow underside is strongly wrinkled, with gill-like veins running down the short stem. The flesh is thick, with a pleasant apricot scent, and bruises orange to red. The true Chanterelle produces a pinkish yellow spore deposit unlike the deadly *Cortinarius* species.

FOUND *often in moss, it is associated with pines and spruce but also with oak, beech, and birch.*

gill-like blunt veins

white to pale yellow flesh

wavy, cap margin

SECTION

depressed cap centre

cap 2–12cm wide

short, solid stem

NOTE
Although the Chanterelle is edible, it has some highly poisonous look-alikes. Some are more scaly and may have a violet flush on the scales. Others are paler and bruise reddish brown.

SPORES *Ochre-yellow.*
FRUITING *Summer to late autumn.*
OCCURRENCE *Occasional to common; widespread but becoming rarer.*
EDIBILITY *Edible and tasty.*
SIMILAR SPECIES *Deadly Webcap (Cortinarius rubellus), which is deep orange with rounded or pointed cap, and banded stem; Fool's Webcap (Cortinarius orellanus), which is bright orange with a rounded cap – both have brown spores and are highly poisonous.*

Smoky Spindles

Clavaria fumosa (Clavariaceae)

This is an unbranched, club-shaped, greyish ochre fungus. If unbroken, the narrow fingers taper to a point. The flesh is thin and fragile, crumbling easily on collection, and older specimens have hollow fruitbodies. Occasionally growing singly, the species is usually clustered tightly around a central base.

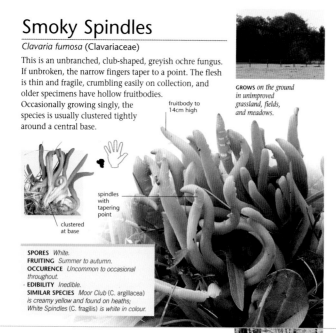

GROWS on the ground in unimproved grassland, fields, and meadows.

fruitbody to 14cm high

spindles with tapering point

clustered at base

SPORES White.
FRUITING Summer to autumn.
OCCURRENCE Uncommon to occasional throughout.
EDIBILITY Inedible.
SIMILAR SPECIES Moor Club (C. argillacea) is creamy yellow and found on heaths; White Spindles (C. fragilis) is white in colour.

Golden Spindles

Clavulinopsis fusiformis (Clavariaceae)

A club-shaped species of grassland, Golden Spindles grow in clusters or dense tufts. The mature fungus is bright golden yellow, gradually becoming brown from the tapered tips as it ages. The smooth surface is often laterally compressed, sometimes with a groove along the length. Slightly tapering bases fuse together, often below the surface. This species is dry to the touch.

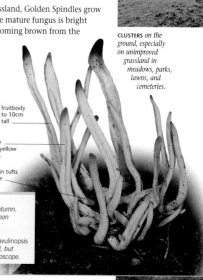

CLUSTERS on the ground, especially on unimproved grassland in meadows, parks, lawns, and cemeteries.

fruitbody to 10cm tall

club-like golden yellow spindles

fused in tufts at base

SPORES White.
FRUITING Late summer to late autumn.
OCCURRENCE Occasional to common throughout.
EDIBILITY Inedible.
SIMILAR SPECIES Other yellow Clavulinopsis species are not generally clustered, but difficult to tell apart without a microscope.

Giant Club

Clavariadelphus pistillaris (Clavariadelphaceae)

One of the largest of the club fungi, this species has a swollen, club-shaped fruitbody. Its surface varies from smooth to slightly wrinkled or fissured. The colour is yellow-ochre to pinkish ochre or lilac, staining darker red-brown when bruised.

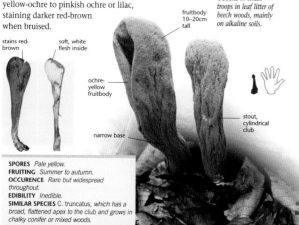

OCCURS in small troops in leaf litter of beech woods, mainly on alkaline soils.

fruitbody 10–20cm tall

stains red-brown

soft, white flesh inside

ochre-yellow fruitbody

narrow base

stout, cylindrical club

SPORES Pale yellow.
FRUITING Summer to autumn.
OCCURRENCE Rare but widespread throughout.
EDIBILITY Inedible.
SIMILAR SPECIES C. truncatus, which has a broad, flattened apex to the club and grows in chalky conifer or mixed woods.

Rosso Coral

Ramaria botrytis (Ramariaceae)

The Rosso Coral has a very stout, sometimes massive central base with thick, short branches subdivided into shorter, very small tips. The central trunk and branches become cream-ochre with age. The thick white flesh has a sweet, fruity fragrance. It is known to cause stomach upsets in some cases.

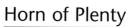

APPEARS in leaf litter in mature broadleaf woods, especially beech. Favourable conditions lead to growth in large numbers.

cauliflower-like appearance

fruitbody 5–15cm tall

cream to pale brown branches

purple-red tips

whitish central stem

SPORES Ochre.
FRUITING Summer to autumn.
OCCURRENCE Rare, widespread throughout the southern British Isles.
EDIBILITY Edible.
SIMILAR SPECIES R. formosa, which is a brighter orange-pink without contrasting tips, and is poisonous.

Wrinkled Club

Clavulina rugosa (Clavulinaceae)

This usually simple, club-shaped, white to cream species occasionally develops antler-like branches. Visibly wrinkled and uneven, the fruitbody may taper slightly towards the base. However, there is no differentiation between a head or stem. The solid flesh is soft but not brittle, and is the same colour throughout. Though edible, it is not considered worthwhile.

SEEN in groups, rarely singly, in leaf litter in woods, especially among conifers.

fruitbody to 8cm tall

sometimes branched fruitbody

wrinkled surface

single white to cream club

solid flesh

SPORES White.
FRUITING Autumn.
OCCURRENCE Common and widespread throughout.
EDIBILITY Edible.
SIMILAR SPECIES C. argillacea, which is never branched; C. cinerea, which is grey and C. cristata, which is white – both are smooth.

Horn of Plenty

Craterellus cornucopioides (Cantharellaceae)

The distinctive Horn of Plenty is difficult to mistake for any other species. The pale whitish grey outer surface is finely wrinkled and has a frosty white bloom. The flesh has a peppery, spicy flavour and a sweet aromatic odour. The fungus can be difficult to spot amongst leaf litter but when it is found, it will usually be in large numbers. It dries well and can be ground to use as a spice or flavouring.

FOUND, often in large troops, in leaf litter of broadleaf woods, on rich, alkaline soil. Frequently on slopes in deep leaf litter.

hollow fruitbody

SECTION thin, fibrous flesh

grey-brown to black inner surface

hollow trumpet-shaped fruitbody

whitish bloom on outer surface

fruitbody 3–10cm tall

SPORES White.
FRUITING Summer to autumn.
OCCURRENCE Widespread and often abundant throughout.
EDIBILITY Edible.
SIMILAR SPECIES C. cinereus, which has more distinct gill-like ridges or wrinkles on the outer surface.

Southern Bracket

Ganoderma australe (Ganodermataceae)

At times a massive bracket, this perennial species forms broad, semi-circular shelves, building up a new layer of tubes each year; the flesh is very thick where it joins the tree. Its rich reddish brown upper surface lacks granules but is irregular and lumpy. The tubes and pores are pale cream and bruise reddish brown, while the tough flesh is a dark red-brown.

GROWS *on old stumps and standing broadleaf trees, such as beech, oak, and lime, rarely on conifers.*

fibrous, dark brown flesh

SECTION

powdery layer of spores

fruitbody 10–60cm wide

SPORES Brown.
FRUITING All year round.
OCCURENCE Common throughout.
EDIBILITY Inedible.
SIMILAR SPECIES Artist's Bracket (G. applanatum), which is thinner, with paler flesh, often with pockets of whitish tissue.

Birch Polypore

Piptoporus betulinus (Fomitopsidaceae)

The Birch Polypore is the cause of death of a great many trees. The fungus starts as a round, brownish ball emerging from the trunk, and later expands to form a kidney-shaped bracket. The leathery upper surface is pale brown, while the blunt margin is white. The white flesh is corky and fragrant. Despite its pleasant smell, it tastes bitter and is inedible. One of the few bracket fungi that is host specific, it is hardly ever absent in any birch woodland.

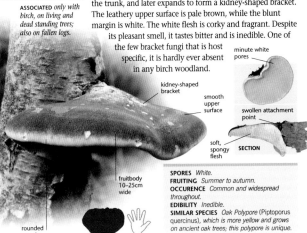

ASSOCIATED *only with birch, on living and dead standing trees; also on fallen logs.*

kidney-shaped bracket

smooth upper surface

minute white pores

swollen attachment point

soft, spongy flesh

SECTION

fruitbody 10–25cm wide

rounded margin

SPORES White.
FRUITING Summer to autumn.
OCCURENCE Common and widespread throughout.
EDIBILITY Inedible.
SIMILAR SPECIES Oak Polypore (Piptoporus quercinus), which is more yellow and grows on ancient oak trees; this polypore is unique.

Chicken of the Woods

Laetiporus sulphureus (Polyporaceae)

Bright yellow when fresh and forming large, tiered clusters of fan-shaped fruitbodies, Chicken of the Woods is one of the most spectacular and easily identifiable bracket fungi. When very young, the fruitbodies are almost orange with a meat-like texture. However, they decay quite rapidly – the colour fades to pale buff and the soft flesh becomes cheesy and crumbles easily. This fungus is often considered edible when young, but can cause stomach upsets for some so it should be treated with caution. This adverse effect is thought to be an allergic reaction with rapid onset and affects about one in ten people.

SEEN *on living trees, rarely on dead trunks. Commonest on broadleaf trees such as oak; also on yew.*

bright yellow bracket

SECTION

soft flesh

NOTE
Do not forget to look upwards at tree trunks when foraying for fungi. Despite their size, tree fungi, such as this one, are often missed by gatherers who have their gaze fixed firmly on the ground.

fan-shaped fruitbody

bracket 10–50cm wide

fruitbody in tiered clusters

SPORES White.
FRUITING Late spring to early autumn.
OCCURENCE Very common, widespread throughout.
EDIBILITY Edible when young, but can cause stomach upsets.
SIMILAR SPECIES Giant Polypore (p.488), which is never bright yellow, and always grows at the base of trees; Oak Polypore (Piptoporus quercinus), which is rare, is yellowish brown and has white pores.

Blushing Bracket

Daedaleopsis confragosa (Coriolaceae)

This species is unusual for its pores, which vary in shape from small and round to elongated and maze or gill-like. The species forms annual brackets, which are semicircular, with an uneven upper surface, often zoned in shades of reddish brown or yellow-brown. When old and wet, the entire bracket becomes dark red then blackish brown. The tough flesh is white and corky. The pores are pale cream to greyish and bruise to a dull reddish pink, especially when young. It can be hard to accept that specimens with gill-like pores are the same species as those with small round pores, but this can be confirmed by bruising.

FOUND *on old stumps, logs, and branches of broadleaf trees, especially willow, causing a white rot; common in damp areas, along streams and near bogs.*

bracket 5–15cm wide

lumpy, irregular, zoned surface

round to irregular pores

thick, corky white flesh

red bruise

reddish brown tube layer

SECTION

SPORES White.
FRUITING Summer to winter.
OCCURENCE Common and widespread everywhere.
EDIBILITY Inedible.
SIMILAR SPECIES Oak Mazegill (Daedalea quercina), which is more robust and grows on oak or chestnut; Hairy Bracket (Trametes hirsuta), which is thinner with a hairier surface and rounder, greyer pores.

NOTE
A variety of this species, D. c. tricolor, has a deep red-black bracket with extremely thin gill-like tubes. It grows on beech or cherry trees.

Hen of the Woods

Grifola frondosa (Bjerkanderaceae)

This species produces large compound clusters of fruitbodies. The fleshy, pale grey individual brackets arise from a common stem, becoming brown when old. Each bracket is tongue-shaped, with radial fibres or furrows forming darker streaks on a pale background. Grown commercially in Japan where it is known as *Maitake*, it is claimed to have medicinal benefits.

ABUNDANT *in large compound clusters at the base of living broadleaf trees, particularly oak.*

brown mature fungus

bracket 2–8cm wide

fruitbody to 50cm wide

pale grey upper surface

common stem

SPORES *White.*
FRUITING *Summer to autumn.*
OCCURRENCE *Occasional and widespread.*
EDIBILITY *Edible when young.*
SIMILAR SPECIES *Giant Polypore (right), which produces larger, fan-like brackets; Umbrella Polypore (Polyporus umbellatus), which produces umbrella-shaped brackets.*

Giant Polypore

Meripilus giganteus (Bjerkanderaceae)

The Giant Polypore lives up to its name and typically produces massive tiers or rosettes of soft, fleshy, fan-like brackets arising from a common basal stem. The brackets are ochre-brown, the pores whitish, and all parts of the fungus bruise grey to blackish. It always grows on or close to the ground, at the base of trees, around stumps, or on buried roots.

GROWS *at the base of trees and around stumps, with oak and beech, but also with a variety of other species.*

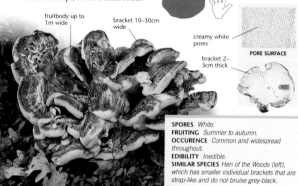

fruitbody up to 1m wide

bracket 10–30cm wide

creamy white pores

PORE SURFACE

bracket 2–3cm thick

SPORES *White.*
FRUITING *Summer to autumn.*
OCCURRENCE *Common and widespread throughout.*
EDIBILITY *Inedible.*
SIMILAR SPECIES *Hen of the Woods (left), which has smaller individual brackets that are strap-like and do not bruise grey-black.*

Beefsteak Fungus

Fistulina hepatica (Fistulinaceae)

This edible, soft-fleshed bracket looks like a bright red clown's nose when it first emerges from its host tree. It rapidly expands to a tongue shape, becoming a darker blood-red, sometimes oozing red droplets when fresh. On the underside, the pale yellow pores become reddish with age and bruising, and are easily separated. The red flesh is soft and thick, exuding a red juice which, together with its distinctive marbled, meat-like appearance, gives the species its common name. Acid- to sour-tasting when old, the Beefsteak Fungus is best consumed when young and fresh.

It is much prized by the furniture industry for the attractive brown rot it causes on host oak trees.

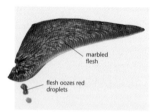

FOUND *singly or scattered on host trees, especially oak but also sweet chestnut. Most often found on living trees but also occurs on dead, fallen, or cut wood.*

marbled flesh

flesh oozes red droplets

NOTE

Cut in half to observe the soft, marbled, red interior with its red juice reminiscent of rare beefsteak. It used to be called "Poorman's Beefsteak", which indicates that its slightly sharp taste is not as good as real beef.

kidney-shaped, blood red bracket

sticky upper surface

bracket to 25cm wide

SPORES *White.*
FRUITING *Summer to autumn.*
OCCURRENCE *Occasional to common, especially in the south.*
EDIBILITY *Edible.*
SIMILAR SPECIES *Resin Bracket (Ganoderma resinaceum) and Cinnamon Bracket (Hapalopilus nidulans) both have hard, woody flesh and are inedible. Beefsteak Fungus is the only red bracket fungus with a soft, fleshy fruitbody.*

Stinkhorn

Phallus impudicus (Phallaceae)

The best-known member of the *Phallaceae* family, the Stinkhorn is also one of the smelliest, often smelt before it is seen. The odour can carry over many metres and it may be difficult to track the fungus down. The smell, when very diluted, is reminiscent of hyacinths but is more unpleasant as one nears the fungus. Hatching from a large white egg, lined by a gelatinous substance, the stout white stem is spongy and hollow. It is topped by a thimble-shaped, honeycomb-like cap, covered with the greenish spore mass. Unhatched eggs placed on damp tissue, under a jar, will often hatch in a day or two.

SEEN *usually close to old stumps and dead wood, in both broadleaf and conifer woods, also in sand dunes.*

large white egg

SECTION

papery skin

stem inside egg

thimble-shaped cap

fruitbody 15–20cm tall

cylindrical stem

SPORES *Olive-brown.*
FRUITING *Summer to autumn.*
OCCURRENCE *Very common throughout.*
EDIBILITY *Edible in egg stage.*
SIMILAR SPECIES *Sand Stinkhorn (P. hadriani), which is usually found on sand dunes, has a pinkish lilac egg and its cap is larger in proportion to the stem.*

NOTE

In temperate zones, there are rare cases where this fungus has a short, lacy veil hanging from below the cap. In the tropics, there are species where this veil is greatly expanded.

Brown Puffball

Bovista nigrescens (Lycoperdaceae)

This fungus is easily recognized by its spherical shape and fairly large size. When immature, it is white and smooth with a sterile basal pad attached to the ground by a cord. As it matures, it becomes shiny brown-black with a ragged slit or pore through which the purple-brown spores are dispersed. At this stage it is light, like polystyrene, and is often found detached from the ground.

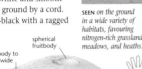

SEEN *on the ground in a wide variety of habitats, favouring nitrogen-rich grassland, meadows, and heaths.*

spherical fruitbody

fruitbody to 9cm wide

papery brown-black skin

SPORES *Purple-brown.*
FRUITING *Summer to late autumn.*
OCCURENCE *Common and widespread.*
EDIBILITY *Edible when young and white.*
SIMILAR SPECIES *Grey Puffball (B. plumbea) is white and peeling, becoming lead-grey when old; Meadow Puffball (Vascellum pratense) has scurfy spines with a short stem.*

Stump Puffball

Lycoperdon pyriforme (Lycoperdaceae)

The very young fruitbodies of the Stump Puffball are covered in granular spines, but these are quickly shed to leave a soft, smooth surface. At the base of each fruitbody is a white, root-like strand. Unlike other puffballs, this species always grows on rotten wood, usually in very large clusters.

GROWS *in large, dense clusters on rotten wood such as stumps, buried wood, or fallen trunks.*

cream to buff when young

opening for spore-release

fruitbody 2–3cm wide

smooth surface

root-like strand

SECTION

SPORES *Brown.*
FRUITING *Summer to winter.*
OCCURENCE *Very common throughout.*
EDIBILITY *Edible when young and white.*
SIMILAR SPECIES *None – although other Puffballs may grow on rotten wood, none has the distinct, root-like strand at the stem base.*

Giant Puffball

Calvatia gigantea (Lycoperdaceae)

PREFERS *nutrient-rich sites in fields and hedgerows, and often near manure heaps, amongst nettles or other nutrient-loving plants.*

This impressive fungus is easily recognized by its sheer size, ranging from that of a small football to the size of a sheep – for which it has reportedly been mistaken. It is generally round but with irregular lobes and occasional fissures. When immature and edible, it is creamy white, with firm white flesh throughout and a thick leathery skin that can be easily peeled away. It may have white cords where it is attached to the ground. As it matures, the Giant Puffball becomes yellowish inside, eventually becoming dark olive-brown, and drying out to become very light and polystyrene-like.

fruitbody to 50cm wide

creamy white when immature

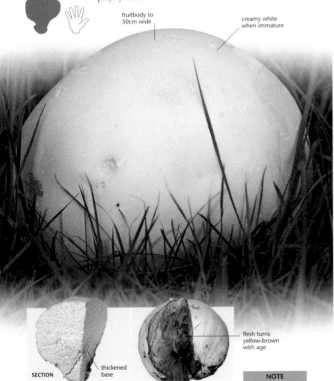

flesh turns yellow-brown with age

SECTION

thickened base

SPORES *Olive-brown.*
FRUITING *Summer to autumn.*
OCCURENCE *Occasional and widespread throughout.*
EDIBILITY *Edible only when young and white.*
SIMILAR SPECIES *Mosaic Puffball (Handkea utriformis), which is smaller, pear-shaped, with a granular to scurfy appearance. It also has a much more obvious broad stem at the base. Other puffball species can reach fairly large sizes but all have scurfy, warted, or spiny surfaces.*

NOTE

Dung heaps and nettle beds are likely spots to find this fairly uncommon species. The Giant Puffball should not be eaten unless the flesh is firm and white throughout.

Collared Earthstar

Geastrum triplex (Geastraceae)

FOUND *in small troops in broadleaved woods, along roadside hedgerows, in scrub, and on sand dunes.*

This is one of the largest and most common earthstars. Young fruitbodies are onion-shaped with a distinct point on top. When mature, the woody outer surface splits and opens out into a star, revealing the puffball-like inner ball which contains the spores. It has a distinctive collar around the ball, hence the common name. There are a number of *Geastrum* species in Britain, many of which need specialist literature and a microscope for accurate identification. The structure of the opening through which spores are released is very important as is whether the central ball is stalked or not.

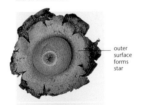

outer surface forms star

onion shaped when young

fibrous hole

puffball-like inner ball

thick, raised collar around inner ball

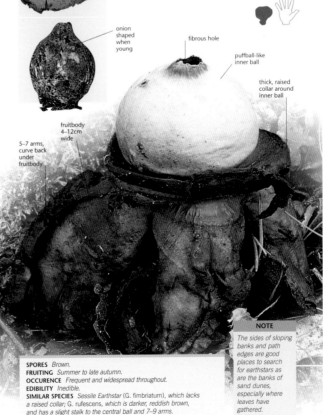

5–7 arms, curve back under fruitbody

fruitbody 4–12cm wide

NOTE

The sides of sloping banks and path edges are good places to search for earthstars as are the banks of sand dunes, especially where leaves have gathered.

SPORES *Brown.*
FRUITING *Summer to late autumn.*
OCCURENCE *Frequent and widespread throughout.*
EDIBILITY *Inedible.*
SIMILAR SPECIES *Sessile Earthstar (G. fimbriatum), which lacks a raised collar; G. rufescens, which is darker, reddish brown, and has a slight stalk to the central ball and 7–9 arms.*

FUNGI

Common Earthball ☠

Scleroderma citrinum (Sclerodermataceae)

At first glance this might be confused with a large puffball, but the scaly yellow surface is distinctive. The fruitbody is much heavier and, if cut in two, reveals a thick, fleshy layer containing a dense black mass of spores, which are released when the fruitbody falls apart. It also has a characteristic smell of old rubber.

GROWS *singly or in small groups with broadleaf trees on pathsides and banks, in acid woodland and heaths.*

scaly, yellowish surface

fruitbody 5–15cm wide

dense black spore mass

SECTION

SPORES *Dark brown.*
FRUITING *Summer to late autumn.*
OCCURRENCE *Very common and widespread throughout.*
EDIBILITY *Poisonous.*
SIMILAR SPECIES *Potato Earthball (S. bovista) prefers less acid ground and has a smoother, greyer surface with a thin skin.*

Yellow Brain

Tremella mesenterica (Tremellaceae)

Like a soft, gelatinous flower, this edible species forms irregular, wrinkled, and folded flabby fruitbodies. The colour varies from almost white or translucent to bright golden-yellow. When dry, it shrivels to become hard, tough, and dark orange, but revives with rain to continue spore production. Spores are produced all over the outer surface.

FOUND *usually on fallen wood of broadleaf trees and piles of brushwood; parasitic on crust fungi species.*

white specimen

wrinkled lobes

fruitbody 3–8cm wide

SPORES *White.*
FRUITING *Autumn to winter.*
OCCURRENCE *Frequent and widespread throughout.*
EDIBILITY *Edible.*
SIMILAR SPECIES *T. aurantia is a similar colour, but is larger, more leafy, and parasitizes Hairy Stereum (Stereum hirsutum).*

Small Staghorn

Calocera cornea (Dacrymycetaceae)

The bright yellow to saffron-orange Small Staghorn appears as gelatinous, rubbery fingers on old wood. These are occasionally branched but usually single. Slightly sticky when wet, they dry to a deeper orange with a very hard and brittle texture.

SEEN *singly or in clusters on broadleaf or conifer wood, such as trunks, fallen branches, cut wood, fences, and steps.*

fruitbody to 1cm tall

bright yellow or orange fingers

branched clubs

deeply embedded in wood

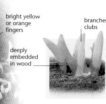

SPORES *White.*
FRUITING *Summer to winter.*
OCCURRENCE *Common and widespread.*
EDIBILITY *Inedible.*
SIMILAR SPECIES *C. glossoides, which has a distinct head; Pale Stagshorn (C. pallidospathulata), which is flat with a pale tip; Clavaria species, which grow on the ground.*

Jelly Ear

Auricularia auricula-judae (Auriculariaceae)

A distinctly ear-shaped fungus, Jelly Ear sometimes has a lobed surface. Velvety brown on the upper side, the inside of the "ear" is greyish and often deeply veined. When fresh, it has a firm feel, like cartilage. However, it shrivels to a crisp texture in dry weather, swelling up again after rain. Jelly Ear is often found in clusters or tiers, rather than singly, and can get quite large and floppy in wet weather when it is sometimes tinged greenish by algae. A very similar tropical species, *A. polytricha*, is extremely popular in Chinese cookery and medicine.

PREFERS *standing trees and fallen wood; prefers elder, but can be found on most broadleaf trees such as beech, ash, and willow; occasionally also on conifers.*

fine velvety upper surface

bracket 4–15cm wide

veined lower surface

velvety brown outside

greyish inside

SPORES *White.*
FRUITING *Year round.*
OCCURRENCE *Common and widespread throughout.*
EDIBILITY *Edible, but dried out fruitbodies should not be eaten.*
SIMILAR SPECIES *Tripe Fungus (A. mesenterica), which grows in bracket-like tiers, and is noticeably zoned greyish brown on the upper surface; brown Exidia and Tremella species, which are also gelatinous but lobed and brain-like, and are inedible.*

NOTE

If you find what you think is Jelly Ear on elm, check whether the upper surface is zoned grey-brown. In this case, it is likely to be the inedible Tripe Fungus (A. mesenterica).

Jelly Rot

Phlebia tremellosa (Meruliaceae)

When growing on the underside of logs, this species is often flattened and crust-like against the surface, but it can form narrow shelves or irregular caps several centimetres across on the sides or top of a log. These are soft and rubbery to the touch, whitish and hairy on the upper side, and yellow-orange and minutely wrinkled on the underside. When dry, they can become very tough and leathery. The margin of the caps is usually white and irregular in shape.

INHABITS *the rotten wood of fallen trees, both broadleaf and conifers, creeping over the surface.*

shelf to 15cm wide

top turned green by algae

SPORES *White.*
FRUITING *Autumn to early winter.*
OCCURRENCE *Uncommon but widespread throughout.*
EDIBILITY *Inedible.*
SIMILAR SPECIES *Other crust fungi lack the dense, tiny wrinkles on the underside and are not as rubbery in consistency.*

Morel

Morchella esculenta (Morchellaceae)

One of the most well-known edible species, the Morel is collected in large numbers in Europe, Asia, and America. Many of the morels for sale in markets are imported from India and Pakistan. The large, sponge or honeycomb-like cap is a bright ochre-yellow to reddish brown, very crisp, and brittle. The cap is fused at the base to the club-shaped, white or pale brown stem. When cut in half, one can see that the cap and stem are completely hollow. When young, the cap is darker brown with white wrinkles and takes two weeks or more to mature.

FOUND *among herbaceous plants in open woods, especially near dying elms, ash, and old apple trees.*

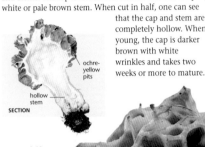

ochre-yellow pits

hollow stem

SECTION

honeycomb-like cap

cap 5–12cm wide

paler margins

	NOTE
SPORES *Ochre.* **FRUITING** *Early summer to late autumn.* **OCCURRENCE** *Locally common and widespread, especially in the south.* **EDIBILITY** *Edible and tasty when cooked.* **SIMILAR SPECIES** *M. elata has grey black conical caps with more vertical ridges. Numerous Morel species have been described by taxonomists, however, most seem to be forms of this very variable species.*	*Compare the depressed pits and ridges of this edible species with the wrinkles of the potentially poisonous False Morel (below).*

White Saddle ☠

Helvella crispa (Helvellaceae)

White Saddle is probably the commonest and most conspicuous of the saddle fungi. Although it varies in size, it is usually large. The stem is white with deep, irregular ridges and furrows, somewhat like a celery stalk, while its spore-bearing cap is cream to pale buff, with irregular lobes. White Saddle is a relative of the morels but, unlike them, it is an autumn-fruiting fungus. This species is said to be eaten in some parts of Europe after drying or repeated boiling. However, it is actually poisonous and best avoided.

GROWS *singly or in troops among leaf litter in broadleaf woods, often on disturbed ground along roadsides or tracks.*

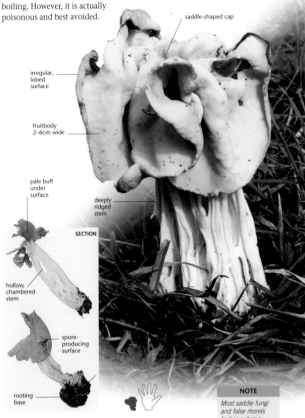

saddle-shaped cap

irregular, lobed surface

fruitbody 2–6cm wide

pale buff under surface

deeply ridged stem

SECTION

hollow, chambered stem

spore-producing surface

rooting base

	NOTE
SPORES *White.* **FRUITING** *Late summer to autumn.* **OCCURRENCE** *Common and widespread throughout.* **EDIBILITY** *Poisonous.* **SIMILAR SPECIES** *Elfin Saddle (H. lacunosa), which is similar in shape and size but has a grey-black cap; Pouched False Morel (Gyromitra infula), which has a smoother stalk and brown cap. A number of smaller Helvella species are difficult to identify.*	*Most saddle fungi and false morels fruit in autumn, whilst the true morels fruit in spring. The true morels also have caps which are honeycomb-like, not merely lobed and irregular.*

False Morel ☠

Gyromitra esculenta (Helvellaceae)

Although widely eaten, False Morel can be dangerously poisonous, even deadly. It has a distinctive wrinkled red-brown cap folded back over a short, strongly furrowed whitish stem. The chambers of the hollow stem can be seen in cross-section. The very thin cap is fused to the stem at irregular intervals. False Morel is known to contain a poison destroyed by cooking.

SEEN *in conifer woods in sandy soils or in wood chippings in spring and early summer.*

wrinkled, brain-like cap

cap 5–15cm wide

hollow stem

SECTION

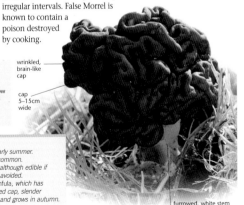

furrowed, white stem

SPORES *White*
FRUITING *Spring to early summer.*
OCCURENCE *Locally common.*
EDIBILITY *Poisonous, although edible if expertly cooked – best avoided.*
SIMILAR SPECIES *G. infula, which has a simpler, saddle-shaped cap, slender whitish lavender stem, and grows in autumn.*

Orange Peel Fungus

Aleuria aurantia (Otideaceae)

Resembling a piece of orange peel, the underside of the bright orange fungus cup is covered in short, downy white hairs. The margin is inrolled, becoming more flattened and wavy with lobes at the edge with age. The vivid colour may fade in older specimens with thin, brittle, and pale flesh. A short base, which may be off-centre, attaches the cup to the ground.

GROWS *in groups, often in large numbers, on bare ground or grass; favours disturbed man-made sites such as dirt or gravel tracks.*

whitish underside

inrolled, wavy margin

vivid orange upper surface

cap to 12cm wide

short, stem-like base

SPORES *White.*
FRUITING *Summer to early winter.*
OCCURRENCE *Common and widespread.*
EDIBILITY *Edible.*
SIMILAR SPECIES *Scarlet Elfcup (Sarcoscypha austriaca) is scarlet; Orange Cup (Melastiza chateri) is smaller; Scutellinia species have a fringe of hair at the edge.*

Dog Tooth Lichen
This strange looking life form is a lichen –
a symbiosis between a fungus and an
algae. The greyish body, or thallus, of this
Peltigera species is irregularly shaped and
has hair-like projections on the underside.

Cladonia coniocraea

Cladonia coniocraea (Cladoniaceae)

This lichen forms extensive patches, made up of tiny grey green leafy scales with erect fruiting stalks that are usually pointed and often curved at the tip; on occasions the tip ends in a very narrow cup. The stalk's surface is covered in grey-green powdery particles. This lichen is very resistant to pollution and can occur in towns as well as rural areas.

COMMON *on decaying stumps, at the base of acid-barked trees, often in woodlands and parks.*

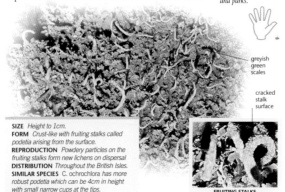

greyish green scales

cracked stalk surface

SIZE *Height to 1cm.*
FORM *Crust-like with fruiting stalks called podetia arising from the surface.*
REPRODUCTION *Powdery particles on the fruiting stalks form new lichens on dispersal*
DISTRIBUTION *Throughout the British Isles.*
SIMILAR SPECIES *C. ochrochlora has more robust podetia which can be 4cm in height with small narrow cups at the tips.*

FRUITING STALKS

Dog Lichen

Peltigera canina (Peltigeraceae)

FOUND *on dry calcerous and sandy soil; also occurs on damp, mossy rocks and trees, and on healthy acidic soil.*

Consisting of large leafy structures that are attached lightly to the substrate by small roots called rhizines, members of the genus *Peltigera* are easily recognized. It is, however, often difficult to identify the exact species. Some have a shiny upper surface while the surface is dull and matt in others. Colours can vary from green to grey. *Peltigera canina* has a grey brown upper surface while the lower surface is fleecy, resembling a shagpile carpet. Its spore-producing capsules consist of reddish brown discs located on the wavy edges of the leafy lobes.

leafy lobe

red-brown capsules

root-like growths on underside

SIZE *Rosettes from few to 25cm in diameter.*
FORM *Flat and leafy rosettes.*
REPRODUCTION *Spores produced from shield-shaped structures called apothecia which occur on ends of the leafy lobes.*
DISTRIBUTION *Commonest in northern and western parts of the British Isles.*
SIMILAR SPECIES *P. membranacea, which has a felted upper surface that is light grey when dry and brown when wet, and a white to tan undersurface with a network of veins and many tufted bottle-brush roots.*

NOTE

The name Dog Lichen comes from the spore-producing structures, or apothecia, which resemble rows of dog's teeth. Dog Lichen often occurs in garden lawns, indicating that there is poor drainage.

Oak Moss

Evernia prunastri (Parmeliaceae)

Lichens that are attached only at the base are called fruticose and *E. prunastri* is the commonest in this group. It has no official English name but is known as *Mousse de Chene* (oak moss) in France. It has a strap-shaped body, with fork-like branches hanging down from the basal attachment. The upper surface of the branches is grey-green but the undersides are white. This distinguishes members of the genus *Evernia* from *Ramalina* species, which are grey-green on both surfaces. Oak Moss had many uses in the past. It was once ground up with rose petals to make a hair powder to whiten wigs and kill off head lice.

FOUND *on trees, shrubs, soil, and fences; early colonizer of twigs and shrubs in towns; sometimes occurs on rocks.*

flat, irregular branches

grey-green above

white below

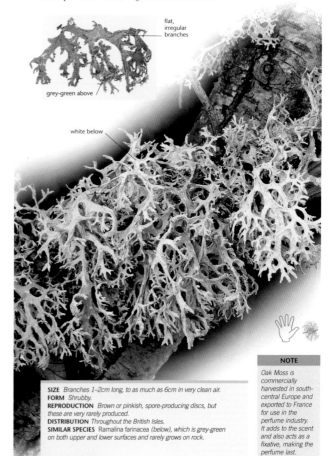

SIZE *Branches 1–2cm long, to as much as 6cm in very clean air.*
FORM *Shrubby.*
REPRODUCTION *Brown or pinkish, spore-producing discs, but these are very rarely produced.*
DISTRIBUTION *Throughout the British Isles.*
SIMILAR SPECIES *Ramalina farinacea (below), which is grey-green on both upper and lower surfaces and rarely grows on rock.*

NOTE

Oak Moss is commercially harvested in south-central Europe and exported to France for use in the perfume industry. It adds to the scent and also acts as a fixative, making the perfume last.

Ramalina farinacea

Ramalina farinacea (Ramalinaceae)

This dry grey-green bushy lichen has flattened branches and is attached by a simple holdfast to the bark of branches, trunks, and twigs. Both sides of the flattened branches are grey-green. Soralia, which are circular broken areas on the surface of the branches, expose powdery patches that contain fragments of algal and fungal particles.

GROWS *on twigs and branches in fairly sheltered, well-lit habitats.*

floury patches

irregular branches

CLOSE-UP

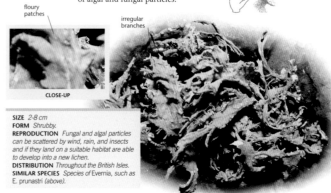

SIZE *2-8 cm*
FORM *Shrubby.*
REPRODUCTION *Fungal and algal particles can be scattered by wind, rain, and insects and if they land on a suitable habitat are able to develop into a new lichen.*
DISTRIBUTION *Throughout the British Isles.*
SIMILAR SPECIES *Species of Evernia, such as E. prunastri (above).*

Sunburst Lichen

Xanthoria parietina (Teloschistaceae)

The most common yellow-orange lichen, the Sunburst Lichen is characteristically, though not exclusively, maritime. It is tolerant of both salt spray and nitrogen enrichment, and so is often best developed around favoured perching sites for seabirds. It also contributes to the characteristic lichen colour zones of yellow and grey lichens at the high water mark upwards on rocky cliffs; these give way to black *Verrucaria* lichens in the tidal zone.

GROWS on rocks and trees along coasts and inland, including walls, roofs, and tombstones.

bright orange-yellow thallus in the open

orange fruiting disc with pale, raised margin

SIZE *Patches to around 10cm wide; often merge together.*
FORM *Leafy.*
REPRODUCTION *Orange fruiting discs, mostly in the centre of the leafy lobes (thallus).*
DISTRIBUTION *Throughout the British Isles.*
SIMILAR SPECIES *Several Caloplaca species, including C. marina, which are maritime and orange, but crust-forming, lacking raised leafy lobes.*

NOTE
Lichens have a long history of use in the production of dyes. Sunburst Lichen produces a yellow or orange dye. Because of its yellow colour, in the medieval period it was thought to be a cure for jaundice.

Map Lichen

Rhizocarpon geographicum (Rhizocarpaceae)

Map Lichen consists of a very distinctive glossy yellow green crust sitting on a black plate of tissue containing the reproductive structures. The crust is made up of individual parts called areoles. Angular in shape, each areole is outlined by a black margin so that the crust with its black network resembles crazy paving. Small, black spore-bearing structures are usually very abundant within the network. With its conspicuous colouring and patterning, it is often possible to recognize this lichen from a distance.

FORMS mosaics across the surface of hard acid rock, especially in upland areas; rare in the lowlands but occasional on roof slates and tombstones.

CLOSE-UP

cracked, yellow-green mosaic

irregular green patches

SIZE *Individual crusts 2–3cm in diameter.*
FORM *Flat crust.*
REPRODUCTION *Small, slightly concave black spore-bearing structures about 1–2mm in diameter.*
DISTRIBUTION *Throughout the British Isles.*
SIMILAR SPECIES *Rhizocarpon lecanorinum, which is matt rather than glossy on the crust surface, and has crescent shaped areoles distinguish; it is uncommon, confined to hard acid rocks in upland areas.*

NOTE
As Map Lichen quickly colonizes newly-exposed rock surfaces and has a known rate of growth, it is often used in a technique called lichenometry, used to estimate the age of exposure of a rock surface.

Lecanora conizaeoides

Lecanora conizaeoides (Lecanoraceae)

This lichen is characterized by small, greenish yellow, saucer shaped, spore-producing structures on the surface of the grey-green crust. These resemble "jam tarts", with the margins sometimes slightly crimped, and covered with powdery granules. Closely associated with sulphur, this fungus was rarely seen in Britain before the Industrial Revolution.

OCCURS on trees, fences gate posts, and can occasionally occur on walls, rocks, and soil.

coarsely granular crust

SIZE *Varies enormously.*
FORM *Crust-like.*
REPRODUCTION *By spores from spore structures on surface of crust.*
DISTRIBUTION *Throughout but declining in many areas since sulphur dioxide levels have fallen.*
SIMILAR SPECIES *L. polytropa has a yellow green crust and jade green spore structures.*

Brain Lichen

Diploicia canescens (Physciaceae)

Brain Lichen forms a white to pale grey crust with clearly defined marginal lobes and a fine powdery covering. The centre of the crust is much darker and is covered with pale floury reproductive patches (soralia). It is common in southern and eastern Britain in dry nutrient enriched habitats, such as trees in pastures grazed by stock, farmyard walls, and rocks used as perches by birds.

FOUND on calcareous rock surfaces, walls, and nutrient enriched trees.

marginal lobes

powdery covering

SIZE *Rosettes up to 5cm across.*
FORM *Flat crust.*
REPRODUCTION *Mostly vegetative; spore-bearing structures are rarely seen.*
DISTRIBUTION *Throughout, but much more common in the south.*
SIMILAR SPECIES *Solenopsora candicans has spore-bearing black discs surrounded by white margins and lacks soralia.*

FUNGI

Glossary

Many of the terms defined here are illustrated in the general introduction to each plant or animal group. Words in *italics* are defined elsewhere in the glossary.

A

abdomen In mammals, the portion of the body between the thorax and pelvis; the segmented, third section of an insect's body in which digestive, excretory, and reproductive organs are located; rear main section of an arthropod's body, except in myriapods, where there is only a head and a trunk.

achene A dry, one-seeded, non-splitting fruit, often with a *pappus*.

adductor muscle(s) The major muscle(s) that run between the two halves of a bivalve mollusc and draw them tightly together.

adipose fin A fleshy *dorsal fin* that lack spines or fin rays and is found only in members of the salmon family.

adnate Used to describe *gills* of fungi that are joined to the stem by their entire depth.

adnexed Used to describe *gills* that are narrower where they are attached to the stems.

aestivate To undergo a period of dormancy during summer.

alternate Leaves borne singly, in two vertical rows or spirally.

anal fin A medial fin on the belly of a fish that provides stability and steering.

antennae Paired sensory appendages attached to, and projecting from, the head of an insect and some other invertebrates.

anther The male part of the flower that bears the pollen.

apical spur A blunt, spine-like structure at the end of a leg segment, usually a *tibia*.

apterygota Primitively wingless insects. The smaller subclass of the class Insecta.

aril A fleshy, often brightly coloured, coat on a seed.

asexual Of reproduction without separate sexes, reproduction occurring by *parthenogenesis*.

auricled With small, ear-like lobes.

awn Stiff bristle-like projection often found on flowers.

axil The angle between two structures, such as the leaf and stem or the midrib and a small vein of a leaf.

B

baleen A fibrous substance that grows in the form of plates, which hang from a whale's upper jaw and are used to filter food from water.

barred With marks crossing the body, wing, or tail.

basic soil An alkaline soil with a high pH.

benthic Associated with or living on the bottom of a body of water.

bipinnate Twice *pinnate*, i.e. with the divisions themselves pinnately divided.

bloomy Covered with a thin blue-white layer which can be rubbed off.

blowhole The nostrils of whales, dolphins, and porpoises, positioned on top of their heads.

boss A rounded projection on a petal.

bract A small, leaf-like structure found at the base of a flower stalk or in the *cone* of a conifer.

bracteole A small leaf-like organ at the base of secondary branches of the flower stalk.

breach To leap out of water (usually the sea), landing back in it with a splash.

brood A generation of individuals produced by a *species*.

bulbil A small, bulb-like organ that breaks off to form a new plant.

burr A woody outgrowth on the trunk of some trees.

buttressed A tree with a fluted or swollen trunk that aids stability in shallow rooting conditions.

byssus threads Tough, hair-like threads, secreted by molluscs to anchor themselves to rocks or other *substrates*.

C

calcar In bats, a hollow *spur* extending from the hind limbs and helping to support the membrane between these.

calcareous Consisting of or containing calcium carbonate.

call Vocal sound often characteristic of a particular species, communicating a variety of messages.

calyx The collective name for the *sepals* of a flower.

capsule Dry fruit that splits open to disperse ripe seed.

carapace The shell-like *dorsal* surface that covers part of the body of some crustaceans, tortoises, and the *cephalothorax* of arachnids.

caste Any group of individuals in a colony of social insects that are structurally or behaviourally different from individuals in other groups, as seen in Isoptera and some Hymenoptera.

catkin An unbranched and often pendulous flower cluster of a single sex.

cell A space on the wings of a butterfly or moth, defined and bordered by veins.

cephalothorax The front section of an arachnid made of the head and *thorax* fused together.

cerci (sing. **cercus**) A pair of sensory appendages at the rear end of an insect's *abdomen*.

chelicerae The first, usually pincer-like, pair of appendages on the *cephalothorax* of an arachnid.

cirri (sing. **cirrus**) Long double-branched appendages used by barnacles for gathering particles of planktonic food.

cladode A modified stem that looks like a leaf.

cleistogamous Used to describe self-pollinating flowers, whose petals and sepals never open.

clitellum The thickened portion about one third the way along the body of a sexually mature earthworm, which secretes the egg sac.

cocoon A silk case made by the fully grown *larvae* of many insects just before pupation.

colony An aggregation of social insects sharing a nest. A group of nests of a highly social bird species, especially seabirds, but also others such as the Sand Martin and Rook.

columnar Taller than broad, with parallel sides.

compound Describes a leaf divided into *leaflets*.

compound eyes The eyes of arthropods, which are made up of many light-gathering units called ommatidia.

cone The fruiting structure of conifers. In horsetails, the spore-bearing reproductive structure produced at some stem tips.

corbiculum The pollen basket of honey bees, being a concave, shiny area on the hind *tibiae*, fringed with stiff hairs.

cornicle One of a pair of spout-like structures on the back of an aphid's abdomen which carry defensive secretions.

cortina Fine, cobweb-like threads usually joining the cap margin of a fungus to the stem.

covert A small feather in a well-defined tract, on the wing or at the base of the tail, covering the base of the larger flight feathers.

coxa (pl. **coxae**) The first segment of an insect's leg, joining the rest of the leg to the *thorax*.

crepuscular Active at twilight or before sunrise.

critically endangered Facing an extremely high risk of global extinction.

cryptic Describes patterns and colours that make some species difficult to see in its habitat.

cuckoo A species in which the *larvae* develop eating food stored by another species for its own larvae.

cultivar A selection made by humans and maintained in cultivation.

cuticle A general term referring to the outermost layer or skin of fungal *fruitbodies*.

cyme A flower cluster with lateral branches, each ending in a flower.

D

dabble To feed in shallow water, with rapid movements of the bill, sieving water through comb-like teeth to extract food.

deciduous Describes a tree that is leafless for part of the year (usually winter).

decurrent Used to describe *gills* that join the fungal stem and extend downwards along it.

dimorphic Occurring in two distinct forms: sexually dimorphic means that the male and female of a species look different; otherwise indicates two colour forms.

disc floret In the Daisy family, a flower in the central part of the flowerhead, whose petals are fused into a tube.

diurnal Active during the day.

dorsal Referring to the upper surface or back of a structure or animal.

dorsal fin A medial fin or fins on the back of a fish that provide stability and steering.

double flower Describes a flower with more petals than in the normal wild state, and with few, if any, *stamens*.

drey A squirrel's nest.

drone A male honey bee.

drumming Sound made by woodpeckers with rapid beats of the bill against a hard object, or by a snipe, diving through the air with vibrating tail feathers.

drupe A fleshy fruit whose seeds are surrounded by a tough coat.

drupelet One of several small *drupes* joined together.

E

ear tuft A bunch of feathers on the head of an owl, capable of being raised as a visual signal and perhaps to assist camouflage.

eclipse The plumage of male ducks that is adopted during the summer, when they moult and become flightless for a short time.

elytra (sing. **elytron**) The rigid front wings of beetles, modified as covers for the *hindwings* and not used in flight.

endangered Found in very small numbers, in a very small area or in a very restricted and declining habitat, so the future security of the species is in doubt.

epicalyx A ring of *sepal*-like organs just below the true sepals (*calyx*) of a flower.

evergreen Describes a tree that always bears leaves.

eye patch An area of colour around the eye, often in the form of a "mask", broader than an *eye-stripe*.

eye-ring A more or less circular patch of colour, usually narrow and well-defined, around a bird's or animal's eye.

eyespot A distinctive eye-like marking, typically on the wings of some insects, especially butterflies; its function can be to alarm and deter a potential predator.

eye-stripe A stripe of distinctive colour running in front of and behind a bird's or animal's eye.

F

fall petal In the Iris family, one of three outer petals that droop down.

family A unit of classification, grouping together related units called *genera*. For example, the *species* Amanita muscaria belongs to the *genus* Amanita, this is placed in the family Amanitaceae.

femur (pl. **femora**) The part of an insect's leg corresponding to the mammalian thigh.

filter-feeder Fish or some invertebrates that feed on minute particles that are filtered from the water, for example, by passing over gill rakers.

flight feather Any one of the long feathers on a bird's wing (*primaries* and *secondaries*).

floret One of a group of small or individual flowers usually clustered together to form a *flowerhead*.

flowerhead A cluster of *florets*.

forewing The front part of a wing, including the outer *primaries*, primary *coverts*, and *secondary* coverts.

form A term applied to certain *species* that occur in two or more different colour variations across the species' range.

free gills Used to describe *gills* that do not attach to a fungal stem.

frond The leaf of a seaweed or fern.

fruitbody A general term for any *spore*-producing fungal structure; more correctly called a sporophore.

fry A stage of the fish life-cycle referring to newly hatched fish.

G

gall An abnormal plant growth caused by a bacterium, virus, fungus, mite, or insect.

gastrovascular cavity The chamber in jellyfish, sea anemones, and corals that functions both for digestion and gaseous exchange.

gemmae An asexual reproductive structure in liverworts and mosses that detaches from the adult plant to form a new plant.

genus (pl. **genera**) A category in classification: a group of closely related species, whose relationship is recognized by the same first name in the scientific terminology, e.g. *Larus* in *Larus fuscus*.

gills The thin, flattened, *spore*-bearing structures of cap and stem fungi. Also, the respiratory organ in fish, molluscs, insects, crustaceans, and amphibians.

glume Small scale in the *inflorescence* of a grass or sedge.

H

habit The shape of a plant.

halteres The greatly modified hind wings of Diptera insects which serve as balancing organs.

hemimetabolous Developing by incomplete or gradual metamorphosis, such as in Orthoptera and Hemiptera insects. Immature stages are called *nymphs*.

herbaceous Non-woody plants, dying back at the end of the growing season and overwintering by means of underground rootstocks.

hibernation A period of dormancy undergone by animals, typically during the winter months.

hindwing In birds, the rear part of the wing, including the secondary feathers, especially when it has a distinctive colour or pattern; in insects, one of a pair of back wings.

holdfast A root-like structure that anchors seaweed to rocks but does not absorb nutrients like a true root.

holometabolous Developing by complete metamorphosis such as in Coleoptera and Diptera insects. Immature stages are called *larvae*.

hybrid The result of cross-breeding between two species; usually infertile.

hybridization The interbreeding of different *species* or *subspecies*.

hymenium A layer of fertile, *spore*-producing cells spread over *gills*, *tubes*, *spines* etc.

I

indusium (pl. **indusia**) Tissue covering a *sorus* on a fern *frond*.

inflorescence A group of flowers on a single stem.

inner wing In a bird, the inner part of the wing, comprising the *secondaries* and rows of *coverts* (typically marginal, lesser, median, and greater coverts).

intertidal The zone of shoreline between the high- and low-tide marks.

J

juvenile A bird in its first plumage, that in which it makes its first flight, before its first moult in the autumn.

K

Keel petal The lower, fused petals of a *peaflower*, folded and curved like the keel of a boat.

L

lancet A lance-shaped muscular projection on the face of a horseshoe-bat.

larva (pl. **larvae**) The immature stage of an insect that undergoes complete metamorphosis.

lateral line Sensory system of a fish that runs along the side of the body and detects pressure waves in the water.

leading shoot The *terminal* shoot of a main branch.

leaflet One of the divisions that make up a *compound* leaf.

lek A gathering of birds at which males display communally, with mock fighting, while females choose which one to mate with.

lenticel A small pore found on shoots and fruit through which air can pass.

ligule A flap of tissue, often located at the base of a leaf.

lip A protruding petal, as in members of the Orchid and Mint families.

litter (leaf, needle) The carpet of fallen leaves or needles and other rotting organic matter in broadleaf or coniferous woods, parks, and gardens.

localized More than 90 per cent of the population occurs at ten sites or less.

locally common Abundant in particular parts of its range; even though it may be scarce or rare in other parts.

lodge The den of certain animals, especially beavers.

M

macro-moth A term commonly used to distinguish certain families of usually larger moths from the other families, called *micro-moths*, which are generally less easily identified.

mantle A fleshy layer of tissue that surrounds the body of molluscs. In many species, the outer cell layer of the mantle secretes the shell.

maxillary palps A pair of segmented sensory mouthpart structures in insects, used to taste food.

melanic A colour form, often very sporadic, within a species' range of variation, which has an increased amout of black or dark pigmentation.

mericarp A one-seeded portion of a fruit formed by splitting from the rest.

mesothorax The middle section of an insect's *thorax*, carrying the middle pair of legs and, usually, the front pair of wings.

metatarsal tubercle A prominent hard swelling under the hind foot of many species of frog and toad.

metathorax The rear section of an insect's *thorax*, carrying the hind pair of legs and, usually, the hind pair of wings.

micro-moth A term commonly used to distinguish certain families of usually smaller, and less easily identified moths from the *macro-moths*.

midrib The primary, usually central, vein of a leaf or *leaflet*.

migrant A species that spends part of the year in one geographical area and part in another, moving between the two on a regular basis.

mine A variously shaped hollow space between the upper and lower surface of a leaf caused by a feeding insect *larva*.

moult The shedding and renewing of feathers in a systematic way; most birds have a partial moult and a complete moult each year.

mycelium (adj. **mycelial**) The vegetative body of a fungus (usually below the surface) formed by a mass of fine, thread-like cells called hyphae.

mycorrhizal The symbiotic relationship between a fungus and a plant, in which the fungus penetrates the plant and exchanges nutrients with it, often to their mutual benefit.

N

native Occurring naturally in a particular region.

naturalized A non-native plant or animal, introduced by human activity into a region, and now forming self-sustaining populations in the wild.

nectary A nectar-secreting gland.

nematocyst A specialized stinging cell of cnidarians, which can be discharged to trap prey.

neurotoxin Highly dangerous poisons which affect the human central nervous system.

nocturnal Active at night.

nose-leaf A thin, broad, membranous fold of skin on the nose of many species of horseshoe-bats. It varies greatly in size and form.

notched Used to describe *gills* of fungi that turn abruptly up, then down, as they join the stem or to describe a petal with V- or U-shaped indentations.

nymph The immature stage of an insect showing incomplete metamorphosis, such as Hemiptera and Orthoptera (Exopterygota) insects.

O

obovate Egg-shaped, broadest above the middle.

ocelli Simple light-receptive organs on the head of many insects.

ochrea A papery, tubular sheath around the stem of some plants, notably docks.

operculum A horny or calcaerous plate attached to the foot of certain gastropods, which exactly fits and seals the shell aperture. It protects the snail from desiccation and to a certain extent, from predators.

opposite Borne in pairs on opposite sides of the stem.

orbital ring A thin, bare, fleshy ring around the eye, sometimes with a distinctive colour.

order A category in classification: families grouped to indicate their close relationship or common ancestry; usually a more uncertain or speculative grouping than a *family*.

ossicle A single calcified component that makes up the skeleton just under the epidermis of echinoderms.

outer wing In birds, the outer half of a wing, comprising the primaries, their coverts, and the alula, or bastard wing (the "thumb").

ovate Egg-shaped, broadest towards the base.

ovipositor An organ, often tube-like, for laying eggs.

P

palmately compound Fan-shaped and divided into *leaflets*.

palps A pair of segmented sensory appendages associated with an insect's mouthparts.

panicle A branched flower cluster, with stalked flowers.

pappus A tuft of hairs on *achenes* or other fruits, which aids wind dispersal.

parapodia (sing. **parapodium**) The flap-like locomotory appendages on the body segments of polychaete annelid worms, which usually have bristles.

parasite A species living off the body or tissues of another species and giving nothing in return in many cases.

parotid gland One of a pair of wart-like glands located behind the eyes in many amphibians, particularly conspicuous in toads. It may produce a noxious secretion.

parthenogenesis Reproduction without the need for fertilization.

partial veil A layer of tissue stretching from the cap margin of fungi to the stem; it may form a cobweb-like veil or a membranous ring.

peaflower A flower, usually from the Pea family, with sepals fused into a short tube, and with a usually erect upper petal, two *wing petals*, and two *keel petals*.

pea-like Describes a flower structure typical of members of the Pea family, with the *sepals* fused into a short tube, and usually with an erect upper petal, two wing petals, and two lower petals forming a keel.

pectoral fins Paired fins on the side of the body of a fish

that aid manoeuvrability and braking.

pedicellaria Tiny, two- or three-jawed organs on the surface of an echinoderm that keep it clear of encrusting organisms and parasites.

pedipalps In arachnids, the second pair of appendages on the *cephalothorax*. They are tactile organs also variously used for handling and killing prey, and in male spiders, are organs of copulation.

peduncle In fish, the fleshy base of the tail fin; in plants, the stalk of an *inflorescence*.

pelvic fins *Ventrally* positioned paired fins that aid manoeuvrability and braking.

periostracum A thin layer of protein that covers the outside of the shell of many molluscs such as gastropods and bivalves. It can be tough and horny, thin, or even hairy.

persistent Not falling, but remaining attached to the plant.

pheromones Chemical "messengers" released by an animal in order to attract a member of the opposite sex of the same species.

pinnate Describes a *compound* leaf with the *leaflets* arranged as in a feather. Pinnately lobed leaves have lobes, rather than leaflets, arranged in this manner.

pinnule Subdivision of pinna on a *pinnate* leaf or *frond*.

plankton Microscopic organisms that drift in the sea. There are two types, phytoplankton (plants), which are photosynthetic and zooplankton (animals).

pneumostome The respiratory opening of an air-breathing land snail or slug, which connects to a simple lung.

polymorphic Having more than two forms.

polypore Common name for fungi with woody or tough *fruitbodies* and with a *pored*, tubular *spore*-producing layer.

pores The openings of the tubular *spore*-producing layer on fungi such as boletes and *polypores*.

prehensile Able to curl around objects and grip them.

primary Any one of the long feathers or quills of a bird, forming the tip and trailing edge of the *outer wing*, growing from the "hand".

proboscis The coiled but extensible "tongue" of a butterfly or moth.

proleg The unsegmented leg of an insect *larva* (different from the segmented thoracic legs).

pronotum The *dorsal* cover of the first segment of an insect's *thorax*.

prothorax The first segment of an insect's *thorax*, carrying the front pair of legs.

pterostigma A coloured panel near the front edge of insect wings.

pterygota Winged insects. The larger subclass of the class Insecta.

pupa The stage in the life cycle of a butterfly or moth that follows on from the *larva* and from which the adult insect emerges.

Q

quadrilateral cell A particular four-sided cell in the wings of certain insects.

R

race *See* **subspecies**.

raceme An unbranched flower cluster where each flower is clearly stalked.

radula The toothed, file-like feeding structure found in the mouths of most molluscs (not present in bivalves), which is used to graze or rasp food.

rare Found in small numbers or very low densities.

rank A linear arrangement of leaves – 2-ranked leaves are arranged in opposite pairs along a stem; 4-ranked leaves are arranged in opposite pairs, each pair at right angles to the pair next to it.

ray/ray floret The outer, distinctively flattened flower of a daisy-type *flowerhead*.

recurved Curved backwards or splayed out.

relict species A species that has survived while other related ones have become extinct.

reticulate Possessing or forming a slightly raised net- or mesh-like feature, such as in some fungi.

rhizome A (usually underground) thickened stem which serves as a food storage organ.

rhizomorphs Thick, cord-like strands of *mycelium*, looking rather like roots.

ring-zone A zone at the top of the stem of a fungus where a *partial veil* was once attached.

riparian Occurring on the bank of a river.

rostrum The tubular, slender sucking mouthparts of insects such as the Hemiptera. The prolonged part of the head of weevils and scorpionflies. In crustaceans, a projecting anterior part of the carapace that extends forwards in front of the eyes.

runner A stem that creeps along the ground, forming roots at intervals and eventually giving rise to separate plants.

rut An annually recurring condition or period of sexual excitement and reproductive activity in male deer.

S

saprophyte a plant which feeds on rotting vegetation in the soil.

scale(s) Tiny, flattened plates that cloak the wing surfaces of most butterflies and moths. In fungi, pieces of surface tissue (often on cap or stem) which break away or peel back.

scape A leafless stem bearing flowers.

scapular Any one of a group of feathers on the shoulder of a bird, forming an oval patch each side of the back, at the base of the wing.

scent gland A gland inside the body of bugs and other insects that produces a secretion, often for defensive purposes.

scutellum The *dorsal* cover of the rear part of the middle or rear section of an insect's *thorax*.

secondary Any one of the long *flight feathers* forming the trailing edge of the *inner wing*, growing from the ulna or "arm".

selection see *cultivar*

sella A saddle-shaped anatomical structure on the face of a horseshoe-bat.

semi-evergreen With few leaves retained over winter.

sepal The usually green parts of a flower outside of the petals, collectively called the *calyx*.

sett The burrow of a badger.

sex brand A patch or line of scent-emitting scales that is found on the forewing of a male butterfly.

sheath Tubular structure around a part of a plant, such as a leaf base round a stem.

siliqua A fruit of the Cabbage family, long and linear or pod-like.

simple Describes leaves not divided into *leaflets*.

siphon(s) Tube-like structures through which oxygenated water and suspended food particles flows in (inhalant siphon) and water and wastes flow out (exhalant siphon) of the body of certain molluscs.

song Vocalization with a character particular to the individual species, used to communicate a claim to a breeding territory and attract a mate.

song-flight In birds, a special flight, often with a distinctive pattern, combined with a territorial *song*.

sorus (pl. **sori**) A distinct group of minute, *spore*-producing structures on the *frond* of a fern.

spadix A fleshy *spike* with many unstalked flowers.

spathe The large, hooded *bract* that encloses a *spadix*.

spawning The process of laying and fertilizing eggs in fish and amphibians.

species A unit of classification that embraces a group of genetically similar individuals, members of which are capable of reproducing with one another and of producing viable offspring.

speculum A colourful patch on a duck's *hindwing*, formed by the secondary feathers. In plants, a shiny, shield-like patch on the petals of some orchids.

spike An unbranched flower cluster, with unstalked flowers.

spicule A slender hard structure, which is often needle-like.

spines Tooth, peg, or spine-like structures over which the *spore*-producing layer of fungi is spread.

spiracle The breathing holes of insects, leading to the tracheal system.

spore The basic unit of reproduction in many non-flowering plants such as fungi, ferns, and mosses.

sporangium (pl. **sporangia**) Minute spore-producing organ on the underside of the *fronds* of ferns.

spur A hollow, cylindrical or pouched structure projecting from a flower, usually containing nectar. In animals, it refers to a pointed, projecting structure on the limbs.

stamen Male part of a flower, composed of an *anther*, normally borne on a stalk (filament).

staminode An infertile, modified *stamen*.

standard petal The upright, upper petal of a *peaflower*, often larger than the others.

stigma The female part of the flower that receives the pollen.

stigma-ray A *stigma* that forms a star with radiating branches.

sting The modified *ovipositor* of some Hymenoptera insects, used for injecting venom.

stipule A leaf-like organ at the base of a leaf stalk.

streaked With small marks that run lengthwise along the body.

striation A longitudinal groove or mark.

stridulation The act of producing sound, usually by rubbing two parts of the body together.

stroma A tough, woody or fleshy structure surrounding the *spore*-producing openings of certain fungi.

style The part of the female reproductive organ that joins the ovary to the *stigma*.

submarginal Used in the context of a band of colour, or perhaps a row of spots, that are found on the area of a wing just inside the margin.

subshrub A small perennial with some stems that become woody.

subspecies (abbrev. **subsp.**) A category of classification, below species, defining a group within a species, isolated geographically but able to interbreed with others of the same species.

substrate The material or organism on which a species grows; underlying soil or sand.

suckers Shoots arising from below the soil at the base of a tree.

suckering Producing strong, fast-growing shoots directly from the roots.

superciliary stripe In birds, a stripe of colour running above the eye, like an eyebrow.

symbiosis Different species living in an association that brings mutual benefit.

T

tarsus (pl. **tarsi**) The foot of an arthropod. It is attached to the end of the *tibia* and is made up of several tarsal segments.

tepal Petals and sepals that cannot be distinguished.

terminal Located at the end of a shoot, stem, or other organ.

tertial Any one of a small group of feathers, sometimes long and obvious, at the base of a bird's wing adjacent to the inner *secondaries*.

thorax (adj. **thoracic**) In insects, the middle section of an adult's body and the one to which the legs and wings are attached.

tibia (pl. **tibiae**) The lower leg segment of insects; the shin of mammals.

tooth fungi Fungi that have their *spore*-producing layer spread over pointed teeth, spines, or pegs.

tracheae (sing. **trachea**) The internal airways of arthropods.

tragus In most bats, a small cartilaginous flap in front of the external opening of the ear.

tree-line The elevation in a mountainous region above which trees do not grow.

trifoliate A leaf made up of three distinct leaflets.

troop A colony or scattered group of fungi, usually individuals, not clumps.

tubercle A raised, wart-like structure on the surface of an arthropod.

tubes In fungi, fleshy or woody, cylindrical or tubular structures, usually gathered together in a layer and in which the *spore*-producing layer is spread.

U

umbel A flat-topped or domed flower cluster with all the stems originating at the same place.

umbo (adj. **umbonate**) A bump or hump, usually at the centre of a fungus cap.

universal veil A layer of tissue completely surrounding the fungus; the veil may be thin and cobweb-like, thick and skin-like, or even glutinous and sticky.

upperwing The upperside of a bird's or butterfly's wing; in birds, it is clearly exposed in flight but often mostly hidden when the bird is perched.

V

vagrant An individual species that has strayed beyond the usual geographic range of its species.

variegated Having more than one colour; usually used to describe leaves.

varietas (abbrev. **var.**) A naturally occurring variant of a species.

vector An intermediate host that carries and transmits a disease organism.

veil A layer of tissue which protects a fungus especially during some early stages of its growth. See also *partial veil* and *universal veil*.

venation The pattern of veins.

vent The area of feathers between the legs and the undertail *coverts*, surrounding the cloaca.

ventral The under or lower surface.

vestigial Of a structure that is greatly reduced in size and often non-functional.

volva Remains of a *universal veil* left at the base of the stem of a fungus as a sack-like bag or scaly swelling as the fungus expands during growth.

vulnerable Facing a high risk of global extinction.

W

warren A series of interconnected underground tunnels in which rabbits live.

wing petal The lateral petals of many flowers, particularly orchids and *peaflowers*.

wingbar A line of colour produced by a tract of feathers or feather tips, crossing the closed wing of a bird and running along the spread wing.

Index

INDEX

Acknowledgments

Dorling Kindersley would like to thank the following people for their help in the preparation of this book: Michelle Payne, Lydia White, and Gina Fullerlove at the Royal Botanic Gardens, Kew, Miezan Van Zyl and Tamlyn Calitz for editorial assistance, and Neil Fletcher for additional photography.

Picture Credits
Dorling Kindersley would like to thank the following for their kind permission to reproduce their photographs:

Key:
(a-above; b-below/bottom; c-centre; f-far; l-left; r-right; t-top)

Alamy Images: Sébastien Baussais 1tl; blickwinkel 71ftl, 458; David Chapman 76tr (bat); Nikki Edmunds 33c; Martin Fowler 438; Geophotos 48–49t; John La Gette 462br; Paul Glendell 33tc; Chris Gomersall 1br; Ian Goodrick 69crb; Greenwales 38–39t; imagebroker 1bl; ImageState 308; Angela Jordan 422–423; Tom Joslyn 4, 164; Roger Kennedy 35crb; Stephen Lewis ARPS 29bl; Matthew Mawson 69bl; David Norton 2–3; Realimage 34–35tc; David J Slater 1tr; Trevor Smithers ARPS 51ca; Mike Spence 31cr; THP UK Nature 166cr (terrapin); Scott Tilley 230; David Tipling 31bc, 69bc; **Ardea:** Pat Morris 182cla; **Photo Biopix.dk:** J C Schou 446, 473ca; **britainonview.com:** britainonview.com 62–63tc; Joe Cornish 8–9, 24l, 43tr, 48tl; Nick Hawkes 354–355; David Sellman 51tc; V K Guy Ltd/ Paul Guy 48bl; **Laurie Campbell Photography:** Laurie Campbell 92–93, 98–99, 178–179, 198–199, 226–227, 290–291, 300, 334–335, 348–349, 358–359, 492–493; **Corbis:** Niall Benvie 47fclb, 52t; Chris Warren/Loop Images 26–27c; WildCountry 56–57b; **David Fenwick (www.aphotoflora.com):** 105br, 178cr, 306clb, 306cr, 306fcl, 307cl, 308bl, 308br, 308fclb, 320fcrb, 337cr, 337fcr, 344fcla, 384fcla, 394cla, 440bl, 440fbl, 440fclb, 442fcra, 443cr, 443cra, 443fcra, 444cra, 445cr, 445fcr, 448bl, 448br, 448cb, 448cl, 448fclb, 448fcr, 448fcrb, 449br, 449cr, 449fbr, 449fcr, 452br, 452cr, 452fbl, 452fcra, 452tl, 453cr, 453cra, 453fcrb, 454bl, 454br, 454cl, 454cr, 454cra, 454ftr,

455bl, 455cl, 455cra, 455fbr, 455fcla, 455fcra, 455ftr, 456cra, 456fbr, 456fcl, 456fclb, 456fcrb, 457bl, 457cl, 457cla, 457clb, 457cr, 457fbl, 457fbr, 457fcl, 457fcla, 457fcra, 457fcrb, 457ftr, 457tl; **Neil Fletcher:** 344ftl, 390bc, 390fcrb, 449cr, 452cla, 452fcla, 455fcla, 457fcr; Neil Fletcher 450–451; **FLPA:** Andrew Bailey 146–147; Richard Becker 464–465; R. Dirscherl 179cr; Jef Meul/Foto Natura 238–239; Jan Vermeer/Foto Natura 260–261; **Getty Images:** Peter Adams 62fbl; Scott Barbour 71bc; Ben Hall 63bl; Paul Harris 27fcrb; Andrew Parkinson 36–37tc; Hans Strand 446–447; David Tipling 42–43t; **Chris Gibson:** 105crb, 306fcra, 307cla, 308crb, 320br, 320fbr, 320fcrb, 337cr, 384cla, 384ftr, 390fcrb, 394fcla, 442fbr, 445bl, 445cl, 445clb, 445fcl, 445fcrb, 445tl, 452cr, 452cra, 452fcr, 452ftr, 453fcra, 453ftr, 454cr, 454fcr, 455cl, 455cla, 455fbl, 455tl, 456bl, 456br, 456fbl, 456ftr, 495cra; **Frank Greenaway:** Frank Greenaway 80–81; **hedge-rose.co.uk:** David Penrose 36tc, 66–67tc; **Tony Howell:** Tony Howell 28–29tc, 46–47t; **iStockphoto.com:** 27bc, 35fbl, 38–39b, 41clb, 53tc, 62bc, 69fbl; **London Aerial Photo Library:** London Aerial Photo Library 22–23; **Andy MacKay:** 206br, 206cr, 206fbr, 206fcr, 210cra, 210fcra, 223br, 223fbl, 223fclb, 224cla, 224tr; **The National Trust Photo Library:** Joe Cornish 12–13, 16–17, 27tc, 27tr, 30–31tc; David Noton 27c; **Natural Visions:** 178fclb, 182cl; Heather Angel 176crb, 177cra, 177crb, 178br, 178cr, 178cra, 179cl, 179cla, 179clb, 179fbl, 183cr, 183fcla, 304crb, 305cla, 305fcla, 306cl, 309fcr, 394tl, 442cr, 443bl, 495bl; M & J Bloomfield 443fbl; Simon Brown 178cla; Doug McCutcheon 455cr; **naturepl.com:** Ingo Arndt 31tc, 35; Niall Benvie 28bc, 44fbl, 47cra, 48cl, 60–61t; Dave Bevan 71br; Barry Bland 43crb; Jane Burton 28bl, 63tr; Pete Cairns 43bc, 51cr, 53bc, 53c, 55t, 56–57tc, 124–125, 328–329; Philippe Clement 48fclb, 53cla; Andrew Cooper 40clb; Christophe Courteau 28crb; Sue Daly 32br; Adrian Davies 48fclb (Mushroom), 62crb; Geoff Dore 14–15; Georgette Douwma 28fcl, 310–311; John Downer 64b; Tony Evans 26br, 31tr; Laurent Geslin 68bc; Chris Gomersall 32tc, 33ftl, 35clb,

50–51t; Paul Hobson 49tr, 163; John Waters 51bc; David Kjaer 6–7, 27crb, 58br, 84–85; Willem Kolvoort 31cra, 170–171; Brian Lightfoot 58c (woodcock); Neil Lucas 322–323; Tim Martin 43ftr; George McCarthy 53, 67bc, 71fbl; Duncan McEwan 47tr, 54cb, 68tc; David Noton 18–19, 65bc; William Osborn 44t, 60–61b; Mike Potts 46c; Colin Preston 54–55b; Reinhard/ARCO 56c; Michel Roggo 170; Jose B. Ruiz 66br; Geoff Simpson 28fcla, 62ftl; Jason Smalley 59b, 66tc; Gary K Smith 64–65tc, 66c; Kim Taylor 36–37b, 56l; Mark Taylor 35crb (Crab); Dan Thory 58–59s; David Tipling 47bc, 194–195; Colin Varndell 65fbl; Will Watson 40fbl, 45tr; Mike Wilkes 34bl; **Alan Outen:** 176cr, 177cr, 178clb, 178fcra, 179crb, 306br, 307bl, 308br, 308fbl, 344cla, 442bl, 442cl, 442cla, 442cra, 442fbr, 443, 443fcl, 443fcla, 444bl, 444fcra, 445br, 445cra, 445fcr, 445fcra, 445ftr, 448cr, 448cra, 448fbl, 448fcl, 448fcra, 448ftr, 449cla, 449clb, 449cra, 449fcla, 449fcra, 449fcrb, 449fcra, 449ftr, 449tc, 452bl, 452br, 452cl, 452crb, 452fbl, 452fcla, 453cla, 453crb, 453fcla, 453fcrb, 453tl, 454rcb, 454fclb, 454tl, 455clb, 455crb, 456fcl, 456tl, 457cr, 457cra, 457fcl, 494cla, 494clb, 494crb, 494fbr, 495br; **Photolibrary:** 308fbr; **Photoshot / NHPA:** Jim Bain 34br; Laurie Campbell 29cb, 31bl, 54tr; Stephen Dalton 45bl, 68c; Guy Edwardes 20–21; Helio & Van Ingen 43c, 120–121; Ernie Janes 28fbl, 28fbr, 45cb, 66bc; Yves Lanceau 32fbl; David Middleton 45cl; Julie Royle 38cb; Eric Soder 242–243, 434–435, 470–471; Robert Thompson 28ftl; Roger Tidman 68–69t; Roy Waller 31br, 31crb; **Photoshot / Woodfall Wild Images:** Andy Newman 280–281; **Mike Read:** 183cla; **Robert Harding Picture Library:** Jean Brooks 428–429; **John Robinson:** 160bl; **rspb-images.com:** 105fcrb, 111tl, 160cb; Peter Cairns 60l; Jan Haladay 38tl; Ben Hall 54c; Steve Knell 166cra (snake); Chris Knights 73–74; Mike Lane 98, 160fclb; David Norton 166crb (newt), 340; Richard Revels 232crb; David Tipling 70; Roger Wilmshurst 112–113; **Dragiša Savi :** 452fcl, 455br, 456tca, 456cl, 456fcla, 494fcl; **Roger Snook:** 442fbl, 444, 444cr, 444crb; **Robert Svensson:** 442br, 442cl, 442cr, 442fcr, 443cl,

443fbr, 444cl, 448fcl, 449cla, 449clb; **www.UWPhoto.no:** Jon Olav Bjørndal 176cl; Vidar Skålevik 174c, 179cra; Erling Svensen 175ca, 175crb, 182br; Rudolf Svensen 174cra, 176cla, 177bl, 177cl, 178crb, 182bl, 182crb; **Jason Venus:** Jason Venus 74

Jacket images:
Front: **Alamy Images:** Tim Graham (main); ImageState cla; **naturepl.com:** Ross Hoddinott clb; Kevin J Keatley fclb; William Osborn fcla. Back: **Alamy Images:** Arco Images tr; Tim Graham c; Tom Joslyn br; Juniors Bildarchiv fbl; Keith M Law bl; David Tipling ftr; **Corbis:** Natalie Fobes tll; **naturepl.com:** Chris Gomersall fbr; Mike Wilkes ftl. Spine: **Alamy Images:** Tim Graham

All other images © Dorling Kindersley For further information see: www.dkimages.com